AMY VANDERBILT'S ETIQUETTE

Books by Amy Vanderbilt

AMY VANDERBILT'S EVERYDAY ETIQUETTE
AMY VANDERBILT'S COMPLETE COOKBOOK

AMY VANDERBILT'S ETIQUETTE

Drawings by
Fred McCarroll, Mary Suzuki, Andy Warhol

DOUBLEDAY & COMPANY, INC., GARDEN CITY, NEW YORK

As this is an etiquette book for all Americans, I have for the sake of interest used a wide variety of names. If any of these happen to belong to real people, living or dead, it is sheer coincidence.

A.V.

Drawings on How to Make a Bed, courtesy American National Red Cross. Drawings on How to Eat a Maine Lobster, courtesy of the Maine Development Commission.

Library of Congress Catalog Card Number 78–171326
Copyright ©, 1952, 1954, 1955, 1956, 1958, 1963, 1967, 1972 by The Daisyfields Corporation

TO MY HUSBAND
CURTIS BRADBURY KELLAR

PREFACE

This book was first published in 1952 after five years of writing and research. In the intervening years it has undergone constant revision as letters from my readers indicated a need for amplification or new material. Aside from these revisions which have accumulated over the years, special additions to this new nine-year revision totaled some 120,000 words.

Perhaps no careful author of any book that has become an established reference work is ever satisfied. When the first book was published a reviewer in the New York *Times* wrote, "Future historians will owe her a great debt." This is definitely a complex subject, constantly changing, a reflection of our times with changes sometimes dramatic, sometimes minor, but always in need of recording.

This major revision has been much more difficult to do than was the first major one ten years ago because the sixties and early seventies have been a period of social upheaval. I have certainly had to consider the Sexual Revolution which in many cases merely reflected what many people were doing all along but were not prepared publicly to admit. There has been a great change in language and the way we handle it. I have had to take cognizance of new, and rather general, forms of expression which have had, to say the least, a leveling effect upon upper-class speech. Many things once automatically considered unshakably correct have been changed drastically under direct assault by the young, forcing the Establishment to take a second or third look at the way it was clinging to some conventions. Men's clothes and sometimes appearance, for example, underwent such a transition back in time and forward into the future. I like it, with reservations, as men become freer in their expression of fashion and less conformist.

Since the last major revision, I have remarried and with this new good marriage acquired five stepchildren, two boys and three girls. My husband is Curtis Bradbury Kellar. I also have one daughter-in-law and one step-daughter-in-law. I am warmly involved with my big family and they with me. The problems, aspirations and ambitions of these young people who range from teen-agers to young marrieds, frequently relate to those of some 50,000 people who write me monthly through my syndicated newspaper column, my column in the *Ladies' Home Journal* (of which I am Contributing Editor) and television and radio on which I appear from time to time.

Owners of the book at the time of the second major revision have about doubled in nine years to over 2,500,000. Many of those early brides now have children nearly ready for junior high. Many young people whose parents gave them guidance with this book are now taking me with them to college. Almost everywhere in the world I go, the book is known and my name with it. (It is also published in Spanish and Portuguese, and my column even in Chinese.)

Changes are occurring in our society fairly rapidly and with them this book will change, too, as necessary. The need for etiquette, for social guidance, is basic and always has been although the ways in which we approach the subject vary from generation to generation, sometimes several times within a generation depending upon the state of the world. Without these guidelines we cannot properly relate one to the other and show the consideration necessary in a civilized world.

In the passage of the years many people have helped me. I shall be forever grateful to all of them and to others who help me still.

Gracie Square   A. V.
New York City
1971

INTRODUCTION TO ORIGINAL EDITION

Who needs a book of etiquette? Everyone does. The simplest family, if it hopes to move just a little into a wider world, needs to know at least the elementary rules. Even the most sophisticated man or woman used to a great variety of social demands cannot hope to remember every single aspect of etiquette applying to even one possible social contingency. The human mind is so constructed that even if a person were to read through a book such as this from cover to cover he could retain only that information that had interest for him at the time of reading. Consciously, at least, the rest would be discarded as irrelevant to his way of life. But let some new way of living open up for him—a move from city to country, a trip to a new part of the world—and his etiquette becomes his *reference* book, ready to piece out his own store of information.

You might imagine that the writer of an etiquette book would certainly know everything in it and therefore have no need for it as reference or guide. But even this is not the case. After ten years as an etiquette adviser, five years of writing this book—five years of interviewing dozens of authorities in their own fields for material to be incorporated here—I, too, can remember only those details that have or have had relevance to my own way of living. If you asked me, for example, some detail of a wedding in a faith other than my own, I might have to refer to my own book. The information is here—the result of my research—but in the writing of such sections I made no attempt to memorize all these details. However, in this book, I, like you, have such information in simple, complete form all in one place, and it can be readily found if needed.

The word "etiquette" for all the things I have tried to discuss is really inadequate, yet no other will do. It covers much more than "manners," the way in which we *do* things. It is considerably more than a treatise on a code of social behavior, although all the traditional information still of value has, I feel, been included in a way that is simple and concise, shorn of mumbo-jumbo and clearly learnable. For we must all learn the socially acceptable ways of living with others in no matter what society we move. Even in primitive societies there are such rules, some of them as complex and inexplicable as many of our own. Their original *raison d'être* or purpose is lost, but their acceptance is still unquestioned.

Change in etiquette usually comes slowly, just as changes come slowly in the dictionary. The analogy applies, too, in that it is not necessarily social leaders who bring about such changes, but rather the people themselves who, through slighting certain forms for a long enough period, finally bring about their abolishment or at least their modification.

Inventions, wars, political upheavals, legislation, all, of course, have repercussions, sometimes immediate, in the field of etiquette. In certain Moslem countries *purdah,* the centuries-old veiling of women in public, was abolished by law overnight. Think of the social adjustment that was required! What had been rigorous social custom now became *illegal.*

Etiquette, too, is obviously geographically influenced. In cities thousands of families live under one roof, yet most never speak to one another on meeting. In the country not to speak to one's neighbor on encountering him would be very rude. In some parts of the South girls are quite accustomed to young men asking for late dates, a date—usually with an old beau—following one that may end at about eleven. Elsewhere such behavior might be considered questionable.

In young countries—and ours is certainly one when you think in terms of Paris's two thousand years—etiquette books have an important place. The physical and economic changes the country undergoes inevitably bring about fairly rapid social changes. The people who first come to virgin country usually arrive as workers, for every hand is needed, living facilities are at a premium, and there is little if any of the leisure or money necessary for the immediate development of an aristocracy. That is why all old American families such as mine have strong and simple roots here. Some of them may have brought with them the drawing-room manners of older civilizations, but they found that many of the niceties of living required adaptation—or else had to be discarded—in this vigorous, busy young land.

My great-great-grandfather, who "read law," was one of the founders of the Bank of Manhattan Company and a man of parts, as they used to say in those days. But in the tradition of his father and grandfather, Hollanders both, he was manually proficient and he had a proper respect for whatever work he did. He seems to have owned a number of "shoe manufactories," and I do not doubt that he could apply a sole with the same expertness that he used in some of the fine mahogany furniture he made for his family and which I still use. On the facing page is his advertisement in the *Diary; or Evening Register* of Wednesday, April 9, 1794.

My own line of descent from the first Vanderbilt to settle in America— Jan Aoertsen van der Bilt, who had a farm near Flatbush, Long Island— has been strongly Dutch, but I have a good admixture of Irish, English, and French blood. That and my partly European education, my fairly extensive traveling here and abroad, my years as a writer, as an etiquette adviser, and in business have given me a flexible attitude toward etiquette which is reflected, I am sure, in everything I have written on the subject.

WEDNESDAY, April 9, 1794.

OLIVER VANDERBILT,

At his Boot and Shoe Manufactory No. 7, the corner of Smith and Princefs-Streets,

TAKES this method, to return his thanks to his cuftomers, for their generous encouragement in the line of his bufinefs, and hopes by his fteady attention and abilities to ferve, to merit the fame. He has lately difcovered a method, which effectually prevents the prevailing evils fo common in the prefent mode of making boots which are thefe, the folding or running down behind and breaking above the counter and in the tongue, which frequently caufes almoft new boots not only to look bad, by caufing pieces to be put in them, but by running down wears very uncomfortably He continues to make, and has for fale, the following articles, wholefale and retail. viz.

	£.	s.	d.
Finifhed boots of Englifh ftuff - -	3	0	0
Do. tanned, brain and oil dreffed buck fkin legs - - - - - -	3	0	0
Do. American calf fkin, or cordiwan legs	2	16	0
Second quality ·do. do. do.	2	10	0
Stout ftrong boots · - -	2	4	0
Bootees of Englifh legs - -	2	5	0
Do. of American do. - -	.1· 18	0

I have a respect for people who do things with their brains and with their hands, who are not afraid of hard physical and mental work. I respect, too, people who are unpretentious yet mannerly, considerate and honest, forthright yet kind and tactful. I dislike display and foolish expenditure in the sense of what Veblen called "conspicuous waste," that is, spending to impress those who have less, as well as to impress associates. I dislike *chi-chi*.

I believe that knowledge of the rules of living in our society makes us more comfortable even though our particular circumstances may permit us to elide them somewhat. Some of the rudest and most objectionable people I have ever known have been technically the most "correct." Some of the warmest, most lovable, have had little more than an innate feeling of what

is right toward others. But, at the same time, they have had the intelligence
to inform themselves, as necessary, on the rules of social intercourse as related to their own experiences. Only a great fool or a great genius is likely
to flout all social grace with impunity, and neither one, doing so, makes the
most comfortable companion.

It is my hope that this book answers as fully and simply as possible all
the major questions of etiquette and most of the minor ones too. It is the
largest and most complete book of etiquette ever written. Like a dictionary,
it will have few cover-to-cover readers aside from my meticulous editor,
Marion Patton, the copy editors, and the proofreaders. But this undoubted
fact does not in the least disturb me, for a reference book such as this
has a long and much-thumbed existence. It can become a reliable friend
to whom one may turn many a questioning glance over the years and
get a helpful answer. It can put down roots and become an integral
part of the family, even be an objective counselor to the children as they
enter their teens.

It is axiomatic that as we mature and grow in years and experience we
must be able to meet more demanding social situations with confidence and
ease. This book contains, I believe, explicit information on every possible
social problem one is likely to encounter in modern social living.

Westport, Connecticut   AMY VANDERBILT
1952

CONTENTS

Part One

THE CEREMONIES OF LIFE

THE CEREMONIES OF LIFE

Every life, even that in a primitive society, has its ceremonies great and small, religious and non-religious. We observe small ceremonies when we say "good morning" and "good night," when we celebrate a birthday or attend a graduation. But the important ceremonies of life have to do with its beginning—the ritual of circumcision of the Jews and the Mohammedans, the Christian baptism or dedication of the child, the youthful years of courtship and marriage, and life's finale. People are born, are married, and, at length after a more or less ceremonious life, die. And everywhere friends, neighbors, and relatives take cognizance of at least the major ceremonies affecting each of us.

Of all life's ceremonies that of marriage is the most touching and beautiful. This is the long anticipated climax of girlhood—and boyhood, too— the doorway to true maturity, the farewell to parents as protectors, the acceptance of responsibility. Madame de Staël wrote, "Without marriage there is no happiness in love." Love seeks completion and the protection of marriage and the family.

All people everywhere rightly make a ceremony of marriage. They proclaim it publicly with a variety of rituals devised to impress its enormous importance on the hearts and minds of the participants and witnesses. All marriages should be solemn and well-proclaimed, with the vows exchanged in a dignified, suitable setting.

Whether the bride wears a lovely bridal gown or a simple cotton frock makes, of course, no difference in the dignity and impressiveness of the ceremony. I believe it is good and valuable if parents and friends gather together to witness the marriage in the traditional way and that it take place —preferably under some religious auspices—in the bride's place of worship or in her home. The elaborateness or simplicity of the wedding is of no real consequence. It is the spirit in which we marry that is truly meaningful.

Ceremony is really a protection, too, in times of emotional involvement, particularly at death. If we have a social formula to guide us and do not have to extemporize, we feel better able to handle life.

If we ignore ceremony entirely, we are not normal, warm human beings.

Conversely, if we never relax it, if we "stand on ceremony" in all things, we are rigid. We must learn which ceremonies may be breached occasionally at our convenience and which ones may never be if we are to live pleasantly with our fellow man.

Chapter 1

CHRISTENINGS

When the Baby is Christened

Usually only infants and very young children are given godparents, among those Protestants believing in baptism. When a child for some reason is not christened until he is eight or nine years old, presumably at the age of understanding and able to read the service with the clergyman, he may accept the sacrament on his own cognizance. His parents are present and he usually receives a baptismal gift of some significance.

Invitations to the Christening Invitations to a christening are always handled informally, by brief note, by phone, by telegram, or in person and should go only to those believed to be really interested in the event by reason of their relationship to or close friendship with the parents. Here is an example:

Monday

Dear Gertrude,
Cornelia is being christened this coming Sunday at church. Will you stay after the regular service for the ceremony and then join us at home for lunch?

Love,
Norma

Even such an informal note is not necessary if a guest is readily reached by phone.

Dressing the Baby for the Occasion The armful of petticoats and the long, embroidered christening dress are lovely but definitely a luxury, as the modern baby in everyday life is free of such bundling. If you have a christening gown that's been handed down or can borrow one or are given one, use it by all means, but a short white dress for a little baby—the kind all newborn babies receive from someone or other—will do for the christening. And shoes, even those little silk-topped and soled ones, are not necessary either. The baby wears white booties in cold weather and can be barefoot when it's warm. If he needs a bonnet and coat, it can be of any baby color, or white, but both are removed, as noted, before the ceremony.

What Others Wear   Adults and children attending the christening, whether at home or in church, dress as for church.

Godparents and Their Responsibilities

Godparents chosen, according to the custom of various denominations, from among close friends and occasionally relatives of the baby's parents are preferably of the same religion as the parents. Or, if they are not, they must be willing to answer the baptismal questions in the prayer book to serve at an Episcopal christening. Catholic children must have Catholic godparents. And Catholics may not serve as godparents to a child of another faith.

Godparents about the same age as the parents, or younger, should be chosen very carefully from among one's oldest and closest friends, as the association itself should be long and close with the child. In the service the godparents promise to oversee the spiritual education of the child and see that he is confirmed. They have an implied responsibility of parenthood, should the actual parents die before the child reaches maturity (although legal guardian arrangements are usually noted in wills). Once asked to serve as a godparent, a friend is virtually bound to accept.

The godparents need not be present at the christening but may be represented by proxies, who, too, are chosen from among close friends. Often various friends and relatives invited to the christening bring gifts to the baby, but the godparents always present him with something he can use and perhaps hand down to his own children—a silver porringer, a mug, or knife, fork, and spoon set. One of my children received a magnificent engraved Sheffield hot-water plate, fine for keeping his baby food hot but also fine for his eventual bachelor quarters. The plate will be excellent for hot hors d'oeuvres.

Sometimes the godmother—but not necessarily—furnishes the christening gown. This is the custom in the Russian Orthodox Church. The godmother dresses the baby and takes it to the church (with the godfather) where the christening gown as well as a white cloth (kryzhmy) has a special place in the christening rites. The christening gown need not be expensive but should of course be suitable for the occasion. The Orthodox godfather buys the cross, also used in the christening rites. Among the Orthodox it is a great privilege to be asked to be godparents and to decline the invitation is considered very rude.

Among the Greek and Russian Orthodox, especially the Ukrainian branch, children are given a token of recognition by their godparents on their birthdays. This is usually a greeting card. At Christmastime godparents expect a visit from their godchildren at which children receive a gift in celebration of the "holy supper," a festive meal prepared especially for Christmas Eve.

It is common in the Russian Orthodox church for a mother to say to her child, "If you misbehave, I will tell your godmother!" A godmother, in turn, will say to her godchild, "I gave you my promise in church to guide you. This was done in the presence of the priest who blessed you (and myself) so it is my duty to explain things to you you do not understand, or that you have to learn." To be disrespectful of one's godparents is unthinkable in this denomination. At the wedding of such a godchild, the bride's godmother has the first say in many decisions, but after the wedding, the duties of the godparents cease. This is generally true in other denominations.

Many godparents have a warm relationship with their godchildren throughout life. On the other hand, increasingly, godparents cease to take their responsibilities very seriously. Many may not have any contact with the children once they have reached their majority and the responsibilities of the godparents are over.

Some people are asked to be godparents over and over again. They should not accept such responsibility lightly, nor should they any longer, in most denominations, feel unable to refuse the honor politely if they already have a godchild or godchildren. A tactful reply might be, "I already have one (or more) godchildren. I do take the responsibilities seriously and I feel that I cannot accept the honor of being a godparent to still another child."

Church Christenings

If the christening is to take place in church, arrangements are made with the clergyman and the time set. As babies are not always too happy about their christenings, it is best for them to be brought to the church just before the event is to take place. The godparents arrive either with them or shortly before and take their places near the font in front of the clergyman, with other friends and relatives nearby.

If the baby has been dressed in cap and jacket for the trip to the church, the outer things are removed and, if the church is chilly, the baby is wrapped in a white afghan and handed to the godmother, without his cap. As the clergyman takes his place, the congregation stands. At the proper moment in a Protestant ceremony the godmother hands the baby to the clergyman and, when asked his name, pronounces it very carefully. Only the baptismal names are given, for example, Stephen John, not the surname. In the Catholic ceremony the godmother or a nurse holds the baby over the font to receive the holy water. If other than a godparent holds the baby, spiritual contact by the godparents is established by the godparents touching the child during the ceremony. If the name is at all complicated, it should be written down for the minister and handed to him just before the start of the ceremony, as the baby's baptismal name becomes his legally.

After the close of the service the clergyman signs the baptismal certificate, usually included in a little commemorative book where there are spaces for the names of the godparents, the parents, and the various witnesses to the ceremony. At a Catholic christening the baptismal certificate is not necessarily presented at the close of the ceremony but is available anytime. It is required for the child's first Holy Communion, for Confirmation, and for marriage.

The Clergyman's Fee   As with other church sacraments, there is never any required fee, but parents usually do hand the minister an envelope containing an appropriate amount, anywhere from five dollars to fifty dollars or more, depending on whether or not the christening is to be followed by a large luncheon, tea, or reception—to which the clergyman and his wife or the priest must be invited. Of course, particularly on Sunday, they may find it difficult to attend.

The Christening at Home

The baby is more likely to enjoy his christening if he may go through the short ceremony in the comfort of his own home, with as little change in his usual routine as possible. Some Protestant denominations permit home christenings. Catholics do not permit home christenings except in case of dire emergency before the administration of last rites.

The requirements are a pleasant, flower-decorated room with space for the assembled guests, a small, waist-high table on which is set a silver bowl to be used as the font. If the table has a high patina, it is often left bare, or it may be covered to the floor with damask. The base of the bowl may be placed within a circlet of delicate, white babylike flowers—sweet william, gypsophila, white violets, anemones, lily of the valley, or even fern. At a late afternoon christening followed by tea, white tapers in silver candlesticks, lighted of course, are suitable on the table if they don't crowd the arrangement.

At the home christening the clergyman is not necessarily in vestments, but if he is to dress he is shown to a special room. If the christening is followed by a reception he changes into his street clothes immediately after the ceremony before attending the reception.

If very young, the baby necessarily appears only briefly—just long enough for the ceremony. If he is older, and sociable, he may enjoy watching the celebration of the occasion by his elders from some quiet corner, where he may be occasionally admired but not disturbed by his well-wishers. He may even be able to enjoy a grain or two of his christening cake.

Refreshments after the Ceremony

Champagne, plain or in a delicate punch, has replaced the traditional caudle cup at christenings. But at an afternoon christening a good dry sherry or, in winter, a hot mulled cider or wine might be very welcome.

A morning or early afternoon christening is sometimes followed by a luncheon, often buffet. But whether a tea or a luncheon is given, the food is more or less the kind one serves at wedding receptions. There is some kind of festive beverage for toasting the baby's health, and the christening cake. The godfather proposes the first toast.

The cake is a white cake with white icing. It may have white icing decorations and often bears the baby's initials or name and sometimes the date of the christening.

It should be kept in mind that this is a celebration in honor of the baby, following a formal religious ceremony. It has a character quite different from a cocktail party and should be kept on such a plane that even the most conservative baby could not object to the behavior and bearing of his elders.

Chapter 2

DEBUTS

In Victorian days, when young girls up to the age of about eighteen were closely guarded at home, their debuts or formal introduction to their parents' friends in society had real meaning. World wars for a time had a sobering effect on debuts and there was a trend away from the individual lavish, often enormously expensive, presentation of a young girl by her family. The institution of mass debuts where a group, sometimes large, of girls is presented publicly for the benefit of some charity became established.

With the steady rise of personal income, the increasing entrance of newcomers to established social circles, there has been actually an increase in interest in debuts both private and public. Many communities that never had debuts now have their own cotillions, assemblies, or balls at which favored daughters are presented, with some debutantes bowing at several assemblies or cotillions at home and perhaps one or more in other cities where their families have social connections. Many of these are preceded by small private functions. Even in New York some newly established debutante balls, such as the International Debutante Ball, have become accepted and established rather quickly. As mass debuts these days are charity affairs with the debutante's family making a contribution, they do serve a useful purpose besides giving a girl a chance to wear a beautiful dress—usually white and diaphanous, though pastel colors are often permitted by the committee. Substantial expenditures for flowers, food, wine, liquors, music, invitations and other things required for ceremonious presentation are important factors in the continuance of the debut. There is even the suggestion that the debut as a status symbol has value to the fathers—business and professional men who pay all these expenses.

It looks as if the formal debut, like the formal wedding, remains a dream that well may become a reality for any girl whose family has the price and ambition to so launch her. The top debutante lists are still difficult for a girl to make, but there is now a wide variety of possible presentations in major cities around the country, with new groups springing up every season. In a number of urban areas, for example, Black groups have established their own debutante cotillions run in a formal dignified manner with all the protocol of the long established ones.

In the outrageous twenties, and even during the thirties, there were huge private debuts—especially in New York—whose cost and elaborateness were positively vulgar. Fifty thousand dollars for a debut was not an eye-popping sum by any means, and even this amount was superseded many times over by two internationally publicized debuts in the sixties. And all this fuss for young girls who had been seen around in night clubs and all the most prominent restaurants and resorts almost since their emergence from pigtails!

While the private debut still occurs occasionally, it is usually in the form of a dinner party or perhaps a dance at home or in a hotel. The dinner party, which is uaually given for the girl's friends rather than for those of her parents, may be given by her mother—or grandmother or other sponsor—together with the mother of another girl, as a joint effort. However, the afternoon reception or tea during the winter and spring college holidays has its adherents, and is growing in popularity.

It used to be that the debut coincided with the end of a girl's school days at about the age of seventeen or eighteen. Today, however, with most girls going on to college, the debut when it occurs is merely a break in the educational procedure. It is rather meaningless now as an announcement that the girl is on the marriage market, for with four years ahead of her of increasingly difficult college courses, the girl, if she is sensible, awaits the completion of her education before marrying. For this reason, or some other, many a girl who is socially eligible to make her debut chooses not to.

The Small Private Debut

Some socially well-entrenched families in such cities as Boston, Philadelphia, and New York, still choose to bring their daughters out privately at small exclusive functions at which their daughters are formally introduced to their own circle of friends with a minimum of publicity, and that most conservative. The debutante then enters into the debutante activities of her friends and may or may not be presented at one or more mass debuts. The debutante at such a debut in the evening may wear a bouffant dance dress, usually white, and her mother's formal evening dress may be dark in color but preferably not black. Both may wear some hair ornament—flowers or a diadem, but not hats. The father, in full evening dress, does not stand in line but, as at a wedding, usually hovers in the vicinity to act as host. Friends of the debutante, in dresses similar to hers, who have been asked to "receive" with her do not actually stand in the line, either. They just feel a little more important and, at a sit-down supper, are seated with the debutante. (For details of formal dance see "Formal Dances at Home," page 429.)

The Debutante Tea

The debutante "tea" is more properly a reception, as it is often followed by dancing, which naturally requires gentlemen, and the gentlemen, in turn, often prefer something stronger than tea. In this case, the tea table ceases to be the central theme and must cede honors to the bar. If the debutante tea dansant is in a club or hotel, champagne or cocktails may be passed by waiters or a table may be set up with a punch such as "Fish House."

There is a receiving line consisting of the mother of the debutante, or whoever the sponsor may be, and the debutante herself. Sometimes her father is in line for a short while in the beginning. She carries her father's bouquet and displays her own flowers in a floral background where she and the hostess stand, usually before a fireplace. Even though it may still be daylight, the curtains are drawn and the candles lighted. The debutante wears the kind of dress a bridesmaid would wear, usually white but perhaps a pale color. Her mother, or sponsor, wears a cocktail dress in a color other than black, preferably something fairly neutral, and they both are gloved but hatless. The debutante may wear a flower in her hair.

The debutante, as at an evening debut, asks numerous young men to act as ushers and tries to arrange it so that there are approximately eleven men to every ten girls. Some of her best friends are asked to "receive" with her. They wear fluffy, semiformal dresses, and perhaps the debutante may possibly give them identifying corsages, but they do not stand in line. They do, however, stay throughout the reception.

After all guests have been received the debutante may join the dancing, usually accepting her first invitation from her father.

Guests who must leave before the receiving line breaks up, wait their chance on the side lines, then say a brief "good-by and thank-you" first to the hostess, then to the bud. But every young man present at a tea dansant should seek a dance with the debutante, and well-bred young men remember to ask her mother as well as other older ladies present.

Fathers and Escorts

At debutante balls and cotillions, the girl being presented is sometimes escorted by her father, sometimes by her escort, depending on the custom of the particular group. In either case, the father and the escort wear tails and properly white kid or bleached chamois gloves, although I have also seen white cotton knit gloves worn (less successfully). Other men at debutante balls may of course wear tails and of course previously this was the custom for all male guests. Today, however, the majority not taking part in the actual presentation wear black dinner jackets in tropical weight.

Flowers for the Debutante

In New York, at public debuts for charity, the debutantes do not wear flowers although they have received them prior to the dinners or the functions that precede the public debut. In other communities, for example Dallas, the girls making their debuts are given many flowers. In some communities, florists who have a list of all the debutantes know what each debutante "still needs" in the way of flowers and also whether it is customary for them to receive corsages or baskets. In York, Pennsylvania, for example, a debutante may receive literally hundreds of corsages and arrangements. In one case the corsages were tacked on an enormous fan in a ballroom, and also to the wall, white floral arrangements were placed on each debutante's table. Each debutante wore a corsage, the gift of her escort.

The Coming of Age Celebration

Some girls who choose not to make their debuts prefer instead a very special party when they come of age. This party has many of the attributes of a debut without the many hectic, associated activities. Here is an engraved card invitation to such a party. The size is $5\frac{3}{4}'' \times 4\frac{1}{2}''$, and at the top there is an embossed crest.

In honour of the 21st Birthday of
Miss Margaret Carol Wilson
Mr. and Mrs. William Henry Wilson
request the pleasure of your company
at a small dance
Wednesday, the fifteenth of June
at nine o'clock
Hyde Lane
Wilton, Connecticut zip code

R.S.V.P.

Gifts to the Debutante

In addition to her flowers a debutante does receive gifts from close friends and relatives. There is a very wide range of possibilities—real jewelry of some kind, pearls—oriental or cultured, charms, gold-plated house key, diamond bracelets (from parents), fur coats, bonds, stocks, convertibles, watches, fine books (often specially bound), perfume. I often give quality boxed stationery with an unmarked die so that the debutante may choose the monogram she wants and, of course, such paper will be very useful for her many thank-you notes. During the debutante season, the debutante is constantly on the go and therefore has need of long white kid evening gloves and all kinds of evening accessories. Jeweled evening heels that can be attached to any evening slippers make a charming gift. Other possibilities are evening wraps, fine white initialled handkerchiefs, credit for limousine service (this may be a boon indeed) or a gift certificate at a top hairdresser's.

Chapter 3

COURTSHIP AND ENGAGEMENTS

Eventually, in the course of things, a girl begins to narrow her interest in young men to one young man. A fairly long courtship and a brief engagement seem to be a safe formula. The courtship period is casual and informal, without pledges on either side. It gives each a chance to know the other better—and yet make a graceful exit if that seems expedient.

Wherever possible, a girl should receive an attentive man in her own home and not see him exclusively in the artificial atmosphere of the theater, restaurants, and other places of amusement. He needs, if possible, to evaluate her with her family, or at least in her own home, and to see her with her friends, to help him decide whether or not life with her would be comfortable and companionable as well as romantically satisfying.

If her relationships with her family are good and happy, no girl need be ashamed to bring a suitor into the most modest home, even if he be from a more prosperous background. And, conversely, a man should be highly suspicious of the girl who does not wish him to meet her family and her intimate friends. It is important, too, for the girl to know and become familiar with his background and interests.

It is impossible for a man and woman to know whether they are really suited to one another if they spend all their courtship time in the exclusive company of each other. Each should give the other an opportunity to expose to searching consideration his best and worst sides. They should see each other in the give and take of family life, or at least among close friends with kindred interests. Otherwise a resulting marriage is in for rude shocks and accusations of, "If I'd known such and such I'd never have married you!"

Meeting a Man's Family and Friends

If a girl is taken to meet a man's family before he has said anything definite about marriage, she should be careful to be friendly and interested, but not *too* interested. Often a man is chary of introducing a girl into his own circle before he has very nearly made up his own mind about her, because either she or his family and friends might assume a seriousness about the relationship that may never develop. If he is wise, he might warn his family in advance not to jump to conclusions. And the girl must pretend not to hear any little inter-family raillery concerning John and herself. Nothing frightens a man more than presumption on the part of a woman. If ever a woman needs to be obtuse with the male it is when he is courting her but has not yet declared himself.

Gifts before the Engagement

A man's gifts to any girl other than a relative, before the engagement is announced, should be relatively impersonal. In other words, they should never admit—or imply—intimacy or be so costly or conspicuous as to cause talk. He might give her a scarf, gloves, or handkerchiefs, but not a dress, underthings, pantyhose, or fur of any kind. He might give her a book, but not an expensive set of books. If she's a bachelor girl with her own quarters he might give her a cocktail shaker or a toaster, if she needed or wanted one, and he knew her well enough, but never a nightgown or anything so intimate. He would, of course, pay for her taxi but never embarrass her by trying to pay the grocery or other household bill at the door or in a shop where they happen to be together. It is quite unsuitable, even after a formal engagement announcement has been made, for a young man to present a girl with a hope chest (What would he do with it if the engagement is broken?). The girl should buy one herself (or it should be a gift from relatives) if she really wants one. To do anything that puts a girl in an untenable position is to be less than a gentleman.

The Exception Is Liquor While a man visiting a woman at her own home may not pay for groceries or other household supplies should they happen to be delivered, he does pay for anything, such as liquor or food, he has ordered sent in, just as he would if he were the host in a restaurant. If, with his hostess's permission, he has ordered a special dinner sent in from a caterer, instead of taking her out, he takes care of the check. If he feels he has accepted her hospitality too often and wishes to replenish her bar supplies, he may do so—within reasonable limits. And always with her permission.

Refusing a Gift A too-intimate or too-expensive gift is sometimes offered by a man who just doesn't know any better. If a girl receives such a gift she should be tactful. She should not show it nor try to explain it. She should, instead, return it to the donor with some such remark as this, "I know you didn't realize it, but I couldn't possibly accept such a gift from you, much as I appreciate your kindness in wanting to give it to me. A *little* present would be better." If she does this in a kindly way he won't be too embarrassed, and she won't be compromised.

The Conference with Father

These days people feel it is their right and privilege to become engaged and to marry without the prior permission or sometimes even the knowledge of the bride's parents—or of the groom's. However, a wise couple will always discuss their plans for marriage with their respective families, and a young man should seek an interview with his prospective bride's father. She in fact might arrange this for the young man when she first mentions her plans to her father, by asking her father when it would be convenient for him to meet with his future son-in-law. A girl's parents, especially if they have been supporting their daughter, but even if she has been self-supporting and living away from home, have the right to know just how her fiancé proposes to take care of her after the marriage, in short, what his income is and his savings, if any, and what may be his future expectations. This conference is a good time to discuss these matters and others, such as where the couple plans to live, or any medical problems that might have a bearing on the father's consent.

Many a young pair vastly overestimate their ability to get along on the income available to them once they leave their parents' homes. They have little or no idea of what it costs to run even a simple establishment in the way they have been accustomed to living. A businesslike talk with the bride's father or perhaps a conference with all four parents can help start a young marriage along the right path, particularly if the couple is still in school and is frankly dependent upon one or both sets of parents for support. If the bride's father knows, for example, that the attractive and promising young man Mary wants to marry has only five hundred dollars in the bank, he may be able to augment that amount with a substantial cash gift in lieu of an elaborate wedding. Or he might plan a very practical present, such as a major furnishing item for their living quarters.

I once knew a debutante who, given her choice of a $30,000 wedding or the cash, chose the wedding with its twenty bridesmaids, full orchestra, champagne, several hundred guests and all the attendant expense, and then went to live in a one-room apartment with her young husband, whose salary was one hundred twenty-five dollars a week and whose savings were nil. Most brides don't have such a choice—or so little sense, either—but they can be helped to face reality with the counsel of older advisers.

In the event that either or both sets of parents objects strenuously to the proposed marriage, a big effort should be made to counter these objections in sane and rational discourse. If even this fails, then perhaps outside help should be sought from a clergyman, marriage counselor, or even a psychiatrist. A couple who completely disregard their parents' wishes concerning their ensuing marriage, may soon find themselves in a very isolated and untenable position.

It is very comfortable to start married life on a sound financial basis. If you are marrying on a shoestring, there is no shame in admitting it to one's family and intimate friends. In this way the inevitable presents can have a more practical aspect, especially if the engaged couple prepares a list of the things needed—from a toaster to dinnerware—and leaves this list, providentially with their parents.

Calling on the Bride's Parents

Another expected custom in connection with the engagement is for the parents of the prospective bride and groom to meet before the official announcement of the engagement. If they are not already close friends and if distance doesn't make it impossible, it is customary for the prospective groom's parents to pay a friendly, informal visit to the bride's family. Especially at the beginning of this meeting, no other family members should be present, except the bride and groom. In these days it is preferable to write or phone first to set a date for this important meeting. If no actual visit is possible, a phone call in which the groom's mother introduces herself and expresses her own and her husband's happiness about the forthcoming marriage may substitute, but even when this is done a letter from the groom's mother to the parents of the bride is correct and reassuring. Should the groom's parents not understand this convention then those of the bride should not stand on ceremony but make the initial call themselves, if necessary. If the groom's family travels some distance to pay this visit it is probably best that they stay elsewhere than the home of the bride's family, although the bride's family may offer to make hotel reservations for them nearby. This formal visit or letter is then followed by an invitation from the bride's family or the visit is formally returned. A letter may also be sent in acknowledgment of the letter of welcome.

So-called "Engagements"

It would seem axiomatic that you can't be engaged while still married to someone else. It is improper to announce an engagement while either member of the future union is still in the throes of divorce, movie and jet set dispatches notwithstanding. And for a woman to wear or even accept a man's engagement ring, even without announcement of an engagement, while her divorce from his predecessor is still pending or while his own divorce is pending is the height of bad taste.

Behavior During Engagements

If young people didn't want to make love most of the time during the period of their engagement it wouldn't seem normal. Everyone around them is conscious of how they feel and, up to a certain point, touched by their ecstasy. But if this joy becomes too tactile, onlookers are visibly embarrassed. Good manners always dictate that men and women be restrained about public demonstrations of their physical feeling toward one another.

While it is my conviction that decisions about premarital sexual relations are a private matter which each couple must decide for themselves, a couple do have obligations toward themselves, society, and their parents. First, they should exercise considerable discretion in their conduct. And second, any girl thinking of taking this important step, be she engaged or not, should consult a gynecologist, or at least her family doctor, to receive preliminary instruction about contraception. It may surprise you to learn that in one state alone one out of every four girls is pregnant when she marries. It is not possible to estimate how many of these marriages are forced. But it is wise to note that necessity is not a good basis for marriage, and that not all engagements lead inevitably to marriage.

If these rules seem hard and conventional to modern young people they should remind themselves that the engagement is a trial flight which can easily end in a crash landing. It is best to follow the rules, for few young, love-bewitched people are invulnerable enough to bring down social criticism without harm to their relationship.

How Long Should an Engagement Last?

It is wise for a couple to fix a date for the expected marriage, as a too attenuated engagement is hard for both, but particularly hard for the girl should the marriage not take place and her other possible suitors slip out of her circle. Except under extraordinary circumstances, a formal engagement should not last more than six months and most are three months or less. With so many young men in the Service and even where the couple may have an agreement between themselves, it is best to hold the announcement of the engagement until quite close to the date chosen for the wedding. And any man or woman who lets the engagement run into a matter of years for any reason whatsoever is not a good marriage risk—at least not for that possible partner.

Is an Engagement Irrevocable?

Engagements were made to be broken. Never, if you have just become engaged, assume that the engagement will necessarily terminate in marriage. If more engagements were honestly viewed before marriages are entered into there would be far fewer divorces. A man or woman should never be made to feel that by virtue of the exchange of an engagement ring he or she is irrevocably committed to the appointed marriage. This does not mean that an engagement should be lightly entered into or lightly broken. But an engagement is a tentative thing. It means, "If all goes well between us, we hope to be married at a later date."

The Engagement Ring

Many a modern bride eschews a diamond or any other engagement ring. If she does want one, she should help choose it, with the kind of wedding band she wants in mind. If her wedding ring is to be wide, she may decide that it would be more attractive to have that inset with small diamonds or some other stone, making it engagement-and-wedding ring in one. Two rings on one finger don't always make an attractive or comfortable combination. Sometimes an eager fiancé, buying an engagement ring without his bride-to-be, selects one that can't be worn with an ordinary wedding ring, so that after she is married the bride can wear her engagement ring only if she takes off her wedding ring, or she must have a new wedding ring made to fit under the engagement ring setting. If an engagement ring is given, the wedding ring should be of the same metal. It is the wedding ring that is worn first on the third finger when both rings are worn.

How Much for the Ring? We used to believe a young man should buy the finest engagement ring his circumstances permitted. If the engagement is to be fairly long and if a ring seems very important to the girl, she should have a ring. What it costs, whether or not it is a diamond, what size the stone is—are all irrelevant. Any girl worth her salt prefers a ring her man can afford to one for which he must go into debt or which his father must buy. On the other hand, she will gladly accept a family heirloom, if she is offered it, in place of a new ring. If the girl has a ring or stone in her family it is quite proper for the young man to have it reset at his expense and give it to her. It is possible she may really prefer some other article of jewelry, even when money is no consideration—a watch, bracelet, or pin.

If No Ring Is Given If a girl does not receive an engagement ring for one reason or another, her engagement may still be formally announced. If her friends ask, as they sometimes do, "Let us see your ring!" she can explain quietly that she has chosen another symbol of the engagement, or she will have her engagement and wedding ring combined in one band, as many do.

The Wedding Rings

Although the bride may help select her wedding ring, she does not see it again until the wedding.

The wedding band is usually engraved on the inside although the engagement ring is not. Arrangements should be made to pick up the engraved ring about one month before the wedding. Usual inscriptions are "J.W.M. to A.P." and the date, with the groom's initials first. If the band is wide, there may be room for anything else that may seem apropos. The modern bride doesn't worry about the occasional removal of her wedding ring— especially if she has one set with jewels that need professional cleaning.

If the groom wishes to wear a wedding ring, he should select one that is plain gold and definitely masculine. It is engraved as a gift from his bride "A.P. to J.W.M." with the date and, if the bride wishes, any phrase or motto that means something to them both. The groom's ring is the bride's gift to him. Today the wedding-ringed husband wears his ring on the third finger of the left hand, the same finger the bride's ring encircles.

Guard Rings The wearing of guard rings is a matter of personal taste. If you choose to wear one because you have the kind of fingers that look more attractive with wide bands, it may be set with diamonds, semiprecious stones, or even with rubies, emeralds, or sapphires. A woman may even prefer to wear two guard rings, one above and one below the wedding band.

A guard ring set with precious stones makes a nice gift for a memorable anniversary. But if the wife wants one, there is no reason she cannot purchase it for herself.

Joint Checking Accounts

It is possible for the engaged couple to have a joint checking account or a joint savings account to take care of gifts of money that may come in after the announcement of their engagement. Such an account would read "Mary Anne Parker and/or John Talbert." The couple are then called joint tenants and have what is known as rights of survivorship. If one dies the other gets whatever is in the account. Joint accounts are usually not set up until just before the wedding is to take place. This is wise because, in the case of a broken engagement, complications may arise in returning money given by friends and relatives, particularly if some of it has been used for the purchase of household furnishings and so forth.

Checks presented before the wedding may be made out either to the girl alone, "Mary Anne Parker," or to them jointly, "Mary Anne Parker and/or John Talbert."

Engagement Parties

Engagement parties are given by the parents of the bride-to-be or by a relative of the bride acting for her parents, usually just before the newspaper announcement of the engagement. The couple does not give such a party for themselves, unless the bride has no family to sponsor her. Invited to them are those closest to the couple—relatives and friends of both families, young and old. Occasionally, if the fiancé is not present, the party is limited to women guests and may be a luncheon or tea. Teas are also appropriate with men included if they are scheduled for a weekend. It is proper to serve sandwiches, either open or closed, and salad at this type of tea. Sometimes it is an evening reception, dinner, or "at home."

Since the announcement is usually planned to be made as a "surprise" sometime during the party, invitations generally do not hint at the real occasion. If the groom is a stranger in the community, invitations might be on the parents' joint visiting cards with "To meet Mr. Robert Brown" written on them in black ink. Or they could be engraved or printed blank invitations with that or any other information concerning the party filled in.

The news of the engagement is made known in various ways. At a luncheon or tea, women guests may be met at the door with a basket of individual flowers, such as carnations, to which are attached double cards with the two names, "Betty and Tom," or if one or the other is quite unknown to the majority, the names in full. Also the young couple might receive with the host and hostess, although a formal receiving line is not necessary. At many parties in the East the young man is introduced to small groups at the party rather than in a general introduction.

In some parts of the country great ingenuity is shown in the disclosure of the news. At smaller gatherings, especially family dinners, a toast to the couple often serves this purpose nicely and is proposed by the girl's father, at the end of the meal, in champagne. If a minister or priest is to be present to bless the couple, this is best done immediately following the father's announcement. This would be true at either a sit-down dinner or a buffet reception.

The bride-to-be may have her engagement ring on her finger at the announcement party. However, she does not officially show it to her friends until the announcement is made either by her father or in some other way if the surprise element is to be maintained. An engaged girl may give her fiancé an engagement gift after she has received her ring. It is usually something of a personal nature, such as gold cuff links, a watch or watch chain (for evening wear), or studs.

Guests at an engagement party may or may not, as they wish, bring gifts. Linens, household appliances, jewelry, lingerie, are all suitable.

Announcing the Engagement in the Newspapers

The engagement of a young couple is announced in the newspaper at the time of the engagement by the parents of the bride. (For exceptions see "Complicated Relationships," page 25.)

Here is a complete engagement announcement.

CYNTHIA ANN TALBOTT
TO WED ASA G. SANTOS

Mr. and Mrs. Loring Talbott, of 10 Low Place, announce the engagement of their daughter, Cynthia Ann, to Mr. (optional) Asa Griggs Santos, son of Dr. and Mrs. José Santos of Caracas, Venezuela. (Note that the groom's name is spelled out in full in this press announcement, and it is stated whose son he is. No mention is made in the engraved wedding invitations or announcements of the groom's parents.)

Miss Talbott is a graduate of The Hewitt School and of Vassar College. Mr. Santos is a senior in the Yale School of Medicine and a member of Phi Beta Kappa. The wedding will take place in June.

In the news story just given as an example, Low Place is, let us say, in the town in which the paper is published, so it is not necessary to give more than the street address.

If the time of the wedding is within one to three months of the engagement, the month the wedding will take place is mentioned. If no date has been set for the wedding, or if there will be a lapse of time of more than three months, then the announcement should read, "No date has been set for the wedding." It is not necessary to include the names of attendants, or the time and place of the ceremony in your release, even if the announcement is made very close to the date of the wedding.

How Much Information in the Engagement Announcement? If an engagement is between very prominent people the engagement announcement may carry all the family information about the couple. But usually the engagement announcement is brief and the more detailed information, if it is considered newsworthy, is carried by the papers at the time of the wedding. But when more details are given with the engagement news they are usually repeated when the wedding is reported, so if you think the papers will use them with either or both stories, furnish them yourself; don't leave it to telephone reportage.

In a situation where the bride has a title, such as doctor of dentistry or doctor of medicine, this title in its abbreviated form, for instance, Dr. Alice Landau, not Doctor Alice Landau, may be used in newspaper announcements of the engagement only if the bride announces her own engagement. If her family issues the announcement her title is not used, upon the first mention of her name which reads "Their daughter, Ann Reeves Tuttle." Thereafter when her profession is mentioned she is referred to as Dr. Tuttle.

Some newspapers have standard forms to be filled out for announcements. Society editors will supply these on request.

The Release Date When an engagement is of sufficient news importance to warrant straight news and perhaps press association coverage to other cities, it is best to decide on the date you would like to see it appear in all your city's papers simultaneously. Then you furnish it to each paper in written form one day, or, preferably more in advance with the notation FOR RELEASE MONDAY, FEBRUARY 6TH typed in the upper left-hand corner in capital letters. To the city editor, to whom such a release should be directed, this means that you have put the same limitation on all other releases furnished his rival papers. If in his estimation the announcement does not merit regular news coverage, the city editor will route it through to the society editor, to whom such announcements are ordinarily sent. Weeklies need engagement and wedding announcements three or more days before their publication dates.

Choice of the Release Date Why so many people send in their wedding and engagement announcements for the Sunday papers, I don't know. That is one way to have your cherished notice attenuated and lost in a sea of other notices or dropped entirely, because of the competition from announcements the editor may consider more newsworthy for one reason or the other. Even if your notice does get into the Sunday paper, it is very likely that your friends will fail to see it because so many are published that day. And the possibility of a picture being used on Sunday is very slight indeed—again because of the competition. But Monday is a slow news day.

An engagement announcement sent to an urban paper for hoped-for Monday release should be so marked (FOR RELEASE MONDAY, FEBRUARY 6TH) so that it won't get into the Sunday paper by mistake. It should arrive at the newspaper office sometime Saturday, preferably in the morning before eleven. Wedding announcements should be timed to reach papers so the news can appear as soon after the wedding as possible. It is quite usual for early editions of city papers to publish details of an important wedding that will take place later in the day. It is convenient for the paper to have the story all set and ready to run before the wedding occurs. Wedding news that arrives very late must be very important to make the paper. Announcement information may be sent only to the paper of the bride's family's choice, or to all local papers, or even to the wire services' regional outlets, if you like.

Identifying Your Releases If you send news to the paper or to radio stations, always place your name, address, and telephone number in the upper right-hand corner of the page. This is so the editor will know who stands back of the story and to whom he may turn for additional information, if needed. Unidentified stories are often discarded by editors, unless they wish to bother to check the information by phone.

In a household where there is a social secretary, her name and title, Miss or Mrs., together with the address and telephone number appear on social announcements from the family. Or the father of the bride or engaged girl may have his own secretary prepare and send out the information. She can refer to him or to the girl's mother any requests for additional information. Any member of the family or a close friend may act as spokesman with the press, but the bride or bride-to-be does not send out her own notices under her own name, even though she may prepare them for someone else to send for her. She may, of course, answer questions from the newspapers herself, but it is more usual for editors to call her parents for added information, if they are available for comment.

It is also a good idea to put some kind of heading on the news story so a busy editor can see at a glance what it is about. To look professional, the head should space out to the same number of "characters" for each line. Each letter and space is a character in the count. For your purpose you needn't be too accurate about it.

Sending Pictures If you wish, send a picture of the engaged girl with the announcement. The picture should have a caption attached, not written on the back of the picture. Type the information, "Miss Cynthia Ann Talbott whose engagement to Mr. Asa G. Santos is announced," on a piece of 8½"×11" typewriter paper. Then paste the caption so that it folds over the picture. Enclose the picture, accompanying release, and protective cardboard in a mailing envelope and send "special" to papers of your choice or, better, have delivered by hand to either city or society desk as the news seems to warrant. It is unusual for engagement pictures to be used in the paper, since wedding pictures are so much more interesting, so don't be disappointed if yours doesn't appear.

If the groom has lived in another city and his parents are still there, a duplicate copy of the announcement, with or without a picture, is sent to them or to their newspaper.

Is the Man's Picture Furnished? Wedding pictures often include the groom, but pictures used with the engagement announcement usually do not include the fiancé. However, when the principals are page-one news the paper will usually request a picture of the fiancé if it does not have one of him in its files or "morgue." For example, if an unknown college student became engaged to the daughter of one of the wealthiest men in the country the papers would certainly consider the young man worth a picture and might, in fact, go to some lengths to secure one, if it wasn't furnished with the announcement from the family.

Different Pictures to Competing Papers Newspapers prefer, if possible, to receive pictures that differ somewhat from those furnished to the other dailies in the same town or city. When the girl selects her pictures from the proofs, she should keep this in mind and try to choose several poses instead of having just one printed. Pictures for the press should be furnished on glossy stock, 8″×10″ size for easy filing. It is presumptuous to ask the paper to return them after use—or even if they don't use them.

Don't "Edit" the Release If you are a newsworthy person it is probable that all leading newspapers have a file of information on you or your family. If an announcement of your marriage is going to the papers and you have been married before, do not omit that information, as some paper is sure to include it, perhaps to the irritation of others that didn't check their files more carefully. The information does not have to be played up, but it is part of the story. A line or two at the bottom of the story can cover it: "This is Mrs. Morgan's second marriage. Her first husband was Robert Henry from whom she was divorced last year. She had two children by this marriage, Patricia and Ogden Henry."

The polite phrase "from whom she was divorced" is better than "whom she divorced," which sounds accusative. Even if her husband divorced *her*, the fact is never stated in social announcements. Never, ". . . Robert Henry who divorced her last year."

If the Files Are Wrong One reason it is a good idea to furnish complete family information, if it will be of interest to the papers and if they are sure to publish it anyway, is that very probably there is some incorrect information in the newspapers' morgues. When a person or a family is prominent, clips, sometimes extensive ones, are kept on all his or its published activities. If one story or item appears and some information in it is incorrect, that goes into the file, too, perhaps to plague the family or individual regularly from time to time as what he does makes news. I was once referred to as the niece—or perhaps it was the grandniece—of Mrs. Cornelius Vanderbilt, which I am not, but I expect to see that reference turn up from time to time because it is in many newspaper morgues.

Complicated Relationships

Deceased Parent or Parents If both parents of the bride are deceased, the engagement may be announced by a close relative, a guardian, or a friend. The word "late" should precede any reference made to either of the parents. If one parent has died and the remaining parent is not close to the child, or is one who prefers to ignore their relationship, the announcement may be issued by another relative, but mention of the living parent should be made in any newspaper releases.

If the father or mother is deceased, and the other parent has not remarried, the announcement might be worded:

Mr. (or Mrs.) Eldon Hartwell Crosby announces the engagement of his (or her) daughter, Ellen Ragland, to Mr. (optional) Gordon Allen Dayton. Miss Crosby is also the daughter of the late Mrs. (or Mr.) Crosby, etc.

An announcement that gives the deceased some identification of his or her own is the following:

Mr. James Muncie announces the engagement of his daughter, Julia, to Edgar Allen Finley. Miss Muncie's late mother was the former Geraldine Pew, descendant of General Custis Pew, one-time business associate of Abraham Lincoln, etc.

If the father is deceased and the mother has remarried, the announcement reads:

Mr. and Mrs. Paul Johnston of 1020 Columbia Heights, Brooklyn, announce the engagement of Mrs. Johnston's daughter, Althea Frances Warren, to Alfred Martin Otis (optionally "Mr."). Miss Warren is also the daughter of the late Clarence Edward Warren, etc.

Should the mother be deceased and the father remarried, one method of handling the announcement is as follows:

Mr. and Mrs. Ralph Eggleston announce the engagement of Mr. Eggleston's daughter, Judith Anne, to Thomas Randolph Turner (optionally "Mr."), etc.

If the daughter has never known her real mother, the announcement might be:

Mr. and Mrs. Ralph Eggleston of Sutton Place South announce the engagement of their daughter, etc.

Divorced Parents When parents are divorced, the mother usually makes the announcement, but the father *must* be mentioned in the story. Even in the case of the second marriage of a divorced or widowed daughter it is appropriate for the mother (if she is also divorced) to make the announcement if she so desires. In the case of a second marriage however, the woman (particularly if she is older) always has the option of announcing her own engagement, if it is announced at all, jointly with her new fiancé. A typical announcement by a divorced mother who has not remarried should read:

Mrs. French Weeks (a combination of the mother's married and surnames) of 1125 Park Avenue announces the marriage of her daughter, Pamela, etc. Miss Weeks is also the daughter of Mr. George Ranson Weeks of Asheville, N.C.

If this form is used, no mention of the word "divorce" is necessary as it is clear that the parents are divorced and it is assumed, unless otherwise noted, that Miss Weeks lives with her mother.

If parents are divorced and the mother has remarried, the announcement reads:

Mr. and Mrs. Clifford Jones Stoddard announce the engagement of Mrs. Stoddard's daughter, Miss Pamela Weeks, etc. Miss Weeks is also the daughter of Mr. George Ranson Weeks of Asheville, N.C.

If it is the parents of the groom who have been divorced a similar formula is followed in both the engagement and wedding announcements for the newspapers.

Mr. Rank is the son of Mrs. Alston Rank of Nashville, Tennessee, and Mr. Morris Seale Rank of Atlanta, Georgia.

In rare cases when the father makes the announcement of his daughter's engagement or marriage, it is worded the same as when announced by the mother.

If the mother is remarried and her daughter has known only her step-father, the announcement might be:

Mr. and Mrs. Clifford Jones Stoddard announce the engagement of their daughter, Miss Pamela Weeks, etc.

If a girl whose parents were divorced and whose mother has subsequently died has been brought up by her aunt and uncle, the announcement of her engagement reads like this:

Mr. and Mrs. Seth McClure of 7 Fifth Avenue announce the engagement of their niece, Miss Sally Guthrie, to Mr. (optional) Penn Snyder, Jr., son of Mr. and Mrs. Penn Snyder, also of this city (often the fiancé's complete address is omitted from the engagement announcement). Miss Guthrie is the daughter of Mrs. McClure's late sister, Mrs. Broadhurst Guthrie, and of Mr. Joseph Guthrie. (This indicates that Sally's father was divorced from her mother at the time of her mother's death and that he has married again. To call her the daughter of Mr. Joseph Guthrie and the late Mrs. Guthrie would be, in effect, to kill off his second wife.)

If a girl has a stepmother with whom she feels closer to than her real mother and the announcement is being made by her father and stepmother, her own mother should accept the fact that she should be merely an invited guest at an engagement party at which the stepmother is the hostess. Her real mother has the option of giving a separate party to announce the news to her friends.

Separated Parents   When parents are legally separated, engagement announcements are made in the name of the parent (or relative) with whom the bride lives. This is usually the mother, who must still use her husband's name, i.e., Mrs. Allen Smithton, *not* Mrs. Joan Smithton.

Adopted Children   When a child has been adopted by a couple, taken their name, and been brought up as one of their own children, there is no reason why the adoptive relationship need be mentioned in the engagement or marriage announcement, even if the fact is generally known. But if the child bears another name it is necessary.

Under special circumstances, sometimes a bachelor or an older, unmarried woman adopts a daughter who may or may not have taken her adoptive parent's name. In such cases the engagement notice reads:

Miss Wilhelmina Bosworth announces the engagement of her adopted daughter, Miss Sybil Frank, etc.

or:

Dr. Orrin Metcalf announces the engagement of his adopted daughter, Florence, etc.

In the case of an underage orphan fond of his or her state appointed legal guardian, it may be mentioned in the newspaper article that the bride or groom is, "the ward of Mr. Alton Dodsworth."

Legally Changed Name   Occasionally you see an engagement announcement or a notice of a marriage where some mention is made of a legally changed name. For example:

Mr. and Mrs. Josef Greenberg of 50 Central Park South announce the marriage of their daughter Dorothy to Robert Harris, son of Mr. and Mrs. Chaim Hirsh, also of this city. Mr. Harris changed his name legally.

This clears up Mr. Harris's status but is not strictly necessary so long as the notice states that he is the Hirshes' son. The reader will assume he changed his name, something he has a perfect right to do with or without legal recourse. And if the change did not go through the courts, it is certainly not necessary to mention the name change and the term "changed his name legally" is not used.

The Bride on Her Own   When a woman has reached "a certain age" she has the choice of letting her parents or some relative, such as her brother, if her parents are dead, announce her marriage or of doing it in conjunction with the groom. Formal engagements between people, one of whom, at least, has been married before, are rarely announced. The publicized engagement period does seem the prerogative of youth, along with the bridal veil and orange blossoms. Older or divorced people usually make a simple announcement of their marriage. If a joint announcement is to be made, it reads:

Mrs. Prime Holden of 8 East 10th Street and Mr. Rutherford Tyng of Princeton, New Jersey, announce that their marriage took place Saturday, April 3rd, at the Church of the Ascension, Baltimore, Maryland. Mrs. Holden, the former Elsbeth Finn, is the daughter of Mr. and Mrs. Clarence Finn of Baltimore. Her marriage to Mr. Harry Holden of Tulsa, Oklahoma, was terminated by divorce last year. (Sometimes the last line needs merely "was terminated by divorce.")

Mr. Tyng, son of Professor and Mrs. Rufus Tyng of Princeton, is an instructor in mathematics at Princeton University, where his father heads the Physics Department. The couple will make their home in Philadelphia.

If the Engagement Is Broken

If notices of an engagement have appeared in the newspapers and the engagement is subsequently broken, additional notices are often sent, though not too hastily. Lovers quarrel, but they also make up. The announcement, if sent, is brief and to the point:

Dr. and Mrs. Richard Shawe, of 66 Riverside Terrace, announce that the engagement of their daughter, Celeste, to Mr. Bertram Farmer, has been broken by mutual consent.

As engraved engagement announcements are not sent out it is not necessary to retract the announcement to one's friends except in the most casual way—in conversation, in letters, "by the way, Bert and I broke our engagement recently." It is not necessary or wise to go into the reasons for a broken engagement outside of the family circle.

If a girl decides to break her engagement she returns the man's ring, although legally it is hers to keep—a gesture that would certainly be considered mercenary. If her fiancé dies no one would expect her to return the ring to his family, if he has one, although if she does not know them well and has received a family heirloom as an engagement present she should at least offer to return it. If she has been given a new ring she can continue to wear it, but not on the engagement finger. She may wish to have the stone reset in some other piece of jewelry. She is not required in this unfortunate instance to return any gifts she may have received from family or friends but she may well wish to do so.

Returning Gifts Gifts that she may have received from friends are returned to them with tactful notes of explanation. For example:

Tuesday

Dear Helen,
You will be sorry to learn that Bob and I have broken our engagement. I'm returning your sweet gift, separately, with great regret.

Love,
Marion

In the case too of an annulment which takes place very shortly after the marriage, any gifts that are unused should be returned. But where the annulment takes places after a considerable lapse of time, it isn't often practical or possible to return wedding gifts.

How Not to Announce or Break an Engagement It is a travesty on marriage when young people, often under direction from press agents, "announce" their engagements or the breaking of them in night clubs or restaurants. Such announcements should come from the girl's parents through formal notice in the press if the families are of sufficient interest to warrant publication of the news. Of course, an engagement may be announced at a party, possibly in a restaurant—but not in a night club. If an engagement party of some kind is given—a luncheon, tea, or dinner—it is more usual for it to be given at the bride-to-be's home and it is limited to the immediate families and very close friends.

Chapter 4

WEDDING INVITATIONS AND ANNOUNCEMENTS

Preparing the List

It is the bride's family that sets the size and style of the wedding, according to the wishes of the bride herself, unless these seem totally unreasonable. No family should go into debt over an extravagant wedding not in keeping with their daily life style. For very small or informal weddings engraved invitations are not necessary. The bride may call, wire, or write personal invitational notes in these cases. If, however, a large wedding is decided upon, the necessary invitation lists must be started almost as soon as the engagement is announced or this vital clerical chore will still be hanging fire during the complicated arrangements for such a wedding.

The groom and his family must co-operate by furnishing their invitation and announcement lists as early as possible, so the bride may combine them with her own usually larger lists, remove duplications, and, if necessary, shorten the lists with the help of both families. The groom's family should be allowed one half the total number of invitations, unless the majority of his relatives and friends live at a considerable distance, in which case a smaller proportion of the invitations may suffice and a larger list for announcements substituted. In either case, the proportion should be agreed upon by the groom and his family.

When the groom's family supplies its list, the complete names and addresses of all those to receive invitations should be clearly spelled out, just as they will appear on the envelope. For instance, the list should read, "Mr. and Mrs. John David Cates," and *not*, "Mr. and Mrs. J. D. Cates," or, "Cates, Mr. and Mrs. John David." Zip codes should be furnished with all addresses.

For a large formal wedding many more people receive invitations than can possibly accept. Even close friends and relatives at a great distance are informed by means of the invitation that the wedding is taking place. The list should include all relatives of the bride and groom, all close friends of both families, neighbors, old family retainers, business associates of the two fathers and of the groom and, of course, of the bride, if she's a career girl and will continue her work. But wedding invitations should never be sent indiscriminately to casual acquaintances of either a business or a social nature. These people often feel obligated to send a gift, and this is an imposition. If one wishes to invite superficial business associates and customers to the ceremony only, this may be done verbally or through the posting in a place of business of the invitation. And, incidentally, invitations should be sent *through the mails* to the parents of the groom, members of the wedding party, and the minister and his wife. These are treasured as mementos of the occasion. The mother of the bride might wish to enclose a short note in the invitations or announcements to the groom's immediate family to the effect that she thought they might like them for sentimental reasons. Parents of members of the wedding party should receive wedding invitations but do not necessarily have to be invited to the reception if it is limited in size. If an attendant is married, it is customary to invite his wife, although he should not expect to be seated with her at the reception, nor must she necessarily be included in the rehearsal dinner. He should not expect that his children be included in his invitation. It is not necessary to invite a friend for each unmarried person invited to the reception. If you do wish unmarried persons to bring an escort of their choice, you should either ascertain the names and addresses of the preferred escorts from the persons, and send them separate invitations, or include a personal note in your friends' invitations (written of course in black ink) saying, "Please bring Mr. Robert Brown," or "Please bring an escort." No one, by the way, should ask to bring a friend to a wedding reception unless the friend is to substitute for a husband or wife or some family member actually on the guest list. An engaged girl may ask that her fiancé be included, and an engaged man may ask to have his fiancée placed on the list.

The full list is then broken down into (1) those who receive invitations to the wedding, (2) those who will receive a reception card in addition, (3) those who will receive announcements and "At Home" cards, if any.

Ordinary three-inch by five-inch file cards with two sets of alphabetical indexes and two convenient boxes provide the best method of compiling a working list. Cards of different colors may be used on the finished list to indicate quickly into which category each name falls, but the usual method is to write in colored pencil an initial on the top right- or left-hand corner of each card—"C" for ceremony, "R" for reception, as well as ceremony, "A" for announcement.

In filing the cards follow the alphabetical procedure, don't just put all the A's or B's together or duplications will be hard to locate. Using such an easily expansible—or contractible—file is better than just typing up lists on sheets of paper or entering names in a notebook under alphabetical headings where they may end up a thicket of crossed-out names that will make addressing confusing.

The second file box should hold "Acceptances" and "Regrets" so that when the reception preparations are made a fairly accurate count may be had, with some allowance made for last-minute changes. Both acceptances and regrets should be filed alphabetically, too.

Invitations to Those in Mourning

People in mourning are included in the wedding invitation list, and may accept just as they would attend church services or continue to sing in the choir. If their bereavement had been very recent, they might attend the wedding but not the reception, always a gay social function. It is even possible for one in mourning to be in the bridal party. If she's a bridesmaid she dresses exactly as the rest, and a mourning usher or best man never wears a band on his sleeve (a custom occasionally seen). All the attendants are considered to be in wedding uniform, their own problems and personalities subjugated for the day they are in the service of the bride and groom. This is understood by everyone, and only if bereavement has been very recent and very close is it sometimes necessary for an attendant to ask to be excused, not because of possible criticism, but because his own obvious sorrow might cast a shadow on the happy day.

When Should Invitations and Announcements Be Sent?

Wedding invitations, unlike ordinary social invitations, are sent as much as four weeks in advance of the wedding and never less than two. Ideal timing is probably to mail them three weeks in advance to guests nearby and four weeks ahead to those coming from a distance. Engraved invitations take time and should be ordered at least seven or eight weeks before they are to be sent out, with consideration given the time it will take to address outer and inner envelopes. One may of course pick up the envelopes in advance so that the addressing can be completed before the invitations arrive. Announcements, ordered at the same time, are not, of course, sent out until after the marriage has taken place, but, if possible, they should be ready for mailing immediately after the ceremony, so that news of the marriage in the papers does not too much predate friends' receipt of the announcements.

Engraving and Stationery

It is far better to write personal letters or inform your friends of your marriage by phone than to have your invitations and announcements printed, rather than properly engraved. Of the various types of lettering available, the least expensive, and the most used, is graceful script. It costs no more to go to a really good, fashionable stationer for your announcements or invitations. There you will see styles of engraving such as the shaded, or shaded antique, Roman currently in vogue. There are slight variations from time to time, but essentially the engraving procedure is rigidly conventional. Do it right, or don't do it at all.

Paper and Envelopes Use the best paper you can afford for announcements or invitations. People do look at the quality of paper, and many inspect the envelopes to see the name of the stationer from whom you ordered. The name of a good stationer embossed under the flap of the envelope lends a certain cachet and costs nothing extra.

The most distinguished wedding paper is the traditional ivory or ecru. Pure white is now seldom used. Some good stationers are showing papers in deep or off-beat light colors, for example, avocado green with white engraving, salmon with silver, etc.—for, I assume, the totally nonconformist bride who by the same token will probably dispense with wedding gown and veil. I am merely reporting this minority preference.

Needless to say, the engraving is always in black and on the first page of the double sheet. If the bride's family has a coat of arms, a small crest, shield, and motto may be embossed—not die-stamped—in color as on ordinary stationery at the top of the first page. However, this is not done if a woman, *alone,* makes the announcement or issues the invitation. If the bride's family has no coat of arms, she may not use the crest of her husband-to-be until they are actually married, but, even then, if her family issues announcements, the husband's device may not be used on them, although the bride's family's may be (see "Heraldic Devices," page 615). If the couple themselves make the announcement, the husband's full coat of arms may be embossed.

Two envelopes are usually used for wedding invitations and announcements, although only one may be. Where two envelopes are used, the inside one is unsealed (and must not be gummed), and is placed in the outer envelope so that it faces the flap. A well-known stationer urges its customers to include half-tissues with large invitations that must be folded to be inserted in the envelope. This is to prevent smudging. On small invitations that do not require folding, tissues may be dispensed with.

The length of the names, the style of lettering, and, in this case, whether or not plate-marked paper will be used has much to do with the size of the paper you choose. There are many acceptable variations, but a fairly standard size is seven and one-half inches by five and one-half inches for a folded invitation or announcement. Smaller announcements or invitations which may be inserted into the envelopes unfolded are also correctly used, but if reception or "At Home" cards are to be enclosed, it is possible they may never be seen if the unfolded style is used.

It is of course possible for a bride, especially one with an attractive or exceptional handwriting, to choose to write all of her own invitations. In cases where this is done, one should use only the highest quality fold-over stationery, preferably white. Black ink should be used.

How to Address the Envelopes

The addressing of wedding invitations, and announcements is rigidly prescribed. Abbreviations are not permitted except in "Dr.," "Mr.," "Mrs.," and "Jr." (or "Lt." when combined with "Colonel," etc.) or in an initial of a name if you don't know it in full. The names of cities and states are written out. When an invitation or announcement is being mailed in the same city as that in which the wedding is taking or has taken place, it has been customary to omit the name of the state. However, in expanding America, where mail delivery is much more difficult than formerly, it is becoming a matter of necessity for the state to be included as well as the zip code in the address. For instance:

Mr. and Mrs. Cedric Moore McIntosh
1886 Shore Road
Chicago, Illinois zip code

Where there are several members of a family to be invited, avoid the phrase "and family." On the inside envelope is written:

Mr. and Mrs. McIntosh
(NO CHRISTIAN NAME)
Belinda and Gordon
(IF THE CHILDREN ARE UNDER AGE)

But if there is an adult daughter or son or other woman or man in the household you wish to invite, she or he must receive a separate invitation. Anyone over eighteen should receive a separate invitation:

Miss Margaret McIntosh
1886 Shore Road
Chicago, Illinois zip code

The inside envelope reads:

Miss McIntosh

If there are two sisters write:
The Misses Agnes and Ann McIntosh (or Misses Agnes and Ann McIntosh) and on the inside envelope The Misses McIntosh (or Misses McIntosh) with no address, of course, on the inner one.

Two grown sons (over eighteen) receive one invitation if they live at the same address. They are addressed as:
The Messrs. Keith and Ian McIntosh (or Messrs. Keith and Ian McIntosh) with simply The Messrs. McIntosh (or Messrs. McIntosh) inside.

In the case of a person who possesses a doctorate (a Ph.D.) and who usually uses his title, the envelope should be addressed to Doctor, or Dr., depending on the length of his name.

If you are sending an invitation to two persons of the same last name both of whom are medical doctors, you address it to, "The Doctors Smith."

Women who are widows or are separated are addressed as, "Mrs. George Hart."

Return Addresses It is now essential to have a return address on a wedding announcement or invitation, but this should not be engraved or printed on the flap, though it may be embossed, a somewhat expensive procedure. An alternative would be to have stickers printed—black ink on a white background—to be placed in the upper left-hand corner on the envelope (preferred by the post office) or on the flap in the back, or you could write it inconspicuously in black ink. Black ink, by the way, and never a ball point pen, should be used in addressing envelopes.

Stamps The dignity of a wedding invitation or announcement, it almost goes without saying, requires first-class postage. Stamps should be placed carefully, not stuck on any way at all. The necessarily careful addressing and stamping of the envelopes requires that the work be started before the bride or her family is worn out by bridal preparations.

Penmanship It is also traditional for the handwriting (in black ink) on the envelopes of wedding invitations and announcements to be obviously feminine and, if possible, of the rounded, clear, English style affected by social secretaries. The address, of course, may never be typed. If no social secretary is used for a large wedding, friends or relatives may be called on to help, but if more than one person does the addressing, the handwritings should be as similar as possible.

Wording of Formal Invitations

Invitation to Church Ceremony

Dr. and Mrs. Grant Kingsley
request the honour of your presence
at the marriage of their daughter
Penelope
to
Mr. George Frank Carpenter
on Friday, the eleventh of June
One thousand nine hundred and seventy-one
at twelve o'clock
St. Mary's Church
San Francisco

If the girl's father has a title he should use it on the invitation. For instance, a judge would probably issue an invitation as "Justice and Mrs. Thomas Ward Preston," although a judge in a lower court may optionally use "Mr."

Mention of the year is optional bordering on unnecessary on an invitation but obligatory on the announcement of the marriage. When the year is mentioned, I prefer to see it in the form, "One thousand nine hundred and seventy-two," but it is possible to include it as, "Nineteen hundred, and seventy-two." The word "honour" is always spelled in the old way. The phrase "honour of your presence" is always used for invitations to a church ceremony. If the ceremony takes place elsewhere than church or synagogue one should use the phrase, "the pleasure of your company." No R.S.V.P. (optional abbreviation R.s.v.p.) is used where the invitation is for the church ceremony alone. The Reception Cards, if any, carry the R.S.V.P., even for a wedding tea if desired, although invitations to tea do not normally require a reply.

In a large city where there are many churches and the one where the marriage is taking place is not in the category of a landmark, the church address is engraved under the name of the church in this way:

Emmanuel Church
1122 South Moore Street
Denver, Colorado zip code

House numbers are usually given in figures, but if the street number in the invitation or announcement is short, it should be written out—"Five" or "Sixteen," although with the complexities of the modern postal services, this amenity is perhaps better dropped.

The time of the ceremony, traditionally on the hour or on the half hour, is usually written out. If it is to be on the half hour the wording reads "at half after four" or sometimes "at half-past four." If the ceremony is on the quarter hour, the wording is "at quarter before four" or "at quarter-past four." If the wedding is to take place the day after Daylight Saving Time becomes effective, the bride may, if she wishes, have "Daylight Saving Time" added to the invitation.

The word "junior" is written without a capital, but it now is abbreviated more often than not, just as "Doctor" is. But then it is "Jr." with a capital "J." With certain engraving—London script—it is usually abbreviated as "Jun." and numerals are used for the date and time of the ceremony.

Sometimes the "On" is omitted so that an invitation may read "Friday, the ninth of June," but simplification of the form reduces its dignity. The invitation may also read, as another option, "Friday, June ninth."

In the wedding of a Catholic to a non-Catholic it is optional to include the information that the ceremony will be a nuptial mass. If you do include this information, and perhaps it is best to do so in order to inform friends who might not know from the name of the Church (Episcopal or Roman Catholic), you may either phrase the invitation, "at the nuptial mass in which their daughter," or include the phrase at the end of the invitation above the mention of the church.

Uncertain Date Under special circumstances it is possible to have wedding invitations engraved with the date left blank to be filled in at the proper time with black ink. This is the solution for example when the date of the wedding depends upon military leave, quite often not known to the exact date sufficiently far in advance to permit the engraving of invitations.

By the same token, if wedding invitations have been engraved already and a change comes in the groom's military orders, an engraved card may be added to the invitation, or a printed card if there is not time for engraving, reading along these lines: "The date of the wedding has been changed to Saturday, the twenty-second of August at four o'clock due to the change in the groom's orders." The same information may be telegraphed of course if necessary and friends of the bride can help her phone wedding guests if the change comes too late to inform people by mail.

The Girl with a Title If the bride is a doctor of medicine or of dentistry, she does not use her title in an invitation issued by her parents. Such an invitation reads:

Mr. and Mrs. George Frank Carpenter
request the honour of your presence
at the marriage of their daughter
Helena

If, however, the wedding invitation is issued by friends or perhaps a guardian, then the bride's name is given as Doctor Helena Carpenter. This is done also when the bride and groom, perhaps both doctors, issue invitations or announcements. The latter would read:

Doctor Helena Carpenter
and
Doctor James Howard Patterson
announce their marriage, etc.

If a girl has a doctorate in some other field outside of medicine or of dentistry, and uses her title professionally, she may choose to use it socially as well. If she is accustomed to using her title and she is issuing her own invitations, then she has the option of calling herself "Doctor" or "Miss" as she prefers. Of course if she is titled and her husband-to-be is not, it might be more discreet if she did not flaunt her accomplishments at this particular time. In the invitation and announcement the title is spelled out as "Doctor" but it appears in its abbreviated form, "Dr." in any newspaper reports.

The Girl with the Same Name as Her Mother If a girl has the same name as her mother and has for convenience's sake been known as Helen Preston, second, she does not use this appellation in her wedding invitations or announcements, since her mother's name, as it must be used in the form, could not possibly be confused with her daughter's.

The Divorced Mother's Invitation If her mother is divorced such an invitation reads:

Mrs. Fenwick Kingsley
(The MOTHER'S MAIDEN NAME PLUS THAT OF HER DIVORCED HUSBAND)
requests the honour of your presence
at the marriage of her daughter
Penelope
etc.

When the Parents Are Legally Separated Invitations and announcements are in the name of the parent (or relative) with whom the bride lives— usually the mother who must use her husband's name, i.e., Mrs. John Kingsley, not Mrs. Ada Kingsley.

The Remarried Mother's Invitation If the bride's mother, widowed or divorced, has remarried, the invitation may read:

> Mr. and Mrs. Roderick Merrill
> request the honour of your presence
> at the marriage of Mrs. Merrill's daughter
> Penelope Kingsley

Sometimes a remarried woman issues the invitation to her daughter's wedding in her name alone, as:

> Mrs. Roderick Merrill
> requests the honour of your presence
> at the marriage of her daughter
> etc.

When the mother has remarried and divorced again, she issues the invitation using her maiden name plus her last married name, e.g., Mrs. Hayden Browning. The girl's father's name does not appear on such an invitation except in the case where he is giving the reception. Then, he may enclose a separate reception card with his name (and that of his present wife, if he is remarried) and R.S.V.P. with his address.

The Foster Parent If a child has lived a long time with people who have not adopted her, but who wish to give her a wedding and make the announcement, the invitation best reads:

> Mr. and Mrs. Joseph Post
> request the honour of your presence
> at the marriage of
> Miss Alice Lamb
> (OBSERVE THE INCLUSION OF THE TITLE, "MISS" BEFORE HER NAME.)

When the Father or Others Issue the Invitation If the daughter after her parents' divorce has made her home with her father, her grandparents, her aunt, brother, or other relative or guardian, the person whose home it is makes the announcement jointly with his or her spouse. For example:

> Commander and Mrs. Charles Simonson
> request the honour of your presence
> at the marriage of their granddaughter
> etc.

or:

The Reverend and Mrs. Myron Cyrus Kingsley
request the honour of your presence
at the marriage of their sister
Penelope Kingsley

In this form the bride's last name is used to show she is Mr., not Mrs. Kingsley's sister.

If the bride's brother is unmarried and he issues the invitation, it reads:

The Reverend Myron Cyrus Kingsley
requests the honour of your presence
at the marriage of his sister
etc.

If the bride's father is a widower he issues the invitation. Also if he is a divorcé and his daughter has lived with him, he issues the invitation, although he may choose to do the more graceful thing and permit the bride's mother to do so for the sake of convention, even if she and her daughter rarely see each other. An invitation from a father alone reads:

Dr. Grant Kingsley   (OR DOCTOR)
requests the honour of your presence
at the marriage of his daughter
etc.

If the bride's sister is issuing the invitations they read:

Miss Cordelia Kingsley
requests the honour of your presence
at the marriage of her sister
Penelope Kingsley

Only if the wedding is being given by a close relative is the relationship shown in the invitation. If cousins, friends, or a guardian issue the invitation, the connection is not shown.

EXCEPTION: The stepmother issuing an invitation for her stepdaughter uses that term in the invitation and announcement, whether or not she has remarried. In this last instance, the lines would read:

Mr. and Mrs. Roland Campbell Potter
request the honour of your presence
at the marriage of Mrs. Potter's stepdaughter
Marcia Rhodes, etc.

The announcement in the paper should include, "Miss Rhodes is also the daughter of the late Mr. Herbert Jackson Rhodes and the late Gwendolyn Morris Rhodes" (no "Mrs.").

Double Weddings of Sisters In a double wedding if the brides are sisters, the elder sister is mentioned first and the invitation reads:

Dr. and Mrs. Grant Kingsley
request the honour of your presence
at the marriage of their daughters
Penelope
to
Mr. George Frank Carpenter
and
Felicia
to
Mr. Amos Reynolds
etc.

Double Wedding of Cousins or Friends If the brides are cousins or just friends, the invitation could read:

Dr. and Mrs. Grant Kingsley
and
Mr. and Mrs. Claude Roen
request the honour of your presence
at the marriage of their daughters
Penelope Kingsley
to
Mr. George Frank Carpenter
and
Marie Rose Roen
to
Mr. Gregory Pardee

Here the older bride is mentioned first, with her parents, but when the brides are more or less the same age the order is alphabetical. However, when there is a great difference in age between the two groups of parents or if, for example, one bride's invitations are issued by her grandparents, it is the older sponsors who take the precedence. Titled parents, too, take precedence over non-titled ones in an invitation to a double wedding. While such an announcement as this is possible, it is more probable that each bride would prefer to have her own invitation, even for a double wedding. Separate invitations also make reception acceptances simple to handle. It is possible to indicate a double wedding by engraving the two separate invitations, vis-à-vis on the inside of the double sheet.

The Bride on Her Own Occasionally a young bride has no close relatives or friends to issue her invitation for her or make her wedding announcement. In this case, as with the older bride who wishes to make her own announcement or issue her own wedding invitation, the form reads:

The honour of your presence
is requested at the marriage of
(or "WEDDING RECEPTION OF")
Miss Cordelia Kingsley
(NOTE "MISS")
to
(OR "AND")
Mr. Winthrop Cass Bowers
etc.

The bride who has established herself in a career or profession under a different name may have her invitation engraved with her professional name beneath her real name:

The honour of your presence
is requested at the marriage of
Miss Cordelia Kingsley
(Delia King)
to
Mr. Winthrop Cass Bowers
etc.

The bride with her own resources may perhaps choose to issue her own invitations, or if she and her husband-to-be are sharing the cost of the wedding between them, they may issue invitations and announcements jointly.

Wedding Given by the Groom's Family

Mr. and Mrs. Perry Coates
request the honour of your presence
at the marriage of
Miss Laura Lee Mercer*
to their son
Mr. Trimble Coates
etc.

The circumstances would have to be very special indeed for the wedding to be given by the groom's family—and those circumstances very well understood by intimate friends of both the bride and the groom. To give remote examples, if the families were old friends or distantly related or if the bride's home were far from the city in which the wedding is to take place and her own parents could not be with her, then she might properly accept her future mother-in-law's invitation that the wedding be given at the groom's home. But she should never flout convention and suggest such

* The "Miss" is used when the givers of the wedding are not relatives.

a thing. And unless she is very sure of her welcome in the family she would be better off with a quiet church or registry ceremony and no attempt at a formal reception. Instead, she might ask the witnesses, if any, to the home of a close friend, if she has one nearby, who might act as hostess for anything from sherry and biscuits to breakfast, tea, or champagne, depending on the hour of the ceremony. Or, if she has an apartment of her own, she can have any unpretentious breakfast, tea, or reception she can manage herself, acting as her own hostess.

The Divorcée The older woman who has been divorced does not send engraved wedding invitations, although she may invite a few close friends and relatives to a small ceremony. She or her family may or may not send announcements.

The Very Young Widow A very young widow may have engraved wedding invitations issued by her family or by herself. If her family issues them, they read:

Mr. and Mrs. Sydney Myers
request the honour of your presence
at the marriage of their daughter
Sylvia Ann Kiser
to
etc.

Here her late husband's name is used with her given names, although some prefer to use the clearer form "Sylvia *Myers* Kiser." Note that she is *not* "Mrs. *Sylvia*," always an ugly appellation. It looks worst of all on a wedding invitation.

If a young widow is issuing her own wedding invitation, preferable, I feel, it reads:

The honour of your presence
is requested at the marriage of
Mrs. Maximillian Georg Kiser
to
etc.

The Older Widow We sometimes see an invitation from an older widow in which she is referred to as "Mrs. Catherine" so and so, the idea being that there may be some lack of propriety in the use of her dead husband's name in the invitation to her wedding to his successor. Throughout her widowhood there has been no impropriety in continuing the use of her late husband's name. No matter how long she remains a widow, she is, properly, Mrs. John Jones, not Mrs. Catherine Jones. Why, when she does remarry, should she subject herself to the indignity of being "Mrs. Catherine Jones" and on an engraved invitation, at that! No—let such an invitation read:

The pleasure of your company
is requested at the marriage of
Mrs. John Jones
to
etc.

If it is a church ceremony the first line reads, "The honour of your presence . . ."

If a widow has remained reasonably close to the family of her late husband she may send them an invitation to the wedding. If she doesn't choose to do this, however, she should certainly send them an announcement.

Invitation to the House Wedding

An invitation to a house wedding carries the R.s.v.p. (or R.S.V.P.), as a collation will be served afterward and the number of guests needs to be known. Otherwise the house wedding invitation reads the same as the one to the church except that the second line is changed to "the pleasure of your company." The house address is used in place of the name of the church:

at
1339 Belmont Terrace
Montclair, New Jersey zip code

If the wedding, with its reception, takes place in a club or hotel, it is indicated in this way that the R.s.v.p. is sent to the bride's home:

at
The Carlton House
New York

R.s.v.p.
1066 Hicks Street
Brooklyn, New York zip code

If the daughter lives far away from her family, and the wedding is being held in her new town of residence, but her family is issuing the invitation, it may be inconvenient to direct the responses to her family's home. In this case the invitation should include the girl's name, Miss Jones, and her address under the R.S.V.P. This same device may be employed in the sometimes awkward situation where the groom's family's home is being used for the ceremony.

Invitation to the Outdoor Wedding

If you have planned an outdoor or garden wedding, there is always a chance that it may rain. Because of this possibility, alternate arrangements should be made indoors, and the invitation should have engraved in the lower right-hand corner:

> In case of rain
> the wedding will be held
> in the
> (NAME OF CHURCH, ADDRESS IF NECESSARY)

Wedding at Friend's Home When the wedding itself is held, for some reason, in the home of friends, the invitation is in the name of the bride's parents, even though they cannot be present. If the parents are not living the bride may either issue the invitation herself (see "The Bride on Her Own," page 40) or have her friends as sponsors do so. In the latter case the form is:

> Mr. and Mrs. Angus Work
> request the pleasure of your company
> at the marriage of
> Miss Penelope Kingsley   (NOTE MISS)
> to
> Mr. George Frank Carpenter
> on Friday, the eleventh of June
> One thousand nine hundred and seventy-one
> at four o'clock
> 600 Rose Lane
> Waco, Texas zip code

R.S.V.P.

Combining Invitation to Church Ceremony and Reception

If all those at the ceremony are to be invited to the reception the wedding invitation may read as follows and no reception card is necessary:

> Dr. and Mrs. Grant Kingsley
> request the honour of your presence
> at the marriage of their daughter
> Penelope
> to
> Mr. George Frank Carpenter
> on Friday, the eleventh of June
> One thousand nine hundred and seventy-one
> at twelve o'clock
> Saint Mary's Church
> San Francisco
> and afterward at
> "The Gulls"
> Belvedere

R.s.v.p. (OR, LESS USUALLY, "THE FAVOUR [NOTE SPELLING] OF A REPLY IS REQUESTED," OR IF PREFERRED THE ANGLICIZED VERSIONS, "PLEASE RESPOND," OR "KINDLY RESPOND."

If there are to be two receptions, one at the church for all the guests and another following for family and close friends at the bride's home or at a restaurant or club, the wedding invitation should read as the above with the following after the name of the church:

And afterward at the reception
in the parlors of the church

Appropriately, a separate engraved card would be included for those invited to the more intimate reception.

The Separate Reception Invitation

Sometimes an invitation to the wedding reception is engraved on the same kind of double sheet usually used for the wedding invitation. This is useful where there may be only an intimate wedding ceremony, for which no engraved invitations may be issued, followed by a large reception. Such an invitation reads:

Dr. and Mrs. Grant Kingsley
request the pleasure of your company
at the wedding breakfast of their daughter
Penelope
and   (NOTE THE "AND")
Mr. George Frank Carpenter
on Friday, the eighth of June
at one o'clock
"The Gulls"
Belvedere

R.s.v.p.

The Late Reception Invitation

Occasionally a wedding reception is given some time after the fact of the wedding by the bride's family, often by the family of the groom, or by both together. It is awkward, and not advisable, to give an evening reception on the same day as a formal morning or noon ceremony. But, a young couple might be married in one city away from their parents and their friends and return to their parents' community for a reception after the honeymoon. The following form is often used on an engraved separate reception card for a reception that will take place when the bride and groom have returned from their wedding trip. It may be issued either by the parents of the groom or by the parents of the bride, or, as the following, by the bride and groom's families jointly:

In honour of
Mr. and Mrs. George Frank Carpenter
Dr. and Mrs. Grant Kingsley
Mr. and Mrs. John Price Carpenter
request the pleasure of your company
Saturday, the third of November
at eight o'clock
Four Sprucewood Lane
Lakewood, Illinois

R.s.v.p.
Mrs. Kingsley
Ten Toddy Hill
Morristown, Ill. zip code

A reply to this invitation would be:

Mr. and Mrs. David Roy Sturgis
accept with pleasure
the kind invitation of
Dr. and Mrs. Kingsley
and Mr. and Mrs. Carpenter
for Saturday, the third of November
at eight o'clock

An informal alternative particularly good for the case in which much of the groom's family cannot attend the wedding because of distance, but where the couple will make a visit to his family's home some time after the wedding, is for his parents to send out their joint visiting card with the phrase, "To meet Mr. and Mrs. George Frank Carpenter," written in ink on the face of it. They should then write the day and time below their names, and if they wish, an R.s.v.p. This should all be done in black ink.

Foreign Wedding Procedures

It would of course be quite impossible here to go into the full details of the national customs concerning weddings in every country. However, there is one important factor that should be made clear. If the wedding is being given by the bride's family in another country where English is not spoken, and you, as the groom's famly have supplied them with the names of people whom you would like to receive invitations, do not expect the bride's family to have a separate set of invitations printed in English to go to your friends. Since in most other countries wedding announcements are not used, you should provide the bride's family with a list of those to receive invitations which includes your friends who would normally receive only announcements in this country. The likelihood of any of these people attending such a wedding is almost nonexistent.

If the groom and his foreign bride are to return to this country after the ceremony to live, you might breach custom to the extent of including an At Home card with the wedding invitation. These could either be mailed to the bride's family to be put in with the invitation or sent separately by you.

In any situation where your son or daughter will be married in a foreign country and you feel inadequately versed in the country's customs, by all means do not hesitate to question your future son or daughter-in-law's parents about your role. It is far better to appear a little overanxious about acquainting yourself with their procedures than to risk a serious breach of etiquette because you are embarrassed to admit that you are ignoring them.

Enclosure Cards

The Reception Card When not all those attending the wedding are to be invited to the reception a reception card of the same stock as the invitation and about half the size is included with its tissue. In the case where children are welcome at the ceremony but not at the reception, one may put only the parents' names on the inner envelope containing the reception card, thus indicating that the children are not to be brought to the later event. The reception card should not bear a crest, shield, or motto, and may read:

Dr. and Mrs. Grant Kingsley
request the pleasure of your company
at the wedding breakfast
following the ceremony
at
"The Gulls"
Belvedere

R.s.v.p.

Note "pleasure of your company," as this is now a social occasion.
When the reception is to be held in the home of friends the card reads:

Dr. and Mrs. Grant Kingsley
request the pleasure of your company
at the wedding breakfast
following the ceremony
at the home of
Mr. and Mrs. Curtis Platt
Turkey Hill Road
Belvedere

The favour of a reply is requested to
"The Gulls," Belvedere, Michigan zip code   (THE BRIDE'S HOME)

If a mother or father alone issues the wedding invitation, the reception card must include the name of the spouse if the divorced or widowed parent has remarried. A reception card bears the name of host and hostess.

In the difficult situation where the divorced mother issues the invitation, but the father who has remarried is giving the reception, a reception card can save much unnecessary embarrassment. Let it be handled this way. The invitation itself reads:

Mrs. Dickerman Green
(THE MOTHER'S MAIDEN NAME PLUS HER MARRIED NAME)
requests the honour of your presence
at the marriage of her daughter, etc.

The reception card reads:

Mr. and Mrs. James Oliver Green
request the pleasure of your company
immediately following the ceremony
in the Terrace Room of the Plaza Hotel
Fifty-ninth Street and Fifth Avenue (optional)
R.s.v.p.
1070 Park Avenue
New York, N.Y. zip code

Dinner Following Reception When a wedding reception following say a four o'clock wedding is to be followed by dinner, it is advisable to say so on the wedding invitation. Otherwise those not understanding that dinner will be given, too, make other plans and the bride may find that she has half the number of dinner guests that she expected. The way this is done is to use the phrase either on the invitation itself or on the enclosed reception card, "Reception and dinner immediately following the ceremony."

Pew Cards, Train Cards, and Plane Cards Today it is fairly rare for an invitation to include either a train card or a pew card. If pews are to be allocated it is preferable that pew numbers not appear on the invitation but for purposes of efficiency be given out after acceptances are received. It is much more usual for the bride's mother and the groom's mother to send their visiting cards along with the wedding invitation to those special friends and relatives they wish to seat in reserved sections "Within the Ribbons"—bride's section (one or two pews) to the *left,* groom's to the *right.* Such a card should read:

Groom's Reserved Section   (HANDWRITING—BLACK INK)
Mrs. Norman Snowden Carpenter

A train card makes sense if a private car has been reserved to take guests for a main point to and from the wedding. Then the card is enclosed in those invitations going to guests likely to go by train, and they, in turn, present it to the conductor in lieu of a ticket. Otherwise, it is expedient merely to enclose a regular train schedule for such guests and let them make their own arrangements. A train card, if used, may read:

A SPECIAL CAR WILL BE ATTACHED TO TRAIN LEAVING GRAND CENTRAL STATION 3:01 P.M. FOR STAMFORD. TRAIN RETURNS FROM STAMFORD AT 6:35 P.M.
PLEASE PRESENT THIS CARD TO THE CONDUCTOR

A plane card might read:

Transportation is being provided
to Wilmington
Guests are requested to be at the
Palm Beach International Airport
on July the eighth at eleven A.M.
Eastern Standard Time
The return flight will leave Wilmington
at ten P.M. Eastern Standard Time
the same day
Please present this card

For a country or suburban home wedding the kind of rustic map often printed for the assistance of guests coming by car may be offset reproduced on high quality bond paper in a tone similar to that used in the invitation and be enclosed with it.

Church Cards Only at very large and fashionable weddings in big churches ordinarily filled with sight-seers is it sometimes necessary to have church cards. They should be without the crest, shield, or motto, if the device is used on the invitation, and should be engraved in the same manner as the invitation and on the same stock. They mean that the church has been closed to the public for the period of the ceremony and only bearers of the cards will be admitted. Such cards read:

Please present this card
at St. Patrick's Cathedral
Thursday, the first of March

Note that here it is usual to abbreviate "Saint."

Response Cards Printed response cards are frequently advertised to be enclosed with wedding and reception invitations, but I deplore their use except under business circumstances and, as noted, for debuts. For example, if a reception is being given to honor an important member of the firm who is retiring, a response card will help the firm's publicity staff, necessarily concerned with many other activities, to expedite matters. Here they are necessary timesavers. Enclosing these response cards in wedding invitations seems to indicate that the sender of the invitation feels that the recipient would not know how to reply properly to a formal invitation.

When there has been no response to a wedding invitation within, say, two weeks before the wedding, it is proper to send an ordinary postcard, handwritten or printed, which says:

We have had no reply to the wedding invitation of Alice Sands Harrison to Mr. Alfred Cooke Stone which will take place on Saturday, September seventh at three o'clock. Will you please phone or post your response as soon as possible? The telephone is Area Code 212 868 2139. The address is 25 Sutton Place South, New York City, New York zip code.

The bride's mother's name should appear printed at the top, if possible. If so, no signature is necessary. If few people are involved, the bride's mother may phone instead and it is also permissible for members of the family, or for friends, to phone the delinquent ones. Invitations do not always arrive.

At Home Cards   At Home cards are often in wedding announcements, less often in invitations to weddings and receptions. If they are in the invitations, they may never bear the name of the couple for the bride has not yet taken her new name. They give the new address of the couple. Smaller than the reception card, they are, however, of the same style as it, with abbreviations and without a coat of arms or a lozenge (see "Heraldic Devices," page 615). They carry the correct postal address in detail:

At Home   (OR THIS MAY BE OMITTED)
after the first of August
(CAPITAL "A" FOR "AFTER" IF FIRST LINE IS OMITTED)
Ten Washington Square South
New York, New York zip code

or:

Will be at home
after the third of November
Thirty-two Morgan Avenue
Bethlehem, Pennsylvania zip code

When the couple will be moving to a very distant place to which it is difficult to send presents, or for which no definite address is yet known, the At Home card can read:

At Home
after the tenth of May
Calcutta, India
% Pepsi Cola Company
India Office
500 Park Avenue
New York, New York zip code

When At Home cards go out in the announcements, they may optionally read:

Mr. and Mrs. Kurt Samuels
after the third of November
Ten Washington Square South
New York, New York   zip code

Recalling Wedding Invitations

If after wedding invitations have been sent out the wedding is called off, guests must be informed as soon as possible. They may be sent notes, telegrams, printed or engraved cards (when there is time for the engraving).

Dr. and Mrs. Grant Kingsley
announce the marriage of their daughter
Penelope
to
Mr. George Knapp Carpenter
will not take place

A telegram is signed by those who issued the invitation. It would read, "The marriage of our daughter Penelope to Mr. George Knapp Carpenter will not take place. Dr. and Mrs. Grant Kingsley." A telegram to a close relative would be less formally worded and carry the familiar signature.

Telephone calls may also be made in this case. These calls are made in the name of the bride's mother by any friend or member of the family willing to do so.

Death in the Family   When a death occurs in a family that has issued formal invitations is it necessary to recall the invitations? It certainly used to be, but our ideas have changed very radically on the subject of mourning. Certainly no bride would want to go through an elaborate wedding ceremony followed by the festivity of a large reception within a few days of her mother's or father's death or of the sudden death of the groom's mother, father, sister, or brother. The death of a very old person, a grandmother or grandfather, rarely calls for the postponement of a wedding these days, but it all very much depends on the feelings of all involved.

If after a family conference it is decided to recall a wedding invitation because of a death, the guests are notified by wire, by phone, or, if there is time, by printed cards in the same style as the invitation. They may read:

Mrs. Grant Kingsley
regrets that the death of
Dr. Kingsley
obliges her to recall the invitations
to the wedding of her daughter
(THE NAMES ARE OPTIONAL)
Friday, the eighth of June

Such notification does not mean, of course, that the marriage won't take place. It may, instead, be a quiet family ceremony on the original day planned. The bride may even wear her bridal gown and have one attendant, but without a crowded church the full panoply of bridesmaids and ushers would be senseless.

Postponing Weddings

If a wedding is postponed and a new date has been set guests may be informed by telegram or sent a new *printed* invitation done in the style of the original engraved one. It reads:

Dr. and Mrs. Grant Kingsley
announce that the marriage of their daughter
Penelope
to
Mr. George Frank Carpenter
has been postponed from
Friday, the eighth of June
until
Friday, the seventh of September
at noon
St. Mary's Church
San Francisco

Replying to Formal Wedding Invitations

Formal, engraved invitations to a church wedding do not require answering. But if a reception card is included or if a separate invitation to the reception is received, then one answers in the traditional form in response to the R.s.v.p. on the lower left of the card or invitation. If you receive a formal invitation to a tea or reception and there is no R.s.v.p., it means technically that the hosts are ready to entertain all who come. No reply is expected.

However, if you cannot attend it is polite to send flowers and/or a note. The reply to an invitation which includes an R.s.v.p. should be written in longhand on one's best conservative notepaper in blue or black ink with the wording and its spacing taking the form of engraving. An acceptance reads (as it does for any engraved invitation):

Mr. and Mrs. Morrow Truitt
accept with pleasure
Dr. and Mrs. Kingsley's
kind invitation for
Friday, the ninth of June
at noon

A regret follows the same form (but see acceptable alternative below). It reads:

Mr. and Mrs. Morrow Truitt
regret that they are unable to accept
Dr. and Mrs. Kingsley's
kind invitation for
Friday, the ninth of June

A more detailed regret states "why" in this way:

Mr. and Mrs. Morrow Truitt
regret (OR REGRET EXCEEDINGLY) that
their absence from the city
(OR A PREVIOUS ENGAGEMENT)
prevents their accepting
Dr. and Mrs. Kingsley's
etc.

In each case, of course, the envelope is addressed, for the reply to Dr. and Mrs. Grant Kingsley, using the names and address exactly as they appear in the invitation. It is acceptable ordinarily to address a reply to the hostess only.

The wedding may be that of your most intimate friend or of your closest relative, but if you have received an engraved invitation you answer it in formal style. If one is going to decline an invitation and the third person response seems too limited for the expression of sincere regret it is best to enclose a personal note more fully explaining the circumstances. The format of the formal reply should also be followed.

In an acceptance it is well to repeat the hour but optional to repeat the full details of the invitation. If a joint ceremony and reception invitation is received and no separate time is given for the reception beyond, "following the ceremony," it is acceptable to use that phrase in your reply instead of the time of the ceremony. But the simple form given is acceptable in all cases except that of a "regret" to the White House (see "Receiving a White House Invitation," page 816). If the full form is used in an acceptance most of the wording in the invitation is repeated:

> Mr. and Mrs. Morrow Truitt
> accept with pleasure
> Dr. and Mrs. Kingsley's
> (OR DR. AND MRS. GRANT KINGSLEY'S)
> kind invitation to
> the wedding breakfast of their daughter
> Penelope
> to
> Mr. George Frank Carpenter
> at one o'clock
> "The Gulls," Belvedere

A fully written out regret does not repeat the place or the hour, merely date.

When one of a couple accepts the invitation and the other regrets, the form is as follows:

> Mrs. Robert Allen Whittemore
> accepts with pleasure
> Mr. and Mrs. Josephson's
> kind invitation for
> Saturday, the sixth of June
> Mr. Robert Allen Whittemore   (OPTIONAL)
> regrets exceedingly
> that he will be unable to accept

When one wishes to substitute a different family member for the one specified in the invitation (because, for instance, the husband is ill, and a grown son can attend in his place) do as follows:

> Mrs. Gordon Ashley and Mr. Gordon Ashley, Jr.
> accept with pleasure
> the kind of invitation
> etc.

If younger, or teen-age, children receive invitations to a formal wedding in the same envelope as their parents, the reply should indicate either the acceptance of all parties, or the acceptance by either the children or the parents.

If everyone can attend, the reply reads:

Mr. and Mrs. Robert Jones
and their children
(OR, OPTIONALLY, Brenda and William)
(NO MR. IF UNDER 18 BUT USE MISS FOR GIRLS)
accept with pleasure
the kind invitation
of Mr. and Mrs. Jackson Brown
for
Saturday, the sixteenth of October
at four o'clock

If only some members of the family can attend, the reply reads:

Brenda Jones
William Jones
accept with pleasure
the kind invitation
of Mr. and Mrs. Jackson Brown
for
Saturday, the sixteenth of October
at four o'clock
Mr. and Mrs. Robert Jones
regret that they are unable to attend

It is always a great compliment to receive a wedding invitation. As I have said, it never requires an answer unless it includes an invitation to the reception, but it is a gracious thing for the recipient to write the person to whom he feels indebted for the invitation—the bride's mother, father, the bride herself, or the groom or his family—about his happiness at the forthcoming event. Such a letter, as it is not in direct reply to the invitation, which needs none, is couched in the usual social form, not in the third person. It might read:

Honolulu
April 8

Dear Jack, (to the groom)

It was wonderful to get the impressive news of the wedding. I'd give a lot to be there, as you and Alice know, but I shall drink a toast to your happiness on that day and hope for a quick trip to the mainland soon, so I may enjoy the sight of you at home together at last.

With warmest regards to you both,
Burt

An alternative to this letter is to send a telegram expressing your congratulations on the day of the wedding. The telegram should be addressed to the young couple and is most effective when it is co-ordinated to arrive just after the ceremony. Often telegrams of this sort are read aloud by the best man during the reception.

Of course, engraved wedding invitations are expensive, and, if they must be limited for economy's sake, some who should receive them, such as brother George in Cincinnati or the members of the bridal party, who would certainly like to keep them in their memory books, may have to be satisfied with their oral or written invitations. It is safer to omit the younger than the older generations, since the latter are more likely to feel slighted if they are not treated to all the formality connected with the event, relatives or no.

Responding to a Foreign Wedding Invitation Formal invitations to weddings abroad in another language are increasingly common. In many other countries it is customary for a wedding invitation to have two panels, one side an invitation from the bride's family, one side an invitation from the groom's family. When responding to such an invitation, reply only to the family from whom one presumes one has received the invitation. You should reply in English, using the proper formal reply for either an acceptance or a regret.

Recalling a Formal Acceptance

If you have accepted an engraved wedding invitation and then something occurs that makes it impossible for you to attend, you may write a formal regret, send a telegram, or telephone your excuses, but a valid excuse must be given. You certainly may not back out of an accepted invitation because a more attractive one has arrived. Illness, death in the family, or a sudden business trip are acceptable excuses. A regret, following a previous acceptance, may take this form:

> Mr. and Mrs. Morrow Truitt
> regret that the sudden illness
> of Mrs. Truitt
> prevents their attending
> the wedding on
> Friday, the eighth of June

Invitations and Replies to Informal Weddings

A small wedding does not require engraved invitations—in fact, they may seem pretentious. Instead, the mother of the bride may write short notes of invitation, telegraph or phone the relatives and friends who are to be invited to the ceremony or the reception or both.

If the bride's mother is dead her father or some close relative, preferably an aunt or grandmother, issues the invitations. Or she may even issue them herself if she has no close relatives. Often, after such informal weddings, engraved announcements are sent to friends and relatives at a distance, but never to those who have been invited to the ceremony or the reception. An informal invitation to a wedding may be phoned—or it may be written on the household's conservative notepaper, in blue or black ink, this way:

> "The Beaches"
> Meriden, Connecticut
> April 6, 1971

Dear Marion,

Faith is being married here at home to Ronald Ward, Saturday, April 17, at four-thirty. We do hope you will be with us and will be able to stay for tea, afterwards.

> As ever,
> Helen

For such an invitation, just such a short note, giving the time and place of the ceremony or, if the invitation is being issued only for the reception, the time and place of the reception is all that is necessary, and it is taken for granted that the invitation will be promptly answered. Informal invitations may be sent on very short notice, if necessary, but the usual two weeks in advance, as for ordinary social invitations, is customary.

Reply to an Informal Wedding Invitation A reply to an informal wedding invitation is sent immediately, usually in the form in which it was received. If it was a telegram and the time before the ceremony is short a wire goes in reply. If the invitation came by phone or note a reply by either means is correct. In phoning an acceptance the recipient asks to speak to the sender of the invitation or, if someone responsible answers the phone, leaves the message, "Mr. and Mrs. Wainwright accept Mrs. Samuel's invitation to Miss Consuela's wedding on the fifteenth." A note in reply would read:

> Tuesday

Dear Lenore,

We are happy about Consuela's forthcoming marriage and are delighted to be included. We'll drive over and will stay at the Inn where I have already made reservations. Until Saturday week.

> Love,
> Maud

Wedding Announcements

Wedding announcements, which are mailed the day of the wedding so that they are received the following day, as previously noted, are sent only to those not invited to the wedding. It is possible to send an announcement to a large group, such as a faculty or the staff of an office, by addressing it to the organization and asking that it be posted on a bulletin board. Announcements read:

Dr. and Mrs. Grant Kingsley
have the honour of announcing
(OR HAVE THE HONOUR TO ANNOUNCE)
the marriage of their daughter
Penelope
to
Mr. George Frank Carpenter
on Friday, the eleventh of June
One thousand nine hundred and seventy-one
(MUST GIVE YEAR)
Saint Mary's Church
(OPTIONAL TO MENTION)
San Francisco

It is not technically necessary to respond in any way when one receives a wedding announcement. All one need do is enter the information in one's address book. However, it is always nice to send a little note expressing one's best wishes for the success of the marriage to whomever one feels indebted for the receipt of the announcement.

Variations of the Usual Wording

The Mature Bride The mature bride may issue her own announcement. For example:

Miss Jane Charlotte Spencer
and
Dr. Elliot Squires Jackson
announce their marriage
on Friday, the eleventh of June
One thousand nine hundred and seventy-one
New York

Remarriage of Divorced Persons to Each Other Occasionally people who have been divorced eventually remarry each other. When this occurs, no formal announcements are sent out, but friends are informed of the good news by word of mouth, by letter, and by telegram. No formal announcements are released to the press. In such instances, often children are involved, so the reunion of the couple should be made almost as if the schism had never existed.

Military and Naval Forms for Wedding Invitations and Announcements

Noncommissioned Officers and Enlisted Men often prefer to use only their names with the branch of service immediately below. For example:

Dr. and Mrs. Grant Kingsley
request the honour of your presence
at the marriage of their daughter
Cordelia
to
Winthrop Cass Bowers (NOTE, NOT "MR.")
United States Marine Corps

but

Winthrop Cass Bowers
Staff Sergeant, United States Marine Corps

is correct, too.

Regular Officer U. S. Army or Navy Only where the officer's rank is Lieutenant Colonel or above in the Army (or above Commander in the Navy, Merchant Marine, and Coast Guard) does the title appear first:

Capt. (OR CAPTAIN) Winthrop Cass Bowers
United States Navy

In either case it is optional to mention the branch of service, though the regiment is omitted. It may read:

Captain Winthrop Cass Bowers
Artillery, United States Army
(OR, UNITED STATES AIR FORCE)

Reserve Officers on Active Duty If officers are of the Army and Navy Reserve it is only when they are *on active duty* that they use their titles on wedding invitations and announcements. Otherwise, they are "Mr." It is modern to abbreviate the titles, just as "Dr." is more often than not abbreviated. If the following form is used, the title is usually written out:

Dr. and Mrs. Grant Kingsley
request the honour of your presence
at the marriage of their daughter
Cordelia
to
Winthrop Cass Bowers
Lieutenant, Army of the United States

For a Reserve Officer on active duty the phrase "United States Army" changes to "Army of the United States."

Retired Regular Army and Navy Officers High-ranking Army and Navy officers retired from regular service keep their titles in civilian life. Their names on wedding invitations, announcements and engraved forms read:

Commodore Vincent Ludlow Bird
United States Navy, Retired   (NOTE COMMA)

or

Lt. General Packard Deems
United States Marine Corps, Retired

Retired or Inactive Reserve Officers (*Colonels or below*)   Do not use their former titles, socially or otherwise.

The Bride in Military Service   Uses her military title in wedding invitations and announcements with the identifying branch of the service as do men in service. When she is marrying a man in the armed forces, the service appears beneath each title.

Chapter 5

WEDDING GIFTS

Must One Send a Gift?

People who receive invitations to wedding receptions send a gift if they accept but need not necessarily send one if they regret. If they are close enough to either family to be invited to the reception, though, they usually will want to send a gift whether or not they will be present. If you are invited to a double wedding and know only one of the couples involved, it is necessary to send a gift only to the couple you know and then actually only if you accept.

Suitable Gifts

There are two important things to keep in mind when you are considering bridal gifts. First, remember that you are buying this gift for someone else whose taste and needs may be quite different from your own. And second, never feel you must "match your gift to the circumstances." If you are the bride's former teacher, living on a small salary, don't feel you must give a gift well out of proportion to the amount you should spend, just because the bride will have a big wedding and perhaps live on a lavish scale. Lovely gifts need not be expensive. A knowledgeable friend who knows old glass or silver can give a present that will really be treasured spending anywhere from a dollar to five dollars for it. A gardener with the knack for it might make a dream of an indoor rock garden and take it to the young couple himself. With shears, old maps, or floral wallpaper and some glue, clever fingers can transform a metal wastebasket into a most useful and decorative receptacle for the new living room. And how about a charming scrapbook ready for the clippings about the engagement and the wedding—or perhaps already containing them as you have gathered them yourself? Such gifts have real sentimental value and show you have given affectionate thought. They have something money can't buy. One of my own wedding gifts was a single, lovely covered dish of old Meissen removed from her own china shelves for me by an old girlhood friend of my mother. It was the nucleus of my modest collection of old Meissen, and I never forget who gave it to me, whereas I sometimes come upon one of many silver dishes and serving forks and wonder who sent it, although I did keep the proper record at least until all gifts were acknowledged. And it is a good idea to keep this record permanently. People are always flattered if you point out the gift they gave and which you are using.

Very appropriate in this day and age is a gift styled to the particular wants, needs, and life style of the couple themselves. It is even possible to supply a couple with a carte blanche for a day's (or more) rental of an automobile if you know they are planning to rent one during their honeymoon. Perhaps you know of some particular interest the bride and groom share. Maybe it is football, or the theater. In that case, why not provide them with a pair of tickets and some appropriate dinner reservations for a date a few months in the future, when some of the wedding excitement will have died down. A few volumes with which to begin a library— a good dictionary and a gourmet cookbook, perhaps even this etiquette book, for instance, are all appropriate.

Gifts of money in cash, checks, or bonds are often presented in the names of both bride and groom the day of the wedding either before the ceremony or before the reception. If a couple prefers to receive gifts of money, because they are moving to a distant place soon after the wedding and can't afford to transport heavy or delicate items, it is best to let the word get around through the bride and groom's mothers. There is really no graceful way to include this information with the invitation. If a couple in this situation does receive actual gifts it might be nice for one of their parents to investigate low-cost ways of having things shipped and volunteer to assume this cost as part of their gift. If checks are sent previous to the wedding, like all wedding gifts sent before the marriage, they are made out to the bride-to-be alone.

Government bonds are popular wedding gifts, and rightly so. If an E bond is sent before the wedding it is made out to the bride alone. In this case, by government requirement, her name on it must read "Miss Barbara Barton." If a government bond is to be sent after the marriage, which is more usual, it may read "Mrs. Barbara Barton Johnson," or "Mrs. Barbara B. Johnson," or "Mrs. Barbara Johnson," but never "Mrs. John A. Johnson." Registered bonds or securities, however, are made out in this way. Before marriage, "Barbara Barton" (no "Miss"). The middle name may be added or the middle initial especially if this is her usual signature. After marriage, bonds or securities given jointly should read properly and legally "John A. and Barbara B. Johnson."

Registration for Wedding Gifts

It is possible for a bride-to-be to choose her silver and china patterns (with the help of her fiancé, please! He has to use them for the rest of his life too) and "register" her choices at a local department or specialty store. In this way she can be assured of getting things that she really likes and needs, and the likelihood of duplication is reduced.

Whereas it is perfectly within the bounds of good taste to register, it is quite outside socially tolerable behavior to advertise this fact. No girl should allow the store at which she is registered to send out notices to her guest list that she is registered there. This is rank commercialization and the height of bad taste. If a girl has registered she must trust her mother and close friends to spread the word. Any really considerate guest will have made some effort to find out what the girl wants, and many will appreciate the convenience of being able to buy the bride something they know she wants and will use.

Gifts to the Groom

Gifts are always addressed to the bride before the marriage, even when close friends of the groom send them. If no "at home" card is in the invitation they are sent to the home of the bride, if it is certain that they will arrive after the wedding or if they are sent in response to an announcement. Of course, if one knows exactly where the couple's future home is to be the gift may be sent there, if it is certain someone will be present to receive it should it arrive while the bride and groom are still on their wedding trip.

Your Cards with Gifts When you send your wedding gift enclose your card (if you have no visiting card a simple enclosure card, not a greeting card, is suitable) with a brief line of felicitation at the top, in black ink to match the engraving. You address your gift to the bride in her maiden name if it is certain to reach her before the wedding. Gifts sent after the wedding—if sent in response to an announcement—are addressed to "Mr. and Mrs." If the gift will arrive after a wedding to which you were invited, send it with a short note of explanation in a sealed envelope if it is sent from a shop. You might write:

Thursday

Dear Betty,

Sorry this is so very late.

We have been traveling. I wanted you to have this from our favorite wedding-gift shop, so I waited until we returned and I could choose it myself.

Love,
Virginia

Gifts at Receptions

In some country areas where parcel-post packages must be picked up at the post office, it is quite customary for guests to take wedding gifts to receptions. A gift table is set up and gifts noted in the bride's book by a friend or member of the family. It is preferable that they not be opened at the reception. This prevents misplacement of cards, possible breakage in re-transportation, and hurt feelings on the part of guests who may have sent their gifts to the bride's home. If the bride insists on opening these gifts at the reception some member of her wedding party should be stationed near the church entrance to collect the gifts as guests arrive. She should wait to open them until everyone has gone through the receiving line and partaken of refreshments—probably just before the cake-cutting.

Display of Wedding Gifts

A formal display of wedding gifts is less often seen now, although it is still good taste to exhibit them. If the reception takes place at the bride's home, the gifts may be shown at a tea before the wedding or placed on display on white damask-covered tablecloths in some room of the house, so guests may view them during the reception. It is a good idea to take out a floater insurance policy to cover the accumulation and subsequent display of gifts. Where there are many valuable gifts private detectives are engaged to guard them.

Cards are now removed from gifts displayed, and gifts of more or less like value are grouped together to discourage comparisons. Checks are recorded on cards which are propped up for display. They read, "Check, $100" but the donor's name is not given, though the bride or groom often reveal the information, as checks usually come from close relatives. If the couple should receive some other gift of which they are especially proud but which would be impossible to display, such as a sports car or even a house, they may try to secure a miniature and display that or they may prepare a card mentioning the item.

If the Gift Is Sent after the Wedding

While wedding gifts should arrive, if possible, well before the wedding to allow for their display should the bride so desire, in actuality many arrive after the wedding has taken place—sometimes months later. Such gifts, if they are monogrammed or initialed, bear the married initials of the bride or the husband's crest and are addressed to the bride and groom, not to the bride alone, as are gifts arriving before her marriage actually takes place. Large silver pieces should not be monogrammed as they are sometimes duplicated and have to be exchanged.

The Bride's Thank-you Letters

Even if the bride does not know the senders of the gift, who may be particular friends of her husband's, or even if she knows them very well, and has thanked them verbally, she herself must write the thank-you note just as soon as she possibly can—within two or three weeks certainly, after receipt of the gift. It is wise for the bride to keep a record of gifts received. She will find that she will refer to it many times during her married life, even long after thank-you notes have been written. Thank-you notes should never be written on Mr. and Mrs. cards, nor on cards that say "thank you" on the top fold. They should be on good-quality, conservative note paper or on informals which, if engraved or imprinted, should carry the bride's name or initials alone. At a large wedding, where hundreds of gifts must be personally acknowledged, an engraved card may be sent immediately upon receipt of the gift. It reads:

> Miss Penelope Kingsley
> wishes to acknowledge the receipt
> of your wedding gift
> and will write a personal note of
> appreciation at an early date

If the card is to go out shortly after the wedding, it may carry the married name of the bride alone:

> Mrs. Thomas Robert King
> wishes to acknowledge the receipt
> of your wedding gift
> and will write a personal note of
> appreciation at an early date

Stereotyped letters are never worth reading. You know just what they are going to say the minute you see a first line that begins, "It was so kind of you to send the lovely cake plate." If you were thanking Aunt Mathilde face to face, would you say anything so stuffy? Wouldn't you be more likely to say, "What a lovely cake plate!" Here is how you can put such spontaneity in a thank-you note:

Thursday

Dear Aunt Mathilde,
The lovely cake plate arrived safe and sound. I always wanted Dresden and now I have a piece with which to start what I hope one day will be a real collection. Frank is very enthusiastic about it, too. When you see us in our new little apartment I think you will like the way I've used it in our decoration.

Love,
Frances

Your letters and you should be just alike. It's foolish to make the written expression of your personality old-womanish and out-of-date if you talk like a nice, alert, and friendly person. It is a nice touch to mention your husband-to-be's joy in the gift in the course of the note.

When a gift has been received from a couple, the acknowledgment may go to the couple, "Dear Mr. and Mrs. Brown" or, and I prefer this myself, to the woman only, "Dear Mrs. Brown," making sure that reference is made to her husband in the body of the note. Addressing Mrs. Brown only is a holdover from the English custom where even engraved invitations are sent in the wife's name alone. One never addresses a couple as "The Browns" or writes, "Dear Browns."

Thank-you notes for wedding presents are signed, "Sincerely," "Cordially," "Love," or "Affectionately" (if the bride knows the sender well), "Mary"—or "Mary Kerr" with her new surname to someone to whom she would not be "Mary" or to whom such a usual first name would not be definitive. A joint signature, "Mary and Bill," is too awkward and should not be used. You use your husband's first name and middle initial with "Mrs." on the necessary return address.

Thank You Notes for Gifts of Money   When gifts of money are to be acknowledged, the sum is usually not mentioned. Such a letter might read:

Dear Aunt Martha,

To say that we were happy to receive your check is to put it very mildly indeed. Our budget is tiny and we still need things for our apartment, despite all the lovely gifts everyone has been sending us. Your generous check will go right into a rug for our living room from which Arnie will no doubt take much pleasure in watching Sunday afternoon football games. When you see it, you'll be very pleased, too, I know.

Love,
Allison

Returning Wedding Gifts

When an engagement is broken or a wedding does not take place, the gifts must be returned to all senders with brief and tactful notes of explanation. (When an annulment takes place almost immediately after the marriage, any gifts that may be returned unused should be.) Gifts should never be returned direct to the stores. Only when the prospective groom has died is it proper for the girl to keep wedding gifts—and then only if she is strongly urged to do so, in some cases, by a donor whose gift may have a sentimental rather than monetary value. She should not keep gifts intended for a joint household that will never be. If a wedding has been postponed for any reason, gifts are not returned unless after a reasonable length of time the marriage still does not take place. In the event that the marriage lasts a brief time, the gifts legally belong equally to both. Socially, however, it has been customary to allot all wedding gifts to the bride except those explicitly given to the groom. It is of course proper to return to the donors any jewelry or heirlooms received from the groom's family. Other gifts are not returned to the senders unless, perhaps, they have not been opened and used.

The Couple's Gifts to Each Other

On or just before her wedding day the bride receives some personal gift from the groom—usually something to wear of permanent value. Loveliest is a string of pearls, but the modern bride—if her husband can afford it— may think in terms of a mink coat or her own car. A piece of heirloom jewelry, a fitted traveling case, or a watch are all possibilities—very expensive or fairly inexpensive ones, as the groom's circumstances permit.

The bride, in turn, makes some gift to the groom, too—a silver dresser set, cuff links, her wedding picture in a silver frame, or anything of somewhat lasting quality for which he will have personal use.

Chapter 6

THE TROUSSEAU

Many of us wish that fashion did not change so often, but the fact that it does has made the matter of her trousseau much easier for the modern bride. Her grandmother was expected to bring with her enough clothes to last at least a year, along with all the linen, bedding, pots and pans—enough to set up housekeeping from scratch. Today's bride, even when her personal allowance permits a lavish wardrobe, seldom buys more than enough clothes for the first few months of her married life—with the exception, of course, of her lingerie. Fashions change too fast. In fact, they change even in the matter of household linens, and Americans move frequently, especially in cities. That's why few of us have hope chests kept from our early teens any more. Instead of collecting a lifetime's supply of embroidered linens, we buy what we need and what we have room to store, replacing these things as needed with linens that suit the taste of the moment.

In fact, the very word "linens" is now a misnomer. Linen sheets which used to be *de rigueur* for the bride's household trousseau are seldom seen now, and a good thing, too, as they needed daily changing to look fresh and inviting and were difficult to iron, whereas good-quality percale keeps its finish and stands up better in home or commercial laundering. And no-iron sheets are a blessing.

Who Buys the Hope Chest—If Any

If a girl wants a hope chest, she rarely, as I have said, starts one in her early teens. She is more likely to consider one when marriage is in prospect. Actually, a hope chest isn't necessary. Many girls prefer to put what they are collecting in a bottom drawer or in a piece of furniture that might very well suit their future home better than the conventional hope chest. Some might even decide to store linens and other things in an antique trunk, now greatly prized, redecorated.

If a hope chest is bought at all, it is bought by the girl's family or she buys it herself. The boy she is going with, or is engaged to, definitely does not buy it. Should the engagement be terminated and the girl have to return the hope chest, what would the young man do with it? He certainly could not offer it to another girl, and there is something very lugubrious about a former fiancée using a hope chest given her by a man she is no longer going to marry.

Must Everything Be White?

It is a sound idea to choose white sheets for the trousseau linen. Colored sheets are dramatic but they must be planned for each room and can't be used interchangeably as can basic white sheets. Unless she knows exactly what her decorative scheme is going to be, the bride should introduce colored sheets and pillow cases, if she wants them, only after she is settled in her home. She may find her new husband had decided opinions concerning sleeping between pink or yellow sheets, with or without rosebud borders. He may be strictly a white-sheet man.

Good white percale or fine cotton top sheets may, of course, be attractively monogrammed in color with one or more of the bride's initials. If one is used, just the first initial of her new name is now usual. If three are used, the middle one is today likely to be that of her maiden rather than her second baptismal name. There should be some reason for the color—it should match the blankets or pick up a decorative note in the room. But in my opinion the most luxurious monogram of all is done in white, on white, doubly impressive by its subtlety.

While white sheets are always basic, the modern tendency is to treat bathroom linen as part of the decorating scheme. All-white bath linen, therefore, seems a little dull, although white linen guest towels can never be in too great abundance even when bath towels, face towels, and washcloths in terry may combine two or more colors to suit the particular bathroom.

The thing to remember when deciding on colored bath linen is, again, that the towels, like colored sheets, cannot always be used interchangeably. They must all match or at least co-ordinate when hung together in a bathroom. Fingertip guest towels are best in white or may match the bath towels or their initialing. Gray bath towels with maroon monograms might be attractively accompanied by maroon fingertip towels with matching monogram in gray. But an ill-assorted collection of towels, no matter how fresh, in any bathroom makes for a "busy" decorative scheme.

What Does the Bride Provide?

Today's bride still comes to her husband with a dowry, too—the clothes for her honeymoon, as many nice underthings as she can afford or as are given her by her family and friends, and as much in the way of household linens and kitchen equipment as she can manage. If she has a bank account, too, so much the better. But many a bride, married without fanfare or much advance preparation, comes to her husband with little more than the clothes on her back. And the couple acquires what is needed for housekeeping as the home is furnished, with the husband footing all the bills, if necessary.

But the bride who can afford it still brings with her a lavish dowry of household linens—enough to last through their first few years of marriage, at least, and geared of course to the way she and her husband will be living. Here is a basic list for a household trousseau, expansible or contractible, of course, according to the size of home the couple will have and the scale on which they will be living—and, too, depending on the bride's resources.

Basic List

Linens   6 sheets for each bed (three top and three bottom, if they are to be hemstitched or monogrammed)

2 pairs of blankets for each bed
1 quilt (preferably eiderdown) for each bed
6 pillowcases for each bed
1 bedspread for each bed
6 bath towels for each bathroom
6 matching or co-ordinating face towels for each bathroom
6 matching face cloths for each bathroom
1 shower curtain for each bathroom with liners if the curtains are not fully waterproof
6 guest towels for each bathroom
1 doz. kitchen towels (the handblocked or printed ones are fun)
1 doz. glass towels (fewer if you have a dishwasher)
1 bath mat to match each set of bathroom towels
1 dinner-size damask or linen tablecloth in white or pale colors, to overlap table not less than 12″, not more than 18″, with 1 doz. matching napkins, dinner-size (this is optional now as many prefer place mats with appropriate dinner napkins and rarely use a large linen cloth)
3 luncheon sets for daily use with matching napkins
2 tray cloths
2 tray sets with 2 napkins each (one napkin for the tray, one for the toast)
1 doz. cocktail napkins (optional—good quality paper ones are just as acceptable)
2 or more sets of practical table mats in straw, cotton, woven matting or any of the modern, tasteful materials used for the purpose with matching or contrasting napkins (white luncheon napkins, simply hemmed, go with everything)
1 quilted mattress cover for each bed
1 blanket cover for each bed

Kitchen Equipment   (Often provided by showers)

4 paring knives	1 canister set
1 kitchen carving knife and fork	set of mixing bowls

measuring spoons
measuring glasses
kitchen scales
1 bed tray
1 serving tray
4 pot holders
6 kitchen aprons (if the bride will officiate)
vegetable bin) if not
bread box) built in
4 nylon sponges for dishes and counters
broom and dustpan
1 dry mop
1 nylon mop (for floor washing)
carpet sweeper (vacuum can be a wedding present or bought after marriage, but carpet sweeper is useful for quick cleanup)
step-on garbage can
kitchen stool
sieve
frying pans (large and small)
griddle
covered kettle
teakettle
custard cups
electric mixer
waffle iron (a sure shower gift!)
flour sifter
rolling pin

ladle
funnel
meat grinder
cooking spoons, one wooden
jelly molds
vegetable parer
kitchen teapot
dish drainer
folding steps
2 sets covered icebox dishes
bread knife
apple corer
colander
casserole
muffin tins
cake tins
egg beater
electric blender
toaster
cookie sheet
large and small pitchers
bread board
can and bottle openers
chopping bowls (large and small)
spice sets
grater
coffee maker
paper towel holder with towels

Glassware and China (These are usually gifts and the bride should state her needs, when asked. Breakage is very heavy and good glass expensive to replace.)

1 dozen or more water glasses
2 dozen ice-tea glasses
1 dozen sherry glasses
1 dozen cordial glasses
1 dozen or more wine glasses
1 dozen champagne glasses, solid stems (Optional. All-purpose wine glasses are preferred by connoisseurs.)

2 dozen old-fashioned glasses
2 dozen cocktail glasses
2 dozen highball glasses
1 dozen sherbet glasses
1 dozen punch glasses
(Optional. All-purpose wine glasses may substitute.)
12 juice glasses

China for a Simple Household   (Some of this china is now in the "fine" category so far as styling and appropriateness and even price are concerned. Chosen with care it can mix with your fine china, too.)

1 basic set utility china (optional)—may be pottery or some one of the "unbreakable" wares such as Melamine, which in best quality and styling can often mix with "fine" china
1 set fine china (optional)

If no matching sets are to be used:
8 breakfast plates
12 breakfast coffee cups or mugs (allowing for breakage) not necessarily matching plates, but if plates are patterned, cup should be solid color, in blending tone (for coffee lovers there are jumbo cups)
8 breakfast butter plates
8 egg cups or small dishes for eggs (milk glass reproductions of setting hens are amusing for the purpose)
8 cereal dishes
1 covered dish for toast (may be in any color that looks attractive with breakfast plates, or may be silver or silver plate)
1 small platter for bacon, pancakes, etc., to match or blend
1 small creamer
1 sugar bowl
1 large creamer for cereal
12 dinner plates (if matching set is not used)
12 butter plates in plain china, such as white or bordered Wedgwood, or in ruby, amber, green, amethyst or clear glass to blend, if matching set is not used
3 vegetable dishes, may be silver or silver plate or match set
1 small platter, may be silver
1 large well and tree platter, silver or silver plate
1 sauce boat with saucer, or bowl for gravy, may be silver, match set, or in blending china
1 ladle for gravy, may be china, silver, or glass
1 bread plate, or tray, may be silver, china, or wood. Basket should be wicker. Bread board is pleasant for informal meals. (Queen Victoria used one on her table as an example of thrift—bread was cut only as needed.)
Condiment dishes, may be china, fine china, pottery, silver or glass; antique or modern. Cut glass is back in favor.
1 water pitcher, may be silver, modern or antique glass, antique china or pottery, such as Majolica or any of the glazed wares for informal use.
2 sets of salts and peppers, may be silver but may also be china, glass, or pewter, antique or modern. Gourmets like wooden pepper and salt grinders.

8 cream soups (optional)

8 soup cups (optional)

8 individual covered casseroles (very useful and may be used, informally, for soups)

8 thin teacups for afternoon tea

8 tea plates, need not match and can be in any fine, blending china or in glass

8 demitasses preferably in fine china but may be glass or, for a completely informal household, pottery

1 teapot

1 coffee pot or coffee maker

1 round serving platter or stand for molded desserts, cakes, and pies, may be china, glass, sometimes silver

8 dessert plates, may match set or be in any fine china, glass, or, informally, pottery

8 "English" dessert dishes, deep enough for baked apples, sauced puddings, etc., though these are often successfully served on a flat plate, as is ice cream

1 serving bowl for desserts, fruits, occasionally for salads

1 salad bowl with serving fork and spoon—the choicest, seasoned wood is best

6 individual table ash trays. May be silver, pewter, antique or modern china, glass, pottery (for informal tables along with shells).

Silver Silver has been associated with weddings since the time of ancient Greece. And a fortunate association it is, too. The bride's family usually gives her her flat silver, and the groom's family gives a silver tea service, a silver tray or a silver after dinner coffee set as a wedding gift.

If having a silver tea or coffee service will create a storage problem in small quarters where it can't be on display, the groom's family might better give a china service or, perhaps, broadloom if that is a paramount need of a young couple on a slender budget. It is nicer, of course, for both families to give enduring things such as silver or fine china, but many young couples would prefer checks to use only in part to start purchases of silver or fine china on a budget basis, adding to their stock as their living quarters and their social activities grow.

Whether or not she is to receive her flat silver all at once or purchase it a setting at a time, the bride should choose her pattern and monogram as soon as her invitations are out, so friends who wish to give her silver may match their gifts. She may register her silver pattern and that of her china and glass at shops from which it will probably come. This will be of much help to her friends. Silver serving dishes and platters don't necessarily match the flat silver but should be in a harmonizing style. Loveliest are the old Sheffield platters and serving dishes, plated of course on copper, but there are many modern pieces in sterling or, more usual, plate, in a variety of classic patterns that complement flatware.

If it is out of the question for a bride to have even a starter set of sterling, a fine quality of plate in a simple pattern will do. But, given a choice between a complete set of even the best plate and a four-place setting of sterling, the wise bride will choose the sterling, adding to it on anniversaries and other gift-giving times. Sterling is a permanent investment requiring no upkeep or replacement. It always has a company complexion and will be just as acceptable and beautiful twenty or thirty years after the wedding.

Styles in silver are fairly stable. Heavy embossed or repoussé silver, which is hard to clean, is better avoided for the simpler, more modern, patterns. But if you have inherited heavy, heavily-decorated silver, it is heartening to know that you can still add to your set, as the great silversmiths still produce for these familiar open-stock patterns. And often you can pick up extra forks, spoons, and knives at auctions or old silver shops. In fact, a friend of mine, with no family to give her silver and a slim budget on which to start, deliberately chose one of the lovely, decorative old patterns, buying it secondhand, and from time to time picks up six spoons or a dozen salad forks in antique shops and elsewhere at half the price they would be new from the silversmiths that have been making them for a century. And, as with all fine sterling, their beauty increases with use and the years.

A dozen of everything in all-sterling flatware is ideal, but a young bride can do very well with four or six place settings consisting of dinner knife, dinner fork, salad fork, butter knife, teaspoon, and dessert spoon. The teaspoon will be used for consommé and cream soup, for desserts in small containers, for grapefruit or fruit cup, as well as for tea or coffee. The dessert spoon will do for soups in soup plates and for desserts served on flat plates. She will need two tablespoons and two extra dinner forks to serve with, a carving set, a cake knife and, of course, after-dinner coffee spoons.

If her budget is limited she should avoid purchasing flat silver that is used only occasionally—fruit knives and forks, oyster forks, iced-tea spoons, fish forks and knives, cheese scoops, and the like. If ancestral silver is to be used, it is probable that some of these things will be missing anyhow and substitutes will have to be found.

A word of warning to the bride who rejects offers of sterling silver when she marries in favor of household furnishings she feels she needs more. *If you don't get your sterling now, you may never get it.* Once a family starts growing, its constant needs too often absorb funds we thought would be available for something so basic as sterling. So we "make-do" over the years with ill-assorted cutlery, deceptively inexpensive because it wears out. Then come the important little dinners, as a young husband gets up in the world. We push a chair over a hole in the living room rug, put a cushion under the pillow of the sofa with a sagging spring, and distract the guests' attention from the pictureless walls by charming flower arrangements. But there is nothing that can be done about the shabby flatware, which, somehow, is still with us, even though it was bought just to tide us through the first year in the tiny apartment. But then, of course, the baby came.

Never again in her lifetime will a girl find her family and friends in such a giving and sentimental mood as they are at the time of her wedding. At no other time will it occur, very probably, to any of them to give her so much as a silver ash tray. But at the propitious moment they think of sterling silver as *the* gift for the bride as part of her dowry—as it should be. So, though she starts married life without as much as a roasting pan, she should be able to lay her table—if it's only a bridge table—with the kind of silver she'll be proud to see on whatever table the future has in store for her.

Right from the start, it is the wife's task to set the tone of the family's living. And one's everyday living should differ very little from that presented to guests. We are all strongly influenced by things around us. What family doesn't deserve the sight of an attractively set dinner table, even when guests aren't present?

Should Gifts of Silver Be Monogrammed? The bride should decide how she wishes her silver marked, then, if it is given to her in a complete set, it arrives already monogrammed. If friends give her flat silver from a chosen pattern, it is better to send it unmonogrammed, in case she receives many duplicates. Hollow ware and trays should be sent unmonogrammed to make them exchangeable.

How Should Silver Be Marked? In hope chest days a girl began collecting her silver piece by piece, long before a knight even appeared over the horizon. It was monogrammed with her maiden initials or the single letter of her last name—or with her family's crest, and it remained her personal property. After she was married, or if her husband's family presented silver, that silver was marked with her married initials or the single initial of the new family—or with her husband's crest. This meant differently marked silver used on the same table. And while this is very usual, especially when we have inherited silver, many brides prefer unity in monogramming. The bride often has her silver marked with her new initials, or the single initial of her new name or with her husband's crest, if they both wish.

Ornate initialing or monogramming has given way to simple markings, usually suggested by the jeweler as being in harmony with the design of the silver. Sometimes triangles or inverted triangles are used, with the bride's initials or her first initial and the groom's combined with his last initial. If the bride, or groom has a surname preceded by "Van" they may use only the "V" or "Van" plus the first letter of the rest of the name, for instance, "Van B." This could be N (his last name)—

J P (their two first initials)—or

J F

G

(her maiden initials in an inverted
triangle or with her first two initials at the base).

If the man is Junior, this may or may not be included in a monogram, depending upon the design. When certain silver is initialed, for example a man's cigarette box, the "Jr." is included.

Wedding silver is not marked with the husband's monogram unless the silver is for his personal use, a dresser set, a desk set.

Chapter 7

PREPARATIONS FOR THE WEDDING

No bride, no matter how much her heart is set on it, should go ahead with plans for a formal wedding without the groom's complete acceptance of all it entails. An elaborate wedding should have professional management, if possible, so the wedding day doesn't arrive with the bride harassed and tearful and the groom wondering why he ever consented to such a thing.

A formal wedding is a beautiful and impressive ceremony if everything has been done on schedule—the gowns delivered on time, every last detail of catering attended to, and the bride with the last two weeks to rest as much as she can, although during this time there will be a rehearsal with a dinner or supper following. And the bride may have a tea at which she will show her presents to close friends, if gifts are not to be exhibited at the reception.

"Modern" Weddings

Young people have been rethinking, or perhaps I should say refeeling, some of the traditional things about the way we live, only in some cases to decide to change some cherished custom radically. I am never against change if it is good. Etiquette does change from generation to generation. Sometimes it changes quite drastically. Usually, however, changes come very gradually. Before we change something that is precious and valuable in the way we've been doing things, we need to examine why and whether such a change would be to the good. I'm thinking particularly of the wedding ceremony, a serious, beautiful and necessary part of our tradition. To marry, one must go through a certain amount of ceremony within our religious beliefs and within the civil code. Religion has always taught that marriage with ceremony is more meaningful. The procedure should be serious, sensitive, and witnessed with respect. There have always been people who wanted to get married in balloons, on television, on camel back or in some other attention-getting fashion, and by this I mean attention in the notorious aspect.

There is little doubt that young people are reassessing many things in our society, and rightly. Some have decided for this reason or that that the customary procedures of the wedding are not for them and make sometimes wild, and sometimes tasteless, departures, expecting perhaps, and often succeeding, in getting into the newspapers or onto television or on radio because what they have done is not the accepted norm. Many young people are writing their own marriage services, finding clergymen to deliver their words, or are delivering them themselves. They borrow from philosophies and religions other than their own but how often do they achieve anything like the dignity of the words of most traditional services. Some of the words, some of the procedures they have insisted upon have been either banal or downright offensive in some cases, in the view of the elders of the community and even of many young people themselves. The important thing to note is that for the main part no great contribution has been made to the ceremony of the wedding even when these amateur efforts have had a certain amount of bathos and tenderness.

If the couple does or says something in its desire to be different that literally outrages mature members of the congregation witnessing the wedding, have they not created a scandal where beauty should be? Should exhibitionist behavior distress those who have assembled to see a beautiful ceremony? Fortunately most brides, and grooms too, want the kind of wedding of which they have always dreamed. They are in the great majority. Perhaps in a future edition, I will say that a bride may indeed go barefoot or bare bosomed when some of these things that seem unsettling now settle into a pattern. I am not against breaking the social rule if there is a good reason to do so. I codify the changes from time to time. One that has crept up on us very gradually and which is now established is the fact that the bride certainly does not need to wear gloves any more, and most do not. Many changes will come, some of them precipitously. As I've said, I am never against change that is good, that makes a contribution to our way of living with one another. The ceremony of the wedding is one of our most beautiful and valuable of all ceremonies. I am glad that most brides still desire its beauty and dignity.

The Visit to the Clergyman

The bride has the prerogative of selecting the officiator (minister, priest, rabbi, judge) for her wedding. She is usually married by her own clergyman. The exception comes when the groom himself is a clergyman, or the son of one, then usually his choice is the bride's. Where the groom is not the son of a clergyman and wishes his own clergyman, pastor or clergyman friend to have a part in the ceremony, it can be done only with the consent of the officiating clergyman. The second clergyman then usually serves in a subordinate capacity (i.e. the betrothal rather than the marriage vows), although other compromises are possible.

It is desirable for a bride to be married in her own parish. Where arrangements must be made for a religious ceremony, with or without the use of a church for the wedding, the bride and groom together visit the clergyman and discuss the hour of the ceremony, the music, the kind of gown the bride will wear (very short sleeves are sometimes not permitted), and any church regulations that must be fulfilled or local customs considered.

The couple should have more than one possible date in mind when they visit the minister to avoid disappointment.

Most ministers prefer to see the bride and groom before the ceremony to be sure there is no impediment to the union about to take place. But sometimes in a small non-church wedding, where the principals are well known to the clergyman, the mother of the bride makes arrangements with the family's own clergyman to perform the marriage on the day chosen.

Special Problems Protestants who have been divorced may have some difficulty marrying in church, especially if they have been divorced more than once. Some ministers make the distinction that they will remarry only the "injured party" in a divorce. They require that divorced persons present the credentials permitting their remarriage. In most states there are blood tests and a necessary "waiting period" (see the World Almanac) between the issuance of the license and the marriage. Ministers are not permitted to waive this period. If it must be waived because of some emergency, a civil procedure must be followed before the marriage can take place.

Choosing the Place for the Wedding

If the bride feels that she wants a wedding which is too large or too formal for her parish church she should investigate the possibility of availing herself of the facilities of a nearby cathedral of her own denomination, or of a cathedral in a city where she may be living at the time of her engagement. The girl's home town is usually chosen because it means that more of her friends and relatives will be able to attend and that her mother will be able to share the burden of wedding planning with her.

If the wedding is to be held in a public place such as a hotel, restaurant, or club, it is best to have several comparable places in mind that fit your budget and other requirements.

If the home towns of the bride and groom are widely separated, one should consider having the wedding in the home town of the bride and a later reception in the home town of the groom given by his parents or other relatives or possibly even by friends. It is unusual to have two ceremonies to suit the demands of each of the sets of parents, even if one be civil and one religious but this is sometimes done.

Choosing the Time of the Wedding

The time of day considered fashionable for weddings differs in different parts of the country. In New York many fashionable Protestant weddings take place at four, four-thirty, or five in the afternoon. Evening weddings are relatively rare in the East but fashionable in many other parts of the country (see below). Their own Sabbath, Christian or Jewish, is usually not chosen for a wedding day by brides of these faiths (religious Jews may not be married on the Sabbath—Friday sundown through Saturday sundown—or on High Holy Days and major festivals) nor is Lent by Christians, at least not for religious ceremonies. It is not considered good taste for Christians to have even large home weddings during Lent, though, of course, simple marriages with or without a clergyman do take place during these forty days of penitence.

Formal and informal Catholic weddings usually take place in church at a nuptial mass which may be said at any hour a mass is permitted. Early morning weddings are frequently followed by a wedding breakfast. Weddings which take place later, at eleven or twelve, are also followed by wedding breakfasts—really lunch. No Catholic wedding takes place after seven at night, except in the case of great emergency—grave illness, perhaps, or possibly the sudden arrival of military orders for the groom-to-be.

Protestant morning weddings are usually simple and informal with the bride wearing a dress or suit, not a wedding gown. Wedding breakfasts—again really lunch—may follow. In some parts of the country Protestant weddings sometimes do take place at noon, that is, truly formal weddings with a bride in full bridal array and the groom and his attendants in cutaways.

The Evening Wedding Evening weddings take place mainly in the South and West. They may be formal or informal and may take place in church or at home. The preparations and procedures follow those of the daytime wedding. (For dress, see "Dress for the Wedding," page 106.)

The Mature Bride

If a woman has reached her late thirties, then marries for the first time, should she wear a wedding veil and have a formal wedding? Many women of nearly forty today look very much younger. If such a bride feels she can still wear the bridal gown on which she's planned so long and still look her very best, let her wear it. She may find ivory, champagne, or pale blue more becoming than pure white. But if she plans to have bridesmaids and most consider that her close friends, presumably of the same age, may not look *their* best in the traditional costumes of bridesmaids, she may decide to wear the prettiest covered-up cocktail dress she can find, or the most becoming traveling suit, and forgo the luxury of a wedding gown and formal wedding. It is good strategy for such a woman to choose her attendants from among her contemporaries. Every bride should look her best and few women of this age are going to shine if surrounded by much younger women.

Church Preparations

Decorations Decorations in the church may be limited to suitable altar flowers—where decorating of the altar is permitted—for a small wedding or may be extensive and expensive, despite the desired simplicity of effect. Sometimes only the aisle posts on the *reserved* pews are decorated, even for very formal weddings. But a clever florist can do impressive things with boxwood, palms, ferns, and various available greenery, with or without flowers—which, if used, need not be white.

You will be wise to speak to a florist very soon after you have chosen the date and place of your wedding. For a florist to do his best work he needs ample time to prepare, and besides, there are just so many weddings he can do on any given day, and it would be unfortunate for you to be disappointed in this respect. When you speak with him be specific about how much money you are willing to spend for floral decorations both at the ceremony and at the reception. With this information firmly in his mind he will be better able to create a floral design in keeping with your budget and you will not be unpleasantly surprised with a bill for which you are unprepared.

In general, it is wise to remember that churches are often dimly lit and that very subtle shades of flowers will go unappreciated in this setting. Blues and lavenders are particularly to be avoided unless they gather support from contrasting colors used in the arrangement.

An effort should be made to co-ordinate the reception flowers with those used at the ceremony. And of course it should be remembered that flowers play a purely supporting role in a wedding so they should never be so elaborate or inappropriate as to overshadow the bride and the rest of the wedding party.

Canopy and Carpet The canopy from the curb to the church door for formal weddings is not used much today, but the church aisle is often carpeted by the florist when he decorates the church. Or immediately before the procession starts and after the bride's mother is seated (and no one should be admitted after she starts down the aisle), two ushers starting in either direction roll the canvas covering, if one is to be used, down the aisle. The canvas is not centered. If the bride is to go down the aisle on her father's right arm, the canvas is slightly to the right. If she is to go down on his left arm, the canvas is placed slightly to the left. This serves as a protection to the bride's train and is left down until all the guests have left. The florist, or whoever furnished the canvas, removes it.

Wedding Music It is necessary to discuss the wedding music with the officiating clergyman and the church's music director or organist, as various rules apply. In some churches soloists are not permitted, in others only rigidly prescribed music may be played by the organists. It is never in good taste for a bride or groom to attempt to sing at their own wedding. The *Lohengrin* Wedding March is traditional in the processional—the thrilling "Here Comes the Bride!"—with the Mendelssohn March from *Midsummer Night's Dream* for the recessional, but many brides prefer other music, often Bach. Such variations should be approved by the organist who will be concerned not only with its appropriateness but with its suitability to the cadence of the processional and recessional. During the entrance of the guests most churches permit a wide range of music, but it is best to keep to the accepted classics and to avoid sentimental, popular music that might take away from the dignity of the occasion. Be sure to discuss each selection with the organist, however—don't just "leave it up to him" or you may find that some of the permitted secular music is not your own taste at all. There is a fee of anywhere from twenty-five to forty dollars or even more for organ music in church depending on the community and the church with additional fees for soloists or choir if they are used too. The sexton is sometimes the source of all such information, especially in large churches or cathedrals, but more often the clergyman is.

Other Preparations

Wedding Photographs Although I give more detailed instructions for your formal bridal portrait later on, this is a good time to remind you that if you want attractive "candid" or formal pictures from your wedding which will give you lasting pleasure, you should arrange for them now. Probably after your announcement has appeared in the paper you will receive letters from several photographers offering their services. It is wise to take the time now to visit several of these people to compare prices, services, and quality. They will be able to suggest ways in which you can organize in advance what pictures should be taken so that you do not lament after the wedding that a record of any cherished moment was missed through inadequate planning. Color photographs are now more reasonable in price, so perhaps you would prefer a few really outstanding color pictures to a larger quantity of black and whites.

The bride's family usually pays for these photographs, but it is a great courtesy to the groom's family if they are asked what shots they would particularly like to have taken. They of course pay for any prints they order for themselves. Let me urge you here to put this important matter in the hands of a professional. It is an imposition on any guest if he is asked to take pictures at a wedding since his pleasure as a guest and duty as a photographer are bound to conflict at times. Besides, it can only create hard feelings if you are not satisfied with his work. These pictures can only be taken once, and they can be the most meaningful mementos of this occasion, so try to prepare to have them done correctly.

Wedding Guest Booklet As soon as possible after preparations for the wedding are begun someone should be commissioned to purchase the album that you will use for your Wedding Guest Book (it can, of course, be a shower gift). Having a guest book is becoming an increasingly popular procedure. Any attractive album with sufficient space for all of your guests to sign would be suitable, although albums designed specifically for this purpose are available.

Wedding Programs One custom in connection with weddings that I deplore is the use of printed programs which may have chatty comments about the members of the wedding, pictures, etc., and are distributed to guests at the church ceremony. These programs have a very unfortunate commercializing effect, and turn a sacred ceremony into a mere entertainment. No girl should agree to the use of these, no matter how lengthy, complex, or unique her ceremony may be.

Wedding Reception Music While the actual day is relatively far away, and things are still in the planning stages, you should make inquiries about the inclusion of music at your reception. Unless you are having a very large and very formal ball after your ceremony, a three-piece combo should be all that is necessary for dancing and incidental music. Consult with friends and family to see what musicians they may have used whom they would recommend, as good bands or combos are usually booked far in advance, especially during the popular wedding seasons.

Such details dealt with early are easily resolved. Left until the last minute they can be tension-provoking, and if postponed too long, may even prove to be insurmountable problems.

Putting up Guests

In the days of larger houses and more commodious apartments, it was usual to put out-of-town members of the wedding, the groom's parents, and close relatives at the bride's own house, with neighbors, and friends. Today hotels and motels mostly must take over this function. In the case of the groom's parents, if they are coming from out of town, the bride's mother writes or phones and offers to make a reservation at the hotel or motel of their choice—or she suggests one if they don't know the community. It is then usual for them to take care of their own hotel bills, but the bride's parents may assume them if they wish and are able to do so. And they, of course, still find them quarters with relatives or friends or put them up in their own home if they have the room. Out-of-town bridal attendants are accommodated the same way, but where hotel expenses are involved, it is usual for the groom to assume those of his attendants and for the bride's family to assume those of hers, if they can manage this financially. The arrangements should be perfectly clear to the attendants at the time they are asked to participate.

Expenses of the Bride's Parents

Often today the groom and his family offer to share some of the costs that have traditionally been the burden of the bride's parents. For instance the long established Midwestern custom of the groom's family giving the rehearsal dinner or supper has been spreading to other parts of the country. Also, particularly among some Jewish groups, the groom's family will volunteer to share the cost of the liquor at the reception and half the cost of the bridal pictures. However, only if the groom's family volunteers to help should this matter be discussed. The subject of sharing expenses should never be broached by the bride's family. Often too, today, the bride and groom themselves pay for the cost of their wedding where doing so would be financially difficult for the bride's family.

Engraved invitations and announcements

The bridal outfit and, though it is no longer expected, the costumes of the
  bride's attendants if money is no object

Bridal photographs (but see preceding paragraph)

The bridal consultant and social secretary, if needed

The bride's trousseau

The household trousseau

Cost of bride's premarital blood test for license

The bride's "maiden dinner," if any

All the cost of the reception

Flowers for the church and the reception

Gratuities for off-duty traffic policemen or others asked to direct traffic at
  the site of the wedding

Corsages for the bride's mother and grandmothers, if they wish to wear
  them.
    (No guest wears a corsage)

Flowers for the bride (SEE FOOTNOTE), her attendants, her father's boutonniere
    (No male guest not in the wedding party wears a boutonniere)

Bridesmaids' party (although this may be given by the bridal attendants,
  relatives, or friends)

Gifts for the bride's attendants

The groom's wedding ring if it is to be a double-ring ceremony

Music at the church and at the reception

Sexton's and organist's fee. Choir fee

Carpets, ribbons, awnings, tents—anything of the kind often rented for
  large weddings and receptions

Fee for the church rental, if any

A limousine for the bride, at least, and other cars for the transportation
  of the bridal party to and from church

A wedding gift of substance, usually silver, or a honeymoon trip
Hotel bills for out-of-town attendants when they can't be accommodated
   by the bride's family, relatives, or friends
Transportation for the bridal party from ceremony to reception, if necessary

Groom's Expenses

The groom, responsible for his bride once the vows are said, presumably
provides the transportation from the place of the reception to the locale
of the honeymoon. Sometimes of course, the bride's family does this
especially if the honeymoon is their gift to the couple. One father I know
had a helicopter pick up the bride and groom on the family's lawn so
they could make connections with their flight abroad.

The wedding ring
The marriage license and cost of the groom's premarital blood test
The bride's flowers (the bridal bouquet if she wears a bridal gown. or a
   corsage. Going-away corsage if any may be the heart of the bridal
   bouquet, or supplied separately). *See Footnote*
His own, the ushers' boutonnieres, and that of his father
Corsage for his mother and grandmothers if they wish to wear them
The ushers' gloves, ties, and collars
Gifts for the ushers
The minister's fee (unless the wedding is so costly and what the groom
   could afford so small in comparison that the bride's father might figure
   a generous stipend for the clergyman in his over-all costs for the
   wedding). Tips for the altar boys.
A wedding gift for his bride—something for her to treasure, usually jewelry
His bachelor dinner if any
The entire cost of the wedding trip (unless this is a gift from the parents)
His own wedding and wedding trip clothes
The home into which they will move and the equipping of it with its
   major furnishings
Hotel bills for his best man and ushers if they are from out of town and
   cannot be accommodated by his family, relatives, or friends

Ex-Husband's Responsibility Concerning the Wedding

When his daughter marries, does the girl's divorced father have a financial
responsibility in the matter? This is a matter for individual solution, depending on whether or not the father has been paying alimony, has
perhaps made a substantial settlement upon the mother which is intended

NOTE: In large formal weddings the bride's flowers and those of the bridesmaids are
considered part of the entire wedding expense and thus borne by the bride's parents.
It is becoming customary, however, for the groom to send the bride's bouquet, though
she selects it, and to provide, of course, his own and his father's and the best man's
and the ushers' boutonnieres. In some communities the groom pays for the entire
bridal party flowers as well as for corsages for both mothers if they wish to wear them.

among other things to take care of such contingencies. In the latter case, the father may feel that he need not pay for any portion of the wedding. On the other hand, no matter what the circumstances, he might feel inclined to do so. Very often, a remarried father offers to give the wedding reception whether or not the daughter still lives with her mother or has her own apartment. These are all things to be individually arranged.

Chapter 8

THE WEDDING ATTENDANTS AND THEIR DUTIES

The very simplest wedding must have at least one attendant for the bride, but an elaborate wedding may have as many as eight or more bridesmaids, a flower girl, perhaps a junior bridesmaid, a maid *and* a matron of honor, or very occasionally two maids of honor or even two matrons who share their services to the bride at the altar. No bride or groom should ever feel duty-bound to choose as an attendant any person in whose wedding he or she may have served in a similar capacity. Friends should understand that relatives should first be chosen for these honors, and beyond that, it is the bride or groom's preference, and never a tit-for-tat obligation, which determines this choice. No explanations ever need be given.

In the management of complex weddings one thing is most vital—the bridal attendants must be on time for the fittings for their gowns, for their appointments with the photographer if photographs are going to be taken prior to the wedding (a sound idea), to the showers and pre-nuptial parties for the bride alone and for the bride and groom. One flibberty-gibbet bridesmaid who can never get anywhere on time, who cannot make a note of her appointments, can throw out all the nicely laid plans of the most efficient wedding consultant. Being a bridesmaid is almost as romantic as being a bride, but it does have definite responsibilities.

Maids and Matrons of Honor

The bride usually chooses a sister as maid or matron of honor, or, if she has none, a close friend. Although a groom may, under some circumstances, choose his father as his best man (see page 89), the bride never chooses her mother as her matron of honor since the bride's mother already has her own complicated function in the wedding party. As I've said, she may have both maid and matron of honor or, very occasionally two maids of honor or even two matrons—one could be her sister, the other a friend. A matron of honor may be a widow or a divorcée, but it is preferable that she not be considerably older than the bride—at least not in a large formal wedding.

Both maid and matron of honor each have a specific part in the ceremony. In the processional the matron of honor walks down the aisle just before the bride. The maid of honor may precede the matron or may walk at her side, whichever the bride or the minister wishes. The bride may ask one or the other to hold her bouquet during the ceremony. Or, the matron of honor, who will be next to the bride, may take it from her, pass it to the maid, who at the end of the ceremony passes it back to the matron to return to the bride. The matron of honor may lift the bride's veil just before the ceremony if the wedding is Roman Catholic, and then replace it, if the bride's father wishes to kiss her farewell when he leaves her at the chancel steps. Where there are two maids of honor or two matrons of honor, the bride decides which one is to assume the duties of chief attendant. Generally, if one is her sister, it is her sister who performs these duties. As the recessional begins, the maid and matron of honor together straighten the bride's train and then follow the bride and groom down the aisle, the best man escorting the matron of honor and the head usher escorting the maid of honor.

The two honor attendants assist the bride and her mother in any way they can during preparations for the wedding. They may help compile the guest list, address invitations, or run any last-minute errands.

Bridesmaids

Bridesmaids, who may be young matrons, are chosen from among the bride's close friends and usually are not noticeably older than she. They are sometimes much younger than the bride, often children, especially in Canada and England. If the groom has a sister of suitable age, it is customary to ask her to be a bridesmaid although not necessarily an honor attendant. Bridesmaids are expected to supply their own transportation to the wedding if they are from out of town. However, the parents of the bride arrange transportation of the bridesmaids, who frequently dress together at the bride's house, to the ceremony and the reception. They see that each bridesmaid has a safe way to get home (or at least to where she is staying) from the reception.

The "Junior Bridesmaid" or "Maiden of Honor"   There is occasionally a place in the wedding party for a girl between the ages of ten and fourteen. She is known as the "junior bridesmaid" or "maiden of honor." As junior bridesmaid in the procession she walks in front of the bridesmaids. If she is to be maiden of honor she precedes the bride if there is no maid of honor or matron of honor. If there is either of these then she precedes the maid or matron of honor. If the bridesmaids are paired with ushers in the recessional, the junior bridesmaid may either walk alone or be paired with an usher who is not too tall (if she is short). A great discrepancy in age is not important and she would undoubtedly be very thrilled to be escorted if the other girls are (this is optional) in the recessional. Where there is no maid or matron of honor and only a maiden of honor, the latter may perform the duties of the bride's chief attendant although I think that it is too much of a strain for a girl so young and prefer not to see her have this responsibility.

The Best Man

The groom chooses his ushers and best man. The best man is usually a brother, if he has one. If a brother does not serve, the groom's closest friend usually does. If the best man is to be chosen from among several close friends of the groom, he must be a good executive if it is to be a large formal wedding, for his duties are legion. It is well to invite the best man and ushers to participate in a wedding a full two months prior to the ceremony. This permits men who live at a distance to make necessary arrangements.

The ushers and best man provide all their own clothes for the wedding with the exception of their ties, collars, and gloves if they are to be worn, which are furnished them by the groom. If, perchance, money is of no consequence to the groom he might volunteer to pay for the rental of his ushers' clothes, but they should certainly not expect him to do so. The groom, or the best man should ascertain the sizes of ties, collars and gloves and should have these items delivered well in advance of the wedding. At the bachelor dinner the groom's gifts to his ushers and his best man are at each table place—but never the clothing accessories.

The Groom's Father as Best Man   Very occasionally, especially if he has no brother, the groom asks his father to be his best man. If the father is very young-looking this does not seem too incongruous, but it is best to keep the wedding party at the same age level as that of the bride and groom.

Duties of the Best Man   The best man has always had an important role in all weddings. In ancient times, when marriage was by seizure of some girl outside the tribe, the best man was chosen for his brawn and bravery, as he was needed to fend off the bride's male relatives and, later, to prevent the bride's escape from the groom. Today, while his duties are less vigorous, they are nevertheless extensive at any formal wedding.

The best man is adviser, messenger, valet, secretary, and general factotum to the groom. He takes him firmly in hand from the very start of preparations for the wedding, seeing to it that he is fitted for his wedding clothes, if new ones are to be made for him—or if they are to be rented (quite usual)—that he has the ties, collars, and gloves for the ushers, that he confers with the bride on the needed flowers for ushers and for her bouquet and his boutonniere, all of which the groom usually pays for, though she orders (see flowers for the wedding party, page 84). He is entrusted with the task of finding accommodations for out-of-town guests and any attendants who need a place to stay.

He rounds up the ushers for the rehearsal and sees that it goes off according to schedule. In fact, it is a good idea if the groom and best man work out in advance a time schedule for the rehearsal and for the day of the wedding itself. He remains with the groom all day before the ceremony, traditionally even rousing him in the morning. He helps the groom dress, making sure there are extra collar buttons ready in case of emergency, laying out all the items of his wardrobe, seeing that his boutonniere is in his buttonhole. The best man and groom should discuss the transportation of the bride and groom to the reception. They go alone usually, at a formal wedding, in the limousine that brought the bride and her father to the ceremony.

The best man sees that the marriage license is in the groom's inside pocket and the wedding ring safely on his own little finger or in his vest pocket. He should have reminded the groom that marriage licenses are good for a limited time only and have helped the groom to plan the procuring of his so it was validated not too far in advance. He should see too that the bride and groom have had the necessary blood tests. He is also one of the witnesses, along with the maid or matron of honor, who signs the wedding certificate. He makes sure that he, himself, has the clergyman's fee. It should be remembered that most clergymen depend upon this honorarium as a necessary supplement to their comparatively small incomes. The fee should be gauged according to the size and style of the wedding and can range from at the very least twenty-five to a hundred dollars or more. If the groom feels he cannot afford this much, the best man might tactfully approach the father of the bride or groom for a contribution. Altar boys should be tipped by the best man in the groom's name, but only a dollar or two. The clergyman's fee should be in a sealed envelope to be tendered quietly before the ceremony, so this important gesture won't be overlooked. The tips and fee may be in cash, but if it is a check, it should be made out to the clergyman and not to his church or synagogue. Roman Catholics and many prefer contributions to the church. The matter should be discussed. Priests are not as dependent upon this stipend as clergymen of other denominations.

The best man has the ushers at the church at the appointed time—an hour before the church ceremony, or three quarters of an hour before at a home ceremony—and the groom in the vesting room a good half hour before. No bride should ever be kept "waiting at the church."

After the ceremony the best man joins in the recessional, escorting the maid or matron of honor, then hurries to the place of the reception, perhaps driving some of the bridal party, to take up his duties concerning the couple's luggage. This must be placed in the going-away car or assembled in a spot safe from pranksters. He gives car and baggage keys and baggage checks, sometimes the hotel key, if any, to the groom after he has changed into his traveling clothes. He may have helped make honeymoon reservations and often arranges to have wine or flowers waiting in the couple's room when they arrive.

At the wedding reception the best man hovers in the neighborhood of the groom, acting as his secretary, reminding him to say something special to the bride's Aunt Mathilde, who is about to come down the line. If the reception is a seated one, the best man is placed to the bride's right, proposes the first toast to the couple, and reads any congratulatory telegrams. If there is dancing, he dances with the bride, both mothers, and as many bridal attendants and guests as possible.

When the bride and groom are ready to dress for their departure the best man again valets the groom and sees that nothing has been forgotten. He fetches both sets of parents and any other close relatives for the private farewell upstairs. Then he clears the way through the guests for the bride and groom, who, all good-bys to their families said, race through a rain of confetti or rose petals (rather than rice, let's hope) to the waiting car or cab (also scheduled to be there at the exact moment by the best man). Then, and then only, does the hard-working aide relax and join in the fun. You can see why the best man does not stand in the receiving line.

Ushers

The groom's ushers should be chosen from among his intimate friends and close relatives. He is not obliged to ask his brother or brothers to serve, but it is usual. He frequently asks at least one brother of the bride. Once asked, a man cannot refuse such an honor except for a serious reason.

In a big church it is necessary to have enough ushers—more than bridesmaids—to seat the expected guests. The rule of thumb is to have one usher for every fifty guests to be seated. When calculating this figure assume that only three quarters of the invited guests will attend. In the processional and recessional the extra ushers walk together. However, if a big church is chosen, it is not necessary to invite enough guests to fill it, as part of the body of the church near the altar may be enclosed with boxwood or other greens to make a small chapel for the ceremony. Ushers seat only invited guests, and do not permit outsiders to be seated until all expected guests are in place. It is possible to have a church wedding without ushers, but it would be difficult to manage in any but a small church or chapel.

Ushers may be married or single, but it is unusual for a husband and wife to serve together, except at a double wedding where the first couple married may act as best man and matron of honor for the second.

When married men act as ushers or matrons act as bridesmaids their husbands and wives must be invited to the wedding, but they need not be asked to sit at the bridal table, which is, officially, only for the bridal party and even excludes the parents of the couple.

Occasionally a relative of either bride or groom is chosen to be a junior usher. This is certainly all right but it is preferable for him to be in his late teens so that he is able to perform the duties of a regular usher. A very young boy, perhaps twelve, looks rather ridiculous escorting adults down the aisle unless he is exceptionally tall and mature for his age and it would be incorrect to dress him formally.

Duties of Ushers   The duties of ushers at a church wedding are quite definite, but ushers at a home wedding serve in a more or less honorary capacity as there is little, if any, formal seating to do. Usually, standards, flower decorated or not, are placed so they will mark off with white ribbon the areas where guests are to stand. Immediately after the ceremony it is the ushers' work to remove the ribbons and standards, so guests may leave.

Ushers should arrive at the church an hour before the ceremony, leaving their hats and outer coats, if any, in the vestry but donning the gloves, which they wear in the performance of their duties within the church. In the vestry they receive their boutonnieres—furnished by the groom—which are their badge of office and should be in place before the ushers enter the church. One usher may be designated by the groom to notify him of the bride's arrival.

Ushers group themselves to the left of the door inside the church, preferably in the vestibule if it is large enough. The "head usher," usually a brother or other relative designated by the groom, tells them of any special seating instructions he has received from the bride's mother. Each of them should be armed with a list of guests to be seated in reserved pews, but as guests rarely forget they have been honored by being assigned seats, these lists are rarely referred to unless, if pew cards were issued, a guest forgets to bring his. Unrecognized guests are asked their names and should themselves say "friend of the bride" or "friend of the groom," or the usher may ask the question so that they may be correctly seated—on the left of the church for the bride, on the right for the groom. If as the church fills up it seems likely that the seating will not be balanced, the ushers seat later-arriving guests on the side that has fewer filled seats, regardless of the guest's status. The head usher should watch to see that seating remains uniform.

Ushers should be gracious and seem unhurried even when, at a big wedding, they must seat a great many people. Bustle and self-importance are most inappropriate in church, so the groom should choose his attendants from among his most dignified friends, whose social presence can be counted upon. For, while an usher actually receives each guest and speaks a few gracious words as he goes up the aisle, he must not be too exuberant or, himself, more than part of the background of the principals—the bride and groom.

An usher does not allow a lady to find her seat unescorted. If several guests arrive in a group, he offers his right arm to the eldest lady, and the others in the group follow singly, women first, and are seated together by the usher. If two women arrive at the same time, the younger steps back and permits the elder to take the usher's arm while she waits his return or accepts the services of the next available usher. If a lady arrives with an escort, an usher still takes her to her seat while her escort follows a few steps behind.

A male guest entering alone is seated by the usher, who naturally does not offer his arm unless the man is very aged and might have trouble negotiating the aisle alone. If two men arrive at the same time the usher walks down the aisle with the elder and the younger man follows so that he may be seated at the same time.

Children—that is, girls and boys under fifteen or sixteen—follow along as their parents are ushered up the aisle. If there is time for such extra courtesy, an usher may escort a girl slightly under this age—to her obvious delight.

Seating the Mother of the Bride and the Mother of the Groom Five minutes before the mother of the bride is seated one of the ushers seats the groom's mother who should be at the church in ample time before the start of the ceremony. Since she is escorted to her seat by an usher, her husband, if he is with her, follows her down the aisle. She is seated in the first pew on the right—not necessarily alone. Other of her children or perhaps the grandparents of the groom may be with her. The groom's mother, however, must have the end seat on the aisle and if anyone else sits with her, there must be room left for her and her husband. When there are no ushers, the groom's father escorts his wife to her seat.

The head usher escorts the bride's mother to her seat, and her entrance, always carefully timed, is the signal that the processional is about to start. When there are no ushers, some male member of the family should escort the mother of the bride to her seat. It is after she is seated that the church doors are closed and the canvas, if any (necessary, actually, only if the bride wears a long train) is laid. The head usher and one other have the honor of rolling down the canvas. After the bride's mother is in place no one else may be seated by ushers. The bride's mother too need not sit alone or only with her husband. She may well choose to share her honored pew with the bride's grandparents or close friends or relatives. Here too, however, the mother of the bride should be near the aisle, and space should be left so her husband, or whoever escorts the bride, may join her after his part in the ceremony. Any latecomers must wait outside until after the ceremony is over or quickly seat themselves on aisle seats in the back of the church if the doors have not been closed.

After the bride's mother is seated and the canvas, if there is one, is down, two designated ushers, starting with their left feet first, walk together up the aisle to the last reserved pews where white satin ribbons have been carefully folded and laid alongside of the decorated aisle posts. They pick up the entire bundle and, again in step, walk the length of the pews, as rehearsed, drawing the ribbons behind the aisle posts in a straight line, placing the loop at the end of each ribbon over the last aisle post.

The ushers are then ready to take their places at the beginning of the procession. Ushers always go up the aisle in pairs, but in the recessional it is optional for them to pair with the bridesmaids, if there is an equal number. The procedure is decided by the bride and the clergyman in the rehearsal.

After the recessional the ribbons are left in place until the mothers of the bride and groom and at least some of the reserved pew guests have been escorted out. After the first few have gone down the aisle ushers often take out groups in order to clear the church more quickly. It is an extremely ill-mannered guest who, despite the ribbons restraining him on the aisle side, leaves from the far side of the church before the reserved pew guests have been escorted out and the ribbons removed.

Complications in the Seating of Couples' Families   When divorces among the bride's family make the traditional seating procedure inappropriate, here are some suggestions to follow. If the bride's parents are divorced, but neither has remarried, it is best for the father after escorting his daughter to return to the mother's pew, if they are friendly. Otherwise he returns to the third pew behind her. This is where a remarried father's wife is seated, if she attends. This is the appropriate seat too for a girl's mother and her new husband, if any, when a girl lives with her father and a stepmother who has assumed the mother's role in the planning of the wedding.

In the event that a brother or uncle is giving away the bride he should return to sit with the mother of the bride in the first pew. It is always the bride's mother, or whoever is acting for her, who is first escorted out by the head usher.

If the groom's parents are divorced they may be seated together, if willing, in the first right pew, or the mother may be in the first alone or with her new husband. Her former husband is seated alone or with his new wife in the second or third pew. In these honored pews may also be seated children of the family, grandparents or intimate friends, if desired.

If one of these solutions seems to fit your situation, it is recommended that you discuss the matter with all those involved and settle upon whatever is least disturbing to all.

At the Reception   Ushers' duties are not over once they have completed their schedules at the church. They must see to it that the bridal party is transported to the reception, if there is one, well in advance of the first guests' arrival, and they should arrange transportation for any reception guests who may not have it. They have limited time to attend to these details, because, although they do not stand in the receiving line, they should be on hand as soon as possible for the wedding group pictures, which should be taken while everyone is still relatively fresh and can be accounted for. And as no guest should arrive and have to wait to be received, you can see that there is split-second timing even here.

At the reception the ushers, at last, may relax and enjoy themselves. At a large formal reception caterers take charge of refreshments, but at a small one the ushers may help serve guests. They aid and abet the couple in a smooth getaway as the reception draws to a close, after the bride has thrown her bouquet to the waiting bridesmaids when she goes to change to her street clothes.

Gifts Ushers, as members of the wedding party, always give gifts to the bride, individually, before the wedding or together give the couple some major gift from them all, with contributions to the fund tactfully geared to the circumstances of the least affluent usher. A silver tea tray, a chair, or coffee table—things the new household needs—are appropriate and better than separate gifts from each usher, as men are often uncertain as to what constitutes a suitable wedding gift. If ushers wish to give a personalized gift they might consider a silver tray bearing their signatures and the initials of the couple. They are often visibly relieved if the bride, when asked, has a concrete suggestion.

Military Ushers In a service wedding where the groom is a commissioned officer—and only if he is—brother officers in uniform acting as ushers make the arch of swords for the bride and groom outside the church if the weather is good. At naval military weddings the naval officer wears only his sword belt, not his sword. At the end of the ceremony the ushers proceed down the aisle with the wedding party, assist the guests outside, then buckle on their swords and at the command "Draw Swords!" from the head usher unsheathe their swords (blades up) and make the ceremonial arch for the bride and groom and for them only—to pass through, then sheath their swords at the command "Return Swords!"

At a West Point wedding, there may be both saber bearers and ushers, or there may be only ushers who may act also as saber bearers. If civilian ushers are used, they escort the parents of the bride and groom in the recessional. If there are only saber bearers the parents leave unescorted, and the arch of swords is formed first at the foot of the chancel steps and again outside.

Civilian and military personnel are sometimes together in a bridal party, but where some ushers and perhaps the groom are required to be in uniform others conform to the proper formal dress for the time of day and season.

Military ushers, because their swords are worn on the left side, offer their right arms to the bridesmaids at all times, and the bride stands to the right of the bridegroom when he is in full dress uniform. All ushers, civilian and military, in the recessional must then be on the right if they are paired with bridesmaids.

At an Air Force wedding the groom does not wear his saber, nor do the ushers. Only saber bearers who are commissioned officers or cadets can wear the saber at an Air Force wedding.

Military personnel never wear boutonnieres, even at weddings.

Since military etiquette on this point is so complex and so rigid, I suggest you consult the head of your branch of service for any helpful booklets he might have on the subject of military weddings. These no doubt will answer any additional questions that you might have.

Gifts for Bride's Attendants, Ushers, and Best Man

Both bride and groom give their attendants some lasting memento of the occasion—the groom at his bachelor dinner, the bride at any convenient time before the wedding (usually a week in advance) when all her attendants are together. The gifts are usually silver or gold—something that can be engraved with the date and the initials of the recipients and are something of lasting value. Desk accessories—silver staplers, paper weights, or letter openers—are suitable for both maids and ushers. Brides often give charms for bracelets or tiny gold or silver pencils or silver snuff boxes (now used for pills). Gifts for ushers should be all alike, as are those for the bridesmaids. The chief attendants receive the same kind of gift varied a little in design or size, a larger stapler, initialed or a letter opener and scissors set for the best man, say, and a bracelet or cultured pearls for the maid or matron of honor instead of a charm.

Going to the Church

Bridesmaids always meet at the home of the bride before going to the church. They may dress there, if that seems advisable, or arrive dressed. If they are from out of town it is the duty of the bride's mother to find them accommodations either in her own home or with friends or, failing that, at a hotel. The bride's family pays hotel bills for these attendants where they are incurred as part of the cost of the wedding. The groom does the same for his ushers or best man, if he possibly can, when they are from out of town and can't be accommodated by his family.

At the bride's home the attendants receive their bouquets. Attendants should all be assembled a full hour before the ceremony and able, if necessary, to aid the bride in her dressing and her mother with the last-minute preparations for the reception.

The mother of the bride leaves the house first. She rides alone or with one or two bridesmaids making sure she keeps room in the car for her husband to ride to the reception with her. The bride, alone with her father, always rides in a special car, whose driver, or chauffeur, wears a white boutonniere. The car's tires, if not white-walled, are freshly whitewashed. The bride is very careful not to sit on her wedding gown or crease her veil. In some new churches there is a bridal dressing room, where the bride puts on her gown. She arrives at the church, ready except for her gown and veil, at least an hour in advance of the ceremony, in this case so guests will not see her. The wedding consultant, if any, assists her as do the bridal attendants, who also may prefer to complete their dressing at the church.

At a large wedding where the traffic will be heavy, the bride's family notifies the local police precinct which may be able to send additional traffic patrolmen. If they cannot, or even if they can, the family frequently hires off-duty policemen or regular uniformed men to park cars and direct traffic. Rates for this work, of course, vary in different communities. The same procedure is used at debuts and other large functions, private and public. With the help of these men, as each car arrives it moves on to a designated parking space. The bride's car, however, remains in front of the church just where it dispatched her and her father, until she re-enters it with the groom.

If an Attendant Drops Out

No attendant asks to be excused from the bridal party except for some very good reason—illness or such a recent death in his or her immediate family that burial does not take place before the wedding day. In any case, the bride or groom is faced with a difficult problem in trying to replace the missing attendant. It may be easier for them to leave the bridal party as it is and let the uneven usher walk alone, if it's a man who's missing, or the extra bridesmaid precede the maid or matron of honor alone in the processional. The friend who is asked at the very last minute to fill in at anything so formal as a bridal procession may well be accepting at considerable inconvenience, while wondering why he was not asked to be a member of the wedding from the beginning.

Chapter 9

PRE-WEDDING PARTIES

There are a number of customary parties given before a wedding in many sections of the country. If the groom cannot be present during this period of festivities, an escort from the family or wedding party should be provided for the bride. These pre-wedding parties of course can be gay and exciting and certainly express the joy and happiness surrounding the impending event. If parties are given in the bride's honor she should write thank-you notes to the hostesses immediately after the event has taken place. It is a nice gesture for her to send flowers as well, although it is not necessary, particularly if the expense is too great. A very important word of caution, however. Too many parties preceding the wedding, or parties too closely scheduled, can be exhausting to everyone concerned. If many people suggest parties, the wise bride urges them to join forces. A sensible program of entertaining can make this time memorable for all and especially for the engaged couple.

The Bridesmaids' Party

In some communities the bridesmaids band together to give some kind of special party for the bride a week or more before the wedding—aside from the usual showers. This may be a luncheon, a tea, a dinner, or in some cases even a cocktail party. The guest list may include only the bridesmaids and honor attendants, or the groom, best man, and ushers may be included along with their respective wives and husbands. As a matter of fact the party may be extended, if the hostess or hostesses wish, to include friends and relatives.

Party for Out-of-Town Guests

At big weddings where a number of out-of-town guests are expected, some kind of party is often planned by the friends of the bride for these guests before an afternoon or evening wedding. Such entertainment is usually a lunch, or, of course, a brunch. Occasionally, as circumstances indicate, it might be a dinner following a wedding where the reception was early and simple and late departing planes or trains again might leave guests with time to fill.

Bridal Teas

It is a nice tradition for some close friend of the bride's family to give a tea in honor of the bride-to-be. These teas, which are usually planned for the afternoon, have a feminine guest list, although the men in the wedding party, and especially the groom, may put in an appearance toward the end. It is standard to have close friends of the bride pour, although it is proper for relatives to pour as well, and particularly those from out of town who may have no other role in the wedding. (The wearing of hats by the pourers is no longer usual.) In a case where the mother of the groom is not well known in the bride-to-be's community, it is a good idea to have a receiving line if many guests attend so that the guests at the tea will all be able to make the acquaintance of the groom's mother.

Bridal Showers

Showers are popular in many communities and a practical and attractive way to help a bride set up housekeeping—but senseless if she comes from a family that "has everything." For the basic idea of a shower *is* practicality—the bride's closest friends give her utilitarian things—kitchen supplies, linens, cooking equipment, staple groceries, pantyhose, all to form a little nest egg of needed articles with which to start off her new life. It is possible, if the bride is going to be living far away from the site of the shower, to specify a "greenback" shower. In this case the money should be affixed to the branches of a tree or plant to make it more festive. Each bill may be twisted in such a way that the denomination is not visible. (See The Money Tree, p. 174). Showers are usually given a month before the wedding. It is nice for those planning showers to consult others who may want to do the same. It is often a financial hardship on friends who are invited to four or five showers for the same girl. It is more considerate for the sponsors to join forces in one or two showers instead. One or two showers as a matter of fact is the sensible limit, and the bride does have the right to discourage friends who wish to do more than this. Showers are not given for second marriages.

Showers if any may be given by any close friend, usually a member of the bridal party. Often they are given by the maid or matron of honor, if she isn't a sister or other relative and if she lives in the community and has the facilities for entertaining. It is the hostess' obligation to inform the newspapers about the shower if she feels that it is newsworthy. She should also know the bride's clothing sizes in case anyone asks. This type of information cannot gracefully appear anywhere on the invitation. Showers are never given by members of the bride's or groom's immediate families, but a cousin may give a shower. It is, however, acceptable for members of the bride or groom's families to offer financial aid to those giving showers, and they may even offer the facilities of their homes, so long as the showers are not given in their names. Showers are supposed to be a "surprise" to the bride, who supposedly has no idea that an invitation to a tea for her might mean that she is to be showered with gifts. She is usually quietly consulted as to her needs. The guest of honor should arrive on time, and should introduce her hostess to anyone she may not already know.

Gifts for Showers Shower gifts are mostly inexpensive, as the bride's intimate friends usually give her wedding gifts as well—though in some cases it is perfectly possible that the shower gift and wedding gift will be combined, as in the gift of an electric toaster or waffle iron at a kitchen shower. Guests at a shower always take a gift. As only the closest friends of the bride are asked, it is usual—but not obligatory for invited guests to send a little gift when they cannot attend. This means that showers are somewhat limited in size. No bride has one hundred intimate friends. People from out of town, other than grandmothers or close relatives who might be flattered to receive the invitation, are rarely invited to showers. Of course, if the hostess has erred in asking a mere acquaintance of the bride to attend a shower for her, then the recipient of the invitation is under no obligation either to attend or to send a gift. She must, though, in all courtesy, reply to the invitation. It is usual to invite the mothers of the bride and of the groom, although not obligatory. If they are invited, they too should bring little gifts.

Joint Showers for the Bride and Groom

In some communities the custom of giving joint evening showers is growing. And the men—among them the ushers and best man—give special little gifts to the groom, usually a poor neglected soul in the wedding setup.

For a joint shower it might be more entertaining to plan a picnic or even a modest buffet dinner than the usual tea or cocktail party. It would be a good idea in these instances for several couples to get together and share the expense of the party. A suitable invitation might be on an informal rather than the fill-in type invitation and might read as follows:

Mr. and Mrs. Ralph Allen

Dr. and Mrs. John Kaufman

(On the inside)

For

Joyce and Alex

A Shower

Saturday, September 12th, at 6 P.M.

"Fair Winds" 17 Oak Street

R.s.v.p.

Mrs. Allen

100 Pine Street

Oakland, Calif.   zip code

The groom might receive handkerchiefs or ties or garden tools if the couple is to have a house. It would be poor taste, however, to give a joint shower in which the bride received anything so intimate as lingerie. Here is a list of possible gifts for *joint* showers:

Bride	**Groom**
pantyhose	ties
linens	socks
Limoges door handles and switch plates	shirts
canned goods	handkerchiefs
cosmetics	barbecue supplies
soap	home desk equipment
kitchen utensils	ash trays
interesting dish towels	pipestand
records or tapes	records or tapes
cookbooks	tools
closet accessories	garden equipment
bathroom equipment	books
gloves	wines and liquors
sewing materials	liqueurs (a very nice idea)
plastic container for paper cups	garden seeds
for bathroom or kitchen	games: Scrabble, Monopoly,
movie camera and film (a fine	chess
"group" gift)	

It is necessary, of course, for shower-givers and guests to get together on themes, colors, and the bride's needs. It is even advisable to ask the bride what type of shower she would prefer. If she is to have a kitchen with red accessories, a kitchen shower should have all gifts geared to the theme— even to a red step-on garbage can or folding stepladder. If either bride or groom is to receive things to wear, exact sizes should be ascertained. The kind of shower should be chosen that permits even the most short-of-money bridesmaid, who is involved with her own expenses of the wedding, to make her own gay contribution, if only a dime-store pot-holder. Gifts should all be assembled, wrapped, and perhaps screened off, before the bride arrives. Any later-arriving guests present theirs personally. The bride opens all gifts at the designated time—usually before the refreshments, which are simple. The bride's verbal thank-you's when she opens her gifts are usually sufficient (but follow the local custom), though she should write a brief note to anyone who sent a gift but could not come herself. You are never expected to send a gift to a shower to which you are not invited. Shower guests should be at least invited to the wedding if not the reception, unless the wedding is to be very intimate, including only attendants and the immediate families of the couple. But perhaps it is a better idea, if you wish to give a party to introduce a bride to people who cannot possibly be invited to the wedding, not to make this type of party a shower. A tea or any event at which presents are not expected is more suitable. You cannot expect a bride to invite members of your family to her wedding just because you have given her a shower at which they were present.

If the wedding is called off, the bride should return the gifts received at the shower or showers.

Proxy Showers

If a young man is being married in a distant place and friends of his family would like to give a shower for his bride-to-be, or if a girl is being married abroad as sometimes happens, a proxy shower can be arranged. In fact, in any instance where the guest of honor cannot attend her own party, a proxy shower is in order. In these cases, the gifts are collected at the shower and the wrapped, unopened presents are shipped in a carton or crate to the absent recipient, or are held until she can open them in person, even if this will be after the wedding. Showers of this sort are particularly appropriate for a young man in the Service who is marrying a girl from abroad and bringing her back to this country to live. It helps her to feel welcome in what are very strange circumstances. The hostess who gives a proxy shower would do well to explain the nature of the shower in a personal note, or make her invitations by phone, rather than trying to convey this complicated situation in the commercially available fill-in invitations.

The Bachelor Dinner and "Maiden Dinner"

Two or three nights before the wedding—certainly not the night before—it is still customary but not obligatory for the groom to give a bachelor dinner to his best man and ushers and perhaps many or few other men friends, usually in a private dining room of a restaurant or club or in the groom's bachelor quarters if he has them.

We usually forget that the groom, too, probably enters marriage with some trepidation, and therefore the bachelor dinner, no doubt, serves to bolster his courage. In past generations it was supposed to allow him a final fling, and it produced a certain "morning after" in everyone attending. It is unusual, to say the least, for a man who is marrying for the second time to have a bachelor dinner.

Today, with pre-marriage relationships on a more relaxed plane, the groom has less need, perhaps, to blow off steam at his bachelor dinner, and, if he has one at all, it is likely to be a quiet stag affair, distinguished, of course, at the end by the expected toast to the bride. For the toast the groom rises and with him all the men at the table. He raises his glass, traditionally filled with champagne, and says simply, "To the bride." Each man drains his glass (normally, champagne is sipped, of course) and replaces it on the table, instead of snapping its fragile stem as was formerly customary. Many restaurants well understanding the bachelor-dinner urge to break the glasses to honor the bride are still willing to provide the cheapest possible glasses, billing the host for the breakage if it does occur. But any modern bride will feel just as honored if the glasses remain intact, I am sure.

Today's bride is, especially in smaller communities, very likely to make her own farewell to the single life by dining with her bridal attendants or alone with her best friend. Customarily she always spends the night before her wedding with her immediate family. If she does give a "maiden dinner" it usually takes place the evening of the bachelor dinner in some restaurant or club or in the bride's home. At this time, if she wishes, she can give her attendants their gifts and propose a toast to the groom.

The Rehearsal Dinner

It is becoming more and more popular for the wedding rehearsal to be held in the late afternoon the day before the wedding, followed by a rehearsal dinner, which may be scheduled for six-thirty or seven o'clock.

In some sections of the country, mainly the South and Midwest, but increasingly in the rest of the country as well, it is customary for the groom's parents to give the rehearsal dinner. However, a close friend of either family or another relative may ask to entertain. Often the rehearsal dinner is a stand-up buffet with no fuss at all, other times it may be a relatively formal dinner at a club or restaurant.

Seating for the rehearsal dinner can be handled with the bride and groom alone at a small table at the top of a "T" formation. The maid or matron of honor would be to the groom's right and the best man to the bride's left, followed on one side by the head usher next to the matron of honor, and then perhaps the clergyman's wife. On the opposite side could be the second head usher and possibly the mother of the groom. The father of the bride would sit to the right of the mother of the groom. A mother of the groom who is a widow and who wants to be hostess at this event might ask some close male relative in her age bracket to accompany her and to serve as host. If you cannot have a "T" formation, place the host and hostess at the head and foot of the table with the bride and groom together in the center along one side and work from there. Place cards are usual when eight or more guests are present.

The rehearsal dinner need not be elaborate, and it is the hostess alone who determines the size of the invitation list, but all members of the wedding party, both sets of parents, and the clergyman and his wife must be included. It is not necessary, but it would probably make the dinner more enjoyable for those concerned if the spouses of married members of the bridal party and the fiancés of at least the honor attendants were invited. If however the spouses or fiancés of attendants cannot be included they should not feel slighted and should do their best not to promote discord about this comparatively minor issue. If the dinner is large enough to include them, relatives or wedding guests who have arrived early from out of town might enjoy participating in some of the pre-wedding festivities. A large party, however, should be avoided as the rehearsal is tiring and it is difficult to know exactly when it will be over.

In many cases where there will be no chance to do so at the reception, the bride is toasted at the rehearsal dinner. It is customary at weddings and rehearsal dinners in this country for the men to do the toasting. The best man should lead with a few spontaneous words while the others stand to honor the seated bride and groom. The bride does not usually return the toast to the groom, nor does she toast herself at the moment the others do by drinking with them. Occasionally, the bride may want to return the toast and may stand and say as she might at the reception, "To my darling husband," or "husband-to-be."

The marriage license should be signed at this time to simplify matters the day of the wedding. It is then entrusted to the best man who, on the morning of the wedding, also receives the wedding ring along with the clergyman's fee in a sealed envelope.

A Cake Cutting

A charming old southern custom that I would like to see revived is that of a post-rehearsal "Cake Cutting" in place of the rehearsal dinner. This party is frequently given by the maid of honor and consists of buffet-type food (salads and sandwiches with as many side dishes as you want) and the cake with any beverage.

The first piece of cake is cut by the bride or the bride and groom, just as it would be at a wedding reception. The advantage of this type of party is that it is friendlier and more intimate and that it can be briefer than a lavish rehearsal dinner which can go on far too long considering the exhausting day everyone faces on the morrow. Particularly if you are not going to have a reception at which a wedding cake is going to be served (if, for instance, you are just greeting guests at the rear of the church after the conclusion of the ceremony) you might consider this lovely traditional substitute.

Pre-Nuptial Receptions

It is sometimes desirable, for a variety of reasons, to hold a party before the wedding has actually taken place which in many ways resembles a wedding reception. This type of event is particularly useful when the couple is marrying in a place which is far distant from, for instance, the groom's home, but to which they will be making a visit before the ceremony. In this way his parents can take advantage of this opportunity to introduce their future daughter-in-law to all of their friends and relatives who would not be able to make the journey to the distant wedding. The invitation for such a party might look like this:

In honour of
Miss Ann Jeannette Carr
Dr. Lucien Russell
Mr. and Mrs. Arthur Russell
request the pleasure of your company
Sunday, the sixteenth of June
from four until seven o'clock
The Roof
St. Regis Hotel
New York, New York

Please reply to
405 East 55 Street
New York, N.Y. zip code

This kind of invitation, which could either be the fill-in type of engraved invitation available at better stationers or a fully engraved one, maintains the necessary degree of formality but discloses that the reception is for a couple who is not as yet married.

Chapter 10

DRESS FOR THE WEDDING

The Bride's Dress

For a formal winter wedding in church or at home the bride wears a full-length bridal gown in a variety of possible materials—satin, velvet, taffeta, chiffon, tulle, and lace. All of them—except the velvet—can be worn for a summer wedding, plus a wide variety of summer cottons, from organdy to dimity.

The formal wedding gown is usually white or ivory (though delicate blue or pink are sometimes seen) with or without a full-length veil of tulle, lace, or other sheer material. A fingertip veil is often used on even the most formal gown, but a veil may be dispensed with entirely by the bride, in favor of a flower circlet on her head. In a simple country church, however, I saw a charming bride go to the altar in a formal gown but bareheaded, because she never wore a hat of any kind. It was what was for her the natural thing. I cannot recommend, however, many of the attention-seeking departures some young brides introduce intended to shock the spectators at a time that should be serious and full of respect.

For a traditional formal wedding, a wedding gown should follow a certain decorum—neckline conservative and sleeves preferably long. If the sleeves are fairly short, this necessitates the wearing of long gloves, which may not be removed during the ceremony. Instead, the gloves are rolled back to the wrists or the under seam of the ring finger is ripped, so the bride can bare her finger to receive the ring. The bride who chooses a long-sleeved gown doesn't wear gloves, and even with three quarter sleeves gloves are not necessary. The bride's shoes are white silk or satin (and she should be sure to wear them around the house for a few days before the wedding so they will be comfortable when it counts most), her orange blossoms are preferably artificial and wiltless, but any jewelry she wears is real and more or less functional. She might wear a strand of pearls or a simple pin or clip, but she wouldn't wear even a tiny diamond studded watch or bracelet. She might wear simple pearl earrings or small gold ones, but she would avoid chi-chi. In place of a bridal bouquet (usually furnished by the groom) the bride may carry a white prayer book, with or without a flower or ribbon marker. If she wears her engagement ring to the altar it is on her right hand to facilitate the slipping on of the wedding band on her left ring finger. On the wedding day, at least, it should not be overshadowed by the engagement ring.

At an informal church or home wedding the bride may wear a street or floor-length wedding gown and a short veil or a simple dress or suit (not black) through noon, a dressmaker suit or covered-up cocktail dress, later. In fact, at less formal and traditional ceremonies there is now great leeway in bridal attire, anything from mini, midi, and maxi lengths to full, skirtlike pants. The wearability of the outfit after the wedding is considered.

Should the Bride Wear a Family Gown? It is traditional in some families that each generation's brides wear a family gown that has served this romantic purpose before. But no one should assume that a bride will prefer to carry on such a tradition or even wear her mother's own gown rather than have her very own. Again, it is the bride who should decide, and any suggestion that she wear other than her own gown should be very tentative indeed. No family pressure should be permitted, for a bride certainly has the right to make such an important decision herself. And if she decides in favor of a modern gown, it is the obligation of her mother to protect her from criticism by unthinking Aunt Nellies. The best way to store the gown, veil, or train, is the traditional method of folding tissue paper between the folds of the material and storing in a cool dry place. But there are companies that advertise that they specialize in the preservation of historical costumes and which supply detailed information.

How Practical Should a Wedding Gown Be? Most brides abandon any thought of practicality when choosing a wedding gown. If a great deal of money goes into it, they like to think that it may become a family heirloom their daughter and granddaughters will wear. However, modern living has created its own storage problems, and it is better, no doubt, to choose the kind of gown that can be remade by a clever seamstress into a dinner or evening dress. If a white dress the first year or so of marriage seems a little obvious, it can very well be dyed. If it is to be dyed, the dyeing should take place before the remodeling, as the fabric will probably shrink. It is more practical to save the veil for future generations than the dress, as wedding veils change very little, while dresses change considerably.

Superstitions Most brides like to follow the age-old superstition that they must wear "something old, something new, something borrowed, and something blue." Some walk down the aisle with a shiny dime in place of the traditional sixpence in their shoe. Most brides, however, scoff at the idea that bad luck will befall them if they rehearse their own weddings, and they rarely have "stand-ins." Rice, sometimes painful when thrown too enthusiastically at weddings, is usually replaced today by confetti or rose petals furnished by the bride's family. Anything of the sort should be thrown only outside the church. The old shoes tied to the bridal car and thrown after it (a dying custom) are said to represent the stones thrown at pursuers when marriage was by capture. No modern bride worries about seeing or talking to the groom before the ceremony on the day of the marriage.

The Mature Bride

If a woman is marrying for the first time, no matter what her age, she is entitled to wear a white gown with all of the traditional trappings. However, many older women find that pure white is too harsh for their hair and skin coloration, and they feel a little precious wearing a veil. It may be more becoming for the bride to choose an off-white (perhaps oyster or champagne) gown and for her to dispense with a veil and settle instead for a tiny headcovering, if any. There is no reason for a bride not to choose any color in which she feels she looks well, except of course a true red or black, for her wedding dress. Nor is there any reason, if she feels more comfortable, why she can't wear a covered up cocktail type dress or even a soft suit, rather than the traditional wedding gown, gearing the formality of her outfit to the time of day of the wedding. In making her choice, however, she should keep in mind that her husband-to-be may be disappointed if she does not conform as much as possible to his idea of the traditional bridal costume.

The Bride's Formal Wedding Pictures

Formal photographs of the bride in her bridal costume are rarely taken the day of the wedding but, instead, after the final fitting of her gown. If they are needed for newspaper reproduction it is preferable that they be furnished well in advance of the wedding day. These particular photographs are never candids.

Trousseau shops often arrange for formal bridal photographs to be taken there before the gown is delivered. Or the bride may have her picture taken at home a few days before the wedding. Growing in popularity is candid photographic coverage, often in color, of the wedding. This is best planned and executed by a professional photographer who works from a "script" to give all-day sequence to the great event. It is up to the individual bride and groom whether they choose to take formal pictures with their parents on the day of the ceremony. If the wedding is in a church and it is desired to photograph the ceremony, it is necessary to get permission to do this from the clergyman who will officiate at the ceremony.

A bride should avoid heavy make-up and, for her photographs especially, be cautious with eye shadow, mascara, and dark lipstick. False eyelashes, if worn, should be light and feathery. Very light make-up produces the loveliest bridal pictures. A cautious bride will try out several hair styles that she is considering wearing for her bridal pictures and for her wedding for several weeks prior to the date of her wedding. She may even arrange a series of beauty-parlor appointments so that the experimenting can be controlled by an expert.

The cost of the wedding pictures is borne by the bride's family. In some Jewish circles, however, the groom's family is expected to offer to pay for half the wedding photographs, as I have indicated earlier. This is something that must be worked out on an individual basis. The bride usually presents a formal wedding photograph, or an enlarged candid, to the mother and father of the groom. Her own parents make the selections that they wish and theirs is the responsibility of furnishing pictures perhaps to grandmothers, friends, and relatives, although very probably the bride and groom alone will have the album of candid pictures of the day if they have been ordered. The groom's family, if it desires any additional pictures than those given them should be business-like and offer to pay for them.

Dress of Groom and Best Man

The degree of formality of the men's clothing at a wedding is determined by the type of costume worn by the bride. All men in the wedding party, even the fathers of the bride and groom, wear the same style of clothes as the groom and best man, unless they are in uniform, in which case the fathers wear formal clothes like any civilian usher.

Formal wedding clothes, even shoes, are frequently rented these days, and when this is so it is essential that arrangements for them be made approximately three weeks in advance to allow for the necessary tailoring adjustments. Trousers, for example, should break slightly above the shoe tops, the jacket collar must hug the neck, and for a well-turned-out appearance at least a half-inch of white cuff should show below the sleeve of the jacket.

The groom's boutonniere is distinctive from those of the other men in the bridal party—lilies of the valley or a gardenia preferably and a breast pocket handerchief is not worn. Pink carnations are sometimes seen since Prince Philip wore one at Princess Margaret's wedding.

Gloves During the Wedding The groom and the best man wear their gloves until they get to the altar. The best man then removes his right glove to pass the ring to the groom at the proper moment. The groom removes his right glove to accept the ring, each man holding the glove in the left hand during the procedure, and in the recessional. Then they may put them in their inside breast pockets, or hand them to an usher. The sexton instructs the wedding party on how to handle these moves. To simplify matters in some churches the sexton suggests that the groom and best man go gloveless during the ceremony.

Gloves, if worn, should be removed for shaking hands, and for eating and smoking at the reception. Gloves are becoming an increasingly less common part of wedding attire. Ushers never wear them if the groom and best man have dispensed with them.

Ushers

Ushers dress like the groom and best man, although lapel facing, fabric types, stripes on trousers, and shirts usually differ. All ushers should be dressed identically in terms of style, although variations in fabric are permissible. Their ties, which the groom gives them along with their gloves and collars, should be different from those of the groom and best man, whose ties should differ slightly from one another anyhow. Actually, if ushers are renting their outfits it is often wiser for them to rent their accessories as well. The groom can probably find a more useful and less expensive gift for them. If he is giving them their accessories, the groom may also wish to give them formal suspenders—necessary to make formal trousers hang properly. Their identical ties may be gray four-in-hands instead of ascots, and are worn with a turned-down collar. The collars may be attached to the shirt or separate. When attached they are soft and a little less formal than a separate collar, which is starched. When the collar is attached, it should be a plain, not buttoned-down, collar.

Summer Weddings

Summer weddings present some special problems. By definition, no summer wedding is considered truly formal. White or gray flannel-like materials and any good-quality white suit or navy coat may replace the cutaways for formal wear when the bride is in full regalia. The groom may also wear a stroller and striped trousers if he wishes to be more formal. This can be worn with a white linen or gray doeskin vest. If the men choose to wear cutaways it is wise in summer to select them in one of the lightweight miracle fibers. The tie is blue, the shoes black, the collar stiff, turned over. No gloves. Also for such a wedding a white linen suit or a suit in light wool or one of the miracle weaves, in white or beige tones, may be worn with a light tie and white or black shoes. White jackets and gray flannels (or gray trousers in permanent press fabrics that look like flannel) are now seen, too. With white Edwardian suits, pale blue shirts usually look much smarter than white ones and white shoes more appropriate than black. Ties should be wide.

For an evening summer wedding white dinner jackets are an appropriate substitute for formal attire. If cummerbunds are to be worn, they should be black, as should ties. No hat is necessary. In making your decision about a "formal" summer wedding, do consider that a dinner jacket can be just as hot as tails made of a summer-weight material. White dinner jackets should not in any case be used for city weddings.

At the summer garden wedding it is becoming increasingly popular for the ushers and best man to wear white suits. When these are worn for a wedding, shirts are not necessarily white but may be, for example, blue and white striped or solid blue and the ushers' ties which may be any color in a light summer silk should be chosen to go with the style of the suit. The Edwardian cut looks best with a wide or medium-wide tie, for example. The groom and the best man wear ties of a different color from those of the ushers but each wears the same color, for example, a shade of blue but the pattern may possibly differ. Their shirts match and if colors are chosen they must be similar to those of the ushers—solids, say, if ushers's shirts are striped. Shoes with white suits may be either black (which are rentable) or white (white are not and might be considered a luxury for the ushers to buy for themselves). I know of only one rental house that presently rents white suits, but because they are becoming very fashionable, the ushers might not object to buying them if they can't be rented. This is certainly an important matter to be discussed with the ushers.

Military Wedding Attire For a military wedding, as for any other, the groom gauges the formality of his uniform to the degree of formality of his bride's dress and to the time of day. The rule of thumb is that the "full dress" uniform is the equivalent of "white tie" wear, and the "mess dress" is equal to "black tie" attire. Both of these are considered very formal and should not be worn before six o'clock in the evening. The "service blue" uniform is the equivalent of a conservative business suit and is best chosen for a daytime wedding, be it formal or informal. If a man is asked to serve as an usher at a wedding in which he will be wearing a uniform while others will be in civilian clothes, he should suit his attire to that of his civilian comrades in accordance with the above guidelines.

Bridal Attendants

The maid or matron of honor may be dressed in slightly different fashion from the bridesmaids, although that trend is not so prevalent as it used to be. If there is to be both a maid and matron of honor they may be dressed alike, or within the proposed slight variations that follow. The honor attendant's dress may be of the same design but a different color or the same color but a slightly different design. Or all attendants' dresses may be alike with different flowers or headdresses distinguishing the maid or matron of honor. An attendant should not feel put upon if she knows that the bride is borrowing her bridal gown but still requiring her attendants to buy theirs. This is often done. Attendants' dresses are chosen in fabrics to complement that of the bride's dress. For example, if the bride's dress is silk the attendants' dresses would not be cotton. Unusual but beautiful is the wedding in which all the bride's attendants wear white. Prints are now permissible. This is especially dramatic if all the bridesmaids are children as they were in Princess Margaret's wedding. It is not recom-

MEN'S WEDDING DRESS

	Suit	Shirt	Tie
Formal Daytime (up to 6 P.M.)	Cutaway (most formal) with gray vest, gray striped trousers	Any wing collar shirt with an ascot Starched fold collar or the usual broadcloth shirt with cuffs with the four-in-hand	Ascot (gray in che stripes, solid) w wing collar. Fo in-hand (styled check) with fol collar
Formal Evening (after 6 P.M.)	Tail coat (full dress), white piqué or waffle weave waistcoat	Starched shirt, wing collar	White piqué or waffle weave
Informal Morning or Afternoon	If the bride wears a veil: Single-breasted gray or black stroller, striped trousers, gray vest	White shirt, fold collar, french cuffs	Gray tie
	If the bride doesn't wear a veil (and optionally when she wears a short one with no train): Business suit in blue, black, Oxford gray	White shirt, white fold collar	Tie in a conservati color
Informal Evening	White or black (preferably) dinner jacket, single-or double-breasted black cummerbund or vest (If bride wears street dress—groom wears dark business suit.)	White pleated shirt, turned down collar	Black

hoes and Socks	Hats, Overcoats and Gloves	Jewelry
ck (plain—not wing-tipped or perforated) ck socks	Silk hat (if any), gray gloves	Black or white pearl or onyx. Gold or silver cuff links— no colored stones
ck patent leather shoes ck socks	Opera or high silk hat (if any), white doeskin or chamois gloves Black Chesterfield (velvet collar)	White pearl or really fine old or antique gold studs
ck (plain) shoes ck socks	Homburg, if any hat at all, gray gloves	Black pearl or onyx
ck shoes ck socks	Derby or Homburg, gray gloves	Black or gold
ck patent leather ck socks		Black or gold
ck shoes ck socks		

summer wedding dress, please see page 110.

mcndcd that rcd bc choscn as thc color for the attendant's dresses. Some headcovering is still used but not always obligatory for the attendants—either hats, Juliet caps, or flower headdresses. The bridesmaids and maid or matron of honor may wear street-length dresses even though the bride's dress is long. It is not recommended however for the bridesmaids to be in long gowns when the bride is in a street-length dress, however informal their long gowns may be. The slippers of all attendants are alike in fabric and style, but the maid or matron of honor may wear slippers of a different color to match her dress if it is another color. In the formal wedding party only the bride may be gloveless, and then only if her sleeves are relatively long.

If there is to be a "junior bridesmaid" or "maiden of honor," her costume should go well with those of the bridesmaids and yet should be suited to her own years. There is no reason why her dress can't be the same color as that of the other bridal attendants. Her dress should be very much like a dancing-school dress, probably full of skirt and with puffed sleeves and a simple modest neckline. Even her headdress need not be too much like that of the bridesmaids, especially if theirs is relatively sophisticated. Often a wreath of flowers seems most suitable for a girl of this age. Her shoes should be the sort that she would normally wear to dancing school, perhaps black patent, one-strap slippers. Unless she is tall for her age, a girl from ten to twelve looks better in socks than than in stockings.

Flower Girls, Page Boys, and Ring Bearers   Flower girls, dressed in picturebook style, are more often seen in formal weddings than page boys and ring bearers, possibly because little girls are more amenable to "dressing up." Little boys tend to think their manhood impugned by frilly blouses and satin knee breeches or long, tight velvet trousers of the Dickens era. A page boy or ring bearer may wear a dark blue Eton suit or, if in a summer wedding, a white linen suit with short or long trousers (but *never* a miniature version of the ushers' formal wear). If period costumes are not used, a flower girl may be dressed in a party dress of white or a pastel shade that matches or complements the bridesmaids' dresses. She may wear white or colored slippers, which, with a colored dress, may match or contrast. Her bouquet should be diminutive—or she may carry a basket of rose petals, which she scatters in the aisle as she precedes the bride in the processional. Her headcovering, if any, is usually a flower circlet or a flower clip. She also wears short white gloves which may be cotton. She may or may not be in the recessional, but if she is, she walks directly behind the bride and groom. It is permissible to have two flower girls. They walk in front of the bride in the processional as they would if there were only one.

The flower girl is not expected to attend bridal parties, which would probably bore her, but her mother is invited to attend and both her parents are invited to parties for the bridal couple.

The ring bearer (chosen by the bride, as he is part of her entourage) carries the bride's wedding ring—for safety's sake not the real one—on a little, white satin pillow. The real ring is usually snug in the best man's pocket, or on his pinkie—and many a cautious clergyman wears a spare on *his* pinkie for emergency use. The ring is fastened to the cushion with light silken stitches, especially if precaution has been thrown to the winds and the real ring is borne by the child. If the ring bearer carries the actual ring, then he will necessarily have to remain with the wedding party during the ceremony. If he has been used merely for effect, however, it is quite simple for him to leave the procession as it reaches the mother of the bride's pew. As the small attendants are usually under seven, it is sometimes hard for them to stand still at the altar throughout the ceremony, so it is safer if they join the bride's mother and are not in the recessional.

In the processional the ring bearer precedes the flower girl if there is one or otherwise walks directly in front of the bride and her father. If he is in the recessional, he pairs with the flower girl and they come down the aisle together. If the attendants are not paired, the ring bearer precedes the flower girl or girls immediately following after the bride and groom.

Pages, who may be boys or girls or one of each, are usually under seven, too, and about the same size. They must be big enough to carry the bride's formal train and of course if she is not in such formal dress, pages are not needed, nor are they always used even when the long train is worn. They appear in both processional and recessional, unless they are too small and restless in which case, just before reaching the altar, they step into the bride's mother's pew and take no further part in the ceremony. Pages and ring bearers as well as the flower girls are considered the bride's attendants. She therefore presents them each with some small suitable token of the occasion—a tiny bracelet for the flower girls, identification bracelets for the pages and ring bearer. As with parents of flower girls, parents of these attendants are invited to parties preceding the wedding and to the rehearsal dinner and the reception. Mothers of these attendants should be included in pre-bridal parties.

Pages and very young flower girls appear briefly at the reception if at all, and then firmly in the charge of their parents. The bride and groom should make a special effort to thank them before going on to the reception if they are not to be included at all in the festivities.

Candle Lighters or Altar Boys   Usually the candles to be used during the ceremony are lit by some member of the church staff. However, in some sections of the country and in some churches young boys who are members of either the bride's or groom's family perform this service. Generally the candles are lit just before the mother of the bride is scatcd. This custom does vary from church to church, and it is well to check with your clergyman or the sexton of your church beforehand. The boys wear what they would to church or Sunday school if they are too young for formal dress—fourteen is the youngest I like to see boys wearing formal dress. Navy blue or gray flannel suits with white shirts, dark ties, dark plain socks, and black shoes are suitable for weddings in cool weather. In hot weather, white linen or linen-like wash and wear suits with white shirts, dark ties, and black shoes are worn.

For an informal wedding, attendants, if any wear the same kind of clothes as the principals, geared to the season, the place of the ceremony, and the time of day.

Flowers for the Wedding Party

The groom's boutonniere is, as I have mentioned before, traditionally a spray from the bridal bouquet and is usually lily of the valley, if in season. But his boutonniere differs from that of the best man and the ushers. Ushers' boutonnieres should not be red.

The bridal bouquet is usually white, although, especially with pastel bridal gowns, sometimes other pale-colored flowers are included. It may encircle a going-away corsage if the flowers come from a florist skilled at making these corsages-within-bouquets so they merely untie when the bride wishes to toss away the rest of her bouquet. The corsage included in the bridal bouquet saves the groom the expense of a separate corsage and "fills out" the bouquet at no extra cost. The bride, even in a street dress, may carry a bible with a flower marker.

The attendants' bouquets are usually Colonial or wrist bouquets, more graceful to manage in a procession than the old-fashioned arm bouquets. If attendants and bride are in street-length gowns, corsages or cascades, as well as wrist or hand bouquets, may be used. They may carry white flowers, just as the mothers of the bride and groom may wear them, if the flowers are not the same as those in the bride's bouquet. It is nice for a mature woman to pin a corsage at the waist of her dress, or even on her handbag. No mother of a bride need feel compelled to wear a corsage, if both she and the mother of the groom can agree not to do so.

Actually the attendants' bouquets may be anything seasonal that complements their gowns. At a beautiful Christmas season wedding all the attendants were in white velvet and carried wrist bouquets of poinsettias. A country garden wedding might find the bridesmaids carrying Colonial bouquets of purple or blue iris or blue cornflowers—or even field daisies.

I do not like to see the use of artificial flowers anywhere in a wedding. If attendants' bouquets seem like too great an expense, or if you fear their wilting, use ingenuity in the choice of flowers. A little bouquet of trailing ivy is inexpensive and will stand up very well in hot weather. It is even possible for the attendants to carry just one stately flower, such as a gladiola or a long-stemmed rose, rather than a whole bouquet.

What the Parents and Guests Wear

The bride's mother has first choice of color for what she wishes to wear to her daughter's wedding and the mother of the groom consults with her before buying her own gown. The mothers of the bride and groom should wear dresses of the same length and general style. At a formal daytime wedding the mothers of the bride and groom may wear soft suits or ensembles in pale or pastel faille, taffeta, satin, or silk, or any delicately colored taffeta, satin, or silk covered-up cocktail dress or suit. A tasteful print would be fine, too, but probably prints would be overwhelming if both mothers wore them. It is perfectly acceptable for a bride's mother to wear a dress already in her wardrobe, even one she has worn to the wedding of one of her other daughters. She may choose to have some restyling done on it, if her daughter feels slighted. No mother of the bride, or of the groom for that matter, should feel bound to wear a pastel or highly conservative outfit. She should wear what looks best on her. But she should remember that on this day particularly, she is there to complement, and not to compete with, her daughter.

At a formal evening wedding the mothers may wear long- or three-quarter-sleeved dinner or evening dresses in any color but black or red. Accessories should not be black, although white is permissible, and some headdress is usually worn, but this now depends on the custom of the particular congregation—perhaps a twist of tulle, a mantilla, a stylish flat bow, or an evening hat. Although hats are no longer considered essential, no woman should ever feel embarrassed because she has worn one, as is proper at a daytime wedding, and a majority of the women guests have not. If the bride's mother has worn a stole for warmth, she should wear it to her seat. Gloves are required for everyone. Women guests dress for the time of day and the occasion and black may be worn at both daytime and evening weddings by guests. The rule that only the bride may wear white at a wedding is no longer an applicable one; women guests may wear white dresses, but not resembling the bride's dress, if they wish, especially in very warm weather.

When the groom wears formal day or evening wear the father of the bride and the father of the groom dress as he does, as do all the male members of the wedding party. Men guests at a formal daytime wedding may or may not wear cutaways or sack coats with striped trousers, as they choose. Younger men usually wear dark blue or Oxford gray suits. At a formal evening wedding men related to the family wear white tie, as do many older men, but it is usual for young men to wear dinner jackets if they are not actually in the wedding party. It is increasingly common during the summer or in warm climates for wedding guests to wear colored dinner jackets, although I still prefer tropical weight black ones.

At informal weddings guests wear conservative church-going clothes suitable to the season. The women wear hats (if the congregation requires it) and gloves. Women guests, incidentally, do not wear flowers, and men guests do not wear boutonnieres. This is the prerogative of the bridal party.

Chapter 11

THE REHEARSAL

All weddings with more than two attendants must be rehearsed two or three days before the event and at the convenience of the clergyman, or in large churches the sexton, who must be present with the organist and any other participants.

Which Arm Does the Bride Take?

This is always settled at the rehearsal and depends on the preference of the minister. It is more convenient at a formal wedding for the bride to go up the aisle on her father's right arm, so that when his role is completed and he must return to the left front pew to stand with her mother he does not have to cross over the bride's train but will be already on the convenient side. However, some ministers prefer the other procedure in which the bride comes down the aisle on her father's left arm. (In all recessionals the bride takes the groom's arm and ushers offer their arms to bridesmaids if this pairing procedure is followed.) The clergyman's ruling is the deciding one.

The Processional

Ushers are paired, as are bridesmaids, so that the shorter ones precede the taller. They learn that they do not actually "march" but walk in time, slowly, left foot first down the aisle, keeping four pews apart, and after a little coaching they manage to deliver the bride to the chancel steps at the moment the music stops playing. The bride, no longer afraid to rehearse at her own wedding, counts eight beats of the music before she follows the attendants on her father's arm (preferably the right one).

No words of the Service are spoken during the rehearsal, although the minister (or the sexton) indicates at what point each member of the party plays his role. The best man learns just when he must produce the ring from his vest pocket or, better, his little finger. The maid or matron of honor notes at what point she takes the bride's bouquet or prayer book. The bride's father—or in some cases her mother—learns when the bride is to be "given away" if this is to be part of the ceremony.

ALTAR

Processional, *Christian Ceremony*

Reading from top down: Bride and her father. Sometimes father is on bride's right (*see text*).

Flower girl or ring bearer, if any, or ring bearer and flower girl, ring bearer preceding flower girl.

Maid or matron of honor. If there are both, they may walk together or the younger may precede the elder.

Bridesmaids. Shorter ones precede taller and are paired according to height.

Ushers. Shorter ones precede taller and are paired according to height.

At the chancel steps: best man, groom, clergyman.

If there is a junior bridesmaid, her place is between the flower girl (or girls) if any, and the maid or matron of honor.

If there are pages they follow the bride and carry her train.

The Recessional

Most rehearsed of all will be the ushers, who, if it is to be a large wedding, will have real work to do. Two ushers, chosen for the honor, will be shown how to handle the ribbons and, if there is to be one, how to lay the canvas at the right moment. It is at the rehearsal that bride and clergyman, or sexton, decide how the recessional is to go. Bride and groom always lead in the recessional, but it is optional whether or not the ushers and bridesmaids pair up or return as they were in the processional, but this time with the bride's attendants immediately following the couple, in the proper order, then the ushers walking together. If there is an uneven number of ushers the extra man may walk in the middle (*see illus.*) and the second variation of the recessional is preferred. I prefer to see the attendants paired in the recessional, if possible, as such pairing after the ceremony seems symbolic of other possible romances springing from this wedding—as so often happens. However, it is necessary to clear the pairing of the attendants with the clergyman. Some don't permit it.

In the recessional the father is missing—he has joined the mother in the first pew as soon as he has given the bride away.

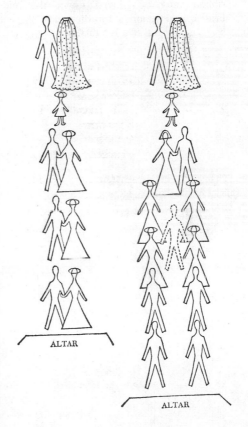

Recessional, *Christian Ceremony, Optional Arrangement*

RIGHT PANEL, *Reading from top down:* Groom and bride. In a service wedding men are on bride's right. In other weddings this is sometimes done too (*see text*).

Flower girl or page, or pages, if any, or second honor attendant, if any. Best man and maid or matron of honor. Ushers and bridesmaids paired.

FAR RIGHT PANEL, *Reading from top down:* Groom and bride.

Flower girl or second honor attendant, if any. (Very small children do not appear in recessional necessarily.)

Maid of honor and best man. If there are two attendants, matron of honor is escorted by the best man, the maid of honor by the head usher. If there is an extra usher he is placed somewhere in the center of the recessional so that he is not the "tail on the kite."

When There Are Two Main Aisles

When a church has two main aisles one may be used for the processional, one for the recessional. When each is given the same importance the pew posts are decorated exactly alike. If it is decided that one aisle is to be used for both processional and recessional, the other aisle is used only for seating of guests and is not specially decorated. If one aisle is chosen, the grouping at the chancel is on the side of that aisle. When both aisles are given equal importance the grouping at the chancel is as it is for a church with a center aisle. If it can be arranged, I like to see the parents of the bride and groom seated in the choir stalls on either side of the altar, with the bride's family on the left and the groom's family on the right. If this cannot be managed, however, the bride's family may either be seated in the pews on the far left or a dividing ribbon may be placed down the middle of the center pew and the bride's and groom's families may share the center front row.

Chapter 12

THE WEDDING CEREMONY

Procedure during the Ceremony

In Christian wedding ceremonies the left side is the bride's, as one enters, the right, the groom's. The family and friends of the bride are, therefore, on the left of the church, and the groom's are on the right. When the wedding is held at a great distance from the groom's hometown and he will be having significantly fewer guests, the ushers should arrange the seating evenly.

As the bride approaches the chancel the clergyman stands at the entrance to the altar and the groom, facing slightly into the nave, is on the right, ready to step forward to assist the bride up the chancel step

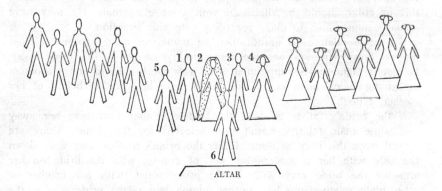

Grouping at the Altar, *Protestant Ceremony:* 1. Groom, 2. bride, 3. bride's father, 4. maid or matron of honor, 5. best man, 6. clergyman. Figures far left and right, ushers, bridesmaids. NOTE: In the Roman Catholic ceremony the bride's father joins her mother in the first pew as he reaches it. He does not give the bride away. Otherwise the grouping at the chancel is the same, with the addition of an acolyte (*see text*).

or steps. Below and behind him a little to the right is the best man. On the left of the chancel as the bride approaches stands her maid or matron of honor in the same position as the best man. Ushers, if any, are lined up below the choir stalls on each side of the chancel with the maids of honor usually in front of them and on a slanting line. In a small church it may be necessary to place only two ushers on the chancel steps, one left, one right, the rest on the floor of the church, flanking the chancel, but many variations of these groupings are used.

Giving Away the Bride

In Protestant ceremonies the father stays at the chancel until the question is posed as to who gives away the bride. He then places the bride's right hand in the hand of the clergyman and responds, "I do." Just as it is the right of a girl's real mother to announce her marriage, so it is the right of her real father to give her away, if he is capable. Step-fathers should not be afforded this honor if a girl's real father is alive and willing and able to take part. There is no graceful way for both a father and a stepfather to participate in the ceremony.

Should a girl's father be too ill or infirm to walk down the aisle, but well enough to wish to participate in the ceremony, he can be brought in from the vestry in a wheelchair just before the seating of the mother of the bride. The bride in these cases may either go down the aisle accompanied by her mother or by a male member of the family, or even alone, and join her father who would be waiting in the group at the altar or seated in the first pew, to give her away. Any situation this irregular should be discussed with your clergyman. He may have valuable suggestions to make regarding a specific situation.

If a male relative (a grandfather, an uncle, an older brother, a close mature family friend) has the responsibility of giving the bride away, he merely stands in his appointed place with the bride and at the moment of "giving away" answers, "I do," or he may answer "on behalf of her mother, I do."

If the bride's father is dead the bride's mother may give her away —if some male relative hasn't been selected for the honor. There are several ways this may be done. Either the bride's mother may walk down the aisle with her daughter—but not, of course, with the bride on her arm—or the bride may walk in the processional, with her brother or other male relative and her mother joining her as the bride reaches the left front pew. Sometimes the bride walks alone in the processional and her mother joins her as she reaches her mother's pew. Still again, a male relative will escort the bride to the chancel steps and when the clergyman asks who is to give the bride away the mother nods from her traditional place or, just before the words are to be spoken, is escorted to the chancel by the best man, who steps down for the gesture, and she then places the bride's right hand in the hand of the clergyman. She may stand to the right of the bride's escort until the ceremony is concluded, and then be escorted by him back to her pew before the recessional begins or be escorted by him directly after the "giving away" to her pew. The ceremony then continues with the vows, the ring, etc.

If a bride is marrying far from her home and none of her relatives will be able to attend to give her away there are several alternatives. The bride may arrange with the minister to dispense with this portion of the ceremony altogether. On the other hand, if she is marrying where members of the groom's family will be present, she may ask her future in-laws to suggest some close male relative of their family to whom the honor of giving away the bride would be appropriate.

Another modern and attractive departure I have seen at Congregational wedding ceremonies, but which might be—with the clergyman's permission—inserted in any Protestant ceremony is as follows. The bride's father, when asked who gave away the bride, replied, "Her mother and I do."

These procedures are necessary only in those ceremonies—the Episcopal, for example—where the one who "gives the bride away" actually places her hand in the minister's.

Giving Away the Mature Bride In the weddings of previously married brides—widows or divorcées—it is not necessary that they be "given away," and this portion of the ceremony is often omitted, just as it is in civil ceremonies when there may well be no designated attendants, merely legal witnesses.

But the older woman who has a church wedding usually chooses to be escorted to the church by some male relative or close family friend, also male, although she may arrive with the best man, the groom, and her own attendant. She does not walk up the church aisle, but waits with the groom, best man, and maid of honor in the vestry until the clergyman is ready, then is escorted to her place at the chancel by the best man, while the groom escorts the maid or matron of honor.

In some ceremonies—namely the Catholic and the Episcopal—the bride and groom follow the clergyman to the altar and may kneel at an indicated point in the ceremony. They are followed by the maid and matron of honor, if there are both in attendance, with the maid on the immediate left of the bride and the matron on the far left of the bride, so that it is the maid who assists with the bouquet and veil. The best man on the immediate right of the groom is followed by the ring bearer, if any, at far right, a few feet behind. When the clergyman asks for the ring, the best man produces it from his vest pocket or, better, his little finger. In the Catholic service he proffers it to the groom, who hands it to the acolyte, who in turn gives it to the priest, who blesses it. In the Protestant ceremony—and the Episcopal service or some variation of it is often used in Presbyterian and Congregational churches, too—he hands the ring to the groom, who gives it to the minister for the blessing.

During the blessing of the ring—or, if preferred, as soon as maid and matron of honor (or just the one attendant) are in place—the bride hands her bouquet or prayer book to the attendant chosen for the honor, so that her left hand will be free to receive the wedding ring.

At the Altar Rail, *Roman Catholic and Episcopal Ceremony, Optional Arrangements:* 1. Priest, 2. acolyte (*Roman Catholic service*), 3. bride, 4. groom, 5. best man, 6. matron of honor.

NOTE: In elaborate Roman Catholic ceremonies the entire wedding party sometimes enters the sanctuary in a large church. In some churches this is not permitted and only the bride, groom, priest, and acolyte enter the sanctuary.

As soon as the marriage service is completed the bride turns first to the maid or matron of honor for her bouquet and to have her face veil, if she has one, lifted. If the maid or matron of honor finds that holding the bride's bouquet and her own becomes too confusing, especially when the veil must be lifted, a small table may be placed to the left of the altar to hold the maid or matron of honor's bouquet. Or, the bride may hand her flowers to the junior bridesmaid before ascending with the groom into the chancel and then, as the bride descends for the recessional, the flowers may be handed back. She then turns, and, although this is not part of the ceremony, receives the groom's kiss if they have decided to kiss at the altar (see "When Does the Groom Kiss the Bride?" page 127), and the good wishes of the clergyman, who usually shakes hands with both bride and groom.

The bride then turns and takes the groom's right arm, and—after the maid of honor has adjusted her train—together they lead off in the recessional.

When Does the Bride Take the Groom's Arm? In the wedding ceremony, although the groom takes a step or two forward to meet the bride and may take her arm to assist her to kneel, if that is part of the ceremony, optionally, the bride does or does not take the groom's arm or place her hand in his until the moment in the ceremony at which this is indicated. In some ceremonies the clergyman places the bride's hand in the groom's, in others the father—or sometimes the mother—makes this symbolic gesture. At other times the bride needs her hands free to arrange her gown for kneeling, to hand her prayer book or bouquet to her attendant. The groom may assist her to rise from a kneeling position, but she should not touch him until the proper moment.

When Does the Groom Kiss the Bride? At large formal church weddings it is not usual for the groom to kiss the bride at the altar after the clergyman has congratulated the couple at the end of the ceremony. But if the couple is to receive in the church vestibule or if the marriage takes place at home, the groom always kisses the bride immediately following the ceremony, as no one may kiss the bride before he does. The clergyman, if he has long been an intimate of the family, may be the next to have the privilege, but on the receiving line the bride is kissed only by those who really have the right to offer this intimate form of salutation. Gay blades and old codgers, impelled to kiss the bride merely because they think custom sanctions it, should check their exuberance and wait for the suggestion, if any, to come from the bride—or the groom. The latter might be heard to say, "Darling, this is Alfred, my old roommate—remember—and he's dying to kiss you, of course. So I'll permit it—this once!"

The Double Ring Ceremony

When both bride and groom give each other rings the question often arises as to who holds the groom's ring until the proper moment. It is the maid or matron of honor who is in charge of the groom's ring just as the best man is always responsible for the bride's until the moment the groom slips it on her finger. The bride's attendant wears the groom's ring for safekeeping. If it won't stay on any finger it should be tied with a small white satin ribbon to her sash or belt, her bouquet or her left wrist, so she can get it off easily.

A man's wedding ring was customarily worn on the right hand, but in recent years, when the double ring ceremony became very popular during wartime, the ring was placed on the man's left hand. So now it is worn on the third finger of either the right or left hand, whichever the bride and bridegroom prefer but usually on the left hand as the bride wears hers. The groom's ring is always a gift from the bride. As it is gold and preferably perfectly plain, it may not necessarily match hers, as it used to. Most weddings are double ring ceremonies but the husbands do not necessarily wear the rings they receive.

The Double Wedding

Double weddings with the brides in formal wedding gowns are most impressive. Sometimes the brides are sisters who wish to marry at the same time, occasionally cousins, or just close friends, although in some denominations the brides must be related. The double wedding does not, of course, have to be formal, and the brides, whether in formal attire or in simple traveling suits or street dresses, need not be dressed alike.

In a formal double wedding if each bride and groom have separate attendants it is necessary that they have the same number and that the costumes of the brides' attendants at least harmonize with each other.

Sometimes sisters have the same attendants. The brides may act as maid and matron of honor for each other, or each may have separate honor attendants. The grooms, too, may act as best man for each other, or each have his own best man.

In a double wedding all the ushers are paired according to height in the processional. They are followed by the elder's bridesmaids, then her maid or matron of honor, then comes the senior bride on her father's arm, followed by the bridesmaids of the younger bride. After them comes the maid or matron of honor of the younger bride, then the bride herself on her father's arm, unless she is a sister of the elder bride. In that case a brother or other male relative escorts her. In the case of twins, the twin who was born first receives the privileges of the elder sister and is escorted by her father first and married first. However, it is possible for the father to escort both girls down the aisle, if he does so one at a time.

In the recessional the elder bride, who was married first, leads down the chancel steps with her groom and is followed by the younger bride with her groom. The attendants follow in the proper order—those of the first bride, first, or paired with those of the second bride if an equal number makes it possible. Otherwise, they leave as they arrived.

If a church has two aisles, each bridal party may have its own, timing the entrance and exit together.

All the ushers of both groups must be identically dressed, even when the bridesmaids' costumes differ for each bride. The only time, by the way, ushers may ever be dressed differently is when civilians and military men serve together.

The mothers of the brides are escorted up the aisle by ushers in the usual way just before the ceremony begins, with the mother of the elder bride coming first. In entering the first pew they leave room between them for the fathers.

It is advisable, by the way, even if the brides are sisters, for each to have her own wedding cake so that no conflict arises over which couple should cut the cake.

Differences in Religious Ceremonies

It is interesting to see how essentially alike the marriage services of different religions are. Most Christian ceremonies are similar with but minor differences. As the Christian ceremony developed from that of the ancient Jews, there is between Jewish and Christian ceremonies a definite similarity.

It is particularly gratifying to observe that increasing numbers of Reform rabbis and ministers are now recognizing these similarities and are agreeing to officiate in the joint blessing of interfaith marriages. Even the Catholic Church is bowing somewhat on this matter. A nuptial mass is now permissible in marriages between Catholics and baptized

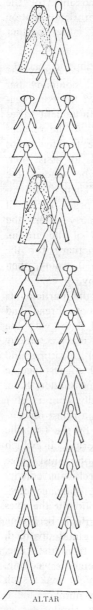

Processional at Double Wedding, Christian Ceremony, Optional Arrangement

Reading from top down: Younger bride with father or substitute (*see text*) if brides are sisters.

Maid or matron of honor of younger bride.

Bridesmaids of younger bride.

Senior bride and father.

Maid or matron of honor of senior bride.

Bridesmaids of elder bride.

Ushers paired according to height.

Recessional at Double Wedding, *Christian Ceremony, Optional Arrangement*

Reading from top down: Elder bride and groom.

Younger bride and groom.

Maids and matrons of honor of both brides, paired.

Ushers of elder bride paired with bridesmaids of elder bride.

Ushers of younger bride paired with bridesmaids of younger bride, or they may go out as they came in.

ALTAR

ALTAR

non-Catholics if the local bishop approves. It is even possible for the non-Catholic to invite a Christian clergyman of his own denomination to offer a sermon, prayer, or blessing in the home of either partner after the nuptial mass.

The Roman Catholic Ceremony In the Roman Catholic ceremony the father does not give the bride away, although he does accompany her up the church aisle. Sometimes, depending on the custom of the congregation or their own wishes, he kisses his daughter (her chief attendant raises her veil, if necessary, for this purpose) before leaving her. As he reaches his own pew he steps into it, leaving the bride to make the few steps to the altar with the bridegroom, who comes forward to assist her. The ring is received from the acolyte, the ringbearer who tenders the ring on the cushion, or occasionally from the best man. There is no established rule on this. The ring is blessed first by the priest before it is given to the groom. Sometimes the entire wedding party enters the sanctuary for the service, with the bride on the left arm of the groom. Some priests prefer that only the couple enter the sanctuary for the blessing of the ring (with an acolyte managing the bridal train), then return to the chancel steps for the balance of the ceremony.

It is now permissible, although not yet common, for the participants in a nuptial mass to receive communion consisting of both bread and wine. Formerly only the celebrant was permitted to take both, with the communicants receiving only bread. A guest at a nuptial mass ceremony should follow the customs of the congregation in regard to sitting and standing. For further instruction about the nuptial mass I suggest people go to a Catholic bookstore and acquire any relevant reading matter there.

Marriages of Catholics and non-Catholics are occasionally (but rarely) performed at home or elsewhere by special permission, with a priest officiating. Civil marriage involving a Catholic is not recognized by the Catholic Church. In mixed marriages performed by a Catholic priest, in which one is a Catholic and one a non-Catholic, the non-Catholic must agree not to impede the Catholic mate in the exercise of his religious convictions. It is not usual for a Catholic priest to perform the marriage ceremony unless at least one of the two participants is Catholic. In the eyes of the Church if you are converting to Catholicism your life is beginning anew. Consequently a non-Catholic who has been married and divorced, but is converting to remarry, is actually marrying for the first time. Technically such a person could have a large, formal, white wedding. But the dictates of common sense and social pressure might make such a move inadvisable.

Jewish Ceremonies The Jewish religion has three denominations—Orthodox, or traditional, whose rituals go back many centuries; Conservative, which is less strict; and Reform, which is most lenient of all and has among other things no interdictions concerning food. A friend once told me that in her opinion the very beauty and impressiveness of the Jewish wedding ceremony must be a vital factor in holding Jewish couples together. The Jewish divorce rate is lower than that of the average American community.

A rabbi of an Orthodox or Conservative synagogue will not marry divorced persons who have received only civil decrees. A religious divorce decree is also necessary. Reform Judaism gives religious recognition to a civil divorce and therefore does not require, in addition, a religious divorce.

Before the ceremony the bride usually receives the wedding guests in an anteroom of the place where she is to be married. Seated with her attendants, she sees all but the groom before the ceremony. In liberal temples, however, she may even see him.

The Orthodox wedding ceremony begins with two benedictions—"The Betrothal Benedictions." This is followed by the Ring Ceremony; then the reading of the marriage contract—"Kesubah," which is in Aramaic. The "seven marriage benedictions" are then read.

At Jewish weddings—Orthodox, Conservative, and Reform—music for the processional is usual and briefly for the recessional. Selection of the music depends on the couple's taste. Frequently, for involved Jews, it is Israeli or Hebrew music. A cantor is not necessary at a Jewish wedding but he frequently does take part in the wedding ceremony especially in big weddings, chanting not singing. There are no vocal solos at Jewish weddings. Instruments may vary from the organ to the violin or woodwinds. Sometimes the music is on tape. Cantor's fees for participation in the ceremony run from $25 to $50 or more depending upon the elaborateness of the ceremony. The organist—or other musicians—is compensated according to individual arrangements.

When the Orthdox ceremony is held in a synagogue the bride stands to the groom's right before the Ark of the Covenant, which corresponds to the altar, with its cross or crucifix, of most Christian faiths. The bride wears the traditional wedding gown and veil in a formal ceremony —exactly like that of the Christian bride. She has the same attendants, too—maid or matron of honor and bridesmaids if she wishes. Sometimes both fathers and both mothers take part in the ceremony and in the processional accompany the bride and groom. Grandparents may participate in the ceremony in this way as well. In fact there is no prescribed limit in the Jewish faith on the number or nature of attendants a bride may choose to have. In the recessional both mothers and fathers may walk together side by side. (*See illustration.*) However, a girl contemplating having an extraordinary number of attendants should remember that they will only serve ultimately to distract attention from her own position of prominence.

In the Jewish ceremony it is usually the right side of the synagogue or temple, as one enters, which is the bride's, the left, the groom's.

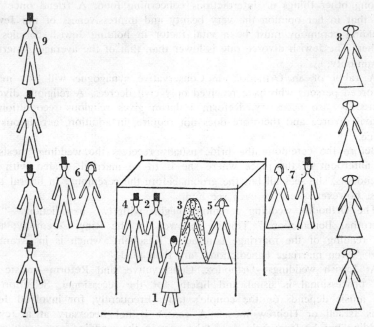

Orthodox Jewish Ceremony at Altar, *Optional Arrangement:* 1. Rabbi, 2. groom, 3. bride, 4. best man, 5. maid or matron of honor, 6. groom's father and mother, 7. bride's father and mother, 8. bridesmaids, in aisle, 9. ushers. NOTE: The arrangement of the wedding party is not a matter of rabbinical law but of social custom, hence it varies. For example, parents may be under the canopy if there is room. Sometimes only the fathers take part, and their placement is optional.

However, this varies according to custom. In Reform practice, the right side of the synagogue, as one enters, is reserved for the groom's family and the left side for the family of the bride. Whether or not the ceremony takes place in a synagogue, the couple is wed beneath a canopy supported on standards and symbolizing home. Under the canopy with them stand the rabbi and, usually, their two principal attendants. If the canopy or *chupah* is large enough, the four parents stand beneath it too, otherwise they stand outside the fringe. Next to the rabbi, who faces the bride and groom, is a small covered table containing two cups of ritual wine and, for the Orthodox and Conservative ceremonies, two glasses wrapped with a snowy napkin. The service begins with the blessing of the wine. The service is in Hebrew and Aramaic in the Orthodox and Conservative synagogues. By law in some states, however, it is in English, with the rabbi's address to the couple either in Yiddish or in the language of the congregation. For, as not all Catholics understand all

Orthodox Jewish Processional and Recessional, *Optional Arrangements*

Processional *Reading from top down far left:* Bride's mother, bride, bride's father.

Flower girl or page, if any.

Maid or matron of honor.

Groom's mother (*left*), groom, groom's father.

Best man.

Rabbi, not in processional or recessional if ceremony takes place in a temple or synagogue.

Recessional *left:* Bride and groom.

Bride's parents.

Groom's parents.

(Flower girl or page not in recessional, necessarily.)

Maid or matron of honor and best man.

Rabbi. NOTE: In Jewish ceremony the *left* (many rabbis prefer the right) side is the bride's. Attendants, if any, come up the aisle, paired, before the rabbi and *may* form a guard of honor through which the procession walks.

the Latin of their services, so Jews do not necessarily understand Hebrew and Aramaic. In the Reform practice most of the service is in English, only a few of the blessings are in Hebrew, and only one glass is used.

After the wine is blessed the rabbi passes one glass of wine to the groom, who takes a sip and gives it to the bride. Then comes the ring ceremony with the ring, in the Orthodox ceremony, always plain gold. The best man hands it to the rabbi, who, in those states that require it, says in English, "Dost thou take this woman to be thy wedded wife?" receiving the usual responses in English. Then, in the Orthodox and Conservative services, the ring is placed on the bride's right index finger directly by the groom, though any time after the ceremony she may remove it and place it on what our Western society considers the proper wedding ring finger. In the Reform service the ring is placed on the bride's left ring finger.

The ring ceremony is followed by the rabbi's short address in English (or the language of the congregation) to the couple on the sanctity of marriage and his own personal interest in their future welfare.

Then comes the ceremonial drinking of the second glass of wine by both bride and groom. The Seven Blessings, followed in the Orthodox and Conservative services with the crushing of a glass beneath the foot of the bridegroom, symbolizes the sacking of the Temple of Jerusalem and is an admonition to the congregation that despite the happiness of the occasion all should remember and work for the rebuilding of Zion.

The reception-with-collation that follows Jewish weddings is exactly like other receptions except that a special nuptial grace is always offered after food.

As in the Catholic ceremony, the Jewish does not require the father to give his daughter in marriage. In the Reform service, the father escorts his daughter on his right arm up the aisle to the groom who, with his best man, awaits her at the altar. In the Orthodox and Conservative ceremony both sets of parents accompany the bride and groom respectively to the altar, taking their places under or near the *chupah*. It is not required that anyone except the bride and groom stand under the canopy. In the Reform service the parents do not stand up with their children. It is becoming common in both the Reform and Conservative ceremony for the groom to dispense with walking up the aisle and to come onto the pulpit platform instead by stepping out with the rabbi and best man from the platform doorway.

In Orthodox and Conservative Jewish weddings all males in the assemblage must cover their heads. They wear the traditional skull caps or their own hats. Synagogues have skull caps available in the vestibule for men who arrive without their hats. In Orthodox synagogues men and women do not sit together, and in the Reform temples men do not wear hats. Single women in Orthodox synagogues optionally wear head-covering, but the heads of married women are covered by hat, shawl, or wig. In Conservative synagogues all women regardless of marital status are urged to wear hats and to dress in a manner appropriate to a religious sanctuary.

In the Reform service the wedding canopy is not required, no glass is broken, and the rabbi does not read the marriage certificate in Aramaic.

No Orthodox or Conservative rabbi ever officiates at a mixed marriage and many Reform rabbis will not. However, though Jews do not seek converts, the non-Jewish partner in a proposed mixed marriage may go through a period of instruction and then be taken into the Congregation as a Jew. Any rabbi may then perform the marriage.

As I stated earlier, particularly among Orthodox Jews recently of European origin, the groom's family often pays for the liquor at the reception and shares the cost of bridal photographs. Otherwise, the distribution of costs remains the same for both Jewish and Christian weddings.

The Christian Science Ceremony As Christian Science readers are not ordained ministers of the church, merely elected officers, they may not perform the marriage ceremony. When members of the Christian Science faith are married, the ceremony is performed by an ordained minister of the gospel, legally authorized to perform such a duty, or by the proper legal authority. Christian Scientists oppose the use of alcoholic beverages. Many do not serve them in any form, even the mildest, at wedding receptions despite the presence of non-Christian Scientists.

Eastern Orthodox Weddings The Eastern Orthodox Church, the Holy Eastern Orthodox Catholic Apostolic Church, has numerous followers among White Russians, Greeks, Rumanians, and various Mediterranean groups in this country. It has many ceremonial forms similar to those of the Roman Catholic Church but does not acknowledge the Pope as its spiritual leader.

The bride and groom must fast, make their confessions, and take Communion. The ceremony is celebrated without Mass and always takes place in either the afternoon or evening.

In the Eastern Orthodox Church the ceremony does not take place at the altar but before a table placed in front of the sanctuary toward the center of the church. Relatively few of these churches have pews, a modern development, and guests must stand or kneel before and throughout the hour-long service. None but vocal music is permitted, and the bride enters to the special wedding hymns sung by the choir. The procession is like that in other Christian services. The father of the bride gives the bride away, then returns to the pew with her mother.

In the Eastern Orthodox service the mystical number three, representing the Trinity, has great significance. The double ring ceremony is used—with the rings placed on the right hands of the bride and groom. The priest blesses the rings three times at the altar, then places each ring first on the bride's finger, then on the groom's. Then the best man exchanges the rings three times on the fingers of the bride and groom. Just before the final vows are taken the priest binds the hands of the bride and groom together and leads them three times around the table, which holds the Bible, or Scripture, a cross, a chalice of wine, candles, and flowers. After the final blessing the choir chants "Many Years" three times, then the recessional starts.

Throughout the ceremony the bride and groom hold lighted candles symbolizing the light of the Lord. During the ceremony the priest places gold crowns on their heads.

These are only the highlights of this richly impressive ceremony, usual in all Eastern Orthodox unions. Only during emergencies is the ritual ever shortened.

The Church makes divorce difficult and insists on a religious decree. Remarriage of divorced persons is permitted.

The Quaker Ceremony Today a Quaker marriage ceremony may see the bride gowned traditionally and veiled, but these simple, unpretentious people believe in the renunciation of worldly display. Their ceremony is as plain as their meeting houses and impressive in its quiet sincerity.

A Quaker wedding may take place in the meeting house or in a private home but notice of intention to wed is made by the couple at least one monthly meeting in advance of the date they have set. It is necessary for at least one of them to be a member of the Society of Friends. It is usual for the parents' permission to be appended to the letter of request, even when the couple is of age. After the letter has been read at the meeting a committee of two women and two men is appointed to discuss with the bride and groom, respectively, the "clearness to proceed with marriage." The committee may discuss marriage and its obligations with the couple just as a minister would, for originally the Quakers had no appointed ministers but instead gathered together in Quaker silence, speaking up in meeting as the inner spirit moved them to express themselves. (In some meetings there now is a regularly appointed minister, especially in the West.)

The committee submits a report on its conferences with the couple to the monthly meeting. Overseers are then appointed to attend the wedding and to advise the couple on the marriage procedure.

On the wedding day bride and groom come down the aisle together—or there may be the usual wedding procession—and take the "facing seats," the benches that face the meeting. After the Quaker silence the couple rises and takes hands. The groom says words to the effect that "in the presence of God I take thee . . . to be my wedded wife promising with divine assistance to be unto thee a loving and faithful husband as long as we both shall live." The bride repeats the answering vow. The couple is then seated again, and the ushers bring forward a table containing the Quaker marriage certificate. This is then read aloud, signed by the bride, groom, and overseers, and later officially registered. The regular Quaker meeting follows.

At the next monthly meeting the overseers report that the marriage "was carried out to the good order of friends." Divorce among Quakers is rare.

The Mormon Ceremony There are two kinds of marriages among the Mormons (members of the Church of Jesus Christ of Latter-day Saints). The first are those that are performed in temples of the Church by those holding the holy priesthood. In pronouncing the couple man and wife, the priest declares them wed, "for time and for all eternity," instead of, "until death do you part." Children born to parents so married are believed by the Mormons to belong to them in the eternal world by virtue of such marriages. These marriages are always referred to as temple marriages. All brides married in the temple dress in white and wear veils, although they may have previously been married.

There are also civil marriages performed by bishops of the Church or any other accredited person. Later, if the couple has complied with the requirements of the Church in their daily living, they may enter the temples of the Church and be married for time and for all eternity despite previous civil marriage.

Following temple or civil marriages, receptions for bride and groom with family and invited guests are usually held in the cultural hall of the church, or in the home of the bride's parents. In some communities there are special reception centers where such receptions are held.

Mixed marriage, although not encouraged, is permitted. Civil divorce is recognized but divorce is rare among those married in the temples. The Mormon Church takes no stand against remarriage.

The Home Wedding

Nicest of all weddings, if space permits, is the home wedding. The largest room, usually the living room, is selected, cleared for the ceremony, and an altar improvised before a fireplace or at some other focal point in the room, preferably at the greatest distance from the entrance or entrances. Seats are usually not provided.

If the room is large and the company numerous, "ribbons" are put in place just before the entrance of the bride's mother and the groom's mother to preserve an aisle. At large weddings a small section for the parents and immediate relatives is roped off on either side of the altar, bride's family to the left, groom's to the right.

Where there is a staircase the bride descends it at the first strains of the wedding march; otherwise she and the bridal party congregate outside the entrance to the main room before the music begins. This is only, of course, if the guests are numerous enough, the house large enough to permit a formal wedding if she wants it. Otherwise the bride wears a street-length or floor-length wedding gown and a short veil or a simple dress (never black or true red) or suit at noon, a covered up cocktail dress with a hat, or a dressmaker suit, possibly satin. Her attendants dress similarly.

At a very small wedding there may be no music at all and the bride may be in a street dress or suit. She need not make the usual dramatic entrance but after the clergyman has taken his place merely step before him for the ceremony. A collation is always served at a home wedding. It may be the same room as that in which the wedding took place or in the garden or on a porch. A large table is usually moved against a wall and set with the wedding cake as a central theme.

A wedding, of course, may take place out of doors if the climate is sufficiently dependable or if alternative arrangements have been made. Sometimes the witnesses to the ceremony are limited and the reception is large, and often in summer, out of doors.

Receiving at a Home Wedding At a home wedding there is no recessional unless a formal receiving line is to form elsewhere in the house or in the garden. Where there are many guests and space is limited, the receiving line, if there is to be one, is best located in a small room such as a hall or dining room with both exit and entrance to facilitate the flow of traffic. Guests should be able to pass on in to a larger area where they may congregate and have refreshments. In simple home weddings it is usual for the bride and groom merely to turn around at the altar, *after* the groom has kissed the bride, and receive informally with the bridal attendants.

The Rectory Wedding

Sometimes a couple will choose to be married in the rectory of their church. The simple ceremony takes place in the clergyman's study or in his living room, often before a fireplace. The bride makes no entrance as she would in a formal home wedding, and she wears a suit or a street dress and hat or some equivalent headcovering if the denomination requires or requests it. The groom wears a dark suit or in the country in summer white or gray flannel-like pants and a blue coat or a white jacket (not a dinner jacket) with gray or blue flannel-like pants or a light tropical suit—never slacks and sports jacket. In all cases he wears black shoes.

A few guests may be present, but usually the party is limited to witnesses and parents. Sometimes members of the clergyman's household act as witnesses, and the couple has no attendants. The bride does not have flowers sent for the decoration of the rectory.

After brief preliminary instructions, the bride and groom stand before the clergyman, the bride to the groom's left. Unless the bride's father or a substitute for him is present the "giving away" part of the ceremony, where it is usually used, is done by the bride herself. Bride and groom stand hands at sides until the clergyman asks the question, then she places her hand in that of the groom preliminary to their being joined as man and wife. Afterward the couple receive the congratulations of the minister, then kiss, if they wish. Before leaving the rectory the groom, if unattended, remembers to leave an envelope for the minister containing an appropriate fee—appropriate, that is, to the circumstances of the couple.

Sometimes a couple wishing the privacy of a small rectory wedding do have a reception at a hotel or at the bride's home. In either case, it is never formal, and the bride and groom stand side by side and receive their guests. Later they do not separate as they probably would at a party but remain together to function as host and hostess on this great day.

The Clergyman's Wedding

The wedding of a clergyman presents certain problems not covered in discussions of usual weddings. If he has his own church, synagogue, or temple the bride may wonder if his entire congregation must be invited to the wedding and, if so, how the invitation is tendered. And where does the marriage take place, in his own place of worship or hers? Then there is the question of the clergyman's son's wedding and that of his daughter. Where and when do such weddings take place and who officiates? Who gives a clergyman's daughter away if her father performs the ceremony? What, too, does a clergyman wear to his own wedding? These questions have come up sufficiently often in my correspondence for me to cover them briefly here.

First, a clergyman, like any other groom, is married in the church, temple or synagogue of his bride by her own clergyman or any other place of the bride's choice such as her home or the home of friends. If her place of worship happens to be his own, then they may be married there by some other clergyman of his faith, his superior, a friend, or a clergyman from a neighboring parish or congregation. Sometimes, if he has an assistant, he is married by him, but someone of his own rank or higher usually would perform the ceremony.

A clergyman usually chooses the morning hours up until noon for his own wedding, avoiding (as a matter of convenience among Protestants) his particular Sabbath. He wears his clericals, if they are customary in his faith, not his vestments. If the hour chosen should happen to be late afternoon, four-thirty, he may wear morning dress or, depending on the season, other suitable clothing (see "Dress of Groom and Best Man," pages 109, 112, 113), with or without the clerical collar and rabat depending on his denominational custom.

A clergyman-father performing the marriage for his daughter cannot give her away, where this procedure is called for in the ceremony. Instead, she is escorted at a formal wedding by an older brother, a brother-in-law, a godfather, an uncle, a grandfather, or a family friend. After delivering her to the groom her escort may step back and into the first pew on the bride's side or remain to give her away. When the clergyman asks the question concerning the giving in marriage the bride's mother steps forward and places the hand of the bride in that of the clergyman or in that of the groom, depending on the denominational custom.

In a very small community and in a church, synagogue, or temple that is unusually well-attended, a clergyman might announce his forthcoming marriage from the pulpit and invite the congregation to attend if the marriage is to take place in his own house of worship. But so informal a procedure, though it seems to be followed occasionally, risks the exclusion of some members who might not have attended services on the day the announcement was made. More correct is the sending of individual invitations of some kind (see "Wedding Invitations") to the entire mailing list. The reception, of course, could be and is really expected to be limited to close friends, associates, and relatives of bride and groom. In a small community where a bride, for extenuating reasons (no relatives of her own, for example), might come from a distance to be married in

her husband's own church, synagogue, or temple, the people of the congregation might give the reception, especially if the couple's joint circumstances were modest.

A clergyman whose son is marrying is usually given the honor of conducting the ceremony in the bride's place of worship with the bride's clergyman assisting. If the bride's home is at considerable distance from his own
the father's congregation does not usually expect to be invited en masse,
though various active members of the congregation might well be included
in the invitation list.

A clergyman's wife should feel free to give a shower for any member
of the congregation to whom she feels especially close, although of course
she does not give one for a relative. A clergyman, by the way, is not
expected to proffer a gift for every couple over whose wedding he officiates.
He may of course give gifts to relatives or close friends.

Elopements and Civil Ceremonies

The Elopement A friend of mine with three lovely daughters gave the
first a traditional big wedding with no expense spared—including that of a
dance band for the reception for more than three hundred. His other
daughters, of course, were attendants, and he told them they'd better
make the most of their day of glory as one big wedding was all he could
stand—and we can sympathize with him. "My other daughters can expect
just a good strong ladder on a nice moonlight night," he warned.

There are elopements and elopements, of course. The kind we don't
like to see is the one where parents have not become reconciled to the
marriage and the couple runs off in defiance of parental displeasure. The
young people should both work very hard, if necessary, to win all four
parents over to the match. A runaway marriage where there has been
bitter objection can start a couple off very defensively.

Then there is the elopement that is frequently a great relief to all concerned, when, because of social position, an elaborate wedding is expected.
Sometimes a girl—or her groom—cannot bear the idea of all the complexities and pressures of a big wedding, and, once they have announced
their intentions and received the blessings of their friends and parents,
they go off and are married—in a religious ceremony, I hope, for civil
ones can be very dreary—with two friends as witnesses, perhaps, or even
two strangers provided by the officiating person. They then phone or
wire their families and friends to whom only the day of the elopement,
not the fact of it, will come as a surprise.

The bride and groom with a wide, expectant circle of friends do better to
elope in this way than to try to have a small wedding from which they
would find it difficult to exclude so many people close to them—friends
whom they might greatly prefer to the relatives who must be asked, for
example.

Gifts for Elopers? Sometimes formal announcements of the wedding are omitted after elopements, but more usually they are sent, even if as much time as six months or a year has elapsed since the ceremony, with the place of the marriage always stated and the date and year. If a civil ceremony has been performed, only the name of the city or town appears. If the couple was married in church, it is optional whether the church is mentioned. If, as happens, a baby is very much on the way, announcement of the wedding is perhaps better made informally. Very early first babies happen these days with not-surprising regularity with the "situation" openly and unapologetically accepted by most good parents and relatives.

Strictly speaking, any couple for whom wedding invitations were not issued should not expect wedding gifts, even if they send formal announcements of the marriage. But of course close friends who receive the announcements and many relatives will want to send gifts. If an elopement is a second—or third—marriage for bride or groom, no gifts at all should be expected, although again there will be friends—usually of the less married or not previously married partner—who may wish to send gifts. But once you have given a wedding gift, even to your dearest friend, you cannot be expected to give one for a second marriage, too.

Parties for Elopers? If the bride's parents or some close relatives or friends would like to give a party for a couple who has eloped some time after the news of the marriage has been made public, this is acceptable. However, the party should in no way resemble a formal wedding reception, and the girl should certainly not appear in a wedding dress. Any friendly, informal gathering at which the recent bride and guests would gear their dress to the time of day is in order. A receiving line would not be suitable. It is inappropriate to give a post-wedding shower or any other kind of party at which the bride would be expected to appear separately after the wedding has taken place. Guests invited to such parties should not feel obligated to bring gifts, though some well may.

Civil Marriage For a civil marriage in a registrar's office or in a judge's chambers the groom wears a dark business suit and the bride wears a simple street length suit or dress, never a wedding gown. She wears a corsage if she wishes, or carries a prayer book, with a flowered ribbon marker, instead of carrying a bouquet, and before the brief ceremony begins she removes her gloves and places them with her handbag. The couple does not kneel during such a ceremony. They should limit themselves to one attendant each, with their attendants acting as witnesses. Where there is no best man and witnesses are garnered from the office staff, the groom quietly hands the officiating person a sealed envelope containing the fee before the ceremony—anywhere from ten to twenty-five dollars or more, depending on the circumstances. Where a high-ranking official—a mayor, governor, or Supreme Court judge—has performed the rite as a special favor to the families involved, no fee is offered but a gift is sent after the ceremony—again depending on the circumstances. Anything from a case of scotch to a bottle or so of fine champagne or perhaps a fine pipe or a humidor of good cigars might be appropriate.

It is also preferable to give a gift, not money, if the judge performs the ceremony in your home. It is also a nice gesture to invite the judge and his wife to any reception held after such a ceremony, just as you would the minister and his wife. If you are having a sufficient number of guests to warrant it, a receiving line could be held at such a reception.

Driving to the Reception

If must be remembered that after the wedding ceremony and before the reception the bride and groom must ride alone—no bridesmaids, no parents—in the car.

If There Is No Reception

At a small church wedding not followed by a reception the bride often receives with the groom, her mother, and the bridesmaids in the vestibule of the church or on the porch—if there is one in a country church. The groom's mother, if she is unknown in the community, may stand next to the bride's mother, who is always first in line, and have guests introduced to her before they pass on to bride and groom. Or, if she is known, her place is a little beyond the bridesmaids. The father of the bride may or may not stand in line, but he usually circulates in the neighborhood of the receiving line to share in the glory of the great occasion. The father of the groom does not receive with the others when there is no formal reception.

Chapter 13

THE WEDDING RECEPTION

At a formal reception the mother of the bride is always first in line, as hostess, usually just inside the door. However, should the wedding take place in the groom's mother's home territory where she will know substantially more of the guests, she could stand first in line. Next to her, optionally stands the father of the groom, then the groom's mother, and, last, optionally the bride's father. Then, a little apart, begins the line of the bridal party—the bride to the groom's right, the groom, the maid or matron of honor, and the bridesmaids. Or the bridesmaids may be divided so that half are on one side of the bride with the maid or matron of honor and the other half alongside of the groom. If there is a flower girl old enough to stand in line without getting too restless (pretty unlikely, I should say) she stands next to the groom. Members of the wedding party retain their gloves on the receiving line, as preferably do women guests going through the line. The line remains intact until all guests have been greeted, then the mother, as hostess, leads the group to the bride's table and the parents' table. The ushers and the best man do not stand in the receiving line.

Whereas it was once unthinkable to serve any refreshments to people before they had been through the receiving line, with the size of weddings on the increase and the receiving line lasting sometimes several hours, it is now possible to arrange to serve at least some champagne to those guests waiting to go through the line. They should not of course proceed through the line itself with glass in hand. Small tables should be strategically placed to receive empty glasses. It might be wiser if the wedding is to be a really large one (and guest lists sometimes number in the hundreds) to dispense with the receiving line altogether and simply have the bride, groom and attendants make an entrance before the assembled guests with a fanfare of music and applause.

Another solution is for the two sets of parents to station themselves at opposite sides of a room with the bride and groom elsewhere and informally greet the guests as they circulate freely. These are among the acceptable modern departures.

I have even heard of the solution where the parents at a large reception will begin receiving before the bride and groom have arrived at the reception especially if they are being detained for wedding pictures. In short, anything you can do to make the receiving line more pleasant and less like an ordeal, and any changes you can make that will discourage guests from skipping the receiving line altogether, which is quite rude, are in order. If you do dispense with the line, an effort should be made for the hostess to extend a welcome to her guests and for the couple to be introduced, however generally. Perhaps the best man could introduce the bride's mother over the public address system and she could dispense with the amenities in this way.

It is sometimes possible to arrange to hold the receiving line at the back of the church, if this is where the reception is to be. But permission must first be obtained from the clergyman for this.

Must Fathers Stand in Line?

At very formal receptions it is usual for the fathers of the bride and groom to stand in line, but not obligatory, especially if the father of the groom is a member of the community. But the fathers stay in the neighborhood of the receiving line, if not actually on it, to make introductions to see that guests are directed to the refreshment tables.

If the father of the groom is quite unknown to the bride's friends it is better for him to be in the line with the bride's father, so he will feel a real part of the important proceedings.

Who Receives in Place of the Bride's Mother?

If the bride has no mother to receive for her at her reception her father may receive just inside the door as the host, or he may request a female relative, an aunt, cousin, or grandmother, to receive with him. If this relative is not actually a member of the household the father may be first in line, introducing the guests to the honorary hostess as they file past, "This is Dorothy's Aunt, Mrs. Malstrom. May, Mr. Jordan, one of our neighbors."

Receiving Line Complications

For the sake of the bride, divorced parents who have not remarried may choose to stand together on a receiving line. It would be quite inappropriate for a couple either of whom had remarried to appear together on a receiving line. This problem can often be circumvented of course since the father's place in line is not mandatory. Any new spouse of either parent, except a stepmother who is the hostess at the reception, attends as a guest and does not receive.

Conversation and the Receiving Line

No one really listens to what you say on the receiving line, as a friend of mine once dramatically proved by muttering something utterly incongruous

Receiving Line at Wedding, *Optional Arrangement:* Bridal party before fireplace banked with flowers, or possibly in front of picture window.

1. Mother of bride, 2. father of groom (*optional, see text*), 3. mother of groom (*optional, see text*), 4. father of bride (*optional, see text*), 5, 6. bridesmaids, 7. maid or matron of honor, 8. bride, 9. groom, 10. bridesmaid, 11. bridesmaid. NOTE: Whatever arrangement, the bride is on the groom's right except when he's in uniform. The best man is *never* on the line. Exceptions: Occasionally in the receiving line the bride must stand on the groom's left for convenience' sake. In this case the line must be routed so that the bride is reached first by the guests. If the groom's father acts as best man, he then may be in line.

as he made his way. You must seem cordial and happy to be where you are. As a couple proceeds through the receiving line, the woman preceding the man, the woman's name is given to the announcer first. The bride's mother—if she doesn't know you—has received your name from an announcer. "*Mrs.* Markham, *Miss* Borden (teens and beyond) *Mr.* Mc-Sweeney, John De Matteo, Ann Shapiro (pre-teens)" are the names given to the announcer, who then gives the pre-teens the courtesy titles of "Master" and "Miss" on introduction. On repeating their own names in the course of going through the line, men, boys, and little girls give their full names without a title. You then pass on to the groom's father, or mother, or whoever is next in line, mentioning your name and if you are someone of particular importance, such as a great-aunt, mentioning the relationship. To each you say, during the brief handclasp, "How do you do," or "Lovely wedding," or "So happy to meet you." To the bride you offer "best wishes" and to the groom "congratulations." (Don't *congratulate* the bride. Offer your felicitations.) Your pause before the bridal couple may be perceptibly longer, but you must never hold up the receiving line with long-drawn-out dissertations. You may be able to get the couple's ear sometime during the reception—but even then remember that you are only one of many who deem it their privilege to have a word with the bride or groom.

If no one announces you as you approach the line, announce yourself. Don't assume that the bride's mother, who has perhaps seen you only a few times, is going to remember your name at a time like this. Help her out by saying, "Peter Gossett, Mrs. Kingsley. Such a beautiful wedding!"

Gloves may be removed once the line is broken up. The bride with long sleeves or three-quarter sleeves these days frequently doesn't wear gloves and the bridesmaids therefore may choose not to wear them on the line. Hats, if worn, may also be removed once the reception gets under way.

How to Address the Bride If you are on first-name terms with the groom and you are an older relative or family friend, it is expected that you call the bride by her first name. If you are a contemporary of the groom's and on a first-name basis, it does not necessarily follow that he wishes you to be on the same basis with his wife unless she suggests it, especially if you and he merely work together. He may be "Bob" to you, but, especially if your social contact with her is to be very slight, he may be pleased that you address his wife as "Mrs. Jones" unless you are urged to do otherwise.

What Does the Bride Say? The bride tries to make each acknowledgment of a guest's greeting sound warm and personal. She repeats the name, if possible, "Mrs. Osborn—so very nice of you to come so far for our wedding," or "Cousin Hattie, the coffee table is exactly what I needed!" Unless she is unusually poised and calm, however, she is safer not trying to remember who gave her what or where strangers to her have come from. She will have to write her thank-you notes anyhow, but the clever bride will contrive to make everyone imagine that she remembers each gift, in detail, and that she has been waiting impatiently to receive this particular felicitation and present the guest to her new husband or vice versa, if he or she is unknown to him.

What Does the Groom Say? The groom, usually, less happy than the bride over the necessity of the receiving line, is often less than verbose. He says "Thank you so much" or "Lovely, isn't she?" or "So glad you could come" before he introduces the guest to his wife, if introduction is needed—otherwise he passes him along with a "Here is Tom, Angela," or, "Darling, you know Mrs. Osborn."

But the groom, no matter how uncomfortable he may feel at this last necessary formality of his wedding, must look happy at having to greet even a seemingly endless line of guests, when what he needs after all he's been through is a tall drink and his bride to himself, or so he thinks. This is his first public appearance as the head of the house, and he is at this moment as much on display as the bride—in some ways more so, as the guests had a better chance to see the bride during the ceremony than they did him.

Photographs at the Reception

If photographs are to be taken of the bridal party it is usually best for the photographer to wait until the receiving line is formed and gone through and the ceremony of the bride cutting the cake is over (but sometimes the photographs must be taken beforehand). This eliminates what can be an awkward wait between the wedding itself and the reception. While the bridal party is then being photographed the parents can look after the guests at the reception as it proceeds.

It is unthinkable to try to sell photographs from the wedding to guests, although the bride may want to have copies made and give them to her attendants or close relatives. Should a guest request a duplicate of a picture, however, he would be expected to offer to pay the photographer direct.

Flowers at the Reception

Flowers at the reception should be considered as part of the bride's family budget. They may be as simple as little arrangements of ivy, or, as I saw once, Mother Carey's chickens, or lush arrangements of elaborately arranged flowers in any suitable colors, perhaps those of the bridal bouquets. Sometimes the bride places her own bouquet on the bridal table. The bridesmaids may place theirs at their own places. The table on which the wedding cake is placed may be decorated with ferns or other leaves. Sometimes palms make a background for the receiving line, especially in a hotel or club. Greens of various kinds, simple branches of dogwood or magnolia can be very much more effective than elaborate and pretentious arrangements. Artificial flowers are unthinkable at a wedding. Better a single real rose or bunches of field flowers.

The Wedding Guest Book

Stationers, department stores, gift shops all sell wedding guest books. They are not a requirement at weddings, but they certainly make a very nice and sentimental souvenir of the occasion. An ordinary guest book will of course do as well with someone to preside over it to see that as many guests as possible sign. Signatures are the proper social names, not "Bill and Betty Smith." Such a record of the wedding calls for proper formality, so "Mr. and Mrs. Joseph Sterling Smith," is the expected and definitive thing, written of course legibly. Years later would the bride necessarily remember "Helen and Joe?" These books are often used as a source of addresses as well, so you should co-operate and provide your complete address if it is requested. Comments, if there is a place for them, should be appropriate, never flip. The person presiding over the guest book may be a young sister or friend (gloveless) perhaps too young to be in the wedding party, or it may be an older family friend, or even a young brother who enjoys the importance of such a position. It is perfectly acceptable to ask people to sign the book, not wait for them to notice its presence.

Gratuities at the Reception

It is customary that at any reception held in a club or hotel the bride's father's costs per head include gratuities for waiters, waitresses, and all others connected with serving the guests. Consequently, guests should never have to tip anyone at a wedding. In addition, the bride's father usually arranges to take care of gratuities for cloakroom attendants in advance, and a sign to this effect is placed by the management at the cloak room. If you have made such an arrangement, check to see that this sign is in plain sight, so that guests will not feel that you have overlooked this nicety of wedding-reception etiquette.

The Wedding Breakfast

The wedding breakfast is actually lunch—three courses. When guests are seated it includes a soup course, such as hot clam broth with whipped cream or possibly fruit cup or seafood cocktail, a main dish, such as sweetbreads *en broche* with green peas and potato balls, plus small biscuits and lettuce salad. For dessert ice cream in fancy molds, petits fours or tiny petits fours glacés, demitasses, and, of course, the bridal champagne or at least a fine white wine to be served with the luncheon, sometimes both.

When the wedding breakfast is served buffet and there is no way of seating guests, even at small tables, the first course is usually omitted and the collation limited to two courses. There may be something like whole salmon mayonnaise with wilted cucumbers and dill, green salad, ice cream, not necessarily in forms, little cakes, demitasses, and a good white wine or champagne, or both.

The Table for the Parents

At a wedding buffet, breakfast, or supper there may be a table for the bride's parents if there is a special bride's table, but not otherwise. It is larger than the guests' tables and is the same except for place cards. Placement of guests is as follows: father of groom to right of bride's mother, who is the table's hostess. Opposite the bride's mother sits the bride's father with the groom's mother to his right. The other guests at the table may include the grandparents of the bride and groom and the clergyman and his wife. If a high-ranking church official performed the ceremony, or a judge or mayor, he is always placed to the left of the hostess and his wife, if present, sits on the left of the host. Very distinguished guests are seated at this table, but essentially it is for the parents and a few of their close friends and, possibly, close relatives.

In cases where a divorce has taken place the divorced parents are not seated together at the parents' table unless they are exceptionally friendly. Another table with prominent guests might be arranged for the non-host parent and his new spouse, should he have one. Perhaps in cases where this will cause hard feelings the parents' table should be left out altogether.

Seating at Parents' Table, *table optional* 1. Bride's mother, 2. father of groom, 3. father of bride, 4. mother of groom, 5. important officiating clergyman's wife, 6. officiating clergyman (*or see text*), 7, 8, 9, 10, 11, 12, 13, 14, friends of parents.

The Bride's Table

At large formal receptions there is a bride's table, especially decorated with white flowers and with the tiered and iced wedding cake in front of the bride and groom—the groom with the bride on his right. Only members of the wedding party—the maid or matron of honor to the left of the groom, the best man to the right of the bride—are expected to sit at the bride's table, but if some of the attendants are married it is courteous of the bride to include their mates, unless it is certain that they know enough people present to enjoy themselves anyhow. But it is preferable for the unity of the bridal party to be kept even at the bridal table. The bride and groom have no place cards at their seats.

Even when the guests are served buffet, the bridal table is waited upon. The bride is served first. If it can be arranged, the maid or matron of honor is served almost simultaneously. Then the groom is served, and the waitresses work their way out from the center to the ends of the bridal table. As soon as the champagne appears, the best man proposes the first toast to the bride, with other toasts following as the guests are inspired to offer them—not forgetting, I hope, one to the groom. If you wish to have a blessing given at the reception to the bridal couple, perhaps it could be arranged for the best man to give it in his role of master of ceremonies. It might be awkward for your clergyman, seated at a parents' table, to bless the couple seated at their own table, but discuss the matter with him. He may prefer to manage the matter in his own way.

The Bride's Table, *seating optional, see text. Reading from left to right:* Usher, bridesmaid, best man, bride, groom, maid or matron of honor, bridesmaid, usher.

When There Is No Bride's Table

When food served at a reception includes no more than two courses—say chicken salad and ice cream—the dishes may be served in part, at least, from a buffet table whose major decoration is the wedding cake. When there is room, guests, either serving themselves or being served by the caterer's men or waitresses, may be seated at small tables—bridge tables are usual at a home reception. But often they eat standing, with the only service the clearing away of the plates and the passing of the punch or champagne.

When there is no formal bridal table at which all the wedding party—except the parents—are to be served together it is pleasant for the bride and groom alone to be provided with a small table to which they may retire for refreshments after receiving. Although the guests may have been to the buffet table for food and have had several rounds of champagne before the weary bride and groom have a chance to get off their feet for a few minutes before going on with their duties, guests must wait until the bride has finished eating before the cake can be cut and dancing can begin.

It is better to serve guests with champagne or punch just as each leaves the line if it hasn't been offered while the lined formed and to make refreshments immediately available than to wait until the bride is through receiving hundreds of guests—at a large reception—before there is any sign of food. Many wise people prefer a little food with champagne or punch as a stabilizer, and there are always guests who must leave early or who have dinner engagements. For them, too, it is preferable to have refreshments early rather than late, as the food at a wedding reception is rarely geared to substitute for a regular meal—with the exception of that at a wedding breakfast. It is possible at a modest and informal wedding to use paper plates, napkins, and tablecloths. And it is always possible at a home wedding even of a more formal and elaborate nature to use paper plates to serve the cake.

Wedding Toasts

A bride to whom a toast is offered—and the first comes from the best man, the second from her groom—remains seated and either lowers her eyes modestly, or if she wishes, looks adoringly at her bridegroom. She does not drink the toast at the moment that the others do, but a minute or so later, and, although the others usually at least try to drink the toast in one drink, she may take a modest sip. If she feels very comfortable about it, she may wish to return her husband's toast to her in a very simple fashion, perhaps saying, "To my darling husband." She may merely stand, raise her glass to his and toast him with her eyes. This is the exception in the matter of women's offering toasts. If you have a special cup reserved for the wedding it should only be used when the groom toasts his bride.

The first toast by the best man should be very brief or, if he feels comfortable on his feet he may say a few spontaneous words perhaps about his long friendship with the groom if that's the case, perhaps tell some suitable anecdote concerning the couple, but he should be tactful and careful, however, and not say things that would cause embarrassment at such a sensitive time. He will probably have spoken informally to others in the wedding, asking if they wish to offer toasts and calling upon them at the appropriate moment. The father of the bride, perhaps the father of the groom, perhaps a grandfather would be in this group. One of the most charming toasts, more of a peroration, was given by the bride's grandfather, a man with a talent for speechmaking, at a wedding I attended. He nevertheless did not speak at too-great length. Many people are embarrassed when asked to give toasts and it is a good idea for the best man to prepare them for the request. If they seem diffident, he can always say that a mere, "to your great happiness," is really sufficient. Toasts at a wedding are usually limited to the bride and groom, but if someone should toast the mother of the bride, or the mother of the groom, or anyone else, that person just smiles, holds his glass and drinks after the others have drunk the toast. If the groom and bride are toasted together, they should behave in a unit as each would individually. Toasting should not be unduly prolonged. The father of the bride is expected to say something loving about his daughter, and about his happiness at acquiring a son, but again it does not have to be lengthy. Generally speaking, a few spontaneous warm words are much better than something that is read or sounds well-rehearsed.

The Wedding Cake

The tiered wedding cake may be a caterer's dream or it may be made in the kitchen of the bride and be as simple or as elaborate as the cook can manage. It need not be topped with the miniature of the bride and groom, as is so often seen, but may be covered with charming sugar flowers in pastel colors with pale green leaves. Or it may be decorated with a pastry tube in white and pastel icing or plain white. The most popular cakes are the silver cake, which is made with the egg whites alone and is light and airy; the gold cake, a yellow pound cake, which is richer; and the dark, rich fruit cake, which is the most expensive of all. It should have nothing "written" on it with icing, however. This sort of decoration is reserved for birthday cakes. The occasional exception is the "ring cake"—a wedding cake baked in the shape of the wedding ring and which may have the bride's initials, first, then the groom's to the right, in the icing on the "band." Often little bridal favors are baked in the cake to tell fortunes but these are difficult to obtain and, in some states against the law in commercial baking as a possible danger should they be swallowed.

Cutting the Wedding Cake   At the end of the repast the bride rises— and with her all the gentlemen at the table—to cut the cake. Usually the guests are told that the propitious moment has arrived and gather round.

If the groom is in uniform the cake is cut with his dress sword, undecorated. At a civilian wedding a silver cake knife is used, and it may have its handle decorated with a streamer of white satin ribbons knotted with bridal flowers. The bride cuts only the first slice, with the groom's help, and she and the groom share it. Some member of the family, a knowledgeable friend, or a domestic employee then cuts and apportions the rest of the cake for service to guests, usually with ice cream. The tiered, decorated cake is cut as follows, after the bride and groom's slice has first been taken. A long sharp knife is inserted vertically through the cake at the base of the second tier and a core is cut all around the second tier. Subsequent slices are then taken from the first layer. When the first tier has been completely served, then the second tier of the cake is cored in the same way and then cut. The very top tier, which may or may not have the traditional bride and groom decoration—sometimes pastel icing flowers are used, for example—is gently lifted off, wrapped, and preserved. It can be stored in the freezer, of course (with the icing removed), for the first anniversary of the couple. If it is to be stored without freezing, it may be wrapped in a brandy-soaked cloth and stored in an airtight container. The remaining layers, after the top tier has been lifted off, will be small but may still be cut in wedge-shaped pieces. In this case, start with the top layer and work down. At second marriages, by the way, wedding cakes may be used but the decorative bride and groom or white bell should not be used at the top. The cake is traditionally a white cake, but it can also be a fruit cake, and I know one pretty bride who insisted that it be chocolate. But whatever the interior, the outside is always white, although it may have pastel decorations (usually flowers). One lovely cake put out by a master caterer is literally covered with pastel flowers and leaves, and skips the bride and groom or wedding bell on the top.

Boxed Wedding Cakes   Real black fruit cakes, wrapped in foil and boxed in tiny, white, satin-tied boxes, are a luxury these days because of the hand labor they entail. But they are a charming gift to her guests for the bride who can afford this extra but no-longer-necessary expense. They make a very nice gift, incidentally, for some close friend or relative to provide for the bride in lieu of a more traditional gift. Too, a friend or relative who is a good cake-baker might make the groom's cake (see *Amy Vanderbilt's Complete Cookbook*) and wrap and box it as her gift to the bride.

If boxed wedding cake is to be given, it is essential that one is at each place at the bridal table and that some one person, friend or retainer, be designated to give them out to departing guests.

As everyone knows, wedding cake placed under the pillow of a guest brings prophetic dreams. And a bride who looks serenely into a long and happy future with her husband puts aside boxes of her wedding cake to open on her major wedding anniversaries. She may even be able to nibble a piece with her husband when she reaches her Golden Wedding, and enjoy it, too, for good fruit cake grows mellower with age.

Music and Dancing at the Reception

It is not essential to have music at a wedding reception, especially if quarters are small and guests numerous. The choice, if there is music, is a trio—a man who plays both piano and accordion, a violinist, and a guitarist might make a happy combination. If the pianist also is an accordionist the trio is able to move through the rooms or over the lawn, as the case may be, serenading bride, groom, and guests.

For very large weddings, where space permits, a full orchestra with a leader is sometime seen—but this is doing things in a very pretentious manner, even when the orchestra can convert into a dance band after the receiving line has broken up.

During the actual receiving of the guests the music is restricted to light classical selections. After the line has received all the guests and dispersed, dance music and popular songs are played and possibly sung by the musicians.

The Groom Gets the First Dance with the Bride As no one but the groom must kiss the bride first, so no one may dance with her before he does. Dancing does not start until the couple has had a little rest and refreshment, and then, at the signal, the groom bows his bride onto the floor and she, gathering up her train, if any, and veil, if long, on her right arm, has the first dance—usually a waltz. The couple goes once around the floor as onlookers applaud. This dancing by the bride and groom need not last a long time, nor need it be a chore for anyone involved. The guests do not expect a professional performance. Then the bride's father leads out the mother of the groom and the groom's father dances with the mother of the bride. Attendants join in, candid camera pictures are shot, and finally the guests enter the dance floor, as they desire.

The bride never forgets to dance with her father, and with the father of the groom, who should ask her just after she has danced with her own father (he may even cut in), or the groom with his mother and with his bride's mother. The bride, after dancing with the fathers, dances next with the best man and then with each of the ushers. Guests may dance with the bride after all her "obligatory" dances are over, but they should not insist, unless she seems still daisy-fresh and really interested in remaining on the floor.

If you want to encourage your guests to dance, it is best if you work out in advance an arrangement whereby ushers are paired with bridesmaids for at least one or two numbers. People will dance if they see others dancing.

After the bride has thrown her bouquet, dancing may continue, but usually it begins to come to a close and guests start leaving. It is only the hardy late-stayers who remain to see the bride off.

It is a pleasant custom for the bride and groom to tour together the tables of their guests although it is not necessary, as they should have greeted everyone on the receiving line.

Throwing the Bride's Bouquet

The bride's bouquet (and sometimes her garter—usually blue) is traditionally thrown to the assembled bridesmaids just before the bride goes to dress for going away. The bride often retains a flower or two for pressing. The girl who catches the bouquet is, as we know, the next to marry.

The bride's garter may be thrown to the assembled ushers, rather than the bridesmaids. If this custom is to be followed, the bride wears one garter, which she then keeps for sentimental reasons, and gives the other before the ceremony to a bridesmaid who turns it over to her when it is time to throw the garter. The catching of the garter by an usher means alternatively that he will have good luck and laughter for his whole life, or that he will be the next to marry, as with the bridesmaids and the bouquet. In either case, it is only the bridesmaids and ushers who participate in the attempt to catch the bouquet or garter, not the guests.

Occasionally, if some dear relative, such as a grandmother, can't attend the wedding, the bride does not throw her bouquet but sends it to the person who has had to stay at home—with everyone understanding and sympathizing with her action.

Problems of the Divided House

If the parents of the bride are separated but not divorced they issue a joint invitation to their daughter's wedding and take their accustomed part in the ceremony as if there were no difference. For her sake, too, both officiate at the reception.

Sometimes when divorce has taken place the mother gives the wedding and the father the reception. If he has not married again, he stands first in line to receive the guests. If he has remarried, his wife acts as hostess. If the bride's mother should attend the reception under the latter circumstances, as might well happen in some instances, she comes as a guest, as she cannot stand at the side of her former husband in his new home and share the duties of hostess with his wife. If, however, her former husband has not remarried she could stand with him on the receiving line in his home, acting as hostess for the occasion, whether or not she has remarried. In this case, as it is his home and not hers, he precedes his former wife on the line.

If the mother, divorced, gives both wedding and reception the father usually gives the bride away, calling for her at her mother's house in the bridal car. If relations are very strained some other male relative may give the bride away, or her mother might if her father is not to attend the wedding. Whether or not he is remarried, he sits in the second or third pew on the left side of the church and, if remarried, may be accompanied by his new wife. She, in turn, may go with her husband to the reception if relations are friendly, but neither she nor the bride's father receives.

If the bride's mother has remarried, her husband sits with her in the first pew on the left and the bride's father sits behind them with *his* wife in the second or third pew. If the remarried mother gives the reception her husband stands with her on the line and the bride's father, if present, attends only as an important guest.

It is far better to err on the side of too-friendly relations between divorced people on their child's wedding day then to have them remind all present by their stiff attitudes of their own failure in marriage. It must be the bride's great day, and even if her parents have been long divorced and long remarried they are to her forever a unit—the unit that produced her. She needs to feel, if possible, that on this day they are brought together if only briefly by this great common interest, the wedding of their child, and confident that the readjustment they have all had to make has been the kind that will provide future serenity in her own marriage.

Conduct of the Wedding Guests

As we have seen, formal weddings are complicated affairs and the person receiving an invitation to the reception must reply immediately, although one to the wedding alone, of course, requires no reply. It is important for the bride's family to know as soon as possible how many guests are to attend the reception, so the caterer may receive the necessary instructions for this reason.

A guest invited to attend the reception makes his own arrangements to get there, either in his own car or by taxi, or he asks friends he may encounter at the wedding to let him ride with them. The bride's family is not responsible for guests' transportation to or from the reception, although ushers do try to find transportation at least for honored guests who may not have their own. If you do not drive and would need to in order to attend the ceremony or the reception, you can call the bride or her parents and ask if they know anyone who is attending from your neighborhood who might have a car. But this really should be a last resort, since the bride and her family have enough to think about at this time.

Dress The guest dresses according to the time of day and the formality of the wedding. (See "What the Parents and Guests Wear," page 117.) Unless he or she is actually a member of the wedding party, flowers are not worn.

It is quite incorrect for men to wear any form of evening dress—tuxedos or tails—during the daylight hours, even for a wedding. Evening dress is never worn before six o'clock, although sometimes it is necessary for a man to be seen in formal dress somewhat before this hour but only if he's in transit.

At the Church The guest aids the work of the ushers by arriving at the church fifteen to twenty minutes before the ceremony or, at a large wedding, even earlier if pew cards are not issued. It is disappointing to arrive so late that all seats permitting a full view of the altar are taken.

Each guest, man or woman, is met in the church vestibule by an usher who seats each in turn or in groups where all are to sit together (see "Duties of Ushers"). As each guest joins an usher he says, "Friend of the bride" or "Friend of the groom," as the case may be, so that he may be seated on the left or the right side of the church. If he has a reserved seat, he presents the card that has been sent to him to the usher, or tells him his name if he is not recognized. At a formal wedding with ushers on duty no invited guest seats himself.

After the guests are seated in the pews to which they have been escorted they may talk briefly in low tones suitable to church. They should not move about among their friends, wave, or turn around to talk to friends in rear pews. After the bride's mother is escorted to the front left pew no other guests are seated and the church doors are closed. As the wedding march begins, all guests rise and, customarily in Episcopal and most other Protestant churches, turn slightly toward the bride's aisle and await her appearance on her father's arm. In most services all remain standing throughout, bowing their heads if bride and groom kneel or kneeling with them if that is customary. A stranger to the ritual goes as far in following it as his own religious customs permit. If it is not the custom of his own church to kneel, he can at least bow his head over the back of the pew in front of him and stand and sit when others do the same. A Protestant at a Catholic wedding is not expected to make the Sign of the Cross, but a Christian man at an Orthodox or Conservative Jewish wedding would be considered irreverent if he did not wear a hat. For the same reason Protestant married women whose own churches do not require head covering in church do cover their heads, in an Orthodox or Conservative synagogue, so as not to offend.

After the ribbons are in place no one may leave his pew, even if there is possible egress to a side aisle. Ushers escort the bride's mother and honored guests immediately following the recessional, before the ribbons are removed. Other guests leave unhurriedly by themselves only after the ribbons are removed, either by the center or side aisles.

At the Reception As guests arrive at the reception they join the waiting line, staying together in family groups, if possible, and never seeking refreshments until they have been officially received, in order, first by the bride's mother, unless it is clear that champagne or something similar is being served to them while they are waiting to go through the line. (See "Conversation and the Receiving Line.")

At large weddings there are always many people from out of town who do not know each other. And, as the parents of the couple are busy on the receiving line and introductions cannot be made in a general way by members of the family in so large a group, it is up to strangers to make themselves known to those in whose immediate neighborhood they find themselves standing or sitting. The host's roof is sufficient introduction.

It is always more tactful for a young girl to approach either an older woman or a girl her own age than for her to speak first to a young man. And a young man shows his breeding by speaking first to an older man or woman, in the hope that he will be taken in hand and introduced to attractive girls. All that is necessary is for an outsider in the group to join others in a casual manner and, when conversation permits, introduce himself or herself with a brief, identifying phrase. "How do you do? I am Nancy Penny (not 'Miss Penny' if she's a young girl, though a married woman would say '*Mrs*. Moore' to simplify further introductions, or possibly, 'Helen Moore—*Mrs*. Moore') from Cleveland. Helen (the bride) and I went to school together." Or, "May I introduce myself? I am Joe Choate from Don's (the groom's) office. I'm afraid I don't know a soul here." Any agreeable guest approached in this way will stay and talk and perform introductions or, if he's in the same boat, at least be grateful for company.

Guests may stay until after the bride and groom's departure, if they wish, but if they do stay to see the throwing of the bride's bouquet no woman guest—and never a man—should make any attempt to catch it if there are bridesmaids. It is traditionally thrown to the unmarried girls in the bride's retinue. Bridesmaids and other attendants are expected to stay until most of the guests have left, since they are, in a way, co-hostesses with the bride's family.

As on any other occasion when he has been entertained, the wedding guest seeks out the host or hostess before his departure. He need not write a "bread and butter" letter, call, or send flowers to the hostess after the event, but if he is a close friend he may feel that so festive and joyous an occasion calls for a brief little note of appreciation—just a line or two to the effect, "The wedding was wonderful. Thank you for inviting us"— or a phone call to the bride's mother—or to the person to whom he is indebted for his invitation.

Congratulatory Telegrams

Friends and relatives unable to attend the wedding ceremony and extend their congratulations in person may send a telegram to the couple, timed to arrive during the reception. It is the best man's function to read such telegrams to the bridal table.

You need not worry about sending a telegram to the couple just because the bride's name is better known since all of the arrangements have been made by her father. Hotels or restaurants maintain lists which record the purpose of the function being held in any room on its premises, with all the necessary names involved.

Congratulations should always be addressed to the couple, not to the bride or groom alone. A telegram may read: "Congratulations and a long and happy life together, love, Aunt Lucy and Uncle Joe," or any other warm, personal message. Attempts at levity are usually out of place and, reduced to telegraphic prose, often seem tasteless no matter how well meant. The seriousness of the occasion should be carefully respected. Such congratulatory telegrams, incidentally, really should be answered. As someone aptly said to me, "If a friend thinks it is worthwhile to send me such a message, I don't see why I should not reciprocate and express my thanks." Actually, a postcard from the honeymoon is enough, or a telephone call when the couple returns.

Second or Delayed Wedding Receptions

A new custom, that of a second wedding reception following the one immediately after the ceremony, is being followed by many brides. The need for this seems to arise sometimes when the bride, perhaps working in a distant city and perhaps marrying a man from that city, decides to be married there usually at a small ceremony attended by her immediate family and that of the groom. Occasionally, the groom's family will lend their home for such a wedding, following it perhaps with a small reception. The second reception then takes place in the bride's home city or town, so that all those who were not invited to the wedding or who could not attend can meet the bridegroom. The second reception conversely may take place in the groom's home town if the bride and groom plan a trip there shortly after the wedding and honeymoon and if many of the groom's family and his parents' friends could not travel to the first reception.

If this second reception is comparatively formal, the bride may wear her wedding gown, but not her veil (a symbol of virginity) as there will be elapsed time between the wedding ceremony and the reception. If engraved wedding invitations are sent out for the ceremony, invitations to the second reception may be enclosed or optionally they may be sent separately two weeks before the reception is to take place.

These second receptions may also be quite informal, with informal invitations phoned or put into the mail. There may even be a wedding cake displayed on a small separate table before being served. If the party is informal there is no receiving line but everyone should meet the honorees. Sometimes the groom's family gives this party, inviting, of course, the bride's family which should certainly attend if possible.

Chapter 14

SECOND AND SUBSEQUENT MARRIAGES

With one in four marriages ending in divorce, and with women frequently outliving their spouses, second marriages for one reason or another are becoming increasingly common. And as second and subsequent marriages proliferate, so do the procedures and ethics concerning them grow up and change. At one time few churches would sanction remarriage of divorced persons, and brides absolutely could not wear white. Today, to meet the changing situation however, churches and communities are revising their stand on second marriages. Much of the opprobrium connected with second marriages, especially in view of their statistically excellent chances for success, has been lifted. However, important distinctions still exist between first and second or subsequent marriages, and an enumeration of them makes things easier for all involved.

What Constitutes a Second Marriage

The single determining factor as to whether a marriage is to be considered a second marriage or not is the previous marital status of the bride, and only the bride. An oft-married groom will probably avoid such frivolities as a bachelor party but if it is his bride's first marriage, she is entitled to all the trappings of a formal first-time wedding, should she desire them.

Any woman however who has been married before, no matter how briefly or unhappily or how long ago, and who is marrying again, is having in society's eyes, a second marriage. It is not realistic or useful for a girl of twenty who had an unfortunate marriage at sixteen and who feels ready to marry again to pretend that her former marriage, even if it were a secret and short-lived one, never took place. By doing that she would be attempting to unlearn exactly the lessons her first marriage taught her which no doubt had an effect on preparing her to undertake the second, and let us hope more successful, one. In the case of an annulment, a person so involved may legally be considered as one who has never married, but socially it is another matter. Discretion and honesty are advocated particularly in this delicate situation. No woman should ever try to hide the fact that she has been married, although she may not wish for some reason to advertise it.

Engagements before Second Marriages

Since most second marriages are small and informal, requiring much less planning than formal first-time weddings, engagements, if announced to friends at all, are usually brief and quite close to the date of the wedding.

No one in the midst of divorce proceedings should simultaneously plan remarriage. Such haste is tasteless and often foolhardy. A decent interval should elapse with perhaps therapy or other counseling seriously undertaken before any remarriage.

No formal announcement of an engagement for a second marriage is actually necessary, although the bride may choose to write or call friends and relatives to inform them of her intention to remarry.

Invitations for Second Marriages

Invitations for second marriages whether for widows or divorcées are telephoned, telegraphed, sometimes given by word of mouth if the ceremonies are small and simple, or handwritten. For example:

September 15

Dear Helen and Bob,

Richard and I have set the date. We'll be married, quietly of course, at St. Andrews in the chapel, Friday, October sixth at five-thirty with just the family and a friend or two. Please let me know if you can be with us and afterward at a small supper here—

Fondly,
Marion

Reception Invitations

Reception invitations, on the other hand are engraved if the reception is to be sufficiently large as to make this expense worthwhile. Such invitations may also be written, as may the wedding invitations, by a calligrapher. Separate reception invitations, say in the case of a young divorcée or a young widow, may be issued by her parents in this way:

Dr. and Mrs. Grant Kingsley
request the pleasure of your company
at the wedding reception of their daughter
Penelope Franklyn
and
Mr. George Frank Carpenter
on Saturday, May eighth
at four o'clock
Hotel Mark Hopkins, San Francisco

R.s.v.p.
15 Shady Road
Belvedere, Calif. zip code

An older couple issuing such an invitation jointly:

Mrs. Samuel Franklyn
and
Mr. George Frank Carpenter
request the pleasure of your company
at their wedding breakfast
on Friday, May seventh
at half after twelve
Hotel Del Coronado, San Diego

R.s.v.p.
Three Mark Lane
Santa Barbara, Calif. zip code

Wedding Announcements

Engraved wedding announcements of a second marriage may be sent, and in fact, this is the best way to publicize the event, since engraved wedding invitations are not used. Announcements, which may be sent to a wide list even when the reception is small, should be mailed the day of the wedding, or as soon thereafter as possible. The bride may have her parents make the announcement, or, particularly if she is divorced, she may do it herself with her new husband. In the first instance, the announcement reads:

Mr. and Mrs. Francis Dorian Kipling
have the honour of announcing
the marriage of their daughter
Anita Kipling Benson
(maiden name, plus former married name)
to
Mr. Arthur Townley Bryant
Saturday, the sixth of March
One thousand nine hundred and seventy-one
New York, New York

In the second case it reads:

Mrs. Kipling Benson
and
Mr. Arthur Townley Bryant
announce their marriage
Saturday, the sixth of March
One thousand nine hundred and seventy-one
New York, New York

The Divorcée's Announcement   If a divorcée is young, her parents issue the announcement of her wedding:

Mr. and Mrs. Sidney Myers
have the honour of announcing
the marriage of their daughter
Sylvia Ann Kiser
to
Mr. Robert Miller
on Thursday, the tenth of June
One thousand nine hundred and seventy-one
Rumson, New Jersey

Or, the divorcée may issue her own announcement, in conjunction with her husband:

Mrs. Myers Kiser
and
Mr. Kurt Samuels
announce their marriage
on Thursday, the tenth of June
One thousand nine hundred and seventy-one
Rumson, New Jersey

Gifts for Second Marriages

The bride who has been married before, whether she is widowed or divorced, technically should not expect wedding gifts, although in actual practice many people do give them. Individual circumstances need to be taken into consideration. If the bride is a young divorcée who perhaps eloped the first time and did not have a formal wedding with the usual wedding gifts, close friends at least and relatives will probably wish to give her gifts on her second marriage. If the bride has been married before and the groom has not, the groom's friends and relatives will very probably send wedding gifts to the couple. When the groom has been married previously and the bride has not, it is perhaps too much to expect his friends or any but the closest relatives to send gifts. Perhaps none will feel impelled to send them.

Preparations for a Second Wedding

Because some clergymen are still reluctant to marry divorced persons, it is important that a divorced person visit a clergyman as soon as possible after deciding to remarry. Perhaps the clergyman will not be willing to approve a church ceremony, but will be willing to perform the marriage in his study or elsewhere. All of these points should be brought up in the discussion. If he refuses to perform the marriage at all, and the couple wants very much to have a religious ceremony, they may approach a clergyman of another, more permissive denomination, who would be willing to perform the ceremony whether or not either is a member of his congregation.

Since second weddings, even those held in a church, are small and simple, floral decorations and music are actually not necessary but if used should be minimal, as there is usually no processional or recessional in a second-marriage ceremony. I have on one or two occasions seen a remarrying widow escorted in a simple processional by a son or family friend and accompanied by her matron of honor. And the couple did have a simple recessional with their attendants, receiving then in the vestibule. One of these weddings was in a Presbyterian church, one in an Episcopal church. The clergyman is actually the final authority in such departures.

Attendants at Second Weddings

It is proper at a second marriage for the couple to have only one attendant each who may even be the sole witnesses of the ceremony. In other second marriages, usually those of widows rather than divorcées, particularly those taking place in church, ushers may be needed to seat guests. Bridesmaids are never included. The two attendants' duties are similar to those of the maid or matron of honor and the best man at a first marriage.

As with attendants at any wedding, the bride and groom in a second wedding present their attendants with some remembrance of the occasion. The bride might give her attendant some small but attractive piece of jewelry, and the groom might give his attendant cuff links or any other personal gift of lasting value as well as his tie which should either be the same or a slightly different version of his own. If they have rented formal wear, the groom provides the best man's collar and boutonnieres for them both.

Children at Second Weddings

The children, if any, of the couple's previous marriages may witness the wedding if the couple are both widowed. If one or the other has been divorced, the matter of the children witnessing the ceremony is a delicate matter. In general it seems better that quite young ones not do so, but older ones may well be included depending on individual circumstances. The children, however, may certainly attend the reception.

Entertaining before Second Weddings

Since the reason for giving showers before a marriage is to help the bride furnish a household with an adequate "dowry" and since the divorced or widowed woman has already established such a household, parties of this sort are not usual before a second marriage. A possible exception might be the remarriage of a girl whose previous marriage had been an elopement with few or no resulting wedding gifts. An older woman marrying for the second time should not expect or encourage showers, although prenuptial teas, luncheons, cocktail parties are quite usual. Rehearsal dinners are not necessary as the ceremony in second marriage is so simple. (Ushers, if any, arrive an hour in advance to receive their instructions.) Small parties—

aside from showers—before second or even subsequent marriages are quite usual. They may be given by close friends or relatives and may be buffets, cocktail parties, luncheons or even barbecues with invitations sent either on fill-in engraved invitations or on ordinary fill-ins. Formal parties of any kind should be avoided before the marriage, but a formal reception may follow it and if not given by the couple themselves, may be given by relatives or friends. Gifts are never usual at these parties as they might be for a similar one for young people marrying for the first time.

Dress for the Second Wedding

Whereas once it was absolutely taboo for a woman marrying a second time to wear a white dress, this is now acceptable, provided the dress does not resemble a wedding gown. Depending upon the time of day and the degree of formality of the wedding, the bride may wear anything from a simple suit to a long gown in any color she finds becoming except true red or black. The second-time bride may carry a very simple bridal bouquet if she wants to, without orange blossoms although I have no objection to a spray of lilies of the valley. Actually, however, for a second marriage a prayer book, perhaps with a flower marker, or even a single flower may be more appropriate. Corsages are much less worn than they used to be. Many second-time brides prefer to omit the flowers, even though the groom does wear a boutonniere.

Anything even mildly resembling a veil should not be worn by the second-time bride. It is not necessary in most cases for her to wear anything on her head if she doesn't wish to, but if it is the custom of the particular congregation such a bride may choose to wear a bow, flower clip or an attractive hat in keeping with her outfit. A cage veil that in no way resembles a bride's veil in another possibility.

The groom's clothes, whether or not he has been previously married, should be keyed to the degree of formality of his bride's dress. At an afternoon wedding taking place before six o'clock, he does not wear formal evening clothes or even a tuxedo. His most flattering dress of sufficient formality, is the stroller, the "new" Prince Edward, or the cutaway. At a small wedding at which only the witnesses may be present and perhaps a member or so of the family, he might wear a dark business suit or in summer a light or even a white suit. A groom in military service may wear his uniform and, indeed, may be required to in time of war, and this is also true of any members of the military witnessing or taking part in the wedding even in a civilian chapel. His attendant dresses in the same manner as he does. The bride's attendant wears the same kind of costume as does the bride, and it should not be in any way a typical bridesmaid's gown.

Guests at a second marriage wear clothes suitable to the time of day as they would at any other wedding.

Second-Wedding Ceremony

The actual ceremony for a second wedding is greatly abbreviated from that of a first-time wedding. There is usually no processional or recessional. The bride in a church ceremony usually enters, following her attendant—but usually not escorted—from the vestry door to find the groom and best man already at the altar. In the case of a young girl, her father or another older male relative might still escort her and give her away, although this part of the ceremony is ordinarily dispensed with for a second wedding. The ceremony should be as brief and as dignified as possible with all procedures discussed in advance with the clergyman who will perform it. In a home, hotel, or club wedding, the procedure is equally simple with the bride perhaps briefly escorted by a family friend, a mature son, or possibly her father. Music, if any, is never traditional bridal music—no usual Lohengrin or Mendelssohn. Solos are best avoided.

Reception for the Second Wedding

Since this is a social event, it may be large and impressive if the bride wishes. If it is large, it necessitates a receiving line. The bride and groom greet people informally as they arrive, but neither set of parents, nor even the attendants stand in line.

It is permissible to have a wedding cake without the decorative bride and groom or white bell or lettering of any kind on top. In every other respect, a second-wedding reception can be just like the first. And in cases where the bride did not have a traditional ceremony the first time she married and could not have one the second time, a large reception is an excellent solution. Any reception, however, should be in keeping with the dignity and decorum of the occasion. The term "second marriage" in all the foregoing refers, too, to subsequent marriages of divorced or widowed persons.

Remarriage of Divorced Persons to Each Other

Occasionally people who have been divorced eventually remarry each other. When this occurs, no formal announcements are sent out, but friends are informed of the good news by word of mouth, by letter, and by telegram. No formal announcements are released to the press. In such instances, often children are involved, so the reunion of the couple should be made almost as if the schism had never existed. In keeping with this, a couple who has been through such a parting should plan to celebrate their anniversary on the date of their first marriage.

Chapter 15

THE HONEYMOON AND
POST-WEDDING CALLS

Somewhere at some time I remember reading a stiff-necked interdiction against the term "honeymoon." Supposedly "wedding trip" is better usage. In French the term for this carefree period of adjustment is *"lune de miel,"* literally "moon of honey," and there is historic significance in the term. In Europe, in some countries, the couple drank a special beverage, or mead, called metheglin, a honey wine, for a month after the wedding—hence the "honey moon."

The modern honeymoon is much simpler, and usually much shorter, than that of previous generations. My mother's lasted three months and included a trip on horseback through part of the Rockies. In the 1860s a honeymoon could encompass a whole summer and might include the entire wedding party—at the bridegroom's expense. The depression following the Civil War put an end to such extravagance, fortunately, or it still might be the expected thing for the groom to take his and his bride's attendants along on what should be a most private holiday.

Where to Go and for How Long

The place and duration of the honeymoon must depend on the amount of time available and the financial resources of the groom—for this is his expense. Unless, of course, either his or her parents, or perhaps both together, are able to give the couple a honeymoon as a wedding gift. A trip to Europe or a world or Caribbean cruise is, barring the interruption of war, a standard wedding gift on the part of parents who can afford it.

Even if both bride and groom must go back to work immediately after the ceremony, as so often happens in this tense society of ours, some sort of quiet getting away together should be planned at the earliest possible moment, before the two are caught up in the whirl of conjugal responsibilities. For suburbanites a weekend in a nearby city can be honeymoon enough, if only that time can be spared. For city dwellers, a trip to the country may accomplish the same thing—a chance to be more or less alone during the first awkward stage of marriage, a time free of routine chores and of relatives and well-meaning friends. I really do not recommend that any couple skip the honeymoon altogether, no matter how much of an extravagance it may seem. It may prove their one and only time in marriage for some years to come when they can just escape together, when people will be respectful of their desire and need for privacy.

Anything too different from the sort of thing each is used to may be a dangerous choice in the way of a honeymoon. A new husband who loves to walk would make a mistake in choosing to introduce his bride to the rigors of distance hiking if she's never trod on anything but city pavements. Too many adjustments should not be made at once—to marriage, and, at the same time, to a strange and perhaps too demanding environment or activity. Neither partner should take along a pet on the honeymoon. Pets can be jealous creatures—and provoke jealousy. The couple should choose the kind of place where both will feel comfortable and where, if they want it, there will be some sort of diversion available in the company of other young people. It is helpful if the honeymoon isn't too—sometimes embarrassingly—private, for it then eases the couple gently into married life as it really is, not two on an island of love and kisses, but two as a unit in a community of friends and neighbors.

The Arrival Telegrams

Upon arrival at the honeymoon spot, the young couple should immediately dispatch telegram or cable to the bride's parents announcing their safe arrival and thanking them for all they did to make the wedding beautiful. Then it is equally thoughtful for the couple to send a wire to the groom's parents notifying them of safe arrival and thanking them, too, for their help in making the wedding go well. Instead of the telegrams, of course, the couple may phone both parents if they prefer, but even on such a private occasion they should not just drop out of sight without making these gracious gestures.

Where Will They Live?

With very few exceptions, it is a very bad choice for a young couple to plan to live with either set of parents, even on a temporary basis. If their parents live well the young people may be reluctant to start out in the more modest kind of home they can provide for themselves. It is safer for the marriage if the newly married people, if necessary, share the home of strangers rather than that of either of their families. It is difficult for even the most understanding parents to think of their children under their own roof as anything but children. Even the youngest husband needs to *feel* he is the head of the house.

Post-wedding Calls

In the days when formal calling was *de rigueur* everyone asked to a wedding was expected to call on the bride's mother within three weeks after the wedding and on the bride and groom within a reasonable time after they had returned home, especially if they had issued "at home" cards.

In actuality, if these formalities were rigidly carried out in our modern society it would make for considerable confusion. Imagine the mother of a bride, after a large, elaborate wedding to which anywhere from three to five hundred guests have come from far and wide, having to receive them all, or at least the women representatives of families, within three weeks after the last bit of confetti has been swept out of the hall! She'll want to talk over the wedding with many of her close friends, who would call or, more probably, phone her in the natural course of events. But to be at home to so many! And the poor bride! It will be months before she has her home running in any proper order. If she's like the average American girl, she knows less than nothing about housekeeping and is either just learning to cook or is trying her best to act mature with a probably part-time helper, if any, whose very functions she hardly knows. Into the middle of all this, and with wedding gifts still being acknowledged, no doubt, step two or three hundred callers? Ridiculous today.

As a matter of fact, the bride's mother, who has gone through considerable in preparation for even a small wedding, expects to hear from no one who attended the wedding and reception, with the exception of a few close friends and relatives who let her know, by calling, dropping her a note, or phoning, how well everything went and how pleased they are at the new addition to the family.

If the bride and groom settle down in a new neighborhood they do not expect their parents' friends who came to the wedding to come from another community to call upon them. They can hope that their immediate neighbors will call, in time, usually in a most informal manner. The local clergyman, in a small community, is certain to call.

The modern bride doesn't stand on much ceremony these days. If she's just fallen heir to a country house and finds its intricacies too much for her, she may merely poke her head through her neighbor's hedge and beg for advice, long before the neighbor has decided it is about time to run in and make herself known. It is certainly simpler to say to a neighbor, who may not yet be conscious that *you* are the one who's just taken the Murphy house, "How do you do? We've just moved in up the street. I'm Margaret Tillman. I wonder if I can ever achieve a garden like that?"

Of course, if a bride moves to New York, she may live in the same apartment house twenty years without knowing more than the face of the apartment holder next door if *he's* in residence that long, although this traditional urban restraint is fortunately beginning to break down, especially in cooperatives and condominiums where tenants have real reason to communicate. But most newcomers *must* make every effort to establish contact with others so they can begin a social life.

By the way, if you are have a social function and are inviting a couple that you know to be newlyweds, it might be kinder for you to seat them together. This custom can be followed for up until a year after the wedding. If a hostess does separate a recently married couple, the husband still dances first with his wife, as is expected throughout the marriage, and then later with his dinner partner and, of course, his hostess. Couples, even newly married ones, should try not to overdo togetherness, however.

Chapter 16

WEDDING ANNIVERSARIES

Today, most couples celebrate their wedding anniversaries in some quiet way as they come along. Some special attention is often paid the tenth, and usually the following are really celebrated with one's friends: the twenty-fifth, the fiftieth, and the seventy-fifth. Wedding anniversaries are celebrated only when both spouses are living. An anniversary which occurs when one of the spouses has died may be quietly recognized by friends and family by the sending of flowers or notes in remembrance of the day, but it can hardly be celebrated as a joyous occasion under the circumstances.

The same formality attends the wedding anniversary invitation as the wedding itself. Invitations may be, of course, engraved or handwritten, or telephoned. For any anniversary celebration from the fiftieth on it is possible to have at least the years (if they are included on the invitation) and even the entire invitation plate printed in gold lettering. The fortieth (which calls for rubies) is sometimes engraved in ruby red and addressed in black. The twenty-fifth (silver) may be engraved in silver, addressed in black. The invitations may or may not mention the occasion, in the latter instance merely asking friends to dine on the particular evening. Anniversaries, by the way, are not necessarily celebrated on the actual day, or even during the actual month when the wedding took place, but the participants may adjust the date to suit the weather or their own convenience.

If the dinner is a formal seated one, the hostess, if other than the "bride" should be placed to the left of the "groom," for the "bride's" place is to her "groom's" right.

There is no set rule about a receiving line at an anniversary celebration. The degree of formality of the celebration is naturally a determining factor. If engraved invitations are sent, there may be a receiving line with the "bride" first and then the "groom" followed by any surviving or available attendants from the wedding. Sometimes (best I feel) only the couple receives. One or both may receive if long standing seems too difficult, or chairs may be nearby to be used as needed.

Formal Invitations to a Wedding Anniversary

1921   1971
Mr. and Mrs. Roland Purdy
request the pleasure of
the company of
Mr. and Mrs. Robjohn*
at a dinner to celebrate
the fiftieth anniversary of their marriage
on Saturday, the twentieth of February
at eight o'clock
850 Park Avenue
New York, N.Y. zip code

R.s.v.p.

or:

In honour of
the fiftieth wedding anniversary of
Mr. and Mrs. Roland Purdy
their sons and daughters
request the pleasure of
the company of
Captain McMurray*
at dinner
on Saturday, the seventeenth of February
at eight o'clock
850 Park Avenue

R.s.v.p.
Mrs. Gibbs Purdy
88 Cricket Lane
Larchmont, New York zip code

This form is used where listing of all children would crowd the invitation.
or:

Mr. and Mrs. Gibbs Purdy
Mr. Allan Nye Purdy
request the pleasure of
the company of etc.

Many seek to put the phrase "Please omit gifts" on this invitation, feeling that they have all the household furnishings and accessories they can ever use. However, I feel that people attending such a celebration should feel free to take a gift or not, as they please. You should not

* Handwritten

deprive them of this opportunity to express their affection for you. Gifts need not be expensive, handmade ones are often most appreciated. Naturally whenever gifts do arrive in the presence of guests who have not brought them they are not opened. If it is strongly felt that the request not to bring gifts should be made, it should be made informally and preferably never be put in any way on the invitation although I have known of at least one exception to this rule that seemed necessary as the celebration was enormous. If such a line must be included, I prefer to see it on a separate printed slip not engraved on the invitation.

Replies to Formal Invitations to a Wedding Anniversary

Mr. and Mrs. Robjohn
accept with pleasure
the kind invitation of
Mr. and Mrs. Roland Purdy
to dine (*optional*) *
on Saturday, the seventeenth of February
at eight o'clock

Captain McMurray
accepts with pleasure
the kind invitation
of Mrs. Gibbs Purdy
for Saturday, the seventeenth of February
at eight o'clock

Anniversary Photographs

For important anniversaries such as the twenty-fifth, the fiftieth, and the seventy-fifth, group photographs can make a precious souvenir. Usually they comprise all the children with their spouses, and all the children and possibly grandchildren that can be gathered together. For historic purposes, it is wise to inscribe all of the names and the ages of the youngest on a sheet to be attached to the reverse side of the photograph. The photograph should then be nicely framed for the couple.

Wedding Anniversary Gifts

Gifts should not actually be expected on an anniversary, except between husband and wife, but of course they may be given by close friends and family members who wish to give them. Greeting cards and telegrams are usual.

There is a tradition for the giving of wedding anniversary presents, especially on major anniversaries, though, of course, it need not be followed. For example, if for some reason the couple has received few gifts

* If "to dine" is omitted, use "for" Saturday instead of "on" Saturday.

of sterling silver, crystal, glass, or linens, the first three anniversaries are excellent occasions on which friends and relatives can help make up these deficiencies. Changing times, new fabrics, and products make it advisable to extend the list somewhat.

1st	paper, plastics (can be furniture)	13th	lace or perhaps a sheer lacelike wool article
2nd	cotton, china	14th	ivory or agate
3rd	leather or any leatherlike article	15th	crystal or glass
		20th	china or occasional furniture
4th	linen, silk, rayon or nylon or other synthetic silk	25th	silver
5th	wood and decorative accessories for the home	30th	pearls or personal gifts
		35th	coral or jade
6th	iron	40th	rubies or garnets
7th	wool, copper, or brass	45th	sapphires or tourmalines
8th	bronze or electrical appliances	50th	gold
		55th	emeralds or turquoise
9th	pottery, china, glass, or crystal	60th	diamonds or diamondlike stones, or gold
10th	tin or aluminum	75th	diamonds or diamondlike stones, or gold
11th	steel		
12th	silk, nylon, linen		

The Money Tree

Money trees are very popular for anniversaries. The collection of such money, instead of gifts, especially for people who have been married many years and have all the worldly goods they want, is a sensible idea. It may permit a couple married twenty-five or fifty years to take a little trip or buy something special they have wanted. Here is the procedure:

Although nothing is on the invitation concerning a money tree, a slip may be inserted which reads something like this. "If you should wish to give a gift, we hope that you will contribute to a money tree we are planning. Contributions may be sent to Mrs. Robert J. Jones, 16 Poplar Drive, Minneapolis, Minnesota 55422." This information may be given out to anyone who calls the sponsors of the party to see what gifts might be welcome.

It used to be that fifty-cent pieces or silver dollars were taped to a money tree for the twenty-fifth anniversary (of course gold pieces are out of the question for the fiftieth). With silver dollars and fifty-cent pieces both difficult to find now, most money trees are done with bills taped to the "tree"—a real branch sprayed with white or silver or gold paint, or an artificial tree. Sometimes the bills are tightly rolled like cigarettes and attached with appropriate colored ribbons, sometimes they are enclosed in silver or gold envelopes but usually they hang free. If an artificial Christmas tree is used for the purpose, the bills may be taped to regular Christmas tree ornament hooks so the tape will not destroy the "needles," of the tree. If the invitation is sent by the couple themselves, such a slip suggesting a money tree may not be enclosed, but the friend in charge could get in touch with the guest list by phone or by note saying that contributions to the money tree would be appreciated rather than other gifts.

When the couple is quite elderly, it is difficult for the wife to write thank-you notes for the gifts received. Such needed notes may be written by a daughter or daughter-in-law which could read along these lines:

Dear Mr. and Mrs. Needham,

My mother and father (or mother and father-in-law) enjoyed your gift of (name the gift, but if it is money, do not state the amount) at their anniversary party. They have asked me to thank you warmly.

Sincerely,

Reaffirmation of Marriage Vows

In some communities it is becoming increasingly popular for a couple to reaffirm their marriage vows after being married a number of years. This service may take place with only the couple and the minister or rabbi present or with several couples reaffirming their vows at a regular service, not necessarily on any wedding anniversary. The couple should dress in their regular Sabbath clothing. There is no standard ceremony for this procedure so that they may adapt something to their unique circumstances, so long as it includes the repeating of the marriage vows. Their children may be present, but only as guests. No one stands for the couple.

Sometimes the whole marriage is re-enacted with certain exceptions, for example among Conservative Jews with the exception of the marriage contract and the ring ceremony. This re-enactment of the wedding may be in a temple or in a church, at home or in a public place such as a hotel with as many of the original attendants present as possible and in the case of a fiftieth or sixtieth wedding anniversary, with the children and grandchildren in attendance. The ceremony, whether it be a re-enactment, a private blessing or a blessing during the course of a worship service, perhaps with other couples, with or without music, may be followed by any private celebration the couples wish to have. The wedding cake may be duplicated and toasts be offered. In all of this, it is important to consult the clergyman involved before making plans.

Some clergymen are not enthusiastic about either re-enactments or re-affirmations and instead offer a brief service of thanksgiving for a happy marriage, the blessing of the children. One Episcopal rector explained to me that he likes this better than the "reaffirmation of vows" explaining that if vows have been hallowed by many years of love and fidelity, they do not need to be reaffirmed. When God has blessed a marriage with happiness, it is a beautiful thing to express joy and gratitude at the family's place of worship on an anniversary. The same clergyman said he did not like the idea of a wedding dress being worn for such a ceremony, or the attendants taking part except as part of the congregation, and I must say I agree with him. When you think about it, the original vows taken at the time of the marriage are not tentative ones. They should not really need reaffirmation, although certainly at a ceremony of thanksgiving for a happy marriage the participants would strengthen the vows made originally and be grateful for the happy years.

Sometimes when vows are to be reaffirmed, a new ring may replace a well-worn one or the original one may be incorporated in a new setting. A completely new ring could be blessed, I am sure, with the clergyman's approval.

Chapter 17

FUNERALS

It is not strange that when man faces the mystery of death he turns to religion for comfort and help. There are many civil marriages, but it is almost unheard of for us to bury the dead without at least a prayer. However unrooted we may be in our religious beliefs, the time of death turns us to the formalities of religion, to the clergyman, the priest, or the rabbi to perform the final, dignified rites.

The family's responsibility when death occurs is partly religious, partly social, partly legal.

Immediate Procedures When Death Occurs

Every family should have an "emergency" file in its strongbox. In this file should be listed the name of a funeral director to be called when the need occurs. If the family owns a burial plot or a mausoleum, the deed should be in the file, as it will be required by the funeral director. If one or more members of the family prefer cremation, a note to that effect should be in the file, even if the request has been placed in the will. A copy of each birth certificate should also be in the folder (the Board of Health supplies photostatic or certified copies for family records at a small cost). Also included should be the names and addresses of all close relatives and friends who should be informed.

If these things are kept all together, whoever is placed in charge of the funeral—often a relative or friend—will be able to handle the many details. Without the birth certificate, for example, he would have difficulty in supplying the necessary information for the death certificate.

It is also important that a list of all bank accounts, social security numbers, bonds, notes, and mortgages of the various members of the family be listed, together with a notation on the whereabouts of safe deposit boxes, insurance policies, and wills. Many a friend or relative put in charge of a funeral has been in considerable doubt as to how much expense he should incur for the estate.

The name and address of the attorney or attorneys drawing the will or wills should be on file, and the person in charge of the funeral should notify the lawyer before the funeral takes place.

When death occurs and a doctor has not been in attendance, or when the person's religious beliefs preclude medical care, the county medical examiner—in some states the coroner—must be called to determine the cause of death and issue and sign the death certificate. This notification properly takes place before the calling of the mortician, who may not act without the medical examiner's permission.

Arranging the Funeral

Whoever is chosen to make funeral arrangements should not be, if possible, any of the most bereaved. Our attitude toward funerals has changed very much for the better, and we now readily accept the fact that an elaborate funeral whose cost will leave the family in serious debt does shallow honor to the deceased. But a frightened young widow, unable to see ahead and perhaps ill-informed on her late husband's finances, can't be expected to make objective decisions concerning the various costs of the funeral.

For a long time the trend has been toward simple funerals, even among people who can afford elaborate ones. No one but the funeral director knows or cares about the fine details of caskets and their relative expensiveness or inexpensiveness. In fact, many people of sensibility shudder at the pretentious ugliness of expensive caskets, remembering that great heroes are often buried in simple, clean-lined pine boxes.

Whoever undertakes the responsibility of the funeral should realize that he or she is entering into a business contract—and under highly emotional circumstances—where those most involved may be of little help in making important decisions. Where expense must be regarded, he should discuss the necessity with the mortician and make as many decisions as possible himself. It is sometimes months before funds can be released for payment of bills he will incur, and in complicated cases it is sometimes necessary to get the court's permission to pay them. Therefore, all these matters must be handled with great care and conservatism.

If the deceased or his family has had some continuing religious affiliation, there is no problem concerning the choice of a clergyman to officiate. Otherwise a clergyman of any faith may, with the family's permission, be asked to read a burial service. When the funeral takes place in a city and the interment is in a family plot at considerable distance, one or more members of the family or its representatives goes with the body to the place of burial and a local funeral director must usually be retained to handle the interment. He asks a local clergyman to conduct the brief service at the grave. A local florist may supply one or more fresh floral offerings.

Clothing for Burial

Among many people, especially among Orthodox and some Conservative and Reform Jews, the shroud is still used for burial. Otherwise, the person in charge of the funeral delivers to the funeral director the kind of clothing the deceased would have worn to worship, choosing for older women soft materials in solid, quiet tones of lavender, blue, beige, gray, or taupe, with long sleeves and a high neckline. Evening dresses are unsuitable, and black is rarely used. Young girls are often dressed in white. Children are dressed as for Sunday school.

Clothes furnished for men should be, too, the kind they would have worn under conservative circumstances, usually something from their existing wardrobe. A cutaway is suitable, or a dark blue or a dark gray or Oxford suit. Evening clothes are not suitable, nor are sports suits, although in the summer a white linen or any light tropical weave suit may be used.

People are no longer buried with their jewels, although many are with their wedding rings. Directions concerning rings or earrings (in pierced ears) are expected by the funeral director.

Hanging the Bell

The custom of hanging the bell goes back to the days when doorbells were bells with clappers hung on or adjacent to the door. When someone died, the clapper was muffled in cloth. This later developed into ribbon streamers in white, purple or black, with white or purple flowers. Like mourning, the bell hanging was for the protection of the bereaved, so that anyone approaching the house would do so with quiet dignity.

Today, few hang the bell. And it is never done except when the funeral is to take place in the home. When a family still wishes to adhere to the old custom it so instructs the funeral director, who orders the flowers and has them hung just below the doorbell of either apartment or private house.

Where the Funeral Takes Place

The telescoping of our living quarters has brought into existence more and more "Funeral Homes"—some simple and functional like the old-fashioned funeral parlors, where a funeral was held only if there was no suitable home from which it could take place, others elaborate establishments with their own private chapels and pipe organs. Today it is very usual indeed for a funeral to take place in a mortuary chapel even when home facilities are quite adequate to accommodate a large attendance at the services.

The use of the funeral home is usually included in the over-all cost of the funeral, with the ocasional exception of a charge for music.

If the funeral takes place at home, the largest room is usually selected, one preferably which can be shut off from the rest of the household. Folding chairs are provided by the mortician.

Death Notices

The person in charge of the funeral prepares the death notices, which are then inserted, often by the mortician, in one or more morning papers, in large cities, and, if thought advisable, in any evening papers that carry these notices. If the death takes place in a suburb the notices are carried by the nearest large dailies likely to be read by friends of the deceased. These notices are placed at regular space rates, and when it is desired that friends in distant cities be notified publicly the line is often added "Chicago (or Houston) papers please copy." Such out-of-town papers then may run a news item on the death.

When the person who died has been very well-known socially or otherwise it is probable that major papers in his city already have a prepared obituary on file which may need merely to be brought up to date through telephone checking with a member of the family. Each paper has an editor in charge of this kind of news, and the placing of the obituary notice is his cue to get the facts from a family representative, if the paper considers the death generally newsworthy.

As in the case of weddings and engagements sure to be considered news, it is wise for someone familiar with the details of the deceased's important activities to prepare that information in written form as soon as possible, as such news runs the day of the death or, at the latest, the day the obituary notice first appears. Although the information is usually called for over the phone, it is certainly better to have it written out for ready reference, as in many cases all papers call, as well as the wire services. Additional stories, when a person has been prominent, often run on the actual day of the funeral.

A paid death notice may be phoned to papers selected, but it should always be *read* from carefully checked information. Where it is given over the phone the newspaper's classified department usually calls back for recheck, to be certain the notice is legitimate. The form is:

Volkman—Lawrence Karl, on November 23 (year optional), husband (or beloved husband) of Helen Schroeder Volkman (his wife's maiden name is always given to aid identification) and father of Louise and Peter Schroeder Volkman (the daughters are listed first). Funeral at (name of church and address, if necessary), at 2 P.M., Tuesday.

Sometimes, especially when there was no generally known preliminary illness, the word "suddenly" may be added after the names of the immediate family. If a man was married his wife is always listed first, not his parents, whose names, in this case, usually do not appear in the paid notice but who are mentioned, of course, in news stories, if any.

A woman's death notice reads:

Jardine—Diana Minor (her maiden name), wife (or beloved wife) of, etc. If the funeral is to take place out of town, friends are so notified in the death notice "Funeral at Emmanuel Church, Rye, New York. Train leaves Grand Central at 1 P.M."

The age is usually not given in the death notice, except in the case of a child. It is often mentioned in accompanying news stories, but need not be, especially in the case of women.

The Eulogy

A eulogy may be given by the clergyman or by a close friend or relative, usually male, of the deceased, when the clergyman did not know the deceased personally. Essential details, human little highlights of the person's life should be furnished by those close to him. Fulsome praise should be avoided and a little humor where applicable can often give real meaning to what is being said.

Attending a Funeral

Unless the words "Funeral Private" appear in the death notice, any friend or acquaintance of the deceased or his family may attend the services, as do interested strangers if the funeral is in church. Close friends or relatives may ask the person in charge of arrangements for permission to attend the interment if they are able to provide their own transportation or if there seems to be adequate room in the funeral cars. They should be very certain that their presence at so difficult a time will be of real comfort to the immediate family, which usually prefers to be alone with the clergyman at the last brief rites.

Sending Flowers

Sometimes the death notice reads "Please omit flowers," and this request should be scrupulously respected. At some Protestant funerals the family prefers that the casket have one floral offering, that of the family.

It is important, however, to know that one *never* sends flowers to an Orthodox Jewish funeral. Often they are not desired at a Conservative or a Reform funeral. And it is preferable not to send them to a Catholic church as they may not be taken into the church (only the family's one spray and occasionally an altar arrangement are permitted). However, flowers are often sent to the funeral home and go to the cemetery even though they may not enter the church. In Episcopal funerals, too, only the family's flowers enter the church, others may be arranged in the vestibule before going to the cemetery.

When flowers are sent to a funeral a plain white card is attached with the name of the sender, "Helen Murray" or "Mr. and Mrs. Frederick Wallace," or a visiting card (a husband-and-wife card) may be used with a line drawn through the names in the case of intimate friends and the message, "Deepest sympathy from Jean and Hugh," written in ink. The envelope is simply addressed to:

> The funeral of Mr. Lawrence Karl Volkman
> Silvan Funeral Home
> 13 Morton Street
> Greenpoint, New York zip code

Where the funeral is to take place in church but the body is at a funeral home, friends may choose to send flowers immediately on hearing of the death, and to the funeral home, if calls are being received there, or to the church in time for the funeral. In the latter case the flowers are addressed to:

> The funeral of Mr. Lawrence Karl Volkman
> Emmanuel Church
> 5 Hawthorne Avenue
> Rye, New York zip code
> Funeral 2 P.M., Tuesday

Cards sent with funeral offerings should include the name and address of the sender on the back of the card if a plain florist's card is used. This is of assistance in the family's acknowledgments.

Flowers after the Funeral　It is a growing custom for close friends to send flowers to the family of the deceased sometime during the weeks following the funeral (except to Orthodox Jews). They should be addressed to the woman who is head of the household and the accompanying card should avoid reference to the bereavement. Instead it may read: "Kindest thoughts from us all, Peggy and John Wilder." The surname is used only if necessary for identification if all are on a first name basis.

Mass Cards

Many Catholics prefer mass cards to flowers. When a Catholic dies his friends and relatives, Catholic and non-Catholic, go to a priest and arrange for mass to be said for the soul. The priest accepts an offering for the mass and presents the card, which he has filled in, to the donor stating that a mass is to be said for the repose of the soul of the deceased, its method of celebration—High or Low—and sometimes indicating the exact time of the mass. The card is given or sent by the donor to the family of the deceased, usually before the funeral. A tray is usually provided at the funeral home for callers who have brought mass cards. These masses may be arranged, too, for a year after the death on its anniversary or at any time immediately after the death has taken place.

Mass cards are available in a number of forms. The one in my files reads, on the front cover, "In Memoriam," and inside, left:

> Sacred Heart Church
> Georgetown, Conn.
> With the Sympathy of

On the facing page, it reads:

The Holy Sacrifice of the Mass
will be offered

_____

for the repose of the Soul of

_____

The Rev. _____

Funeral Calls

Now that the mortuary chapel has so much replaced the home in the laying out of the dead, people are often confused as to where they are expected to make their funeral calls. If they are close friends or relatives they may call both at home and at the chapel if they wish, signing the register at the funeral chapel. The register is signed in formal fashion—Mr. and Mrs. John Brown—not Betty and John Brown and the husband or wife signs for both. They don't each sign separately unless they visit the funeral parlor separately. The reason the signing is done in this way is that after the signatures have been seen by the family, some of these calls may be acknowledged by brief note by someone representing the family, not necessarily anyone knowing that Betty Jones is properly Mrs. John Jones. The names should be signed very legibly, for some of the scrawls that confront families are impossible to decipher and many frustrations and hurt feelings can result because of this thoughtlessness.

Although funeral calls need not be acknowledged and customarily are not, sometimes the family wishes, in special cases, to make acknowledgment of such a call, especially if some have called when no immediate member of the family could be present to receive condolences. Some family representative should be present during the afternoon and early evening when calls are likely to be made.

The Funeral Service

It is a matter of family choice whether a casket is left open or closed before the funeral. At State funerals the open casket is optional, but it is always closed during Service for Episcopalians and Jews. At Catholic services, which must take place in church, the casket is open only for the clergy and occasionally for a high-ranking layman.

Pallbearers Among Christians pallbearers are always men, and today, merely honorary in that they seldom actually carry the casket and serve only at large funerals of distinguished *men*. There are never less than four and rarely more than ten chosen for this honor from among those personally and professionally close to the deceased. Jews have honorary pallbearers for both men and women.

The pallbearers are usually chosen by the person in charge of funeral arrangements, after he has received suggestions from various members of the family. Pallbearers do not volunteer their services. They wait to be asked. When a funeral takes place at a funeral home there is generally no charge for the professional pallbearers. When they go to a church, however, the hourly charge is incurred. This may be one reason a family asks good friends to serve. These men should be young and strong, able to shoulder the often heavy casket. At many large and important funerals, professional pallbearers do the actual work. Honorary pallbearers, all men, may number as many as twenty. The family itself should be represented among the pallbearers, and the other men chosen must accept the honor unless there is some very valid reason for refusing, such as illness.

Sometimes the casket is already in place before the altar and the floral offerings are arranged on and around it by the time the congregation gathers. In this case, just before the start of the service, the family may file in from the vestry and into the front pew, usually to the right of the center aisle, or, more usually, may enter from the front of the church just before the start of the service. The honorary pallbearers sit in the front pews to the family's left. At the end of the service after the family has retired to the vestry, the pallbearers, walking two by two, are first to leave the church, marching slowly in front of the casket if it is to be carried from the church at that time, or marching out slowly alone and into the waiting cars that carry them with the family to the cemetery.

If the casket is carried into the church the pallbearers precede it, marching slowly, two by two, and stepping into the left-hand first pews as they reach the front of the church.

Pallbearers who have come from out of town and who may not be able to make their funeral calls upon the family before leaving often call briefly at the vestry, before or after the service, to pay their respects.

Ushers and Seating Arrangements   While the mortician has men in attendance at every funeral who may act as ushers, and the sexton in a large church has a staff for the purpose, it is preferable that men relatives likely to know many of those attending the funeral act in this capacity. In church, like wedding ushers, they escort those attending the service to their seats but do not offer their arms, except to the old or infirm. A woman being escorted to her seat either by the usher or her husband walks on his right. Ushers do their best to place relatives and close friends toward the front of the church, keeping the front left-hand pews free for the honorary pallbearers or, if there are no pallbearers, for themselves. When there are no honorary pallbearers the ushers selected by the family precede the casket in the same manner as the pallbearers, or march up the aisle, two by two, just before the service is to start. They march down the aisle at the end of the service ahead of the casket, if it is carried out, before the rest of the congregation leaves the pews.

At Roman Catholic funerals the family does not enter from the vestry but follows up the aisle in the order of relationship to the dead when the casket is carried into the church, preceded by altar boys, priest, casket, and pallbearers. After the service they file out the same way behind the casket. On occasion this procedure is followed in Protestant churches.

Funerals are not encouraged in Orthodox synagogues. They take place only when a rabbi or some other dignitary dies. Therefore, Orthodox Jewish funerals are usually held in mortuary chapels or at home, with the men and women assembling side by side, the men with covered heads, the married women with some headcovering.

Memorial Services

Sometimes for a variety of reasons, either the expressed wish of the deceased, or the difficulty of making public funeral arrangements, a memorial service takes place after the funeral, usually within a few days or weeks, but sometimes as late as a year after. In one case of which I know, a woman who had a home with her husband in Paris died there, but expressed in her will the desire to have her cremated remains buried in the spring of the year at her summer home in the United States. At that time a memorial service was held in the small church in the community and a few close friends were invited, by brief note or telephone, by her husband to attend. Such services usually take place in church, but might be held elsewhere, for example at home in a garden or at a club or organization with which the deceased was identified. A few flowers are provided by the family or close friends for an altar or an arrangement. Usually the service consists of a period of meditation. In large churches the mourners meet in a small chapel. There is often carefully selected classic background music—Bach is a favorite. Sometimes there is a choir or a solo rendering of the deceased's favorite hymns or other music.

There is usually a brief eulogy either by a clergyman or by a friend. The mourners are then received briefly by the family, say a few words of consolation, and depart.

Those attending memorial services usually wear ordinary street clothes, the women with or without hats according to local custom.

Cremation

Cremation may be preceded by regular funeral services in the same manner as is burial. Usually just a few close relatives and friends go to the crematorium, where a further brief service is conducted. Subsequently the family is notified concerning the availability of the cremated remains. Their care or disposal is regulated by various state laws. Sometimes, according to individual circumstances, they are interred in the family plot, placed in an individual niche in a public columbarium, or dispersed following a specific request in the will of the deceased.

Interment and Grave Marking

The minister, rabbi, or priest goes along with the family and pallbearers, if any, to conduct the brief graveside service.

A grave is marked with the name of the deceased and the date of his birth and death and, frequently, his family relationship, "beloved father of," "beloved son of." In the case of a woman the inscription would read Sarah Morris (or Anne) Harrison (no "Mrs.") beloved wife of Francis Lee Harrison, 1920–1970. Women who have been married more than once are buried with, or in the plot provided by, the most recent husband. Single women's names are engraved in full—Sarah Anne Harrison (no "Miss"). Sometimes a line or two of epitaph is added. The footstone or monument bearing this information is ordered by the family from a monument maker shortly after the funeral at minimum cost, but, of course, elaborate monuments with sculptures can run into thousands of dollars. The monument maker installs the monument or marker at no additional fee. If no monument or footstone is to be erected, the funeral director, if instructed, can place on the grave at time of interment a simple bronze plaque costing considerably less than a footstone and bearing the essential data. Some cemeteries require these for all new graves.

Most cemeteries provide perpetual care of graves as part of the purchase price, but families usually visit and tend their plots from time to time, especially among Christians on Memorial Day, Easter, and Christmas, and arrange for special care of plantings. Any fresh green plant however simple or even a single flower is preferable to plastic or other imitation flowers or plants.

Fees to the Clergyman, Sexton, Organist, Vocalist

It is usual for the minister to be given a fee for his services. Sometimes an appropriate amount is sent to him by the funeral director, who includes this expense on his bill. More often it is sent by a member of the family in a letter of appreciation for his comfort and help.

The amount should be based on the family's ability to make a contribution. Simplicity of the funeral is today no indication of lack of funds. And certainly if the funeral has been large and expensive the officiating clergyman should not receive less than seventy-five to one hundred dollars. For the average funeral he usually receives from ten to twenty-five dollars. When checks are sent they are made out to the clergyman rather than to the church, as these fees are expected to contribute to his own expenses. In the Catholic Church fees are set by the Church according to the type of Mass. The family is informed during the arrangements of the amount it is to pay.

The sexton in a large church is on the church payroll and devotes full time to church business affairs. He may receive up to twenty-five dollars for opening a big church and overseeing the work of his assistants at a large funeral. In a small church this office, if it exists, is voluntary, but the sexton usually is sent a fee, approximately fifteen dollars, which, if his own circumstances permit, he may contribute to the church. The organist and vocalist, if one is used, receive a similar amount.

Acknowledgments for Flowers

If the funeral takes place at home, some member of the family makes a careful note of the flower offerings as they arrive, removing the cards and recording, either on the back of each or in a notebook, a description of the flowers, "yellow roses" rather than "roses" or "dark red carnations" rather than "sheaf." The flowers of those nearest and dearest should be placed close to and on the casket, even when those from civic organizations or others are more impressive.

When the funeral takes place at a funeral home the funeral director's staff collects the cards and makes the necessary notations for the family. At a church funeral some member of the family arrives in time to place the flowers and remove the cards when the coffin is to be in place before the start of the service.

Flowers, donations to a charity in memoriam, and mass cards should be acknowledged within a reasonable length of time. Morticians usually supply, as part of their service, engraved acknowledgment cards, foldover or flat, to be sent out by the family. If a friend or relative helps in writing a line or two on the acknowledgment cards, and this is quite permissible, she should thank whomever she is writing to in behalf of the bereaved and sign her own name. While a handwritten note is preferable, it is understandable that when hundreds—and in the case of large public funerals—thousands —must be sent, these acknowledgment cards may be used.

When there are no relatives of the deceased, the executors of the will often handle the funeral arrangements. The acknowledgment cards they send are usually indefinite and might read:

Your message of sympathy on the death of Mr. (full name) is greatly appreciated.

or

Your most kind expression of sympathy is deeply appreciated.

or

Your kind expression of sympathy is gratefully acknowledged and deeply appreciated.

The note acknowledging flowers, mass card, charity contributions, or a telegram need not be more than a few words, such as:

Dear Mr. Scott,
     You were kind indeed to think of us at such a difficult time. Your violets were beautiful and comforting.

                                        Sincerely,
                                        Helen Volkman

Acknowledgments to Clergy, Pallbearers, Ushers

Shortly after the funeral a member of the family or a representative of the family should write a personal note to the officiating clergyman, thanking him for his spiritual solace and help. This should be sent separately from the fee for his services, which is usually best handled by the funeral director if the clergyman accepts a fee for this service. If an offering is being sent to the church or memorial fund, it should be sent separately from this note to the clergyman. Honorary pallbearers also receive prompt notes of appreciation of their services, which may be written inside engraved acknowledgment folders if these are used—a virtual necessity today when literally hundreds of letters and telegrams of condolence may be received. The same folders may be used in the writing of the necessary notes of thanks to close friends and neighbors who offered their assistance before and during the funeral.

Letters of Condolence and Replies

Social letters of condolence, always handwritten, need not be long. In fact, "Deepest sympathy" may be written in blue or black ink on your visiting card. This is most acceptable when you do not know the people very well. Whatever condolence is sent must be sent very promptly. Telegrams are often sent and follow the usual telegraphic form:

DEEPLY SHOCKED AT YOUR SAD LOSS. ALL OUR SYMPATHY. LOVE.
>   HELEN AND TOM BURNS

(Surname may be used for identification if you are on a first name basis.)

You address your letter to the widow of the deceased, or the most bereaved, otherwise to the parents or a sister or brother of the person who has died—always addressing the nearest relative, whether or not you are acquainted. This may sometimes be a couple, but your decision on whom to address or whether to address them jointly depends mainly on what seems to be appropriate under the particular circumstances.

In expressing sympathy to a family on the loss of someone you have not known well, it is sufficient to send your visiting card with the phrase "With deepest sympathy" written at the top. The card is mailed to the most bereaved (to the wife, for example, in the case of a deceased husband, to the parents on the loss of a child) but the phrase "and family" never properly appears on the envelope. If you wish your condolences to go to the whole family, you use instead a phrase such as "Our deepest sympathy to you all."

To do nothing when a friend dies is heartless. If news of the death comes to you tardily, it is never too late to extend your sympathy by a personal call, by sending flowers to the bereaved after the funeral, by writing a warm and helpful note.

To the mother of a friend you might write:

Dear Mrs. Volkman,

It is several years since I have seen Larry, but it was with a real sense of loss that I heard the news. We were very close at college, as he may have told you, and have always kept in touch with one another even though we lived at such a distance.

I hope when I am in New York again that I may call upon you and, if possible, be of some service.

Most sincerely,
Gregory Burns

It is better to avoid the words "died," "death," and "killed" in such letters.

It is quite possible to write the kind of letter that will give a moment of courage and a strong feeling of sympathy without mentioning death or sadness at all. For instance:

Dear Jeanette,

For me Gale will remain the happy, dancing child I saw for the first time on her fifth birthday. She will always be with us in spirit.

Lovingly,
Mary

If you are writing a letter of condolence from a business office to someone related to a person you have known mainly in business the letter may be dictated and typed.

In replies to letters of condolence one may write at any length one wishes, but it is quite understandable that the note be brief, even to a close friend. Today it is usually on plain white rather than on the rarely seen black-bordered paper. Mourning paper is unusual now in the United States and quite unnecessary. Informals are frequently used.

Printed Sympathy Cards

Printed cards of sympathy, available everywhere, should really not be sent to bereaved persons. Instead, depending upon the situation, one sends flowers and frequently a brief note as well on white paper in blue or black ink. Even the sending of flowers alone is not enough in the case of the loss of a close friend or relative. Funeral calls and notes, or both, are still needed.

Contributions to Charity

Sometimes in the funeral notice it is requested that flowers be omitted and that friends send contributions to some specified charity instead. Checks should be made out to the charity mentioned and sent with a notation that the amount be contributed in memory of the deceased. The charity then sends the donor an acknowledgment (which may be used for tax purposes) and notifies the family of the deceased of the contribution, usually not mentioning the amounts. It is then proper for some spokesman for the family to write a brief note thanking the donor for his memorial gift. If someone who has not seen the notice interdicting flowers inadvertently sends them, he should let the family know that the slighting of their wishes in the matter was not intentional.

Food after the Funeral

In rural communities in particular, it is a kindly custom for neighbors to prepare food for the family of the bereaved for service after the funeral to the family, close relatives, and friends who may be detained. In large cosmopolitan communities where there are many restaurants and catering services, there is no such need. However, as one clergyman wrote me, "At a time when so much is professionally done and when we speak of the 'high cost of dying' any touch of neighborliness of this type is much appreciated. With many families today, unprepared to accommodate even small groups, it makes unnecessary going to a public restaurant for meals."

Among the Jews, the custom of friends and neighbors supplying food is much more common. A rabbi friend has supplied me with the following information: "Among Orthodox and Conservative Jews it is customary for the immediate family to return to the home of the mourners immediately following the interment of the deceased. Friends in the community come to the home of the mourners at eventide and for seven days thereafter for the purpose of participating in a worship service. As you probably know this is called 'Shivah,' when the mourners of the Orthodox persuasion do not leave their homes for any business or social contacts for seven days following the death of a loved one. It is customary for neighbors either to bring food or to help prepare the meals. The degree to which this is done varies with the national origin of the person.

"Reform Jews return to the home of the mourners immediately following burial for a brief worship service. This religious service in the home is optional, and is conducted by the Rabbi or a layman at the suggestion of some member of the family. Reform Jews refrain from business and social contacts for a maximum of three days following the demise of a loved one. I have found that Reform Jews follow the usual American custom of receiving fruit baskets or flowers. However, if the family is too broken up, considerate neighbors will bring in food or prepare it."

Mourning Dress

Visible signs of mourning—the widow's bonnet, the black clothes even for little children—are, happily, almost never seen these days. We all mourn the deaths of those we love, but the healthful thing is to accept the loss as well as we can and gradually make our adjustment to the life we must live without this beloved person.

Black has lost much of its meaning as the badge of bereavement ever since, in World War I, Chanel decreed that all fashionable women should mourn with her for her own war-loss when she launched the "little black dress," which has since become an essential of the wardrobe. Prior to that women seldom, if ever, wore black except for mourning.

Black dresses from the regular wardrobe and in a dull material are often (but not necessarily now) worn by women members of the family at a funeral. Children wear Sunday-school clothes in quiet colors or white. Someone usually divests dresses to be worn at funerals of any bright-colored ornaments, but they may be trimmed with white. Pearls may be worn and any functional pin of silver or, possibly, dull gold or an heirloom piece of jet. Simple pearl button earrings are acceptable, but any costume jewelry, diamond rings, or bracelets should be dispensed with, at least for the period before and during the funeral, in deference to conservative feelings in these matters.

The black chiffon veil is often worn by the bereaved women at a funeral, for protection. These are difficult to find today so often are borrowed. They may certainly be dispensed with and so may hats. Stockings worn with black dresses at funerals need not be black. Ordinary street clothes such as one would wear to church are acceptable, too, for family members as well as for others attending a funeral. Mourning is never worn, even for the funeral, by Christian Scientists.

Men of the family wear cutaways for a large church funeral or dark business suits in navy or Oxford, with black shoes and socks, black or gray ties and white shirts. Boys wear dark blue or gray suits, white shirts, dark blue or gray four-in-hand or black knit ties. At small, simple funerals any conservative street clothes are worn with subdued ties.

The Traditional Idea of Mourning   Essentially, the wearing of mourning (not necessarily black—it is white in the tropics) was to give protection to the family as well as to honor the dead. In great families even the retainers were often put in some degree of mourning, and social activities even for tiny children were rigidly circumscribed for as much as two years. It was frequent for the older women in the family, especially elderly widows, to remain in mourning, more or less, for the rest of their lives, a custom that is still common in some Latin countries.

We have discarded the harsh idea that a strong will to live happily in spite of personal loss is sinful and disrespectful to the dead. We have developed a more positive social attitude toward others, who might find it difficult to function well in the constant company of an outwardly mourning person. In time of war it is often advised by governments that the putting on of mourning by war-bereaved families is an aid and comfort to the enemy and a decided detriment to home morale. Another reason, I believe, for the little use of mourning today is the rapid spread of news. When death does occur everyone concerned is quickly informed by telephone, telegraph, and the daily papers. There is little possibility that the bereaved family will not receive tactful consideration on all sides, and it need not publicly proclaim its loss by the wearing of black, the use of black-bordered note paper, the strict withdrawal from any merely social activity. Today when a girl returns to her office desk the day after her mother's funeral wearing her usual work-a-day clothes and a man goes forth after the death of his son without an armband to proclaim his grief, their co-workers know and understand. And no one considers that they mourn any the less.

A widow continues to wear her wedding ring if she wishes to, and most do, especially if she has been happily married and whether or not she has children.

The widow refers to her deceased husband as, "my late husband."

Restriction of Activities

Those who have just lost someone close to them naturally feel disinclined toward public festivity. Scheduled events, such as weddings, are, however, permitted to take place (see pages 32, 51). Most of us pursue, or try to pursue, our usual social course within a week or so after a funeral in our immediate family, with our own feelings and convictions governing our behavior rather than "what people might think."

Today we go to small dinner parties, to concerts and the opera, to the theater and the movies. We play games, including cards, listen to the radio, watch television, and read novels, all as an aid to regaining our ability to function normally. We try to remember that our own state of mind affects those around us and aids or interferes with their ability to face life's daily problems.

The activities of young children should never be restricted after a death has occurred in a family. Children have, if anything, even more need to run and jump and play when their parents are weighted with sorrow and strange things are happening in the house. The fact of death must be faced by everyone, and children, unless they are very tiny indeed, cannot be shielded from it. They can understand the tears and the immediate grief, but continuing sorrow is not the pattern of the normal child. Let him run off his tension in uninhibited play and noise—away from the mourning house if there are those who cannot understand a child's needs.

Resumption of a Social Life

The lonely widow or widower wishing to face realistically the problem of deep personal loss today is, after about three months of widowhood, ready for open dating with members of the opposite sex and may well have been seeing women or men friends quietly as soon as the need for human companionship evidenced itself. Modern men and women approve such emotionally healthful reaching out for reassurance. In a small, conservative community such dating is possibly limited at first to evenings at home, movies, the theater, musical events, walks and drives, small parties with other couples. Often, today, remarriage during widowhood takes place in much less than the formerly prescribed year. In cities where life is more impersonal there is less likelihood of criticism than in small towns. But here again mature people can best decide what is best for them in their particular circumstance. In general neighbors are happy to see widowhood end, so long as remarriage does not seem ill-considered and hasty.

Christmas and Greeting Cards after Bereavement

People who have had a death in the family are frequently concerned as to whether or not Christmas cards should be sent within the year. Their friends are equally concerned as to whether or not mourners should receive Christmas or other greeting cards. The sending of Christmas cards to people in mourning, if the bereavement has not been too recent (a matter of days or weeks, for example), is today quite usual, but the cards that are sent are restrained, often religious. Behind this thinking is the very human need for these sorrowing people to communicate with their friends, to wish them joy even at a time when their own is muted. The great holiday seasons are very important emotionally to us all. When we are sorrowing, we make the sorrow unbearably bitter if we shut our hearts to happiness around us. Contributing in whatever way we can to that happiness leads us toward sound emotional health if this means merely wishing happiness to other people. By the same token, people in mourning should not be ignored at the holiday times of the year. The cards and wishes they will receive should be restrained and tasteful. If the bereavement is immediately before such a holiday as Christmas, the family refrains from sending cards (cards of course may be already in the mails) but friends try to do what they can to make the holiday at least tolerable. Gift giving, especially where children are concerned, takes place as scheduled. Such gifts are expressions of love and affection, particularly needed at such a time.

Part Two

DRESS AND MANNERS

Part Four

DRESS AND MANNERS

DRESS AND MANNERS

Good manners and appropriate dress are, or should be, part and parcel of gentle people. Notice the word "appropriate." Clothing need not be expensive or of the finest needlework or tailoring, but it must suit the occasion on which it is worn. We are not born with the knowledge that curlers are poor taste in public, that boisterousness is out of place in church. Precept and example show us how ladies and gentlemen should look and act. And feel. Outward conformity to a code is never enough.

The finest rules for behavior are to be found in Chapter 13 of First Corinthians, the beautiful dissertation on charity by St. Paul. These rules have nothing to do with the fine points of dress nor with those of superficial manners. They have to do with feelings and attitudes, kindliness, and consideration of others. Good manners have much to do with the emotions. To make them ring true, one must feel them, not merely exhibit them.

Chapter 18

MEN'S CLOTHES

A man these days is certainly more comfortable, and his clothing, even for the relatively conservative, more colorful and varied. He goes to business, in a collar-attached, often colored or striped, shirt, in a suit which may differ greatly from the Oxford, navy, or black one his father considered a gentleman's business uniform. His hat, if any, may be a soft, snap brim or a rolling Homburg, and is unlikely to be the derby, a headgear not universally becoming. He is no longer a dun-colored bird. Even if he is cautious about the use of color in town (if he's not completely sure of his taste), he can indulge his long inhibited love of it in undergarments whose patterns and colors often rival Tahiti's sarongs. His slacks and jump suits at home, his bathing outfit, his pajamas, his clothes for active sports, his country wardrobe may all proclaim a peacock—if he can get away with it gracefully. But he'd better be able to live up to it.

It takes a good figure, perfect carriage, and tolerable looks as well as an inborn style for a man to wear some of the modern clothes well. If he hasn't these attributes he's better off minimizing his defects by sticking at all times to conservative habiliments designed to call no special attention to themselves or him.

Suits

A man's profession, the kind of work he does, must necessarily influence his choice of dress. If he's a gentleman farmer, an artist, or a writer and rarely goes into the larger cities near his home, he may get along nicely with one sack suit, filling out his wardrobe with slacks and sports coats to please his fancy and satisfy his needs. Such a man may even look quite appropriately dressed if he comes to town attired in his customary clothes—a sports jacket and slacks or peaty tweeds—if he keeps to such masculine haunts as his club, men's bars, offices, or the homes of his understanding friends. He is dressed *informally,* albeit quite possibly more expensively than some on whom he might call. So attired he does not belong in pretentious restaurants, at receptions, dinner parties, funerals, weddings, or directors' meetings.

A man whose professional or business life takes him on frequent trips to parts of the country where life is less formal than it is in New York, and where his activities may take him more out of offices than in them, is justified, too, in wearing slacks and a sports jacket or tweeds to town if his travels will carry him more or less immediately out again. Slacks and sports jackets and, of course, tweeds are more and more worn for travel, as rumpled they look less unattractive than does a sack suit. A commuter, who comes in for a short day—a half holiday, say—and who has no plans for any appearances in town that require a more formal outfit, can conceivably choose to wear slacks to his office. But the wearing of this costume indicates the country gentleman who invades the city, if only for a short time. For a city dweller to choose it for office wear when he is not planning to leave the city that day seems posey. For other than executives to select such a costume for office work in a cosmopolitan community might seem pretentious to an employer. Although there has been great relaxation of this rule for younger men especially in banks, shops, lower-echelon jobs in publishing and advertising, in top, conservative organizations and many professional offices the rule continues.

The Business Suit

The suits a man wears to work should avoid being too distinctive in pattern, fabric, cut, or color unless he has a tremendous wardrobe from which to draw. I remember one young executive with whom I shall always associate a sharkskin suit, although he may have had several others with which to spell it. But he had to wear it much too often. As sharkskin can't be cut on the easy lines of tweed or Cheviot, my mind always sees him poured into that piscine garment.

It is safer to be dressed for any business occasion that might occur than to go to the office in clothes that might be out of place if an important client should turn up or a vital meeting be called. The beloved rainy-day suit looks shabby when the sun comes out at noon, the old tweed jacket throws a man off stride if he's suddenly precipitated into a group of men wearing well-tailored suits.

In winter, worsteds, flannel, the softer tweeds, Saxony, and Cheviots are office wear. In spring and summer, gabardines and the various lightweight miracle fabrics are correct, with more latitude in the matter of mixed outfits. The man who must work in town in the summer is permitted clothing comfort—within reason. In these days of air conditioning he is often expected to keep his coat on at his desk, however, especially if he's an executive.

His suit colors may be gray, black, any of the toast browns, grayed greens, blue. The strong reddish-browns (except in Harris tweeds), the yellow-greens, and the strong green-blues had better be bypassed except in an extensive wardrobe. A man's suit should be of good enough quality to last four or five years, if he alternates it with at least three others of the same quality. If any one suit is too assertive it automatically telescopes his wardrobe. The same is true of a too vibrant plaid, a too broadly striped one, a very pale color, or a check that doesn't fade into gray at a short distance, or too shaggy a tweed.

The single-breasted suit, most popular now, does not require a vest but one may of course be worn. Even for the most conservative business occasions, the vest, if worn, need not match the suit in fabric or color. The black-and-white, black, blue, and white, or black, white, and yellow-checked Tattersall waistcoat on light ground flannel is correct even with plaid or pin striped suits, as is the natural-color chamois waistcoat (weskit). It takes a man knowledgeable and easy with his clothes to wear them well, however. False moves with a tie, a shirt, or socks can make the wearer of a contrasting waistcoat look like a drummer. Fancy waistcoats call for careful selection of shirts, paisley, foulard, or solid color ties. They may be the sole accent note of the costume or with careful co-ordination only one of them. The unsure or the very conservative man lets them be the sole accent color. The bottom button of the vest is nearly always left unbuttoned.

The double-breasted suit, according to authorities on men's wear, will never go out of style. Periodically it makes an attempt, as it is now, at a fashion comeback and some very well-dressed men have never abandoned it. The modern double-breasted suit has soft construction. It needs to be very carefully tailored to measure. It can be most unbecoming to the man of less than average height or to one who, though tall enough, has too generous a girth or too short a waist. It must be kept buttoned when a man is on his feet. It is worn without a vest.

If it is worn by a short man with a short or large waist the broadening effect of the suit's cut foreshortens the wearer. But a man with less than an Adonis figure can wear the double-breasted suit if the buttons are not so far apart as to carry the eye to the outside outlines of the figure, and if the broadened shoulder line is on the conservative side and begins high enough to give an illusion of waist. Slanting the top buttons outward helps the effect. Lengthening the coat doesn't usually simulate height. On the contrary, it shortens the legs. The length of the coat is determined by the shape of the man. A suit coat should always be long enough to cover the seat of the trousers, but on a short man it should not ordinarily be longer than that, no matter what the current fashion. A man who is tall and very thin looks better dressed in a coat of medium length. A too short one puts him on stilts, and one too long accentuates his thinness. Whatever the length decided upon it should hang evenly all the way around, never hike up in the back. Even a readymade jacket should conform to the figure so as to avoid this unattractive sight.

A man's jacket must fit close around the neck so that anywhere from one half to approximately one inch of shirt collar shows in back, depending on the style of shirt. A man should know that sleeve lengths can be very deceptive, that it is the yoke of the shirt that seems to determine the actual sleeve length. In trying a new brand of shirts, not made to order, it is wise to try on the shirt, not go solely by the length of sleeve given. Even then some imported shirts in particular may shrink somewhat so that the sleeve length after the shirt is washed is even with the sleeve of the jacket instead of a good half-inch below. Too much cuff showing is better than too little. On the other hand, the shirt sleeve should not show above the cuff itself. The collar points when not buttoned down must appear perfectly even from a front view, never ride askew.

All trousers hang better when suspenders are worn and when a minimum is carried in the pockets but most ready-made business suits have no provision for suspenders these days. Formal trousers must be worn with suspenders as there is no provision for a belt. The carefully groomed man limits his trouser pocket contents to his small change and his keys. The keys should be in a flat key case. A used handkerchief, folded as flat as possible, can be returned to his hip pocket, but his wallet there may make an unsightly rear bulge (and may be an invitation to pickpockets who are not deterred by a button). A distinguished man I know, noted for his excellent taste in clothes, once told me that he carried an absolute minimum in his suit pockets so his clothes would fit as they were tailored to fit. He pointed out that a man who must take along with him the familiar assortment of papers, checkbooks, pens, pencils, photographs, credentials, and the wealth of small-boy items he manages to collect would make a better appearance if he carried most of them in a brief case rather than on his person.

The trousers of the sack suit may have cuffs or be pressed straight down, depending on preference. If they are tailor-made and cuffless, the bottoms should be finished so they can be turned up in stormy weather. Length of trousers is again a matter of individual taste, but, fashionably, those with permanent cuffs should hang straight and not break over the instep. Plain uncuffed trousers should be slanted in back so that they are approximately one and a quarter inches longer there than the front. The trousers width should be medium, avoiding the sloppiness of the English "bags" and the excessive narrowness of the Continental trouser leg. A good tailor will proportion them to the size of the shoes a man is wearing as well as to the size of his thighs so they will have the right "look." The short man improves his appearance by wearing his trousers cut fairly high, comfortably above the hipbones.

Refinements of Tailoring The notch on the collar of a business suit should be almost a right angle and the lapel in recent years has tended to be cut a little broader—about ⅛ to ¼ inch wider—than the collar, especially on a single-breasted coat. On double-breasted suits the lapels are definitely wider than the collar and are frequently slightly peaked instead of right-angled but should always avoid the pixylike exaggerated peak.

Side pockets, except occasional patch pockets, should have flaps (which for good grooming should aways be worn out). Trouser pleats if worn may be long on the tall, slim man, but on the average or short man unpressed pleats not too generous, extending a few inches below the waistline, are more becoming. The buttonhole on the left lapel should be usable. In custom-made suits it is sensible to have the sleeve buttons completely functional, so the cuffs may be turned back if desired. British tailoring features this, together with colorful suit linings meant to be seen occasionally.

Business Suits *Left:* Good shoulder line merely improves slightly on natural contours except to correct defects—such as one shoulder lower than other. *Right:* Exaggerated waistline, sleeves too long, wide lapels. Not recommended. This is often teamed with impossibly athletic shoulders and an over-long coat. Theatrical.

The Morning Coat or Cutaway and Accessories

This is an expensive accouterment for a man who does not lead a fairly active social life, but it is often a necessary one. It is the proper costume for a really formal daytime wedding, when the bride wears a veil and has bridesmaids. It is the usual costume of the church usher. In fact it may be worn at any daytime function, until six o'clock, that makes a special attempt at being impressive or festive—a wedding, a public funeral, a debutante tea, a formal call at the White House or at a governor's mansion, a concert, a formal christening, a city church service especially at Easter or Christmas, any daytime ceremony.

Many a man who owns a morning coat rarely thinks to wear it, yet its acquisition need not be the extravagance it seems. Once acquired, formal daytime dress should be worn frequently, so a man feels at ease in it. His coat need not be the cutaway but, more modernly, may be the short, single-breasted black or Oxford stroller, unless the suit must be bought especially for a formal wedding or other use where the wearer is expected to be attired the same as other members of the group who already possess cutaways. But where all the ushers, say, are buying (rather than renting) new morning coats for a wedding, it might be better to suggest the short and, I think, more wearable jacket to be worn with the usually, but not necessarily, striped trousers.

In winter the waistcoat, which may be single-breasted or double-breasted, may be pearl gray or light or darker tan, or may match the black or Oxford gray of the coat.

Shirts worn with the morning coat should be with single or French "double" cuffs, white with pleated or plain bosom. The collar is wing or turndown, again depending on whether one is dressing like others in a group or not.

The Ascot in a variety of materials from rep silk to broadly striped grosgrain, in grayed effects, checks, or plain black, white or lavenders (more mature), is the formal type of tie but the four-in-hand is often worn, and always worn in black for funerals. With the stroller, the four-in-hand suits its somewhat lesser formality. With the Ascot, a pearl pin or an antique or modern gold scarfpin set with moonstone, amethyst, or other light stones is worn but is nowadays usually dispensed with on the four-in-hand. Pearl studs are *de rigueur* for the shirt, and gold cuff links—which may even be large, striking antique, jeweled ones—fasten the cuffs.

The boutonniere may be any small, suitable flower—a dark red or white carnation, a cornflower, or bridal flowers at a wedding (orange blossoms, white violets, gardenias, lilies of the valley, etc., with the groom alone wearing a sprig from the bride's bouquet). At a funeral mourners do not wear boutonnieres. White ones may be worn by ushers and pallbearers.

The correct hat with the morning coat is the black silk hat, although in England the gray topper is frequently worn at Ascot and for coaching. In summer, ushers in morning coats usually go hatless. Black socks, plain or ribbed, preferably over the calf are worn with black calf, plain-tipped oxfords. Except at funerals, the black socks may be figured or clocked in white. Shoes are black calfskin.

Garters and suspenders are conservative gray or black-and-white, the handkerchief pure white, the scarf gray, white, or black, and the gloves light gray mocha, except at a funeral where dark gray suede gloves are substituted.

The Dinner Jacket and Accessories

A man, especially a young man, may be able to do without a morning coat, but he needs a dinner jacket (even if he never owns a tail coat) if he is going to have an active social life in sophisticated circles. Here is a suit that should do duty for five years if it is well chosen, of good quality, from a good men's shop, if ready-made, or carefully tailored by a recognized tailor in conservative, tropical-weight black. As for dark red or other colors in dinner jackets which may have seasonal popularity, it's better to shun them unless he has an extensive evening wardrobe. No girl wants her beau to turn up in a red jacket, no matter how excellent the cut and quality, every time she goes dancing or dining with him. Whereas his one black dinner jacket, the fully accepted evening uniform of the semifestive male, is never too remarkable.

Modern dinner jackets are usually single-breasted, and are worn with a single-breasted black or matching brocaded vest. The waistcoat may also be of marseilles (or marcella), or black silk, ribbed or figured. Small braid matching that on the trousers may trim the vest in a custom-made suit and possibly the breast pocket in an Edwardian style. It is fastened with self-covered or smoked pearl buttons, not links. The vest is always dispensed with with a cummerbund (silk, rib-hugging sash which hides the top of the trousers), but this somewhat dashing accessory is no asset to a gentleman of expanded girth. The cummerbund in now best worn in black or possibly (with the colored worn with matching ties) maroon, or midnight blue. The cummerbund is particularly attractive, and certainly more comfortable, in summer and may be topped by a summer dinner jacket (in the country and suburbs) in white, with or without lapels or shawl collar in the same fabric. The double-breasted dinner jacket, not often seen now, is worn without a vest.

A shawl collar, considered more casual, is preferred by many now. The facing of either the shawl collar or the notched collar may be satin, grosgrain, or of the same fabric if the jacket is white. Dinner jacket lapels may be more peaked than those of business suits but should avoid eccentricity.

The lines of a dinner jacket should be about the same as those of an easy, comfortable business suit. Avoid the too-fitted waist and the too-narrow Latin-style trousers as well as the absurdly built-out shoulders, although some padding is advisable for most men.

Trousers It is not entirely necessary to have a different pair of trousers (always uncuffed) to be worn with a tail coat, as there is only a shade of difference between the braid on the trousers worn with full dress and those meant for a dinner jacket. Specifications differ very slightly over a period of years, but, generally speaking, the braid for full dress is double or triple width while that on dinner jacket trousers is narrower and usually coarser.

Sometimes a very broad braid in satin finish is worn with dress trousers, and at times some men affect no braid at all on trousers with a dinner jacket (though there is some possibility they might be accused of aping their butlers, if any—who wear no braid).

For a man with heavy social duties two pairs of trousers to go with his dinner jacket and one pair of full dress trousers might be an economy. But the average man, unless he has pretensions to being a fashion plate, can get along with one pair of evening trousers, matching his dinner jacket and to be worn, as needed, with it or his full dress coat.

The Shirt A revolution has been taking place in the matter of the proper shirt to wear with a dinner jacket. Rarely, if ever, is the old, and to some torturous, "boiled shirt" and stiff collar seen these days. Even for quite formal occasions the best-dressed men wear white shirts, pleated, with a soft or lightly-starched front, and turned down collar attached and in summer, even button-down collar shirts with buttoned wristbands. Soft dinner shirts may even have the usual ocean pearl buttons but can be had to accommodate small real pearl, onyx, gold, or small smoked pearl studs (two or three of them). Cuff links may match the studs, or, if a man possesses them, he may wear handsome antique or modern jeweled ones.

The Tie The tie for a dinner jacket is always a bow in black dull silk, rep, grosgrain (seldom), or satin. Maroon rep is sometimes worn but, if so, looks better in summer with matching cummerbund and a dark red carnation. Occasionally one sees an evening tie with a small colored figure, a club tie. This is permissible for members of the club but not for others. Butterfly bows, sometimes in velvet or unusual fabrics, black or colored, a style imported from England, are seen on the less inhibited. Butterfly bows in standard fabrics are generally seen.

The Boutonniere As a dinner jacket is a semiformal outfit, there is leeway in the selection of boutonnieres, although the carnation in red or white is most popular. White flowers other than carnations usually seem bridal, but certainly a miniature dahlia in white or any other color would be quite suitable, as are cornflowers, pinks, strawflowers, holly, or snowberries (in the right season) or any little flower—even a tiny orchid or modest gardenia—that can go through an evening in such service without early collapse. The flower is worn without any backing of greens.

Any woman would prefer no boutonniere at all to one of the permanent-duty feather ones. (Of course, the wearing of a decoration, such as the Legion of Honor, precludes the wearing of a boutonniere.) How would any man like her to wear a corsage of imitation orchids? There is always the tender implication that the woman a man is escorting has placed the boutonniere in his lapel with her own hands—as she very often does.

Shoes and Socks Black patent leather oxfords or pumps are traditionally worn. Practically, however, many men are wearing soft black calf evening shoes or even, in the continental fashion, black suede. The Duke of Windsor pioneered the wearing of soft black slip-on shoes back in 1958. Socks should cover the calf. They either have an elasticized top or are worn with garters.

The Tail Coat and Accessories

This is the winter, formal evening outfit of the, usually urban, gentleman— "white tie," it's called on formal invitations. A man wears it to the opera— at least to the opening if he is in a choice seat or when he sits in a box with others similarly attired, for example, with members of The Opera Club at the Metropolitan—to an evening wedding (which rarely occurs in New York), to formal dinners where it is requested, although the modern hostess knows that many men do not possess this garment and will either stay away if it is required or ask if they may wear "black tie." It is worn at balls, evening debuts (but here, especially if the hostess hopes for a turnout of young, dancing men, a choice of "black or white tie" may be given on the invitation), and for any elaborate evening entertainment particularly a ball, although black tie will frequently turn up with white at such an occasion. The escorts of the debutantes and the debutantes' fathers wear tails, however. The host at a dinner party, at home or not, is never incorrect when so attired, when the hostess has given a choice to the men of black or white tie. It is possible that a man might be requested in some communities to wear a tail coat to a formal evening wedding in the summertime, but generally speaking it is winter wear. At a formal banquet where a degree of formal dress is "optional," that is white tie or tails, guests of honor, speakers, men on the dais properly choose tails.

Like the dinner jacket, the tail coat is black. The trousers worn with it may be the same as those for the dinner jacket, for economy's sake, or have the somewhat wider, finer braid usual for full dress. The lapels are satin or grosgrain, always conservatively peaked and never the shawl collar sometimes seen on dinner jackets. If he can possibly afford it, a man should have his tail coat made to order, unless he is of average proportions, because it is almost impossible to alter a ready-made tail coat so that it fits as if it were made for him. A man somewhat under average height may shun the tail coat, because he feels it makes him look shorter. Yet if the tails are proportioned to his height by an expert tailor the suit can seem to give him several inches in height. A ready-made tail coat— or a rented one—for such a man can make him look like a small boy masquerading in his father's clothes. But, tailored to fit, "white tie" can give any man a special dignity and distinction as do no other clothes.

The Waistcoat, Tie, and Shirt The full dress waistcoat is always white —piqué or marcella, with white or antique pearl buttons which may be inserted like studs for washability. It is made with or without a revers and with the bottom cut on the straight line preferably—although this is usually possible only on the custom-made suit with high-rise trousers—and is worn with a white piqué bow tie. The stiff or "boiled" shirt now has a wing collar attached and is worn with one or two studs (small white pearl, gold, platinum, or certain antique studs with light colored stones permissible).

Boutonniere, Gloves, and Muffler For full dress the boutonniere is, for conservatives, always white, usually a carnation, unless for a wedding, ball, or other very festive occasion when small gardenias are suitable. Dark red carnations are often favored, too. Prince Philip wore a pink one when he served at Princess Margaret's wedding, however. Very occasionally white boutonnieres (usually carnations) are worn at funerals by men acting as special ushers or honorary pallbearers to distinguish them from the other men present—the same reason ushers wear boutonnieres on Sundays. The boutonniere used to indicate a member of a dance committee or some such distinction. White kid gloves or bleached doeskin are now worn only when specified or when the tradition of certain balls, such as the assemblies, calls for them, although some super-fastidious men don them for dancing (rare now), to avoid having to place a moist hand on a woman's bare back. Gloves, if any, worn on the street are gray doeskin. The muffler worn with formal dress is white silk, woven or knit, initialed, possibly, in black or white—in fact, all formal evening accessories are unrelieved white or black or a combination of these as, for example, in garters and braces, which may be white or black with contrasting woven or embroidered design in black or white.

Shoes and Socks Shoes worn with the tail coat are more formally black patent leather oxfords or pumps. Socks are solid black silk or nylon, plain or ribbed. If they are not worn with garters they should be over-the-calf length.

Overcoats for Formal Wear

Practical for the average man is the black, Oxford gray, or dark blue chesterfield with a black velvet or self collar. The chesterfield is equally useful for day as for semiformal or even formal evening wear but many a man settles for his raincoat.

The black satin-lined evening cape, an elegant garment, is still seen on gentlemen who take their clothes very seriously and who like to keep alive the niceties of Victorian dress. It is usually tailored to measure but is sometimes featured by the best men's shops in lush seasons. Once you own it, you can presumably wear the same cape the rest of your life with complete confidence.

Formal Hats

There is nothing more elegant than an opera hat, the proper headgear for tails (silk hat for the cutaway), but this elegance is too seldom seen. Men tell me that at balls, where men's most formal wear—white tie—is more likely to be seen, there is frequently a checking problem insofar as tall hats are concerned. Also, very young men do not wish to make the investment in such a hat and in general prefer to go hatless. Other men sometimes substitute the black Homburg or a black soft-brimmed fedora to wear with white tie as well as with dinner jacket, if they wear any hat at all. With a dinner jacket in spring and summer, gray felt snap-brimmed hats of the dressy variety are also seen, and with dinner jackets very occasionally one sees a straw sailor with a black band.

When Not to Wear Evening Clothes

It is not correct—no matter what you occasionally see—for a man to wear dinner jacket or tail coat in the daytime.

The only other possible uses for evening wear in the daytime are an audience with the Pope and certain Continental State functions when full evening dress is worn, not a dinner jacket. Evening clothes should not be worn before six o'clock, unless, for example, a man is leaving the city for a suburban dinner or vice versa and can change only at home. But even this means he would be likely to emerge in his bedecked state between five and six. The ideal is not to appear in dinner or evening clothes in broad daylight, although in spring and summer this is usually quite unavoidable.

Dinner jackets are now permissible for guests in formal evening church weddings. The wedding party, however, wears full dress. Black or white jackets only, according to the seasons, are preferable. In New York, even in summer, tropical-weight black dinner jackets are preferable for all formal evening occasions, as they are in Europe.

Ties, Handkerchiefs, and Jewelry

Ties, Evening and Otherwise Not every man is dexterous nor can every man, attiring himself for a social evening, be valeted. Hence, into being came the pre-tied bow tie, for evening as well as for day wear. It seems to me a sad little invention, like the old-time celluloid shirt and the sleeve garter that, I gather, compensates for the ill-fitting shirt sleeve. However, I suppose the pre-tied tie is better than a self-tied one that is askew most of the evening. The new butterfly ties, however, do seem impossible for a man to tie himself and thus they come pre-tied. This would be appropriate for an Edwardian-style dinner jacket. Most men wear bow ties so seldom they have little chance to practice tying them, but a man with a nimble-fingered wife has no excuse for turning up with his bow tie in a dreary little lump or in the startling butterfly perfection of some of the pre-tied ties. If a pre-tied tie must be the choice, be careful to wear it with a turned down collar if it has an observable fastening in the back, otherwise the coat collar will eventually ride down enough during the evening to reveal this little sartorial deception.

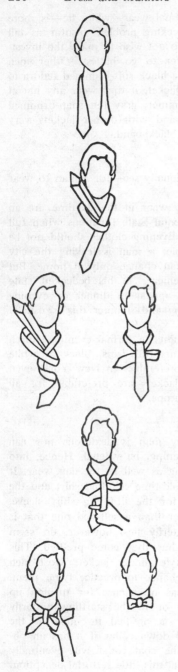

How To Tie a Tie

Place the tie well under the collar. Place the ends of the tie so that the wider end (the one in the left hand) extends 1½″ below the narrower end.

Cross the longer end over the shorter one and pass it through the loop.

Take the hanging shorter end, double it up to form the front loop of the bow, placing it across the collar points. Hold the front loop between thumb and forefinger of the left hand. Pass the long end down over the front.

Place the right forefinger, pointing up, at the base of the hanging part. Pass up behind the front loop.

Push the resulting loop through the knot behind the front loop. Even ends and tighten gently.

The daytime tie, usually a four-in-hand, is developing into an often gaudy creation which is giving the long color-repressed male a chance to exhibit his taste—or lack of it—in the choice of ties suitable for his wardrobe. While I deplore the "poached egg" and hand-painted, as well as the explosively geometric schools of tie design, I suppose it is the privilege of the male to wear them. It used to be that women who knew little about men's canons of taste were responsible for the gift purchase of such ties, but there is an alarming trend among men themselves to buy and wear such horrors.

If a tie has any design but a variation of the stripe, the paisley, the polka dot, or the small square, it had better be of exceptional quality and style, with cost no real indication of either. Any woman will tell you that it is much easier to combine one or more plain colors with not more than one figured one than to combine several figured ones, which takes some knowledge of color and design values. It is quite possible for a man to wear a colored, striped shirt, a Tattersall waistcoat, a Glen plaid suit, and a bright, figured tie and a fancy handkerchief, but he needs either innate or acquired taste to do so. A man who is not sure of his color sense is safer wearing plain colored or white shirts with a suit that is either striped or plaid, plain ties and shirts with "horse-blanket" sports jackets or patterned suits, a single bright accent rather than several. This is, admittedly, the ultra-conservative point of view. There are men who can wear bright green suits with pink shirts and sunburst ties and still look all right, I guess—but not to me.

Ascots are suitable for daytime wear—with sports clothes. These are of two varieties. One is made from a silk handkerchief folded in a triangle, tied around the neck, and tucked into the shirt front. The other type of ascot is a long narrow silk scarf made especially to be tied in a looped-over fashion and tucked into the shirt. Ascots are worn with the top shirt button open and may or may not be fastened with a stickpin.

A very tall man should be careful to have ties that are long enough. This may mean in extreme cases finding shops that cater to tall men. A tie of normal length on a man 6'3" can look as strange as too-short trousers.

There is nothing shameful in being either color blind or, let us say, color unsure. It is only the foolhardy male who, knowing nothing about color harmony, goes right ahead and buys his clothes without any attempt to co-ordinate them acceptably—and without seeking advice. Perhaps it was the lack of opportunity to wear bright colors for generations that has made the male uneasy in the presence of the wide assortment of colored and figured garments he finds even in the most conservative shops. He sees even his most reactionary friends attired in colors and color combinations quite unthinkable except in Bohemian or Broadway circles a few years back, and he wonders if he'll have the audacity himself to brighten up the old routine of the blue, gray, or brown suit with the white, blue, gray, or tan shirt and the plain blue, brown, maroon, or (more daringly) green ties that have been his safe choice for so long. Perfectly acceptable males are wearing yellow, for example, and not only in canary waistcoats in the hunting field or in the generations-old chamois ones. They wear yellow wool mufflers and, in the country, yellow knit gloves and cheerful bright yellow wool socks and dress and polo shirts along with such colors as coral and rose until recently the prerogative of women. The old maroon tie in variations of pattern is always good, but the reddest of red ties now appear on sound, aggressively masculine men and with good effect, too, and so do red striped shirts, some with bold striping. Green suits and hats, always considered tasteful in English and Continental tailoring circles, have captured the imaginations of the most conservative American ones. Green clothes need still to be chosen with caution and with a careful eye to a man's coloring. If he has a sallow, yellowish cast to his skin he can look mighty bilious in a green hat or suit. Forest green, gray green, and Lovat green are the safe ones to choose in wools and felts and go best with the well-tanned skin that has underlying color. The pinkish skin with ruddy accents can wear the various greens, too.

If a man decides to put a little more life into his wardrobe, he will find that women will approve and, with their usually more developed color sense, be able to advice him if he feels he needs advice. They will be able to help him find what is right for *him*—irrespective of what Jones at the club turned up in yesterday. It may be some comfort for him to realize that men have dressed so dully and conservatively for so long that the frequently startling changes now going on in men's fashion circles (and there are male style leaders who exert a considerable influence on what men wear, you know) go almost unnoticed, and not only by other men but even by the more fashion-conscious women, the majority of whom know nothing of what is considered good, tasteful male attire from a technical standpoint. But women, generally, know what "looks good" on their own or other males, and many a man who has improved his financial and social position over the years gets some help from his wife in the selection of his clothes. Many men, in fact, leave entirely to their wives the purchase of handkerchiefs, socks, underwear, and shirts and ask their wives to go along when they are choosing a ready-made suit or overcoat or selecting material from which they are to be made.

Handkerchiefs I feel about decorative silk handkerchiefs for men exactly as I do about chiffon squares for women—they in no way replace the good white linen or lawn handkerchief and, when worn for decoration, must not be used for the handkerchief's true function—for wiping one's face after exertion or blowing one's nose. Such handkerchiefs must, usually, be dry-cleaned or at least very cautiously washed, so they are not suitable for sanitary purposes at all. In fact, they may be knotted around the throat for sports wear rather than worn in a breast pocket. A man with a cold or an allergy need never apologize if he carries in his pocket a little pack of tissues, but their use does not preclude his obvious possession of a fresh handkerchief as well. Tissues, once used, are carefully discarded.

When a handkerchief with a colored border or initial is worn (and avoid these, of course, with formal day or evening dress unless, on an initialed handkerchief, the initial is in black or white) the color should be geared to the socks and tie, preferably. A man wearing a gray suit, a light gray, white-striped shirt, a maroon figured tie, and maroon wool socks would be better off choosing a handkerchief initialed in maroon rather than one with a gray initial.

The handkerchief in a man's breast pocket is supposed to be a clean, completely unused one, folded and placed casually so that it shows about two inches above the edge of the pocket. This is best achieved by picking the handkerchief up by its center, shaking it, and tucking it point down in the pocket. A silk handkerchief is handled the same way, but the handkerchief is placed in the pocket so that the center makes a casual puff at the top of the pocket. To be avoided are the geometrical points or even what I call the television fold which allows an inch to be seen in a straight line with no points and often with an initial showing. This is better for department-store dummies than for living males. Once a handkerchief from the breast pocket has been used (after the spare one in the hip pocket has been exhausted), a man is not supposed to put it back in the same pocket, because it is no longer suited for display and stuffing it down out of sight produces an ugly bulge. The Englishman shoves it up his sleeve (not a bad idea), but the carefully groomed man does not make himself a walking laundry bag by carrying two soiled handkerchiefs. He shifts one to the bottom of his brief case or his desk drawer, to be taken home for laundering. A man who travels a lot on his job does well to locate a good hand laundry near his office where he can have laundered the extra supply of handkerchiefs, shirts, and underwear he keeps in the office to take care of unexpected out-of-town trips or freshenings-up he may want to do when he goes directly from the office to a social engagement. Even the very young executive can usually find a bottom desk drawer or the back of a file drawer—or, better, his locker—where such accessories may be kept. Let him not be embarrassed over his little caches—some top executives keep entire wardrobe changes in their private offices and have dressing rooms attached to private baths, where they may groom themselves as is expected of them.

Initials on Handkerchiefs I like initials or monograms (two or more initials) when they are not too ostentatious. If only one initial is to be used on a handkerchief or on any other article of men's apparel, it must be his last initial (the reverse is true of initials on women's handkerchiefs). Initials should never be machine done—they should give a custom-made look to clothes. In buying handkerchiefs be sure the initials are hand-embroidered and the hems hand-whipped or hemstitched, the material of good quality.

A man spoils the effect of otherwise good grooming by bringing out a handkerchief that is sleazy or not immaculately clean. If a man asks a woman what constitutes good quality in handkerchiefs she will gladly show him what to look for in buying his own. Then he might go through his present collection and consign to use in spading the garden all those he bought in vending machines when he ran out of handkerchiefs on various business trips. Or give them to his young son whose ability to lose all handkerchiefs promptly will solve the problem of how to get rid of them.

Initials on Clothes and Various Articles   The rule for monogramming or initialing of handkerchiefs applies, too, to those on shirts, pajamas, and leather articles. Initials should never be ostentatious. If a man has his shirts custom-made and wants a monogram in white or color (and it should never, in this case, be a single initial [the last one] as is often used on handkerchiefs), he might have it put on the sleeve about three inches above the cuff rather than on the shirt front or pocket. Two or three little block initials—white, maroon, black, gray, or blue, preferred—are better than a scrolly monogram with an embroidered border. Initials on leather articles, such as a brief case or portfolio, are quite functional and should be readily readable, not just a fancy decoration. As only a man's family, intimate friends, or servants see him in his pajamas, he might have a fancy monogram in any color his heart desires, if he wants. It is usually placed on the left breast pocket. To monogram or initial everything one owns, from a car to a pipe, may seem feminine, so it's a good idea for a man not to let the women in his family overdo it in giving him monogrammed gifts.

Jewelry   What jewelry a man has should be of precious metal, good, simple design, and as expensive as his pocketbook permits. When he adds up the sums he has paid for the male equivalent of "junk jewelry"— tie clasps, tie pins, tricky cuff links, make-do studs, collar buttons, and watch chains, all of which eventually lose their plating or drop their ersatz stones—he will see that the gradual acquisition of good jewelry is good business as well as good taste. Before hurrying into the nearest men's shop and paying five dollars or more for brightly plated cuff links, because the last pair, costing the same, looks like something from the dime store, he might look through the jewelry his father or grandfather wore. He may find a beautiful pair of heavy gold links or some intricately enameled ones that he couldn't buy today from a dealer in antique jewelry for a hundred dollars or more. These "old-fashioned" things are often in far better taste than the machine-made jewelry most men must wear, either for lack of the price of anything better or because they don't know that heirlooms like these are never out of fashion. Today an Eastern man generally doesn't wear diamond rings or stickpins, but he may find an old-fashioned stickpin that will be really distinguished in an Ascot tie—even if it does have a tiny diamond somewhere in the setting.

Never discard these things on the ground they're not "modern." In the West and Southwest many men, Eastern educated or not, wear a hefty diamond ring or stickpin perhaps as a status symbol. It is far from frowned upon because of its sartorial splendor.

If a young man's social life is relatively limited by the exigencies of bringing up a family, he might consider that some day he may be a man whose clothes are all made to order and who will be able to find the leisure for the kind of social life that almost requires such niceties as real jewelry. Grandfather's heavy gold watch chain may not look like the delicate platinum one someone else received when he served as best man at that expensive wedding, but it will have meaning to a grandson and even give him a little edge over the young man whose granfather had no gold watch chain to leave him and who has had to work up to a platinum one himself.

A man with a big, long-fingered hand can wear a ring better than the man with a short pudgy one. If he has an antique seal ring—usually heavy gold with a coat of arms or a well-devised monogram—it may be worn on the little finger of either hand, although he's less likely to wince in handshaking with hearty individuals if he wears it on the left hand. When a ring with an emblem is worn—a Masonic ring, for example—it is usually worn facing the wearer. A ring with a stone, if worn at all, should be flat and preferably unfaceted, set in a simple gold setting. Some class or fraternity rings are so badly designed that a man often discards them a few years after graduation. There is no reason why when a very young man demands a ring (usually as he enters prep school) that it can't be tasteful enough for him to wear throughout his lifetime if he wishes. To be avoided are such things as "Chinese style" initials, imitation rubies, garnets, or emeralds set in the signet. If the ring is not going to be especially made for the boy don't overlook the pawn shops or the little jewelers who sell antique jewelry. There may be found the kind of man's ring (or studs or watch chain) of which he will never cease to be proud.

Wedding rings for men came into considerable use during World War II, and it is probable that the men who started wearing them will continue to do so influencing present bridegrooms to follow suit. It used to be thought incorrect for a man to wear his wedding band on any but the little finger of his right hand, but the modern wedding-ringed husband prefers the same finger the bride's ring circles—the fourth finger of the left hand. And it does seem to me that his wearing it there does make it seem unmistakable that he is a "married man." His wedding ring by the way is a gift from his bride.

Rings worn on the index finger or on the second finger are just plain theatrical and affected, no matter how they were worn in Victorian days or by some effete gentlemen.

Watches and cigarette cases may be gold, silver, enamel, steel, or platinum, and the cigarette cases should not be set with precious or semi-precious stones. Wrist watches, unless of delicate design and without a leather strap, are less likely to be worn with evening clothes. Instead, a thin watch, in gold or platinum, on a thin gold or platinum chain (or grandfather's good gold chain, which may be monumental but impressive) is worn. If any ill-advised woman should try to give a man a platinum chain with tiny diamonds between the links, he should return it to the jeweler who was talked into making it and go to Palm Beach on the proceeds or put them on the nearest fast horse.

Divorcés and Widowers' Wedding Rings   A man who has been divorced removes his wedding ring if he was married in a double ring ceremony. A widower either removes his or chooses to continue to wear it until his re-engagement.

What Every Man Should Know about Vests, Socks, and Shoes

The vest is, quite obviously from the look of the back of it, a piece of apparel to be worn under a coat. The suit with a matching vest is more formal than the vestless business suit. If a man does remove his coat, when given permission to do so for reasons of comfort, he should remove the vest, too, unless it is the rare probably custom-made kind with a back. If he is wearing suspenders it is better to keep his coat on or, if he happens to have on a belt, too, to unhitch the suspenders when he removes coat and vest. A coatless man is more agreeable to the eye than one in a vest or one whose suspenders show. Need anything be said about the abhorrent custom of wearing sleeve bands? If a man can't buy shirts that are the right sleeve length, he should have the sleeves shortened or have fewer but better shirts, custom-made.

White cotton or lisle socks are never worn except with white bucks, country loafers, or sneakers, teen-agers excepted. Heavy white wool socks, on the contrary, may be worn with country shoes and clothes—with tweeds, flannels, linen suits, or wool slacks—and for active sports. Argyle socks, preferably in dark patterns, have invaded urban areas and may be worn quite appropriately with such business suits as Glen plaids, wools, cheviots, flannels, and tweeds. Socks should be chosen with an eye to the tie worn, but exact matches are more cautious than interesting. A well-dressed man when in doubt chooses black socks. All dress socks should be worn over the calf with elasticized tops or garters. It is most important that "suit socks" not be worn with sports clothes such as shorts. Shorts require wool or cotton casual socks. Bermuda shorts may be worn quite formally with knee socks, jacket, and tie and are occasionally thus seen in cities like New York, but commonly in the Caribbean, and Bermuda in particular.

Shoes   There was a time when a rigidly well-dressed man would have looked askance at the wearing of brown shoes with a blue suit. The ultra-

conservative still wear black shoes with a blue suit, but brown are certainly correct, and with any tweed or rough-surface mixture more suitable,
in my opinion. I'll grant that a hard-surface blue serge might conceivably
limit one to black shoes.

Brown shoes are also worn with all the varieties of gray with the exception
of Oxford, which looks better accompanied by black. But many well-
dressed men wear brown cordovans with it successfully. Gray suits are
more conservatively teamed with black shoes, but many men wear black
shoes in the country, which once was considered definitely brown-shoe
terrain.

Suede shoes in brown reverse calf or buckskin are permissible in the city
with tweeds, and the monk shoe, moccasin, and rough brogue, once
solely country foot covering, are seen in the city with tweeds or slacks.
Internationally minded well-dressed men have been wearing black suede
shoes with dinner jackets. Much easier on the feet, they say, for long
standing and for dancing.

Alligator shoes (simulated now), even black ones, are properly worn only
with sports clothes and even then they are not for the most conservative.
Alligator belts (simulated), in black or brown, may be worn with business
suits, and black ones even with a dark suit in the evening unless the
occasion is rather formal in which case a plain black calf would be more
conservative.

Colored patent pumps in white as well as brown, maroon, red, blue dark
green, and even more sophisticated colors are part of the new leisure men's
fashion revolution. I see no objection to them with the right leisure
clothes.

White shoes, especially for tropical wear and warm weather anywhere, appear again, as do two-tone shoes such as brown and white, which had
a long period in the fashion doghouse. It is difficult to find a shoe that
looks right with the informality of the summer suit made of seersucker
or the various cotton mixtures so needed in our cities in the hot weather.
The black or brown monk's shoe or moccasin seems nearest to being acceptable, especially as the cotton suit coats are now often worn with gray
or brown-tone flannels or with gabardine slacks in a variety of muted colors
from sand and grayed greens to slate blue. Cotton-mixture suits in white,
often cut Edwardian style, team best with white shoes, especially patent
or woven leather. They are worn in the city as well as in the country now
in the practical drip-dry fabrics. They call for contrasting often even deep-
toned shirts.

Formal shoes fall into two categories, the patent, bowed, dancing pump,
and the laced patent evening oxford. The pumps are worn with tails, at

home with a smoking jacket, or with a dinner jacket. However, as noted under "Suede shoes," there has been a departure in the past few years in favor of black suede shoes for formal wear, a choice that is a little more recherché than the now quite accepted plain front, dull calf for evening shoes. These are often the slip-on type. This radical change in men's fashion now even has the cachet of the Duke of Windsor. They are preferred over the other types when the wearer expects to dance. The laced patents should not be pointed in toe or spade, and they look better without a toe cap. Black oxfords worn with morning coat should have a plain tip and preferably should be calf, avoiding the heavy-duty look of black street oxfords. These are the shoes in which a man is married when he dons the full regalia of a morning coat. Patent shoes of any sort would seem too frivolous for such an occasion. Nor are they suitable for funerals.

The Hatless and Gloveless Man

Frequently in winter you see even well-dressed men going gloveless and hatless. Perhaps they feel hardier that way, but an ungloved hand is, in the winter, usually a chapped and roughened one.

Only the man whose hair stays put should attempt to go hatless in town. If he has no hair, he'll probably look better-dressed wearing either a lightweight felt or some kind of straw hat. The traditional sailor is becoming to any man with a good figure, medium to tall in height, and preferably with a long or oval face. But let him be careful not to choose one with a band associated with a club or fraternity to which he does not belong. These color combinations can't be patented by the organizations in question, but wearing such a band when not entitled to do so makes one seem like a gate crasher. Before a man buys a band, he would do well to ask the clerk if it does belong to some specific group. Adorning a hat band with fish flies on bright little feathers is amusing or, if he's the type and can afford it, he may choose bands made entirely of pheasant feathers.

Going hatless to formal affairs, to city weddings, to funerals, even to business calls is a matter of personal preference now. Yes, there are men who affect a certain boyishness by going hatless winter and summer, rain or shine, but if a man wears a suitable hat, he is always right. This can't be said if he barges in everywhere hatless. Especially if he accompanies a well-turned-out woman.

The Tieless Man

Certain ways of dressing that may be tolerated regionally are not appropriate for travel into urban, particularly Eastern, centers. I mean specifically the dress shirt unbuttoned at the neck and without a tie, a turtleneck sweater or a sports shirt buttoned or unbuttoned at the neck but worn with a business suit or even with a sports jacket where other men are attired in shirts with ties. The best Eastern restaurants will not permit a man to enter in this half-dressed fashion and properly so. Such deshabille destroys others' feeling of special occasion—the luxury they are paying for in patronizing top restaurants, for example.

The Turtleneck

The turtleneck *sweater* worn with a dinner jacket was never considered right even by the avant guard. The well-tailored turtleneck *silk shirt* had acceptance, but anything less sophisticated looked hopelessly careless. The subject well may be academic now, though those who have them may persist until they wear them out.

The Daytime Overcoat

For town wear with business or semiformal daytime clothes the blue, black, or Oxford gray single-breasted chesterfield is always right unless the business suit is, say, a heather mixture or any rather woodsy tweed becoming to certain big-boned men. The chesterfield goes with the smooth surface fabric or herringbone, but tweeds need a more loose-lined topcoat, not only for comfort's sake but for congruity. Popular today is the single- or double-breasted camel's hair, Vicuna or cashmere in navy, black, Oxford, or possibly natural, which has a dual life for daytime and evening, especially on younger men.

Bad-weather Wear

Whenever possible, waterproofed shoes are preferable to rubbers for street wear in bad weather, but where rubbers are necessary the kind that covers just the sole of the shoe certainly looks better. For heavy duty in the country, elk-hide boots are more attractive than bulky galoshes, but these or rubber boots must be the choice of the commuter in snowy weather. Raincoats and hats (or plastic protectors over hats) are more practical than umbrellas, but there are times when every man needs to carry an umbrella. It should be large and black with a wooden crook handle and should be carried furled in its case when not in actual use. It may have a gold or silver initialed band on the shank of the handle.

The Raincoat The good old British raincoat, belted trench-coat style or fly-front, has been taken to the heart of the American male, who, like his English cousin, wears it as a light extra topcoat in the city or country, rain or no rain. In London this practice makes more sense, as any bright day is likely to turn into a rainy one before teatime, anyway. There is one injunction I should like to make—that the American not wear his raincoat when it is so dirty it embarrasses the women he escorts. An Englishman feels that his raincoat *must* be dirty—in fact, I am sure he tramps on a new one before he wears it for the first time—but in the United States a dirty raincoat is just a sign of careless grooming. In fact, it's just as repulsive as any other garment worn once too often.

Informal Wear in the City

Because of the increase of sports facilities in urban areas and the large numbers of people who on weekends and holidays converge from the city upon the surrounding suburban and country area, there is much more wearing of informal clothes by men on city streets outside of business days and hours. The sensitive man knows, however, where to draw the line between appropriate formality and restrained informality in cities. He might, without offense to anyone, wear a conservative, knit sports shirt, buttoned at the neck, without a tie, odd jacket, corduroy or other casual slacks, comfortable buck shoes or other casual footwear for an afternoon museum tour with his family if they are also in sports clothes. He might also wear a V-neck stevedore sleeveless sweater or knitted vest with a business suit unless the suit is a dark one that would be worn for semiformal evening occasions. He would draw the line on wearing this costume to a symphony concert unless it was held outdoors under quite informal circumstances. He remembers always to dress in the same style as the lady he is escorting. When there is any doubt, he makes a conservative choice.

What to Wear When

Proper dress is much less strictly defined these days. A man sometimes discovers that he is quite unsure what to wear on certain occasions, for example to a cocktail party followed by a buffet. It is much simpler if possible if he lets his wife determine the garb either by checking with other women going, or with her hostess. He then dresses in something appropriate to what she has decided to wear. If he is a bachelor he can call his host and say simply, "What would you like me to wear?" if he is not familiar with the customs of the household. Perhaps slacks, a colored sports shirt, and an ascot or just an open-necked shirt may be just the thing in a suburban or country area or even in a big city depending on the circumstances. On the other hand, he may be expected to wear a dark suit (which incidentally need not be navy any more but could be oxford or even chocolate brown). The traditional white shirt for informal evening wear is never wrong but it can be somewhat unimaginative. In sophisticated areas many men choose not to wear white shirts even under such circumstances. Shirts may be boldly or conservatively striped, solid blue, or any pastel color. In some cases they may be in dark colors plain or striped especially in the summertime if a white suit is worn. Men who have made a wrong choice in dress either in overdressing or underdressing for the occasion, can be just as uncomfortable as women are under the same circumstances. But if you do find yourself inappropriately dressed for the occasion, it is better not to apologize or explain but to carry on as if everybody else is wrong and you are right. I read a story in the *Reader's Digest* once about two men from our State Department who called on the

Japanese Ambassador at six o'clock and found him in dinner jacket. The Ambassador looked at them, asked to be excused, and said that he'd be back soon. They took the opportunity to rush to their apartments, change into dinner jackets and return. When they got back, they found the Ambassador in a sack suit. This kind of thing can be carried to ridiculous extremes. Every man should strive for, as the objective of his sartorial efforts, the knowledge that he is dressed in an appropriate way. When in doubt, check. When there is no way to check, take a chance. When wrong, relax. You'll know better next time.

Wearing Decorations

The Legion of Honor   Most countries grant various orders to distinguished citizens and non-citizens who have performed some outstanding service to the State. Among those often seen internationally are the various buttons and ribbon of the French Legion of Honor (Légion d'Honneur).

There are five grades of the Legion of Honor, each distinguished by its insigne as follows:

First Grade, Knight (Chevalier): Red ribbon at buttonhole, worn from the buttonhole to the outer edge of the left lapel.

Second Grade, Officer (Officier): Red rosette in buttonhole.

Third Grade, Commander (Commandeur): Red rosette on silver bar.

Fourth Grade, Grand Officer (Grand Officier): Red rosette on silver and gold grosgrain covered bar.

Fifth Grade, Grand Cross (Grand Croix), highest rank: Red rosette on gold grosgrain covered bar.

The highest rank that a woman has achieved in the Legion of Honor is that of Commander (Commandeur) and there is no regulation preventing a woman from rising higher. Women wear the red ribbon of the Knight on tailored suits, sewn on the left lapel just as men do. On street dresses they may wear it through the collar or neckline on the left side.

The insigne of Commander is pinned to the left shoulder as flowers would be.

For formal wear, women Commanders wear a white-lacquered five-pointed star on a circlet of gold attached to a large red ribbon worn necklace fashion.

Male Commanders for formal wear wear the same cross on a gold circlet on a large red ribbon tied around the neck beneath the white tie.

The Grand Officer has for formal wear a ten-pointed silver plaque worn on the left side of the breast. The Grand Cross (generally given to sovereigns and chiefs of state, occasionally to commanders in chief) is worn with red sash draped across the chest from right to left.

Holders of various ranks of the Legion of Honor may use the following designations or initials after their names: Knight ✸; Officer (O.) ✸; Commander (C.) ✸; Grand Officer (G.O.) ✸; Grand Cross (G.C.).

Rules for Wearing Decorations by Civilians A U.S. civilian possessing any U.S. war decoration wears it on the left side, always above those granted him by any other country.[1] Other decorations are worn in the order in which they are received, except that those of any one country are always grouped together. This is true even when one has been received after a decoration from another country has been awarded.

The possessor of many decorations need not wear them all at the same time on formal occasions. But an American possessing an American decoration wears it at any time that he also wears a foreign one, with, as has been noted, the American one always taking precedence.

American decorations are worn in order of their particular importance, irrespective of when they were bestowed. Foreign decorations are worn in order of their bestowal, irrespective of their relative importance.

The rule that foreign decorations are worn according to order of bestowal has the following exception: at a reception or dinner abroad in honor of a foreign official or any distinguished citizen of a foreign nation, any decoration an American has received from that country takes precedence over his other foreign decorations for the occasion.

Medals of Patriotic Organizations

A man or woman belonging to several patriotic societies, such as Sons or Daughters of the Revolution, and having medals signifying the fact, should not wear all these medals to a meeting of one of the organizations. The only one worn is that of the society which is meeting. Usually the medals are miniatures, but sometimes very old members own and wear full-sized ones. When a person is dressed formally, however (women in full evening dress, men in white tie), it is correct to wear a set of miniature medals from all the organizations to which he belongs. Miniature medals are not properly worn with black tie.

---

[1] Exceptions: The Medal of Honor and the Presidential Unit Citation ribbon are worn on the right. With evening dress the Medal of Honor is worn on a broad blue ribbon around the neck, hanging just below the tie. The Presidential Unit Citation ribbon is worn, by both men and *women*, on the right, in miniature, for full evening dress. The Navy, in uniform, wears even these decorations on the left.

Chapter 19

THE WELL-GROOMED MAN

The well-groomed man looks clean, his clothes fit him comfortably, his shoes are well shined and their heels in good order, his tie is neatly tied so that it covers the collar joining and the short end lies well under the longer one if he's wearing a four-in-hand. If he ties his tie in a Windsor knot, the knot should be small and tidy, not theatrically large. If he wears a bow tie, it should not be a droopy little blob or pre-tied if this can be avoided.

If he can help it, the well-groomed man never wears a suit the second day without having it pressed, unless it is of a material which shakes out overnight. To facilitate this, he hangs his trousers over the bar of a valet stand when he takes them off or puts them immediately in their hanger— one for each pair of trousers. His coat is hung on a hanger or on the valet stand and buttoned so it will fall into shape.

A fastidious man never wears the same shirt, underwear or socks the second day, and he is never without a clean handkerchief. He keeps his nails clean and short with the cuticle pushed back. If he has his nails professionally manicured, they may be buffed but should never have any colored or even colorless polish applied.

A man who's unduly hirsute should have his barber clip the hairs in his ears and nostrils (but, of course, for safety's sake, never tweeze them). If his eyebrows run rampant they can be cautiously weeded out to give him a more groomed appearance, although any tweezing should be restricted to stray eyebrows or to the heavy hairs between the brows—a man's brow line should never be thinned or obviously shaped. Mustache, sideburns or beard, if any, should be kept well-groomed, their style chosen to complement his face and suit his daily life.

For the unbearded man with the blue jowl there seems to be no other course than that of a twice-daily shave. Powder doesn't really cover that bristle. The husband who gives himself a shaving holiday on a day at home is in the same class as the wife who doesn't put on her make-up or take her hair out of curlers until afternoon.

The well-groomed man never allows his hair to get so shaggy his new haircut is all too apparent. His hair is trimmed as often as necessary for the current style he affects. He has it scissor-trimmed, not clipped, so as to avoid an ugly ridge across the back of his head. His sideburns should be scissored rather than closely clipped or shaved. They are needed to give balance to his face. If he is bald he should realize that letting his side or back hair grow long enough to drape stickily over the bald spot deceives no one and usually produces a peculiar parting in the hair. And, let him be sure his bald pate is washed as often as he washes his face, because it is just as vulnerable to dirt.

I have a particularly soft spot for bald-headed men because so many of them suffer so obviously and needlessly from what they consider a handicap. Anthropologists have pointed out that baldness is usually hereditary and while it is a secondary sexual characteristic of the male, it is not a sign of virility. Scientists have pointed out, too, that eunuchs are very seldom bald. On the other hand, we associate luxuriant hair with femininity. And satyrs are depicted as bald. Perhaps women's intuition tells her these things, because you rarely find a wife concerned over the baldness of her husband. If he could understand this, he would sweep his hat off on the street, not lift it timidly or touch the brim in an effort to keep his secret shame to himself. And when he goes to a photographer, he will not insist on being photographed with his hat on—a dead giveaway. Instead, he will get help in making up his bald spot for the occasion, so that it will not be highlighted in the picture. Any woman can show him how this is painlessly and quickly done.

Recent advances in medical science have offered help to *some* bald men with the use of local application of male hormones, or in *selected* cases by means of hair transplants, although not all men can be helped by the latter. More specific advice as to the feasibility of these treatments is best obtained by consulting a dermatologist.

Some men perspire quite heavily, winter and summer. If this perspiration is excessive enough to stain his suits under the arm a man should have recourse to any of the commercially available deodorants and perspiration checks offered for both men's and women's use as a supplement to his regular deodorant. (If hatbands show perspiration marks they should be changed as often as necessary.) Daily or sometimes twice-daily baths or showers should be routine for any man, but for the heavy perspirer they are obligatory with a good soap. No cologne or powder can possibly cover the need of thorough daily cleansing.

Mention of cologne brings me to the observation that custom has changed in this respect, too. Not so very long ago no American he-man would have considered using a bit of cologne on his handkerchief or after his bath. A man didn't use perfumes—or so he pretended. But American men, nevertheless, were inundated in a sea of ill-blended effluvia—violet hair tonic, mint, lilac, or carnation after-shave lotion, lilies of the valley or some such in their talcum, pine or geraniums in their bath soap. Now there are matched sets of these preparations for men or mercifully odorless items that won't conflict with a little good-quality men's cologne or clash with their women's perfume. True cologne, spicy and fresh, was always used by well-groomed men and women abroad, and there are many muted scents that suit even the most masculine male a lot better than do the violent odors in many popular hair tonics and lotions. Used restrainedly, simple colognes and toilet waters of the spicy variety (one at a time) are attractive for men and increase the impression of careful grooming.

Most men's hair does need some dressing to keep it in place, but daily application of such preparations eventually leaves the hair heavy, sticky, and inclined to pick up odors of tobacco smoke, even if a man doesn't smoke himself. Every shower should have handy to it a bottle of shampoo. Just letting the shower soak the slightly soaped hair is not enough. Hair that has been heavily oiled needs several soapings and rinsings. Using liquid castile or a detergent shampoo prevents bits of soap from sticking to the hair.

The man who wants to make the proper appearance wears clean clothes always—even those items which by some are considered proper only if well dirtied up. Most men look better after their new hats begin to conform to the shape of their heads, but the battered old hat, no matter how dear to the wearer, contributes a careless rather than the hoped-for casual effect. As for shirts, they must be clean daily. It is good for a man to cultivate a very necessary vanity—the kind that is well this side of fussiness, of course.

My grandfather used to say that he judged a man by his shoes. Perhaps he was saying that our external effect is often the only one most people see and judge us by.

It takes time and care for a man to dress well. He can't do so if he throws his clothes over a chair at night and gets up so late in the morning he hasn't time to give any thought to what he'll put on. He grabs a shirt from the drawer, puts it on before choosing his suit for the day, lifts a tie from the rack with no consideration for his socks, shoves his feet into his untreed shoes without undoing the laces, gulps his breakfast, hustles into his topcoat—which hasn't been pressed all season—puts on his hat and is off. His pockets are bulging with yesterday's handkerchiefs, his heels need lifts, his hat could do with a blocking or at least a brushing. He's a pretty average American businessman. If he ever does catch sight of himself in the mirror, he decides that nothing can be be done about it anyway. He hasn't a valet, he hasn't time, and very probably—or so he imagines—hasn't the money.

One of the best-dressed men I know went through a period, after years of military service, when he had two presentable suits, one pair of gray flannels, a sports jacket, two pairs of shoes, one tie, a gabardine raincoat, and a snap brim brown hat. The clothes he had he bought with great care and paid as much for each item as his budget could stand. His shirts were all light blue, classic collared. They were all quality pima cotton. He washed them himself at the local self-service laundry and learned to iron them himself without starch, like a professional. Not for him the less satisfactory drip dries, except for emergency travel. Both his suits were gray—one a flannel and the other a fine Glen plaid. His tie was blue, red, and white, always pressed, always spotless, and worn with the air of a club tie whose style and color would always be the same, too. His hair was always well-trimmed—and he learned to trim it himself to save money. He alternated the wearing of his two pairs of shoes and kept them handsomely shined and carefully repaired. His handkerchiefs were plain white linen, always fresh. His clean shirts he hung on hangers to keep the collar tabs and the cuffs from rumpling.

There is more to good grooming than good, clean clothes, of course, but cleanliness, neatness in dress have much to do with the outer integration of the man. Taste in dress is innate in some, acquired in others—but it can be had by any man who wants it. Top business and professional men usually dress well because certain standards of dress are set them by the circles in which they move. But money alone doesn't determine the final effect.

Cosmetic Defects   There are men who, if they look in the mirror except to shave, either fail to notice certain obvious cosmetic defects or else think that it is effeminate to consider them seriously. Among these are chapped lips, blackheads, pimples, unsightly moles, dirty, stained teeth, and scaly scalp. Ordinary yellow vaseline or a bit of cold cream applied nightly or in the morning will relieve chapped and cracked lips. Blackheads and pimples may be in the province of a dermatologist if they are very evident, but thorough scrubbing of the face with hot water and plenty of soap at least once a day may stimulate the skin so it can police itself. A good barber or a loving wife using a sterile comedo extractor and a hot towel can keep blackheads at bay if utmost care is taken. Pimples should not be opened, especially on the face, as a resulting infection can be serious. Instead they should be dried up with a lotion or salve for the purpose. If true acne occurs, see a doctor about a possible change in diet or other corrective regimen. A diet high in fats and carbohydrates can be a cause of this unsightly disfigurement. Moles, especially if they interfere with shaving, should be removed surgically or by the electric spark or other accepted method by a regular doctor treating such things, not by a barber or cosmetician. Barber treatments of really serious scalp disorders will probably make the situation worse. A dermatologist should be consulted. All scalps are somewhat scaly. Daily brushing (not too vigorous if hair is thinning) with clean brushes helps carry this flaky refuse off, as does a careful weekly shampoo. Even a bachelor can learn to clean his combs and brushes as often as necessary in a solution of ammonia and cold water or even simpler, a solution of bicarbonate of soda and water (ordinary baking soda).

Unattractive Teeth   Some teeth gather tartar because of smoking, some because of improper and hurried cleaning, and some for reasons no dentist can determine. Teeth that do stain in this way should be professionally cleaned, probably every three months, otherwise the tartar gathers mouth acids, causes unpleasant breath, and, if not removed, can loosen teeth by causing pyorrhea. Aside from this medical reason for having clean teeth, there is certainly the cosmetic and social one. You may have the kind of teeth that don't show when you smile or talk, but do show—perhaps in all their dreariness—when you laugh. And your breath depends on the condition of your mouth and teeth to an important extent. Offense here can have a deleterious effect on business, social, and, yes, especially love life. Don't let your oral hygiene go unchecked. See your dentist and dental hygienist as often as they deem necessary and learn, as an adult, how to wash your teeth and how to keep the spaces between your teeth free of food particles through the use of dental floss or dental picks (the professional kind dentists suggest) preferably after each meal (that wonderful invention the Water-Pik is available in a travel version, too). There is no nostrum that can disguise the need for dental attention or hygiene.

Chapter 20

A MAN'S MANNERS IN THE
BUSINESS WORLD

The encouraging thing about etiquette is that it can be learned, that it doesn't necessarily have to be bred in the bone—though that is, of course, the way it would come easiest.

Professor Arthur M. Schlesinger, Jr., of Harvard in a learned discussion of etiquette throughout American history points out that Andrew Jackson, elected to the presidency in 1828, was our first President not in the Adams-Washington aristocratic tradition. He was the son of a desperately poor Scotch-Irish immigrant, who through native ability rose to highest office, correcting his rough manners as he went along to such a degree that, as Schlesinger puts it, he "excited the admiration of both friend and foe by his urbane and courtly demeanor."

Knowledge and instinctive practice of accepted good manners does not, of course, make the gentleman. A real gentleman, a man with a heart for the kind, considerate, decent thing may have no manners at all, in the usual sense. Polished manners and a scurrilous character can well be encountered in the same individual—just as a man may dress like a gentleman as a result of careful imitation, yet be far from a gentleman in his daily actions. At the same time, it is highly desirable from a social and business point of view for every man to know and practice the accepted manners of his time—to err, perhaps, on the side of punctiliousness in such things.

Learning to make good manners almost innate makes life easier at home and in business. Young men who want to become executive material must do more than apply themselves to the technique of their jobs. They must school themselves in social as well as in business manners if they went to get ahead. They must learn how to dress, how to conduct themselves on various social and business occasions, how to communicate their ideas to others in concise, well-chosen language.

We have all known successful businessmen whose grammar was bad, whose taste in clothes was atrocious, and who broke every rule of good manners, if indeed they knew any existed. But this is doing it the hard way.

It takes considerable business or professional genius to overcome the destructive effect of boorishness and uncouthness. Top executives, if they must endure these drawbacks in a key man, are uncomfortable and apologetic concerning him. Often such a man is replaced, if he can be, with another who fits more smoothly into a growing business. The day of the hell-for-leather individual in American business is passing, if it isn't completely over.

I have often noticed that the great corporations invariably practice a most formal business etiquette. Their façade is imposing, they employ well-dressed, soft-spoken receptionists, they provide private offices and inter-office communications to cut down unnecessary noise and traffic. They usually exercise considerable control over the behavior and appearance of their employees for the sake of improved efficiency and of their public relations.

In such offices you don't see men put their feet on desks or sit around with their hats on and their coats off—although in some offices there is relaxation concerning coats during the hot weather. But even so, employees are expected to don their coats when leaving their desks to welcome visitors, to go elsewhere in the building, or to attend conferences. In the latter case, they may remove them again at the invitation of their superiors and with the permission of any women executives present.

When Does a Man Rise?

Gone are the days of the quill pen and communication by letter only. Business pace is fast, and the courtly manners of old-time business offices are often impractical now and few expect them.

In business a man does not rise when his secretary enters his office to take dictation, although if she is newly assigned to him as his personal secretary he does rise to greet her and to shake her hand.

He rises if he has a woman caller—unless she is a job applicant for a non-executive position. If he is on the telephone or dictating when she enters, he nods, indicates a chair, and rises when he has concluded his conversation, which he makes as brief as circumstances permit. If he must receive other phone calls, during the course of the interview, he excuses himself each time for the necessary interruption.

If he is at his desk and a superior, man or woman, enters, he rises and remains standing until his guest is seated or leaves.

If a male co-worker enters his office, he does not rise unless, perhaps, to greet him after an absence, for gentlemen *always* rise to shake hands—even with a man—or excuse themselves for being unable to do so for some reason.

It is courteous for a man to rise for any man caller except a job applicant in the non-executive capacity. He certainly rises for all "gentlemen of the cloth" and for men very much older than himself, although, if seated, he may acknowledge an introduction to another contemporary joining a group of men, merely by nodding or saying anything that seems to come naturally such as "Happy to see you here," or "Nice to see you," or even a smiling "Hello."

If a woman executive is in the group joined by a man, the man who makes the introduction rises, unless he is the chairman (who *may* remain seated by virtue of his dignified position), as do the other men at the meeting if the group is of reasonable size. Otherwise, only the men in the immediate vicinity of the woman to be seated rise for specific introductions if any are necessary. If an introduction would interrupt the meeting, the man next to the nearest chair rises to seat the woman, unless he is in the midst of a report or discussion. A general introduction of the woman to the group may be made, if convenient, by the chair, "Gentlemen, this is Miss Helena Coyle, from our advertising agency." In such introductions it would only cause confusion for all to rise as would handshaking.

Who Precedes Whom?

In leaving a room in a business office a man always steps back to allow his superior to go first if the other is about to leave too, or, if there seems to be some delay, asks permission to go first. From the standpoint of superiority, the top executives certainly have the privilege of leaving before their inferior women employees, but I have noticed that, even in business, most gentlemen step aside, no matter what their capacity, to permit the women present to go first, even women in non-executive capacities. It's not a bad idea, for if a man gets into the habit of stalking through doors ahead of his secretary he is likely to forget that women take precedence in this respect in social life. It is difficult to have one set of manners for business and another for home.

The rule that a woman precedes men through doors is a set one, with the exception that a man goes ahead if the couple is walking the length of a train, opening the heavy doors and holding them open until the woman passes through. He also enters an *unlighted* room first to put on the light. A woman, however, passes through a revolving door first after the man has set it in motion for her unless there is no doorman and such an exit might put her momentarily on a dark or slippery street. The man may well suggest he go first in order to assist her.

Smoking in the Office

A superior, man or woman, calling upon another employee may, of course, smoke without asking permission, but an outsider may not smoke in the office of someone else unless he is asked to do so. It makes a bad impression for such a caller to ask permission to smoke if he is there in his own behalf, asking for, say, a contract, a job, or an introduction. And especially is it bad if the person on whom he is calling is not smoking himself.

A Man's Secretary

A really experienced and urbane executive keeps his relations with his secretary on a friendly but purely business basis even after years of association. In informal offices a secretary is often now called by her first name, especially in small towns where everyone knows everyone else. But to the outsider—and, remember, such businesses may grow to be big, impersonal corporations in time—it often seems less than businesslike and sometimes a shade too intimate for a man to call his secretary "Mary" instead of "Miss Jones," at least in office hours. The temptation is for everyone else, in and out of the office, to call her Mary, too, so that she is deprived of the dignity of her title. When everything goes smoothly it may be comfortable enough for a man to call his secretary by her first name and—as is often the case in these instances—for her to reciprocate by using his first name, but it is very difficult if Mary must be corrected about something or has to be fired.

If in your office a first-name precedent has already been set, at least refer to the women on your staff as "Miss So and So" to visitors to the office. Let it be, "Miss Ross will show you out, Mr. King," not, "Mary will show you out."

The Pretty Secretary   It is only human for a man to want his secretary to be neat, attractive, and, if possible, pretty. He has to look at her all day long. But the more attractive she is, the more, for his own and her protection, he must treat her with careful, polite objectivity. The quickest way to trouble, a straight line into the maze of gossipy office politics, is for a man to pay more than business attention to his secretary. If it happens that both are free to have some social life together, if they wish, they should still maintain formal relations in the office if their efficiency is not to suffer. Even at that, it is difficult for the woman, especially, not to show others that she has her boss under rather special control.

Lunching and Dining with One's Secretary   A secretary has a right to lunch as she wishes, in welcome solitude or with some friend in or out of the office. For her employer to make a frequent practice of asking her to lunch with him so he can catch up with his work is slave-driving. Occasionally, it may be a good idea for a man to take his secretary to lunch for business or purely social reasons, to smooth their working together, but it should always be kept in mind that it is easier to work with those with whom we do not have a close emotional tie.

If a man and his secretary are traveling together, the man may well offer to take his employee to dinner if otherwise she faces dinner alone. But he should be careful—if he is married or she is—to avoid any but the most dignified restaurants. If a married man takes his secretary to a night club, for instance, or some honky-tonk, whether or not they actually eat a meal, they are both open to some suspicion should they be observed by someone from home.

There is a delicate difference in the relations between a man and a woman associate in his business and a man and his secretary. Society might well feel that a secretary could not safely refuse purely social invitations from her employer, except at the possible risk of her job. A woman executive associate has more leeway. Supposedly she can control any difficult situation that might arise. She might well go to a night club in a strange city with an associate with whom she is traveling, although if one or the other is married, she would not do so at home unless others were in the party or there were some definite business reason for going.

Traveling with a Secretary

Making Hotel Reservations In making reservations at a hotel for an executive and his secretary, the firm name should be used, not the executive's nor the secretary's, although it is correct for some other person in the organization to make the reservation if it is more convenient for return mail or telegrams to be addressed to an individual. Such a reservation might read:

HOTEL BLACKSTONE
CHICAGO, ILLINOIS
PLEASE RESERVE TWO SINGLE ROOMS THIS FIRM'S DR. ROGER GIDDONS AND SECRETARY MISS ELLEN PRINCE FOR DECEMBER 9. CONFIRM.

> WM. TRAVIS, TRAFFIC MANAGER
> HUTTON BROTHERS
> 444 MADISON AVENUE
> NEW YORK

Although such a message makes it clear that the two should be assigned to different floors, a mistake, if it is made by the reservation desk, should be tactfully corrected by whoever signs the register if other rooms are available. If they are not, there need be no reason for panic. *Honi soit qui mal y pense,* which could be translated that you are your own best protection.

How Should They Register? It is usual for a secretary to check into the same hotel as her employer, so she will be available when he needs her. As his secretary, she may sign the register, "Henry Murray," with his firm name and address (rather than his social address) and beneath that, "Miss Bernice L. Wisner, secretary, same address." The clerk, unless asked to do otherwise, will usually assign the two to different floors. If the employer signs the register, he signs the same way, giving the business address and making his secretary's relation to him clear by entering the information on the register. Any verbal explanations to the clerk may embarrass all concerned quite unnecessarily.

Does a Secretary Need a Chaperone?   It is obviously impossible for a secretary traveling with her employer to insist on a chaperone or to refuse to take dictation in a hotel room. It is not always possible for either a man or woman executive to secure a hotel suite, even if such extra expense is willingly borne by a firm, and it is often necessary for dictation to be given when executives travel.

A man should not hesitate to ask his secretary, traveling with him, to take dictation or do other office work in his room, though not in hers, once the rooms have been made up. (If it is impossible to get the chambermaid to do the room in time, at least the bed should be pulled together, not kept open.) The door should be unlatched, although it is not necessary now that it be open.

An employer may order lunch (but preferably not breakfast) in his room for his secretary and himself if necessary to conserve working time, but not drinks. He should not ask his secretary to dine with him in his room if it is at all possible for them to go to the hotel restaurant or some other one. Even while working, he should, preferably, keep his coat on while his secretary is present, and she should be careful to be as completely groomed as she would be in her office at home. Needless to say, no man should ask his secretary—or even a public stenographer—to take his dictation when he is not fully dressed, unless he is ill and the fact is well-known.

The Executive on the Telephone

In a personal service organization—one that depends on its daily contact with others for its business—an executive should answer his own phone, if at all possible. Many a deal has been queered by a snippy secretary's self-important announcement to the telephone caller, "This is Mr. Brown's *secretary* speaking. What did you want to talk to him *about?*" It is always that awkward and infuriating past-tense phrase, too. Mr. Brown is probably right there swaying back in his swivel chair and quite able to pick up the phone himself. If he's any kind of an executive, he can dispose of unwanted callers with tact and dispatch and he does not run the risk of cutting off his business blood supply.

But in case a man or woman executive is really busy, actually out of the office, or for the moment can't be disturbed, it is vital in almost any kind of business for the intermediary to handle the call in a way that will not hurt the firm's public relations. If the secretary can say, "Oh, Miss Johnson, Mr. Brown will be so sorry to hear he missed your call. I can't reach him just now, but where may he call you? Or is there something I can do?" Humanly enough, many secretaries build up their employers' importance in their own minds in order to bolster their own egos, and this reluctance to let the outside world—no matter how important the call—at the Great Being is all too apparent. In all my years of business experience I have yet to see anyone who really wanted to do business with an executive through a secretary.

Where the procedure is absolutely necessary in order to conserve a busy person's strength and time, the utmost discretion must be observed by his go-betweens, from the switchboard operator to the executive's secretary. And it is a business axiom that the bigger the executive, the more approachable he is. I have always found it much easier to deal with the heads of corporations than with third assistant vice-presidents.

May I Ask Who's Calling?　A busy executive, trying to protect himself from constant telephone interruptions, frequently instructs his telephone operator or his secretary to ask, "May I ask who's calling?" When the caller identifies himself to the board or the secretary, he is politely given the needed information, "He is on the phone at the moment but as soon as possible I know he will want to call you back" (this to an important client, the executive's wife or business associate). In a day of most hard-pressed executives, it *is* often a matter of selecting those calls that can be returned within that day. Therefore, if a caller is unknown to the secretary who is anxious to protect her employer, she may safely ask, "Is this a personal call?" If the caller says it isn't, she may then add, "May I ask your organization?" It is a rare jewel of a secretary who, knowing that her boss is not available or should not be disturbed, who will say, "I can't reach him just now but if there is anything *I* can do—" If she sounds warm and pleasant, she should be able to take many telephone call burdens off her boss's shoulders. With direct dialing, a great many top executives now answer their own phones and thus are particularly vulnerable to the demands of the telephone. When the phone rings, a man replies, "Patterson." His tone is businesslike and the person on the other end is thus encouraged to make his business short. If he can't talk, the executive may certainly say so, if the conversation threatens to be lengthy. He may say, "I'm so sorry I can't talk now." (He doesn't need to explain why.) "What would be a good time for me to call you back?" Or simply, "May I call you back?" Business calls, if possible, should be kept very brief. Irrational though it may be, callers—some of them important—calling a number become irritated at the person being called if they get a constant busy signal.

Instant Intimacy　A secretary does not answer her employer's phone by saying, "Alice Jones's office." Instead she says, "Miss Jones's office." No matter what she calls her boss, she does not say for example to a stranger calling, "Bob is out now. I'll have him call you back." Even if she does call him by his first name, she says instead, "Mr. Roberts is out at present. I'll have him call you back." She does not refer to herself by her first name to strangers, but says, "This is Miss Jones's secretary," and optionally adds, "Miss Peterson."

"What Was the Name?"　This maddening past tense phrase is one that should be discarded by receptionists and secretaries. This extended-pinkie school of speaking has irked me for years. When somebody says to me, "What was the name?" my overpowering desire is to say, "Was and *is* ————." The proper expression is "May I have your name, please" or "May I say who is calling?" though I prefer the former as obviously the person must be told who is calling on him or her.

When Relatives Visit the Office

Men or women in offices, whether as business principals or not, should discourage members of their families from using the office facilities in any way. Even when staff members or other executives seem polite enough when relatives of their associates come in to use the office because of its convenience on trips to town, the interruption is often resented. If secretaries, bookkeepers, or the office boy are enlisted in any way in the service of such outsiders, they should be compensated for their trouble, and they should never be taken from their appointed tasks for such errands or favors without the consent of their immediate superior.

Convention Badges

Where is a convention badge worn? A woman wears hers as she would a corsage, on the left. A man does likewise. Women do not enjoy wearing badges with heavy pins which may mark their clothes, but prefer the adhesive variety, better in my opinion for both men and women. Men like even better the kind of badge that will slip in the breast pocket.

Women's badges should bear their titles, Miss Anne Green, Mrs. Nancy Brown (if that is the way the employee is known in the company), or Mrs. John Brown (Nancy, may be added parenthetically if it seems advisible) if she is merely accompanying her husband at a convention. The name of the company also appears on the badge or label. Such badges are not normally worn outside of the building where the convention is taking place.

At one successful convention very small badges were given additionally to the women for evening wear. These bore just the first and the last names, for example, Mary Green. The badges were decorated with small rhinestones. This was helpful as all of the men were on a first-name basis through the business hours, whereas their wives were often meeting other husbands and their wives for the first time. Normally, however, badges are large and names are typed in large type in black or lettered with black felt markers so they may be readily read even by people who wear just reading glasses.

Office Donations

A constant demand for money to cover all sorts of situations in offices from the birth of a baby to the retirement of a secretary, can be a great burden and a real annoyance to staff members. The best way to handle this, perhaps within a department, is for the group to agree to a small contribution each payday from each employee who wishes to contribute to a fund. If the amount is kept small—say, twenty-five or fifty cents—nearly everyone will be willing. One employee should be responsible for the collection of the money. An accounting of collections and disbursements should be made at agreed-upon periods, perhaps every three or four months. Each time a gift or flowers are purchased, all involved should be told how much has been spent. Usually there is a ceiling on collections—fifty to one hundred dollars, depending on the size of the office—at which point collections may cease until the fund reaches an agreed-upon low point. Usually the amounts spent on the gifts depend on the length of time the employee has been with the firm. There are other methods of handling this difficult problem, but this is one I have found works well.

Is It Necessary to Meet Socially with One's Business Associates?

From the employer's standpoint it is rarely essential—except perhaps in a small community—for him and his wife to pay serious social attention to the families of junior executives. Business luncheons, an occasional drink, perhaps, with a younger man, or a few rounds of golf often suffice. Executives who are too close socially often work less well, rather than better, together, for they lose their objectivity or at least feel they should repress it.

It is a good thing in business to be able to speak out fair and valuable criticism without thought of close friendship. Staff promotions, too, are better handled when the owners are on relatively formal terms with all employees rather than intimate with a chosen few. To paraphrase Ben Franklin, "Love your business associates but don't pull down your hedge."

From the viewpoint of the employee, we might consider this. If, for example, your business superior invites you to a social cocktail party at his home, it is rather a point of courtesy to accept the invitation—even if you don't drink. In all correctness, though, the invitation should be phoned or written to your home and not extended at the office. It also holds true that other gatherings involving the families of business associates should be arranged through the wives. Men may make tentative plans, but, properly, the wife follows through in issuing the invitations. Making social engagements, after consultation with her husband, is part of the woman's responsibility in the household.

Tipping Answering Services

Men—or women—in business for themselves frequently employ an answering service. At Christmas time operators at answering services do expect a tip from subscribers. If a subscriber has twenty-four-hour service, the lowest usual tip is five dollars per girl, with a possible contribution to the kitty for relief operators. A subscriber with limited service, say only mornings, or during certain hours, should determine the number of operators on his account and tip each one a minimum of five dollars with perhaps more to any girl or girls who have given extra service and perhaps here, too, something for the kitty. One check may be sent to the company itself with the indication of how it is to be divided, or individual checks may be sent to the girls with or without a greeting card.

Letters of Resignation

Resignations from business firms are usually given in person but even then are frequently followed, for the sake of the record, by a brief, polite note of resignation, stating the cause of the resignation only if it in no way reflects on the firm. Such a letter is always pleasant, even if the parting has been stormy.

June 1, 1971

Mr. Abel Cressman
Premier Products Ltd.,
99 Lake Street
Green Bay, Wisconsin zip code

Dear Mr. Cressman,
   It is with great regret that I must tender my resignation as vice-president after so many years with Premier. As you know, I have long wanted to locate in New York and an excellent opportunity to do so has presented itself.
   I am leaving with the warmest regard for you and my fellow officers. I hope to renew the bond whenever I pass through Wisconsin, which may be frequently, as my new duties call for considerable travel.

Sincerely,
Robert Murray

Business Letters of Introduction

It is perfectly proper to ask for a business introduction. A man might introduce a business friend by giving him his business card with "introducing John Brown" written on it in ink (the same phrase for a woman includes her title, Miss or Mrs.). Then the introducer would write his friend in the out of town firm:

October 1, 1971

Mr. John F. Campion
Crestview Paper Products, Inc.
1815 Water Street
San Francisco, California zip code

Dear Mr. Campion:
   Mr. John Brown, a valued customer of ours, will be in San Francisco about October 20th and I have given him a card of introduction to you.
   We would greatly appreciate any courtesies you may wish to show Mr.

Brown. I think that he would be most interested in going over your plant. Perhaps you will have an opportunity to lunch with him at Fisherman's Wharf.

Thanking you for whatever you may do to make his stay pleasant, I am,

Cordially,

Peter Stapleton

Chapter 21

THE MASCULINE GRACES

Sending Flowers

Too many men use little or no sense in the sending of flowers. Confused, they buy something expensive and therefore, they believe, impressive, but it may be quite unsuited to the occasion or to the costume the girl is wearing. A corsage of purple orchids looks foolish at a football game, whereas a shaggy chrysanthemum, a bunch of violets, or orange calendula, or even a charmingly arranged spray of bittersweet would be in tune with her sport coat, lap rug, and boots. Even a non-wearer of flowers would enjoy these. Actually no corsage is necessary and many prefer not to wear them.

A woman is much more impressed when a man makes an effort to find out what kind of flowers she would prefer than if he just leaves it up to the florist. A man sending flowers should take into consideration that there are some women who prefer, for one reason or another, never to wear flowers, but who, of course, enjoy receiving them for use in decoration. The woman who is not a flower-wearing type usually feels uncomfortably impelled to wear flowers sent to her even when she considers them unsuitable for her costume or her personality. Many women, in big cities particularly, never like to wear flowers with evening clothes but they may make exceptions for flowers for day wear—a little bunch of violets on a suit, an occasional spray of discreet small orchids. Men should cultivate the ability to observe these little preferences among the women they escort and when in doubt should ask.

If a man can't determine for himself whether a girl is the orchid or gardenia type and can't bring himself to ask her what she plans to wear, he is safe in sending white flowers—lilies of the valley, gardenias, chrysanthemums (for daytime wear), rosebuds (but they are perishable for an evening of dancing), carnations in a tight little round bouquet. But he should be careful not to have so many flowers in the corsage that a delicate gown will be pulled out of place by the weight of it. And for a short girl, never, under any circumstances, should a corsage of more than one or two orchids be sent. A girl with taste—and a taste for orchids—would prefer one little green, yellow, or white spray orchid to half a dozen ostentatious purple ones. But, orchids or cornflowers, corsages should be free of ribbon trimming, and rose corsages should not have any greenery but their own as background.

Flowers are worn various ways with evening clothes. If they are to be worn on the shoulder for dancing, the right shoulder keeps them fresh longer. A girl with her hair in a French twist or a chignon might prefer a bright red or pink camellia or a single gardenia for her hair rather than a corsage. A girl under five feet might prefer a small arrangement to be worn on her back décolletage—rather than one to be crushed at the waist or on the shoulder during dancing—or a tiny nosegay to pin to her gloves or bag. Tall girls can stand the big impressive corsages men love to buy, but little girls often abhor them. And big girls may well, too.

Flowers should be arranged in corsages so that they will be worn the way they grow, with the heads up. They should be sent with several florist's pins so they can be anchored firmly in place.

Bouquets of flowers should always be sent with some thought of where and how they will be arranged and, if possible, of the room in which they might be placed. Several dozen towering dahlias, chrysanthemums, or gladioli, sans container, will not always be welcome in a hotel room, in the compartment of a train, or aboard ship in anything less than a suite. A potted plant is impractical for a transient. Flowers—corsages or arm bouquets—sent to trains and planes are usually just a burden to the recipient.

It is a very nice thing, however, to send flowers for decoration to a girl who is giving a party. It is considerate to tell her the flowers will be coming so that she won't buy more. And it is important to get them there early on the day of the party. I once knew a charming gentleman with imagination enough to do that. He filled my apartment with flowers the afternoon I was giving a large cocktail party—and sent along his Filipino butler, too, to help out.

A man who is laying siege to a girl's heart does well not to systematize his flower-sending. I knew one man who could be counted on to send two dozen long-stemmed red roses every Saturday, rain or shine. And another who might send a gay red geranium in a simple clay pot or turn up with a single gardenia in a twist of green waxed paper—or a new recording or some fresh catnip for the kitten—one never knew. Any woman could tell in a minute which was the more interesting man.

Lateness

If one is meeting a lady at an appointed place, lateness of five to ten minutes is acceptable, but it is always better manners to be there slightly before a guest's arrival. Greater lateness than this can be acutely embarrassing to a lady, and if some emergency has arisen an explanatory message should be sent, if possible.

Lighting and Offering Cigarettes

If he is seated or standing near her in a social group, a man leans over and holds a light to a woman's cigarette, if she has made the gesture of taking one herself. A thoughtful man, though he be a non-smoker, carries matches for this purpose or even a lighter.

If a man wishes a cigarette himself, he must first offer one to the ladies in his immediate proximity, or at least to the one to whom he is talking. If she doesn't smoke, and he remembers the fact, he needn't make the offer, but if she says, "Not now, thank you," he should offer her a cigarette each time he takes one himself. A man or woman refusing a cigarette should never make a speech about it, although anyone may say, simply, "Thank you, I don't smoke."

Hands Off!

Other than permissible instances (see Manners on the Street), men should avoid touching a woman publicly in a way that might seem offensive. Where he might throw an arm around another man in conversation, he avoids doing this with a woman. He does not poke her in the ribs to make a point—nor does he do this to a man either if he has any sensitivity. Playful gestures of pushing or punching he might do with another man he should never indulge in publicly with his wife let alone show in this way that another woman attracts him sexually. If fondling takes place in public at all it should be discreet, unembarrassing to the most conservative in the group.

Shaking Hands

A handshake is as much a part of personality as the way we walk, and although we may modify and improve a poor handshake if someone calls our attention to it, it will still usually be just like us, assured or timid, warm or cool.

Bad handshakes include the bone crusher—the grip that makes the other person, especially a woman wearing rings, wince. Or a limp, damp handshake that seems to say, "I am not really happy to meet you at all!" Or it may be the kind of straight-arm shake that seems to hold the other person off, or the octopus grip that draws you inexorably toward the shaker, who never seems to want to let go. Then there's the pump handle, or country bumpkin shake, and the very Continental style—reserved for women—which, though not a hand kiss exactly, is cozy and overlong, ending in an intimate little squeeze. Most repulsive of all the practices by men and women (and much worse for men) is the handshake wherein the shaker offers only the tips of his fingers with his hand somewhat elevated.

The good handshake is elbow level, firm and brief. A man, except under business circumstances, does not offer to shake hands with a woman unless she makes the move first. Outdoors, it is no longer necessary for him to keep her waiting awkwardly while he removes his glove, nor need he apologize in this country (but better, abroad) for taking her hand with his glove on. A woman does not remove her glove to shake hands except with the President, head of church, or head of state. Whether he is shaking the hand of a man or a woman, the shaker must look the person he is greeting firmly in the eye and, at least, *look* pleasant, if he doesn't actually smile.

In the breezier Midwest and West men often do not stand on the traditional formality of waiting for a woman to offer to shake hands before offering their own, but in Eastern, conservative circles, they should expect this. Frequently women, upon introduction, merely bow and make no attempt to shake hands. Of course, the tactful woman who had planned to bow and finds a man's outthrust hand in front of her, takes it despite the convention. Here is an exception to the rule. When a man is a host either in his office or his home, he offers his hand in a handshake to all guests, male or female, upon their arrival and upon their depature. As a guest, he always seeks to shake the hand of his host and his hostess upon arrival and upon departure, even when the circumstances are relatively informal.

Hand Kissing

In this country hand kissing is an intimate rather than a social custom. But an American man encountering a French *married* woman, for example, who extends her hand to be kissed will certainly feel foolish if he doesn't know the technique. He should take her fingers lightly in his, palm upward, *bow* slightly over her hand (not lift it to his level), and touch his lips to the back of it, not really implant a kiss. His eyes may salute her, too, and she should look at him with becoming attentiveness. It is an assumption of great—and sexual—intimacy to kiss the palm of the hand, no matter what certain ill-bred foreigners do in taking hand-kissing liberties here for which they would be ostracized at home—all because *we* don't know the rules. It is not correct to kiss the hand of an unmarried woman unless she is very definitely "of a certain age." It is plain silly for an American man in our own social circles to affect hand kissing. On the other hand, he should not stiffly insist on shaking hands in circles where hand kissing is usual—here or abroad.

It is important to note, however, that the traditional hand kiss is a formal gesture. It is never done on the street. As a Frenchman explained to me, "I wouldn't do it in a drug store or at a cocktail party for fifty, and I wouldn't necessarily kiss the hand of even a distinguished woman whom I had known for many years—on the other hand, I just might. It's rather a delicate matter."

A Man's Hat

A man's hat should sit more or less squarely on his head, not be pushed toward the back or tipped too jauntily to the side. It should never distort the natural position of his ears. But the way a man wears his hat is very personal, like his walk, and tells the world quite a lot about his image of himself—"square," dashing or cautiously conservative.

In the corridors and elevators of public buildings a man may keep his hat on his head. In crowded public elevators he is more considerate to keep his hat on, as holding it in front of him will require more space. If he approaches an information desk where a woman is sitting, it is polite of him to touch his hat when asking directions, though he need not remove it until he has actually entered an office. The same gesture—that is, of touching his hat but not removing it—is expected of him if he accidentally jostles a woman in some crowded place. He touches the crown of a soft hat or the brim of a stiff one, such as a derby or a sailor, but he does not actually lift the hat off his head for such encounters. The schoolboy yanking of the fedora brim, instead of gracefully touching the crown as if to lift the hat, has a certain servility about it and should be avoided. A man may well, however, greet another man with a casual salute in which the side of the hand touches, or nearly touches the brim.

In greeting a woman friend in the street or in some public place, once she has bowed first, a man actually lifts his hat from his head, turning his head slightly toward the woman and smiling, if he wishes, but not stopping unless she stops first. He must certainly not stop dead in his tracks and stare after her. If they do stop and talk, he should guide his companion out of the way of traffic after shaking hands—if she has made the first gesture to do so. He may return his hat to his head without apology if they are in the open and the weather is bad. If he has been smoking on the street he usually holds his pipe or cigarette (never a cigar on the street, please) during the course of a conversation, but if he joins a lady and continues to walk with her, he may continue his smoking and it is no longer necessary to apologize. He should never, however, talk with a cigarette or pipe in his mouth.

Conduct in Public Conveyances

A man touches his hat but does not look more than briefly at a woman to whom he gives up his seat. He then stands as far away from her as possible and does not look in her direction. It is certainly not expected that a tired businessman relinquish his seat in a crowded conveyance to any woman who happens to strap-hang over him (but let his conscience be his guide). But decency dictates that he give it up to a tired mother with a young child or a baby in her arms, to a pregnant woman, or to an old or crippled one— or to an old or disabled man. The relaxing of the rules has led to too many men jumping up for pretty girls who can well stand on their own two feet, while women who obviously need seats are left standing. Needless to say, no boy or girl should occupy an unreserved seat on a public conveyance when older women or women with babies in their arms are standing. A boy touches the brim of his hat and moves away from the person, man or woman, to whom he gave his seat. The person to whom the seat has been given says, "Thank you," but never opens a conversation with his or her benefactor.

If a man gives up his seat to a woman accompanied by another man, both men should touch their hats without actually removing them.

Alighting from Conveyances Men sometimes mistakenly allow the women they are accompanying to go first when alighting from various conveyances. This is incorrect as the man should go first in order to assist the woman to alight. Strangers, however, have no responsibility in the matter, letting women alight as best they can, unless it is obvious some difficulty is involved. A man may help a woman with baggage or a small child if no driver or conductor is on hand to do so, but he must be very casual in such offers of assistance, open no conversations, and, once he has helped, not seek to prolong the contact unnecessarily.

Elevators and Escalators In a crowded public elevator a man, even if accompanying a lady, leaves his hat on his head. In an apartment house elevator or residential hotel elevator—unless he is burdened with packages —he probably would remove it when ladies enter. People in a crowded elevator step aside or step out to let those in back exit and, while a man accompanying a woman tries to exit first in order to turn and assist her if necessary, this is not always a very practical solution and expediency must be considered.

In self-service elevators a woman alone pushes her own button, or a man in the elevator may ask others (particularly women) which buttons they wish pushed if he happens to be nearer the board. In a crowded elevator at any time it is not a matter of "ladies first" in getting off. Similarly, in business elevators men do not usually stand aside to let women on unless they are escorting them.

A man escorting a woman stands aside and lets her go first up an escalator unless for some reason he might be needed at the top to assist her off. In descending an escalator, the man usually goes first in case the woman should misstep, or perhaps become dizzy on a long descent.

Summoning or Sharing Taxis If his time allows for the courtesy, a man waiting for a taxi permits a woman waiting in the same place to take the first to stop, but he never offers or asks to share it unless, of course, he has some acquaintance with the woman and they are going in the same direction. If his acquaintance is very slight and the woman is perfectly willing to share the cab (when there is obvious difficulty in getting one), each pays his portion of the fare, with the one getting out first paying the fare up to that point and leaving the usual tip. Under the circumstances, conversation is not expected, and it is never opened by the man.

If her escort summons a cab for a woman whom he is unable to accompany to her destination, he asks the driver what the approximate fare will be and pays him in advance, including the tip. He does not thrust the cab fare at the woman. If the appointment was a business rather than social one, he has no such responsibility, but, on the other hand, if the woman wants a cab, she should ask him to summon one and she should pay her own fare.

A man should never ride part way with a woman in a taxi, whether they have been on a social or business appointment, and leave her with the whole fare, if he alights first. If he has ridden in the cab at all, he should be willing and able to pay the entire fare. For a man to put a woman into a cab she has not requested with the assumption that she has enough money with her to pay for it is to place her, perhaps, in an embarrassing position.

A Man's Bow

A man's bow, a slight, graceful inclination of his body from the waist up, is the grown-up version of the boy's dancing class hand-on-heart one. He must not merely duck his head or, worse, pull in his chin in greeting, like a turtle, or give it a backward jerk, like a wet dog. He must modify to modern usage the courtly, sweeping bow of the knight-errant, and the only way he can master it is to practice it in front of a mirror until he knows how he looks. His bow must then become as much a part of him as his skin and should be so geared as to be suitable for men and women alike. It should be a democratic bow, as gracious to the little girl down the street as to the British Ambassador.

You must return any bow directed to you, whether or not you know the person bowing, or whether or not you have a friendly feeling toward the bower. Sometimes a person bows under the assumption that he knows you— and such a bow you must return, though if you are certain a mistake has been made you do not stop, if you can pretend you haven't seen the other person hesitate, in order to save him or her embarrassment. You never "cut" another individual who greets you publicly, no matter how much you may wish to do so. There are other ways of protecting yourself from unwanted acquaintance without doing that.

It is accepted that a woman bows first, but in this crowded world, today, a woman usually prefers to have the man indicate by his expression that he expects her to bow if she doesn't at the moment recall him—perhaps not in that place or under those circumstances. This is particularly true in the business and professional field, where it is hard to distinguish those we have met or had introduced to us from those we merely recognize because we see them so often in the places we frequent. A suburbanite may not instantly recognize a neighbor if she runs into him on a city bus and may feel very embarrassed later because she has failed to bow after he has looked directly at her but without showing he knows her. In this case he might have avoided the awkwardness by stepping toward her and saying softly, "Good afternoon Mrs. Curtis. I'm Ralph Peterson. We live near you." She then is able to cover her confusion by saying, "Oh, yes. I know!"

Manners on the Street

In America it is customary for a man to walk on the curb side when accompanying a lady on the street, but the rule is not so hard and fast as it used to be. In Europe (except in England where the custom is the same as ours) the man walks on the woman's left, which may, of course, be the inside. When a man is accompanying two ladies he may walk between them or, conservatively, on the outside, moving to the center position to assist both across the street. He does not usually offer his arm to a lady, except to an elderly or infirm one, in the daytime, although he does do so at night or in bad weather. He offers his arm to assist her across the street but does not propel her by the elbow. The only time he does touch her elbow is when he is helping her *up* into a conveyance. If he precedes her—for example, down a train step—he offers her his hand to steady her descent. He may never take *her* arm. A man may offer his arm in the daytime to a woman on a crowded street or in a crowded place in order to keep them together. He may also take her hand and draw her after him through a crowd. He always precedes a lady through a crowd to make a way for her.

Who Holds the Umbrella? A man holds an umbrella over a woman in the rain if they are of relatively equal height. If the man is very tall and the woman very short, obviously the sensible solution is for the woman to hold her own umbrella and the man his—or he walks without protection.

An umbrella should never be a hazard to those nearby. A furled umbrella should be carried at the side or tucked under the arm. When in a public place, an umbrella should be held close to the body. This is particularly important if the umbrella is wet.

An unfurled umbrella should never obscure the vision of the carrier.

Doors A man should always assist a lady in going through a door. He usually approaches the door first, opens it and lets the woman pass through first. However, if it is a very heavy door, it seems sensible for the man to open the door and go through first in order for him to have a more secure hold on it as the woman passes through.

In encountering a revolving door, the man should first stop the door, allow the woman to go in, and then follow her and push the door for both of them. If they are going out into the dark street, though, he should precede her before going into the revolving door and adjusting it so she may enter.

Kissing in Public The Victorian gentleman shook hands gravely with his wife and family if he met them in a public place. But now, if it is usual for us to kiss our relatives or close friends, we do so, in greeting and farewell, in public or not, so long as the gesture is sufficiently brief so as not to attract the attention of passers-by. The senseless public kissing when women meet, particularly those who see each other frequently, should be discouraged. From the way they go about it, it is obvious each is afraid of getting lipstick smeared on her careful make-up or having her hat, if any, knocked awry. But if you feel like kissing out of real affection and pleasure at seeing someone, go ahead, so long as you avoid too public a display of your emotions. Even boys and girls who have no romantic attachment for one another sometimes kiss in public, on occasion, without anyone being embarrassed by their spontaneity. It isn't the kiss, it's the too obvious enjoyment or prolongation of it that should be avoided in public places. Lovemaking should be a private pursuit. Of course, if a man does greet a woman in public with a kiss, he must remove his hat entirely.

Making Apologies In disturbing anyone by passing in front of him or her—if there is no other course—say, "Please excuse me," or "I beg your pardon," or "I'm sorry," not the curt, imperative, "Excuse me," "Pardon," or "Sorry." Where possible, ask permission to pass first—as in a theater row —don't barge past people or over their feet without first giving them a chance to make way. In this country it is usual to pass in a theater row with your back to the people you are passing. In Europe you face them—but this we consider too intimate.

Opening Conversations A gentleman does not open conversations with women he encounters in public places or conveyances unless there is some sound reason for doing so. If a woman leaves her seat in a hotel lobby and forgets her fur piece, a gentleman picks it up and goes after her with it. As he catches up with her, he touches her arm lightly, hands her the forgotten scarf, tips his hat, and turns away immediately, as she thanks him.

Careful about Names Never call out a woman's name in public place, or in conversations use the names of friends, clients, or employers where they may be overheard by strangers. Talking in public places should always be keyed low, though it must never seem too intimate, either, where a woman companion is concerned. A gentleman does nothing to make a lady conspicuous in a public place.

Delicacy in Money Matters

In handing anyone a check, it is always considered more courteous to fold the check so the amount does not show. Such checks might be a salary check to a household employee, a charity contribution handed to a neighborhood solicitor or possibly a gift check handed to someone when a greeting card is not available. The amount given should be a personal matter between you and the person to whom the check is handed.

The Bachelor's Social Problems and Obligations

At first glance, from a feminine standpoint at least, the bachelor seems to have no problems whatsoever. He may be fat, bald, poor, homely, and dull, but someone will corral him as a dinner partner. The bachelor to the desperate hostess seems as rare and wondrous as the cigar store Indian and as worthy of collecting. A hostess without an almost inexhaustible list of fairly presentable bachelors on her list is really up against it.

The superior, highly eligible bachelor, of course, needs but to keep himself in clothes. Just enough to cover him decently, at that. Unlike his unmarried sister, he need give no thought at all to his appearance, as his appearance at all is enough. Everyone knows that a man can always marry even if he reaches 102, is penniless, and has all faculties gone. There is always some woman willing to take a chance on him.

However, bachelors, I am told, really do have problems. One of them told me all hostesses treat all bachelors like supernumeraries. "They invite me to fill in at their dinners at the last minute, never thinking I might like, for once, to bring a girl of my own. I always get stuck with someone's unwanted relative. I am expected to fetch her and take her home. And act exhilarated during the proceedings."

Bachelors tell me, too, that motherly women assume they are lonely, especially over weekends, and invite them to spend such free time in the child-ridden country or suburbs, but neither provide attractive, young, feminine company nor suggest that they bring some along.

It can be very expensive to be a bachelor if the young ladies he escorts insist on going to night clubs and to the to-be-seen-in restaurants. If he says frankly he can't afford such places a girl with any sense will settle for places he can afford. Actually, he may sensibly return to the time-honored custom of calling on a girl at home and leaving the responsibility of feeding her up to her or her parents.

Despite the bachelor's frequent feeling that he is being put upon—true in many cases, I'll admit—he does have one or two obligations. For example, the well-bred, polite man replies promptly to invitations and follows through with a note of thanks to his hostess immediately after having been entertained overnight or longer. When he has been a guest for the first time at someone's home or party, it is thoughtful of him to write a note to the hostess or at least phone her within a week, even though when he left the party he thanked her. (But this courtesy is rarely encountered.)

Frequently, bachelors wonder how they can repay hostesses for repeated hospitality when they themselves have no facilities for entertaining in return. It's a nice gesture to arrive occasionally with a gift—books, candy, nuts, glacéed fruit, or an assortment of cocktail snacks. A theater, opera, or concert invitation to host and hostess is also an excellent way to repay hospitality. Most bachelors can manage cocktail parties.

Bachelor on the Phone   A bachelor answering his home phone merely says, "Hello." If he has a servant or servants, they answer, "Mr. Robinson's *residence*" even though it may be an apartment. Any friends answering for him in his absence merely say, "Hello" as he does. They do not use the phrase a servant would use.

A Few Brief Reminders

Do not—

enter a room before a woman unless it is dark and you wish to make it ready for her

fail to precede a woman down a staircase but follow her up unless she is entering a dark hall or room

seat yourself while women are standing

seat yourself unless asked to do so

speak or bow to a woman before she has given some sign of recognition (There are exceptions, of course. A man passing a very good friend on the street or in some public place, and being sure that she had not seen him, might catch up with her and place his hand lightly on her arm or, if they are on a first-name basis, might call "Mary" softly when within hearing, but never "Miss Thayer!" as no woman wishes to have her name publicly called out.)

smoke without first offering a cigarette to the woman you are accompanying, then not without her permission if she refuses. Don't smoke either so near to a woman as on a train or at a crowded counter that the smoke might annoy her. Do not smoke pipes or cigars in any close quarters without first asking if it will disturb those in your immediate vicinity.

call any but your contemporaries or children by their first names

keep your hat on while talking to a woman (unless asked to replace it) or fail to touch your hat or to lift it when necessary

let a woman carry anything that is too heavy such as a suitcase. You may be more comfortable and so may she if she carries fussy little packages. You are not expected to carry her fur scarf or fur coat for that matter, unless she is ill or infirm.

take a woman's hand, touch her face or body in the course of conversation, nudge her or take her arm except to help her up *into* or *out of* vehicles or, if really necessary, across the street

speak intimately of any girl or woman to other men

fail to pull out a woman's chair for her or fail to serve her or to see that she is served first

speak of repulsive matters at table

criticize another's religion, belittle his race or country, or refer unnecessarily to his color in his presence

enter any place of worship without removing your hat (if its removal is expected) and without speaking in reverent tones

laugh at the mistakes or misfortunes of others

fail to give due respect to a clergyman of any faith, to a woman of any religious order

fail to come to the aid of a woman trying to put on or take off her rubbers or boots.

fail to help a woman tie a shoelace that has come undone.

Chapter 22

THE WELL-DRESSED WOMAN

The best-dressed women I know pay very little attention to the picayune aspects of *fashion,* but they have a sound understanding of *style.*

There are smart women who haven't changed the length of their skirts materially in twenty years, whose hats are always more or less the same shape although they vary in color and material with the seasons. Such women often wear their hair exactly the same way from girlhood on, wearing it short or long as most becomes them, despite current agitations one way or the other. We may envy such women. They have such a sure sense of what is good for them. They save time and temper assembling their wardrobes. Often they are considered among the best-dressed women in the world, although they might not make the famous list because, while they have style, they are superior to mere fashion.

This sureness is, sad to state, not for all of us. Instead, we are pushed hither and yon by the shallow dictates of fashion, often to a degree that is truly wasteful and silly. While fashion, if you can afford it, is fun, it is no fun to feel you must discard an expensive dress you have worn only a few times because it is no longer "high style." Unless you can really afford it, or because of your position must afford it, it is better to avoid all the expensive aspects of radically new fashion ideas until they have been sifted enough for the sound ones to emerge and have a fair existence.

The basic wardrobe has a theme which often carries through from year to year. If you have one winter cloth coat you must consider its color as your guide for all the seasons you wear it. The same is true of the accessories you bought for it. Such long-range planning means that you can buy better quality, for the investment is to be spread over more than one season, as it must be if you are an average woman not engaged in the fashion business—which lives on quick changes.

The Smart Shopper

The well-dressed woman is relaxed about the planning of her wardrobe because she does it well in advance and allows time for necessary shopping. She never waits until she wants to wear an outfit to go shopping for it. At all times she has in her wardrobe something acceptable for all social occasions she is likely to encounter.

I know several clever women who are well dressed on sale merchandise, but they are a distinct exception. The way they do it is to locate the things they want, possibly try them on before they go on sale, and then note, via their charge accounts, prior notice of a public sale. They then buy only those things they know they want. Never, in desperation, do they buy something just because it is cheap. They know that sale merchandise usually has something wrong with it when it has been so marked down. The best bargain is nearly always fresh merchandise.

End of the season clothes buying is rarely satisfactory. If you resort to it, you will seldom find the size and color you really want. You won't get satisfying wear out of what you do select for by next year this bargain will be last year's style. A New York stylist says this is like buying children's clothes too big so they will grow into them, only to find by the time they have grown into them the clothes are worn out.

The well-dressed woman does not buy her wardrobe in a piecemeal fashion but at the beginning of each season gets out all of her clothes, discards those things that take up closet space without being worn for one reason or another, decides what needs remodeling, shortening, lengthening, or other alterations, then, with a picture of what she needs firmly in mind, goes to her favorite stores or couturiers. She does not discard basic standbys of her wardrobe that have given good service and that are becoming. Instead, she integrates them into a wardrobe for the coming season, adding a new belt here, a scarf there, a fresh jacket or costume jewelry to make something old and beloved look new and fresh.

Planning the Basic Wardrobe

Colors The woman who has no basic color scheme in her wardrobe must have considerable money in order to be well dressed. She will need many more accessories than the woman who plans each season's clothes around what is still good and usable in her existing wardrobe, who has accepted the idea that there are certain basic colors becoming to her and to which she should adhere if she wishes to dress well on a controlled dress expenditure.

Basic colors are black, blue, brown (with all its variations), and gray, possibly green and wine. On the first four a good wardrobe can be built, allowing for much variety. The last two, as basic colors, are more limiting, except for a season or two. This doesn't mean that you shouldn't buy a plum or wine suit or a green one, but you should accept the fact that after two seasons such suits are readily recognizable if worn too frequently and that if accessories are bought to match them they will not be easily worn with other colors.

It is the interchangeability of accessories that makes for interesting variety in the wardrobe, not a large number of dresses and suits. Even extravagantly well-dressed women follow the basic plan, sometimes never varying the basic color from season to season.

As a young girl's taste in clothes develops, she will find that she turns again and again to certain accent colors because they make her prettier or happier. Eventually she is guided almost unconsciously to these colors, and variations of them, in choosing, say, a print dress or perhaps flowers for her spring hat. She will have decided early which of the basic colors go best with the accent colors she likes to wear, and she will buy her shoes, bags, belts, coats, and hats in basic colors that will complement or match anything she is likely to buy.

Coats The wise shopper will select a coat in a basic color that complements her wardrobe. Remember, too, that too-fitted coats have a shorter life than looser ones.

For summer wear, a loose-fitting white or natural or even perhaps a yellow or red camel's hair or vicuna coat is a basic that will have years of use if it is bought in a classic style. A black evening wrap is a sound conservative choice, but it is surprising how well one in flame red will go with almost anything a blonde or brunette is likely to wear in the evening if she doesn't go out too much, and especially if she has a dressy fur coat for a change-over.

If only one fur coat or jacket is possible on your budget, let it be a dress coat—preferably three-quarter- or full-length, with a shawl or roll collar. Avoid the high-fashion models. Mink in good quality is a long-term investment, and the new youthfully styled Persian lamb, the new muskrats in mink tones, sheared beaver, and skunk (for a jacket) are among the hardier furs that should have a life of at least five years. Check with your local conservation society before making your choice of furs. When you consider that a good cloth coat is expensive and more likely to show wear or go out of fashion in less time than this, a fur coat might well be a better buy in a cold climate. You consider its cost as amortized over five years or even longer if you are careful.

If you live in a cold climate and in the country, a tough fur sport coat is often a better long-term investment than even the heaviest cloth coat suitable for bad weather—the upkeep is small and it *looks* warm. Among the best for the purpose are mouton (processed lamb), lambskin, sheared or long-haired raccoon, ranch mink styled for sportswear, pony skin (suitable for town, too). And many of the new fake furs are well styled and becoming as well as practical. Even women (and men) who can afford real fur wear them. Almost a uniform for both men and women in smart country places is the trim, windproof, lambskin- or pile-lined belted coat of gabardine or a windproof fabric in basic tones. A well-tailored fabric raincoat makes a good extra topcoat between seasons.

If your budget is limited, beware the spring coat. It is often too high-styled and relatively too expensive for the use you will get from it. If your climate calls for some slight protection in early spring, a fur piece or little cape, jacket or blazer or a variety of handsome wool stoles will have a much longer life and be usable day and evening. A classic camel's hair or cashmere or a good simple, tailored coat and a dual-duty raincoat will be of use spring, summer, and fall for many seasons.

Jewelry Today costume and real jewelry may be worn together if this is done tastefully. The late Helena Rubinstein had a priceless collection of real jewels, yet she wore them with the "frankly fakes" and laughingly boasted that one couldn't tell one from the other. With all the imaginative designing in today's costume jewelry, regardless of price, we have come a long way from the day when "a lady" limited herself to a modest string of pearls or a locket.

Sterling or silver-plated jewelry, even when set with semi-precious stones, is more suitable for casual wear unless it is a prized heirloom or reproduction. In this case it can be worn with informal afternoon or "at home" clothes. When set with rhinestones, clear or colored, it should be worn only for dress-up occasions. This applies to gold or gold-plated jewelry as well.

Silver and gold jewelry if delicately designed can be combined. For example, gold and silver chains as a necklace or belt can liven up a dark dress. I do not suggest, however, combining a silver necklace with a gold bracelet.

Matching sets of jewelry are often given as gifts. These consist of a necklace and earrings with perhaps a bracelet or ring all in the same pattern. These should never be worn at one time. Break it up. Wear the necklace with the ring, or earrings with the bracelet. Along with this you can wear a simple watch and wedding band. Two or three rings, particularly if in all-gold or gold and pearl, can be worn in good taste. This goes for bracelets, too. But then don't wear the necklace.

Costume jewelry watches set in bracelet bands which are usually reproductions of the real thing may be substituted for bracelets. Sport watches are not worn with late-day clothes. By the same token, that is the only time to wear jeweled watches, whether they are real or fake.

Fashion is an ever-changing thing. Whatever it dictates, a good rule to follow is to avoid overdecoration at any time. It is preferable to be understated in dress than to look overdressed, overdecorated. Remember that, unfortunately, it is always the tall, thin young woman the designer has in mind. The fashion pages are proof of this. If you are anything else, beware! There is nothing more pathetic than an older, plump matron trying to look like a teen-ager. Use your full-view mirror objectively, as if you were seeing your image for the first time. When you have finished front and profile, be just as critical from the rear view. If the stranger before is to your liking, you are ready. If not, or you are not sure of the image, start again. The *mirror* is your best friend.

Hats If you are a country dweller your need for hats is usually limited. Instead, you need scarves, colorful bandannas, berets, a hunting cap for your belted sports coat, a duck snap brim, if you're the type, and possibly a good dress hat or two each season that will carry you smartly into town on your occasional sorties into the more sophisticated world of clothes. In winter a becoming fur hat, well made and expensive, to go with your dress coat—to match it or its scarf, collar or muff, or to contrast—say, a mink hat and muff with a black Persian lamb or broadtail—can have long and fashionable life. The original investment is high, but you are sure of getting a hat that can take hard winter weather, stay on your head in a high wind, keep you warm, and be becoming for as many seasons as you will wear your coat. Its style can be varied from time to time by an adroit milliner, but, here, if there ever was one, is a basic hat.

More and more women are going hatless especially in America's increasingly hot summertime. For poolside and at the beaches they wear an amusing collection of inexpensive straws, cotton kerchiefs—especially if they have bleached hair that needs to be protected from the very hot sun. In convertibles, on boats, and whenever the wind is a problem, they keep their hair in place with chiffon scarves, amusing caps and a variety of attractive nets. At church, at weddings and funerals, headcovering may now be very slight: anything from a velvet bow to some little decoration attached to a headband, half veil, or a birdcage veil simple or decorated, but increasingly even this token "hat" wearing has given way in most churches. There are women who love hats and enjoy wearing them, but whether a woman wears a hat or chooses not to is no longer a matter of social import summer or winter. Much depends on the custom of the community and the group with which one travels. (For the wearing of a hat in synagogues and temples see p. 134.)

Suits Every wardrobe needs at least one good wool or tweed tailored suit. It should be cut on classic lines, so that with minor shortenings and lengthenings from season to season it will be good for from five to seven years—or even longer. A cheap dressmaker suit, cut in the latest fashion and color, is an extravagant abomination. A high-style dressy suit is a short-run extravagance, nice only if you can afford it.

The perfect tailored suit can be worn both in town and in the country with a change of accessories. Shoes may be walking pumps for town (not high heels), and ties, brogues, moccasins, or any other solid country shoe out of town. Beware the effect of too light a shoe—in color and heft—with a dark tweed. The feet should be darkly shod, too, to furnish a base for the soundness of the suit, but there are times when fashion does decree the light-colored shoes, perhaps in bone with dark tweeds and wools.

Too-sheer blouses look just as bad as too-delicate shoes with tweeds and heavy wools. A slipover sweater or wool shirt or some heavy fabric with body is best with tweed for the country. In the city a simple, non-sheer tailored blouse, in any suitable matching or contrasting color, with a round collar or a turnover collar on a shirt neckline is most appropriate.

Underthings Underwear should be simple, easily washable, and of excellent quality, devoid of imitation lace, sleazy ribbons, and machine embroidery. Hand-made real silk or fine nylon underwear is lovely, but machine-made underwear of good quality can do nicely, too, in a well-conceived wardrobe.

Nylon, unless it is the perforated knit variety, is hot in summer as perspiration cannot evaporate beneath it readily. Sheer cotton, fresh and crisp (it now can be found with drip-dry qualities) every day, is the coolest during a hot spell. Some of the miracle-fabric combinations, dacron and cotton for example, stay remarkably fresh and launder easily. Fine quality silk, if you can find it—and afford it, well-made, with strong, French seams, costs a lot initially but can last years with careful laundering.

The most comfortable girdle is the two-way stretch, which allows free body movement and which is made at least partly of Lastex or Lycra. Its loose weave permits evaporation of perspiration. Any girdle that pulls you in unnaturally, into some semblance of the currently fashionable figure, is likely to make you so uncomfortable and irritable that any striking effect your new clothes can make is nullified by your tense expression. If you are conscious of your girdle, it's the wrong one for you. The most you should ask of a girdle, anyhow, is that it hold in your stomach somewhat, give a smooth line to your hips, and support your stockings. If it does more than that it is merely displacing fat—pushing it from one spot, say your abdomen, to another, to your thighs or your diaphragm. And don't think the new bulges don't show. Pantyhose support, preferably, can free many women from the "upholstered" look.

Brassières have come a long way. For problem figures there are many solutions—everything from carefully wired bras (the wire should never press on the soft tissues) to completely seamless contrivances that literally create a new figure. No woman need look droopy today, either in a dress or a bathing suit, or flat-chested either. Ready-made clothes fit better if the bust line is something like the ideal—even if this approach to perfection is considerably helped along by uplifts or falsies or both. Heavy, over-large, pendulous (and painful) breasts may be safely reshaped by plastic surgery done by a qualified surgeon. The augmentation of breasts by silicone prosthesis (a silicone bag containing a thick silicone liquid) is also a procedure approved by the American Medical Association. This pliable implant gives a natural look to the breast upon movement.

Dresses Here, considering to what a degree fashion plays a part from season to season, we can talk about line and fabric, color and suitability, rather than what is current at the moment. The basic rules of good grooming don't change.

The first rule is to accept what you are. If you are under five feet five or so—with small bones, the heavy, masculine fabrics and bulkiness of line are never for you, no matter how much they are in style at the moment. You should dress to the lines of your body. If the line from the hip to your knee is relatively short, even if you have moderately long legs and an average waist, you will look overdressed in heavy tweeds, loosely cut clothes, large inverted or box pleats. Any next-to-the-body wools should be very light-weight. Dress coats should be somewhat fitted, or if loose only moderately loose, or you will seem lost in bolts of material.

Most ready-made clothes are designed for the model figure—the long-legged, long-thigh-boned, and long-waisted type who can drape herself in a portiere and look chic. The little woman, or even the medium-height one should choose clothes which have been scaled to her proportions, or she should have her clothes carefully altered to suit her figure, first avoiding too heavy fabrics and too dramatic lines.

On the contrary, the tall, very thin, rangy creature should usually avoid too fine, too closely fitted materials and concentrate on bulky, rough-textured fabrics, loose line, pleats, bold plaids and stripes, contrast in skirt and blouse, tall, even staggering hats, and those handsome, tongued brogues that make the little woman seem rooted to the good earth.

A short or middling woman should strive for continuance of line. A red hat, a white jacket, and a navy skirt will cut her in three pieces. She can have the patriotic effect, if that's what she yearns for, by having jacket and skirt the same blue, by having a white blouse relieve the neckline, and by trimming her blue hat, if she wears one, with a red cockade and carrying a not too large red bag.

Large, obvious accessories—such as huge bags, bulky gloves, big costume jewelry—and bright box jackets, heavy embroidery, enormous hats are only for big women, preferably the big-boned ones. A slender, medium-height woman can get away with one of these things at a time, occasionally, but she should beware of the dumpy effect they can give.

Evening Clothes

Evening clothes for small and medium women should follow the body line and not be of heavy, bulky, or too stiff fabrics unless the wearer is very slender. Chiffon, satin (even heavy slipper satin), crepe, velvet (for the slender), moiré, taffeta are all suitable if simple in line and very restrained in trimming. Trains, panniers, bustles, wide sashes, bordered fabrics, and bouffant effects, when in style, tend to cut height and increase girth, as do all bold, two-or-more-color effects. The tall woman can wear heavier, bolder materials, unless she is heavy. In the latter case darker tones, lighter weight materials, smaller, but not tiny, patterns are more suitable.

Pants dresses and pants suits for evening wear have become very popular and may be worn just about anywhere an evening dress might be worn. I have seen them at the opera, at parties, and in restaurants. Most restaurants now permit them, but I would call first to make sure. Pants dresses are really for all the tall slender figure, and the woman planning on buying only one evening costume would be wiser considering a dress whose style will outlast pants.

Women who wear pants suits, or pants of any kind, should be careful that they are properly tailored to their figures, never too tight for easy movement and always the proper length. If they are worn cuffless, they should be 1¼ inches longer in back than in front, clearing the ground and showing the heels of the shoes.

Except for the very social woman, an evening dress is a luxury worn only a few times during a season. If a new dinner or evening dress is velvet its season is very short indeed—it begins to look outmoded by late December or January when the new Palm Beach prints make their appearance and it is not smartly worn after the weather becomes springlike. Prints are worn now throughout the year in a variety of materials.

The best choice for an evening dress, if it is to have real use, is crepe, chiffon, or the various laces in a becoming color. It can be worn in any season and can be changed by various accessories—a scarf, a bright sash, or colored elbow-or-longer evening gloves in doeskin or cotton doeskin or glacé kid, loosely fitting and with bracelets (but never rings) worn over them. Such gloves are now usually removed during the evening, otherwise the hand of the glove is pushed back over the wrist when one eats or drinks and the gloves should be removed entirely at the dinner table. To be avoided, usually, are embroidered or fancily stitched gloves and any made of weird materials such as silver or gold tissue or, to anticipate wildly, fur fabric. Gloves should be background, not bull's-eye, for a costume—except on an entertainer.

A wise woman never discards an evening or dinner dress that's been becoming to her, no matter how often she's worn it around home. If she goes first class on an ocean liner or cruise ship she will want to dress for dinner most nights, and a well-chosen evening dress five years old can look brand new to people who have never seen it before. Good evening clothes for women approach the uniform and date very slowly.

Dinner or Cocktail Dresses A dinner or cocktail dress for a woman depends very much on the community in which she lives and the activity in which she is going to indulge. In many places, including New York, such a dress today is a cocktail dress of some kind, short and sometimes very very simple with only the fabric differentiating it from a dress than can be worn during the day. Sometimes not even the fabric differs from that of good daytime clothes. The dress may be anything from a jersey top (often black) and a matching wool skirt to a silk or satin dinner suit of street length. It could quite possibly be a simple sheath in an elegant material or a soft wool dress in a jewel color or black. The at-home kind of dinner dresses may be floor length—full or slender, in dark colors or bright, with long sleeves, short ones, or none at all. In sophisticated communities a dinner dress or dinner suit for street and theater wear can well be long if that is fashion's seasonal dictate, but for all practical purposes they usually are street length. If they are elaborate in fabric or treatment, they may in many instances double for simple evening clothes.

Luxury Furs

Sable, mink, ermine, chinchilla are all luxury furs to be treated with respect and worn on appropriate occasions only. While mink is sometimes treated as a sports fur—used as a lining for tweed, for trimming, or combined in some way to give a sports effect—it is essentially, like sable, ermine and chinchilla, a dress fur. While ermine might be worn by a bride in the day-time over her wedding gown, it is essentially an evening fur for wear with evening clothes. The very delicate and expensive chinchilla is also best worn in the evening or if in the daytime only with dressy clothes and simple ones at that, for it is a most decorative fur usually cheapened by too much jewelry, a too-festive hat, a too-glittery gown. Stoles of mink and sable must be chosen with great care—if at all. Scarves, however, in proper proportion, can be worn even by short women who are not particularly slim, but no woman just because she can afford it should load herself down with a large mink coat or a long mink or sable scarf as some kind of status symbol. A successful New York career woman, seen in a mink coat that literally dragged on the ground, replied to the sugges-tion that she have it suitably shortened, "When I pay $10,000 for a mink coat, I'm not cutting anything off!" Many women have this approach to the matter and I deplore it. And better no mink than cheap mink. Imita-tion furs should be frankly fake and handled by good designers.

Fur scarfs are best worn at night over cocktail or evening dresses, even aboard cruise ships and in the tropics, where air-conditioned rooms make wearing them comfortable. In climates that are cold or cold at night in the summer, or where air-conditioning is ubiquitous, they are frequently worn. They are useful over dressy daytime clothes, but inappropriate worn with slacks and obvious sports clothes. Summer cottons or linens, unless designed for cocktail or evening wear, look better topped with wool or self-fabric jackets when extra warmth or a covered-up look is needed.

Chapter 23

THE FASTIDIOUS AND WELL-MANNERED WOMAN

A Practical Beauty Routine

A woman is well-groomed when she looks fresh, neat, clean, and well-pressed. This means a daily, and often twice daily, shower or bath, fresh underwear and stockings or pantyhose daily or twice daily, competent home or professional hairdressing at least once a week, well-manicured hands, no chipped nail polish, runless, wrinkleless stockings or pantyhose and shined or clean foot-supporting shoes at all times, even for housework.

Beauty care must be on a regular schedule, not just when social activities are planned. Excess hair must be kept invisible by one method or another at all times. Feet, pedicured and with toenails painted or not, must be kept soft and attractive, knees and elbows must receive their regular attention with emollients, and eyebrows be kept neat, though not obviously plucked. A good deodorant must be used daily or on recommended schedule.

Hair must be brushed morning and night with a clean, firm brush and combed with a good comb that, like the brush, is frequently cleaned in cold water and ammonia or a solution of baking soda, then warm suds. A dirty comb or brush is as repellent as a bath towel used beyond its initial freshness.

A well-groomed woman is carefully girdled, if necessary, from the time she gets up until she undresses for the night. If she has heavy work to do she protects her hands with rubber gloves or work gloves and uses hand cream. For dusty work she covers her hair with a clean kerchief and she wears clean aprons or smocks to protect her clothes. Her handkerchief is always clean and when not in use, safely on her—not left on chairs or tables around the house or office. Tissues are practical and perfectly acceptable. They should be used once or possibly twice (for the larger ones) and immediately discarded.

The fastidious woman understands how much the appearance of her hair has to do with that of her whole person. If her hair is fine and hard to manage she arranges it many times a day, if necessary, to preserve the required neat look. There are on the market hair sprays that obviate constant hair-rearranging. She has her coiffure styled in the way that stays neat and attractive longest, and she never combs her hair or does her nails in public. Hair curlers *in public* are "uncultured."

House Dresses

It is far better to wear a simple house dress, a clean one daily or a washable knit, if you must do housework, than to wear sweaters and skirts of wool or other dresses or slacks that must be dry-cleaned, unless you make up your mind to send them to the cleaners the minute the first spot appears (and if you are caring for young children, this may mean fresh outer clothes daily, an expensive proposition). There are dark winter cottons and dresses and pants in miracle fibers that are perfect for housework. You can make them in a becoming style, or have them made, with matching work aprons and feel like a well-dressed "lady of the house," no matter what dirty work you're up to.

Changing for Dinner

Every woman should change for dinner, if only into a clean house dress. Dinner is the high point of the day, the forerunner—it is to be hoped—of a free evening. Every little girl should be clean and in fresh clothes, even if they are just clean pajamas and bathrobe for nursery supper, every night, so that the idea of changing for dinner is inculcated at the earliest possible time. Fresh clothes and make-up, even if you are to be alone with the children for a simple meal, are psychologically sound and bring a needed change in the day's pace. Fresh grooming for evening is one of the criteria of gentility.

Make-up

Our idea of what's permissible in make-up has undergone a drastic change in recent years. The young frequently eschew most of it except eye make-up entirely but imagination can run rampant in make-up for day *and* evening.

Lipstick should follow the natural lines of the mouth. Colored or colorless nail polish is more usual than not, although it is attractive to see well-groomed, healthy nails that have merely been buffed.

Mascara, once used only at night by some women, is frequently worn day and night and in a variety of colors, from blue, green, and purple to various shades of brown or black. Heavy black mascara is often hard-looking, but the others, properly applied and of the non-smear variety, can help the appearance very much, especially that of a person with pale lashes as does the correct application of eyeliner. (Beware it *under* the eye. It can make you look hard.) Eyebrows, if they need darkening, should be lightly rubbed with an eyebrow pencil the reverse of the hair growth, then brushed back into place, never drawn on. Eyeliner can be used adroitly with an upward stroke, especially at night, at the far corners of the eyes to give them depth and to elongate them, but the line should be blurred with the finger tips.

Wonderful things can happen with eye shadow, properly chosen for your eyes and appropriately applied. The wrong color, inept application, can make you look dead tired and ten years older. The right color, the correct recommended application for your eyes can give your eye color depth and make your eyes sparkle, as well as seemingly to enlarge the eye and correct certain little defects. Very young teen-agers should eschew it, older ones use it only for special ocasions. It is grown-up stuff.

Rouge, when used (and the older we grow the older it makes us look), is often best *not* on the cheeks. It can bring a glow to some faces if it is lightly applied above the eyelid, shading toward the temples. A little brushed on the vertical planes of the nose bridge, on the chin or the ear lobes can play nice tricks, but experiment is needed.

It is often more youthful to leave all but the nose unpowdered and to allow a little shine in your face. A little eye cream or petroleum jelly on the eyelids will keep a youthful look whether or not eye shadow is used. A good cream or liquid powder base on older skins keeps make-up fresh and minimizes skin defects, lines and shadows. Special make-up sticks properly applied where lines appear—the sides of the mouth, under the eyes—can give a more youthful effect.

A pocket-sized magnifying make-up mirror is a requisite for every woman. It should be consulted regularly.

False Eyelashes False eyelashes now come in a dizzying variety of styles, shapes, textures, and colors. It takes instruction and experimentation to learn how to apply them correctly, how to choose the ones that are best for your eyes. They come now for both upper and lower lids and they may be had in half-lengths, possibly for daytime wear, in light and heavy lashes, long and feathery or short and practically indistinguishable from your own or obviously and fabulously fake. They can be a great ego-builder. I don't like to see them on anyone too young or very much too old, although I knew one very chic old lady who wore them until her eighty-fifth year, the time of her demise, and I couldn't imagine her without them. Obviously heavy theatrical eyelashes on thin, delicate old eyelids can look ridiculous, but fine ones, carefully applied, not obvious can be something else and worth considering.

There are eyelashes for the lower lid, too, which for some may seem like too much trouble but perhaps might be a morale booster for others. False eyelashes have become so generally accepted that their price has fallen to the point where you can now buy them in variety stores. The best are made of real hair, some are of mink hair, some of nylon. There are special cleansers for them and they may be kept clean by having the, preferably surgical, glue delicately picked off with the fingernails after each using. The removal of false eyelashes is very important. They should never be yanked off because they could very well take off some of your own eyelashes, too, so injuring them that they might never regrow. The best way is to moisten a washcloth in hot water, gently apply it to your eyelid then carefully peel off the eyelashes. They may be cleaned then or after they dry. Each set should be put in its own box for protection until the next wearing. One hazard I find in wearing eyelashes is the constant use of surgical glue tends to lighten your own eyelashes, so the use of mascara when you are not wearing the false eyelashes becomes necessary. When you have a clean face at night you may have to endure a rather blank look in time. There are nighttime false eyelashes, but this seems like taking entirely too much trouble. Even the eyelid should have some time in the day to rest from make-up of any kind.

Perfume   It is not wise to select a perfume solely on its fashionableness. It may very well not be for you. A good general rule is that very young women, women with blonde or light hair, find light floral fragrances more suitable than heavy exotic ones. It is a grave error to choose a perfume one likes and wear it from morning until night so it has no mood-changing effect either on yourself or on those around you. One really needs a wardrobe of perfumes and colognes and even of toilet waters. The lighter or simpler ones for ordinary day wear, and the more complex ones for dressy afternoon and evening wear. Such colognes and toilet waters are used at bedtime (and why not).

A woman who chooses one perfume and literally bathes in it, wearing it in all seasons with all clothes, is being banal as well as old-fashioned. She may even get to a point where she doesn't smell it any longer on herself. The same perfume at all times cannot reflect our moods or complement our clothes. Any perfume or cologne we do use we should like, realizing that even some supposedly "good" perfume can change with our individual body chemistry into something offensive or nearly offensive to others. If in doubt, ask your husband or your friends. There is one small, very nice restaurant to which I go frequently but my pleasure in its excellent food is greatly dulled by the fact that the proprietor inundates herself with a well enough known perfume which unfortunately seems to take on a chemical after-odor which one can literally not get out of one's nostrils. As she is a large woman, and the restaurant is small, her use of the perfume constant, you can imagine how this can interfere with the pleasure of dining.

When a new perfume comes out that interests you, try a bit from a tester bottle on your wrist. Even if it smells attractive, don't buy it. Wait an hour. It may change to something you cannot bear, or if you tend to have allergies, it may cause a rash. Or your husband may detest it. Even if you still like it after a little time has passed, buy only a small bottle or possibly buy the cologne first (but this may not be the ultimate test).

Perfume is such an intimate thing, and perfume you don't use is a waste. It should never be bought in large, economy-size bottles, but in small amounts and kept away from bright light. Do not try to "save" it. It must be used or it will deteriorate. It should be applied only to the skin, not to furs or fabrics. Favorite spots are the lobes of the ears, behind the ears (but be sure you have no allergy to it), the hollows of the throat, the bend of the arm, between the breasts, at the wrist. Don't overdo it, but on the other hand don't be too timid. Finally, be sure that it is your kind of perfume, not just something that *everyone* is wearing. In fact that might be a very good reason to avoid a newly introduced perfume.

Sunglasses

A psychologist has said that people in sunglasses always seem to be staring. To some they have an absolutely furtive look, so it is a good idea when being presented to someone to remove your sunglasses as the eye-to-eye contact is important if we are to reveal our personalities to others. For this reason too, and because they do obscure vision, we remove our sunglasses indoors. The person who wears sunglasses, for example, at a night club seems very affected although it is true that some women and some men, also, have the lenses of their sunglasses ground to their own prescription and thus the actual need for glasses is disguised. People who wear sunglasses indoors, however, do tend to make others feel uneasy as their eyes tell us very much about what they are thinking, how they are reacting, and we count on this to read others' expressions.

Cosmetic Defects and Plastic Surgery

Excess Hair Unwanted hair, that which is not routinely removed after the bath, as necessary, should be professionally removed as soon as it appears or, if fine and downy, bleached. Even quite young girls often have excess facial hair which causes them embarrassment, yet it is simple and tolerably painful to have it removed by electrolysis. Unattractive hair lines or too heavy eyebrows can be permanently corrected the same way. The operator should be recommended by the family doctor, as inexpert, careless work can cause infection and scarring.

Hair removal over large areas, such as the legs and thighs, is lengthy and expensive, but, where necessary, certainly feasible and often advisable. It should never be tweezed, especially around the mouth or nose, not only because tweezing injures the roots and may make permanent removal by electrolysis most difficult, but because there is often the possibility of very serious infection. The wax removal of hair is centuries old and, properly done, satisfactory.

Moles and Warts Brown hairy moles, unless they begin to grow or are subject to constant irritation, are harmless and need be removed only if they really constitute a blemish. Often they are considered natural beauty spots. But when they are unattractively placed or in danger of irritation they should be removed by a competent doctor, not by a beauty operator. The commonest method, which is quick and painless, is for the doctor to cauterize them with an electric cautery after first anesthetizing them. After one or more treatments, they turn black and drop off, leaving, usually, an indefinable scar. Hairy moles should never be tweezed, though the hairs around them may be carefully cut off, as needed.

The horny warts that are so familiar on children's hands sometimes appear on those of adults, along with the difficult-to-treat palmar or plantar warts on hands or, in the latter case, the soles of the feet. These warts often disappear without treatment, but sometimes respond to X ray or acid, professionally administered, as does the common child's wart. Many warts do not disappear unless treated with the electric needle or cautery after local anesthesia. Some are treated by cryo-surgery (freezing with liquid nitrogen) or by application of chemicals.

Birthmarks, Malocclusion, Needs for Plastic Surgery There are various kinds of birthmarks, some not in the least disfiguring, and all usually subject to modification by make-up or correction by X ray or plastic surgery. Birthmarked infants now usually receive CO_2 (dry ice) or liquid nitrogen treatments which eliminate or greatly reduce the newly made marks.

Many a girl or even older woman can improve her appearance by having protruding or crooked teeth corrected by orthodonture. Although this is an expensive and lengthy proposition—taking usually two years in most cases—it often pays for itself in lessening decay and delaying of gum troubles, not to mention the increased self-confidence resulting from an often dramatically improved appearance.

Plastic surgery has made fantastic strides as a result of two world wars. Its cosmetic uses are really wonderful. It corrects ugly, pendulous breasts, usually during fairly brief hospitalization, it reduces pendulous arms, lifts faces, all usually with the minimum of trauma, as the surgery is connected with a sound rather than sick organism. Truly disfiguring noses are tailored to one's face, protruding ears are fastened back, bags removed from under the eyes, puffiness from above them, and harelips made whole, all to the benefit of the ego. But this delicate work must be done, of course, by real experts approved by one's own doctor, members of recognized medical and surgical societies. Most of our physical defects need only the correction of our point of view, however, and plastic surgery, dramatic as it is, is not always advisable or really needed.

All surgery has of course potential hazards, physical and mental, and should not be entered into casually.

How to Sit Comfortably and Gracefully

You never see a product of Victorian days sprawled in a chair. Women influenced by the austere etiquette of that time will invariably select the straightest, most uncompromising-looking chair in the room and sit on it, spine straight, hips flush with the back of the seat, feet parallel and flat on the floor. It was taught that a lady never crossed her legs or sat with her stomach protruding.

Today with fewer and fewer uncompromising chairs being manufactured, we are more or less forced to lounge as we sit. Sofas—the modern ones—are often so deep that the only way we can get back support is to boost ourselves onto them with our feet sticking straight out in front of us or curled as gracefully as possible under us. If we have short legs, we have a terrible time with most modern furniture. It throws us into unlovely attitudes, and sometimes we can't get up without help.

On entering a room, try to select a chair or sofa that suits your height and figure. If you are overweight and short you will not look your best on a high spindly chair that leaves your feet dangling and causes you to bulge over the seat. If you get down into one of those modern bucket seats you will need a strong arm to get you out again. If you sit on a sofa with a wide seat you must perch on the edge—which makes both yourself and others uncomfortable—or more or less sink back into the depths until you can be helped up again. Those low, deep-seated chairs, if they do not have bucket seats, are good for you but bad for a long-legged woman, who has no alternative but to stick her feet straight out in front of her or else sit jackknife fashion.

In sitting, be sure to look at the chair before bending your knees. Before your knees bend, the back of your leg should actually come in contact with the chair. When you have received this indication of the chair's position, you should bend your knees, lean forward slightly and go gently into the chair, maintaining careful contact with the floor. This way, if the chair is deep or tippy, you won't be thrown backward or forward.

The deep, wide sofa, modern style, is supposed to accommodate your entire thighs and all or part of your legs. The position of the cushions is an indication of where your spine is supposed to be. But if you are not supple, avoid such Turkish traps. If you do sit on them, don't flop, then squirm back into position. Instead, seat yourself on the edge, then, placing your hands on the sofa, ease yourself back with a lifting motion. A woman is more comfortable on such articles of furniture if she has on an evening-length skirt, slacks, a pants suit, or lounging pajamas. But sometimes it is possible to rearrange the pillows on such a couch so that there is less width and it can be used comfortably by someone who does not wish to lounge.

Crossing the legs is no longer considered masculine in women, but there are good reasons to avoid it as much as possible. First, unless one has slender legs, it creates unattractive bulges on the leg and thigh crossed over. Secondly, when skirts are worn short, crossed legs can be indecent or at least immodest. Thirdly, it is said to encourage varicose veins by interfering with circulation. So if you do cross your legs habitually, change the cross from left to right and from right to left at frequent intervals. It is much more graceful to sit, model-style, with the toe of one foot drawn up to the instep of the other and with the knees close together, if one wishes to vary the position of the feet. Further, crossing the legs *is* informal. It should not be done at the dinner table, which would be very awkward, or when one is sitting on a dais or applying for a job where leg crossing might make either an immodest impression or one that is too casual.

When the legs are crossed attention should not be called to the fact by bouncing the free foot. And skirts should be full enough and long enough not to make the position a burlesque on how a lady should look seated.

When Women Wear Hats

The wearing of hats by women today is for the most part purely a matter of personal preference. Among Christian churches neither the Roman Catholic nor the Protestant Episcopal makes any point about hats any more. In some small communities, in some parishes, individual pastors make an effort to encourage hats on women for divine services, but most have given up, knowing, especially among the young, such recommendations are virtually useless, that many women required to be hatted would in preference stay away from church. This does not mean that any woman or girl who wishes to wear a hat to church, to a wedding or a christening, may not do so. In fact, many women still feel uncomfortable not wearing a hat to church.

In Reform temples there is no effort to get women to wear hats. In Orthodox synagogues there is a regulation that married women must wear some form of headcovering, but this may well be a wig, and a modern one, not a sheitel. Even in Conservative synagogues the matter is governed by the wishes of individual rabbis, many of whom are quite permissive in the matter.

Even at daytime functions at the White House there is more hatlessness than otherwise. The majority of women international travelers go hatless except perhaps on a winter trip to a cold climate where fur hats are attractive and practical. Whereas women wearing hats with street clothes at functions such as meetings, women's lunches, usually kept their hats on throughout, they may today very well choose to remove them especially in the country or suburbs. What women today wear hats in their offices, as used to be *de rigueur* at *Vogue* for editors? This does not mean that a woman who chooses to wear a hat in a group of hatless women needs to conform by checking her hat with her coat. Before six o'clock she may if she wishes, wear it and later, too, if she's still in street dress or if she enjoys wearing some frippery of a cocktail hat. It would certainly seem unusual today to see a woman sitting at a private luncheon table with her hat on unless perhaps she's an older woman lunching with her contemporaries.

Hats when worn to the theater or any other indoor entertainment should, unless they are very close to the head, be removed when the performance starts. Wearers of Afro coiffures or Afro turbans not meant to be removed should seat themselves in back rows if possible as should any woman with an obscuring hat which she wishes to keep on. If a woman is asked to remove her hat by someone having difficulty seeing beyond her, she should do it immediately with murmured apologies. Any woman preferring to keep her hat on when other women are hatless, or have removed their hats, may certainly do so without an apology such as "My hair is a mess!" Those women who feel a hat is part of every daytime costume at least—and there are still some—are entitled to their opinion and should not be made uncomfortable by the hatless ones. Hats still have many uses—to cover one's head in the sun, to keep it warm in winter winds, to give protection perhaps against the rain. A hat is not necessary in most courts (required though, with gloves, still at Buckingham Palace for daytime functions) any more, but you may wear one if you wish. Milliners are still in business although they are wisely diversifying. There will always be women who will find hats very becoming—and others who can't abide them under any circumstance. Both may be comfortable now and fashion dictates from time to time that hats are still "being worn."

Wearing Gloves

The most formal gloves, dress gloves, are white kid in short, medium, or long length. They are worn only with a dressy costume. Considered the utmost in luxury because one wearing is usually all that is possible, they must be discarded at the first sign of soil. White doeskin gloves are less formal, but some people have success with the washable variety.

Formal wedding gowns are usually designed with long sleeves that cover the back of the hand or with three-quarter sleeves so that the bride does not have to wear gloves. If she does wear them, the ring finger has its seams slit and the fabric is turned back so that the wedding ring may be slipped on easily.

Although bracelets are sometimes worn over evening gloves, rings should not be.

White or beige cotton gloves, fresh and attractive, are worn in the spring and summer with clean changes always quickly at hand. Kid, chamois, pigskin as well as wool are worn at other times of the year with wool, of course, least formal but in some styles nevertheless for street wear. Avoid a bad color match in gloves, or a poor choice in a complementary color if you wear colored gloves at all. Gloves in the neutral tones—white, black, beige tones or possibly navy, depending on the costume—are much safer. Navy gloves if worn should match either bag or shoes, not both, but neutral beige need not be matched to either shoes or bag and with a navy costume would look much more attractive than navy gloves. Black, especially kid, gloves, incidentally are considered in the same way that neutral ones are and may be worn with navy or with brown or any bright color, but not preferably in hot weather.

It is not necessarily true that if one goes hatless, one also goes gloveless. While generally speaking, hatlessness is now a matter of choice, most conservatively groomed women do wear their gloves in urban downtown areas with street costume because they do perform the function of keeping the hands clean. But even this is changing and especially among the young in spring and summer there is much glovelessness even in the cities. Gloves should, however, be worn under formal circumstances and especially with evening clothes, at least when one is coming and going.

Gloves have almost disappeared in the suburbs and in the country except for church, for weddings, and similar occasions. Women are following men in this respect; they wear gloves when the weather calls for it and not otherwise. It is a fashion loss. The fastidious woman likes clean white or beige cotton gloves even on the hottest day to keep her hands clean in downtown areas. I can understand her not wearing them in the country or suburbs or small city neighborhoods when she does her daily shopping, however.

I have long noted now that even at the most fashionable charity balls in New York, few women wear gloves for dancing and practically no one turns back the hands of gloves for cocktails. Instead, gloves are taken off and either put in handbags, or more practically, checked with coats or furs. Certainly no escort wants to carry them in his pocket. The result of this changing custom means that many women now go down the receiving line ungloved whereas those receiving under formal circumstances are usually gloved—another sign of changing times. Increasingly, one finds that the women on the receiving line, especially at afternoon formal functions decide to dispense with gloves. If one or two do, then all must. A woman approaching the reception line with her gloves on, keeps them on even though the receiving line may be gloveless as traditionally a woman's gloves are part of her costume. However, the right glove is removed if she is shaking hands with a head of church or state.

Few women now keep their gloves on throughout a church service (they must be removed for communion services) as handling a prayer book or hymnal with gloves on is awkward and uncomfortable. For the same reason, a woman does not keep her gloves on throughout a club or board meeting. A woman speaker might approach the podium with her gloves on, but she would take them off before handling her notes. Gloves, too, look very odd on television and are usually dispensed with entirely. Gloves must always be removed for dining and in taking of refreshment such as hors d'oeuvres. For smoking and for drinking it is preferable to remove the gloves entirely, but at very least to remove the right one or roll it back.

Although glove etiquette has changed very much and continues to change, I still like to see gloves worn to church, while shopping in the inner city, in public places under dress-up circumstances, and for parties and receptions.

For outdoor sporting events gloves are needed only in the winter, with the exception of a golfer's glove.

In court a woman being administered the oath does not remove her gloves if she is wearing them as they are considered part of her costume. When serving on a jury it would certainly be more natural for her to put her gloves in her handbag.

In the summertime it is rare to see gloves in suburban areas except under formal circumstances. In resort areas they are not worn at all. In European cities, even in cosmopolitan Rome, Lisbon, and Madrid, you see few gloves in hot weather. But in Paris, in London and even in New York you do see them still on well-dressed women in the downtown areas. The very young, however, frequently don't bother with them at all.

Choosing gloves for a pants suit can be a problem which is why many women wearing them choose to go ungloved except in winter.

The omission of gloves means a great deal more hand washing and nail cleaning, just as wearing barefoot sandals requires more than once-a-day ablutions if people are not to be offended by dirty feet.

The trend to glovelessness may well reverse itself in seasons of relative fashion elegance.

Entering Taxis and Cars

Low-slung taxis and cars sometimes make it difficult for a woman being accompanied by a man to enter first, especially if her skirt is tight and short, if she is in evening clothes, or for any other reason. It is now perfectly proper for her to say, "Will you please get in first?" The man should do so quickly, seat himself to her left, and perhaps offer his hand as she enters and, if there is no doorman, reach over and close the door. If the car or taxi subsequently pulls up to the curb in a way that doesn't leave the man seated on the curb side, he must excuse himself and cross carefully if he can in front of the woman to assist her out if there is no one else to do this.

On entering a taxi it is perhaps more graceful to put the left foot on the floor first, instead of trying to enter with head and shoulders first. Then, with the foot on the floor, insert the body sideways in a semisitting position. In a very low-slung sports car when the top is down it is possible to seat oneself sideways on the seat, feet on the ground, then, legs together, lift the feet into the car. When the top is up, the preceding directions for taxis work best.

On leaving low-slung cars or taxis, slide along the seat until you can put one or both feet on the ground when the door is opened. Then lower your head and ease out.

Courtesy Toward the Handicapped

There are many ways that people can be handicapped—physically, emotionally, culturally. The best way to understand what the problem is is to relate to the particular handicap. Just a few minutes of covering your eyes so that you cannot see can give rise to anxiety. Putting cotton in your ears so that sounds don't come through clearly will help you understand just a little of the problems of the deaf person. Think how you would feel as a culturally deprived young person, if seemingly unfriendly and unsympathetic people threw complex words and phrases at you which nothing in your background or school experience gave you the ability to understand. What if you didn't even know the language? When you next get into your car, think how it might be if you couldn't drive it without a special steering wheel. Perhaps the only real way of understanding anything is to put oneself in the other's place.

People who are handicapped in any way have problems themselves and often create problems for other people. Physically sound individuals feel a helplessness and sometimes an embarrassment when they are confronted with the reality of a blind person's problems. They may find it very difficult to act normally when they can't make themselves understood to someone who is totally deaf.

We must recognize, of course, that some people with handicaps learn to accept them with exceptional grace and anticipate our awkwardness and help us overcome it by putting us at ease in many ways. I have noticed this particularly in regard to blind people. I remember a blind man picking up a beautiful little statue and saying to me, "Have you seen this? It's lovely, isn't it?" He was "seeing" it with his sensitive fingers. It is very true that handicapped people frequently compensate for their disabilities by developing extra sensitivities normal people may lack. Close your eyes, ask someone to put in your hands an object you haven't seen before and see how well you can describe it—blind.

In recent years much excellent work has been done with the handicapped of all kinds. Banks have found that the deaf can endure the constant clatter of the check-processing machinery perhaps better than most people with normal hearing. The blind can be trained for many technical skills. Sensitive hearing aids are available in many guises. Corrective glasses, eventual sight via television for the blind, are all here or in the believable future as are increasingly realistic prostheses. The people who need these things usually adjust to them well and quickly. As one lovely girl who had had cataracts removed said of her new compensating glasses, "They make everybody look beautiful." Her eyes were indeed as big as saucers. Mr. J. C. Penney, the late great American merchant, at the age of ninety-four, admitting that his eyesight was failing, remarked, "But my *vision* was never better."

The Blind Here is how you can help the blind person.

Offer him your arm. Don't take his. Don't propel him. He can tell from the motion of your body, how to move.

If you go with him to a restaurant, put his hand on the back of the chair. He will know how to seat himself.

Don't hurry him. If he hasn't been to the restaurant before, describe what it looks like—the flowers on the table, people in the room. Don't worry too much about your choice of words. A person may have been blind since birth, and while to you it is perhaps impossible to describe what the color red is, he will have his own conception. Other people have been blind only part of their lives and to them there is memory of the physical world and its superficial appearance.

Treat the blind person like an adult, not like a helpless child. If he wants help in cutting his meat, adding cream or sugar to his coffee, he will ask you. Many blind people take great pride in the fact that they can do these things very well for themselves. If the blind person does seem to want aid, it may help him to know that the vegetables are at the "nine o'clock" or "six o'clock" position on his plate, the meat at "twelve o'clock" or whatever.

Because a blind person can't see you, don't make the mistake of diverting your attention from him during conversation. Treat him as if he were a sighted person. He can tell by the tone of your voice whether you are really attentive to him or not.

Don't startle blind people. Identify yourself when entering a room where a blind person is. Don't come in on little cat feet. Let him know when you are leaving a room. Don't just wander out.

Be careful not to disarrange the furniture from the positions a blind person may have memorized. Don't leave doors ajar or drawers open. Be sure that hallways are clear of clutter. If there is a hazard, tell him about it.

In giving directions, put yourself in his place, directing him left or right according to the way *he* is facing.

If the person has a guide dog, do not treat him the way you would your own dog. He is there for a specific purpose, to be constantly alert to his master's needs. On him, his master's life depends.

Never talk "over the head" of a blind person or make asides that he can't comprehend. Again, put yourself in his place. Say, "We were laughing about Julia's hair. She got caught in the wind and it looks as if she just got out of bed!" Never let him think that you are laughing at *him*.

Treat the blind person always as a fellow human being. He does not want to be reminded of his handicap any more than does any other handicapped person.

The Deaf Studies of adult deaf people indicate that they have a great feeling of alienation and for this reason they may seem aloof, disinterested, when actually through their deafness they feel isolated. It is up to others to make him feel part of the group.

Vision, it seems, is not a sufficient substitute for hearing, for the deaf person must concentrate very hard to find out what people are saying to him. When he looks up to scan the room, it interrupts his concentration on the sound being directed to him and which he may be desperately trying to catch. Even with an efficient hearing aid, deaf persons can be in grave difficulty if too many voices come at them at once, for example, at a cocktail party. They may find chitchat difficult or almost impossible. They must rely on other people in many ways we don't think of immediately—for example, to tell them the telephone is ringing, that someone is at the door.

Again, don't treat a deaf person as if he were a backward child. If he has been deaf a long time, he has developed acute sense of what people really mean no matter what they seem to be saying. He watches your face as well as your lips, so don't turn away. Even with a hearing aid, he needs to *see* what you are saying. Enunciate clearly but in a perfectly normal tone of voice at a normal pace in order to help him. If he has become totally deaf, he must depend on your lips and has been taught to read lips that speak in a normal way, so don't distort the motions of your mouth or shout at him. On the other hand, don't mutter. Sometimes, as with a person who doesn't know your language well, it may be necessary to say a thing in several ways to make yourself understood. Do this without impatience.

A person in whom increasing deafness has become very apparent to his friends and who has finally decided to accept a hearing aid, is helped if they accept it, too, without comment or apology. Nearly everybody is embarrassed at first at having to reveal that he needs such a crutch whether it be dentures, a toupee, a cane to help a faltering step, glasses for distance vision not just for reading. I know a man who was so immeasurably improved in appearance by his glasses that he chose to wear them even when they weren't necessary—and his admiring friends encouraged him to do so. Of course, hearing aids are miraculous these days, some of them almost invisible or so disguised for example in glasses frames that we need never know about them if the wearer doesn't wish to inform us concerning them. In the final analysis acceptance is what is needed here, by the person who must adjust to the disability, by those around him who must adapt themselves to it as well. Courtesy, consideration, and empathy are all called for.

The Snooper

Snooping is such a basic discourtesy that sometimes we assume that everybody knows about it and would not stoop to snooping. Unfortunately this is not true. Anyone who rides a bus or train, or even an airplane, well knows it. If some stranger tries to read your paper over your shoulder, or is fascinated by the book you are reading and it bothers you, close the newspaper or book and look off into space for a few minutes. If, when you resume reading, the over-the-shoulder viewing continues, close the newspaper or book again and look at the person, perhaps with raised eyebrows. This may not work, but in that case change your seat if you can. If *that's* impossible, either abandon your reading or say, "Would you mind? I really don't enjoy anyone reading over my shoulder."

Offensive, too, is the straying of a visitor's eyes to letters or papers on a desk or table, or, of course, the picking up of a personal letter which may inadvertently have been left in view. Even parents should be courteous in avoiding this, although they might say to a son, "You left a letter you received in the kitchen. Is it something you want me to read?"

Family members must feel secure no one is prying, that their individual privacy is respected. That this is assumed by well-bred people is evidenced by the long-standing rule that the word "Personal" should never be placed on a letter going to anyone's home. This notification is suitable only for mail directed to business offices.

A Woman's Manners in the Business World

However competent she may be in business no woman should conduct herself in any but a dignified feminine manner. The brusque, unwomanly woman is anything but attractive in or out of business. And, equally, of course, the overly-feminine, coy female is just as uncomfortable to have around.

One time after I had addressed a directors' meeting the chairman, seeking to be complimentary, said, "We enjoy having her with us. She's just like one of the men." I was not complimented and replied, pleasantly, I hope, "Mr. X, I may be able to meet with you on your own ground professionally, but I am not like one of your own men and have no desire to be." He got the point and from that time on I had my place and the men had theirs. My professional standing was improved, and my femininity politely accepted. Every woman who refuses to become "one of the boys" in business and who insists she be treated as a lady in the human rather than in the drawing room sense does her share toward a better understanding between the sexes.

Business leaders are quite conscious of the fact that women in business are also pulled in the direction of domesticity. Either they are in the marriage market, with few exceptions, or involved in the dual and difficult role of marriage plus a career. Today more married women than single women are in business. They are there to earn their livings or to help out the family income. And most of them have the complete management of their homes as well.

The married woman with a job in and out of the home is working under pressure, even if she is efficient and relatively relaxed about both home and job. There are always the unpredictables to cope with—Johnny's measles, the maid who leaves without notice, her husband's possible transfer to another city. A woman must be superlatively good at her job to give her employer full value while working as well as a head of a family. Her personal problems must be kept carefully in the background, and she must necessarily work more efficiently on her two or more jobs than does the man by her side, who traditionally is always protected against personal encroachments upon his business or professional life.

The woman who runs a job and a home often feels she deserves all kinds of special consideration from both her family and her employer. Of course she never can get it, because, despite the material benefits her job brings, her family is always resentful of mother's time away from home and her employer or associates are necessarily coldly objective about her ability on the job. "Miss Barnes didn't get that report done for Mathewson because her husband's home with the flu" seems an untenable excuse to someone paying well for Miss Barnes's supposedly undivided attention.

It's hard to face this, but no woman can find happiness in putting career above her husband and family. Once she has taken on woman's natural responsibilities, whatever work she undertakes must be done in a way that deprives the family the *least*—for some deprivation they must endure if she works at all. Once encumbered she must have something very special in the way of talent to offer an employer to make hiring her worthwhile, at least while her children are young. Everywhere we meet women who seem to overcome the difficulties of the dual role, but the hard truth is that the average young woman with young children may well fail at making a happy home while working full time.

With this in mind let us go on to the problems of women in business.

Secretarial schools send forth their fresh young graduates well equipped with elementary rules of office etiquette. As a result the American secretary is usually a well-mannered, poised young woman. The girl who has not gone through business school, however, and who comes to a firm even in a junior executive capacity often has much to learn.

Appearance Appearance is of primary importance, of course. Neatness and quietness of apparel are important. Conservative hairdressing, make-up and a minimum of jewelry are equally so. Low-cut dresses, front or back, decorated stockings, exaggerated heels, Mandarin nails, tight sweaters, and overwhelming perfume are taboo. Although it is now acceptable for secretaries and other women personnel to go without stockings in the summer months in some areas, there are delicate questions that arise concerning this practice. Are legs slim and well tanned, are they free of hair and blemishes—varicose veins, broken blood vessels? Such things, like heavy arms, are better covered up in an office despite hotter weather and the permissiveness of fashion. Unfortunately, the girl who sheds her stockings usually sheds her girdle or the support her pantyhose gave her, and the result for some is not always trim and businesslike.

Many offices have found it necessary to make rulings concerning boots, slacks, shorts, and pants suits, in the office. Boots when they are worn should be replaced during working hours with shoes, not scuffs or bedroom slippers. In some office situations slacks of various kinds or pants suits may be practical or even necessary, but the employers' decision in the matter must be accepted without argument.

Promptness Employers are paying for time on the job, so women executives, junior or senior, should get to work promptly and once in the office start the day with a minimum of primping and colloquy in the restroom. Make-up repair should be in private, never at a desk, except in a private office.

Taking Orders One of the most important things a woman in business can learn is to take an order and carry it out. This requires listening to the order without interruption, then asking any necessary questions that may clarify it. The woman who cultivates the ability to listen, to grasp instructions, and to carry them out without chatter or argument gets on in a man's world.

Office Introductions A secretary or typist working at her desk is not expected to rise for an introduction to a woman caller in the office or the boss's wife. A smile and a polite bow are sufficient. If the president of the company, or say, the chairman of the board, should enter the office, and is introduced, then such an employee does rise as this is a business situation and she would need to be attentive to any request that might be made of her.

Praise or Blame An employee, praised for work well done, should accept it with a modest, "Thank you." A reprimand should not be countered with all kinds of excuses. If there is a valid excuse, it should be preceded by, "I am sorry this happened," then the excuse should be brief and to the point, courteously offered.

Smoking and Eating in the Office Most organizations have rules concerning smoking on the job and eating at desks. If smoking is permitted, women should smoke in such a way that it does not interfere with work output. A chain-smoking woman is much more likely to be criticized than is a man with the same habit. Candy eating or coffee drinking, when permitted at a desk, should be done during a work-pause, then wrappers or containers removed from sight.

Telephone Calls Even a well-placed woman executive limits her incoming and outgoing telephone calls. Social chitchat in an office annoys other workers and, even when indulged in by an employer, sets a poor example.

Personal Letter Writing and Callers Personal letters should not be written on office time, unless they are done during lunch hours. Friends and relatives should be strongly discouraged from visiting employees or even top executives. When such a visit does occur it should not be made a general social occasion.

The Woman Executive

A woman who achieves executive status of some kind must guard against being dictatorial at home as well as in the office. Men meet with their frustrations on the way up but not to the same degree, that is, on the ground of sex, as do women. Therefore when a woman does arrive she tends to become irritatingly important. When she gives an order she wants action, and never mind the human element. It is very hard sometimes for a woman to continue to be warm and feminine and kindly once she has received business or professional recognition. Actually, she needs all these qualities more than ever if she is to keep on advancing and if her marital chances or relations are not to be harmed.

The very important woman is a tempting target for a jealous male associate. She rubs him the wrong way, threatens his position, overrides his suggestions, and tramples on his pride. She forgets the feminine graces and cajoleries and tries to meet him man-to-man. This leads to inevitable defeat. If women in business would only remember that they are *women* in business they would meet so much less resistance from men. No amount of professional conditioning will ever overcome the very real fact of femaleness.

Attitude Toward Other Women It has been said many times that women have difficulty as executives because they treat other women business associates as implacable rivals, as if they were competing on a sexual rather than an intellectual level. This does seem to be true, that there is little real solidarity among some women. I believe that with woman's increasing sense of security a more generous attitude toward women co-workers has started to come too. At any rate, it helps to be conscious of the competitive feeling and thus make an effort to modify it. (See "A Man's Manners in the Business World.")

When the Woman Pays the Bill Occasionally in business it is necessary for a woman executive to pay entertainment or other bills for men clients or to take their share of checks when lunching with men business associates. In all cases (for the sake of the man) a woman tries to avoid a public display of her financial arrangements. Onlookers cannot know the circumstances, and men are easily embarrassed by a career woman's usurpation of their traditional role. Even if she is lunching a junior executive, it is courteous to allow him the dignity of seeming to pay the bill.

The arrangements for the preservation of male pride can be made in several ways. With an important client, whom the firm wishes to entertain but who would certainly not permit a woman to pay the bill, the obvious solution is the selection of a restaurant where the firm maintains a charge account for entertainment purposes. Even the tip is included in the bill, and the woman signs the check on the way out. She may ask the room waiter in advance that the check not be presented at the table but be left for her at the desk. When such tact is not necessary and the co-worker or client are on easy terms, the woman can quietly say to the waiter when it is time for the check to be presented, "Please give me the check." Having a credit card is an easy solution for the woman executive. In this case the bill is signed and even the tip can be added to the check. When women executives entertain other women for business reasons, the woman or women being entertained should learn to accept such entertainment gracefully and not squabble over the check if it has been made clear that one is definitely the hostess.

The Single Woman

How to Make Friends in a Big City Men have less trouble than women adjusting socially to big city life because, presumably, they are aggressive, while women are supposedly passive in such contacts. A girl living in, say, New York, after being brought up in a small town, can grow very lonely, waiting until she is asked out by the all-too-few unattached males she may meet in her office or elsewhere. A young man need not be even passably attractive to have as much social life as he wishes in such a metropolitan center. The competition for him, at least as an escort, is often keen, even if his prospects are meager and his spending money minuscule.

The girl who can surround herself with some sort of home background has the best chance of a full social life in a big city. Entertainment outside of the home is so expensive that a girl who has a home to which a man may come and be entertained has a better chance than the siren who lives in a hotel room and must be taken out continuously to meals, movies, theaters and night clubs. Such a girl costs too much and is too wearing. And, even if she is really interested in a man, she never gets to know him as she should in such an artificial atmosphere. The less beauteous girl with a stove and fireplace of her own has the advantage.

Take Precautions Urban communities in particular are growing increasingly dangerous for single women—for any woman. A woman living alone should never post her name and address in a public place or list her first name, only the initial, in the phone book or on the apartment directory. If possible, she should choose an apartment with a doorman or one where all visitors must be announced. Escorts should call for her if possible and, on taking her home, escort her to her own door, not merely leave her in the lobby of her apartment building. There is always possible danger in a young woman's speaking to strange men and where it is occasionally done, the acquaintanceship should proceed on a very conservative basis and any future meeting preferably made when others are present. Blind dates, especially in cities where it is difficult to check social credentials, are chancy, to say the least.

Should a Girl Live Alone? Living alone in a big city is for most girls who try it a disillusioning experience. Even if they are able to find and furnish—and support—attractive apartments all by themselves, they find that the drawbacks to living alone are, among other things, loneliness, inertia concerning household chores, and lack of at least implied protection.

A girl with her own apartment in a city is not insured against loneliness. Often she tries to be out every night or to have guests to combat loneliness. If she does stay home alone she listens for the telephone, and if it doesn't ring she feels abandoned. If she takes advantage of her ability to act as a hostess and invites a young man home to dinner she runs the risk of not being able to keep the rest of the evening on the easy, pleasant basis she desired. Too many young men, finding themselves in a girl's bachelor apartment without the steadying presence of other guests, imagine that more than conversation is expected of them.

Teamwork The girl who has a good time in New York or other large cities is the girl who lives co-operatively. She finds one or more other congenial girls (preferably not more than two) approximately her own age, and together they rent a furnished or unfurnished apartment, which they run on the basis of their individual capabilities.

As often as they wish, such girls cook at home, thus keeping down expenses and eating better meals. They have more social life with men, because they can freely invite attractive ones they meet to come to their home without fear of being misunderstood, as there can always be a "roommate" at least in the background to dispel any mistaken ideas. And, on nights when there are no dates or prospects of them, the household tasks can be done cooperatively in short order and can be relaxing rather than annoying. Too, by pooling their expense money such girls can usually afford a little outside help for heavy cleaning.

Such living can prepare girls, who have always had everything done for them at home, for future homes of their own if they go about it in the right way. They can learn what it is to serve dinner guests, to manage a budget, pay household bills, and meet regular obligations such as the rent. They learn, too, how to divide the labor so that no one person does most of it.

Choosing a Roommate When a girl decides to share an apartment with another girl she should try to find someone from more or less the same background as her own, preferably a long-standing friend whose crotchets and personality she knows all about. They should have approximately the same income and be able to share the financial responsibilities of the venture on an even basis. If the income of one is considerably larger than that of the other, the living should be scaled to the lower of the two incomes so there never need be the feeling that one girl has more right to the place than the other.

If possible, the apartment should have at least two rooms, with the bath accessible to both the living room and the bedroom. A floor plan that requires anyone entering the bath to go through the bedroom is poor for sharing, as the girls' social activities are not always simultaneous A girl who must sit up when she's sleepy because her roommate is entertaining is not going to enjoy such an arrangement for long—especially if she has fewer dates than her friend.

Finances In such a shared apartment there is usually one girl who is better at money matters than the other, or who has more time for these details. A budget must be worked out, and a part of each salary turned over each week to the treasurer for necessary disbursement. One girl should never carry the other, but all debts should be settled with alacrity if the working arrangement is to prosper. The most important obligation, the rent, must be paid promptly each month and receipts kept if cash has been paid. Food bills for shared meals are evenly divided, but each girl takes care of her own extra entertainment costs.

The lease for such an apartment is better taken out in the names of the co-operating lessees, where the landlord is willing. But where he prefers one signee, the other tenant or tenants should hold a brief written agreement on the length of their shared tenancy and the terms of it from the holder of the lease. It is also well to have duplicate or triplicate lists of all the belongings and effects in the apartment that are being shared, with a notation as to ownership, whether joint if they were bought out of pooled funds—and what the cost was—or individual. Such a businesslike view right at the beginning helps to keep the arrangement on an even keel, and, in the event one girl decides to leave for one reason or another, it makes her responsibilities clear.

Such a shared home needs house rules, too, drawn up by the participants. Perhaps the girls will agree to let each have one set night to have the apartment alone without the other or others. Maybe one night will be put aside as a "no visitors" night, when hair can be set, bureau drawers straightened, and the housework finished up. Certainly essential tasks must be assigned—the cooking, the bedmaking, dusting, and cleaning, laundry, shopping, and bookkeeping, the division of the chores dependent on the amount of time each girl can give and her abilities.

A little box by the telephone should remind visitors to pay for their own calls and encourage the girls to deposit their tolls for out-of-town calls right away or at least make a record of who made them. Only the base rate for the telephone should be equally shared by all.

If all the rules of courtesy are followed, such living can be most congenial. It can lead to a full and happy social life, with good possibility of marriage, even in a crowded unfriendly city where the competition for the eligible males is much fiercer than it would be in the small town that seemed to offer little in the way of career or romance.

Does Becoming a "Joiner" Help? Suppose for some reason, perhaps her inability to find a congenial girl with whom to share a home, a newcomer to a large city must live in a girls' club, a boardinghouse, or a small hotel. What are her chances of having a pleasant social life? Unless she makes some definite and continuing effort to meet people, even a pretty, attractive girl may be lonely during her free hours.

Before going to a place like New York, Washington, or Chicago to work, young people—men and women—should attempt to find someone who can give them social introductions in their new home. It makes much difference if there is someone to take a stranger in hand and see that he or she meets others of the same age and background. If there is at least one real home where such a stranger may go occasionally, it can help him find his own niche among new friends.

If there is no one at all to whom one may go in a big city for advice and companionship outside of working hours, the next best thing is to find one or two groups one can join. But to become a "joiner" in the sense of mapping out a continuous plan of activity in an effort to escape loneliness may mean that with so much to do a newcomer really enjoys nothing, gets to know no one well enough in her rush from club to club and classroom to classroom.

A church with a real and youthful social life can bring sound interests, as the stranger is always welcome and can quickly be made to feel at home in familiar activities. A hobby group is a sure way to find congenial friends. Adult education courses keep free hours busy and productive and may lead to new skills and friends. A college club—any group that brings something of a former background into the new life in the city—helps orientation.

Often an out-of-towner feels a little awkward at first in a metropolis. After a while she will realize that a certain polish may be acquired. Anything that makes her feel she "doesn't belong" can usually be corrected, from a broad regional accent (helped by diction lessons) to ungainliness on the dance floor or an unsureness about clothes. The "Ys" abound with all kinds of self-improvement courses for people who suffer from feelings of inadequacy one way or the other. Such courses are of great help, especially in big cities where on all sides others press for advantage.

Big Cities Are Stimulating Once the effort to break in socially is made, the newcomer finds most big cities culturally stimulating and financially rewarding, as small towns can rarely be. A city like New York is full of people expressing or trying to express a wide variety of talents,

talents for which there may have been no market at home. One needs only to make oneself a small part of the profession or business that appeals to find satisfaction and a feeling of "belonging," even in a city of nearly eight million. And once this feeling is achieved, the stranger is one no longer but able to realize that New York, especially, is made up of millions like himself who came from other places in the world. One may walk for miles in the city before finding a true "born New Yorker," and it is rare to number many among one's friends.

Chapter 24

WHAT'S WHAT IN VARIOUS SPORTS

Customs and Taboos

Sportsmen have very stiff notions of what constitutes a gentleman, and unless you know these shibboleths you may be guilty, in your enthusiasm over a sport new to you, of offending, of being classified as a boor rather than, more fairly, as a mere ignoramus. Sportsmen are notably intolerant about non-conformist behavior.

In playing all games and pursuing all sports in a team or group you must abide by the accepted rules—unless, of course, the majority of players or participators agrees to relax the rules in some way or adopt other ones pro tem. For example (to the horror of experts), some people on their own badminton courts prefer to score in the manner of ping-pong rather than use the regulation scoring as set down by the American Badminton Association. They do this because they think the ping-pong scoring speeds up the game and is easier to keep track of for both spectators and players. But on neighbors' courts where the usual rules are well-established, they follow them and allow their host the privilege of keeping the more complicated score. To be safe, before plunging into any sports activity find out beforehand from a friend and active participant what the accepted practices and traditions are in the group you're planning to join.

Golf

Golf courses fall into two categories, the private club to which one must be invited by a member and the public course open to all upon payment of a fixed green fee and caddy fee. On both public and private courses the caddy fee varies greatly as does the greens fee.

At a private club guests usually pay their own greens fee and caddy fee. At the "nineteenth hole" (the bar) it is usual among men to throw dice to see who is going to pay for a round of drinks, but almost as frequently each player picks up his own check.

At the first tee there is no special order of precedence except that a guest or guests would be asked to tee off first and a woman or older player would usually be given the first drive. Another method is for each player to toss his ball over his shoulder with the one that goes farthest determining the first player. Tossing a coin is another popular way to settle the matter. Thereafter, the winner tees off first. Sometimes on crowded courses, when eight or ten players arrive at the first tee at once, there is a ball slide into which players are expected to place their first ball as they step onto the green. When their ball emerges it is their turn to tee off. This system was devised to obviate dissension at the first tee. A player who is unaware that it is used, however, and who does not put his ball in the slide may miss out on the play entirely or at least be delayed.

Two players supposedly take precedence over a foursome, which must necessarily play much more slowly. It is good golf manners for a foursome to allow a twosome to play through. On the other hand, a twosome that is playing a leisurely game always permits a businesslike foursome to play through. Any other combination of players, from the lone golfer to the "gang"—over four—must allow the twosome or the foursome precedence. On many courses, especially public ones, only twosomes or foursomes are permitted on crowded weekends.

Even non-golfers should know the rules concerning quiet as a player tees off. Other players should stand still—not even make practice swings with their clubs nor speak to their caddies as another player addresses the ball. When a ball is lost other players in the group help look for it, but the search is never drawn out to such an extent as to hold up the play—a few minutes is enough. If he wishes, a player who has lost a ball may go on to the next hole, leaving his caddy to make a further search.

Great care must be taken not to tee off when others are in line with what a player hopes will be the flight of the ball and certainly never until the players ahead have each had their second strokes. The warning "fore" may not carry sufficiently against even a light wind. It should be used infrequently. Instead, a player should wait until golfers immediately ahead are well out of range.

Clothes for Men On warm days in spring, summer, and fall, the most comfortable attire is Bermuda shorts and a loose knit sport shirt—more often in one of the synthetic fabrics. In winter a regular tucked-in sports shirt with a light pullover is the conservative choice with slacks in pleasant weather. In cold weather a windbreaker or leather jacket is worn over a sports shirt with or without the addition of a pull-over. Socks, summer and winter, are best in wool—argyle, white or bright colors such as canary. Hats are always of the sports type, a snap-brim, unbound felt, a rough straw, a cap or a turned down duck hat such as is worn in sailing. Shoes should be regular cleated golf shoes.

A golfer wears one glove—on his left hand if he is right-handed and on the right if left-handed. It is always leather, especially made for golf of very, very thin leather in brown, black, cream, white, or beige.

Clothes for Women Bermuda shorts or shorts with the wrap-around skirt front (short shorts are permitted in many clubs now), colorful man-tailored shirts and bright matching knee-length socks are seen on links everywhere.

Older women who feel that they are not at their best in shorts may prefer the classic shirtwaist dress for golf. This may be of cotton, linen, or one of the synthetic fabrics, loosely cut for swing action, pleated at the waist in back and fastening down the front. The regulation golf glove for women comes in all the usual colors plus red, pale blue, yellow, etc.

The short knee-length skirts or Bermuda shorts or pants or pants suits are fine for spectators. Culottes for players or spectators, unless they are meticulously tailored and worn by a slim-hipped woman, can be an unfortunate choice.

In cold weather a loose pullover sweater worn with a shirt and a comfortably cut wool or flannel skirt is best. A loose tweed jacket or a windbreaker may be worn on top if you choose to play when it's *that* cold. Good English lisle hose may replace the usual anklets or be worn with them. Thin wool stockings are a good idea. The reliable, soft round felt hat in a neutral color or brown is helpful on a windy day.

Any club, club-head cover, or other equipment found on the golf course should be carried back to the clubhouse and turned in to the pro or the caddy master.

Tennis and Badminton

A sociologist—or a psychiatrist—could glean considerable information about any tennis player's personality defects by watching his behavior on the tennis court. There is something about this game played in its sun-baked, circumscribed area with its inevitable gallery that spotlights character more quickly than any other except badminton. In these games each man stands revealed, even in a game of mixed doubles. He has plenty of room in which to throw a tantrum—or his racket—lots of space in which to yell and hurl taunts at his opponent, many opportunities to cheat when there is no referee and his word as a sportsman and gentleman decides whether ball or shuttlecock are "in" or "out." There is sufficient opportunity for watchers to observe the apologist whose "bum serve" is loudly explained by all kinds of things except his lack of technical skill at the game. We see here the man whose anxiety about himself carries over to the court—a man who doesn't dare to lose a game and who, if he does come out the loser at the end of the set, derives none of the relaxation the game should supply, but only adds to his inner anger and aggressions.

People cannot be taught by rules alone how to behave in any game so that others will not be disturbed and inconvenienced by their actions. This is because what a man *is,* he is most likely to express in the way he plays, and no list of rules is going to change the unconscious attitude he brings to the game. But if he can't or won't get in tune with the rules, social pressure usually effects his compliance with them. No man can play tennis, badminton, or table tennis by *himself* as he can play golf, hunt rabbits, or shoot clay pigeons. He needs at least one opponent, and if he is consistently objectionable as a player he finds everyone worthy of his mettle either hostilely unwilling to play with him or else having other commitments— often suspiciously far into the future. When this goes on too long an intelligent man finds out what's wrong with himself, the boorish one quits the game —and then belittles it—and the stupid or unyielding one resorts to playing with the professionals—at a fee—or with any members of his family unable to say him nay.

Here, then, are the rules of the tennis or badminton court, and many apply equally well to many other sports—even the British cricket. In fact, the phrase "it isn't cricket" has come to epitomize all things unfair and uncomfortable to others in social, political, business, and even amorous behavior.

1. Come decently attired to the court, in clean, acceptable clothes appropriate to the game.

2. If no court is immediately available, await your turn courteously, making no attempt to disturb a play setup until a set has been completed by those in possession of the court and there is ample indication that a determining set is not to follow. If a set of singles has just been played, any suggestion that the court be given over to doubles must come from the players already on the court, although on a crowded day any considerate players would make such a suggestion, even if the club rules didn't require fair sharing of the courts on Saturdays, Sundays, and holidays.

3. Inexperienced players should not demand to share court space with crack players on crowded days, but should team up with those in their own class. If weekends and holidays are the only times they can practice or learn the game, they should try to occupy the courts either very early or late or at any time when others more proficient are not waiting for them. But fast, able players, in turn, should be satisfied with fewer sets on busy days. If they play more than three, they should break up the foursome to include some fresh player or players

4. Each court is an island. Keep your activities and remarks and conversation within it, so as not to disturb other players or make a boiler factory of the clubhouse porch or the side lines. Spectators, presumably duespayers too, have the right to watch the game without being jolted by loud hoots of triumph, yells of despair, swearing, shouted imprecations, racket throwing, or other unseemly exhibitionism.

5. Toss rackets for first serve, or choose any other method of deciding pleasantly who should start the service, but don't assume the service yourself, unless asked to do so. A first serve, unless you know your opponent expects and can meet vigorous competition from the start, should be a moderate or slow one to indicate that this is a pleasurable game of give-and-take you are initiating, not a would-be one-sided slaughter.

6. If the sun will be in the eyes of a player or players on one side of the net, you may offer to take the sunny side in the initial game yourself, especially if you have invited your opponent to play, or determine the side each takes by toss.

7. Don't alibi your game in any way. Play as well as you can, except in a friendly game against a decidedly unworthy opponent and then if you do relax out of fellowship and to make the game a little more interesting and encouraging for him—or her—don't be offensively obvious about it. If you let anyone beat you—or nearly win—never say so. Don't take the wind out of the other fellow's sails. Leading on a coming player this way may develop him into exhilarating competition later on, to your own advantage.

8. Be a cheerful loser and a modest winner. Don't crow over your triumphs or sulk or exhibit anger over your defeats. If you are constantly defeated and feel angry or discouraged about it to such a degree that the game is not a pleasure to you or your opponents, take more lessons, play only with other players in your class or change your game to something else that suits you better physically or emotionally than this exacting, competitive game. Insisting on playing a game for which, after a fair amount of time, you show no natural aptitude is frustrating to you and annoying to all but the most complacent opponents.

9. While spectators have their rights, they also are subject to rules guaranteeing the rights of the players. Spectators should make no comments, critical or otherwise, from the side lines during the course of play. They must not distract the players by invading the court for any reason or dodging past the back line while play is in progress. They should not lean on the posts, climb on the fence, leave the gate open, or touch the net. They should not throw anything into a court or behind it—such as a burned-out cigarette —as this can cause a player to fall or miss a shot. Drunkenness is no more desirable on a club porch than it is on the court itself. The function of a tennis club is to provide playing opportunities for members who expect to play tennis. Any spectators there happen to be, from small boys to old gaffers, must respect the players' right to play without interference or distraction from the gallery.

10. When you ask your opponent to keep the score you have no alternative but to accept his count. If you know he has colored the scoring to favor his own side, you are privileged not to play with him again or, at least, not to permit him to keep score again, but don't make an issue of it publicly or even privately.

11. At game and set, thank your opponents or opponent. You needn't apologize for winning nor explain why you lost—a matter that is usually obvious enough. It's not necessary, Wimbledon style, to leap over the net to show the winner how magnanimous you feel about being trounced. In fact, easy give—and especially—easy take seems the essence of good sportsmanship in social games. Even where stiff competition for the sake of a cup or other honor is involved the same rules of courtesy hold sway.

Clothes for Men White clothes are so traditional on the tennis court that it is obvious that there must be a reason for them. Dark colors, even in lightweight cotton or other fabrics, under a beating sun would absorb the rays, while white deflects them. That is why white clothing is worn in the tropics. The extravagant white flannel trousers that used to be *de rigueur* for the well-dressed tennist are certainly dreadfully hot, despite their lack of color, but that is because of the weave rather than the weight of the material—and the same may be said of the white ducks that have always been considered correct. Pale yellow and pale blue, however, are now being allowed on the courts in competition play by the U. S. Lawn Tennis Association.

Most men today prefer the knee-length English or even quite short tennis shorts, in white or sand, to the more conservative flannels or ducks for both badminton and tennis. They are comfortable and look good on most men. They should not be too short. An initial investment in shorts of excellent quality, properly tailored will mean a long-run saving. In buying them, look for durable, closely woven material, slide fasteners, reinforced seams, the absence of metal on fabric belts or half-belts, and a hem that is generous enough so that it won't fray out at the first hard laundering. Don't try to substitute white or tan bathing shorts for tennis shorts. The shorts are worn with white wool anklets, with or without a cuff. Wool socks, as a matter of fact, are superior at all times of the year to rayon, cotton, or nylon for any active wear, because they allow for the evaporation of perspiration. (Some men even wear very sheer black wool evening socks, ribbed or plain, for dancing, for this reason.)

Any comfortable white, light yellow, or light blue sports shirt or a polo shirt permitting full play in the shoulders and arms is worn on the court for the warm-up, if the player wishes, or to be thrown over his shoulders, or donned, when he comes off the court. White, pale blue, or pale yellow (to match costumes) wool socks are preferred, even in the hottest weather, as affording the best protection to the feet against the pounding on the court.

The tennis hat is usually soft white duck, sometimes with a green underbrim to protect the eyes from glare. Such hats are usually washable, although to see those worn by most men, you wouldn't think so. Tennis shoes are the flat, rubber-soled, heelless ones developed originally for the game. Wearing any other type of shoe, rubber-soled or not, generally calls forth a severe reprimand from the grounds committee and removal of the offender from the court.

Lawn tennis courts should not be torn up by leather or composition soles, either, but rubber-soled shoes or other types than the tennis shoe are often worn for badminton.

Clothes for Women If she's playing in competition a woman wears white, pale yellow, or pale blue for tennis or badminton to keep from distracting other players on adjoining courts with bright colors. She may wear shorts—knee-length or above—loosely fitted for real playing comfort. Really classic is the short-skirted, pleated tennis dress in white, pale yellow, or pale blue cotton piqué or broadcloth, linen or sharkskin, knee-length or shorter, round or slightly V-necked, sleeveless or short-sleeved. To keep the hair and sun out of her eyes she wears a white duck or flannel green-lined visor or tennis cap, or just a clean, white linen sports handkerchief tied in a bandeau, or a simple ribbon. Shoes must be white, flat-heeled with rubber soles. Regular tennis shoes—sneakers—are best with white or the new-regulation pale yellow, or pale blue anklets to match the rest of the costume. Socks are preferably light wool for comfort, but with one-inch leeway in the toes to allow for foot expansion during play. For badminton there are special shoes, which provide a little more support than sneakers. Hair flying loose, clanking jewelry, uncomfortable shoes or socks, shorts that are too tight can all ruin anyone's game.

Yachting and Sailing

The word "yacht" comes from the Dutch verb *jagen,* to hunt. Essentially a yacht is a pleasure craft, a light sailing vessel meant for racing, but the term can refer to any pleasure craft that is not propelled by oars, whether it derives its power from the wind or from steam or electric power.

There are numerous yacht classes, some distinguished by the class mark on the mainsail—the Star, International, Atlantic, Lightning, all racing classes—several by meters and others by their length. Yachts of the same class usually race together or, if they are unevenly matched, they are raced on a handicap basis.

Anything over one hundred feet is technically a ship. All sailboats—with the exception of skiffs (light rowing or skulling boats)—are correctly called yachts, but seasoned yachtsmen casually refer to anything under sail as a "boat" and to themselves as "sailors." To refer to one's own sailboat, whatever its size, as a yacht, seems pretentious. Technically, a boat is actually a dinghy, a launch, tender, rowboat or skiff, none of which is in the yachting, or racing class.

A fanatical sailor spurns any auxiliary power in a sailboat, preferring to get in and out of harbors and yacht basins under sail and take his chances on a homeward-bound wind. When yachtsmen become fathers and there are children aboard to consider, this fanaticism is often tempered for a time and a "kicker" is added to the gear—at least until the children can be taught to sail.

The past few years have seen an enormous rise in boat ownership and it seems that every lake, river, and inland waterway is gaily dotted with all manner of craft. Newcomers to the pleasures of sailing should be careful to observe all the rules of safety. These are clearly set forth, along with other pertinent information, in an excellent booklet called the United States Coast Guard Recreational Boating Guide, Coast Guard publication 340. You can get a copy by writing to the United States Government Printing

Office, Division of Public Documents, Washington, D.C. 20402. Price is 60 cents per copy.

Being a Good Sailor Because the space aboard a boat is circumscribed, the rule of the sea concerning neatness must be observed by guests. Everything must be shipshape. No one should come aboard except on a large yacht with a stiff suitcase. Stowable gear is always canvas. Guests on any owner-sailed boat should be prepared either to lend a hand or to find a way to keep out of the way, especially at those crucial times when the sails are being hoisted or lowered, the course is being changed, or a jib is being broken out. Guests who have never been on the sea before can learn to do the small jobs such as pumping out the bilge or polishing the bright work.

Smoking aboard a small boat must be limited to the times when the boat is on its course—that is, for working hands. Cigarettes must not be thrown on the decks and stamped out or tossed over on the windward side, which would cause the sparks to fly back aboard. Garbage, too, must never be disposed of to windward or, of course, in a yacht basin or harbor.

On large yachts with a paid hand and crew, guests do not fraternize. Their relations with the crew are formal, and they call the men by their last names. A professional captain is called by his title and is treated with respect due his highly technical calling. On a very large yacht the stewards who attend the cabins and saloon are called either by their last names or simply "steward."

No one, needless to say, should dive overboard except from the stern or sides of the boat and then only with the captain's permission and only, too, when there is a tow line out the back if the boat is under sail. At all times the captain is responsible for the safety of the passengers.

Clothes on Board What one wears aboard depends on the size of the yacht and where it is tied up.

A man invited to lunch or dine aboard a large yacht (with a saloon and cabins) tied up at a city club would wear just what he would wear in town. If he is to join the same yacht at an out-of-town mooring he would wear suitable country clothes and rubber- or rope-soled shoes and some kind of cap or hat that would not blow off in a wind. Warm sweaters, even in mild weather, are essential and shorts, preferably of the longer variety are often comfortable. They may be worn in the more formal fashion with knee-length, cuffed wool socks or, less formally, with short athletic socks and the kind of shoes I have just described.

On smaller yachts under fifty feet, or even on those over fifty feet where there is no paid crew, male guests (and sometimes female ones) should be prepared to lend a hand. This requires hardy clothes—never brand new ones. Duck, sailcloth, or denim trousers are best with T-shirts and pullover sweaters, pea jackets, or wind-resistant jackets. For sailing in sloppy weather parkas are ideal; otherwise a raincoat, preferably an oil-skin with hat, is a necessity. Socks are best in white or light wool. Sunglasses or a sun-peak cap are advisable as a shield against the glare. Sunburn cream or lotion is needed, too, even, for most, when the skin has acquired a protective tan, for sunburn hazard is far greater on the water than on land. If the boat is very small, it is a good idea for a man to wear bathing trunks under his trousers, if he plans to swim.

A woman's best guide, as always, is what the hostess, if any, is wearing. On a big craft, with regular captain and hands, ordinary country cotton, flannel, or gabardine sports dresses are suitable as are shirts, jackets or sweaters, and slacks or shorts with rubber-soled shoes to prevent marking of the deck. A sweater or a sport coat, a bandanna, beret, or snap brim duck hat are advisable even if you start out on a hot day in a relative calm. A bathing suit and cap may be welcome. If the yacht is to put ashore at a club for dinner, inquire as to the advisability of taking a simple dinner dress and accessories. There may not be room aboard for such refinements—or no one may wish to bother with them. On large steam yachts with cabins you take the kind of clothes you'd take for a cruise, good country clothes, shorts and slacks if you wear them. Nicely tailored blue knit or flannel, linen, or cotton slacks or a gray or blue or white knit or flannel skirt or one in linen or cotton of some kind with a jersey and a jacket or blazer are comfortable and appropriate daytime wear. On an elaborate ship, ports of call and duration of the voyage determine your wardrobe. Inquire what others are taking. Any ship-side wardrobe should be reduced to an absolute, functional minimum, be of materials that won't need constant attention and stow away in limited space, if necessary.

On small boats women are suitably attired in blue denims or shorts, cotton shirts, socks and sneakers, and a bandanna or cap for the hair. Sweaters as well as a raincoat or slicker will come in handy, too. Bathing trunks, dungarees, chinos, or shorts are all good male attire, along with cotton shirts, rope-soled shoes or sneakers. A good windproof jacket will get plenty of use. If the boat is very small, it is a good idea for a woman to wear a bathing suit under her shorts or slacks, if she plans to swim.

To be deplored are the costumes I've seen—usually on tyros at sailing—at some of the marinas. Even on small boats hard-soled shoes, high or hard heels, nylons, elaborate coiffures, Hollywood style make-up are all sadly out of line and betray a lack of knowledge of boating and yachting traditions.

Rowing and Canoeing

The person who is rowing or paddling the boat gets in first. He takes his place, in the case of a rowboat, facing the stern and in the case of a canoe facing the bow. At this point the passengers step in, assisted if necessary by the rower, who holds his craft against the dock and extends a steadying hand. In debarking, the rower beaches or ties up the boat, and, if a man or boy, jumps on land or the wharf to hand out the women passengers. The prime requirement of the passengers, of course, is never to rock the boat. Each must sit quietly in the seat assigned to him and not change seats during the journey except with the rower's permission and under his direction. The rower is in effect the captain of the boat and responsible for the safety of his passengers. No one in any boat should litter the waterways with anything including cigarette butts. Occupants should not trail their hands in the water, as this creates a drag. Where circumstances warrant, the boat should be equipped with life jackets, for example in a rushing stream, in the ocean or in a deep lake. They are always advisable when children are aboard. Life jackets made of Kapok should not be sat upon as this mats down the Kapok and may destroy the jacket's buoyancy in time.

Riding

More people are riding horseback in this country today than ever before. They are riding, of course, for pleasure, and although the big stables are much less in evidence, there are many more one- and two-horse owners, many of whom board their horses or even keep them in their garages.

Riding is a sport for people of all ages. Many young and not so young new riders are coming into the sport with no background whatsoever as to its conventions, and rules of safety.

A horse is an individual. Some are skittish, some passive, some reliable, some so unpredictable they require a highly experienced rider. Never mount a strange horse without first inquiring as to its disposition and experience.

When riding in a group be very careful if you are on a kicking or biting horse. Do not ride too close to the others. If he is a kicker, see that he sports a red ribbon on his tail as a warning. Keep a horse-length behind the person in front of you and avoid crowding other animals on the path. Never be diffident about refusing to mount a horse you feel incapable of handling. If you wish to gallop when the others are walking, trotting, or cantering, explain this to the other riders and ride your horse at their pace far enough in advance of the group so that a sudden gallop will not disturb them.

When coming upon another group, slow down until you are past. Don't pass other riders at a gallop which could cause their horses to break into a gallop as well. On a narrow path slow down in passing until you are well ahead of other riders. Slow your horse to a walk when you approach roads.

Accidents can happen if someone dismounts momentarily and others don't rein in until he has remounted. In fast riding on woodland paths watch for low limbs on trees, holes, or logs in the path and warn those behind you.

Keep your horse well in check as you are approaching home. Sometimes a horse may make a break for the stable and others will follow.

Hacking   Hacking is informal riding in the country, the kind of riding many young people have taken to. The dress is very casual—blue jeans, sweater, open-neck flannel shirt, typical country clothes worn preferably, of course, with boots. Boots are proper protection and are relatively safe. Sneakers, loafers or bare feet are not.

There are, however, correct and traditional hacking clothes for men and women which consist of a single-breasted tweed coat with back vent. Breeches are in buff, canary, tan, or rust. The waistcoat in cold weather is either checked or plain, single-breasted. Shirts are tailored in wool or cotton, possibly button-down, worn either open or with a tie (which in turn should be well secured). A turtleneck sweater may also be worn, in hunting yellow or any of the leafy muted colors. For this kind of riding the boots should be brown and as long and as narrow as the leg can accommodate. They may be laced field boots. A tweed cap on a man, soft felt hat or scarf on a woman are preferable, but for safety's sake, particularly when one is riding alone, one is well advised to wear a hunting cap. For hacking, either breeches or jodhpurs are worn. They fit the leg tightly, Indian fashion, and are worn with jodhpur boots under them which have a strap around the ankle. These boots are also worn with slacks or trousers for informal wear by both men and women. With jodhpurs, knitted shirts, turtleneck sweaters, tailored sports shirts, with or without a tie, are worn, with the formality of a tie usual in city park riding, but not obligatory there. Stocks are not worn for informal riding, but ascots, properly secured, are often worn with collarless shirts. Suitable gloves are required in leather, cotton, or string, lined or unlined, the latter advisable in wet weather particularly. In warm weather just a shirt may be worn, with short or rolled sleeves and open collar. A waistcoat alone is not worn. There has been much relaxation in the matter of garb for city riding so you now see riding in shirtsleeves there, although the purists frown.

Western Riding   In western riding the stock, or working saddle, is used with a horn in front to which may be attached the lariat. The stirrups are covered (tapadero) to protect the legs in brush country. The reins are held in the left hand, leaving the right hand free for work with the rope. To the rider of an English saddle, a stock saddle seems like a rocking chair for it is very secure.

Western boots have a high heel. The toe is pointed.

Western wear for riding can be very elegant and quite expensive, but Western boots, sturdy pants (not necessarily riding pants at all), work shirt in wool, flannel, or cotton, a bandanna and a broad-brimmed hat (which may be a handsome and expensive Stetson in felt or straw with a brim to shade the eyes) complete the costume. For warmth in the mountains and protection against rain, a slicker or jacket or even a sweater may be added.

The men who handle the horses are called wranglers, never cowboys. In riding with a wrangler who is the leader, never pass him.

As in all safe riding, keep one horse-length between your horse and the one in front of you. Careful respect for gates is more important in the West than it is in the East. The fences not only mark boundaries, but often restrain valuable herds. When a gate is opened by the wrangler, the following riders ride through slowly until all are through with adequate space between the animals. All then wait until the wrangler has closed the gate and resumed his position at the head of the line. It is not only incorrect riding manners to ride ahead of the wrangler, but unsafe. Even if you are a good rider, the rest may not be able to control their horses as well.

Only when there is room on the trail for horses to come abreast should you allow yours to do so and then only at a walk. Horses may kick if a rider comes too close to their heels, dangerous to both you and your horse.

Keep your horse up with the others. If you feel unable to keep up with a fast ride, say so in the beginning and ask to be placed with a slower group.

Your hat and your scarf should be well secured. If you must put on a jacket or slicker, don't do so while in the saddle. Dismount for this purpose, preferably telling the rider ahead so that he'll slow down if necessary and not let you get too far behind. Or wait until the whole group stops for this purpose or some other.

Don't try to carry anything in your hands or strapped to you, or around your shoulders. If you take a camera, picnic lunch, blanket, or sweater, have the wrangler secure them to the saddle.

Do not smoke except at cigarette breaks. Break used matches and finished cigarettes. Be sure that they are cold before you throw them down.

If you are an inexperienced rider, do not go out on the trail for the first time without instruction. If possible, get to know your horse and his idiosyncrasies. Don't feed him sugar or apples until instructed on how to do it safely. Keep away from your horse's hoofs. They are highly dangerous.

Fox Hunting Fox hunting is always formal, even for children. Any infringement of the rules of fox hunting etiquette is intolerable to those who take this very special sport seriously.

Fox hunting etiquette is much like other etiquette in that it is based partly on the rules of safety. Furthermore, there are traditional customs which are not always explicable but which should be followed nonetheless out of deference to the conventions.

Those riding to hounds are known as members of the Field. The Master of the Hunt can be compared to the captain of a ship, requiring the greatest deference. Each member of the Field rides up to greet the

Master at the meet. At the end of the hunt, they thank him for permitting them to participate. The hunt staff consists of the huntsman who hunts the hounds assisted by the whippers-in. The Master directs the staff and is followed by members of the Field.

No one except the huntsmen and the whippers-in are permitted to precede the Master over a fence or across country. Followers should take particular care not to override the hounds or injure them in any fashion. If the pack suddenly changes direction, the riders must pull over and make way, keeping their horses' heels away from the hounds.

A command from the Master, "Hold hard!" is an absolute stop signal. At this point there should be no attempt to jockey for a better position in the Field. When the hounds are drawing or casting, nearby riders should be quiet themselves and cause their horses to stand quietly.

Riders on a strange mount or one that may be difficult are expected to keep to the rear of the Field.

No special courtesy is shown to women riders, who are expected to comply with the rules of courtesy for the Field in general. In the event, however, that a man is thrown, it is a man who is expected to help. Women need to pause to help only in the event that the rider in trouble is a woman and no man is available to assist her.

Riders should be alert for a glimpse of the fox. Anyone who sees it should alert the hunt staff immediately. It is, however, only the experienced hunter who should shout the traditional "Tally ho." For others, it is better to remove their hats and hold them out with a straight arm pointing in the direction the fox has taken. The rider whose horse has refused an obstacle, pulls the animal to one side and waits for others to jump before bringing his horse around to make the attempt again. The last member of the Field riding through a gate opened for the hunt must be sure to close it.

Novices in the hunting field are often children under instruction who are thus expected to keep to the rear of the Field. They must stay with the group and avoid turning the fox or riding over posted or seeded land.

Hunts do ride over private property, usually by pre-arrangement. Closing gates, avoiding riding over tilled fields or damaging crops, avoiding littering, all encourage the owners to leave their land open, not to "post" it.

The Spectators Watching the hunt is almost as exciting as being a member of it, but spectators can cause havoc, especially if they follow the hunt by car. If they do this, they should park well out of the way of the hunt, avoid loud talking, honking of horns, using of flash bulbs close to horses or hounds. They must never in any way impede or interfere with the hunt either at the meet or in the Field.

To Join a Hunt Various hunts have differing rules in the matter of guests. In some one must be an overnight guest of a member in order to be allowed to cap, but in most hunts all that is necessary is for the person wishing to be a guest to write to the M.F.H. (Master of Fox Hounds) or secretary for permission to join the hunt. He does not need sponsors. The cap is a fee paid by the guest invited to join and should be sent or given to the Hunt Secretary before the start of the hunt.

Some hunts require that those seeking to be regular members of the hunt live in the area and be landowners. Others require that one cap first as a guest. If a guest caps three times and is not asked to join the hunt, if that is his objective, he should not cap again until the following season. He may be blackballed or the Field may already be full.

Hunt Colors   Every hunt has its distinctive colors. Not all members wear them. Those who have been regular members of the hunt and have proved themselves in the Field are invited by the M.F.H. to wear the hunt colors which are then shown in the collars of their hunting coats. The honor extends also to buttons which are usually dark bone with the special insignia of the hunt.

Hunting Attire   If you are invited to join a hunt and plan to hunt more or less regularly, special hunting clothes are called for. But if you are just to be an occasional guest of the hunt you certainly wouldn't invest in a formal outfit. Instead, it is permissible for you to ride in your usual jacket and breeches with a white, collarless shirt and well-tied and anchored stock with an appropriate plain gold safety pin (worn horizontally), white or buff chamois or calf gloves, plus the hunting derby. Cuff links, if worn, are plain. The stock is said to have been designed to act as a bandage or sling in case of accident, and thus is a truly functional bit of men's wear still. The plain safety pin is used when necessary to secure a sling or bandage. If the Master of the Hunt is a great stickler for form, he may frown on your informality. Ask your host or the hunt secretary to determine his stand on the matter before you accept. If you have had no experience with cross-country riding and jumping, do not accept a hunting invitation.

Formal hunting dress, whether worn by amateurs or by the professional hunt "servants," is rigidly prescribed. The "pink" coat cut as a frock coat or cutaway (shadbelly) as worn by male members (or the Mistress of Fox Hounds) of the hunt, is actually vivid scarlet. It may be worn only by those receiving a special invitation from the M.F.H. (Master of Fox Hounds). Although each hunt has its own colors worn by the master and staff, only fully qualified members of the hunt are invited to wear them on their coat collars. Others wear standard riding clothes. Riding breeches in white, canary, buff, or brick are worn with black or dark blue coat, according to the specification of the hunt club. Brown boots are never worn with formal hunt attire. Only black calf boots are correct. With scarlet coats black calf boots with tan tops are *de rigueur*.

The hat worn with a pink coat is a high hunting silk hat. A black riding derby which is shallower than the street derby is never worn with the pink coat, and the hunt cap is worn only by juniors (under eighteen), or the hunt staff, M.F.H. or ex-M.F.H. The waistcoat is a Tattersall or canary wool flannel, or may be of any distinctive color adopted by the hunt.

Skiing

Skiing requires careful instruction from professionals or friends, preferably professionals. The tyro skier is a menace to himself and others if he blunders onto a difficult run or discards his poles Swedish style before he is ready. He must do his practicing when well rested on the simpler slopes preceding practice runs with the required limbering-up exercises and behave as modestly as the beginner in other sports in the presence of accomplished skiers. It is tiring for one whose muscles are unaccustomed to the effort, but the beginner must herringbone up the slopes or use the ski lift and not walk up, breaking the crust and making the slope perilous or unusable for others. As he makes his precipitous way down the trail, he shouts "track" to warn others of his approach stopping on the way if someone nearby seems to need help. On the slalom run, when he graduates to it, he is thoughtful to put back any gate poles he dislodges—right away, not on his ascent. His conduct on the ski lift should say very plainly, "I'm a beginner and I want to learn the rules of this sport." If in his embarrassment at being a beginner he acts the cutup, he will be considered crass, to say the least. Generally speaking, this is a sport that must be learned on locale, although it is sometimes possible to take a few lessons from professionals indoors. If you decide to learn to ski, don't spoil the fun of professional skiers or of others out of your strictly amateur class. Mind your own quiet business and take your lessons seriously, or there is a fine chance that you may break your neck.

Here are some rules for the beginning skier, and even the seasoned skier: Ski with courtesy—give the other skier a break if he is faster and more experienced than you. Ski only according to your ability; don't try to show off. Never ski when you are tired, or count on "just one more run" when it may be getting too dark. Keep your eyes off the tips of your skis and watch out for worn spots that may have iced up. Never ski alone. Keep yourself in good physical condition. Check your equipment regularly, and always be sure your release bindings and straps are adjusted. If you must stop in the middle of a run, do so out of the line of traffic, at the side of the trail. Rest after meals before skiing again. Be quiet on the lifts. If you come on a skier who seems to be hurt, don't move him. Remove his skis, cross them upright in the snow as a marker, and get the Ski Patrol.

Since in ski resorts you simply live in ski clothes, it is essential that they be warm and comfortable. The traditional costume is relatively the same both here and abroad. Stretch-pants, black and blue for men, often bright colors for women, are the general choice. These are worn with ski sweaters or hooded parkas—all covering warm, warm underthings. A warm cap is necessary, too, especially on sunless days, along with two pairs of wool socks (these are put on before the trousers are put on) and usually two pairs of mittens or gloves with the outside pair of some water-repellent material. Sunglasses or goggles ar a must. This ski outfit for both men and women is good for many other winter sports such as tobogganing and hiking on snow-covered roads.

In many resorts spectators are almost as numerous as actual skiers. Women wear either ski suits or well-tailored wool slacks, wool shirts, and heavy wool sweaters. For watching, a three-quarter or full-length parka or sport coat and ski pants or heavy slacks seem best to provide warmth. Heavy fur coats, except suitable fur parkas, are not comfortable because of the weight, which hinders climbing. This is also true of ski boots. The spectator fares better with low, warmly lined boots.

After-ski clothes remain simple and comfortable. Women wear anything from well-tailored pants in wool or velvet to long wool skirts or pajamas, jumpsuits or wool dresses. Colors are varied, both bright and dark, and clanking jewelry accents most outfits.

Skating

Almost anyone can skate if he has strong ankles. I've seen babies skating almost as soon as they learned to walk, and I've seen men and women in their seventies showing a gay blade. It all depends on how you go about it. There's always the skater who looks as if he's skating to a fire—round and round he races, frightening all the timid ones. There's the old gentleman in the middle of the rink performing graceful figure eights and bothering no one. There's the little boy on the double runners shuffling a foot or two at a time while clutching desperately at a hockey stick held by his father.

The clothes you wear for skating should be warm wool or wind-resistant and waterproof material. Ski pants or slacks are comfortable for skating, with jackets or sweaters for both men and women.

On an indoor rink you soon find your place among the slow or fast skaters —the fast ones are usually on the outside of the rink, and heaven help you if you stray in their path. As on the street, a man takes the outside position when he's accompanying a lady. Tripping a skater through your own awkwardness or foolish interference is grounds for mayhem. Loud shouting or games of tag disturb the philosophical skaters on a metropolitan indoor or outdoor rink, and usually an official puts a stop to them if they occur. If you cut any capers, be sure they are graceful ones that will be appreciated by the inevitable onlookers.

Generously proportioned women would do well to eschew the ballerina-type costume. It is only for the young and shapely. For others, good, active-length wool skirt, slacks, knickers or ski pants or pants suits are best, with a sweater or jacket and wool stockings (lisle wool stockings with wool ankle socks are appropriate).

Snowmobiling

There are 1,600,000 American families who have taken to snowmobiling and the sport is accelerating, and with it the injuries related to it. States in the snow areas have already passed or are passing laws regulating these machines which can cause noise pollution, air pollution, and general bad feelings among residents in invaded areas.

The code of ethics published by the The U. S. Snowmobile Association should guide the owners of these machines. Here it is.

Code of Ethics for Snowmobilers

1. I will be a good sportsman. I recognize that people judge all snow-mobile owners by my actions. I will use my influence with other snow-mobile owners to promote sportsmanlike conduct.
2. I will not litter trails or camping areas. I will not pollute streams or lakes.
3. I will not damage living trees, shrubs or other natural features.
4. I will respect other people's property and rights.
5. I will lend a helping hand when I see someone in distress.
6. I will make myself and my vehicle available to assist search and rescue parties.
7. I will not interfere with or harass hikers, skiers, snowshoers, ice fisher-men or other winter sportsmen. I will respect their rights to enjoy our recreational facilities.
8. I will know and obey all Federal, State and Local Rules, regulating the operation of snowmobiles in areas where I use my vehicle. I will inform public officials when using public lands.
9. I will not harass wildlife. I will avoid areas posted for the protection or feeding of wildlife.
10. I will stay on marked trails or marked roads open to snowmobiles. I will avoid country travel unless specifically authorized.

Surfing and Water Skiing

Both surfing and water skiing are rough sports that attract more men than women. They require great co-ordination and should not be undertaken by anyone who is not a strong swimmer, as both activities initiate in deep water, the skier, being towed by a power boat, and the surfer swimming out with his board into deep water before surfing in.

Both sports require open water, free of boat traffic and swimmers.

Taking off with a skier in two requires that the operator of the boat start in low speed so as not to throw the skier off balance. Not until he has risen from his crouched position should the boat be accelerated and then it should be kept at an even speed calculated to maintain the skier's balance with the boat keeping a straight course, never zigzagging. Turns must be wide and gentle for skiers who are less than professional.

The boatman must watch his skier, stopping immediately if he falls, and returning to see if he wants to continue or stop. In surfing there is always danger from the heavy surfboards, both to the surfer and to anyone close by in the water. A surfer and surf board separated can mean an accident if the errant surf board hits a swimmer or collides with another surfer. The surfer, finding the wave that takes him into shore should not be imperiled by another surfer taking off in front of him.

Beginner surfers are like ski bunnies and should keep with others with similar limitations until they have attained real ability.

The costume for both of these sports is, of course, a bathing suit or bathing trunks, strong and functional ones. One of the hazards is the sun beating down on the water, no matter how cool the sportsman or woman may feel. Even the experienced surfer going out for the first time during a season without adequate protection from the sun will find it even more of a hazard than the heavy board that has been separated from its owner, and of course the water skier runs the same risk even if he finds himself more in the water than out of it.

Swimming

Swimming in the same ocean does not give a man the right to force his conversation or attentions on other—usually feminine—swimmers or sun bathers. Exhibitions of water-splashing, porpoising, wrestling, and sand-throwing, often engaged in by very young men to attract feminine attention, usually make them offensive in the very eyes of those they seek to attract, and certainly make them loathesome to the run-of-the-beach bather in search of a little peace.

When swimming, you do not swim beneath the diving board, for reasons that should be perfectly obvious, or jump off a raft into the midst of water-treading or floating bathers—instead you slip off backwards to create the least possible backwash. A man should be perfectly objective about his figure before deciding in favor of extremely attenuated costumes.

Any woman less bony than a shad looks ridiculous in a bra-top bathing suit and one that doesn't at least partly cover her thighs. If she has anything even slightly resembling a rubber tire around her middle, let her choose a bathing suit that will cover, or better, mildly control it, as do well-cut Lastex suits. The dressmaker suit is a boon to less than perfect figures. The bikini is for perfect figures only and for the very young. To swim is to make a very public appearance. Legs and underarms should be meticulously groomed, and feet should be carefully pedicured.

Hunting and Shooting

In fishing and in duck hunting, you hear much about the need for being quiet so as not to frighten off the quarry. Low conversation is permissible in deep-sea fishing but not in surface fishing, as fish can hear and they feel vibrations such as are made by throwing an empty beer bottle into the water, by rocking the boat, by banging of any sort. Ducks' hearing is very acute, even when they are high above the blind. Fish take fright at violent movement, if they are surface swimmers. It takes a certain philosophical state of mind, a rigid self-control to make one a good fisherman or duck hunter, and especially an acceptable companion in these enterprises.

If you hunt in the deer-shooting season, you must not wear a white shirt or show a white handkerchief—or anything else white, for that matter—for it might be mistaken for that little patch of white on a deer's tail and so call forth a shot by another hunter stalking game in the same terrain. Loud talking or even noisy movements that frighten away the game limit not only your own possibility of making a kill but that of other hunters. In bagging small game, such as partridge or grouse, determine the legal limit before setting out and stay within it. It is not good sportsmanship to go over the permitted bag, even when there is little possibility of being caught at it. In shooting small game, never fire until the birds are on the wing, never shoot down a treed animal or one in cover, never horse in a fish without playing him on the line—give all a sporting chance to escape. In a wild turkey shoot, the sportsmen often camp under the trees in which the birds have roosted for the night, but any man who tried to wing one before it left the roost would be considered no gentleman. When you are working with dogs, wait until they have flushed the birds well out of cover and never shoot too low or you may pepper the dogs instead of the birds.

Guns, even in the hands of experts, are dangerous weapons. Look well before you aim, check the position of others in the party before you shoot. Carry guns, when not actively hunting or shooting, with the safety catch on. In the field, except when actually shooting, and en route, carry them with the muzzle down or with the gun over the shoulder with muzzle pointing up, or "break" the gun. Unload your gun when you enter the shooting wagon or car and when you stack it. Never lean on a gun.

In shooting with dogs, give orders only to your own. If another hunter's dog retrieves for you by mistake, don't take the bird from him yourself. Ask the owner or the handler to do so, as game retrieved by a dog is considered the property of the dog's master rather than of the man who shot it down. Also, a hunting dog must, more than any other, be a "one man dog." He is not a pet in the usual sense but a work dog and should receive his orders and his commendations only from his owner or handler, from whom he is trained to expect both. Shooting is like tennis in one respect— you don't take another man's shot. If a bird comes within range of another huntsman's gun, leave it to him. Don't "reach" for it, even though you, as a better marksman, are certain he will miss it.

Clothes Comfortable, loose-fitting clothes—corduroys, flannel shirts— are good masculine attire. A red hat, a patch of red for the sleeve or back of a jacket, or even a red handkerchief knotted around the cap, is a necessary safety device. Sporting-goods shops also sell little packets of red tissues for hunters now. The use of white ones is dangerous. High-laced boots, waterproofed, are needed for marshlands and snake country. Otherwise any heavy, comfortable shoes cushioned by wool socks will do. A hunter who goes into a blind inadequately prepared to withstand hours of cold and damp will be *persona non grata*. If you have never owned long woolen underwear, prepare to wear it now—and if you're a novice, maybe two pairs are better than one. A man in a blind who complains unendingly of the cold because he isn't dressed for it is in the same class as the pariah who ruins the fishing trip because he has not developed the fisherman's quiet philosophy of "watchful waiting" and can't sit still for what may prove to be fruitless hours without a catch.

Upland shooting where birds are flushed by dogs and fly in front of the guns at some distance from the hunters permits the wearing of other than neutral colors. A gay flannel shirt may be worn with khaki breeches laced below the knee or with regular riding pants. Comfortable leather boots, field boots, or those high-cut, or moderately high-cut elkhide, waterproof boots with leather, not rubber, soles are needed. Wool socks prevent blisters, and cautious people wear a thinner pair inside heavy ones. In snake country, for example in Florida and Georgia, boots should always come just below the knee. (You learn to look down each time before taking a step, too.)

For clay pigeon shoots, dove shoots, and turkey drives (in open country, not in the Florida or Georgia woods) women will find that an English wool or tweed walking skirt with jacket or loose pullover sweater (over a collared round-necked white blouse) is often worn instead of breeches or pants.

If a hat is needed, it is, again, the trusty neutral soft, unbound felt with a dull-colored ribbon. Hair should be very neat, in a net if it is likely to fly loose.

In thickly wooded country briar-resistant trousers are advisable and white duck jackets are sometimes worn, or white duck visored caps, for visibility. Otherwise, for safety, you can tie a clean, white, man's handkerchief around the left, or shooting, arm.

For big game hunting—deer and moose—neutral-toned, heavy-duty breeches, boots, and hunting jacket are necessary with either a red hunting cap or a red patch on the back of the jacket or a red handkerchief tied around the shooting arm. Again, white must not be worn, as a flash of white might be mistaken by another hunter for the white of a deer's tail.

In the matter of terminology, one "shoots" other birds but "hunts" ducks. You "hunt" deer and other four-footed game. The serious hunter and fisherman may cling to the superstition—as does the actor stepping on-stage—that you spoil his luck if you wish him good luck as he starts out.

Distress Signal People handling guns should know the distress signal—three shots fired at three-second intervals.

Bowling

One of the most popular sports today, and one which the entire family can enjoy together, is bowling. Bowling of course is a very old game. Excavations in Egypt have revealed that some form of this game was played as early as 5200 B.C. And of course we all remember Washington Irving's reference to it in his unforgettable Rip Van Winkle adventures. Introduced into this country by the Dutch settlers, bowling, or nine pins as it was then, has acquired enormous popularity over the years. Today the game is played with ten pins and since it doesn't require great physical strength appeals to a wide age group. Men find that well-tailored slacks and sports shirts that allow for good freedom of action are most comfortable. Full skirts or culottes are recommended for women, along with short-sleeved shirts to permit the arm to swing easily but many wear shorts, slacks, and jumpsuits for comfort and ease of movement. Special shoes are required for bowling—the left sole is made of leather, the right sole of rubber. Shoes may be rented at the lanes for a nominal fee, but bowling *aficionados* have their own and many have their own bowling balls.

As in every sport there are certain rules and procedures that the courteous player follows to allow for maximum enjoyment of the game for himself and others he is playing with, and as a safeguard from possible injury. Here are a few of them:

When two persons are bowling on adjoining lanes, the bowler on the right shoots first.

Don't use another person's ball without permission. After all you wouldn't think of using another person's tennis racket or putter without permission.

Remain on the bench quietly waiting your turn. Don't feel free to give advice to the bowler who is ready to shoot, unless it is asked for of course. And move up promptly when it is your turn.

Don't wander from your own lane on to your neighbor's as he is getting ready to shoot. You will distract him and very likely spoil his shot.

Make sure that your shoes are clean and have nothing on the soles to mar the approaches.

Bowling from behind the foul line is part of the game. Disregarding it brings a penalty, which will not make you the most popular member of your team.

Excessive "body English" is distracting and can even be dangerous if you collide with another bowler.

Let's Not Be Too Casual

Big cities increasingly are offering sports activities that require the appropriate clothing, clothing that is certainly more comfortable than traditional city streetwear. However, bathing suits worn to and from pool and beach areas, for example, should be properly covered and not just by short beach coats. Slim pants worn for skating in the park are fine for restaurants there, but are inappropriate for formal restaurants where others are suitably dressed.

The Sauna

Particularly relaxing after sports is the popular sauna. As saunas are becoming a community commonplace with saunas being built into existing houses as well as into new ones, the necessity for etiquette rules is obvious.

The word, pronounced properly "sow-na," is the Finnish word for "bath." The heat in the sauna can rise as high as 240° but most sauna habitués, I believe, find 200° pleasant. Those saunas which have shelves at various levels have the greatest degree of heat at the top. Some people finish off a sauna by standing upright to get the maximum heat at the end.

A home sauna—and they are proliferating throughout the country— is much more responsibility than a home pool. Saunas may have either dry or moist heat, the kind with low humidity more popular.

Not everyone should take a sauna any more than everyone should dive into a pool or race from end to end. Check your doctor. It is said that people in their young and middle years, free of disease, should be able to take as much as one sauna a day, or possibly two, but you must accustom the body to sauna-taking. Therefore, the owner of a home sauna has great responsibility. A guest, for example, taking a sauna in your home without medical approval, possibly after having imbibed a few cocktails, could have some unpleasant effect from it for which he might choose to hold you responsible.

No matter what you have heard, the sauna is not the place to sober up.

In Finland people have been taking saunas since infancy and continue to take them until very advanced old age. As saunas become more and more a part of the American scene, probably we can do the same, but in the meantime, a house with a sauna needs careful supervision of this excellent addition.

Every sauna should have a thermometer and a door that opens outward with non-metal handles, or if the handles are metal they should be covered with something such as terry cloth. There should be a timer so that the lone sauna-taker will know how long he has been inside. It is wise to have a thermostat that shuts off automatically after a certain period of time. Saunas should never have locks. In Finland there is no mixing of the sexes in the sauna except in family groups, but here mixed groups take their saunas lightly draped in Turkish towels.

About thirty minutes is as long as anyone should stay in a sauna, with beginners emerging after five or ten minutes to take a warm shower, followed by a cold one and perhaps a little rest before going back in. Experienced sauna-takers who react well to the routine take an ice cold shower after ten minutes sometimes, but not always, preceded by a warm one. A sauna should always be finished with a cold shower, although it is not necessary, of course, that you jump into an icy lake or stream. Interestingly enough, after a proper sauna the body temperature is so high that no shock or chill results on contact with cold. The procedure may not be recommended for somone with heart, vascular, or respiratory disease, or any other disease which causes restriction of activity. But there is great medical disagreement on the subject and people with any of these problems should follow the instructions of their own doctors in the matter.

As the major principle of the sauna is to induce relaxation and a sense of well being, you cannot rush in and out of it. A sauna should be followed by some rest. It should never be taken when you are ill. It is unwise to take any vasodilating drug (since they intensify the blood-pressure-lowering effect of the heat) or any drugs for that matter that impair judgment or affect emotions. You should never drink or smoke in a sauna, or do any exercise.

The body in the sauna should be unrestricted by anything more than a turkish towel—even a bathing suit is inadvisable. In a private sauna some conversation may go on in a group, although it is really unwise because one is supposed to relax and all conversation takes effort. In a public sauna, silence should be observed. Don't read or work. Lower the light to dim.

Jewelry, watches, glasses, etc., should not be worn because they become very hot. Slippers should be left outside the door. Don't go into a sauna after exercise; wait until your pulse has come back to normal. Don't rush the end of your sauna. Allow at least twenty minutes for the final shower and rest period before dressing.

It is important not to go into a sauna, or to allow anyone else to go into it, without letting someone know you will be there alone. If possible, put a pane of glass in the sauna door. A red light should indicate that the sauna is on and possibly in use. Young children should not be allowed to take saunas alone or invite their friends to do so without their own parents' permission.

As saunas do tend to flatten coiffures, women find that saunas should be scheduled before hairdressing appointments or a hair spray that resists humidity should be used. If you do put your hair up in curlers before going into the sauna, use the light plastic or plastic covered kind with no exposed metal that will heat up. If you have just used public saunas and decide to have one in your own house, get the small definitive book, "Sauna: The Finnish Bath" by H. J. Viherjuuri (Stephen Greene Press, Brattleboro, Vt., $3.95). The American edition lists all sauna manufacturers and suppliers in this country.

Chapter 25

THE SOCIAL PLEASANTRIES

"Gifts of Love"

"Gifts of love" are thoughtful mementos given for no particular reason except perhaps for the joy of giving. They may foster good community relations but primarily are only to bring a ray of happiness to others. A new neighbor gets that wonderful feeling of being "in" when almost every woman in the neighborhood comes to the door with a small offering—flowers or vegetables from back-yard gardens, a plate of cookies, or a basket of fruit.

An amusing gift for friends—both to make and to give—is a booklet depicting their lives or some part of them. Cartoons, pictures, and headlines or snips from advertisements are surprisingly applicable to people and incidents concerning them when cut out and pasted in sequence.

Daily papers or magazines may be exchanged among neighbors—along with jars to use in canning. Scraps of material may be valuable to some for rug or quilt making. A single flower taken to a new homemaker or just to someone special is a "gift of love" from the heart.

A Guide to Tactful Conversation

In greeting people we say, "How do you do?" We do not really expect an answer, but it is all right to reply, "Very well, thank you," even if it is a blue Monday and you feel far from well. No one wants a clinical discussion in response to this purely rhetorical question. In fact, you may answer Socratically with "How do *you* do?"—expecting, and getting, no answer. In farewell, say simply, "Good-by," or something you really feel, such as "Let's meet soon again" or "It was so nice running into you." Don't use some current banality such as "Good-by now." It is obvious it is *now* you are saying "Good-by"—not an hour previously nor an hour hence. Watch these clichés. Up to a point they can lend a little color to your conversation, but they can easily become second nature, so that you seem to be a person of little imagination, one suffering from a sad poverty of language. These innocuous slang expressions sound particularly inept from a grown man or woman, unless one is using them quite consciously and in fun.

When to Use a First Name

Be slow to use people's first names and try to let the other person take the initiative. A man must never call a woman of his own circle by her first name unless he is asked to do so. Usually she indicates her willingness to be on a more familiar footing simply by calling him by his first name without any explanatory preliminaries but she may say, *"Do* call me Joan."

If a much older man or woman calls a much younger man or woman by his or her first name, that does not, of course, indicate that the junior should return the familiarity, although if the relationship continues over many years it is possible that in time it will be appropriate for the younger person to call the older one by his or her Christian name, but even then it is best to be asked to do so.

If You Cannot Remember Names

No one is ever pleased if you say, "I know your face—but I just can't recall your name." Tactful people who aren't infallible about names work out a technique for coping with these bad moments. If you are warmly greeted by someone whose name—or maybe whose face, too—you can't recall, say something harmless such as, "Nice to see you" or "You're looking well." Then while looking quite attentive, let the other person do the talking until he or she gives a clue as to identity. Let us hope he doesn't ever say, "You don't remember me, do you?" for your own expression should always indicate you remember him well and favorably.

If you have trouble remembering the names that match the faces, always help out the other person who is probably suffering from the same thing. Never say, "Do you remember me?" or "You don't know who I am, do you?" Instead, in greeting people you haven't seen for some time or whom you are meeting outside of your usual place of encounter, identify yourself quickly and gracefully, "How do you do, Mr. Burton. I'm Joseph Bye of Arbor Mills. We did a little business together last fall." Or, when a woman has stopped and is obviously confused as to who you are, "I'm Joseph Bye, Miss Fox. We see each other at the Advertising Club." It is certainly more modest and tactful to assume that you aren't remembered than to presume that you are. I well remember the effect on me when my partner at a public dinner sat down, turned to me, and said, simply, "My name is Hoover." It was Herbert.

Sending or Presenting Flowers

A gift of flowers sent in celebration of a special occasion such as a wedding anniversary, Christmas, Thanksgiving, Easter, is usually addressed to the couple. Flowers sent or presented by a guest before a dinner party, or perhaps in appreciation of one, are directed to the hostess. Flowers brought by the guest are presented to the hostess, or if this is impossible, are given to someone else (a servant, for example) for her. It is a difficult matter at a big party for a hostess to receive her guests, unpack and arrange flowers in any way to do them justice. It is considerate to send flowers the morning of a party—and flowers from your own garden, if possible, can be a perfect choice—or perhaps several days after when her party flowers will have faded. When the occasion is a big one such as a wedding anniversary celebration, an open house, it is considerate to let a hostess know that she may expect flowers from you so that she will not order too many herself. Too many flower gifts can be overpowering.

Some knowledgeable hostesses call prominent florists when they believe they are going to have a large influx of flower gifts and may wish to be notified when such gifts of flowers are ordered so that they may stagger their receipt.

Men may be sent flowers. A plant for a man's office makes an excellent gift if it is a suitable one such as a hardy and decorative fern, colocasia or more familiarly "elephants' ears" or hydrangeas. Your florist can best advise you on this when he knows where the plant will be used, how much light it will get, etc. Men may receive gifts of flowers and plants in hospitals but they should be chosen with an eye to their masculine appeal. Jerusalem cherries, zinnias, carnations (not pink), chrysanthemums, long-stemmed roses in vivid colors, jonquils and iris, are better than sweetheart roses or other more feminine offerings. If you are ever stumped for a gift for a tiny baby who seems to have everything, send small-scale flowers for the nursery —Tom Thumb roses (especially for little girls). And Japanese gardens fascinate children and adults equally. They are particularly attractive for convalescent patients and for people who must stay long in a hospital as such gardens require virtually no care.

When funeral notices carry the line "Please omit flowers," flowers sent after the funeral to some member of the family can be very comforting even when you have made a contribution to charity if that has been requested. (See page 182).

Personal Questions—What Are They?

Sometimes I feel that understanding of what constitutes a personal question is innate rather than acquired. There are people who seem to have been born tactful and others who, no matter what they are told or how often they offend, consciously or unconsciously, continue their stream of personal questions to the discomfort of all those with whom they come in contact.

We should not, for example, ask the cost of everything. If your neighbor wishes to volunteer certain information in the course of conversation—the amount he paid for his house, the cost of his son's school tuition, how much he paid for his new lawn mower, that is his privilege, but we should not ask these intimate questions unless there is some very valid reason for doing so. If you plan to send your child to the same school, you might ask the tuition your neighbor pays, but even then you might embarrass him, as some private schools have a sliding scale based on the parent's ability to pay, the desirability of the child from a scholastic or other standpoint, etc., and if he pays less than the regular tuition he may well be annoyed at the question.

Unless you have some business reason to do so, you shouldn't ask a man or woman the amount of insurance he or she carries, the amount of the mortgage or rent, the salaries of the servants. You might ask a man's age— though many men are less than anxious to divulge that information as they pass forty—but you never ask that of a woman over twenty-one, except for official reasons. Even then, the courtesy of letting her say "over twenty-one" usually is accorded a woman—except by the U. S. State Department, the various Motor Vehicles offices, and other sternly realistic representatives that must know all. So even though many women are frank about their ages—sometimes aggressively so—it really is no one's business, and it is, I think, a permissible conceit for anyone to shave off a few years if her face doesn't belie the amputation. But in her very late years a woman usually takes a belated pride in her longevity and brags that she is eighty-nine or ninety—except a great-aunt of mine who at ninety-six refused to admit it and blithely said, when queried about her great age by a caller on her birthday, "Oh, I guess I'm about ninety." (She lived to just three months short of one hundred.)

Most women are equally sensitive about their weight and dislike being asked to name the figure, with which they are doubtless displeased.

Men and women of less than average height are often diffident about references to the fact. Surprisingly enough, it seems to me, very tall men usually are far from flattered at references to their height, and, of course, no very thin or fat man likes to have his deviation from the norm commented upon in public, no matter how much inured he seems to friendly raillery. The very fat and the very thin are sensitive people, easily hurt.

Many of our ways of thinking are changing, so that a six-foot girl today might not bat an eyelash if you asked her how tall she is. If she carries herself straight and tall, is not afraid of high heels and dramatic hats, you can be sure she has no complex about her height. If she goes around in flat heels, walks stoop-shouldered, and wears itsy-bitsy accessories, you can be equally certain she'd hate to be asked her measurements and that to her such a question would be highly "personal."

And while practically all American girls—and men, too—have big feet these days, many women like to pretend their feet are smaller than they actually are, in deference, perhaps, to the Victorian idea that small hands and feet denoted gentility. A woman who wears a 10½ D might get on the defensive if you asked her shoe size.

I'd never ask my best friend whether he or she had dyed hair, false teeth, a wooden leg, or a glass eye no matter how apparent these things may be. I wouldn't ask anyone who his legatees would be or how he had made out his insurance, how much money he had in the bank or how his marriage was going.

Dangerous Topics of Conversation

You may be Helen Burke's most intimate friend, and she may have half-confided in you many times that she and Herbert are not getting along any too well. But for you to ask her a direct question as to the status of her relations with her husband is dangerous business. If you are cast in the role of confidante, willingly or unwillingly, avoid asking direct questions or referring to a former confidence when perhaps the crisis that precipitated it may have passed. All married people have their moments of incompatibility. Never take them seriously until and unless you see separate residences established. And mentioning any such acrimonious scenes to which you may have been witness is a good way to close the doors to reconciliation between the couple. Somehow if all her best friends keep reminding Helen that Herbert's behavior has been unforgivable she will find it harder to forgive than if no one but the most discreet among her friends is mutely conscious that there has been a little fuss.

When people are angry and abusive toward some friend, associate, or member of their family, don't take sides. Listen, refrain from expressing an opinion, and stay objective, though vaguely sympathetic. If angry friends ask for, get, and take your advice they will not like you better. On the contrary, they may resent your interference, well-meaning though you may have meant it to be. The role of mediator is hard and thankless, and most of us are not really equipped for the task.

Change of Partners

Divorces and deaths change relationships. Upon seeing people you haven't seen in years, be cautious with your questions and guard your expression if one member of the couple looks unfamiliar. He or she may be a new partner to the marriage, or be drastically changed by the loss or gain of weight, the graying of hair, a radically new hair color, or just the inevitable passage of years. Don't blurt, "I would never have known you" or, "I thought you were still married to Helen." And remember, too, you have changed in the interim.

How to Parry Direct Questions

Personal questions can be unsettling unless you develop enough sophistication to cope with them gracefully. Sometimes they are brutally asked with intent to wound. A naturally witty person knows well enough how to reply. An author who was asked by a jealous contemporary, "Who *wrote* your book for you?" replied, "Who *read* it to you?" This is the Socratic question-for-question defense which had best be left to professionals.

The safer way is to pretend that no offense was meant—and often the poser of personal questions is just a blunderer and doesn't really mean to be malicious. If you are a woman who does not care to advertise her age, whether it be twenty-five or forty-seven, you might reply to someone who asks how old you are (when it's none of his business), "You know, the women in my family have always been ageless and I like to keep it that way." Women are expected to lie about their age, anyhow, so even if you bared your sensibilities and told the truth the chances are your interrogator would, mentally, add another five or ten years.

When no tactful answer seems to suffice and the personal probing goes on, the only solution is to be quite frank. Say, without getting angry, "I know you don't realize it, but that is a personal question I don't feel willing to answer." If he then takes offense, he deserves to.

That Word "Lady"

The word "lady" is suitable in the discussion of etiquette—"A gentleman stands behind a *lady's* chair until she is seated," but the use of it in conversation is very limited, unless we wish to imply our own humbler position.

A woman caller being announced in an office or in your home by an employee—or at home by a child—is a "lady," not a woman. A secretary will announce, "There is a lady to see you, Mr. Zachary. Here is her card." Or, "There is a Miss Long to see you. She's from the Grolier Society" (if she's presented no card). A child at home would say, "There's a lady to see you, Mommy."

A secretary or other white-collar employee never says—at least not in the hearing of the caller—"There's a *woman* here." Neither, ushering in the caller, does she say, "You may come in, lady." Instead, she says, "Please come in," adding the visitor's name, if known.

In a shop no one should ever use the word "lady" to a customer to get her attention, although a clerk in referring to the customer in speaking to someone else it is proper to say, "This lady would like to know if we carry——" In cases where a man or woman, no matter what his or her station in life, does not know the name, or doesn't wish to use the name of a woman to whom it is necessary to direct a remark, it is proper to say "Madam," never "Miss," unless the title is followed by her last name.

I have heard men in high business positions say, as a domestic properly does, "Please come in, *Miss* (to an obvious 'Miss')." Even with office personnel whose names they don't know, they should not use this form of address. A pleasant "Come in" is all that is necessary.

Remember, the King of England in his abdication speech referred to Wallis Simpson as "the *woman* I love." The word used properly has great dignity and meaning. A man, speaking of his wife, should refer to her as a "woman" to his friends, as a "lady" only to tradespeople and various others in service capacities. He may say to his new client, "I'd like you to meet my wife sometime—a charming *woman*." To the station porter he should say, "Will you help the *lady* over there with the bags while I buy the tickets?"

A woman does not refer to herself as a "lady" to her social equals. She does not call on the new neighbor explaining she is the "lady" next door. Instead, she says, "I am Mrs. Birch, your next-door neighbor." To the meat dealer in the chain store she might say, "I am the *lady* who ordered the turkey last week," but I like better the more democratic, "I ordered the turkey last week." From your way of addressing him, the tradesman can see for himself how you should be catalogued.

How about "Miss!"?

Whenever possible the word "Miss" as a summons to someone whose name you don't know should be avoided. If you are being served by a waitress and fail to catch her eye, "Waitress!" is better than "Miss!" If you are trying to catch up with a woman friend in the street, never call out her name—which might embarrass her. Certainly you can't call "Miss!" after her, although if you are near enough and are on a first-name basis, you might call her first name softly in a crowd, if you fail to catch her attention any other way.

Salespeople nowadays avoid "Miss" in speaking to customers, although many well-trained ones say "Madam," if necessary, except to a very young girl. It is undignified for a matron, however young, to be spoken to as "Miss" by someone waiting on her—"Will you try these for size, Miss?" The "Miss" should be omitted and if any title is used, it should be "Madam." A customer, failing to catch a salesperson's eye, may call out "Miss," however.

The Use of Ma'am and Sir

The use of "Ma'am" is disappearing and is little used in the North except by displaced Southerners or servants of the old school. In the South you still hear it and in some areas there is a strong effort to keep the custom of having children and, of course, servants address adult women as "Ma'am." I don't endorse this. I feel that Mrs. or Miss together with the surname is properly respectful for everyone for all parts of the country.

In the Ivy League prep schools and colleges the use of "Sir" between students and their men teachers is taught. I like it and I also like it between young men and their superiors or older men. This is still considered good usage in big business and conservative social circles.

Introductions

In America when men are introduced to each other they shake hands standing, without, if possible, reaching in front of another person. They may smile or at least look pleasant and say nothing as they shake hands, or one may murmur some such usual, courteous phrase as "It is nice to meet (or know) you." To which the other may reply, "Nice to meet you" or merely "Thank you."

In shaking hands, men remove the right glove if the action isn't too awkward because of the suddenness of the encounter. If they shake hands with the glove on they say, "Please excuse (or forgive) my glove." If the introduction takes place on a ballroom floor and the men are wearing white kid gloves (very little worn these days except by fathers and escorts at debuts), the right glove is not removed, even for an introduction to a lady, and no apology is made. The purpose of the glove, in this case, is to prevent damaging the ladies' gowns with a (possibly) perspiring palm.

Men who meet or are introduced to each other outdoors do not remove their hats unless a lady is present. Nor do men who know each other raise their hats when they pass on the street unless they are escorting ladies. When a man is introduced to a lady he does not offer his hand unless she makes the move first, as it is quite correct for a lady merely to bow in acknowledgment of an introduction—in fact the usual thing. But of course no lady ever refuses a proffered hand and we should know that European men are taught to take the initiative in handshaking. Neither is it correct in this country, as I've said elsewhere, for a woman to remove her glove to shake hands except with the President, head of church, or head of state. The words of the introduction between a man and woman go this way: "Mrs. Gardiner, Mr. Longstreth." Or, "Mr. Longstreth, I would like you to meet Mrs. Gardiner." Or, again, and more formally, "Mrs. Gardiner, may I present Mr. Longstreth." Never introduce the woman to the man unless he is a head of a church, the President, a governor, a mayor (under official circumstances), or a foreign head of state. Foreign ambassadors are introduced *to* ladies. There is much less handshaking in this country, less between women, and women and men, than between men. A hostess, however, greets all her guests and bids them farewell by shaking hands, and all guests should seek to shake the hand of the hostess and the host on being received and saying farewell.

When introducing someone to a group, for example at a cocktail party, it is not necessary to do a large-scale introduction. When there are more than five or six people present, introduce the guest to those in his immediate vicinity. As he moves along he introduces himself to other guests.

When women are introduced to each other and one is sitting, the other standing, the one who is seated does not rise unless the standee is her hostess or a much older or very distinguished woman or perhaps a friend she has not seen in a long time. The rising of one woman for another in this country indicates great deference. It is often a delicate matter to decide whether or not a woman is sufficiently older than oneself to be worthy of the gesture. If not, she may be offended rather than honored. Any young girl in her early teens, however, should rise when introduced to any matron and to any older man of her parent's circle, but she shakes hands only if the older person so indicates. Of course, any woman seeking employment rises when presented to her prospective employer, male or female, and permits the interviewer to make the move to shake hands, or not, as he chooses. A woman also should rise when being introduced to her hostess, host, or to the guest of honor.

A woman or man introducing husband or wife to another person says, "This is my husband" or "May I introduce you to my wife?" A man's wife would, however, be introduced *to* a much older woman, to a woman of great distinction, or to an elderly and distinguished man.

Neither spouse refers to the other socially as "Mr. Brown" or "Mrs. Brown." Nor does a man say "the wife" or "the missus." "My wife" is the courteous term.

No one properly says "Charmed," "Delighted," or "Pleased to meet you" when presented to anyone. In fact, under ordinary circumstances a casual "Hello," or "How do you do?" (to which no answer but a repeated "How do you do?" or a smile is expected) is sufficient. A spontaneous "It's so nice to meet you" or "I am *so* glad you came" or even "I have heard so much about you" is fine when it is really meant— but it is never obligatory. All introductions may be acknowledged with a pleasant glance and a slight bow except those between men, where a handshake is usually expected.

Introducing Doctors and Others of Special Distinction The hostess can simplify matters for guests if, when she is entertaining a doctor even under circumstances where everyone is to be on a first name basis, she introduces him as "Doctor." Doctors are used to giving their names with their titles. A doctor under such circumstances usually comes forward and says, "How do you do, I'm Dr. Noyes—Stephen." He realizes perhaps subconsciously that people are a little embarrassed if they accept him as a layman only to find some time later that he is a doctor. For the same reason a hostess who is entertaining a woman whose professional name is different from that of her husband, explains in introductions, "Mrs. Remington is also Melissa Murray, the sculptress." Husbands of celebrated women are quite used to having their wives addressed as "Miss" in social circumstances by people who know them only under their professional names. The thing that every professional woman of note herself tries to avoid is having strangers call her husband by her own name instead of by his. Sometimes an explanation by the hostess before such guests arrive is a tactful way of handling this.

Dancing

Duty Dances At any dance, each man guest asks the hostess to dance at least once and also asks her daughters, if she has any, or her women house guests. A well-brought-up young man seeks out each lady of the household, including house guests, at a private dance, even grandmother, if she is present, and courteously asks for a dance. The phrase he uses is, "May I have this dance?" or "May I have the pleasure of this dance?" Between very young people this is often abbreviated to "Dance?"

A man always leads the way to the dance floor to make a path for the woman he is with. If the room is clear they may walk side by side. At the edge of the floor she steps forward and faces him in the dance position.

At a supper dance those who have come together sup together. It is the expected thing. As suppertime approaches a girl's escort seeks her out if she is dancing with someone else and at the appropriate moment says, "Shall we have supper?" At seated suppers hostesses should not separate dates.

Refusing a Dance   No lady need dance with anyone if for some reason she doesn't care to. But she must always be polite in her refusal. If she is hoping for another partner she may say, "Thank you, but I don't believe I'm free right now." Or if she is tired she should say so, "Thank you, but I'd like to rest a little. Won't you join me?" (if she really wants him to). At a large dance where there is a floor committee or stag line a man can always signal adroitly when he thinks he has danced enough of a duty dance.

Girls, of course, get stuck too during interminable dances when no one asks to cut in. If no relief seems in sight either partner can suggest leaving the floor, usually under the pretext that there are too many couples dancing, that a drink, or a talk, or a walk in the air might be more fun. If either partner feels inept at a particular dance and the music strikes up in that tempo that is another quite acceptable excuse for sitting out a dance. But a man never escorts a girl from the floor and leaves her unaccompanied.

Husband's Obligation to His Wife   When a man escorts his wife to a dance, his obligation to her as an escort is the same as it was when he was a single man. He dances the first dance with her, sees to it that she is never left alone, and has the last dance with her, too. He is obliged to dance with the hostess at least once and with any woman guest of honor. In leaving his wife to do this, he sees to it that she either has a dancing partner or is seated with other people. If the party is a supper dance, he escorts his wife or sees to it that someone else, perhaps the man with whom she is to be seated, is taking care of her. Ideally, husbands and wives at such functions both circulate and do not stay glued together all evening.

Chapter 26

THE SMOKING PROBLEM

Cigar Smoking

There are men who will agree with me—and most women will, too—that cigar smoking has certain definite perils, esthetically. To me a large fat cigar in the mouth of a young man has about the same effect on his appearance as would a pince-nez. The smaller, slim, mild cigars seem preferable. At least it seems to discourage the unattractive habit of a man's leaving a half-smoked cigar around for later relighting. And a small cigar is usually treated like a cigarette and not allowed to stay overlong in the mouth. A chewed cigar end, only too apparent when the cigar is removed during the course of conversation, is enough to repel all but the most hardy females. If you do smoke cigars, treat them as if they were cigarettes. Don't exhale vast and, perhaps, offensive clouds of smoke. Remove the cigar when you talk, take brief puffs to keep the cigar dry and relatively sightly. Be sure a large enough ash tray is at hand before you start, so that you won't get cigar ashes all over the floor, furniture, and yourself. Never even ask to smoke a cigar during a meal (I suppose some men might). At table bring out cigars only at coffee time and even then, when the cigarettes are passed, be sure to ask if your stronger-odored cigar is permissible. Ask for a larger ash tray if the cigar you are to smoke is a large one. Do not smoke cigars on the street.

If you are smoking your cigar in the living room, you will be considered very thoughtful if you don't leave the butt in an ash tray. If you know your way around the house, put the dreary remains in the garbage can. Or, first running it under water, wrap it in paper and drop it in a waste basket. Of course, if servants are on hand to empty ash trays the minute they get overcrowded, one cigar butt more or less will make no difference. But it will make a terrific difference in a party-crowded room where all the ash trays fill rapidly and are not being emptied as soon as desirable.

The truth is, the man who is a constant smoker of heavy cigars stains his teeth, lips, and fingers to a degree seldom encountered in cigarette smokers. But any heavy smoker—whether of pipes, cigars, or cigarettes

—should at least be conscious of the fact that his over-all powerful odor of often stale tobacco can be very offensive, especially to women.

Heavy smokers—men or women—should be sure their clothes and they themselves are frequently aired. They need at least one thorough shampoo a week and regular trips to the dental hygienist to remove stains from the teeth. Finger stains can be taken care of at home with a few drops of peroxide on the nail brush or a rubbing over with pumice stone. But yellow-stained fingernails just have to grow out, I gather.

Every animal—including us, has his own special natural odor. Ours should be an attractive one, but it is easily distorted into something less than attractive by oversmoking, overdrinking, or too great consumption of certain foods—fatty ones, for example. Delicate colognes and perfumes should enhance our natural odors, not overshadow them. Scrupulous physical cleanliness and a cultivated fastidiousness about our habits, such as smoking and drinking, will make us more attractive.

It is well known scientifically that humans, as well as animals, are attracted or repelled by the odor of another person even when they are not actually conscious such odors exist. Perhaps we have more in common with the hound than we imagine.

The Pipe Smoker

Pipes are generally becoming to most men of any age—and with cigars are more in evidence as many men face the truth about the harmfulness of smoking cigarettes particularly. Cigars and pipes are the lesser evils.

But the pipe smoker must watch his manners, too. Pipe cleaning is a messy operation even in the hands of an expert and should be done in relative privacy. The discarded contents of the bowl and the used pipe cleaner should be quickly disposed of, not left in the ash tray to befoul the atmosphere. And if the smoker feels the necessity to improve the pipe's draw through loud sucking or blowing, or whatever it is that's so noisy, let him step outside the door, unless he is quite alone at his task. Small, neat evening pipes may now be smoked at formal dinners with the hostess's permission. Small pipes are also smoked on the street now, but the more dramatic ones are best avoided under these circumstances.

There is pipe tobacco and pipe tobacco. It's safer perhaps to go by the judgment of friends in the matter of which blend to choose than to pick one by taste alone. It is not possible that tobacco that smells so bad can taste that way, too. Let your friends' pleased or pained expressions when you light up be your guide.

When Not to Smoke

With smoking so common, we sometimes forget there are times and places where one never smokes, even though not so reminded by a "No Smoking" sign. Members of the assemblage in any religious ceremony taking place at home, a wedding, a christening or a funeral, do not smoke—just as one doesn't smoke in church or, if he has any consideration, in elevators. Getting into an elevator "palming" a lighted cigar or cigarette is threatening yourself or fellow passengers with possible burns if the elevator becomes crowded or there is an accident.

You may not smoke in an airplane while the "No Smoking" sign is lighted, although you may when the plane has reached a certain altitude and the sign goes off. Some planes now properly have no smoking sections.

Smoking is not allowed in court or in most public meeting places such as concert halls, movies, department stores, and theaters except in sections set aside for smokers, Some of the best restaurants prohibit smoking or restrict it.

You do not smoke on buses, streetcars, or trains unless you are seated in a smoking section, so labeled. Do not even pass through non-smoking areas carrying lighted pipes, cigars, or cigarettes.

You never walk, smoking, into a sickroom or into a nursery. In a sickroom, if the patient is smoking, you may smoke if invited to do so and are careful not to leave ashes and butts behind you to make the atmosphere unpleasant. It is incredible how many people not only smoke while visiting a young baby in his nursery but also use any available receptacle for the ends of cigars and cigarettes—from silver porringers to diaper pails—with no thought at all for the baby's possible reaction to the ensuing fumes.

Business firms have varying rules concerning smoking, but, even when employers don't consider the matter important, employees seated where they receive visitors to the office should not smoke on the job. Where office employees are permitted to smoke at their desks, they should not allow ashes and butts to pile up in receptacles but should dispose of them from time to time—and not by dumping them loose into the waste basket. Some employers, in desperation at the amount of time lost if employees are allowed to smoke in rest rooms only, permit smoking on the job. But a cigarette or cigar resting on the edge of a desk can ruin the finish. Close work interrupted by drags on a cigar, pipe, or cigarette can suffer badly, and production can be slowed down to the point of serious inefficiency if the worker is a constant smoker.

Women should not smoke while walking on city or town streets, although on open country roads they may if they wish (being careful to put out matches and cigarettes carefully before discarding them, to prevent fires). Unattractive is the woman who insists on smoking while driving—especially if she leaves the cigarette in her mouth (which also makes her look very tough).

No one riding with others in a taxi or automobile should smoke without permission of the others. And used matches and butts should not be ground out on the floor. If no receptacle is provided, snub out the light against the sole of your shoe and discard the butt out the window. Do not throw lighted cigarettes or cigars out of the window, not only because they may start a fire or burn a passer-by, but because the wind may blow sparks or the smoke itself back into the car and cause damage. This poor practice can also bring a stiff fine.

If you smoke on a sailboat, flip your ashes or discard your cigarette on the side the sail is on so the wind won't blow sparks or ashes or butts back into the boat.

Chapter 27

CLUBS

Men's Clubs

A good club is not a social necessity, but it is a social convenience. It is, usually, a place where one meets men of similar interests and background, a comfortable *pied-à-terre* in town where a man can stay overnight, put up another man guest, receive messages and entertain in private, if he wishes, as if he were in his own home.

Any man with enough money to pay the dues can list a long string of clubs after his name, even a long list of the best ones if he stands muster with the membership committees. But the man of substance prefers to be associated with usually not more than two main clubs, one in the country and one in town, depending on his interests. He avoids taking membership merely for the prestige in a number of clubs in whose affairs he can take little or no part.

Actual, active identification with his club is to a man's benefit, because it permits him a say in the running of it. Absentee, inactive membership, widely practiced, means that a club is taken over by a small clique that runs it for its own benefit and often against the interests of the membership as a whole. Furthermore, if he really understands what his club represents, what the thinking is as reflected in the by-laws, a man can protect himself against being classified as something he really is not, by fighting what he doesn't like or getting out.

Joining a Club It is part of our snobbism that we don't want to join a club everyone can join. For that reason, a man never openly asks that he be put up for membership in any of the exclusive clubs, although he may tactfully indicate his interest to members among his friends. Then, if he seems eligible, they may propose him, first making sure that he understands what membership entails as to initiation fee, dues, rules, and regulations. It is, of course, highly embarrassing to the sponsor or sponsors if the proposed new member is rejected for any reason. Their explanation to him of such a rejection must be accepted gracefully and without probing. It is often possible for him to qualify for the same club later, especially if his reaction to the first refusal has been sporting. It is an axiom that it is easier for a well-introduced stranger to get into a good club than a well-known man-about-town who's had ample opportunity to gather enemies as well as friends.

Tipping in Clubs In the major clubs the employees are tipped by the members at Christmas, or at the holiday time members may contribute to a kitty for the staff. In addition, most clubs now add a service charge to all bills. Guests of members do not tip unless they have been put up at the club, though the service charge is usually added to bills. Resident guests or members using private rooms for large parties may, if they wish, tip additionally the employee with whom they have had the most contact—on the same scale one would in a first-class hotel.

Proposing and Seconding In large clubs new members are usually proposed by letter, although sometimes the proposing is done in a brief interview with the club secretary, who then usually posts the name, with the names of the proposer and seconder, after the suggestion has cleared the membership committee. The posting of the name gives members who might object to the inclusion of the proposed member a chance to protest to the board of governors. Such protest is often verbal to one or more governors or, preferably, by letter to the board of governors, stating one's objections to the proposed member. These objections are, supposedly, kept confidential and should be. It is foolish not to make them if they are merited and thus possibly admit a member who will not be agreeable.

Letters of Proposal and Seconding A friend writes to the board of governors of his club to propose a new member somewhat in this manner, including relevant material:

September 15, 1971

To the Board of Governors of the Town Club
Gentlemen:

It gives me much pleasure to propose for membership my friend Dr. Norman Benson, Jr., a former college classmate. Dr. Benson is a graduate of Dartmouth College and of Harvard University where he received his M.D. His late uncle, Judge Timothy Way, was a long-time member of the club.

Dr. Benson is married (to the former Lola Ferris) and lives at 800 Park Avenue. He is chief of research staff of Botts Pharmaceutical Company at 700 Fifth Avenue. He is in his early forties, a good squash player and a sound man in every way.

I hope you will agree that he would be a most desirable member.

Respectfully,
Norris Lanson

321 Park Avenue
New York, N.Y. zip code

The seconding letter merely states that the writer is seconding the proposal and adds a few words of commendation, general or specific. It is always wise for a sponsor to get more than one other member to endorse his candidate for admission to the club if there seems any possibility of refusal. Often outsiders who can vouch for the candidate—his clergyman, his banker, or his lawyer—write to the board. Also, the sponsor sees to it that the proposed man meets as many of the board of governors as possible in brief calls upon them at their offices. The candidate makes these calls alone, after the sponsor has made the necessary appointments. He meets usually four governors in this way, two of whom are on the membership committee.

The Letter of Objection   Voting on the candidate takes place in committee, with two blackballs counting against admission and no explanation required. All objections have usually been weighed before the election meeting. So any letter to the board is sent soon after the posting of the name. Such a letter should be reserved, but explicit enough to permit the board of governors to consider your objection properly. It might read:

January 12, 1972

To the Board of Governors of the Town Club
Gentlemen:
   It has come to my notice that Mr. —— has been proposed for membership. In my opinion Mr. —— indulges much too frequently and heavily in alcohol. I have seen him garrulous and contentious to a degree that would, I am sure, disturb our relatively conservative membership.

Sincerely yours,
Signature

62 Sutton Place
New York, N.Y.   zip code

Putting up a Guest   Most club by-laws have a limitation on the number of times any guest may be admitted to the club over a certain period. They also limit the length of stay of a house guest, in most cases to two weeks. Only out-of-town guests may be put up at a club, not local residents.
   A letter putting up a guest is addressed to the club secretary. For example:

February 6, 1972

To the Secretary of the Town Club
   I should like to put up my business associate Mr. Thomas Putney, of Chicago, for the week of March 14th. Will you be kind enough to send

him a membership card to our Chicago office, whose address is on this letterhead.

Sincerely,
Norris Lanson

321 Park Avenue
New York, N.Y. zip code

It is well understood that a member never asks to have a guest put up who for some reason would be quite ineligible for even non-resident membership in the club should he wish to join. A member would not ask to put up a prominent Socialist in the Union League, for example.

Resigning from a Club The loss of an influential member from a club is usually regrettable. If he is resigning "in protest," that is known by his conduct in the club prior to his resignation. His actual letter of resignation is brief and merely for the record. If he must resign after bills for dues for the new year have been received, he pays his dues even if he does not plan to use the club. A letter of resignation is always formal and makes some polite excuse for not continuing membership. For example:

June 16, 1971

To the Board of Governors of the Town Club
Gentlemen:
Pressure of work makes it most difficult for me to take advantage of club privileges at all this year. I should like to resign with the thought that at some later date I might be able to continue the many pleasant activities and friendships the club afforded me.

Most sincerely,
John Robert Barbour

321 East 76th Street
New York, N.Y. zip code

Guest of a Private Club A guest of a member must never "take over" a club. He should make himself agreeably inconspicuous and no more criticize the service, the furnishings, or facilities of the club than he would criticize these things in his host's own home. As in a private home, too, he asks permission to use the outside telephone, as he is required to give the member's name to the operator who is making the call. If he makes out-of-town calls or many local ones, he asks for the charges and quietly reimburses his host. He should not attempt to entertain his host in the club but should take him elsewhere, except possibly for a drink. Members, by the way, do not pay for meals and drinks at time of service but sign checks submitted and pay their bills monthly.

Men's clubs sometimes have certain rooms or sections where they may entertain women guests or where women friends or members of their family may meet members or lunch or dine without them. These facilities should not be used without the express knowledge of the member, who then arranges for the courtesy. The bill is signed by the guest, who places beneath his or her signature the member's name. The bill may then be settled later with the member, if that is the understanding. No tip is left, as a service charge is included.

Also, in most men's clubs, there are rooms for members only. Guests are expected to meet members in the public rooms, only, by appointment.

Women's Clubs

Women have far fewer resident clubs than men have. In formal clubs where there are full facilities the rules are much the same as those governing men's clubs. In such organizations as the Junior League, dedicated to social service, there are in addition certain work requirements before a candidate is eligible for membership. Membership in the Junior League, by the way, is by invitation only.

The Women's Club in communities throughout the country concerns itself at least in part with local improvement. It is usually tied in with the national organization, the General Federation of Women's Clubs, and open to any local resident who wishes to join. There are, too, many special interest clubs, many of them affiliated with such larger entities as the Garden Clubs of America, the League of Women Voters of the U.S., and the various women's divisions of political and fraternal organizations, all of which are of social and civic importance.

How to Obtain Membership In such clubs as these it is perfectly proper for an interested woman to write the club secretary and ask for a membership blank. Or she may be taken to the club as a guest of a member, who then asks the secretary to give her a membership blank. Dues are usually nominal. They should be paid promptly, and, as in a very formal men's club, one pays her dues anyhow if the bill for them has arrived before a letter of resignation has been received by the club.

In all women's clubs that make any pretense at formality the parliamentary procedure is followed. Women members should familiarize themselves with the rules, so that the business affairs of their club may be conducted in a dignified and efficient manner. (See "Simple Parliamentary Procedure.")

The Elective Clubs Such organizations as the Daughters of the American Revolution are elective to the extent that a candidate's qualifications for membership are rigidly fixed—in this case certain ancestral participation in the American Revolution. Anyone who believes she qualifies may apply for membership, and her application is then passed upon after the necessary historical checking.

Club Teas It is usual for women's club meetings to be followed by afternoon tea, with the tea presided over by one or more club officers, who thus serve as hostesses. The tea table, always properly covered with a white cloth, is set up with a silver tea service at one end, the water kept boiling by a spirit lamp. Cups and saucers are arranged within reach of the hostess, each cup on its saucer and a teaspoon to the right of the handle. For a limited number of guests the cup and saucer is stacked on a small cake plate with a tea napkin (usually paper) between saucer and plate. Generally only finger foods are served, so no fork or butter knife is needed. For very large teas the cake plates are stacked at the other end of the table with napkins between, or adjacent to, them. Guests go for their tea to the person pouring, telling her whether they wish sugar, lemon, or cream, then pick up their plates and serve themselves to little tea sandwiches or cakes. Frequently coffee is served at one end of the table and tea at the other, with a hostess presiding over each beverage.

Guests usually take their tea standing and place their empty cups and plates on a sideboard or serving table for removal by committee members or available waitresses. As at any reception, one speaks to anyone who happens to be standing near, whether or not one has been introduced. The chatting women do not necessarily introduce themselves to each other but may, saying merely, "I'm Mrs. Petersen" (*not* Kitty Petersen). The other need reply simply "Mrs. Antonio," adding, perhaps, "It's nice to meet you."

Women's Listing of Names On club letterheads women's names are listed with their titles Miss Anne Brown, Chairman; Mrs. *James* McGee, Entertainment Committee. A married officer or committee member signs such letters Agnes Sorensen (maiden name or middle name or initial optional) Blake and below it parenthetically (Mrs. Robert Blake). It is completely incorrect for club women who are married to assume that within the club they would be known as Mrs. Agnes Blake. Professional women who use their professional names in their work will, of course, in a professional club list themselves by their professional rather than social names.

With the ever-increasing status of women in business and the professions, more and more women who retain their maiden names for their professional lives (something I always recommend) do encounter problems of duality. Well-known and respected in her own field, a woman may find that socially, too, when she is with her husband people tend to refer to her and to introduce her by her professional name. I have known only one woman who ever insisted on her professional name, preceded by Miss, in her social life as well. She was never known by the name of her husband. He, in turn, always introduced her as "Miss" even though he himself had a very distinguished name. Most women in such a situation certainly prefer to use their husbands' names socially. In a social group, however, Helen Hayes might very well make everyone more comfortable by introducing herself as Helen Hayes MacArthur, rather than just Mrs. MacArthur. Hostesses, too, are often well advised to so introduce professional women under social circumstances as this can often avoid embarrassing situations.

Sometimes for a professional woman there are times when both her professional name and her social name need to be listed. An example of this was in a society page photograph caption in the New York *Times* of the famous artist, Helen Frankenthaler. She was so listed in connection with a photograph headed, "Art Lovers." But the *Times* parenthetically placed after her name: "(Mrs. Robert Motherwell)." Her husband, of course, is a very distinguished artist, too, and such a solution is a good one. In a listing for sponsors for a charity, or other money-raising event, where a prominent wife's name is needed, the couple may be listed in this way: Mr. and Mrs. Francis X. Harper (Ann Morgan).

Country Clubs, Beach Clubs, and Yacht Clubs

Under "Men's Clubs" and "Women's Clubs" I have discussed the procedures of becoming members and of resigning from clubs. The rules for behavior in all clubs are much the same, with consideration of others of major importance. In the section, "What's What in Various Sports," I discuss specific rules in sailing, tennis, swimming, etc., for spectators and participants.

If you move into a community, it is best to inquire tactfully whether or not it is necessary to be proposed for membership to any local clubs that interest you. In general, community clubs are fairly informal, and one may apply to the club secretary for membership without being proposed by a sponsor and seconder. Yacht and golf clubs maintained by the municipality are open to all able to pay the small fees or dues for maintenance.

Country and beach clubs are always family clubs and thus necessarily more relaxed than formal town clubs. The family uses them during summer weekends and sometimes in the winter, too. During the summer the younger generation—infants with their nurses, sitters, or mothers, the subteens and teen-agers—takes over during the week. From Monday to Friday there is not much point in trying to keep the noise down to a bearable level, except late in the day when adult members may wish to use the club, too. Infants obviously need their own little paddling corner, safe from the older children. All the children need some adult supervision even when there is no water. They must be taught early to use their own equipment, to return borrowed toys, boats, rafts, balls, and other things when they have finished using them. They should not be allowed to dig up turf or courts, throw sand, or misuse anything in the club house.

Weekends, when weary adults hope for some relaxation, children must settle for less than the full facilities of the club. Parents with young children should try to keep them away from the club on Saturdays, Sundays, and holidays to give older people a chance.

Club bills should be settled promptly and dues never be allowed to accumulate. Even club members in good standing should remember they are there by sufferance, by tacit consent. The club itself with its rules and its bylaws creates an atmosphere wherein even a founder member has the status of a guest the minute he steps on the grounds.

Club Guests Most family clubs have few regulations concerning the bringing of guests, but good taste and good sense enter into consideration here, too. No one should bring so many guests that the facilities of the club are thereby taxed insofar as the members are concerned. For example, no member with consideration will fill all the badminton or tennis courts with his guests to the exclusion of members. Limited guests over weekends should be an unwritten rule if guests are to use the club facilities such as locker and steam rooms, game courts, pools, beach, or golf course. If they are invited to be spectators, that is another matter, but they should always be the kind of people the club might welcome as members. A private club is no place on which to inflict one's own private little social crosses.

Manners in Public Places

Loud and inconsiderate behavior in public places, on beaches, in parks, in playgrounds, at spectator sports, has always been considered bad manners because it does not take into consideration the feelings and needs of others. Public conveyances or the street, for example, are not the places to play transistor radios. Others may not wish to listen. At spectator sports where most people are paying close attention to the play, people who are noisy among themselves or inconsiderate in entering or leaving, can spoil the pleasure of people who, like themselves, have paid for admission. Parks are for all of the people, not just for those who want to take part in some physical activity there and may be noisy. If you are considerate of others you will confine your noisy activities to areas set aside for handball, jogging, football, etc. There is so little privacy, peace, and quiet left in this world; be sensitive to other people's need for it even if such a need has not perhaps yet evidenced itself to you.

Littering The worst manners, the greatest disregard for the sensibilities, the safety, the sensitivity of other people are exhibited by those who litter, by people who wantonly destroy nature by pollution, and destruction of various kinds. Just cleaning up the litter careless people create costs U.S. taxpayers some five hundred million dollars annually. Urban communities spend nearly three hundred million dollars of that amount just for street cleaning—and we still don't have clean streets. Another one hundred million dollars must be expended for the removal of litter from the highways, and our highways are a disgrace nonetheless. Additional millions are spent cleaning up our forests, parks, beaches, waterways, park fountains, national monuments. In all, the cost of public litter removal added to the cost of private clean-up now approaches a billion dollars a year. Every twelve minutes a home in the United States is destroyed or damaged by fire starting in rubbish and litter. Litter on the streets and in homes causes the rodent and insect population to proliferate. Litter gets into our streams, rivers and into our oceans, endangering swimmers, fishermen, boaters, killing marine and plant life. Litter spreads decay, ruins property values, disgusts foreign visitors, discourages tourists and new industries.

Litter is mainly a matter of individual thoughtlessness, Keep America Beautiful tells us. People feel no personal responsibility for the appearance of their streets, their highways, the countryside in general. They leave a trail of trash behind them that says very plainly and clearly, "I am not a person of culture. I have no sensibility. I don't relate to my fellow man. I am a boor." The litter in this country is created by millions of individuals. Only individuals can stop it. When you see somebody throwing a used cigarette pack on the sidewalk, don't hesitate to ask him to pick it up. Be pleasant in your request. If he refuses and you love your country, pick it up yourself. If there are not enough trash cans in your area, keep after the local government until you get them. Dispose of your garbage in such a way that it does not scatter or attract rodents. Don't permit trash to collect in your house, especially in out-of-the-way places like cellars and attics. Teach your children to respect their environment. As it is now, we are choking on it. This can be a beautiful country again if each one of us every day makes the effort to achieve this ideal.

Chapter 28

MANNERS AT TABLE

A man or woman may take on a superficial patina of breeding, but it is very difficult to overcome slipshod table manners. And poor manners at table can be a real deterrent to social—and even business—progress.

Gentle people are often acutely embarrassed by the table manners of those with whom they find themselves eating. A carefully bred wife may suffer much inner torture because her husband—always when manners seem very important—forgetfully leaves his spoon in his cup, waves his fork during conversation or absent-mindedly licks his fingers. It is the job of a good wife to help an ambitious husband overcome these poor manners in a tactful way if she can—not solely because they offend her and are a poor example for the children but because good manners can help him advance in his work or profession. Of course, it is sometimes the other way around, and people are even less willing to overlook bad table manners on the part of women, who are expected to be fastidious about such things.

Some of the things necessary to know about behavior at formal meals are discussed under "The Guest at Formal Meals." But there are many more:

Who Is Served First?

The hostess is *not* served first unless she is the only lady at the table or is alone with her husband and children. If grandmother or even a young girl guest is present, the dishes are first presented to her after inspection by the hostess. When the hostess is serving at least part of the meal from in front of her place, with or without the aid of a servant, she is served next to last and her husband last. For her to serve herself earlier will mean her food will be cold and her filled plate in the way.

When to Begin Eating

After several people have been served, guests begin eating, so their food will not be cold. For example, guests may begin eating after three people at a table of six have been served. If the hostess sees them hesitate she should urge them to start. But children wait, if they are old enough to understand, until at least several guests have been served before beginning to eat, too. When children are alone with their parents it is considerate of them at all meals but breakfast to wait until their parents begin eating before beginning themselves, unless they are told to go ahead. And, except at breakfast, the polite husband waits until his wife has been served before beginning himself to eat.

The Use of the Knife and Fork

Knives and forks may be used American or Continental fashion, but a combination of the two systems is now often seen and is quite acceptable. Even when one uses the American zigzag method, it is sensible to convey food one has just cut to the mouth with the fork in the left hand, if one wishes. In other words, if you have cut off a bit of chop, it is not necessary, even conservative American style, to lay down the knife, place the fork, tines up, in the right hand and convey the meat to the mouth. Instead, one may use the fork in the left hand, with the tines of the fork down cutting only one or two pieces of meat at a time. Also, in eating a bit of bread and gravy—by impaling the bread on the fork (in either hand), tines down, and sopping up the gravy—it is now more usual than otherwise to convey the bit to the mouth with the fork tines down rather than up. Of course, nothing that would leak off the fork—apple pie or other things needing a shoveling technique—should be eaten this way. Elbows should be kept close to the sides, not flapped, wing fashion so as to avoid intrusion upon one's neighbor. In the European fashion, food eaten with fork and knife is piled with the knife on the back of the fork, held in the left hand, and pressed down so it won't fall off—or in the case of meat, impaled on the tines. The fork is then conveyed to the mouth, upside down, with the left hand.

The fork is never "cleaned" by wiping it on the knife or a piece of bread or on the edge of a plate. If it is not in use it is returned to the plate, not held in the air during conversation.

The Dessert Silver

The spoon and fork or fork or spoon alone which may be needed for the dessert course may be placed, along with the dessert, on the plate. I prefer, however, to have the table set with the dessert implements placed above the dinner plate—with the fork, tines up facing right, and the spoon above it—bowl facing left. There is occasionally some puzzlement as to where to place the dessert spoon after one has finished—in the dessert dish itself or on the service plate. Much depends on the size of the dessert dish in relation to the service plate and on the general shape and height of the dessert dish itself. For example, when you are served a dessert in a stemmed glass on a service plate, obviously the dessert spoon should not be left in the glass but should be placed on the service plate at the right. On the other hand, if you had a pudding-type dessert served in a plate that resembles a soup plate or sauce dish, there would be no reason why you cannot leave the spoon in the dish when you have finished. It may of course be placed on the service plate, to the right, if you choose and there is room.

Drinking Beverages at the Table

In drinking any beverage at the table, a sip is never taken until the mouth is empty and has been wiped with the napkin. This keeps cup and glass rims free from food marks. Hot beverages best tested with a spoon are sipped once from the spoon which is then placed on the saucer beneath the handle.

The Napkin

Napkins are placed on the lap—entirely open if they are lunch-size or in half if they are dinner napkins. Guests wait until the hostess has taken up hers before placing their own. Napkins are tucked in only for children or on airplanes. They are never refolded by a guest and family members do so only if napkins rings are used. At the end of the meal, napkins are gathered and laid casually to the left of the place setting. If rings are used, they are given, usually, as I have noted, only to the family. A guest staying over should have a clean napkin each meal. Napkins reused are as incomprehensible to me as beds which have only one sheet changed. There are so many more sensible ways to economize but this fashion is changing for ecological reasons. Drip-dry or no-iron napkins are in favor and napkin rings for family and guests (even for one use) for environment conscious people.

Tipping of Dishes

The tipping of soup or dessert dishes is acceptable if the plate is tipped away from the eater, not toward him.

The Handled Soup or Bouillon Cup

Soup or bouillon served in a handled cup or even in a small cup-size bowl (Oriental fashion) may be drunk. If there are dumplings or decorative vegetables or other garnish floating on top, these may be lifted out first with the spoon before the soup is drunk. Noodles or other things which may be in the bottom of the cup are spooned up after the liquid has been drunk.

Testing Liquids

Coffee or tea may be tested for heat or sweetening by one sip from the spoon, then drunk. If it is too hot, it must be allowed to stand until it is tolerable—it may not be blown, spoonful by spoonful, until it is cool enough to drink. The spoon, after it has been used for tasting or stirring, is placed on the saucer to the right beneath the handle.

Token Portions

If you are serving yourself from a buffet, you need not take anything you don't like, if there is a wide enough choice of food. If the main dish contains an ingredient you simply cannot eat or dislike intensely, take at least a token portion and disguise the fact by adding more of other things such as rice and salad. Don't mention your dislike to the hostess unless she notices, and then make light of the matter so she won't feel she must get you something else. You can always eat something when you get home or on the way home if you are starving. I once saw a woman of great culture go through an entire New England shore dinner without actually eating a thing except her salad and dessert, merely by pushing things around on her plate. She was dreadfully allergic to seafood and nobody there knew it, including the eagle-eyed hostess. If you are not eating at a buffet or a dinner such as the shore dinner where you are served everything automatically, you take from the dishes offered you the things you like and take only token portions of what you don't like and these of course you need not eat. Do avoid taking large portions of food you have no intention of touching for this is not only wasteful but may make the hostess think there is something seriously wrong with what she has offered you.

"Stirring" Food

Nothing should ever be stirred up or mashed into a conglomerate heap on the plate. Gravy—unless it is a gravy in which meat, fish or other protein is incorporated (rarebits, curries, blanquettes, chilis, etc.)—is never poured or ladled onto rice, noodles, or other than meat on the plate. It is an insult to the cuisine to inundate everything on your plate with gravy—or with that American favorite, catsup. If you want to eat your potatoes with gravy, you dip a forkful into the gravy that has escaped from the meat.

The Left-handed Person

The left-handed person learns to adapt to a right-handed world, thus at the table he should not expect any special consideration. He leaves his place setting as it is. If a hostess or the family can place him at the end of the table or alone at one side of the table, he will of course be more comfortable eating. Cultivating ambidexterity will make his life easier.

Rearranging the Table

No diner, even a left-handed one, presumes to rearrange the placement of the table nor pushes away his plate after completing his dessert when dessert dishes are not necessarily removed as guests sit over coffee and perhaps liqueurs.

Conserves and Jellies

Conserves and jellies (jam and marmalade are for breakfast and tea) may be served at dinner or lunch with meat and are placed on the side of the plate, as are horse-radish, cranberry sauce, apple butter, relish. They are incorporated onto the fork as the food is taken into the mouth. Hard sauce is placed on the side of the dessert plate and incorporated with the pudding with dessert fork or spoon. Dessert sauces are ladled onto the dessert. Liquid sauces (mint, Chateaubriand, Worcestershire, etc.) meant for the meat are poured only onto it.

When Food Is Too Hot

Too hot foods taken accidentally into the mouth are never hastily spit out in any way but are quenched with a drink of water or other liquid at the table before being swallowed (exception to rule against drinking with anything in the mouth).

"Spoiled" Food

Nothing, not even a bad clam, is ever spit, however surreptitiously, into a napkin. But it is sheer masochism to down, for the sake of manners, something really spoiled, once you have a goodly mouthful. Anyone with experience in those foreign countries where such things are common knows it is better to seem unmannerly than to brave ptomaine or worse. Certainly, a partly chewed mouthful of food looks unappetizing to one's dinner partner if it has been necessary for you to deposit it from your fork on the side of the plate. It should be screened, if possible, with some celery leaves or, perhaps, a bit of bread. And, in taking it out of your mouth, try not to look as if anything were the matter. After all, if you were eating stewed or canned cherries, you would place the pits in the spoon with which you were eating, then place them on the side of your plate without anyone thinking the procedure disgusting.

Accidents at the Table

Even the most careful eater occasionally has an accident at table. If food is spilled, for example a bit of jelly or sauce, you may quietly retrieve it with any convenient utensil—butter knife, fork, or dinner knife—and place it at the side of your plate. Occasionally a bit of food or liquid will spill or drip onto a dress or tie. In such a case the best thing to do is to use a clean knife or spoon to lift off the offending substance if it hasn't soaked immediately into the fabric. Do this quietly and without apology. Then take the corner of your napkin, dip it into your water glass, and lightly rub the spot. After you have taken all of these precautions, forget it. We all have these moments, it is comforting to remember. The real social *gaffe* is in making a mountain out of such a molehill.

Swallowing the "Wrong Way"

If food should become stuck in your throat this is no time for formal manners. A half-inhaled piece of food which blocks the air passage can possibly cause death in about eight minutes. Don't let anyone slap you on the back, which might cause you to inhale it further. Get up without apology and leave the table immediately, getting somebody to come with you. Open your mouth wide and either reach into your throat yourself or let the other person do it, being careful not to push the food further down into the throat. Keep your fingers well to the side of your throat and try to hook the food, pulling it away from the danger area. Do not feel that you must return to the table to be polite. This is a very frightening experience and you should rest and recover. If it isn't really as simple as this, sometimes artificial respiration is necessary. Waiting for a doctor or an ambulance *can* take too long.

The prevention of such accidents is important. The ingestion of large amounts of alcohol can anesthetize the swallowing muscles and of course impair judgment on the amount of food taken into the mouth. The wearing of dentures sometimes causes miscalculation on whether or not food has been sufficiently chewed before being swallowed. It is important, therefore, to cut food into small bites, to put a small amount of food into the mouth at one time and to chew thoroughly before swallowing, especially if the meal has been preceded by cocktails or served with wine.

Sneezing

At the table, if you have no time to reach for a handkerchief or a tissue, cover your face with your napkin although otherwise a napkin must never be used as a handkerchief. If you must sneeze in a public conveyance or an elevator and haven't time to reach your handkerchief at least cover your face with your hand and turn away from others if possible.

Often, in other situations, a sneeze comes so quickly that you can't reach for a handkerchief or a tissue. In this case, place your hand before your mouth and nose to hold back the droplets which otherwise would go into the air around you. A paroxysm of sneezing in the course of a play or concert would require your leaving the hall. If it happens when you are standing or sitting with a group, you should certainly turn away. It is not necessary to apologize profusely. A simple, "I'm sorry" (unless you are at a performance) suffices. Do not try to suppress a sneeze by pressing your upper lip with your forefinger if this possibly can be avoided. A sneeze should be allowed to occur, doctors say. You should, however, do the best you can to keep it from being loud and disturbing.

Food in the Teeth

If food gets wedged in the teeth and can't be dislodged with the tongue, don't use a fingernail but on leaving the table ask for a toothpick. Dislodge the offending bit in private. If this is a frequent problem it is wise to carry your own emergency equipment. There are little triangular toothpicks in packets like matches. They are called Stim-U-Dents and are available in drugstores. They are handy to have.

Blowing One's Nose at the Table

If the nose must be blown at table, it is done as quietly as possible, without excuse to draw attention to the fact.

Speaking with Food in the Mouth

Nobody today bothers to completely empty the mouth before speaking at the dinner table, despite the injunction to children, "Don't speak with your mouth full." Certainly the mouth should not be full when you are trying to talk, but waiting to speak until every bit of food is out of your mouth delays conversation interminably. It is possible to learn how to speak while eating and still be inoffensive. Certainly no food should be in the front of the mouth, and the mouth should never be too full. If anyone directs a question to you when your mouth is full, naturally you must wait until it is at least partially empty before replying. The other person can easily observe your dilemma and should wait quietly, preferably with eyes averted until you are ready to reply.

Burping at Meals

Burping or belching should not be considered "rude." It is nature's way of getting rid of gas and, medically, suppressing it may be harmful. If you must, cover your mouth with your napkin. Polite people at the table will pretend it didn't happen. If anyone seems thoroughly surprised you might murmur a quiet, "I'm sorry" as you would with a loud sneeze, which also should not be suppressed, although it should be covered with a handkerchief. But if *that's* impossible, at least with your napkin. A napkin, however, even a paper one, should not be used as a handkerchief at table, as I've said before. It may be used if necessary only to prevent the spray of a sneeze from going any farther than your nose. It may be used to cover a sudden cough if you don't have time to reach for your handkerchief.

"Foreign Matter" in Food

Foreign bodies accidentally taken into the mouth with food—gravel, stones, bird shot—are removed with thumb and forefinger, as are fish bones and other tiny bones. If a gnat gets into a beverage or some other unappetizing creature turns up in or on a diner's food, he fishes it out, unobserved (so others won't see it and be upset), and then either proceeds or leaves the drink or dish untouched, depending on the degree of odiousness of the intruder. A gnat or a tiny inchworm on lettuce shouldn't bother anyone, but most fastidious people draw the line at a fly or worse. If the hostess notices an untouched dish, she may say, "Do let me serve you a fresh portion," and she has the dish or drink removed without remarking clinically as to the need for the move. Or if a servant notices, she asks if the guest would like a fresh serving. In a restaurant, if host or hostess does not notice (and both should be alert for this sort of thing) that something is amiss, the guest may tactfully murmur to the waiter that the dish or drink needs changing—preferably when host or hostess's attention is directed elsewhere.

When You Need Silverware

Your own wet spoon should never be placed in a sugar bowl, nor your butter knife in the jam or butter dish. If the serving utensils have been forgotten, pause long enough for the hostess to notice what's happened. If she doesn't, ask for what you need.

Tasting Another's Food

Sometimes a couple dining in a restaurant wish to taste each other's food. This is informal but permissible, though only if a fresh fork or spoon is used, with the possessor of the dish then handing the "taste" implement, handle first, to the other person. The other must not reach across the table and eat from a companion's plate, no matter how many years they have been married. If one of the two has had included some item—say french fried potatoes—in his order and doesn't wish them, he asks the waiter to serve them to the other, if desired—he doesn't take them on his plate, then re-serve them.

Seasoning

It is an insult to the cook, professional or not, to shake salt and pepper indiscriminately over food that hasn't even been tasted first for seasoning. This is unattractive at a home table, in a restaurant or anywhere else, and for some a poor health practice.

Using Bread as a "Pusher"

A bit of bread, if available, is used to push food onto a fork—never use the fingers. At formal dinners when bread is not served one may always switch to the Continental style, if one is adept, and chase the peas onto the back of the fork held in the left hand, pressing them down before conveying the fork, upside down, to the mouth. Or, holding the fork in the right—or (French and Italian fashion) left—hand, tines up, on the plate, one may guide difficult food onto it with the side of the knife.

Leaving the Table

If you must suddenly leave the table because of feeling ill, or needing to go to the bathroom, no explanation is necessary, merely a nod to the hostess and the request, "May I be excused," is sufficient. When you return to the table—if you do—no explanation is needed or expected. Take your place without comment.

No one should leave the table unless specifically excused until the hostess has put down her napkin, perhaps glanced at the host, a guest or a member of the family before preparing to rise. She may say something such as "Perhaps we should go into the other room" once she has the necessary attention. The guest places his napkin at the left of his plate and prepares to rise with the hostess, with the man on her left assisting her if she is not assisted by a servant.

Reaching at the Table

Reaching at table is now preferred to asking neighbors to pass things one can well take up himself, but one should not have to rise out of his seat. When passing the salt and pepper, pass them together so that they do not become separated at the table.

Smoking at Table

If one must smoke at table, it should be done after the service of dessert, not between courses. And the lone smoker should certainly ask the others if they mind if he smokes.

Conversation at the Table

Conversation and laughter should always be modified at table. Loud guffaws are disturbing at any time but worse from a dinner partner. General conversation, though it should never fall to a too confidential tone between diners, should never be so loud that the hostess cannot make herself heard, if she wishes to address the table. As it is she who guides the conversation, it is necessary for guests, even at a distance, to watch her for possible conversation breaks in the general talk. The modern hostess no longer does what her Victorian predecessor did—that is, at some point halfway through dinner "turn the table" by turning and talking to her dinner partner on the other side, with everyone, no matter where he was in his conversation, expected to break off and turn in the same direction to talk to the partner on *that* side. Instead, well-bred men and women talk pleasantly across a narrow table and whenever a partner on one side seems disengaged may draw him or her into the conversation on the other side. No two partners ever allow themselves to become so engrossed in conversation as to exclude everyone else, especially partners on the ofher side, throughout dinner. And it is the host and hostess's task to prevent such a thing.

What is deemed proper table conversation today? Almost anything except highly controversial (religion, politics) or squeamish topics (accidents, illness, operations, nasty scandal, unaesthetic things), but many sophisticated people are able to discuss once taboo-at-table subjects in a manner that is quite inoffensive, because they know how to employ polite euphemisms in the same or a foreign language—being sure they are comprehensible, of course, to the others at the table. A foreign language unknown to everyone at the dinner table should not be spoken together by others in the group except perhaps for a quick and necessary phrase or so. Unless of course the certain guests know only a foreign language but then they should be seated together and the situation explained to other guests.

Bad Language

Normal conversation today can certainly be studded with what not too long a time ago was considered abnormal language. Not only is the context of our conversation so free that it is virtually without taboos, but words once confined to the locker room appear freely on the lips of some of the most delectable young women. The injunction, "Watch your language!" is meaningless because young people in particular don't seem to know what language to watch. What shocks us does not shock them but seems to be a perfectly reasonable way of expressing themselves. Four-letter words once anathema now appear in the public press, in the movies, on the stage, in generally available books. The underground has surfaced. Most of the acceptable euphemisms are scorned. Much of this may be healthful, more of it is offensive to fastidious people.

It has always been true that words that are offensive in one culture can be perfectly acceptable in another. Words with shock value now can relatively shortly become non-abrasive through constant repetition. Even nice old ladies are no longer shaken by an overheard four-letter word, however they may disapprove. The hostess still has the responsibility of making an evening as pleasant as possible for all of her guests. If she finds conversation growing unpleasant and uncomfortable for some of her guests, she may certainly take a guest or guests whose language seems excessively offensive aside and say something like this, "I wonder if you will be a little careful. There are people here tonight who are conservative. I know you don't realize that the words you are using or some of the subjects you are introducing will offend them, but the truth is that that is the case. I hope you will help me to make their evening pleasant, by using more conventional language." If this doesn't work, a hostess can certainly separate guests who obviously are unsympathetic. To teen-agers (your own or others') you can explain that even though many adults use such expressions, they are not acceptable in your house. Explain to them that these are ugly words, that they offend many people of sensibility, that they are particularly unattractive coming from children or from women. If you keep calm about it and don't show shock, you may be more effective. Among the young particularly, the very words you are inveighing against may shortly be out of style because they have lost their value as attention getters.

Posture

Elbows on the table are permissible between courses but not while one is eating.

Sit at table as you have been taught—with the base of your spine against the back of your chair and your feet flat on the ground. Never sit at table eating with your legs crossed. Men staying in the dining room after a formal dinner for cigars and liqueurs and coffee often do push their chairs away from the table and cross their legs and relax. Chairs should not be so placed or tipped during the course of a meal (and should not be tipped at any time).

The hands between courses were once, in this country, properly held gracefully in the lap, a posture which today seems a little stiff and priggish. There is no reason now why the right hand may not stay in the lap when not in use and the left wrist be laid lightly on the table continental-style so long as one does not lounge. This seems to me much more graceful and natural than the old "hands in the lap" ukase.

Taking Portions from a Serving Dish

When a serving dish is passed with toast or patty shells beneath some food in a sauce, one takes toast or patty shells, too. While their function is sometimes to absorb excess liquid (toast beneath poached eggs), they may, of course, be eaten, cut with fork or fork and knife, never in the fingers.

When a dish is presented with serving fork and spoon, the spoon is used to cut or take up a portion, the fork is placed on top of it for the transfer to the plate. Where food is already portioned—for instance, planked steak—the guest takes the whole portion, does not (in this case) scrape off the potatoes and take just the steak although once the portion is on his plate he eats what he pleases.

Additional Butter

In eating potatoes or other vegetables, if additional butter is desired, it is taken from one's own butter plate with the lunch or dinner *fork*. The butter knife is only for the buttering of breads or corn on the cob.

How to Hold Cups

A handled cup is held with the index finger through the handle, the thumb just above it to support the grip, and the second finger below the handle for added security. The little finger should follow the curve of the other fingers and not be elevated affectedly. It is incorrect to cradle the cup in one's fingers if it has a handle. This is done only when the cup is of Oriental style without handles.

How to Hold Glasses

Large, stemmed glasses (water or wine goblets) are held with the thumb and first two fingers at the base of the bowl. (Exception: If they contain chilled white wine, they are held by the stem so as not to heat the wine with the fingers.)

Small, stemmed glasses are held by the stems. Tumblers are held near the base, but, except by a child, never with both hands. A brandy snifter, of course, is held in the palms of both hands to warm the liquor. The delicate fragrance is inhaled, and, finally, the contents drunk, almost drop by drop.

Saying Grace

The saying of grace is, unfortunately, not the daily matter it used to be. But in many homes throughout the land grace is said. It is heard after the meal—on Friday night especially—among religious Jews. In most Christian homes the grace-saying ceremony is often limited to such great feast days as Thanksgiving, Christmas, and Easter, but, especially in rural communities, grace is frequently heard at the main meal of the week, Sunday dinner. It is usually said, at least on Sunday, in clergymen's homes.

A guest at the table is often given the honor of saying grace. Sometimes a child is asked to say it, or it is the expected privilege of the head of the house (i.e., father—mother is head of the table).

Grace is usually said after everyone is seated and before anything—napkins or even water—is touched on the table. A guest, of course, waits for the hostess's signal before unfolding his napkin, thus he can tell whether the table is waiting for all to be quiet so grace may be said. Heads are bowed and the grace is said by one person at the table who may be designated by the hostess, with the "Amen" intoned by all. A clergyman at the table is usually asked to say grace. In Orthodox and Conservative homes all say ritual grace. In Reform Jewish homes the father or someone designated by him says the grace with the "Amen" intoned by all. Christian graces, like prayers, may be extemporized, of course, but there are many lovely, familiar ones.

Here are two for children—the first an old Scotch one suitable for all religions:

> Thank you for the world so sweet
> Thank you for the food we eat
> Thank you for the birds that sing
> Thank you God for everything.

Blessing for a Christian home:

Bless this food
And make us good
For Jesus' sake.
Amen.

In religious Jewish homes after the father leads the general prayers before food, a child may say this grace:

May the All Merciful bless my
father, my leader, the master
of this house, and my mother,
my teacher, the mistress of
this house.

Here is the most familiar grace of all, acceptable to all religions:

For what we are about to receive,
Lord, make us truly thankful. Amen.

An eighteenth-century grace from Charles County, Maryland, is for Christian homes:

O Lord, forgive us our sins and
bless these refreshments in
Christ's name. Amen.

A simple one for a guest is Ophelia's blessing from *Hamlet:*

God be at your table.

Various denominational prayer books, too, give graces.

Catholics are instructed in the saying of grace both before and after meals. A Catholic grace before meals is:

Bless us, O Lord, and these Thy
gifts, which we are about to receive
from Thy bounty, through Christ
Our Lord. Amen.

A clergyman who is a guest at a public function is also usually asked to say the grace.

How to Eat Various Foods

Artichokes A finger food. The leaves are pulled off, one at a time, the fleshy base dipped in the accompanying sauce, then dexterously pulled through the teeth to extract the tender part. The inedible part of the leaf is then placed at the side of the plate so that by the time the choke (the fuzzy center) is reached there is a neat pile of leaves which, if the artichoke is very big, may be transferred in part at least to the butter plate, for greater convenience. When the choke appears, it is held with the fork or fingers and the tip of the knife neatly excises this inedible portion. Then the reward of all the labor comes—the delicate *fond* or bottom of the artichoke, which, if large, is cut in manageable bits, then dipped in sauce and enjoyed thoroughly.

Asparagus It is not taboo to eat this in the fingers, but it is messy if sauced, so a fork is better. Use the fork to separate the tender part from the tougher end of the stem, then, again with the fork, reduce the edible part to manageable lengths to be dipped in sauce. Do not chew up and then discard, however delicately, the tougher ends, though you may bite off anything edible that remains on the ends by holding them in your fingers, not with the fork.

Bacon Very crisp bacon may be eaten in the fingers if breaking it with a fork would scatter bits over the table. Bacon with any vestige of fat must be cut with fork and knife and eaten with the fork.

Birds', Frogs' Legs Tiny birds, such as squab and quail, and the bones of frogs' legs may be eaten in part with the fingers when the legs or wings are so small as to defy all but the most expert trencherman. Such small bones are held in the fingers by one end while the other end is placed directly in the mouth. The impression of gnawing the bone must be avoided. It is no shame, by the way, for a lady confronted with a squab or half a broiled chicken to ask assistance from the gentleman with her in disssecting it— unless perhaps she's at a formal dinner. This is better than running the risk of having the meat land in her lap or, on the other hand, going hungry, if she is really inept.

Cake Sticky cake is eaten with a fork. Dry cake, such as pound cake or fruit cake, is broken and eaten in small pieces. Tiny confection cakes (served at wedding receptions, etc.) are eaten in the fingers. If they are in a paper frill, they are taken frill and all just as chocolates or bonbons are. Large cream puffs, Napoleons, and éclairs, all treacherous as to filling, are eaten with a fork.

Celery and Olives Celery and olives are on the table when guests are seated if there is no service; or they are passed by a servant during the soup course. They are no longer considered essential even at a formal dinner. They are taken in the fingers, placed on the side of the plate or on the butter plate (and see "Salt"). Olives, if small and stuffed, are popped all at once into the mouth. If they are large and not pitted, they are taken in the fingers and nibbled around the pit. If, however, they are part of a salad and have become involved with dressings or salad ingredients, they are eaten along with the salad with a salad fork. If they are merely garnish on a salad—or on a sandwich—they are eaten with the fingers.

Chicken (*Broiled and Fried*) Under formal circumstances in sophisticated social circles here and abroad, chicken must be eaten with fork
and knife except at picnics. However, I have been in cities in which it is
considered perfectly proper for people in evening dress to pick up chicken
bones. I prefer to see chicken eaten in the conservative way except under
obviously informal circumstances. It is wise, even if you always eat chicken
under informal circumstances, to teach children how to cut and eat
chicken that is broiled or fried. With the increase of world travel, they
are certain to encounter circumstances where informal chicken-eating would
be inappropriate. Chicken bones are not put into the mouth but are
stripped with the knife while being held firmly by the fork. Joints are
cut if one's knife is sharp enough and it can be done without lifting
the elbows from the normal eating position. The best way to manage a
broiler if you are served half a one is to separate the leg at the joint,
with the fork holding it in place and the knife cutting into the connective
tissue. With the fork, then hold the leg in such a way that the meat may
be sliced with the grain, cut into manageable amounts, and eaten. Do
not cut more than two or possibly three pieces at one time. Whatever
chicken cannot be removed with a fork and knife is left. Chicken is not
picked up in the fingers except under the most informal circumstances.
Small chicken legs with the bone end in frilled paper or foil that one
sees at cocktail parties and buffets are, of course, meant to be eaten with
the fingers and one holds them with the frill. Chicken croquettes should
be cut with the fork only, as are all croquettes and fish cakes, then
conveyed to the mouth in manageable pieces.

Rock Cornish hens are eaten with knife and fork. The joints are cut
with the legs dissected from the carcass. The meat may then be removed
with the knife and fork and the wings are treated in the same way.
Then, with the fork in the left hand, impale the breast and slice the
meat from the breastbone. On a small bird, just one slice will usually
accomplish this. If the birds are very small indeed, tiny leg bones (only)
may be taken in the fingers if the hostess so indicates by eating in the
same manner.

Chops Pork or lamb chops even when they are served with a frilled
paper on the small bone end are meant to be eaten with knife and fork,
not taken up in the fingers unless very tiny lamb chops are served this
way at a cocktail party, when, of course, they are meant to be finger
food, like tiny chicken legs served at cocktail parties the same way or
with the bone wrapped in foil. In eating a chop, impale the plump end
with the tines of your fork (upside down) and with your knife, cut out
the center eye. Cut this, one or two pieces at a time into bite-sized pieces.
Then with the knife and fork clean as much meat as you wish from the
remaining bone. The frill end may be held with the fingers (but kept
firmly on the plate) to facilitate cutting from the small bone. Only under

very informal circumstances are such bones taken up in the fingers. The actions of the hostess are the guide.

Corn on the Cob This is only for informal eating and, unless one's teeth will not permit, is best eaten on the cob, with the fingers of each hand firmly in control on each end. A long ear may be broken in half, but only a row or so at a time is buttered and seasoned, never the whole ear at once. Salt already mixed with butter, pepper, and perhaps paprika and shaped in little pats or balls may be provided by the considerate hostess, but a mixture of salt, butter, and pepper may be made, unnoticeably, on the side of one's plate, then smeared a little at a time on the corn as you are eating it. If the corn is to be cut off the cob, the cob is held on one end with the left hand and the kernels cut off a few rows at a time with the dinner knife (which had better be sharp for the purpose). The kernels are then seasoned and eaten a forkful at a time, as one eats peas. There are small silver spears or cob holders for holding corn, but if they are provided you are quite free to ignore them for the more trustworthy fingers-directly-on-cob technique. When they are used, cob holders usually come implanted in the ears of corn. It is also possible to place them to the left of the table setting. In a sense they are "forks."

Eggs, soft-cooked An egg cup is frequently used to serve soft-cooked eggs especially abroad. It is placed on a service plate, and the egg is served in the cup with its small end up. To eat the egg, crack the shell, using the blade of a knife in a sharp horizontal stroke. The egg is then eaten right from the shell with a spoon. If you prefer, you may ask for a small dish for your eggs, instead.

Fish Small fish, fried, are usually served whole (though cleaned) with head and tail (smelt, sunfish, butterfish, etc.). The head is cut off first, then the fish is held in place with the fork and slit with the tip of the knife from head to tail and laid flat. The tip of the knife is then inserted under an end of the backbone, which with the help of the fork—in a serving motion—is gently lifted out, bringing with it many of the tiny bones in the fish. This skeletal material is laid on the side of the plate or possibly on the butter plate. The balance of the fish is then cut with the fork, or with the knife, if need be, for manageable portions. Any tiny bones still in the fish when it gets into the mouth, after being thoroughly cleaned in the mouth, are taken in thumb and forefinger, and are laid on the edge of the plate or on the butter plate if there is one. There is no objection to anyone hardy enough eating the head, and very tiny fish, such as whitebait (too small to clean), are eaten head and all in one bite. Never one for enjoying the sight of a fish-eye on my plate or in my chowder, I prefer to have even boiled fish (cod, haddock, salmon) come to the table with the head removed, but it is quite proper to serve it whole, with a lemon filling the gaping maw. And in oriental countries, especially, a fish eye is a great delicacy offered first to honored guests as is a sheep's eye in Arab countries.

Fruit *Apples and Pears* Informally eaten in the hand, but at table they are taken onto the fruit plate and spirally peeled, or quartered with a knife, then peeled. The sections are then cored and eaten with the fingers or with the fruit fork. Lady apples, tiny as crab apples, are eaten in the fingers like plums.

Apricots, Cherries, Kumquats, Plums Apricots, cherries, plums are eaten in one or two bites, and the stones, cleaned in the mouth, are dropped into the cupped hand and placed on the side of the plate. Kumquats are bitten into or eaten whole depending on size.

Halved Avocados In their shells these are eaten with a spoon, scooped out and taken spoonful by spoonful, with the dressing (perhaps lime juice and powdered sugar, or a little lake of French dressing) provided. Halved or quartered avocados in salads or on fruit platters are eaten with the fork after being broken into manageable bites.

Bananas Very informally (at picnics and by small children) bananas are peeled down with the end of the skin as a protective holder. When eaten at table from a fruit dish they are peeled, then broken as needed into small pieces and conveyed to the mouth with the fingers. Or, particularly in Europe they are cut through the peel into manageable lengths, then each segment peeled, with the knife and the fork holding it in place on the plate. Each section is then eaten with the fork, not taken up in the fingers.

Berries Eaten with a spoon. Large strawberries are sometimes served whole with their stems on. These are grasped by the stem and dipped in powdered sugar on the plate, then eaten in one or two bites, with the stem remaining in the fingers. Or they may be impaled on a fork and dehulled with the fruit knife, then eaten with the fruit fork.

Grapes Cut a bunch or section of bunch from bunches in bowl with knife or scissors (never absent-mindedly pull off grapes from centerpiece or arrangement of fruit). Eat one grape at a time, after placing bunch on serving plate. Grape skins, if you can't eat them, should be cleaned in the mouth but not chewed, then removed in the cupped hand with the pits and placed on the side of the plate. Or, holding the grape with the stem end to the lips, pop the inside into the mouth and lay skin on side of plate—if they *will* pop. Grapes, despite rumor, are not peeled except in the course of culinary procedures.

Grapefruit Eaten, halved, with a pointed fruit spoon. Sections should be loosened with grapefruit knife before serving. Do not squeeze out juice at table, except *en famille* if the family can stand it.

Mangoes Wits say the only place to eat them is in the bathtub. But they may be used in a fruit bowl and eaten at table, even though the best way to serve them is peeled, quartered, pitted, and chilled. A whole ripe (spotted) mango should be cut in half with a sharp fruit knife, then quartered. Then, with the quarter turned skin up and held in place with a fork, the skin should be carefully pulled away rather than peeled from the fruit. The juicy sections are then cut in one-bite morsels. Finger bowls or at least paper napkins are necessary, as this fruit stains badly.

Melons such as honeydew, Persian, and so forth, served in the half, quarters, or eighths are eaten with a spoon. Peeled and sliced melon, free of seeds, is eaten with the fork, or under some circumstances informally with the fingers. Papaya is often served with its black seeds as many people eat them.

Oranges Peeled with a sharp knife in one continuous spiral (if you're adept), then pulled apart into segments and, if the segments are small, eaten segment by whole segment. If segments are large they are cut in half crosswise with the fruit knife and eaten with fingers or fruit fork. Navel oranges are sometimes more easily eaten if the skin is quartered, then pulled down toward the navel and pulled off. The navel is then cut off and the orange segmented or cut in slices and eaten with the fork. At breakfast, oranges may be served halved like grapefruit, with the segments loosened, and are eaten with a fruit spoon.

Peaches Halve, then quarter with fruit knife. Then lifting the skin of each quarter at an edge, pull it off. Eat sections in small pieces with fork, preferably, as peach juice stains table linen.

Whole Peaches or Pears in Wine or Syrup This Continental dessert is served with a fork and dessert spoon. The fork, taken in the left hand, tines down, may be used to keep the whole fruit in place as the spoon cuts off manageable bites. If it is served with a dessert spoon alone, the spoon must be used with great care to prevent the whole fruit from skidding out of the dish or splattering the wine or syrup. The soft flesh of the fruit is eaten with the fork rotating the fruit to make it available. When only the dessert spoon is served, then the dish itself is rotated with the left hand to make the fruit manageable in its standing position. The core is left in the dish, although the wine or syrup may be spooned up.

Persimmons Often served as a first course with the top cut off well below the stem and the base cut flat so the fruit stands firmly on the plate. Grasping the persimmon with the left thumb and index finger, scoop out and eat a spoonful at a time, keeping the shell intact. Avoid the skin which, unless dead ripe, is puckery. The large pits are cleaned in the mouth, dropped into the spoon, and then deposited on the side of the plate. Persimmons in salad are peeled and quartered—too difficult a procedure to attempt at table, and persimmons in a fruit arrangement firm enough to be decorative are likely to be all but inedible anyway. They should be dead ripe and slightly spotted.

Pineapple Eaten with a spoon if served cut-up for dessert. If served on flat plates in quarters or eighths, peeled pineapple is eaten with a fork, after being cut with fruit knife.

Pomegranates The seeds used as a garnish or alone are eaten with a spoon with the tart pulp cleaned from the seeds in the mouth then the residue dropped delicately into the spoon and placed at the side of the dish. If the fruit is served halved, you hold the half with the index finger and the thumb and extract the seeds carefully with a spoon, eating one or two at a time in the manner described above.

Stewed or Preserved Fruit The pits or bits of core of cherries, prunes, plums, apples, etc., eaten in compote form with a spoon are dropped into the spoon, then deposited on the side of the plate.

Tangerines Stripped of their skins, segmented, and eaten in the fingers without cutting or breaking the segments.

Watermelon If served cubed and chilled (often in white wine), eaten from a compote with a fruit spoon. Otherwise eaten with the fork sometimes with the help of the knife to cut the ripe fruit a mouthful at a time from the green rind when the fruit is served in large half-round sections. If seeds are present, the fruit is taken seeds and all into the mouth, then the seeds are cleaned in the mouth, dropped into the cupped hand, and placed on the side of the plate, entirely dry.

Ice Cream Ice cream, depending on how it is served, is eaten with a small spoon, a dessert spoon and fork, an ice cream fork and spoon, or ice cream fork alone. When ice cream or sherbet is served in a sherbet dish, it is eaten with a small spoon. When it is served for example as Baked Alaska, it is eaten with a dessert spoon and fork, or possibly with an ice cream fork and spoon (the fork being used in the left hand to guide the portion onto the spoon). If ice cream is served in a neapolitan slice or in scoops on a dessert plate, it is eaten with a spoon and fork—spoon right fork left—when the dessert is presented or the dessert spoon and fork may be above the place setting throughout the meal (see page 402). Ice cream served together with cake on the same plate is eaten with a fork and spoon.

Meat Meat that is served in one large piece or slice—such as steak or a slice of ham—is cut with a knife and fork and each piece impaled with a fork, tines down. It may be conveyed to the mouth this way or the fork may be transferred to the right hand and the meat conveyed to the mouth, tines up. Meat such as hash is scooped up with the fork, possibly with the aid of the knife held in the left hand.

Parsley and Other Garnishes Parsley, dill, watercress, mint, and other greens used as garnish may be eaten with the fork as part of the dish, or if clear of sauces, dressings, and so forth, in the fingers. Decorated lemon slices, or wedges of lemon, are meant to be squeezed over the food they accompany. This may be done through a gentle pressure of the fork, or the fruit may be picked up in the fingers if it is not covered with sauce or melted butter. In very smart restaurants lemon halves or quarters are served masked with cheesecloth to prevent squirting of the juice when the lemon is squeezed. When this hasn't been done, a way to prevent squirting is to pierce the slice of lemon with the tines of the fork. This ruptures the juice cells, thus preventing squirting. You may also, when squeezing lemon on food, use your hand, palm toward the fruit to protect your clothes.

Pickles and Radishes Whole pickles are taken with the fingers, as are radishes. Sometimes you will see pickles of various kinds served with a pickle fork. Use it if you wish to serve yourself, but it is not necessary to do so. Pickles are never conveyed from the serving plate directly to the mouth (nor is anything else where a serving plate is provided) but are laid on the side of the dinner or lunch plate or butter plate. (And see "Salt.")

Pizza Pizza is usually served in a pie-shaped wedge. Informally it is eaten in the fingers gently held together so as not to lose its filling. More formally it is eaten with knife and fork.

Potatoes *Baked* These should be rubbed with fat before baking and be presented immediately on coming from the oven, a cross having been cut neatly on the top to allow the escape of steam and to permit the pre-service insertion of a lump of butter, plus a sprinkling of salt and paprika. Then it is simple to hold the potato with the left hand while one explores its innards with the fork. But if a baked potato is presented whole it is taken from the dish with serving fork and spoon, then broken apart with the fingers for buttering and seasoning. The butter is taken from the butter plate with the fork—not with the butter knife. If one wishes the skin may be cut up with a knife and eaten with a fork (never cutting it up in pieces all at once, any more than one would meat). If the skin is unwanted, the mealy part of the potato is eaten right from the skin with each portion seasoned just before entering the mouth. Except for a child, *do not* scoop out all the potato, set the skin aside and mash the contents all at once with butter and seasoning. A baked potato presented in foil (often the case in restaurants as foil baked potatoes bake faster and keep hot longer—but never taste as good) is eaten from the foil.

Chips Eaten in the fingers.

French Fried Eaten with the fork after being halved with the fork, if necessary. Poor manners to hold any food with the fork and nibble off a manageable mouthful. The exception is shrimp.

Shoe String If really dry and impossible to eat with fork, may be eaten in the fingers. Gravy-soaked french fried or shoe string potatoes are always eaten with a fork.

Salad A quarter of iceberg lettuce may be eaten with knife and fork, though gourmets and nutritionists both frown on the cutting of lettuce in salad preparation. Lettuce for mixed salad should be *broken* in bits and mixed at the last minute—to preserve the vitamin content.

Salt and Pepper If there is only one saltcellar on the table (as there is when a condiment set is used or when there is a master salt), the salt with the pepper is always sent down the table to the honored guest, if there is one, or to the hostess before making the rounds of the family. Pepper and salt sets that are not individual are always kept together in the passing, but pepper grinders may be passed without the salt. If salt is needed for dipping radishes or celery or for corn on the cob it is placed on the edge of the plate, *never* on the table cloth. If open salts are used and no salt spoon provided, use a clean knife to take salt from a common container. If individual open salts are at each place, salt may be taken between thumb and forefinger. Individual salt and pepper shakers are centered in front of the dinner plate. Salt is at the right, pepper left.

Sandwiches Small tea sandwiches and canapés are taken in the fingers and bitten into or, if bite-size, placed whole in the mouth. Double- and triple-decker club sandwiches, though served cut crosswise, are eaten at least with the *aid* of knife, and fork. If they are not too unmanageable, they may be cut into fourths and eaten in the fingers. Otherwise, they are eaten with the fork, after being cut into small bits.

Seafood *Clams* (*steamed*) The steaming process is supposed to open the shell completely but sometimes doesn't. If a shell is not fully open, take it up and bend it back with the fingers. If this doesn't work, forget that one—do not use a dinner knife or fork as an opener. With shell fully open, take the shell in the left hand just over the dish and with the right hand lift out the clam by the neck. Holding the neck with the right hand, pull the body of the clam from it and discard the neck sheath. Holding the clam by the neck with the right hand, place the whole clam first in melted butter or broth, or both alternately, then in the mouth in one bite. As empty shells collect, remove to butter plate or shell plates provided (and as clam-eating of this kind is always informal, it is an excellent idea for the hostess to provide platters or bowls for empty shells as well as plenty of paper napkins and finger bowls with hot soapy water afterward). Do not spoon up remaining liquid in soup plate—it may be sandy—but drink the broth separately provided in a bouillon cup or small bowl (but not if it is in a little dish which is meant for washing off the clams). If clams are fried, eat with fork after breaking into two pieces if necessary. As these are greasy they should not be taken in the fingers, even by the neck.

Lobster and Hard-Shelled Crabs (*broiled or boiled*) The claws of both of these require dexterous handling. They should be cracked in the kitchen but further cracking at table (with a nutcracker) may be needed. Then the shells are pulled apart by the fingers and the tender meat extracted carefully so, if possible, it comes out whole. A nut pick is useful for this, but an oyster fork may do it, too. The claw meat, if small and in one piece, is dipped in melted butter or, with cold crab or lobster, in mayonnaise, then put all at once into the mouth. Larger pieces are first cut with a fork. The green material in the stomach cavity, called the tamale, along with the "coral" or roe in the female are delicacies and should be eaten with the fork. The small claws are pulled from the body with the fingers, then the body-ends placed between the teeth so the meat may be extracted by chewing (but without a sucking noise). The major portion of meat is found in the stomach cavity and the tail and is first speared, one side at a time, with the fork, then with the help of the knife, if necessary, lifted out and cut as needed into mouthfuls, then dipped in sauce or mayonnaise with the fork.

Crab "fingers" Served often as hors d'oeuvres are picked up by the small end of the shell with the meaty end dipped in the sauce and sucked out.

Mussels Served pickled or smoked on toothpicks as cocktail titbits and are thus taken via toothpick directly to the mouth. Served shells and all in a variety of soup styles, too—Moules Marinières (Mussels mariner style) in a soup dish with a delicate thin souplike sauce redolent with garlic. The mussels may be picked out with small oyster fork provided, but it is easier and just as correct to use the shells containing the mussels as small scoops. Pick up with the right hand and, placing the tip of the shell in the mouth gently (and silently), suck out mussel and sauce, then discard shell onto butter plate or platter provided. When shells have been cleared from dish, eat balance of sauce with spoon and bits of French bread used to sop up sauce, then conveyed to mouth with fork. Italian variety of this dish has tomato, is eaten the same way, often as a main dish with salad. Fingerbowls are advisable, or pass the little, packaged wet towels, or individual small rolled cotton or linen napkins or even terry fingertip towels that have been rung out in scented hot water, oriental style.

Oysters and Clams (*half shell*) Hold the shell steady with left hand and, using oyster fork, lift oyster or clam whole from shell, detaching, where necessary, with fork. Dip in cocktail sauce in container on plate, if desired. Eat in one mouthful. (Yes, this includes the big Chincoteagues.) Never attempt to cut them and don't take in two bites or more. Oyster crackers may be dropped whole in sauce, extracted with oyster fork and eaten. Several oyster crackers at a time may be dropped whole into the sauce, extracted with the oyster fork, and eaten. Also when eating oysters on the half shell, it is quite acceptable to pick up the shell after eating the

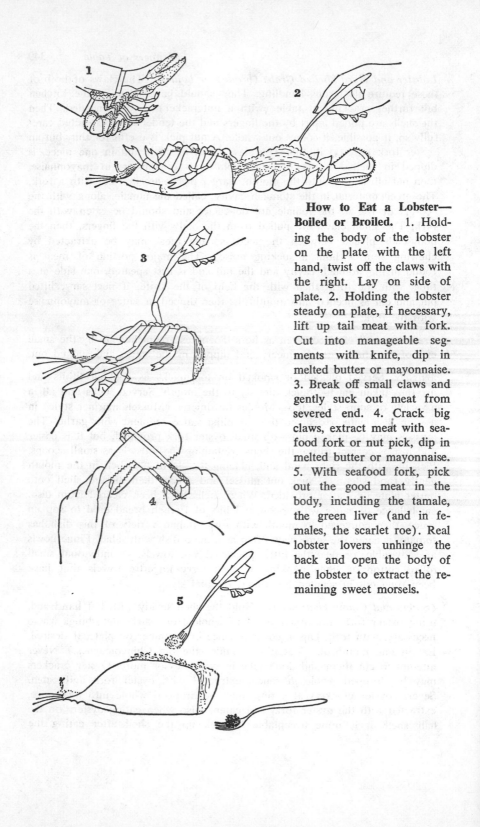

How to Eat a Lobster— Boiled or Broiled. 1. Holding the body of the lobster on the plate with the left hand, twist off the claws with the right. Lay on side of plate. 2. Holding the lobster steady on plate, if necessary, lift up tail meat with fork. Cut into manageable segments with knife, dip in melted butter or mayonnaise. 3. Break off small claws and gently suck out meat from severed end. 4. Crack big claws, extract meat with seafood fork or nut pick, dip in melted butter or mayonnaise. 5. With seafood fork, pick out the good meat in the body, including the tamale, the green liver (and in females, the scarlet roe). Real lobster lovers unhinge the back and open the body of the lobster to extract the remaining sweet morsels.

oyster to drain the liquor into your mouth. This should be done gracefully after the oyster has been eaten by picking the shell up between thumb and forefinger. If a chip of shell should get into your mouth while eating, remove it unobtrusively with thumb and forefinger.

Shrimps, Scallops, Oysters (fried) Eaten like fried clams, except that oriental fried shrimp (french fried with the tails on) are to be taken up by the tail with chopsticks if you're adept, or with the fingers if you are not, and dipped in sauce, then bitten off to the tail, which is then discarded. Unshelled shrimp are lifted in the fingers, shelled, and conveyed whole to the mouth.

Shrimp Cocktail Where shrimps are too large to be eaten in one mouthful, impale them on the seafood fork and bite off a manageable bite. Re-dip the remaining portion in the sauce, eat the balance. Do not attempt to cut the shrimp in half on the small service plate beneath the cocktail cup as this undoubtedly would be disastrous.

Snails Usually served on a hot metal plate. A special hinged holder with which to grip the hot snail shells is usually provided (or hold the shell with your napkin protecting the fingers), as snails must be dug out. The holder grips the shell with the left hand while the right pulls out the snail with a pick or oyster fork. Snails are eaten whole, like raw oysters. When the shells have cooled, it is proper to tilt them into the mouth to get the garlic butter and snail liquor, or one may sop this up with bits of French bread, which are then conveyed to the mouth with the fork.

Sherbet When sherbet is served with the meat or fish course, perhaps in a relatively flat dish, it is entirely proper to eat it with the same fork one is using for the main course. However, if a spoon is provided, it is also correct to use the spoon instead of your fork. When sherbet is served as a topping for fruit salad, the salad fork is used. A spoon is usually provided if the sherbet is in a compote.

Soup It is acceptable to tilt the soup plate (away from yourself) in order to get the remaining soup. When small crackers are served with soup such as oyster crackers, they may be added to the soup. Larger soda crackers should not be crumbled into the soup and are best kept on the plate and eaten with the soup. The exception to this would be when eating chowder. In this case the water biscuits served with it are meant to be crumbled into the soup.

Using Chopsticks The enormous popularity of Chinese and Japanese restaurants and the great interest in the service of oriental foods at home makes it at least interesting to be able to use chopsticks correctly, as oriental food seems to taste better when eaten with them.

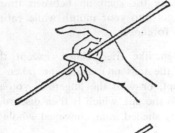

Pick up the chopstick almost as if you were going to hold a pen, but place it at the base of your thumb with the third and fourth fingers supporting it about one third up the chopstick, leaving your index finger free to use as a lever.

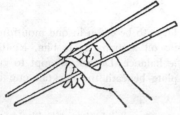

Now place the top chopstick in a parallel position, held firmly with the thumb and index finger. Practice picking up an imaginary grain of rice. (You should be able to pick up a real grain when you're adept.)

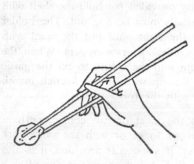

The first chopstick always remains firmly in position in the crook of your thumb, and held there by your third and fourth finger. The top chopstick is used as a lever and should move freely. You use the pair as pincers to pick up any food you wish. Don't be embarrassed to ask your oriental waiter to help you get started. Eating oriental food with a fork is no crime, but it is not as much fun. The Chinese invented the fork but returned to the chopstick.

Spaghetti The *aficionado* knows that the only graceful and satisfying way to eat real Italian spaghetti (which comes in full-length or perhaps half-length rounds) is to eat it with a large soup spoon and a fork at least when it is served as a course (the pasta) by itself. The spoon is placed in the left hand more or less upright in the plate (or often platter) of spaghetti. The right hand uses the fork with the tip of the prongs against the spoon to wind the spaghetti into a manageable mouthful. It should not drip off the fork. The forkful of spaghetti is then conveyed to the mouth while the spoon remains in the hand and on the platter. As with any sauced dish, it should be eaten without stirring the spaghetti, grated cheese, and meatballs (or other garnish) all together, infant style. The timid way to eat spaghetti is to cut it into small bits with knife and fork and eat it with fork alone. Thick macaroni can't be eaten rolled on a fork so readily and is better cut with a fork as one goes along. Remaining sauce of each dish may be eaten with a spoon or sopped up with small bits of bread, which are then eaten with a fork. Some Italians protest the only way to eat spaghetti is with a fork alone, letting it drip and fall as it may. When in Rome—or Naples—follow your leader. It's a moot question at best.

Toast, Hot Breads, and Bread Sticks Toast and the various hot breads —scones, English muffins, Parker House rolls, and so forth—may be buttered whole while they are hot, then broken or cut with the butter knife to be eaten in manageable pieces. Long bread sticks should be broken and buttered, if desired, over a small area. If unbuttered they may be left whole and nibbled.

Tortillas These are laid flat in the left hand or on a plate, filled slightly with *frijoles* (kidney beans) or other appropriate mixture, rolled up and eaten like a rolled sandwich, endwise.

Chapter 29

OUR COMMUNITY RELATIONS AND INTERFAITH COURTESY AND UNDERSTANDING

If we know nothing of our neighbor's beliefs or background we may unwittingly offend him. If we have only a vague idea of his religious customs and taboos we may seem discourteous by our failure to respect them in our contact with him.

Courtesy is a superficial name for actions that can have a very important place in the character building of a human being. Both children and adults should know about the often unthinking cruelty inherent in intolerance of other religions than their own. And how intolerance often stems from our primitive suspicion of anything that is different or not a part of our own experience.

Many educators believe that one way to help children and adults toward better relations with their fellow man is to give them some knowledge of others' beliefs and customs as a purely educational activity, not with the idea of disturbing their own religious affiliations. There are important differences and similarities between denominations, between the belief of the Roman Catholic and that of the Jew—and among Jews themselves—between what the Quaker believes and what guides the Buddhist or the Greek Catholic. If we think less of the *differences* and inform ourselves of the *similarities* I believe we will have a warmer, more understanding attitude toward our neighbors.

The wise parent, I feel, teaches his child that no matter what people's beliefs are, all who follow religion are seeking the same thing, the strength to be good. Or what in their religion teaches them is good and worthy in their day-to-day communion with their fellow men.

Our country may be predominantly Protestant, but the lives of all our minorities are intimately connected with our own, many in very subtle ways. If our Italian tradesmen shut their shops to celebrate the Feast of St.

Anthony, we may be affected. For that day at least we must find other places to shop, just as on Yom Kippur much business throughout the country slows down or stops or is in some way affected—through the absence of personnel or the closing of some key business houses. If every fourth or fifth person we meet on St. Patrick's Day is wearing the green, we are conscious of the Irish-descended among us, of their predominantly Catholic adherence.

Every community has its minorities. A Methodist is in the minority in an Irish or Italian neighborhood. A white man is in the minority in the Chinatowns or in the Harlems of America. The key to comfortable community life is courtesy—true courtesy that respects the rights and feelings of *all*. Courtesy and friendly knowledge about your neighbor help prevent tensions. As America grows and cities proliferate we'll need, more and more, to use courtesy in our community lives. Without it there is no comfort, safety or decent living.

Should a Christian Send a Christmas Card to a Jewish Friend?

I think that depends on whether the friend is a deeply religious Orthodox Jew or one who thinks of Christmas and perhaps celebrates it, especially if he has children, as the national, gift-giving holiday it has at least in part become. It is perhaps better to avoid cards illustrating the Nativity. Many Jews now send non-religious Christmas greeting cards and give and receive gifts, despite the strong disapproval of the majority of their clergy. Christmas trees in a Jewish home are considered universally by all Rabbis, Orthodox, Conservative, and Reform, as well as by many Jewish people, as being in exceedingly bad taste. According to this belief a Christmas tree can mean nothing to a Jew, and if it does not have a religious significance it is an affront to Christians.

Dietary Laws of Various Religions

What about food restrictions of Jews and the fast days of Roman and Greek Catholics and some Episcopalians? What about Lent? As almost everyone knows, some Catholics do not eat meat on certain days during Lent, Advent, and throughout the year. During Lent most Catholics and many Protestants keep certain Holy Days through special church attendance and fasting. Individuals often make token personal sacrifices by giving up candy, smoking, or other non-necessities of life as a form of self-denial during this period.

If a Catholic is to be your guest on Ash Wednesday or Good Friday, it is considerate to plan your meal around non-meat dishes, if such a solution is acceptable to the majority who will be at table. On the other hand, to abandon the roast beef everyone has been looking forward to in favor of fish is, perhaps, to make the guest uncomfortable. The hostess in such a situation should offer him a substitute for meat. But for a non-Catholic hostess never to consider this problem with Catholic guests is thoughtless, to say the least. When special food must be served a guest, whether he be an abstaining Catholic or Episcopalian, a non-shellfish eating Jew, or a man with an ulcer, or a cardiac on a salt-free diet, let it be done without drawing the table's attention to the fact.

An Orthodox Jew has many rigid restrictions concerning food and its preparation, but naturally no non-Jewish home is equipped to follow them. However, it is important to know that people who at home keep kosher will usually not feel free to eat the following foods away from home: any fish that is without gills, fins, and scales—the scavenger fish such as eels; any seafood, and this includes oysters, crabs, lobsters, mussels, clams, crawfish; reptiles—turtles, for example; or pork in any form. On the other hand, never assume that your Jewish friend adheres to the traditional restrictions. It is better to ask. I have known Conservative Jews who, as my guests, would condone the garlic butter on the steak, eat baked ham, but refuse a lobster. Reform Jews have no food restrictions, but they do fast on the Day of Atonement.

Moslems, many of whom are racially Semites, have many of the same food restrictions. They may not eat pork in any form or shellfish. The old religious leaders knew the peril of eating improperly cooked or cured pork, the danger of trying to keep it without refrigeration, so they forbade it. The equally perishable shellfish they prohibited too, not on the ground that there was anything basically impure about it, as I understand it, but because unless it was handled in a most sanitary way and eaten almost as soon as it was caught it was dangerous.

It is interesting, too, that the mere proximity of these foods to permitted foods is forbidden. In my own home, we often give buffet suppers when there is a large crowd. Among my guests on one such occasion was an old friend, an Arab sheik. Both a ham and a turkey were on the buffet table, and, as the meat was carved, someone passed the sheik a plate containing a slice of ham and a slice of turkey. He sat politely with the plate of food untouched until I noticed what had happened and took the plate from him. Then, not completely understanding the problem, I merely removed the slice of ham and returned the plate with more turkey. Still he ate nothing, and when my attention turned to him again I realized at last what was the matter. The whole plate had been "contaminated" by the ham. I got a clean plate and served him again, omitting the ham, of course, and all was well. As he was a devout Moslem, my friend did not take alcohol in any form, although some Moslems do, and many smoke, although the Prophet forbade smoking as well as drinking. In place of occupying himself with a cigarette, the Moslem will often run his prayer beads through his fingers as he talks with friends or he will consume interminable cups of the sweet, thick "Turkish" coffee drunk demitasse without cream.

Religious Holidays

The first day of Lent, Ash Wednesday, is kept by the Catholics and the Episcopalians, particularly, and their churches have special services on that day. Then both Catholics and high church Episcopalians may be seen with a smudge of ashes on their foreheads where the sign of the cross has been made by the officiating priest with ashes from the preceding Palm Sunday's palms burned for this Holy Day.

On Palm Sunday, the last Sunday before Easter, you will see Catholics, Episcopalians, Presbyterians, Methodist-Episcopalians among the worshipers coming from church with palm leaves or strips of palm to commemorate the palms carried on the entry of Jesus into Jerusalem.

No matter what our own religious beliefs, in heterogeneous America we are conscious of many of the major religious festivals—Ash Wednesday, Palm Sunday, Good Friday, Easter, Christmas. In some areas we note Chinese New Year with its paper dragons on parade, its firecrackers to warn off evil spirits, Russian Easter and the New Year that follow the Gregorian calendar in the Greek Orthodox Church. We are conscious, too, of the traditional Jewish Holy Days—Hanukkah, which corresponds in time to Christmas and is an eight-day festival of lights and gift-giving; Purim, the festival held in the spring, celebrates the victory of the Jews over the tyrant Haman; Passover, the seven- or eight-day festival of Freedom, celebrates both the liberation of the Jews from Egyptian bondage and the hope for universal freedom, which some day may come for all the children of men. This is a time of joy and great preparation, new clothes for the family, special feast food, and (in Orthodox and Conservative homes) the hunt by the father for any leaven in the house—with mother always arranging for him to find it. This symbolic hunt commemorates the fact that in the Passover the Children of Israel were ordered to flee Egypt, as is told in the Bible, without taking time to leaven their bread. Then, of course, there are Rosh Hashana, the Jewish New Year, and Yom Kippur, the Day of Atonement. And in big cities, at least, it is possible that we might meet a Moslem who, though in Western clothes, is keeping a special one-month period like Lent, Ramadan, as did a Persian prince I knew, by wearing a mourning band on his arm and leaving his collar open at the neck. He fasts from sunrise to sunset, denies himself, and ends the period with a happy festival.

Ceremonies of Many Faiths

There are many similarities in our various religions and sects. Both Roman Catholics and Episcopalians celebrate the Circumcision because the baby Jesus, like all Jewish boy babies of religious parents, on his eighth day of life was named and circumcised with the appropriate ceremony. Among religious Jews (and Moslems, too) the day of circumcision is the same day as the boy child's naming. On this day, like many Christian children, he is given godparents. (Non-ritual circumcision is now practiced very generally, whenever the obstetrician deems it necessary, regardless of religious beliefs, or where parents desire it as the health measure the ancient Jews believed it to be.) A girl receives her name when her father goes to synagogue as soon as possible after she is born, usually on a Sabbath (which is from Friday at sunset until Saturday at sunset). He recites a little prayer at the altar and states her name. Jewish girls of Conservative or Reform congregations may have godparents, too, like their brothers.

In Reform congregations it is customary to offer a prayer and state the name of a child, whether male or female, at the earliest service of worship that both parents can attend after the child's birth. This is done regardless of the fact that the boy child may have been named during the rite of circumcision.

In the Reform temple confirmation for boys and girls takes place at about sixteen years of age. The children are confirmed as a group in a solemn and meaningful ceremony usually on the Feast of Weeks, or Pentecost, which comes seven weeks after the first day of Passover. Bar Mitzvah for boys of thirteen is optional. Conservative congregations have both Bar Mitzvah for boys of thirteen and Confirmation for children of sixteen. There are, however, variations in Conservative congregations depending upon the views of individual rabbis. Some confirm both boys and girls. Some have Bar Mitzvah for boys of thirteen and confirmation only for girls of sixteen. Still others have also inaugurated the ceremony of Bat Mitzvah for girls of thirteen to correspond to that of Bar Mitzvah for boys of thirteen.

Among Catholics the baptism—which joins the child to the Church—takes place as soon after the birth of the child as possible, during its first month of life, usually on a Sunday afternoon. Catholic children have just one set of godparents. Some Protestant denominations permit two godfathers for a boy or two godmothers for a girl. And some wait until the child is of an age to understand the baptismal ceremony before performing it. Other Protestants don't baptize at all.

Catholic children often receive multiple names, one of which is that of a Saint, perhaps that of the Saint on whose day he was born. These names are not always all used when the child grows up, but they are his officially, nonetheless, even though he may use a shorter form of his name for legal and social purposes. Greek Orthodox children have just one given name. A Jewish child of traditional background is rarely "Jr.," "2nd" or "3rd" because it is not customary for Jews to be named for living people. If any meaningful name is used, it is usually that of someone recently dead, although the Biblical names are popular among Jews, too.

The children of Congregational parents may be baptized at any age, and godparents are not traditional, though permissible. Often Congregationalists of Episcopal or Lutheran background like to have godparents for their children.

Some Baptists—depending on whether they are liberal or conservative—dedicate their children to the Church soon after birth. Actual baptism with complete immersion takes place any time after the age of twelve, when the individual is believed to be able to make a free-will decision to come into the Church. After this, as in most of the "gathering" denominations, he is elected to Church membership.

Presbyterians baptize at any age, without godparents, then, after the age of twelve, the individual is elected to the Church. There is no confirmation. Lutheran baptism is similar to that of the Episcopalians, with the child having at least one sponsor. As with Episcopalians, the Lutherans accept the child into the Church at the time of baptism and confirm the pledges, made by the godparents at the time of baptism, when the child is twelve years old. The Eastern Orthodox confirm at the time of baptism in early infancy.

Methodists baptize at any time, and the child has at least one sponsor. The parents make a statement at the time of baptism promising to bring up the child in the Christian way of life. Then as the child approaches adulthood, any time from twelve on, he is prepared for admission to the Church through an affirmation of faith.

Quakers do not have a christening ceremony and neither do Christian Scientists.

Particular Courtesies

Does a Protestant walking with a Catholic lift his hat, too, as he passes a Catholic church? He may if he wishes, out of courtesy, but no one would expect it.

Does a non-Jew attending a wedding in a synagogue wear his hat if the congregation follows the old custom? Of course he does. (And yarmulkes are provided in the vestibule for those who come hatless.)

How does one reply to a Quaker who uses "thee" and "thou"? The use of "you" would be more natural, I believe.

Should the Christian Scientist kneel at the funeral Mass for a friend, or should he merely bow his head as is his usual custom?

These are difficult questions for any one to answer. We might say, "When in Rome . . . ," but there are religious practices such as crossing oneself, lighting votive candles, or repeating the Creed that seem out of place or even hypocritical in one for whom such rites or statements of faith are not usual.

It is not necessary to stretch courtesy to the point of offending one's own conscience, yet one may stay within the form of the service one is attending, sufficiently to show proper respect for the traditions and rules of that particular house of worship, standing when others stand, bowing the head at least when prayers are said, covering or uncovering the head as is customary.

Communion, except among Catholics, who administer it to children before confirmation, is usually not taken by those who have not been confirmed, although in some Protestant churches the individual minister may administer the sacrament to the baptized at his own discretion.

In some Protestant churches the single chalice used in the Communion service of the Episcopalians has given way to individual cups of sacramental wine or, with some denominations, grape juice.

Or it has become customary for those taking Communion to dip the wafer in the cup (intinction) instead of touching the chalice to the lips. There are other variations used under certain circumstances. However, in many parishes such modernization of the ceremony, though now permitted, is not really welcomed.

In taking Communion in a strange church take your place, without gloves, if in this church the wafer is placed in the palm, on the left of the rail—when it is given at the altar—so you may observe the custom of the church before accepting the sacrament or cup yourself. Catholics never offer Communion to non-Catholics, and in the Catholic service only the priests partake of the wine.

What is the meaning of the Greek letters IHS which we see on Catholic and Protestant altars and the INRI often seen especially on crucifixes? IHS is the Greek contraction of Jesus's name in that language. INRI stands for Jesus (Iesus) Nazarenus Rex Iudaeorum, Jesus of Nazareth, King of the Jews, and is used only by Christians. The sign of the fish stands for Jesus, too, for the letters of the word in Greek for fish, *ichthys,* are the same as those in the Latin phrase for "Jesus Christ Son of God the Saviour."

On their confirmation day, the day which for many is the day they join the church, you will see little girls of eleven or twelve walking to or from Catholic, Greek Catholic, and some Protestant Episcopal churches all in white, wearing miniature wedding veils and carrying flowers. On the Jewish boy's Bar Mitzvah you see him dressed as soberly as the Christian boy who goes to his confirmation at about the same age. His sister in the Conservative temple may have her Bar Mitzvah, for which she, too, dresses in white, although she is not veiled. The basic idea for all is the same, the admission of the child to the church or temple after a period of special preparation for the ceremony, a marking of a certain spiritual maturity and acceptability to the elders.

In some parts of our country the largest minority consists of Orientals. Many are Christians, both Catholic and Protestant, especially among the Filipinos and Chinese. Japanese conversion is still fairly rare.

One of the important things the Jews gave to many religions, including the Christian, is the Sabbath. Before the Mosaic law (that man should work six days and rest the seventh, the Sabbath) was handed down, men and women of the world then worked from daylight to darkness without having a specific day of rest. In fact, the expected thing was that they work a full seven days. The Sabbath, set aside for physical and spiritual replenishment, doesn't fall for all of us, not even for all Christians, on the Sunday of the Julian calendar. Seventh-Day Adventists, for instance, celebrate it on Saturday. In many places of the world, Japan, for example, there still is no Sabbath. Religious worship may take place daily or several times daily before household shrines or in special calls to prayer. Work often goes on around the clock, seven days of the week, and these peoples' places of business stay open even when they are transplanted to predominantly Christian Sunday-Sabbath communities unless local ordinances forbid it.

As the Christian Sunday is not the Sabbath of religious Jews, you will often find Jewish businesses in Jewish neighborhoods open on Sunday but closed on Saturday, for the convenience of their regular customers and to permit employees and business owners to attend religious services.

Clerical Dress

Greek Catholic, Roman Catholic, high church Episcopalian priests and some other Protestant ministers wear the clerical collar and rabat (pronounced raby) outside of church. However, there is much leeway in some denominations in this matter, especially for sports wear. Rabbis do not wear the clerical collar and neither do Christian Science readers. Members of Catholic and Protestant brotherhoods and sisterhoods wear their garb all or most of the time with the priests increasingly wearing secular dress for sports, vacation periods and recreation. Catholic sisterhoods are rapidly approaching the secular in their garb in the name of ease of movement and relationship to the laity.

Catholics, in general, carry and display the crucifix. The simple cross is more often used by Protestants, though the crucifix is used in many Protestant churches. When the cross is worn as jewelry, it is always the plain cross, or the Coptic one sans crucifix.

Both Catholic and Protestant brotherhoods and sisterhoods are celibate, and some high church Episcopal priests take vows of chastity. Confession, too, is not limited to the Catholic Church but takes place as well in high church Episcopalian services.

Chapter 30

THE NEW CITIZEN AND HIS
PARTICULAR PROBLEMS

Our Attitude toward Newcomers to the U.S.

Every generation has its immigrants. Many of us are descendants of the Irish who emigrated here during the potato famine in the nineteenth century, of Italians who came to supply our labor pool or bolster our artisan class in the nineteenth and twentieth centuries, of early Dutch settlers dissatisfied with opportunities at home and who came to trade and colonize in New Amsterdam. We are all, no matter how impressive our family trees, descended from immigrants of one kind or the other, if we are Americans. Even the American Indian is now known to have emigrated here from Asia.

Millions of us are the children or grandchildren or great-grandchildren of those who took refuge here to escape political, social or economic upheavals in their own lands or who fled from religious persecution. The Pilgrim fathers, now so revered socially as ancestors, were the first refugees, fleeing religious persecution, just as in the twentieth century refugees from Hitler—Protestants, Catholics, and Jews—sought not only the right to worship as they please among us but the very right to stay alive. The Pilgrims faced the Indians, who, being here first, resented any encroachment on their hunting grounds. Every new settler today has us to face— the entrenched Americans, who, like the Indian tribes, forget sometimes that they came (or their grandfathers or great-grandfathers) to this land of opportunity because, for some reason or other, things were not good at home. It is only natural for every man to regard the stranger, the possible economic encroacher, with a wary eye. But we need to remember our own sources and realize that the vigor and progress of the country is stimulated by each such influx of new Americans, who bring with them talents, trades, ambition, and even wealth America can use.

Let's examine some of our attitudes toward refugees in our century.

One hears the criticism "Why do they all have to live in one neighborhood—all the Italians, all the Poles, the Scandinavians, all the French, the Germans, the Jews, the Mexicans, the Cubans, the Puerto Ricans, the Blacks in tight little settlements?" The answer is that our ancestors, even if they came here at the time of the founding of our country, tended to do the same thing—for reasons of solidarity. The melting pot that is America doesn't immediately gobble up the new citizen or the one whose color differs from that of the majority. Any American who was born abroad must, of necessity, have mixed feelings about his new homeland. The old living patterns, morals, social habits, and language are all part of him, and it is his children or perhaps his grandchildren who will first have the feeling of being uncomplicatedly "real Americans." Even after generations of assimilation there tends to be this gathering together of Americans with like backgrounds—the Irish in Boston, the Germans in St. Louis, Milwaukee, and Chicago, the Italians and Jews and dozens of other ethnic groups in New York, the Cubans in Miami, the Scandinavians in the Midwest, the Pennsylvania "Dutch," (really German) in Pennsylvania. Newcomers, quite understandably, gravitate toward these centers, where they can hear their own language, eat their own food, go to their own houses of worship, and receive assistance in their adjustment to a new and strange—and often unfriendly—land.

It is true that the young do move out and into other circles, through marriage or business opportunities, but it is human and understandable that the older and less adventurous often prefer to make their way in a more familiar atmosphere although this cohesiveness is becoming less observable than it was in cities as older neighborhoods gave way to modern housing developments.

We should all remember that, no matter how American we are now, our ancestors, even if they were English speaking, had their own problems of adjustment here too—physical, social, and economic. Even well-bred English who settle here today feel our hostility or experience our ridicule of their manners and customs—as any English-born bride of an American can tell you. So it isn't language that is the principal difficulty at all. It is just the perversity of human nature. We all hate to move over, as others had to move over for us.

Becoming an American Citizen

Becoming a naturalized American citizen is a great honor—but also a great responsibility. The candidate for citizenship must fulfill certain rigid, moral, political, and to some extent intellectual requirements before going through the necessary legal procedures. Someone becoming a citizen might ask you to "sponsor" him. This usually entails appearing in court and swearing that you have known your friend at least five years, that he has never had difficulty with the law, etc. Most questions are brief and answered simply. To be a sponsor you must yourself be a citizen and if naturalized have your papers with you. After the more serious ceremonies, there may be a gay party given by friends to fete the new citizen.

It is thoughtful of you, as a sponsor, to give the newcomer a small gift—preferably something "American" that will help him as he continues to adjust to American customs, ideals, and manners. This gift might be a framed copy of the Declaration of Independence, a dictionary, an American etiquette book, or an American flag.

What Do They Think of Us?

All our new citizens or citizens-to-be have their own opinions of us, collectively as well as individually, and some of them quite unflattering. We are said by some Europeans to be noisy—which some of us are—screameaglish, that is, insular in our point of view, unsophisticated, often vulgar, and, worst of all, lacking in culture and inherent good taste.

These things so often said of us by foreigners are to some degree true, but not all so reprehensible as some of us in our indignation may feel. We *are* a very young country in the eyes of older, wearier civilizations—hence our frequent naïveté. We Americans are in the process of developing a culture of our own, and some of it we have adopted from all the peoples who have come to make up our country. Our language, taken from the English majority among our settlers, is in many ways quite different from the English of England, because it has been influenced by the melting pot. Our music, our art, our literature are all trending toward a recognizable American culture. The fact that we are young and learning—and yearning— should not be held against us. But we, in turn, should not feel superior to the older, established cultures and rich traditions, understanding and appreciation of which can make our own lives immeasurably more interesting.

Differences in Manners

Tucking-in the Dinner Napkin In this country the napkin is never tucked in at the collar or in the vest, but must be put on the lap and opened lengthwise so that it is folded double across the knees. As it is used throughout the meal to dab the mouth, the napkin does come out of its fold but it should not be shaken out that way at the start of the meal (as you sometimes see waiters do). At the end of the meal or if, for any reason, you must leave the table during the meal, place the used napkin casually, not refolded, to the left of your fork. Little children may have their napkins tucked-in to save their clothes, however.

Silverware The placing of silverware on the table here is quite different from the placement in Europe (see "Table Setting"). The dinner knife is always on the right side of the plate, and the necessary forks are on the left, with the one to be used first at the far left. If an oyster fork is used, however, it often appears on the knife side. When your dinner plate is to be removed either for a second helping (when the host carves at the table) or to go to the kitchen, place the fork and knife you've been using side by side on the right side of your plate with the blade of the knife facing in and with the prongs of the fork up. The knife should be placed on the right of the used fork.

The American and Continental Use of Knife and Fork I see no real reason why a person who all his life has employed the Continental style in using his fork and knife should change to the American, unless he feels needlessly self-conscious about the difference when he's eating with Americans. Here, the knife is used for cutting and is never used to pile food on the back of a fork which then, European style, is conveyed to the mouth upside down and with the left hand. In America the fork is mostly used in the right hand, so that it corners the food by itself with little or no help from the knife, whose function ceases after it's cut the meat (and here potatoes may be cut, too). A bit of bread may be used to coax the food onto the fork or to blot up gravy (but then the gravy-soaked bread must be conveyed to the mouth by the fork). The knife may be used to steer food onto the *front* of the fork but, if you are eating American style, never convey the fork to the mouth upside down with food *packed* on the back, though you may use the fork this way with a manageable mouthful, say, of waffle, impaled on the prongs. The knife must be left, preferably blade in, on the right side of your plate when you are not actually using it or with the point toward the center, blade left.

If you are eating in the Continental fashion, knife held in the right hand, fork left, the utensils are not used to gesture with and are placed on the plate when not in use or when the plate is being passed for refilling. The utensils are not held in the hands of the diner during this latter procedure, any more than they are in the American style of eating.

The Use of the Toothpick In Europe if a bit of food catches in one's teeth at dinner it is considered by many proper to remove it adroitly with a toothpick, using a table napkin as a screen. In America, and among many cultured Europeans however, one suffers. If you can't dislodge the offending bit with your tongue (and even such maneuvers must be unnoticed by the assemblage), leave it there until you can remove it in privacy. If something desperate happens—such as a bit of oyster shell threatening to puncture your gum—excuse yourself quietly from the table and make no report on your excavations when you return. The well-mannered person never inquires, even by the lift of an eyebrow, as to why someone else has left the table.

"Thank You" Many who come here knowing some English have learned it from English governesses, tutors, or instructors. They may never become conscious of many little Americanisms, ignorance of which can cause some social confusion. In America when you are asked, either at table or elsewhere, if you want something and you say "Thank you," this means you *do* want what is offered. In England it means the opposite.

Here it is expected that you will say "Yes," or "No, thank you." A shake of the head is all that is necessary if you are offered something you do not wish by a servant at table although you may say, "No, thank you" to him or her quite properly.

Acknowledging a Compliment   Americans often disconcert the foreign-born by exclaiming, "Thank you!" when given a graceful compliment. This is an Americanism, of course, and the Continental manner of acknowledging a compliment—a gentle, protesting smile—is quite acceptable here also.

Introductions and Salutations   In English the wife of a man bearing a doctorate does not receive his title as she does in some other languages although in Germany where it used to be customary this is now out of use except perhaps among the elderly. She is merely Mrs. So-and-So, not Mrs. Dr. So-and-So. This applies to letters addressed to her, as well as to oral address. If in introducing her you wish to indicate that Mrs. So-and-So is the wife of a doctor, you say so. "May I present (if you are introducing her to another woman older than herself or of her own age and social status) Mrs. So-and-So. Her husband, as you may know, is Dr. John So-and-So." For further information on introductions, see "Dress and Manners."

Who Is "Doctor"?   Europeans, by the way, tend to use doctorates, socially, more freely than we do. In America we commonly address as "Doctor" only persons holding the following degrees: M.D. (Doctor of Medicine), D.O. (Doctor of Osteopathy), D.D.S. (Doctor of Dental Surgery), D.D. (Doctor of Divinity), and, optionally, Ph.D. (Doctor of Philosophy), and Sc.D. (Doctor of Science). The latter doctorates, along with LL.D. (Doctor of Laws) are sometimes courtesy rather than professional titles and thus are usually not employed socially unless the holder uses the title in his profession. Veterinarians, chiropodists, and chiropractors (in some states) who actually hold professional degrees use the title "Dr." both socially and professionally. If a woman has a doctorate of her own she is known professionally as Dr. Mary Smith and may socially be, according to her own desire, either Mrs. John Smith or Dr. Mary Smith. This latter is awkward if her husband is not a doctor, too, for addressing them jointly is difficult. It would have to be Dr. Mary Smith and Mr. John Smith, much too awkward on a letter addressed to both of them, thus Dr. Mary Smith would be well advised to be Mrs. Smith socially. If both are doctors, however, both using the same surname, the joint address is simpler. The form is The Doctors Smith, or The Drs. John and Mary Smith with the former preferred. If the wife practices under her maiden name, there is no choice but for her to be known socially as Mrs. Smith (unless she prefers to be an out and out Lucy Stoner and never embrace the name of her husband socially).

Using the Phone The Continental is frequently puzzled about the accepted way of using the phone in English—just as the American is often struck dumb if he must cope with a foreign operator or try to make himself understood in another language by means of the phone alone. When the phone rings, pick it up and say "hello." It is not necessary to announce your own name to the person calling. If you, a man, are calling someone else you do, of course, announce yourself by saying *"This is* Mr. Paris" or, if you feel a need to identify yourself more clearly, "This is Jacques Paris speaking," *not* "Here is, etc.," European style. Give your whole name without Mr., if the person himself answers and is your social equal. You do this even when you do not use each other's first names in conversation. If a woman answers with whom you are on a business basis, you announce yourself as Mr. Paris, no first name. If your name is rather usual, it may be necessary to add your first name or your business affiliation—"Mr. Jones of the telephone company." If a servant answers you say, "Mr. So-and-So is calling," giving your first name, too, only if your last name is rather common.

A woman calling on the phone announces herself to someone she does not know as Mrs. Paris or Miss Paris. If her name is very usual, she must of necessity say, "Mrs. *Patrick* Smith" or "Miss *Alice* Jones." For business calls her business affiliation may be enough, for example, "Miss Jones, Hurlbutt School." In suburban and country communities in the United States, a woman calling another woman socially whom she does not know on a first-name basis usually announces herself on the telephone to another woman of her social group (but not to tradespeople) as "Norma Paris." She may find it necessary for identification to add her husband's name, "Mrs. Jacques Paris." In cities, more formality is usual, and she announces herself as "Mrs. Paris"—"Mrs. Jacques Paris," if necessary. This is advisable if the person you are calling does not know whether you are Mrs. or Miss.

In the United States the old British form of telephone greeting between men—"Black of the National Bank calling"—is infrequently heard. Here it is usual for a man calling another man to announce himself as "George Black." To a woman he says "Mr. Black" in a business call (with identification if necessary) John Black in a social one.

If you give a number to the operator orally a zero is pronounced "o." If you are spelling a word or name, the "z" is pronounced "zee" in America, *not* "zed" as in England.

Greetings Don't translate your reply to the polite greeting, "How are you?" into "Fine, how's yourself?" Instead you should say, "How are you?"—answering the question with a question, as the whole greeting is a formality anyhow, or you may reply, "Fine, and how are you?" or "Very well, thank you—and you?"

The Use of "Lady" and "Gentleman" In conversation we do not refer to a woman of our own social status as a "lady" or to a man as a "gentleman." Don't say, "I went next door to see the lady who lives there." Say, "I went next door to visit Mrs. Brown." You might add that she is a "charming *woman*" or that someone else is a "nice *girl.*" Somehow the term *"young* lady" doesn't fall into the same servile classification as does that of "lady." In speaking of a male friend it is preferable to say that he is a "fine man" rather than that he is a "fine gentleman," as the latter phrase places you a step below him socially. Again, however, the use of the adjective "old" or "young" furbishes the word. You might refer to a "fine *old* gentleman" or a "gay *young* gentleman" and still indicate that they are of your own circle.

A child, however, in referring to a grown-up says, for instance, "Mommy, may I offer the candy to this gentleman?" or "Does the lady always carry her doggie with her?" When a child knows the names of his parents' friends he should refer to them as Mrs. or Mr. So-and-So, if old enough to master surnames. I know a little boy of four who, if he forgets your name, refers to you simply as Mr. or Mrs. "Somebody." Very young children in America are often permitted to call their parents' intimate friends by the names they hear their parents use—"Joe" or "Mary" —because we may never use "Mrs.," "Mr.," or "Miss" alone without the surname as one does so simply in foreign languages. As children grow older they tend to decide for themselves where such intimacy is unwelcome and where it is preferred. To insist that a child call older people who are familiars of a household "Aunt" or "Uncle," when there is no reason for such a title, seems foolish and often irks the child.

Using First Names Americans are very quick to use first names. This usually makes those of European and other backgrounds uncomfortable, especially when the last name is not given at all or is merely mumbled and never mentioned again. If using first names on introduction is difficult for you, follow your usual more conservative custom and use titles. If someone indicates that this is unfriendly, explain gently that it is difficult for you to use first names so quickly. If you object to being called by your first name, you may say so. If you continue to use titles yourself for such situations you will find others will usually give you the dignity of yours. Not everyone likes "instant intimacy." You will find that Eastern and Southern communities are more conservative in this matter, Western and Southwestern generally informal.

Changing Your Name

What justification is there for changing your name? If you are handicapped with a name that is almost impossible for English-speaking people to pronounce or spell—some of the Russian, Polish, or Slavic names are good examples—or are the possessor of a name that may leave you open to possible ridicule because of its association (Schicklgruber) or its connotation in English, you may do well to change it. Beware however of picking a surname at random only because its first letter is the same as that of your own. A man with a strong accent and the pleasant Italian name of Guglieri, who wearies of the way Americans mangle it, makes a mistake if he hits on—to be a little far-fetched—Gallagher, a typical Irish name. The combination of an Italian accent and an Irish name might make him the butt of many jokes.

Wherever possible simplify your name (the Welsh name Ijams to Iams is a good example) if need be, rather than choose a totally new name, for example, Szurovy to Surovy, easily spellable for us. Such a change permits you to keep your own identity, too. Try to have your name match your background. It should not be too obvious that your name has been changed, if it's to fit you comfortably. If you go too far afield in your selection of a name people will have trouble associating you with it. If a man named Otto Schmeller, to choose a Germanic name at random, settles on Arthur Washington when everything about him is Germanic, including his accent and appearance, he will find his new name more of a handicap than he thought his original name to be.

Who Can Help with Your Name?   First, don't change your name just to become Americanized or because the naturalization clerk suggests some banal name or names to you which you seize on without careful consideration. A name is important. If you change yours, get help in choosing one that fits. Don't be afraid to keep the name you were born with, even though it is a little difficult, if you like it. You may come from a distinguished family abroad and, in your heart, want to remain identified with it. America is peopled with men and women who bear other than Nordic names. I'd rather have a difficult name any day which, once mastered, is not easily forgotten, than one so common it has no distinction at all.

If, after talking the matter over with your friends and family, you decide to change your name, discuss it further with a librarian, a genealogist, or an English teacher, so you will find the name that suits you best. Try wherever possible to keep your original first name. If your friends call you Hans or Rudolph or Jean, it will be confusing if your new legal name is anglicized to John, Ralph (let us say), or James, and when you bring old friends together with new ones, or with business acquaintances, there will always be the impression of duality. However, when it is essential to change your first name completely or to anglicize it in some simple way, be firm in your request to old friends to call you by your new name. It is amazing how quickly the new name can take hold and the old one actually be forgotten by people who called you by it for years. It will be more comfortable for everyone if you use your name both in business and socially.

How Do You Announce a Change of Name? When people change their names by legal means there need be no more confusion about it than there is when a woman changes her name to that of her husband. A formal announcement may be sent to friends and business associates to simplify matters, or you may let everyone know informally by letter, as the occasion arises, or casually in conversation. A formal announcement reads like this:

Mr. Casimir Wojciechowski
announces that by permission of the court
he has changed his name to
Cass Wiecks

A graceful announcement of the change may be made in a way that includes the juniors of the family, too. It is not, by the way, necessary to secure a court order to change your name, so long as you can, if challenged, prove you had no intent to defraud. A family adopting a new name may do so this way:

Mr. and Mrs. Ulrich Uhrmachermeister
Miss Gerda Uhrmachermeister
and Master Karl Uhrmachermeister
wish to inform you that they have adopted the surname of
Urman

If first names have been changed you should list all the changes so the announcement reads:

Mr. and Mrs. Ulrich Uhrmachermeister
Miss Gerda Uhrmachermeister
and Master Karl Uhrmachermeister
wish to inform you that they have adopted the names of
Mr. and Mrs. Richard Urman
Miss Gertrude Urman
and Master Charles Urman

The phrase "wish to inform you that by order of the court they (or he) *will be known as*" is also used.

Simple white cards are engraved with or without plate marking in black script or in any of the restrained English-style types. Where a very small list makes engraving of the cards extravagant, you may choose to have them printed, but the formal style should be the same. It's a serious matter to change one's name, and the procedure should be treated with due dignity.

If no such formal announcement is made, seasonal greeting cards, if usually sent, could be signed "the Urmans (formerly the Uhrmachermeisters)," but here again dignity should be the objective.

The New Citizen and the English Language

English with an Accent Many foreign born who become American citizens may find it impossible to lose an accent—a matter of little importance, I think, for foreign accents in English can be very attractive. It is the very rare American remember who learns to speak another language without accent. While there are methods of "de-accenting" the foreign born, it is not the accent itself that is of concern but the ability to make oneself understood and even to achieve real fluency in the language by thinking in it.

The new citizen has at least a beginning understanding of his new language. It is more than courtesy to his adopted country that impels him to continue to study it carefully, even after his papers have been granted to him. If he is satisfied with a small vocabulary and a few idioms, or if, after many years in the country, he continues to translate his own language literally into English, he will continue to be considered a "foreigner" despite his American citizenship. He will have difficulty expressing his ideas fully in his business or profession. His children may feel some embarrassment at his unfamiliarity with English.

If you, as a new American, speak as much English as possible even with business associates of your own original nationality, you will find that you do begin to think in English and can express yourself readily. If, however, your social life is spent largely with those of your own original nationality, something quite natural because of a community of interests, you may for years make the same errors as they do in speaking English. You may also lose the ability to hear the important differences when you speak with native-born Americans—presupposing, of course, that they speak correctly themselves.

Foreign Words in English It isn't easy to know what foreign words have become anglicized and which have not except by listening to the pronunciation of cultured people. Even here it is possible to become confused, for in England the French word *"garage"* has gone native and becomes the ugly "ga-rahge," with the accent on first syllable. "Hors d'oeuvres" is pronounced in the French way. "Valet" is preferably pronounced as it is spelled, although in the Middle West if you phone for valet service in a hotel the operator will probably correct you—"Vallā service?" she will query. But you may rightfully stick to your pronunciation, backed by even the Oxford Dictionary, which, by the way, can sometimes lead you sadly astray on American pronunciation. "Chauffeur" becomes "shofer," losing its French twist somewhat, while "aide-de-camp" is pronounced as if the words were English. "Buffet" is pronounced as the French meant it to be and is never anglicized.

Writing Letters When you write a letter and use the form of address "My dear So-and-So," you are, in the United States strange to relate, using the more formal not the less formal term. In writing to intimates say, "Dear So-and-So," not "My dear." In speaking, too, if you say "My dear John," or "My dear fellow, would you pass me the salt," you are being patronizing rather than affectionate.

If you are writing to someone very intimate you close your letters with something less formal than "Cordially." You say "Yours," "With love," "Love," "Affectionately," "As ever," "Always," or some other phrase to indicate your closeness.

How to Welcome Overseas Guests

Overseas guests in the United States have been much fewer proportionately than American visitors abroad, but the tide is turning due to the efforts of our government to attract foreigners to our shores. Let us hope that we will develop and exercise the courtesies we have ourselves enjoyed on our visits abroad. Here are some suggestions that may help.

Invitations In issuing our invitations to people from abroad, we must be very specific. Our geography is vast and confusing to foreigners. Many understandably cannot really conceive of the distances between our cities, of the time it takes to get from our cities to our suburbs. They need to receive specific information. If we live in Boston and our friends are landing in New York by ship, we should tell them just how long it will take them to get to our homes, what transportation means are available, and the cost. Many visitors are on very much smaller travel budgets than we could travel with comfortably. Where we can meet them or provide transportation in some other way, it is courteous and considerate to do so.

Foreign-speaking guests often find directions most difficult to understand over the phone, just as we have the same problem when we are abroad in non-English speaking countries. Wherever possible, write directions, invitations, and other communications to them legibly. If you use a typewriter for any of these, however, you should make some slight apology mentioning the difficulty people have in reading your handwriting, for example. Although it is proper to use the typewriter here for social communications (with some exceptions) it is not usual abroad however practical the idea might be.

As part of our plan of orientation for foreign visitors, it is helpful to provide a map or maps and local guide books that may be available— and these are still fairly rare, but material is being developed with the visitor in mind.

Dress Someone who has not been here before may have quite a misconception concerning the clothes that he will need for a visit to an American home. If your household is informal and you live in a community where the wearing of a dinner jacket or a cocktail dress over a weekend is unlikely, then be specific in your suggestions on what your guests should pack. I have had European men guests uncomfortable and ill at ease for a weekend in the American countryside or suburbia because they brought with them only white shirts and business suits with black shoes.

Entertainment Plan for your guests' entertainment but don't provide so many activities that you will all be fatigued and your guests will be left with a feeling of confusion over what he has seen. Most visitors appreciate, just as we do abroad, the opportunity to visit American homes and participate in the activities there. After all, restaurant and other public entertainment is much the same in cosmopolitan centers everywhere, whereas church fairs and suppers, country auctions, visits to historical points of interest, boating on local ponds, or swimming at local beaches or at someone's pool may much better reflect the quality of our living and provide memories and friendships that can be savored by our foreign friends upon their return home.

Meals Plan good American meals for them. Don't attempt to produce their own cookery in an effort to make them feel at home. They want to feel *away*. Remember that American kitchen appliances and all our conveniences may puzzle a foreign visitor. Explain how things work. An American self-service elevator with its strange markings can be just as confusing to an Italian as the Italian lifts that demand a coin are to us. The guest who is used to wine at dinner may miss this pleasant custom in a household where ice water is usual and in this case, even though the service of wine is not your own custom, it is pleasant to provide it unless for some reason you cannot.

Even if meals in your home are not served according to a rigid schedule, it is well to let your foreign visitor know what time he can expect his next meal, as foreigners eat meals of different quantities and at different times than we do. For example, a cup of coffee and a piece of toast may be all you want for breakfast at eight o'clock, but a guest, a Scot, for example, used to eating heartily at that hour will be very hungry indeed by twelve and if lunch in your household is a "raid the refrigerator" affair, he may well be starving by dinnertime. Let him know roughly when you serve meals and approximately what your plans are for the day ahead. "We'll just grab a sandwich for lunch before we go to the museum" will be enough to let him know whether or not he should help himself to another muffin at breakfast. Our meals tend to seem hurried indeed to a European used to leisurely dining.

Let your foreign visitor contribute. Food offers a wonderful way to do so. If you are preparing a meal, invite your guest to look on and watch American methods. Your frozen foods or your electric can opener, your commodious refrigerator, or your stove with its timers and automatic devices, may delight even a male visitor. Exchange of recipes or mutual instruction in cooking methods can be a fascinating way for you to get to know each other.

Gifts Most foreigners come to us bearing gifts. When we visit them abroad we usually leave with gifts from them. We can remember this pleasant custom and send them away with some remembrance, however simple, of their visit.

Part Three

HOME ENTERTAINING

HOME ENTERTAINING

An Albanian proverb goes, "Every guest hates the others, and the host hates them all." Too much entertaining is exactly like that, with no fun intended.

It is a good thing for a family to set aside its home for itself and its friends. When guests are invited to break bread for other than purely friendly reasons the entertainment is too often a failure, unless it so happens that such business acquaintances turn out to be congenial. A good rule to follow is: don't try to do business over your own dinner table.

So entertaining at home should have no strings attached. Occasionally we all accept invitations we prefer not to accept and thus incur a social obligation we must repay. The successful hostess never includes too many new or difficult guests at what should be an intimate little dinner. Eight people who never saw or heard of each other before—and hope never to see or hear of each other again—can do social violence to the most adequately planned evening.

If host and hostess themselves can, through the careful selection of their guests and through sufficient advance preparation, look forward with pleasure to an evening or a weekend, then the party is virtually assured of success. Whether trained servants present platters of peacocks' tongues or the hostess herself dishes up a good spaghetti dinner is quite immaterial. If the house looks as if it expected and welcomed guests, if the host and hostess are relaxed and smiling, the guests will feel at home and at ease, no matter what superficial accouterments of entertaining may be missing through necessity or design.

Entertain and enjoy it!

Chapter 31

INFORMAL ENTERTAINING

The Company or Semiformal Dinner Party

The truly formal dinner in all its stiff elegance is not what the average American thinks of as formal dinner. What we encounter most in the way of special entertaining is the semiformal or company dinner for which the household puts its best foot forward. This is the seated dinner of four to eight guests (who may or may not be in evening dress) or even more, depending on the dining room's ability to contain them all comfortably. Entertaining at home of more than eight at dinner usually must be buffet style or at bridge tables, informally.

Invitations Invitations to the company informal dinner are usually phoned or are given by word of mouth, and, of course, may be extended by informals or calling cards (see "Invitations, Acceptances, and Regrets," page 570). The hostess always tenders the invitation. On occasion, for convenience's sake, her husband may do so *in her name,* where close friends are concerned. For example, if he is a commuter and the friends are in the city he may phone them for his wife. He says, "Mary would like you to come to dinner on Friday at seven-thirty. Black tie." A hostess who asks her men guests these days to wear black tie in the suburbs or in the country, however, is very optimistic. She is safer to suggest that her women guests wear cocktail dresses and let the men come in their preferred dark suits, especially on a week night.

A hostess who is telephoning an invitation should keep in mind that it is sometimes awkward to press for an immediate answer as it is always wise for a husband and wife to discuss such invitations and come to an agreement about them. The wife can always say, "Will you let me call you back. I don't have my calendar right here and I'm not sure whether we have anything on that evening or not." Of course, if she knows they are free and is sure that her husband is as eager to go as she is, she may accept promptly. But she must be sure that she is not accepting an invitation her husband would prefer to regret. It is also up to the wife, especially at the very festive times of the year, to see that their social engagements don't overly fatigue them both. It is always acceptable to say, "No, Joan, I would love to accept but we are going out three times that week and I just can't accept another invitation. I promised Joe. I hope you will ask us soon again."

Invitations to company dinners are not lightly treated. The hostess obviously is going to considerable trouble, especially if she has little or no help. Guests should not disappoint her at the last minute without a believable excuse such as illness. Neither should they ask to bring another guest, with the possible exception of another single man for whom most hostesses have need. It's the wise hostess who sends out a reminder if she has issued her invitation by telephone. This may be simply these lines written on the third side of an informal that bears her name: Reminder—Dinner Thursday, April 12th at 7:30. Then, if her address is not on the informal, she should add it complete with apartment number if the couple lives in an apartment. Such reminders may also be written on visiting cards in black ink at the top with the address lower right if it isn't on the card. The wording can be quite telegraphic. Engraved fill-in reminders are also available for this purpose at good stationers. They read in this way:

This is to remind you that

Jane Saunders

expects you for *dinner*

on *April 3*

at *7:30*   o'clock

Reminder cards need no reply unless, of course, the person invited has mixed up her dates, become ill, or has some emergency that makes it impossible to attend the function for which she has accepted the invitation.

Greeting the Arriving Guests   No guest should be allowed to arrive without greeting. Both host and hostess should be on duty in the living room five minutes or more before the appointed time. When an invitation is issued for seven o'clock, guests may arrive at that hour, promptly, or up to ten or fifteen minutes later. At a large dinner party lateness of as much as half an hour is virtually expected in metropolitan communities, but frequently in the West and Midwest when a dinner invitation is for seven, guests begin to arrive at six-thirty as it is assumed that they are to be seated at dinner at seven or shortly after.

Once dinner is announced the hostess should not be expected to wait more than a few minutes for late-comers, unless one includes the guest of honor, who ideally should never be late but without whom it is certainly peculiar to sit down. If the lateness is really very serious, guest of honor or no, the hostess proceeds with the dinner. A late-comer enters the dining room as quietly as possible, goes briefly to the hostess (who remains seated so as not to disturb the table), makes an apology, and sits immediately in the indicated place. If the late one is a woman, the man to her left rises, or semi-rises, to seat her. Any long explanation of the reason for the lateness is uncalled for and should never draw in the others at the table. The hostess, no matter how she really feels about it, always minimizes the inconvenience to her as well as to the other guests. She says something such as, "It's really quite all right. I knew you would expect us to go right ahead."

Entering the Dining Room Where dinner partners have not been assigned by card (see "Formal Dinner" for example of place card) the hostess, when the meal has been announced, usually leads her women guests into the dining room with the men following, the host bringing up the rear. The men step forward and hold the chairs as the hostess indicates where each lady is to sit—with the woman guest of honor placed to the host's right and the male guest of honor placed to the hostess's right. Gentlemen seat the ladies to their right. At an informal or family dinner there may very well be one less man than women. The hostess in this case may seat herself or is seated by a servant or by the gentleman guest of honor, if any, if there's no man on her left to seat her. For parties of more than eight, place cards simplify this little procedure. Where everybody knows everybody else, these place cards may carry just first names. Otherwise they read Mrs. Benton, Mr. Cunningham, Mrs. Smith. If two couples with the same surname happen to be at the table, then the cards of course must read Mrs. Robert Smith, Mr. James Smith. Titles are always simplified, Justice Goldfrank (not "The Hon. Gerald Goldfrank, Justice of the Supreme Court"). The title "Hon." is not used on place cards. Instead, "Mr.," "Mrs." or "Miss" as the case may be is used with the last name. Even at a smaller party cards should be used if the hostess is likely to become flustered or forgetful of names—she must never resort to a little memorandum at her own place, as did one nervous hostess I knew.

Newlyweds and Engaged Couples Newlyweds and engaged couples should not be separated in table seating arrangements, although they may be seated vis-à-vis if this makes for a better seating plan. After the first year of marriage newlyweds may be separated. At large parties, any couples requesting to be seated together, or at least at the same table, should be accommodated if possible.

The Menu for the Company or Semiformal Dinner Party   The season, naturally, must be considered in planning dinner for guests. Availability of produce and meats, too, is a factor, as is the seasonableness of the weather. Foods with rich sauces are less appetizing in hot weather. In winter a main dish *en gelée* would seem unsubstantial.

In my cookbook, *Amy Vanderbilt's Complete Cookbook,* I have given a variety of menus for guest meals. The recipes for important guest dinners as compared with those for buffet suppers show the degree of difference in the choice of food. A simple buffet supper suitable for the family or, very informally, for guests, for example, includes carrot sticks, raw cauliflower, cheese-garlic dip, baked limas, baked ham, sliced peaches, pearl onions, peeled sliced tomatoes with minced chives, charlotte russe, and coffee. Whereas an important guest dinner menu is given as follows:

DRY SHERRY   PÂTÉ DE FOIE GRAS   TOAST TRIANGLES
CELERY AND CHICKEN CONSOMMÉ FLAVORED WITH
CELERY SALT
QUAIL, SQUAB, OR SQUAB CHICKEN ALEXANDRA
JELLIED CRANBERRY SALAD MOLDS WITH LETTUCE HEARTS,
THINNED MAYONNAISE
WILD RICE   BRAISED BELGIAN ENDIVE
LEMON SOUFFLÉ WITH LEMON SAUCE
COFFEE

The informal dinner consists of an entrée of some kind, which may be hot or cold soup and which may be served in a handled cup, pottery bowl, or cream soup bowl, whereas at a formal dinner, soup is always in a flat soup dish. The main course may be fish instead of meat, since usually not both are served. Second helpings are often offered. At formal meals they never are. Salad may well be served at the same time as the main dish rather than as a separate course. There is dessert, and after-dinner coffee is often served at the table with dessert or just following it and is usually poured by the hostess (who adds sugar and cream for those who wish it) and passed around, though it may be poured in the kitchen if there is a waitress and passed on a tray with cream and sugar.

Arranging and Setting the Table

Today there is infinite variety in place mats and in table coverings of all kinds. A damask cloth in white or color, always the most conservative choice, may still be used for an informal dinner, but place mats are more usual. Candles are on the table and may be colored, rather than the white of the formal table. There is a centerpiece (which, if the table is against the wall, is centered against it rather than in the middle of the table), and it may consist of flowers, greenery, silver, a ceramic or porcelain of some kind. A small table may have to dispense with a centerpiece entirely and use its main serving dishes—a lovely tureen, a handsome casserole—as focal points of interest. Artificial flowers and leaves are being used even by the most conservative hostesses now. Sometimes they look absolutely real and are frequently mixed in with real flowers and leaves. Other times they are frankly "fake" and meant to look so, and chosen with very great care can be most attractive, as are of course many charming dried arrangements. And certainly in a dark area where nothing would grow, a well-fabricated plant can be attractive. Even in households where the cost of fresh flowers is not an important consideration, many hostesses have lovely arrangements of imported handmade flowers of silk or feathers that can be much more expensive than the real things would be, and which are indubitably more practical in certain circumstances. It takes taste, however, to select the right artificial plants or flowers. Avoid like the plague anything that looks cheap and tawdry.

The old idea of white cloth and white napkins, matching fine china, clear matching crystal kept solely for "company," made for monotony. Hostesses who made a fetish of such things often had set company dinners, too, devoid of imagination and deadly dull. Actually there is considerable precedence for gay dining cloths. Those of the early Saxons were bright crimson, gold-fringed.

At today's informal or semiformal dinner the guests may sit down at a bare, gleaming table, on occasion. Napkins may be almost any color, almost any material. Thick pottery mugs may be used for the summer iced tea, or frosty beer may come on in beer glasses, tankards, steins, or even large Burgundy glasses. The dishes, the glassware, and the table

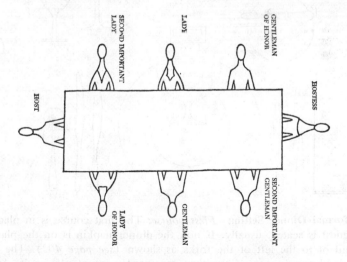

Seating at the Company or Semiformal Dinner Party

covering if any, are more likely to be geared to the choice of food than to the fact that this is a company dinner.

Imagine the visual effect of cold boiled scarlet lobsters in a big wooden mixing bowl in the center of a round table covered with fringed woods-green cloth. Think of the mayonnaise in yellow and turquoise majolica, the chablis in chunky clear glass, the napkins big, lobster-printed paperlike cotton bibs. The salad, of course, is served in individual wooden bowls, and the dessert is chilled mixed fruit—whole red cherries, rosy pears, purple plums, crackling apples on a bed of crushed ice. Such a dinner is a far cry from grandmother's hushed Victorian party meals. And a lot more fun for everyone.

At a semiformal company dinner party the silver is preferably sterling, but at a wholly informal or family dinner it may be a good plate or any of the wood or plastic-handled tableware in common use, so long as it is in good condition and usually all matching. Whatever the "silver," it is placed one inch or so from the edge of the table at place settings that are equidistant from one another on a table laid with care and precision. The napkin is placed on the place plate, unless the first course is in place, and then it is to the left of the forks, but it should not obscure them, nor should the silver be obscured by the plate. On an informal table the other appointments are geared to the size of the table, the amount of service available—which may

Informal Dinner Setting   *First course:* The first course is in place when the guest is seated, usually. If not, the dinner napkin is on the place plate instead of to the left of the forks as shown (*see page 402*). The seafood fork is shown in one of the three accepted ways of placing it. Ash trays are needed but many hostesses do not offer cigarettes now.

Second course: Informal dinners are very elastic. They may have as few as two courses but are usually limited to five. The soup course may well be omitted, especially if an appetizer is served first. At informal dinners the soup need not be served in the traditional flat soup plate.

Third course: The salad is usually served with the entree for simplicity's sake. The knife is optional, depending on the type of salad and whether or not cheese is served.

be none at all—and to the number to be seated. At a small, round table, for example, a centerpiece may prove impractical if meat and vegetables are to be served at table. Perhaps all the table can conveniently hold at the center, in addition to the food, are the candlesticks or a single candelabrum. Candles may be in any color but should be above eye level and, if they are on the table at all, lighted but then only if the room is darkened (though unlighted candles with wicks charred for easy lighting may be in any room as decoration when not in actual use). The silver is whatever is needed for the meal, though many prefer to introduce the dessert silver with the dessert. Otherwise dessert spoon and fork or spoon alone may be above the plate (illustrated). The knives are usually limited to two—one for an appetizer, if any, one for the meat, as the informal dinner rarely has

Fourth course: The salad course may be served separately as a fourth course and, especially when accompanied by a cheese tray, may replace dessert.

Fifth course: When dessert silver is not in place above the place plate at an informal dinner it comes in on the dessert plate, or is so placed and passed with the dessert by the hostess from her place. When the dessert is in place, flanked by the silver *on the plate,* it is left that way. If the silver is on an empty plate with or without finger bowl, the guest places silver left and right of plate (*see illustration of dessert service and text*).

more than four courses. If salad is to be served with cheese a salad knife is needed. The silver is placed traditionally, that needed first, farthest right and left of the plate. The forks are usually two, for meat and salad, occasionally one more for an appetizer, but never more than three at once. The salad fork is inside the meat fork, unless the salad is served as a first course in which case it is the first fork in the setting. At informal tables iced tea or iced coffee may be served but not at the same time as wine and either may be followed at the conclusion of the meal by demitasse if the hostess wishes. The iced tea spoon is placed to the right of the knives. Sometimes the iced tea or coffee is on its own small serving plate, sometimes placed directly on the (treated) table or on a small coaster. For iced coffee, cream and sugar are passed. Iced tea at a meal is best served sweetened and lemon-flavored and poured from a pitcher at the table over ice.

Spoons for soup or fruit are on the table, to the right of the knives. If hot coffee or tea is to be served at the table, during the meal or with or after dessert, the spoons for it are on the saucers, to the right of each cup handle.

Butter plates and knives are used with the butter knife placed in a variety of ways—across the top of the plate, blade toward the user, across the top of the plate, tip toward the center of the plate, or occasionally parallel to the knives, blade to the left (illustrated).

Salts and peppers on an informal table may be in a wide variety of materials, from the wooden salt and pepper grinders of the gourmets to Victorian condiment sets with their pressed or etched glass and silver containers for salt, pepper, paprika, red pepper, mustard, and vinegar. At a large table a salt and pepper for each two guests is convenient. Little open dishes may be used, glass or crystal, even ceramic or pottery. They should be freshly filled, and unless there are individual salts and peppers for each guest little spoons are needed. It is well to remember that any salt cellar with a silver top must have the top removed and the threading washed completely free of salt after each use or the threading will corrode and the diner will get much more salt than he bargains for!

The informal diner expects to smoke at table if he is a smoker at all. Individual ash trays are best, but one larger one for each two guests is acceptable, too. Increasingly hostesses are ceasing to furnish cigarettes at the table, although they do provide ash trays and matches. Guests who do smoke expect to provide their own brand of cigarettes. The hostess, in not providing any herself, delicately dissuades her guests from smoking at her table. Today in many cases the smokers are in the minority and should, for this reason, be particularly considerate of non-smokers around them.

Wines at an informal meal are usually very simple—at most two, perhaps sherry with the soup and one dinner wine throughout the meal. Wine glasses are placed in order of use. The sherry glass is above the knives, the wine glass to its right in a variety of positions (illustrated). Sometimes the sherry glass is removed with the soup, sometimes it stays until dessert. At an informal table the dinner wine glass remains throughout. Sometimes, depending on the menu, beer replaces wine. It may follow sherry, but no sweet wine or liqueur should follow it. It is served in tall, cone-shaped beer glasses, in mugs, steins, or any tall glass.

Sometimes demitasses are served at the table by the hostess or even hot tea, after the meal, at the table. The spoons are on the saucers, to the right of each cup handle.

Dinner Service with One Maid

Pretension is so very uncomfortable. If a family has just one servant it is foolish to try to turn her into cook-waitress-nurse and lady's maid. Rarely these days do servants stay on one job the years it requires to function flawlessly at it. Pretrained servants coming on to a job are equally hard to find. The best thing in a one-servant household is for the mistress to face the fact that she cannot expect too much.

Entertaining causes extra work. Some of the added chores such as making the butterballs or decorated pats—these cut with a warm knife from a quarter-pound bar and made festive with a bit of mint, parsley, fresh herbs, or a sprinkling of paprika—and canapés have to be taken care of. Too, preparing the dessert, getting out the extra glassware, dishes, and silver and cleaning it, if necessary (special pieces can be sealed away in pliofilm, by the way, to appear bright as new for parties) are other things to be considered. A hostess is expecting too much of one maid, except, of course, when the family is small and adult. But there is still the usual routine of the household before party preparations can begin. Perhaps extra help is needed from outside, either during the day or to wait on the table and help with the cleaning up.

A company dinner that is to be both prepared and served by one maid should be kept fairly simple—three courses. Having a freezer makes it easy to have some dishes prepared in advance. Canapés may be frozen, then thawed or put in the oven (for those requiring broiling) just before the guests arrive and so may the dinner rolls. Frozen vegetables cut down on preparation time. The dessert—even pie or cake—may come from the freezer.

If you have no freezer, use the freezing compartment of your refrigerator wisely. It can store a dessert for a dinner party a day or more in advance, and it also can yield the vegetables. Rolls may be of the brown-and-serve variety or little glazed dinner rolls from the bakery. Don't ask Anna to bake fresh rolls, along with everything else she has to do.

A simply prepared solid piece of meat for carving at the table or to be passed from a platter cuts down work. A roast, steak, broilers, or chops are more convenient for a dinner than fried chicken, veal scallopini, fried fish, or seafood. Avoid foods that require last-minute preparation and prompt consumption—fried things and soufflés for example. Roast beef is everybody's favorite, and everyone, too, likes steak, plain or dressed up. But steak is difficult if dinner has been preceded by more than three cocktails. It just can't be held indefinitely. If there is any doubt about the exact time of sitting down to dinner, roast lamb, roast pork, roast veal, baked ham, roast chicken are far wiser choices than steak or roast beef.

The First Course   If a first course is to be served at the table (it could have been served in the living room and at such a dinner it may be omitted) a place plate is in place with the folded dinner napkin on it or the first course is actually on the place plate. In summer the first course may be vichyssoise, in winter a fish ramekin or hot soup in a bowl, a cup, or in a flat plate, with the folded napkin to the left of the forks. For utmost simplicity, if there is no first course, the heated dinner plates, if the course is hot, are at each place.

A first course may be served by the maid once guests have been seated and have opened their napkins (but napkins are not touched at a seated dinner until the hostess takes up hers). All serving procedures described are intended to simplify work, save steps, and speed service. The maid comes in from the serving pantry or kitchen with the soup or other entrée in her left hand, and at a dinner of no more than eight, beginning with the lady at the host's right (never with the hostess), she serves counterclockwise, ending with the host. Everything is served to the *left*. Or, if there is no first course and place plates are on the table, she exchanges the place plates for heated dinner plates, taking off the place plates with her right hand to the guest's left *or* right and putting down the hot plate with her left on the guest's left side. Then she brings in the main dish and sets it before the host if it is to be carved. She passes it (first showing it to the hostess for inspection) to the woman guest of honor, at the host's right, if it is a made dish such as a casserole or if it is meat or fish that has been portioned in the kitchen. This is balanced on her left hand on a clean, folded napkin, steadied, if necessary, with her right. Then she brings in the vegetables, one dish in each hand on the serving napkin. (A two- or three-compartment dish is excellent here, too.) She offers first the dish in her left hand, then that in her right. In each dish is a serving spoon and fork face down with handles toward the person to be served. Forks may be omitted if the vegetable is something like peas. However, with a vegetable like asparagus or a vegetable that actually needs to be lifted, both implements are provided. Asparagus, by the way, is often on a folded linen napkin in the dish if a sauce is to be served separately, otherwise it must be well strained before being placed on the platter. Sometimes toast, too, is used as a moisture-catcher for asparagus, and by the way should be taken up by the guest when he serves himself, and may be eaten.

The dish or platter should be held at a level comfortable to the guest, never too high and never so far to the side as to cause him to twist around in his chair. Sauces or gravies should be served immediately after the dish they accompany. Hot dishes should be very hot, cold ones chilled. No luke-warm gravies, tepid chops, or cold biscuits.

If the Host Carves When carving of meat is done at the table, the carving set with the sharpener is placed to the right of the carver above the place setting, so that when the roast is brought in the implements will be to the right of the platter. The maid stands at the host's left. Either she has removed his place plate and put before him a stack of hot dinner plates or he has before him one hot plate which he fills and which the maid then takes with her left hand and places before the guest of honor, first remov-ing his hot plate with her right hand, to the left or right. She then returns to the host, puts the new hot plate in front of him, serves it and gives him another. The host ladles on to each portion the accompanying sauce or gravy or this may be passed separately by the maid before the vegetables. Or she may place it on the table to be passed by the guests.

If the host has before him a stack of hot plates the maid may stand at his left and take one filled one at a time, or two, if the table has been set with no place plates. Or she may let the host pass the plates right and left, as convenient, and she may bring the vegetables from the kitchen and serve them. With one maid, this is the best way to serve when the meat is carved at table. It assures that the food will be served hot.

If the Hostess Serves When the hostess is to serve there are hot-plate mats, if necessary, in front of her place and to her right are arranged serv-ing forks and spoons needed, the fork nested in the spoon. Silver (or china or glass) ladles for sauces are in the sauce when it is served, and the bowl or boat is on a serving plate. When jellies or condiments are in place on the table, to be passed, the spoon or fork for them is next to them on the table and is placed in them by the first person taking up the dish. A made dish or one to be portioned at the table, such as baked fish, may also be placed before the hostess. Or the host may serve meat or fish, and the hostess serve the vegetables. The maid first receives the plate from the host, takes it to the hostess's left for vegetables, sauces, or gravy, then serves it to the guest of honor (the woman to the host's right) and so on around the table counterclockwise, serving the hostess in the regular order as she reaches her, unless she is serving (in this case the hostess is served just before the host who is served last). If the dining room is so tiny as to make any service awkward or if the maid is inept at service, the best thing is to let her bring in the dishes for the host and hostess to serve, remove them at the right time, crumb the table, perhaps pour the water, and serve the dessert and after-dinner coffee, letting it go at that. Better no service than the bumbling kind. A tea table or serving cart may certainly be used. If it is placed at the hostess's right, it can greatly simplify the matter of service and prevents the overcrowding of the table with serving dishes.

Serve Left, Remove Right? At my school in Europe each girl had to wait on table certain days in the week. Everything was served to the left

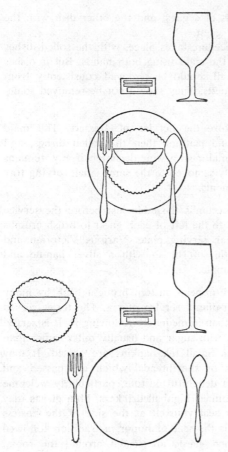

Dessert Service *Left:* The dessert service is placed before the guest this way: finger bowl (optional except at formal dinner and lunch) on doily (optional) and/or small plate, flanked by dessert fork and spoon on dessert plate. *Below left:* Guest rearranges dessert service like this: doily and finger bowl (including small plate, if any, *see text*) upper left, fork left and spoon right of dessert plate awaiting service of dessert. Informally demitasse may be served with dessert, either from the kitchen or poured by the hostess at table and passed (*see text*).

and, formal style, *removed* from the left. This was to teach us how to train our servants when we had our own households. The removal of plates from the left is strictly correct, but in America to speed service with limited help it is quite permissible to serve *left,* remove from the *right.* If this is done, however, the waitress never reaches in front of a guest to remove from the *right* anything such as a butter plate on the guest's extreme *left.* These things are removed from the left, always. Conversely, she never reaches from the guest's left across to the right to take off water and wine glasses, but removes these always from the right.

Serving and Removing Two Plates at a Time Where a service plate need not be considered, particularly after the table has been cleared for dessert, two plates at a time may be served. This is done by placing one dish with the right hand to the left of a guest and the other dish with the left hand to the right of the next guest.

In removing dishes the same procedure takes place, with the soiled dishes being removed right, or left, with the maid using both hands. But if dishes are being removed from the left, all should be removed consistently from the left, so as not to confuse the guests. They should not be removed sometimes left, sometimes right.

Clearing the Main Course Before the Service of Dessert The maid first removes the serving dishes and platters, then the soiled dishes, and finally the condiments. At an informal meal a wine decanter, if any, remains on the table. Unused silver is quietly removed to the same small serving tray that will accommodate the condiments.

Crumbing the Table The maid crumbs the table just before the service of dessert. A folded napkin is used to the left of each guest to brush crumbs either onto a small tray or a clean serving plate. Various Victorian and older crumb sets are used—a little soft brush with a silver handle and miniature silver dust pan, for example.

After-dinner Tea A delightful European custom brought back by many who have lived abroad is the after-dinner service of tea. The tea is served an hour or so after dinner, rather than immediately following it. It is served in the living room in thin teacups, with sugar and usually milk, rather than cream, if desired, or lemon slices. Small tea napkins are passed. It may be accompanied by little cookies or shortbreads, which are passed and placed on the saucer. Late tea is a delightful custom, particularly welcome to those guests who are not after-dinner highball drinkers. Men guests may assist in the service of tea. Never seat yourself at the side of the hostess without special invitation, as this is the seat of honor, a tradition followed especially in Latin countries. When guests are seated around the room, they come forward to take the teacups from the hostess—she does not rise to serve the guests.

Hot evening tea may be served, too, Russian-style in tall glasses with lemon slices and lump sugar. For those who wish, it can be laced with rum or brandy. But whichever way it is served, the important thing is that the tea be properly made in the first place.

After-dinner Coffee or Demitasse At the end of dessert, the coffee may be served at the table, with the hostess pouring, adding cream and sugar as indicated, and passing the demitasses to guests, or after-dinner coffee may be served in the living room. Incidentally, many people do not like black coffee, and it is certainly inconsiderate for a hostess not to offer cream (or a cream substitute) with after-dinner coffee on the ground that it is unfashionable *not* to drink demitasse coffee black. How can fashion dictate what pleases the palate? When a second cup of coffee is desired, the guest picks up the cup and saucer together and passes it to the hostess for refilling. If there is a servant, she takes up the cup and saucer with the left hand and the coffee is poured behind the diner's back with the right hand. She then replaces the cup and saucer on the table at the diner's right.

The Buffet Supper

There are several ways to serve a buffet meal—guests standing (large receptions), seated at one table, seated at small tables, or sitting any convenient place and taking plates on their laps. If the group is small—six to eight people—and the dining table large enough, the table may be laid with cloth or mats, silver, wine glasses, napkins, salt, pepper, nuts, candelabra, ash trays, and cigarettes (if the hostess wishes), and filled water or iced tea or coffee glasses (in summer) but no service plates.

The buffet foods are placed on the sideboard or a serving table along the wall, and guests form a line at one end, pick up their plates, and either serve themselves or are given servings from the main dishes such as baked ham, turkey, or a casserole by the host, hostess, or servant. Guests usually serve themselves to the secondary dishes, to buttered rolls, salad, cheese, and relishes, then take their places at the table. The guests, on finishing the main course (and "seconds" are quite expected), place their soiled dishes on the buffet table, from which they are cleared to the kitchen. Dessert is then brought in and served at table or the buffet by the hostess or each guest may serve himself and go back to the table.

Where the buffet meal is not seated at a main table, guests take their filled plates to any convenient spot in the living room or other indicated place. There bridge tables may be set up (see "Setting the Table for Card Table Service") or coffee tables may be available for those who dread to balance a plate in their laps. It is not necessary for all to be served before those arriving first start eating, though two or more guests usually form a group and eat together.

Any wine or after-dinner coffee at an informally seated buffet is passed by servant, host, or hostess. At a very large party a guest may help himself to wine or coffee, although it is usually poured for him. If all guests are seated together, wine may be passed in its bottle, with each guest pouring his own into the glass at his place, the men pouring for the women.

The Buffet Table

A buffet table is always informal in that, from it, guests serve themselves. But it can certainly have the aspect of formality when it is spread with damask, beautifully decorated with flowers, and sparkling with the finest silver, china, and glass. At a presidential reception in a foreign country I saw such a table with serving platters on one side—and footmen ready to serve from them and actual place settings for guests opposite. The guests in full evening dress ate standing before settings that included glasses for two wines.

Usually, however, a buffet table is much less elaborate. Instead of places being set, the table, opened to its full length, is placed in such a way that guests may serve themselves easily. Sometimes the table is against the wall. Sometimes it is built up beneath a covering cloth, or cloths, into tiers for a *smörgåsbord*. Often a buffet table is bare, or it may have a bright linen cloth. Great leeway is permissible in a buffet setting, so long as it is not crowded. Large serving dishes are placed so they balance one another. Platters are complete with serving spoons and forks. Plates are in stacks near the main dishes and napkins are placed, one overlapping the other, in

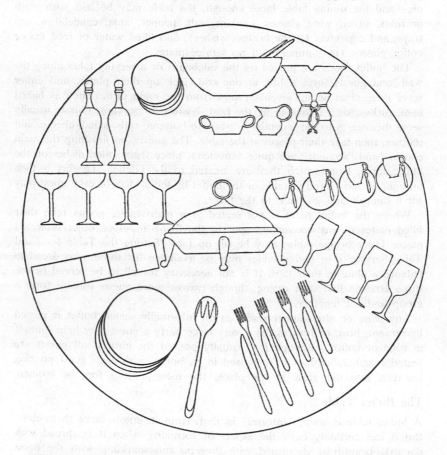

Setting the Buffet Here a round table, always friendly, is shown with a buffet setting for a garden supper. Round tables look best when silver and other things in the arrangement radiate from the center. A buffet should not be too crowded. Additional serving tables may hold anything else necessary if the main table is not large enough.

any agreeably symmetrical fashion. (Illustrated.) Service plates may be used instead of dinner plates and may prove very helpful when there is a large choice of food. I like to see forks and knives (if necessary) arranged in neat rows, forks first, about an inch from the table, and I like to avoid any fanciful arrangement of them—an arc, for example. A pepper grinder and a salt grinder or salt cellar of generous proportions belong on a buffet table. Nearby are ice water and glasses or cold beer or a container with assorted bottled drinks in cracked ice. Or wine may be passed. It is pleasanter to clear all serving and other dishes before bringing on dessert. This may be portioned, or guests may serve themselves. Demitasse is poured by the hostess or guests may serve themselves from the buffet.

Dinner and Supper

The words dinner and supper are not interchangeable. Dinner is the main meal of the day. In Europe it is always in the middle of the day except when there is formal entertaining. The evening meal, following midday dinner, is supper or, in England, high tea, a relatively simple meal of usually not more than three courses and built, more often than not, around a main course of cold sliced meat.

In America we usually follow the midday dinner plan only on Sunday, if then, since it is unusual for an American businessman to return home for his noon meal as the European so generally does. Our suppers, therefore, come on holidays or Sundays or after dances or other special evening entertainment or after an afternoon wedding. A supper table is set as for informal dinner with whatever silver is indicated by the menu. Buffet meals served in the evening are always referred to as suppers, never dinners, which are *served* meals.

Maidless Entertaining

It's a dull life without friends in one's home. Therefore the woman who gives up servants, or who never has depended upon them, must strongly resist the idea that entertaining without at least day-help is impossible, or at least very difficult.

Most households have no outside help whatsoever. It is the rare thing to have a full-time houseworker, rarer still to have anything approaching the full staff of even upper-middle-class living in the last century. But we can't all entertain away from our homes, and where the cost of outside entertaining is immaterial, it is still the warmer, friendlier thing to entertain in one's own home often, no matter how simple the hospitality must be.

It is obviously impossible for a woman doing all her own work and tending several nursery-age children to conduct her home on the same lines as her neighbor does who employs both cook and butler and whose half-grown children are away at boarding school. But such differences in household management occur constantly in the same neighborhoods and on the same streets. The woman with the small children does not, today, hesitate to invite her neighbor to tea or dinner merely because she cannot entertain her with traditional formality, the kind of formality that at one time was expected in upper-class neighborhoods.

If one must simplify one's living, it is important not to feel apologetic about it, or even try to explain it. Put away silver that is not regularly used, pack away the huge damask tablecloths for some easier time and use table mats instead. Streamline each room by removing from it all dust-catchers, keeping ornaments to a minimum especially in summer. Slipcover the furniture with washable fabrics. Make the kitchen so attractive that work-saving meals served there—breakfast and the children's lunch—will be cheerful. Convert lost space in cellars and attics into play and work areas, to save traffic in the more damageable parts of the house.

Avoid the tension and trouble of extra preparations for company entertaining by living, daily, approximately the way you do when guests are present. This way, we cease to think of guests in terms of much extra effort, and so include friends more often in the family circle. Inviting one or two guests at a time this way makes living more agreeable and creates diversion for the family without too much work for the hostess.

The Let's-get-it-over-with Idea   The kind of entertaining whose object is to pay off as many obligations as possible all at once is usually a social failure, even if it does accomplish the objective.

The cocktail party with guests elbow-to-elbow, unable to make ordinary conversation heard above the din, is an unbeautiful American phenomenon wise people avoid. If cocktail parties are to be the solution, let them be small and manageable—and more frequent. The cost of materials will be no more, and the saving in wear and tear on the furniture and nerves will be very great. For more information about cocktail parties see the section on Entertaining.

The buffet meal is often the best way for a staffless household to entertain six or more guests, but, again, too large a crowd defeats the purpose of social entertaining. Guest and host should be able to enjoy each other, not be separated most of the time by the very weight of the crowd.

Managing a Sit-down Dinner without a Maid   There is absolutely no use, in a servantless household, in trying to duplicate at the table the kind of service one would have with a trained staff. Multiple courses that require the hostess to spend most of the mealtime rushing back and forth from the kitchen defeat the very idea of relaxed, effortless entertaining that should be the goal of a servantless home.

English-style service, with all the food for the course on the table or on adjacent serving tables within reach of host and hostess, is comfortable and intimate. The system is often followed in households employing an adequate staff, so if this must be your method of serving meals never feel embarrassed.

The active participation of host and hostess in serving food to guests at the table creates a fellowship that is often lacking at a table waited upon by butler or waitress. The constraint necessary when servants are in constant attendance is missing, and dinner becomes a friendly, leisurely matter, with no need to finish promptly so the table may be cleared by employees anxious to complete the day's work.

It is important, however, to so organize such a meal for entertaining that the family enjoys itself, too, and the guests never feel that host and hostess are trying to double as butler and waitress. The host, for example, does not rise to pour wine for each guest though some insist on this little rite still. Instead, he pours a little of any bottled wine in his own glass, tastes it, serves the guest on his right, then passes the bottle to the gentleman nearest him on the left, who in turn serves the lady to his right, as her wine glass is nearer to him than to the host. The other glasses are filled by the gentlemen, but without reaching or rising. The glass of the host is filled last.

If soup is desired, the easy way is to serve it from a tureen at table. Or filled soup plates, optionally, on service plates, may be in place when guests enter the dining room. Then, as many guests are confused by the ritual of the service plate, unless a servant has charge of it, service plates should be cleared with the soup plates, even if it does mean leaving a blank space in front of the guest for a few minutes. The hostess, actually, should not try to function as a maid would. Serving soup without service plates is the easier French way.

In small quarters where the dining area has been reduced to an absolute minimum the table is often unable to hold all the accouterments of a well-set dinner table that would be expected in a more commodious, though still servantless, dining room. If placing the roast on the table for the host to carve, family style, crowds the table, let him carve it in the kitchen or on the sideboard and place the carved portions on a serving platter furnished with serving fork and spoon. The platter is then passed around the table by the seated hostess, each guest serving himself. The meat dish and the serving dishes containing vegetables are then placed on a nearby serving table or tea table (if they can't be accommodated on the table), in a position, if possible, to be reached without the hostess leaving her place. This serving area also is used for clearing the first course, if there is one, without taking the hostess out of the room.

(At breakfast or luncheon, bread or rolls may be passed already thinly buttered, so that a small table won't be crowded by butter plates.) At family dinners bread is often not served, although crackers may be passed during the soup course and are placed on the serving plate beneath the soup or bouillon. A dinner roll, unbuttered, may be on or in the napkin on the service plate. Butter formerly was never served with the roll at dinner, but in recent years it has been accepted that most people don't really enjoy a dry roll and even at formal, served dinners a butter plate and pat of butter or a serving of margarine are often in place.

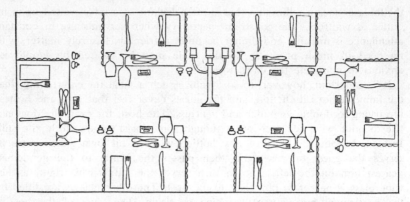

The Sit-down Buffet This is the most comfortable way to dine buffet. The dinner table is set as usual, with the exception of place plates and serving dishes. On the table are all the silver needed, ash trays, salts, peppers, candelabrum, napkins, glasses for water and wine, possibly place cards and flowers. Guests serve themselves at the buffet, then take their seats at the table. Close-up shows informal placement of dessert silver.

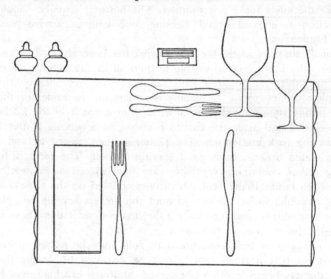

If a tea wagon is used as a serving adjunct guests pass their plates to the hostess, who refills them or at the end of a course, without obvious scraping, stacks them on the tea wagon, placing used silver on the top plate. After the salad course, if it has been separately served (but it is easier to serve it with the meal), all the things that were used at the meal—vegetable dishes, condiments, cruet set, unused silver, salad plates are passed to the hostess. Bits of bread are inconspicuously gathered up by each guest and placed on the used plates being passed to the hostess but the hostess does not crumb the table.

When the clearing has been completed for the dessert course, with no one but the hostess, if she must, having to rise, the table should have on it just the cloth or place mats, wine glasses (if a dessert wine is to be served or if a white wine is being served throughout dinner, including dessert), water glasses, and ash trays, nut and bonbon dishes, if any. Dessert silver may be placed on the dessert dishes before they are passed, or placed on the table at the beginning of the meal, above the dinner plate, Continental style. Finger bowls are dispensed with. The used dessert plates are usually not cleared if coffee is served demitasse around the friendly table.

Suggested Menus for Maidless Dinners   As I've mentioned before, graceful efficiency is easy if courses served at table are reduced to an absolute minimum. That means the main course with salad and dessert. What about a first course? If you must have one, let it accompany cocktails, sherry, or appropriate wine in the living room. One good idea is to place oysters half-shell on a large platter of cracked ice. Place small serving plates nearby, with oyster forks, horseradish, and cocktail sauce, and let each guest help himself. Serve with oysters a chilled dry sauterne or Rhine wine instead of cocktails. Thin slices of buttered white bread cut in strips are good with this, or the usual oyster crackers. It is not difficult, by the way, to learn to open oysters with a regular oyster knife— the heavy steel kind—or you can use a beer can opener very effectively, too. (See *Amy Vanderbilt's Complete Cookbook*, page 344.)

The same sort of thing can be done with shrimp. Shell them *first* (Chinese style—it's easier), remove the black line, cook them in a small amount of bouillon, covered, with a bay leaf and a few black peppercorns. (Save the bouillon for stock.) Serve them on a platter, each impaled on a toothpick, surrounding a dish of cocktail sauce or one of mayonnaise, curry powder, a minced onion, to taste.

Hot fish ramekins or scalloped fish in shells or even antipasto can be served in the living room with cocktails or wine, too. Clearing the empty dishes on a tray from the living room before seating the guests for dinner is simpler than having to leave the dining table to clear dishes from there.

Any substantial hot hors d'oeuvre can double nicely as a first course. Many are simple to make but so effective and delicious that they give the impression that hours have gone into their preparation.

Many people, too, serve soup or bouillon in the living room in cream soup or bouillon cups. The course can be borne in on a tray, and guests can consume it sitting or standing.

A main course that is reduced to one dish is ideal for the kind of entertaining we have been discussing. If you are sure all your guests like it, a curry is festive and satisfying. Curried lamb, veal, chicken, or shrimps can be served on a mound of fluffy rice. It is good accompanied by small dishes of chopped peanuts, grated coconut, chutney, and chopped hard-cooked egg. A mixed green salad in a generous-sized salad bowl completes the course.

Other good possibilities—much liked by men—are deep-dish chicken pie cooked with peas, baby onions, and potatoes, beefsteak and kidney pie with potato crust or with a pastry crust and the potatoes combined with the meat. Old-fashioned chicken pot pie with dumplings and new peas needs no apologies, either, nor does a fine fish and potato chowder served with garlic French bread and plenty of green salad.

Cookbooks and Recipe File Every woman who runs a home needs more than one cookbook. She also needs an indexed recipe file. Not to refer to such adjuncts to good housekeeping is to limit the meals, company and otherwise, to a few stereotyped patterns. By using good cookbooks often and by building an interesting recipe file we can get away from the monotony of twenty-one meals a week.

There are many specialties easy to make that put interest into ordinary meals, yet many women hesitate even to try them. I'm thinking of popovers, homemade cream puffs (fine as a base for leftover meat or chicken, creamed, or they make a delicious dessert filled with ice cream), homemade soups in infinite variety, hot hors d'oeuvres, soufflés of all kinds, potatoes in the dozens of different ways they can be served, other than baked, boiled, and fried.

Proper acquaintance with interesting cookbooks, plus practice, can prove to any woman that it is possible to entertain frequently without the expenditure of much, if any, more money for food than one would use in the average, unimaginative family meal-planning by a routine-weary homemaker. The thing is to forget the routine things and explore the byways. Try königsberger klops instead of hamburger, ham jambalaya instead of cold, sliced, baked ham, potatoes boiled in bouillon and dill instead of in plain water, a meat loaf made with beef liver instead of ground beef. And thinly sliced apples or a cup of blueberries will do a lot for those ready-mixed pancakes that do save trouble.

The Informal Lunch

The term "luncheon" is not properly used in conversation, as it is supposedly reserved for formal and ceremonious use. A servant announces, "Luncheon is served," but the hostess might turn to her guests and say, "Shall we go in to lunch, now?" Hotels and restaurants use the term, but unaffected people use the verb "to lunch" instead. "Yesterday I *lunched* with Muriel," not "Yesterday I had luncheon with Muriel." In writing, especially in etiquette books, lunch and luncheon are more or less interchangeable, however.

As at breakfast, the basic silver for lunch is always a fork and knife, whether or not both are actually needed. To this is added a spoon for soup or appetizer, if needed. The table may be covered with a lunch cloth, elaborate or simple, depending on the degree of formality. But, as is the modern fashion, it is more likely to be set with place mats. Water is in the goblets at each place, or may be poured. The centerpiece can be simple garden flowers, a ceramic or porcelain ornament, or an arrangement of fruit. There are ash trays, cigarettes, and matches at each place—unless the hostess is unalterably opposed to smoking at any meal. Butter plates are always used. Luncheons are usually limited to three courses—which may be soup (in cream soup or bouillon cups rather than soup plates) or appetizer such as shrimp cocktail or paté, a main course often combining meat and vegetable (shepherd's pie, casserole, stew, curry), salad with cheese or simple dessert, often with a fruit base. Sometimes there may be only two courses—a main dish, such as a cold sea food plate, and dessert.

Lunch is an excellent time to serve simple dishes almost everyone likes, yet which are not exactly "party" fare. At an informal lunch in the winter the following would all be appropriate as the main course, preceded or not by an appetizer: fish chowder, French potato soup, bouillabaisse, *pot-au-feu* (all served from a tureen and served in generous portions in soup plates), baked macaroni and cheese, baked beans with salt pork served with raisin brown bread, tripe, potato and chipped beef or ham casserole, corned beef and cabbage, or frankfurters, sauerkraut, and mashed potatoes, eggs Benedict, scrambled eggs with kidneys and whole hominy or hominy grits, pancakes with creamed lamb, and rice, tomato, and ground meat casserole.

Dessert silver may be on the table above the place plate or on the dessert plates, passed by maid or hostess.

Lunches may also be served buffet and are conveniently done that way even for only a few guests when there is no service at all or inexpert or limited service. The food is placed, buffet style, on the dining room table or on the sideboard if it is to be eaten elsewhere, or the table may be set with place settings and the guests may serve themselves from the buffet, then seat themselves at the table. Service is limited to the removal of plates and to the replenishing of dishes as necessary.

When salad appears at lunch it is often not served as a separate course but may come to the table in a wooden bowl to be mixed and served— perhaps in small wooden bowls—to the delectation of the guests. Or it may be an "arranged" salad placed at the luncher's left immediately following the service of the main course if there is a maid. If there is no maid such a salad is often in place as the guests sit down and may be eaten by the guest with the first course, if any, if he wishes.

In California it is popular to serve the salad first as an appetizer. It is beautifully done, often in individual wooden salad bowls or abalone shells in place as guests are seated.

In summer iced tea, iced coffee, iced chocolate, or a tall fruit beverage may be in place on the lunch table before guests are seated. At informal

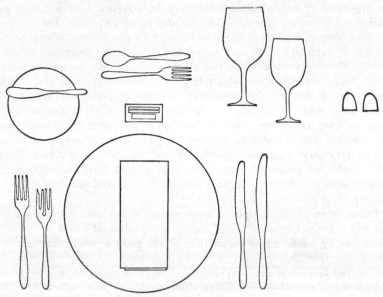

Informal Lunch and Dinner Setting Without first course (or with first course served after guests are seated): Dinner napkin is on dinner plate (or on service plate if one is used) when guests sit down, as at a formal dinner. Note optional placement of dessert silver above the place plate, easy when serving is done by the hostess or when service is limited. Many hostesses who no longer offer cigarettes at table do take the precaution of placing ash trays as shown above in case guests bring their own cigarettes.

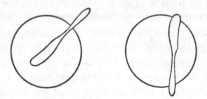

Optional Placement of Butter Knife: Two of the three ways the butter knife may be placed on the butter plate. The third way is shown in many of the place settings illustrated and is more usual.

luncheons hot tea or coffee may be passed during the meal or with dessert. Or demitasses or large cups of coffee, for those who prefer them, are served after dessert at the table.

Lunch in a household with one maid is simple—at most three courses, sometimes, in consideration of dieters, only one.

The first course, which may be soup or an entrée, is in place on a place plate as the guests enter, hostess first to indicate the seating. Soup is served at lunch in a cup, bowl or covered casserole. However, if it is to be the main course—a thick soup such as bouillabaisse or French potato soup—it is often served in flat soup plates from a tureen, with thick slices of French bread, fresh or toasted, in the semicut long loaf with garlic butter. Butter plates are on the table, and the maid either passes a variety of breads, often small hot ones, or places the bread basket or dish on the table for passing among the guests. A long French loaf may come to the table on a cutting board with a bread knife.

When summoned, the maid removes the soup and place plate together from left or right and immediately replaces them with the plate for the following course, which may be a salad plate arranged in the kitchen or a luncheon plate with an individual casserole on it or a warm plate for a dish that is to be passed or served by the hostess.

She then brings in the main dish, if there is one to be served, and either holds it on the flat of her left hand on a folded napkin, serving to the left of each guest, or places it in front of the hostess, then stands to the hostess's left to receive the filled plates. In small dining rooms or where the maid is less than perfection it is much simpler for the hostess not only to "dish" the main course but to hand around the plates herself, serving the lady on her right first (but never serving as a domestic would). Better complete informality than ceremony that doesn't quite come off.

During the main course the maid pours water, when needed, and perhaps wine. In the summer, iced, sweetened, and lemon-flavored tea or water and wine are placed on the table, so the guests may help themselves at the hostess's suggestion. If iced coffee is served, hot coffee is poured over ice cubes into the glasses at the table and sugar and cream are passed either by the maid or by the hostess, so guests may add either or both to taste. At the end of the main course serving dishes are removed first, then the plates, left or right, then the butter plates, bread tray and condiments. The water glasses remain and so do wine glasses if wine is to be served through dessert. If sherry was served with the soup the sherry glasses are usually removed with the soup. Before the dessert comes in the table is crumbed.

Dessert at an informal lunch depends on the season and on the menu, of course, up to that point. A rosy baked apple stuffed with nuts and raisins or topped with fluid or whipped cream, fresh cut-up mixed fruit in season, what I call the nursery puddings—tapioca, rice, rennet, cup custard, cornstarch, farina—all are pleasant at lunch. When men are present a sound fruit pie is always a good choice, as is fruit and cheese, but the fussier desserts such as charlotte russe or meringue glacé usually seem better suited to dinner.

Dessert may be portioned in the kitchen and served, left, to each guest, with dessert spoon and fork left and right on the plate, or the dessert implements may be at the top of the plate throughout the meal, European style.

Or the dessert, say, mixed fruit, may be served by the hostess who has to her left the plates on which to serve it. Either the maid stays to place one plate at a time before the hostess from a stack at the left or the hostess does this herself, placing the dessert silver from the neatly arranged spoons and forks on her right before passing each dish right, then left. Hot tea, never served after iced tea, of course, or after iced coffee, is served by the hostess at the table. If it is convenient and she has the equipment she may make it right at the table over a small electric burner or, traditionally, over a spirit lamp. Or, more usual, the teapot is brought in from the kitchen on a bare tray with the necessary cups and saucers, the sugar, milk, hot water, basin, and lemon slices. (See "How to Make Tea," page 405.) The little ceremony of making tea is always reserved to the hostess, who, in turn, unless there are many at table, hands each cup directly to each guest, right, then left. She may add "cream" or lemon and/or sugar as indicated by the guest, or these may be passed separately by the maid. Tea is never, never served in the kitchen and passed on a tray. It should be made with loose tea leaves, never with what Louise Andrews Kent (Mrs. Appleyard) refers to as "the mouse in the teacup," a tea bag. These little horrors are, I suppose, a necessity of cafeterias, but they do a great disservice to tea.

There is no further disturbance of the guests by the maid while tea is being drunk. Tea is one of the most pleasant digestives. Its good offices must not be hurried by a busy little maid clearing away the dessert dishes.

The Informal Tea

Afternoon tea as a gentle means of relaxation should be encouraged in this country. Surely it is a pleasant, and incidentally inexpensive, way to repay small social obligations, even though husbands, unless they happen to work at home, can rarely be included.

Invitations to simple teas at home are usually given personally by the hostess or by phone. For elaborate teas a calling card or an informal may be sent but this would be done only for some special occasion. For debutante teas the invitations are engraved. (See "Invitations, Acceptances, and Regrets," page 570.)

The actual tray on which the tea is served has no cloth, although the table on which it is placed usually does. (See "Service of Tea, page 438 and "How to Make Tea," page 405.) All silver should be gleaming. Tea plates are in a stack, a folded napkin between each one. On the tea tray are the following: pitcher of hot water (for those who like diluted tea), teapot in any heat-holding material, silver or silver plate being the most decorative, a bowl for waste leaves, sugar, milk (not cream), lemon slices with pick or small fork, tea knives and forks if necessary, cups and saucers, conveniently stacked if necessary, buttered thin bread, jam, cookies, small cakes, tarts, or pastries, sugar tongs for lump sugar.

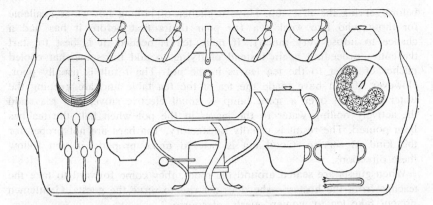

Setting Up the Tea Tray   The tea tray is always set up without a cloth and with all the things on it arranged in pleasing symmetry. *Shown lower left to right:* Teaspoons (optional, otherwise on saucers as shown), basin for leaves, teapot on alcohol lamp, cream (really milk), sugar, sugar tongs, hot water. *Upper, left to right:* Tea plates stacked with tea napkins, tea cups with spoons shown on saucers to right of handles, jam pot, lemon slices stuck with cloves.

One dresses for tea according to neighborhood custom. In the country and even in the city a pants suit might be appropriate or a wool dress or suit. In some houses and with some people a simple daytime dress might seem more apropos. In the summer a fresh cotton or linen such as is worn in hot weather is correct. Hats are optional.

How to Make Tea   One thing we prepare badly in this country is tea. Consequently, we think that the tea is at fault, that compared to coffee it is a characterless beverage. Anyone who has drunk tea prepared by the Chinese or the English knows what a fallacy this is.

The first rule in making tea is to have the water actually boiling. It must bubble-boil three to four minutes and then be poured immediately over the tea leaves. Tea made with water under the boiling point does not have its flavor liberated and is flat and insipid. The tea made in most restaurants and at drug store counters is tasteless, because the water for it is drawn from the coffee urn or from kettles kept hot for some time and is not fresh water, *freshly* boiled.

When the water is actually boiling scald out the teapot so that the metal, china, or pottery is heated through. Then *dry* the pot and set it near the heat to keep hot. Now measure one teaspoon of tea for each cup to be served. Pour in the boiling water, cover the pot and, if you have one, use a tea cosy, although there are excellent sturdy pots of various kinds that keep the tea piping hot. Let it steep three to five minutes. Stir before serving the first cup. Have a pitcher of boiling hot water available for those who like weak tea (or pour theirs first before it has had a chance to infuse very much). If more tea is needed, it is best to start the entire procedure again instead of trying to add the somewhat cooled pitcher of water to the tea leaves in the pot. The result is usually poor. However, if you have made the tea at the tea table and are keeping the water at a boil over a spirit lamp or small electric stove, you may add the actively boiling water to the leaves in the pot when half the tea has been poured. The result is usually satisfactory. Tea bags are not proper for this kind of service. Good tea is easy to make properly if you follow these directions.

When guests are seated around the room, they come forward to take the teacups from the hostess—she does not rise to serve the guests. Gentlemen present take tea to women guests, of course.

The Kinds of Tea   The dark teas—sometimes with a little green blended in—are good for daily use. But there are delicious—and sometimes very expensive—mixtures one should try in tea-taster amounts to find preferences. It is well to know that people who know tea never put milk in a green tea (makes it *look* unappetizing), though they sometimes use lemon. The flower teas such as jasmine are horrid with milk in my opinion and also so special they should not be offered to conservative tea drinkers. If you serve them, it is wise to offer an alternative tea at the same time unless you are sure your guests like them. The herb teas, tisanes, are sometimes greatly liked, often as a nightcap, and are usually best with honey as the sweetener but because they are green teas, not with milk. Among the easier to find (always in drug stores) are peppermint tea, camomile tea, and anise. The latter is very good, I think, steeped in hot milk, strained, and sweetened with honey as a nightcap. Children and invalids—and people coming down with colds—often particularly enjoy these tisanes.

Coffees

Coffees, or as they are also known in New Orleans, coffee parties, take place in the morning any time from 10 A.M. until noon. At present they are regional in character, a familiar form of entertainment in the South and Southwest in particular, but deserving of wider attention. In Dallas young housewives told me they liked them because they permitted a little bit of manageable social life during the hours when young children were in school. They are simple for the hostess to handle and, like a formal tea, permit the guests to arrive at any time within these hours, stay as short a time as twenty minutes, and depart. Coffees are not necessarily held in private homes but are also given in hotels, clubs, and so forth. Depending upon the group and the kind of household giving the party, coffees vary between the fairly formal and the fairly informal. In New Orleans, for example, older women often wear hats and of course gloves, and younger women frequently go hatless both summer and winter, but do properly wear gloves at least in winter.

Refreshments at coffees can be anything from a simple bit of coffee cake to an elaborate offering of a very special coffee menu, which incidentally can well include such refinements as café brûlot and a fine tea and sherry. In fact, the elegant Pontchartrain Hotel in New Orleans uses interchangeably their menu for teas and coffees. It follows:

TINY HOT BISCUITS WITH CRUMBLED BACON
GRILLED CHEDDAR CHEESE AND HAM ON MELBA TOAST
BROILED OYSTERS WRAPPED IN BACON
ROLLED AND TOASTED ASPARAGUS SANDWICHES
BOUCHÉES OF OYSTERS ROCKEFELLER
FRENCH BREAD ROUNDS WITH MUSHROOM PÂTÉ
FRIED SHRIMP ON TOOTHPICKS
SOUTHERN PECAN PIE
LEMON MERINGUE TARTS
HOT STICKY BUNS (SCHNECKEN)
HOT BLUEBERRY MUFFINS
CHEESE STRAWS
COFFEE OR CAFÉ BRÛLOT AND TEA (DARJEELING)
SHERRY

At a less elaborate home coffee this type of thing can well be served simplified and could include one or more hot hors d'oeuvres in addition to some finger sandwiches such as white meat of chicken, cucumber, cream cheese and chopped pecan or possibly tuna fish or an additional cheese item.

Invitations to coffees are phoned, are sent on visiting cards or informals or on the fill-in type of invitation. Like teas, they do not usually request an R.s.v.p., but even when they don't it is always convenient for the hostess to know how many are coming and I recommend that a response either by phone or note be made.

Cocktail Parties

Cocktail time is usually from five-thirty to seven. On Sundays and holidays, especially in the country, cocktails are often served before the lunch or noon dinner hour, not necessarily followed by a meal at the home of the host and hostess.

Any hostess who gives a large cocktail party where many guests are jammed in a relatively small area may expect a certain amount of damage. The space should be cleared as much as possible of footstools, *objets d'art,* delicate plants, small children, and pets. Large, inexpensive ash trays should be provided in every spot where a careless one might feel prompted to abandon a cigarette.

The Service of Cocktails   Cocktails being served by a bartender or by a member of the family, are never served first to the host and hostess, and neither the host nor the hostess should greet the first incoming guest with a cocktail in hand. Hors d'oeuvres equally are passed first to guests, next of last to the hostess and finally to the host. A coaster may be at hand for the drink, together with a cocktail napkin, or quite appropriately a paper cocktail napkin may be wrapped around each glass as it is served.

A table or bar should be set up, close to the festive scene, where drinks may be mixed and picked up. If you are planning on having help in tending bar, it is wise to have one bartender for thirty people and two bartenders for more than thirty. The "bar" may be a pantry, a porch, the dining room—or any place but the kitchen if a meal is also in progress of preparation. It is inevitable that most of the male and some of the female guests will stay in more or less fixed positions in the vicinity of the refreshments.

On or near the bar should be a continuous supply of *clean* glasses and a tray, too, for the used ones. People are supposed to keep track of their own glasses at cocktail parties in anticipation of refills, but they never do. A wise hostess equips herself with three times the number of glasses as guests. Such glasses need not be expensive at all.

No cocktail party ever ends on schedule. The people you expected to stay on for dinner frequently disappear early, probably because they can't wait out the bores who refuse to depart without one more drink. The experienced giver of cocktail parties plans to have dinner out to give himself a good excuse to clear the decks at a fairly definite time. He is, of course, under no obligation to extend a dinner invitation to those remaining, but it usually works out that all the stragglers go along if the dinner place is a restaurant and there the men share the check. The host and hostess wishing to avoid the cocktail guests who linger until midnight providentially make outside dinner engagements at friends' homes where they cannot take last-minute guests. Or, failing such an escape hatch, they bring out a cold supper when the party has dwindled.

Supplies   For such a party, the rule of thumb formula calls for three drinks per guest. If you know that the party will stretch out longer, it is wise to be prepared to serve more, although generally you can figure that one fifth of liquor will serve six people.

A proportionate amount of your stock should be allotted to the various types of beverages you plan to serve and needs to be governed by local consumption patterns and your own knowledge of your guests' preferences. Young budgeters, of course, need make no bones at all about their inability to supply a wide range.

The commonest cocktail party supplies, however, are these and usually in this order although tastes differ in various parts of the country: scotch, Canadian whisky, American blended whisky, bourbon, gin, vodka, and rum. These usually come in fifths (25.6 oz.) or quarts (32 oz.). A fifth will make 17 drinks or cocktails measured in a 1½ oz. jigger. A quart will serve 21 drinks or cocktails measured the same way.

A Word of Warning As this is a personal book, I am going to be personal. Although I very occasionally find it necessary to give a cocktail party, I do so with reluctance and extreme care. It seems to me that for every social drinker who can go to a cocktail party and remain attractive, there seem to be several others who manage to be insulting, indiscreet, boring, or occasionally much worse. I am not against alcohol. As the foregoing pages indicate, I believe that its very cautious use can contribute to pleasant social intercourse. I am conscious always of its dangers. I have quoted from the American Council on Alcohol Problems that (alcohol) "in small doses . . . relaxes tensions, dulls inhibitions and decreases the powers of self-evaluation and rational self-control. In heavier drinkers it progressively impairs mental and physical faculties such as sight, hearing and muscular coordination."

One in every fourteen drinkers becomes an alcoholic. When that happens, society generally is affected and many involved people are troubled, inconvenienced, sometimes to the point of desperation.

I never let the cocktail hour run on and on. I try to have dinner ready for serving shortly after the second drink has been offered and I let my guests know when we are going to dinner.

It is an important rule to have plenty of appetizers as "blotters" so that people will not be encouraged to drink on empty stomachs. If I know that a friend has an alcohol problem, I try to avoid inviting him to a cocktail party, but if I must ask him, I see to it that there are substitutes for alcohol available to him. I cannot be his conscience, but I can be his friend.

When I give cocktail parties, I have definite hours for them. When the time comes to close the bar, we close it. If we have friends or acquaintances who do not behave well as a result of attending a cocktail party of ours, we do not invite them again—at least not to a cocktail party.

Informal Dancing at Home

Large dances at home are becoming rare except for weddings, when an orchestra may be brought in and a dancing pavilion erected. In many homes there are occasions when the rugs may be rolled back and the room cleared for dancing to the radio or phonograph or to the music of an accordion.

Graduation parties often are built around a home dance. Porch or living room floor is sprinkled with wax or even corn meal, a refreshment table is set up, music of some sort provided, and the evening is under way. Punch is the most suitable beverage at a dance as it is a pre-mixed drink and refreshing between dances. Nothing is served with it, but a dance is usually followed by a late supper, simple or elaborate as the occasion demands.

No matter what the age group, certain rules are always followed at dances. A man or boy always asks his hostess for a dance during the evening. And he literally dances attention on the girl he has brought to the party, dancing his first dance with her and seeing that she is never without a partner or never left alone on the sidelines. A girl has the obligation of paying proper attention to the man who has brought her, not allowing herself to be whisked away the minute she enters the door, never to see her escort again during the evening until it is time to be taken home.

A host tries to dance with each woman guest at his party sometime during the evening. In a small group if some of the men do not dance he dances first with a guest, then with his wife if she has not been asked to dance. If all wish to dance, host and hostess often start off the dancing.

No guest, of course, leaves a dance without a brief farewell to host and hostess. A man who has come alone always asks his hostess if he may be of help in escorting an unaccompanied lady home. A hostess never allows a lady to go home alone, although if everything else fails, she may see to it that she is safely in a taxi or, if driving herself, that she phones upon her safe arrival home. All guests, men and women, shake hands with both host and hostess upon leaving.

Open House

An open house is an informal gathering of friends and neighbors by card, by phone, and by word of mouth. In smaller communities where virtually everyone knows everyone else news of a coming open house is often announced in the local papers and the community knows it is welcome to come without a specific invitation. An open house is often given before a large wedding or the day afterward if many people have come long distances for the event and the parents of either the bride or groom wish to entertain them in this way. Too, an open house is frequently given as a housewarming.

At an open house the time is given to span as many as four or five hours—with invitation hours sometimes staggered to control the flow of guests. People call to pay their respects, have some light refreshment, punch and small cakes, sometimes buffet and highballs, and leave. Twenty minutes to half an hour is as long as a guest should stay. In this way hundreds may be entertained modestly or elaborately, as the hosts wish. Paper plates and cups are usual and guests often serve themselves.

Housewarmings

Housewarmings are a delightful way to get friends together and at the same time allow you to satisfy their understandable curiosity and indulge your pardonable pride in showing off your new home. Since housewarmings are usually informal, couples may give their own, as in the East, or friends may ask to entertain for them, usual in the Southwest.

Individual circumstances depend on how soon after moving the event should be scheduled or whether it should be a surprise if given by friends. I rather discourage the surprise element, which may not be wholly appreciated by a couple caught at their worst—even if friends and relatives come bringing all the food and other necessities. However, having a housewarming before everything is perfect is half the fun. Otherwise the occasion may become too formal.

As many guests as the house can comfortably accommodate are usually invited. Or there may be a series of housewarmings. People usually bring inexpensive gifts, something "for the house" such an initialed matches or cocktail napkins, decorative dish towels, potted plants, fresh flowers, playing cards, groceries or beverages, or gadgets perhaps for the kitchen, bathroom, or garden.

Depending upon the kind of party one decides to give, refreshments may range from pretzels and beer, or coffee and doughnuts, to very hearty fare. A buffet supper with casseroles preferably that can be prepared ahead of time and eaten with a fork alone is nice.

Entertainment may vary, of course, but it is most often just talk. Sometimes on informal occasions like this, adult parlor games are fun or groups will want to sing, dance, or play cards.

Setting the Table for Card Table Service

The amount of silver on a card table should be at minimum, because service at small tables is always relatively informal even at a big party. A crowded table is always unattractive. If wine is being served, you may omit the water glass, European style, and have water available to any who want it on a convenient serving table. If iced tea or coffee is to be served, water glasses are omitted and the beverage may be passed on a tray or be in place when the guests sit down. For supper or luncheon, tea or regular coffee cups may be at the right of each bridge table setting, with a spoon on the right-hand side of the saucer. Each table may have its own pot of tea or coffee, or the beverage may be poured by whoever is serving. Also to prevent crowding, hot buttered rolls may be passed and placed on the luncheon or supper plate instead of on a butter plate. Where there is limited service with one servant, or none at all, a warmed service plate is used for service of a hot entrée and the first course, if any, is in place when the guests seat themselves. Too many courses and too inconsequential food served at bridge tables—when there is a pretense at serving a full meal—is a mistake. A hot-dish pad in the middle of each table can hold one substantial hot dish from which guests can serve themselves. Or the tables can be used for a sit-down buffet supper, with guests serving themselves as they wish at the buffet table.

Much fussing over the service at little tables makes for confusion and destroys the feeling of intimacy they give. Even if you have a waitress, keep the service at bridge tables very simple. Plates are removed with both hands, not one at a time, and courses are limited, usually to three. It is a good idea to have salad, arranged on each plate, as a first course, or to pass it with the main course—say of spaghetti and chicken livers. Finger bowls are not advisable and rarely seen in such informal serving, as the removal of them from the dessert plate creates a crowded table, already burdened with ash trays, salt and pepper, possibly nut or candy dishes, cigarettes, and beverage.

On bridge tables a luncheon napkin is on the service plate or, if a first course is in place, to the left of the plate. In the evening if more than a dessert is to be served dinner-size napkins are used. Attractive, large and substantial paper ones are quite acceptable if the hostess runs the household herself and the labor or expense of doing up a number of large dinner napkins is of some consequence. But attractive no-iron ones are everywhere available—and non-polluting.

Drop-In Luncheons

In the West I encountered a very interesting and useful form of entertaining—the drop-in luncheon. It is mainly a form of women's entertainment, but it could be adapted to a mixed group very nicely. The idea is to set up a buffet luncheon, usually quite simple and attractive, and to serve it continuously from 12:30 until 2 P.M. Guests, often business and professional women or homemakers with busy schedules, drop in during those hours, choose what they would like to eat, consume it usually standing and chatting with their friends before departing. Guests stay either for the full length of the luncheon or depart immediately after consuming their food. The drop-in luncheon may be as large as the hostess wishes, or limited to two or three friends who all have the same problem in common—lack of time—but who enjoy such an opportunity for social contact with others at lunchtime, however brief.

As the drop-in luncheon is informal, invitations are always informal, either telephoned or extended by fill-in invitations or brief notes. A "thank you" at the door by each departing guest is all that is expected.

Chapter 32

FORMAL ENTERTAINING

The Formal Dinner

Few homes in the land these days can accommodate the traditional thirty-four guests at one dinner table. Who indeed has the space to store all the silver, glassware, and china for such dinner parties, and where are the trained men to serve them, one man to each three guests? Queen Victoria's dinners required three servants to each six guests. Present-day monarchs have one footman to each four or five guests.

Important hostesses today feel that formal dinners at home are best replaced by smaller, more frequent semiformal and quite informal dinners or, if occasion really seems to demand formal dinners, that they be given in a private suite of a hotel or fashionable restaurant. However, as the occasional formal dinner does take place, let us see how the hostess must marshal her forces for such an undertaking.

First, she must have the room to seat all her guests at one dining table. The minute she deviates from this arrangement, or makes do with female help at table, her dinner can no longer be considered formal.

Then, paramount, of course, is a chef or real *cuisinière* who can turn out *to perfection* the food that, of itself, proclaims a formal meal. Finally, she must have a butler who will function as major-domo, commanding his men—trained footmen perhaps hired for the occasion but preferably true house servants rather than restaurant waiters recruited for the event. These are usually best supplied by a catering service, along with any additional kitchen help that may be needed. Of course all must be properly attired (see "Dress and Duties of the Household Help," page 523). The hostess who can give such a dinner with only her own staff is fortunate indeed.

Just before the arrival of her guests, usually a few minutes before eight, though sometimes formal dinners start at eight-thirty, the hostess checks the dining room and gives any last minute instructions to the butler. He, in turn, makes his tour of the footmen and inspects their apparel, their shoes, hair, and fingernails. In earlier times such serving men wore white cotton gloves, because of the danger, as one writer put it, of a dirty thumb in the

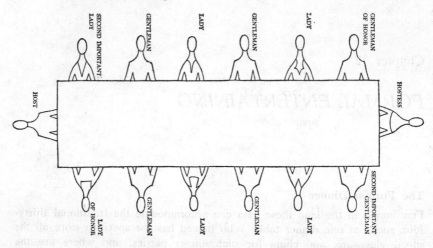

Seating at Formal Lunch and Dinner and the Informal Dinner Party
soup. The butler sees to it that there are no dirty thumbs or anything else
that can't pass muster.

Arrival and Introduction of Guests at the Formal Dinner As he removes his coat and hat each gentleman takes the small envelope bearing
his name and containing the name of his dinner partner from a conveniently placed hall tray. If the lady is unknown to him he arranges to
be formally introduced before dinner is served. At very large dinner
parties there is often a table diagram in the hall, and he should locate
his and his partner's seat on this before going in to dinner.

At such a formal dinner the "roof" is not sufficient introduction, and
guests must be formally introduced to one another. Obviously at very
large functions guests necessarily meet only a limited number of other
guests.

Entering the Dining Room At formal dinners the host offers his right
arm to the woman guest of honor and leads the way into the dining room
followed by the other guests, teamed, with the hostess and the male guest
of honor entering last. Host and hostess stand behind their chairs, and the
hostess indicates (if no diagram has been provided) where each guest is to
sit, or, at a long table guests may find their own place cards. Husbands
and wives are usually not seated together although the hostess does
attempt to seat together men who have escorted women to the party,
just-engaged people, and those who have been married for not more than
a year. Ladies approach their chairs from the left and sit from the left.
Gentlemen seat the ladies to their right, women sitting immediately even

though the hostess has not yet been seated. Men, however, all stand
until the hostess has taken her place and she is in turn seated by the
male guest of honor on her right, who seats first the woman on his right
and then the hostess. If there is a butler in attendance, she is seated by
him. When place cards are on the napkins for a formal dinner, the guest
removes the place card and puts it at the top of the service plate so
that it may still be read by those on either side of him who may not
have caught his name.

Seating   The seating at formal and informal dinners at which guests are
present is the same. Host and hostess are seated more or less opposite
each other, with the hostess preferably near the entrance through which

Formal Place Card   Monogram, in this case, in gold with matching
border. Name of guest is handwritten without given name.

the food will appear. To the right of the host is placed the honored woman
guest. If a young engaged girl is to be feted, for example, she is given this
place despite the fact that older women are present. If among the guests
there is one woman who has come some distance and is rarely a visitor to
the household, it is she who would be given this place of honor. Ordinarily,
among people who see each other frequently, the hostess places to the host's
right any woman who has obvious seniority over the rest or, if none has,
any woman guest who will bring out her husband conversationally if he
needs special incentive. To her own right the hostess places the husband
of the guest of honor, if there is one, the man who has come the greatest
distance and is an infrequent visitor to the household or a man who may
be a little shy or difficult conversationally.

To the host's left is placed the next most important woman guest and to
the hostess's left, the next most important man guest.

At a long banquet table host and hostess need not sit at opposite ends but may sit across from each other at the center. The same seating of guests of honor maintains, however.

Place Cards at the Formal Dinner At each place will be a guest's name. The cards are usually plain white with beveled edges gilded, although in a household using a heraldic device the host's full coat of arms may be embossed in gold or the crest alone without the motto may be used. A widow or an unmarried woman may properly use only a lozenge for menu and place cards. (See "Heraldic Devices" page 615.)

Place card names are written "Mrs. Roberts," "Miss Sweeney," "Mr. Prudhomme" at formal dinners. At diplomatic dinners titles are abbreviated —H.E. (for His Excellency) the Norwegian Ambassador, the Secretary of Defense, if necessary—but it is always more gracious to write out such titles. A congressman, a member of the UN Secretariat, a foreign dignitary entitled to "The Honorable" before his name, does not have this written on a place card. Instead, the card reads "Mrs. Black," "Mr. Scarlotti." Place cards should be written legibly in large characters in black ink so they may be easily located without the use of glasses for those who need them. At very large business or charity functions mainly, place cards are sometimes typed, but this is not advisable for private or especially diplomatic functions, although it is occasionally seen. For special occasions—Christmas, a golden or silver anniversary—place cards might be written in red, green, gold, or silver, but black is the usual choice.

Menus and Menu Cards Menus are printed, occasionally engraved, in script, or written in scriptlike handwriting in black ink, frequently in French.

They may or may not carry a heraldic device. The menu is in its holder at each place, but one is always in front of the host and hostess and others are placed down the table with one for each three guests.

The Formal Dinner Table

The silver at a formal dinner must be sterling (gold plate at the White House!) placed, as is silver for all other meals except buffet, about one inch from the edge of the table, each piece lining up at the base with the one next to it. The silver should not be obscured by the place plate. The large damask dinner napkin, folded, is on the place plate, no matter how decorative the latter may be. But the place plate, if it is pictorial, is carefully arranged so that the design is toward the diner.

It was traditional that no butter plates or butter knives appeared on a really formal table, as breads that were passed were placed directly on the tablecloth. The hard dinner roll, unbuttered, was in or on the napkin or to the left of the place plate as the guests were seated. Today, however, even at the most formal meals one frequently sees butter plates. Undoubtedly

GOURMET DINNER

THURSDAY, OCTOBER 20, 1960

THE PLAYERS CLUB

Dom Perignon
Magnums
1949

CAVIAR

*

CHICKEN BROTH

*

Wehlener Sonnenuhr
Auslese
1953

BROILED BAY SCALLOPS

*

Chambolle Musigny
1934

**SCOTCH GROUSE
WILD RICE**

*

Niersteiner Kanzberg
Beerenauslese
1953

**STRAWBERRY PINEAPPLE
KIRSCH COMPOTE**

*

Chateau de La Grange
Jonzac, Charante
Cognac
1893

COFFEE

Formal Place Setting   The dinner napkin is on the service plate as the guest is seated. Shown are the usual number of glasses for formal dinner: water, sherry (for soup course), red wine for entrée, dessert wine. Sometimes there is also a white wine for fish instead of sherry, sometimes both. Occasionally just champagne is served throughout the meal as the only wine. Note in this illustration the oyster fork is shown with the other forks, an *optional* arrangement, but no more than three forks may be in place at one time. In this case the salad fork and knife (if needed) will be put in place when the salad course is served. At a really formal dinner there are no ash trays on the table. There is no smoking until the service of dessert has been accomplished (*see text*). Butter plate is optional.

the dry roll did not seem palatable to some diners despite the richness of an elaborate menu.

Silver and settings must be exactly arranged, just as they are for all settings except the buffet. A crowded table is never attractive, but a crowded formal table is impossible to serve. There must be a foot or more between each guest, the space accurately measured. But there should never be so much space between guests that conversation becomes difficult. At a long narrow table with few guests the seating is arranged so that host and hostess sit opposite each other at the center of the table with guests grouped right and left of each and with the ends of the table unset.

At a formal dinner all serving is from the kitchen or pantry, so no serving implements are on the table. As the guests sit down there is a

Alternative Placement of Silver Here the silver is arranged for a first course of salad, California style. In the top illustration note that although the dinner knife and fork are the prescribed 1″ from the table edge the salad silver is paired with them at the junction of the handles. Below, the more usual arrangement is seen with the handles all lined up evenly 1″ from the table edge.

centerpiece, usually of flowers, with four silver candlesticks, one at each corner of an imaginary rectangle described about the centerpiece a comfortable distance from the place plates. Or there may be one large candelabrum (sometimes wreathed with flowers at the base) with its several branches holding tall, lighted white tapers. If the table is large, there may be two candelabra spaced carefully equidistant from the centerpiece the long way of the table.

At each place, in addition to the place plate, the butter plate, and the napkin, is the following silver: knives, to the right, never more than three—for appetizer, if necessary, fish, and meat or for fish, meat, and salad (if cheese is served with it or if the salad is difficult to eat solely with a fork). If more than three knives are necessary the additional one is put in place at the time the course is served. To the left are the forks, also never more than three at a time, one for the appetizer, if any, one for the fish, if needed, one for the meat, or the first for the fish, the second for the meat, and the third for the salad. If a fourth fork is needed for salad it is placed when the salad is served. If there is an oyster fork it is usually placed, not with the forks, but on the side with the knives with the tines of the fork placed, upward, across the soup spoon or parallel with the knives. With the exception of the spoons for soup or melon there are no spoons to the right of the knives, as at *all* settings, except buffet, silver is placed left and right so the diner works from the outside in toward the plate in choosing his implements. At a formal dinner, coffee is served demitasse and the spoons are in place on the saucers to the right of each handle. Dessert spoons with their forks are in place, spoon right, fork left, on the dessert plates when they are brought in. Sometimes the finger bowl, on a doily or on a finger bowl plate or on both, is on the dessert plate, too. Sometimes the finger bowl is presented with fruit silver after the dessert.

On the formal table individual silver or silver-and-crystal salts and peppers are, pepper first, directly above the place plate or a little below the line of the glasses, with one set for each two guests. At a large table larger sets may be used rayed out, pepper above, salt below, from the corners of an imaginary rectangle around the centerpiece. Open salts and peppers require little sterling, ivory, or mother-of-pearl spoons. Where many sets are used on a formal table they need not match but they should be somewhat alike—not "modern" with Victorian. Mustard pots are not set on a formal table but are passed, if needed, on the butler's tray. But I have even seen beautiful silver pepper grinders—two or more—on formal tables, where the hostess is one who makes a fetish of freshly ground pepper.

Formal glassware need not be in matching sets, but all glasses for a particular wine should match each other and all glasses chosen should look good together. A host might have a set of antique or modern light-green-bowled hock glasses for Rhine wine and like to see them used on a formal table with the, otherwise preferred, clear glass. Wine glasses may be large or small, but many who love wines like to see a generous one for red Burgundy, handmaiden of the equally substantial meat course. Beer is not served at strictly formal meals.

Glasses are placed in order of their use above the knives (see illustration) in a variety of ways. Each is removed with the course it accompanied with the exception of the dessert wine glass, which remains through the fruit and demitasse (when these are served to the gentlemen at table). At a formal dinner champagne may be the only wine served after the service of sherry with the soup.

On the really formal table there may be no ash trays and cigarettes at all during the meal. Or, as is becoming acceptable, in front of each guest is a small silver or porcelain ash tray, with two cigarettes laid horizontally across the top and a small box or book of matches below. The match box may be silver, containing tiny dinner matches, or a plain gold or silver or sometimes black packet of book matches may be used, the smaller the better. Otherwise, cigarettes and cigars are passed with the coffee. Sometimes the butler brings cigarettes in silver cigarette boxes and individual ash trays on a serving tray with a lighted taper or sometimes a large silver lighter and passes them to guests after dessert, lighting each cigarette and placing the ash trays to each smoker's right.

The Service Begins The butler takes his stand behind the hostess. He moves from this vantage point only when a footman needs direction or when he, himself, pours the wine. He actually serves food only if there is not sufficient additional staff to do the serving, and then serves the main dishes only.

In a smaller household a butler and a footman can efficiently serve a formal dinner for from eight to twelve guests. If he is quite adept, with adequate kitchen support a butler alone can handle a formal dinner for eight. At dinners larger than twelve it is necessary to have duplicate serving dishes presented simultaneously to each six or seven guests. In this way all food will be served so that the guests may eat more or less at the same time and hot food will be properly hot. The service begins with the lady at the host's right, and at a large dinner dishes are presented simultaneously to the ladies nearest, right and left, of the hostess. Butler, if he serves, and footmen present dishes with the left hand, right hands behind back.

At a very large dinner it is, naturally, not possible to wait until each guest has finished eating before the clearing of plates begins. In lavish service where a man was behind each chair, for instance at royal banquets, each plate was removed the minute the diner indicated by placement of the silver that he had finished with it. Today, the butler directs the removal of plates, or begins the removal himself, when the majority has finished, by-passing the slower diners, but there must be no sense of hurry and certainly clatter or audible staff directions.

At only one period is there ever a moment when there is not a plate before a guest. That is just before the service of dessert. Until then, beginning with the place plate with its folded napkin upon it, there is always a plate. Sometimes there is still another on top of it, as in the case of, say, a crabmeat cocktail which would be in a stemmed double container, the "suprême" glass (sometimes silver) surrounding the "liner," on a small service plate. This complete unit is placed on the place plate. It is replaced, on the place plate, with the soup course—always in a flat dish. At the end of the soup course place plate and soup dish are removed, and, at a formal meal, removal is *only* from the left, except for those parts of the setting that are on the guest's right. As the place and soup plate are removed together, the warm plate for the fish course is immediately substituted. After the fish course has been removed the *"rôti"* appears, always hot, though not necessarily "roasted" at all. It is always completely arranged on a beautifully garnished platter or platters, often with its accompanying vegetables, such as tiny pan-roasted potatoes. Or green vegetables follow on a separate serving dish, sometimes on the partitioned kind where vegetables such as new peas, julienne carrots, and buttered pearl onions may each occupy a section. The whole course is passed to each guest who takes what pleases him but (at a formal dinner) nothing is offered a second time, aside from water and wine replenishments.

In Victorian days a sherbet, or "sorbet," followed the roast or came between entrée and roast as a separate course. In some locales this custom is still in vogue, though the sherbet usually appears with the meat or fish course and is eaten with the fork.

Where there are plenty of servants the finger bowl may not come in on the fruit plate but may be brought on its own serving plate, replacing the used fruit plate before the guests leave the table for coffee. Otherwise, at a formal dinner, fruit plate, fruit knife and fork, finger bowl, and doily arrive as one unit. (See "Presentation of the Finger Bowl," page 434.) I note that now even at the Waldorf's formal dinners there is no presentation of the finger bowl and it is becoming rare in private houses.

Leaving the Dining Room   At the end of the fruit course, the hostess catches the eye of the lady of honor or some other lady at the other end of the table, bows, and slowly rises. The gentlemen rise and, where there are not enough men servants, assist the ladies. The hostess then indicates where coffee is to be served. English style, the men are served at the dining table with cigars, port, liqueurs, and demitasses, the latter offered today with cream and sugar, though once it was *de rigeur* to serve *café noir* at a formal dinner. Or the men may escort their dinner partners to the living room, then leave them for the library or wherever else the men are congregating for coffee. The women then have coffee and liqueurs alone and, before the men return, repair their make-up. Or, Continental fashion, men and women leave the dining room together with each man helping the lady in the chair to his right (and, if necessary, to his left), offering her his arm and proceeding to the living room where they together enjoy coffee and liqueurs and smoking. This is the pleasanter method, it seems to me, and helps prevent that dismaying banding of men together that so often occurs at American dinner parties.

Departing after the Formal Dinner   Except for some very good reason discussed previously with the hostess, no guest may leave after a formal dinner in a private home in less than two and a half to three hours and even then, not until the guest or guests of honor have departed. At formal public dinners guests who must leave early go quietly either before the speeches begin or between them, never while a guest of honor is speaking or while a national anthem is being played. Those who must leave, leave by the nearest exit without stopping to talk or bid farewell to guests encountered en route, except to bow briefly.

Tipping members of the staff to get one's coat and hat in a private home is never done in the United States.

The Formal Luncheon

Today, although the formal lunch at home is rare, it does occasionally take place, especially at country places, resorts, and in diplomatic circles.

Invitations to a formal luncheon are usually telephoned, but those to official luncheons are engraved. At official luncheons and at Sunday, Saturday, or holiday ones, men and women guests are usually equal in number; otherwise a formal luncheon is essentially a feminine occasion.

Again, a formal luncheon is not possible without an adequate household staff. A hostess may not serve it herself, although if butler or houseman is lacking a waitress is quite acceptable at a formal lunch, though not at a formal dinner.

Greeting Guests The guests are met at the door by a servant who indicates where coats may be left. He or she then usually precedes the guest to the living room (unless all guests know the house well), walks to within speaking distance of the seated hostess, and announces the guest's name. The hostess rises in greeting, but there is no formal receiving line.

Sherry and "biscuits" are often served. Occasionally cocktails are served before luncheon, but usually the hostess offers an alternative of vegetable juice of some kind.

After all the guests have assembled, the butler or waitress announces luncheon. The hostess leads the way with the guest of honor, if any, and the others follow along in any convenient manner, with any gentlemen present *not* offering their arms as at a formal dinner. If there are no place cards the hostess from behind her chair indicates where each is to sit, with the guest of honor at her right. If a host is present and the guest of honor is a woman, she is seated, of course, on his right.

Place Cards and Menus At official luncheons both place cards and menus may be used, and place cards at other formal luncheons are convenient when more than eight are to be seated. The place cards (those for host and hostess are omitted) are placed upon the folded napkin, which is, in turn, *on* the service plate. A menu card, engraved or handwritten, is placed in its holder or flat on the table, either one for each place or one for each two or three guests. There should be one before the hostess and another before the host if he is present.

Arranging the Table Damask cloths are not used at formal luncheons. Place mats of the more formal variety, often white, or an embroidered cloth which does not overhang the table are customary. The silver must be sterling, the china and glass of the best quality.

There are no candles on a luncheon table, but there are flowers or some other centerpiece. Butter plates are used, even at a formal table. Most formally, the butter is passed, rather than being in place when the guests sit down. The butter is in decorative curls or decorated balls or pats, or, if neatly sliced off a quarter-pound bar, is usually decorated

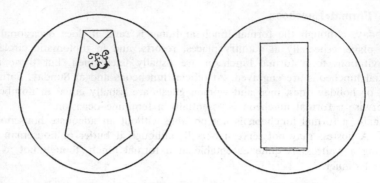

Folding of Napkins *Left:* There are many ways to fold napkins (*see text*), but simplicity is usual now. To dramatize initialed dinner napkins, first arrange napkins with loose edges upward on the plate. The fold of the napkin will then form the point of a triangle. Now fold over the loose edges to form a small triangle above the monogram, then fold under the other two points of the napkin to make the arrangement shown. Lay flat on service plate with the point of the napkin toward the diner. Monograms on napkins are, of course, meant to be seen. A napkin is folded to display them. (Incidentally, an embroidered initial looks best when the embroidery is ironed on a spongy surface such as turkish toweling which permits the initial to be raised.) *Right:* The simple fold of a large dinner napkin. The square is folded over left into a rectangle and placed flat on the plate with the edge either on the left (more conventional) or right. In picking it up, the diner takes it by the upper left-hand corner if the fold is to the right and by the right-hand corner if the fold is at the left. A large dinner napkin should not be completely unfolded but merely spread across the lap. A small hard roll may be placed in the fold or on top of it, or to the left of the forks, but increasingly, even at formal dinners, rolls are on butter plates and served with butter.

in some way, perhaps by a bit of parsley or other herb. Various hot breads are passed during the meal.

If the table is large, decorative dishes of fruit, candies, or nuts may be spaced down the length of the table. A large epergne may contain both fruits and flowers, and on a long table the flower motif could be repeated in tight little low flower arrangements strategically placed.

The luncheon napkin is smaller than that used for a formal dinner. It is folded with an eye to the usual corner monogram (see illustration). It has been folded by the laundress in a square. This square is folded into a triangle with the embroidery at the top. Then the other two points of the triangle are folded in under the napkin, which is then

Formal Luncheon Setting *First course:* Crabmeat cocktail in suprême glass is in place as guests are seated. Seafood fork is placed in one of three accepted ways (*see Informal Dinner Setting*), to the right of knives and parallel to them. The iced-tea spoon above the service plate may be placed to the right of the knives. The salad knife, optional, depends on the type of salad and whether cheese is served (*see text*). Napkins are to left of forks.

placed on the place plate, monogram up, of course. The napkin may also be folded in half lengthwise, as it comes from the linen supply, so that it forms a neat rectangle. This is placed on the place plate with the fold either on the left or right.

At the formal luncheon no food is portioned or carved at the table but is brought in and passed.

If soup is served the soup spoon is at the right of the knife or knives (not more than two). If it is to be the less usual four-course luncheon, with the soup followed by an egg dish or fish, there is a small knife to the left of the spoon and next to it the larger knife for the main course. If it is a three-course meal beginning with an appetizer, the soup spoon is, of course, omitted. On the left of the plate go the necessary forks, not more than three, appetizer fork, meat fork, salad fork, with the one to be used last on the inside. The exception is the oyster fork, which usually goes on the knife side, either parallel to the knives at farthest right or slanting over with the tines upright and in the bowl of the spoon. Forks and spoons for dessert are not included on a formal table but are brought in with the dessert.

Butter plates are used on a formal luncheon table in the usual place (illustrated), with the butter knives in any one of the three accepted positions (illustrated). There are rarely more than two wines, often only one, and glasses for each wine may either match or just go well together for the two wines.

Second course: At formal luncheon of four courses the salad is served with entrée, have creamed chicken and mushrooms with border of puréed peas in a ramekin. Salad may be served in place of dessert. The iced-tea spoon is at right of knives (*but see above*). Dessert silver is brought on dessert plates (*illustration of dessert service*).

If the hostess wishes, individual ceramic or silver ash trays with their complement of cigarettes and matches (see illustration for formal dinner) are at each place, or cigarettes may be passed at the end of the dessert course or later in the living room after service of demitasse. Neat, "dress" pipes are now acceptable even in town in mixed company at any time other men are smoking cigars. No gentleman would light a pipe in the middle of any meal—or a cigar, either—even though many thoughtless people take the table cigarettes (if they are there at all) as an invitation to smoke between courses or even while eating. This can never fail to offend a hostess whose cuisine makes any claim at all to excellence.

The Food As people prefer lighter luncheons today, even a formal luncheon is limited to a maximum of four courses, more usually three. The food should be chosen for its seeming simplicity and deliciousness. Each course should balance well against the one to follow. There is expected to be a certain distinction about the food for any formal meal, and that for a formal luncheon is no exception. Menus are frequently written in French, and the service must be as faultless as the linen and silver.

A possible winter menu for a formal luncheon could be:

Consommé à la princesse

Red snapper à la dauphine

Pommes duchesse   Salade de concombres

Fromage de Roquefort

Fruits assortis

Café

Usually not more than two wines are served at a formal luncheon, but one throughout is correct, too. Sherry, at room temperature, may be served with the soup (but not with fish). It may be poured from a decanter by the servant, who, however, must not lift the glass from its place. The sherry glass is at the upper left of the knives, with the glass for any subsequent wine to its right. (See illustration of place setting for the formal luncheon.) A dry white wine is served with the fish, and possibly a liqueur after the coffee. Champagne, for some very special occasion, could be the only wine, served from soup to dessert or introduced with the entrée.

A suggested summer menu for a formal luncheon:

Bisque d'écrevisses

Filet de volaille glacé à la Périgordine

Tomate nouvelle farcie   Choufleur à la Polonaise

Asperges froids sauce vinaigrette

Pêches à la crème

Café

A well-chilled white wine might be served throughout the meal. Sherry could be served with the soup, but, as it is fortified, it is not always the best choice on a hot day.

The Formal Tea

Occasionally there is an official tea or perhaps a large tea for a visiting celebrity where the guests are mainly feminine. In these cases, formal tea follows a traditional pattern. (See also "The Debutante Tea," page 12.)

The Table and Lighting The tea table must be large enough to accommodate two services on trays, at opposite ends of the table, one for tea, the other for coffee or chocolate. On the table, too, are placed, buffet style, the necessary cups, small plates, and silverware as well as the special tea foods. The tea table, opened to its ultimate length, may be set in any convenient room to which passage to and from is easy and where groups may stand about, or occasionally sit, and have their tea with access to the food, which they serve to themselves. (See also "Club Teas," page 323.)

On the table itself is a white tea cloth, but the trays, usually silver, are bare. Each beverage service—a large urn is usual for coffee, a samovar good for the tea—is presided over by a hostess. The tea is set up farthest from the entrance, the coffee closest to it. At a large tea the hostess herself often reserves her energies for seeing that her guests enjoy themselves, and she delegates the actual "pouring" to two friends well-acquainted with the ritual, or at very large teas, teams of two that relieve one another. These ladies seat themselves at opposite ends of the table before the trays and serve each guest as he appears. The conversation may be limited to "Sugar?" or "Cream?" (actually this is, or should be, milk or nearly so, but it is usually referred to as "cream"), "Lemon?" In a crush, the guest may volunteer this information, and during a lull he may stand by and exchange a few courteous words with the "pourer," who despite the honor is probably in for a dull period. The guest always says, "Thank you," on receiving the proffered cup. It is permissible to return as many times as one wishes for more tea, coffee, or chocolate, but one waits until any who have not yet been served have received theirs before asking for more.

Very occasionally at a large tea, the tea, chocolate, or coffee are poured at the table but passed by servants on trays. This is not very satisfactory. The rule is that the tea should come directly from the hands of the pourer to the receiver, that it should be made, if possible, before one's eyes, as it was in the days when the kettle came directly from the hob and the guests had the pleasure of watching the steam rise and the full fragrance of the steeping tea filled the room.

Of course, if gentlemen are present they may offer to get tea for the various ladies, but a tea is, essentially, a self-service repast, and aside from the receiving of the cup from the hands of the tea-maker, guests are expected to help themselves to the various things upon the table.

The room in which formal tea is served is always artificially lighted, with the curtains drawn as if for an evening entertainment. Candles, tall and white, are most formal and, of course, most becoming.

The Food Tea refreshments are quite different from those served at a cocktail party, and it is not wise to try to combine the two. People who love tea begin with some simple, bland thing like thin, very fresh bread with butter and jam. (For this plain bread and butter the crusts are left on, for sandwiches they are removed.) They may pass on to more complex combinations, such as watercress sandwiches, chopped candied ginger and cream cheese sandwiches, little hot, toasted cheese rolled sandwiches, open-faced rounds of crab or lobster mixture on soft white or graham bread—the tea kind of food, not the cocktail appetizers.

Bidding Farewell There is no obligation on the part of a tea guest at a formal tea to stay more than the half hour needed to consume his tea. He has chatted with anyone taking tea in his immediate vicinity, not necessarily introducing himself first if he is a stranger. He has thanked the "pourers," if they are courtesy hostesses, as he received his tea, so in leaving he need not approach them again. If his hostess is not pouring he seeks her out for a few appreciative words in farewell. He also says good-by to the host if there is one. If the hostess herself is pouring she does not, in this case, rise to bid a guest farewell. She bows from behind the tea table, offers her hand, perhaps, smiles, and says a few words. The guest may be shown out by a member of the family, but more likely he makes his departure alone.

Formal Dances at Home

The very formal dance or ball at home, frequent in the "season" abroad in the great houses, is increasingly rare here because of our telescoping living arrangements. Still, mainly in the South, the Southwest, the Midwest, and sometimes in the Far West there still exist the houses that can accommodate large numbers of guests—and hosts and hostesses who enjoy giving such elaborate parties. They begin late, and invitations state the hour as ten-thirty or eleven (rarely on the quarter hour for formal invitations). They really get under way around eleven-thirty. (See page 573 for dance invitations.)

The exterior of the house is always specially prepared for the occasion. A red carpet usually runs from curb to front door and there is an awning. A floodlight is on for the convenience of arrivals. The family chauffeur assists guests from their cars, and there may be private detectives or a policeman to protect arriving, bejeweled celebrities, all most formally attired.

A caterer and florist have taken over the house. There is a room set aside for racks on which coats are to be checked, and a caterer's man in house livery gives each guest a ticket for articles checked as he enters. A gentleman accompanying a lady accepts her ticket and, on leaving, collects both garments. In an extensively staffed house there may be a rack in the ladies' dressing room under the supervision of a ladies' maid. In the gentlemen's dressing room a valet may be in attendance, but in any case checks are given. When house servants perform these duties they are not tipped in this country unless they perform a special service of some kind. Even when a caterer supplies these racks and an attendant, the attendant is not tipped at a private party.

Guests approaching the line give their names as "Mrs. Smith," "Miss Brown," "Mr. Cortright" to the butler or announcer as they enter the ballroom, ladies preceding the gentlemen of course. Most formally ladies keep on their gloves, as do the ladies of the receiving line, but this rule is often not followed now. Gloves are removed or turned back for light refreshments, but always removed for a complete meal. Hostess and guest of honor, if any, stand together receiving until the last guest seems to have arrived or until supper is served—about one o'clock. The host, as at a wedding reception, stays in the vicinity of the line and introduces guests to one another whenever his kindly offices seem necessary. He may actually stay in the line briefly early in the evening. The hostess, too, has had the foresight to invite a stag line of ushers, theoretically one *extra* man to each nine or ten girls, and they wear identifying white boutonnieres which are usually awaiting them on a tray in the hall. Ushers come early and stay late and see to it that there are no wallflowers.

As extra men are always welcome, those invited frequently phone the hostess and ask for permission to bring a friend. If such men arrive without their sponsors they say to the hostess on arrival, "George Whitman asked if I might come. I am Andrew Tierney." Needless to say, no one, not even a friend of a friend, should "crash" any private party. To prevent this, many hostesses include in their invitations admission cards which must be presented at the door.

As at all formal affairs, the "roof" is not sufficient introduction. A man who has not been introduced to a girl may not ask her to dance, but of course he may ask someone to introduce him. An usher may ask a girl to dance even if he has not first been introduced, but that is because he is an acting host. In going on the ballroom floor a man leads the way through the crowd and once arrived stands ready to receive his partner. In crossing the floor to leave it he walks with the girl to his right. Then, if there is a crush, he goes first, as in a restaurant where there is no headwaiter, to the group where he found her or to the refreshment table or to her waiting next partner. He never leaves her stranded.

Supper At a formal dance or ball, supper is always served either buffet or at small tables supplied by the caterer. There are never place cards, and guests seat themselves as they wish, usually with friends. A girl's escort always takes her in to supper. Ushers see to it that unescorted girls are seated in congenial groups with young men who will serve them supper.

Abroad, sometimes the reception line re-forms for "good nights" when it is time to go. But in this country, after a dance or ball, this might mean that the guest of honor, if any, might have to stay on duty until dawn. Therefore after the receiving line breaks up at a late party, it does not re-form. Guests say "good-by" to host and hostess if they are still about or to any member of the family, and, of course, a debutante stays up until the last guest departs.

"At Home"

An "at home" is a formal reception of some kind—often a tea or even an evening reception at which a buffet meal is set up. Cards are sent to one's visiting list with the words "at home" written on the face with the date and the time (see page 575 for engraved examples). A reply is usually requested. This kind of entertainment is suitable for wedding anniversaries.

Chapter 33

THE GUEST AT FORMAL MEALS

When a guest receives a formal invitation to lunch or dine he should know the procedures of this kind of stylized entertainment. If he knows exactly what to expect he can be at ease. It is only the unknown that tends to shake our poise. Let us examine the guest's part in formal entertaining.

When a butler or waitress is serving at table, the persons served pay sufficient attention to the service to be ready to take their portions when dishes are presented to them (from the left) and, at a crowded table, to move aside, left or right, slightly, to aid the service or removal of dishes— the latter virtually always to the right, except for butter plates.

Second Portions At formal luncheons or dinners second portions are not properly offered (or asked for) because of the usual multiplicity of courses. But at meals where they are offered, any guest who wishes more may serve himself from the proffered dish or platter even if other guests have abstained. The hostess then takes at least a token amount to keep him company, or she has eaten so slowly as to have a little left on her plate from which to eat while any guest consumes a second helping.

Guests Do Not Assist Unless asked to do so by the hostess, a guest does not assist in the service of anything at the table while there are servants in attendance. He never stacks dishes nor hands an empty plate or glass to a servant but permits these to be removed or replenished for him. At a formal meal there should be no need for those at the table to pass anything. There should be salt and pepper, ash trays, matches, cigarettes (if the hostess wishes) at every place, or at every other place. Bread or rolls are passed at luncheon, or rolls are in place on or in the napkin at a formal dinner or to the left of the plate, if they are served at all.

Smoking at Table It is poor manners for a guest to sit down to a table, formally set or otherwise, with a lighted cigarette in his hand. At a formal table he may well find no place for the ashes or finished cigarette (if the hostess takes pride in her cuisine) and will be forced to leave the table with his cigarette or ask for an ash tray. At formal dinners cigarettes are usually not placed on the table until the dessert is served, if then.

Greeting Servants at Table   A guest at table pays no particular attention to the servant waiting upon him. He never carries on a conversation with even an old family retainer while being served. He may, however, quietly say, "Good evening" or "Good evening, Johnson" (or "Nellie") as the butler, houseman, or waitress approaches to serve him, if this is the first time he has seen him (or her) since entering the house, and then only if he has been a frequent guest.

The Token Portion   A guest takes at least a little of everything offered him at a formal dinner or luncheon and makes some pretense at eating it. This is done so the attentive host or hostess will not imagine he has been overlooked in the presentation of dishes. It is necessary neither to eat every bit on one's plate nor, again, to leave a little so as not to seem gluttonous.

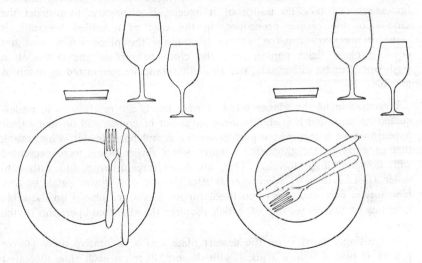

The Placement of Used Silver is optional—either of these two ways best assures that the plate, when removed, will have the utensils firmly upon it. The method on the left is used in *informal* service when plate is passed for second portions.

Placement of Used Silver   When a plate of food has been finished or the diner has had all he wishes, he places the fork and knife (but only if he has used one or both) on the right side of the plate, sharp side of the blade facing in, the fork tines up, to the left of the knife. They should be so placed as not to slide off as the plate is being removed. Dessert spoon and fork are placed on the empty plate, as they were when the plate was presented, that is, fork on the left, spoon on the right with tines of the fork up and facing, with the bowl of the spoon slightly toward the center of the plate, and securely enough so they won't fall off when the servant picks up the plate. No used silver is ever placed on the table or left in a cup. A soup spoon is left in a large soup plate. An iced tea spoon is left in the glass if no service plate is beneath. Unused silver at the place is left on the table, to be removed to a tray by the servant before the dessert course.

Crumbs and Spilled Food When there is full service, crumbs and bits of bread are left on the tablecloth by the guest and are removed by the servant when he or she crumbs the table. But if any semiliquid, such as a bit of jelly or sauce, has been dropped on the cloth, the guest, at the time, if he sees it, quietly retrieves it with some convenient utensil—butter knife, fork, or dinner knife—and places it on the side of his plate. If anything is spilled while a guest is being served, then the servant attends to it. The guest should make no more than a murmured apology, if any, and the hostess should take no notice of it except, if necessary, to instruct the servant in the proper procedure. In the case of a spilled beverage, it may be necessary for the servant to remove the place setting and put down a clean linen napkin over the cloth or replace the mat with a fresh one. But on either side, the accident should be minimized as much as possible.

Presentation of the Finger Bowl Finger bowls are rarely seen in under-staffed or unstaffed households these days, but of course still do make their appearance in homes where perfect service is still possible. (It is interesting that as early as the thirteenth century silver finger bowls were presented with flowered linen towels.) They are filled three-quarters full with cold water (but see below) when served after dessert, and flower petals or tiny blown-glass fish, etc., are often used. Finger bowls are placed on the table in either of two ways, one of which requires the slight co-operation of the guest.

If the finger bowl is on the dessert plate and a decorative doily (never paper) is placed before a guest with dessert silver on each side, the guest is expected to lift bowl and doily and small glass plate adroitly with the right hand and place it in front and slightly to the left of his place setting. He then removes the silver and places it, fork left and spoon right of the plate. If the finger bowl is presented with no silver flanking it, this indicates that there is no further course and the guest does not remove it from the plate. Very occasionally, a small underplate on the dessert plate, topped by doily and finger bowl, is intended for use. For example, strawberries Romanoff is a difficult dessert for a flat plate. The menu or the hostess gives the cue.

In using a finger bowl, the guest dips in the fingers of one hand, then of the other, lightly, then dries them on the napkin on his lap, but all so briefly as to avoid the impression that this is a serious ablution. He may, too, of course, touch his lips with his moistened fingers, then pat his lips lightly with his napkin, which he then places, unfolded and unarranged, to the left of his place. He never leaves it on his chair or tosses it onto a plate.

Finger bowls, even without service, are almost necessary after the serving of boiled or broiled lobster or steamed clams. In this case, they are filled three-quarters full with warm water which may be soapy. As a different and rather novel idea to replace the use of finger bowls after lobster and such, the hostess might borrow the Oriental custom of passing a flat dish or basket containing small napkins or terry towels wrung out in hot, scented water.

The thing before an Oriental-style meal is to pass refrigerated scented towels on a tray so that guests may refresh themselves before eating. These are used to wipe the hands and may be discreetly applied to forehead as well as to mouth in very hot weather. This is not a substitute for cleaning up before dinner, however. Used napkins, lightly folded, are replaced on the tray.

The Signal to Rise   As coffee is not served at the table to gentlemen and ladies together at a formal dinner, the guests should be ready for the hostess's signal to rise at the end of the fruit course. If the gentlemen stay in the dining room for coffee, cigars, pipes, and liqueurs they move up in a companionable circle near the host—and all stay. For one robustious Lothario to make off after the ladies is considered bad conduct. And in equally poor taste is the young lady who leaves the gentlemen with a reluctant backward glance. Needless to say, if the gentlemen move on to the library for coffee no lady allows herself to be persuaded to join them. Historically, the stories that are sometimes told at these stag moments after dinner are unfit for shell-like ears, and, at any rate, the other ladies would frigidly resent such a defection. As insurance, perhaps, against any such encroachment on masculine preserves, the doors were locked upon the gentlemen after dinner in the early nineteenth century, and it is said many never did eventually "join the ladies."

Chapter 34

SPECIAL PROBLEMS OF SERVICE

The Steak Knife The steak knife is placed on the table where the regular knife would ordinarily go. In very formal service, where there is a butler or waitress, or in an elegant restaurant for example, the place setting has a regular knife and when the guest is served with the steak, the butler or waitress replaces the dinner knife with the steak knife.

The Placing of Teaspoons Teaspoons are not put on the table with the fork and knife, unless they are to be used in place of bouillon or cream soup spoons or for grapefruit. Otherwise they are placed on the saucers of tea and coffee cups on the side opposite the cup's handle (always to the right). At breakfast the cups and saucers, with their spoons, may be grouped around the coffee at the right of the hostess or on the sideboard, English breakfast style, or at the right of each place setting.

After-dinner coffee spoons, like teaspoons, are placed on the saucers before the coffee is served, whether at the dinner table, after dessert, or, formally, in the living room.

Incidentally, demitasse spoons need not be reserved just for the service of demitasse. They are also used in the service of desserts served in very small ceramic or porcelain ramekins used for service of *mousse au chocolat* and other delectables. They may be used also for the Italian dessert *zabaglione,* which is frequently served in a small wine glass but may be served in any small, preferably glass dish in a very small portion, as it is rich.

The Iced-Tea Spoon In the setting of the table the iced-tea spoon is placed to the right of the knife. As iced tea is usually served without a small service plate beneath it many are puzzled as to what to do with the spoon, once the beverage has been stirred. When there is no plate beneath the drink the long spoon is left in the glass, with the handle held toward the far side with the first and second fingers while one drinks. This is an admittedly awkward procedure but the only possible one if there is no small service plate. Certainly a wet spoon may not be laid on the tablecloth or place mat. The same is true of straws, which are left in the glass.

Serving Water at Meals At an informal meal where there is a cold beverage to be drunk in place of water—milk, iced tea, iced coffee, or iced chocolate—water glasses are not always placed on the table. At a formal meal, even when wines are being served, the water glass is placed at the tip of the knife with the wine glass or glasses slightly below and to the right of the water glass (see diagram). Incidentally, it is not necessary to serve water when you are serving wine. Europeans do it only on the insistence of Americans. (It's pleasant, however, to offer water sometime during the evening after dinner, preferably in fine, small tumblers.)

At family meals where there are no guests and service is limited or missing completely it is acceptable to omit the water—and usual to omit it at breakfast—if the members of the family do not ordinarily take it at meal times. But if guests are present water glasses are usually in place (but see above). The water, chilled, may be poured—in fact, usually is poured—before guests sit down, and, if there is service, butler or waitress replenish glasses as needed throughout the meal from a pitcher of ice water on the serving table or sideboard. Otherwise guests serve themselves from a pitcher on the table, or the hostess offers it from a pitcher on the sideboard.

The Service of Margarine It used to be that margarine, if used in a household for reasons of economy, was never served to guests and butter was especially purchased for entertaining. That attitude is no longer justified since margarine is now considered the equal of butter by most people.

When soft margarine is used instead of margarine sticks, it does pose some problems of service. No matter what you see in the ads, the little tub in which it comes should not be put on a properly set table. Loaves of French bread may be liberally spread with the soft margarine, sprinkled with herbs of choice (for example, garlic salt, dill weed), and then wrapped in thin aluminum foil and heated in the oven. Less-than-formal dining certainly permits the presentation of spread bread if the slices are cut diagonally and arranged attractively on the plate. No problem here of soft margarine on the table. A good solution, and one that I have used, is to put the soft margarine in individual little ceramic or porcelain ramekins, the kind that are used for the service of butter in France. These go on the table either directly above the place setting, or at the point of the knife. The butter spreader is placed on the butter plate. If hot biscuits are to be passed, even simpler is to spread them in the kitchen, if you are using soft margarine. Soft margarine may be melted and passed at the table for use on corn. Little dishes of melted margarine may be at each place when hot lobster is served, just as butter would be.

The Service of Tea   Hot tea is always gracefully served by the hostess or a woman friend acting for her, never by servants, except perhaps at an enormous tea. When tea is served informally at the luncheon table it is passed down the table from hostess to guests, not passed on a tray by a servant. Aside from the traditionally ceremonial aspects of tea-serving, tea is never poured out, then passed several cups at a time, the way coffee may be, because it cools very quickly. Instead it is always taken by the guest directly from the hands of the hostess or the woman friend or relative acting for her.

Actually, the only formal service of tea is the service of afternoon tea in the living room or elsewhere with due ceremony, eggshell-thin cups, the finest silver, and most delicate napery. But why worry about such formality when many people would enjoy tea at other than four or five o'clock and without the kind of preparation that makes tea-drinking a special and sometimes troublesome occasion. Tea may be served informally at any time of the day or night, so long as it is served hot, if it's supposed to be hot, and made properly with actively boiling water so it will not be the poor apology for a beverage it so often is in this country (see "How to Make Tea" page 405).

Candy at the Table   At a formally set table that is long enough, bonbon dishes may be placed between the candelabra and the end of the table place settings, but they are not essential. Candy may be passed after the dessert or with the coffee, usually informally around the table after it has been brought in and placed on the table in a bonbon dish or sometimes in a decorative box. It may be formally presented, of course, too. It should not be nibbled by the guests before dessert time if it is on the set table, though salted nuts, of course, are. When a piece of candy is selected, it is taken frill and all and the selection should be made quickly. Many people appreciate such a little morsel of sweet in place of a rich dessert these days.

At holiday tables decorated for special occasions nuts and candies are often in little party favors at each place, especially at a family affair where there is a mixed group of children (who feel cheated without something of the kind) and adults. Little paper boxes or baskets at each place never seem suited, somehow, to even the most relaxed adult dinner, but then I can't bear paper hats and streamers at New Year's, either.

The Service of Food on Trays   Tray cloths or special tray mats or doilies are placed only on trays used in the service of meals—high tea, breakfast, luncheon, supper, or dinner (in bed or on individual trays on the dining room table or any convenient and attractive spot). Cocktails are served on bare trays with alcohol-proofed surfaces. A glass of water requested from a servant is brought on a small bare tray, just as a card or a letter is tendered on a bare silver salver. After-dinner coffee is on a bare silver tray, and tea is poured into cups—placed directly on the bare tea tray, which may be of course on a set table.

A man or woman dining alone might prefer a tray in the library or on the porch rather than sitting alone at the table. Or a hostess might find it much more efficient to have weekend guests served breakfast trays in their rooms than to try to keep things hot in the dining room until all filter down.

The Fine Damask Cloth The height of formality is a good damask tablecloth with matching dinner napkins. Well-equipped households have several of these, one at least large enough to cover generously the dining table that is opened to its fullest extent. It should overhang not less than twelve, not more than eighteen inches.

Such a cloth is a luxury in that it can seldom be used more than once. It must never be put on the table with the slightest wrinkle or stain—far better to use table mats. It should be over a table pad or silence cloth, and it should be placed so carefully that the center fold is exactly down the center of the table, lengthwise, with the fold in the cloth tentwise to the surface of the table. In some establishments, where an expert laundress does up such cloths at home—a hard job—and the storage space is sufficient, the cloths are rolled on a cylinder to avoid any creases at all. Once on the table, the cloth's ends should be equal and so must its sides.

While pale pastel damask is acceptable, damask that has the design in one pale color and the body of the cloth in another should be avoided. The beauty of damask is always its elegant simplicity and the sublety of the woven design.

A too fancy tablecloth is like a too assertive rug—in color or design— in that the things that go on it must be keyed to it rather than be used against a quiet background.

Garnishes Food should never be overdecorated, and whatever garniture there is should be perfectly edible. The obvious exception is the frill on the bone of a chop or chicken leg or the frill around the crown roast of pork. There is nothing modern about these, by the way. They go back to the days before the carving fork and were meant to protect a lady's hand from grease when she took up the bone in order to cut off a portion for herself. Today we use such frills sometimes to hide the bare bone where the meat has drawn back in roasting or frying. They are *not* an invitation to pick up the bone in one's fingers.

It is well to explain to a husband who carves that whatever is on the plate with the fish, roast, or chops, steak or other meat should be apportioned too. He should not shove aside the parsley or the watercress, the thin lemon slices, perhaps neatly cut out in some way on the rind. Nor should he ignore the sauce on the dish. Of course, a serving spoon should be placed with his carving implements to facilitate the serving of gravies and sauces on the serving plate.

What constitutes garniture? Anything that trims the dish—minced parsley, capers, fried eggs on veal cutlets (schnitzel à la Holstein), a lump of appetizingly melting butter, a sprinkling of paprika, a grating of nutmeg, chopped, sliced, or quartered egg, strips of pimiento on asparagus vinaigrette or perhaps on a white fish such as sautéed filet of sole. Buttered breadcrumbs (à la polonaise) are also a garnish, as are the onion rings for hamburger. The cook should avoid garnishing *every* dish, as this defeats the attempt at surprise. She should also learn different ways to garnish standard dishes. Spinach need not always be served in the leaf with quartered hard boiled egg. It is better in the opinion of many if it is finely chopped, then thickened (keeping its own juice), flavored with garlic salt and nutmeg, seasoned with butter and a pinch of sugar, and served with little croutons browned in butter or sometimes in bacon fat. Or it may have a garnish of crisp, crumbled bacon and chopped egg.

In garnishing a platter the cook strives for pleasing balance. If a rib roast is on a large silver tree platter her eye must tell her—and this takes practice—just where the parsley or watercress shall be and how much is needed to make a setting for the roast without crowding the platter.

Continental style, a whole boiled fish is served with the head on and with a lemon in the fish's mouth. As the head is not served, the lemon is not, either. The same is true of suckling pig, served whole with the head and with a bright red apple in the mouth. Actually, I have never cared to see food served in too anatomical a fashion.

When Are Place Cards Needed? Place cards are a convenience to the hostess who is seating more than eight guests or possibly as few as eight. They may be used at any time—at a festive breakfast, at luncheon, at seated buffet suppers, and, of course, at large formal dinners.

Such cards, if everyone is going to be on a first-name basis, may read "Bob," "Susie," "John" etc. Otherwise they read "Mr. Anderson," "Mrs. Montgomery," "Dr. Burke." Sometimes they may read "Mary Simpson," "Jim Burke," "Carole Anderson," especially if there are new people in the group who may not know all the last names. Black ink is most legible for place cards, but under informal circumstances colored inks or even felt markers may be used in any color the hostess desires. For a formal dinner, however, black always looks best. For anniversaries such as the silver or the gold, gold or silver inks are often used as are red or green for Christmas. Place cards are in holders directly above the plate, or if they are the folded kind they may be used without a holder in that same position. The flat kind may be placed directly on the napkin, which in turn may be on the dinner plate if no first course is in place, although there are many optional arrangements of napkins in informal and semi-formal table settings.

Extra Guests at the Dessert Course   An easy way to expand your entertaining painlessly is to invite a manageable number for dinner and then additional guests to join you for dessert and coffee in the living room. But, of course, it is not necessary to include for dinner or even dessert all the guests you may have invited for the evening. Some may be invited much later than others, although nine o'clock is usually the latest for which such an evening invitation is given.

Chapter 35

THE RITUAL OF DRINKING

Drinks for Guests—Cocktails and Highballs

If you are having people to dinner, mix only one kind of cocktail and offer, in addition, sherry, and scotch or bourbon or rye and soda—with vegetable or fruit juice for possible teetotalers. On-the-rocks drinks— bourbon, scotch, martini, vodka martini, and consommé (for the teetotalers) are very popular and of course painless to make. Old-fashioneds are a nuisance to fix for more than four or five. The safest choice seems to be martinis, which have the virtue of being relatively inexpensive, more or less foolproof as to concoction, and mixable well in advance. In fact, they may be bottled and stored full-strength for a week or more in the refrigerator—but don't bother to save diluted ones. They may also be varied—a tiny pearl onion in the glass instead of the usual unstuffed olive makes a gibson. Cocktail mixes, bottled or in some cases frozen, are convenient to have on hand.

A martini should always be dry, never sweet. It should have a twist of lemon peel in the container in which the martini is stirred, or the peel may be twisted over each glass so a bit of oil drops in. Some experts insist that the ingredients be stirred all in one direction with the cracked ice—never shaken—but as I, with many another woman, am unenthusiastic about martinis (except for their convenience), I cannot say whether this is really vital. I have even seen a very knowledgeable gentleman of the old school shake his martinis vigorously, with a loud snort at all the talk that they must be stirred.

A prominently placed home bar, with the makings of a wide variety of drinks on demand and a host who can oblige, takes away the emphasis on dinner and puts it untastefully on what should be only an incidental procedure. Only at a really large party should more than one kind of cocktail be served at home, and then the host is usually not acting as bartender.

Esoteric cocktails should be avoided at dinner parties unless you are certain your guests have such preferences. An alexander, for example, would be a poor choice, especially with men present. Fancy mixed drinks are usually frowned on by men, though beloved of some women who like to order them in restaurants. But the standard cocktails are the wisest choice—and don't let the person who mixes them do so without following an exact formula. Nothing is so horrid as a martini with too much vermouth or an old-fashioned with too much bitters. A bacardi, a margarita or daiquiri that is sickish-sweet will kill appetites for the best-conceived dinner.

Generally, gin and tonic, vodka and tonic, rum cocktails, and beer are preferred in hot weather to whisky cocktails. Eggnog is a cold weather specialty and is not served before dinner. It is an afternoon drink, always served with fruit cake and sweet biscuits, usually on New Year's Day.

Such drinks as hot buttered rum, glög, hot spiced wine are winter between-meal drinks often served after outdoor sports. They do not properly precede dinner.

Rum-and-Cola, tom collins, punch (milk punch perhaps excepted), bishop, bowles, swizzles, juleps, spiced wines are afternoon or evening libations, not appetizers before dinner. Stingers are served liqueur-fashion as a digestive after dinner.

You make no mistake when you choose one of the following cocktails to serve before a dinner party—martini, bacardi, or daiquiri (especially in summer), whisky sours (good any time and well-liked by both sexes), manhattans and old-fashioneds (with a minimum of garnish for male tastes).

Cracked ice—easy to make with a canvas bar bag and mallet or a little ice-cracking machine—makes cocktails cold fast without undue dilution. One exception is the julep, which requires crushed ice and plenty of it.

In punch, an old-fashioned, or any tall drink such as a collins served with garnish, a stirrer is offered so that the guest can extract flavor from the garnish by pressing it gently against the side of the glass. The garnish is not taken up and eaten in the fingers. A cherry, olive, or onion that isn't impaled with a toothpick (for easy eating) is sometimes gracefully tipped into the mouth, but it is unattractive to see people fishing out a garnish from their drinks with their fingers.

Mainly about Wines

The subject of wines is a fascinating one—so fascinating that mountains of material have been written on it, thus frightening more than instructing, I sometimes think.

In Victorian days no gentleman of fashion could possibly be ignorant of all the fine points of vintage and temperature, vintner and *endroit* of the wines at his table. He kept a proper wine cellar and tended, or had tended, each precious bottle on schedule. He knew enough not to permit his butler to wipe off a fine old, dusty bottle of, say, Chateau Mouton Rothschild of a superlative year and wrap it in a napkin to hide the details of its lineage from interested diners. Red wines never are. His fine sedimented wines were kept on their sides at proper temperature and never put upright even before service. They could be decanted into beautiful clear glass decanters, slowly after the cork had been eased— not yanked out—until the sediment was reached. Or they could be poured from a cradle or wine basket that held the bottle almost horizontal so that wine and sediment would not mix. However, a simple and quite satisfactory way of dealing with sedimented reds is to stand them up in the dining room by midmorning of the day of the dinner. This room conditions and obviates decanting or basketing. Red table wines which have been confined to bin welcome a chance to breathe before pouring. Uncork them an hour before dinner.

The *table* wines are those served at meals. The reds range from the hearty, full-bodied French burgundies (in infinite variety), the more delicate, ruby red, tart clarets to the blushing vin rosé, so light in body that, unlike the others which are served at room temperature or slightly warm, it is chilled and thus is most agreeable in warm weather. Of the myriad American varieties of dark red full-bodied wine, most with French names, not all, naturally, are burgundy, though burgundy they are often commonly called merely because they are red. I think it is advisable to know a little more than that about wines. The major wine merchants are interested in improving your wine education. Go to one and ask him to explain to you the fine points of difference in the red wines. Compare those pressed from the cabernet, the true grape of French clarets, with the delicate bouquet of some of the fine table wines from vintners in California's Livermore, Napa, Soma, and Santa Clara valleys.

Dry Reds The dry red wines are those whose sugar content is low —red chianti, berbera are among the many types. These are preferable for service during main courses, although sweet red wines, and even some of the sweet sauternes, are said to be becoming popular in America as dinner wines—but mainly, I suspect, in the less pretentious restaurants and, I suspect, too, at the insistence of the ladies. But people who know food—and wines—will tell you that a sweet wine served before or during a meal takes the edge off the appetite and so defeats a dry wine's whole function, that is, to supplement rather than overshadow the food.

Dry Whites It has become acceptable in our more simplified way of living to serve one dry white wine, if we prefer, throughout a meal, even as an accompaniment to red meat. But on a more elaborate basis for dinner it is pleasant and formal to serve sherry with the soup, a dry white wine—perhaps hock or chablis—with the fish, chicken, brains, sweetbreads, or seafood, and a dry red or sparkling burgundy with red meat, duck, goose, or game.

At luncheon the one-wine theme is delightfully carried out with an alsatian, a moselle, a white chianti, or white orvieto, all imported. Or their American counterparts—reisling, sylvaner, semillon, pinot blanc, traminer, and the Ohio and New York State white wines—all merit consideration as do the South American rhine types and, of course, the true rhines, of which some, like some of the liebfraumilchs, are worth much penny-scrimping in other directions.

Sweet Reds The sweet red wines are dessert and between-meal wines. They include port (excellent with nuts and cheese), the sweet sherries (neither of which are ever referred to, properly, by the way, as sherry *wine* or port *wine*), muscatel, and madeira.

Sweet Whites The sweet white dessert wines include malaga, semidry champagnes, white port from Oporto, Portugal (very delicious and not enough known), tokay, and angelica, an American dessert wine originated in California.

And then there are the delicious homemade wines, white and red, whose acquaintance should be made by those gentlemen who enjoy showing off their culinary talents. What better way than to learn to make grandmother's dandelion, elderberry, or blackberry wine, or even to brew a real, authoritative ginger beer, English style? Old cookbooks give all the essential directions.

Filtered Domestics Some American wines are excellent, some poor— just as some imported varieties from the wine countries fit into both categories. Judicious experimentation is highly recommended so you may find what wines suit your needs, your palate, and your pocketbook most adequately. Experts tell us that there is less sedimentation in American red wines but that this isn't to their credit, as overfiltering to remove the sediment robs them of some of their character.

Wines in Place of Cocktails The true gourmet is horrified at the blatancy of cocktails before exquisitely planned and executed meals. He much prefers wine with canapés, *foie gras*, or caviar. Chablis—really a French white burgundy—is commendable in place of cocktails, as is a chilled dry (American—the French ones are sweet) sauterne. Most elegant, of course, is champagne, straight if it's the best imported, as a champagne cocktail if it lacks final excellence. Any of these, including the champagne, may be refrigerator cooled at about 45° for home service, as this is a less drippy procedure. And a partly used bottle of champagne or any other white wine, restoppered with a *different cork* will keep for weeks in the refrigerator, and even champagne will stay lively for days the same way (and good for champagne cocktails), though such refrigerated wines should not be allowed to freeze.

Partly used bottles of red wine should be recorked and kept in a cool place, rather than in the refrigerator. If they start to turn sour before they can be used, never discard them but permit them to turn to wine vinegar, being careful to leave the "mother" in the bottle to effect this chemical change. A little from a bottle of wine vinegar added to leftover dry red wine will start the vinegaring process.

Port, sherry, and madeira are all available dry, as well as sweet, and the dry types are all suitable for service in place of cocktails. A good dry sherry is usually served from a chilled bottle rather than from the decanter at cocktail time.

Both dry port and sherry are good with bitters—orange or Angostura—in place of a cocktail. Dubonnet and vermouth at room temperature and served with a twist of lemon peel appeal to many palates, as does Amer Picon, but Dubonnet may be served frappé, i.e., with finely crushed ice in a cocktail glass, and the vermouth makes an attractive pompier high-ball, or vermouth cassis, to those who prefer appetizers low in alcoholic content. A vermouth cassis is made with 1½ to 3 ozs. of French dry vermouth (it's the Italian that's sweet and which is not good alone as an appetizer) plus ½ oz. of crème de cassis (a French black currant liqueur) plus lump ice and club soda, in a small thin highball glass filled ¾ full and gently stirred.

In some South American countries a cocktail party is called "a ver-mouth," and vermouth you get—no cocktails! And in Europe if you order a martini you may well get vermouth and no gin.

Storage of Wines All table wines should be stored on their sides, to keep their corks moist (and uncrumbling), in a cool cupboard, away from the light and from steam pipes. A wooden wine rack to hold them reduces chance of breakage, but they can be placed sidewise on narrow shelves of any kind. Wines with plastic corks may be stored upright.

What Kind of Glasses You may be the possessor of your grandmother's benobbed and overlaid green hock glasses or handsome ruby wines and will certainly want to use them. But any connoisseur of wines will hold out for the use of clear thin glass for all wines, as wine itself is sufficient decoration. The table wines should be served preferably in a fairly large glass—just under goblet size and more than twice cocktail size. They should be shaped to bunch the bouquet under the nostrils—in other words, the rim should be narrower than the base of the bowl with the exception of V-shaped (they *needn't* be this shape—any 3-oz. stemmed glass will do) sherry glasses, which, by the way, are the only ones to be filled almost to the brim. Others are filled about one-half or two-thirds to permit the inhalation of the bouquet. Champagne glasses are best without hollow stems, which are decorative but which permit the warming of the drink, as a chilled white wine is always grasped by the stem. (Red wine is drunk with the hand grasping the bowl to warm the wine.)

To Decant or Not Sherry served with soup or between meals (this the sweeter type) may be decanted, though service from a good bottle is always right, too. Tequila, aquavit and vodka (not wines, of course, but served often enough straight from the refrigerator, ice-cold as an appetizer) are not decanted.

Claret, madeira, and port may be decanted, though many like the appearance of the bottle—especially if the vintner's name means anything. All but the claret (unstopper this, by the way, an hour before serving) are safe in the decanter almost indefinitely, though sherry may begin to cloud up if decanted and not kept fairly cool.

Burgundy is not decanted but served from a wine cradle or at least from its side if it is an imported, sedimented type. It should be brought into the room and unstoppered an hour before serving. American filtered types may be served decanted or from an upright bottle. Sparkling burgundy, however, is served chilled in its own bottle, upright like champagne. In very hot weather these wines are served "cellar" temperature, cooler than the room, though not chilled.

White sparkling wines are served from their own bottles, upright and slightly cold but not chilled.

Liqueurs and Cordials Liqueurs are usually served at room temperature with the exception of crème de menthe (green or white), which is served frappé or in a stinger, though any cordial, especially a fruit one, may be served frappé, especially for ladies, or for all in the summertime—try Southern Comfort or cointreau frappé, for example. Liqueurs and cordials are served after dinner with or following demitasse. A fifth of cordial or liqueur will provide approximately 25 one-ounce servings.

Pouring of Wines A decanted wine may be poured first into an honored guest's glass (the lady to the right of the host)—though the host should check flavor sometime before serving. At a big party where there are many small tables set up, a good idea is to have a bottle of wine on each table with one man at each table serving it. An undecanted wine, which might harbor traces of cork, is poured—just a little of it—into the glass of the *host* or, if there is no host, into that of the *hostess* to drain off bits of cork, if any. Host or hostess left with bits of cork in his or her glass is not expected to finish the pouring on top of cork after others have been served. A servant, if present, pours off the bit of wine-with-cork, or if there is no servant the cork-receiver may carefully lift out the offending bits with, say, the blade of a clean knife or a spoon and lay the bits on the side of his plate. Or he rises, glass in hand, and empties the offending inch in the bar or kitchen.

To Prevent Spilling To prevent spilling a drop of wine on the tablecloth when pouring from a bottle, turn the neck of the bottle gently before lifting the mouth away from the glass. The bottle mouth may also be wiped with a clean napkin between servings.

How to Open a Bottle of Champagne

The best way to serve champagne is to first chill it in the bottom of the refrigerator for one and a half to two hours before you wish to use it—don't keep it in the coldest part. Never freeze it! Wine coolers are not at all necessary for they make the bottle wet. The bottle has to then be wrapped in a napkin where the label may not show and the bottle becomes awkward to handle. If you are new at champagne opening, do it in the kitchen where your guests won't make you nervous. Open the bottle before an audience if you wish, but in either case be quite aware of the little loop of wire on the side of the cork. If you simply untwist this and pull it up, the whole wire bridle will come right off. Then remove the disk of metal over the cork. Be extremely careful to handle the bottle gently, otherwise on opening you'll cause an explosion, which, although anticipated by people, is not good.

Now that the wire is off, hold the champagne at an angle with the bottom of the bottle toward your chest, taking care to point the neck of the bottle away from the chandeliers and your guests. Then slowly ease the cork with your thumbs or else give it a quick twist with your fingers. Although the timid hold a napkin over the cork, this is not necessary if you feel you have command of the situation. The effervescence of good champagne will help lift the cork and with a little practice you can remove the cork without losing a drop of champagne. If there is too much effervescence, just insert an iced teaspoon into the neck of the bottle and it will stop immediately.

A bottle of champagne can serve from six to eight people, so to pass it down the table might embarrass guests who do not know exactly how much to pour for themselves. The easiest way to handle the pouring is for the host to walk down the length of the table and serve the champagne, with fitting ceremony. After pouring each glass, he should turn the neck of the bottle gently to prevent any drops from falling on the tablecloth.

Toasts

Weddings, christenings, bachelor dinners, engagement parties are always occasions for toasts. But there are other occasions—formal dinners, anniversaries, birthday parties, intimate dinners—where men, in particular, may wish to propose a toast. While it is nice to be able to extemporize gracefully on such occasions as the rare man can, it is pleasant to know most of the standard toasts and to be able to tender them with ease.

The person toasted, if present and if not the President of the U.S. or other high dignitary, usually returns a toast. A woman, except when she is a bride, usually accepts the compliment of the toast simply with a smile and lowered eyes, remaining seated if the others stand and holding her wine, but not sipping it until the toast has been drunk. In fact, the person toasted never touches the drink to his or her lips until the others have drunk the toast, otherwise he or she would be drinking to himself or herself, an immodest procedure.

A man drinking a toast across the table to his dinner companion may do so merely by catching her eye and raising his glass. He doesn't rise unless others are at the table and there is a real occasion—such as her birthday—to propose a toast to the lady. If the two are alone the gentleman may actually say the words of some gay little toast, *"A vos beaux yeux* [To your lovely eyes]" or suggest they drink together "To a wonderful evening" or "To happy times."

A dinner chairman at, say, the Republican National Committee dinner would propose the first toast to the President. The President, if present, merely remains seated and bows slightly in recognition of the standing toast by the others.

Important toasts, to rulers, to the President, to a bride, etc., are properly drained at one drink. The glasses used often to be thrown in the fireplace or at least snapped at the delicate stem, but today no dishonor to the toasted one occurs when the glasses are, sensibly, left intact. It is, by the way, rude to the point of insult to refuse to drink a toast to anyone. If you can't drink wine, you pretend to do so. A toast with water is supposed to be no toast at all, but this is the solution arrived at by King Gustav of Sweden, by principle a teetotaler. Therefore, toast in water if you wish, or if you can't drink wine, you may pretend to do so. It is not really correct to toast with cocktails, but a toast with punch or beer, ale or whisky is usual.

In England some drinks still have a bit of toast placed in them in the traditional style. In drinking a toast, one had to drain the cup to get the "toast," which, saturated with the drink, sank to the bottom. Toasting is a very old custom, indeed, predating the Caesars.

Many charming toasts to women are in French or other foreign languages because toasting is the expected thing abroad, relatively unusual—except for special occasions—here. If you can't master a toast in a foreign language so it sounds the way it should, don't attempt it—translate it into English, and it will be appreciated just as much. But it is convenient to understand what these familiar toasts in other languages mean. In addition to the one I've given, there are many more, often heard. Commonest are:

"À votre santé!" (Fr.) "To your health!"—suitable for anyone, of course.
"Sköal!" (Swed.)—"Your health!"
"Prost!" or "Prosit!" (G.)—"To your health!"
"Here's to your good health and your family's good health, and may you all
   live long and prosper!"—from "Rip Van Winkle," by Washington Irving.
"May you live all the days of your life!"—Swift.

FIVE REASONS FOR DRINKING
If all be true that I do think,
There are five reasons we should drink:
Good wine—a friend—or being dry—
Or lest we should be, by and by—
Or any other reason why!
—HENRY ALDRICH, c. 1700

At a small private dinner a toast may be informally proposed by anyone as soon as the first wine has been poured. The company stands only if the toaster rises. More than one toast may now be drunk with the same glass of wine—though a toast in champagne is often drained at one drink, especially at wedding receptions. Toasts are not drunk with liqueurs, although the dessert wines, sweet sherry, port, marsala, or angelica, would be suitable.

At public dinners toasts are not proposed until the end of the meal just before the speaking begins. The first toast is proposed by the toastmaster, and others may be proposed—with his permission—by honored guests at the dais but not by members of the general assembly.

Chapter 36

ENTERTAINING INDOORS

I never fail to be somewhat alarmed at the extent of my correspondence from people who want to know how to entertain their guests after dinner or luncheon. "What games should we play?" they ask.

Now an occasional game of bridge, canasta, mah-jongg (which still has its devotees), backgammon, or even poker can be enjoyable if everyone is in the mood, but certainly I'd like to be warned before accepting an invitation to dinner that it is to be followed by serious bridge. I wouldn't want any hostess to count on me for a fourth, for I asserted myself concerning ritualistic parlor games long ago.

The best after-meal entertainment though is stimulating conversation. Constant, organized card playing can kill off any attempt at conversation in a group of people who regularly see each other. They may have their bridge luncheons and suppers for years and never really get to know each other at all or get very much out of such meetings.

Of course, the nervous hostess and the awkward, inexperienced host are terrified of just an evening of "conversation." They feel they must do something. They rush around filling glasses, dumping ash trays, pulling up chairs, fiddling with the radio dials, or, willy-nilly, turning on the television.

The good hostess is careful to invite people who have some common thread of interest. She tries to have one, at least, known to be an eager conversationalist. Even if he spends the evening talking interestingly about himself, he can save the evening in a group of semimutes. People are always at their best, anyway, talking about themselves and their experiences. The adept hostess knows how to get them going and how, when others grow restless, to turn the conversation so that everyone else gets a chance to put in his oar. Above all, a hostess should not, herself, feel she must provide all the conversation, no matter how witty or erudite—or capable at conversation—she is. The essence of good conversation is to get others to talk.

Conversation

The talk-talk kind of conversation does little but fill time better left unfilled. The chatterbox, usually feminine, rattles on very often because she is really ill at ease socially and in this way tries to make herself felt.

In conversation it is not really necessary to have a ready opinion on everything. On the contrary, good conversation develops opinions and thus depends on an ability to listen as well as to express oneself.

The bane of every hostess's life is the guest who falls into complete silence, who won't be brought into a conversation, but who, on the other hand, remains in the company. Such people feel shy, superior, or plain tired, I have often found, and should not be forced into conversations they are plainly trying to avoid. Often they enjoy themselves just listening, or they will suddenly come alert and make an interesting contribution later on.

An ability to converse comes with general social ease. The relaxed person, comfortable in his surroundings, is able to parry the conversational ball with little assistance. He should be himself and not try to fit his conversation in some stilted way to the company. If he finds himself well beyond his intellectual depth he can be an alert listener and he can ask a question now and then. His companions will usually be only too pleased to enlighten him.

A host and hostess should try to develop skill in bringing out their guests conversationally. They should know, or find out, the interests and hobbies of each and bring together those with kindred interests. From then on they keep the conversational fires kindled by helping the quieter guests to express themselves from time to time.

A hostess should never try too hard to get her party going. If she relaxes and lets her guests become acquainted, general and group conversation will normally develop. I know one hostess who carried clenched, in one hand, a little black notebook containing the tag lines of what she deemed appropriate stories. Whenever a lull came in conversation she would leaf nervously through it and come up with a story. She succeeded only in making her ineptness as a hostess even more apparent.

No two evenings of conversation are ever alike, even with the same people. An open fire, the preliminary of a good dinner, music perhaps, the little ceremony of evening refreshments—all help to make people comfortable together and expansive.

Conversation at Table

Modern notions of what constitutes proper dinner table conversation are drastically different from those that prevailed in Victorian and even later times. It was once thought that politics, religion, illness, accidents, scandal, were not fit subjects for the dinner table. I concur within reason. Certainly if everyone at the dinner table is known to have the same political beliefs, a discussion of politics is not out of line. Even when some hold different views, a political discussion could be interesting and many times is not wisely avoided. A good hostess, however, watches the conversation and tries to prevent acrimony by changing the subject if there seems to be some danger of serious contention at the table. Even religion need not necessarily be taboo. It can be a very pleasant subject of conversation at the dinner table or elsewhere. To be avoided, of course, would be attacking anyone concerning his religion, either at the table or elsewhere.

Impersonal conversation is, at best, dull. A healthy give and take, warm expression of one's feelings and opinions, the accounting of interesting personal experiences, all means lively social intercourse. People are increasingly themselves, more relaxed in their contacts with other people. Even argument may make lively interchange so long as barbed and painful personal remarks are avoided. Expression of differences of opinion is healthy and interesting at the dinner table or anywhere else.

Ice Breakers

Occasionally, however, even the most astute hostess will find gathered under her roof—perhaps at a birthday party where relatives and friends are of varying ages—a group of people it is difficult to entertain. In this circumstance games are often very helpful as ice breakers. "The Game" is very popular even among intellectuals. "Ghosts" is also entertaining. I remember playing it in the country when our electric power went off for four hours and we wearied of trying to read by candle, lamp, and flashlight. Even a spelling bee can be fun in a large crowd of young and old. A book of games is probably an excellent addition to anyone's home library.

Music in the Evening

Good music is often a stimulus to conversation if it is kept in the background. If everyone, or nearly everyone, is interested in music, classical or otherwise, the hostess may ask if certain records or special programs will be welcome. Then conversation may—or may not—cease. Many a delightful evening with friends can be spent with hardly a word exchanged if all are listening to music.

Few people can or want to talk against the blare of the radio or the glare and chatter of the television screen. If you plan an evening of radio, bridge, poker, or television, say so and give any guests who prefer a different evening the opportunity to leave approximately one hour after dinner.

Television

The hostess with a television set should never assume that her guests are willing or eager to look at it. It is safer to assume that callers came to talk with their friends, not to enjoy their television.

If unexpected guests arrive during the course of a telecast that the family is obviously enjoying, the hostess may say, "We like this program and look at it each week, so I hate to shut it off, but perhaps you would like to see it? If not, let's go into another room and any of the others who care to may join us." It is certainly not fair, for example, to drag father away from a championship boxing match, if that's what he's glued to, to help entertain Mr. and Mrs. George, who just dropped in from the next block. What probably happens is that Mrs. George and the hostess retire from the din and the two men have their television.

If the hostess, on the other hand, has television in mind as a means of entertaining expected guests, she should tell them so in advance. If they consider a whole evening of watching television lost, they have an opportunity to refuse the invitation. They wouldn't hesitate to say they don't feel like a movie. They may even be quite frank and say, "We hardly ever turn on our own set, except for a program or two we occasionally enjoy. Please ask us some other time when you're planning something else."

Guests who do accept a television invitation are ill-mannered, however, if once settled they keep up a continuous chatter that prevents the others from hearing what's going on. Trying to keep up conversation while watching television is impossible. They should be still and look and listen or remove themselves thence.

Playing Bridge

If it is agreeable to a majority of the guests—enough to make up tables— to play bridge after dinner, the tables are set up as needed half an hour or more after coffee has been served. It is always best, when possible, to put the bridge players off by themselves in another room if at least half the guests prefer to talk. If space permits, the tables can be set up during dinner and placed in such a way that it doesn't seem essential for every guest to take part. It is quite possible for two or more guests not wishing to play to have a pleasant evening by themselves in a roomful of bridge addicts. But unlikely, I should say, and of course kibitzing is very dull indeed. The desire of the majority decides the evening, but non-participating guests should be helped by the hostess to do something they enjoy—to listen to the radio, read a book or the evening papers, play chess, or take a walk if they must stay to the end.

No one should play cards against his own desire or he will probably make a miserable partner. No hostess should worry about a guest who has named his preference for evening entertainment. I once had a non-bridge-playing friend who spent his evening with me in the kitchen learning how to make a delicate dessert soufflé, while his wife played bridge with an interest he couldn't even feign.

Setting Up Tables Bridge tables should not be covered during play. The surface should encourage the easy deal of the cards. Two packs of unused cards, or at least very fresh ones, should be on each table, with a score card and a well-sharpened pencil with an eraser. When luncheon or supper is to be served on the tables, the tables are then covered with square luncheon cloths, preferably in damask, cotton, or linen and as alike as possible and usually matching in color, although contrasting pastels might be attractive.

Behavior During the Game   My own feeling is that bridge is a game you should play well or not at all if the others are skilled players. You may be beautiful and witty, intelligent and glamorous, but if you sit down to a table of bridge with only a faint interest in and a hazier understanding of the game itself you make yourself worse than foolish. Very few people like to teach the game as they play. So if bridge is played much in your circle, go to a professional teacher and learn the latest methods. Read the bridge columns in your daily paper, and study a good book of modern rules. Don't let yourself be persuaded to sit in at a serious game whose progress your own inept playing will only hamper.

Not everyone, by any means, has a real feeling for cards. If you are one of those that no amount of teaching can improve, let it go. You will not be a social leper if you prefer to sit by and knit or read while the others really enjoy themselves. It is just as irritating to good players to have someone with poor card sense join them just to be agreeable as it is to an excellent tennis player to have a halfhearted one inflict himself on a game of doubles. You can't be too modest about your card playing. Always state frankly whether you are considered a good, middling, or poor player, and let the others decide whether to risk you. They, in turn, may very well suggest another game in which you may be more skillful. Certainly if you are to play any card game with a partner for stakes you are honor bound to explain your card status, even if *you* can afford to lose.

If you do play bridge, be attentive to your partner's signals and exercise judgment in taking bids away from him. Even if you are dummy, sit by quietly and pay attention to the play. Don't carry on constant chatter with the players at your table or with others in the room while you are playing.

Bridge seems to breed its own disagreeable mannerisms—the player who "takes all night" to make up his mind which card to play, the drummer-on-the-table, the slammer-down of the trick-taking card, the chair-teeterer, the whooper who takes loud pleasure in the opponent's defeat or discomfort. Then there is the historian who does an autopsy of every game, mainly to show how the others would have played their cards had they been he. Bridge is no different from other competitive games in that the rules of sportsmanship are the same—play quietly as well as you can, and win or lose without making your opponents feel uncomfortable.

Playing Cards for Money

A host or hostess planning to follow dinner with poker or bridge for money should say so when he or she issues the invitation. If a certain number of players are actually required and one guest, for reasons of his own, prefers not to play for money it can create an awkward situation.

Few of us like to admit, publicly, that we can't afford to gamble. We don't even like to admit that, if we play, a certain limit must be placed on the stakes. The danger, in that event, is always that as the heat of the game gets us we tend to permit a raising of the stakes with a possibly ruinous result. No one should enter any game of chance with the thought that he will win. He should, instead, face frankly the thought that he has an excellent chance to lose, and he must predicate his refusal or acceptance to play on that premise.

It is not good sportsmanship to agree to play for stakes that are possibly perilous to you and then be unable to pay off to the winner in the necessary, casual manner. Many people as a matter of principle always say, "We don't play for stakes," even when they can well afford to lose. If you are young people on a budget, play for stakes, if you enjoy the thrill, only if you are budgeted for the losses. Never anticipate the possible gains.

The Pay-off If you play for stakes, be prepared to pay off your losses then and there, preferably in cash. If you get beyond your depth and can't meet the obligation at the game's end, tell the winner when he may expect your check in full settlement. And don't make it necessary for him to remind you of your obligation. If you don't pay he can't go to law about the debt but he can ruin your reputation for decent sportsmanship so that others will be warned not to play for stakes with you again. The moral is always: *If you can't afford to lose, don't play for money.*

Chapter 37

ENTERTAINING OUT OF DOORS

Picnics on Your Own Grounds

There are picnics and picnics. There's the kind you may see at Southampton, with dowagers sitting gingerly under beach umbrellas, the food being served by their chauffeurs. On the other hand, a picnic to be a good one does not necessarily mean that sand be in your sandwich. But it is more fun done in a quite informal, albeit, comfortable style.

The picnic on your own grounds probably makes use of a barbecue. The equipment can be anything from a simple charcoal burner on wheels to a handsome barbecue with wrought-iron grills, an oven and a chimney to blessedly take away the smoke. Whatever it is, so long as it's fire you can depend on the men to enjoy tending it.

With outdoor cooking facilities it is easy and pleasant to entertain relatively large groups at home. But, as with buffet, it is important to have a comfortable place for guests to eat the food so appetizingly prepared within view. A round table is very friendly. Sometimes one can be built around a tree well to leeward of the fire. Or a long pine picnic table with benches is convenient. An old-fashioned heavy oak or walnut round table with extension leaves may, with luck, be found at a secondhand shop and rubbed down, painted, and waterproofed for an outdoors picnic table.

The adept-at-picnics hostess uses colorful, partitioned plastic picnic dishes or sturdy, waterproofed discardable paper plates, also partitioned. They hold foods safely and cut down table clutter by making it possible to put meat, vegetable, and salad attractively on one plate. And men, I think, are more comfortable with such a sturdy plate—plus a place to put it.

While the old stand-bys of hot dogs and hamburgers are perfectly acceptable at a picnic, guests are usually grateful, especially if it's a picnic supper, to be served something a little more substantial and partyish. There is nothing better, of course, if the budget permits, than charcoal-broiled steak and baked or fried potatoes (these with onions). Charcoal-broiled chicken is another favorite. Spareribs, southern style, may be prepared outdoors or in the kitchen. Like the chicken, they should be eaten "in the rough." Finger food including, of course, corn-on-the-cob is most enjoyable at picnics.

Picnics Away from Home

Automobile picnics—with the food eaten by the side of the road while the party is en route, or at some planned destination such as the beach— require special equipment. The confirmed picnicker usually invests in a hamper—the basket kind is light and long-lived—and equips it, or buys it equipped, with picnic "silver," plastic or aluminum plates and cups, a vacuum bottle or so, and a corkscrew and beer opener. Waterproofed paper bags for leftovers, paper napkins, and such are a wise precaution if there is no time to burn trash and then to see the fire well out. Don't be litterbugs!

The Art of Packing the Picnic Hamper   It's an art to pack a picnic hamper with the kind of food that makes the picnickers glad they didn't stay home. Cold fried chicken or little cold veal or ham pies, English style, make delicious out-of-hand eating. Chicken or potato salad in a glass jar combine easily at the picnic spot with crisp lettuce which has been brought separately in a damp towel and like the other foods mentioned are, to my mind, more palatable than a much-traveled sandwich. Warning here: any creamy salad or sandwich, anything mixed with egg or mayonnaise, transported to a picnic should be kept safely cold either in a vacuum container or ice packing. There are all sorts of good things that can be put in picnic jugs and served piping hot hours later— spaghetti with mushrooms and chicken livers, for instance, or baked beans or even thick fish chowder.

If you are going to a distant picnic ground, it is preferable to take food in vacuum jugs and bottles rather than to light a fire, unless specific camp sites have been set up in safe places. Or, if there are really able woodsmen in your party who can manage a camp fire so it doesn't smoke up the guests and ruin the food, be sure every spark is extinguished with water or loose dirt before you leave. And obliterate all signs of your presence so others may enjoy the woods or beach as you have.

Alfresco Meals

Eating outdoors in pleasant weather is a delightful and relaxing thing and, of course, needn't resemble a picnic in the least. Alfresco meals are merely less formal, even when they are served, with fewer courses and those substantial ones. A luncheon in the garden, with no picnic atmosphere at all, would be set out under the trees or on the terrace table on colorful mats or a luncheon cloth, with matching or contrasting napkins. A first course of tomato juice or vegetable juice cocktail, or a combination of either with clam juice, might be passed with crisp crackers before the guests are seated. Already arranged salads of chicken or lobster and tall glasses of iced tea could be in place before the guests take their places. The hostess or a servant clears this main course—perhaps onto a rolling tea table—and the dessert is served and passed by the hostess. Even where service is available, host and hostess function informally in serving their guests and servants are not kept constantly in attendance to spoil the rural effect.

Barbecues

In summer and in our warm climates the barbecue is one of the most popular forms of entertaining and one in which the men of the family shine. Barbecue equipment comes in all sizes and varieties, from the simple hibachi that can be used in a city one-room apartment to an elegant gas or charcoal barbecue for installation on a patio or in a large living kitchen for year-round use.

A barbecue is always informal. Paper plates and cups or durable plastics are sensible and attractive. Fingers come before forks and paper napkins should be in plentiful supply. As in any entertaining, don't try to manage more guests than you can comfortably serve. Keep the menu simple, the food plentiful, and in keeping with the method of preparation. Barbecues are hearty and masculine in feeling. Gelatin molds, ice cream, *bombes,* layer cakes don't belong here. Authoritative stews, chowders, thick steaks, shish kabobs, garlicky green salad, tomatoes eaten out of hand are among the appropriate offerings. In my cookbook, *Amy Vanderbilt's Complete Cookbook,* there is a section on barbecues that includes recipes that I've used myself many times—barbecued chickens (fine for a large group) and beef, corn cooked in its husk, ash-roasted potatoes, and other barbecue delights. Forget the cocktails and fancy hors d'oeuvres and settle for pretzels and cheese served with ice cold beer packed in a wheelbarrow full of cracked ice, along with Cokes and other soft drinks. Serve coffee in heavy mugs to keep it hot. Desserts should run to fresh fruit such as watermelon simply quartered or sliced to be eaten out of hand.

At a night barbecue two things are essential and romantic—firelight and group singing. And let us hope the site has been well mosquitoproofed.

Swimming Pools and Pool Parties

The families with swimming pools are getting to be almost as common as two-car families. The ownership of a swimming pool incurs certain obligations. Rules are vitally necessary to prevent accidents and to keep the pool from being a neighborhood nuisance. In many communities there are ordinances which properly require pools to be enclosed so that small children or wandering pets cannot fall in by error.

If you are building a pool, be sure that it is within sight of the house. An isolated pool invites accidents.

For Pool Safety: Keep the pool gate locked. Each user of the pool should be required to lock the gate whenever he leaves the area.

Do not swim alone. Do not permit children to swim in the pool unsupervised. The supervisor should be able to effect rescue if necessary. Do not permit your own children to swim in another's pool unless this safety law is followed.

Have life preservers or floats available at each pool. Require very young children who are not capable swimmers to stay at the shallow end of the pool and even then to wear life preservers, unless a strong swimmer is immediately available.

Prohibit roughhousing, running, or jumping near the pool. Do not allow sharp objects in or around it.

See to it that even strong swimmers among teen-agers always have supervision to prevent stunts that might cause accidents. Keep a sharp eye on the use of the slide and diving board, ruling out unorthodox use.

Avoid permitting very young children to swim with older ones, as accidents can happen in this way.

Don't let small children using floats or toys go beyond their depth.

Remember a small child can go under without having time to call for help. Watch for trouble.

Do not permit anyone who is under the influence of alcohol to use your pool. The same is true of anyone who is ill or overtired. You are responsible for keeping accidents from happening.

When you go away, cover the pool to keep it clean and to keep out uninvited guests. Cover it in winter for general safety. Keep it clean and chlorinated either by using a service or doing it yourself. A dirty pool is a menace.

For your own comfort and that of your neighbors, keep these things in mind.

If you are a new pool owner, you may tend to be too generous with the pool. Letting your friends and neighbors use it ad lib is a great mistake. Make it clear that the use of the pool is by invitation only, with the possible exception of some time convenient for yourself when the pool may be open to children of the neighborhood who must, of course, use it under proper supervision.

Require that guests help keep the pool area clean. Have them bring their own towels (and take them away) or if you wish to provide towels, require that the towels be put in the proper container after use. Make it clear that showers are required by children before they use the pool. (You may assume that an adult has bathed that day.)

Require that people in wet bathing suits remain in the pool area, not wear wet suits into the house.

See to it that the last persons using the pool remove any playthings or floats still in it, store chairs, etc., for the night and generally restore order.

Be sure that children using the pool are doing so on your invitation. Do not permit them to bring unknown children whose parents may not know where they are. You are responsible for such children even if they wander in uninvited. The law says you are maintaining an "attractive nuisance."

If you are having a pool party, tell your neighbors about your plan so that they may be forewarned. On ordinary occasions insist on keeping the noise around the pool at a minimum if you are close to other houses.

Do not permit family or guests to swim at night unless your pool is well lighted and a strong swimmer is present—and sober. Never let any-one swim alone at night, no matter how competent he is. Many drownings have taken place in this way.

Don't start building a pool with all the attendant noise and mess without forewarning your neighbors. Give them, if possible, some idea of when the pool will be completed. Try in every way to make up to them for any possible inconvenience.

Do not open your pool in any season without being certain that your liability insurance is in full effect. Owning a pool creates hazards, even (or perhaps I should say especially) the uninvited pose legal problems in case of accidents.

Chapter 38

HOSTS AND GUESTS

Who Invites Whom

Whenever a couple is entertaining together, it is the hostess who issues invitations and accepts them. She is, in effect, the family's social secretary. If her husband, under informal circumstances, should receive an invitation for the couple, he must always say something such as, "I'll have Mary call you about this" or, if it is a telephone call, "Will you speak to Mary?" This is not only a courtesy to the wife, but it prevents confusion in the matter of invitations.

In issuing invitations to someone you have met in another person's house, you must include your host and hostess in the first invitation to the people you met there. Of course if the host and hostess decline, you are free to ask their former guests alone, but explain that you did invite the couple who introduced you.

Last-Minute Guest No one should consider a last-minute invitation an insult. True, in some cases they need to be very carefully handled. A hostess who is giving a dinner party for eight, only to have one guest drop out, should ask a replacement with great care, being perfectly frank to say why the invitation is coming at the last minute and it should be asked of a trusted friend, not a stranger. A neighbor or close friend should not feel diffident about offering last-minute invitations. It is a pleasant thing at the end of a long day to find that you have plenty of food and energy to entertain a guest or two who may well feel equally delighted to put aside dinner plans and join you. This kind of spontaneous entertainment is much more attractive than the planned kind.

Arrivals and Departures

The time at which one arrives at a dinner party differs in various parts of the country. A man escorting a woman to dinner needs to discuss with her what time he will call for her in order to get her to the dinner party within the permissible period of "on timeness." In New York City this means fifteen minutes to half an hour beyond the time given in the invitation. Anything later than that requires an excuse. Being exactly on time or a little before the hour usually proves embarrassing, with guests likely to say, "Oh, are we the first?" Every guest tries to avoid this. In Washington in diplomatic circles, the time appointed is the time to arrive, not five minutes before and not five minutes after. In other parts of the country, most frequently the time given in the invitation is the time the guests are expected to arrive, allowing five or ten minutes. I have found in some places in the Midwest, in small towns, the time of the party actually means the time when dinner will be served and guests arrive as much as half an hour before the appointed time. When in doubt, ask.

The street door is opened to guests by some designated member of the family. At a dinner party, for example, in a one-servant family it is unlikely that the servant can attend the door as well as serve and prepare the meal.

Whoever opens the door takes the guest's coat and hat and leads the way to the living room, stepping back to let him enter. The hostess excuses herself to any guest she may be with, rises, and comes forward to greet the guest, man or woman. The host comes forward, too, and both host and hostess shake hands with the newcomer. This same little ceremony is repeated when the guest departs.

Often there is an awkward pause in conversation when a new person is introduced into the group. Large-scale introductions in which the possibly already somewhat self-conscious stranger is introduced to many people all at once, and vice versa, should be avoided. Instead, when there are more than five or six present, introduce the new guests only to those in his immediate vicinity, after host or hostess have greeted him. From there on as he moves about he introduces himself to those he hasn't yet met, or someone to whom he's been talking takes him in hand and presents him to others he may find congenial.

Seeing the Guest Off   Whether a servant or the host or some other member of the family sees a guest to the door, the door is never closed until the guest is actually under way, on foot or by car. In apartment houses a servant or the host summons the elevator and waits until the guest has entered it before closing the apartment door. If the elevator is a self-service one, he pushes the ground-floor button after the guest has entered. Where there is no doorman, of course, the host or servant sees the guest into a taxi or asks other departing male guests, in the case of a woman, to extend this courtesy. If a taxi is needed, host or servant phones the doorman as the guest prepares to go or asks the elevator operator to see that the guest is taken care of.

Where There Is No Host   A single woman entertaining alone without servants delegates the role of host to some male guest—a relative or close friend—at a party, or if it is a party of women and there is no servant to greet guests at the door a friend may be asked to do so, so that the hostess will not have to leave her guests every few minutes at a large party to go to the door. The friend, if he or she doesn't know the guest, introduces him or herself and leads the way to the living room. Or if many guests are arriving all at once, the person at the door indicates where coats are to be left and guests, when ready, find their own way to the living room and greet the hostess before joining any friends who may be present.

Should a Guest Be Called For? If a guest is coming for a visit to the country and the hostess knows the time of his expected arrival but has said nothing about meeting the train or bus, then the guest is expected to get to the hostess's home by any available public transportation. The guest does not phone and ask to be met unless some transportation breakdown or great delay has occurred.

A guest, already resident in the country where transportation is necessarily by car, doesn't ask to be called for unless every conceivable way of getting himself to the hostess's house has failed. If transportation is really a difficulty, the matter should be mentioned at the time the invitation is tendered, and the hostess may then suggest that the guest be picked up, either by someone else coming by or by the hostess's own car. Or she has the opportunity of withdrawing the invitation under the circumstances. Certainly the guest who must be picked up and returned by the hostess must be very attractive indeed to justify the inconvenience, if it really is one.

The Extra Woman

While an extra man is a boon to a hostess, an extra woman can be either a problem or make a problem for herself. It is considerate of a hostess inviting an extra woman to a cocktail party to give her permission to bring a man or to suggest that she come with another guest or guests invited, and this may be a couple or even another woman. It is dreary for a woman alone to arrive at a cocktail party which has started on its merry way, particularly if she knows few, if any, there. The lone woman departing from a cocktail party needs the hostess's consideration, too. Someone—the host, another member of the family, a departing couple, or single man—should see that she either gets a taxi or is safely in her own car if she is driving. The woman who must, or who prefers to, arrive alone should have a fictitious reason to leave early if pairing—so usual at cocktail parties—seems unlikely in her case. Sad, indeed, is the lone woman who stays at a cocktail party to the bitter end, hoping some interesting male will turn up, only to depart well past the dinner hour obviously dateless.

The problem of the lone woman at dinner parties is much simpler. The dinner party hostess usually does arrange for an equal number of men and women and even perhaps for an extra man or two. Especially if country driving is concerned, it is of course more gracious for the hostess to arrange to have either a couple or one of her men guests pick up the lone woman, if this is at all possible, especially if driving conditions are bad and the guest might have to drive herself perhaps in evening dress. At the close of the evening, the hostess sees to it that such a woman guest has an escort home, if only with another couple. A woman who drives herself to such a party and drives home herself should be asked by the hostess to phone upon her arrival home.

Acting Host for a Bachelor Girl

The man, other than a relative, who is asked to take on some of the responsibilities of host at the home of an eligible woman may open the door to guests and see them off, fetch chairs, mix drinks, help serve, and clear dishes where there are no servants and, in general, help make the guests comfortable. If he does seem very much an intimate of the household in this way, there is, possibly, some speculation concerning his exact relationship to the hostess. To allay such speculation, a bachelor girl may designate more than one "acting host" from among her men friends. But if only one serves, he is careful to leave with the last guest if it is late in the evening. Even if the relationship between "host" and hostess is quite intimate, a gentleman must always go to elaborate lengths to avoid anything that might appear to be compromising. Even an announced engagement doesn't free him of this obligation.

The Host's Seat

There is an unwritten law that no guest ever preempts the host's seat either at the dining table (which would be very unlikely indeed) or in the living room or library. There is usually one seat that has the look of the host about it. Being displaced from his accepted seat makes any host uneasy, may even bring out a feeling of hostility toward the guest, male or female, who preempts it. A careful guest about to sit down, and in some doubt as to which chair is the host's, asks, "Is this your chair?" The host may say something like, "Oh, it's all right, take it." But the wise guest takes another.

In the dining room the hostess's chair is inviolate. It is usually, and most practically, the one nearest to the kitchen door, but as she seats her guests, it is unlikely that someone might seize her position of authority.

How a Guest Takes Leave

It is never necessary to make elaborate and lengthy excuses for leaving a party. A reluctance to leave should always be shown by one's manner or words, of course, no matter what kind of time you've had. One may say, seeking out the hostess first, "I'm so sorry but I must leave now. It has been such a pleasant evening." If it is still a reasonable hour, your hostess will probably reply, "Oh, can't you stay a little longer? We hate to have you go!" If you really wish to stay after such urging, do so, but you are under no obligation to and may, instead, gently and at least seemingly reluctantly go on your way, again without meticulous explanations. Even if other guests seem entrenched for the night, your hostess may be silently blessing you for your good sense in leaving at a reasonable hour.

When a man guest wishes to leave early he excuses himself to the group in which he finds himself without stating his intention of leaving and, going quietly to the hostess, makes his farewell. If saying farewell to his busy host might break up the party, he may say, "Do say 'good night' to Fred for me" to his hostess. He then is shown out to the street door by a member of the staff or some member of the family. If he is an intimate of the family, he will probably see himself off. The hostess will go with him at least to the door of the living room.

An early-departing woman guest leaves in the same tactful fashion, except that the host or some male member of the family must be summoned by the hostess to see her to her car or to a taxi if there is no servant to take her in hand after the hostess has escorted her to the living room door.

The guest of honor, if he or she cannot stay through the duration of a party or function, makes this clear to the hostess, "I'll have to leave by eleven to catch a plane." The presence of the guest of honor used to mean that the guests could not leave until the guest of honor did so, and under important diplomatic circumstances, this rule is adhered to if at all possible. At public banquets, for example, even when the President is a guest of honor, however, people do slip quietly away before his departure if they must, although they would not leave early from a private dinner before the President.

A departing guest leaving before the guest of honor excuses himself to his hostess and if possible bids farewell to the guest of honor and the host very quietly. An important guest of honor surrounded by people would, of course, not be interrupted while one departing guest slips away early. The hostess might say afterward to the guest of honor if it seems necessary, "Mrs. Patterson has a long drive home tonight so she left early and said how much she had enjoyed meeting you and hopes to see you again." At the normal departure time, when guests show indications of leaving, the hostess and the guest of honor stand attentively, ready to bid the guests good-by. The host is in evidence, too, as much as possible in the midst of his various duties of seeing people off.

Thank-you Notes

In the deep South I find that a thank-you note after a dinner party is mandatory in some communities and some Southern hostesses are offended if they don't receive thank-you notes for cocktail parties. In other sections of the country the host and hostess are thanked as the guest takes leave. It is a courteous gesture to call the next day or within a day or two and very briefly repeat one's thanks. However, a word of caution. If the dinner party was a particularly large one, the busy housewife may be driven to distraction accepting a barrage of telephone calls. In this case a brief thank-you note is a much better idea than a telephone call. Of course if the party was for you, then you, as the guest of honor, *must* write a thank-you note.

Thank-you notes of any kind should be written as soon as possible while spontaneous words still come easily. A thank-you note written many days or weeks after the fact, seems cold and unappreciative no matter how it is couched.

Problem Guests—Do's and Don'ts

The Self-invited Guest How much responsibility does a hostess have toward a self-invited guest, one who drops in without warning at mealtime —other than at teatime, which is traditionally open house? Aside from exercising her usual courtesy, the hostess has no definite obligation toward such a guest. She may invite him to stay to the meal, or she may quite unembarrassedly not do so if it is inconvenient. If he or she shows no sign of going, she says, "I do hope you will excuse us. Our dinner is ready. We're busy this evening or I'd ask you to join us. But perhaps some other . . ." If she gives in, time and time again, to these thoughtless people who arrive, I am sure by intent, at mealtime, she might as well open a boardinghouse. Of course, there is always the exception—the quite intimate friend who feels free to invite himself or herself occasionally. Life would be dull if all meetings were strictly by appointment.

Taking Strangers to Your Friends' Homes Another deplorable habit is that of taking your own guest—or more often several ill-assorted guests—to a neighbor's home in the evening or at cocktail time without even so much as an advance warning. Your guests may be charming people, but your neighbor may have a headache and wish fervently for an evening to himself in the bosom of his family. If you turn up with your crew and he is obviously without the slightest excuse to escape you, you have done a thoughtless thing. You probably won't even think to offer to leave after twenty minutes or so but will make yourself at home by his fireside and with his best scotch, no doubt, till far beyond what he hoped would be his bedtime.

Under such circumstances and with a frequent offender, it is certainly justified for the host or hostess to take aside the ringleader in this assault on their privacy and say something like this, "It was nice of you to bring the Snodgrasses over, but Joe (or Mary) has had a hard day today and there are a couple of things we want to go over this evening before I get him (or her) to bed. I know you understand and do let us *know* [hint!] when the Snodgrasses visit you again and perhaps we can plan a little something."

Try to train your friends to call you before dropping in, without or with friends. If they wish to bring friends, they should explain who they are. Many a difficult situation could be avoided if we could ward off uncongenial people in time.

Suppose Bill Adams next door calls (because you've trained him to do so) and says, "Say, Mary, my cousins, the Mears from Philadelphia, are here for the weekend. I'm desperate. You know what they're like. May I bring them over and we could listen to some of your long-haired music? That will interest them." You can always say you're busy (no explanation required), and how about taking the Mears for a brisk walk or to the movies. Given advance notice, you are not required to receive anyone in your home you do not wish to see. If they arrive unannounced, you can dispose of them in any tactful way after twenty minutes or so by treating them as formal callers.

Inviting a Guest to Another's Party There is practically no excuse for breaking an engagement for a formal dinner party—not even the sudden arrival of your favorite aunt. Extra women, even attractive and relatively young ones, are anathema to the hostess who has slaved over getting a man for every woman invited to her dinner. But even a decrepit "extra" male may be very welcome to her, so give her a chance to reject or accept him, but, in either case, go yourself even if your guest has to spend the evening at your home playing cribbage. If he has any upbringing he knows all about the sacredness of such an engagement, arranged a good two weeks, usually, in advance.

It is less heinous to ask to have your house guest included in a cocktail party, a buffet meal, or an informal dinner, unless you have observed your hostess's home to be small and ill-staffed or running under her power alone. Sometimes just one extra guest, especially one with nothing in common with the others, can put a drag on the best-planned little party.

If, when you are invited, you know you will have a house guest, give the hostess a chance to invite you some other time, instead. Say, "Laura, I'd like to so much, but that week Aunt Belle will be with me and I'm not at all sure she'd fit in." Any hostess with aplomb knows just what to do with that opening. Let's hope she means what she says, either way. There is little that makes a hostess more ill at ease than the presence of a guest she would have preferred not to include. And the guest suffers, too.

The Guests Who Won't Go We all know the sitters. They are the ones who want a nightcap after all sensible people have indicated a desire to call it a day. If it's Saturday night with no workday ahead for father, there's little hope. But there is one thing a host can do. He can rather pointedly not join them in that one more drink. This ought to make them drink up fast— but I don't guarantee it.

If the guests really are impervious to all delicate hints, such as the gathering up of used glasses and ash trays and the host's reluctance to put another log on the fire, the hostess can always say, "Joe's been working pretty hard lately and I (or the doctor) want(s) him to get plenty of sleep weekends. So let's send him to bed now." The inference being that she'll stick it out on the sofa if it takes all night.

There are inveterate talkers and serious drinkers who won't even notice old Joe's departure but, usually, this technique works. The one unbreakable rule is that the hostess must stay, even though the host, as breadwinner presumably, may be excused after a decent interval. The only exception is when the guests are house guests. If, as I have mentioned elsewhere, they are intimate friends, they may stay on in the living room, talking or listening to music or playing cards, after their hosts have retired at a relatively early hour. But they should not make so much noise as to keep the rest of the household awake. Other than intimate friends or relatives take the host's or hostess's lead concerning bedtime.

The Guest with a Dragnet   We are all acquainted with the guest who no sooner arrives than he's on the telephone making contact with all his friends in the area. While this is permissible within reason, if the guest is from a distant point, his attention should be directed to his host and hostess and the plans they have for him. He may not invite other friends to call upon him at his host's home. He may tactfully mention that he knows someone in the vicinity, and if the hostess makes the suggestion herself that the friends be invited for some time during his stay, she may invite his friends herself, by phone. The guest may speak to them first, then introduce his hostess who extends the invitation.

Under certain circumstances a guest may be asked to be excused to make a brief call in the neighborhood, but he should not involve his hosts in it nor ask for transportation. Host and hostess are on duty in their own home while entertaining and should not be asked to chauffeur their guests on various personal errands.

Again because a guest must focus his attention on his hosts, he may not ask any friends in the vicinity to invite him, with his hosts, to their home. An exception might be someone whom his hosts have expressed a real desire to meet or whose gardens they would greatly enjoy, for example. A guest then might ask permission to call with his hosts. Or if his hosts are new in the neighborhood and are really anxious to meet neighbors with whom he is well acquainted, the guest could ask his friends to call upon him at his hosts', if he feels he will be promoting a mutually attractive future association. The thing to avoid is any suggestion that what his hosts have to offer in the way of entertainment is meager compared with what he could have at any number of nearby friends' and why not just join up with the friends and have a really good time?

Problem Drinkers   Many of us number among our friends a certain number of problem drinkers of whom we may be fond but who are difficult and often unpleasant to entertain at home. Where others stop after a social drink or two before dinner or in the evening, these people who have the alcohol habit to a dangerous degree go right on drinking. How far can a host or hostess go in an effort to control the situation?

In discussing this all too common problem with some of my wisest friends,

I found that the best course seems to be to consider the problem drinker among one's guests right from the start. Bring a cocktail shaker into the living room or out onto the terrace before dinner with just enough for two drinks for everyone or pass a tray of highballs you have prepared at the bar or in the kitchen. Do not place bottles and soda so guests can mix their own. After dinner, optionally, again pass one highball or possibly two, then lock the liquor cabinet and say nothing whatsoever about the possibility of any more alcoholic refreshment. The moderate drinker rarely will take more than one highball after dinner, if any. The immoderate drinker must not be allowed to ruin the evening for everyone else.

This procedure I have outlined does not, of course, attempt in any way to reform the uncontrolled drinker, who has probably arrived sufficiently "fortified" so that even these rationed drinks take considerable effect.

Should others present voluntarily forget alcohol to save the problem drinker from himself? I think not. But at the same time no one should urge alcohol on someone who is trying to stay within reasonable limits.

The most agreeable solution, naturally, would be to omit from our guest list anyone who is a problem drinker. But, as this is rarely possible for business or family reasons, the only thing we can do, as hosts and hostesses, is to keep a sharp eye on the source of supply, keep track of each round, and lock up all alcohol, including wine and beer, after a reasonable amount has been dispensed.

The Obnoxious Guest The hostess with any experience avoids asking a guest who might well turn out to be a thorn in the side to other guests present. If it is necessary to entertain such a burr, she restricts others present to her immediate family, whose reaction she hopes she can control with signals. She does not take a chance of fitting such an unpredictable guest—if she knows about him or her—into an otherwise intelligently assembled group.

When it does happen that a hostess finds she has erred in asking someone highly and unamusingly contentious to a party, she and the host must spend the evening trying to keep the conversation away from explosive topics—explosive to the particular guest. If he gets under way, and others are growing angry or hurt, the host or hostess breaks in with, "Perhaps we'd better continue this some other time," and then attempts a diverting technique. Best of all is to give the arguer something to do. If you have a game room, get someone to take him on at table tennis. Or take him for a brisk tour of your grounds, ostensibly to show him something, but really to get him to work off his aggression physically. If this can't be done, get the troublemaker into a card game or get him to show off some specialty of his, magic or card tricks, piano playing or tap dancing. A man or woman who feels mean and aggressive in company can often be brought pleasantly into the group by being permitted to shine in some acceptable way. A clever hostess can say in the midst of a heated argument, "Joe, we can't all follow you in debate, but I know *I'm* dying to hear you beat out some rock music." He takes this much better than other methods of shutting him up, because, interrupted in the midst of an argument, he can save face by immediately doing something to attract favorable attention.

Making Your Overnight Guest Feel at Home

City apartments and suburban homes are growing ever smaller. Perhaps in time there will be no such thing as the overnight guest. As it is now, it's a rare house that has a guest room. If the guest gets a room to himself at all, it is usually a room ordinarily devoted to sister Susie or to mother's sewing and mending. Never planned for a guest's comfort, it seems geared to send him on his way in despair first thing in the morning.

The Extra Touches That Count Wherever you tuck him or her, be sure your overnight or weekend guest has the following:

Night clothes, including bathrobe and slippers
Face towel, wash cloth, bath towel, soap
Razor, shaving cream, clean brush and comb, deodorant
Adequate bedclothes—more than adequate if there's any doubt
A bed light for reading
Current magazines, a mystery, or any preferred bedtime reading
Facial tissues, cold cream, toothbrush and toothpaste
Enough pillows to permit reading in bed
Ash trays, though put your foot down about in-bed smoking
Hangers for clothes, including trouser-skirt hangers
A bedtime snack—offer it anyhow but a dish of fruit, a plate, knife, and a paper napkin add cheer on a bed table, and a hot drink—bouillon or hot milk (the guest may prefer it skimmed)—in a vacuum bottle is a thoughtful addition.

The Well-appointed Guest Room If you can set yourself up a permanent guest room and do not have to tuck the guest into the pull-out couch in the library or on the sun porch, here are some additional desirable attractions:

A full-length mirror with a make-up mirror, attached or separate, that shows the sides of the face
Free drawer space, enough of it so a weekend guest needn't dress from his bags
Shoe racks and trees, hat boxes or stands, clothes brush, spot remover, sewing kit
Manicure equipment
A well-equipped shoe-cleaning box
Radio, possibly a portable TV
Writing equipment of all kinds, including post cards (stamped)

Hamper or laundry bag
Drop-down ironing board and folding iron
Luggage rack and bed tray
Aspirin, milk of magnesia, Q-tips
"Don't disturb" sign
An electric hot pad or hot water bottle
Scrap basket

Beds for Guests   Never assume that a couple who are your guests would prefer twin beds to a double bed or vice versa. In planning a guest room from scratch it is probably more sensible to choose twin beds, preferably the kind with a double headboard so that couples used to the security of sleeping in one bed won't feel isolated in twin guest beds. It is thoughtful, if you have only a double bed for guests, to ask a couple if they would prefer single sleeping arrangements—if you can shift things around and provide them. Many couples, unused to sleeping on one bed, no matter how commodious it may be, spend sleepless nights when so forced to share a bed together.

Turning Down Beds   In a well-staffed household it is the duty of the chambermaid to turn down beds for the night. If a party is in progress and the guest room or the master bedroom is to be used as a cloak room, it looks better to delay the removal of the spread and the turning back of the covers until after the party is over. Then, if the servants have retired, the hostess should prepare the guest's bed for the night, although under the circumstances a thoughtful guest will attend to the matter himself or herself but, please, according to Hoyle.

A double bed which is to be occupied by one person has the spread removed or neatly folded lengthwise at the foot of the bed if it is very light and won't be a weight on the feet. If it is removed, it is not tossed on a chair but is folded neatly to preserve its freshness and to keep the room restfully in order. The top sheet, which should extend as much as twelve inches over the tops of the blankets, is turned, with the blankets, in a right angle with the center of the bed forming the perpendicular side of the resulting triangle. This turn-back should be on the side from which the guest is expected to enter the bed. If two people will occupy the double bed, turn back the other side the same way, on the other side of the bed, so that you now have two right-angled triangles with the center of the bed a common side. This makes a neater effect than does the more usual method of simply turning back the coverings half way down the whole bed.

The pillows, which have been pressed into a roll under the bedspread, should be plumped up and resettled on the bed with the borders to the outside edges of the bed, seams toward the center. If a bolster has been used, it should be removed and sleeping pillows substituted. If you have a closet or chest in which to place unneeded bedding for the night, you will help create a restful atmosphere by getting the bolster out of sight. If you use a day bed, try to create space in drawers, closets, or built-in ends to house the box spread and the cushions, so that they may be kept out of sight during the time the bed is used for sleeping.

If You Live in the Real Country Country living often has specific problems that should be promptly explained to guests—aside from the matter of transportation.

If your hot water supply is limited, for example, it is important to explain that to a weekend guest so he won't waste water by taking overly prolonged showers or letting the water run while shaving, for example, as he might in the city.

If you have a septic tank or cesspool, you need to explain that insolubles such as facial tissues and cotton should not be thrown into the toilet bowl but should be placed in the bag-lined wastepaper basket you have provided in each bathroom. If the guest is going to help around the house during his or her stay, explain that with such plumbing facilities a minimum of such household aids as ammonia and chlorine must be put down the drains because they inhibit the necessary growth of bacteria in the tank, bacteria which in turn consume the waste and make it unnecessary to have a septic tank cleaned out more than every few years—and that's an expensive process.

If you are turning a country house (or even your city home) over to a guest or guests, even for so short a time as overnight, don't imagine he will know exactly what to do in the event of an emergency. Suppose there is a power failure, or the telephone wires go down in a storm, or the furnace goes out, or the oil burner breaks down? What if he needs a doctor or the police or the firemen? At all times, every home should have prominently placed near a telephone the following information to aid family, servants, and possible guests in-charge in case of an emergency.

Instructions in Case of Emergency

Fire: Pick up phone. Say "I want to report a fire." (Or use the firehouse number, if given.) You will be connected with the nearest firehouse. Give your name, the exact address—floor and apartment number, if any—and the nature of the fire, general, localized, stove, or whatever the origin may be, if you can determine it. The fire department may be able to instruct you on what is to be done until they get there.

If there is no phone available, run to the nearest fire alarm (explain its location). Pull it and *stay* there, or have someone else do so, to give the firemen the address when they arrive.

Fire Extinguishers: Explain their location in your home and how to, use and on what kind of fire to use specific ones.

Police: Pick up phone and say "I want the police." Speak to the desk sergeant.

Doctor: List your various doctors—pediatrician, if any, general practitioner, your dentist, and your veterinarian if you have pets—with their addresses and telephone numbers.

Plumber:[1] List name and phone

Electrician:[1] List name and phone

Repair Man:[1] List name and phone

Laundry: List name, address, and phone

Dry Cleaners: List name, address, and phone

Tailor: List name, address, and phone

Beauty Parlor: List name, address, and phone

Household Employment Agency: List name, address, and phone

Drug Store: List name, address, and phone

Liquor Store: List name, address, and phone

Names of People to Call in an Emergency: Explain who they are

Husband's Business Address and Number

Wife's Business Address and Number if any

School Address and Number

Fuse Box: Give location in house and place where extra fuses are kept. At the box itself, have a diagram of what fuses serve what rooms and utilities. Instruct servants and members of the family on how to change fuses. It is frequently impossible—and certainly unnecessary—to summon an electrician to perform so simple a service. If you have a circuit breaker explain how it works.

The Weekend Guest

Invitation and Reply for a Weekend Visit In extending a weekend invitation it is very necessary to be specific about the date, the time you are expecting the people to arrive, and whether or not you will be able to meet them if that is necessary. In replying to a weekend invitation it's a good idea to mention both the time and date of your arrival so that no misunderstanding is possible.

August 3rd

Dear Nell,

Will you, John, and the children spend the weekend of the 21st with us? There's a train that leaves town at 12:30 which we plan to meet. A convenient one going back that others will be getting leaves at 11:30 P.M. on Sunday and we will get you to the train of course. We'd be so happy to have you.

Love,
Molly

---

[1] If your city home has a superintendent he may be in charge of these matters. If so, list his name and apartment number.

August 5

Dear Molly,

We'd love it. Count on us on the 12:30 on the 21st complete with children.

As ever,
Nell

Let's take the country hostess, in this case, who plans to have guests for the weekend. Unless she runs the equivalent of a hotel, it is vital that she know long before the weekend just who is coming and when, so she may apportion her beds and plan the entertainment. If everyone says airily, "Oh, I'll call you Saturday morning," or "Let's see what the weather's like— maybe we'll be out," she may be left high and dry with one lonely bachelor and a large leg of lamb on her hands or she may be flooded with guests— because of the sunshine—and have to make one small chicken do for Sunday dinner. In the real country there is no such thing as a delicatessen open twenty-four hours a day and not everyone has a freezer, especially not people who, themselves, go to the country only on weekends. So, then, the first requisite of the guest is that he respond to his invitation promptly and permanently and be specific as to when he'll arrive. To accept and then later turn down an invitation to the country because of a cloudy sky is to belittle your hostess's ability to entertain you, no matter what the weather. Or it shows that you are more interested in the terrain than the people.

Arrival and Departure   The hostess herself should suggest the time of the guests' arrival and any guest or guests who can't make the train or bus indicated should at least offer to get themselves from the station to the hostess's house by cab. Otherwise the host, hostess, or, if he exists, the chauffeur may have to make countless trips to the station where one would have done. For the same reason, the hostess, who is herself run by the railroad's timetable if she's a country dweller, can certainly suggest the time of the guests' departure so that all can make the same train in something less than breakneck speed. Any guest who drives himself to the country weekend and removes himself the same way is doubly blest if he offers to bring and return other guests from his own bailiwick.

Gifts to the Hostess   If you are a frequent guest at a home, you are not expected to take a gift to the hostess each time, but on the first visit for a weekend it is thoughtful to do so. And throughout the year, if you go often, take an occasional gift. This gift need never be elaborate or expensive. In fact, if it is obviously beyond your means it will embarrass everyone. Many women are pleased if you take some small gift to the children rather than to them. Children are so often pushed aside by all the grownups on weekends this little sop to their presence is helpful—maybe a box of lollipops, a book, modeling clay, a game, or a soap bubble set.

Men, in particular, seem to be at a loss as to what constitutes a suitable gift to a weekend hostess. Taking her flowers is often like carrying coals to Newcastle, but if she has a collection of house plants she will always be pleased to have one more. African violets, geraniums, especially the rarer ones such as rose or lemon, begonias, that charming little plant, the pick-a-back (that should always be watered from the saucer beneath it, like all fuzzy-leafed ones), or a hydrangea are all welcome. An original gift in the early fall is a dozen or so tulip or narcissus bulbs. Go to a good seed store and buy the best varieties and be sure you know the color so she can plan her border accordingly. You may not know a daisy from a cactus, but you can get all kinds of agreeable information on gifts suitable for your country hostess, if you will describe her garden to the man at that florist shop, greenhouse or seed store. At the moment I can think of nothing nicer than a spring weekend guest arriving with a few pansy plants to set out in the annual border. They wouldn't cost as much as the usual fancy box of chocolates and would give pleasure for weeks to come. There are estates you might visit, however, that have their own greenhouses, and their own corps of gardeners might think you presumptuous if you turned up with a box or two of pansies and might let them wither, out of sheer spite, behind the carriage house.

Thinking up a gift for such a hostess, for one who seems to have every material thing, is always challenging. There's little use just buying something *expensive*. Anything you might think of she probably has. In such a case, I usually fall back on gourmet foods, things like imported English ginger beer, a smoked turkey, Stilton in port, or a brace of partridge. For some reason, people who have all the money in the world to buy any food they wish esteem such rare and relatively expensive specialties. A hostess may have a famous cellar but she will love you extra well if you turn up with a dusty bottle of fine champagne or one of Lacrima Christi.

In every well-appointed household things are always wearing out or getting broken. If you're an observant person, note well what a house needs if you are a frequent visitor. Perhaps the bar could stand a more efficient bottle opener or corkscrew—in fact, extra ones are received with joy in most homes. If the summer season is coming on, maybe a dozen or even half a dozen commodious beer glasses will anticipate eventual breakage of those in current use. Maybe the place could use a little bird house or a bird feeding station, some large ash trays, pretty aprons—who ever has enough?— a poultry shears (for the host's convenience in carving—especially duck), or some cocktail napkins. Gay books of matches in quantity, and with the covers initialed or not, fit in anywhere. Some of the things you can get in stationery departments make pleasant gifts—memo pads for the kitchen or the telephone stand, office-style pencil sharpeners (wonderful for a boy's room or a study), those lovely Swiss, floral post cards or thank-you notes, paints and crayons for the children or their art-yearning elders. Gifts of books are good if you are sure of your hostess's reading taste. The latest novel, chosen for its hot-off-the-griddle quality and nothing else, may just offend her sensibilities. A non-fiction book on some subject that interests you may bore her. If she's an enthusiastic cook, she can never get enough cookbooks. If she gardens, the newest gardening book will always interest her. If she loves music, a symphony she doesn't already own or some unusual records—European or South American imports—or new pressings of Caruso may be fine.

Think twice before you take your hostess something that will just clutter up her house and which, because of your frequent presence, she won't be able to tuck away or, in desperation, discard. Many of these white elephants grow in gift shoppes. Be careful in choosing pictures or actual furnishings for another's house—in fact, I wouldn't do it unless I had the hostess with me.

The bathroom suggests many suitable little gifts—big, fragrant cakes of bath soap to a friend you know very well, luxurious little guest cakes of soap (I remember some shaped like succulent strawberries that once delighted me in someone's powder room), bath salts, if they are not from the bargain counter in a drug store but are, too, in the luxury class, bath cologne, bath oil, bubble bath, or a pair of hand-embroidered guest towels in a color that will blend with the bathroom's color scheme or in good, safe white linen or practical terry.

A thank-you gift may be sent, of course, after your visit. It is sent either to the hostess or jointly to the husband and wife, but separate gifts to husband and wife are never sent except by a very intimate acquaintance if the sender is a woman.

If you are a guest in the country you can give yourself instead of a money-costing gift and be blessed for the thought. You can arrive with the news that you would like to rake the leaves, help build the rock garden, mow the lawn, or clear the brush—if you know any of these activities are on the calendar. In a help-short household you can offer to get a meal if your talents lie in that direction, paint a boat, take the children on a picnic, do odd jobs around the house, or wash the car—all this, of course, if you know your host and hostess well enough to take official notice that these things are in need of being done if someone just had the time to do them. I don't mean to suggest that you should imply in any way that the lawn's a mess, the meals terrible, the children underfoot, the house and its accouterments falling apart from lack of attention, all of which may be quite true.

Whenever you offer to do any such personal things, you must do so with great diplomacy, giving the idea, if possible, that the suggestion that the things should be done by someone came from the hostess or host themselves. For instance, if you're a woman—or one of those rare males who can get a good meal without wrecking the kitchen and calling for a score of helpers—say something like this, "I think you said Ida would be off Sunday afternoon. Let me get Sunday night's supper, won't you? I've found out where I can get some good clams for a chowder." If you want to put on an epicurean feast that will make more work for the hostess in the getting of ingredients she doesn't already have in the house, your offer may not be received in too grateful a spirit unless you fetch the missing things yourself.

What Clothes to Take   The good guest arrives on time and knows, or quickly finds out, when he should leave. If he doesn't know the customs of the household and neighborhood he's visiting, he should find out in advance what wardrobe is expected of him. Find out if you are to dress for dinner, if you will need tennis, golf, riding, or swimming outfits. It is sometimes possible for a hostess to equip a guest for these various activities out of the family wardrobe and game closet, but she prefers to have you come equipped with your own things.

The size of the house and the bank account of your host are no indication at all of how his family entertains in the country. On some large estates the entertainment may be quite formal, with dinner jackets and dinner dresses the expected thing every evening except Sunday. On the other hand, taking a cue from the host and hostess, the guests may wear sports clothes all day and continue to wear them at dinner, fresh clothes preferred, of course, but still sports clothes—sweaters and skirts or slacks of flannel, wool, silk, gabardine, or cotton sports dresses for the women, slacks or even Bermuda shorts and sports jackets for the men. It is not "correct" to sit down at many tables in the evening in such informal attire, but in many, even elaborate, country homes it is an accepted and comfortable custom. Never be embarrassed to ask your hostess what you are expected to wear for dinner.

But how do you find out what to bring? You ask your hostess or your host by phone or by note when you accept the invitation, "Will I need my dinner jacket?" or, for a woman, "Should I bring a short or long evening dress or will I need a cocktail dress? What are you planning for us—shall I bring along my tennis racket, my swimming or riding things?" When, for some reason, it isn't possible to ascertain these things in advance it is better to be safe than sorry—pack dinner clothes, take your tennis racket or your skis, as the case may be. Men should take a dark suit for dinner, if dinner jackets aren't worn but slacks won't do. A woman should take at least one cocktail dress for the weekend and one or two non-sports-type dresses suitable for dinner. It is better to have your clothes a little on the formal side than overly casual. I am thinking of a suburban dinner party I once attended where the men wore dark suits and the women appropriate silk dresses. One male guest, a well-known "character" about town, came to the table without his coat and sporting bright red suspenders. His theatrically casual appearance may have been forgiven by his hostess, who knew, and was amused by his idiosyncrasies, but to the others who didn't recognize his peculiar genius he was boorish.

Rules of Behavior   The rules for country and city weekends are about the same. You are prompt for meals, you let the hostess plan the activities and you fall in with those plans as well as you can. If she projects a long walk and you are a poor walker, she will understand if you prefer to stay home with your book. If you are the only guest, she will counter with a more suitable activity you can share with the family or maybe, mercifully, she'll take them on their brisk walk and leave you in peace.

I am an advocate of the English style of entertainment—I don't believe in the close organizing of guests' activities but like to let them entertain themselves in whatever manner that pleases them most. If they want to sit up listening to recordings with other congenial guests until four in the morning, I feel no compunction against going to bed myself and telling them to enjoy themselves without me. If they prefer to lie in hammocks, sleep late, or read in the garden instead of attending the hunt breakfast or the local fair, it's all right with me, so long as the entertainment, whatever it is, wasn't planned especially for them. If they turn up for meals on time or skip them entirely (if they don't request sustenance at odd hours—although they are free to raid the refrigerator), I am quite happy. But I realize that more rigid hostesses might be put out, to say the least, by a guest who felt so much at home as to say he wanted to sleep late or go to bed early. She couldn't leave him, with good conscience, to munch an apple during his sun bath while everyone else went blueberrying. She might even feel forced to stay home with him or make everyone else go sun-bathing to keep him company, which, alas, was not at all his idea.

There are people who can't stand having their leisure time organized to the nth degree—and I am one. And the hostess who works so hard at keeping every guest unremittingly busy having a good time is usually so tense and full of drive she spoils everyone's fun. On the other hand, someone has to be at the helm, to see that everyone is comfortable and that entertainment of some kind is at least available, to keep down domestic insurrections by getting people to the meal table on time to keep soufflés from falling and hollandaise from curdling. Why is it that, despite adequate warning of the approaching dinner hour, all men disappear "to wash their hands" the moment dinner is announced—while the soup and the ladies' heels cool?

Greeting Servants   If you are a familiar of the house you are visiting you may say, "Good afternoon, Perkins," to the butler or houseman who opens the door and greet by name other servants you recognize if you wish. Housemen and butlers are usually addressed by their surnames, chauffeurs preferably by their surnames but often by their proper names (never nicknames). Maids and cooks are "Ella," "Katherine," or "Katie," whichever they prefer, although in some formal households the woman servants are called, English fashion, "Murphy," "Keene," etc. Chinese men servants are called by their last names, which, Chinese fashion, are always given first. A man who tells you his name is Fu Wang expects to be called Fu, his last name. Housekeepers are often dignified by being called "Mrs. Jackson" or "Miss Lang" by the staff and their employers, as is the cook, very often, in a house with a large staff. But she is often called simply "Cook." To the staff the butler is always "Mr. Perkins," for he is the household's executive officer. A chef is "Chef" or else is referred to by his surname alone. A French chef is usually "Monsieur Robert" (his first name).

Professional People in a Household   A registered or practical nurse, is, preferably, "Miss Cranford," never "Mildred," though sometimes "Nurse," especially if visitors don't know her name. A governess, tutor, or companion is "Miss Romano," "Mr. Robertson," "Mrs. Grayson," and a social secretary is accorded the same courtesy.

In many long-established country communities where a small household's help is drawn from neighboring homes, employees (more often in the "mother's helper" or housekeeper category than not) are frequently called "Mrs. Willis" rather than "Mary," because the calling of such neighbors "Mary" would encourage the use of the employer's first name by the employee or else make the employee feel herself to be in a class socially to which, in the eyes of the community, she does not belong. Young baby sitters are usually called by their first names, a mature woman is Mrs. Ferguson, unless she is socially on a first name basis with the parents. However, to the child, she should be, unless she prefers otherwise, Mrs. Ferguson.

Tenant farmers are "Mr.," though a hired hand or handy-man gardener may be "Peter." A full-time or visiting professional gardener is "Mr. Swenson," not, usually, "Ole."

Pets   The pet owner thinks his dog, cat, monkey, or canary is the most delightful pet. Some people actually identify with their pets so criticism from an outsider can be taken very personally indeed. If the dog's ancestry seems very vague, never refer to him as a mutt, or to a cat of dubious ancestry as an alley cat, or refer to obvious infirmities or shortcomings.

Never speak to him in any but courteous tones. Let the owner give the orders if any. If you are a pet owner, consider that not all people will like your pet or perhaps any pet. Some people, for example, are allergic to cats, and the host or hostess inviting a stranger should perhaps mention the fact that they have a cat or cats. A guest who is an ailurophobe should be quite frank in saying that he would prefer you to have the cat or cats out of sight during his visit. People who love animals, on the other hand, can totally disrupt a family's routine by insisting on feeding a dog or cat or pet monkey at the table when this is something strictly forbidden in the household. Animals should be trained to stay out of the dining room at mealtime. Allowing a cat to sleep on a bed or a chair when this is not permitted, or to urge a small dog to jump up in welcome can also be infuriating. Guests who wish to travel with a pet should forewarn any hostess before taking the pet. A hostess who has her own pet, or who has allergies, may well have to insist that the pet be left at home or put in a kennel, and no guest should take offense at the suggestion. Do not attempt to approach a pet without the owner's permission. A tiny animal such as a Chihuahua, normally friendly, may be very nervous and give a nasty nip to a stranger who comes at him suddenly. Pet owners who encourage their pets to "kiss" them should understand that others who like animals perfectly well find this disgusting and unhealthful. They are quite right in holding off overly affectionate animals. They may not enjoy having the family's house cat sit on their laps. Any guest left alone with an animal should respect the owner's instructions concerning him—not let him out of the yard, leave the bathroom door open so he can get to his litter, cover the bird cage at bedtime, etc.

Handling Catastrophes Catastrophes, small and large, can happen when one is a guest and especially do these little contretemps trouble the bachelor who breaks a piece of bric-a-brac in his bathroom. He doesn't just dump it into the waste basket and say nothing. He quietly discusses the crime with his hostess and offers to replace the particular piece, never offering money in replacement, however. Good taste dictates that she in turn make little of the incident even though the piece in question was a bit of mercury glass of her grandmother's. If he is wise, the bachelor finds out exactly what it is he has broken and then, with the help of a knowledgable friend if necessary, makes some attempt at replacement if not then and there, at a future convenient time. He should not rush out and buy *any* replacement, especially something she would be most unlikely to use. He should realize that some things are irreplaceable for sentimental or other reasons and should vow to be more careful in the future and to be particularly nice to his hostess.

If a guest requires any personal item such as shaving cream or a new toothbrush and asks someone in the household to get it for him or phones for it himself, he pays the bill and his hostess lets him. Aside from these things and of course the telephone bills, he does not try to cover the monetary portion of his entertainment. If his host and hostess invite him out to dinner, he assumes that they mean to pay the bill and doesn't wrangle with them about it. On the other hand, should he, a relatively long-staying guest perhaps, invite them to dinner, they should expect that he will pick up the bill and shouldn't make an issue of it.

How to Infuriate Your Hostess Bachelors, no matter how attractive, seem to bring with them on weekends somewhat heinous faults. While the things I'm about to discuss seem rather masculine failings, they are by no means entirely so. Many a non-housekeeping or just thoughtless girl can set a hostess's teeth on edge the same way. For instance:

Using cups, dishes, and decorative ornaments, not meant for ash trays, as ash receivers or throwing dead cigarettes in the dregs of tea, coffee, or cocktail. If the hostess hasn't put ash trays on the dinner table it is probable that she prefers to have you smoke after you leave the table, but if you feel very much at home you may ask for an ash tray—but please wait until dessert has been served, even if ash trays and cigarettes have been provided. Smoking throughout the meal is messy and an insult to the cuisine. It seems to indicate a background of lonely living. Good talk and good food should be comfort enough. When you do smoke at the table, ask permission of the hostess first unless she is smoking, too. Flicking ashes onto the floor, into vases, and into the fireplace, followed in the latter case by the butt, *sans doute,* is something else that will not endear you to your hostess. If you don't see enough ash trays around, ask for one, don't improvise. The fireplace, lighted or not, that is turned into a garbage incinerator by the guests is not exactly an attractive hearthside. Be conscious of the fact that as a guest you may, these days, be the *only* smoker and thus offensive in your habit even when you think you are being reasonably considerate.

Leaning back on the rear legs of your chair. If your hostess owns antiques she hates you doubly for this. Do it, at the risk of your neck, with the kitchen chairs or garden ones, preferably those of cast iron, but sit on the others as they were meant to be sat on.

Putting your shod feet on the bed or on an upholstered chair. There are times, places, and rooms where feet may find some level other than the floor, but watch where you put them and let the house owners lead in any such informality.

Using the table silver for purposes other than that for which it was intended —drawing on the tablecloth, opening clams. Now that isn't at all farfetched. One of my best silver knives bears the ineradicable scars it received while being used as a clam opener by a guest who got a steamed clam that hadn't unhinged itself in the cooking process. I had it resilvered but the deep marks can't be removed.

Standing on the furniture to reach something. Every well-equipped household should have a kitchen step-stool. Your full weight on the loveseat springs (and by the way, don't sit on the arms of chairs no matter how tender your motives) may cause them to collapse in despair at such treatment.

Leaving the bathroom in a mess. Not every household has a chambermaid lying in wait for you to emerge from the bathroom so she can tidy up after you. In there somewhere, perhaps under the basin or in a cabinet, is a can of cleanser and a cloth or brush for cleaning the porcelain. Use it instead of leaving a childish ring in the bathtub. Men should clean the basin too of their shaving lather and bits of beard (run the soap under the water, too, to clean it of lather).

If you have been provided with a towel rack in the bathroom instead of in your room, use it, folding the bath towel first in three, lengthwise, then neatly over the rack. If the rest of the towels are folded in another manner, try to duplicate it. If you are using a guest hand towel, discard it in the hamper if one is available or refold it neatly and lay it somewhere to be discarded. Don't leave used towels and washcloths thrown around the bathroom or draped over the bathtub or basin. This makes the room unpleasant. Leave it as you found it or better (if you have been preceded by a guest who has never been told these things).

Disciplining the children. Never reprove a small child in front of its parents —let them do it if they deem it necessary. Child-raising methods are different now than those to which you were exposed yourself, very probably. If you don't like children, see your friends away from their home or wait until the children are somewhat grown before you weekend. Happy, healthy children must make a certain amount of NOISE. If you can't take it or the family can't isolate it, stay home.

Giving orders to servants or disrupting them in any manner. If you have been told that Mary will be glad to help you in any way, give her something to press, if it's unavoidable, but remember all guests make extra work for the household. If it's a one-maid household and you know how to press, ask to use the ironing board yourself, but never when the kitchen is in an uproar. A good rule is to keep out of the kitchen unless you've been invited in. Many a good cook has left in a huff because a guest has made a highhanded invasion of her sacred domain to show her how real tea *should* be made or to tell her, in a friendly way mind you, what's the matter with the coffee. Some people really do things like that. Be even more polite to servants than to your friends. Rudeness to those who have much less than we have is the mark of a person who was not raised with privilege. The good people of this world are born with a kindly understanding of others' problems and, no matter how they prosper materially, treat everyone else, especially domestic employees, in a decent democratic manner without being either condescending or overfriendly. While servants want to be treated in the same way as any other kind of employee, they often resent the jocular, personal remarks sometimes made by guests—usually the male ones. Any servant will enjoy an appreciative word about his or her work, a tip for extra consideration, an occasional personal gift from a frequent visitor— never liquor—but cigarettes, candy, toilet water, playing cards, a mystery story, writing paper, and stockings or pantyhose (from a woman only) are all good choices.

Strewing papers, turning down book leaves. If you are reading the papers— especially those monster Sunday papers—in the library, living room, on the lawn, sun porch, or in your bedroom, for goodness' sake keep them neat. When you finish, put all the sheets in order and fold them in the proper fashion. Place them in a magazine rack or on a table, don't leave them on a chair or on the floor. Even if no one else is going to read the papers after you—and how can you be sure of that?—it's easier to store them if they are nicely folded, and this keeps the room inviting. Many households, especially country and suburban ones, keep newspapers for housekeeping purposes or save them to aid various causes, such as the Boy Scouts, who put on waste-paper drives from time to time. Crumpled and torn paper is hard to handle this way. As for books, anyone who turns down a leaf to mark a place or bends a book back to make it stay open is out-and-out destructive. Let him read paper-bound books, but it is good to treat them decently, too, so others will enjoy them. They are easy to mail to friends or to pass on to the hospital wards or club rooms. Why destroy them?

Rising early. You don't come on the hearty ones so much any more, some-how, but sometimes a weekend houseful gets an early riser who is up and out for a walk before the family knows Sunday has come around. Let him go quietly, that's all, I say.

The breakfaster-in-pajamas. If the family breakfasts weekend mornings in dressing gowns, pajamas, nightgowns, you are free to do so too. But don't take the informality so much to heart that you fail to comb your hair, wash your face and teeth, and generally make yourself attractive. No woman guest should appear too *negligée* or with her hair unarranged (neat, newly braided pigtails are all right, if you're the type, or a ribbon around your hair) and her face unmade-up, if she's in the habit of using make-up—and most of us are. Be sure your dressing gowns or negligees are fit for public appearances. Otherwise get dressed. Don't stay in this temporary costume a minute longer than the others in the group. But it is better to come to the breakfast table so attired, but freshly groomed, than to keep everyone else awaiting breakfast, if you haven't been called in time. But ask permission first. If you prefer to dress fully or if you should because the others have, ask them not to wait breakfast for you. Remember you may be inter-fering with the routine of the household if you delay getting to the table too long.

Hunger Pains The weekend guest sometimes is weak from hunger be-tween meals, or so it seems. Fruit, nuts, candy left around in containers are meant to assuage such hunger pains, and it is not necessary to ask the host-ess's permission before taking them. Most hostesses attempt to overfeed the guests, but sometimes it's the schedule of meals and the guests' own eating habits that make it hard to get from meal to meal without someone wanting a snack. If you can't bear more than fruit juice and coffee for breakfast on Sunday—or any other day—it will be difficult to get through until dinner-time at night in a two-meals-on-Sunday house, quite a comfortable arrange-ment for the others who have had a well-rounded late Sunday breakfast. In this case, ask for a sandwich and milk to tide you over when hunger hits you. Offer to make it yourself, as Sunday schedules, even in fully staffed households, are sometimes sketchy. Whatever you do, clean up after you and make as little public hue and cry about it as possible. If something to eat or drink before bedtime is your usual habit, ask for it quietly, if it isn't offered—maybe others will be delighted you brought up the matter. There is little more pleasant than an informal, friendly snack in the kitchen late at night with interested excursions into the refrigerator. But, again, clean up afterward. The servant—or the hostess—who's finished the last dish and put it away won't want to face a pile of cups and saucers, dishes and silver on the early morning after.

How to Help with the Household Routine Whether or not you lift a hand around your host's home while his guest depends very much on the staffing of the place and the personality of the hostess. There are fastidious housekeepers (I am one) who would rather have you sit with your hands folded than see you stack their fine Wedgwood china and waltz with it to the kitchen when you're the type who puts it, scraps and all, into the dishwater. There are hostesses who are (I think rightly) distressed when all their guests rise as one man—or woman—and start clearing the table, just as everything was going so well, conversationally. A good hostess wants the mechanics of meal-getting and serving to go as smoothly as possible. If you want to help—if she's obviously bogged down—fall in with her system. She's captain of the ship. Never mind how you've always washed the dishes. Maybe you never had anything like these dishes and this crystal to wash, and it does make a difference.

If you do offer to do the dishes in a household without help, your hostess assumes you will do it in proper fashion. She may even leave you completely alone with the task—often a grave error, considering possible breakage and inferior washing where tyros or untrained housekeepers are concerned. But there is a right way, and no housekeeper, no matter how careless she may be herself, will be offended if you treat her dishes with this respect:

How to Wash Dishes If you are using an electric dishwasher—God bless the inventor—get proper instruction from whoever knows how to operate the particular model you're to use. Then do your brief work and be grateful.

For the usual and much disliked hand dishwashing there is only one correct, really sanitary method. Scrape the plate scraps into a garbage can or automatic disposal unit, onto several folds of newspaper (which you later roll up and discard) or give the contents to the pets, if so instructed. Save all food from the serving plates, putting it whenever possible into covered refrigerator dishes. Don't store it in the plate in which it was served unless the dish is plastic, Pyrex, or pottery, and then only if there is enough food left over to make the use of so much storage space sensible. Save cold coffee and leftovers from butter plates for cooking use if the hostess approves. Clean bits of butter can go in a refrigerator dish or in a piece of wax paper.

If you have only one sink to work with, rinse each dish in running hot water, then stack before beginning the real washing. Remove any garbage from the sink, clean the porcelain if it has absorbed grease from the rinsing. Now run in the hottest water your hands can stand (maybe there are rubber gloves to be had) with enough soap powder or detergent to do a good cleaning job. Never put pots, pans, glasses, silver, and dishes in together! Do the dishes first, rinsing each as it emerges. Place them in the dish rack to dry by themselves or pour scalding water over the washed but unrinsed dishes once they have been stacked in the dish rack. This is really more sanitary than towel drying, according to the American Medical Association, in case anyone is unduly critical. You will need to dry the silver well, otherwise it will spot or rust. Don't put plastic-handled knives, forks, and spoons into the water. Wash just the metal part with dishcloth, dish mop or plastic sponge. Otherwise the handles will eventually come off.

Unless there is some limitation on the hot water—and if it is heated by a separate heating unit there may be—wash the glassware in fresh, clean hot water with plenty of detergent, then rinse in hot water. Washing it in with the dishes will often streak glassware, and no amount of rubbing with the towel will improve the situation. Let it dry itself. This prevents lint sticking to the glass. To test your efficiency, hold the glass up to the light. You can see that running glasses under a stream of cold water, bachelor-girl-and-boy fashion, isn't acceptable. Who wants to encounter a lipsticked rim? If you are working with hard water it may be particularly difficult to produce sparkling glassware. A bit of automatic dishwater detergent—or ammonia—may aid you in your handwashing.

A special blight on the guest who offers "to do the dishes," then leaves the greasy pots and pans for the hostess. Pots are washed last, first rinsed of any food that may be sticking to them. They should be scoured inside and out wherever necessary. A good dishwasher leaves the bottom of the pot as shining as its sides. Pots should be rinsed and dried, preferably over a low flame, or with paper toweling, not with the best glass toweling. They should be put away, if possible, nesting if they are meant to nest, but it is better to leave them on the top of a stove or cabinet than to tuck them in some odd place where the cook can't find them at hand when she wants them.

The dish towel should be placed over the draining dishes, when you have finished, to keep dust from settling on them. If you know where to put the dishes and silver when they are dry, put them away, exactly as you found them, if your hostess has an orderly cupboard, not stacked any old way. If the cups have hangers, put them on all facing in one direction to minimize breakage. In putting away kitchen cutlery, be sure it's perfectly dry or it will spot or rust. Leave the kitchen like the laboratory it should be— drawers and cupboards closed, dishcloth hung on a rack or neatly folded over the sink, broiler pan back in the oven, all counters wiped up (with the dishcloth or a sponge, not the dish towel!), the stove shining and with all the burners turned off. A really good housekeeper sweeps the kitchen after each main meal to repel rodents and just to be neat and clean. Sweepings should go into the trash can, not out the window or into the yard.

Making Beds If you're a guest it's better to leave your bed strictly alone unless you are perfectly sure you can make it up at least the way you found

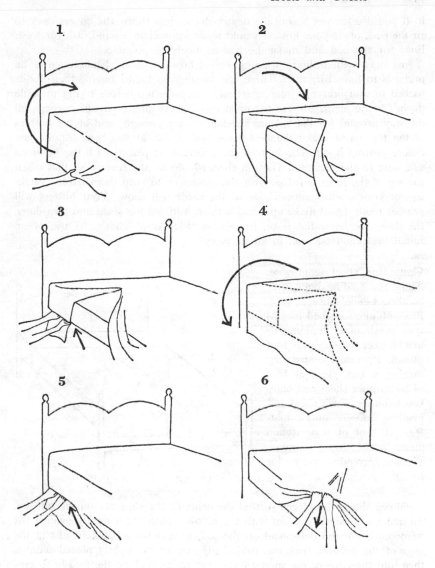

Making a Bed, *placing the under sheet.* 1. Grasp sheet as shown, raise. 2. Let fall on top of mattress. 3. Tuck in hanging part of sheet smoothly. 4. Drop corner of sheet. 5. Tuck under, being sure to catch fold coming down over head of mattress. 6. With fists uppermost, hands together, pull diagonally and tuck under, holding onto roll as far as it will go. Repeat this along entire length of bed.

it. If you are leaving before the next bedtime, just throw the covers back to air the bed, or, if your hostess would really appreciate a hand, ask for fresh linen for the bed and make the bed as nicely as possible.

Any man with military training knows how to miter sheets, even if he pretends to have forgotten. There are people who loathe having their sheets tucked in and prefer to tear apart any bed so made before trying to settle down for the night. But for the most part, sheets mitered at the corners, all the way around for the bottom sheet if it's big enough, and at the bottom of the top sheet make the best-made bed. Look at the hems of a sheet before putting it on. The bottom sheet should be placed with the hemmed side next to the mattress. The top sheet should be the reverse so that when the top of the sheet is folded over the blankets—to keep them from scratching, of course—the smooth side of the sheet will show. Your hostess will grit her teeth if you make up a bed with an initialed top sheet and turn down the sheet so the initial is on the wrong side—now what's the use of an initial that can't be seen in all its glory?

Center top sheet lengthwise. Allow for folding back over blanket. Leave loose at foot. Place blankets on bed lengthwise at shoulder height. Allow blanket to hang over foot of bed. Provide toe space by making a box pleat at foot of bed, upper sheet and blankets together. Tuck sheet and blankets loosely under mattress at foot of bed. Retain pleat. Make loose corners. (Pleats provide space for toes.)

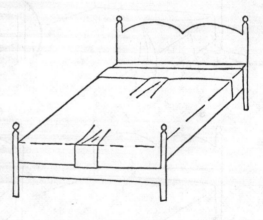

Pillows should be placed so that the hems of the slips are on the outside. To make a bolsterlike effect with the pillows, push them tightly against the headboard, put the bedspread on the bed, turn down a top fold just at the edge of the pillows, tuck this folded edge under the tightly placed pillows, then fold the edge of the spread back over them, tucking the fold in to give an unwrinkled appearance. The bedspread should hang evenly on the sides and on a bed without a footboard is usually best left hanging loose to cover the springs. The quilt, if any, is either put away for the day or folded attractively at the foot of the bed. One way to do it is to fold it in half, end to end, place it on the bed, then indent the folded side so the quilt looks like half a bow knot. Don't ever put a quilt under the bedspread—that gives a lumpy, unmade look to the bed.

Duties of the Overnight Guest in the City

Most city-dwellers live in apartments. And in apartments the guest room is becoming archaic. The living room, the library, the dining room, or a child's room must serve for the occasional overnight guest in the usual city home. Because of this lack of privacy, overnight guests in town are usually just that. Weekends are usually too difficult for all concerned, and longer stays an impossible strain on the household. An overnight guest in a city apartment should leave as promptly as possible, be as neat as if he were operating from a footlocker aboard a naval transport, observe a strict meal-and-shower schedule and prompt rising and retiring hours compatible with the family's living.

He should not treat the apartment-dwelling friends as if they were running a hotel for his convenience, open all night and with latchkey freedom. He is a guest even on a daybed, and if he merely wants the convenience of a stopover in town, without any social obligations involved, the real place for him is a hotel.

The Guest and the Telephone   A guest, whether for an hour or a week, should never use the telephone when adult members of the family are present without first asking permission. "Mind if I use the phone?" may well be enough, but then the guest must be meticulous about charges. When making out-of-town calls, it is possible to have them charged to one's home telephone or telephone credit card. In doing this, it is important that you tell the hostess that this has been done. Optionally, of course, one may ask that charges be given when the call is concluded. The amount for the call then must be left and brought to the hostess's attention. Many people don't seem to realize that local calls are usually not on a limitless basis and therefore the telephone should be used even locally with restraint and money should be left to cover the calls one has made. A household with only one telephone line should not be cut off from the outside world too long by any one caller. The considerate guest limits his call to five minutes unless he has specific permission to use the phone for longer calls, perhaps at a time of day when there is little phone traffic.

Sometimes it is necessary for a guest to answer the phone. He does not do this as if he is a servant of the household. Instead of saying, "Mrs. Smith's residence" he says merely, "Hello," and then summons someone to the phone or takes the message as the case may be. If he is asked who is speaking, he says, "This is Mr. Roberts, a guest." If the guest is a woman, she gives her name as "Mrs. Gordon," not as "Nancy Gordon." A guest alone in the house does not give out information concerning the household on the phone to someone he doesn't know, any more than a child or servant would. He says perhaps, "Mrs. Jones isn't here at present. May I take the message?"

Appreciation and Reciprocity The weekend guest leaves nothing behind for the host or hostess to send on to him. For overnight or longer visits, a guest, and this includes the single male, should send his hostess a note of thanks immediately, if possible or certainly within the week. A wife writing this for the couple, mentions her husband in the body of the note although she signs just her own name.

Part Four

HOUSEHOLD MANAGEMENT

HOUSEHOLD MANAGEMENT

This section is written mainly from the point of view of most of us. The day of the complete staff, of formal entertainment, except in a limited way, is about done. The most exclusive men's tailors in the country say they have no ready-made liveries any more because there are no longer customers to support the department. The very few establishments with permanent men servants must have liveries made to order.

This is the day of the electric dishwasher, the storage wall, the dining ell, the deep freeze, buffet meals, day workers, cleaning services by the hour, unionized bonded help, sitters, the automatic washing machine, the dryer, and nursery school instead of Nanny.

Actual living space has become so expensive and difficult to obtain, that nonessentials in household furnishings are automatically ruled out in many a home. There are usually no attics, no pantries, and often no cellars for storage in the ranch houses that have mushroomed all over the country. The one-level floor plan itself is designed to make it easier for a woman to do the housework without a servant. All this simplifies our living and, necessarily, our entertaining. It usually means that, even if we can afford help, we have no room for a servant to live in if we could indeed find one. Women with no previous domestic talents have found it necessary to develop at least the fundamental ones.

In many ways it's better, but whether we like it or not we can never go back. We must master the new ways, the new mores, and the new skills. I have tried in this section to show how this can be done most effectively.

Chapter 39

FAMILY MEALS

Breakfast

Breakfast is a simple, informal meal—unless we wish to make an occasion of it (wedding breakfasts, hunt breakfasts, etc.). It is the one meal where it is often not even expected that all the family and the guests, if any, eat at the same time. And even in a well-staffed household it is not a served meal, except in a sketchy sense.

For ease of service, breakfast is often served on individual trays at the table with each tray containing individual salt and pepper, a covered portion of toast (covered with a linen napkin or a china or silver dome), coffee or tea cup with the spoon on the saucer, knife, fork, butter plate and butter knife, fruit or fruit juice, cream and sugar, napkin to the left of the fork, jam, the breakfast dish and—especially when the tray is taken up for breakfast in bed—a simple low flower arrangement.

The Breakfast Table For the breakfast table the centerpiece may be simple flowers, a green plant in a silver or copper urn, or a convenient Lazy Susan. The table is usually bare except for place mats, but on a beautifully surfaced table or in a breakfast nook where the table has a composition top even these may be dispensed with. The silver at each place consists of a small fork and knife, a dessert-size spoon for cereal, if needed, a butter knife on the butter plate, and a teaspoon on the saucer beneath the coffee cup or to the right of the knife to the left of the cereal spoon. Coffee cups may be before the hostess or at each place to the right of the knife. Jam or marmalade is served in a small serving dish or silver-topped or other decorative jam jar on a small service plate, with a spoon on the right side of the plate or in the jar or dish. Fruit or fruit juice is at each place on the breakfast plate. Water is at each place in tumblers, at least when guests are present.

When there is service the maid pours the coffee and asks each person how he wishes his eggs. If there is something else offered, plates may be arranged in the kitchen and served individually. If everyone is ready at once, a platter of, say, bacon and eggs may be passed or griddle cakes

The Breakfast Tray always has a tray cloth or place mat, usually linen. It may have its own special china. *Shown top left to right:* Simple low flower arrangements if space permits, jam jar, toast or rolls in napkin or under dome, sugar and cream. *Below, left to right:* Butter plate, napkin, breakfast plate with cover for food upon it, salt and pepper, water glass, juice glass (serving plate under it optional), coffee cup with spoon to right of handle, coffeepot. The morning paper in an upright holder if room on the tray.

and bacon. Or foods may be kept hot on the sideboard along with the coffee, either over alcohol lamps or in electric *bains-marie*. Toast may be made on the sideboard or at the table if it is not brought in from the kitchen on a covered dish or beneath a napkin. The napkin is laid on the plate, the buttered or unbuttered toast on top, then the corners of the napkin are folded to cover the toast.

Breakfast is the one meal at which it is permissible to read the paper, mail, or anything else that suits our fancy. Many people are totally unable to function conversationally early in the morning.

Family Dinner

If just the family is at table, let us say mother, father, and three children, the serving is usually handled by both mother and father, with father serving the meat and the mother the vegetables. It is pleasant to vary the serving sequence if all three children are of the same sex, with the oldest one not necessarily always being served first, and the baby last (unless his meat has to be cut for him, for example). If the children are of mixed sexes, the girls are served before the boys as they will be when they are grown up. The father passes the dinner plate with the meat on it up to the mother (usually passing on his right if there is a child

At Breakfast the first course, stewed fruit, is in place on the breakfast plate. Tumbler is used for breakfast water. Coffee spoon may be on saucer as shown, or at right of knife. Dry cereal is placed above place plate. Hot cereal is served from the kitchen.

Informal Family Dinner The first course may be in place before the family sits down, in this case fruit cup. If the first course is soup, it may be served from a tureen with plates being passed.

able to pass the plate there). The mother adds the vegetables and passes the plate on to the child she wishes to be served first.

In both serving and clearing the table, a serving cart or perhaps a small table close at hand is of great help to the mother. Empty plates may be passed up and prepared for removal to the kitchen with one plate if necessary designated for scrapings (but this procedure should always be done as unobtrusively as possible, preferably below the level of the table). A hostess with no maid cannot be expected to serve as she would, removing two plates at a time.

In this kind of maidless service, soup or first course is usually on the table when the family is called. Soup, in this nice friendly way, can be served from a tureen in front of the mother. Milk if it is served is replenished from a pitcher, never from a bottle or carton. Commercial food containers are not placed on the table with the exception of catsup or other condiment bottles or jars.

The alternative way to serve a family like this without a maid is to have the food on a buffet or side table, English fashion. And a very good idea it is, too, especially if you have an electric hot plate. In this case the meat is either carved in the kitchen or carved at the buffet with the father—or the carver—filling the plates from the vegetable dishes there. Salad may be passed at the table or may possibly be in place when the family sits down.

Chapter 40

FURNISHINGS IN THE ESTABLISHED HOUSEHOLD

How to Form Your Own Tastes in Selecting Furniture

Many a fine and helpful book has been written on the subject of house furnishings. Many magazines deal well and extensively with the subject. If your taste is unformed, perhaps because you've never given the matter thought, you can and should learn from these sources. But best of all, move with your eyes and senses alert through the loveliest homes you can find. You might start with a trip to Charlottesville, Virginia, where Jefferson's majestic "Monticello" will prove an inspiration and delight. Drink in the colors of the walls, of the handmade brick, of the furniture whose patina has deepened with time. Enjoy the surprising freshness and frugality of the muslin curtains, the depth of the boxwood, the body to the silver. Then go to Williamsburg, to Mount Vernon, to Sleepy Hollow Restorations in Tarreytown, New York, to the Richmondtown Restoration on Staten Island, to New York City's Metropolitan Museum of Art, and Museum of Modern Art, to antiques shops, to modern galleries, to the great silversmiths and glassmakers, to the beautiful homes in your own community that may be opened each year to the public through co-operation with the garden clubs.

Keep a scrapbook, collect swatches of material and samples of color. Develop your own taste from what pleases you in all this. Then build your own home around what you have learned with the help, if you wish, of a decorator. But never let a professional superimpose his taste on yours. You will never be comfortable in your surroundings if you don't understand them and if, no matter how perfectly conceived from a decorating standpoint, they don't seem in the least like you.

Never decorate in haste, trying to complete the whole picture within a four-wall frame at once. Homes grow from the outside in. We need to live in them a little and in relation to what belongings we have with which to start, before we know what is right for the house and for us.

Planning a Graceful, Comfortable Room

Do not be misled by those who preach the necessity of "period." Nothing, to my mind, is duller than a room, modern or ancient in genesis, all keyed to one static note. Good modern rooms come to life with old glass, a piece or so of antique furniture, an old painting, a time-honored rug, a brass from ancient Syria or Ceylon. A room graced by antiques will be more comfortable for its present-day roomy sofa and its freedom from froufrou.

Whatever you do, remember that some things must be of as recent vintage as your purse will allow—sofas, beds (which if old may be lengthened, equipped with box springs and innerspring mattresses), kitchen and laundry equipment. The living room must have one or more really comfortable chairs, preferably with some equipment, such as a hassock, that permits elevation of the feet. The sofa should be as big as the space will allow and have adjacent a coffee table for ash trays, drinks, a book or so, and flowers or ornaments. The furniture should be grouped with a main center of interest—the fireplace or the view—and subsidiary groups for conversations among two or three, so that they can join, without moving, conversation in the main group governed by the placement of the sofa or sofas.

In good decoration a room should never look too new. Do not fuss if you can't have every piece of furniture freshly reupholstered at one time. It will seem more comfortable for an occasional bit of genteel shabbiness.

Do not be misled by the vagaries of fashion in decorating. A good room can remain exactly as it began for many, many years, with occasional necessary refurbishing.

The most livable rooms reflect the interests and hobbies of the owners. A friend of mine, proud possessor of a New York brownstone, has a pleasant masculine study whose chief decorative motif is a large airplane propeller over the Victorian marble fireplace. My friend is an aviation engineer and to him a propeller is just as beautiful, I suppose, as one of his Manets. At any rate, it looks right in the room because it expresses *his* interest, not one some decorator has thrust upon him.

Choosing Furniture to Fit the Individual   Most important, our surroundings should take into consideration our physical appearance. The possessor of a six-foot-two, big-boned husband is plain silly to expect him to sleep comfortably in a spool bed she hopefully imagines is big enough for two. The small couple make themselves smaller still—if it matters—by surrounding themselves with massive furniture in large, open rooms with high ceilings. The plump family spills over on the seats of gilt salon chairs and looks even plumper in rococo rooms.

Selecting the Right Colors   Colors are most important of all. Never try to live with a color you don't like and couldn't wear. This goes for men, too, who are notoriously uneasy in juxtaposition to pastel, fussy-feminine *décor*. To be good, pleasant, and satisfying, a living room should have shades or variations of each primary color—red, yellow, and blue. Our eyes unconsciously seek these colors. Of course they include all the greens, shades of rose, orange, gold, and dozens of possible combinations. Beware the startling and work up from the rug or the floor color.

Linens

Monogramming Bed linen, special bedroom linen such as handkerchief and lingerie cases, tray sets, and bathroom linens are marked with the married initials of the mistress of the house. In modern usage these are her first initial, the initial of her maiden name, and the initial of her married name. Helen Fulton Jameson has initials HFJ. No longer is the old usage popular whereby her initials would be HMJ, for Helen May, her baptismal names, Jameson.

These personal, feminine initials may be as simple or as elaborate as a woman may wish. But as good household linens may last a decade or more, it is well to remember that simple things hold up best, fashionwise. While this traditional monogramming is followed in the master-suite linen, there is no reason why private bathrooms of other members of the family—for example children—could not have individually monogrammed towels. And so may a husband with his own bath.

Downstairs linens, except those for lavatories, are usually marked in the same way silver and glass are when they are acquired during the course of the marriage—with the initials of both husband and wife in a monogram, in elaborate lettering or in a simple triangle, or with a crest or crest and motto for small pieces and coats of arms or larger, decorative monograms for large pieces (see "Silver Marking").

Four complete linen changes for each bed and four complete towel sets for each bathroom are usually adequate so that there is always a complete change of linen ready for each bed.

Nursery Linens Linens for the nursery should be simple and sturdy. Coarser muslin or percale for sheets—eight per bed for the wetting ages— and terry cloth accessories stand up under the necessary heavy laundering. Cotton knit bottom sheets—four to six—with elasticized corners that fit snugly over mattresses are excellent for cribs and youth beds, for they stay in place and, of course, require no ironing. The no-iron fabrics are great time-savers. Children's towels and washcloths—four of each, minimum per child—are best tape-marked, but they may be marked with a single machine- or hand-embroidered initial (that of their surname) or with a first name, "Stephen," or a nickname, "Patty," sometimes amusingly machine-stitched in bright colored script.

Children should never be surrounded with ultrafancy bedroom accessories that can't take good, hard wear. I prefer simple white muslin curtains, rickrack trimmed, cottage style, to starched organdy, dimity, or dotted swiss. Denim, ticking, woven, or candlewick bedspreads are better than those of delicate fabrics. As much as possible should be washable.

Table Linens What kind of linens you regularly need depends very much on the living quarters you occupy and the life you lead. If your "dining room" is a tiny foyer of a small city apartment, dining must, of necessity, always be informal. Place mats are the best solution here—four or five sets, including one or two for breakfast, should be enough. A gay linen cloth or so will ring an occasional change. If you own a large house, beautiful linens, silver, glassware, and china, you may still live informally because of your inability to get the servants who understand formal entertaining or even those willing to be instructed in it. The trend is toward more and more relaxed living. It is both thrust upon us and, in most cases, gratefully accepted. Formal entertaining of all kinds is either on the wane or already gone and, like the value of the nickel, I don't see how it ever can return.

Modern hostesses set their dinner tables wherever it's convenient or particularly appealing. On a cold winter night a round table drawn up before the fire in the living room or library may seem ideal. In summer, dinner on a terrace, even one opening off a bedroom would seem inviting. Some people have all their summer, spring, and early fall meals on a porch or, weather permitting, fully out of doors. One of my friends has made a lovely, green dining place beside his dammed-up river. Built-in storage space houses simple dishes, glassware, and "silver." An old-fashioned ice box functions nicely at hand. The tablecloth is checked cotton or shiny green oilcloth. The whole family trails down, even for breakfast. The dining room in their little remodeled farm house is forgotten except on rainy days.

In one of the largest town houses I know the hostess is famous for entertaining in her huge, Victorian kitchen. On Sunday she dismisses her servants, dons an apron, and goes to work on one of her delicious specialties— spaghetti with clam sauce, chicken cacciatore, New England baked beans and ham with brown bread or thick, sizzling steaks with tender, pan-steamed onions, and bursting, hot baked potatoes. She could entertain in her dining room with all the éclat in the world, and she has the staff with which to do it. But everyone loves her kitchen fests. And she really enjoys herself.

Actually, variety in the service of meals makes them interesting. I would not care to dine formally every night—nor buffet-style every night, either. Dinner always served on the same china, with the same candlesticks or candelabra on the table, the same style of table covering, shows lack of imagination. Kitchen meals may be delightful as well as easy but it is easy for a harried career-housewife to slip into this make-do arrangement too often.

Formal Table Linens Truly formal dinners require full-sized cloths, that is, large enough to provide a generous overhang on the table for which they are intended. Damask ones, not necessarily white but often pastel for formal dinners, should have self-color woven designs or simple bands. Large dinner napkins (approximately twenty-four inches square) should be hand-hemmed and match the cloths. Damask cloths are placed over silence cloths, felt mats that fit the table exactly. Delicate linen cloths with embroidery and lace are placed over a bare table. Large dinner napkins to match such cloths should be very simple. All machine-made lace should be rigidly avoided. Many hostesses eschew the fully covered look for formal tables, now preferring beautiful lace mats on even bare, handsomely finished tables protected at place settings with small heat-resistant rounds on which service and other plates are set.

Finger bowl doilies are not necessary even at the most formal dinner, but if they are used they should be of fine linen or real lace. Paper ones are not correct.

Doilies in lace or embroidered linen are also needed for the bread tray used for dinner rolls, melba toast, cheese sticks, crackers—all dry finger foods—and for the plate on which petits fours are served. Except at formal meals these may be paper.

Informal Table Linens As a ménage develops it will become more and more apparent that the most useful pieces of table linen are place mats. They may now be used at any meal and are more popular than table-cloths. They cut down on laundry and reveal the wood of a beautiful table. They are available in very wide variety with the almost too-practical plastic ones best relegated to the kitchen, dinette or terrace. Fabric ones are best hand washed in cool water and mild soap and ironed on the wrong side so that they will hold their shape.

Most place mats are large enough to hold only the silver and a plate. The rest of the place setting, for example the butter plate and any needed glasses, goes on the bare table with the glasses sometimes on coasters. Sometimes, as with a large round mat, there is room for the glasses and sometimes even the butter plate on the mat. Very smart as a place "mat" is a small square of woven hemp, a round of cork or some other material on which the plate alone may rest. The table otherwise is bare. This is effective only, of course, on a highly polished beautifully grained dining table (and see Formal Table Linens).

If it seems likely that no use will ever be found for the two damask banquet cloths that were among the wedding presents, the clever woman will either sell them or convert them into four dinner cloths, two or three of which she may have dyed a pleasant dark color, such as ruby red or amethyst. Her napkins may remain white or be dyed to match or contrast. Out will go the table runners and the dresser covers, the embroidered rounds meant for occasional tables and only Heaven knows for what else. Off to the Thrift Shop will go the faded linens that seemed worthy of saving but are never quite presentable enough to put on the table, and they might well be accompanied by the giftee nightgown cases, the cross-stitched napkin cases.

China

Formal China   China for the formal dinner is fine bone china or porcelain, never earthenware. Occasionally it is fine glass, antique or modern. One famous collector of early American glass has a complete set of Diamond Point, which, of course, could appear proudly on the most formal table.

But even on a formal table with fine china it is not necessary, nor even usually very attractive, to have a matching set turn up course after course. The effect may be varied with, say, antique oyster plates in iridescent oyster white on service plates of blue and white Copeland, followed by the fish course on lovely, fish-decorated Limoges. The dinner plates could be of the set, if one owns one, in any of the old or modern fine chinas from Lowestoft to American Lenox, perhaps in the gold and white wheat pattern. The salad course for formal dinner is always on a flat plate, perhaps on a beautiful clear or frosted glass in color, never in individual bowls, and is passed, with or without cheese and crackers. In the Victorian era the cheese tray was passed between the dessert and demitasse.

The main thing to remember, at either a formal meal or an informal one, is that all the place plates at a single course must match. Serving dishes and butter plates may be silver or of a fine blending china or glass, but need not match the set. Butter plates, as I've said elsewhere, are now seen at the most formal kind of dinner.

Informal China   Into this class falls almost any receptacle for food placed on the table. It includes sea shells to hold deviled dishes or to be used as outdoor ash trays, the Mexican glass salad plates, pottery ramekins and those in fine china, the everyday dinner plates (and one should have enough so that the same plates don't turn up night after night). In this group are the pitchers in pottery, china, glass, brass, copper, pewter, and silver that are part and parcel of every household. Serving dishes that come from stove to table are informal but may appear without a blush at the nicest company dinner. Wooden salad bowls, large and individual, belong here, along with wooden pepper grinders, nutmeg graters, salt grinders not used on really formal tables. Platters may be in wide, wide variety from great round porcelain or pottery wall hangings occasionally put to use, to wooden cheese trays and the tole trays which often can double as platters.

Butter plates are informal and come in dozens of materials from pewter and wood to ruby or amethyst glass. It is often more attractive if they don't match a dinner or luncheon set.

Glassware

Fine Glassware   Of all a young bride's household possessions the most fragile is the fine glassware and, though she is at first perhaps unaware of the fact, very expensive to replace. After a few sad experiences she learns to use it only when she herself is willing to wash it and put it away in its special storage section. A growing family makes so many demands upon an inelastic budget that somehow the broken sets seldom get filled out again. Therefore, fine glass, of all luxury furnishings, must be given the most special handling.

Perforated rubber mats or hard rubber racks in sinks help cut down breakage and chipping. Pliofilm covers over glassware help avoid extra washing, and washing of crystal glass should be done by hand. In hard water a detergent, possibly the same one you use in the dishwasher if the water is very hard, and perhaps a water softener in addition lessen the need for dangerously hot water. Glass must really sparkle. It should be rinsed in fairly hot water, hot enough so that the glass will dry without being toweled. When necessary, polishing may be done with a linen glass towel.

It is frustrating indeed to try to set a table for guests only to find that there is one too few really good glasses or that the best wine goblets have chipped rims here and there. By carefully husbanding her best glass, the wise hostess sees to it that she has at all times eight or more matching glasses for water and eight or more for one or two wines. A dozen or more really good cocktail glasses and eight nice sherries should be kept apart from the regular glass supply of the household. Twelve good highball glasses should be reserved for those special occasions when the hostess can't afford even to *feel* apologetic about such minor matters. Fine liqueur glasses are cobweb-frail and should be stored well away from casual gropers in the bar shelves.

Wisest of all is the careful hostess's habit of washing her party glasses herself after a late party, not leaving them to be done—probably carelessly—with the breakfast dishes.

The young homemaker who did not receive the kind of fine glass for which she yearns as her home takes shape, yet is appalled by the price of new glass, should patronize the auctions, treading carefully at first to learn what quality is and what the glass she sees would bring when new. The contents of estates out of town are more likely to yield what she wants than the auction rooms in town.

Glassware for Everyday Use   The established household usually includes children, and children mean breakage of glassware. Open-stock, inexpensive, heavy glass should be used for children's meals. Plastic and other unbreakable wares are attractive and sensible.

Along about the fifth year of marriage wedding glassware is often about gone, sad to state, except for the little-used fine glass such as champagne glasses, although these are particularly short-lived because of their delicacy. Glasses used in the summer for beer and for iced drinks have a very high mortality. They fall onto stone floors, are tipped

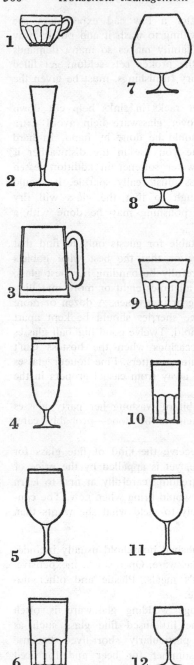

Glassware

1. Punch glass, 1½ oz. Fill ¾ full.

2. Pilsener glass.

3. Beer mug. Shape optional.

4. Iced-tea glass. Shape optional.

5. Water goblet. Shape optional. Preferable at table for luncheon and dinner. Fill ½″ from top.

6. Water tumbler. Fill ½″ from top. Preferred for water served away from table except at breakfast.

7. Large brandy, approx. 8 oz. Fill only ¼ from the bottom.

8. Small brandy, approx. 2 oz. Fill only ¼ from the bottom.

9. Old-fashioned glass, 3 to 4½ oz. Fill ¾ from top. Use for all kinds of "on the rocks" drinks.

10. Juice glass, 3 to 4 oz. Shape optional. Fill ½″ from top.

11. Large bowl for white wine. Fill ½″ from top.

12. Crème de menthe frappé, about 4 oz. For stingers, too, and any frappé, such as Old Southern Comfort frappé or apricot frappé. Or a frappéed liqueur may be served in an ordinary cocktail glass. Fill about ¾ full.

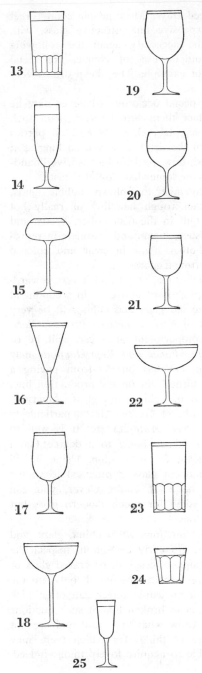

13. Delmonico or whisky sour (but ordinary cocktail glass will do).

14. Stem whisky sour or parfait glass. Fill ½″ from top.

15. Hock or Rhine wineglass, sometimes with green bowl, occasionally decorated (antique specimens). Should not be used except for hock or Rhine wines. Any table wineglass may be substituted. Fill ½″ from top.

16. Traditional sherry. Fill ½″ from top.

17. Optional sherries. Fill ½″ from top.

18. Cocktail glass, 1 oz. or more. Shape optional.

19. Large bowl glass, 4 oz., for red table wine.

20. A balloon glass, wider and larger than a wineglass—as much as 18 or 19 oz.—is used for either white or red less expensive wines. It is sometimes used for beer or even martinis on the rocks. It is not used with other wineglasses. Fill to not more than ½. Milk may also be served in it.

21. Optional glass for table wine, 1 oz. or more. Fill ½″ from top. For white wine, port, and red table wines, Irish coffee.

22. Champagne glass, solid stem preferred. Used for frozen daiquiris and champagne cocktails too. Fill ½″ from top. Champagne may also be served in an all-purpose wineglass, tulip-shaped (see illustration 11, on opposite page).

23. Highball glass. Shape optional. Fill ½″ from top.

24. Shot glass, 1½ oz. For whisky.

25. Liqueur glass, 1 to 2 oz. May be used for liqueur brandy too.

over on the terrace, fall from ill-balanced trays. Most people soon forget their pride and replace them with inexpensive but attractive glass, with the realization that replacement will be necessary again the following season, anyway. Very practical for outdoor use, of course, are metal glasses—hammered or spun aluminum for example. They keep drinks very cold and are indestructible.

It is wise to put on a high shelf for special occasions whatever may be left of the fine cocktail glasses and replace them with heavier, open-stock ones in a pleasant pattern or in a simple, plain glass. At cocktail parties few give any notice to the glass in which the drink is served so long as it is the right shape and size. To be avoided, however, are inexpensive "hand-painted" glasses and overdecorated ones in somewhat doubtful taste.

In making replacements it is well to remember that blown "bubble" glass, interestingly irregular, cannot stand either rough handling or really hot water. It must be washed by hand, not put in the dishwasher. Pretty and practical are some of the plates, sauce dishes, sugars and creamers in reproductions of cut and pressed glass and other items in clear and colored glass which abound in variety and department stores.

One of my own hobbies is old glass and china, and I find it very rewarding to discover the things I love in antiques shops and even in secondhand shops. A little study on how to recognize old glass and china will be very worthwhile. Ruth Webb Lee's *Handbook of Early American Pressed Glass,* kept for easy reference in the glove compartment of a car, will be of help in such treasure hunts. Her *Antique Fakes and Reproductions* may keep an "antiquer"—once the collecting but has bitten—from paying a sky-high price for something now being turned out on the production line. In the library are all sorts of books on old china and glass, American and European as well as some of the books of George Grotz, particularly *Antiques You Can Decorate With, The New Antiques* etc. It is well to remember that antique blown glass, too, is perishable to a degree (satin glass, for example) and was mainly meant for decoration. Using it will prove disappointing, but early pressed and cut glass is practical to collect and use and makes for an attractive table. If you're clever, you can have it at prices no higher than those asked for much modern glass but beware the many meritricious reproductions.

It is a good idea, too, to patronize the auctions when china, glass, and other household items need replacement. Go early enough to inspect the merchandise, however, and do not buy chipped, cracked, or crazed glass or china. Dealers who go to auctions are usually interested only in the more valuable pieces of old glass, so that an astute buyer can often pick up fairly modern glass and even fine china in broken lots at such auctions at a fraction of its original cost. If you know what you want and are not distracted from the search by the allure of things for which there may be neither use nor space, you may be able to acquire lovely things indeed.

When expensive glassware does become chipped in the rim, if the chip or crack is not too deep it should be taken to someone specializing in grinding down glass. The cost runs around a dollar per glass—much less than the replacement value of most, and saving them this way often keeps a set intact. Collectors' magazines often have ads of these and other fine repair specialists. They are also listed in classified directories.

Chapter 41

EMPLOYER-SERVANT RELATIONS

The Hiring of Servants

Work with Your Employment Agency It is best, I believe, to hire domestic help through an accredited employment agency with whom you regularly do business. The agency checks the applicant's references and lets you know what amount of work is expected in each category at the current wage. The agency helps you determine what is fair and expected in the matter of time off and vacations. If differences you can't seem to handle satisfactorily arise, a good agency will act as mediator between you and your employee, in the hope of keeping you a satisfied customer.

When complaints are put on a businesslike basis instead of being constantly tossed at a bewildered or resentful employee the results are often good. If you have a complaint to make—about wastage of food, lack of promptness, about attire or the handling of some household job—interlard the complaint with an encouraging remark before and after. For example, "Mary, I thought your service tonight was very good indeed, but I'd like you to be a little more careful about your sleeves. Be sure, if you shove them up for work in the kitchen, that you push them back in place and fasten the cuffs before you begin to serve. You always look so nice in your dress uniforms if they are quite in order." (Three-quarter sleeves now available for dress uniforms avoid this common problem, by the way.)

The potential employer should keep in mind that the hiring of household employees is on a different basis from that of a generation ago. Domestic service has many drawbacks from the employee's standpoint, not the least of which is the thoughtless and unbusinesslike manner in which servants are often treated.

When you interview, have in mind, or better, have a list of the minimum duties you will require. Do not be vague in this first interview, full of enthusiasm over the pleasant job you are offering, and forgetful of the unattractive aspects every job holds.

Wages State exactly when the salary is to be paid—weekly, semimonthly, or monthly. It is usual for the monthly wage to be given, but, if the employee wishes to be paid by the week, it is important to make it clear that the monthly amount is not merely divided by four, as so many seem to think it should be. To arrive at a weekly wage from the monthly figure, multiply the monthly wage by twelve and divide by fifty-two. This is the way it is done in the business world, as there are four extra pay days a year. If you pay by the week—basing your pay on a four-week month every month you are overpaying an employee one full month's wages. Be sure your prospective employee has a Social Security number and explain that you contribute one half of the Social Security deduction for the employee's future welfare. Do not agree not to withhold Social Security, an offense. To pay it all yourself, as some applicants insist, is foolish and unfair to the next employer, who may well be unable to afford such a gesture. Such additional compensation—and it is that—is taxable to your employee, anyhow, something she should understand.

Your Requirements   At the beginning of an interview, state the possibly difficult or unattractive things about the job first, or the things to which some domestic employees object. If, for example, you require a health certificate—and you should, especially with children in the house—say so immediately. Your interviewee may not wish to go into the interview any further—which settles an important point. If she has no health certificate and wishes to go to your doctor for examination, you yourself should pay the doctor's bill and wait the necessary time, usually three days, for results of chest X rays and Wassermann tests before taking on the employee even on a temporary basis.

It is better to conduct an interview in your own home, showing the applicant the house and explaining your requirements if after the first few minutes he or she seems a possibility. If you interview in an agency office, do not commit yourself until the applicant has seen your home and had explained to her, graphically, what will be expected. She should be satisfied, too, that the quarters you offer are as you represented them.

Where a servant sleeps, the privacy and comfort you can afford him or her are very important. If it is necessary for a nurse or maid to share a room with the baby, say so immediately. And make some arrangement for her to have occasional use of another room of the house or apartment for the entertainment of friends, if only on your own evenings out.

The Interview   Try to set the locale of your interview of a domestic at home in surroundings in which she will be more at ease than she might be in your drawing room. Choose a study, your office, if you have one, a sunroom, dinette, servants' sitting room, or even the kitchen if it is free and there are not other employees to overhear what is being said.

Establish immediately the employer-employee relationship. Put the interviewee at ease, but do not offer him or her a cigarette unless, if you hire him or her, you are going to permit smoking in your presence and on the job. Remember that everyone undergoing a job interview is likely to be self-conscious and not at his best. Know, too, that no matter how your questions are answered and what the first impression is, you cannot know how this potential employee will work out until you see the quality of his work.

The questions you ask depend on your own family and household situation. You can usually guess an applicant's approximate age, so it is not usually necessary to ask it, though you may. If you are interviewing many possibilities, jot down your impressions and the answers to your questions as you see each one, so you can make comparisons later.

If you have children with whom the applicant will be in contact if she is hired, it is not only necessary to ask her feeling about children but, if the answer is satisfactory, to see her with them and to see how they react to her. Often a child's response to an adult is more acute than yours can be. If the baby takes an instant dislike to a woman applying for a job as a nurse, don't hire her. The baby knows best. People who like children seem to telegraph that information to the younger generation by their warmth and unaggressive friendliness. Beware the efficient, scientific woman who knows all about children but whom children detest at a glance. Better to have an easygoing, ill-educated "Nanny" with love in her heart.

Be sure you are always in charge of the interview, that you aren't being interviewed yourself! Of course, an applicant for the job you offer has a right to ask a few questions herself, and, in fact, you should encourage her to do so. But never in desperation hire someone who has put you on the defensive, who, in effect, will do you a favor by taking the job. Such a woman will shortly be running you as well as the household, whether or not she is younger or older than yourself. In regard to age, by the way, some women make it a practice to employ only those younger than themselves so they can maintain executive control. Executive ability should not depend on seniority. It is quite possible for a young employer to employ a woman or man twice her age, so long as she knows, and knows well, how the job should be done and has the ability to see that it *is* done.

In describing the job never minimize the duties you will expect. Don't say "light laundry" when all the family's wash is to be done at home. If you have no dishwasher and the person you are hiring will be responsible for the dishwashing, say so. If you expect windows to be washed and heavy cleaning to be done, describe the work in detail and save yourself trouble later. If you are in charge of the baby but plan to leave him with the maid a full day or more a week, establish that right away. Don't say she will have no care of the baby and then turn him over to her, unannounced, when she has many other things to do. Where small babies and their care are concerned, household matters often have to wait.

Among the questions you should ask are those concerning drinking and smoking. Make it clear that you will not permit drinking on the job. And make it clear, too, that you will not permit drinking on time off if work suffers as a result of drinking off the premises. If you permit smoking, establish in what parts of the house it may take place. Do not allow it during the course of actual work or you'll have burned table tops, holes in the rugs or linoleum, and ashes in the food.

It is usual in this country to permit servants to eat the same food as the family eats with the exception of expensive delicacies such as pâté de foie gras, candies, out-of-season foods, and other things the mistress may wish to buy only for entertaining or her family's own use. Where privilege is abused and special foods disappear in the kitchen before the family sees them, the only answer is a locked food safe, or pantry, Continental style.

What Recommends You as an Employer?   An applicant for a domestic job wants earnestly to know—whether or not knowing how to ask—what kind of person is hiring him. Tell the applicant, reservedly of course, what you can about yourself and your family, what hours you keep, how much entertaining you do, how much you are away from home, how long other servants have been in your employ. If your employees stay a long time with you and leave only for good cause—such as marriage—say so. Most people prefer to work for kind, generous employers than for those who may pay better than standard wages but who are mean and faultfinding and who have a record of rapid turnover in help.

How Good Are References?   The average employer who must let a servant go usually gives her a reference. Ask for these references when you interview. Usually you can tell whether they are perfunctory or genuine recommendations. If no address or phone of the reference-giver is forthcoming or the employment referred to was too far back and the explanation as to the interim occupations too vague, be very wary. Even when a written recommendation is unequivocally good, it is best to check it by phone, not, of course, in the presence of the applicant. People are more willing to tell you the faults or quirks of their former employees over the phone than in letters.

The Part-time Worker   If you have part-time workers, it is virtually imperative that you get verbal recommendations from other employers. Many such workers, gotten through agencies, are floaters about whom the agencies know very little. You are better off finding someone who does such work for a friend who will vouch for her honesty and thoroughness, because, very probably, you will have to entrust her with a key and, perhaps, if you work yourself, rely on her doing her work without any direct contact with you.

Introducing the New Servant to the Household

In introducing a new servant into the household, all members, including the males and even the baby, have the newcomer introduced to them, never the other way around. Children below their teens are called by their first names by servants, unless they are titled. In formal households children in their teens may be called "Master James" or "Miss Ellen," except by old family retainers who have known them from infancy or early childhood and who may be privileged at least until the children reach their majority. Children's nurses, governesses, and tutors call children by their first names, except titled children (and sometimes even then if the children are not of royal blood).

Wherever you can accord household employees the dignity of their surnames, do so. Many capable people have left the household field because of what they feel to be the indignity of their loss of identity. It is sometimes wise to begin a well-trained, full-charge houseworker in your one-servant, busy home as "Mrs. Childs" rather than "Nora" and to start her as a housekeeper rather than as maid-of-all work, at least in appellation. Her morale may rise as a result, and children, especially, may immediately accord her relatively more respect, as may her friends. Don't however, force such a change upon her if she's more comfortable being called just "Nora," as I have seen happen, too. But just being "promoted" to the executive classification has often persuaded a wavering Nora to stay in household work rather than desert it for the factory where she is, in her own point of view, accorded dignified treatment. Every human being needs to feel important, especially Nora—wages or opportunity for saving, quite aside.

Introducing Servants and Guests

In introducing guests and servants the servant is always introduced to the guest in this way, "Mrs. Hansen, this is Mona, my personal maid. She's going to look after you, too, while you are here, so call upon her if you need anything." You do not complete the introduction. If you call your visitor by her first name and have not had an opportunity to straighten out the guests' identities with the servants, say, "Sigrid, this is Mona, etc." Then to Mona say, "Mrs. Johanson will spend the weekend with us and will be in the North Room." That takes care of the identification of the guest. In very formal households Mona will call her "Madam" or "Ma'am" rather than Mrs. Johanson, but it is increasingly acceptable for household employees to use such titles with their employers and with guests.

How to Furnish a Maid's Room

If a maid's room is furnished like a bed-sitting room she will probably feel more comfortable in it and can have an occasional friend in to visit her— a practice you should encourage, so that she feels part of the household in at least a one-room home of her own. But her personal guests should certainly not have the run of the house or appear too frequently. She will never feel as free and as much of an individual as if she "lived out," and you must put yourself in her place. Give her as much freedom as her personality and integrity seem to merit, but never let down your regulations as to dress, punctuality, and manner or you will find yourself with the kind of problem only dismissal will solve.

If you are a kind and fair employer who treats her domestics as she would like to be treated were she in their place, you will occasionally be taken advantage of, but you will also have a better chance of keeping your employees. Constant domestic turnover is hard on you and very hard on your family. For that reason a pleasant, willing employee who may not be completely competent is better in the long run than a household martinet who must be handled with kid gloves and who makes everyone uncomfortable.

The Bed Anyone who has slept—or tried to sleep—on a hard, lumpy bed knows how he feels the next day. Therefore, no maid's room should have as its bed some family cast-off that can't possibly provide a decent night's rest. If you have doubts about the comfort and cheeriness of your servant's quarters, try them yourself and see if they would induce you to live in them, were you in your employee's place.

Accessories The modern maid's room needs a radio, perhaps a television, air conditioning, if necessary, a comfortable chair or so, some place for writing letters, for storing clothes. It must have a good bed, light, adequate heat and bedding, and as attractive general surroundings as you are able to provide. And you must see that the room is kept as spotless and orderly as the rest of the house. Many a servant, obliged to keep the rest of the house clean and tidy, lets her own room go. Her morale will be better if she must keep her own room attractive, too, and she should be encouraged to take pride in it as her part of the home. It must not be just an untidy place in which she can flop on her time off.

It Is Your Job to Teach and Direct

It is a rare servant who arrives in your household perfectly trained. If he or she is unique in having undoubted ability for the job it will still be necessary to train him or her for your job. And you can't expect the job to run itself without direction—and often some aid—from you.

The nagging employer who is never pleased with the cook's work but who can't cook herself will never have her household running satisfactorily so long as she remains ignorant of how to do the things she demands of her servants. Not unless she employs a managing housekeeper who, having these household arts at her fingertips, knows exactly how the household is going at all times.

It is hard to be sympathetic to a servant's problems if you have no real conception of what they are. If necessary, can you rise at seven or before, prepare breakfast—sometimes several breakfasts at differing hours—wash the dishes, clean the house, do the laundry, take care of the children, prepare and clean up after lunch, answer the phone, do the ordering, answer the door, cook and clean up after dinner, and sit with the children afterward—all the while looking neat and clean yourself and keeping a civil tongue in your head? Many women, who had always formerly had servants, have found out what it is like to do all these things day in and day out without much relief from monotony. And they also found out, perhaps, why generous wages and time off were not enough to compensate for the drudgery.

Are You Your Own Managing Housekeeper?

If you have a one-employee household and a busy family it will certainly be necessary for you to give your maid some systematic assistance, as well as careful supervision.

You will probably save money by doing the supply shopping yourself if you have a practical knowledge of cost and quality in food. Telephone ordering from charge-account stores is convenient but expensive. In some shops it is customary to rebate to the servant, who brings her mistress's business, a percentage of the monthly bill—which, in turn, is padded to take care of the rake-off. If you cannot afford runaway bills, watch these details. If you permit telephone ordering, have the kitchen save the sales slips for you. Be sure each package is checked to see that it contains each item for which you have been billed. Omitting items in a package, but billing for them, is another way some unscrupulous merchants gouge households whose servants do the ordering and, through connivance or carelessness, overlook such omissions. Don't be embarrassed at checking up. Your employees will respect you more if you are not "easy."

If you have a maid-of-all-work, you may decide you can help the household run more smoothly if you do the routine upstairs work every morning—if your own time permits. This may mean making the beds, tidying up and dusting. You may designate as your job—and in this you will be wise—the dusting or washing of valuable ornaments in the house. Perhaps you will make the day's dessert. It is probably certain that you will do the family mending—or arrange to get it done outside—attend to repairs, put out clothes for dry cleaning, keep drawers and closets tidy, and, unless you can hire someone to help take the burden off Mary, help in most of the regular work when you have guests.

Keep Your Dignity Try from the beginning of your relationship with a domestic to establish a dignified employer-employee relationship. Make your orders clear, and, whenever possible, put them in writing. From time to time review the work in a friendly manner, giving censure, encouragement, and praise, as needed. Avoid an apologetic attitude when telling an employee what must be done or improved. In your own manner and tone of voice, assume that what you are saying will be acted upon without difficulty or argument. Adult treatment of domestics usually results in responsible, adult behavior on their part.

How to Write Notes to Servants and Tradespeople

Notes left or sent down to servants should always be pleasant and clear. Criticisms should be made face to face wherever possible. If you have a part-time maid you rarely see, it may be necessary to leave a note of criticism from time to time, but it had better be tactfully phrased. The same thing said to her with a pleasant expression on your face will be much more tolerable. But such a note could read:

Emma—

When you do the silver today, will you use a little brush on the raised design so that no polish remains? It helps, too, as you know, if you wash it afterwards in hot water and suds before shining it. I do want it to look especially nice tonight as I am having guests.

Also, while you are working with the polish, will you be sure to go over the light switches and the bathroom faucets and soap recesses.

A.V.K.

This note implies that Emma has been a little remiss previously, but it should not make her annoyed. Try not to state a criticism except indirectly, unless you are there to hear what the servant has to say about it. There are often mitigating reasons for poor domestic performance.

A note for a tradesman may use the same initial signature or simply be signed "Mrs. Knowles." For example:

Oil Man—

Please don't disturb me today. Just fill the tank and leave the slip on the porch table. I'll sign it and mail it in.

Mrs. Knowles

Don't Pry

In all things that don't concern you or your family or that don't affect her job, a servant's life and activities should be her own business. In personal matters, don't give advice unless it is asked. The salary she earns is hers as inviolably as that of your husband's secretary. But if she gets into financial difficulties to the extent that her work suffers, that is your business and she may welcome or at least need some suggestions from you on how to manage her affairs. Help her, with your own care concerning expenditures of household funds, to value thrift and to seek security through regular saving of some portion of her earnings in addition to her Social Security.

Time Off

In various communities the days for time off and the amount of free time differ. But your staff needs time off on one shopping day at stated periods as well as on the usual Sunday afternoon and evening. You should not dictate that a maid spend the night in on her free days, so long as she is on the job on time the following morning or whenever it is she is expected back. You should not, except in unavoidable emergencies, change her time off without adequate advance warning. She has, it is hoped, some social life too, which, because of the restriction of her job, must be carefully arranged beforehand. It is unfair to her to tell her, suddenly, that you want her to stay in Thursday afternoon, without finding out if it is just as agreeable to her to take some other afternoon on that occasion. Normally, have regular days for time off and keep to them. If possible, offer your job on an eight-hour work basis. A job that is nine to five for housework may call for family adjustments but it will be much easier to fill. It is a future probability as is unionized household help.

Answering Calls and the Use of the Telephone

A maid employed in the home of a couple answers the phone by saying, "Mrs. Greer's residence." In a man's residence she would answer, "Mr. Greer's residence." In all cases the word *residence* is used even though it may be an apartment. A member of the family merely answers "Hello."

Where you have unlimited local service, servants should be given telephone privileges in moderation. They should not make or receive so many calls that their work is seriously interfered with or the family can't use the phone when it needs to. Records of out-of-town calls by servants should be kept and the toll charges either deducted from wages or settled at regular periods.

Extension of Credit

The employer who constantly gives an employee advances on his or her salary is doing no kindness. Everyone has an occasional emergency, of course, but no employee should be allowed to be constantly in debt to his employer. Such a practice encourages credit-buying and charged expenditures to a degree that the employee may be spending more than he or she makes. The existence of unpaid debts, especially to an employer, makes for a poor relationship, fraught with resentment. Avoid such situations by making your statement of policy concerning loans-against-salary, right at the beginning of employment.

Workmen's Compensation

By all means carry insurance to cover the possible injury of employees in your household. And check with your insurance broker or your state employment office on what other insurance may be necessary or advisable.

There are personal liability policies issued by major companies that protect the householder against what might be financially crippling liabilities incurred through bodily injuries, sickness, disease, or death to employees, guests, or even casual visitors such as delivery boys on your property. If a housemaid falls from a stepladder, her injuries, under such a policy, are covered by the medical clause. If she sues, the employer is covered by the liability clause.

Social Security Deductions and Withholding Tax

Domestic employees are specifically exempted from the withholding tax but any employee who is paid cash wages of $50.00 or more in a calendar quarter comes under the Social Security law. A calendar quarter is a three-month period ending March 31, June 30, September 30, or December 31. Disregard the value of food, lodgings, clothing, car tokens, and other non-cash items furnished to houschold employees. A cleaning woman, for example, who has been paid cash wages of $50.00 within a calendar quarter on one job must have Social Security payments deducted by her employer, who of course pays an equivalent amount to the Social Security fund on a quarterly basis. Since both you and the employee are liable under the law for non-compliance, you should obtain the employee's Social Security number before he or she starts to work. It is best to deduct the tax weekly if the employee is on a weekly basis, and by check, noting the amount of deduction on the face of the check. If wages are paid in cash, the amount of the tax must be taken out and entered in the household books, together with the employee's Social Security number and home address.

Beginning with the first calendar quarter in which you pay taxable wages to one or more household employees, you must file quarterly returns reporting the employees' taxable wages and remit the Social Security tax due for the quarter. The tax return and payment must be submitted no later than the last day of the month following the end of the quarter.

The law requires each employer to furnish to each employee a written statement of wages and employee tax for each calendar year on or before January 31 of the next year. If a household worker's employment ends before December 31, the employer's statement should cover the part of the year through the last day of employment, and should be furnished within thirty days after the day on which the last payment of wages is made to the employee. Form SS-14, provided by the Internal Revenue Service, may be used as the statement.

Permanent workers in a household who are not domestics or independent contractors—social secretaries, secretaries—are subject to withholding tax as well as to Social Security tax and these deductions must be taken from pay checks and reported quarterly.

Dismissing a Servant

It is always more efficient—and kinder—to give a servant another chance whenever possible than to be a hair-trigger firer. In business the careful office manager does everything possible to avoid wasteful turnover of personnel. Even if help is readily available, it takes time to train a strange servant in the ways of your own household, and despite excellent references, verbal and written, there is always the unknown factor of how he or she will work with you and with your other employees if any. Give me, anytime, a pleasant, cheerful, co-operative worker who's perhaps not quite perfect rather than a rigid paragon of virtue you hate to face in the morning.

There are times, of course, when a second chance might prove foolhardy, and circumstances must be considered. I once had a wonderful German country girl who came home once or twice noisy and considerably tiddly from beer drinking. She was genuinely repentant, and the slips were very infrequent over a period of several years. On the other hand, I had a Chinese houseman who was as quiet and respectful as a mouse but who somehow never seemed to be able to get his work done. Eventually I discovered he consumed nearly a quart of whisky a day—his own, it is true—and had been doing so for twenty years without ever being really drunk. He was a real problem, and I couldn't let him stay on.

In some of the places where I have lived abroad it is freely assumed that all the servants steal, given the chance. Firing servants for light fingers would mean a dizzy turnover of help. Instead, everything tempting is kept under lock and key and home-going servants are checked out like workers in a gold mine. Here, however, we usually feel uncomfortable and resentful if we are certain a servant is involved in even minor pilfering, and once guilt is certain it is usually better to let the employee go rather than try to circumvent him.

The employee who wears you out with his or her contentious reactions to routine orders is also usually not worth wasting your effort on, unless you are veritably desperate for help. Such people are usually resentful and hostile about the fact that they must do household work, and the only way they *can* do it is their own way. They usually get on better with bachelors or certain household-unconscious career women than with an employer who really knows what she wants. Just be sure, before throwing in the sponge, that you are not piling too many conflicting orders on such a servant and are not, perhaps, expecting too much. It helps to write everything out in proper order, and it is even better if the employer has an exact knowledge as to the length of time each of these assignments should take, all legitimate interruption taken into consideration.

The Letter of Reference

Withholding a letter of reference is a very serious matter. Whether or not a servant leaves of his own accord or is discharged, he should have one unless your experience has been very bad indeed or the employee has left without notice. Another employer, in many instances, may find your ex-employee satisfactory—perhaps because her own requirements are much simpler. At any rate, you can usually write a letter that gives the worker a chance to earn a living elsewhere and which doesn't make you feel like a hypocrite. The thing is to write all the good things you can and omit mention of the bad. An experienced hirer can read between your lines and make her own decision, probably after phoning you for details concerning your obvious omissions as to honesty, sobriety, neatness, promptness, and training. In writing a reference for someone who has been unsatisfactory, keep in mind that for someone else he might be at least adequate.

Such a letter might read, on your house paper and preferably in your handwriting:

[No salutation, definitely *not* "To Whom It May Concern" unless a butler or managing housekeeper is writing the reference]

Hilde Dummkopf has been in my employ several weeks as a general houseworker [if it's been at least two, stretch your conscience] and has proven cheerful and prompt about her work. She is kind and patient with children and a good cleaner. I found her sober and honest. She is leaving me because our requirements call for someone with experience enough to proceed without supervision much of the time. But it is with real regret that we are parting with Hilde.

This letter covers the essential points of sobriety, honesty, and disposition and anyone, except possibly Hilde, will understand that here is a girl who is untrained and probably disorganized and who certainly should not be let near a stove unless her mistress stands behind her, as there is pointed omission of her cooking. Consider that many a woman will be content, indeed, if she can get a maid-of-all-work who is good with children, patient, prompt, and a good cleaner. And another employer's idea of good cooking may differ fantastically from your own.

Careful employers are always concerned, or should be, about sobriety, length of previous tenure, honesty, disposition, and ability or at least willingness to learn. They also wish to know why the person has left or been discharged from the job. Wherever discharge has been necessary, give the worker benefit of the doubt, and consider that under other circumstances things might have been quite different. If you cannot, honestly, say anything constructive, or some very serious infraction has occurred, withhold the reference. Never give an unreservedly enthusiastic reference to any employee who has proved to have serious faults, especially where morals are concerned.

When you find it really necessary to withhold a reference, say reluctantly to the departing one, "Hilde, I am sorry, but I am not able to give you a reference." Say why, of course, if an explanation seems necessary, but usually she knows only too well.

When you can really give an unreserved reference, don't be too formal and restrained, give the employee a good chance to better himself in the next job by being explicit in your praise. For instance:

[No salutation]

Mary Washington has been with us for the past five years as cook, and I can recommend her highly. She is sober, pleasant, honest and in five years was never late or absent from the job. We are most regretful that she is leaving us now that we are moving to the country. We wanted to take her with us, but she prefers to stay in the city near her family. I shall be most happy to answer any inquiries about Mary at any time.

> [no closing]
> Henrietta Forrest Bates
> (Mrs. Mark J. Bates)

If the letter is not written on house stationery with the address at the top and on the envelope (left unsealed), the date and address may be written at the top right, as in an ordinary letter, or the date may be top right, and the full name of the employer may be written, with the address, in the lower left-hand corner:

Mrs. Mark J. Bates
12 Prospect Street
Forest Hills, N.Y.   Zip code

But, of course, she signs the letter, too.

Giving References over the Phone   If someone calls you to get additional information concerning a written reference you've given, you can be somewhat more frank, but again, if possible, try not to be damning.

If you have omitted "honesty" in your list, say, perhaps, "We were careless about leaving loose change around and it disappeared, but if you keep that in mind, maybe James would work out for you." If "sobriety" is the issue, perhaps you can say, "I suppose we should have locked the liquor cabinet but we didn't and there were several rather embarrassing experiences with Theresa. But perhaps she's learned her lesson now. I had no such report from her previous employer and I checked carefully." Let the decision rest with the interviewer after you have been rigidly fair in giving facts. But do not withhold any truly important information.

Chapter 42

DRESS AND DUTIES OF HOUSEHOLD HELP

Most of us do our own work or make do with occasional or regular part-time help as I've said above. There are indeed, however, some households run with full staff, which have some of the facilities still for the kind of gracious living once quite usual among those who could afford it. (All previous editions of my book, dating from 1952 and which can be found in most public libraries, carry detailed information on a complete house-hold staff and its duties.)

Most of us don't want to live this way any more even if it were possible. I remember a delightful story about one of the richest men in the country with a large estate in Westchester, New York. A British titled guest assumed, of course, that he would have a valet. The guest put his shoes outside the door and retired fully confident that they would be shined by morning. They were—by his host.

The General Houseworker

Few families today can afford a staff of servants, and even the general houseworker, employed full-time, is becoming rare except in the upper in-come group and not always found then. Most families with even much better than average income just can't afford her—if indeed they can find her.

If you are among the relatively few who can afford a full-time maid—or who must have one whether or not you can afford it (and sometimes it is necessary, especially when there are young children, to have help even at the sacrifice of other things)—you must not expect the impossible of her.

Some women, perhaps previously without help at all, or long without it, become suddenly complacent when they finally are able to hire someone and expect to achieve, without lifting a hand to help, a perfection in their homes that has been expediently foregone up until then. They may expect a houseworker to do all the things they have themselves done—and done perhaps not too well—and to add to her duties certain frills of service that only overwork and irritate the poor maid to the point of dissatisfaction with her job. In desperation, if she doesn't quit, she may inflict a kind of bumbling slowdown on her employer that is worse than no help at all.

See also "The Baby Sitter," page 683.

The Live-in Couple

It is the rare household these days that boasts of a butler, that well-trained, English-style servant whose duties are quite circumscribed and who is chief-of-staff in an establishment. More usual is the couple who share responsibility for running the household.

Where a man and wife work as a couple in a small household with perhaps a nurse as the only other staff member, or no other staff at all, the man may be referred to as a butler but he is more properly a houseman because of his very general duties. He will assist his wife with all the household work, help with the dishes, possibly drive, wait on table, answer the door, and in the country often do some outside work on the grounds.

Answering the Telephone and the Door   He or she answers the phone, saying, "Mrs. Sawyer's residence." In a man's residence, the servant answers, "Mr. Sawyer's residence." In all cases the word residence is used even though it may be an apartment. The houseman or maid takes messages and relays them to the member of the household for whom they are intended. If a guest is to be called to the phone, the servant so informs the hostess, who tells the guest, if they are together in the same room.

He or she opens the door to callers and, if necessary, asks who's calling. She no longer opens the door, card tray in hand, but has one ready on the hall table if a card should be tendered. Even with family friends he recognizes, a servant is careful not to commit himself at the door as to whether the person inquired for is actually at home, unless he knows the guest to be expected. He says to a social caller, "Will you be seated, please (indicating a hall or anteroom chair). I'll see if Mrs. Moore is home."

Dress   A houseman for dress wear appears in black trousers, black shoes and socks, white shirt, black bow or string tie, black or gray alpaca jacket or white linen or cotton (with oriental men servants particularly preferring the latter the year round). For heavy work the man of the couple is often attired in practical work clothes, such as tan washable trousers with matching shirt open at the neck. He is not expected to wear a jacket. If he is the family chauffeur, as well, he changes into chauffeur's uniform when driving members of the family or transporting guests but all this is today very flexible indeed with a dark suit often substituting for a uniform and the cap frequently dispensed with in country or suburban areas particularly, or worn only when there are passengers in the car.

The woman of the couple, whose main domain is the kitchen although she does the chamberwork as well, wears either the preferred morning uniform in colored no-iron (preferably) cotton with comfortable and practical bib apron, white or black shoes with adequate support and neutral stockings or pantyhose. Slippers, scuffs, sandals should all be prohibited, for they can cause falls and fatigue. Rubber soles can cushion against non-resilient kitchen floors, but area mats or other floor covering should be provided if necessary. Long standing on hard floors can cause or activate varicose veins. Any woman should work in her own kitchen to check on its comfort and convenience before asking another to take over the task.

The daytime uniform is not necessarily changed to the afternoon and evening uniform until just before the service of dinner because of the many duties of the cook-houseworker, although at least an hour's rest should be provided during the afternoon. Today's evening uniform is also preferably no-iron in a good grade of cotton or miracle fabric in whatever color the household prefers, not necessarily the ultra-conservative black or gray. An attractive color—warm yellow, deep green, brown or maroon may be preferred by the worker. (Prohibited should be the wearing of the woman's own clothes as unsuitable to the job.) The afternoon uniform is covered during kitchen work with an enveloping work apron to keep it clean but this apron is replaced for dining room service with a white serving apron. Sleeves are now three-quarter rather than long and may have attached cuffs for easy care.

Caps are rarely seen outside Hollywood extravaganzas and the wise employer will avoid asking her household employee to wear one. The uniform, on the other hand, is practical, saves the workers' own clothes, and gives a sense of unity and order to the household.

Consideration Most of us work in a nine-to-five world, a forty-hour week, which in industry is beginning to be telescoped into a four-day work week with the ten-hour day. The family lucky enough to be able to employ a couple should be conscious of the fact that the old ways of such employment cannot exist today. However it is managed, depending on the family's requirements, the objective should be a five- or five-and-a-half-day week for each member of the couple, together or separately as they wish as can be arranged. Often it works better to get in extra help for parties or if hours are to be extra long and duties complicated, additional compensation for overtime. To ignore these human needs is to contribute to the complete drying up of the household-help market.

A live-in couple must be able to live comfortably in the quarters provided. Radio is essential and so is at least access to television. Air-conditioning where needed is also to be assumed. Some areas should be provided where a couple may entertain if they wish at times convenient to the employer and without, of course, disturbance to the household. Reasonable use of a car is often expected.

Where a houseman or maid does all of the work, he or she cannot be expected to be on duty in the dining room throughout the meal, and, actually, many families prefer not to have servants in attendance in the dining room. Instead, they are summoned by buzzer or silver bell when one course is completed and another is to be served or when more water or other beverage or bread should be passed again. An alert servant knows approximately when these replenishings should be and appears from the kitchen without being summoned.

The Chauffeur

In most modern households a full-time chauffeur, where this relatively *rara avis* still exists, is expected to do more than drive the car or cars and care for them when they are privately garaged. Usually he doubles as butler or, in the country, as gardener or stableman. For this reason, the traditional chauffeur's livery with its leather puttees and uncomfortable coat is seldom seen. Instead, most private chauffeurs now wear a plain Oxford gray or black single-breasted suit, usually three buttons, with a white shirt, semisoft collar and black four-in-hand, black shoes and socks, brown heavy driving gloves. For summer, he wears exactly the same kind of suit in the same color but in a lightweight miracle fabric. The usual chauffeur's stiff-visored cap is retained. The chauffeur's black or Oxford overcoat, double-breasted and round-collared, is still worn, but fur collars are much less seen, as chauffeurs, even in town cars, are usually under cover.

Chauffeurs are often on seven-day duty, on call day or night. The family must modify its own demands so that within this period the chauffeur receives the equivalent of a full day and a half of time—an occasional evening with no expectation of call and free mornings to counterbalance late nights. A tired man is an unsafe driver.

In those states that renew drivers' licenses merely on payment of a fee a chauffeur's employer should see to it that the chauffeur receives a thorough physical check-up at least annually, especially if he is an older man.

The Managing Housekeeper

A housekeeper is not a servant but an executive in household management. Sometimes she is a well-educated woman who comes into a motherless household and takes full charge, with or without additional help. She does all the household buying, its hiring and firing, its meal planning, bookkeeping, and, if necessary, she prepares the meals, takes full care of the house, and supervises the children. She is treated as a social equal and often has meals with the family. She wears her own dark clothes.

Only very large "establishments" these days, such as the White House or a Governor's Mansion, and a few large, private homes have managing housekeepers. They are knowledgeable, educated women, well-versed in homemaking and able to supervise all the household service and purchasing, with or without the assistance of the household's mistress.

Such a housekeeper is always "Mrs. Todd," not "Mary." She has her own attractive apartment (or she may live out) and directs the household from a convenient "office" near the service quarter. Her meals are served to her by the waitress, footman, or butler. She associates and may often have meals with a registered nurse within the household or with a governess, tutor, companion, or social secretary but not with the servants over whom she has charge. She sometimes eats with the family, especially in a motherless household. The hiring of governesses, social secretaries, gardeners, valets, cooks, and butlers is done by the housekeeper although the employer might wish to interview the housekeeper's final selections.

The Companion

Many gentlewomen in reduced financial circumstances turn to the profession of "companion." They are never servants but live in households as members of the family. Their duties usually concern only one woman member of the family who needs friendly company. A companion is often a friend or relative. She should be a good and cheerful conversationalist and a good reader, enjoy parlor games, and be able to adjust herself readily to the needs of someone else. Often she is expected to undertake light nursing duties, mending, and personal shopping.

A companion has meals with the family or on occasion with any other congenial professional person in the household, rather than alone.

She wears her own clothes and dresses for dinner whenever the family does so. If she accompanies her particular charge to formal entertainments, she, too, wears formal evening dress.

The Social Secretary

The private social secretary is almost but not quite an anachronism. She is sometimes expected to live in the household she serves at least part of the time, especially when the family travels to various fashionable resorts. Her social life is often theirs, yet her paid status makes her participation strictly at the suggestion of her employers. At other times she must be available, appropriately dressed, for anything from a beach picnic—in her dual role as companion—to dictation of letters from her employers. The modern social secretary is an expert typist, usually takes dictation, and has a cultivated handwriting, rounded, legible, and of the English school. She is expected to be able to compose both social and business letters and to write them in longhand or on the machine as the situation demands. Her hours and her days off are usually dependent upon the household's plans.

Where a household employs a social secretary, much of the business it transacts passes through her hands, so she must have a head for figures as well as for the social graces. In a very high income family her financial activities may have the supervision of a visiting accountant. She keeps the books, handles the payroll, pays the bills, takes care of insurance, balances the accounts, and keeps careful records for income tax purposes.

In a household where there is no managing housekeeper, a social secretary, where engaged, is often expected to take on this role, as well. She is responsible for the planning of meals, especially those at which entertaining is done, unless the mistress assumes this duty. She may do the hiring and firing and in general she keeps the household in smooth running order.

When the family entertains, the social secretary, with the hostess, makes up the guest list, issues the invitations, compiles the replies, often orders the food and all the party accouterments just as the mistress would if the secretary were not there to take these details off her hands. She usually has her meals alone and is in no way treated as a servant. She wears her own clothes, chosen with her duties in mind.

The public social secretary often has a small organization which works with her on the management of social events such as debuts, weddings, dances, and balls. She works out a guest list with the hostess on the committee—and even supplies a list in some cases—issues the invitations for those giving the party, collates the replies, often works with caterers and florists, and is present with her staff, if necessary, to check the guests at the door at large parties and receptions. She charges a fee for her services and, in addition, may have an arrangement whereby she receives a percentage of various suppliers' bills.

The Cook

In the household boasting a professional cook, this important personage does virtually nothing but cook. The kitchen is her domain. She keeps it clean and sees to it that it is completely stocked at all times, whether she does the marketing or is just responsible for making out the shopping lists. She confers with the mistress of the house, or the housekeeper, on the daily menus. The cook provides her own white cotton dress and wears white shoes and neutral stockings.

Chapter 43

GRACIOUS LIVING WITHOUT SERVANTS

A Routine for Managing the Household

I know many women who can afford full-time help who forgo it in these days of high wages and often quite inferior performance. They have faced the fact that the whole domestic employment situation is changing rapidly and that eventually the live-in worker will be rare indeed. Daily workers, instead, will do the work of each household, probably in four- or eight-hour shifts, where full-staffing is maintained. Outside professional cleaning services with bonded workers are the answer for many households.

With such electric equipment as dishwashers, mangles, automatic washing machines, power vacuums, home freezers, electric waxers, and modern clock-watching stoves, easy-care fabrics, no-iron bedlinen, an intelligent, organized mistress can do the work of even a fairly large household more quickly and efficiently than can the average, often truculent maid-of-all-work. And the mistress will respect the equipment.

Heavy cleaning is usually more efficiently done by men day-workers where they are available, so the functional, servantless household often runs very smoothly indeed, even when there are small children. The meals are always a problem, of course, but even there a mistress who likes to cook and who prepares delicious meals in a relatively effortless manner can run a more agreeable household than does the woman who must depend entirely on the somewhat doubtful ability of her cook-house-worker.

Every household has its own specific requirements and thus its own schedule, but unless some daily plan is followed even in a servantless household good housekeeping is almost impossible.

In Victorian days, and earlier, the fine china never went to the kitchen for washing. Instead, a pan of dishwater and one of rinsing water were brought to the table after a meal and the dishes were washed and put away in their special china cupboards—or else returned to the table for the next meal. So, too, for the sake of efficiency, the lone homemaker can start her day the night before, by setting the breakfast table after she finishes the dinner dishes at night.

Everything that helps avoid the morning rush is advisable. It is important to start the day without hurry and tension, then things will seem to go in their proper, ordered way. So it really does help if the breakfast table is set the night before. Some even prepare the orange juice, grapefruit, or other fruit (if the prepared fruit is covered the vitamin loss is very slight). The next day's menus should be decided upon, perhaps written out as a guide, so that, in the sleepy early morning, preparation of the breakfast can be more or less automatic.

Most important is to avoid the last-minute search for mittens, schoolbooks, rubbers, caps, and father's brief case. These articles can be assembled the night before, or at least their whereabouts checked upon. Of course, they should all have their special place, but as it takes years of training to get children to "put things back," it is certainly not a good idea to count on everything being where it should be.

The whole family should be urged to arise early enough for a leisurely start on the day. There should be time for father's second cup of coffee, his pleasant walk to the station, his morning romp with the baby. If mother is to become family chauffeur, breakfast should be eaten by all at the same time so she has a regular, peaceful meal, too, and time to clear away the dishes, if not perhaps to wash them, before taking father to his train or the children to school.

Laundry It takes approximately twenty-five minutes for one load of wash to run through an automatic washer. Be sure, however, that you read the labels on all new purchases for proper washing instructions. Various fabrics require different lengths of time for washing. And if laundry is done at home, it is easier to do some laundry each day than to allow it to collect so that a whole morning must be devoted to the laundry project. If there is no dryer and there are hanging facilities in the cellar or elsewhere, it is not necessary to wait for sunshine. Where much laundry is done at home however an electric or gas clothes dryer is a virtual necessity in many households at least for winter weather in the North.

In a large household with little or no help, ironing tends to collect. An automatic ironer may be the solution or neighborhood inquiries may possibly turn up one or more women who will pick up ironing to do at home or who will come in for a few hours on this task. Easy care fabrics especially in children's wear and underclothes become increasingly necessary.

Daily sorting of laundry is another timesaver. This means that as the soiled laundry goes to the laundry room it is immediately put in separate hampers. Hampers are labeled "Woolens," "Lingerie," "White," "Colored," "Baby," etc., according to requirements. First chore of the morning, after breakfast is over, is to load and start the washing machine. If it is loaded the night before, it can be started before breakfast so that clothes to be sun-dried—weather permitting—can be put out early.

Cleaning Routine   As the kitchen is the heart of the house, it should never be left untidy while other chores get prior attention in the morning. The best plan is to finish the kitchen first, then proceed to bedmaking (see "Making Beds," page 486), if it is not possible for each member of the family to air and straighten his own room and make his bed before reporting to breakfast (the ideal arrangement in a servantless household).

After beds are made and bedrooms tidied, bathrooms are cleaned and put in order, then the living room tidied (if this was not done the night before—and certainly the family should help). Now, with everything in order, dishes washed, and beds made, dusting and floors come last.

When all the work is done by the mistress of the household one room each day or at least once a week is chosen for thorough cleaning. This room, then, on the early schedule is ignored, except for bedmaking, if it's a bedroom. The objective, is, of course, to set the entire house to rights as soon as possible, so that if further housework must be abandoned for the day, as so often happens, or unexpected visitors arrive, there is at least order, if not perfect cleanliness.

The room chosen for thorough cleaning, whether by a day-worker or the mistress, if first disassembled as much as is practicable. Furniture is pulled away from the walls, scatter rugs or carpets are rolled up, orna-ments are removed from shelves, pictures taken down, draperies are folded back or taken down.

All walls and woodwork are cleaned first. Modern vacuums are good at getting at dusty surfaces, cornices, cobwebs in corners or on the ceiling. Everything washable should be washed as time allows—window sills, shelves, even furniture finishes benefit from careful going-over with a clean, soapy, not-too-wet cloth or nylon sponge occasionally, followed by thorough drying and waxing. As all dirt falls onto the floor as one proceeds, the floor is done last if it is to be washed and waxed or vacuumed. Floors to be swept are done before the dusting, obviously. Whether the floor is to be washed depends on its surfacing, but waxed wooden floors respond well to an occasional thorough cleaning with one of the modern cleaning waxes or a solvent such as turpentine (after sweeping). The waxer is used only after the freshly applied wax is quite dry. Old wax should be removed from time to time anyhow, even from linoleum, tile or vinyl either with soap and water, a detergent, or a recommended liquid cleaner. (Windows should be open if the mixture is combustible!) In corners and inaccessible spots the floor should be lightly scraped with a paint scraper, steel wool, or a dull knife.

When the cleaning is finished, the room should be put in perfect order, not left for later reassembling. Too often schedules can't be completely adhered to in busy households, and it is dismaying to think of cleaning things to be put away, pictures to be rehung, and rugs to be put down at the end of a long day.

On sketchy days the minimum housework should consist of meal-getting, dishwashing, bedmaking, bathroom cleaning, and room-tidying. To neglect any of these things until day's end means coming home to an uninviting house and, usually, a feeling that a free day is hardly worth it.

Division of Labor

Women's Lib aside (and it does make many important points, at that), the division of labor between husband and wife, mother and children, becomes increasingly important as women seek more complete expression and life fulfillment. There should be no reason why the mother of a household should have all the backbreaking chores, previously labeled solely "women's work." I know a father of seven children who cheerfully takes on the family laundry chores, taking the huge load to a public laundry when they are traveling and reading a book as it runs through. Another man, a busy doctor whose wife works as a teacher, puts the laundry through the washer and dryer when he comes home for lunch (as she does not). Many a considerate husband has learned how to iron his own shirts to his satisfaction to save the wear and tear of commercial laundries, not to mention the expense—as well as his wife's energy. Teen-age boys and girls, and the younger than teen-agers, can and should be given chores to lighten the work of mother, who increasingly needs—and has come to expect—time of her own to rest, read, pursue some outside activity, and thus be a more interesting and happy woman than she would be as a household drudge if the rest of the family never lifted a hand to help. Although this is a very new idea to many women, especially older homemakers, a family conference can sometimes clear the air where resentment and fatigue have been building. Actually, the family that works together in a co-operative fashion has stronger bonds than the one in which everybody goes selfishly his own way.

Part Five

CORRESPONDENCE

CORRESPONDENCE

The art of letter writing has certainly been neglected as telephone and telegraphic facilities have spread. I cherish little notes from some of my old lady friends in their eighties, because they know how to turn a sprightly phrase in even the briefest notes while some of my contemporaries freeze up at the sight of note paper and put down only the most stilted expressions.

If you think of letter writing as conversation put on paper, it's much easier to produce a readable missive. We used to be told that it was ill-mannered to talk about ourselves and what we were doing, but to keep social letters on a high, impersonal level is to make them dull. While the "you" beginning may seem more courteous, here, too, it is usually impossible to go on in that vein indefinitely without growing stilted, especially if your correspondent is at a distance and you really haven't too good an idea of what he's doing or thinking. Everyone likes to talk about himself and is usually more entertaining when he talks about what he's doing and what's going on around him, what touches him and moves him, than he is if he struggles to keep his comments away from strictly personal matters. Gossip belongs in social letters, gossip in the friendly, interested sense about friends in common, about births, deaths, successes, and little disappointments. These are the things you would tell a friend face to face, so why bore him with talk of the weather when what he wants to know about is you?

A bowing acquaintance with other languages and certainly a sound knowledge of our own are aids to stimulating correspondence and conversation. I hope the lists—which do not pretend to be complete—at the end of this section prove helpful in showing how both writing and speaking can be more colorful and exciting.

Chapter 44

STATIONERY AND LETTERS

A Woman's Social Stationery

When you choose your social stationery there are various factors to be considered. If you are a woman, is it for your personal use, or for the use of the entire household? If the latter, it should be of a comfortable size for a typewriter or for a man's handwriting—or for a woman's if hers happens to be large—monarch size, usually single sheets which fold twice. The post office prefers that the envelopes be at least 3" by 4½". If it's for the whole family it should obviously be more or less neutral. Any conservative color will do, white, gray, blue, tan, usually with cut rather than deckle edges. The paper may have a simple colored border, in a sound plain ink—nothing iridescent or metallic. A die-cut city paper is more conservative than one for the country. It carries just the address and, if you wish, the telephone number, at the top center of the paper. The envelope usually has on the flap just the address with the apartment number, unless the sender lives in a house when just the street number suffices. Often the return address is simply handwritten. In either case the zip code is included.

A revolution has occurred in colors of women's stationery. Ultra-conservative white, gray or pale blue is still necessary for restrained correspondence. White paper or a white foldover card or a white engraved correspondence card are all proper for replies to formal invitations, for example. A conservative paper is right for letters of condolence, for introductions, formal notes of thanks. Otherwise a woman may use any social stationery she wishes. All the bars are down on bright colors, even violent colors or even psychedelic combinations with co-ordinating ink. I know a number of smart women whose papers with red borders and engraving or die-cutting are used with red ink and not just during the holiday season. The interdiction concerning it for regular use is over.

If any heraldic device (see "Heraldic Devices," page 615) is used, it should be small, engraved in one color. It may be centered at the top of a double or single sheet or in the upper left-hand corner. If a device is used, it is better to let it stand alone, not complicate the paper with an address. The envelope alone may carry that on the flap.

Paper bought with a single initial engraved, printed, or cut out is better avoided. Engraved initials may be used either in a decorative arrangement in the upper left-hand side of the sheet or in the upper center. They should not be so large as to dominate the paper and should be in one color. Engraved initials may be die-cut.

Country paper is usually very relaxed and informal. It can carry considerable information—anything the householder thinks necessary. As it is often "family" paper, the color is usually chosen that will suit all members— white, gray, blue, gray-green, some variation of tan—which can be printed or engraved in the basic colors such as black, maroon, blue, brown or forest green to match the paper selected. Ink to match the engraving, for example green ink with forest green engraving, would be effective although a man might hesitate to use house paper with co-ordinating fuchsia ink. Many men, however, today do use green ink as well as brown, blue, and black.

The telephone number is nearly always included on country paper and may even be pointed up by a tiny drawing of a telephone. Sometimes country papers carry maps to aid the visitor from town.

Every home, city or country, needs a special, excellent grade of white (preferably not engraved) note paper, standard note paper size and usually double fold, for handwritten letters of condolence. Many people of good taste prefer such paper, too, for replies to formal invitations. Dark blue-black or black ink should be used. Return addresses including zip codes are now used in such correspondence.

Printed versus Engraved Stationery   It is nice, indeed, to have some stationery specially engraved for occasional use. But, considering the cost, it is impractical to carry on all one's personal and business correspondence on such paper. For this reason, most well-equipped households and most busy women with much correspondence to take care of have a secondary utility paper of no pretension whatsoever. I have mine done, a thousand sheets and envelopes at a time printed in dark green. The same kind of single-sheet paper with unlined envelope may be bought at any department store stationer or by mail with blue or black printing of a simple name and address, complete with zip code, almost by the pound. The name (Mrs. John Jones not Mrs. Mary Jones), address, and often the telephone number appear on the paper, upper center, and the name and complete address are printed on the envelope flap. If you are not married, Miss does not necessarily precede your name on the paper but should be on the envelope if you have them printed also. However, if the stationery is engraved, it is quite expensive to have another die made just for the envelopes, and people assume that when no title appears, Miss is correct. This kind of stationery does well enough for all routine correspondence.

Lined Envelopes   Even the finest quality paper, engraved, is frequently unlined. A lining, if used, is most conservatively a plain, darker shade of the same color as the paper is pleasant, as is a conservative contrast—a blue lining for white paper. The plaids and the polka dots amuse the youngest set, along with the magenta ink, the facsimile signatures, and the daisy borders. But adult papers are growing increasingly fanciful, too. Let your own taste be your guide and use discretion in selecting your paper for conservative purposes. For fun, a wardrobe of papers is a good idea.

Inks Everyone, I think, needs conservative blue and black ink, but especially designed papers are often designed to co-ordinate with colored inks for correspondence between friends where almost anything goes. Some women have almost trade-marked stationery color combinations. I have one friend who uses the typewriter for nearly all correspondence. Her paper is tan, her typewriter ribbon brown and she signs her name with brown ink. Green ink is also very usual when it co-ordinates with the paper. And, as I have said, red has acceptance now but not for men. I still don't like purple ink, although I have known some very proper old ladies to pen their notes with it, which may explain my prejudice. It does seem elderly. But I cannot say it is incorrect. The use of felt-tipped pens is informal and of course permissible on informal stationery.

Personal letters should not look too arty. As do many of his friends, I treasure those from the late Hendrik Willem Van Loon, with the delightful elephants or little Dutch scenes in crayon on the envelopes, but genius can do many things unbecoming to the rest of us.

I would even go so far as to warn against the ultrafancy new typewriter type that looks like handwriting but this is a personal prejudice. Why should typewriting pretend to be anything else but? As for handwriting personal letters, with certain exceptions I'll note, it may be just as well to avoid it if you can unless your penmanship is beautifully clear.

Woman's Social Stationery

TELEPHONE NUMBER (OPTIONAL)

SCARLETT MORRISON
LIPPINCOTT SQUARE,
PHILADELPHIA, PENNSYLVANIA   ZIP CODE

Type is Engravers' Roman. The 8×10 paper size is useful for large handwriting or for typewritten letters. Same die used on envelope flap. Or new die includes "Miss" (more expensive). The name on the letterhead may also be preceded by "Miss" for both social and business stationery. The use of a telephone number on social stationery is optional but unusual.

Die-cut Note Paper. An appropriate combination of colors might be French blue with die in darker blue, silver, and white. Border of paper light blue and white. The monogram may also be centered. Envelope carries flap (see also, "Stickers" on facing page) address: 15 Whippet Lane, Toledo, Ohio zip code, for a house; Mrs. Elton Gow, 119 Lake Ravine, Ohio zip code, for an apartment with the apartment number listed if necessary, i.e., 12C. The name may be used with the address of a house, too, in the same form as it would be used on the face of a letter, Mrs. or Miss. A good size for this paper is 5¼ × 6¾.

ELYSIAN FIELDS
NEW LONDON
CONNECTICUT ZIP CODE
(TELEPHONE NUMBER OPTIONAL)

Lozenge of Social Stationery. Type is Microgramma Extended. The lozenge might be in blue, gold, and black on blue-and-gray bordered white paper which is 5⅜ × 6¾. Address in matching blue.

House Paper

 Westbury

 Water Land, 755-0113   *Cedar Hills*

 Old Westbury, N.Y. Zip Code

Type is Bernhard Modern Italic. Paper size is 5⅜ × 6¾.

Stickers While return addresses are still printed or engraved on the flap of a social envelope, the post office likes return addresses on the front to speed the mail. When the return address is engraved or printed on the flap, the sender can facilitate matters by using a small printed return address alone, if feasible, as well on the upper left-hand corner

Man's Social Stationery

STEPHEN JOHN KNOX
14 BANCROFT PLACE, N.W.
WASHINGTON, D.C. ZIP CODE

Type is Engravers' Roman. The 7¼ × 10¼ size is suitable for typewriter or longhand.

Norman Bell
14 East Fifty-second Street
New York, New York Zip Code
Plaza 5-0000

Type, Typo Script, is in black. Size of paper is 7¼ × 10½.

of the envelope. Or, if his return address is not printed or engraved on the envelope's flap, he may write his return address (including zip code) on the face of the envelope, upper left, as small as possible.

A man does not precede his *return* address by the title "Mr." A title is used only if he is Doctor, Captain, The Reverend, etc. A woman always uses her title on a return address.

A Man's Social Stationery

A man's social paper should look masculine—in size, in color, and in quality. He sticks to cream, white, or gray with engraving or printing in black, blue, dark green, or perhaps maroon. He may use his initials, die-stamped in color or in simple block form at the top of his stationery or upper left, or his name, Geoffrey Lansing (no Mr., of course, but his professional title if he has one), with or without the address.

Or, he uses the address, upper center, alone, with or without his telephone number. If he has the right to use a crest, he may have it engraved in color, upper center or to the left, but in this country for an American citizen, male, it seems pretentious. If he is "Jr." he may or may not include this in his monogram, depending upon how it is designed. For best results consult a top stationer and follow his advice. (See "Men's Correspondence Cards," page 578.) For highly informal correspondence light brown paper with black or brown printing or possibly engraving is also seen in memo pads or writing pads with matching envelopes.

"Personal" Business Stationery

Business executives often have their own personal stationery, which may bear no relation at all to the firm's. The best of this is in heavy white bond paper, sometimes watermarked, with an engraved or printed address:

40 Wall Street

New York, N.Y. zip code

Office of the President (title often omitted)

This is the generous size of a man's note paper, usually a single sheet. Women in business use this size, too, for personal notes dictated in the office. For such paper, engraving or printing is done in black or, for a woman, in any conservative color she likes such as forest green, maroon, or blue.

Envelopes carry the sender's name (on a man's paper) without the prefix with the exception of Captain, Doctor, The Reverend, etc. The address should be complete with zip code. Sometimes a suite number is added, though if an executive is important enough to have his own stationery, he is usually important enough to be listed on his building's board. A woman executive does use her title, always, on her return address as she does in social correspondence where possible.

Business Firm's Stationery

The best business stationery is white, even when it is the "personal" business stationery of an executive, the kind used for notes of a more or less personal nature sent from the office.

Good white bond paper in the standard 8×10 size with standard envelopes is best for business correspondence because it takes erasures well and fits standard file folders without dropping out of sight or extending beyond the confines of the folder. However, many business firms and business and professional people have speeded up their correspondence through the use of small-sized stationery for brief letters and memoranda—$5 \times 8\frac{1}{2}$ for example. The use of name-imprinted memorandum sheets where correspondence is heavy is also helpful interoffice and for use between correspondents well known to each other. This saves the typing of the address, salutation and close.

A firm should not try to save money on the stationery with which it faces the competitive world. It should not permit its letterhead to be designed by the office boy, either. It is worthwhile to have a simple, attractive letterhead laid out by a typographical expert. It should, if possible, be devoid of photographs, drawings of the plant, slogans, and extensive lists of officers' names. Lettering or printing is preferably in one color. Simple, clear black on white paper is effective, but increasingly color is used. To save the reader's effort, the letterhead should list the telephone number, including area code, in parentheses, the zip code, and the cable address, if any.

The envelope should have the name and address of the firm, simply designed, in the upper left-hand corner. The post office dislikes any return address on the flap, especially on business stationery.

Certain businesses in the advertising, publicity, fashion, and novelty fields

Business Stationery

> **DOROTHY PALMER LEIGH**
> INTERIOR DESIGNER
> 30 EAST 44TH STREET
> NEW YORK, N.Y. ZIP CODE
> MU 1-0000

Professional Woman's Stationery. Type is Light Gothic. Paper size 7¼ × 10½. Preferred business practice is to use same die on both the paper and on the flap of the envelope (or upper left on the face of the envelope).

> **SHIRLEY LANG**
> 1 WEST FIFTY-FOURTH STREET
> NEW YORK, N.Y. ZIP CODE

Business Woman's Personal Stationery with office address. Type is Light Gothic Extended. The paper size, 5¾ × 7¾, is large enough for the typewriter. The title may be used, also; Miss Shirley Lang.

WILLIAM AUSTIN BENJAMIN
THIRTY ROCKEFELLER PLAZA
NEW YORK, N.Y. ZIP CODE

Man Executive's Personal Stationery with office address. Type is Light Gothic Extended. Paper size 7¼ × 10¼.

DOUBLEDAY & COMPANY, INC. *Publishers*   277 PARK AVENUE, NEW YORK, N.Y. 10017   TEL: 212 TA 6-2000

Well-designed Business Letterhead with full information, including phone. Size 8½ × 11.

may feel leeway is called for in the matter of stationery. If they begin their business life with highly unconventional attention-calling stationery, they may live to regret it if they grow to important proportions.

Signatures on Checks, Legal Papers, and Letters

A woman who signs herself M. L. Gibbons (except to a domestic—and I'm not fond of it there either, preferring Mary L. Gibbons) seems a little masculine, to me, even on a check. A check signature may carry her given and maiden name plus her married name if her married name is a common one and her first one usual, too. For example, Elizabeth Green might better sign herself Elizabeth Grainger Green.

With the increasing automation of banking, the depositor's number means as much as her name. If you are a married woman there is nothing you can do, I find, to avoid the use of your given name preceded by "Mrs." on your imprinted bank check as well as on your bank statements coming to you each month. This is the way the bank's statement stencil reads. Increasingly we will have to put up with this insult to proper social nomenclature.

If a woman has a career and is married, her personal checking account may carry either her married or her maiden name and she may use either as her legal signature. She often pays her income tax under her maiden name, if she uses it in business, because she receives most of her income under that name and is known to the government as a tax source by her business name.

I think it a good idea, when possible, for a woman to use her maiden name in business and thus keep her business and social life completely separate. This is a well-established American custom and eliminates being addressed socially as "Mrs. Mary Jones"—an insult to her husband—instead of "Mrs. John Jones." If a married woman does not want to use her maiden name in business, she may sign her name "Mary Jones" and type under it "Mrs. John Jones," but this may lead to clerical problems in the office. Thus more and more married business women are calling themselves *Mrs. Mary.* I dislike it but must accept it. The practice should not be carried over into such a woman's social life, however.

A woman should not sign business letters just Jane Woods, for example, or Mrs. Gordon Woods alone. A postcard order with no salutation could read, however, "Please send 1 doz. Green Star toothpaste. Charge my account. Mrs. Gordon Woods [address if not printed on card]." If she is leaving a note in a milk bottle for the milkman, she may sign it "Mrs. Woods." But she should never sign any letter, business or social, with a "Miss") or beneath her name. I prefer to see the married name used in full parenthetically, not simply as Mrs. Gordon because it sometimes happens that the careless reader imagines that, although she signs herself "Jennifer Woods," she is perhaps Mrs. Gordon, rather than "Mrs. Gordon Woods," as she meant to indicate. It is better to make it very simple and clear. If she is single she signs her name "(Miss) Jennifer Childress." If her signature is impossible to read she should type or print under her signature: (Miss Jennifer Childress).

When a married woman lists her name as an officer of a woman's organization, she should use her social form of address, Mrs. John Jones, not Mrs. Mary Jones unless her club is a professional one calling for the use of her professional name.

A man does not put (Mr.) before his name unless his name is one that might be mistaken for a woman's name, for example Marion, Carol, or Beverly, or if he is writing out a self-addressed and stamped envelope. In the listing of his name on social lists, for example as a letterhead as one of the sponsors of a charity ball, he is listed by title, Mr. John Jones. In business listings, for example as a company officer, he is John Jones.

In signing a social letter, sign it with one name even if it expresses joint interest or thanks. A thank-you note looks odd signed, "Affectionately, Betty and Joe." If Joe wants to send a message, let there be reference to the fact in the letter. "Joe and I both enjoyed ourselves so much." Or, "Joe joins me in thanks for the lovely weekend. Cordially, Betty." Joint signatures are suitable only for telegrams, greeting cards and post cards. For example: Wish you were here! Edith and Bill.

If your name is very usual and you are writing to someone with whom you are on first-name terms, but who may not be able to identify your first-name signature too readily, sign yourself "Dorothy Preston," not just "Dorothy," for the recipient may know three or four Dorothys who might be writing such a letter to her. Even if such a letter is typed the signature must be handwritten.

Illegible Signatures Perhaps little can be done about improving a signature that has evolved, or rather deteriorated, into an illegible chicken track. You can help people with whom you deal by having stationery with your name and address printed on the envelopes, by using name and address stickers on envelopes, or by typing or printing your name beneath your signature together with your title—Miss or Mrs. (and very especially so if you have a name like Marion, Leslie, or Cecil, which may be masculine or feminine), by having your personal checks printed at slight cost with your name and address at the top or on one end, and by using correspondence cards with your name, address, and, optionally, telephone number printed on the top. You will save your own time as well as that of business people, and you will prevent costly delays and mistakes.

Ms. for Mrs. or Miss

Some secretarial schools advise the use of the abbreviation to cover situations in which one does not know the title of a woman to whom he is writing—whether it is Mrs. or Miss. I do not advise this abbreviation. It should be assumed that a woman whose name is not preceded by the definitive title is "Miss." That has always been the assumption in business and in the social world. To clarify matters, it is always advisable for any woman who has a name that might possibly be mistaken for a man's name to precede her signature with (Miss) in business or (Mrs.).

In the dictionary Ms. stands only for manuscript. Where one must address a letter to a person whose name could be either masculine or feminine, the use of this "Ms." would be useless at any rate. When in doubt as to the sex of the addressee it is forgivable to omit the title entirely—Carol Jones and use the name in full as a salutation "Dear Carol Jones." Of course it is much more courteous to make a great effort to find out what the proper title is. In business, and socially, it is generally incorrect to omit the title in addressing an envelope.

Dropping the "Jr." and Changing Other Suffixes

A man who is a Jr., a II, a III or possibly a IV, usually needs to take action when the preceding holder of the name dies. A "Jr." usually drops the "Jr." unless there would be what I call a confusion in history. In other words, if the father were so well known and perhaps he himself is so well known that to drop the "Jr." might cause public confusion. As the man who is called "II" is not named for his father but for someone else, perhaps an uncle or a grandfather of the same name, he drops this suffix on the death of the holder of that name unless there is a possibility, too, of a confusion in history. (See page 578 under "Men's Correspondence Cards.") When such a suffix is dropped usually nothing is necessary other than the notification of people as the occasion arises, for example, voters' registration, banks, the Internal Revenue Service. This last provides a space on the income tax form in which you indicate whether or not the name under which you are submitting your return this year is the same as that used last year. Social Security, of course, concerns itself with numbers primarily. A man with a "Jr." on his name, or any other suffix, does not change his Social Security number on dropping the suffix. There should not be any problem about stocks and bonds either, I am told. A man merely signs his name now without the suffix. I know one well-known man who dropped not only the "Jr." from his name after his father died, but his middle name as well. He made no explanation to anyone. In a short time his "new" name was well established. Checks received under the old name are endorsed that way and below the endorsement, the new name. It's as simple as that. It is good to remember that legally one may call oneself anything he pleases so long as there is no intent to deceive.

The Use of Senior

When a man drops the "Jr." upon the death of his father, and lives in the same town, or perhaps even in the same house, as his mother, his mother to avoid confusion adds "Sr." to her name. She does not become "Mrs. *Mary* Smith" but as a widow should, retains her husband's name becoming in this instance "Mrs. Charles Russell Smith, Sr." Father and son, working together in the same organization, with the son a "Jr." cannot properly call themselves "Jr." and "Sr." in written form. The father is Robert Loveman Brown and the son Robert Loveman Brown, Jr. A call coming into the office switchboard, however, might elicit the response from the operator, "Junior or Senior?"

Sequence of Pages in a Letter

The envelope determines how a single sheet of paper is to be folded for insertion, in one or two folds. Either way, the writing goes from top down, then again from top down on the other side, never crosswise of a single sheet. When a double sheet is used for a short letter the sequence is to write on page one, finish on page three. If all four pages are used they may be in the usual sequence, one, two, three, four, or the letter may go from page one to four, then be folded flat and the balance written on paper sidewise down the full folded-out page with the sequence of pages numbered. The sequence is not important but two things should be remembered: writing should not be written over, Victorian fashion, in the opposite direction, and if the envelope is transparent a protective sheet should be used if page four is readable through it.

Sequence of Pages in an Informal

If an informal has a monogram or the name printed or engraved in the center of the first side, nothing is written on that side and the note begins, if it is a short one, on the inside below the fold. If it is to be a long-enough note, it may begin at the top of the page when the informal is laid flat with the fold in a horizontal position and may follow on to the last page. An informal is exactly that. It doesn't necessarily require salutation or formal close. It may be as brief as this: We'd love to see you Saturday. Expect us at seven. Mary Ann.

Addressing Social Envelopes

Addresses on social envelopes may be typewritten or written by hand depending on whether the letter within was typed or handwritten which determines the matter. Handwriting on the envelope should be orderly and legible, with names either preferably written in full in formal social address or initials omitted entirely. Either Mr. James Nathan Webster or Mr. James Webster, not Mr. James N. Webster, common in business usage. If an initial normally precedes the name and the full name it stands for is never used then it must necessarily read, Mr. J. Nathan Webster.

In a social address commas are omitted and there are no abbreviations. City and state occupy separate lines. An imaginary margin on the right-hand side may be perpendicular so the last letters of each line line up with those above this way:

> Mrs. Ralph Webster Crooks
> 62 Morningside Drive
> Las Vegas
> Nevada zip code

or:

> Mrs. Ralph Webster Crooks
> 62 Morningside Drive
> Las Vegas
> Nevada zip code

The latter is much easier to achieve.

Many people follow these rules very loosely, yet achieve distinguished envelopes. Small numbers may be written out—"Ten," "Twenty," "Eighteen." More complex numbers are nowadays put into numerals in consideration of the postman.

Addressing Mail to Children When she is under sixteen, a young girl is addressed as "Susan Priddy." When she's over sixteen she is always "Miss" on cards or correspondence. In addressing a letter to a young man use "Master" through age twelve only. In his teens and until he is eighteen, when he becomes "Mr.," he is just "John Jones" on his cards or mail addressed to him.

Return Addresses Return addresses are a necessity today on everything from post cards to formal invitations (see Chapter 4, "Wedding Invitations and Announcements"). The post office asks that these return addresses be in the upper left-hand corner of the envelope so that it need not be turned over in the sorting. Return address stickers may be used, or on formal invitations and correspondence the address alone, including appointment number if necessary (*not* Mr. and Mrs. John Catterwood Smith) may be written in very small handwriting or printed in black ink, upper left. A man in adding his return address does not precede his name with Mr. or The Hon. Clergymen use The Rev. or Dr. as the case may be and medical and military men use their proper form of address on the return. A married woman uses Mrs. John Jones in her return address, not Mrs. Mary Jones (unless she uses her name this way professionally and this is a business letter). An unmarried woman precedes her name on a return address by Miss. The possible exception— on engraved stationery where the same die is used on the paper as on the envelopes for an unmarried woman, it is very expensive to have the plate re-engraved to include the Miss. It is assumed, therefore, that she is Miss if her name reads Christine Burnside on the envelope. In religious brotherhoods a return address reads John Patrick Murphy, S.J., but in the sisterhoods the name is preceded by Sister with possibly the letters of the order following.

Change of Address

If you change your address, notify all your friends and business correspondents promptly. The Post Office Department has a change-of-address card. Or you may have a post card printed. If you live formally, you may send out engraved cards, 3×5 inches, enclosed in envelopes. The printed post cards might read:

> The John Browns have moved to
> 625 Locust Street, New York, N.Y. zip code
> New telephone Plaza 0-0000

These cards do not have to be signed but may, of course, have a personal message added. Engraved cards might read:

Mrs. John Brown
has changed her address to
280 Park Avenue
New York, New York zip code
Telephones:
Plaza 0-0000   Eldorado 0-0000

To be doubly certain people remember the new address, address stickers might be made up with the top line reading "New Address." These could then be put on the back of every letter, stuck onto personal stationery bearing the old address, or given to friends to put beside your name in their address books.

The Use of "Personal," "Please Forward" and "Opened by Mistake"

It is always assumed that a letter sent to a person's home will be opened only by the addressee. It is therefore rude to other members of the family to mark such a letter "Personal." If, however, you are addressing a purely social, and perhaps quite confidential, letter to a person in his or her office where there is likelihood that mail is first opened by a secretary, then the use of "Personal" in the lower left-hand corner of the envelope is permissible.

If you know only a former address, not the present one, of the person to whom you are writing, you may write in the lower left-hand corner of the envelope, "Please Forward."

In our urban areas, where many people live in large apartment buildings, there is often more than one resident having the same last name. This often creates the embarrassing situation of your receiving and opening another person's mail. In this case, you reseal the envelope, mark it, "Opened by Mistake," sign your name, and mail it for the post office to redeliver. Do not attempt to deliver it in person. Legally, this will protect you in the event the mail is lost.

The Use of "Mesdames"

The French word Mesdames is used in writing only in addressing a group of women. For example:

The Women's Christian Temperance Union
Address
Mesdames:

The title is not preceded by "Dear." The substitution of the word "Ladies" in this case seems awkward and is not recommended.

The Use of "Messrs."

"Messrs." is the abbreviated form of the French for "Misters." It should be used only for letters addressed to brothers, never as an address for father and son. It is always used instead of the English word. In sending a Christmas card or a wedding invitation to two young men in a family which include several others to whom you do *not* wish to address the card or invitation, you write, "The Messrs. Guy and Donald Parsons." If there are merely the two brothers in the family you may address them as "The Messrs. Parsons" or simply "Messrs. Parsons." (See "Wedding Invitations and Announcements," page 30, for further information on this point.) This form is usual in the United States, rather than the awkward English "Mr. Guy and Mr. Donald Parsons."

Stamps on Envelopes

Stamps should be affixed neatly, particularly so for formal invitations where the appearance of the envelope is very important. In foreign countries where a head of state, religious leader, or some venerated person is used on a stamp, it is considered exceptionally rude for anyone to place the stamp in any but the upright position in the right-hand corner of the envelope. We have never paid very much attention to this rule in this country, but when you think about it, it is not a courteous thing to stand past Presidents on their heads, or to affix our flag upside down.

Letters That Must Be Handwritten

Although the typewriter has come into social use, there are a few limitations on its use for such correspondence. Preferably, no matter how illegible your handwriting, it is used in letters of condolence, but of course exceptions must occasionally be made. If you are writing a condolence letter from a business office to someone related to a person you have known mainly in business the letter may be dictated and typed.

Informal notes on invitations may be typed, but never formal ones, nor notes of invitation to a small wedding. Letters of congratulation—on the birth of a baby, on a girl's engagement, of felicitation to a girl on her marriage—all should be handwritten as are most thank-you notes unless the "thank-yous" are part of a long chatty letter. People with social secretaries dictate much of their correspondence, but even the busiest people usually take the trouble to write such notes as these in longhand.

Social Letter Writing

The Correct Form for Social Letters   If no engraved or printed address appears at the top of the paper the writer writes her return address in the upper right-hand corner, unless her address is well known to the recipient, thus:

876 North Main Street
Walpole, Massachusetts zip code
February 6th (year optional)
(sometimes the date appears,
lower left on the last sheet
below the signature)

Dear Natalie,
    Affectionately (or Sincerely, As ever, Cordially, Love, Lovingly,)
                                            Prue

February 6th
  (optional placement of date)

How to Get Started A quick plunge instead of a slow approach is better for any letter, business or social. Get to the point quickly in a business letter. In a social letter start with something that will lead the reader on.

If you have unpleasant but necessary news, try to prepare the way for it tactfully. Don't write, "Uncle Joe died suddenly last night and the family asked me to tell you immediately." Instead, write, "Something has just happened that was a great shock to us all and which will be, I'm afraid, to you, too. I am sorry to have to tell you that Uncle Joe, who hasn't been at all well lately, etc." Again, in such a painful instance, try to think what you would say to this person in his presence, and use the same form.

Bread-and-Butter Letters The thank-you for entertainment is obligatory after any overnight stay as a guest and is written to the *hostess*. I prefer even the briefest little thank-you note to a laconic "Thank you for the lovely weekend" scribbled on a visiting card and mailed to a hostess, although, mind you, such a thing is quite correct. A little more human, something that indicates a little more thoughtfulness, is a note, handwritten if your handwriting is legible, typed if it is not, but in any case graceful and friendly:

                                        Monday
Dear Mildred,
  Your party and the entire weekend, as always, were great fun. I enjoyed meeting the Le Beaus and found them just as stimulating as you promised. In fact, just talking to M. Le Beau stirred me to dig out my French grammar again. Frank, who had a fine time, joins me in hoping we will see you and Tom here soon.

                                    Love,
                                    Josephine

Thank-you Notes for Entertainment A note to someone who has never entertained you before, or with whom you are on formal terms, might read:

Saturday

Dear (or more formally, [in this country but *not* in Great Britain where "My dear" is the intimate form] My dear) Mrs. Goodrich,

We have always wanted to see "High Ridge" in the peony season and so enjoyed your invitation last Tuesday, especially as you served cocktails in your really lovely garden. Thank you so much for including us.

Cordially, (or Sincerely yours or Yours truly)

Josephine Mason

Here, because she knows you are Mrs. Fielding Mason, you don't put that information parenthetically under your signature, of course.

Technically, it is not necessary for you to do more than thank a hostess orally as you leave a luncheon, tea, or dinner party if you are not staying the night or longer. But if it is obvious that the hostess has gone to much trouble to arrange entertainment especially for you, it is certainly decent of you to drop her a line of thanks or to telephone her to express your appreciation and necessary indeed if you were guest of honor. It is a little irritating to a hostess when she has gone to great lengths to entertain people to have them depart with a brief word of thanks and not send her any word again for weeks, months, or sometimes years. Yet that is what happens today, especially in our busy cities, now that the party call has disappeared. But the little party note, even if it is on your card, takes the party call's place if you have a certain sensitivity about such things. Even when you are entertained at dinner very often by the same people, it is courteous at least occasionally to bother to write a few words of appreciation, or to phone your thanks preferably not the next day if the party has been a large one for an especially nice time. And to send a little gift to someone who entertains you often and whom, perhaps, you have no way of entertaining—at least in the same manner—is another pleasant way to say thank you.

Do not, however, send printed cards of thanks for anything. But you may use those charming little floral-bedecked informals or post cards, so long as no sentiments are printed on them. There is no objection to a post card (especially ones specially printed for you) between old friends if they will speed up a thank-you for a happy time together and if they are used informally. You can hardly put intimacies on a post card for anyone to read. I'd never use even an imported floral or art post card for a thank-you for overnight entertainment unless I enclosed it in an envelope, and even then it should go only to a close friend, as others would expect more formality. To be avoided especially are informals that actually have "Thank You" printed on them. They are no substitute for a brief handwritten note.

Thank-you Notes for Gifts If a gift is given in person, the recipient gives his thanks then and there, though, of course, if he wishes to write a note after the donor has left, it makes a nice, spontaneous gesture and I find they are really expected after baby or bridal showers. Thank-you notes should be sent just as soon as possible after the receipt of the gift, within a week preferably. A thank-you for such a gift may go on an informal or on a single sheet of paper or on a correspondence card. No one expects more than a few words, but they should sound sincere and really appreciative. Just the day of the week will do for the date, upper right or lower left below the signature. For example:

Dear Jon,
The melodious little alarm clock was exactly what this household needed. Now Allen won't have to rush to the station mornings without his coffee. Next time you come you'll see what a reformation you have wrought!

Cordially,
Nina

Tuesday

When gifts of money are to be acknowledged, the sum is not mentioned. In some households especially where both husbands and wives work, husbands have taken to sharing some of these chores. As this is usually the duty of the woman of the house, it remains a delicate situation for the man to handle. A man might write a brief note, even one dictated from the office on his executive stationery reading:

Friday

Dear Mary,
Consuela has just arrived home with the baby. You know what that means! She was concerned about getting to all her thank-you notes promptly so I offered to tell you she—and our new son—enjoyed your pink carnations very much. We all thank you and hope you and Sam will soon be able to view the handsome new member of our family.

Sincerely,
Gerald

When You Retire A graceful note of thanks should be written to fellow employees and associates who have perhaps contributed to a handsome retirement gift when you leave your firm.

Dear Henry,
This is just to tell you how much I've enjoyed our working together over the years. I do want to thank you for your part in that memorable farewell party and for the handsome set of matched golf clubs. Many thanks.

Sincerely,
John

Greeting Cards We are the largest users of greeting cards in the world. Many are charming, amusing, and clever and they fill almost any communication need. They must be chosen and sent with discretion, however. A funny card showing a wrecked house with the legend, "Wow! What a party!" is not a proper thank you to conservative people for entertainment or even for highly informal ones without at least an added few lines. Cruel, unkind, or tasteless cards should never be sent. There is no place, for example, for that horrid offering, a card that offers congratulations on a divorce or for cards announcing a divorce. Greeting cards with envelopes should be sent first-class mail. They do not require a reply. When they have come perhaps from someone you haven't heard from for a long time, a reply if only on a post card is considerate and helps to keep open the lines of communication, so important in this busy world.

Any greeting card should have a return address including zip code to aid the post office.

Greeting cards for people who are ill should be selected with greatest care. You don't of course send a "get well" card to someone who knows he is not going to get well and everyone else knows it, too. There are greeting cards that can bring cheer without being tactless. When in doubt about the propriety of sending a greeting card, send a letter or flowers, or a gift, instead. In some circumstances, the less said the better. There are, however, many attractive cards that can cheer someone hospitalized even when the prognosis is bad, but they must be chosen very carefully.

When a great many greeting cards have been received, for example in the hospital where replying to any of them would be a problem for the sick person a reply is not necessary nor expected. A greeting card—at Christmastime or for a birthday—from a friend one hadn't seen for a long time, might call for a reply if only a few lines but, generally, greeting cards do not require a response.

Telegrams Telegrams today no longer strike terror in the heart of the recipient for they are bearers of all kinds of news and are used for many casual purposes. They may issue an invitation, postpone a wedding, congratulate parents on the birth of a child, transmit a birthday greeting, or convey a message of condolence. They speed business offers and reassure friends and family of safe arrival. They do not necessarily require any reply unless they bear the legend "Reply Requested." It is considerate to reply to telegrams of condolence or felicitation by note however simply. No zip codes are used in telegrams.

"Angry" Letters If you are angry, be very careful how you express your anger in a letter. Remember it may travel many miles and that circumstances, or just time, may change your feelings materially. Almost as soon as you have posted an abusive or ill-tempered letter you may wish it back. We all need to have an outlet for our anger from time to time. Write exactly how you feel about something, let yourself go and be furiously vituperative, then "sleep on it." The next day rewrite such a letter and, in calmer tones, say anything that needs to be said. Try to begin your letter with praise, if possible, and end it the same way if you can. How?

Wednesday

Dear Genevieve,

It isn't often that I have any reason to complain about your treatment of the children. In fact, I sometimes think you are, if anything, too likely to overlook their faults but . . .

And end it:

I hate to bring this whole thing up and really wouldn't have except that it was troubling me very much, probably quite unnecessarily. I am sure you, who are usually so very considerate, can help me prevent such a thing happening again.

Get things off your mind. Anger that isn't expressed sometimes makes us vaguely or definitely anxious or depresses us. But, if you can, rehearse what you plan to say. Write it out, let it cool, then see if that is really what you want to say in the way you want to say it. Wasn't that putting it pretty strong? Was it really that way? Couldn't there be extenuating circumstances? Everyone has his bad day and perhap you are damning a good friend or neighbor for life for something you could clear up with a firm, courteous objection. For instance:

A Letter of Complaint to a Neighbor

June 12th

Dear Mr. Robbins,

You will be sorry to hear that our baby was snapped at yesterday by your dog. I am sure it was the baby's fault, as the dog is normally a friendly animal, but your children do bring him here unleashed and it isn't always possible to keep an eye on him. I wonder if you can ask the boys to leave Rags at home—at least until the baby is old enough to understand he mustn't pull a dog's tail.

With kindest regards to you and Mrs. Robbins,

Cordially,
John Doe

Letters of Apology Occasionally there is need to send a letter of apology. Such letters should really be notes explaining some remissness, such as the sudden canceling of a dinner or failure to keep an appointment, though telephoned or telegraphed word has probably preceded the letter. Apologies of a more serious sort are difficult and sometimes useless to put in a letter. When some grave misunderstanding has arisen it is better, if possible, to settle it in person, as even the most carefully couched letter may merely add fat to the fire.

A note of apology need not be too definite. If you had sudden guests drop in the evening you had promised to play bridge with friends who were not near neighbors, you would write a note something like this if you had not been able to reach your hostess in person by phone:

Wednesday

Dear Carol,

Hope you received my message in time to get another couple for bridge Tuesday night. We had counted on it but had some guests from out-of-town show up unexpectedly just before dinner. Let's try again for next week. Will you plan to come here? Please let me know.

Love,
Ruth

Love Letters Love letters are sometimes bombshells. It has often been said that nothing should go into a letter that couldn't be read in court. It seems hard to regard so tender a passion with so suspicious an eye, but life can sometimes distort the tenderest sentiments into something else. Letters are often opened by mistake, or by prying hands. A gentleman should never write anything in a letter which might damage a lady's reputation if his words should be read by someone else. Promises of undying devotion might give an unfriendly reader the impression of intimacies that had never occurred. Even where love is eagerly reciprocated, expressions of it are best not entrusted to the mails unless they are couched in asbestos phrases. Some of the greatest writers of all times have been able to write the subtlest love letters in such a way that the loved one may read anything he or she wishes into the words. But they are written, too, so that no direct promises are made, no reputations put in jeopardy, no intimacies exposed to ridicule should the letter fall into hands other than those for which it was intended.

Letters of Social Reference and Introduction Letters of social reference are never baldly requested by anyone, and the wise friend never gives one except obliquely. That is, she may write to friends in a community to which a close friend is going and ask them to look him up, stating why she thinks they may have something in common. This leaves a delicate matter entirely up to the friend-at-a-distance and gives her some protection, should entertainment not be convenient at the time. Otherwise, if a letter of introduction is actually written and presented she has little choice but to entertain the stranger in some way as a courtesy to the writer of the letter. Thus, never write letters of introduction for people you know only casually and never send them to those you know just slightly unless you are sure of performing a service to those who will be obligated to entertain for the people you introduce. Give such letters only after mature consideration, for you are guaranteeing your friend's behavior and social acceptability. For this reason never allow a friend to extract such a letter for a friend of his own. The oblique introduction goes this way:

Dear Margaret,

Our dear neighbors here, the Lionel Downings, plan to spend several weeks at The Rock, which seems to be fairly near you. While they are the sort of people who make friends easily, it might be interesting to you both if you could get together during their stay. Both Lionel and Anne play golf well and I think you'd enjoy a foursome. Don't feel this is a "must," of course. I haven't obligated you in any way and if you do call and introduce yourselves it will be a pleasant surprise for them.

Love,
Margery

A direct letter of social introduction has some point, perhaps, if a close friend—and only a close friend—is going abroad and you would like to make his social path pleasant for him where you have friends. You might then furnish him with a letter which he would personally present with his card on making a formal call or, if more convenient would mail with his card on which he had written in ink the name of his hotel. If his time is limited he may telephone and explain that he has a letter of introduction. A woman using such a social letter always mails it. She may present a business letter, however.

The direct letter of introduction might read:

My dear Henriette [this is the European *intimate* form of address]

This will introduce one of our dear friends, Henry Welsh Lanier. I could not let him go to Paris without at least the promise of a glimpse of you. He won't be there very long, something you are sure to regret the moment you all meet. How I envy him the chance to visit you and Paris in the spring.

Love,
Paula

The letter is given the traveler, unsealed, with the name of the friend to whom it is to be presented on the outside:

Madame
      Simon de Nouilly
Courtesy Mr. Lanier
(or Courtesy of)

The address, presumably, is in his address book. The letter should be accepted and sealed in your presence without being read. If you send the letter of introduction through the mail to the person who will present it, enclose it in its own unsealed envelope.

It is becoming common for people to say, even to chance acquaintances, "When you're in St. Louis, do call my good friends the Chases. Any friend of mine is a friend of theirs. They'll treat you royally." And doubtless on a dull evening this far from intimate friend will do just that. And the Chases, not considering this a casual matter, will put themselves out considerably for your sake. Try, always, to leave the initiative up to those in the home territory if you would keep their friendship. Sometimes, however, it is expedient to do something like this if people are traveling on an irregular itinerary and don't know exactly when they will arrive at a stated place. In this case write your friends, "My good friends the Milton Petersons are traveling in California this spring and I have taken the liberty of asking them to let you know when they are in San Francisco. If it is convenient do let them see your cliff gardens. They are ardent gardeners."

Writing to a Celebrity

No writer, author, public officeholder, artist, musician, or other person singled out because of his accomplishments is ever offended by your words of praise, oral, or written. He may even be stimulated by, and interested in, your criticisms decently given, if you care to give them. He may or may not reply to you depending on the warmth of his personality or the lack of it. He may actually not have the time to take care of such correspondence, especially if he has no secretary. But don't hesitate through diffidence to express yourself, if you feel you have something you'd like to say to such people. Encourage the expression of such response in your children, too. One of my sons at age eight read a charming children's book by a famous writer who had just made his first venture into the juvenile field. Much to my surprise, my son said, "I want to write that man to tell him how much I like his book." He'd never suggested such a thing before but was quite unself-conscious about writing to someone he didn't know. We got pencil and paper, and he printed his own little letter which, with the help of Who's Who, I sent off to the correct address. Within two days back came a charming reply, which we all treasure and which will be kept in that particular favorite book for grandchildren to enjoy, too. (*Stuart Little*, by E. B. White.) I am sure the author enjoyed the bit of sincere appreciation, sent so spontaneously, quite as much as we enjoyed his delightful reply to a worshipful small boy.

Everyone, I am sure, enjoys appreciation of what he is trying to do if the words he hears or reads are sincere and given without thought of possible benefit to the giver of them. You need never feel constrained to keep your reactions to yourself. Even the President of the United States wants to know what you are thinking—even if you aren't necessarily thinking his way. Let's try some of these letters I'm talking about:

A Letter to the White House

(Your address
Date in full)

The President of the United States of America
The White House
Washington, D.C. zip code, U.S.A.

Mr. President: (or, less formally, My dear Mr. President, and the tone of
     your letter can decide which you wish to use.)

Your address to Congress last week brought us new confidence in the
quality of your leadership. While my wife and I are not members of your
party and have previously taken issue with you on many measures you have
endorsed, we now feel that your recent actions have shown us that we have
been wrong in some of our judgments. I believe, sir, you are on the road to
converting two hitherto hidebound opponents to your party's platform.

I have the honor to remain,

Very Respectfully,
(signed) Cyrus Tweedsworth

A Letter to an Author

(Your address
Date in full)

Lake Meadow, Illinois zip code
Miss Gertrude Prince
Dogwood Heights

Dear (or more formally, My dear) Miss Prince:

Your new book, "The Dinner Bell," certainly deserves the best-sellerdom
it has achieved so quickly. It gave me so very much pleasure I wanted to
tell you so. I am recommending it to all my friends as the best thing you
have written. Let's have more about the Judge family.

Sincerely,
Lisette Ford Bowens
(Mrs. Martin Bowens)

Writing to a Public Official

Express your appreciation when you feel admiration for something someone
has done, even if you don't know that person or have any hope of knowing
him. If you disapprove of legislative activities or of pending bills, say so,
too, to your properly delegated representative. It is senseless to vent your
fury on your friends when there are—in Congress, or in your state or local
legislatures, or other bodies—representatives elected by you who must listen
to you, pro or con, concerning their actions. Here is a letter to a Congressman:

June 1, 1971

The Hon. Paul Burns Tyng
House of Representatives
Washington, D.C. zip code

Dear Mr. Congressman (or Sir, or Dear Sir):

May I add my protest to those that are pouring in upon you concerning your recent attack on the Moreland Bill (H.R. 267). I believe the passage of this bill is vitally necessary to the proper safeguarding of interstate motorists, and I urge you to reconsider your stand.

Sincerely,
(signed) Julia S. De Palma
(Mrs. Guido De Palma)

So much righteous indignation which could be a vital and intelligent power in our legislative bodies is wasted by people who have no idea that they have a right and a duty to inform their Senators, Congressmen, their Mayors, and even the President himself, if they are so minded, of their own convictions concerning such vital matters as pending legislation. If you don't know the names of your state's Congressmen and of its Senators, call your local paper or library for the proper information. A post card or a telegram (composed by you) will register your protest or support. A telegram, properly addressed, is even suitable to send to the President. Do it this way:

THE PRESIDENT
WASHINGTON, D.C. (No zip code is used in telegrams.)
RESPECTFULLY URGE VETO JENNINGS BILL DISCRIMINATING AGAINST SCHOOL TEACHERS.

BURTON WHEELER GAINS
PRINCIPAL, LAWTON HIGH SCHOOL
BRIGHTON, KANSAS

In wiring the President or any other officeholder, always prepay the wire even where the telegraph company might slip up and accept a collect wire to such an individual. A Congressman might feel called upon to accept the charges because you are a constituent, but he has only limited funds for office expenses and will not appreciate your adding to them.

Always identify yourself if you hold some position, and, if possible, indicate in your wire what your interest is, if you have a biased one. Never misrepresent your interest or you may find yourself in an embarrassing position. If, as the wife of a man who will be deeply affected by the passage or non-passage of a piece of legislation, you appeal for or against it without stating your personal stake in it, it is possible you might be asked to testify for or against the pending bill. Also, your communication might be published, and your vested interest immediately revealed. Congressional committees are always very interested in what is behind a mass protest or support of a bill and whether or not activity has been professionally organized.

Offensive Communications   You may be indignant or downright furious at something your representatives in Congress or in the state legislature have done but never send an abusive letter or wire. Try to be as objective as possible and to consider the respect the office deserves, even though you may at the moment consider the holder of it ill-advised, to say the least. An offensive, possibly libelous, telegram is usually refused by the telegraph company. A scurrilous letter can bring a libel suit, although if your Representative should reply in kind—and some have been known to do so—his congressional immunity prohibits legal retaliation by you. He can call you all kinds of a liar, special pleader, fellow traveler, or whatever suits his fancy if you attack him. But you are vulnerable to his wrath if you overstep the bounds of decency and at least relative respect in addressing him. Again it is the office that is protected against abuse, not the man.

Don't Telephone   A protest to a legislator by telephone is useless unless you, for some reason, have the privilege of talking to him personally. Put your reaction into writing. If he knows his business he will answer you, often with a brief personal letter or at least an acknowledgment of some kind. Before berating him or requesting he vote this way or that, determine what stand he has already taken on the matter. The League of Women Voters, your local newspaper, your local or national political headquarters all have this information, down to the most recent details. It is embarrassing to write a letter to a Congressman only to receive assurance by return mail that one look at his record shows he is on your side and has been battling all along for the cause you urge him to support.

Discouraging Correspondence

We all from time to time hear from old schoolmates, people we knew years back and with whom we are not truly interested in continuing a correspondence and who, frankly, we hope we may never have to see again. I remember a very wise man once saying to me that we all receive letters which are best left unanswered, and some such letters are. The kindliness in most of us, however, urges us to reply to the letter from the woman we met at that resort hotel fifteen years ago and who may have been sending us Christmas cards ever since. Some such letters are of course greatly welcome and we know exactly how to answer them. Others pose a severe problem. It is probably best to acknowledge such a letter, but in a way that discourages further communication. How do you do this without being hurtful? Analyze first why the letter was written to you. Realize that as people get older, they sometimes grow more sentimental. Anything might have inspired this unexpected letter—an old song or seeing a snapshot or even financial need. It is kind to respond but if you are absolutely certain that this is not a person with whom you wish to continue correspondence, reply somewhat along these lines:

Dear George,

It was a great surprise to hear from you after all these years, and pleasant of course. We enjoyed hearing about your family.

Unfortunately, I don't have the time to write more at length as our lives are very complicated (we have four children) and much as we'd like to, it is not always possible to keep up old friendships. Perhaps we'll run into you sometime. In the meantime, thank you very much for writing to us.

Cordially, (or Sincerely,)

Don't include snapshots or anything else that might encourage further communication. Sign your own name, not jointly with your spouse (never recommended except on post cards, greeting cards and telegrams).

Christmas Cards

I think the spirit of Christmas is destroyed when a man and his wife sit down and address hundreds of engraved or printed Christmas cards, partly for business reasons, partly because they know that they themselves will be deluged with other hundreds of cards at which they scarcely have time to glance once the holiday season is upon them. But they will display the deluge, nevertheless, as a proof of their vast and friendly acquaintance.

When Christmas card sending begins to take on such gargantuan and impersonal proportions the time has come to take stock. You will not become a social pariah if you don't send a single Christmas card. If you don't send any at all a great many people will probably cross you off their own swollen lists with a sigh of relief, and like you none the less. If you pare your list to distant friends and leave out the close-by ones to whom you may wish a Merry Christmas in person, that makes sense, too.

If business and friendship have become so intermingled in so social a thing as Christmas card giving it is wise to separate the two anyhow. If business Christmas cards must be sent—and I have never seen much logic in that practice—let the business send them, not the executive and his wife. Better "The Jones Company (or Roy Jones) sends warmest wishes for a Merry Christmas and a Happy New Year" than "Mildred and Roy Jones wish you, etc.," especially when Mildred Jones is not a part of the firm and probably is unknown to most of the firm's clients.

The frenzied sending of Christmas cards to everyone who sent *you* cards the year before or who may be expected to send cards this year is really senseless. It takes courage to abandon the custom and to send cards, only if you want to, to those people whom you are not likely to greet in person. I would infinitely prefer a card with the warmth of a signature and perhaps a little message for me alone to the most ornate engraved card.

It is, as they say in German, *gemütlich* to have a photograph taken of your children of the family together or of your house, your pets, or a beloved part of your garden to send to really interested friends, who will often keep such historical cards year after year. These needn't be elaborate at all. They may even be printed on post cards and sent without an envelope, with or without a personal message. They needn't even be Christmassy. Everyone will understand that you are sending a little sentimental keepsake because it is a friendly time of year. A handwritten "Merry Christmas" is all that is needed. You never send such personal cards to people who would not possibly be interested in little Alex's first attempt to stand alone. Others may be sent little holiday informals with a note inside, or any engraved or printed Christmas card in good taste. Religious cards, unless recognizable Art—for example the Raphael Madonna—are often bathetic. Simple cards, not necessarily expensive ones, are best and should always be given the dignity of first-class postage.

Addressing Christmas Cards Christmas cards should always be addressed to a husband and wife even if the sender knows only one of the couple. When a card is sent more or less for business reasons it may be sent to a man or woman's office, to him or her alone. Where a business and social relationship exists which has included the wife or husband, then the card, even a firm's card, may be sent to a home address, addressed to both husband and wife. In this case where the woman is in business under her maiden name, she should be addressed jointly with her husband—Mr. and Mrs. Robert Clawson, preferably not at home as Miss Caroline Carter.

Signing Christmas Cards The British tradition, which we follow in many things, is that the man's name comes first in a signature on greeting cards or in an engraving or imprinting of these names. That is, John and Mary Jones rather than Mary and John Jones. I prefer it this way in engraved or imprinted material, but I feel it makes no difference whether in a *signature* on a greeting card the actual writer of the signature puts his name first or second. It is done both ways. If a list of members of the family is to be given, the father's name comes first: Bob, Mary, Helen, and Peter Jobson. The inclusion of the family may also be handled this way: The Robert Meyer Jobsons. If a sister and brother live together, they can send out joint Christmas cards by signing them, Mary Jobson and below that Robert Jobson, or just The Jobsons. On this occasion use red ink if you wish, even on the envelope.

When the suffix Jr., II, or III is used within a series, it is not separated from the name, for example: Robert, Elizabeth, Robert Jr., Jerry. When a name with a suffix is at the end of a series, however, the name and the suffix are separated by a comma, for example: Robert, Elizabeth, Jerry and Robert, Jr. When suffixes are used in greeting cards the family may be designated as The Robert R. Holdens II or The Robert R. Holdens, second. Also correct are the following: The Judson K. Reillys, Jr., or The Judson K. Reilly, Jrs.

Return addresses should be written or pasted on the upper left-hand corner of greeting card envelopes. If you contribute to charities that sell Christmas stickers as a means of raising revenue, it is nice to use the seals on your Christmas card envelopes and packages, to further such worthy causes and encourage others to think of Christmas, too, as a time for impersonal giving as well. Such return addresses on cards from a couple or a family require only the address, including apartment number if necessary. They should not, for example read "Mary and Bob White" with the address.

Women's Business Letters

Writing the Business Letter Everyone has occasion to write a business letter from time to time. A woman's order to a department store, for example, should be a business letter in correct form in order to facilitate the filling of the order. If your handwriting is illegible except to friends, type or print your business letters. Using block letters may seem childish, but it's better, isn't it, than to leave considerable doubt concerning what you are trying to say? A woman signs a business letter as she signs a social one, using her signature, Mary Jones with her title (Miss) added parenthetically if it isn't on her letterhead or typed or printed with her name beneath her signature if her signature is illegible. Beneath a woman's signature, Melissa White, is typed or printed her proper social form of address (Mrs. August White) if this name does not appear on the letterhead.

Simplicity of Language and Punctuation The perfect business letter is shorn of the phrases we used to find in textbooks on English usage. The good letter writer never uses such expressions as "Yours of the fifteenth inst. received and contents noted." Instead he writes, "Thank you for your letter (or for the information)," and goes on, briefly and succinctly, from there, putting in all relevant information and trying whenever possible to limit his communication to one page or less.

Use punctuation skillfully. For example the constant use of the semicolon on any page, handwritten or printed, causes the eye to jump to the punctuation instead of concentrating on the subject expounded upon, just as a "river"—vertical space on a type page caused by inexpert setting—disturbs vision. Where a semicolon can't be replaced by a simple comma, it is often better to rephrase the thought into two or more separate sentences for easier comprehension.

In any writing avoid the use of quotation marks around words which you feel should get special emphasis for some reason—slang words, for example, which you have habitually placed in quotes to show that they are slang. Your correspondent probably knows slang when he sees it and will read your letter with greater facility if it isn't dancing with quotes, underlinings, exclamation points, and those irritating dots that advertising writers use to indicate a blank spot in their thoughts. If you want to use dots, use them as they should be used, to express an unfinished quotation or thought, "The time has come, the Walrus said . . ." "So I told Johnny if he ever brought a toad into the house again . . ." In letter writing I think the dash performs the same function nicely. But avoid having your letter full of dashes, too.

As in the social letter, try to avoid the "I" as an opening word and, instead, use some form of "you," if possible. Keep sentences short. Here is an awkwardly phrased letter:

February 5, 1972

Mr. Max I. Klug
Klug Inc.
600 York Street
Elizabeth, New Jersey zip code

My dear Mr. Klug:

I am chairman of the board for the York Street Juvenile Society and I would like to know if your firm would, as it has on previous drives, be willing to contribute the sum of $500 for this worthy cause which is, etc.

Sincerely,
Jane Doe

Instead of using such a self-important approach, the writer should have thought of herself as face to face with this businessman. Then she might have written as she would have talked, and thus produced a better letter. For example:

February 5, 1972

Mr. Max I. Klug
Klug Inc.
600 York Street
Elizabeth, New Jersey zip code

My dear Mr. Klug:

Your firm has given generously to the York Street Juvenile Society each year at this time when our drive takes place.

As you know, the Society's work is to provide greatly needed facilities for the minor children of working mothers. It furnishes play space Saturdays and Sundays. It gives psychiatric and other counseling to families and individual children needing help.

We are sure Klug Inc. will want to continue its support of this work. I enclose a pledge for $500, the amount you regularly subscribe.

Sincerely,
(Miss) Jane Doe

Ordering from a Department Store   It is frequently necessary to write to department stores, shops, and local merchants.

Here is an example of such to-the-point communication.

(use your address in full)
1482 Cricket Drive
Lake Forest, Illinois zip code
January 22, 1972

B. Coons & Co.
Fifth Avenue at 34th Street
New York, New York zip code

Gentlemen:

Please send me the dressing gown #79 listed in your current catalogue. I would like it in yellow, size 16. My second choice of color is rose. Please charge to my account.

Sincerely,
Jennifer Woods
(Mrs. Gordon Woods)

Use of Post Cards   Post cards are a very useful adjunct to social and business correspondence. Name-and-address printed correspondence cards with or without telephone number make it quick and easy to communicate brief messages to friends, orders to stores. In the latter case, as they bear the name and address (including zip code), the salutation is not necessary in giving the order, for example,

Please send me 6 pairs pantyhose size Medium-Tall in Suntan as advertised in The Press July 12. Charge my account number 000-00=000.

This is then signed as you sign your charge card.

Letters of Complaint   In writing to a business organization of some kind to voice a complaint about merchandise or service, think of the recipient of your letter as another human being like yourself and not just as a representative of an organization. For he will be affected pleasantly or otherwise by the tone of your complaint and inclined, quite possibly, to act less quickly, or not to your benefit, if you are abusive. Even big companies are fallible because of the human cogs in the machine. Most companies want to keep your patronage by making good or at least by apologizing when things go wrong. Let's see how a friendly letter of complaint to a store might read:

786 Decatur Road
Thomasville, Georgia
November 3, 1971

Nu-Fairbanks Seed Company
400 Bond Street
Richmond, Virginia zip code

Gentlemen:

Your company has always given such excellent service that I regret having a complaint to make now. On June 22 you mailed me a package of grass seed I had ordered and which arrived with the carton open and most of the seed gone. I took the matter up with the post office here, and they informed me that the package had not been properly prepared for mailing, nor had it been insured. As the mistake seems to have been made by your shipping department, I am sure you will make good on the order by having the carton more carefully packed before sending it out to me again. Thank you for your attention.

Sincerely,
Jane Doe
(Mrs. John Doe)

If you write politely and make it clear that you expect some adjustment or correction to be made, you will usually get prompt results. Contentious letters and abusive ones sometimes get delayed results or a refusal.

I had a self-important friend whose request for a passport was held up interminably because she was offensive to a government clerk. Somehow her abusive letters and complaints never seemed to get through to the right people. An irritated individual can usually find some way of being uncooperative, especially if he's a little, pushed-around cog in a big machine. Try approaching him with a pleasant letter or a friendly tone of voice and he will be so surprised to hear a complaint couched in such a human manner that he will often find a way to make exceptions in your case. People are people even when they are part of big, often bureaucratic, organizations.

Making Reservations   When travel reservations are to be made, letters or wires may be sent by either the husband or the wife. In either case the term "my husband and me" or "my wife and me" are used to make clear the relationship of those desiring reservations. Such a letter reads:

285 Park Avenue
New York, New York zip code
December 12, 1972

The Manager
Crazy Horse Ranch
Denver, Colorado zip code

Dear Sir:

Will you please reserve a double room with double bed for my husband and me, and a single room for my son for July first for one week? If such accommodations are not available at present please let me know the earliest date you can take care of us.

Sincerely,
Myra Cox Castle
(Mrs. Brion Castle)

On arrival, the husband registers, "Mr. and Mrs. Brion Castle and son," unless the son is grown in which case he is registered separately, George Castle (no "Mr.").

Mrs. Castle traveling with a maid registers, "Mrs. Brion Castle and maid." Optionally, "and maid, Miss Monia Dolonoso."

Wiring Reservations   Husband or wife may wire reservations ahead:

AMERICAN AIRLINES
633 THIRD AVENUE
NEW YORK (No zip code is used in telegrams.)
PLEASE RESERVE TWO FIRST CLASS SEATS TO SAN FRANCISCO WIFE AND SELF FIRST AVAILABLE SATURDAY AFTERNOON FLIGHT. REPLY COLLECT. BRION CASTLE.

In a collect wire the telegraph company has a record of your return address, but it does not accept collect cables. To insure a reply by cable you prepay the reply as well as your cable.

Chapter 45

INVITATIONS, ACCEPTANCES, AND REGRETS

Formal Invitations

Formal invitations, engraved or handwritten on conservative paper, are sent out on a number of occasions—for the formal dinner, the debut, the formal dance, and the official luncheon or reception. They are written in the third person and are sent approximately two weeks ahead of time. A formal invitation should be given that much leeway, but not more (except during the Christmas holidays when the great number of invitations going out often requires early mailing), as the occasion might be forgotten entirely with more advance notice. (For wedding invitations, acceptances, and regrets, see the Wedding Section.)

The Engraved Fill-in Invitation to a Formal Dinner

Mr. and Mrs. Charles Smith Prescott
request the pleasure of
*Miss Wing's**
company *at dinner*
on *Tuesday, the Second of May*
at *eight o'clock*
4 East Eightieth Street
New York, New York zip code

R.s.v.p.

* Italic type indicates handwriting.

When an invitation that asks for a reply is issued well in advance, the hostess is justified in sending out small reminder cards or telephoning those people who have neglected to notify her. Most conservatively such invitations are also on white cards but are sometimes engraved on colored stock in contrasting inks such as green on gray.

Engraved Invitation to a Formal Dinner

Mr. and Mrs. Elliott Harrison
request the pleasure of your company
at dinner
on Friday, June the fifteenth
at eight o'clock
250 Park Avenue
New York, New York   zip code

R.s.v.p.

When friends are issuing an invitation together, their invitation would read:

Miss Francesca Miller
and
Miss Vanessa Abott
request the pleasure of
Mr. William Fuld's
company at dinner
on Saturday, August the ninth
at eight o'clock
25 Fifth Avenue
New York, N.Y.   zip code

R.s.v.p.

Handwritten Invitation to a Formal Dinner   The formal written invitation may be written on any personal formal writing paper, usually white. If the stationery does not have the address at the top the address is written at the bottom underneath the time. A telephone number is never used on formal invitations.

> *Mr. and Mrs. Walter MacFee*
>
> *request the pleasure of*
>
> *Mr. and Mrs. Anderson's*
>
> *company at dinner*
>
> *on Wednesday, September the sixth*
>
> *at eight o'clock*
>
> R.S.V.P.   *Poppy Villa*
>
> *Beverly Hills, California zip code*

For a Dinner in Honor of a Special Guest

> Mr. and Mrs. Gerald Fox Healy
> request the pleasure of
> *Mr. and Mrs. Buxton's*
> company at dinner
> on Monday, September the tenth
> at eight o'clock to meet
> Mr. Johnson Parker

R.s.v.p.
21A Sutton Place
New York, New York   zip code

Invitation to a Formal Dance

Mrs. Richard William Horst
requests the pleasure of
Mr. and Mrs. Thompson's
company at a small dance
on Saturday the thirteenth of September
at half after ten o'clock
Lotus Beach Club

R.s.v.p.
One Silver Lane
Palm Beach, Fla.   zip code

(The wording, "small dance," in the above invitation is often used whether the dance is large or small. But the expression is not necessary.)

When a Guest May Bring Along an Escort

Mr. and Mrs. Gordon Smyth Cummings
request the company of
Miss Melissa McKee and escort
(OR IN THE CASE OF A MAN, MR. MARK MCKEE AND GUEST)
at a small dance
in honour of their daughter and son
on Saturday, June the eighth
at eight o'clock
Edgemere Country Club

R.S.V.P.
14 Apple Tree Road
Larchmont, New York   zip code

Invitation to a Formal Dance When the Reply Is Sent to Social Secretary

Mr. F. Vernon Osborne
requests the pleasure of
Mr. Scott's
company at a small dance
in honour of his niece
Miss Amanda Osborne (Note: Miss)
on Monday, the twenty-ninth of December
at eleven o'clock
Montclair Country Club

R.s.v.p.
Mrs. Van Broeck
8 East First Street
Montclair, New Jersey   zip code

Invitation to a Debutante Dance

Mr. and Mrs. Macy Linde Turner
request the pleasure of
the company of
Miss Lippincott
at a dance in honour of their granddaughter
Miss Charlotte Gilchrist
on Saturday, the fourth of February
at ten o'clock
River House

The favour of a reply is requested
998 Fifth Avenue
New York, N.Y.   zip code

or, if the parents give the dance:

Mr. and Mrs. David Filmore Gilchrist
Miss Charlotte Sue Gilchrist
request the pleasure of
the company of
Mr. Butterly
on Saturday, the fourth of February
at ten o'clock
31 Sutton Place South
New York, New York   zip code

R.S.V.P.   Dancing

Though on wedding invitations the "Miss" is virtually always omitted, it appears on social, formal ones. Note that the phrase "in honour of" does not appear when the debutante's name is listed under the parents'. (The reason for this is that a debutante can't "honour" herself.) For an invitation to a small dance the guest's name is frequently not handwritten and the phrase "request the pleasure of your company at a small dance" is substituted.

Invitation to a Debutante Reception

Mr. and Mrs. David Filmore Gilchrist
Miss Charlotte Sue Gilchrist
At Home
Saturday, February first
at five o'clock
31 Sutton Place South
New York, New York   zip code

R.s.v.p.

An Invitation to an Official Luncheon

Mr. and Mrs. J. Peter Morton, Jr.
request the pleasure of your company
at a luncheon in honour of
His Excellency, the President of Chile
and
Señora de Martinez-Garcia
Sunday, the twenty-third of March
at one o'clock

R.S.V.P.   Aboard
17 Gracie Square   The "Mermaid"
New York, New York zip code   Long Island Yacht Club

The abbreviation "J." is permissible when the first name is never used. If necessary, engraved or printed directions with or without a map may be included.

"At Home" Invitations Occasionally a prominent bachelor of the old school will have formal "at home" invitations issued. The following card indicates cocktails followed by a buffet supper. These cards usually measure 4½ × 3½.

Mr. Frazier Gerard
at Home
Tuesday, July 6th

The Regency   *Cocktails*
                                                   6 o'clock

Older, socially established women still occasionally, too, have their formal "at homes." Cards for them may read:

Mrs. Cornelius Wade Duer
at Home
Sunday, May 4th

Tea and Sherry   R.S.V.P.
                                                   The Plaza

Informal Invitations

Invitations to informal or semiformal dinner parties, luncheon, tea, cocktails, buffet suppers, and children's parties may be extended by visiting card, informal, or may be telephoned. If the hostess desires an answer she writes R.S.V.P. on them. Otherwise, it is omitted but the recipient may certainly reply even if no R.S.V.P. appears on the invitation. On the visiting card carrying a message you may or may not—as you wish— draw a line through the engraved name if the message is signed informally with a first name.

There is now a device growing in popularity for speeding replies to certain invitations. It is suitable for informal functions such as cocktail parties, club teas, college and high school social activities, where it is necessary to know the number of guests expected. It is the line "Regrets only—(telephone number)" added to the R.S.V.P. on informal invitations. It is never on engraved invitations of great formality such as those for a wedding. However, beware of having all your guests R.S.V.P. via the telephone, as everyone who calls will talk for a few minutes, keeping your wire constantly busy.

Informal invitations should be mailed two weeks in advance but at holiday periods five to six weeks may be advisable.

Invitations on Visiting Cards

Lunch
Sunday, June 2nd–1:30
Mrs. Laurence Patton

775 Park Avenue
R.S.V.P.   New York, N.Y. zip code

Cocktails Tuesday
March 2nd, 5–7
Mrs. William Goode Harper, Jr.

10 Park Avenue
New York, N.Y. zip code

Tea
Tuesday, April 16, 4:30
Mrs. William Thayer

14 Maine Street
R.S.V.P.   Garden City, N.Y. zip code

Dinner
Friday, March 7, 8 P.M.
Mrs. John Alexander Klemin

7 Pink Cloud Lane
R.S.V.P.   Locust Valley, N.Y. zip code

Invitations on Informals The "informal" is the fold-over card, once only permissible in white with black engraving, the latter usually from the calling card plate. Today's informals are exactly what the name describes and can be in almost any color and engraved or printed in contrasting colors. Often they bear amusing little maps, sketches of a country home, or initials. They often contain the address and telephone number of the sender, sometimes are gaily bordered, and may be plate-marked. The paper on which they are engraved or printed is often that used in the household's stationery. Colored inks may be used in writing messages on them. Informals have many uses but can't double for calling cards—they are abbreviated stationery and may be used for any short note (except one of condolence, if they are initialled or otherwise decorated for their informality—and the gaiety they have—would be out of place). They may be used for invitations and for birth announcements. A joint informal may be used for sending and replying to informal invitations. It may be enclosed with gifts and flowers or used for Christmas messages. No signature is used here as the joint informal bears two names. Signatures are not necessary either on ordinary informals which bear the name rather than the monogram of the senders.

Cocktails Sunday
Mr. and Mrs. Joseph Asa Benet
Sept. 6th, 4–6

Bayside Avenue
East Islip, New York   zip code

Men's Correspondence Cards Men's correspondence cards, which have the same uses as the woman's informal, do not fold over. They should be 5×4 or larger and should have the man's name or initials and address (optional) and may have an embossed crest at the top. A crest is sometimes used by women, but is not strictly correct. (See "Heraldic Devices," page 615.)

Dinner Friday
Mr. Arthur Paul Banks
Nov. 10, 8 o'clock
Cedar Hills Road
Greenwich, Connecticut   zip code

R.S.V.P.   *Black Tie*[3]

Nov. 3

Dear Sabra,
Won't you and John please join us for brunch, Sunday, November 10th?
Love
Natalie

A Woman's Informal with Monogram

[3] The phrase "black tie" means tuxedo, also more commonly referred to in sophisticated circles as dinner jacket. The phrase "black tie" is not used on formal engraved invitations except those to public events such as charity balls. The supposition is that people receiving formal engraved invitations understand that they are for a formal function and that the time of day indicated denotes the proper dress. Therefore you don't see "black tie" on invitations to debutante dances, wedding receptions, private dinners

46 East Fifty-first Street

Mrs. Humphrey Arden Hanshaw

Tea, Saturday April 12th

4-6

Invitations on the Card-informal The card-informal is frequently used. It is larger and heavier than a visiting card, about 3½″×4⅝″ or 3⅞″× 5⅜″, and unlike the usual informal does not fold over. This card may also have the address in the lower right corner. One style of type may be used for the name and another for the address, but I prefer both in the same type style. This card is also used with the joint names, and has become popular not only for issuing invitations, but also for replying to formal invitations by writing the acceptance or regret immediately below the name using black ink. It is not necessary to repeat the engraved names in the handwritten reply, merely "accept with pleasure the kind invitation of." They are also used with single or joint engraved names to express condolence or extend good wishes—"with our best wishes on this happy oc-

---

with very occasional exceptions. Such an exception might be a Sunday Jewish wedding to which many Christian friends are to be invited. With the hour of the wedding after six o'clock, people might be puzzled as to what to wear on Sunday, which of course is not the Jewish sabbath, thus Jewish Sunday evening weddings are frequently formal, something a Christian guest might not necessarily understand.

On formal fill-in invitations it may be handwritten lower right (in black ink) or on a visiting card used to issue a dinner invitation. It may be written in, lower right, on any handwritten third person invitation on a correspondence card. It may also be used, lower right, on an informal fill-in invitation.

When the words "black tie" appear on an invitation you judge whether women attending wear evening or cocktail dress (and if evening dress, long or short) by the kind of function it is. Generally speaking, an invitation to a large charity ball might say "black or white tie" but "black tie" will be worn by the majority of men. Presently at balls approximately half of the women wear long gowns, those of the ball gown variety, and half short evening dresses. It is a matter of choice. But at very important balls in major cities, it is perhaps better to err on the conservative side and wear a long gown.

casion" again without repetition of the engraved names and in all cases without signatures.

In the case of a man using the card-informal, his name may be engraved with Mr., since the card is usually made up from the plate used for his calling cards.

Invitations and Replies by Telephone

In issuing an invitation to an informal or semiformal dinner party by telephone, a social secretary or a butler may leave the message with employees of the other households. "Will you please say that Mrs. Willott Meegs invites Mr. and Mrs. Carter to dine on Saturday, the eighth, at eight o'clock. Black tie. Mrs. Meegs's number is [give number]." The person taking the message repeats "Dinner at Mrs. Willott Meegs, Saturday, the eighth, eight o'clock. Black tie," and of course writes it down.

The reply by telephone follows the same form, "Will you please tell Mrs. Meegs that Mr. and Mrs. Carter will be happy to accept her invitation to dine on Saturday, the eighth, at eight o'clock" or ". . . regret that because of a previous engagement," etc. The wise hostess then sends a reminder in the form of her visiting card or an engraved reminder card to those accepting. If she uses her visiting card these words are written in ink at the top of the card, "To remind—Dinner, Saturday, April 8th at 8." If the address is not engraved on the card it should be written in the lower left-hand corner. Below is an example of the engraved reminder card—

This is to remind you that
Mr. Douglas Stewart
expects you for *dinner*[4]
on *Tuesday, May 2nd*
at *eight* o'clock
Heatherside Farms
14 Merridith Lane
Manhasset, New York

(in this case the zip code is not necessary but a simple printed or duplicated map may well be—plus a telephone number in case it should be necessary. Alternate routes—train only—may be given should guests not be driving).

In answering an informal invitation by telephone, try to speak to the hostess in person, saying, "We received your invitation for Tuesday and look forward very much to being with you."

If it is necessary to leave the message with a servant, say, "Will you please tell Mrs. Grant that the Bigelows accept her invitation for Tuesday the tenth?" Spell your name and be sure he has understood the message by having it repeated to you. It is unforgivable not to answer an invitation and so keep your hostess on tenterhooks. Giving your acceptance too

---

[4] Italic type indicates handwriting.

casually to a servant or a person especially a child other than the hostess answering the phone, in the expectation that it will reach your hostess, can be equivalent to not answering at all.

Invitations and Replies by Telegram

Formal Invitation

DR. AND MRS. WALDO BURNS REQUEST THE PLEASURE OF DR. AND MRS. RICHARD LIONEL FLANDERS' COMPANY AT DINNER MONDAY JUNE SIXTH AT EIGHT O'CLOCK. BLACK TIE.

Formal Reply

DR. AND MRS. RICHARD LIONEL FLANDERS ACCEPT WITH PLEASURE DR. AND MRS. BURNS'S KIND INVITATION FOR MONDAY JUNE SIXTH AT EIGHT.

Informal Invitation

PLEASE JOIN US AT DINNER MONDAY THE SIXTH.

SUE AND WALDO BURNS

Informal Reply

WE ARE DELIGHTED TO ACCEPT FOR MONDAY THE SIXTH AT EIGHT.

LUCY FLANDERS

(Note the woman, the family's social secretary, replies for her husband and herself.)

Postponing or Canceling an Invitation

Formal Postponement

Mr. and Mrs. Charles Smith Prescott
regret that it is necessary to
postpone their invitation to
dinner from Tuesday, the second of May
to Tuesday, the ninth of May
at eight o'clock
4 East Eightieth Street
New York, New York   zip code

R.S.V.P.

This may be telegraphed, telephoned or even sent in typewritten form by a social secretary if necessary. On a joint card it may be abbreviated still in the third person "regret that their dinner party of May second must be postponed to Tuesday the ninth of May at eight o'clock.

R.S.V.P.
4 East Eightieth Street
New York, New York   zip code

Informal Canceling on a Joint Card

Sorry, we must cancel our
dinner for Tuesday the eighth
but will see you soon, we hope

Mr. and Mrs. Harold Clark Straghan

Accepting Invitations

Invitations are accepted with the same degree of formality with which they are extended. Formal invitations receive a reply written in the third person on the first side of one's most conservative stationery—never on informals or on calling cards. They may also be telephoned or telegraphed. (See "Invitations and Replies by Telephone," page 580.) All invitations should be answered as soon after receiving them as possible. In accepting a formal invitation or even an informal one where a meal is involved, it is better to repeat the day and the hour, so as to be sure there is no misunderstanding.

Following is a written acceptance in the third person. It follows the same general form whether it is to a dance, dinner, reception, or any other formal entertainment. Incidentally, when replying to an invitation from people whose name is followed by Jr., Sr., II, etc., you omit these suffixes in your answer. Note, however, that the reply repeats the date and the time. The envelope is addressed, unlike answers to informal invitations, to *both* the host and hostess, as is the reply.

Mr. and Mrs. Frederick Walter Stevens
accept with pleasure
the kind invitation of
Dr. and Mrs. Newman
to dine
on Saturday, the fifteenth of June
at eight o'clock

When One of a Couple Accepts

If a husband and wife receive an invitation and only one can accept, the acceptance is stated first and the regret follows:

> Mrs. John Sloane
> accepts with pleasure
> the kind invitation of
> Mr. and Mrs. Featherstone
> for Monday, April 8
> at eight o'clock
> Mr. John Sloane
> regrets exceedingly
> that he will be unable to accept

Again, the reply matches the degree of formality used in the invitation.

This is a convenient device in the unhappy circumstance when a couple is separated legally or otherwise, but not divorced. Should a formal invitation come to a couple who has been divorced the only possible solution to the dilemma is for the former wife to write a brief note of explanation to the hostess, merely stating the situation, neither accepting nor regretting. It is then up to the hostess to decide which of the two she wishes to invite. She certainly cannot invite both.

In answering a formal invitation to a "small dance," your acceptance— or regret as the case may be—should omit the word "small."

If the names of several people appear on the invitation or any formal invitation, only the first name or names on the list need be used in your acceptance or regret, unless one name is given to which to reply (very helpful, for example—please reply to Mrs. Cameron, 40 Evergreen Lane). For example:

> Miss Sarah Harrison
> accepts with pleasure
> the kind invitation of
> Mr. and Mrs. Cameron
> for Saturday, the tenth of March
> at ten o'clock

The envelope is addressed to Mrs. Cameron only who is acting social secretary of the group.

Acceptances to Informal Invitations   When informal invitations are sent out on visiting cards or on informals and the date, time, and purpose of the gathering are briefly stated but the R.S.V.P. is *omitted,* the hostess is assuming that you'll come if you can. If you are a busy person, you might at least phone or drop your card saying you'll try to get there. If you don't make it, you've made an agreeable try in that direction, at least, and your hostess is conscious of the fact. Even if you don't get around to replying in time for the event, you might send a card later saying, "Hear the tea was a great success. I wish I could have been there—and thank you. Marie." For such little messages on visiting cards salutation and closing are never used and on informals are not necessary, although the inside of an informal is often treated as if it were note paper. The envelope is addressed to the hostess, as is the reply.

If the informal invitation on a calling card or informal has asked for a reply, of course you reply, as in the following examples:

> *We accept with pleasure for*
> *the 6th at eight*
> **Lucy**

> *Love to come Friday*
> *at five*
> **Laura**

If You Have to Break an Engagement

If an invitation which has been accepted must be broken, the best method is to phone or telegraph the hostess immediately and explain the circumstances. (Such excuses to the White House are written or telegraphed—see "The New Resident in Washington.") The usual social form is: (Telegram) MR. AND MRS. HAROLD CLARK STRAGHAN REGRET THAT MR. STAGHAN'S ILL-NESS MAKES IT IMPOSSIBLE FOR THEM TO KEEP THE ENGAGEMENT WITH DR. AND MRS. PRESCOTT ON MAY SEVENTH.

However, if time permits, you can withdraw your acceptance by sending your visiting or your engraved correspondence card (a joint card if you're married) and writing your excuse on it in black ink.

Regrets

In regretting, as in accepting, an invitation you must reply with the same degree of formality with which the invitation was extended. A formal regret usually states briefly in a word or two the reason for the refusal—"because of their (her) absence from town," "because of a previous engagement," "because of illness"—but it is often better to omit the reason when illness is involved, except in refusing a most important summons such as one to the White House. If you refuse an invitation, you are not obligated to reciprocate.

Regrets to a Formal Invitation

> Mr. Preston Moore
> regrets exceedingly (or simply "regrets")
> that because of a previous engagement
> he will be unable to accept
> Mr. and Mrs. Treadwell's
> kind invitation for the third of August

Regrets to Informal Invitations

> *So sorry I can't make*
> *it the 6th—my parents are*
> *arriving for the weekend.*
> *Francis*

> *So very sorry I*
> *can't join you and*
> *Charles on the sixth—*
> *I'll be in Paris!*
> *Love, Tabitha*

Business Invitations and Replies

It is frequently necessary for business corporations to do semisocial entertaining. The following invitation form may be used for a reception, luncheon, or tea:

> Doubleday & Company
> requests the pleasure of your company
> at a reception
> in honor of
> Miss Amy Vanderbilt
> celebrating the publication of
> the millionth copy of
> Amy Vanderbilt's Complete Book of Etiquette
> on Tuesday, November seventeenth
> from five-thirty to seven-thirty o'clock
> The Penthouse
> Hotel St. Regis
> Fifth Avenue and Fifty-fifth Street
> New York City

R.S.V.P.
Miss Louise Thomas
575 Madison Avenue

The foregoing type of invitation is formal of course and therefore replies must be made in the third person. (Incidentally this invitation was issued in 1961 and the book is now over two and a half million in sales.) Replies may be telephoned or written. The usual third-person reply typed on an office letterhead would be:

> Miss Hope Waring
> accepts with pleasure
> your kind invitation
> for Tuesday, November seventeenth

In place of the usual letterhead stationery, it is advisable for executives to have personalized stationery of good quality for reply to such invitations and for typed letters of condolence to families of deceased business associates, and so forth. Naturally when a secretary replies to formal *social* invitations her employer and his wife receives, she never uses a typewriter or business stationery. Replies should be carefully handwritten with black or blue-black ink on the very best quality white paper. In this case, as in any case, when the time on the invitation allows such leeway, the time is not repeated as it normally is in the response to a formal invitation when often the exact time of arrival is very important.

Chapter 46

CORRECT FORMS OF ADDRESS

In the matter of correct form of address it is vital to be on sure ground. No one likes to be incorrectly addressed, verbally or in writing, and to so err, carelessly, is often to get off on the wrong foot. We all have at least occasional need of this information, for example in addressing the clergy, the military, or members of Congress.

We need to know the differences, too, in British and American forms of address. We should not ever use the American formal form "My Dear" on a letter to a British person with whom we are not on intimate terms. In England, as I have explained, "Dear" is the formal form.

For Americans, British titles and forms of address, with all their complex ramifications, are very difficult to remember, especially as they differ very much from those on the Continent. In England there is no "Count," but there is a "Countess." Earl is the British equivalent of the Continental "Count." I have tried to make all the shades of difference clear in each category. When I asked an English friend how the British themselves keep all these distinctions clear in their own minds she replied, "My dear, when you're born into it, the distinctions seem perfectly simple."

GOVERNMENT OFFICIALS

Correct Forms of Address

In making *formal* presentations for banquets, etc., the form is always that of the full title: "Ladies and Gentlemen—the President of the United States; the Vice-President of the United States; the Honorable James J. Brown, mayor of Trenton; the Honorable Eustis Coates, Associate Justice of the Supreme Court.

PERSONAGE	WRITING TO	IF WIFE IS INCLUDED
The President of the United States	For domestically mailed letter, address The President The White House Washington, D.C. Zip Code	The President and Mrs. Adams
The Vice-President of the United States	The Vice-President United States Senate Washington, D.C. Zip Code	The Vice-President and Mrs. James Home Address
Cabinet Officers[1]	The Honorable Percy Woods Secretary of the Interior Washington, D.C. Zip Code A Woman Is: The Honorable Mary Fortune	The Secretary of the Interior and Mrs. Wood Home Address
The Attorney General	The Honorable Jared O'Neil Attorney General (or The Attorney General) Washington, D.C. Zip Code	The Attorney General and Mrs. O'Neil Home Address
Assistant Secretaries	The Honorable Benson English Assistant Secretary of Labor Washington, D.C. Zip Code	The Assistant Secretary of Labor and Mrs. English (diplomatic) Home Address The Honorable and Mrs. Benson English (social) Home Address
Head of a Division	Mr. John Gray Bureau Address Washington, D.C. Zip Code	Mr. and Mrs. John Gray Home Address
Chief Justice[2]	The Chief Justice The Supreme Court Washington, D.C. Zip Code	The Chief Justice and Mrs. Meigs Home address

1 When cabinet officers are women and husbands are included:
   The Secretary of Labor and Mr. Fortune (diplomatic)
   Mr. and Mrs. John Fortune
   Home address (social)

LETTER OPENING	LETTER CLOSING	SPEAKING TO	INTRODUCING OR REFERRING TO
Mr. President: (business) Dear Mr. President (social)	Most respectfully yours (business) Sincerely yours (social)	Mr. President. In prolonged conversation, occasionally Sir (for men only)	The President, or Mr. Adams
Mr. Vice-President: (business) Dear Mr. Vice-President: (social)	Very truly yours (business) Sincerely yours (social)	Mr. Vice-President. In prolonged conversation, occasionally Sir (for men only)	The Vice-President or Mr. James
Sir: (business) Dear Mr. Secretary or Madam Secretary): (social)	Very truly yours (business) Sincerely yours (social)	Mr. Secretary, Mr. Woods or Madam Secretary or Miss or Mrs. Fortune	The Secretary of the Interior, Mr. Woods. The Secretary or Mr. Woods. The Secretary or Miss or Mrs. Fortune
Sir: (business) Dear Mr. Attorney General	Very truly yours (business) Sincerely yours (social)	Mr. Attorney General or Mr. O'Neil	The Attorney General, Mr. O'Neil. The Attorney General or Mr. O'Neil.
Sir: (business) Dear Mr. Benson (social)	Very truly yours (business) Sincerely yours (social)	Mr. English	Mr. English
Sir: (business) Dear Mr. Gray: (social)	Very truly yours (business) Sincerely yours (social)	Mr. Gray	Mr. Gray
Sir: (business) Dear Mr. Chief Justice: (social)	Very truly yours (business) Sincerely yours (social)	Mr. Chief Justice	The Chief Justice

2 For a State Supreme Court, the same rules would apply, changing, of course, the address to the state capital.

PERSONAGE	WRITING TO	IF WIFE IS INCLUDED
Associate Justice	Mr. Justice Burke The Supreme Court Washington, D.C. Zip Code	Mr. Justice and Mrs. Burke Home address
Speaker of the House of Representatives	The Honorable Mark Ewing Speaker of the House of Representatives Washington, D.C. Zip Code	The Speaker of the House of Representatives and Mrs. Ewing Home address
American Ambassador[4]	The Honorable Frank Peabody American Ambassador London, England	The American Ambassador and Mrs. Peabody[3] American Embassy Home address London, England
American Minister	The Honorable Philip Gordon American Minister to Switzerland Bern, Switzerland	American Minister and Mrs Philip Gordon American Legation Bern, Switzerland
American Chargé d'Affaires, Consul General, Consul, or Vice-Consul	Prentis Gates, Esq. American Chargé d'Affaires, ad interim (or other of these titles) Paris, France	Mr. and Mrs. Prentis Gates Home address
Judges[5]	The Honorable Jackson Adams Presiding Justice, Appellate Division Supreme Court of the State of New York New York, N.Y. Zip Code	The Honorable and Mrs. Jackson Adams Home address

[3] In countries other than England the form is: The Honorable and Mrs. Frank Peabody and the wife of the American Ambassador is Mrs. Peabody. She is only occasionally given a courtesy title socially of "Ambassadress." A woman actually appointed Ambassador is not referred to as Ambassadress, but as Madam Ambassador. A woman appointed as Minister is referred to as Madam Minister.

[4] In presenting American ambassadors and ministers in any Latin-American country always include the phrase "of the United States of America: after Embassy or Legation. Avoid the terms American Embassy or American Legation, even American Minister or American Ambassador. For the latter say, Ambassador of the United States or Minister of the United States. The reason for this is that Latin Americans consider the South American continent and the Central American states "America" too.

[5] Judges of various other courts are also The Honorable, but are referred to as Judge Jones. When this is the case, in presentations and introductions they are:
The Honorable John Jones,
Judge of the Murfreysville Court

LETTER OPENING	LETTER CLOSING	SPEAKING TO	INTRODUCING OR REFERRING TO
ir: (business) Dear Mr. Justice: (social)	Very truly yours (business) Sincerely yours (social)	Mr. Justice or Mr. Justice Burke	Mr. Justice Burke
ir: (business) Dear Mr. Speaker (social)	Very truly yours (business) Sincerely yours (social)	Mr. Speaker or Mr. Ewing,	The Speaker, Mr. Ewing, or Mr. Ewing or The Speaker
ir: (business) Dear Mr. Ambassador: (social)	Respectfully yours (business) Sincerely yours (social)	Mr. Ambassador or in prolonged conversation Mr. Peabody	The American Ambassador, or Ambassador, or Mr. Peabody[4]
ir: (business) ear Mr. Minister: (social)	Very truly yours (business) Sincerely yours (social)	Mr. Minister, or Mr. Gordon	The American Minister, or Mr. Gordon
ir: (business) ear Mr. Gates: (social)	Very truly yours (business) Sincerely yours (social)	Mr. Gates	Mr. Gates
ir: (business) ear Mr. Justice: (social)	Very truly yours (business) Sincerely yours (social)	Mr. Justice	Justice Adams

PERSONAGE	WRITING TO	IF WIFE IS INCLUDED
Lawyers	Charles Edison, Esq. 250 Park Avenue New York, New York Zip Code	Mr. and Mrs. Charles Edison Home address
Foreign Ambassador[6]	His Excellency, The Ambassador of Brazil Washington, D.C.	His Excellency, The Ambassador of Brazil, and Madame Lo Pinto .Washington, D.C.
Foreign Ministers Plenipotentiary and Envoys Extraordinary	The Honorable Theodore Lie Minister of Finland Washington, D.C. Zip Code	The Minister of Finland and Mrs. Lie Legation of Finland Washington, D.C.
United States Senators and State Senators	The Honorable Angelo[7] Cognato United States Senate Washington, D.C. Zip Code	The Honorable and Mrs. Angelo Cognato Home address
Representatives and Assemblymen	The Honorable Lincoln[8] Chadwick House of Representatives Washington, D. C. Zip Code	The Honorable and Mrs. Lincoln Chadwick Home address

[6] Foreign ambassadors and ministers are referred to as Ambassador or Minister, with name of the country, i.e., Ambassador of Ireland, Ambassador of Peru, with the following exceptions: Ambassador of the Argentine Republic, British Ambassador, Chinese Ambassador, Ambassador of the French Republic (informal form of reference, French Ambassador), Italian Ambassador, Japanese Ambassador, Ambassador of the Netherlands, Ambassador of Thailand, Ambassador of the Union of South Africa, Ambassador of the Union of Soviet Socialist Republics, Minister of the People's Republic of Yugoslavia, Minister of the People's Republic of Romania.

Ambassadors are addressed at their embassies, i.e.: Ambassador of the Argentine Republic, Embassy of the Argentine Republic. Ministers are addressed at their legations, i.e.: Minister of Switzerland, Legation of Switzerland. Foreign presidents, ambassadors and cabinet ministers are referred to as His Excellency unless they have royal titles, in which case the royal title is used. Where they have titles such as Doctor, Lord, or Sir, etc., these titles are included.

The wives of all foreign ambassadors and ministers, with the exception of those from English-speaking countries, are given the French courtesy title of Madame and in speaking are referred to as Madame Lo Pinto, or Madame, rather than Signora, Senhôra, Vrouw, etc.

LETTER OPENING	LETTER CLOSING	SPEAKING TO	INTRODUCING OR REFERRING TO
Dear Mr. Edison	Very truly yours (business) Sincerely yours (social)	Mr. Edison	Mr. Edison
Excellency: (business) Dear Mr. Ambassador: (social)	Very truly yours (business) Sincerely yours (social)	Mr. Ambassador	The Ambassador of Brazil, Mr. Lo Pinto, the Ambassador of Brazil, or Mr. Lo Pinto
Sir: (business) Dear Mr. Minister: (social)	Very truly yours (business) Sincerely yours (social)	Mr. Minister or Mr. Lie	The Minister of Finland, Mr. Lie. The Minister, Mr. Lie.
Sir: (business) Dear Senator Cognato: (social)	Very truly yours (business) Sincerely yours (social)	Senator Cognato or (informally) Senator	Senator Cognato
Sir: (business) Dear Mr. Chadwick (social)	Very truly yours (business) Sincerely yours (social)	Mr. Chadwick or Assemblyman Chadwick, or (informally) Assemblyman	Mr. Chadwick or Assemblyman Chadwick

7 A woman is The Honorable Genevieve P. Schuler (always with given name). If husband is included, the form is, socially: Mr. and Mrs. John Schuler, home address. Official invitations read: The Honorable Genevieve P. Schuler and Mr. Schuler, home address.

8 A woman is The Honorable Lucy Butterfield. If husband is included, the social form is Mr. and Mrs. Amos Butterfield, home address. Official invitations read: The Honorable Lucy Butterfield and Mr. Butterfield.

PERSONAGE	WRITING TO	IF WIFE IS INCLUDED
Governors[9]	Honorable Grover Welsh Governor of Connecticut Hartford, Conn. Zip Code	The Honorable and Mrs. Grover Welsh Home address
Mayors	Honorable Joseph Leach Mayor of Portland, Portland, Oregon Zip Code	The Honorable and Mrs. Joseph Leach Home address
PROTESTANT CLERGY[10] Presiding Bishop of the Episcopal Church in the U.S.A.	The Right (or Most) Reverend Peter Flagg, D.D., LL.D. Presiding Bishop Address	
Bishops of the Episcopal Church	The Right Reverend Gideon Carew, D.D. Bishop of Cincinnati	The Bishop of Cincinnati and Mrs. Carew
Deans	The Very Reverend the Dean of St. Matthew's or The Very Rev. John Brown, D.D., Dean of St. Matthew's Cathedral	The Dean of St. Matthew and Mrs. Brown
Archdeacons	The Venerable Charles Smith Archdeacon of Richmond	The Archdeacon of Richmond and Mrs. Smith

9 Only three states—New Hampshire, Massachusetts, and South Carolina—have officially adopted the title, "Excellency" for their governors, but the term may be used as a courtesy in any state, viz.: His Excellency the Governor, Hartford, Conn., if the letter is from within the state. In a letter from outside the state, if his wife is included: His Excellency the Governor of Connecticut and Mrs. Welsh, Executive Mansion, Hartford, Conn.

LETTER OPENING	LETTER CLOSING	SPEAKING TO	INTRODUCING OR REFERRING TO
Dear Governor:	Respectfully or Sincerely yours	Governor Welsh	Governor Welsh or The Governor
Dear Mayor Leach:	Sincerely yours	Mayor Leach or Mr. Mayor	Mayor Leach or The Mayor
Right (or Most) Reverend Sir: (business) Dear Bishop Flagg: (social)	Respectfully yours (business) Sincerely yours (social)	Bishop Flagg	Bishop Flagg or Dr. Flagg
Right Reverend Sir: (business) My dear Bishop (or Bishop Carew) or My dear Bishop Carew: (social)	Respectfully yours (business) Sincerely yours (social)	Bishop Carew	Bishop Carew or Dr. Carew, the Bishop of Cincinnati
Very Reverend Sir: (business) Dear Dean Brown: (social)	Respectfully yours (business) Sincerely yours (social)	Dean Brown	The Dean of St. Matthew's or Dean Brown
The Ven. Archdeacon Smith Venerable Sir: (business) Dear Archdeacon Smith: My dear Archdeacon: (social)	Respectfully yours (business) Sincerely yours (social)	Archdeacon Smith	The Archdeacon of Richmond or Archdeacon Smith

10 All church dignitaries in any formal presentation before audiences of any kind are given their full titles—for example, The Most Reverend Peter Flagg, Presiding Bishop of the Protestant Episcopal Church in America.

Bishops of the Episcopal Church may be married, unless they belong to one of the religious orders of the Church. The social form for a bishop and his wife is The Presiding Bishop and Mrs. Flagg.

PERSONAGE	WRITING TO	IF WIFE IS INCLUDED
Canons	The Reverend Canon Charles Pritchard Thomas, D.D., LL.D. Canon of St. Mary's Cathedral	The Canon and Mrs. C. P. Thomas
Clergymen with Doctor's Degrees	The Reverend Joseph E. Long, D.D.	The Rev. Dr. Joseph E. Lon and Mrs. Long
Clergymen without Doctor's Degrees[11]	The Reverend Frank K. Hanson	The Rev. and Mrs. Frank K Hanson
Methodist Methodist Bishop	Bishop Marshall Reed of the Detroit Area Home address Optionally: The Reverend Dr. Marshall Reed, Bishop of the Detroit Area	The Rev. Dr. and Mrs. Marshall
Mormon Mormon Bishop	Bishop John Richards Church of Latter Day Saints (Address) or Mr. John Richards (Home address)	Mr. and Mrs. John Richard
JEWISH Rabbi with Scholastic[12] Degree	Rabbi Nathan Sachs, D.D. LL.D. Temple Emmanuel[13] Bridgeport, Connecticut Zip Code	Rabbi (or Doctor) and Mr Nathan Sachs (Some prefer Rabbi to Docto Home address
Rabbi without Scholastic Degree	Rabbi Harold Schwartz Beth David Synagogue New York, N.Y. Zip Code	Rabbi and Mrs. Harold Schwartz Home address

11 In addressing clergymen who do not have doctor's degrees, it is wiser to use as an invariable form "Reverend Sir" or "Sir," since this is always correct and will avoid giving offense to the several groups who are used to a particular form of personal salutation.

The use of Father, designating an Episcopal clergyman or a priest who is not a member of a religious order, is a matter of the clergyman's own preference. When Father is used in writing it is usually coupled with the surname of the clergyman—The Reverend Father Huntington, O.H.C., without the Christian name. In direct reference, it is Father Huntington. However, in the Episcopal order of Franciscans, where there is a name conferred by the order—as among Roman Catholic religious orders—it would

LETTER OPENING	LETTER CLOSING	SPEAKING TO	INTRODUCING OR REFERRING TO
Reverend Sir: (business) Dear Canon Thomas: (social)	Respectfully yours (business) Sincerely yours (social)	Canon Thomas	Canon Thomas or Doctor Thomas, Canon of St. Mary's
Reverend Sir: (business) Dear Dr. Long: (social)	Respectfully yours (business) Sincerely yours (social)	Dr. Long	The Reverend Doctor Long
Reverend Sir: (business) Dear Mr. Hanson: (social)	Respectfully yours (business) Sincerely yours (social)	Sir	The Reverend Frank Hanson
Reverend Sir: (formal) My dear Bishop (informal)	Respectfully yours (business) Sincerely yours (social)	Sir (formal) or Bishop Reed (informal)	Bishop Reed
Sir: (formal) My dear Mr. Richards: (informal)	Very truly yours Sincerely yours	Bishop Richards (formal) Mr. Richards (informal)	Bishop Richards or Mr. Richards
Sir: (business) Dear Rabbi (or Doctor) Sachs: (social)	Very truly yours (business) Sincerely yours (social)	Rabbi Sachs, Doctor Sachs, or simply Rabbi	Rabbi Sachs or Doctor Sachs
Sir: (business) My dear Rabbi Schwartz: (social)	Very truly yours (business) Sincerely yours (social)	Rabbi Schwartz or Rabbi	Rabbi Schwartz or Rabbi

be The Reverend Father Joseph, O.S.F., in writing, and Father or Father Joseph in direct reference. Lay brothers are addressed in writing as Brother Charles, O.H.C., and in direct reference as Brother or Brother Charles.

12 All rabbis do not necessarily hold both degrees. In addressing a rabbi, give him whatever degree or degrees he possesses.

13 RABBIS OF THE ORTHODOX, CONSERVATIVE, AND REFORM CONGREGATIONS Rabbis of Orthodox congregations preach in synagogues. Rabbis of Conservative congregations preach in synagogues or temples, depending on the term adopted by individual groups. Rabbis of Reform congregations preach in temples. The term "church" is not used.

PERSONAGE	WRITING TO	IF WIFE IS INCLUDED
Cantor (Chief singer of the Congregation)	Cantor Chaim Levy Beth David Synagogue New York, N.Y. Zip Code	Cantor and Mrs. Chaim Levy Home address
THE ROMAN CATHOLIC HIERARCHY The Pope	His Holiness, the Pope or His Holiness Pope Benedict I Vatican City Rome, Italy	
Cardinals	Patrick, Cardinal Terrance (Archbishop of San Francisco)[14]	
Bishops and Archbishops	The Most Reverent Peter Judson, D.D. (Archbishop of St. Louis) (Bishop of Dallas)*	
Abbots[15]	The Right Reverend Henry J. Loester or Abbot Loester	
Prothonotaries Apostolic, Domestic Prelates and Vicars General	The Right Reverend Monsignor Robert McDonald	
Papal Chamberlains	The Very Reverend Monsignor Robert Ross	
Priest	The Reverend Father James L. Cullen	

[14] Title in parenthesis, for cardinals, bishops, and archbishops, not needed in address, but may be used if desired.

[15] Members of the order of St. Benedict—The Right Reverend Dom Anslem McCarthy, O.S.B., addressed as Dom McCarthy.

ETTER OPENING	LETTER CLOSING	SPEAKING TO	INTRODUCING OR REFERRING TO
r: (business) y dear Cantor Levy: (social)	Very truly yours (business) Sincerely yours (social)	Cantor Levy	Cantor Levy
our Holiness or Most Holy Father:	Your Holiness' most humble servant	Your holiness or Most Holy Father	His Holiness, the Holy Father, the Pope, the Pontiff
ar Cardinal Terrance:	I have the honor to be etc.	Cardinal Terrance	Cardinal Terrance
ar Bishop (Archbishop) Judson:	I have the honor to be etc.	Bishop (Archbishop) Judson	Archbishop or Bishop Judson
ght Reverend Abbot or Dear Father Abbot:	I have the honor to be, Right Reverend Abbot, etc.	Abbot Loester	The Right Reverend Henry J. Loester or Abbot Loester
ght Reverend Monsignor or Dear Monsignor McDonald:	I am, Right Reverend Monsignor, etc.	Monsignor McDonald or Monsignor	Monsignor McDonald
ry Reverend Monsignor or Dear Monsignor Ross:	I am, Very Reverend Monsignor, etc.	Monsignor Ross	Monsignor Ross
verend Father or Dear Father Cullen:	I am, Reverend Father, etc.	Father Cullen	Father Cullen

PERSONAGE	WRITING TO	IF WIFE IS INCLUDED
Brothers	Brother William Shine	
Sisters	Sister Mary Annunciata	
EASTERN ORTHODOX COMMUNION[16] Patriarchs	His Holiness, the Ecumenical Patriarch of Constantinople Constantinople, Turkey	
Archbishop[17]	The Most Reverend Michael Archbishop of Cincinnati Address	
Bishop	The Right Reverend Basil Althos Bishop of Chicago Address	
Archimandrite	The Very Reverend James Papas Address	
Priest[18]	The Very Reverend Nicholas Kontos Address	

[16] EASTERN ORTHODOX COMMUNION Greek Orthodox clergymen choose before ordination whether they are to be celibate or non-celibate priests. All highest clergymen, i.e., archbishops, partriarchs, and archimandrites, are usually celibates.

There are three other patriarchs of the ancient sees of Jerusalem, Alexandria and Antioch. They are addressed, Your Beatitude, as is the Archbishop of Greece.

[17] Metropolitans, who supersede suffragan bishops in rank, are found in large cities mainly among the Russian and Syrian Orthodox congregations but in Greece they function, as well, for the Church of Greece. They are addressed, The Most Reverend Peter, Metropolitan of Boston, etc., and like archbishops are referred to as Your Eminence.

LETTER OPENING	LETTER CLOSING	SPEAKING TO	INTRODUCING OR REFERRING TO
Dear Brother William or Dear Brother:	I am, respectfully yours	Brother William or Brother	Brother William
Dear Sister:	I am, respectfully yours	Sister Annunciata or Sister	Sister Annunciata or Sister
Your Holiness:	Respectfully yours	Your Holiness	His Holiness
Your Eminence:	Respectfully yours	Your Eminence	His Eminence
Right Reverend Sir: (business) My dear Bishop: (social)	Respectfully yours	Your Grace	His Grace
Reverend Sir: (business) Your Reverence: (social)	Respectfully yours	Father James or Father Papas	Father James or Father Papas
My dear Father Kontos:	Yours respectfully	Father	Father Kontos

[18] In the case of a non-celibate priest the form including his wife would be The Reverend Nicholas Kontos and Mrs. Kontos in the U.S. or, abroad, the Reverend Nicholas Kontos and Madame Kontos. At present there are no Greek Orthodox sisterhoods in America, but they exist in Greece and are very similar to those of the Roman Catholics.

PERSONAGE	WRITING TO	IF WIFE IS INCLUDED
BRITISH OFFICIALS AND INDIVIDUALS[19] The King	Communications are sent to the Private Secretary to the King (with the complete address on cables and envelopes only) with the request that the communication be placed before His Majesty the King or His Majesty (name) King of England	
The Queen	Her Majesty the Queen same as for the King	
A Royal Prince or a Royal Duke	His Royal Highness the Duke of Trent, K.G.	
A Royal Princess or a Royal Duchess	Her Royal Highness the Princess Royal Local address Her Royal Highness the Duchess of Trent Local address Her Royal Highness Princess Anne Local address	
THE PEERAGE A Duke, Non-Royal[20]	His Grace, the Duke of Norfolk, K.G. Local address	

[19] It is exceptional for a private individual to address a king, queen, or other member of a royal family. A foreigner should address them only through the regular diplomatic or other proper channel.

It is never correct to address a husband and wife jointly when one, or both, holds a title. All communications are addressed to the husband *or* the wife, with all invitations of course being sent to the wife alone.

An American citizen in addressing any member of a royal family or nobility or any foreign official may use the American form of formal address and close. In England

LETTER OPENING	LETTER CLOSING	SPEAKING TO	INTRODUCING OR REFERRING TO
...lay it please Your Majesty	Yours very respectfully or Yours respectfully	Your Majesty. In prolonged conversation usually, Sir	His Majesty the King
...our Majesty:	Yours very respectfully or Yours respectfully	Your Majesty. In prolonged conversation, Ma'am	Her Majesty the Queen
...r:	Yours respectfully	Your Royal Highness. In prolonged conversation, Sir	His Royal Highness the Duke of Trent or His Royal Highness, Prince Thomas
...adam:	Yours respectfully	Your Royal Highness. In prolonged conversation, Ma'am	Her Royal Highness the Princess Royal
...r: (business) ...ear Duke: (social)	Yours very truly (business) Yours sincerely (social)	Your Grace. In prolonged conversation, Sir	The Duke of Norfolk or His Grace

the form for letter closing always properly begins with "Yours." The term "My dear" is the intimate form of opening, "Dear" the formal quite the opposite of the American form.

20 The eldest son of a duke has the highest family title below his father's, such as Marquess. His wife has the corresponding title, such as Marchioness.

PERSONAGE	WRITING TO	IF WIFE IS INCLUDED
A Duchess, Non-Royal	Her Grace, the Duchess of Norfolk Local address	
The Younger Sons of a Duke[21]	The Lord James Beaumont Local address	
The Daughters of a Duke	Lady Bridget Beaumont Local address	
The Wife of the Younger Son of a Duke	Lady James Beaumont	
A Marquess[22]	The Most Honourable the Marquess of Remington, or The Marquess of Remington (less formal)	
A Marchioness	The Most Honourable the Marchioness of Remington, or The Marchioness of Remington (less formal) Local address	

[21] The terms "my lord" and "my lady" are forms of address used mainly by servants and tradesmen, although the usage is not necessarily menial.

[22] The eldest son of a marquess has the highest family title below his father's, such as Earl—his wife has the corresponding title, such as Countess. The younger son and daughter of a marquess take the title Lord or Lady, respectively. The wife of the younger son of a marquess has the title Lady combined with her husband's full name.

ETTER OPENING	LETTER CLOSING	SPEAKING TO	INTRODUCING OR REFERRING TO
adam (business) ear Duchess (social)	Yours very truly (business) Yours sincerely (social)	Your Grace. In prolonged conversation Madam	The Duchess of Norfolk or Her Grace
r: (business) ear Lord James: (social)	Yours very truly (business) Yours sincerely (social)	Lord James[31]	Lord James Beaumont
adam: (business) ear Lady Bridget: (social)	Yours very truly (business) Yours sincerely (social)	Lady Bridget	Lady Bridget Beaumont
adam: (business) ear Lady James: (social)	Yours very truly (business) Yours sincerely (social)	Lady James	Lady James Beaumont
: (business) ar Lord Remington: (social)	Yours very truly (business) Yours sincerely	Lord Remington	The Marquess of Remington, or Lord Remington, (less formal)
dam: (business) ar Lady Remington: (social)	Yours very truly (business) Yours sincerely (social)	Lady Remington	The Marchioness of Remington, or Lady Remington (less formal)

PERSONAGE	WRITING TO	IF WIFE IS INCLUDED
An Earl[23]	The Right Honourable the Earl of Leeds, G.C., V.O., C.M.G. (business) or The Earl of Leeds (social) Local address	
A Countess, Wife of an Earl	The Right Honourable the Countess of Leeds (business) or The Countess of Leeds (social) Local address	
A Viscount[23]	The Right Honourable the Viscount Bemis (business) or The Viscount Bemis (social) Local address	
A Viscountess	The Right Honourable the Viscountess Bemis (business) or The Viscountess Bemis (social)	
The Family of a Viscount[24]	The Honourable Thomas Bemis Local address The Honourable Mrs. Bemis Local address The Honourable Gladys Bemis	Omission of husband's Christian name indicates she is wife eldest son.

[23] The eldest son of an earl has the highest family title below his father's such as Viscount. His wife takes the corresponding title such as Viscountess. The younger sons of an earl and their wives have the title Honourable. The daughters of an earl have the title Lady combined with their Christian and Family names.

The term "Dowager" is used as part of a title in England to indicate the earliest surviving widow of a preceding peer. She is known as the Dowager Duchess of Wickham. A later surviving widow who might be the widow of the first earl's son, nephew, etc., would be known as Mary, Duchess of Wickham, retaining this usage for life even if the dowager dies.

[24] The eldest son of a viscount and also his wife have the title The Honourable. The younger sons of a viscount and their wives also have the title Honourable. The daughters of a viscount take the title The Honourable with their Christian and family names.

LETTER OPENING	LETTER CLOSING	SPEAKING TO	INTRODUCING OR REFERRING TO
Sir: (business) Dear Lord Leeds: (social)	Yours very truly (business) Yours sincerely (social)	Lord Leeds	The Earl of Leeds or Lord Leeds (less formal)
Madam: (business) Dear Lady Leeds: (social)	Yours very truly (business) Yours sincerely (social)	Lady Leeds	The Countess of Leeds or Lady Leeds (less formal)
Sir: (business) Dear Lord Bemis: (social)	Yours very truly (business) Yours sincerely (social)	Lord Bemis	Viscount Bemis or Lord Bemis (less formal)
Madam: (business) Dear Lady Bemis: (social)	Yours very truly (business) Yours sincerely (social)	Lady Bemis	Viscountess Bemis or Lady Bemis (less formal)
Sir: (business) Dear Mr. Bemis (social)	Yours very truly (business) Yours sincerely (social)	Mr. Bemis	Mr. Bemis
Madam: (business) Dear Mrs. Bemis (social)		Mrs. Bemis	Mrs. Bemis
Madam: (business) Dear Miss Bemis: (social)		Miss Bemis	Miss Bemis

PERSONAGE	WRITING TO	IF WIFE IS INCLUDED
A Baron[25]	The Right Honourable Lord Lancer (business) or The Lord Lancer (social)	
A Baroness	The Right Honourable Lady Lancer (business) or The Lady Lancer (social)	
A Baroness (not in her own right)	The Right Honourable the Lady McGuiness (business) or The Baroness Lancer or The Lady Lancer (social)	
A Baronet[26]	Sir Thomas Riddle, Bart. Local address	
The Wife of a Baronet	Lady Riddle Local Address	
A Knight	Sir John Waugh, G.C.M.G. Local address	
The Wife of a Knight	Lady Waugh Local address	
Member of the House of Commons with Title	Sir Henry Coakley-Smith, K.B.E., M.P. Local address	

25 All the sons of a baron and their wives have the title The Honourable. The daughters of a baron also have the title Honourable.

26 A baronet has the title Sir and the abbreviation for Baronet (Bart. or Bt.) follows his name. The wife of a baronet has the title Lady with her husband's surname only. The sons and daughters of a baronet have no title.

LETTER OPENING	LETTER CLOSING	SPEAKING TO	INTRODUCING OR REFERRING TO
ir: (business) ear Lord Lancer: (social)	Yours very truly (business) Yours sincerely (social)	Lord Lancer (never Baron)	Lord Lancer (never Baron)
adam: (business) ear Lady Lancer: (social)	Yours very truly (business) Yours sincerely (social)	Lady Lancer	Baroness Lancer or Lady Lancer (less formal)
adam: (business) ear Lady McGuiness: (social)	Yours very truly (business) Yours sincerely (social)	Lady McGuiness	Lady McGuiness
ar Sir: (business) ar Sir Thomas: (social)	Yours very truly (business) Yours sincerely (social)	Sir Thomas	Sir Thomas Riddle
ar Madam: (business) ar Lady Riddle: (social)	Yours very truly (business) Yours sincerely (social)	Lady Riddle	Lady Riddle
ar Sir: (business) ar Sir John: (social)	Yours very truly (business) Yours sincerely (social)	Sir John	Sir John Waugh
ar Madam: (business) ar Lady Waugh: (social)	Yours very truly (business) Yours sincerely (social)	Lady Waugh	Lady Waugh
ar Sir: (business) ar Sir Henry: (social)	Yours respectfully (business) Yours sincerely (social)	Sir Henry	Sir Henry Coakley-Smith

NOTE: English officials in England are not addressed as Excellency even when entitled to be so addressed in other countries.

NOTE: A member of Parliament has no special title except that the letters M.P. are written after his name.

PERSONAGE	WRITING TO	IF WIFE IS INCLUDED
Member of the House of Commons without Title	L.T. Needham, Esq., M.P. Local address	
A Privy Councillor with Title[27]	The Right Honourable Sir Percy Harron, Bart., D.S.O., P.C. Local address	
Prime Minister (British)[28]	The Right Honourable Harley Asheden, M.P. Prime Minister, London	
A British Ambassador[29]	His Excellency The Right Honourable Sir Harold Pim, G.C.M.G. British Ambassador Rome, Italy	
A Minister[30]	Edward Matheson, Esq. Envoy Extraordinary British Legation Bogotá, Colombia	

[27] A Privy Councillor is addressed according to his title, preceded by the title The Right Honourable. If without title, he is addressed simply as The Right Honourable, "Mr." in the salutation. (All members of the British Cabinet are members of the Privy Council and as such are entitled to the initials P.C. after their names.) The wife of a Privy Councillor has no title as such.

[28] A Prime Minister (being a Privy Councillor) has the title The Right Honourable in addition to and preceding any other title.

[29] A British Ambassador is addressed according to his rank of nobility, if any, his title of rank being preceded by the diplomatic title His Excellency.

[30] A British Envoy Extraordinary and Minister Plenipotentiary is addressed according to rank of nobility, if any, his title of rank being preceded by the diplomatic title— His Excellency.

LETTER OPENING	LETTER CLOSING	SPEAKING TO	INTRODUCING OR REFERRING TO
Dear Sir: (business) Dear Mr. Needham: (social)	Yours very truly (business) Yours sincerely (social)		
Sir: (business) Dear Sir Percy: (social)	Yours respectfully (business) Yours sincerely (social)	Sir Percy	Sir Percy Harron
Sir: (business) Dear Mr. Asheden: (social)	Yours respectfully (business) Yours sincerely (social)	Mr. Asheden	Mr. Asheden
My Lord (or Sir, according to rank): (business) Dear Lord X, Sir Harold, Mr. Y: (according to circumstances) (social)	Yours very truly (business) Yours sincerely (social)	His Excellency (when at post, Sir Harold elsewhere)	Sir Harold Pim
Sir: (business) Dear Mr. Matheson: (social)	Yours very truly (business) Yours sincerely (social)	Mr. Matheson	Mr. Matheson

PERSONAGE	WRITING TO	IF WIFE IS INCLUDED
UNITED NATIONS Secretary General	His Excellency Pierre Meunier, Secretary General of the United Nations New York, N.Y. Zip Code	His Excellency Secretary General of the United Nations and Mrs. Meunier
U.S. Representative to the United Nations	The Honorable Joseph Bruckner, U.S. Representative to the United Nations New York, N.Y. Zip Code	The Honorable Joseph Bruckner and Mrs. Bruckner

The Use of Esquire

"Esquire" was originally used as a lesser English title. It indicated a knight's eldest son and the young male members of a noble house whose hereditary title was borne only by the eldest male heir. In addressing business or social correspondence to a British gentleman without title, use the abbreviation "Esq." (for Esquire) after the name, but do not precede it with "Mr." or "The Honourable" or, of course, any title such as "Lord," "Sir," or "Dr." A British surgeon, however, is always addressed as "Henry Walters, Esq." and in conversation is "Mr. Walters," not "Dr. Walters." Professional men and those working in the so-called genteel callings—arts, letters, music —and members of the House of Commons and the landed gentry are addressed in writing with "Esq." following their names. Often, too, older gentlemen of standing are called "Squire" in conversation.

In our own country Esq. is used by lawyers in written address to each other, a bit of old-school tradition the Correspondence Review Staff of our State Department is attempting to abolish in those few areas where it still persists. In business and social usage it is courteous for the lay public to follow this custom. If the Esquire is used, it follows the name and is abbreviated Esq. or spelled out in full. The name is then not preceded by "Mr." In the salutation of the letter, however, the lawyer is referred to as "Dear Mr. Jones," and in speaking he is called "Mr." When he and his wife are included in the form of address it is "Mr. and Mrs. Murray Price."

In diplomatic and extremely formal correspondence Esquire is written out.

LETTER OPENING	LETTER CLOSING	SPEAKING TO	INTRODUCING OR REFERRING TO
Dear Mr. Ambassador (social and business)	Very truly yours (business) Sincerely yours (social)	Mr. Secretary General	His Excellency Secretary General of the United Nations
Dear Mr. Ambassador (social and business)	Very truly yours (business) Sincerely yours (social)	Mr. Ambassador	Ambassador Bruckner

English Customs

Where a man's name is combined with his wife's, as in this country, the form is "Mr. and Mrs. Bertram Montgomery," but this form is rare in Great Britain except on joint visiting cards. Engraved invitations are addressed to the wife alone. Inside on the top, or in the blank space provided, is written "Mr. and Mrs. Montgomery." Invitations written in longhand are also addressed to the wife. If a visiting card is used for an invitation the envelope is addressed to the wife alone and on the top of the card is written "Mr. and Mrs. Montgomery" (no Christian name).

Christmas cards and wedding invitations may be addressed "Mr. and Mrs. Bertram Montgomery."

Military Forms of Address

In the modern Army, rank is used in all grades for both men and women in the service.

Doctors in the service have a starting rank of Lieutenant, and common Army usage dictates that they be addressed by this rank, but junior officers are not infrequently called Doctor. Once, however, they reach Captain or above, they are generally addressed socially by the Army title so long as they remain in the Army. Officially they are always addressed by rank.

Chaplains in the Army and Navy are always called, officially and socially, Chaplain, no matter what the military rank. There is no ruling, however, expressed in regulations, which would prevent men from referring to Catholic priests as Father.

Non-commissioned officers are addressed officially by title, i.e., Sergeant for all grades of Sergeants—First Class, Master, Sergeant, etc.—but there is no regulation prohibiting the use of Mister socially.

A Warrant Officer in any branch of the service is called Mister officially and socially.

In the Navy, Commanders and above are addressed socially by their Navy titles. All below that rank are Mister. Properly a Lieutenant Commander is Mister, but recent custom accords him the courtesy title of Commander socially, with his actual status indicated to all by his two and a half stripes.

Any officer in command of a ship, whatever its classification, is Captain for the period of his command, no matter what his usual title may be.

Cadets of the U. S. Military Academy are Mister socially and in conversational references, but Cadet officially.

National Guard and Reserve officers not on active duty do not use their titles socially or in business affairs unless their activities have some bearing on military matters. Whenever the rank is used, the proper designation must follow the name, i.e., ORC or NG.

Socially and in ordinary military use Lieutenant Colonels, Major Generals, Brigadier Generals, and Lieutenant Generals are known as Colonels and Generals, respectively.

Vice-Admirals and Rear Admirals are Admiral.

All officers of the military services retain their rank after retirement.

Chapter 47

HERALDIC DEVICES

What Is a Coat of Arms?

The subject of heraldry is very complicated, and what I shall say here for
the purposes of etiquette is necessarily greatly simplified.

In the twelfth century the custom arose for warriors to emblazon their
distinguishing devices on their shields so they could be recognized as friend
or foe in battle. Armor was, of course, completely concealing when a man's
visor was down as he prepared to engage. His device therefore became his
trademark and was for further clarity also embroidered on the sleeveless
jacket worn over the armor—hence "coat of arms." On his helmet a
warrior wore a crest—say a falcon or dragon, forged to the metal headcovering. The helmet itself might be of a distinctive shape and design.
Today a coat of arms consists of these three elements—the *shield* with its
coat of arms, surmounted by the helmet, in turn surmounted by the *crest.*
To these may be added "mantling," symbolic of the flowing cape or cloak
which was attached to the warrior's shoulders and "supporters," which are
generally animals such as lions, unicorns, deer, or even human beings, and
the motto on a "ribbon." Mantling is mere optional ornamentation but
permission for the use of supporters must be granted by the Heralds' College in London, which is the best-known authority on heraldry. Some
other countries have such governmental heraldic authorities—Holland, for
one, with its *Koninklijk Nederlands Genootschat Voor Geslacht-en-Wapen-
kunde Bleijenburg* in the Hague.

By the sixteenth century many families other than the descendants of
Crusaders and Knights bore coat-armor—hence the term "armigerous families"—and some merely assumed arms. It therefore became necessary for
the Heralds' College, or College of Arms, established by law in 1483, to
make an official "visitation" of all the families in each of the shires and
counties, recording pedigrees and arms. These pedigrees form the basis of
the mass of records collected in the College of Arms in London, England.

If you are of English, Scotch, or Welsh descent the College for a fee
(which may run to several hundred dollars) will examine your claim to the

right to use a coat of arms. Or if that right cannot be established it will for a fee grant you a new coat of arms. If you are of Irish descent you may apply to The Genealogical Office, Dublin Castle, in Dublin, Ireland. If your family is of Scottish descent, the Lord Lyon King of Arms, Edinburgh, will verify your arms or make a new grant.

Although in the United States there is no legal, governmental authority which issues a coat of arms or rules upon your "right" to use a heraldic device, the New England Historic Genealogical Society, 9 Ashburton Place, Boston, Massachusetts 02176, has had a Committee on Heraldry for many years. This committee will examine a claim to the right to bear arms and rule on its validity and, if the claim is found to be authentic and the descent from the armigerous immigrant correct, will issue a certificate to that effect. A small fee is charged for this service. However, the Committee does not "grant" a coat of arms or do any genealogical research. Up to 1962 the committee authenticated nearly eight hundred claims (and rejected many more) and published a "Roll of Arms" listing those which they have accepted as legitimate.

Full Coat   Crest   Lozenge

A complete coat of arms consists of the shield with the appropriate heraldic insignia, called the "charge," on it; in this example the chevron is the charge. A crest consists of simply the insignia (generally quite different from that on the shield) surmounting a "wreath" above the shield, which may be used separately on stationery or silver. A lozenge is a lady's equivalent of the shield (see text) and must be used with a crest.

JONES   BROWN

Mr. Jones marries Miss Brown (an heiress) and their coats of arms are impaled thus:

and this achievement they use during their lifetime. Their son and heir quarters the Jones and the Brown arms, and he and his descendants continue to use the quartered arms.

To determine your family's right to a coat of arms, you need to know not only the full name of your earliest paternal American ancestor, but his connection with an armigerous British (or Continental) family and your own exact line of descent from him. If your name is Clark, Smith, Carpenter (all occupational names) or even such an unusual name as Blenkenship, Hungerford, or Cobleigh, you don't merely ascertain that there were coats of arms for these families and proceed to appropriate them for your own use. It may be happenstance that your name is the same. One Miller family, say, may have the right to use the coat as listed in Burke's *General Armoury,* another, quite unrelated, could not legally use that coat. Using a coat of arms not rightfully yours is like using another's trademark (as a matter of fact, some coats of arms actually are copyrighted in the United States).

The right to use a coat of arms was given in perpetuity to all direct male descendants *of the name.* In the early days of our country it was the younger sons who were more likely to emigrate from Europe than the oldest ones who inherited the title and lands. These younger sons sometimes came alone, sometimes with families, and with limited funds and even more limited experience in the kind of work they had to do in a new, rough country. In a generation or two perhaps former claims to gentility were forgotten, as all struggled together to build the new world. But the male heirs of the name, of direct descent from the original armigerous forebear, still had the right to the coat of arms, a right many a family here today doesn't realize it has.

The Lozenge

A woman who is an heiress or co-heiress (with sisters) of an armigerous family, and having no surviving brothers, has the right to use her father's coat of arms (as may her sisters) in a diamond-shaped "lozenge." (Illustration.) If she marries she may "impale" her arms with those of her husband—the shield is divided in half vertically and his arms are blazoned on the left and hers on the right. (Illustration.) Her children then "quarter" their parents' arms. (Illustration.) Technically, if an "heiress" marries a non-armigerous husband she and her children lose their armigerous standing. An heiress may continue to use the lozenge herself even though she marries a non-armigerous husband. But if she is not an heiress she is not correct in using her family's arms on the lozenge after her marriage.

How Are Heraldic Devices Used?

The most common use of a coat of arms is on an *ex libris,* or bookplate, or drawn or painted ("blazoned" is the technical term) and framed as a wall decoration. It may also be used on stationery if the paper is of the best quality and the coat of arms engraved (in color, if you choose) or embossed. This should appear only on the first sheet, and the envelopes should be stamped in the same fashion as the paper. It is also proper to have the full coat engraved on large pieces of silver, such as a tea tray. The crest only may be engraved on smaller pieces such as flat silver or personal articles such as a toilet set, cigarette case, or compact, or etched on glassware such as goblets and cocktail glasses, or reproduced in wedding invitations and announcements, place cards and menus for formal entertaining.

Although it is improper to use currently the coat of arms of a family other than that of one's father, or, in the case of a married woman, one's husband, it is not offensive to the laws of heraldry or good taste to hang in one's library, hall or bedroom a drawing, painting, or print of the coat of arms of any armigerous ancestor any more than it is to display other heirlooms such as family portraits or flintlock guns. Too pointed display of the coat of arms, however, is something like keeping the Social Register on the coffee table.

A Woman's Use The full coat of arms—shield, crest and motto—or what is known as a "gentleman's heraldic bearings" is never properly used on personal belongings by a woman. Women in medieval days did not normally go forth in battle and therefore did not carry shields. It is proper form in England, to which we look for precedent since we have nothing resembling heraldic authority in our own governmental setup, for a woman to use a *crest* on her stationery, on personal linens, etc., but never a coat of arms on a shield. The lozenge, however, is approved. If a British woman is titled she uses the coronet of her rank above it. But a woman of an armigerous family, especially if she is unmarried or a widow, may use just the crest (illustration) or the coat of arms itself—but only if blazoned on a lozenge. (Illustration.) No woman ever uses a heraldic motto, for these were invariably aggressively masculine and unsuited to feminine social use.

A Married Woman's Use of the Device A woman whose father has a coat of arms, but whose husband has not, shows better taste, actually, in saying good-by to it and its feminine modifications once her family has used it on her wedding invitations and announcements and, if she wishes, on silver her family has given her. A painted coat could be displayed on bedroom or library walls, not too conspicuously, but the device may not be adopted either by her husband or children.

Use on Wedding Invitations and Announcements When the names of a girl's mother and father appear jointly on wedding invitations and announcements it is correct, if the father has a coat of arms, to use it if desired either in its complete form—shield, helmet, crest, and motto or, more commonly, the crest only—embossed without any color at the top of the invitation. If the bride's mother alone—or some woman sponsor alone—has her name on the invitation or announcement she should not use her husband's or father's coat of arms. She may, however, use her crest or lozenge embossed without color.

Silver Marking and the Coat of Arms When the bride's family gives her silver they may mark it with her father's crest and motto without the shield and helmet. Very large plain pieces such as soup tureens, punch bowls, tea trays, etc., may carry a full marshaling—shield, helmet, crest, supporters, and mantling, with the motto on a "ribbon" beneath. If silver is given later to match the original set, it *may* be marked the same way. Silver given at any time by the groom's family may bear his crest. Additional silver purchased by husband and wife during the course of their marriage may, if they wish, have their respective arms, "impaled," on it, but her family device should not be used, except possibly upon her personal silver—toilet articles, cigarette case, vanity, etc. Even on strictly personal objects, however, it is better taste to use her husband's crest rather than her family's. Or, if he has none, to omit it altogether.

Chapter 48

WRITING AND CONVERSATION CAN BE MORE COLORFUL

A Bowing Acquaintance with Other Languages

Once I spent a challenging evening with a well-known writer, who seemed to question every other word spoken. In his adjacent study he had an unabridged dictionary open on a stand. He referred to it at least twenty times in the course of general conversation. It was a rather nervous way to chat, I thought, but the quality of this man's writing indicates that the dictionary is a good, close friend in the best sense. He does not use impressive words merely to seem erudite, but he uses words with an exactitude that is delightful.

We needn't be linguists to get along nicely in cultured circles. We do need to master quite a list of foreign phrases and words, however, so that we do not find ourselves beyond our depth.

In this country moneyed circles are not necessarily cultured ones at all. In Europe cultured people, threadbare professors or not, move in the highest social circles by virtue of their erudition and sophistication. Here, one is more likely to encounter learning at a level below that of millionaires and so-called social leaders. Certainly, to move in the jet set and its equivalent you need to know less than nothing about language—your own or those of contemporary or ancient civilizations.

The kind of society we should seek is that which stimulates us to express ourselves verbally, that spurs our intellectual processes, that make us want to achieve our own ultimate. People who keep us on our social and mental toes are good for us and make us grow spiritually, socially, and, often as an end result, financially. Ours is supposed to be, but of course is not, a wholly democratic, classless society. A foreign student once remarked to a friend of mine that all Americans are in their own minds actually divided into three classes, their own, the one directly above them, and the one just below.

As we mature as a nation, as the world produces more balance between the haves and the have-nots, so shall we each seek our place among people solely on the basis of intellectual and social gifts comparable to our own—because of their congeniality. Actually, money should never be a determinant of "class," and with thoughtful human beings it can't determine real values. But young people should keep in mind that they should prepare themselves to move up, to widen their social circles, to move with greater ease among strangers, to be able to go any place and meet anyone without feelings of social inferiority.

As one form of insurance against the dreaded feeling of "not belonging" among educated people, I urge at least a bowing acquaintance with Latin and French, a slight knowledge, at least, of Greek roots, prefixes, and suffixes, an ability to pronounce German and Spanish words reasonably well.

While it is affected to interject foreign words and phrases into ordinary conversation at every opportunity, it is nevertheless true that such expressions are second nature to many intellectuals and it is more comfortable to be on terra firma with them than on terra incognita. You don't need more than good, native intelligence and a lively curiosity to build an interesting vocabulary. Even a college education is no guarantee that a man or woman can express himself in well-chosen words—he may be too lazy mentally or too unsure of himself.

A friend of mine who had to go to work at fifteen has one of the most excellent vocabularies I know, and he doesn't build it solely by consulting the dictionary from time to time. Instead, he has a flattering way—considering his job as head of a large organization—of asking you, during the course of conversation, what a word you have used means. Then the next time you meet him you will find him using this word correctly and easily in his own conversation. The very fact that you know he has built his vocabulary step by step himself, not just absorbed it as many of us do from our family circle as part of our cultural heritage, makes you admire his continuing drive for self-improvement.

In the following lists of foreign words or phrases which you'll very likely encounter as you enlarge your social circle, I have omitted instruction on pronunciation. I would rather have you hear how a word should be pronounced than simply read it, dictionary-wise. Learn how the word or phrase looks, how it is spelled, what it means, then find someone who can really tell you how it sounds. In this way, with a little practice, you will have made many good, useful, and descriptive phrases and words part of your vocabulary. You won't be afraid to verbalize them if you have learned how to pronounce such words and phrases from someone who really knows and if you have listened for them to crop up in conversation. Be like my friend—if you don't know, ask. People will like you all the more for it. If you hear a man say he's "suffering from Weltschmerz," don't mumble a reply and make a mental note to look that one up in the dictionary sometime—you'll probably forget to, anyhow. Instead, say, "Is that how you pronounce that word? I've been meaning to look it up but now you can help me. I'm not even too sure of what it means." This is certainly better than forming hazy ideas of new words just by listening, then never questioning or looking them up in a reference work. I have a relative who shied from the forthright "pregnant" and substituted her notion of the correct and seemingly more modest French term, which she thought was *ancienne,* actually "ancient," when what she meant was, of course, *enceinte.*

I like what Dr. Calvin E. Gross said when he was superintendent of New York's schools. "Every citizen of this country, whether he pounds nails, raises corn, designs rockets or writes poetry, should be taught to know and love his American heritage; to use the language well; to understand the physical universe; and to enjoy the arts. The dollars he gains in the absence of enlightenment like this will be earned in drudgery and spent in ignorance."

An interest in language—all language—is tantamount to an interest in people. If you go to your Italian grocer and ask him how to pronounce *pizzeria,* he will not only tell you, but instruct you in the making of the specialty, *pizza.* He will be delighted at your interest and will add to your store of Italiana on each subsequent meeting. Borrow your son's Latin primer and ask him to help you on modern Latin pronunciation and you will create a warm feeling of co-operation between you, and a feeling of being needed—through momentary superiority—on his part. Ask help from your librarian by telling her what you want to accomplish.

The library is full of foreign language textbooks, unabridged dictionaries with all kinds of foreign words and phrases, foreign periodicals. Getting away from the notion that English alone is enough for anyone widens our social horizons in a neighborly sense that can embrace the whole world. It increases our own self-esteem and so puts us on a better footing with others. Every added competence increases our social acceptability and makes new friends.

French Words and Phrases

À BAS down with

À CHEVAL on horseback, but also used in the sense that one can consider or look at a thing from two sides

À COMPTE on account, in part payment. You might hear a phrase like this: "Here's a few dollars, *à compte.*"

À DEMI half, by halves, or imperfectly. In the latter sense it is used in this fashion: "That man! He does everything *à demi!*"

AFFAIRE DE COEUR a love affair

À HAUTE VOIX loudly

AIDE-MÉMOIRE quotes or memoranda literally to aid the memory, a frequently used term in diplomacy.

À LA BONNE HEURE Good! Fine! An expression of approval

À LA CAMPAGNE in the country

ALLEZ-VOUS-EN! Be off with you! Used literally and also as we use "Get out" to indicate non-belief.

À MOITIÉ half

À MOITIÉ MOITIÉ half and half

À MON AVIS in my opinion

À OUTRANCE to the bitter end

À PROPOS timely, reasonably

À PROPOS DE BOTTES literally, about shoes. Used parenthetically to indicate an irrelevancy; *à propos* of nothing.

À REBOURS inside out, across the grain, wrong sense and, idiomatically, "Quite the contrary."

ARRIÈRE-PENSÉE mental reservation

AU COURANT up to date

AU LEVANT to the East, also the sunrise

AU PLAISIR awaiting the pleasure (of seeing you again)

AU PLAISIR DE VOUS REVOIR in anticipation of seeing you again

AU PREMIER the first floor above the street floor, our second floor

AU RESTE as for the rest, besides

AU REVOIR until we meet again

AU REZ-DE-CHAUSSÉE even with the street, the ground floor

AU PRINTEMPS in the spring

AVANT COUREUR forerunner

AVANT-PROPOS preface or preliminary

À VOLONTÉ at pleasure

À VOTRE SANTÉ To your health! A toast.

BAS BLEU bluestocking, puritanical

BEAU GARÇON fine, but not necessarily handsome, fellow

BEAUX YEUX pretty eyes, but often means a pretty or handsome face

BEL AMI a beau, a handsome fellow

BELLE DAME an elegant matron, rather than a pretty woman

BÊTE NOIRE stumbling block, bugbear

BIENTÔT soon

BON JOUR good day; how do you do

CARTE BLANCHE without interference

CHEF-D'OEUVRE a masterpiece

CHEMIN DE FER train, also a gambling game

CHERCHEZ LA FEMME Look for the woman. A phrase often used in connection with the solving of crimes.

CLIQUE small group with mutual interests; set. Often used disparagingly.

COMME IL FAUT the way it should be; correct

CONCIERGE desk clerk or door tender, sometimes janitor

COQUETTE a flirt

COUP D'ÉTAT political stroke

COUP D'OEIL a glance

CUL-DE-SAC dead end

CULTE a group following a particular leadership; clique

D'ACCORD in harmony; in agreement

DÉCOLLETÉ low-cut (usually said of a neckline)

DÉJEUNER À LA FOURCHETTE American- and English-style breakfast (requiring a fork)

DISTINGUÉ distinguished

EN FAMILLE together with the family

EN PASSANT in passing

FAUX PAS a social error

FEMME DE CHAMBRE chambermaid

FEMME FATALE an irresistible woman

GARÇON boy, waiter

GAUCHE awkward, left

GIGOLO male, paid dancing partner

GRANDE DAME dowager

HOMME D'ESPRIT witty fellow

HOMME DU MONDE man of the world

HONI SOIT QUI MAL Y PENSE Old French. Evil to him who evil thinks.

JEUNE FILLE a young girl, girlish. (For one of her age, her behavior is certainly *jeune fille*.)

JEUNESSE DORÉE young fashionables

JOIE DE VIVRE exuberance, joy of living

LÈSE-MAJESTÉ high treason

MAÎTRE D'HÔTEL headwaiter

MAÎTRESSE mistress, schoolteacher

MAL DE MER seasickness

MARIAGE DE CONVENANCE an arranged marriage

MAUVAIS GOÛT poor taste

MÉNAGE household

MERCI thank you

MIDI the South, noon. Le Midi— the South of France

MODISTE one who makes or sells fashionable dresses or hats

MON CHER (masculine) *ma chère* (feminine) my dear

MON VIEUX old man (in the complimentary sense—"That's quite a hat, *mon vieux*.")

MOUSSELINE DE SOIE very fine silk muslin

N'IMPORTE it doesn't matter

NOBLESSE OBLIGE one's position implies decent behavior

NOM DE GUERRE a pseudonym by a writer of barbed material

NOM DE PLUME pen name

NOUVEAU RICHE newly rich and considered crass

OBJET D'ART collector's item

ON DIT people say, also literally, one says

OUI yes

PARDONNEZ MOI I beg your pardon

PARVENU a pusher, one who tries to crash into high circles

PETITE AMIE little friend (often used in the sense of "mistress")

PETIT À PETIT L'OISEAU FAIT SON NID Little by little the bird builds his nest. Nothing is accomplished overnight.

PETIT DÉJEUNER French breakfast of coffee and rolls

PIÈCE DE RÉSISTANCE the main dish, the incomparable

PIED-À-TERRE a lodging such as a small city apartment kept by one who lives in the suburbs

POUR FAIRE RIRE to make one laugh (often used sarcastically)

POUR PASSER LE TEMPS to pass the time

PREMIÈRE first appearance of a play, movie, etc.

PRIX FIXE fixed price. A meal that is listed as *prix fixe* includes all courses at the indicated price.

RACONTEUR a (usually) witty storyteller

RAISON D'ÊTRE the purpose

RECULER POUR MIEUX SAUTER to retreat, the better to advance later

RÉPONDEZ S'IL VOUS PLAIT (R.S.V.P.) please reply

ROBE DE CHAMBRE a dressing gown

ROBE DE STYLE period gown

SALON a meeting place for intellectuals in someone's home

SANG-FROID composure

SAVOIR-FAIRE knowledgeableness, sophistication, social awareness, social grace

SAVOIR-VIVRE knowledge of how to live elegantly

SOIRÉE an evening entertainment, usually at home

SOUPÇON a little bit, a suggestion of

SUCCÈS D'ESTIME polite acclaim out of respect alone, often a critical success rather than a monetary one

TABLE D'HÔTE the whole meal at a fixed price

TÊTE-À-TÊTE confidences, intimate conversation between two people

TIENS! an expression of annoyance or surprise. Pshaw! Or, "You don't say so?"

TOUJOURS as ever, always

TOUR DE FORCE a thing accomplished by sheer determination

TOUT DE SUITE right now

TOUT ENSEMBLE all together, complete

VIVRE DE SON SAVOIR FAIRE to live by one's wits

VOILÀ There! Sometimes, "Here comes—" (*Voilà* la Princesse Maude)

VRAISEMBLANCE likelihood, probability

Latin Phrases

AD NAUSEAM to the point of nausea, disgust. We might say, "His complaints went on, *ad nauseam*."

ARS LONGA VITA BREVIS Art is long, [but] life is short.

AVE ATQUE VALE Hail and farewell. This is a phrase that you very likely have noticed many times in obituaries. It frequently appears on tombstones.

CARPE DIEM Make (good) use of the day, seize the opportunity.

CAVEAT EMPTOR Let the buyer beware!

DE FACTO actual. For example, *de facto* government

DEUS EX MACHINA a wonderful, fortuitous and unexpected happening or circumstance that saves the situation

ECCE HOMO Behold the man!

ET TU, BRUTE You, too, Brutus. Caesar said this when he saw his great friend among his assassins. It is used to indicate treachery— sometimes facetiously.

EX CATHEDRA Usually used in connection with a pronouncement from the Pope. Literally, "from his chair" or officially.

EX LIBRIS from (among) the books (of), a bookplate with the owner's name, coat of arms, etc., to be pasted on the inside cover of a book

HABEAS CORPUS A writ or order permitting a prisoner to be produced at a stated time to determine the court's right to detain him. This is a phrase beloved by crime reporters and mystery writers.

IPSO FACTO by the act itself

MARE NOSTRUM our sea. A phrase used politically by the Italians to indicate the Mediterranean. And a phrase particularly liked by editorial writers.

MULTUM IN PARVO much in little

NOTA BENE note well (often seen abbreviated: N.B.)

OBITER DICTUM a conversational aside; in law an incidental decision that isn't binding

OMNIA VINCIT AMOR Love conquers all.

O TEMPORA! O MORES! Oh [the] times! Oh [the] customs! (often used in a pseudo-shocked sense)

PATER FAMILIAS father of the family (very commonly used)

PAX VOBISCUM Peace be with you.

PER CAPITA each individual (actually counted by heads)

PER DIEM by the day, daily. "Department store workers are sometimes paid on a *per diem* basis."

PER SE by itself, intrinsically. "I do not object to television *per se*, but I do object to many of the programs supposedly suitable for children."

PINXIT sometimes seen on paintings after the signature—meaning "painted it"

POST SCRIPTUM the after writing, or thought. Abbreviated by P.S. when an additional message is appended to a letter after the signature. Sometimes when still another paragraph is added a P.P.S. precedes it, meaning *post post scriptum*.

PRO BONO PUBLICO for the public good

PRO PATRIA for one's country

PROPTER HOC because of this

PRO TEMPORE for the time being (abbreviated as *pro tem*)

QUID PRO QUO tit for tat

QUOD ERAT DEMONSTRANDUM The problem is solved, or demonstrated. A term used in Geometry in abbreviated form, Q.E.D. These initials appear at the end of a solved geometric problem but are often used conversationally to indicate that a matter is closed.

RARA AVIS a rare bird, a unique person or thing.

REDUCTIO AD ABSURDUM reduced to an absurdity, silly

REQUIESCAT IN PACE Rest in peace.

SCULPSIT used after the signature of a sculptor—meaning "he or she sculptured it"

SIC thus. Indicates when used parenthetically that the quotation thus used, although quoted as it appeared is, of course, incorrect in some way

SIC TRANSIT GLORIA MUNDI So go the glories of the world; everything's so transient. (Often used)

SINE QUA NON without which nothing (is good or advisable); a necessary condition

STET Let it stand. An editorial indication that something which has been crossed out should be left as it was originally.

SUMMUM BONUM the supreme good

TAEDIUM VITAE boredom

TEMPUS FUGIT time flies

VENI, VIDI, VICI I came, I saw, I conquered. (Julius Caesar's report of a victory.)

VERBATIM word for word (very commonly used in conversation)

VICE VERSA the relations between things being reversed

VINCIT OMNIA VERITAS Truth conquers all.

VIVA VOCE by word of mouth, orally

VOX POPULI, VOX DEI The voice of the people [is] the voice of God.

Familiar Words and Phrases from Other Languages

AUF WIEDERSEHEN (Ger.) Till we meet again.

DAS ALTER WACHT, DIE JUGEND WAGT (Ger.) Old age considers, youth ventures.

DOLCE FAR NIENTE (It.) It's sweet to do nothing.

EINMAL IST KEIN MAL (Ger.) One swallow doesn't make a summer (literally, one time is no time).

GEMÜTLICH (Ger.) friendly, appealing. "That restaurant has a *gemütlich* atmosphere I like."

GESUNDHEIT (Ger.) To your health! Often said if someone sneezes.

GOLD VERLOREN, NIET VERLOREN; MOED VERLOREN, VEEL VERLOREN; EER VERLOREN, MOER VERLOREN; ZEEL VERLOREN, AL VERLOREN (Du.) Gold lost, nothing lost; courage lost, much is lost; honor lost, more is lost; soul lost, all is lost.

GOTT MIT UNS (Ger.) God is with us. God is on our side.

GRÜSS GOTT (Ger.) old German greeting. Literally, God greet you.

HOI POLLOI (Gr.) *the* common people. Don't use the article before it. "That is for hoi polloi."

KAKON KORAKOS, KAKON CON (Gr.) Like from like. (A bad crow lays a bad egg.)

LEBENSRAUM (Ger.) breathing space, space, space to live

NITCHEVO (Rus.) What's the use?

PRIMA DONNA (It.) first lady, used usually to indicate top-ranking woman singer, and frequently to describe a woman who is not a singer but indulges in "temperament"

¿QUÉ PASA? (Sp.) What goes on? What's happening? What's new?

¿QUIÉN SABE? (Sp.) Who knows?

SHIBBŌLETH (Heb.) Now used to mean criterion, identifying word or action. Originally it was a word, meaning "stream."

SKOAL! (Swed.) Good health. Often used as a toast.

WANDERJAHR (Ger.) a year of wandering. University students often took a year off in Europe to discover the world around them physically and philosophically. It is in this sense the term is used.

WANDERLUST (Ger.) a tremendous desire to travel or wander

WELTKRIEG (Ger.) World War

WUNDERBAR (Ger.) wonderful

ZAPATERO À TU ZAPATO (Sp.) Shoemaker stick to your last.

ZEITGEIST (Ger.) spirit of the age

ZUM BEISPIEL (Ger.) for example. Abbreviation: z.B.

Common Expressions from English Literature

In English there are innumerable phrases, many taken out of context, the understanding of which indicates at least a nodding acquaintance with the classics and unfortunately, ignorance of which leaves one very much in the dark, sometimes, as to the meaning of some spoken or written comment. Listen for such phrases, mark them in your reading, and discover their sources.

The information desks of large libraries, your local librarian, a well-read friend, a teacher, the inquiry columns of newspapers, Sunday supplements, and literary publications can help you classify and understand these myriad enrichers of our language. Some of the world's greatest writers have kept journals and notebooks—Arnold Bennett's were minutely kept—in which to record their day-to-day impressions, to capture an attractive phrase, to record a shade of meaning in a word or quotation for possible future use or inspiration. This is an excellent way to improve one's vocabulary.

Some of us are born with good memories and some seem to be unable to remember things easily, at least not exact quotations. Sometimes memory can be trained, but it can always be jogged by notes. Make good use of them in the building of your vocabulary and in collecting a usable background of quotations, allusions, and proverbs. It's pedantic, of course, to stud everything you say or write with such references, but you'll certainly need to recognize them and it is pleasant and interesting to be able to use them without self-consciousness after they have become as much a part of you as your everyday expressions.

It will be impossible for me to list more than a few of the common expressions and quotations, but the following brief list may suggest where you'll find more. The old and new books of the Bible are studded with quotations and references we meet, often unknowingly, every day. Shakespeare contributed immensely to cultured language. *Aesop's Fables, Alice in Wonderland,* Benjamin Franklin's *Poor Richard's Almanack,* Dickens, the great poets, the Greek and Roman legends, folk tales, and fairy tales are among the many, many sources of words and phrases that are dropped into conversations and that turn up with great frequency in our reading.

English Expressions Commonly Used, Their Sources and Meaning

ACHILLES' HEEL   The heel of legendary Greek hero Achilles was the only vulnerable portion of his body. "When we know his background, we can easily detect his *Achilles' heel.*"

A PROPHET IS NOT WITHOUT HONOR, SAVE IN HIS OWN COUNTRY . . .   Matthew 13:57. "A prophet is not without honor, save in his own country and in his own house." Oracles with whom we are on a familiar footing fail to impress us.

AUGEAN STABLE The cleaning of the Augean stable, terribly, repulsively dirty, was one of the tasks assigned to the legendary Hercules. "The place was a veritable Augean stable!"

BARKIS IS WILLIN' From *David Copperfield,* by Charles Dickens. Barkis was willing to—and did—marry Peggotty, David's nurse.

BETWEEN SCYLLA AND CHARYBDIS The Greek poet, Homer, describes two opposing perils—a six-headed monster and a whirlpool—one on each side of the Strait of Messina, through which sailors had to steer their course. The phrase is used to indicate a great dilemma. "I was between Scylla and Charybdis, not knowing which way to turn."

BEWARE THE GREEKS BEARING GIFTS Virgil's *Aeneid.* A paraphrase of the line, "I fear the Greeks bearing gifts." The reference is to the Trojan horse.

BEWARE A WOLF IN SHEEP'S CLOTHING From the Aesop fable about the wolf who, draping himself in a sheepskin, pretended he was part of the flock. "I thought him a friend but he turned out to be a wolf in sheep's clothing."

BILLINGSGATE Invective. Refers to the imprecations of fishwives in England's Billingsgate market. "He was treated to some rare billingsgate."

BLARNEY Cajolery. In Blarney Castle, Ireland, there is a stone which, if kissed, is said to confer a cajoling tongue. "What a lot of blarney"— talk that is pretty obviously flattering. We also say, "He has kissed the blarney stone," meaning he can turn a complimentary phrase neatly— that we enjoy the blarney but don't quite believe it.

BREAD CAST UPON THE WATERS From Ecclesiastes 11:2. "Cast thy bread upon the waters: for thou shalt find it after many days." Literally, good deeds are rewarded in kind.

BROBDINGNAGIAN Giantlike. From Swift's *Gulliver's Travels.* Brobdingnag was the land of giants.

BY THEIR FRUITS YE SHALL KNOW THEM Matthew 7:20. "Wherefore by their fruits ye shall know them." People are judged by what they do.

CAVIAR TO THE GENERAL *Hamlet,* Shakespeare. This means something is very unusual, special, not appealing to most people. "Orchid growing is caviar to the general."

COUNTRY MOUSE Know when you're well off. Aesop tells of the country mouse who yearns for the life of the city mouse, tries it and discovers its perils. "He thought he'd like New York, but he discovered that he was just a country mouse."

"CURIOUSER AND CURIOUSER" Alice's exclamation when she began to grow as she ate the little cake in *Alice in Wonderland* by Lewis Carroll. The phrase is used to express wonder. "Her actions are growing 'curiouser and curiouser.'"

DAMON AND PYTHIAS   From the Greek tale of two devoted friends. "They are a veritable Damon and Pythias."

DARBY AND JOAN   From an old English ballad, "The Happy Old Couple." "It's been a happy marriage. They are a real Darby and Joan."

DAVY JONES' LOCKER   Ancient seamen's expression for the deep, or a watery grave. Jones is thought to be a corruption of Jonah, the prophet who was thrown into the sea. "Captain Kidd's gold is in Davy Jones' locker."

DOG IN THE MANGER   Refers to Aesop's tale of the dog in the manger who, though he didn't wish to eat the hay there himself, wouldn't let anyone else enjoy it.

GORDIAN KNOT   To cut the Gordian knot—to solve a problem by swift, direct action or by evading the conditions. Derives from the classical myth about Alexander the Great's cutting of an intricate knot. "To get through the red tape of Customs was like trying to cut the Gordian knot."

HARE AND TORTOISE   Slow but sure. From Aesop's fable of the cocksure hare who challenged a slow but steady tortoise to a race and was beaten because he idled by the wayside while the tortoise kept his eye strictly on the finish line. "Jones has made a good showing in the primaries, but remember the tale of the hare and the tortoise."

HER PRICE IS ABOVE RUBIES   Proverbs 31:10. "Who can find a virtuous woman? for her price is far above rubies." This whole passage, 31:10–31, "The Praise of a Good Wife," is one of the most often quoted in the whole Bible.

HOIST WITH HIS OWN PETARD   From *Hamlet,* Shakespeare. Hamlet says "For 'tis the sport to have the engineer/Hoist with his own petar." A petard was an ancient variety of bomb. Shakespeare used the former spelling, now obsolete. To be trapped by his own machinations.

HOW ARE THE MIGHTY FALLEN!   Bible. II Samuel, 1:23. Indicates the impermanence of established people and orders. "The Republicans suffered a defeat—how are the mighty fallen!"

IF THE HILL WILL NOT COME TO MAHOMET, MAHOMET WILL GO TO THE HILL.   Usually we hear this quoted "the mountain." From Francis Bacon's essay "Of Boldness." "He may be stubborn but, after all, Mahomet can always go to the hill."

ILL WIND   Usually quoted as "It's an ill wind that blows nobody good." From sixteenth-century Thomas Tusser's poem:

> Except wind stands as it never stood,
> It is an ill wind that turns none to good.

IN THE ARMS OF MORPHEUS   Asleep. Morpheus was the Greek god of dreams. This is a frequently heard, rather coy expression for describing a night's sleep.

LET SLEEPING DOGS LIE   Chaucer in *Canterbury Tales* says, "It is not good a sleeping hound to wake."

LEAN AND HUNGRY LOOK   From *Julius Caesar,* Shakespeare.

> Let me have men about me that are fat,
> Sleek-headed men and such as sleep o'nights:
> Yond Cassius has a lean and hungry look;
> He thinks too much; such men are dangerous.

LET HIM FRY IN HIS OWN GREASE   "In his owen grese I made him frie." Chaucer, *Canterbury Tales.*

LITTLE FOXES   The Song of Solomon 2:15. "Take us the foxes, the little foxes, that spoil the vines." Depredators, destroyers in a sly fashion. "Gossip of the little foxes sometimes destroys reputations."

MILK OF HUMAN KINDNESS   From *Macbeth,* Shakespeare. We use it in an approving sense—"Her kind actions reflected the milk of human kindness."

"MINE IS A LONG AND A SAD TALE."   The mouse's plaint to Alice in *Alice in Wonderland,* by Lewis Carroll.

MUMBO JUMBO   A grotesque idol of a tribe of the western Sudan, object of senseless veneration. When we say, "to me it's much mumbo jumbo," we mean it's incomprehensible.

MURDER WILL OUT   From *Hamlet,* Shakespeare: "For murder, though it have no tongue, will speak with most miraculous organ." Crime can't go undetected. (Shakespeare got it from the *Canterbury Tales,* where Chaucer wrote it "Mordre wol out.")

NEMESIS   Nemesis was an ancient Greek goddess who personified retribution. "He met his nemesis"—he got what he deserved, his just due.

"OFF WITH HIS HEAD!"   The Queen of Hearts' frequently voiced order in *Alice in Wonderland* by Lewis Carroll. This is often used in a joking manner to indicate disapproval.

O, THAT THIS TOO TOO SOLID FLESH WOULD MELT . . .   From Hamlet's soliloquy. Although a somber thought in Shakespeare, this is often used facetiously by the overweight.

POLLYANNA   From the juvenile novel, *Pollyanna,* by Eleanor H. Porter. The expression is used to describe someone, male or female, who is saccharinely optimistic.

SOUR GRAPES From Aesop's fable of the fox and the grapes. The fox, unable to reach the grapes, covered his chagrin by declaring them sour, anyway.

STYGIAN NIGHT Taken from Greek mythology and referring or pertaining to the river Styx, over which souls crossed to Hades; murky, gloomy night. "It was a starless, Stygian night."

TENDER MERCIES Proverbs 12:10. "A righteous man regardeth the life of his beast: but the tender mercies of the wicked are cruel." A phrase used sarcastically, "I would not like to be subject to her tender mercies."

THE BEST LAID SCHEMES O' MICE AND MEN GANG AFT A-GLEY The best laid schemes of mice and men often go wrong. From Robert Burns's "To a Mouse."

THE LEFT HAND DOESN'T KNOW WHAT THE RIGHT HAND DOES Matthew 6:3. "But when thou doest alms, let not thy left hand know what thy right hand doeth." Go modestly about your good works.

THE OLD LADY OF THREADNEEDLE STREET A familiar phrase which refers to the venerable Bank of England.

TROJAN HORSE Something that looks harmless but is really perilous. From Virgil's *Aeneid*. In the Greek siege of ancient Troy, Greek warriors, hidden in a great wooden horse, got inside Troy's walls by this stratagem and overpowered the city during the night.

UGLY DUCKLING From Andersen's fairy tale of that title. The ugly duckling grows into a beautiful swan. Used to predict promise of beauty.

UTOPIA An imaginary island in the book of that title by Sir Thomas More in 1516, epitomizing the perfect social and political state. From the Greek, meaning "no place."

VALHALLA From the Norse myth. The souls of slain heroes feasted in Valhalla, the palace of Odin, which was the final resting place of such illustrious dead. "The hero went to his Valhalla."

VOICE OF THE TURTLE The Song of Solomon 2:12. ". . . and the voice of the turtle [meaning turtledove] is heard in the land." Spring.

Words and Phrases Often Incorrectly Used and Pronounced

ABDOMEN The preferred pronunciation is ăb·dō′měn, ab′do·men

ACCLIMATE Meaning to habituate and pronounced ă·klī′mĭt

ALL THE FARTHER (I am going) Should be "as far as I am going."

ALLOW and ALLOW ME Do not use as a synonym for "agree." It means "permit." The phrase "Allow me" used as a supposedly polite offer of assistance to a lady is classed with "Permit me"—among the Victorianisms. A man offers such assistance without comment or with some more current phrase such as, "Do let me help you with that."

AN INVITE The noun is "invitation."

ARCTIC The first "c" is pronounced. It is ark'tic.

BETWEEN As a preposition used to make comparison between *two* things. When higher numbers are involved use *among*. Ex.: "Between us two," "Among us three."

BUILD or SHAPE These vulgar expressions should never be used to indicate a person's "figure," e.g., "Jane has a good shape."

CAN'T HARDLY No; "can hardly," instead of the double negative.

CARE TO Do not use for "wish to" or "want to" or "prefer to."

CHAISE LONGUE Means "long chair" in French and must be used in the two original words, never shortened to "chaise" (shāz) which just means "chair." Also note it is "longue" pronounced *läwng*, not as our word "lounge."

CONGRATULATE Be sure to pronounce the first "t." Often carelessly pronounced congradulate.

CONSENSUS Use alone. Do not add "of opinion." It means "agreement of opinion or testimony."

CORPUS DELICTI Mystery writers to the contrary, it does not mean "the body" but "the body of evidence in connection with a crime."

DAIS Speaker's platform—pronounced dā'is, not dī'as.

DISTINCTIVE The word means "distinguishing," "characteristic." Some people trying for simplicity translate the French term *"distingué,"* meaning "of distinguished *air*" into "distinctive," which can't be done. "Distinguished" is the appropriate translation, but use of the French term is very common. "She was very *distingué*, I thought."

DRAPES Advertising term for "draperies" or "curtains." It should never be used in conversation.

DROWN-DED No, the past tense of the verb to drown is pronounced *drown'd*

EITHER Two pronunciations (ē or ī) and meaning "each of two."

EXPECTING The phrase "Is she expecting?" meaning "Is she pregnant?" is one of those little evasions that sound particularly vulgar. Even "Is she expecting a *baby?*" sounds odd to the purists. One of them used to rail against the common *"expectant* mother" for what doctors call a "primipara," one who bears a child for the first time. "She may be a woman expecting a child," he would fume, "but she is not an expectant *mother."*

FIFTH Not to be pronounced fith. The second "f" should be heard.

FINE, SPLENDID, EXCELLENT Often incorrectly used in adverbial form (plus the "ly") when they should be used as predicate adjectives referring to the subject. It is "I feel *fine*," "He looks *splendid*," "It really seemed *excellent*." But when these words modify a *verb*, then the following sentences are correct: "The comparison was *finely* drawn." "The music swelled *splendidly* out into the hall." "She rides *excellently*."

FOLKS Don't use for "family." But "folk" (plural for people, nation, race) is correct, of course, in such a sense as this: "The Lilliputians were imaginary folk."

GENT In the same vulgar class as "dearie," "girlie," "tootsie" (unless you're joking), "hubby," "little woman," "old man."

GIRL FRIEND, BOY FRIEND, GENTLEMAN FRIEND, LADY FRIEND True, our language is deficient in words for these combinations. There is something very low class about them all, especially "lady friend" and "gentleman friend." Etiquette has given up over "girl friend" and "boy friend" but in all cases it is better to substitute "man (girl, boy or woman), who is a friend of mine" or "woman friend" or "man friend," "sweetheart," possibly (for young people), or "beau" for any man or boy who is courting a girl. A girl introducing a girl to her mother preferably doesn't say, "Mother, this is my *girl* friend Jeanette." The word "friend" is sufficient, and it is obvious she is a girl. Even if the friend is not present, the use of the pronoun identifies her enough. "Mother, I have a friend at school I'd like to ask over today. You'll like her."

GIVE ME, LET ME, GOING TO, WANT TO Enunciate these words carefully so they don't become, "gimme, lemme, gonna, wanna."

HAIRDO This ugly word has been admitted to American dictionaries because people have trouble pronouncing the more attractive French word "*coiffure*" (kwa·fūr') and get that confused with "*coiffeur*" (kwa·fer), a male hairdresser. Word-sensitive people either use *coiffure* or some substitute, "Have you *arranged* (or fixed) your hair in a new way?"

HIGH-CLASS This is one of those phrases that seem to indicate social inferiority in the person uttering it. Instead, use "good, superior, excellent, distinguished, fine" to indicate something or someone of good quality.

HOLD ON Don't let this disintegrate into the sloppy Hole-don.

HOSIERY This is a shop or trade term for stockings. It should not be used in social conversation.

HOSE Same as above but Pantyhose, having no equivalent, is acceptable. No one says panty *stockings*.

HOSPITABLE Preferred pronunciation is hos'pitable, but hospit'able is also correct.

HOUSE, HOME There is a delicate difference, and the two words are not interchangeable. You may be hunting for a house in which to live, but after you are in it, with your goods and chattels around you, it is your home. In referring to the style of its architecture, however, you would say, "it's a modern house," or, "Our house is the one with the pillars." You are, or are not, "at home," but some other resident of the house would, if in the garden, say, "Mother is in the house," never "in the home" or even "at home," which is in this case unspecific. Mother might well be boating on the pond yet still be "at home" to callers. But if you buy a television set, you have them deliver it to your "house."

INTEREST Pronounced in'ter·est or in'trist. Never pronounced in·ter·est'.

ITCH If your foot itches, you scratch it. Be careful not to confuse "itch" for "scratch." The former is the sensation, the latter the action to lessen it. Of course, both words are nouns, too. You may have the itch. Or you may have a scratch on your hand.

LEAVE ME Not to be used for "let me." Say "let me go" not "leave me go."

LEND You lend something to someone who wants to borrow it from you. Never say "I want to lend it from you." You borrow from and lend to.

LIKE It is colloquial—but ugly—to use *like* as a conjunction, as if it were synonymous with *as*. Not "It snowed like it did in January," but "It snowed as it did in January." Why give in to the vulgar without a fight?

LIMB Don't use as a nice-nelly substitute for the forthright "leg."

LINGERIE Probably one of the most frequently mispronounced words. It is lăn'zh'r·ee' (the "zh"="z" in "azure" and the heavier accent is on the last syllable), not *longeray'*.

LISTEN! UNDERSTAND? I MEAN These words appear far too frequently in conversation. Sometimes you will hear them several times in the same sentence. Listen for them in your conversation and try improving your way of speaking so that you will not fall on these weak devices for trapping your listeners' attention.

LOAN "Have a loan of" is very colloquial. Instead say "borrow."

MAESTRO This is an Italian word used as the most distinguished title for a master of music—a composer, a conductor, or a great teacher. It shouldn't be used for every little tunesmith. It is pronounced "mä·ĕs'trō" in a liquid, rapid pronunciation which, sad to state, sounds to some like "mīce·tro." If you enunciate the second syllable carefully you avoid this.

MANUFACTURE It is surprising how many otherwise well-spoken people turn this into "manafacture." The "u" is pronounced as in "unite."

NEITHER Two pronunciations (nē or nī), followed by "nor." "Neither my son *nor* I could go."

NOTORIOUS To be used only in the sense of "infamous." "The notorious Jesse James" but "the famous Disraeli."

OFF Never use in place of "from." It is never, "I got it *off* him," if you mean he gave it to you.

PARDON ME This is a rude order. One says instead, "Please excuse me" or "I beg your pardon" or "Please forgive me."

PERFECT When used as a verb, the preferred pronunciation is per·fect'. When used as an adjective, it should not be modified by "more" and "most" as it is the superlative. "It's a perfect day," is the ultimate you can say. "The most perfect day" is really meaningless.

THE REASON IS BECAUSE This should be—"the reason is *that*." The "because" is superfluous in this construction.

REFER BACK The word "back" is redundant in this phrase. Say simply "refer," as in the sentence: "The President referred to his previous remarks before Congress." The *re* means back and *ferre*, from the Latin, to take.

RICH, WEALTHY Supposedly it is "manners" to avoid these two terms indicating affluence, and, if one must be used, "rich" (tongue-in-cheek style) is supposed to be preferable. In speaking socially of people, it is more usual to say "They have a lot of money." To me "rich" seems more vulgar than "wealthy," but the dictionary has nothing against either.

SECOND Be sure to sound the "d."

SORE Correct and acceptable only to describe physical or mental hurt, not a state of irritation. "Was she sore at me!" is a vulgarism.

STRENGTH All the letters are pronounced. It is often mispronounced as if the "g" were omitted.

TOMATO It is not more elegant to say "tomahto." In fact, though both pronunciations are correct, "tomāto" is preferred in American dictionaries.

TUESDAY If you pronounce the first three letters almost separately you achieve the correct pronunciation. It is *not* Toos-day.

VASE It seems affected these days to pronounce this as "vahz" instead of "vāze."

WHITE The *h* is pronounced.

YOU'LL HAVE TO EXCUSE ME Instead say, "Please excuse me."

Musical Terms

ADAGIO slowly, also a balancing movement in ballet

ALLEGRETTO musical term meaning quicker than "andante" but not so quick as "allegro"

ALLEGRO musical term indicating speed; brisk, lively

ANDANTE moderately slow, but flowing; quicker than larghetto, and slower than allegretto

ARABESQUE a ballet term meaning to pose on one foot; a musical ornament

AUX POINTES ballet term: on the toes, the half-toe position of the male dancer

BALLETOMANE a ballet enthusiast

BOURRÉE a lively old French dance tune in 4-4 or 2-4 time

COUNTERPOINT contrasting musical themes, neither having dominance in a composition

DOLCE soft and smooth in execution

ENTRECHAT a scissoring of the legs in mid-air with calves touching

FORTE loud, powerful

FUGUE in music, a theme repeated in such a way that the first theme seems to take flight from the repeating one, often played in another octave

GLISSANDO gliding effect of notes sounding in quick succession

LARGHETTO somewhat slow, but less so than largo

LARGO very slow, broad, stately

LENTAMENTE slowly

PAS DE BOURRÉE ballet term: tiny little steps on the toes, suggesting a glide

PIANO soft

PIROUETTE ballet term: to whirl or turn on the toes

PIZZICATO plucked—a direction to players of bowed instruments to pluck the string instead of bowing

PREMIÈRE DANSEUSE a ballet company's principal female dancer

PRESTO at a rapid pace

SUR LES POINTES ballet term: on the tips of the toes, toe dancing, the female dancer's elevated position

TOUR EN L'AIR a complete turn off the ground, in ballet

TOUR JETÉ leap and turn in ballet

Regional Accents

Many experts on the English language contend that the finest English in America is spoken in Boston. That is, I suppose, it most closely approaches English English. But to my ear there are many delightful regional accents I should hate to see disappear in some vast misguided effort to make us all speak alike.

In the various theater arts it is considered advisable to erase regional accents for the simple reason that an actor or actress usually desires to play a variety of parts. A person with a strong southern accent would necessarily find himself typecast in the theater or on radio or television. This problem does not exist for most people, but those who travel or live in a variety of localities find that their original regional accents become more or less cosmopolitan in time or take on the inflections, the tones, the idioms, the slurrings, or the stresses of the place in which they have lived longest. Often the widely traveled, cultured person has no ascertainable accent at all. He is a language-citizen of the world.

Of course there are ugly accents and regional idioms that may well be overcome. But before we condemn, for example, "foist," "erster," and "boid" as pure Brooklynese of the lower strata we should travel to the South, where the same distortions turn up among some of the native-born, politely educated citizens of New Orleans, among other places.

I like accents of all kinds. They help to make people different and interesting. Unless they are real handicaps, professionally, or from the standpoint of understandability, I hate to see them "corrected."

A Well-modulated Voice

The placement of the voice is very important. There are, naturally, all kinds of born speaking voices, some attractive, some unpleasant. But all respond well to efforts toward pleasant modulation. Vigorous people usually have voices to match, and they often wear us out just through the sound they generate. It is difficult to gear them to more pleasing tonal levels, but if they want to improve their voices they can do so consciously.

Childhood is the real time to do something about the tone and quality of the voice. The familiar reminders—"Not so *loud*," "Please *speak up*," "A little *slower*," "Don't *mumble*"—eventually have some effect, if only when the child is on his best behavior outside the family circle. But essentially the child will speak, when he becomes an adult, as his parents and siblings spoke, which may be well or badly—unless, of course, his higher education was completely away from his family. Even then, no change may ever come in his manner of speaking unless some special effort has been directed toward the changing of it, if that seems advisable.

The ideal speaking voice is placed low, is not nasal. If we speak too rapidly what we say loses much of its effectiveness. If we drag our words out in what seems an excess of caution we bore our audiences. If our voices drop at the end of each sentence we tend to depress our hearers. If we speak in a constant burst of enthusiasm we tire others and seem sophomoric. A good speaking voice lifts slightly at the end of each sentence. It is not too rapid, nor too pedestrian. It comes through well-opened lips and from an open throat, from the chest rather than from the neck. Good speech requires good breathing, good posture, and essentially good health, mental and physical. Fear, anxiety and ill-health constrict our vocal cords and make our voices thin and tight or weary. Relaxation makes our voices round and easy to tumble out.

The sound of the voice and the way the language is used is often a deciding factor on the assay of a man's or woman's personality. A beautiful woman, beautifully dressed, carrying herself like a queen can destroy the effect in a flash merely by opening her mouth. A handsome, well-groomed man is ineffective if his voice has a weak, high register.

I once knew a very attractive artist whose wife told me his success as an artist and as a man came as a result of his lowering his high, thin voice to a resounding bass after special teaching.

Part Six

THE FAMILY AND SOCIAL
EDUCATION OF THE CHILDREN

THE FAMILY AND SOCIAL EDUCATION OF THE CHILDREN

The most important phases of etiquette deal with the comfortable living together of the family. The family's politeness to its individual members is vital to its happiness. One face to the world, another at home makes for misery. Of course in the family circle there is always some necessary relaxation of the rules of etiquette, but simple manners are always essential between husband and wife, between children and parents. It is important, too, to recognize the essential from the non-essential in the light of present-day psychology.

Rigid parents can, naturally, insist on a regime of strict behavior at home, but they will, by so doing, lose something very beautiful in the child-parent relationship. And the negativeness that must have some expression is sure to erupt outside the home, at least if the child is to be emotionally healthy. Better to have it at home to a certain tolerable degree than in school or elsewhere, where it may be less understandably dealt with and where it can really interfere with educational and social progress.

It may seem odd to include such things as thumb-sucking and bed-wetting in a book of etiquette. Actually, of course, they have nothing whatsoever to do with the subject of manners. But many people, especially those with no children or those who have raised children a generation or so ago, often contend vehemently that the correction of these things lies within the realm of manners, i.e., of teachable behavior. For this reason I am setting down the modern, pediatric viewpoint, which has effectively demonstrated that we cannot correct the sometimes embarrassing habits of children by treating them in terms of good or bad manners. We must dig down to the basic emotional causes of anti-social behavior.

Parents can help their children learn comfortable social practices by their own attitude toward each other. Again mere correctness of form is not the deciding factor. Warmth of spirit, kindliness in their dealings with one another, generosity, and elasticity are much more significant.

Chapter 49

MANNERS IN MARRIAGE

Understanding the Woman in the Home

Great heat is generated over the discussion as to whether men can ever understand women—especially their own wives. Perhaps it is impossible for most husbands to understand everything about their wives, and it is equally true that even relatively uncomplex husbands are never completely understood by the women they've married. But both husband and wife can try to find the widest possible area of agreement, and each must eventually recognize that there are some traits, habits, anxieties, ambitions, prejudices, sentiments in the other that need to be accepted or made allowance for. That in almost everyone there is some immaturity, no matter what the chronological age may be. At certain periods in their cycles the glands of both men and women stimulate special needs, either for passionate expression or for understanding and comfort.

A few days before the beginning of her menstrual period, for example, the average woman is likely to have one of two moods: the first of great feminine activity—tidying drawers, cleaning closets, or, if she's a business woman, reorganizing her files, cleaning her desk, picking up stray ends of unfinished business. This mood is often fairly intolerable to the slower-geared male, who is especially resentful if the accompanying burst of activity extends to his own domain and results in the rearranging of his tool chest, his desk or his favorite chair. The second possible mood-change is one of deep or moderate and unaccountable depression, which lifts when the period begins. The more high-strung the woman, the more likely this is to be her reaction to the physiological change, just as in the menopausal period the neurotic woman may have physical and psychological upsets the happier woman rarely experiences.

Being married does not give women the right to be brusque or impolite in dealing with their husbands. But the man who does not take the calendar into consideration when he has serious problems or criticisms to thrash out with his wife, is plain foolhardy. If such problems can't wait a day or two, let them be presented very cautiously and quietly, with criticisms preceded by a nicely turned compliment, if possible, and followed by another. Let me give you an example:

Mrs. Birch has had discipline troubles all day with her four-year-old— he's reached that well-known negative stage and she's in no humor to cope with it diplomatically. She knows that force will only defeat her aims, one way or the other—and she's on the verge of the "weeps." Besides, she has a backache and a blemish on the tip of her nose, is pale, has circles under her eyes, her hair is limp, and her feet are swollen. She has a vague headache and a feeling of inability to contend even with the family puppy, let alone Junior. Home comes father, fire in his eye. She's overdrawn their joint checking account, and the bank had called him to make a deposit before three o'clock. (A pox on joint checking accounts, by the way.) Let me spare you the rest—tears, mutual accusations, slammed bedroom doors, father in the guest room for the night. One look at the calendar and Mr. B. would have buttoned up his wrath or worked it off somewhere else (chopping wood, punching the bag, boxing at the gym, weeding are all fine outlets for justified —and unjustified—rage). By next Tuesday he can mention the matter quite safely. Mrs. B. will be prettily contrite and manage to make her husband feel like a big, strong infallible male who never overdraws his account.

The truth is, women are people and should be treated as such, with time out for physiological interferences such as the well-known instability of pregnancy—another period in the female cycle intended by nature to bring out the supposed innate protectiveness of the male. However, many a woman sails cheerfully through those nine months protecting a quaking husband against his own pre-paternal anxieties.

The Agreeable Husband

A man who's easy to live with gets up in the morning in time to get to work without putting the house in an uproar. He does his best to be agreeable on arising, to help the whole family get off to a good start. Or, if he's one of those people who's grouchy before coffee, he explains his temperament to his family, so they'll know there's nothing personal about it. He either accepts what is put before him for breakfast or, if he has special preferences, states them in ample time beforehand. It is difficult for the cook—mother or a paid hand—to change the breakfast order from boiled eggs to hash while father drums on the table and watches the clock.

When things do go wrong at mealtimes he doesn't make a scene. The best cooks have their off moments. At the breakfast table, even when the family is alone, he makes some attempt at pleasant conversation with his wife—who may have a lonely day ahead of her—and with his children of whom he sees little enough as it is. He should make it a rule to avoid unpleasant and acrimonious discussions at the table any time for the sake of the family's collective digestions.

A man should come to meals shortly after he is summoned. It is difficult enough to time a meal for a specified hour, and it is even harder to have to hold it and still serve palatable food. The agreeable husband conducts himself at the table exactly as if guests were present. He is clean, combed, and generally presentable. If he wants to sit down coatless or tieless, unless others are dressed the same way he should ask his wife's permission just as he did in the days when he was trying to impress her. He should limit his smoking—if indeed he still smokes—to the end of the meal, using an ash tray instead of dishes as ash receptacles. (I shall keep driving this point home.)

In all things he should consider himself a partner in the home, not its dictator, he and his wife sharing responsibility in the management of the family resources. He should give his wife some portion of their income for her own use without any strings attached, just as he keeps some funds to use at his own discretion without having to account for them.

Even in physical things—manners, appearance, behavior—he must remember that it is no longer he alone who is answerable for them. Society holds a wife accountable to a large extent for the presence or lack of agreeable attributes in a husband. If his manners are boorish, she is expected to correct them, one way or the other, to help him get ahead. If his clothes are ill-kempt and shabby, the fact is usually attributed to his wife's negligence or lack of thrift. If he's blatantly attentive to other women, society asks where his wife has failed—and it may be right.

A man, for example, host in his own home, rises and comes forward to shake the hand of any guest—man, woman and very often child—who enters. In the latter case, the child who is to be a guest in the household, even a very young child, is punctiliously greeted by his host just as if he were a grown-up.

A man should rise when a woman guest enters the room, perhaps I should say, especially if she is his mother-in-law. If his wife comes home after he does, he rises to greet her just as she properly and lovingly rises to greet him upon his return to the household. They rise to see each other off. A man, of course, does not hop up every time his wife enters the room, but he does so when she makes her first entrance when there are guests and he has preceded her. If she must leave a group, he rises with the other men in the party to bid her farewell, and if possible escorts her to the door and if necessary puts her into a conveyance. A man rises for all introductions to women or to men in his own house or outside.

It seems to me that one of the greatest difficulties a man meets in adjusting to married life is the proper evaluation of his wife's contribution. Most men, while enjoying their work, hate the actual daily necessity of doing it and tend to think of their wives as having comparative leisure because they stay at home. Because of this fundamental misunderstanding, a husband is likely to minimize his wife's problems and not to see the need of adjusting to conditions in his own home as he would adjust in the office.

It is quite true that a woman's work is never done, while the average man, once he leaves his office, shuts his door on his work until the next morning. At five o'clock his wife, instead of having a long and peaceful evening ahead of her, must bathe the children, prepare dinner, make herself attractive for her husband's home-coming, serve dinner, get the children to bed, wash the dishes, and entertain her husband, and possibly guests, for the balance of the evening. Even after she gets to bed she may still have to rise up in the night to attend to the baby or comfort a child with a nightmare. And she never, or rarely, knows what it is to sleep late or get a full day off without at least checking in to see what's going on at home—not if she has a growing family. If she is a career woman she has all these responsibilities, in some degree or other, added to those of her office. And, considering the number of women gainfully employed in this country, this means millions of women on double shifts—breadearners and homemakers. It is not always an enviable outlook for a woman in these days of high-cost and sometimes impossible-to-obtain household help, small quarters, and high tension. A husband needs to lend a hand not only morally but physically.

How a Husband Can Lend a Hand   The old-fashioned paterfamilias, whose dignity would have suffered if he lifted a hand toward the household tasks, is as extinct as the Stanley Steamer. Most modern fathers can change a diaper, feed and burp the baby, take a pulse, figure a temperature, bind a wound, make beds, oversee children's baths, and scramble together an emergency meal. Anything a husband does do, should be done in a spirit of camaraderie rather than of martyrdom. His wife should, I think, try her best to spare him the too feminine chores—washing the dishes, setting the table, or sweeping the floors. But he can and should help, if the household is literally on his wife's back, by picking up after himself and others (a neat bedroom induces rest), helping to clear the table occasionally, taking out the garbage (if there are no small boys around), doing small essential repairs and, if he can, intelligently helping with the shopping—a back-breaking and time-consuming job for a woman if she must use the cash-and-carry system to balance the budget. Any man can be a boon to a household in a nice, unobtrusive, and wholly masculine fashion. But a man who can't or won't see a woman's problems can be hard to live with despite his flashing eyes and all-American figure.

Business Entertaining

"I'm bringing a client (or the boss) home to dinner." How often such news —usually delivered at the last minute—strikes terror into the young wife.

She has not reached that phase of housewifely proficiency where the announcement that the President himself was about to descend for a meal would not fluster her overmuch.

No well-brought-up husband should ever bring *anyone* except perhaps a most intimate friend home to dinner without sufficient warning to his wife. It may be cook's night out—if there is a cook—or "economy night" when the family is to eat the remainder of the roast in a hash. The silver may be due for a cleaning tomorrow but will make the hostess self-conscious before guests tonight. It isn't that the average wife is unable to rise above such unimportant things herself, but she knows full well the critical eye of an outsider can light on these domestic deficiencies and imagine the household has no better standards. And apologizing only makes everything much worse. Every hostess naturally wants her home to look its best when guests come.

These last-minute business invitations are often psychologically correct from a man's point of view. He has made some progress with a difficult associate and feels now is the moment to apply a little personal pressure from the social angle. But he should never ask such an associate home to dinner—and certainly not for the weekend—without forewarning his wife and having her enthusiastic consent to the invitation.

Suffice it to be said that running even a simple household is much more complicated than most husbands ever understand. Often everything goes wrong at once—a crisis with the plumbing, an accident to the baby, trouble with the help, if any, failures in delivery of supplies—a thousand irritating household matters. Of course, all this can also happen when you are preparing for expected company. But when it happens and unexpected guests arrive, it is that much worse.

Business dinners are often best handled outside of a man's home unless he and his wife are really willing and happy to accept the business associate and, necessarily, his wife on social terms. This is very important. Home should really be home—not just a continuation of the office. A man should do all he can to avoid taking into his home business associates whom he and his wife cannot possibly enjoy socially. Instead, he can entertain such people semisocially outside of his home—often to their greater comfort. Perhaps they, too, prefer to keep social and business lives separate. A businessman may invite a client and his wife to a good restaurant for dinner and, unless her presence seems vital, make a tactful excuse for his own wife if she doesn't really enjoy such evenings. Of course he may freely invite the man to lunch alone or with other business associates.

Some husbands—or career wives—will argue that it is of inestimable business value to entertain important clients, prospects, or associates at home. But is it? Good taste prohibits the pursuit of business deals while the quarry is breaking bread under one's own roof. On the other hand, over dinner at a restaurant two men can come together on business matters easily enough, even when one is playing the host for reasons apparent to all concerned.

If business friends from time to time are to be brought into one's home circle, not because of what they can do, but because of what they are as people, that is a different matter. They should not be invited, however, when there are important business matters pending, as it will be too difficult for the host and probably the hostess not to show some strain.

The Agreeable Wife

Until you have been married you can't know what a marriage partner can do, or fail to do, that makes him or her less than attractive to have around constantly. It's a good idea before marriage for two people in love to discuss, good humoredly, all the possible things they would dislike in this close living-together. A man might remember some of his mother's habits that annoyed him or his father and so give any intelligent, co-operative wife a good idea of what he'd prefer her not to do. He might make it clear that he'd hate to see her come to the breakfast table with her hair in curlers—in fact, that he is quite repelled by curlers at any time, even after lights-out at night. And that he couldn't abide the sight of her face oiled with cream.

I wonder how many wives could resist rising up in unholy protest if husbands suddenly took to wrapping their heads up in wire and head rags, greasing their faces, tying up their chins, putting on oiled mittens for the night. If a woman has her own room I suppose she can safely dedicate herself to the pursuit of beauty in her sleep, once she is alone. But if she shares her sleeping quarters she is obliged to make herself an attractive roommate, not a banshee. Experts say that the skin absorbs in about twenty minutes all the cream it's going to absorb, so if you feel your skin needs some lubrication, why not use your bath time or a rest period, when you can be sure of privacy?

Bedtime should be a time for nice, feminine nightgowns, clean faces (traces of lipstick in the morning look very careless to a fastidious male and, besides, think of the sheets), well-brushed hair braided or tied back with a ribbon, perhaps—especially if you have a double bed and want to keep your curls out of your husband's face—and a touch of flower cologne. Isn't this from a man's standpoint more inviting in a wife than utilitarian pajamas, a face covered with grease, hair rigid with curlers?

Meeting Commuter Trains All over America, morning and evening, is enacted the rite of delivering father to the train and picking him up at night. The appearance of the country-staying wife and the city-going husband at these times is often sadly incongruous. Too often the wife is under the impression that no one notices her as she delivers her well-pressed (we hope) husband to the 8:11. She may throw an old coat over her house dress and tie a bandanna over her curlers or her ill-dressed hair.

The baby beside her, if she has no maid to leave him with, may have traces of his morning egg on the face he offers Daddy for the good-by kiss. Mother's shoes as she takes over the wheel may be anything she thought good enough for the approaching morning's housework.

Maybe only occasionally does a well-intentioned homemaker find herself downtown looking this way. But doesn't it invariably happen that if you are not looking as you'd be proud to look you will run into someone you'd rather not see under the circumstances—the man who holds the mortgage or that older woman who made the catty remarks about Johnny? Making yourself presentable on arising, whether or not you are going to make the trek to the station, is always a good investment in self-respect.

A man's last glimpse of his wife in the morning and his first view of her at night should be pleasant experiences. At the station he likes her to compare favorably with the other wives bound on the same errand, and he likes his children to be attractive too.

A man who has been surrounded all day by a trim, well-ordered office staff is never pleased to be met by a sloppy, preoccupied wife and his unwashed, uncombed brood, where any neighbor may see how things are at home. Father's home-coming should always be a respected occasion for which the whole family prepares as best it can, for father is certain to appraise it though he may be unconscious of doing so.

Who Should Manage the Family Income

The responsibility for management of income must be decided on the basis of who has the greater ability—husband or wife—to handle major expenditures. Sometimes—quite often—the wife is better equipped through training and inherent qualities to handle accounts than her husband is. Only in the most hopeless cases, it seems to me, should either wife or husband be denied the right to control some of the family's funds, at least. And even when one partner has an obviously good head for figures, plus the time to handle at least the major bills, it is often wise for the responsibility to be at least divided. On the other hand, a wife who constantly overdraws, lets bills slide, has to borrow constantly to make ends meet, and in general finds it impossible to keep the family's finances in some sort of order certainly needs help in the management of them. A husband, talented as he may be in his own field, may also have difficulty in the handling of money and, if so, should be helped toward the organizing of his obligations. He should be relieved of the detail of expenditure of the family funds as much as possible if his wife is more capable of taking over. But it should be well understood that difficulty in arithmetic is no sign of low intelligence. A general vagueness on the part of, say, a creative artist concerning the mundane matters of existence makes him in no way inferior to his mate who may be able to read a balance sheet at a glance. Their fields of comprehension are different, that is all, although their I.Q.s may be neck and neck.

Living within Your Means   It is never a disgrace to say, "I can't afford it." And when you do have to make such a statement when you have been urged to spend beyond your means, it is certainly not necessary to explain why. Perhaps, in spite of a really generous income, you have obligations about which others don't or can't know—the support of an aged, distant relative, private charities, extensive savings programs or investments. It is never shameful to have to say, "I can't afford it." It *is* shameful to commit yourself to expenditure you know you can't really afford and shouldn't make—just because someone else urges you to go against your own better judgment.

I have real respect for the person who can say without any self-consciousness at all, simply and cheerfully, "I can't afford it." But I hate to hear a long-drawn-out explanation of why. As a matter of fact, we should never demand to know why a person can't spend money on something he says he can't afford unless there is a sound reason for his finding some way to afford it. Then you may, if you feel you should, try to show him that way, quietly and without irritating him.

Joint Checking Accounts   Except for those rare couples who never have any trouble over their family finances and for whom everything rolls along in an ideally smooth fashion, with each careful and accurate about money, a joint checking account is a constant source of possible friction. Invariably one or the other fails to make an entry or list a check drawn, and there is a snarl or worse.

It always seems much better to me for the wife to have the handling of the house money and her own clothes and spending allowance through the use of her own checking account. She can handle such purchases with cash, but this involves more bookkeeping. To have husband and wife each drawing household expenses and their own expenses from the same account often makes for confusion.

Every man and woman needs a certain amount of money regularly to spend as he or she needs without having to give wife or husband, brother or sister an explanation of its disbursement. Once a husband gives his wife her house allowance, out of which she may or may not be expected to get her own clothing and other expenses, depending on what proportion of the family income can be spared, and after he has met obligations such as insurance and dues, he should not be held accountable concerning his own spending of what remains.

Special Adjustments

Annoying Habits   I can think of any number of annoying habits, not exclusively the property of wives, which are mightily unattractive day after day. Do you put the cap back on the tooth paste? Are you careful to screw the covers on various bathroom-cabinet jars when you have finished using them? Do you close boxes, stopper bottles, shut doors? Perhaps doing so is a sign of an orderly mind, but these are certainly things you can train yourself to do if you think of them as being considerate to your mate or your family. A razor, used by man or woman (and *no* woman should borrow her husband's razor!), should be loosened in its holder, rinsed to remove the hairs, and replaced on its shelf. Any discarded razor blades should be carefully disposed of. If there is no slot for them in the bathroom, put them in their envelopes, if you still have them, or wrap them in paper so that anyone emptying the waste-paper basket won't be cut. A used razor blade left to rust on window sill or basin is a proclamation of a careless and thoughtless member of the family.

No one should smoke in bed, ever, because of fire hazard, but where one mate is a smoker, the other a non-smoker, watch particularly the habit of smoking before going to bed or immediately on rising. Dead cigarettes and their ashes in a bedroom can be nauseating, and, if you ask me, any wife who smokes when her husband doesn't takes a long chance with his affections if she permits herself to be a chain smoker or a first-thing-in-the-morning and last-thing-at-night one.

You wouldn't think otherwise fastidious women would fall into the habit of biting their nails or pulling their fingers out of joint, but they do—and so do grown men. These are usually habits carried over from childhood and the nail-biting can be a sign of emotional disturbance in an adult. Nagging—as with anything else—is no help, but reassurance, affection, gentle reminders may be. A happy, relaxed marriage relationship can sometimes perform miracles in overcoming tense reactions to life. A well-balanced diet high in the *B* vitamins and vitamin *A* can assist, too, with the attainment of greater nervous stability. But where chorea (St. Vitus's dance), nervous tics, nail-biting, and other anxious habits are really distressing to the person having them as well as to his or her partner, something can be done about overcoming them through emotional re-education with psychiatric help. If such help is not possible, allowance must be made for them as such motor habits usually cannot be controlled by will power alone.

Suppose you are married to someone who drums his fingers on the table, snaps them while waiting for something or aimlessly draws on the tablecloth with his knife. These are just habits—not necessarily nervous ones. You might tackle the problem by suggesting tactfully that the particular habit is somewhat annoying to you and at the same time asking him to bring to your attention any habits that may be annoying to him. Perhaps you forget to comb your hair before breakfast or you never let your husband finish a funny story, constantly interrupt his reading with conversation, or ask your relatives too often to meals.

All these things can be adjusted between two people desirous of living happily and fully together if discussion of them is friendly. It is better to run the risk of a little immediate acrimony by bringing the matter up when it first annoys than to let the irritation fester over months or years of married life. Out of such little, infuriating things can spring the seeds of actual or spiritual dissolution. There must always be a comfortable balance in marriage, with each partner giving and being given due friendly consideration.

There are times when even the most loved person is viewed objectively by his or her partner, and it is well if on these occasional days of—often silent—reckoning we pass muster in the most important things. But it is amazing how often the little things that are wrong in a marriage can make it less full and beautiful than it should be. We tend to think, "If she really loved me she'd remember I hate to see her nose shiny, she'd take a little more trouble about herself when she knows I'm on the way home." Or, "If he wouldn't make me ask for the house money, wouldn't keep me waiting dinner night after night without phoning to say he'll be late."

The little things that are too often overlooked are sometimes a sign that the whole marriage can do with a check-up. A husband or wife who begins to be careless about grooming or weight, for example, may feel unloved or at least less loved by his mate, rather than less loving himself. The overweight may be just a symptom.

Overweight and Underweight　Many eating habits are social devices to make us more at ease with one another—cocktails before dinner, the eating of the dinner roll as we wait for the first course, the nibbling on mints after demitasse. The thoughtful meal planner provides substitutes for these things for anyone in the family on a reducing or other diet. Self-denial seems less heroic to the dieter if there is a fruit or vegetable juice cocktail for him on the cocktail tray and crisp celery, carrot or cucumber sticks at his place in lieu of bread. It isn't too much trouble to provide him with non-starchy breadsticks or rye wafers. Dry skimmed milk, hot skimmed milk or evaporated milk will taste better in his coffee than cold skimmed milk, a little container of saccharine on the demitasse tray will cater harmlessly to his sweet tooth, if his doctor approves.

There is considerable modern medical literature devoted to the thesis that both underweight and overweight can have emotional causes. Sometimes the underlying factors are very complicated and not easily brought to light, but almost anyone with a weight problem—in either direction—will recognize that anxiety either causes his appetite to decrease and his weight to go down or that in anxious periods he becomes a compensatory eater. He may eat without waiting for his hunger mechanism to prod him, just for the sake of the vicarious satisfaction the mere act of eating gives him.

Many compensatory eaters take to sweets at such times, thus piling calorie on unwanted calorie and so making themselves as unattractive as they secretly feel. It seems obvious that anyone with a proper self-regard does not overeat or undereat to a degree that makes him or her un-attractive. The desire to achieve and hold the proper weight must come from a real, consistent effort to do so if there is a tendency toward wide fluctuations. The happy, healthy, well-adjusted person is usually neither too fat nor too thin. He eats when he's hungry and abstains when he isn't. Food to him is pleasant and necessary, not something to give him satisfactions he misses in life, or something which he denies himself for some neurotic, usually unconscious, reason.

It is useless to try to stuff a member of the family who is sadly under-weight or to limit the intake of another unless we have their real co-operation and can help them find satisfaction and security in their lives. Threats or nagging are senseless and cruel, but the meal planner can be a friendly ally once the individual announces that he wishes to lose or gain and seems ready to make a real effort to do so. He needs co-operation, and he needs bolstering of his ego. Tell him continually how noticeable the difference is from week to week, how much more attractive he is, how much better his clothes look on him, etc. When someone is on a reducing diet at the family board, help him to avoid making exceptions, too many of which will prolong the routine discouragingly. Don't be a tempter. If possible, try to set up a little friendly rivalry, pitting two dieters against each other.

Speaking of Diets Making a to-do about anyone's diet is a bore to everyone except the dieter, who may either delight in the extra attention or squirm under it. But the diet that works best, it seems to me, is the one that is taken as a matter of course by everyone without special comment or commiseration. Most diets are not life-time sentences. They are planned to accomplish a certain result in a specific time. Mary will not forever be denied her strawberry shortcake, so what does it matter if tonight she takes her strawberries plain? John, if he cuts some of the fat off his meat for another month or two, omits bread at dinner and lunch and substitutes fruit for the pies and cakes he loves, will soon be able to take in the desired notch in his belt. Genevieve, if she adds a little of the thick cream to her coffee each time, though she'd prefer it black, and takes that extra slice of bread and butter, may soon have the little padding here and there that will make her a prettier girl.

Both reducing and gaining diets are somewhat of a trial at first, but it is encouraging to know that, if we wish to gain, it is not necessary at all to increase the actual quantity of food we take. It is possible to gain by revis-ing our diets to include the same quantity of food but food of greater caloric value, perhaps taken in more frequent meals. Reducers need to know that they may eat relatively huge amounts of low-calorie foods, to a degree that they need never be hungry, by substituting them for the high-calorie preferences that have been their downfall. But remember, diet-talk for those not dieting is dull business. Let the results do the talking, and the increased personal satisfaction and well-being will be the chief reward.

The In-law Problem

Your Mother-in-law With longevity increasing, the possibility of a newly-married couple having mothers-in-law is greater than it was twenty or thirty years ago. A mother-in-law in her late forties or fifties without enough to occupy her fully, now that her children have left home, can be a source of friction, especially if she is also a widow. Good and secure family relations are among the best gifts a man and woman can bring to marriage. But no family at all is better than an interfering one.

When we marry we literally must "forsake all others" and consider the marriage bond the paramount one. The whole process of growing up is that of growing away from one's parents in the physical sense and to a great degree in the emotional one, too. Young people need the freedom to make their own mistakes in their own way. They really never do believe their elders who want them to accept experience in life vicariously.

Where in-laws are to be considered, especially a mother-in-law who finds it difficult to relinquish hold on her child, the very first steps in the relationship are most important. A young son-in-law, for example, should not be made to feel like a culprit because he can't call this relatively strange and sometimes seemingly hostile older woman "mother." And, perhaps, despite the usualness of the term for her, the mother-in-law doesn't like it either. Both she and her son-in-law may be more comfortable with the modern "Mrs. Brown" or just "Jane" as if she were a contemporary. Then when the children begin to arrive, a pet name usually solves everything, and "Mrs. Brown" or "Jane" becomes comfortable "Nanny" or "Granny"—or any other variation of a child's loving title for his grandmother—to everyone in the household. And somehow with little hands in hers she feels less shut out, more needed in the new living arrangement, and she usually is.

Living in the Same House When it is necessary or advisable for a mother-in-law to live in the same house with a couple it should be remembered that she herself probably feels a certain diffidence if not an actual unhappiness at the upheaval in her own life. She is perhaps less adaptable than she was as a younger woman, used to her own way of doing things and probably to more privacy than seems possible in the new household.

Whenever feasible, she should have her own room, however small, furnished with at least some of her own things. It should be a bed-sitting room so that when she pleases she can get away from the family and have an inviolate place of her own, reminiscent of the home she has left. If certain contributions to the household are expected from her—a hand with the children or the meals—it should never be assumed that she has no plans of her own. Too many little chores constantly dropped on her shoulders without a by-your-leave make her feel imposed upon, and quite understandably. The smaller her own means, the more helpless and frustrated she feels under such thoughtless imposition. Older people (especially mothers-in-law) must always be treated like human beings. Happy ones who feel needed and useful can add immeasurably to a full, complete family life in the secure old-time sense.

Real Troublemakers Sometimes mothers or fathers living with a young couple become impossibly difficult. They either can't or won't adjust to the new arrangement, and they become tyrannical. If the young people have moved into the older person's home, then they may have no recourse but to move out again as amicably as possible, or, if possible, somehow divide the house into completely separate living quarters so there can be a minimum of contact between them and the difficult parent.

When a Parent Requires Financial Support Many young married people have to support one or more parents or at least contribute to their support. During the first few years of marriage especially, a couple needs to live by themselves. It is better for parents to live separately, no matter how simply, to ensure their own independence and that of their children. Whether the dependent parents live with their children or not, their bills should not be paid for them if they are at all capable of managing their own affairs. Unless they are senile, they should be treated like responsible people, and permitted to handle their own expenditures for rent, clothes, food, and spending money. Unless they ask to be relieved of the responsibility, they should have their own checking or savings accounts to which their children contribute at stated intervals. They should know how much money they can count on and when. Even if the income is small and they must keep strictly within it, most old people feel more self-respect managing it themselves.

The very aged seldom are willing to consider that their remaining days are limited. They often have the fantasy that they will outlive those who care for them and then, without means, will be dependent on "charity."

Money in their own name helps them to feel that they have a little more time. And they need to make their own decisions on how to spend it.

Chapter 50

CHILDREN AND THE FORMATION
OF CHARACTER

Baby Showers

Baby showers are not always given when a baby is expected. When they
are given, they are given by friends rather than relatives. In some communities baby showers are often given for subsequent children as well as
first ones and are greatly appreciated. Even when there is no actual necessity
for showers, they are often given just because friends want to express their
pleasurable anticipation of the coming event. Clothes for baby showers are
usually in the layette category and gifts of money for the baby's account
are always welcome. They are presented to the mother in cash, checks, or
bonds enclosed in gift cards. A baby's bond is made out to the child and
his mother—John Joseph Smith *or* Mrs. Joseph Dayton Smith.

Invitations to baby showers are issued by phone, note, or fill-in card.
They are usually given about a month before the baby is expected. More
than one shower for a baby should be discouraged but friends may co-
operate in the giving of the shower.

Thank-you notes should be sent to the guests by the honoree.

Choosing the Baby's Name

Some babies' names are chosen in sheer desperation, it would seem, and
too often they form an unlovely combination with the surname. A baby
who is saddled with a cumbersome family name as a first name, with the
thought that he will be, conveniently, called "Buster" as a little boy, may
never be able to shake his nickname. A sixty-five-year-old "Buster" is a
somewhat ludicrous fellow, no matter how he tries to stand on his dignity.

Be careful that the first name you choose doesn't form some kind of pun
when coupled with the last one. Parents, if they notice it, may think such
a combination of names amusing, but the child probably will find it far
from amusing, once he gets to school. A jaw-breaking first name—perhaps
Montmorency—finds itself teamed with a family name of Drinkwater or
Hasenpfeffer. Or a first name is chosen with little consideration of how it

will sound when spoken aloud with the last name. A child named Brooks Scott will be referred to as Brook Scott because his name, spoken, doesn't indicate the two "s's." Be careful not to elide a child's name this way by having the last letter of the first name the same as the first letter of the last.

A name should strive for dignity and simplicity. If your surname is Gallic, German, or Italian try to find a Christian name that suits it, although most of the short English names such as John, Mary, Robert, Charles, Edward, Andrew, Henry, Ann and Peter go well with almost any surname. But don't overlook the pleasant possibility of giving such a child some variation of these or other good names that are in keeping with the surname. Carlo, Henri, Mara, Marie, Hans, Hannes, Jon, Roberta, André, Andrea, Jeanne, Pieter, Peta, are all possibilities. Many real Scotch or Irish names are strong and fine—Moira, Kitt, Sean, Timothy, Michael, Kim, Sheila, Terrence— but they belong with Anglo-Saxon surnames. Sometimes coined names are very effective. I had a friend who shortened her name, Charlotte Louise, as a child to Charlise and liked that so well she named her daughter Charlise.

Every school roll has dozens of Sarahs, Janes, Marys, Catherines, Susans, Anns, Joans, Elizabeths, and Lindas. Before deciding on a name, talk to as many friends as possible and see if you are about to give your child one that may, at the moment, be greatly overworked. Be extra careful about this if you have a common last name.

How Do You Find a Name? The best place to find a suitable name for the baby is in your own family tree. It is my own feeling that wherever possible it is better not to name a boy "Jr.," because doing so sometimes has the effect of denying him his own full identity during his father's lifetime. He gets "little Tom" or "Junior" or "young Tom" instead of a good name all his own. He can be named for his father without becoming "Jr." if he is named, say, Thomas Briggs Macy instead of Thomas Gordon Macy, and he will then have a middle name that can be used as his first name to avoid confusion.

A little girl should never be called "Junior" even if she is named for her mother. She may come to resent "little Helen," too, and wonder why she couldn't have had her very own name. She may be "Helen II," but that does seem cumbersome. If it is ardently desired that she be named for her mother, it might be better to call her Helen Louise, so that she may use "Louise" to distinguish herself from her mother.

If a careful study of the names used in your family turns up nothing you think sufficiently attractive for the new baby, you can find lists of names in unabridged dictionaries and there are books devoted to possible names, giving their derivations and meanings. We needn't take the meanings too literally. A boy named "Christopher" is, today, not necessarily the child of Christian parents—the name means "one who carries Christ."

Does Your Child Need a Middle Name? Today the simpler a name, the better. With few exceptions, middle names, if used, get lost in a muddle of initials that people can't remember. Is the name Clarence R. Jackson or Clarence E. Jackson? When a man signs his middle name and if it is meaningful—as in Ethan Allen Jackson or, to use a real instance, George Washington Carver—people will remember it and use it. But more often than not a middle name merely elongates and confuses a signature and often weakens the name. Which is stronger—Virginia Jocelyn Framingham or just Virginia Framingham? Be careful a name you have carefully selected doesn't sound like a mouthful of hot potatoes when it is burdened with a middle one in addition to the surname.

Boys' Names for Girls and Vice Versa Sometimes, especially in the South, a girl is given a boy's name when a boy had been expected and a name for him had been firmly decided upon. There are numerous examples of girls named "Charles" or "Peter" or "John" because of the rigidity of their parents, and one shudders to think of the possible psychological effect upon the children who, in name at least, are not allowed to be little girls. The same danger exists for girls whose names are derived from boys' names if their families shorten Andrea to Andy, Maxine to Max, Charlotte to Charlie, Josephine to Jo, Philippa to Phil, Frances to Frank.

There is a similar danger in naming boys with names used more frequently for girls—Marion, Evelyn, Cecil, Jean, Florence, Carol, and Beverly who may have to go through life prefixing an explanatory "Mr." to their signatures.

Children's Clothes

Dressing the Baby Modern babies are dressed for active comfort, not for style. This is good social and pediatric practice. It's usually only the first baby, partly because of the mother's inexperience, who's in danger of being overdressed in weighty and too warm clothes and in overly fancy ones. It's the first baby who gets the lion's share of clothes from friends and relatives, who spend too much on frills and never give a thought to utility and ease of laundering—or to the baby's comfort. Gone are the days of long baby dresses with a matching, lacy slip—except for christenings and even then a short white dress will do nicely. Babies hate hats, so the rosetted ones, the ones with long satin chin ribbons, the layer-on-layer of georgette or organdy lovingly shirred into a bonnet are all a waste of time and money. In the winter, of course, the baby must wear a hat, and it needs to be something he can't pull off and which won't annoy him any more than necessary with bows under the chin. Often his snow suit has a functional hood that keeps his neck and head warm without restricting his movements or giving him something to chew on.

If you could ask a baby, he would tell you he wants clothes that allow a maximum of freedom. A very young baby is constantly having his clothes changed, and they need to be tough and absolutely washable. Little flannel bathrobes with satin binding and fancy trimmings are just silly if they can't go into the tub and after one or two wearings must go to the dry cleaner. Even in a household where money is no particular consideration this is certainly an unnecessary and foolish expense. The various cotton fabrics—corduroy, seersucker, piqué, cotton flannel, cotton jersey, Byrd cloth, and denim are sensible and comfortable.

The tiny infant is best dressed in a terrycloth stretch suit or a cotton knit nightie, and most babies I've seen don't care for the ones that make a restricting bag at the feet (if so the drawstring may be pulled out). Over the nightie goes a cotton sack—seersucker is fine, or cotton jersey or cotton flannel. Fine embroidered wool sacks or silk ones are an affectation, and in one or two washings they will be a shambles anyhow, especially if they've run afoul of some cod-liver oil, a certain eventuality. Under the nightie, with the inevitable diapers, is worn a plain cotton shirt, preferably without buttons or strings. The baby who is tiny through the winter or who lives in a drafty house should have long-sleeved shirts. Otherwise the short-sleeved or sleeveless ones are adequate and should be bought in year-old-size, like everything else for the infant, because the rate of growth of a healthy baby is amazing and the tiny little garments offered for newborn babies in all the shops are rendered useless in a few weeks. All these items are relatively expensive, and friends and relatives should be encouraged to give them along with other clothing into which the baby will grow.

Few babies are put into shoes these days until they are actually walking. Stitched shoes in pink or blue silk will be wasted on the modern baby, no matter how much they appeal to Aunt May. Bootees, large enough to allow for inevitable shrinkage are fine for the infant who is tiny during winter and spring. Innumerable infant sweaters—all size one or larger—are welcomed by any mother and baby.

Satin, quilted coats or comforters are useless to today's baby. Cover him with lightweight, easily washable wool or miracle-fabric blankets. Receiving blankets are very useful, but only if they are relatively utilitarian—several should be in cotton flannel and the others should not be too elaborate because there is always the washing problem. Hand-knit afghans must be washed very carefully by hand and rolled in a towel to dry—a long process and something to consider when you think of the dozens of quick changes a baby needs daily.

One rarely sees today those delicately embroidered "dribble bibs" that were an accouterment of our own clothes-tortured infancy. Current cotton-clad babies aren't constantly be-bibbed, although a good, absorbent bib is vital at feeding time. For these, turkish toweling is best, as it prevents spilled food from soaking through to the underclothing and may be washed without ironing (so very important even if a mother has help, even if she has a baby nurse). Plastic bibs shed liquids onto mother but are useful later when more solid food is taken.

When the baby is big enough—from six months on—he or she goes into creepers or dresses, with overalls for ordinary rough wear (which means most of the time) standard for both sexes. Don't buy something that fits too exactly, for in a matter of two or three weeks it will have to be discarded. In buying baby clothes, take into consideration the weight and length of the particular baby, not just his age. Children's clothes are unfortunately not standardized, so one "size two" may be much smaller than another. An expensive "size one" pair of corduroy overalls may fit the baby from six to nine months and then have to be passed on to a younger child.

Even where there is help, a baby's clothes are often left unironed, except for dress-up ones like starched pinafores and dresses. It is better to keep a baby as clean as possible and sweet-smelling in fresh but unironed clothes than to have mother or a nurse busy most of the time ironing his clothes when there are so many more things that would be better for all, such as an extra hour in the open air.

Keeping the baby as clean as possible makes him feel comfortable when he's very little. But later on as he begins to crawl and toddle it is expected that he will gather considerable good clean dirt, and constant fussing at him over "dirtiness" tends to inhibit his adventurous spirit in an unwholesome manner. Any soiling that doesn't make him uncomfortable is certainly perferable, psychologically, to overstressing of cleanliness. At this time, the bath, often the second for the day, takes place before suppertime, for a baby can't be comfortable going to bed dirty. The warm bath, in which he should be given plenty of time to play, will help him settle down for the night.

Clothes for the Pre-school and the Older Child   In what *style* (the cost of the clothes is unimportant) are the other children of your neighborhood dressed for school and for party occasions? That's the way you must dress your child if you aren't to interfere with his healthy emotional growth. If you make a little Lord Fauntleroy of your son, refusing to crop his charming little curls, or if your daughter wears velvet and taffeta to Sunday school when the other children wear clean, pretty washdresses even in the winter, then you are handicapping them. Children have a psychological necessity to be exactly like the others in their group. If they are made to be different by strong-minded, often highly individual parents, they miss something very important in their development.

This does not mean that you can't mention an eventual goal of tidiness and quality of dress to your growing son when he is at the stage where he won't wear anything but blue jeans, polo shirts, and dirty sneakers or sloppy moccasins. All the other children are at times poured into "Sunday clothes," wearing ties, shined shoes, socks and being expected to have clean nails and combed hair, so he won't feel too discriminated against if you insist on his conforming to community custom on these occasions, too.

From six on—sometimes earlier—he should have something to say about the clothes he wears. If he detests certain colors and textures or styles, try to avoid them. If he wants his hair long and you prefer it reasonably short, try to effect a compromise.

Little girls are likely to be more clothes conscious than boys, and at an earlier age, but not necessarily so. Boys, if they get a chance to express them, have strong opinions on what is "the thing" to wear, and, within reason, parents should shut their eyes to the ridiculousness of current boy and girl clothing fads. Each generation has had its own fads, and to prohibit a child from following what is probably a quite harmless fashion, even if it offends your own and your friends' sensibilities, is to make the child "not belong" with his crowd, a hurtful thing.

Hand-me-downs and Made-overs Even the last child in a large family has the right to at least a few clothes bought especially for him, if it is at all possible. The system of handing down clothes from one child to the next is necessary for most of us, and most children accept this economy in good grace. But a child who from infancy is clad only in castoffs can't develop the necessary pride of possession and of loving consideration he gets from having at least some things that were bought or made for him alone.

Children's clothes that are made over from those of adults should always be of fabrics and colors suitable for a child, and unless the remodeling can be done with an expert hand it had better not be done at all. Children always seem to know when they are being made to wear something that will cause them to be ridiculed by their peers, and they, very rightly, fight against it. A child is often secretly embarrassed at having to wear a coat made out of an old skirt of mother's or a dress concocted from some all-too-familiar garment of sister's. Swapping clothes with other mothers—and preferably with mothers whose children move in different neighborhoods —seems a good solution, for to most small children any article of clothing they haven't seen before is "new" to them.

As children rarely wear new clothes out before they outgrow them, a barter arrangement set up through the Parent-Teacher Association or just among the mothers themselves is a sensible and widely accepted idea now in even upper-income groups. Older children often love to sell their outgrown clothing through such outlets and use the money to buy other new or used things that suit them. Where such swapping is an accepted thing in a community, they don't even mind knowing whose clothes they are getting. In fact, they often are delighted to be able to buy or swap something for a garment or other article once owned by an admired older child. By setting up such organizations and encouraging all groups to contribute and exchange clothing through them, we do a social service that avoids the onus of charity for those children who must get their clothing this way or not at all or whose parents feel this is a sensible way to save money.

When Does the Child Choose His Own Clothes? I believe that a child should be at least consulted on his clothes preferences almost from the time he is able to state an opinion. Where he is making an obvious mistake, he should be guided, but within reason he should not be forced to wear clothes he patently dislikes. He has his own, sometimes quite peculiar-to-us, ideas of what's becoming to him. And consideration of any strong opinions he may have on the subject is only fair if we wish to follow the modern ideal of considering the child as a person right from the start, not just a possession to jump at our superior commands.

His taste in clothes and in other things develops slowly, partly through example and partly through his own character growth, through enthusiasms passionately embraced, then quickly or gradually abandoned to be replaced by others. We can help children find their style by letting them, wherever possible, make their own choice if they seem ready to make one—a brown hat instead of the blue, a rose dress instead of the more practical tan. Mistakes will be made, but then they won't be made a second time if they have caused the child any discomfort.

Children's tastes in good clothes are usually conservative, perhaps because it takes an individuality they haven't yet achieved to choose something which, while still in good taste, is not just like everybody else's. The teen-age girl who, despite gentle advice to the contrary, selects a dress that is too old for her or too impractical for the purpose will, after having worn it, learn the valuable lesson that something that looks fine in the shop under the sales person's blandishments may look all wrong viewed against her existing wardrobe or next to the party dress of her best friend. The older boy who uses up several months of his clothes allowance to buy his first dinner jacket when he really needs school clothes more will learn to regret his hasty decision.

About Allowances

How Much Allowance Should the Child Have? The amount of a child's allowance should depend on what he is expected to do with it and, when he's very young, on what others his own age in his community normally get. A child of wealthy parents should not have more pocket money than the children with whom he regularly associates. But neither are children expected to "keep up with the Joneses" if a large family, heavy responsibilities, or other circumstances make it necessary to give a child less spending money than is customary in the neighborhood. Children are much more realistic than we believe. They can accept all kinds of economies and deprivations if they are told quietly and sympathetically why they are necessary.

Whatever the allowance is, its entire use should not be dictated by his parents, because a child learns to use money intelligently only through handling it himself. If a six-year-old gets ten or fifteen cents a week allowance and is made to put it all in his piggy bank, he gets no idea that the real use for money is as a medium of exchange. He gets the shiny coins and they promptly disappear. The idea of a bank account is much too abstract for so small a child, although he can be made to understand and enjoy saving his pennies—not all of them, only a part of what he receives—to buy something he especially wants. To expect any young child to save, say, for his college education is expecting entirely too much and is asking him to assume at least in part the responsibility of the parent. Instead he should be saving, earning, and spending suitable amounts all along in order to learn how to manage money and to keep him in a favorable status with his friends. The boy who never can "treat," who can't join the kids in a candy store occasionally, because he has to save every cent he gets or earns for some big dim project his parents have chosen for him, is a sorry child and likely to be left out of things.

Give the child a chance to earn some money around his home or in the neighborhood to develop his initiative. Give him a set allowance, expect certain not-too-difficult or time-consuming chores from him, and pay him for extra work you ask him to do. But let him spend his own money as he pleases after he and you have agreed to some saving and spending plan that leaves him leeway to move in his own little world as a sufficiently moneyed individual.

Children treated with this kind of understanding don't squander their money. They nearly always save and nearly always are solvent. They don't attach undue value to money, because it is not used as a weapon against them and they are not told what to do with each penny supposedly freely given them. Taking away some privilege is safer punishment for a serious infraction of discipline than withdrawal of his allowance, because a child's "social obligations" go right on and having no spending money might encourage a resentful child to pilfer or to impose on others in his desire to get the things "all the other kids have." A child wants to be able to depend on his allowance being given to him on a set day and to have nothing interfere with it, if that is humanly possible. To him it is a pay check and what he has planned to do with it is as important to him as the family income is to his father.

Withholding Allowances The only time an allowance should be withheld, if you want your child to have an understanding of money, is when he himself wishes to borrow in advance for an immediate purchase. Explain that loans must be promptly returned and that his allowance will be withheld until his contemplated loan is paid up. Usually he will prefer to save for the purchase, instead—a very good practice to encourage.

If allowances are withheld for the sake of punishment, his share of the family income ceases to be in the proper perspective for the child—instead, it is something he can't count on, which can be given or withheld according to what he thinks of as his parents' whims. An allowance riddled by fines, which are often levied at moments of parental anger, ceases to be the inviolate thing it should be.

There are other ways of punishing a child that are more effective than by using his allowance as a club. When he handles the money which he receives on schedule, money restitutions are often valuable in developing a sense of his obligation. Suppose a child habitually rises late, misses the school bus, and has to be driven to school by a harassed mother or father, thus upsetting their daily schedules. Sometimes the way to cure that is to give warning that the next time it happens the child must go by taxi and the fare must be returned to his mother, out of his allowance—no matter how long it takes. His actual handing over of that money until the debt is paid is more valuable educationally than the complete withholding of the allowance by the parents for the same period. And there is more dignity in such an arrangement for the child, especially if it is all done on a quiet, businesslike basis devoid of scolding and moralizing about promptness. He will get the point very well.

Children's Table Manners

Playing with Food A happy, year-and-a-half-old child may make efforts to feed himself with his spoon. If so, let him do as much as he can in some easily cleanable place, but don't expect him to take over the function immediately and don't let fussy grown-ups annoy him with their admonitions to keep his hands out of his food. A baby who puts his hands in his cereal or dabbles his fingers in his mug of milk is experimenting with self-feeding—not exhibiting bad manners. If he spills some on the tray before him—an inevitable result—don't be in too much of a hurry to clean up the mess, because to him it is delightful. He slides his fingers around in it, and it makes an interesting squishy sound. He likes the feel of it and needs this kind of play whether with mud pies, water or, under such circumstances, his food. A child who dawdles over food once he is competent to feed himself may want to attract his mother's attention so she'll sit with him or perhaps give him a hand with some of the less tractable items, like custard (and why not?), or else he's not hungry. In the latter instance the food should be pleasantly removed.

Must a Child Finish His Food? At various periods in our culture we have heard diametrically opposite pieces of advice, which we, in turn, have drummed or tried to drum into our children. One is that a child must for discipline's sake "clean up his plate" at any cost—even that of an immediately rebellious stomach. No one knows why although it must be akin to the interdiction against "wasting" food whether or not you want it. Another is that it is "rude" to leave any food on one's plate. And then that it is "rude" to eat every last thing—on the ground that one should not be too interested in one's food if he is to be considered well-bred, a rather Victorian concept of nutrition.

Each baby is born with a built-in, well-functioning hunger mechanism. It tells him when he should eat and when he should stop eating. If this mechanism is respected by parents and baby, normal growth and appetite usually follow right along. But interference with this delicate adjustment can cause serious emotional difficulties in a young child that may continue into his adulthood in a very complex manner. Constantly coaxing a child or forcing him to eat beyond his capacity, beyond what his hunger dictates at the moment, puts this mechanism out of commission. It often results in an overweight child or one tense and thin, prone to car sickness and frequent digestive upsets.

Should a Child Choose His Own Food? Suppose someone with quite different tastes from yours dictated every morsel you put into your mouth. Would you enjoy your food or would you feel frustrated and angry? Anger causes digestion to stop dead in its tracks. A chronic state of tension at mealtimes is the cause of many of our modern ills, especially ulcers. Unpleasant mealtimes must be avoided for the sake of the whole family and especially that of the children, whose attitudes concerning food are being set at this time. Insisting that a child eat food he doesn't like (and usually the dislike will pass) is bad for the child-parent relationship. The child knows instinctively mother is not right this time.

But if you let a child dictate what he'll eat and when, won't he fill up on sweets and never eat the things his body needs? There are many modern children for whom no problem about feeding has ever arisen—they are under the "permissive" or "self-regulating" system. Such children are not fussy eaters unless there is some particular reason for the fussiness—teething, oncoming illness, overfatigue—which is respected by the adult in charge. The child is excused from his meal with no comment one way or the other. Conversely, when he eats well he is not praised for eating. Why should he be? It is important that the whole issue of eating to please a parent (or of not eating to displease) never arise and that happy mealtimes geared to the child's food preferences be the rule.

Where a child has a history of tension over meals and has been subjected to rigid rules of manners even in the nursery, he may when introduced to the self-regulating system of feeding start eating his dessert first or refuse to eat anything but sweets. This is because a premium has always been placed on these things—"If you don't eat your lamb chop, you may not have your ice cream!" This puts good, sound lamb chops into the class of something unpleasant but necessary, to be bolted quickly so the "good" child can have the "delicious" dessert.

Psychologists and psychiatrists working with children have found that children who have been exposed to this kind of handling may, once given the opportunity to choose what they want to eat, eat their dessert first. If they do, it's not important, not worth making an issue of, because shortly they will want to be like other people who eat their meat and potatoes first and finish with dessert. In experiments with very young children it was shown over a period of time that children have selective appetites—one day a child may want nothing but string beans for lunch and won't touch his milk. Another day he'll want the meat but not the vegetable on his plate; but careful graphing of such food intake over a period of a week will show that the normal child, allowed to select his food according to his preference, will instinctively consume a properly balanced diet if he has been offered, each day, the various elements in it. If he skips lettuce one day and eats twice as much of it the next, he is getting what he needs, isn't he? The body, given the chance, dictates what it requires for adequate nutrition.

In time, any normal, happy child wants to be like those closest to him. If his mother and father, his aunts and uncles, his older sisters and brothers break their bread into small pieces before buttering and eating it, cut their meat into manageable forkfuls, the littlest one will eventually cease trying to get a whole slice of bread or an entire chop into his mouth at one time. It does no harm to bring a child to the family table as soon as he can stand it and the family can stand him. But to expect him to sit silent like a little statue throughout the long adult meal or wait for late-comers is not to understand the immediacy of the small mind. In time, he'll catch up to our way of doing things. We did not ourselves arrive in the world full-fledged in the complexities of etiquette.

Should Children Be Seen and Not Heard?   It would be a good idea for us to discard many of the old saws to do with the training of the young, and this, the idea that a child, having nothing to say—at least nothing of importance to most adults—should say nothing, is one of them. The ability to carry on a conversation at meals is an art, developed like any other through guided practice. Even the baby at table should have some conversation or attention directed his way occasionally, even if he replies with nothing more than "Goo." Otherwise, he will find some anti-social way of getting attention, such as spilling his milk on the tablecloth or dropping his spoon on the floor. If we have the children at the table at all, they should be treated with the same courtesy and consideration we give to the adults there. Of course children should not be permitted to monopolize the conversation or make everyone else uncomfortable by their noise or messiness.

If because of fatigue or the presence of too many strangers (other children as guests can sometimes upset the applecart nicely) the usually pleasant child begins to make a scene at table, remove him gently and let him have his food by himself, not as punishment but for his comfort—and, of course, yours. In fact, it is better to anticipate such possible crises and arrange, beforehand, to side-step them. But don't scold the child or apologize unduly to the adults about him. "This, too, shall pass." Don't expect too much of him, now.

Older Children at Table Later on, adolescence brings forth in children the same orneriness that we find in the four-to-six bracket. They are a little more amenable to reason but not much, because of their own physical and emotional upheavals. Again, don't exact more than the child can deliver, of manners or anything else. He should be made to understand that meals with the rest of the family are a privilege, that no one member should make the others uncomfortable by bickering, noisy behavior, lounging all over the table, lack of grooming, etc. If it seems impossible to get him to follow the house rules concerning meals, let him eat alone for a while until he is ready to return and conform, within reason. Making every mealtime a battleground of manners is a strain on everyone and usually does no more than stir up defiance in the child. But, while manners are caught, they can also be taught, gently, during the course of ordinary exposure to them.

A child is very interested at around ten or eleven in the reasons behind various food practices. He likes to hear, for instance, that primitive man ate out of a common dish with his fingers, that the Chinese invented the fork, then later returned to the dainty chopsticks so difficult for the Occidental to handle expertly. He is relieved to discover that, while most things on his plate should be eaten with fork or spoon, there are still many finger foods. He hates to seem awkward, so if he is to be confronted, for instance, with his first artichoke when there are guests present, show him in advance how you take off each leaf and dip it in the sauce, how you eat just the tender base of the leaf and place the rest at the side of the plate. Explain about the choke and how to remove it with knife and fork before coming to the reward of the heart.

Children like to eat with their fingers. Give them plenty of opportunity for it with between-meals snacks and in meals out of doors, in spring and summer where they may eat hot dogs, pie, cake, and fruit out of hand, with adults doing likewise. Take no time out for pleasure-spoiling lectures on manners.

Awkwardness in Children Children are beginners. They are starting a job in life. If we expect them to do everything expertly at once we are certainly going to be disappointed. It doesn't help for adults to be affronted or infuriated—as so many of them are—by childish errors at table. We should realize, for example, that awkwardness is increased by nagging—not only awkwardness in children, but in adults. When we are having difficulty in the carrying out of some motor act, criticism embarrasses or irritates us into further awkwardness. If the peas won't stay on Junior's fork, give him a spoon—quietly and pleasantly—and let him use it until he is ready to cope with the fork.

It is important to know that increased, very noticeable awkwardness, especially at table, shown in the dropping and spilling of food, the knocking over of glasses, can be a forewarning of one of the infectious childhood diseases—scarlet fever or measles, for example—which may be followed by

chorea or St. Vitus's dance. But where awkwardness seems to be part and
parcel of the child, then increasing his social poise and skills may help.
Usually it is easier for a child to eat with his left hand resting on the
table next to the plate instead of rigidly in his lap. Most well-mannered
adults keep the left hand on the table gracefully, now. In severe cases
professional re-education, sometimes in handedness, may have to be resorted
to, and for this school and medical advisers need to be consulted.

Children's Hour Any mother of children has known the tension of
finding the child's room in an unholy mess just when the rest of the house
has been made highly presentable. It is easy to get annoyed and downright
angry over this and a temptation to be punitive with the offending child.
The martyr-mother will stiffen (and tense) her spine and attack the offending
area, often doing the job herself while berating the child. How much better
to say instead, "Let's clean this up together." Or, if that is impossible, to
close the door firmly without feelings of guilt and shame. Most healthy
children are messy sometimes and some are messy always. I have had
many moments of agitating over three none-too-neat sons. A friend with
much experience changed my thinking in the matter years ago when he
pointed out when my children were grown I would have firmly impressed
in their memories the recollection of the orderly attractive home in which
they were raised. They would *want*, he said, to create the same kind
of atmosphere for themselves in their own homes. One of my sons is
married now and when the two younger ones visited his bachelor apartment before he was married, they came home complaining that he would
storm at them if they hadn't put their chairs back in the proper places
when they got up or hadn't straightened up the pillows. This was a far cry
from the way he felt about these things when he was in his middle teens.
I see emerging in my college junior son a real interest in the appearance
of the surroundings for which he alone is now responsible. Moral: If
you can't stand disorder you have not created yourself, and can't spare
the time to clean it up or get it cleaned up without a scene, shut the door—
firmly.

The Social Behavior of Children

Teaching Respect for Others' Property The public libraries each year
report thousands and thousands of dollars' worth of damage to books. The
damage is not all done by children, of course, but the damage done by
adults—tearing out pages, dog-earing pages, doodling and scribbling, and
breaking the backs of books—results from the lack of training during
childhood.

A small child cannot be controlled with a constant stream of prohibi-
tions. When he reaches the crawling and toddling stage, breakables like ash
trays and ornaments must be put out of his reach wherever possible and his

activities confined to areas he can't seriously damage. He should not be allowed to play with such things as phonograph records which he is bound to break. He will squall when he is removed from such enticing playthings with the words, "Those are Mother's, you mustn't touch," but in time he will find it not worth his while to turn in their direction, especially if acceptable articles are given him immediately as a substitute. It accomplishes nothing to give him cracked or damaged records to break, for he cannot distinguish between the records he may treat with impunity and those he will be punished for breaking.

A baby should have his own books—with the first ones the undamageable kind. Later when paper books are introduced, they should be looked at only under parental supervision at first. Infant interest is very short, and in a matter of minutes the new book that was so bright and arresting may pall. The baby will throw it on the floor or start tearing out the pages. This should not be permitted. The mother should say, "We don't hurt books. I'll let you see the book later." And the book should disappear until the next supervised reading. If this procedure is followed every time, eventually even a child of one or two will not destroy his books and won't harm those of his parents, should any be within reach. To give a baby old magazines to mutilate, or permit him to harm his own books, is inviting trouble. He can't know the difference between old and new magazines, between his books and his parents'.

When the child gets his first pencils and crayons he should be allowed to use them only under supervision until he learns how they are used and where. The minute interest lags and the crayon starts straying off the paper or coloring book, the little artist's equipment should be gently put away until the next time.

Children should, of course, be taught not to interrupt. A mother can tell a child to wait for just a moment until she is finished with her conversation. However, if her two- or three-year-old interrupts her, the situation is a little more difficult because of the child's more limited ability to understand and to wait. In this case a mother can excuse herself momentarily from her conversation, see to the tot's question, and then continue her conversation.

Twenty-three Guides for Good Conduct   It is often said that the manners of today's children are atrocious. Perhaps many parents are so sensitive to possible criticism that they fail to take into consideration that manners, where actually taught—aside from being almost bred in the bone through proper example—are never successfully imparted through constant nagging or physical reminders (a sharp crack on the recalcitrant elbow at table, for example). Such teaching makes most children resentful and unco-operative. The tension created by such parental tactics is a poor background for learning the social graces, to say the least.

There comes a time when even a headstrong child will want desperately to know how to do the right thing. The time to remind him of the rules of manners is *before* he comes to table with guests, *before* he goes to the party, *in advance* on his boarding the plane. Constant correction of the child in front of others is irritating to all concerned and often reflects the parents' own lack of social poise.

A boy or girl studying American history will be amused and benefited by being referred to George Washington's fifty-four maxims on personal conduct, which for all their quaint phraseology do embody most of the things we all should know about accepted social actions and attitudes. The maxims, by the way, were probably translated by Washington from the original French while he was a teen-ager, himself, and are not believed to be original with him. Any library can turn up frequent references to them.

Aside from Washington, whose advice is so basic as to refer to the picking of teeth in public and reading the letters of others, there are elementary codes of behavior and niceties of manners that should be implanted in all children in their years of close contact with parents, who, it is hoped, follow the same pattern of behavior. What are some of these? I believe a child should eventually come to understand that publicly in "polite society" we do not do the following things:

1. Scratch, pick the teeth, spit, comb the hair, or tend the nails.
2. Chew with our mouths open or with obvious noise or lip-smacking.
3. Leave a spoon in a cup, or eat with a knife.
4. Tuck in a napkin (unless we are very young indeed), lick our fingers instead of wiping them on a napkin.
5. Sit down to a meal unwashed and uncombed or improperly dressed.
6. Fail to greet others encountered in the household when we arise and when we return home.
7. Tilt chairs or push them back from the table with all our body weight upon them.
8. Lounge on the dinner table or put our elbows on it except between courses (and then preferably one elbow at a time, if any) or sit on our spines.
9. Go up and down stairs like elephants and bang doors after us.
10. Pass in front of others without saying, "Please excuse me" or "I'm sorry."
11. Use a flat "No" or "Yes" in answer to questions. Instead, "Yes, Mother," "Yes, Mr. Roberts (or, Sir)." In some instances a pleasant "Yes" or "No" is acceptable. The tone of voice is important.
12. Speak ill of the dead or repeat damaging gossip.
13. Swear in a way that is generally considered offensive (though most children need a list of acceptable "swear words" with which they can blow off steam—perhaps one list for use in the parents' presence, if

absolutely necessary, and another list for away from home where there is likely to be more rigidity in the matter).

14. Put more than a manageable mouthful in our mouths at one time.

15. Burp, belch, sneeze, or cough without attempting to turn away from others and then only behind the cupped hand or a clean handkerchief.

16. Stick feet out into aisles and passageways so people may fall over them.

17. Behave noisily and conspicuously in public places.

18. Enter a room whose door is closed without knocking and waiting for permission to enter.

19. Interrupt a conversation except for an important reason and then only after asking permission to speak.

20. Speak unnecessarily loudly. Chatter incessantly.

21. Walk without actually picking up our feet.

22. Pull our finger joints, drum our fingers or indulge in any similar irritating little habits that set people's teeth on edge.

23. Chew gum except in private or at least discreetly or without snapping on a plane for relief of pressure.

Children and young people (and, of course, all men and women) should know and practice these things as an integral part of their daily lives, eventually without particular consciousness that they are following accepted precepts of gentlefolk.

Instead of constantly reading adolescents and pre-adolescents the Riot Act, let them study a list such as this at times when they seem relatively receptive. Often they will accept what is in books more readily than what they hear, perhaps too constantly, from properly concerned parents.

Calling Parents by First Names In ultra-progressive educational circles parents and even teachers are often called by their first names. The idea seems to be that this puts adults and children on the same level and increases rapport. To me it seems self-conscious, if not, in the case of parents, barbaric. To other children who call their parents "Mother" and "Father," or variations of these honored titles, in the traditional manner, children who substitute "Marie" and "Bill" seem peculiar, unless most in the group do likewise. The mother-father relationship is there, no matter what parents are called. Why shouldn't it be frankly proclaimed for the sake of children and parents? To me, such ultramodern parents and children seem to be missing something very important. And to the uninitiated the children seem like foundlings.

"Making" Children Mind Their Manners There are certain accepted manners which children should be continually encouraged to cultivate. Their attention should be drawn to the fact that, on various occasions mother and father do certain things to be socially agreeable and these courtesies will be expected of them, too, as soon as they are able to cope with them.

The mother who makes a scene with her child because he won't shake hands with Mrs. Smith or thank a small hostess for a party he didn't in all honesty enjoy does little but make everyone uncomfortable. It is far better to say, "Helen, Johnny would like to tell you what a nice time he had at your party. And he hopes to see you soon again," the minute one senses that a child is going to balk at the expected amenities. Most children eventually rise to the social graces in their own good time. In the meantime, they should hear us deliver the courteous phrases for them, without irritation. And they need to be told quietly, before and after social events, what will be expected of them as a matter of course.

If necessary a mother should say in a low voice to her young son with whom she is walking on the street, "Here comes Mrs. Smith, dear. When she stops to speak to me, remember, please, to take off your cap. If she offers her hand, shake it and *look* at her pleasantly." She should avoid giving these lessons in front of others, unless the reminders can be made very privately.

I have never seen a child with well-mannered parents who grew into an adult completely devoid of social grace. But I have seen such a child, in rebellion at constant goading concerning his manners, go through a savage period during which the only conformity with social customs was enforced with damaging tension to both child and parents. Such a nagged child gets to believe he *is* a boor and that nothing can remedy the fact, so he might as well be as primitive as possible, just to show them.

A friend of mine with whom I was discussing these things said he and his wife taught his horde of boys manners by taking them out very frequently, en masse. They quickly saw for themselves that the relatively relaxed manners possible at their family dinner table were not the manners for a fine restaurant in town. They were so thrilled at their parents' including them in grown-up parties that they were most anxious to conform to the code of proper public behavior.

A little friendly review of manners before and after parties and other events to which children go helps, too, to make such things second nature.

Real social polish is usually acquired away from parents, once the essentials have been inculcated. Children need plenty of opportunity to practice what they have been taught at home in the company of other children who are going through the same social exercises. Dancing class from eight to ten and on up is very helpful and for some self-conscious children a virtual necessity. Concert, museum, and theater attendance, the opera, if possible, "Y" classes, Boy and Girl Scouts, all the extra-curricular activities where manners, social form and co-operation can be taught and observed are very valuable, just because the lessons do not come from the often overinsistent parents.

Bad Language Language—its intonation, its vocabulary, its grammar—begins for the child at home. The language of the parents for good or bad becomes his language. If it is bad, it must be modified by his schooling. If it is good, it must be protected against the inroads of vulgarity, the ugliness of senseless obscenity. When children hear shock words and repeat them, they find that they can cause a reaction. The first time it happens, if it is handled well, may mean no repetition of the offense. The best thing is for parents not to be shocked when they hear a four-letter word from a five-year-old, but to take the child aside, and ask the child if he knows what the word means. Usually he has no idea and it isn't always necessary to explain the meaning of the word, but to say quietly, "This is a word that we don't use at home because it is unpleasant and makes many people feel uncomfortable. Instead, if you want to use a strong word, to express your feelings, say something like 'Dammit.' This will shock some people, but it isn't quite so bad as the one that you used and I don't think anyone will mind very much." If something like this is said gently, in a reasonable way, the child usually responds. The child's language which is literally studded with obscenities indicates a disturbed child. You will receive complaints from other parents, from teachers and may have to seek therapy for him. On the other hand, this period often passes if no one gets excited about it. And be sure about your own language before him! Be sure his "bad" words don't ape your own.

Must a Little Girl Curtsy? The stiff, self-conscious little curtsy, against which so many little girls under ten rebel, is not essential to good manners today. It may be required in dancing class but it should not be insisted upon in the living room. It looks Victorian outdoors and ridiculous from a gangly schoolgirl. If a little girl enjoys the dramatic effect of the curtsy before adults in greeting them and saying good-by, as many do, that's fine. But many little girls come through these little social contacts more gracefully if they are just expected to bow or shake hands politely. And they should certainly not be expected to kiss a whole roomful of strangers, or in fact anyone whom it would not be quite natural for them to kiss without being reminded.

The Boy's Bow Even little boys can be encouraged to come forward and, feet together, bow their heads slightly and shake hands with their parents' guests, so long as the occasional neglected courtesy is not made into a crisis. If the tiny boy says "No!" when asked to say "Good afternoon" to Mrs. Smith, Mother can say, "Well, next time I'm sure you'll shake hands, like Daddy." Usually he will want to emulate Daddy right then, if belatedly, if the mother is relaxed rather than humiliated. Sometimes childish coldness to guests is instinctive—they sense the guest does not like children. The warm, child-loving adult rarely has any trouble in such introductions. Children are attracted to them at once. Which is more valuable socially—for a baby to reluctantly go through a stiff little ceremony, or flatteringly crawl onto the stranger's lap?

The Boy's Hat Boys should remove their hats for the same reasons that men do. A man no longer removes his hat upon entering a public or office building, but would do so in a private home or residential hotel. While a school is technically a public building, a boy would remove his hat, as the school has certain rules which govern it, and may almost be considered a boy's second home. This would hold true even in an all-male school.

Extending Invitations Boys or girls, even those in their very late teens, should not extend invitations to other children to meals, for weekends, or for outings of various kinds except through their mothers. A boy of ten or so may phone another boy of his own age and say, "Peter, my mother says I may ask you to dinner and to stay overnight. If you'd like to come, she'll speak to your mother." It is courteous to let the children make the preliminary arrangements, as they invariably have their own plans and preferences in playmates. Mothers should avoid making such arrangements for their children's entertainment without their full consent.

An invitation from a boy to a girl (whatever the age) to visit his home for a meal or overnight should always be extended by the mother in the final stages of the arrangements. This may be done by note, if the children live at some distance, or by phone. In the case of a teen-age girl, the mother of the host writes to her or phones her, then asks to speak to the girl's mother in order to verify the invitation herself.

Children's Introductions A child bringing a strange child home says, "Mother, this is Billy Burnham. Billy, this is my mother." If his mother's surname is different from her son's, he says, ". . . my mother, Mrs. Fellows." The guest says, "How do you do," or perhaps just "Hello." If he is introducing a girl he follows the same form, introducing the guest to his mother as soon as possible after arrival. The mother then leaves the young people to their own devices in their own part of the house or apartment, but, in the case of very young children, she doesn't leave the house. Young teen-age boys and girls are not left without acceptable adult supervision, that is, not solely with servants, except perhaps for short periods.

When a child is a host or hostess at a party or in his home, he offers to shake hands first with an adult. In other circumstances the adult offers his hand first.

Birthday Parties for Children It has long been clear to me that many a small child's birthday party is put on for the pleasure of the grown-ups around him rather than for the delight of the child.

Watch a party for a one- or two-year-old. He sits in the midst of piled-up packages but hasn't the tactile ability yet to open them himself. So some adult unwraps each thing and hands it to the baby. A profusion of playthings is troubling to such a small child. He likes to pick up, examine, and play with one toy at a time in his own fashion. But he is not allowed, on this occasion, to make proper, slow acquaintance of each gift. Too many things and people come at him at once. By the time the cake and ice cream are triumphantly brought forth for his approval, he is probably in tears or has retired in self-protection to some quiet corner to play with some familiar, tattered plaything. He might as well not be at his own party.

There are exceptions, of course, but usually things don't improve much by the fifth or even the tenth birthday. In fact, many sensible mothers, with their children's complete agreement, make birthday celebrations very simple indeed. There are no big parties with magicians, donkey games, Mickey Mouse movies, and other exciting diversions. There is never the inevitable ice cream and cake spilled on the living room rug and the birthday celebrant too keyed-up and goody-stuffed to go to bed peacefully. Instead, perhaps, the older child is permitted the choice of one friend with whom he can do something very special. They may lunch in a restaurant and go to the zoo or on some little trip. Mother goes along and perhaps father does, too. There is never too much of anything—not too much rich food, not too much entertainment.

Very young children can't possibly understand what birthday parties are all about. But as the adults enjoy them, let there be ice cream and a cake after one of the baby's regular meals. Let just the family celebrate with him, with perhaps one other little friend arriving for the cake ceremony. As the baby won't appreciate more than one or two simple toys, let doting relatives give him things he needs—clothes or money for his bank account. If many toys arrive, some should be put away for the inevitable rainy day. They should never be showered on him all at once.

In my experience, most children prefer these quiet family celebrations of their birthdays without too much said about it all in advance. Certainly threats such as "If you are a bad boy, you won't get any birthday presents this year!" should never be used. We don't really mean such threats, but the child believes them, and even when his birthday arrives along with the presents much of the pleasure is dissipated because of his preliminary anxiety.

In the early teens, birthday parties begin to come into their own. Now the children can take real part in preparing for them, making up their guest lists, choosing favors, planning and conducting the entertainment.

What Hours for Children's Parties? Most mothers dislike the birthday party at which their eight- or ten-year-old gorges on ice cream and cake, arriving home at his normal suppertime unable to eat what's been prepared for him. Parties for young children, if they are given at all, should include a normal meal followed by the birthday food. This means that in the five-to-ten group parties should begin at three-thirty or four and terminate with an early supper, so the children will be home and ready for bed by six-thirty at the latest for the little ones and seven-thirty or eight at the latest for the older ones.

The Child's Manners at His Party No child, we know, learns manners or anything else at one fell swoop. So a child who is host at his own birthday party should not be goaded and corrected by an overanxious parent all during the proceedings. If he is old enough, he may be told just before the party that, as he has been taught, it is good manners to greet his guests as they enter, to thank them for gifts (even if they have brought something he doesn't like), to see that they have a good time and first chance at toys and games, and, finally, to bid them good-by and, if possible, to thank them again for coming and for their gifts.

All this ceremony is trying, even for adults at a party, so we should not dissolve in despair if our children forgot a few moves in the complicated game of etiquette. We should remember that the child feels some embarrassment at all this focusing of attention on him. It is normal for him to take a playful poke at some incoming pal with a "Hi, Skinny! I was hoping you'd stay home." Children understand each other. Parents should, within reason, allow them to conduct their social intercourse without censure.

Of course, these occasions are valuable for learning. But correction—by means of gentle suggestion—should come before and after (much after) the party. The parents can watch how their child conducts himself, stepping into the picture only if things get too much out of hand. The next day they may find it desirable to go over some of the things that were less than perfect, taking into consideration that the child was under a strain at the time and that, at his age, it was instinctive for him to try to enjoy his own birthday party to the utmost, guests notwithstanding.

Children's Dancing Classes Etiquette is traditionally taught in dancing classes for young children along with such basic steps as the fox trot, the waltz, the cha-cha, possibly the bossa nova and the tango, along with the current discothèque dances. The girls usually are taller than the boys at this stage and more poised socially.

None of the schools I know of insists on the wearing of gloves by the boys any more, but they must have clean hands. After all, in adult life men no longer wear gloves with evening attire except on rare diplomatic or perhaps debutante occasions. In many classes little girls not only wear white gloves to the classes but wear them throughout the dances. While this may put the little girls on good behavior and look festive, it is rather meaningless today when practically no adult woman any more wears gloves for dancing, although gloves are worn, of course, to the dance. More often than not they are checked with evening coats and not even worn through the receiving line if any. But following the traditional system at least in dancing class they may give the little girls a feeling of one-upmanship and allow the teachers a definitive word. The curtsy is still taught in most dancing classes. It is rarely needed in adult life except in a few parts of the world, but the acquirement of the grace can do no harm.

I do not like to see girls from eleven and a half on in dancing class without stockings. Mothers tell me that girls this age often refuse to wear the little girl socks and that only junior nylons fit them, an expense to which some mothers don't wish to be put. However, as dancing class doesn't take place every day, I think that teachers are correct when they require either socks or stockings. Dancing class for boys and girls is a special discipline, one that will add to their poise and maturity.

The Extension of Dancing Class The ability to dance—really to dance—aside from the fine points of etiquette learned in dancing class can be a joy not only to a very young person but to the adult he will become. Treating dancing class as a dose of medicine that must be taken can defeat the idea of dancing as a joyous experience. When a child goes to dancing class, it is well for the parents to put the information gained to practice outside of the dancing class, encouraging a young son to dance with his sisters or his mother during their travels or on special occasions such as weddings. A daughter learning to dance should have the experience of dancing with her father and her brothers, even when the latter may be no further advanced than she. A child who is frozen in dancing class will benefit greatly by having a few private lessons in an adult school or from some older friend or relative who takes an interest in his progress. The young girl heading for an eventual debut who becomes a really good dancer before the great event will have an advantage over her fellow debutantes who have never really learned to *dance*. The boy who has persisted in considering the dancing class a real bore may find that when he gets to college he may be considered less than wonderful as a date if he doesn't know one foot from the other, and is more or less ignorant of the social graces connected with dancing. A man can express his masculinity quite thoroughly in the way he conducts himself on the dance floor—or he can fumble and misstep and be a drag on his partner. The best way to become a good dancer is to master the art at a young age, so it becomes as natural as walking and a delightful exercise, a happy social accomplishment to be enjoyed the rest of his life.

Special Problems

Taking a Child to the Doctor's Office You need your doctor as a ready ally in coping with the inevitable illnesses and emergencies of childhood. Don't build him up in your child's mind as an ogre through senseless threats—"If you fall, you'll be hurt, and the doctor will have to come, so get down right away!" or "Stop eating that candy or you'll be sick and the doctor will take you to the hospital!" Doctors and hospitals are necessary. Children should know their functions but should never be threatened with them as a method of so-called discipline.

As far as a child is concerned, the doctor should be a familiar friend. The child-wise doctor knows this and, except when quick action is vital, takes time to let the child get accustomed to him as a person before examinations or treatments begin. When a mother can do so without anxiety she should tell the child what is going to happen. "Your throat is sore, so the doctor will ask you to open your mouth wide—like this—so he can see where the trouble is. He will hold your tongue down with a stick for a minute. If you ask him, he'll give you a throat stick to play with. It will come in handy if Teddy gets a sore throat."

Some mothers increase tension if they are present in the examining room, but most mothers can help the doctor materially in calming the child's fears. No good is accomplished by telling even the smallest child that something that will certainly hurt, won't. Instead say—or let the doctor say—"Now this will hurt just an instant but it will soon be over. Then I'll give you a lollipop." Try to make all contacts with the doctor or dentist have a pleasant ending, and do not build up unnecessary tension beforehand by talking unnecessarily about the coming session. The baby who is frightened because of his memory of painful inoculations needs to be reassured by his mother and, if possible, have an opportunity to make friends with the doctor before the next treatment takes place. A favorite toy or a lollipop should be ready to catch his attention and comfort him the minute he can be released. A calm, cheerful mother, not overly commiserative, helps the situation considerably.

The Child in the Hospital   Where an operation is necessary for a child—a tonsillectomy, say—it is important for his mother or doctor to tell him quietly, not too far in advance, just what is going to happen, how long he will be away from home, to what degree it will hurt, and who will be with him. The young child should, if possible, have his mother, or some member of the family, and a favorite toy with him in the hospital at least the first night after an operation, especially when he first comes out of the anesthesia. He should be given a sedative before going to the operating room, if possible, to dim its terrors and, again, if it is permitted, the mother or father should go with him until after he is anesthetized to keep him calm and secure and to pass on the orders of the strange person who will administer the anesthesia. Needless to say, a frightened, anxious parent under the circumstances is worse than a calm stranger. But the right kind of parental reassurance is of tremendous assistance both physically and psychologically. A relaxed, trusting child, sure of a safe outcome for the operation and understanding the need and procedure of it reasonably well for his age, makes the best patient. A frightened child who has built up many nameless fears of an operation about which he's in the dark can cause complications for the surgeon, the anesthetist, and the nurses. An anxiety concerning hospitals and operations may shadow the rest of his life and, of course, delay his immediate recovery. An operation, well-handled in an atmosphere of parental reassurance and patience, can for the small child be something beyond recall a few years later.

Children in the Dark The end of the day should belong to parents and their guests, once the children have been put to bed. But many a family's troubles with a child begin with insistence that the child "learn" not to be afraid of the dark. Fear of the dark is often implanted by thoughtless grown-ups or older children who threaten a little one with the "boogie man." A tiny infant is not afraid of the dark, and its mother may be planting the seeds of trouble if she starts the baby off sleeping in a room which is always kept lighted.

Babies, right from birth, can be trained to sleep undisturbed either by the absence or presence of light. To pull down the shades automatically at nap time for a baby may be to make him too dependent on light conditions in a room. Instead, start the baby sleeping in an unshaded room not overly protected from the usual household noises so he will quickly learn to go to sleep under any conditions. Place his bed so he won't be disturbed by the sun shining full in his face, but don't pull the shades. An older child who has been conditioned to sleeping only in darkened rooms can be patiently encouraged to sleep in a room under different circumstances. If he learns to do so, he is laying the base for better adult sleeping habits.

Night Lights The happy child who has never had a night light normally takes "lights out" in his stride. A child who has been given a night light and then as he grows older is arbitrarily expected to do without it sometimes becomes frightened and prolongs his sleeping preparations endlessly because of a fear he is ashamed to express. Such a child may so infuriate his parents with his jumping out of bed, his demands for a drink of water, his needless trips to the bathroom that he brings undeserved punishment on his head. If continuation of a night light quiets such a child so that he goes to sleep promptly, isn't it better to give it to him than to try to force him to give up his fear by rational explanations to the effect that the dark is harmless?

Many adults are unable to sleep in a room that is completely dark, either because they have been accustomed to a night light since babyhood or because in childhood they were frightened by stories of the terrors lurking in darkness. Fear of the dark, of going to sleep is very usual and human. Think of the prayers that suggest it—"If I should die before I wake," "The pestilence that walketh in darkness." No one, child or adult, should be forced to sleep entirely in the dark if he is unable to do so easily and fearlessly. Showing a little child who is terrified of the dark that there is nothing to be frightened of by switching on a light when his fear comes on is one way to help overcome fear of the dark, if it is to be overcome at all. To insist that a child sleep in a dark room when such devices are ineffective and the darkness keeps him tense and sleepless defeats the whole purpose of putting him to bed and needlessly disturbs him and the household.

Being perfectly matter of fact about lights, one way or the other as the child seems to desire, right from the beginning is the best way to prevent fantasies concerning the danger of darkness. If a child knows he may have a light if he feels he needs it—and on special occasions even a child who has slept happily in a dark room from infancy may want a little light—he will be more secure and less likely to demand a light at all times. The child who is forced to sleep in a dark room, who is punished for not going to sleep on schedule will be a child who, when he does sleep, will have restless slumber and perhaps night terrors that will wake the whole family.

Handling the Shy Child   Most children, even the most confident and happy ones, pass through various periods of shyness. At these times don't use force. A young baby, who until now has been gay and friendly, may suddenly run to his mother and bury his head in her skirt at the approach of a stranger. Don't scold or ridicule in a mistaken effort to teach him "manners." Don't allow the visitor to force attentions on the child, either, but keep cool and objective yourself and direct attention away from him. He will then usually emerge with his normal amount of curiosity about a newcomer and, if let alone, will probably make friends in his own way. It is well to remember that even Daddy, suddenly appearing in hat and overcoat, may look quite different to a young child. Reassure him, lightly, and let him get his bearings himself.

Thumb-sucking, Bed-wetting   Since many parents erroneously think of thumb-sucking and bed-wetting in children, nail-biting too, in terms of bad manners (see the Introduction to this section), I feel that presenting the modern pediatric viewpoint on this may be helpful. It is obvious that no mother wishes to see her child suck his thumb, wet his bed, or bite his nails indefinitely. But all these things are perfectly normal to a greater or less respect in most little children, and growing out of them depends much more on the happiness of the child and his adjustment to the difficult business of life in a grown-up world than on arbitrary "training." A child may be led out of these behavior patterns sometimes, but never coerced out of them by punishment, restraints, or ridicule, though rewards are sometimes helpful.

Some children have a greater need to nurse—for which thumb-sucking is a substitute—than others. Modern pediatricians warn that abrupt cessation of breast-nursing or, later, too early and complete insistence on the cup instead of the loved bottle can cause the child to thumb-suck in a compensatory manner. Even children who have had the most understanding care will, when they come up against frightening periods when something new or undesired is expected of them, begin to suck their thumbs again. Or they may do so when they are overtired, hungry, or under any tension. Most thumb-sucking stops, anyhow, by the time the child is five if no attention is paid to it.

Thumb-sucking in a child over five may be an indication of insecurity and may be helped by increased attention to the child's emotional needs through more companionship with the mother. Sometimes this may have to be done at the expense of a younger—and usually more relaxed—child who needs her less. The thumb-sucker "wants to be a baby." Give in to this desire for a little while through extra mothering. If a new baby has arrived, the older child may benefit from a brief (and private) return to the bottle if he expesses longing for it. If his need is handled understandingly, he will soon be reassured and realize that, while being a baby and dependent is comforting, being his own age and growing up is much more satisfactory. But don't be rigid and peremptory with a thumb-sucking child. Let him get his comfort from you rather than from his thumb.

Most dentists agree that thumb-sucking has little effect on baby teeth, that even if they do become displaced the second teeth push in and correct the malocclusion. If the second teeth are crooked, thumb-sucking isn't necessarily to blame at all and it is foolish to tax the child with the responsibility for it. Even proper nutrition and vitamin supplements don't guarantee straight teeth or even good teeth. Inheritance has much to do with it, although good nutrition and vitamin D, especially, can minimize hereditary tendencies toward crooked or protruding teeth and receding jawline (no sign at all, by the way, of a weak character, and conversely a bull-dog jaw does not indicate either strength of character or tenacity of purpose).

Never hurry any change-over to a more grown-up behavior pattern (such as making the child switch from a bottle to a cup) with a child. Wait until he indicates a readiness for the step.

The Baby Sitter

You and Your Sitter Professional and amateur baby sitting has come into its own as a result of the servant shortage, women's independence, and smaller living quarters that can't accommodate relatives. Unmarried or widowed older women now usually have lives of their own and no longer spend them in return for keep as unpaid handmaidens in relatives' families.

A baby sitter may be a college or high school girl or boy earning spending money, a mature woman, or a young mother interested in taking care of another young child occasionally at the standard rate of pay.

The age and experience of the sitter is usually taken into consideration and sometimes there is a sliding scale—so much per hour if light housework is done, such as dishwashing, bedmaking, and preliminary meal preparation, so much for child care and nothing else, so much once the child is asleep.

How Old Should a Sitter Be?   For daytime care of a small child, with the mother within hailing distance, a child of twelve or thirteen, if responsible, may be satisfactory. A tired mother needing a relaxing bath and a nap might employ such a sitter to watch the baby in the playpen, sandbox, or nursery. But she shouldn't go out and leave the two alone, though she might take the older child on a shopping trip to help with the younger one.

For evening care of a child an older person is needed—a boy or girl in the late teens, known to be stable, conscientious, and really fond of children. For overnight and longer periods, children should be left with an older woman or, if possible—particularly in an isolated country house— with a man and his wife. The mother should always consider that an emergency might occur, with which an immature person might not be able to cope.

Before going out the mother should tell the child a sitter is coming, and if the sitter is someone new she should be introduced into the routine before the mother departs. All instructions—and they should cover any possible emergency—should be carefully written down. If a formula must be prepared it should be written down, too, and the mother should be sure the sitter knows how to prepare it.

Exact instructions concerning meals should be left and a memorandum on what food the sitter may have as an expected snack. The rate of pay should be carefully established before the sitting starts and the sitter paid promptly at the end of the agreed period. Transportation or an escort to her home should be provided for any girl or woman after midnight and, of course, if necessary before.

Should the Sitter Be Allowed to Entertain?   A baby sitter's main interest should be the child or children she has in charge. A teen-ager should not be permitted to have the gang in while he or she is baby sitting, nor should a teen-age girl be allowed to have a boy visit her while she is on the job.

Once the child is asleep, the baby sitter can be permitted use of the television or radio or may study or sleep—so long as the baby can be heard easily if he wakes and calls. Young baby sitters who take too many late sitting jobs night after night are dangerous, because they can fall so soundly asleep that virtually nothing will wake them. Their charges, therefore, have no protection during the parents' absence.

Older women often enjoy having a woman friend or a couple come in during a long, late evening, and, if the habits of all concerned are well-known and there will be no contact between the guests and the children, such visiting is permissible if the baby is within hearing at all times. Of course, there should be no drinking permitted at any time.

Sharing Sitters   If two or more mothers wish to leave their children with one sitter in the home of one of the parents, the amount of pay should be increased in proportion to the added responsibility.

Neighbors Sit for Each Other   The hiring of sitters is often quite a financial problem. In many communities families work out a club sitting plan whereby one mother or father will sit certain nights of the week or month for others in the group, who will reciprocate by sitting for them. Careful accounting must be kept so that there is a fair exchange for each family's sitting time.

Mother Needs a Night Out Too   It is considered a good idea for couples to have two nights out a week, but one of these nights may be stag for each. On mother's night out father should sit with the baby. One of the satisfactions of modern life is the father's increasing, informed participation in the actual physical care of his children. The children feel closer to their fathers, and the fathers learn that even a tiny baby will respond contentedly to their ministrations, awkward though these may be at first.

Divorcée and Widow Sitters   Many divorcées and widows tell me that if their dates did not pay the sitter, they could not go out. Parents without Partners condones this but my strong recommendation is that the divorcée or widow not make a practice of permitting their dates to pay the sitter if they can possibly avoid it. For one thing, young men, particularly, must often watch their own entertainment budgets and to have to assume the cost of a sitter in order to take out a woman may mean that he will look for his dates elsewhere. Secondly, this is actually a responsibility of the mother of the children and obligating herself to her date in matters that have to do with the upkeep of her home can be socially embarrassing. It is far better for divorced or widowed women with children to arrange among themselves to share sitting chores and to share sitters than to ask their dates to take on this financial responsibility.

Chapter 51

THE ADULT-CHILD RELATIONSHIP

Your Manners with Children

Little children—as well as older ones—should always be treated as the individuals they are. A baby in a carriage rightly and usually loudly resents the passing stranger who, placing her face close to his, pokes or tickles him or makes silly, gurgling sounds meant to denote friendliness. If you want to make friends with a baby, be gentle and quiet. Let the baby make the overtures, if any. Don't force yourself upon him or try to take him from the arms of his mother or nurse. Don't make loud noises around him. Never confuse a young child by telling him it's all right to do or have something that his mother has just said he couldn't do or have, even if you are the hostess.

If you are entertaining a mother with a young child, don't disturb the child's ordinary routine any more than absolutely necessary. Don't insist the child is old enough to come to the dinner table if the mother, very rightly, wishes to feed it earlier and without the confusion of strange faces and the expectation of grown-up manners.

A pleasant, adaptable child at home can be turned into a little nuisance while visiting by too much attention on the part of other people, who, after overtaxing and overentertaining him, are then horrified if he ends the day in tears or a tantrum.

A very young child accompanied by an adult on a visit should not be ignored, of course. In fact, if you ignore him, he will soon show you how much he dislikes being overlooked. But he should be treated with dignity and respect—even if he's a babe in arms. He can't possibly understand your standard of behavior, so don't become irritated at his occasional and necessary interruptions of your conversation with his mother.

It is grossly impolite to speak in a foreign language or use obscure phraseology in front of a child with the purpose of excluding him from the conversation. He is usually quite conscious of what you are doing and will respond by making an issue of the matter immediately. If you speak in a perfectly simple and normal way, even of subjects beyond his comprehension, he is usually satisfied, so long as you take his presence into consideration from time to time by directing your conversation to things at his level. To expect a little child to sit at the dinner table with the only attention paid him of a correctional nature, is to expect entirely too much.

Your Tone of Voice

There is nothing so catching as the sharp manner. Have you noticed that children whose parents speak to them in a petulant, annoyed tone of voice speak to others in the same way? Conversely, if a child, right from the beginning, is spoken to with the same politeness and consideration one would give an adult, even where he is a tiny baby and can understand only the tone, not the words, he is usually a gently spoken child. Waspish mothers make waspish children who grow into waspish parents.

Take time and effort, if possible, before any necessary admonition of a child to control your irritation with irrelevant things or toward other people. The smallest child is quick to resent anger unjustly taken out on him for trivial transgressions. To vent one's irritation on the handiest person, especially on a child who does need correction, is human enough. But, if it happens, your relationship with your child will be better if you can apologize. No child thinks his parents are infallible creatures. Children know that parents are often wrong, sometimes make mistakes. It improves our stature as parents if we can say, even to the youngest child, "Johnny, I'm sorry I was cross, just now. You know how it is when people get too tired. They sometimes get cross without much reason." This isn't spoiling Johnny. This is treating him like a real human being and teaching him that the quickest way to dispel another's anger is to admit you're wrong—sometimes even when you aren't completely convinced that you really are.

Conversation with Children

The only way to teach children how to converse is to start very early indeed to include them in your conversation. If they have only a few words of their own, use those words with them, including them in sentences. If the baby says "Hot!" when he sees the fire, say to him, "Yes, the fire is hot. See, Mother puts wood on the fire so it will burn. You mustn't touch the fire, because it is hot. Fire would hurt you." Shortly, baby gets the idea, and he also adds words to his vocabulary, especially if you never laugh at his attempts to do so or repeat his baby talk in his presence, no matter how enchanting it is. He is trying to talk as you do and to do the things you do. He doesn't want to remain a baby forever. Laugh with him, never at him, and encourage him in every little step toward maturity, so long as he makes it himself.

This maturity is a delicate matter. Grown-ups so often make the mistake of refusing to consider a child's chronological age and the fact that maturity usually comes very unevenly. A big child of six may be able to go to the store but may not be able to sit through the long family dinner without being excused from time to time. A very bright child may well be emotionally younger than his actual age in some things. Take these things into consideration and never expect a child to measure up equally well to all standards accepted for his age group. If he is above his age group in certain of his abilities, do not expect him to be so in all of them, nor in his emotional needs.

A child from whom too much is expected, either emotionally or intellectually, grows to feel unable to do anything well enough to please his parents. In self-defense he sometimes refuses to make more than the barest effort to get by academically or socially. Such a child needs encouragement, never ridicule or increased severity.

Teaching Children to Behave

Most children eventually conform to the behavior standards their parents lay out for them, provided those standards are reasonable and attainable. The best way to understand this is to attend P.T.A. meetings and to talk over your children's behavior with other parents. Too often, if we don't do something like this, we get the fixed notion that only our children act like hellions. Actually, the whole business of growing up is a matter of fitting one's real desires and energies—sometimes painfully—into a socially acceptable pattern. All children must go through it and with some it is harder than others—mostly because of the way their parents go about the necessary saddle-breaking.

In social behavior it is much more comfortable to conform to generally accepted standards than to be in a constant state of rebellion. Children can be made to understand that, and they usually accept the logic of it.

Why We Must Have Rules Family life must have rules—although occasionally they should be relaxed for good cause, just as rules outside the family are sometimes relaxed, within reason. Parents must know that children need and want direction. They don't want wishy-washy parents, sometimes easy and sometimes—and most inconveniently—rigidly strict. A little child will say with pride, "I am not *allowed* to visit after school without permission from my mother." The child who is permitted to do anything he pleases is not secure. He is rudderless and shows it by his behavior.

Bedtime Every pre-school and school child should have a fixed bedtime, for which he should be pleasantly but firmly prepared. Give children plenty of advance warning of bedtime—or mealtime. Children's play is their "work," from which they can't be suddenly separated without warning. They have little sense of time, even after they can tell time. It is better to say, "You have just time to put your blocks away—see, I'll help—before bathtime," than to say, arbitrarily, "In twenty minutes, have these blocks put away and be ready for your bath!"

You may be relieved that the end of the day has come and the children will be soon in bed. But if you show it you are in for trouble—dawdling trouble and "drink-of-water" trouble. Children hate to give up, even when they are dog-tired. They are afraid they'll miss something and that all fun really begins when they are out of the way. So they refuse to get out of the way, using all kinds of legitimate and illegitimate pretexts to keep you with them or to rejoin the adult world.

If bedtime trouble regularly crops up in your household, examine your manner with your children at the end of the day, see if it is polite and un-hurried. Be sure you make them feel you still have adequate time for them —again within reason. Keep in mind the bedtime deadline—and have *them* keep it in mind—but be relaxed about it. When the deadline comes, see that they are in bed and arrange your household affairs so that you do have time to hear prayers, tell a bedtime story, or sing a lullaby. One little boy I know learned to relax at bedtime when his mother and he told little jokes together —had what they called a "laugh" time—just before he went to sleep.

When, occasionally, you can't keep this bedtime date with your children, realize their disappointment, substitute a little treat of some kind to make up for your necessary dereliction.

Are Threats Effective? Never make a threat to a child which you don't intend to or can't keep if infraction does occur. It is cruel and stupid to say, "If you do that, Mother won't love you." Or, "If you get out of that bed once more, Mother will go out and never come back." Quite intelligent parents often resort to such threats in desperation, so increasing the anxiety and unmanageability of their children. Parents' love must be inviolable. They cannot always love the *behavior* of their children, and they have every right to take prompt steps to correct it, but they must never withdraw love itself as a means of punishment. To damage a child's love-security is to open the way to his becoming a neurotic.

It is certainly better to use the pleasure-principle than the punishment-principle when dealing with a child. How much more sensible—and effective —to say to a child who keeps jumping out of bed, "Now settle down, darling, and get your sleep. Tomorrow, if the weather is nice, we'll go on a picnic," than to threaten, "If you don't go to sleep immediately, I won't take you on that picnic tomorrow even if it is a nice day." Did *you* ever try to go to sleep promptly, on order?

Where threats are necessary, express them quietly, if possible. "If you do spend all your allowance today, Esther, remember, you will have to wait until next Saturday before you get any more money. And I know you want to buy a new pencil." Be reasonable and mean what you say.

Interference from Friends or Relatives Don't let friends or other mem-bers of the family undermine your discipline. One parent should not know-ingly countermand the order of another. Many a quick-witted child manages to play one parent against the other very nicely, to the detriment of his own character development. If any change in orders must take place, let the parents be in polite agreement. "Joe, I know you asked Bobby to help you clean the cellar, but you and he didn't know I planned to take him to get his hair cut this afternoon and it is the only chance I'll have all week." Not, "I don't care *what* your father says, you're coming with me to get your hair cut!" Family politeness, alone, should prohibit such conflicts, but unfortunately it often doesn't, to the confusion of the child and the irritation of the parents.

Is It a Child's World?

Some modern parents have the mistaken idea that adults no longer count. Parents, too, actually do have their rights and should assert them. No child should be permitted to make the adults around him miserable or to deprive them of all peace, quiet, and privacy. There are—and should be—limits to all adults' patience with children. A child who has discovered that he can ride roughshod over the adults in his family is far from contented with his tyrannical role. Consideration of others comes slowly to the young and must certainly be regularly imposed within the child's ability to understand. And that understanding can be absorbed very early, indeed, if the handling of the child is relaxed and loving. One of my boys at twenty months learned to "put it back" and "pick it up" with obvious satisfaction in response to gentle requests. And, on his own, he threw his apple cores into a scrap basket instead of on the floor.

Habits are fixed through doing the same thing over and over again. If you pick up after your children—scolding as you do so—and expect them to become neat as a result, you are making a sad mistake. A child must go back and do the routine things over and over before they become habits. He needs to be reminded—patiently and firmly reminded—to do the things expected of him. But don't nag. Use charts, stars, rewards of various kinds, praise when he remembers, pleasant reminders when he forgets. Don't get his back up. You didn't learn to wash your teeth, comb your hair, scrub your nails, tie your shoelaces, and wash your face automatically, merely by being asked to do so once or twice.

We Shoot Too High   If our children were always spotlessly clean, never made any noise, were always pleasant when spoken to, jumped up at every request, and never talked back, there would be something very much the matter with them. They aren't born that way, and it is a very long time before they come to believe there is some virtue in what we ask of them.

Healthy children must get dirty. It is part of the business of playing, and the dirtier they get the better they like it. When a child is afraid to get dirty, to put his hands in mud pies, to yell and run with the other children, he's not normal. Adult standards have been imposed upon him to too great effect and to the detriment of his whole life.

There are times when it is better if a child manages to keep reasonably clean—if he's in his Sunday best, for example—but if he does, by accident of course, walk into puddles or slide down a cellar door the world is not going to collapse.

Children all come to the stage when, because of a growing consciousness of the other sex, they want to wash, to keep their hair combed, and to clean their nails. In fact, they want to do all these and other more startling things to a degree that may even alarm you. They begin to memorize etiquette books and to criticize their parents' appearance, behavior, and belongings to an embarrassing degree. But it's all part of their growing up, which, like everything else connected with them, we shouldn't take in too hard and fast a way.

The Treatment of Servants by Children

Children usually reflect our own attitude toward our employees, but there are imperious children who attempt to "get away with" things with servants which would never be permitted by their parents. Servants rightly resent the high-handed treatment they get from some children and should be given full permission to cope with it firmly, short of physical punishment. The chauffeur should know he may say authoritatively to the son of the house, "Johnny, you may not remove tools from the car's tool chest. If we had a breakdown on the road and the tools weren't available, your father would hold me responsible." The cook should be able to keep her kitchen as inviolate as her usually sensitive nature desires. She can't be expected—unless she is unusually agreeable—to keep an eye on the baby as she prepares dinner. She won't be happy, either, if children pour into her kitchen and congregate there while she's in control, or if they are permitted free access to her supplies. She is responsible for the meals and for the condition of her bailiwick. She must be given full—though reasonable—authority within it.

Children who rebel at parental authority sometimes try to take out their anger on servants. It is too much to expect a calm, poised reaction from a maid or houseworker who has just been kicked or reviled by a small child. Children must be made to understand at the earliest possible age that they may not vent their anger or annoyance on those not in a position to fight back, except perhaps at the cost of their jobs. Parents must prevent such occurrences by working out their children's behavior problems themselves, if necessary with professional help.

Chapter 52

ADOPTING A CHILD

Not so long ago adoptions were not announced, because our attitude toward adoption was concerned less with the child itself than with the possible circumstances of its birth. Not with the wonderful fact that a couple wanted a child so much, but rather with speculation as to why they couldn't or wouldn't have one of their own. The very fact of his adoption was often kept from the child until maturity when, presumably, he could stand the shock of such a disclosure.

Today adoptive parents are needed more than ever. Many thousands of children needing those parents live with foster parents or in institutions. Sometimes couples wait for years for just the kind of child they have in mind, then with a change in their thinking, and loving readjustment of their plans, accept an older child who otherwise might never have an opportunity for adoption. There are advantages to this. Such a child is certainly more of a person than is a tiny baby whose very charm can sometimes cloud judgment. He can be studied from a physical and psychological aspect more definitively than can a very young baby. His need is very great and often very obvious. It can be highly rewarding to adopt such a child.

It is no longer true that children have to be "matched" to their adoptive parents. Thousands of warm intelligent people are actively seeking to adopt children of other racial or cultural groups—children of Negro, French-Canadian, Indian, and Mexican origin and of course oriental children orphaned, or half-orphaned, by war. Often the adoption of one child actually triggers the birth of a child of their own to the adoptive parents. Or the adoption of one child is followed by the adoption of two or three more, not necessarily of the same race or cultural background. The Adoption Resource Exchange of North America (ARENA) helps to find homes for all children with special needs. They are an offshoot of the Child Welfare League of America, Inc., 44 East 23rd Street, New York, N.Y. 10010. Interestingly enough, some of the big families of adopted children who may be quite different racially or culturally from their adoptive parents, may occur in families with much less money than love and concern. There is nothing hush-hush about adoptions now, and children are usually told as early as possible that they were "chosen." As someone said to a friend of mine who had just adopted an infant girl, "I have never seen a more beautiful baby. It is wonderful to be able to *choose* your child, not just wait to see what God will send you." The new mother replied, "Yes, that is true, but you know we feel that God did send her to us nevertheless."

While modern adoptions under proper auspices are proudly proclaimed by new parents, there are still certain discretions necessary on the part of friends of such a family. The parents themselves probably know nothing of the actual parents of their child. For the protection of all, this information is locked in the agency file. Nor does the mother relinquishing her child know, usually, who its new parents will be. She knows, however, that it is being placed in a home where it is wanted, where its financial and emotional security has been assured, as far as possible, by social workers investigating all aspects of the adoption.

For this reason, when a new baby arrives via the adoption route we do not exclaim "What a darling! Where did you get her? Why in the world did her parents ever want to give *her* up?" Of course, the adoptive parents are prepared to deal with such thoughtlessness by either polite evasion or as much frankness as they wish. Sometimes they offer the information that the child came from some well-known adoption center.

Later, when the child grows older, outsiders should never assume that in the parents' opinion the time has yet arrived to tell the child of its adoption. This is a matter for the parents to decide and for them to handle. For this reason discussions with our own small children of another's adoption should not be gone into unnecessarily. Children must accept their contemporaries as children like themselves not as set apart by some circumstances of birth.

There has also been relaxation on the old rule that an adopted child must have two parents. In exceptional circumstances single parents might be encouraged to adopt providing they have some family structure. This parent might be an unmarried man or woman who is able to meet the rigid standards. Even religious background is no longer a determining factor, according to the Child Welfare League of America. The age of adopting couples is no longer a barrier and they need not necessarily be, for example, under thirty-five years of age as was once required.

Adoption Announcement

Well-advised parents do make public from the start the fact of adoption. Usually, because of possible disappointment, they do not announce before the fact that they are seeking to adopt a child, but once the adoption is under way they may send out announcements, either before the child actually comes to their home or after its arrival. Parents who have adopted the child privately rather than through a recognized agency, might be better advised to wait until after the legal adoption before making an announcement. Individual notes may be sent to close friends and relatives, of course, or engraved cards, if they wish to send them, may read in a variety of ways.

A plain card engraved in black could read:

> Mr. and Mrs. Robert Shore Lewis
> announce that
> Miss Betsy Anne Lawson
> has been adopted as their daughter
> and will hereafter be known as
> Miss Betsy Anne Lewis

This form indicates the child, not an infant, may be an orphaned relative or one whose parenthood is publicly known and whose name-change by means of the adoption needs to be announced. The same form may be used for an infant baby girl with the omission of the "Miss." Another might read:

> Dr. and Mrs. Arthur George Adamson
> take pleasure in announcing that
> Bruce McKay Adamson
> age 2
> has been adopted as their son.

> Eighteen Fox Lane
> Red Hook
> New York   zip code
> (address optional)

The birth date, of course, is always the actual one of the child, not the date on which he was adopted.

Or:

> Mr. and Mrs. James Stern Harris
> have the pleasure of announcing the adoption of
> Donna Phillipe Harris
> age 3 months

Some adoptive parents use the word "arrived" rather than "adopted" along with the date of birth and the date of placement (but see below). Some design their own unique and personal announcements. Still others use the appropriate announcements put out by greeting card companies. Although an adopted child should celebrate his actual birth date, this date should not be publicized at the time of adoption in any way unless of course there is no real reason to conceal it for example if an uncle adopts his niece or nephew after some family tragedy. But under ordinary circumstances the use of the correct birth date in announcements which will reach the general public is not discreet. Natural parents who placed infants for adoption born that same day might believe that this is their own child. Others who know of such cases may erroneously believe that they know the origin of the child in the announcement, too. In other words, the date in itself publicly announced could possibly start a chain of rumors and unfortunate phone calls or notes affecting the adoptive parents and the child. For this reason it is proper to give the age of the child rather than the correct birth date in adoption announcements of any kind.

The Double Birthday

The adopted child knows soon enough that he is different, because adoption really is different from natural birth in a family. Although the adoptive parents are thrilled about the adoption and wish to celebrate or acknowledge the day the adoption took place, for the child it is a continuous reminder to the public that he *is* different. Therefore, it is probably not wise to celebrate two birthdays, the original one and the date of the adoption. Also, adoption experts tell me, celebration of the original date is to the child psychologically the real acceptance of his natural parents by his adoptive parents and therefore the real acceptance of the child himself. This is the reasoning of the Spence-Chapin Adoption Service in New York, one of the most prestigious services of the kind in the country.

Newspaper Announcement

There is no reason why announcement of the adoption should not be in local newspapers. This may be done in this way. "Mr. and Mrs. James Stern Harris announce the adoption of an infant daughter, Donna Phillipe, age three months." Such a release might be printed in suburban and country newspapers but are better not sent to large city dailies which evidently do not run adoption notices of this kind.

Gifts for Adopted Children

Adopted children receive gifts upon adoption no matter what their age. Babies receive all the usual baby gifts, which may be addressed to them personally or to their adoptive mothers for them. Older children receive gifts in their own new names, if they have been given them. In the latter case gifts may be bonds, savings accounts, clothing, toys—all the things one would give a child on a birthday or festive occasions. Showers are also given for babies who have just been adopted. It is wise for friends to wait until the actual adoption has gone through before giving any gifts of lasting and important value. However, where there is a probation period, showers are also given for babies to be adopted. These are the usual layette needs, but here as in the case of baby showers for other babies, the mother should be consulted as to whether or not she wishes to have a shower for the child and, if so, what her needs are for it.

Chapter 53

TRAVELING WITH CHILDREN

If your children are very young, don't travel with them at all if you can possibly help it. Or, if travel is necessary, try to keep to the usual meal and rest schedule and watch for signs of overstimulation and fatigue. Travel, even with older children, is likely to be tiring for all concerned. What seems like ornery behavior in the small travelers is probably exhaustion. But whatever causes it, it is hard to endure. Hard for the parents, but even harder for those with whom the whole irritated group may come in contact.

I have seen roadside restaurants thrown into an uproar because of small, car-weary youngsters whose parents could not keep them under control any longer. The inevitable spanking, of course, effected nothing but the mollification of the proprietor.

If travel with young children is absolutely unavoidable, travel if you can by car rather than in a public vehicle. If some public transportation system must be used, spend extra, if at all possible, to insure maximum privacy and comfort—a compartment or a roomette on a train, a cabin to yourselves in a boat, or, whenever feasible, plane transportation. Babies take well to the air, and the mother has the expert assistance of stewards and stewardesses during the flight. Air travel shortens the journey. Flight seems to act as a soporific to little children and interests the older ones to such a degree that their behavior is usually exemplary during the trip.

Start Early

Never, if it is humanly possible, start a trip with children in the middle of the afternoon or at the end of their day. Even for grown-ups, traveling early and quitting early makes for less fatigue. In traveling by car or by bus don't push on at nightfall to get to an objective the same night, if it is possible to find a resting place at the usual time for bedding-down the children. The extra expense will be amply repaid next morning when you all start out early again, refreshed and cheerful.

Travel Sickness

Keep the traveling children on ultra-simple meals, away from candy and soda pop. Travel in as relaxed a manner as possible, taking time for orderly departures. Tenseness and hurry on the part of parents are communicated to children, who often react with travel sickness. But some children, under the best of circumstances, throw up even during the course of simple travel. Small, leisurely meals and a minimum of liquids, with rest afterwards, may help.

The airplane technique of having a waterproof paper bag or other disposable paper container handy in the event of air sickness works well when parents are traveling with children. Often the knowledge that something of the kind is instantly available and there need be no hurried flight to window or lavatory, steadies a child. Needless to say, warning a child not to be sick or scolding him afterwards is useless and unkind.

Supplies

In traveling with children do not overburden yourself with clothes, toys, special foods, a medicine cabinet, fancy equipment. If you have a baby's bottle to consider, you can buy a bottle warmer that is attached to the lighter socket of your car or you can take along an electric bottle warmer that plugs into any light socket. Actually, bottles can be left behind and with them the washing and sterilizing problem. There are plastic, disposable bottles, a little more expensive it is true, but worth the difference in convenience. There are also disposable diapers in every drugstore en route, but you should carry with you the lightest-weight cotton ones, with powder for washing them if you need to use them. They dry in an hour or so—but not, please, over your hostess's guest room chair back.

A playpen can double as a crib even for a child as old as three or four, if you are going some place where a crib may not be available. In most inns and hotels cribs are obtainable, but in some of the smaller places there is one crib per floor, or even one per hostelry, so it is well to be prepared for such emergencies. Often a twin bed can be pushed against a wall and so protected with chairs that it serves as a crib. But when in doubt, it is safer to bed a child on a pile of blankets on the floor than to put him in some precarious makeshift.

Travel Clothes

Travel clothes for children should be of the simplest materials—cotton, denim, miracle fibers in the summer. If you are traveling by car, let the soiled clothes accumulate for a day or two, then stop off at a self-service laundry, wash the clothes, have them put through a drier, or hang them to dry on wooden hangers or a portable clothes line in the car as you go on your way. In winter, knit clothes for the little ones, with nylon or other water-*resistant* (not waterproof) underpants for protection, stand up best and are healthful for most babies. Nylon or other miracle fabric underthings, including nighties and pajamas, are a good investment, for they dry instanter and cut down on packables.

Each child should be allowed one favorite toy of reasonable size, one book. Inexpensive toys and books can be added en route, as boredom threatens, and discarded as they become burdensome.

Descending on Friends

It is difficult for any parent to believe his children are not as attractive to others as they are to himself. The grim truth is that others, even relatives, are usually unwilling to accept the inevitable little lapses with good will. Besides, even people who really love children often don't wish to be bothered with other people's, especially without notice.

Never, if you would be considerate, visit even a close friend with your child or children without asking if it will be convenient. This rule should hold even for an hour's visit and even when there are other children in the household with whom your own are friends. Your friend's children may have plans of their own and resent being saddled with another child even briefly. Or they may have just been put to nap only to shoot out of bed again at the excuse of a visitor's presence, to the ill-concealed irritation of the mother.

Never, of course, arrive with your brood unasked and unannounced for an overnight stay with anyone, even relatives. Always remember that all visitors make work and inconvenience for a household, children most of all.

Chapter 54

THE TEEN-AGER AND YOUNG ADULT

Today's teen-ager is a young adult, more mature and responsible, sociologists tell us, than many generations of previous teen-agers. He is nevertheless beset with customary trials and tribulations natural to his age group—disconcerting periods of indecision, self-doubt, other periods of self-sufficiency and superiority. His character and personality are not set but are in the process of being molded. It is a stage where he is not quite on his own, not altogether sure he wants to be on his own, yet resentful of too much parental pressure and old-fogyness. Much of this attitude and feeling will change as he learns how to live with the world, especially with his parents, siblings, and teachers.

Teen-agers are frequently criticized as discourteous, but in my reading of old etiquette books—and my collection goes very far back—I find the same criticism in every generation. I myself don't subscribe to it. There are rude teen-agers but there are many (a majority, I would say) who make a serious attempt at least to be acceptably considerate of other people, including other teen-agers.

Strictness, in itself, is not the perfect answer to the teen-ager's social problems. Any smart teen-ager can circumvent on overly strict parent who thinks in terms of the discipline he or she received as a child, rather than of the effectiveness of it. Along with the firm rules about home-coming and frequent reporting of activities must go an understanding heart and a real friendliness with the teen-ager. It's a wonderful, creative, often troubling time.

Most adults, thinking back, would never wish to go through it again!

Courtesy Begins at Home

Everyone is more or less under compulsion in the outside world to follow certain accepted social rules, whether it be in school or business. It is human, and especially so to the pubescent, to let down a little at home. Parents who are relatively lenient about small courtesies, who don't crack down at every small infraction within the household, often find that they get reports from the community that their teen-agers are indeed courteous away from home. On the other hand, each household needs to have a code of basic courtesies that the adults will practice toward the children and the children should practice toward each other and toward their parents. Parents are wise to overlook seemingly disrespectful outbursts from time to time. The teen-ager who, in a fit of anger, screams at his mother or father "I hate you" may really be reflecting serious doubt as to whether at that moment he is himself loved. As with little children, we need to make it clear that it is certain behavior we dislike or even hate, but that these feelings in no way disturb the essential loving relationship between parent and child. The parent must get across the idea that "I love you always but sometimes I do not love your behavior."

Manners

Teen-agers often feel that they are inhabiting a world of their own in which they can make their own rules. Parents who can break through this fallacy in a gentle fashion can make their teen sons and daughters realize the essential discourtesy to other people, who also have rights, when teen-agers are noisy in public, monopolize the phone, the family car, or any other convenience or possession meant for general sharing.

I have never known a teen-ager who did not need to be reminded about many of the things that careful adults take for granted, such as the need to answer all invitations promptly, to acknowledge gifts graciously and quickly, to show respect and courtesy toward adults, to be protective and kindly toward the younger and weaker.

Teen-agers rightly complain that parents nag. Nagging is irritating and virtually useless at any age, but particularly ineffective between parents and teens. Similarly, accusations call for automatic denial. It is far better, first to get a teen-ager's full attention, to tell him once, and then perhaps to leave written reminders of what you want him to do than to nag, however well-meaning you may be. It is more effective to tell a teen-ager that you know he has done something of which you disapprove than to ask him if he has done so. It is good psychology to teach children that they avert your irritation if they freely confess their misdeeds. After all, what can you do when a courteous, repentant teen-ager says, "I did it and I am sorry." The Biblical injunction to agree with an adversary quickly is very sound and if it were more generally followed, especially between parents and teens, it would avoid a great deal of dissension.

Teens on the Telephone

Ask any parent. One of the worst annoyances teens inflict on their families is telephonitis. Many parents keep their blood pressures down by having separate phones for their teen-agers with the telephone number listed under the children's names, sometimes below that of their parents' under Children's Phone. This is perhaps the best solution if a family can afford it, for it can prevent many annoyances.

Teen with His Own Phone A teen with his own phone ideally pays for it out of his earnings or out of his allowance. If this isn't feasible or possible, he is told how many calls he is allowed if the service is limited, and is required to keep within them. He should be asked to tell his friends not to phone after the family's bedtime or before they get up in the morning. Perhaps there will be other times during the day or the week when parents prefer not to hear that phone ringing and should make the necessary requests of their teen-ager and his friends. Even a teen-ager with his own phone will certainly need supervision on its use if that use interferes with necessary study time or the performance of chores. It must be made clear that long-distance calls must not be made without permission unless he plans to pay for them himself, that the phone is not available to his friends without permission. His friends must be made to understand that all calls to the teen-ager must come in on that phone. When he doesn't answer it, his parents will not. They must not be called on their phone to take messages for the absent one. The penalty for the ignoring of these rules should be, of course, the loss of the phone.

The Teen on the Family Phone Teens have great need to communicate with one another, even when they have just left each other a few minutes previously. This is a phenomenon many parents don't understand, but should try to. A teen-ager who wants *privacy* when he is on the telephone has a right to it. He may be doing nothing more than going over a homework assignment with another boy or girl, but he doesn't want his parents picking up the phone and demanding the use of it or, heaven forbid, listening in. The teen-ager who is reduced to using the one family phone, therefore, needs to have a good working arrangement with his parents as to the hours he may use that phone virtually without interruption from them. If it is a one-car family and father has to be picked up at the train, certainly it should be made very clear to teens and their friends that no calls may go in or out at the time when father is expected to phone.

A little family consultation will make it clear to teen-agers that a phone constantly tied up can cause great problems for adults trying to reach the house. It may well be agreed that at certain times of the day no one is to hang unnecessarily on the phone when there is but one line into the house. Of course if it is a party line, all use of the phone should be carefully restricted.

A parent finding it necessary to interrupt a teen-ager on the phone should do it with courtesy just as he would expect the same courtesy from his child. A great many flare-ups over the use of this essential instrument would be avoided if everyone could remember that simple rule.

Good Grooming

It is a good idea for parents to make quiet note of some areas of deficiency, and then at the appropriate, receptive moment to suggest gently where improvement might be beneficial.

Teen-agers, like the adults around them, are often in such a hurry that they bypass the very things that they have been taught at home. Schools, overcrowded and under pressure to propel their students toward the important goal of college, find little or no time to instruct in the graces, turning this obligation back to the parents. For example, there is an appalling lack of cleanliness, neatness, and attention to such details as well-shined shoes. Grubby hands have long been the prerogative of the schoolboy, but today the schoolgirl gives an amazing disregard for feminine meticulousness in dress and grooming and at school, at least, no one says her nay. Untended hands may well improve upon the gift of a complete manicure kit or permission for regular professional manicures. Here, the mother in particular, without nagging, can help a daughter toward the achievement of order and physical presentability. There may be tears in the face of abrupt unsympathetic interdictions against hair that is too rarely shampooed, almost never brushed, but some guidance should be given concerning the advisability of shining, healthy hair and in some cases simple hairdressing appropriate to school years. Colloquies or agreements with other mothers may put a stop to the wearing of damaging footwear and clothing fads that defy good taste and good sense. No teen-ager wants to be too different from his or her peers and for parents to insist on strict nonconformity is unwise. There is a medium ground here that can be achieved with understanding and patience on both sides.

Make-up Most adolescent girls are unimpressed with their mothers' logical reasons as to why heavy make-up is inadvisable for them. They are even unimpressed with the quite obvious argument that, if at twelve they get themselves up to look twenty, when they *are* twenty no one will believe it. Usually the group is a fairly good criterion, in this case, of what represents the compromises of most of the mothers. Presently both mothers and young daughters seem to agree that the natural look is the one to strive for. A twelve-year-old might feel a little more confident at a party with a touch of natural lipstick or at the very least a lip softener, a touch of powder and her own (but never overwhelming) perfume, but only if *she* wants them. Mothers should resist any pressure to speed the growing-up process. At about fourteen sometimes it is wise to see that a girl gets some professional advice on the discreet application of suitable make-up, perhaps a very little eyeliner for special occasions, never put directly on the inner lid, however. Eye shadow should wait until a later date when a good natural-tone lipstick can be an everyday matter along with special teen products that will cover, and at the same time help along, troublesome complexions. Cleanliness is essential and powder if applied at all should be put on with a clean puff or fresh cotton. Such young skin has no need for powder base or rouge. Rouge, even artfully applied, can make the most charming young girl look déclassée. Lightly applied mascara for parties and special occasions are acceptable now. False eyelashes and more sophisticated make-up should wait for much later. I shall never forget the incongruity of the heavy false eyelashes I once saw on a girl with her teeth in braces.

For a young girl there should be no need of nail polish. Nails that are nicely shaped, cuticles that are soft and carefully pressed down after each bath, fingers free of hangnails, hands that are unchapped, make a better picture than young hands with bright nail polish. Buffing is better than even pale nail polish which tends to break the nails on many people. Young girls are often impatient with polish, too. Chipped or peeling nail polish is no more attractive on teen-agers than on their mothers.

Teen Dates

When does dating begin? Earlier and earlier, it seems. It is often difficult these days to distinguish a twelve-year-old girl from her seventeen-year-old sister if a misguided or overpressured mother permits the little one to dress and wear make-up as her sister does. Physically, each generation's girls are bigger, and this physical bigness often deceives parents into believing that emotional development necessarily follows size.

Boy-and-girl dating may begin at about fourteen on a limited basis—early movies, dates at home of course, various sports, days at the beach, bicycle trips that bring the two home before dark, etc. Steady dating should be firmly discouraged throughout the early teens, because tastes are formed through a variety of contacts.

Every mother of a popular young daughter knows that there are periods when one boy seems to be more in evidence than others. When this becomes quite obvious the family often undertakes to reduce him in status in various ways. Such passing attachments always do seem more of a menace than they usually are and should be accepted with a certain amount of humor untinged with ridicule. Puppy love is serious to the lovers, if a little ludicrous to parents, brothers, and sisters, but it should be respected, for it has its painful aspects. Very few daughters really wish to settle their affections for life on a teen-age boy when it comes right down to it, though the fantasy of undying devotion is very evident for a time.

How Does a Boy Ask for a Date? At what age a boy dates depends very much on the boy himself. And again physical size bears no relation to emotional readiness. Anywhere from fourteen on a boy may be ready to leave the teasing group of boys and go on his first date. His family should be well prepared for the metamorphosis that will occur.

The first sign, of course, is cleanliness. He will suddenly begin bathing without reminders, lengthily combing his hair before setting out for school instead of merely running the comb—or more likely, his fingers—through it. Suddenly his shoes may seem to take on a polish, and he will stop biting his fingernails. He will require two or three times his usual number of clean shirts, and he may even take an unusual interest in ties, socks, and handkerchiefs, hitherto items of no interest at all. He will also begin to agitate about his inadequate allowance and start wondering out loud how he can augment it by a little manual labor. He constantly asks if anyone notices how deep his voice is getting. Of course, none of these things may happen—but if they do, you are lucky parents.

It is usually Mother who sees the signs first. She knows instinctively that her son is about to take his first steps away from her apron strings. Most of what she can do for him she has already done. Soon he will probably turn more and more to his father for counsel, or to some father substitute.

Boys usually don't need advice on how to ask a girl for a date. They bungle through somehow in the early years of dating, eventually acquiring a certain polished technique only experience can bring. Parents can help by showing that they expect their children to date whenever they are ready. They should never force the issue or make the choices for the children.

Boys usually begin by going to games and school dances stag. They yearn from the sidelines, while pretending a vast disinterest in the equally cohesive girls. After a certain amount of this mothers often suggest, "Joe, why don't you take Mary to the game this afternoon?" This is usually met with a derisive snort, but soon, sure enough, Mary and Joe are eating popcorn together in the bleachers. As a result of the motherly approval he needed, Joe has probably blurted, "You want to go to the game tomorrow, Mary?" And Mary has said "Sure." From then on making dates is easy enough.

Embarrassing Moments I remember my mother telling me that on her first date she went all day long wthout going to the toilet because she was embarrassed to ask her date to be excused. He undoubtedly was in the same agony. Boys and girls today are much more natural about these things, and it's a good thing. Still I notice a boy may say very self-consciously, "Will you excuse me while I wash my hands?" He then usually looks at them very pointedly. All that a boy or a girl either needs to say at such a time is, "Will you please excuse me for a few minutes." Everybody knows where he is going, and why not? When a girl leaves the table on such an errand the boy rises. He rises again when she returns to the table. It is interesting that in Latin American countries, he may actually be expected to take her to the door of the ladies' room and wait until she comes out to keep her from possible molestation.

Running short of money can be another possible source of embarrassment but really shouldn't be either. Everybody miscalculates from time to time. A girl should always have some money with her on a date if only "mad money." If a boy finds he doesn't have quite enough money say for a taxi tip, he can always say to the girl, "Can you lend me a quarter? I don't have enough change." Then he should be careful to return the loan when he next sees her. If a girl finds herself without a dime and she is heading for a pay toilet, she should not be embarrassed to ask the boy to let her have one. He will know what she wants it for and in this case he doesn't expect it to be returned. But it is really wiser for her to carry her own dimes.

What if you arrive at a party in exactly the wrong clothes? Don't let it spoil the evening—or the day. If you hold your head up and are obviously having a good time, people may even think that they are wrong and you are right and starting a new style. If you do make any comment about it, make it once and let it go. This kind of thing happens to everybody, too. What if you have forgotten to respond to an invitation promptly, or worse still, forgotten the date? The best way is to admit your error and apologize quickly—and briefly. Sometimes you can't really make amends for these things, which can be great slights, but at least you have done the best you can do. You can promise yourself to be more considerate of others in the future.

In fact one of the greatest protections for anybody is to be able to say, "I did it. I was wrong. I am sorry." Hardly anyone can continue berating you once you have made this statement.

Dates and Money Dating, for boys, does bring with it increased financial responsibilities. While a certain amount of Dutch treating goes on, especially in group entertainment, a boy usually does pay for the entertainment of his special date. If his allowance is not adequate for his participation in the social activities of his high school group and if his parents cannot comfortably increase it, then after-school jobs must provide the difference. And boys should learn early to be unembarrassedly frank with girls about what entertainment they can afford to offer. Pretending to have more money than one actually has is an acutely uncomfortable business, and usually no one is deceived by the pretension.

A boy might say, "Jane, I can take you either to dinner or the movies. Which shall it be?" Jane will probably answer, "I'll ask mother if I may ask you here to dinner. Then we can go to the movies afterward." And, of course, it's perfectly proper for parents to furnish theater, concert, or opera tickets and permit their daughters to ask boys to escort them or for a father or mother to go along occasionally, say to the circus or to a country fair and to pay for everything for both young people.

A realistic attitude toward money is important to teen-agers. It should never be a dominant factor in their relationships. If a girl comes from a moneyed family she adjusts her tastes in entertainment to the young men with whom she goes out and does not selfishly expect them to impoverish themselves in order to be with her. The boy who must make the best of the spending money available to him is likely to turn out much better than the boy with limitless funds who is permitted to run to his parents for all kinds of extras as well.

To help older children and teen-agers manage money and handle it skillfully, some practice is necessary. By permitting them to go out to lunch occasionally, handle the check and figure out the tip, you will help them gain experience in money matters and a sense of responsibility and independence. Too, the teen-ager learns from direct experience more of the social facts of life, that even as a teen-ager he is expected to tip on an adult level. He finds that 15 per cent of the bill is usual except in self-service places. In luxury restaurants if he finds himself the host, he will find that 20 per cent is more in line.

Car Date A boy who has the privilege of the family car for dates, sees to it that it is clean when it goes out of the garage and clean before his parents drive it again—this means inside and out. The car returned with the ash trays full and litter on the floor, the gas tank empty and the oil low, can cause family arguments, to say the least. A car is a lethal weapon and no one getting behind the wheel should forget that for a moment. A teen driver, like an adult one, should check tires for air and for wear and be sure that the car is in proper running condition before taking the responsibility of driving others.

When the boy is driving the girl sits in the front seat with him but not with her head on his shoulder or virtually in his lap. If she is another boy's date and they are riding in the car, she sits in the back with her date. In a car that holds three in the front, only three should sit there. A car should carry only the number of passengers it is meant to carry, in other words, no sitting on laps which can obscure rear vision and thus cause accidents, or possibly call down a police reprimand or worse. No teen-ager should drive when he's been drinking or smoking marijuana. This is not only his responsibility, but the responsibility of his passengers. It is not "chicken" to say that you will not drive with someone who is under the influence of drugs or alcohol—it may be life insurance.

Sometimes it is the girl who has the use of a car—her own or her family's—and her date does not. If her date is a licensed driver and known to be a good one, she may with her parents' permission, say to her date, "Would you like to drive?" If he accepts, it is then incumbent upon him to drive with the greatest care. This means keeping both hands on the wheel at all times and not smoking when driving. Many an accident has been caused by a driver who has had one hand outside the car or his right arm around his girl. In the name of safety and good taste, other passengers in the car avoid rowdy behavior or anything else that might distract the driver from his responsibility.

A boy calling for his date in a car, parks the vehicle if possible and goes to her door to pick her up. If, because of traffic, he knows that he will not be able to go in and parking is difficult or impossible, he phones ahead to tell the girl to watch out for his arrival—he does not honk except perhaps once to let her know he is there. If he cannot leave the car, he at least leans over and opens the car door from the inside. In returning her home, it is increasingly important that the escort see his date safely inside, even if it means parking the car some distance away. Both must be constantly alert to the possibility of danger.

Parents and Dates The girl's parents should meet, if possible, any boy who is going to take their daughter on an evening date. This does not forecast an inquisition. It means that when the boy calls, he should meet the girl's parents or some responsible adult in the family. He should be able to exchange a few graceful words with them, and they in turn should realize that such moments can be acutely embarrassing for the boy. Conversation should be light and casual and not admonitory. Few daughters are so desperate for dates that they accept them injudiciously. And after all, the boy has been willing to show his face at the door.

The Matter of the Key Possession of the house key is a grave responsibility, for a boy or a girl. The family's safety rests upon its being carefully guarded. Upon returning from a date (and not before), a girl, if she has her own latchkey, hands it to the boy so that he may open the door for her and step ahead to be sure that it is safe for her to enter. It is important for him to be particularly alert in apartment house lobbies if there is no doorman in attendance, and tenants enter with keys, not to let his date go upstairs alone in an elevator at night. He should see her to her apartment door, using the same care as he did entering the building. A man always goes first into a darkened room and lights a light if none has been left on.

Does She Ask Him In? Whether a boy is invited in after a date depends on the hour and a girl's understanding with her parents in the matter, and whether or not someone is home. After midnight she should say good night at the door, adding, "I'm sorry I can't ask you in." She should say something of the kind at any hour if no one is at home.

Refusing a Date It is always a woman's prerogative to refuse an invitation from a man. Suppose there is a country club dance. Mary, like every other girl in her group, is dying to go and waiting impatiently for the telephone to ring. The wrong boy calls up. Must she accept, or, having refused, not go to the dance at all if she later receives the invitation she is waiting for? No, she leaves the way open. She says, "Thank you very much,

John, but I'm not quite sure I'll be free that evening. I hope you'll ask me again sometime." Then if she is invited by the boy she hopes will ask her, she may attend without offending the first boy. Or, if she is not invited by someone else, it is possible the first boy will try again a day or so before the party. She should remember it is never necessary for a lady to make detailed explanations as to why she cannot accept an invitation.

Going Steady

I am against going steady until young men and women reach at least near-maturity, and marriage is somewhat in view. I know that in some areas in this country boys and girls begin to go steady at twelve years and in some cases even younger. The prevalence of this custom is frightening educators and sociologists. The pressures in our society that cause young people to go steady at younger and younger years are decried on all sides. The record of teen-age early marriage as a result of this practice is bad. Increasingly, young people are not to go steady at least in their teen years. These years should be free to develop personality and to experiment with different friends and different social situations. Through this they grow in social experience. They learn to make comparisons. They suffer disappointments in people and learn to look for those qualities that are meaningful to them and their own personalities.

The kind of "going steady" that wears itself out in a week or so is not what I am discussing. That kind of crush has been going on for generations and is just adolescent social experimentation, all to the good. The kind of going steady that troubles mature minds is the kind that apes the intimacy and closeness of formal engagements in its exclusiveness of other social contacts. Supposedly this comes about in large grade schools, high schools, and of course later in the colleges from an anxious need on the part of young people for some kind of emotional security and identification with some one person of the opposite sex. It may result from a fear of being alone, of having to wait for invitations on dates, of having to seek out dates, and make the necessary adjustments.

It takes courage to date freely in these important formative years. Sometimes it requires parental pressure to do so and too many parents are being lulled by young sons and daughters who report that this steady dating is what everybody else does. All of those "everybody elses" are building what is sadly called in this country "a pattern of repetitive marriage." I know one despairing parent whose daughter married at the age of seventeen a boy she had been dating exclusively since she was fourteen. The mother said, "Well, it is after all only her *first* marriage." Two young people literally glued together by the pressures of this modern custom are, through unrelieved intimacy, under constant sexual tension. The result is frighteningly predictable to thoughtful observers.

According to the Population Reference Bureau in Washington, annulment and divorce rates are highest and the probability of second and third marriages is greatest among women married for the first time at age nineteen or younger. Among most teen-age marriages not ending in divorce, a greater proportion are rated as unhappy and regrets about marrying are more frequent, according to another study reported in *PTA Magazine*.

Gift Giving

Teen-agers who are going steady, or who date one person frequently, often wish to give each other gifts for birthdays or Christmas. These gifts should be kept impersonal and inexpensive. Records and books are generally safe gifts to give either boys or girls. Boys may give girls jewelry if it is costume jewelry or *inexpensive* real jewelry, perhaps a little pin or bracelet of cultured pearls. Gifts of clothing are not in good taste unless a girl has perhaps knitted a scarf or made some ski mittens herself.

Subscription Dances, School Dances, and Proms

At subscription dances or dances given by a girl's school the girls pay for their escorts' tickets and their own. They may freely ask any boy or boys of their choice to attend with them. The boys furnish transportation and any entertainment, such as midnight scrambled eggs and coffee, on the way home.

At a boy's school the boys, of course, supply the tickets as well as brief transportation to and from the dance, but only occasionally pay for any major transportation for their dates. This is better paid for if possible by the girl herself or her parents.

Often dance programs are used at such affairs, with host or hostess making out the program in advance with dancing partners for his or her guest. The first dance and the last, at least, are reserved for the boy or girl who has issued the invitation. The floor committee sees to it, in non-card dances, that all girls are kept dancing. A boy asks for a dance by saying, "May I have this dance?" Boys on the stag line may cut in without introduction, but once a girl has been cut in upon she should not permit another partner to interrupt the dance. A boy, of course, always thanks the girl for the dance and the girl indicates she has enjoyed it, too, even if her toes have been trampled upon.

Few girls wear corsages these days, but in some communities they still expect them at these dances. Rather than a corsage, a wristlet or a light hair arrangement might be much more welcome as neither is so readily crushed in dancing. A corsage, if worn, should be worn stems down. The girl should pin it on herself. In some areas it is customary for the girls to give the boys their boutonnieres but usually the boutonniere for the boy is included in the flowers for the girl—sometimes as a gift from the florist. The girl inserts it in her escort's buttonhole if he has one, or pins it on his lapel. Local custom should prevail in these things.

Adult Supervision

The chaperone is not quite as dead as the dodo, but she is a very pale reflection of her former authoritative self. At the teen level she still exists, if only as reassuring background, often with her husband and another couple or couples. No school or country club is likely to turn over quarters for a teen dance or party without at the same time furnishing some restraining presence. Parents who permit their teen-agers to have mixed parties without an adult somewhere in the background are asking for and likely to get trouble.

One city at least broadcasts nightly on radio, the reminder to parents, "Do you know where your children are tonight?" as the hours grow late. Teen-agers may give lip-service to the idea of complete freedom, but at the same time it frightens them, especially the girls. Reasonable requirements and regulations are reassuring and show them that their parents do care about what happens. Teen-agers of both sexes need protection against themselves and against vicious gossip. There is still a necessity to "avoid the appearance of evil" and for this reason the protective parent or parent surrogate, whether or not this person is called a chaperone, is at times still necessary.

When we insist on this kind of protection for our children, it is to guard them from possible physical harm in the streets at night, from possible foolishness or from involving themselves in situations from which they are not mature enough to extract themselves.

Just how much adult supervision is necessary for a teen-ager depends on the community and the customs of the child's group. This does not mean that if some parents are dangerously careless, all parents should follow along in their footsteps. But a golden mean can be achieved. Too much protection where other children have relative freedom can set a child off too much from her group.

It is enough for children, once they are beyond babyhood, to be escorted to children's parties and fetched afterward. If mother or nurse does stay she remains very much in the background. The official chaperone in this case is the mother of the child who is giving the party, and her presence is, of course, imperative at all times at very youthful parties. She must be in the immediate background at young teen ones, as well. No child should be permitted to attend a party where no adults are somewhere present, preferably to receive guests with the young host or hostess, be in the background, then see them safely away.

In most communities, and especially in large cities where many children must necessarily achieve independence early, boys and girls in their early teens are allowed to go unaccompanied to lunch, the movies, and theater matinees. Their places of entertainment and their choice of shows should be approved by their parents. They should not be permitted to go to the so-called "bistros," restaurants that are essentially night clubs, to wrestling or boxing exhibitions, to offensive reviews. Later, in the late teens, they may go occasionally to a night club, preferably with their parents, but if they are alone, their behavior should be extra-circumspect.

Can the Group Chaperone Itself?   Many parents feel safe in permitting their teen-age children to go places at night with a group of other boys and girls. This is fallacious reasoning, for the group, once out of sight of parents, may break up into twosomes immediately, with the rules of behavior determined by the boldest. This independent course should be permitted only if the group is going to a specific, approved place and will return at an exact, agreed-upon time. Its whereabouts should be known by the parents at all times, and no unaccountable junketing around the countryside in some boy's car should be allowed. Remember, adolescents want rules and need them. They do not respect the too "easy" parent, or the one who is in bed and asleep when they arrive home.

Sweet Sixteen Parties

The sixteenth birthday is a magic milestone for teens, particularly girls. Sweet Sixteen parties are often large, sometimes quite elaborate and always mixed. Sometimes they are in restaurants or clubs, sometimes almost debutlike in their presentation. I like best Sweet Sixteen parties that are given at home. Here is a formal invitation to a Sweet Sixteen tea. It is engraved on a white or cream card, $6 \times 4\frac{1}{2}$, but I know one girl who wanted pale pink and got it. The following invitation indicates that a Sweet Sixteen party need not be given by the parents at all.

Miss Eleanor Jane Reilly

At Home

in honour of her niece

Miss Margaret Jane Reilly

Tuesday, the twenty-sixth of December

from four until six o'clock

1280 Park Avenue

New York, N.Y. zip code

R.S.V.P.

Invitations for the Sweet Sixteen party, however, are usually issued by fill-in informal invitations which require an R.s.v.p. In sending the invitations to girls whose dates you do not know, add, "Please bring an escort," to the invitation. If you know the boys who are to be the dates, send them separate invitations. Replies should be made as quickly as possible after the receipt of the invitation and follow its form. Simplest on informal invitations is to give the telephone number, which indicates to the guests that they may phone regrets or acceptances. It is usual for the honorée to receive birthday gifts, a little more elaborate perhaps on this important birthday than they would be on others until the twenty-first.

The girl having the Sweet Sixteen party sometimes wears a corsage made of candy. These can be bought from a florist or made at home.

Teen Car Manners

A boy picking up a date when his parents are driving goes to the girl's door, steps in and greets her parents, then escorts the girl to the car. If necessary he introduces her to his parents by saying, "Mother and Dad, this is Bernice" (they, of course, know her last name). He holds the car door open for her and sees that she is seated. On bringing her home, he gets out first, offers his hand palm upward so she can balance herself if she needs to as she leaves the car. He takes her to her door and thanks her for the evening, saying good night to her parents if they are still up. No matter how he really feels, he does express a desire to see her soon again. If the evening has been a catastrophe, he needn't be specific and the girl should not try to pin him down either. He is also careful to thank his parents.

If the boy is doing the driving, he should if possible go to the girl's door to pick her up. If he knows that parking will be impossible, he phones ahead and tells her exactly when he will be outside, that he will not be able to leave the car. She should not keep him waiting. As she approaches the car, he should lean over and open the door for her. If necessary, she may assist him in closing it but wherever possible she should let him perform the traditional masculine courtesies. When they get where they are going, if the boy is able to park, he should exit first, walk around to open the door for the girl and assist her out by offering his hand, not by taking her elbow. (This is done only when he is helping her *up* into a vehicle or guiding her across a street but never otherwise.) The date manners are not necessarily followed during the day in casual driving around town. The girls often exit and enter cars without waiting for special courtesies.

A young man driver must take very seriously his responsibility for his passenger or passengers. He does not permit them to goad him into driving indiscretions of any kind such as drag racing. He must not crowd the car beyond the legal limit or drive while under the influence of liquor or drugs. He may not permit an unlicensed driver to take the wheel. Romantic as it is, he should not drive with one arm around a girl and certainly should not drive while smoking. Holding up the car roof with one hand may look dashing, but it is hazardous. Both hands on the wheel is the rule of safety. A car is a possibly lethal machine. Psychologically it is said to represent an extension of the masculine personality and thus many teen-agers use it aggressively, causing accidents and deaths to such a degree that insurance for young men under the age of twenty-five is routinely uprated. Not so with girls, who, thanks to the same driver instruction the boys get plus natural conservatism, are adjudged safer drivers.

Parents' Permission   In many a family there is constant friction about the use of the car by juniors in the family. Driving a parental car should be considered a privilege rather than a right. Family conferences can establish ground rules which should be respected by all. If a young son or daughter is to be permitted the use of the car, his needs should always be subsidiary to those of his parents. Once permission is granted, it should not be quixotically withdrawn. Parents should be able to make adjustments, too.

A Girl and Her Car   Sometimes a girl has her own car and the boy she dates does not. He may certainly drive in the car with her, but he should not be permitted to take the wheel if the car is registered in her parents' name without specific permission from them because it is possible the insurance might be invalidated in case of an accident. If she is the owner of the car, she may permit any licensed driver to take the wheel, however. She would certainly be very careful not to let her date drive if he has been drinking or is under the influence of drugs. She should be ready to take the wheel back at the first sign of subversive driving and without apology. She can always say, "We are not permitted to speed. Please stop the car. I'll drive now." Better to be square than dead or injured.

When a girl is driving, the young man still shows her the same courtesy as if he were in the driver's seat. The traditional courtesies in the matter are passing but the girl should at least hesitate to see whether a boy expects to help her out of a car before jumping out on her own. Sometimes a boy who has prepared himself for a courteous gesture feels snubbed if the girl barges ahead like a militant woman. Few girls like to be overprotected, but behavior on their part that denigrates the masculine role can also be destructive to the relationship. Men like to think of themselves as strong and protective. Would it hurt a girl hockey player to go along with this notion if it makes her date feel ten feet tall?

Teen Drinking

There should be no place for alcohol in the lives of children. A girl or boy of sixteen or so may possibly be permitted an occasional glass of wine at home with his or her parents to celebrate some event, but regular social drinking at this age should not be encouraged. A teen-age boy or girl younger than sixteen might be allowed a small glass of champagne at a wedding or on New Year's Eve, but only with his or her parents. No child of any age should be allowed to mix or pass drinks.

In all areas there are some teen-agers who do drink, and by doing so show their friends and themselves in a poor light to the adult community. They arrive at parties where no liquor is being served with their own supply. When this situation occurs, the boy or girl giving the party should politely ask these guests to leave. If there is any difficulty a parent, particularly a father, should take the matter firmly in hand. A teen-age party, of course, should only be held when there is some adult supervision.

Children usually look with great superiority on any observed inebriateness of their elders. It might, however, be too much to ask a lively young son to abstain from alcohol until he reached his majority or until he entered college if an example of insobriety has been set by his parents. Yet when we think of the foolish things adults do when intoxicated, despite all their knowledge of the world, we shudder at the too-young adding alcohol to their difficulties.

We hope that our children will not grow into immoderate drinkers as adults, but lectures on the evils of alcohol will accomplish very little. If they have seen alcohol used at home as a pleasant, controlled adjunct to living and never abused, they are likely to follow the same behavior pattern if they are well-adjusted young people.

On the other hand, I have seen overindulgence among boys and girls whose parents have been overstrict concerning drinking. These parents have made such an issue of adolescent experiments with alcohol that their objections have had a too dramatic effect. And sometimes an unhappy young son may use alcohol as a means of compelling attention from a stern, withdrawing father.

The best attitude, I think, is for parents to realize that in most communities a certain amount of drinking goes on among boys and girls in their late teens and early twenties. If they set agreed-upon limits for these young people, instead of prohibiting what they cannot really control, they will be helping their children to responsible maturity—the kind of maturity which considers too much drinking unattractive and socially unacceptable but not a heinous sin. If children can discuss the problem of drinking with their parents quietly and without recrimination on their parents' part, alcohol need be no more dangerous than many other temptations the flesh is heir to—especially in the early years.

Smoking

Smoking is another habit which to most children, even those who come from non-smoking families, represents the wonderful state of being "grown-up." Most boys and many girls, too, experiment with at least substitute tobacco (brown paper, corn silk, etc.) at the age of ten or eleven. Nothing much can be done about that, either, except to get them to smoke the odoriferous things outdoors and to be careful about the matches. But this predictable activity is followed sooner or later by experiments with real tobacco.

When it comes to important habits that can interfere with growth or sleep or nerves, children, even older teen-agers, do *not* have to do what most of the others in the group do. Children who love their parents and vice versa are guided on conduct by parental judgments, if these judgments are given reasonably and in a kindly fashion and if they see daily examples of maturity in the behavior of their own parents.

At the first signs of a child's interest in smoking you might say, "I suppose you may have tried cigarettes. I hope that you are too intelligent to become a smoker. Young people of your age are being reached by the Surgeon General's appeals. Older boys and girls who have already contracted the habit and can't stop, regret that they ever started. More than half the doctors in the United States have stopped smoking. You are surrounded everywhere, especially at school, with educational material on this subject. The best advice is that you not start. Or, if you have started, stop. Either way, your father and I cannot give our consent to your smoking. We must ask that you not encourage other teen-agers to smoke in our house. It is because we love you that we ask these things of you." Then, if the child is obviously smoking or later begins to smoke, reiterate what you have said, and see to it that he gets all of the scientific material available that will make him conscious of the need to stop the habit. And set him a mature example by not smoking yourself.

The Drug Scene

The greatest protection against evil is education. The wise parent never assumes that his child is immune from the temptation to experiment with drugs which seem everywhere available today. There have been instances where quite young children have been offered candy or gum coated with LSD. There was an instance where young people were fed LSD-coated potato chips at a party and this was followed by some deaths. Along with today's open discussion of sex, there must be from a very early age family discussion of the dangers of drugs.

In some communities as early as the fifth grade the drug problem arises in schools. In California alone there are over five thousand first-time arrests each year for possession or usage of drugs mostly involving juveniles.

Young people have told me that they have been under great social pressure in their peer groups to smoke marijuana, to take drugs, rather than be "square." This is a drug-oriented society. Children who are to be saved from this possibly killing choice need warm support and understanding at home and the freedom to discuss their fears and temptations. Perhaps the best book I have read on the subject, and one that answers questions specifically in clearly understandable language, is *The Drug Dilemma* by Sidney Cohen, M.D. (McGraw-Hill). It covers every aspect of drug taking with a summary of drug effects. Shielding one's eyes to the dangers of the drug problem is foolhardy. Every suburban weekend, and every urban one, too, finds young people—even young children—involved in drugs, dangerously driving on the highways, threatening their delicate psyches, courting death. Knowledge is power. Without moralizing teach your children *before* they are exposed to temptation using information on the effects of the drugs that will surely at some time be offered to them. If possible, let them see the results of drug use by involving them and yourselves in existing drug programs in your own hospitals and drug addiction centers. Let them empathize by contributing their services. As a child of an alcoholic knows and fears the effect of the abuse of alcohol, so a child who can actually see what drugs can do to a human being may be persuaded from experimentation. Most important of all in this very dangerous age in which we live, parents should examine their feelings toward their children, and their children's reactions to them. Never before were warm family ties more necessary, the ties of love and understanding.

The National Institute of Mental Health, Chevy Chase, Maryland 20015, is a source of much free or almost free material on drugs. Write them for a list.

High School Graduation

Graduation Announcements and Invitations At some schools graduation announcements are sent prior to graduation and act also as invitations. These have the student's name either filled in or on an accompanying visiting card, usually in this case printed rather than engraved. The card should, for a girl, include the "Miss" and for a boy include "Mr." if he has reached the age of eighteen, otherwise it reads just "John Gordon Smith." Initials are avoided.

Graduation invitations and announcements should be sent only to relatives and close friends who are really interested in the event for many will send gifts.

Guests should arrive at least twenty minutes before the start of the ceremony. The audience usually stands for the processional and recessional, but gets its cue in this regard from the faculty.

Gifts There is a wide range of gifts from which one can choose something attractive and appropriate for a modest sum. Here are a few suggestions:

Fine quality white handkerchiefs, hemstitched or with rolled hems. For a girl, they are initialled with her first initial or her monogram. For a boy, with his last initial or his monogram—never with the first alone.

Ties, socks, gloves, shirts, scarves.

Two tickets for a summer theater or concert performance or a restaurant credit. A girl would welcome one for a beauty parlor.

Printed stationery and reference books such as dictionaries, etiquette books, and cookbooks. A subscription to a fashion magazine for a girl.

Gifts that would cost somewhat more, but have lasting value include:

For the boy, furnishings such as a brush and comb set, cuff links, a desk lamp, a brief case or attaché case. For the girl, a piece of sterling silver in a pattern she may have decided upon if she has started a hope chest, charms, cultured pearls, an evening bag or gloves, a small bedside clock, sheer evening stockings or pantyhose or a gift certificate at a high-fashion store, an overnight case or other luggage. For the girl who is planning early marriage, linen, clocks, silver place settings, china are all things to keep in mind.

For both, a silver paper clip initialled, a good-looking bank—an antique one might start a graduate on a collection of his own, a sterling or leather postage-stamp case, a sterling bookmark or a sterling silver ruler, initialled.

For any graduate, money is a very good gift, as are savings bonds and stocks.

Acknowledging Gifts   The graduate should be careful to acknowledge gifts in writing, however brief the notes, as promptly as possible upon their receipt even where they have thanked the givers personally at the time of graduation. For gifts of money do not mention the amount. The notes should be written on good quality stationery or informals and sent, of course, first-class mail.

Constructive Teen Activities

Volunteer Work   Some years ago, General Alfred M. Gruenther, at a luncheon meeting of editors hearing about the aims and work of the American Red Cross, said that the clue to teen-age happiness and fulfillment hinges upon the new rallying cry. This he said should be "How can I contribute?" rather than the all too familiar "What's in it for me?"

Communities everywhere have need for teen assistance and talent. In some areas the Red Cross reports it has more teen boy workers than girls. Hospitals find that high school age girls are of invaluable assistance as nurses' aides. The aides, in turn, learn new skills and disciplines that will assist them in the choice of a career and teach them to work well with older people. Teen-agers are being offered and are accepting many new opportunities for responsibility in the social-service field. I know one gentle fifteen-year-old who spends every Thursday afternoon after school as a volunteer worker in an orphanage for Puerto Rican babies as part of her school's social-aid activities. She uses the Spanish she is learning in school to communicate with her little charges. She returns home deeply touched by her experience, more grown-up than another girl who at the same age makes no such contribution.

"But how can I do something interesting like that," a teen may ask. The Girl Scouts, the Campfire Girls, the Boy Scouts, the Boys Clubs of America all have community projects on which its members work. For those who qualify, the Junior League has many valuable social-service activities for older teen girls. Churches need baby sitters so young mothers may attend services. Ask in your community how you can help. To be needed, to be able to give of oneself with intelligence is to live fully and to achieve one's fullest potentialities.

Jobs There comes a day when every teen-ager rebels against having to take every cent he needs from his parents even when parental giving is generous and understanding of teen needs and obligations. Holding down a job, earning money is fun even when what you are doing won't necessarily lead to your life work. If a teen-ager knows where he is heading and is able to get summer and other vacation or after-school jobs that will lead naturally to his eventual goal that is fortunate, but all productive work well-performed is valuable discipline.

If he is an earner, it is important to be an intelligent spender and saver as well. Note that I list spending first, for saving and never spending can be spiritually limiting. As I have said elsewhere in this book money is a medium of exchange. It should not be endowed with values it doesn't have. Many teen workers have developed a mature outlook on the money they earn and have put some of it to work for them. Witness the rapid growth of teen-age investment clubs, many of them under the direction of school math instructors. In this way teens learn money management and stretch their imaginations to the potentials of the system under which we live.

How does a boy or girl get a job while still a student? First he or she must evaluate the amount of time available for such a job without neglecting school work. For most, a Saturday or Sunday job or one for Friday night may be all that can be comfortably managed. The range of possibilities is wide. I know teen boys and girls who clerk in supermarkets or in banks, who drive delivery trucks, run errands, work in libraries, baby-sit, tutor, act as file clerks and stenographers, model, work in restaurants and hospitals and sell door-to-door or by appointment a wide range of products and services. Many teen girls are relief operators for the telephone company, a job that is well-paid and highly disciplinary in that it requires discretion, strict concentration, and unfailing courtesy to the public.

Once the teen-ager has evaluated his time and assayed his talents (the latter with the help of family, friends, and guidance counselors) he may find that the fastest route to a job is to ask everyone he knows if there is some opportunity for him. If his school maintains an employment office, he should use its services or apply to the state employment office. Job openings for teen-agers are usually available on a part-time basis in most communities, but the summer plums in camps and resorts must be applied for in a businesslike way months, sometimes years in advance. Today everyone wants a job, not just needy students. Every teen-ager should have the opportunity to earn money and handle a job at some time during these important years in preparation for a lifetime of work ahead, whether or not he actually requires such earnings for his education and maintenance.

The working world is a serious place even for a teen-ager working part time. He will need to conform to the standards exacted of older workers in regard to dress, behavior, performance, and punctuality. It should be a matter of pride on the part of the teen worker that he need never be chided on these things and generally it seems true that the current and coming teen-age groups are more serious minded and stable in this regard than were many such in the past. Teen earnings are at an all-time high and climbing further. Teen spending is an essential pillar of our economy.

Letter of Application and Interview

The letter of application and the job interview are both extremely important for the job-seeking teen-ager. Each presents a different aspect of your personality to your prospective employer. Your letter of application should be written clearly and correctly, and typed (if possible) in the usual business style. Here is an example:

45 Maple Street
Larchmont, New York   zip code
March 15, 1971

Mr. David Parnes
The Parnes Corporation
116 Laurel Avenue
Larchmont, New York   zip code

Dear Mr. Parnes:

In June I will complete my sophomore year at Larchmont High School. I am sixteen years old and I am preparing for a career as a legal secretary. My scholastic average is a B. I am interested in working for your company during the summer and would like to do any type of secretarial work. I type 60 words per minute and take shorthand at the rate of 100 words per minute.

I would appreciate meeting you and talking to you about job possibilities. I am available for an interview any weekday after 3 P.M. and all day on Saturday. My telephone number is MA 3-0162.

Sincerely,
(*your signature in ink*)
Ann Morse (typewritten)

Note that your signature is never preceded by your title, Miss, except parenthetically where necessary (if your name could be mistaken for a man's).

For the job interview be sure you arrive on time. Your clothes should be simple, clean, and neat—a jacket and tie for a boy and a dress or suit, gloves, most conservatively, and shoes with a low heel for a girl or the kind of clean clothes you would wear on the job if you get it. Speak clearly, and answer the interviewer's questions directly. Don't be embarrassed about letting your interviewer know that you are very much interested in working for his company. If you do so with enthusiasm and sincerity, he will appreciate your interest and attitude. When the interview is over, rise and thank the interviewer.

Don't smoke during an interview even if the interviewer is smoking. Gum chewing, of course, would be a mistake.

Appreciation A teen-ager should be careful when he gets a job to thank those who helped him land it. Ambitious people sometimes forget the necessity of looking back to see how they effected their progress. The prompt note of appreciation, the telephone call to report the result of interviews, the continuing contact with advisers and helpful friends of the family all build toward a sound future. These are necessary courtesies in life but also good business. You can never know when you will need someone again. Only you can leave the right impression.

A Special Problem

Despite shrieking headlines from time to time about reckless or mischief-making teen-agers, there are many who are polite, well-mannered young adults. Those who are instinctively courteous to all adults should nevertheless be prepared by their parents for possibly unpleasant experiences.

Young teen and pre-teen boys need to be warned against the male stranger who may seek him out or sit next to him on any public transportation or in other public places and try to strike up a conversation. While such an overture may be perfectly innocent, the boy should be told gently the necessary facts concerning deviates. If any action or conversation seems to be of a suspicious nature, such a boy should find another seat or, if permission to do this is necessary, he should ask whoever is in authority for it. If this request is made quietly and firmly, the person in authority usually understands the situation and makes the adjustment quickly without requiring any explanation. The same action should be taken by any girl or woman who is in any way molested. If she cannot freely change her seat, she should request assistance without calling public attention to the situation. It should be understood that those who approach strangers in such a way are ill and usually quite easily discouraged if the person molested makes the suggested action promptly without violence or outcry.

This same technique should be followed by the boy or girl who is threatened with rowdyism on the part of groups of boys or girls in public places. A quick appeal to the nearest person in authority should be made immediately.

Chapter 55

THE COLLEGE YEARS

The college years mark perhaps the first time that a boy or girl is free from parental supervision. This newly acquired independence is a precious opportunity to acquire and develop habits and attitudes that go toward making the mature human being. An orderly and balanced plan that places the proper emphasis on all the diverse elements that go to make up college life —study, recreation, sports, social activities—is the most desirable, and is largely up to you. These four years can be a marvelous preparation for your future whether it is a career, marriage, or both. Use them wisely.

College Applications

College applications require letters of recommendation from social and other sources. Applicants should always ask permission before giving such a social reference to a college. A call upon the person or a brief note can easily secure this. Perhaps a note might read,

Dear Mr. Gordon,
I am applying to Yale and, as you know, I will be required to give a social reference. As you have known me for a number of years and know my parents, I wonder if you would mind very much if I gave your name on my application.

Sincerely,
Julia Burke

Such delicate requests should not be made of prominent people the applicant may know very slightly merely because such a name might impress the university or college.

Where such letters of recommendation are written to schools and colleges, it is courteous for the institution to make some acknowledgment to the endorser whether a form (not seen by the student applying) was merely filled out or a warm letter of recommendation written, a copy of which might well have gone to the applicant. Here is one acceptable example of a form sent out by a university:

Brandeis University
Waltham, Massachusetts zip code
January 24, 1972

Your communication sent in support of the application to Brandeis University of Mark William Kraus (handwritten) is gratefully acknowledged. It will be placed in the candidate's file and made available to the members of the Committee on Admissions.

(signature)
Director of Admissions

Courtesy and Manners

College living is always public living and thus courtesy toward others is an absolute necessity. There are so many little courtesies—little physical courtesies—that make such goldfish-bowl living more comfortable. The student going through corridors and halls who looks behind him before letting go of a door, a male student who steps aside to let a faculty member or a woman enter a room first, the individual who speaks and moves quietly and does his best to create order instead of adding to the normal confusion in such a community is one who is using and developing social graces so necessary in any society. How important it is to exercise a little verbal courtesy, to express the "pleases," the "thank-yous," the "I'm sorrys," and of course the "may I's."

Table manners among both men and women on college campuses frequently deteriorate to such a degree that parents barely recognize the signs of the social training that they have given their sons and daughters home for holiday periods. The same reason for good table manners at home exists away from home. Considerate table manners aid digestion and add to the pleasure of the meal for all those around the table.

Good table manners pursued in college strengthen a most important social asset necessary for competition in the outside world. Good manners of all kinds neglected in college must be relearned if the graduate is going to move in a world where these graces are considered necessary.

Introductions

Introductions between students in college are usually very informal—"Betty, this is Joe Brown." "Joe, Betty Green." Introductions by students between their young guests and faculty members are given in such a way that the faculty member's name is mentioned first even though he is a male—"President Chaffee, this is Louise Brown, my guest for the weekend." In introducing parents and faculty, the student's mother's name is mentioned first, "Mother, may I present President Chaffee. President Chaffee, this is my mother, Mrs. Wentworth." It is necessary to mention the mother's name when her name is different from that of her son or daughter and a good idea on a large campus when student's names may not readily come to mind. The father is then introduced. "President Chaffee, this is [or may I present] my father." [Optionally: "my father, Dr. Murphy."]

Invitations to Teas and Receptions

During periods at college when there are many guests on the campus, invitations are frequently issued by faculty members to teas and receptions and these invitations are replied to in the same form in which they are issued. Formal engraved or printed invitations require a prompt answer in the third person written on good quality white stationery in blue or black ink, if they require an R.s.v.p. But they may also be phoned.

The Receiving Line   Wherever there are receiving lines at campus functions it is essential for guests to go through them and shake hands. On men's campuses the man goes first and introduces his date, "Mrs. Chaffee, may I present Miss Smith," or on very informal campuses, "Anne Smith." At very large dances where hundreds go through the receiving line, there is not time for such introductions. On a man's campus the man goes first, shakes hands with the first in line and says "Good evening" or "Good afternoon" as the case requires, and is followed by the girl he escorts, who, if there is no time for a brief introduction, gives her name, "Miss Smith," and like her escort goes on to the next in line. At women's colleges the girls go first through the line, followed by their dates, and the same procedure takes place with the man saying, "John Smith" rather than "Mr." On some campuses the receiving line re-forms at the end of the evening, and in this case everyone again goes through it, saying "Goodnight" and omitting the name. No one leaves, except in great emergency, before the guest of honor.

The Male Guest

The male guest on campus today usually gets himself there at his own expense. It is no longer unthinkable, however, for a girl to furnish his transportation if not doing so means that the man she particularly wants to be her escort cannot accept her invitation. If the relationship between them is easy and comfortable enough for him to accept such help, she can easily give it. The same is true of dates on campus for such a man visitor. It may well be that his assumption of all expenses for refreshments, taxis, etc. (even when admissions to various college functions are paid, as always by the girls), might prove a considerable, even intolerable, hardship. Girls increasingly are paying their share and sometimes even more of the expenses without embarrassment or apology on either side. If parietal and other regulations permit it, visiting men often stay at dormitories or in sorority houses, or of course in nearby boardinghouses, motels, and hotels (the latter usually but not necessarily now at their own expense). As few girls wear corsages any more, the problem of the cost of flowers is minor, if it exists at all, but it is a good idea for a man to ask what the custom on the girl's campus is in this regard. And no girl was ever insulted by receiving flowers even if they are not meant to be worn. Flowers can make the most independent girl feel very feminine and desirable. A man who has been entertained on campus by a girl writes her a note of appreciation very shortly afterward. He writes, too, to hostesses who have entertained them as a couple. Such notes need not be lengthy but should be written soon enough after such entertainment so as to sound spontaneous and appreciative. If a man simply cannot write—but he'd better learn—a phone call is better than nothing. A girl who has had a big weekend with a man and hears nothing from him for months or perhaps ever again may well feel very miserable indeed.

Dormitory Living

Students living in a dormitory need to observe carefully the social rules that make living in this kind of group shelter tolerable. Women students in particular are sensitive to the inevitable inconveniences, distraction, and noise of dormitory life. Fraternity and sorority house living has many drawbacks which are best countered by very strict adherence to considerate social rules.

As privacy is so hard to achieve, those who respect it are among the blessed. A closed door, whether it is tagged "Don't Disturb" or not, is an indication that privacy is desired. Even the courteous knock at the wrong time, for example when a student is sleeping at a normal hour for such an activity, can be highly irritating unless the intrusion is for some serious reason. Constant borrowing of money, articles of clothing, books, note-paper, ink, snacks, toothpaste, even with permission, is another bone of contention. Noise and disturbance at night is very inconsiderate. The student who monopolizes any facility to be used by all, such as the bathroom, kitchenette, or the telephone, is headed for social disaster.

It is generous—and expected—that students who are in receipt of manna from home (cookies, cakes, candies, fruit, and so forth) share it. Parents making such gifts should keep this in mind and make their purchases or bake their cookies accordingly.

When irritating situations arise, orderly disciplinary action is the answer. This should be meted out by an appointed or elected authority to whom all such complaints should be made.

Housemothers

College housemothers are few and far between these days at girls colleges. Instead, young married couples frequently little older than some of the students (and often graduate students themselves) are in residence. In the past decade things have changed greatly. University and college students no longer consider that the college should supply the equivalent of a housemother, *in loco parentis*. There are, of course, house rules and agreements on them sometimes are signed by both parents and students.

Parietal visiting, literally visiting "within the walls," is very new in some areas, well established in others. There is either no restriction on visiting hours from the opposite sex or very liberal ones. In effect, colleges and students alike agree that students entering college should be mature enough to conduct themselves according to regulations agreed upon by all.

And these rules are becoming more and more permissive. It is a great responsibility for young men and women of college age to learn to live together as adults. Whether or not all parents agree on all the issues involved, there can certainly be no turning back. Even greater freedom is in the offing with exclusively all-male and all-female colleges bowing out in favor of coeducation.

In a long report by the College Council on women visitors at Amherst, the following appeared: "The changing role of women in our society, their increased opportunities for independence, and the increased under-standing of women's sexual nature and capacities simultaneously raise her to the status of an equal partner and remove much of the need for external protections beyond her own sense of personal integrity. Likewise the extension of time for educational training before young men and women enter upon their careers has meant that they cannot postpone their entry into many aspects of manhood and womanhood until their education has been completed. This has necessarily led to a considerable blurring of those apparently logical stages of development which previous generations regarded as natural. It has meant that general rules give way to more individual and variant courses to maturity." I am in agreement.

Clothes for College

Dress on all-male and on all-female campuses tends to be less formal than it is on co-ed campuses for obvious reasons, although customs, of course, differ in various parts of the country, between Ivy League and non-Ivy League colleges, between urban and country campuses. College catalogues are usually fairly explicit about what form of dress is expected, and insofar as the women's colleges are concerned the matter is well taken care of with the placement of student fashion advisers in the college departments of department stores before the beginning of the fall term.

Many co-ed colleges seem to permit Bermuda shorts and even short shorts on girls. Even where this is so, the girls themselves should have the sense to know that, if their figures can't stand this attire, they should wear skirts. I have seen short shorts and skinny pants on some co-ed campuses, but consider them inappropriate even in women's colleges whether or not there are male teachers. Campus clothing fads differ so greatly, change so much from season to season, that more comment is impossible. Some are fun and harmless, others so inappropriate or po-tentially harmful that faculty, parents, and the conservative element of the student body rightfully frown on them.

One of the most uncomfortable things that can befall a student just entering college is to arrive with all the wrong clothes. The best way to prevent this is to discuss clothing needs for the particular college with someone who has been there in recent years and to choose one's wardrobe accordingly. Most large department stores provide this advisory service before college opens in the fall. Reasonable conformity will be the comfortable course.

Clothes for a College Weekend   Girls who are going to be guests at men's university or college weekends are not always safe in asking their dates what clothes are expected. Men can be a little vague in this matter. It is a good idea to ask, however, what activities are scheduled and of course to take into consideration the geographic placement of the university. One campus will go in for winter sports, another for concerts and dances. Generally speaking, a cocktail dress on the "dressed down" side, a dressy wool, perhaps even a cashmere sweater with a cloth skirt are a better idea than something too fussy. On many campuses, short evening dresses for formal dances are more likely to be seen than long ones, but when in doubt, and your date can't help, ask him for the name of the college hostess and write her. The information may be in a school catalogue or pamphlets issued by the university or college, too.

In winter and spring a simple, easy wool suit with a warm topcoat, if needed, or a sports fur coat are appropriate. Hats are not necessary. Good and appropriate footwear is essential and on most campuses there is plenty of walking. Simple dress pumps with a medium heel are right for daytime dress occasions, but comfortable well-fitting walking shoes of some kind are vital. Take clothes for active sports of course and perhaps pants suits or slacks if they will be needed.

Weekend Expenses

Girls invited to college weekends preferably pay their own fares to and from the college. At the colleges, the boys provide sleeping arrangements for the girls either in fraternity houses where they are residential, the masters' houses, or in other approved quarters including motels, hotels, and boardinghouses. The hosts in Ivy League colleges assume the cost of this overnight accommodation and also that of meals and incidental expenses while the girls are their guests. This practice is well-established and is considered quite correct and usual, although there could arise special circumstances in which it would be impractical or work a hardship on the boy. In the latter situation other arrangements might be made. In non-Ivy League colleges the girls usually pay for accommodations themselves, but in some cases now the expense is assumed by the hosts.

It is understood, of course, that women guests adhere very carefully to all rules of decorum expected by the universities.

Blind Dates

Blind dates are an established fact of college and prep school life. It is best that they be arranged by someone you know and trust to use discretion and who will be, if possible, along with you on the date. Blind dates should never be made with someone who has picked up your name one way or another and called you without the necessary intermediary arrangements. Ignoring this necessary rule can be very dangerous.

In many girls' colleges and prep schools it is a common practice for boys from other colleges, in groups of two or more, to turn up at dormitories and sororities to check at the desk to see if there are any girls who would like to have dates. While some colleges frown on this practice, others feel that it is acceptable if the boys are careful to identify themselves and if the housemother has an opportunity to look them over and make the introductions.

I know of many happy marriages that resulted from blind dates, even of a few that resulted and have been happy when the initial impression on the part of the girl was bad for one reason or another. The participants on both sides in a blind date of course take a chance at least of having a dull evening. Sometimes a blind date gets out of hand. If it does, the girl may certainly ask to be taken home, giving some good social pretense such as a headache. If the boy is unable or unwilling to comply with the request, she should take herself home by any possible means. Remaining with a disorderly, noisy crowd, or putting up with a boy whose behavior is bad for one reason or another, is destructive, possibly dangerous.

A boy who has met a girl on a blind date and is then given an invitation by her for some function or to a party may certainly refuse, but should always do so courteously and seemingly reluctantly.

Sex in College

I doubt very much if every young man and every young woman entering college feels completely adequate in the matter of what he believes will be expected of him sexually in this new exciting and increasingly permissive world. On the contrary, I am sure many young daughters go with feelings of great personal inadequacies, as do young sons. Not to mention the fears and doubts of the parents who in their day probably faced a very different kind of college or university atmosphere where sex, although it of course existed, was not the open thing that it is now. It can be ignored by none. Students who have had good relationships with their parents in regard to this as well as other things can be expected to face the reality of sex in college with the feeling they are able to make their own decisions in the matter. They will not use sex as a reward or as a punishment to prove their masculinity or their femininity. They will accept it as an important fulfilling part of their lives, a matter of private dclight and enjoyment with someone with whom they preferably have close bonds of affection and respect.

Young people, like mature ones, need to understand that they have responsibilities to society not to produce children out of wedlock, not to use their bodies promiscuously with resulting possible damage to their psyches and their health. They need to understand that sex is a great gift to be used with delicacy and understanding. It is a highly personal thing, not to be indulged in because "everyone else is doing it" but because it has meaning for someone who can be embraced without feelings of shame or guilt.

Parents of college men and women in this time of sexual revolution cannot be overprotective. Such an attitude is not only useless but can create seemingly insurmountable gaps between the generations. Parents should be receptive, available, and concerned rather than curious. By the time young people are in college, parents have done just about all they can do in the formation of their character. The rest comes in the painful process of growing up.

What About Rules at Home   Young people who have had freedom—sexual freedom particularly—in college are going to view with confusion the clamping down of harsh rules when they come home to visit. A young man who has lived freely in a sorority house with girls among his roommates as is happening now, will do one of two things if he is told he may not have a girl in his room at home. He will ease around the injunction every chance he gets. Or, he will be home very little. The same is true of a girl who has experienced the freedom of present-day college life. Parents need to understand their children's early experience, experience undoubtedly they did not have themselves at the same age. Generally speaking, our young people are not promiscuous. They develop meaningful relationships which sometimes, but not always, lead to sexual ones. Young people strive to have their relationships natural and they stress that this "naturalness" does not mean that they consider sexual intercourse as the only possible relationship between the sexes. They want to be able to make these decisions themselves along lines worked out by their peers. It is difficult for all concerned.

If possible, the furnishings of college sons' and daughters' rooms at home should follow the lines of a studio or study rather than of a bedroom or, where possible, a student should have a living room of his own where absolute privacy can be assured. Such a solution helps parents contend with the inevitable criticism that can come from some older members of the family either living within the household or visiting.

Parents have a right to their own privacy. They also have the right to be protected from blatant affronts to their own hard-won emotional controls. Often it is not the things that the young people do which produce the upsets in the parents but the way in which they do them. Young people should be expected to be discreet and to show a degree of consideration.

Although all parents have a right certainly to make reasonable rules to be followed within the family, rigid and unrealistic ones have only a destructive effect. Some realistic ones will seek to overcome the fact that unsupervised college living rules out graciousness. Quite different rules in many social requirements at home are reasonable to the parents who have agreed upon them. This means for example that while haircuts may not be imposed, clean, combed hair and clean clothes at family meals are valid enough expectations. The student who has been padding around his faternity house bare- and dirty-footed, perhaps will have some sympathy for his mother if she requests socks and shoes at least in the public parts of the house or at the very least clean feet. A student who has had no obligation to carry on a dinner table conversation with his housemates would be kind to make some effort to communicate with his family for the brief periods in which he sees them. If all of this seems a waste of time, he should think in terms of his future relationships in the world, where lack of communication, sloppiness, bad table manners, and the ignoring of other people's rights are all considered examples of immaturity rather than of maturity. Reasonable conformity can be a pleasant thing for everybody.

Pinning

"Pinning" in college contemporary parlance means "engaged to be engaged." The girl wears the boy's fraternity pin. It means more than the fact that they are going steady. It means that they are contemplating marriage, without the forthright public avowal of a formal engagement. At this stage, parents are not brought together and the parties to the pinning may, in the opinion of some, date occasionally with other people, although on some campuses this is considered beyond the pale. Pinning commitments can be broken much more readily than formal engagements, but suspect is a girl who is pinned too often during her college years and the boy, too, who has become this serious with a whole succession of girls. Pinning is a romantic trial balloon, easily punctured if not taken seriously enough by both parties and kept a highly private and not-too-restrictive arrangement.

Graduation Invitations and Announcements

Invitations to college graduations are usually strictly limited so that they are available only to immediate members of the family. If the student is engaged or going steady, his or her date usually attends the graduation with the family. Announcements furnished by the college may be sent to a wide list but should be sent only to those close enough to the graduate and the family to be really interested in the event, because many, upon receiving such announcements, feel impelled to send a gift. Usually the graduate's visiting card is included in the invitation and should follow the conservative, correct social form—Mr. John Rogers Smith, for a man (note the "Mr.") and Miss Anne Ethel Jones, for a girl. Initials are avoided. It is nicer to have engraved cards rather than printed ones. A man or woman at the college graduate level can find use for engraved cards in his social life, especially if he travels abroad or even in this country.

Invitations and announcements should be addressed in black ink, never by typewriter, and should be sent by first-class mail.

All graduation gifts must be promptly and graciously acknowledged. Informals may be used for this purpose by women (they make a nice gift for the graduate, by the way) but men should use conservative masculine note-paper or a man's informal card (see "Men's Correspondence Cards," page 578). These cards, by the way, also make an excellent gift for a man graduate. If his name is engraved, it should be in full, and although it may carry his home address he may find it more useful without one, and like his *social* visiting card, it includes "Mr." It may be engraved in black, blue, gray, brown, maroon, or dark green with the name centered, at the top of the card on top left, depending on the design.

Woman's Name on a Diploma

Increasingly large numbers of women graduates are married. The question often arises concerning the name to be called out by officiating faculty at graduation under these circumstances, especially when the women students are being graduated with their husbands. It is the name on the diploma that is called out—Gretchen Eleanor Brown or, optionally, Gretchen Lansing (maiden name) Brown, whichever the girl chooses and the latter is more modern. The "Mrs." is omitted, but appears in the program in parentheses before her name as shown on the diploma. A girl who is going on in her profession may choose, of course, to graduate under her maiden name whether or not her husband is on the same campus and graduating with her. In this case, her name on the program is not preceded by "Miss" and the name called out is Gretchen Eleanor Lansing.

Chapter 56

DIVORCE AND SEPARATION

With one divorce now to approximately every four marriages, this social upheaval touches the lives of every one of us in some way. Sometimes, though our own families are happy and intact, we find our children in a school group where most of the children come from broken homes. Our own children may become affected by the insecurity of so many of their associates. A sudden divorce may disturb long-standing business relations or remove from the neighborhood part or all of a family that had been friendly and congenial.

Divorce should never be entered into in the midst of battle but should follow, if all efforts of settlement of differences fail, only after as lengthy a separation as possible. It is not only poor taste but a foolhardy procedure to air one's domestic troubles in public. Even the poorest marriages usually have some roots, and sometimes after a quiet separation it is possible for two people to correct the causes of their difficulty and give those roots a new chance to grow into a sound marriage.

Even separation is, however, a drastic step, which may so wound one of the partners that he may not be able to come to a reconciliation, perhaps because of injured pride.

Procedures and Agencies That Are of Help in Marital Difficulties

Where there are children to consider, one or both of the partners should seek outside, objective help before deciding to part. The causes for separation and divorce are so twisted and complex, so involved with emotions rather than reason, that it takes a wise counselor to bring the problems into proper focus. Where are such wise counselors to be found?

Some progressive churches have marriage counselors, who meet with young people before marriage and help prepare them for the union they contemplate. These advisers, usually psychiatrically trained, are also available for consultation by married couples who are having domestic difficulties.

As it is important that those contemplating divorce seek objective help, they should not take their troubles to their friends who, however well-meaning, often find themselves taking sides. Usually a lawyer should be the last resort, because he is geared for the one kind of action he understands—legal action of one kind or the other. (It does happen, however, that a wise, understanding lawyer who sees some possibility of adjustment will refuse to take a case and suggest psychiatric aid.) A priest, minister, or rabbi may be the right sympathetic counselor, and they are all likely to be necessarily conservative in their suggestions.

Psychiatric or psychoanalytic aid, especially where one or both partners may have a history of previous divorce, may be the most complete answer and, contrary to popular belief, troubled people seeking such assistance are rarely "advised" to divorce. Their consultations or analytic sessions help them make their own decisions and they are cautioned from the beginning against taking any decisive step until their problems can be brought to light and understood. For it is a sad fact that millions of us, divorced or thinking of divorce, could never be happy in any marriage, no matter how perfect the other partner, because of our own inability to lead relaxed and happy lives. Marriage itself is not at fault. But in our increasingly complex world the individuals who enter into marriage need to be more and more adult. People who are anxious, insecure, tense, and frightened find no magic security in the responsibilities of marriage and are inclined to retreat at the first obstacle.

While many communities have no resident psychiatrist or psychoanalyst, many do have psychiatrically trained social workers whose assistance is available either free or for a modest sum. All big cities have practicing psychiatrists and psychoanalysts whose qualifications should be checked on by your family physician and who should be members of a recognized group—such as the American Psychiatric Association or American Psychoanalytic Association.

Throughout the country in the larger cities there are important clinics where patients may live in and receive counsel or analysis at whatever fee they are able to pay, or they may be out-patients, going to the clinic for private or group consultation daily or several times a week.

Information on recognized psychiatrists and psychoanalysts may be had, free, from the National Association for Mental Health, 1800 N. Kent Street, Rosslyn, Arlington, Virginia 22209, from the American Psychiatric Association, 1270 Avenue of the Americas, New York, N.Y. 10020, and from the American Psychoanalytic Association, Menninger Clinic, Topeka, Kansas 66603.

People in difficulty with their marriages do not necessarily require a lengthy psychoanalysis. They may be able to adjust their difficulties after a certain number of consultations with a psychiatrist, accredited social worker, or marriage counselor.

Separation

Trial separation, that is, temporary separation by simple agreement, should never be openly announced even to one's friends. News of it is bound to seep out eventually if it is prolonged but direct questions concerning it should be delicately parried by both parties, because of the possibility of a reconciliation. If the fact of a trial separation has been covered up as well as possible, then it is relatively simple for two people who have had time to consider the gravity of their step to come together again. If there has been a public airing of their problems, reconciliation is usually impossible.

When, even after a trial separation, in which the husband usually has removed himself from the home by his wife's request, it seems unlikely that any coming together again is possible, no step toward divorce should be taken until a legal separation or at least a separation agreement drawn by a lawyer is entered into. A separation agreement still permits the fact of the separation to be relatively unknown if the couple finds a way to keep up the fiction of an intact marriage—by having one or the other remove to another city, for example—as it is merely a formal instrument signed by both parties. It does not go through court channels except in the event of a lawsuit based on its violation or a separation or divorce suit when it may be used as the basis of settlement. In a regular judicial or court separation, both parties go into court, where certain requirements as to the husband's financial contribution and his provision for the children are agreed upon or, in the event of disagreement, settled by the court and entered into the record.

Especially if children are concerned, it is wise and advisable for one or the other type of separation to be entered into, whether or not divorce is actually contemplated, as it settles without haste and by considered agreement important matters of support, division of property, and custody. In the event that the separation has been brought about by the insistence of one partner that he wishes to remarry immediately, it is good sense for the other to insist on separation for at least one year before divorce proceedings may be started. The partner trying to jump from the frying pan into the fire will, nine times out of ten, be grateful for this cooling hiatus, whether or not it results in the patching up of his existing marriage. New marriages hastily entered into after old ones have been dissolved usually end in the same disaster.

If either judicial separation or separation-by-agreement occurs, no public announcement need be made through advertisements in the press, such as "My wife having left me, I am no longer responsible for, etc." This is never *legally* necessary. While he is still her husband, a man is financially responsible for his wife's debts for "necessaries," those incurred by her during the marriage, no matter how much he may protest to the contrary. They may have only their own "gentleman's agreement" concerning the handling of charge accounts and the incurring of obligations.

Only the vulgar announce their separations by way of newspaper interviews, often taking the opportunity to announce their "engagements" to others at the same time. Requests by newspapers for comment on possible separation should be politely denied and any printed rumors pointedly ignored. Many and many a couple which has adhered to this course of behavior has been able to come together and live a long and happy married life even if they did encounter a few rough spots in the road.

When a husband moves out or a wife gathers up the children and returns to her mother, the partner who receives their joint mail punctiliously forwards it to the other but does not give a change-of-address for the other to the postman. Phone calls are parried with, "Mr. Green is away just now, but I can take the message and have him call you." Or his temporary number may be given, without explanation, if the matter seems urgent.

Where legal separation actually takes place, the couple is *still married* though no longer living together. Therefore, the wife is still Mrs. William Green, not Mrs. Robertson Green, the name she may assume if she does divorce her husband—a combination of her maiden name and her married name. She usually wears her wedding ring, especially if she has children.

It is the wife who still replies to formal invitations, whether or not it is she who was left home. She refuses any to which the couple has been jointly invited. She has her own quiet social life, as does her husband, but she should conduct herself always as a married woman should, carefully giving the impression that the marriage is intact and that for some reason that is none of the public's business the couple does not attend social functions together at the moment. Or she may invent a believable fiction. Polite people never press for such information, anyway.

If divorce becomes inevitable, the fact that it is impending should never be publicly announced. A divorce is never a divorce until it becomes final, and even if the unhappy procedure has been entered upon reconciliation is still possible. But even when any idea of reconciliation is firmly over, it is always poor taste for people to announce in a jubilant fashion that they are getting divorced. If they have no sensibilities themselves, they should consider the example they are setting for the young in treating divorce so lightly.

When people are so prominent that their divorce proceedings become news—if they haven't been sensible enough to insist on proceedings behind closed doors—then they should make a discreet announcement to the press.

Divorcée's Change of Name

Only when a divorce is final does a woman change her name from "Mrs. William Green" to "Mrs. Robertson Green." She signs her checks and her letters "Mary Robertson Green," but never, preferably, becomes *socially* "Mrs. Mary Green" although she may use this in business.

The death of a divorced woman's former husband does not change her status or her name. She remains a divorcée and she continues to be "Mrs. Robertson Green." (See also "Divorcées Card and Name," page 764.)

Our Attitude toward Divorce and the Divorcée

Anyone who has read what I have written about divorce knows I believe it can never be cause for rejoicing. It is only the shallow and silly who ever return from the divorce courts in a carnival frame of mind, desirous of public celebration. Whatever our inner relief may be that an impossible situation has been faced and legally, at least, rectified, it is normal and decent to keep our feelings and our experience to ourselves as much as possible. And even close friends should be careful not to assume that a divorce is accepted by the divorcé or divorcée as an unmitigated boon. Actually it is like a painful operation, the necessity for which cannot occasion any joy.

Divorces are never announced formally. The divorcée should write to friends and relatives in distant places and tell them of the divorce. Neighbors and friends should be told.

Any remarks directed toward the newly divorced should be tactful indeed. Friends should not attempt to extract information concerning the proceedings from one obviously unwilling to discuss the matter. And even when a divorced person seems to feel the necessity to discuss the case with sympathetic listeners it is their cue to make only the most noncommittal remarks in return. Such emotional outbursts are often greatly regretted later and the one who gave the confidences frequently feels a certain resentment against those who avidly received them.

Removing One's Wedding Ring

Increasingly, women who are divorced remove their wedding rings even when they have children. This is considered a good therapeutic measure by psychiatrists, making it easier perhaps for the divorcée to accept the reality of her new situation. If she continues to use the "Mrs."—usual when she has children—the absence of a wedding ring indicates her status to new acquaintances. Too, she usually puts away her engagement ring or has its setting redesigned. She then wears it on her left pinkie or on her right hand, not on her engagement finger.

Many young widows particularly choose to remove their wedding rings especially if they don't have children. Others continue to wear their wedding rings, finding it simple enough to say, if they meet someone interesting, something like, "My late husband used to say . . ." in order to reveal their status. Divorced men who wore wedding rings during their marriage should remove them for the same reason a divorced woman no longer wears hers. A widower who had been married in a double ring ceremony may continue to wear his wedding ring, but most younger men, particularly, choose not to.

The Dating Divorcée

The divorcée who begins to date again often feels embarrassed when she runs into people who do not know of her divorce. She feels that they are curious or even bewildered seeing her with a man not her husband. She can react to this either by saying nothing, knowing that her friends will find out in time, or by saying then and there very frankly and promptly, after introducing her date, "I'm sure you do not know that I was recently divorced." (Probably this latter is the better procedure.)

Many divorced people react to the fact of divorce as if it were rejection even when they have sought the divorce themselves. Some attempt to plunge themselves into a whirlpool of social activity. Saturday nights are a bad time for that was "date night," the night a married woman has the security of knowing she will be with her husband at home or out. Instead, the divorcée becomes an extra woman, often not included in community plans for the weekend. Especially if she is newly divorced, she may not yet know available men who might ask her out. She tends to stay home, feeling depressed, doing nothing herself about reaching out toward others.

The newly divorced woman can help things considerably by giving parties herself as she feels up to them, inviting couples she knows with an extra man or two if she can find them. Such men don't necessarily have to be in her mind "eligible" but having an acceptable (if not necessarily romantic) date can give her a feeling of security again. One such contact may well lead her to another that might interest her more. The important thing is for the divorced woman, if possible, to keep in circulation without losing her dignity and without the desperation some new divorcées exhibit.

It may help the new divorcée to think of herself as a widow rather than a divorcée. She has, after all, been through a period of mourning and is facing a difficult adjustment. Dating for her poses new problems that she did not have prior to her marriage. The little flirtatious games of her younger years may seem almost impossible for her after years of marriage. She may make it too obvious that she needs a man—almost any man—and this has the effect of frightening off the very men she might hope to attract. Yet she must come out into the world, begin to live and communicate again. Dating, even when it isn't very exciting, is valuable and necessary to this end.

The divorcée who feels ill at ease when she begins to accept invitations from men, should analyze why she has this feeling. Does she wonder whether or not people are talking about her? Actually, they probably are and they may be curious. If she is discreet, however, in her behavior and doesn't feel compelled to tell everyone she knows all about the dates she has had, she will feel more relaxed. She should merely accept these social sorties as a pleasant and normal part of a single woman's life—and that's what she is now, a *single* woman. In time she will accept her right to date again and stop wondering about what people think.

Some divorcées have the fantasy that because they are divorced, every man they meet—including husbands—think of them as easy conquests. This may very well be true in some cases, as men are certainly men, but the new divorcée's bearing, her language, her conduct, can quickly disabuse the Lotharios in short order without rupturing friendships. These little jousts should not be depressing but should be accepted as compliments to her physical attractiveness. There is little doubt that some men make these "passes" because they think it is expected of them, not because they have any actual plans to follow through. These are just the games that men and women play. They don't necessarily have any serious meaning at all.

A divorcée tends to think of herself as in competition with young, attractive unmarried women, free of the stigma of divorce. It is important instead for her to think of herself as an individual, her own woman—poised and worldly with an understanding she might never have gained without pain. She is vulnerable, sensitive to the problems of others. As such she may attract men who have undergone loss, too, either through divorce or death. She can be and should become a concerned and sensitive listener. Two such people may well fill each other's needs.

Divorcées tend to look at themselves much too critically. In their despair they feel that something drastic must be done and think in terms of physical change of some kind. They are unable to accept themselves as they are. Most of us can do with reappraisal from time to time if it is realistic. The large and small discontents one has with oneself need to be sifted through so there is an appraisal as to what is important and what is not, in any plans for change. Once the decisions are made, they should be followed through to prevent lingering self-disparagement. Sometimes when nothing really needs to be done, a change of a minor kind can lift the spirit. Something so simple as cutting the hair, or letting it grow, changing the hair style or even the color, having a professional analyze her make-up and effect certain changes in her style, can help a woman who feels she just must do something about her appearance. Getting fresh advice on clothes may suddenly make a woman seem more glamorous, helping her to like what she sees in the mirror and giving more self-confidence in facing her new role.

Perhaps more than superficial changes are needed. Often the new divorcée goes to work, perhaps for the first time in many years. Or, if a paid job is not the answer and she must stay at home with young children, she should make a determined effort to broaden her horizons with the reading of good literature, attendance at good theater or special cultural courses if only with a woman friend. She will benefit by doing something physical with her body, for many tensions can be worked out through regular exercise such as gym, dancing, purposeful walking, bicycling.

Depression tends to make people want to lie around and "rest" whereas physical activity stirs up the glands and gives a feeling of well-being. The divorcée—and the widow, too—needs to look outward, not inward in the conviction that the new life can be as good or perhaps even better than the old.

The Remarriage of Divorced Persons to Each Other

More often than most of us realize, people who have divorced each other with heartache and misery decide for one reason or another to try once more to resolve their problems together within the ties of marriage. Such a remarriage is always cause for happiness, yet care must be taken by the participants that good taste is adhered to, especially when there are children who, having suffered from the original upheaval in the lives of their parents and themselves, fear to believe that home will once more mean Father and Mother together. Couples who are divorced and are later remarried to each other celebrate their original wedding aniversary date as though the divorce never took place. The remarriage of divorced people to each other is always quiet, often with witnesses alone. No invitations are issued except by note, wire, or word of mouth, and then only to a few nearest and dearest friends and relatives. No announcements, except by letter or wire, are sent out. Underage children are, preferably, not witnesses to the ceremony. Explanations are brief, and married life resumes, we hope, on a maturer basis.

Part Seven

YOUR PUBLIC LIFE

YOUR PUBLIC LIFE

At some time or other there is an occasion when we must rise to our feet and express ourselves before some sort of group. This public performance may be in the form of an interview we must give or a talk before our local branch of the Audubon Society or a speech on a local radio station, or even an appearance before a large television audience. Whatever the locale, the occasion, or the subject matter, it is good to feel at ease and able to cope with the situation—and upsetting to feel nervous and inadequate.

If we belong to organizations and wish to have our opinions carry weight, we must learn to express ourselves well publicly. If we aspire to office in such organizations, we need to learn through frequent practice to speak well. The quiet member, talented though he may be, is rarely thrust forward into leadership. Part of belonging is active participation in the groups that interest us. It is possible to learn how to participate with poise and assurance.

Part of our public life is, of course, concerned with what others see when we venture forth from the social security of our homes. Can we pay a call with grace and terminate it within the accepted time without being brusque? Can we go into restaurants, theaters, and other public places so that we fit in in a well-mannered, unobtrusive way? If the circumstances of our lives are such that we are more or less public figures, can we treat the press and the public courteously, without arrogance—and also have a real sense of noblesse oblige?

If we are able to do all of these things gracefully we can indeed feel that we can take our proper place in the active life of the community.

Chapter 57

DINING IN RESTAURANTS

Restaurant Reservations

A wife making a reservation by phone or otherwise for her husband and herself and perhaps a group of guests, makes the reservation in her husband's name, as he will be host. A secretary, making a reservation for her employer at a restaurant, makes it in his name even though he and his wife are entertaining together. A businesswoman entertaining either a mixed group or men alone at luncheon or dinner, as hostess, makes the reservation in her own name just as a woman does who is giving a luncheon or dinner without a male host.

Entering and Seating

A man entering a restaurant removes his hat and, if accompanying a woman, excuses himself while he checks it, his coat (a woman usually keeps her on), and any packages or umbrellas they may have been carrying, first guiding the woman out of the line of traffic. The Maître d', if there is one, is addressed as "Mr. Charles" if you know his name, Monsieur Charles, or Monsieur. He need be given no form of address. However, if he steps forward, the man says at least "Good evening." If there is a headwaiter who comes forward to seat them, then the man steps back and lets the woman go first. Otherwise, the man goes first, finds a table, pulls out a chair, and seats the woman, preferably to his right. The choice of the woman's seat, either by the waiter or her escort, depends on the view she will get. She should be able, if possible, to look out into the main part of the restaurant or be by a window with a good view, but she should not be placed where passing traffic may strike her chair. If the table is poorly situated, she should not be facing the rear wall or a swinging door. If the two are to be seated together on a banquette, the table is pulled out at one end usually, so the woman may slide in and seat herself on the man's right, but if she can't seat herself in that position without disturbing others around her or causing her escort to seat himself awkwardly she should sit, quickly, in the nearest available seat.

If there is only one wall seat, the woman takes it and the man, of course, sits in the aisle seat. When there is a group of four the women take both wall seats and the men seat themselves opposite them, husbands opposite their wives, men opposite their dates. If there is no waiter immediately in attendance to assist the women with their coats, their escorts offer this courtesy.

If a young couple is dining with a much older one, the older couple is offered the wall seats and the young couple sit together on the aisle so that the younger man is opposite the older woman.

Where two young couples seat themselves, the women take chairs opposite each other. If one man is the host, he tries to seat himself so the woman to be honored is at his right even if it is his wife—this may be her birthday or their anniversary. No great point, however, need be made over the seating.

Where one woman is accompanied by two men, she seats herself between them, unless there is a divan. In that case she sits on the divan with the man she knows less well. If a woman is doing the seating of other women, she indicates the wall seats for others and takes the aisle seat herself. And although the hostess goes last, guests do not allow themselves to be seated until her arrival for she must direct the seating. Where two women are shown to a booth, the hostess indicates the seat with the better view for the guest. If it is a "Dutch treat" lunch, any much younger woman steps back to let the older take the preferred seat in the booth or on the divan. Otherwise, the one who reaches the table first offers the better seat to the other, unless in a crowded restaurant it seems expedient for her to seat herself as quickly as possible. But she should then offer to place the other's bag and gloves on the seat beside her.

Reading the French Menu

It is nice, but not necessary, to be able to pronounce foreign culinary terms as you encounter them on menus in many restaurants. Often the waiter himself, unless he's French, can't pronounce them any too well, though of course he must know what they mean. But you can easily learn from the following list that *rognons* for example, are kidneys. It is perfectly sensible to ask, "How are the kidneys prepared?" Perhaps they are in a steak-and-kidney pie, or with red wine and mushrooms. You can remember that the word *"hachis"* means chopped-up, hence our "hash." So, *"pommes de terre hachis"* are our old friend, "hashed brown potatoes." A *"pomme de terre"* is, literally "an apple from the earth," so *"aux pommes"* means with apples, whereas *"aux pommes de terre"* means with potatoes. But often on menus the *"de terre"* is omitted. Fried potatoes become *"pommes frites,"* meaning *"pommes de terre frites."*

A girl can always ask her escort to choose a meal for her and leave the deciphering of those French terms to him. And he should know what they mean even if, as I said, he doesn't dare try to pronounce them. If he is confronted with something that stumps him completely he can always say to the waiter, "What is this please?"—but a working knowledge of a French menu is an impressive little skill. It must be no fun at all for a man to feel at a disadvantage before a pencil-poised waiter.

The reader wishing to go further in his French culinary education will enjoy the Escoffier cookbook, for example, which gives recipes for the best-known French dishes. It has been translated into English with no loss of Gallic flavor. It is interesting to the novice cook as reading matter mainly, but the graduate cook, male or female, will find it inspiring. At last count my own cookbook library numbered 300 volumes—not because we use them all constantly but because we like them for occasional reference. A knowledge of food and international cookery helps to add to the pleasantness of life and quite often to metamorphose everyday routine.

À L'ANGLAISE roasted or boiled

À LA BÉARNAISE with sauce of chopped onions, egg yolk, vinegar, oil or butter and seasonings—for meat or fish

À LA BIGARADE with sauce made with orange juice or rind, usually served with duck

À LA BONNE FEMME housewife style; thin meat or fish stock with vegetables. *Omelette à la bonne femme* is made with pan-browned potatoes or onions.

À LA BORDELAISE sauce with Bordeaux wine combined with chopped mushrooms, garlic, shallots, or onions

À LA CAMERANI usually a thick chicken liver soup

À LA CHATEAUBRIAND steak or chops (usually) with *maître d'hôtel* butter

À LA CERFEUIL with chervil sauce; usually with fillet of beef

À LA CIPOLLATA with hot Italian sausage or forcemeat

À LA COCOTTE heated and brought to the table in a shell

À LA CRAPAUDINI chicken, squab etc., with legs and wings removed and the meat flattened before broiling

À LA CRÉOLE with sauce of tomatoes, onions, mushrooms, and peppers

À LA CROISSY OR CRÉCY flavored with turnips or carrots

À LA DAUBE little squares of bacon or salt pork cooked with sliced carrots, onions and turnips

À LA DAUPHINÉ a thick vegetable soup

À LA DAUPHINE with egg sauce

À LA DAUPHINOISE dipped in sauce or batter, crumbed, then French fried

À LA FINANCIÈRE truffle-flavored Spanish sauce

À LA FLAMANDE Flemish style with sliced turnips, Brussels sprouts, and cabbage

À LA GODIVEAU with meat balls, usually of veal

À LA LANGEDOC cooked in or served with olive oil

À LA MACÉDOINE with mixed fruits or vegetables in unusual variety

À LA MAÎTRE D'HÔTEL in the host's style, plain substantial dishes with sauce of chopped parsley, melted butter, and lemon juice

À LA MARENGO with oil and garlic

À LA MARYLAND with a less rich Newburg sauce

À LA NEIGE snowy (as meringue)

À LA NORMANDE served usually with apples

À LA PRINTANIÈRE with spring vegetables

À LA PROVENÇAL Provence-style, with olive oil, garlic, tomatoes and, often, onions

À LA RAVIGOTE in an herb-flavored white sauce made with tarragon vinegar, egg yolk, mustard, and pepper

À LA REINE cream of chicken (soup)

À LA SERVIETTE served in a napkin —corn or steamed clams, for example

À LA TARTARE with a sauce of mayonnaise, chopped olives, and capers

À L'HUILE in oil

AU BEURRE FONDU in or with melted butter

AU BEURRE NOIR with well-browned butter

AU BEURRE ROUX with browned butter sauce

AU BLEU cooked to the blue point —refers to fish

AU GRAS with the fat or, with soups, containing meat

AU GRATIN with a topping of grated cheese and crumbs. Also refers to well-baked meat.

AU JAMBON with ham

AU VERT PRÉ with green herbs. Non-culinary meaning, grass.

AUX FINES HERBES with chopped herbs

BONBON candy

BONNE BOUCHE a titbit

BOUILLABAISSE thick fish and seafood stew, Marseilles style

CAFÉ AU LAIT coffee with hot milk

FOND D'ARTICHAUT artichoke bottom

MONGOLE in a sauce made of tomatoes and puréed peas and beans. Most frequently met with in *potage* (soup) *mongole*.

ROGNONS SAUTÉS sautéed kidneys

VIANDES meats

VOLAILLE poultry

Ordering

When previously arranged luncheons or dinners are given in restaurants or hotel dining rooms, the order is often given in advance by the host or hostess and no menu is handed to the guests by the waiter. Guests accept what is put before them, and, even if they don't care for the host's or hostess's choice in some dish or other, they make at least a pretense of eating it.

The man in ordering always refers to his woman companion as "Madam" or "the lady." Never as "Mrs. Brown" or "my wife," and certainly never as "she." The use of "my wife" or "Mrs. Brown" might be permissible, however, when they are dining in a small restaurant where they are well known, at their country club, or in a resort where they are also known.

If the luncheon is planned on a "Dutch-treat" basis, then the guests should be able to order their own meals. Otherwise, when two or more people are lunching or dining together, one, whether he or she is actually the host or hostess and will pay the bill, takes the initiative and does the ordering after a little consultation. If the group is awkwardly large or the restaurant, at lunch, exceptionally busy, the waiter will take the order from each one. Where a woman is accompanied by a man, it is always assumed that the man is the host and he is expected to do the ordering (except at lunch when she may give her own order to speed the service) after the woman has had a few minutes to look over the menu presented to her by the waiter. He says, "What do you think you'd like to have?" She chooses, preferably, the table d'hôte—the meal in which everything is included in the price of the entrée—and says what she will have, beginning with the first course if there is no extra charge for it. If she orders à la carte—where each item on the menu has its own price—she names only the entrée, the main course, and lets her host suggest a first course to her, as he should. When the woman, out of respect to her host's pocketbook, has not selected a first course even though he has invited her to have one, the man should not order one for himself without first asking her again, "Are you sure you won't join me? I'm going to have blue points." She may then take it for granted that he can well afford the gesture, or in the case of a business luncheon has the time, and she may say, "I believe I'll have something after all," and quickly chooses something that appeals to her.

Where a woman accompanied by a man is asked directly by the waiter what she will have, she looks at the proffered card and then tells her host what she wishes to eat except at lunch when she may order as I've said above. Too, she may, at either lunch or dinner, ask the waiter a direct question if she wishes, such as, "Are the snails prepared with much garlic?" Then, if the answer is satisfactory, she turns to her host at dinner and says, perhaps, "Good, then I'll have snails."

It is sometimes difficult for a woman guest to concentrate on the menu if she is immediately offered suggestions from her host. While the host should have his guest well in mind, he should give her a little opportunity to choose something by herself before he makes any suggestions. If she seems to hesitate, let him say, for example, "I understand they make a specialty of steak here. Would you like a filet mignon?" Or, "How about the salmon? Would you like to try it, too, or does something else appeal to you more?"

As a guest, in ordering table d'hôte avoid ordering the most expensive entrée unless you are certain the cost of the meal is of no consideration at all to the person entertaining you. But don't choose the least expensive things either, lest your host suspect you think he can't afford to entertain you well. Unless, of course, the least expensive thing on the menu, tripe perhaps—happens to be the one thing you really prefer above anything else there. Then you might say, "I'll have tripe. I do like it if it's done nicely, and I haven't had it in quite some time."

If you are dining where foreign food is a specialty or where the menu is in an unfamiliar foreign language, don't hesitate to ask the waiter about a particular dish or how it is prepared. He will also probably be glad to suggest something which is considered particularly good—the *specialité de la maison.*

Omitting Courses   It often happens that women prefer to eat less than do men and, on a table d'hôte luncheon or dinner, really wish to omit certain courses. There is no reason why they shouldn't say so and equally no reason why a man should not accept the course even if his guest does not. Certainly no guest should be urged to eat a course he or she really does not want, even to keep the other company.

Drinks

There is equally no obligation for all in a party to take cocktails or wine just because some do, even if it is only a party of two and the man wishes a cocktail and the woman does not. In this case, whoever wishes the drink should have it without urging the other to join him or her.

Ordering Wine

Where a restaurant meal has been ordered in advance, the wine, if any, is indicated in the order with the entrée, whether meat or fish, determining the choice. A dry white wine is now considered suitable throughout a meal, even a meal with red meat, though traditionally it is served with fish and poultry while a red wine is reserved for meats and game. One wine is considered enough except at banquets or gourmet dinners, where two or even three wines may be used if the host knows what he's about.

Where a restaurant meal has not been ordered in advance, the host or hostess asks for the wine card—or for the sommelier, or wine steward, if the restaurant boasts one (he's the man with the chain and keys). If the party is given by a woman and there are men present, it is usual for her, even if she is expert herself, to ask one of them to select the wine for her. A man may do this gracefully even if he knows little about the subject, merely by saying to the waiter or wine steward, "What do you suggest?" If some of the guests have chosen poultry or fish, the wine steward will usually indicate a choice of white, dry, still wines. It is not at all axiomatic that any imported wine is better than a good domestic one. On the contrary, some domestic wines are far better than some of the cheap, imported ones, and it is a good thing to familiarize oneself with the various offerings, or if unsure, to ask the opinion of the steward or of others at the table who may be informed on the subject.

Various chicken dishes or kidneys are often prepared with red wine, such as burgundy, and if such a dish has been ordered by anyone present it is well to ask if red wine has been used in its preparation. If so, a red wine can quite suitably be ordered if the other orders at the table are for meat.

Champagne can quite properly be ordered in place of cocktails and can be served throughout a dinner and even throughout the evening instead of being reserved just for dessert—although such a champagne should be dry rather than sweet. It may be served with mild cheeses but not assertive ones. The sweet wines, both white and red—port (of course, there is also a dry port), madeira, angelica, sweet chablis and tokay—are dessert wines and should not be served before luncheon or dinner or during them. A dry sherry (Amontillado), served cold, may substitute for cocktails and be drunk during a meal, while a sweet sherry at room temperature, like port, is reserved for dessert or may be taken with a biscuit or a bit of simple cake in the afternoon in place of tea or cocktails.

If You Don't Wish Wine   If, as a guest in a restaurant, or in someone's home, you don't wish to be served the wine, you may check the pouring of it by lightly touching the rim of your glass with your fingertips, without turning, as the waiter or butler leans over you. You may never place your glass upside down to indicate refusal although I have seen busy Waldorf waiters do this after a first refusal to simplify their serving. You may permit the server to pour a little, then raise your hand above your glass, even if you don't intend to taste the wine. This is a better procedure at a small table where a host might notice your empty glass and think you had been neglected.

If you do not take wine, the server, or your hostess, may properly ask you if you'd wish something else—scotch or rye with soda (or with plain water, if you prefer), white wine with seltzer (a Spritzer), or even milk unless it's a very formal meal. It is perhaps a little masculine for a woman to refuse wine and specify a highball, as formerly it was only the men who were asked to state such an alternative if they did not wish wine.

Problems of Service

Although the rule in using table implements is this: Work from the outside in, some restaurants don't necessarily know how to set a table. Where the traditional placement of the silverware is not followed in your judgment and if you find you have used the wrong fork or spoon and are an implement short, ask for another if the waiter does not notice. Don't apologize. If your salad plate has been incorrectly placed on the right and you find it uncomfortable to use it, you may certainly put it on the left, where it belongs, without comment. Never wipe off the silver. This should not be done even in the lowliest of restaurants. If an implement seems less than clean, ask that it be replaced. You will not be able to get it clean with your napkin anyway.

Implements that are not used in the course of a meal are left on the table, not placed by you on outgoing dishes. Tender foods like pancakes, soufflés, and omelets are preferably eaten with a fork alone rather than with a knife and fork unless one is eating Continental style. If you have finished a course and wish the plate to be removed, don't shift it elsewhere on the table yourself. Allow the waiter to remove it.

When sugar is served in little packets, it is permissible to leave the paper on the tablecloth after using it.

Presentation of Dishes

At better class restaurants the food is served from individual serving dishes onto the plate of each diner and each main dish before it is cut into is presented to the host or hostess for approval. Such a dish should really be inspected by a careful host. Is the steak medium-rare, as ordered, or perhaps overdone? Has an error been made in the vegetable order? Is the guest picking at the shrimp cocktail he ordered? Seafood must be absolutely fresh to be safe.

Too much fussiness about the food in a restaurant, too much of the pose of gourmet is boring, but a nice attention to the wants of guests is as important in a restaurant where one is playing host as it is at home. A host or hostess should never assume, even in the best restaurant, that his guests are being well cared for—he must be alert concerning the service and food.

Complaints and Compliments

Any complaints should be made quietly but firmly to the waiter at your table or to the section headwaiter if there is one—and by the host. When necessary, they are made to the captain—or in a small restaurant to the headwaiter—whose business it is to see that things go smoothly at each table. Hot food should be really hot, cold food cold. It is better to send food back to the kitchen—without fuss—than to expect a guest to eat something not up to standard just because you may feel too embarrassed to complain. At the same time, ostentatious complaints about every little thing impress no one, least of all your guests. But if you keep in mind what each guest wanted, you can make little changes or corrections where they are necessary, just as smoothly as you would at home. Any good restaurant appreciates a customer who understands the niceties of dining—and exacts good service. I suspect they secretly despise the man, especially, who will accept any sloppy sort of service and poor seating as good enough because he is intimidated by the atmosphere of expensive chic in which he finds himself.

As opposed to complaints, gracious compliments are appreciated if service has met your expectations. For, don't forget, the establishment's primary purpose is to serve the public in the most satisfying manner possible. Thus, if the owner is there, tell him you have enjoyed your meal and compliment his staff just as you would your hostess in a private home. As you must be served the meal, you do not thank the waiter or waitress in the course of the service unless some special service has been performed, although an occasional "thank you" is quite acceptable. In requesting service use the words "May I" or "please" for example, "May I see the menu again?" or "Will you please pour me another glass of water?" The same rules of course exist at home if you are being waited upon by a servant.

Incidentally, if the proprietor of a restaurant is an acquaintance of yours, it is entirely correct to ask the captain or waiter to let him know you are in. He may not be able to give you more than a very few minutes of his time, however, because he must look after all his patrons. Also, don't be disappointed if he doesn't accept your offer of a drink. If he accepted all offers he received, he would be in no condition to serve as proprietor!

Buffet Service

In some restaurants, especially Swedish ones, and at some private restaurant parties the food is served buffet style. If there are small tables at which to be seated, a man locates one, seats his lady to remove her coat, and asks her if she wishes to go to the buffet with him to select her assortment of foods. The flow of traffic around a buffet table is always clockwise and selection begins with fish at a smörgåsbord, properly eaten separately, and ending with the cheese, also eaten separately. It is expected that several trips to the buffet table will be taken in the course of the meal. After their preliminary selection the man picks up napkins and silver, if necessary, on the buffet table and sees that they both have whatever beverage is being offered. If there are no waiters to do so, he later clears the table of soiled dishes—or takes the lady's dish if they have eaten standing—excuses himself, and locates the dessert. If she has not been left with a group and therefore will have to wait alone at a table, a woman may wish to go along to the buffet table—unless it is too crowded—to make her selections herself. In that case the man goes first, hands her a plate, and indicates to the waiters, if there are any, what she would like to have. Otherwise, he serves her himself, or, especially at a smörgåsbord, she may serve herself with perhaps occasional suggestions from him. He hovers in her vicinity, of course, to see if he may assist her in any way, even though he may be filling his own plate at the same time so as not to leave her too long alone.

When she has an escort a lady does not wait at a buffet table to pick up her own wine or other beverage. That is always the man's responsibility, especially as there is always the danger that someone may knock into the drink-bearer and spill the contents of the glasses. It is always proper for a man in a group lunching or dining buffet, in which there may be unaccompanied women, to ask, "May I get you a drink?" if any of them have not been served by someone else. The sight of women pressing through a crowd to a buffet-bar is not attractive.

Table Hopping

No one seated in a group at a restaurant table should get up to go table hopping, which is insulting to those with whom he is lunching or dining. A man dining in such a restaurant would not ask a woman at another table to come to his table to meet anyone unless that person is a much older and perhaps distinguished woman, or a very much older and distinguished man and circumstances make it necessary for some reason to make such a request. It is the man, on request, who approaches another table to be presented to a woman, or women, but never the other way around.

Stopping By

A woman in a restaurant does not approach another table where men are seated except possibly briefly on her way out, or on the way in as the men must rise or at least half-rise and thus be uncomfortable in her presence. If she must stop and chat, she should seat herself quickly if possible. Even asking the men to sit down will cause them to be embarrassed if she remains standing. A man does not stop to speak to a woman he knows when she is obviously on a date with another man, but he may certainly bow in recognition if she looks expectantly in his direction or bows to him herself. He does not seek an introduction to her escort unless she suggests it. The same rule holds true for a woman seeing a man she knows in a restaurant accompanying another woman.

Presentation of the Check

When the meal is finished the host catches the waiter's eye and says, "The check, please." If he can't catch his eye and the table is in a hurry, he waits until the waiter is somewhere within hearing and then calls out in an ordinary tone of voice, "Waiter!" Just that. In the case of a waitress he says, "Waitress!" not "Miss!" He does not whistle, tap his glass, or say "Psst" or "Hello!" in the European fashion, although, and especially in a European-style restaurant, he is perhaps justified in tapping his glass with a piece of silverware if his table seems to have been forgotten by both the server and the headwaiter and it is imperative that his group move on without further delay. He may not, naturally, rise and fetch the inattentive servitor (though preparing to leave will surely bring him).

When the check comes it is presented on a small plate, face down. The host turns it over, without disclosing its figures to his guests, and looks at it sufficiently long to see if there are errors but never so long and methodically as to make him seem niggardly. It is wise for a host to know approximately what a restaurant's ordinary prices are before going to it. Once there, he should not have to worry about the bill, for if he has judgment, he will not attempt to entertain in a place he can't easily afford.

If there is something obviously wrong with the bill, the host asks quietly for the headwaiter, explains his puzzlement, and accepts the correction or explanation without unnecessary comment. The waiter may have overcharged you, or perhaps the reverse has happened and he has forgotten to charge for something you ordered. In this case it is considerate and obligatory for you to point this out, for most restaurants charge the unpaid-for dishes against him in the kitchen. A host should, of course, never embarrass his guests by making a scene over a bill, or even discuss his dilemma with them. And they, at bill-paying time, should ignore the transaction.

If an adjustment is not to his liking, he still accepts it with good grace and privately decides to boycott that restaurant in the future. But he does not make his guests feel that the evening or luncheon has been spoiled because of such an incident, any more than he would make too much of a point of some mishap in service at home in the presence of guests.

Tipping at Private Dinners

If a man frequents a certain restaurant, it is not necessary for him to tip the headwaiter on each occasion, unless he has had special consideration—worked out the menu in advance with the headwaiter, had his table changed, or ordered some spectacular dish such as crêpes suzette, the completion of which has been presided over by this factotum. The tip is given on the way out. When the headwaiter is also an owner of the place he receives no tip but is thanked on the way out if he shows out his guests.

If one is well known in a restaurant, he may tip the headwaiter—in a popular spot often enough to make himself remembered—as he leaves, as insurance against getting poor tables in the future. Such a tip is quietly slipped into the waiting palm in an unobvious manner, but if the room headwaiter is not at his post he is not sought out by the patron. The tendered tip in an expensive place is usually five dollars. In a less elaborate establishment it is certainly never silver—always at least a dollar. A woman who entertains frequently in favorite restaurants uses the same tipping scale but tips a little less frequently, perhaps on the theory that between times she is often accompanied by tipping escorts.

The wine steward, if his services have been enlisted, receives 10 to 15 per cent of the wine bill in round figures and it should be given to him as you leave the restaurant. Where drinks begun at the bar have been brought with the bar bill to the table later, the bartender receives his 10 to 15 per cent or more depending on the quality of the restaurant.

In restaurants that employ headwaiters for sections—men who do no more than take the order and pass it on to table waiters for execution—no tip is expected by the section headwaiter, unless, of course, special service has been requested in which he has taken some active part. In that case his tip is not less than a dollar bill and may be two dollars if the party comprises more than two people.

A waiter receives 15 per cent to 20 per cent (depending on the place) in round figures. Don't leave pennies on the plate unless they add up to an even amount.

A cigarette girl usually arranges her change to indicate what she'd like to get, but ten or fifteen cents surcharge on a pack of cigarettes is enough and no one need feel like Shylock for picking up the additional change from a dollar bill.

The bus boy is not tipped as the waiter shares his tip with him. In a nightclub or expensive restaurant the attendants in the men's and women's lounges usually put decoy coins on a plate to indicate what they expect in the way of a tip, as does the hat-check girl. Unless some service has been asked, the tip need not be, for instance, a quarter, but can well be ten cents.

Whether or not we like the tipping system, we must consider that the wages of such employees are predicated on their receiving tips, that the tips are part of their salary and part of what we pay for the over-all service. To ignore someone usually tipped, unless he has been blatantly forgetful or rude, is to be unfair. Again, if the cost of going into such places must be minutely considered, we don't belong there at all.

The same tipping system is followed for a private restaurant dinner as for anyone or any group dining in the restaurant proper.

Doormen who perform a service—secure a taxi, summon or bring your parked car—usually receive a quarter or as much as a dollar on a stormy night.

Public Dinners

Tipping at Public Dinners At public dinners there is sometimes (and this is an excellent idea) a small card on each table which reads, "Gratuities have been taken care of by the Dinner Committee." This relieves the guests at each table of any obligation concerning the waiters. If there is no such notice, the waiters, immediately after the service of dessert and coffee and before the speaking begins, come to the host or hostess of each table and place a silver salver or small plate before him or her, often with the murmured explanation that something is expected for the table's waiters. Often a "host" or "hostess" at a table may merely have organized the table, each guest having bought his own ticket. Unless all at the table are personally invited guests, the host or hostess makes no attempt to tip for the whole table and after placing a dollar or a dollar and a half to two dollars (per service for which he or she feels responsible) on the tray, directs the waiter to the gentlemen at the table, each of whom should leave (at an eight dollar to ten dollar per plate dinner) a dollar or a dollar and a half to two dollars for himself and one for the lady he escorts. Women should not be approached for tips if there are gentlemen at the table.

Tipping Strolling Musicians Musicians who stroll through restaurants need not be tipped unless they have been asked to play special selections. Then the tip is a minimum of a dollar and depends on how long the musicians play for the table, with five dollars the usual amount expected for several selections. There is no standard practice concerning this. It varies from place to place and from city to city. Diners should not feel obligated to tip musicians who stop by the table but from whom a special number or numbers have not been requested.

Orchestras playing for charity functions do not expect gratuities. Occasionally, however, the purchaser of the music will enclose a gratuity of five dollars apiece for the members of an orchestra with some words of appreciation for a job well done. This is the exception rather than the rule.

Guests at Public Dinners At official and other public dinners there is usually a private reception for the guests of honor and the officers of the organization sponsoring the affair. Admission to the reception is frequently by card, and a ticket to the dinner does not entitle a guest to attend the reception unless he has been invited to do so.

At the reception there may be a receiving line if many are expected, or at a small gathering the guests of honor may stand around informally chatting with guests who are presented by organization officials or members of the dinner committee. If there is a receiving line, all guests must go through and shake hands. It is rude to bypass a receiving line.

The dinner guests are usually standing behind their chairs before those to be seated on the dais make their entrance. As the guests of honor enter, the assembly remains standing until those on the dais have been seated. On the introduction of a very important speaker, such as the President of the United States, royalty, or a very distinguished woman, the assembly rises, sits again until the speech is over, then rises once more in final tribute. If such a distinguished guest must leave immediately after his speech and before another has begun, the guests all rise and remain standing until he has left the dais.

Dress at Public Dinners It is quite common for the men to appear in dinner jackets and lately, even in dark suits, unless they are seated on the dais, which may still call for white tie and tails. Invitations to some very important public dinners now often read "White or Black Tie," for without that choice being offered, many would refuse to come. Invitations that read "Dress optional" mean dinner jacket or dark suit.

Properly, women wear full evening dress and long evening gloves to a formal dinner (removing the gloves before eating, of course), but here again one more often sees dinner dresses, especially at public dinners, rather than full décolletage. Many women prefer to leave long gloves in the cloakroom rather than cope with them all evening. Few now dance wearing gloves. This may now mean going through the receiving line ungloved, even when hostesses are gloved, an acceptable modern etiquette expedient.

Most sophisticated restaurants now admit women in properly tailored pants suits. Evening pajamas are acceptable in most elegant restaurants. When in doubt, phone ahead.

Leaving Restaurants

After finishing dinner, you may wish to linger over additional coffee and cigarettes. Determine if this after-dinner relaxation is in order or not by whether or not there are others waiting for your table. If it is very late and you are the last party in the restaurant, don't detain the hard-working staff just for your benefit.

If a table has had both host and hostess, the hostess rises, after catching the eye of a woman guest, once the bill has been paid, to indicate the party is ready to move on. Where there is only a host, he rises first, after making some such appropriate remark as "We'd better get started, don't you think?" If he is a gentleman escorting a lady to dinner or a night club and the next stop is home, she must be the one to terminate the evening, although he can say, "Perhaps you'd like to go on somewhere else?" She should take the hint and say, "Oh no, it really is late. Will you take me home, now?" Under no circumstances may she say to her escort, unasked, "Let's get out of here and go to such and such a place," as he would, politely speaking, be required to accept her suggestion. Very young and thoughtless girls sometimes do such things with no consideration of a man's working day or of his pocketbook, demanding to be taken from one night spot to the other, mainly, I suspect, for the sole purpose of being seen there.

When a couple is ready to leave, the man assists the lady with her coat if there is no waiter in attendance who is already prepared to make the gesture. On rising, the man is seen by the headwaiter, who then properly steps forward and makes a path for the lady or ladies in the group to file out after him. If there is no headwaiter, the man goes first, making a path and opening any doors. Once in the lobby, or wherever the checkroom is, he again places his companion out of the traffic, picks up his hat and coat, and holds the door for her to go into the street. If it is late at night or the street is dark, the man may well go out the main door first, with permission, to hold an umbrella or offer his arm the minute she makes her exit. It always looks sad to see women in evening dresses blowing out through a revolving door into a windy street while their escorts lag a matter of seconds or even minutes behind—even when there is a doorman, supposedly, immediately available.

Unescorted Women in Cocktail Bars and Nightclubs

Bar laws differ in various states. In some, women alone are not permitted to sit at the bar in a cocktail lounge but must be served at a table either in the bar area or in the restaurant proper. Unaccompanied women should not seek to be seated in nightclubs although of course they may be part of a party which includes a man or men or possibly a group of women. This good rule is for their own protection as well as for the protection of the club. Women who are traveling may see such local entertainment safely with tour groups. A woman guest of a hotel which has a nightclub may always speak to the manager to see whether arrangements may be made for her to view the show unescorted, and such arrangements usually can be made.

Chapter 58

CARDS AND CALLS

Are Calling Cards Necessary?

Engraved calling cards are a pleasant social convenience, but perfectly nice people have been known to get along successfully without them. It's preferable to do that rather than use printed cards, which are quite taboo. If you are asked for a card, don't fumble for a nonexistent one. Merely say, "Please say Miss Addington is calling." If you have no personal card to enclose with a gift, most shops will supply a plain white one in a matching envelope. Write a little message in longhand and seal it. You won't need a card if you are going to present the gift yourself, unless you're going to a party where it would be helpful to have your gift identified by card. When you call on a friend or neighbor and don't wish to trust a servant's or a member of the family's memory, or if the person to whom you are calling is not at home, ask for a memorandum pad, write a little greeting—"So sorry not to find you here, was in the neighborhood and hoped to find you home"—and hand it, folded, over for later delivery. Above all, don't use prepared thank-you cards or greeting cards for these purposes.

When Cards Are Left While the full ritual of the calling card is these days known by few, and practiced less and less, it is helpful to be familiar with it. Formal calls are sometimes still expected in older and very conservative circles and always in diplomatic and military ones. Instruction in the proper leaving of cards is given in our military academies as part of a young officer's necessary training. The simplest-living family of a small midwestern town may, by reason of the voters' action, be thrown into the formality of the nation's capital. Or we may go abroad and find ourselves in circles where knowledge of such etiquette is expected of us.

There are definite rules for card leaving. Whether or not you cleave to them depends very much upon the formality or lack of it among your own friends and acquaintances. Calling cards are not left at the White House any more. They are now put in envelopes and left at the Office of Protocol at the State Department. They should include the address of the visitor in Washington. Military or diplomatic etiquette aside, the leaving of a card upon a hostess who has entertained you for the first time greatly depends on what is usual in the circle in which she and you move. She might vastly prefer a little thank-you note to having your calling card handed to her by her maid or butler, if she has this rara avis, and followed by you in person if she is "at home." In busy cities the party call is almost extinct, especially among men and career women who, excused by business activities, presumably may find it much more practical and just as gracious to thank their hostesses by means of flowers accompanied by their cards, by a phone call, or by note.

The Size and Style of Cards   Social cards should always be engraved, although business ones may be printed. But even in business an executive who tenders a properly engraved card gives an impression of stability in regard to his job that the man or woman with a printed card does not.

Both business and social cards must follow certain standards of size and style if they are to be in good taste. A salesman once sent me in a card reading, "Mrs. Patrick's little boy Harry," and I have seen a doll-sized card used by a girl publicist which certainly failed to fix her name on my mind. As in all phases of social behavior, avoid the freakish if you want to be comfortable.

Visiting cards may be engraved on parchmentlike paper, whose virtue is that it's so thin it permits the carrying of more cards in your card case or wallet. Card styles change in minor details from decade to decade, and at present even a young girl does not use a plate-marked card and a man never does. A plain white card is supplied for engraving by all good stationers and the major jewelers, and may be in a variety of sizes and in several qualities—all of them standard. A man's card differs from a woman's in width but may be the same length as hers. Among the standard sizes permissible for women's cards are those $3\frac{1}{4}'' \times 2\frac{1}{4}''$, $2\frac{13}{16}'' \times 2''$, with the length of the name determining the size selected. The men's narrower cards, designed to fit standard card cases or wallet sections, may be any of the lengths used for women's cards but are rarely more than $1\frac{1}{2}''$ wide. A $2\frac{13}{16}'' \times 1\frac{1}{2}''$ is usual for a man's card.

Addresses on Cards   It is correct, if you wish, to have your *complete address* engraved in small letters without abbreviations in the lower right-hand corner of your card. But, perhaps because of the this-century insecurity of our living arrangements, only about fifty per cent of engraved cards carry this information. People write on, where desired, an address or phone number. A business card may considerately carry the telephone number, but a personal one does not (but see below). Cards for use in the country frequently are addressless, although the addition of the address is certainly permissable because such cards are often given to city friends, traveling companions, and acquaintances so that the address may be recorded. A telephone number is occasionally included on country cards, just as it is frequently put on country stationery and correspondence cards for the convenience of one's friends.

Engraving Script used to be the most popular, and is therefore considered by some the most correct style of engraving for a visiting card.

Mr. and Mrs. William Malcolm Parks

TYPO ROMAN SCRIPT

It is less of a favorite today but still much used by both men and women. More modern and perhaps better suited to younger people and for business cards are the modified English period types—shaded Roman, Norman, and St. James. Illustrated cards in this section are Typo Roman. Any simple type face is correct, but don't seize on the highly stylized types used in advertising copy. And do avoid the quaint or ornate. Be guided by a top-quality stationer's advice. Never have your cards engraved in other than black ink, and do not have them plate-marked.

Baby Announcements

The traditional and formal way to announce the birth of a baby is shown below. As you can see the baby's card is attached to the parents' joint card.

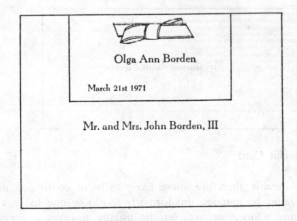

Olga Ann Borden

March 21st 1971

Mr. and Mrs. John Borden, III

But of course the announcement may be made in many ways. Greeting card companies have baby announcement cards of all kinds, some of them delightful. Special announcements may be engraved or printed and some of these are original and most attractive. Here is an example of one such which was engraved:

Mr. and Mrs. Arnold Jones
announce with joy
the birth of their daughter
Diana Margot
on the fifth of June, 1971

A Man's Social Card

A bachelor who does not have his own apartment or who does not live at home with his parents, but who belongs to a club, uses the club address on the left-hand corner of his card, whether or not he has quarters there. If he lives in a residence hotel in permanent style, he may prefer to list that address. But any bachelor's status and living arrangements may change,

```
Mr. Gery Addison Harder, Jr.



The Yale Club .
```

A Bachelor's Social Card showing club address

```
Mr. James John Sweeney
```

A Man's Social Card

and a club address is, therefore, more likely to be of continuing usefulness on his card. After he marries, the formerly footloose one has a choice of listing his home address or not, but he usually reserves it for the card carrying his wife's name, too. If he commutes to the city where his club is situated, he may find it useful to give out a club address where he may receive mail and messages, English style. However, there is some slight danger here that a club address on a married man's card might be construed to mean that he is separated from his wife. He avoids that by not using it without explanation. Or he can get around it by writing in his home address for those to whom he wishes it known. Note the important difference between a man's social card and his business card. His social card carries the "Mr." and includes his full name. His business card does not include "Mr." and may use initials. (See Men's Business Cards)

"Junior, Second and Senior" The use of "junior" on a social card does not, as with the initials "M.D.," preclude the necessity for "Mr." before the name. A man is "Mr. Karl Austerlitz, junior," or, where the name is a long one, "Jr." The first letter of abbreviations of titles is capitalized in forms of address and on cards, but non-capitalized when the title is spelled out in full. On his card usually a man is "junior" only while his father is alive and, of course, only if he bears the identical name. However, if he bears his grandfather's name, which differs from his father's name, he is "the second" during his grandfather's lifetime. If grandfather, son, and grandson all have the same name, the father is, of course, "junior" and the grandson is "third." When the grandfather dies the father becomes "Mr. Karl Austerlitz" and the grandson becomes "Karl Austerlitz, junior" (using "Mr." after eighteen). The use of "second" indicates that the bearer of the name is a cousin, grandson, or nephew of the original holder of it. It is sometimes used when a child has been named for a famous personage who has gone or may go down in history, and there may or may not be any actual relationship. A Roosevelt baby four generations hence might well use the "second" throughout his lifetime if he is christened "Franklin D.," even if he is very remotely related to F.D.R. It is possible he may grow up to be a distinguished personage himself and that the press will wish to refer to him in such a distinctive way. The use of the "second" will help future historians, too, if he does make a mark for himself that would put him within the orbit of the great men of the country.

A son of "Karl Austerlitz, second" or (or II or 2nd) would have to be Karl Austerlitz, "third," but if there is already a "Karl Austerlitz, third" it is courtesy and common sense to break up the sequence and create a new name for the child by adding a middle name of his own. He then needs no suffix. When a man in professional life acquires a title such as Dr., Rev., Canon, and so forth, he drops the suffix unless the man he was named for also had the same title.

When a father and son with the same name are in business together, it is quite all right to refer to the father in speaking only as Senior while referring to the son as Junior. This is done simply to eliminate confusion.

Men's Titles on Cards Clergymen, doctors of medicine (or allied sciences such as psychology, dentistry), judges, senators, mayors, military or naval officers, governors, professors who make teaching their profession and are holders of university professorships—all use their titles on their social cards. It is Doctor Phelps Harvard, Captain Joseph Wiley Coates, The Very Reverend Herman Hoffman (Dean of a cathedral), The Right Reverend Claire Croix (Bishop), The Venerable Percy Prime (Archdeacon), The Reverend Canon Guy Waters, The Reverend Geoffrey Gates, Brother Francis (of a Catholic or Episcopal order), The Reverend Stephen O'Mara (Catholic priest), The Reverend Selig Wise (for a rabbi), The Right Reverend (or The Very Reverend) Monsignor John P. Bowdin (for a Catholic prelate). All of these titles may be abbreviated, if necessary, to prevent crowding the card.

The governor of a state is simply "The Governor of Connecticut" on his card. More sensible but presumably less "correct" is the use of his name, prefaced by "Mr."—not "The Hon." which is never correct on an American card—with "Governor of Connecticut" in smaller type beneath it. A mayor's card follows the same form.

The letters of degrees, no matter how important, are not used on social cards. The holder of an LL.D. has the privilege of calling himself "The Rev. *Dr.* Charles Percival" on his card (spelling it all out if there's room). But the holders of all honorary degrees show better taste in omitting "Dr." on their cards, although they may use the title otherwise socially except in social signatures or on engraved announcements or invitations whose form should follow that of the social card.

Many judges prefer to put their titles in the lower left corner of the card. When they return to private life, they assume "Mr." and "Mr. and Mrs." even though everyone may continue to address them as Judge. "Mr. Justice" is used in the United States Supreme Court and in the Supreme Courts of several states.

Husband and Wife Cards

A joint card used by a husband and wife often carries their home address and is necessarily large enough to accommodate their names on one line. Convenient sizes are 3¼"×2¼" and 3½"×2½" depending on the length

---

Mr. and Mrs. John Murton

3 Wilder Terrace
Westchester, New York Zip Code

---

of the combined names. Because of the necessity of combining much in a small space, titles permissible to use are abbreviated if necessary—"Dr. and Mrs. Grant Simpson"—to avoid crowding the line. It is considered better form for a military or naval officer and his wife to use separate cards for post calls. When an officer has retired from active service he usually does not use a joint card, because the word "Retired" must appear in the lower right corner of his card. A joint card is possible however. It reads:

Admiral Lande Crouse, Retired
Mrs. Crouse

A man never leaves a joint card. If his wife doesn't accompany him on a call he must leave his own card only and may not include one of hers. The woman is properly responsible for the family's social obligations and must make her own calls.

The joint card is used to accompany wedding presents. On formal visits the wife may *leave* such a card upon her departure when not accompanied by her husband but should not *present* it when calling without him. It is included in flowers for a funeral, to a debutante or to anyone to whom the couple may wish to send flowers. It is now used sometimes for informal invitations and in reply to them, as is the joint informal. Joint cards may announce a new address or tell friends you are leaving town for a while if both husband and wife are on equal footing with the people to whom the card is sent. In this case the initials p.p.c. (*pour prendre congé*) are written in the lower left-hand corner. They mean "to take leave." Any thank-you notes must be sent separately, however, as the p.p.c. cards don't in any way fulfill the function of thanks for various kindnesses or entertainment.

A Woman's Social Card

Married Woman's Social Card A wife's card should match her husband's usual use of his signature. If he calls himself "J. Frederick Parks" her card must read "Mrs. J. Frederick Parks," not "Mrs. Jeremiah F. Parks" or even "Mrs. Jeremiah Frederick Parks" unless he prefers to use his name in full on his own cards. If a man has been blessed with a string of names, he'd better drop a few rather than confound the world with a line of initials no one remembers anyhow.

Mrs. J. Frederick Parks

A Married Woman's Social Card

Single Woman's Social Card If your name is Mary Hope Harding and you are known to your friends as Hope, don't call yourself "Miss M. Hope Harding" on your cards—a definitely masculine procedure. Either omit the Mary or leave your name in full, even if it may puzzle a few people. But I prefer shearing names of parts that are superfluous.

Miss Hope Harding

A Single Woman's Social Card

Widow's Social Card A widow shows respect of her husband by keeping his name on her cards and by using it *socially* in every way no matter how long she has been a widow. She is Mrs. George Grayson, not Mrs. Alice Grayson, no matter how long she survives her husband. On legal documents, checks, and in business matters she may be Alice Grayson (but not *Mrs.* Alice). If it is necessary to show the prefix, she signs "Mrs. George Grayson" in parentheses under her signature if she is permitted to do so, otherwise *Mrs.* Alice it must be. If she has a son who was named for his father she does face some dilemma when he reaches the "Mr." age and lives with her or in the same community. The son always ceases to be "Jr." on the death of his father, unless his father was so distinguished a person as to remain even after his death a public figure— John D. Rockefeller, for example. In such a case the son is virtually forced to remain "Jr." and his mother has no problem about the continued and proper use of her husband's name. Where the "Jr." has been dropped and some confusion might arise, the mother may add "Sr." to her name to distinguish herself from present or future daughters-in-law.

Divorcée's Card and Name Increasingly, divorcées—especially those without children and continuing in business or planning to enter business or profession—revert to their maiden names or ask the court's permission during the proceedings to precede their married names by "Miss," or do so later without such permission as a matter of convenience. This solution is certainly superior to a woman's having to accept the inevitable "Mrs. *Gertrude* Glen" or to struggle with the matter of making people understand that she is socially Mrs. Butterworth (her maiden name) Glen (her married name) in spite of the fact that her *signature* is Gertrude Butterworth Glen (See "Signature on Checks, Legal Papers, and Letters," page 544). She may not legally, of course, keep her husband's name after divorce. That is, she may not be Mrs. *Robert* Glen, on her cards or otherwise. Sometimes the divorcée's coupling of her maiden name plus her married name after divorce results in a name so resoundingly long and fancy as to be ludicrous—for example, Mrs. Butterworth Chomleley-Brownell. Where her own maiden name doesn't team well with her ex-husband's, a divorcée is perfectly free to choose some other, preferably family, name to go with it—her maternal grandmother's, for example.

In desperation, many women, especially those with children, merely place the "Mrs." before their *maiden* names, becoming "Mrs. Gertrude Butterworth" or sadly agree to becoming "Mrs. Gertrude Glen" (given name plus married name preceded by "Mrs.") in business and socially—a solution I shall always find unattracive, but one, I must admit, that has been accepted even in the Social Register.

Where a divorcée's children are by another marriage than that from which she has just emerged, she may choose for convenience's sake to return to the name her children bear. It is unusual but sometimes necessary for a divorcée with children to call herself "Miss" socially as well as professionally.

Women's Titles on Cards A woman doctor who practices her profession has a choice, as does any other professional woman, of using her maiden or her married name while following her career. If she chooses the latter, "Dr. Mary Keen" (her husband's name), she obviously cannot be "Dr. James Keen" so "Dr. Mary" she must be. Like any professional woman she may hide her calling under cloak of her husband's name, socially. She may be Mrs. James Keen on her social card, if she prefers, even if she has a practice.

If she uses her husband's name professionally and he is not a doctor himself, it would seem a little belittling for her to use a joint card, which reads "Mr. James Keen and Dr. Mary Keen." A joint card in this case would read "Mr. and Mrs. James Keen." If both are doctors, their joint card should read "Dr. and Mrs. James Keen." A woman physician's card for social purposes should read "Doctor Mary Keen," as whenever possible the title should be spelled out in full—that is, when the length of the name permits. Her business card may read "Mary Keen, M.D."

A woman's card should never read, e.g., B. A. Sorensøn, which not only looks completely masculine but undoubtedly in some cases is intended to look so. A businesswoman should never be ashamed of her sex, nor hide it behind such initials on a card or in a signature. It should always bear her title.

A registered nurse uses the initials R.N. after her name on her business card and business stationery but Miss or Mrs. in social correspondence. When her name is preceded by either of these titles, the R.N. never follows it. It is *never* Mrs. Joan Appel, R.N. merely Joan Appel, R.N.

Is a Girl Ever Jr.?

You hear it and you see it in print, but a girl should never be referred to as "Greta McCarthy, Junior" even if her mother is a very well-known "Greta McCarthy" whose name frequently figures in the social, business, or theatrical news and who, for professional reasons, may also be known as "Miss." It's too bad the parents didn't think to give the poor girl her own identifying name at birth to avert such confusion, but, as it is, the daughter may have her cards read "Miss Greta McCarthy, second" or, if she prefers, "younger" but she can't use the masculine "junior." Of course none of these suffixes is necessary on a wedding invitation or announcement and should not be used. If I were she, I'd invent or exhume a middle name and call myself "Miss Greta *Ann* McCarthy." She certainly needs to do something to keep her mother from receiving her mail, her flowers, her invitations. Even if her mother carefully uses her husband's name socially, it is unavoidable that a certain amount of her mail will arrive addressed to her professional name, since many people never know her other one although they do know her home address.

When You May Send Your Card

Your calling card may go without you any place you might, and in other and less hectic times did, go yourself. Our communities have broadened so much geographically that the average socially popular woman, bearing the responsibility of her family's social obligations, could well spend a highly disproportionate amount of time in the mere traveling from her home to the home of friends or acquaintances on whom she should call. So today she more often phones, wires, or preferably sends her card with a necessarily brief message written on the face. "With deepest sympathy" (to someone bereaved). "It was a wonderful party!" (though I prefer a little thank-you note, on an "informal"). "Much happiness to you both" (to a girl newly engaged).

Your card is a great convenience for gift or flower sending, and no message need be written on it. Where you have charge accounts at a florist's, you may find it very convenient to supply him with some of your cards in their accompanying small envelopes. Remember that your card is a highly personal thing, sometimes an "open sesame," so give it this way only to the most meticulous tradesman who can be depended upon to guard it from misuse. If you are sending the box and write a very personal message on your card, enclose it in its own sealed envelope, if you have one with you, or in one of the tradesman's envelopes. Be sure he places the card directly on the flowers and doesn't attach it in some manner outside, where it is easily lost in the unwrapping. If you plan to deliver the box yourself, have him lay the card in its unsealed envelope among the flowers. On the envelope write "Miss Broderick" or "Mrs. Martin" not "Sue" or "Dorothy." The complete name and address will be on the florists' tag.

Often you see cards with lines through all or part of the name. If you are an intimate "first name" friend and go to a shop yourself to choose flowers or some other gift, you may wish to draw a fine pen line through your name, write a message on the face of the card, and sign it "Betty" or "Joe," as the case may be. I have often seen just the last name and the title "Mr.," "Captain," or "Miss" lightly crossed out, with just the first name remaining. Obviously a married woman or a man with a nickname must cross out all of the name and write "Marie" or "Pete." There is no rule that says this must be done, but when a message is included and friends are intimate it often is. Do not, of course, ask your florist to do this for you. Such pen scratchings should always indicate you chose the flowers or merchandise in person. If you phone in your order to a florist's where you have no personal cards, the florist may write your name and message on a plain white card for you, signing it in any way you wish. The dictated message in this instance should never be embarrassingly intimate, and it goes in an unsealed envelope. If you write such a casual message yourself, you may choose to send it in an envelope whose flap is tucked in rather than sealed.

Using Your Card for Invitations Your calling card is an ever-ready messenger for the issuing of invitations. If you have small neat handwriting, so much the better, for you can restrict your messages to the lower left corner. For example, you may note—Dinner, Tuesday, January 12th at 7:30. Black tie. If you write R.S.V.P. (please reply), the answer must come back to you in written form, preferably written in the third person if the recipient knows his etiquette. However, it is quite customary to answer such semiformal invitations by mailing your own card with a brief message of regret or acceptance—"Looking forward to Tuesday the 12th, 7:30!" (Black ink to match the engraving preferable) or "Sorry we can't come Tuesday." But if you want a speedy answer, so you can reshuffle your guest list if necessary, you just write your telephone number on the card and your intended guest will certainly get the idea. For further information on using the calling card as an invitation, see the Correspondence Section.

How to Mail Cards The post office will loathe you—and probably send you a notice indicating disapproval—if you make a regular practice of sending large numbers of your cards through the mail in the small envelopes supplied with them. Such envelopes require hand stamping and thus slow down the post office's work. It is preferable to enclose such cards in a normal-sized envelope.

When No R.S.V.P. Is Required Here again be guided by the usual practice among your friends. Any large reception, tea—especially a debutante tea—or garden party, for which formal invitations have been issued, does not require a reply unless the R.S.V.P. is included. But if you can't go, it is entirely correct (and in diplomatic and military circles, expected) to send your card and cards of the members of your family through the mail, so that they arrive the morning of the affair. They should be sent to the hostess. In the case of the debutante tea, the cards go only to the debutante's mother or sponsor, whoever has issued the invitations. Write nothing on the cards. Send one of your own, if you are a woman, one of your husband's (or a joint card for you both), and one for everyone in your household likely to have called with you.

How Many Cards Are Left at One Call?

When your hostess is at home, you send in your own card, via the servant who has opened the door, together with that of anyone actually with you (or you may use a joint card if your husband is with you). After you have been received you leave cards from other members of your family on the card tray, which should be in the hall—or in any convenient spot on the way out. You leave one card of your own for each lady in the household—but not more than three of any one card. You leave one of your husband's cards and one of any sons who are of age for each lady and gentleman of the household, including any house guests. You leave your card for women only, but you may leave a joint card for husband and wife. If the hostess herself opens the door you merely lay your clutch of cards on the hall table tray as you leave without comment.

Properly you call upon gentlemen only when you are actually accompanied by your husband or a close male relative living with you. All this is important to remember, or refer to, if you move in military or diplomatic circles. If you lead an average life in a community only mildly interested in these stiffly social matters you can forget it all and use your card in all sorts of secondary ways, instead.

To Ensure Your Card's Delivery If there seems to be some doubt about your card reaching the right person, pencil the name on the top—"For Miss Mary Carson" or "For Mrs. Worthing Frost." This is a necessary precaution if you are calling on one of several daughters or are leaving your card at a hotel desk or with an apartment house doorman.

Men's Business Cards

A man's business card differs from his social card in omitting the "Mr." before his name unless his first name is one which can also be a woman's name such as Carol or Beverly. In this case the use of Mr. would be used to eliminate confusion. It is larger than his social card and for an executive always engraved or printed in black conservative type faces, not script. Salesmen's cards used for advertising purposes may be printed or engraved in colors, but that of the company's top executives should not be.

A business card is approximately 3½"×2" and is engraved, preferably, or printed on fine quality parchment or good white pasteboard. The thinner parchment, of course, permits a larger quantity to be carried at one time, which is an advantage to a business person.

Stephen   Saunders

Sales Manager
Gordon Sales, Inc.
San Francisco, California

John F. Hasty

Williams, Inc.   700 Fifth Avenue and 51st Street
Tel. 0005-3599   New York, N.Y. zip code

A company president's card reads:

Loring K. Peters

President
Peters Engineering, Inc.
Portland, Oregon zip code

Possible variations: the complete address may be given, the telephone may be listed in the right-hand corner, the title may be omitted if the man is known as founder and president of his company.

A representative of the same firm without a major title (vice-president, treasurer, secretary) has his card with the company name appearing first:

Peters Engineering, Inc.

George R. Duffy
Traffic Department
Portland, Oregon zip code

While on social cards initials are avoided, they are common on business cards. In the cards shown, the names could read "L. K. Peters" or "G. R. Duffy." The firm's name always appears exactly as it is registered, although elsewhere on the card everything is spelled out as on a social card. Telephone numbers (advisable), where shown, have the exchange if needed written out, followed by the numerals.

Women's Business Cards

A woman's business card is exactly like that of the men in her firm with the exception that she should be designated as "Miss" or "Mrs."

Miss Lois Severy

President
Publicity Advisers, Inc.
Empire State Building
New York, N.Y. zip code Longacre 3-4098

A widow in business may optionally be Mrs. John or Mrs. Lois Severy. It is acceptable now, however, for widows as well as married women to use their first names on *business* cards preceded by Mrs. and, in some instances, Miss where this title is preferred by an employer or by the woman herself. Computers are making it a virtual necessity. (See also "Divorcée's Card and Name," page 764.)

Social Cards vs. Business Cards

A man's wallet should contain both business and social cards, for his business card may never double for social purposes. Of course, for an executive or a professional man, business and social activities often overlap, but they should never do so obviously. A businessman sending flowers to a customer or client who is in the hospital is making a social gesture (even if he has to do so for business reasons) and should enclose his social card or use a card the florist will furnish. If his connection with the customer is so remote that the latter would not be able to identify his name without that of his firm, he should not be intruding in an essentially personal situation. If a customer is opening up a new place of business, flowers may go from one firm to the other, accompanied by the business card of an executive or representative of the company.

Making and Receiving Calls

In Victorian days and up until the First World War the making of calls was a highly stylized business. The duty fell on the women of the household, who left their husbands' cards with their own. However on certain occasions, such as calls of condolence, of congratulation, or calls on the sick, men often made their appearance and left their cards in person, too, as they still properly may.

A personal call, however, is still necessary to make new neighbors feel at home in small country or suburban communities or even large ones where you have been given the name of a newcomer by friends who would like to arrange introductions for them. This custom is not followed in cities, and in some places in the country it is a neglected courtesy. Today, calls are preferably "by appointment."

All over the country it is becoming the accepted thing to phone first before paying a call, because call-making—when it does take place—quite sensibly is taking on more meaning.

It is a considerate thing to phone any newcomer on whom you plan to call to ask when it will be convenient for her to see you. If she is in the middle of unpacking her goods and chattels and without the leisure or peace of mind to receive you, she will appreciate your not dropping in until she is settled. Even then she might well appreciate a forewarning of your visit. You can do this on very short order the day you wish to call. Don't plan to run into any such household in the morning, as used to be the eleven o'clock custom. Choose the afternoon between three and five or, if it's an informal home and an informal neighborhood, in the early evening after dinner, first making sure you are welcome. If you are a woman, you don't call on a man who has moved into your country neighborhood, but, of course, some male member of the family may call or you may go with your husband or any adult male relative living with you. Also you may phone or write to invite such a man to call on you.

The Call Itself Ask for your hostess at the door during the accepted calling hours that I have mentioned. If the servant says she is not at home, it may mean, merely, that she is not receiving any visitors, a necessary social device not intended to offend. Just leave your card. (But see pg. 757)

If your hostess is able to see you, do not remove your coat or gloves. Leave within twenty minutes.

A man making a formal call removes his overcoat or topcoat and leaves it with his hat, gloves, and stick, if he carries one, in the hall and on leaving he leaves his social card. No visitor trails rubbers, umbrella, or boots into a drawing room, needless to say.

Conversation During Calls No one expects you to discuss any very vital topics while making a social call. The hostess will know why you are there. Light conversation about the party you attended (unless this is a call of condolence), the attractiveness of the people you met, something amusing that has happened, even that conversation piece, the weather, will do. Don't prolong your farewell. At the end of twenty minutes, or at most a half hour, thank your hostess again and leave promptly.

Bringing Flowers Sometimes it is pleasant to take flowers to your hostess if you make no special point about it. Leave them in the hall to be arranged after you've left, or have them arrive with your card after you leave.

The cost of flowers should always be in keeping with your income if money is any consideration, and even when it is not, pretentious bouquets should never be sent where your hostess's quarters may be too small to accommodate them. Two or three gardenias arranged for use in a flat container, or a small fragrant bunch of lilies of the valley or violets may be much more welcome than two dozen towering gladioli. Many florists will send flowers already arranged in containers—a godsend to people who live permanently or temporarily in small quarters.

Calling on the Eligible Man Living under the same apartment roof in a big city with neighbors does not sanction a social call unless some introduction has taken place. You might receive a visiting card from a friend with the notation, "John Oakes, my ex-classmate, has moved to your building. Do look him up!" Even this doesn't suggest you and your husband call on him unannounced—a procedure very unpopular among bachelors in or out of cities. If you are a single woman you might arrange to include such a man when you are having a cocktail party or tea, mailing your card to him or sending it by the hall man or slipping it under his door in a sealed envelope. It might read, on the face of the card, "Cocktails at five, Thurs., Dec. 5th, Apt. 601." It is to be assumed that your friend has told him about you. However, if you feel he may be puzzled to receive an informal invitation this way and might not immediately recognize your name, phone him or drop him a note reading something like this:

Dear Mr. Oakes,

Our friend in common, Gordon Ward, tells us you are now a neighbor in the building. Some friends whom I feel you might enjoy meeting are coming to cocktails this Sunday.

Will you join us around four-thirty in apartment 601?

Sincerely (or, less formally,
Cordially, which is now
an accepted closing, so-
cially and in business)

If you include Mr. Oakes, whom you have never entertained before, on your invitation list for a formal party, remember that he may not immediately recall his friend Ward's promise to make him known to you so you might ask him to call. It is better to invite him to the small gathering first. If you do include him on a party list for which you are issuing formal third-person invitations (which are sent increasingly rarely except for weddings, receptions, debuts, balls), include your card, on which you might write "at Gordon Ward's suggestion," or phone him first. You might say something like this, "Mr. Oakes, this is Jessie Gray, Gordon Ward's friend. I believe he told you I live in this building too. I just wanted to tell you you'll receive an invitation to dinner shortly. I do hope you'll come."

Do not by any chance ask the gentlemen to call on you, unless friends will be present, if you are a woman living alone and are of marriageable age (and when does that cease to be?). The more eligible he is, the more it must seem that the courtesy you are extending him in asking him to call comes at another's request. Never be too obvious in your bachelor-gathering. If he does not accept your invitation, it would be very pleasant of him to send flowers with a note on his card to the effect that he hopes you'll think of him again. From there on it should be his move. He may ask to call on you. If he doesn't, better look elsewhere for bachelors to enliven your parties.

The Bachelor Host and Calls A man living alone who entertains at home, even if he's of high military or diplomatic station, does not receive party calls, phone calls, or even notes or cards of thanks from the ladies who were present. It is the man who must always thank the ladies who have been his guests, although any departing guest says a few graceful words of thanks on leaving. The only exception is when some woman receives with him as hostess pro tem—his mother, sister, or other female relative—and then it is she who should receive the party thanks.

Calls of Condolence You leave your card at the door and do not ask to be received when making a call of condolence, unless you are very intimate with the family. If no tray is offered, step in and leave your card in the hall on a table or chair. Don't hand it to the person at the door. On such a call, where you do not feel you can offer to do more, say to whoever opens the door, "Will you kindly tell [naming the member of the family you know or saying 'the family'] that I called to offer my sympathy?" Such calls are not returned. They should be made within a month after the funeral, but most considerate people make them as soon as the death is known. The call of condolence is about the only call that still seems almost obligatory in all circles where it is at all possible for friends to offer their sympathy this way in person. Where personal calls are impossible, a telegram of condolence may be sent with a request to the telegraph company that it be delivered, not phoned.

Calling on a Public Official Anyone has the right to request to see the President of the United States, the governor of one's state, the mayor of one's city, or anyone else holding public office. Such a request must be motivated by something more than a desire to shake his hand, as all these executives run on split-second timing of their engagements.

Requests to see the President are made to his aide but may be made to the aide through anyone close to the President in an official or unofficial capacity through whom you have a personal approach. A relatively small number of those seeking an audience can receive it, so be sure before making such a request that it *is* only the President who can be of help in the matter. And, if possible, put your request in writing so it can be attended to without a personal audience. Of the thousands and thousands of letters the President receives every year, none goes entirely unnoticed. All those actually requiring a reply receive it. Some come to the President's personal attention and receive an answer from him or from a secretary. Some are referred to other departments of the government for follow-up. Threatening and abusive letters go to the FBI.

Chapter 59

HOSPITALS AND DOCTORS

Hospital Visits

Most hospitals have strict visiting rules. There are certain hours during which private patients may have callers and usually more limited ones for ward or semiprivate patients. Unless there is some valid reason for doing so, never ask for any extension of official hours.

Unless you are a close friend or relative who can really help in the nursing of the patient and are needed, don't stay more than a few minutes on any visit. If the patient is well on the road to recuperation, you may, with permission of the nurse in charge, stay perhaps as much as the full visiting time in the afternoon or evening if there are no other visitors. It is unfair to the patient and to the nurses to cram a sickroom full of visitors. In fact, many hospitals limit the number of visitors a patient may have at one time, and some have enforced quiet periods for patients, especially maternity patients, every afternoon during which not even telephone calls may be received.

Visiting the New Mother A baby is always a matter for rejoicing, and a hospital call on a new mother is the kind people like to make. But childbirth is tiring and the mother needs plenty of rest, and this may be the only time for months that she may really be able to. get it. So, if you call upon her, be brief. A note or a little gift for her or for the baby may be better than a phone call, if she has a phone, and better than a personal visit. Just talking on the phone when your whole body is weary can be fatiguing to the point of tears—especially when well-wishers call in great numbers or stay on the phone too long.

Sending Gifts

Before sending flowers to a person who may be literally blanketed with them it is well to phone a relative to see if more flowers will be welcome. Sometimes, depending on the cause for hospitalization, delicacies are preferred, but be sure the patient is not on some sort of diet that would prohibit fruit, candy, or your best homemade cake or cookies. There is hardly a diet, however, that rules out all kinds of ice cream, and, as hospital ice cream is often dull, a really good permissible ice cream brought in from outside is usually a treat.

Very often to women patients a pretty bed jacket or nightgown, a bottle of eau de cologne, or an armful of pocket-size books that are easy to hold are sometimes more welcome than more flowers. If you do send flowers, it is sometimes better to send them during the latter part of the patient's stay, for in the first days of an illness, bouquets may arrive. And if you do send them, provide, if possible, a container for them because most hospitals have too few vases and those available are usually inadequate in the making of an attractive arrangement. The best thing, perhaps, is to send a flowering plant that needs little care from overworked nurses, or one of those permanent arrangements that do not have to be taken apart each day.

A woman patient in a hospital is always listed as Mrs. Mary Jones, offensive as this is socially. There is no reason why friends writing her letters or sending flowers or other gifts cannot give her name as Mrs. John Jones and put parenthetically after it (Mary). This is what I do and recommend.

If You Are the Patient

When you go into a hospital you are not entering a luxury hotel, no matter what superior accommodations you are able to pay for. Only a few years ago I was in a hospital at the same time a distant relative of mine arrived there for a sojourn with her own table linen, silver, china, personal maid, and all kinds of special equipment to make her feel at home. Even her food was sent in. But I doubt whether, today, even hospitals badly needing endowments would permit such special privilege. In fact, there isn't room in hospitals today for any but the very ill. Stays are often limited for certain things, such as childbirth, tonsillectomies, or appendectomies, unless, of course, some complication occurs.

We are so short of hospitals that it isn't even possible today to name one's accommodations if you are an emergency patient. You may land in a semiprivate room or even a ward, may have to have floor nursing. This means great curtailment of your notions of service. You may not summon the floor nurses as you would a private nurse, and you must consider at all times that you do not occupy the quarters by yourself—the other patient or patients must be considered. Actually, once you get used to the lack of privacy, a pleasant roommate may speed your recovery, although an inconsiderate one can certainly slow it up.

How to Share a Hospital Room In wards your conduct is pretty strictly regulated by the ever-present nurse, but if you are behind the heavy door of a semiprivate room, you may be quite a menace to the recovery of your roommate—sometimes without fully realizing your thoughtlessness. Some hospitals, rightly I think, prohibit the installation of telephones in semiprivate rooms or, if they do allow them, limit the hours they may be used to regular visiting hours. The constant ringing of the phone, from early morning until late at night, and protracted, sometimes alarmingly clinical conversations are a painful nuisance to the other person sharing the room. One smoker can make a non-smoker miserable by filling the sickroom with cigarette, cigar, or pipe smoke. The unremitting noise of one patient's radio or a TV, where it is permitted, can distress the other. Guests who overstay, who are too numerous or too loud in their conversation make it impossible for other patients to have the necessary rest. If you ever find yourself on the receiving end of a hospital nuisance, don't suffer in silence. Explain the situation to the floor nurse or to the house doctor who visits you or to your attending physician, and steps will be taken, one way or the other, to correct the trouble. Your peace of mind is important in your doctor's regimen for you.

You and Your Nurses   Patients often make the mistake of asking a nurse all sorts of questions about their own condition, which nurses are, ethically speaking, not permitted to answer. If you want to know the result of your operation or the state of your temperature, ask your doctor, not your nurse.

Your nurse's attitude toward you should be strictly objective, so don't try to make her your confidante, as you may regret it very much after you leave. On the other hand, don't treat her like a servant—she is a professionally trained person working under the direction of your doctor. She is there to fill your requests, if advisable, but not to take your orders. If you don't like your nurse—and some few, perhaps because of overwork or limited social outlet (nursing is one of the lonely professions), are crotchety—ask your doctor to try to replace her, if possible, with someone less irritating.

If you have a private nurse for a week or more, you pay her bill promptly as tendered. Don't ask her to run errands for you on her hours off.

When she leaves you, you may show your appreciation by giving candy, flowers, perfume, stockings, gloves, handkerchiefs, cigarettes or books. But don't feel obligated to give beyond your means, especially if the hospital cost has been hard for the budget to bear. And to the very occasional surly or sadistic nurse, if it has been your lot to get one, give nothing.

If you have just had a baby and the baby has been kept in the hospital nursery, it is thoughtful for you to remember at least the head nurse there. If you have been a ward or semiprivate patient, it is not necessary to give anything—in fact, it is never *necessary*.

Don't give cash to this professional worker, but when months or even years of nursing have taken place, a bond or bonds or perhaps a special bequest in the case of a death are matters to be decided upon in thanks for patient devotion.

Visiting Your Doctor

If you live in a small community and your doctor has his office in his home, there are various courtesies that should be considered. Even a general practitioner has office hours, and these should be respected. Don't drop in on him before or after these hours just because you are passing his house and think it might be a good time for him to look at Danny's tonsils. If an emergency arises, phone his office, not his home, if your town has an answering service that takes doctors' calls. It is not fair to ask the doctor's wife to take his messages or chase him up at other patients' homes, if by phoning the office, day or night, you can reach him through the service he maintains.

When you do go to your doctor's office, remember that he has little free time for unnecessary conversation, even if he is a personal friend. If he makes a call at your home, if indeed he accepts house calls, don't expect him to give a once-over to all the members of the family without billing you for his additional attention. Offer him, if you wish, a soft drink, coffee, or tea. The conscientious doctor takes nothing stronger on calls because the odor of alcohol on his breath might cause the next patient to doubt his competency, especially in an emergency. Think twice before you call him at night or in very bad weather. Often phone advice will tide you through and save the doctor's energy. Many mothers of young babies pay a doctor a flat fee for one year's care of the child, and this service includes telephone consultation as often as necessary. But calls should, even then, be made during office hours, if possible. A list of questions, prepared beforehand, saves the doctor's time as well as your own.

Professional Ethics   It is incredible the questions patients ask their doctors concerning the troubles of other people. They want to know why Mrs. Kelly is in the waiting room, if her husband is still drinking, if her daughter is going to have a baby. Your doctor has taken an oath not to reveal such professional secrets. Don't ask him such questions, and don't be annoyed when he side-steps all personal questions about his treatment of other patients or concerning his relations with them. Do not pass on to others the names of patients waiting to see a doctor—especially an obstetrician or a psychiatrist. People may or may not wish their visits to such specialists known by the general public.

Medical Examinations   You would think that no man or woman would turn up for a prearranged doctor's appointment without having bathed and dressed in clean clothing. But the reports I have received from nurses and doctors prove otherwise. Evidently, even a Park Avenue practice doesn't protect a doctor from unfastidiousness.

Personal Relationships   It is only human to believe that your doctor, because of his intimate relation with you, has a very special personal interest in your welfare, which he may indeed have. But his interest is basically professional and if he is to serve you best, it should be kept on that basis. Doctors rarely treat their own families because they are likely to lose their objectivity when prescribing for people with whom they have too close a relationship.

The young doctor or the pretty nurse is often embarrassed by the reaction some patients have to the necessarily close physical association. A doctor is often deluged by gifts, many of them silly and useless, from what he terms G.P.s—grateful patients. Be grateful and appreciative of your doctor's care, but never expect more than professional consideration from him and be on guard lest your own warm feelings for him, engendered by the flattering, personal attention he must give your every complaint, embarrass him in any way The best thing you can do to show your appreciation is to pay your bills promptly, be on time for appointments, and take no more of his time than is actually necessary. Any gifts should be simple and impersonal.

Be chary of suggesting any social invitations, unless he indicates a desire for them. A doctor should never be put in the position of either having to see his patients socially or lose them. Again, objectivity between patient and doctor makes for the best professional relations.

Doctors have little enough uninterrupted social life as it is, without having to discuss symptoms with friends, or even perfect strangers, when they do go to a dinner party. If you meet a doctor socially, never ask his professional advice unless you're willing to go to his office for it. It is true that many doctors like to talk "shop" in their free time, but usually not with laymen unless the latter are particularly well informed on scientific matters. Never use a social contact with any professional person to ask advice for which you would be charged if you applied for it under the usual circumstances.

The Psychiatric Patient

In big urban centers such as New York and Chicago, creative individuals in particular who have not had or are not undergoing some form of psychiatric therapy seem on the surface to be in the minority. Psychiatry, psychoanalysis and its language have all become a familiar part of our society. In theatrical circles, not to have an analyst is virtually an admission of failure and here the urge to use the analyst and his findings as conversational and creative material is usual. It is, however, therapeutically unwise and socially tasteless to proclaim this confidential material. It is usually the beginning patient, fascinated by the experience, who feels impelled to tell everyone about it. On the other hand, today almost no one undergoing treatment should be embarrassed to mention the fact if there is reason to do so. The diabetic does not arrive at a cocktail party loudly announcing his illness, but he may have to mention it if some unthinking guest insists upon forcing alcohol upon him if it is forbidden. The analogy is not far fetched. Mental illness, whatever its degree, is a disability which may be acute or chronic, but which, through therapy, may be cured, helped, or at worst made tolerable. The feeling of stigmatization which formerly concerned individuals suffering from psychiatric illness has subsided markedly as the probability of successful treatment has become better known.

This is true of many illnesses formerly considered incurable as hopes for cure have been discovered.

To Be Avoided Here are some things to be avoided in regard to the psychiatric patient.

Never ask a patient what he has discussed with his doctor or how much his sessions cost. Avoid asking how long treatment will last—even his doctor probably can't give a definite answer to that.

Imply neither that his trouble is minor nor that psychiatry is in his case a waste of time. Resist being a parlor analyst. It is easy to take your friends apart, but difficult to repair the damage you may do.

It should go without saying that you should never ask the doctor about one of his patients when you meet him socially.

For the Patient You don't have to make a special point of your medical or dental appointments, nor should you with psychiatric or psychoanalytic ones. If you have a regular session at the same time each day or each week, explain this if necessary to your family and associates in a casual fashion, as is your right.

Never discuss outside of your doctor's office the fact that you have seen and recognized any other patient in the waiting room, and never ask your doctor who his other patients are. The same delicacy, as I have pointed out above, is followed concerning the practice of obstetrics and certain other medical specialties. If this necessary reticence embarrasses you or your family, comfort yourself and them with the thought that it is the strong who have the courage to seek help, and with the doctor's aid to work their way to health and independence.

Chapter 60

SPEAKING BEFORE AN AUDIENCE

Like death and taxes, some form of public speaking comes at one time or another to all of us. We may only find ourselves on our feet at the Parent-Teacher meeting or at our club, but for the uninitiated, the shy, the unsure even this mild public appearance is agony in anticipation and often in actuality.

Extemporaneous speaking is an art fostered by plentiful practice. It is said that George Bernard Shaw, struck dumb when he first tried to speak in public, joined the contentious Fabian Society in England, and on any and all occasions rose to his feet until glibness became through constant practice part and parcel of his personality. Many a seemingly extemporaneous speech has been carefully memorized and lengthily extolled beforehand so that it comes forth smoothly—but not so smoothly as to seem well-prepared.

It is cheering to know from the testimony of experts that people do not wish us to be completely perfect in our delivery. Many excellent public speakers deliberately stumble or stutter occasionally to make their performance seem more humanly fallible. The man who speaks with too much assurance in his own performance sometimes finds his audience somewhat hostile. Perhaps this is because each person in the audience at some time mentally puts himself in the place of the speaker and suffers what he believes to be his diffidence or embarrassment, his strangeness in these surroundings or circumstances. For this reason the speaker starting his talk with too much self-assurance or brashness often finds his audience is not with him at all.

Introducing Your Speech

It takes an audience a few minutes to get used to you, so when you get on your feet you do not immediately proceed to the matter at hand. People are adjusting to your appearance, the tone of your voice, your bearing, and in my opinion they don't actually hear your opening words. I think it is this, rather than the routine dullness of most speech openings, that focuses the audience's attention so slowly on what you are saying. For the first few minutes the practiced speaker, therefore, fills in time with his "Thank you" to the chairman introducing him, calling him or her by name—"Thank you, Mrs. Wirk." Then come his formal salutations, "Mr. President, honored guests [if there are any], ladies and gentlemen." Some speakers, at this point, drag in some pointless joke or anecdote to tide them though what I think of as the inspection period, but as the pre-occupied audience rarely gets the point of it and just laughs auto-matically, it seems better technique to begin with a little appropriate preamble that leads logically to the heart of what you have to say. One way of doing this is to prepare in advance an outline of what you plan to dis-cuss. It is perfectly sound technique to state categorically what you have been asked to speak about and to indicate what you hope to prove or what points you wish to develop, but not at such length as to dull people's antici-pation of your talk. The biggest "don't" in an introduction is don't apologize or excuse yourself—for anything—for not being prepared, for not being qualified to speak on the subject, or simply for speaking at all. Let's hope the first two aren't true! Do be modest but don't convey the feeling that you were forced to speak and that perhaps the chairman or president of the group asked you because he didn't think his audience important enough to find a very good speaker.

Clichés

The speech that is studded with clichés, especially those old saws of public speaking, "I come before you today," "Unaccustomed as I am to public speaking," "I point with pride," "We view with alarm," ". . . and in conclusion let me say," etc., is dreary. More is expected of us since the development of radio and television than the old-fashioned arm-waving oratorical approach. The more natural your speaking voice, the simpler your language and presentation, the more believable you will be.

Using the Voice Correctly

If a microphone is placed before you, it is well if you have noted how the person who introduced you used it. Properly, microphones are tested beforehand for volume and the speaker is told just how to speak into the one presented to him. Because of the wide use of the public address system and of radio microphones, the well-versed public speaker knows he must avoid the shouting that he used to do from the old lecture platform when he wanted to emphasize a point. He knows, too, that he must stand quietly and talk at all times directly into the microphone, which must not be touched or clutched. Turning his head from side to side to take in the full sweep of the audience often partially blots out what he is trying to say. If he raises his voice perceptibly for emphasis, he must step back a little from the microphone to avoid blasting his hearer's ear-drums. But often greater emphasis is made, when a mike is in use, by the lowering of the voice, even to a whisper. This technique, occasionally and artfully used, causes the audience to hang literally on each softly spoken word.

If You Have to Cough

If a speaker must cough or sneeze or blow his nose during the course of a speech, he need not be embarrassed but may think of it as a useful, human diversion that brings a perhaps needed little break in the flow of his speech. He of course turns his head away, especially from a microphone, and excuses himself in the case of a cough or sneeze but not if he blows his nose or takes a sip of water. Some accomplished speakers use the drinking of water as a way of heightening suspense before making some dramatic charge or assertion. "And now I am going tell you something that will shake every one of you, that will bring tears to the eyes of every man and woman in this hall——" (drink of water).

Reading a Speech

No speech should ever be read if you want your audience to listen to what you have to say. It is sometimes quite satisfactory to have before you a written speech the gist of which, at least, and phrases from it, have been committed to memory. But to read it verbatim, unless you are in a radio studio and the reading of a script is required, is to lose your audience at the start. Even if you read well, the audience will be bored and restless if it sees you in the act. Using an outline or notes on small cards held in the palm of the hand is much better and makes for a more believable, more personal presentation of your ideas. Many good speakers use the written speech before them in toto, or better as a reminder or a guide, especially when discussing scientific or political matters or in presenting professional papers, but they make it a point to look up frequently, to develop little techniques that make them at least seem to be extemporizing.

Directing Your Talk

Some speakers find it disconcerting to talk generally to an audience, so before they rise, they select one face, sometimes one they know, and direct the entire discourse to it. This device may be effective for the speaker but works better, I think, if he chooses several faces in opposite parts of the hall and directs his words sometimes this way, sometimes that, to lend a little variation.

The Use of Jokes, Illustrations, and Anecdotes

Jokes and anecdotes, if at all appropriate, do have a function in that they loosen up an audience—and the speaker too—especially at the difficult beginning of a speech. But they are better omitted if a speaker tells a story badly and self-consciously. And if they have nothing whatsoever to do with the case, they are certainly better omitted. Otherwise members of the audience may be so puzzled by the introduction of the stories that they will spend the rest of the time trying to determine the connection and so not hear, as consciously as they should, whatever else you have to say. It is good, in making a speech, to remember that many, many people are not aurally sensitive, that is, they don't easily comprehend what they get through the ears alone. For this reason points need to be made more than once, propositions put in several ways. Wherever possible, illustrate what you are saying visually in some way, with charts, graphs, slides, motion pictures, or some form of illustration in which you take part—sketches, exhibits, instruction in techniques. The action involved breaks up a too smooth presentation and makes the audience feel more at ease—and you will, too. A spotlight pointer where slides or movies are used is the most effective way of calling attention to certain details.

Closing a Speech

Many a speech loses it effectiveness if the closing is too greatly drawn out or if, on the other hand, it is too abruptly terminated. Give some indication that you have said about all you are going to say on the subject a few minutes before sitting down. Many graceful speakers say something like this, "You have been kind enough to give me this amount of time, and, while I could develop this subject to a much greater extent, we are all anxious to hear what the next speaker has to say, etc." Then comes some brief summing-up point or points and a final statement of conclusion, but never say, without preamble, "I guess that's all," or "That's all I have to say." A speech should end on a point the hearer will take away with him, if possible, or on an anecdote that sums up in capsule form part, at least, of what the speaker was trying to say. The best speech stirs action.

Making Your Departure

Often a principal speaker will end his speech and almost without pause make his getaway from the speakers' table. He may have to make a train or fulfill another engagement, and, if so, the chairman should, if possible, prepare the audience for such a sudden departure when he thanks the speaker. The chairman in thanking him should repeat the speaker's name for late-comers or those who may not have caught it correctly before. "Thank you, Mr. Graham Saunders" is better than "Thank you, Mr. Saunders." Otherwise, it is courteous for the speaker to hear out his successors, if any, with at least a show of interest and to linger after the speeches to receive the felicitations or answer the questions of those assembled whenever this seems advisable.

The Speaker's Spouse

A delicate situation arises when the spouse of the speaker is on the dais. If there is a standing ovation, does he or she stand? does the spouse applaud with the others, or just look pleasantly attentive? The speaker's spouse should stand with the others, and usually just looks pleasantly attentive during the applause. At a political rally, however, it is very probable that the spouse would applaud, too.

Dress of the Speaker

Dress of the Man Speaker A man making an evening speech inquires beforehand what those at the speakers' table will wear—business suits, dinner jackets, or full dress. It frequently happens that people at the speakers' table wear full dress and the others at the dinner come in dinner jackets. At public dinners it is never incorrect for the speaker, the chairman, and those at the speakers' table to wear full evening dress, even if the body of the assemblage comes informally attired. For the same reason, a lecturer, a conductor, or any personage making a public appearance in the evening wears formal clothes if there is any possibility of some of his hearers doing likewise. He should set the highest sartorial standard for the occasion so as not embarrass any who come formally attired to do him proper honor.

What to Wear if You're a Woman A woman speaking in the evening wears a long or short covered-up cocktail dress or a formal evening gown, depending on the occasion and on what the majority of women present will be wearing. If she is to open the opera season with an appeal for subscriptions she wears formal evening dress and her finest jewels. If she is to get up in the high school auditorium to explain the functioning of the Girl Scouts she dresses in street clothes and optionally wears a hat.

Clothes so vivid or spectacular that they distract the hearers' attention from what you are saying are certainly a mistake. At the same time you should look your best, being sure that your clothes are not so new and high style that you are at all conscious of them. Overdressing is more likely to be criticized than underdressing for the occasion. For most speaking occasions, when in doubt, wear a good, tailored, but not sport, suit. Most women speak without a hat, or, if they wear a hat, they are careful to choose one that does not in any way shield the face. Shoes should be well-fitting and suitable to the costume, of course.

A professional woman speaker usually wears clothes a little more dramatic than those of her audience because actually she is putting on a performance. The information she received on her engagement through her lecture agent, or directly from the organization retaining her, usually does indicate the type of dress expected. Even if she is asked to wear something equivalent to a cocktail dress, she would not of course wear anything too elaborate or too naked. A well-groomed appearance complimentary to her audience is very much a part of her whole presentation.

Swearing in At any swearing-in ceremony or any ceremony for that matter in which an oath must be taken, a woman need not remove her right glove, and a hat is optional. A man does remove his right glove, if the procedure takes place out of doors, just as he would, if possible, for shaking hands. A woman, of course, does not remove her right glove to shake hands except with the head of church or state, as her gloves are considered part of her costume.

Your Radio Appearance

Many citizens of distinction—and many of no particular distinction—find themselves for one reason or other in a broadcasting studio and confronted with a microphone. Mike fright, like stage fright, is very common, even in professionals, and results in stuttering, stammering, or a positive inability to say anything at all.

The psychological reasons for mike fright are probably very complex. They may have to do with the idea that we are such poor creatures that no one would be interested in what we have to say—about the Boy Scout Drive or whatever. Perhaps the situation is painfully reminiscent of our school recitations. Whatever the cause, there are a few physical and mental tricks I find do help overcome mike fright. Here they are:

Before your turn at the microphone, keep your mind on the individuals before you and off the nebulous millions supposedly listening in. You are going to talk to these few flesh and blood people, who, your reason tells you, are quite ordinary and harmless.

Just as you are about to speak into the microphone, take a deep breath so your first words will not be tight and breathless. Keep your hands and body relaxed and limp. Keep your eyes on one person to whom you are talking, not on the microphone.

Smile as you speak and your words will come more easily. It is hard to be tense if you are smiling. Your outwardly easy manner helps reassure those with you so that they expect you to acquit yourself well, and you do.

Hold your head still about one foot from the microphone, and speak directly into it, trying to attain your usual conversational tone of voice.

If you are taking part in an interview, be sure to let the other person finish his question or answer completely. Overlapping voices in radio create a meaningless jumble for the listener.

Have handy a glass of water, a piece of paper, and a pencil (for doodling if you're a doodler). Sometimes fear that your mouth will become dry and no water be available to you is enough to make you nervous. Have the water on hand before you start. And take a sip or two if you wish while you are on the air. Little breaks in your talk are natural and human. They make what you are saying more attractive to the listener.

If you must read a script in an interview and you lose your place, don't be afraid to say to the person opposite you, "Now where was I? Oh, yes, I was saying, etc." Remember that in ordinary conversation people lose momentary track of what they were saying, too. A too smooth delivery on radio is uninteresting. The ideal is to try to make everything seem unrehearsed and spontaneous.

The Do's and Don'ts of Radio Appearances   Speak in a natural tone of voice.

Don't shout into the microphone or lower your voice—unless for the latter you move closer to the microphone at the same time. Sometimes it is more effective to lower the voice in making a point than to raise it, but it takes some practice to know how to do this on radio effectively.

Don't wear jewelry that rattles or fabrics that rustle.

Don't tap your feet or drum your fingers.

If you must cough, sneeze, or blow your nose, turn aside from the mike and don't apologize. You may use the cough button on the microphone if there is one.

Get to the studio a half hour before your broadcast, if possible.

Go through a rehearsal, if requested, with the same care you will accord your actual broadcast.

If you read from a script, remove clips or staples beforehand, and as each page is completed, drop it gently to the floor. Rustling and turning of pages is clearly audible to the audience.

Watch the studio warning lights. When the light is green, it is all right to talk to others in the studio—you are off the air. But keep alert. When the light changes to red you are on the air, and then you speak on cue only.

If others precede you at the mike, take your place, when your turn comes, very carefully. Don't touch the mike at any time, and if you must seat yourself before it during the broadcast, do so without scraping the chair or jarring the table.

If you have never been on a radio program before, do not hesitate to ask a few questions of someone in the studio before you go on. If you are to follow the engineer's instructions, ask to have the hand signals demonstrated to you. But briefly, here are a few signals with which you are most likely to be concerned: If the engineer, announcer, or interviewer places his hand palm up horizontally and makes a lifting motion, this means "keep your voice up." If he turns his palm down with a patting motion, this means "lower your voice." If he raises five, three, two, or one finger, this means you must finish what you are saying in that number of minutes. If he makes a circle with his index finger and thumb, this means you are doing fine. If he lays his finger on his nose, that means you are finishing right on time. If he "cuts his throat" with his hand, this means the program has been cut off the air. Watch the light at this point—the program may resume and words not meant for broadcast go out over the air.

At the end of the program—if you have stayed until the end—it is courteous to thank your interviewer (if you've been interviewed) for asking you, and to thank the announcer and the engineer as well if they have not already gone on to other things. However, schedules in radio are on a split-second basis, so don't detain artists or staff unnecessarily.

In most radio studios there are "No Smoking" signs, but if others in the studio are smoking nevertheless, before or while the program is on the air, you may do so too if you really believe it will help maintain your poise.

But never do what some misguided amateurs do—take a few cocktails before going on the air in the expectancy that that will help.

If You Appear on Television

The continuing development and changes in television make it difficult to give very much in the way of advice to those likely to appear on television programs.

For studio shows, rehearsals are usual. Scripts are rarely obviously read, although if necessary the text, or notes from the text, may be in large type on a Teleprompter or on "idiot cards" somewhere out of camera range. More often what is to be said is memorized or presented ad lib.

For black and white television, light clothes, preferably unpatterned, are preferred. Sometimes guests are asked to avoid shiny jewelry or trimmings which catch the light and divert televiewers from the subject, but much depends on the type of lighting on the set. In ordinary living room lighting unspotlighted, there is much more leeway in dress. Otherwise, jewelry, such as a shiny necklace, which seems necessary to the costume may be worn if its shine has been reduced temporarily with a film of soap or other substance applied by the make-up department. Women's necklines must not be too plunging (but professionals are given more leeway in this matter). One that is too high, on the other hand, gives telescopic effect to a short-necked, short woman. A hair style should be as simple as possible and so should the lines of clothes, for the television camera can distort the figure and add a good twenty pounds. Color television, like a color photograph, is more flattering, adds perspective. White on women, sometimes pink and yellow are better avoided but much depends on the set. When in doubt, ask. But remember, even when the show is in color many viewers will be seeing it in black and white. For men, blue shirts are always preferred for television, even in evening shirts.

Make-up Everyone receives special make-up for studio television appearances, and at large public dinners and other events to be televised public figures try to meet some of the make-up man's specifications whenever possible. Men should be newly and closely shaven. If their beards are very dark, pancake make-up, not too obvious to nearby guests, can help improve the speakers' appearance on the television screen.

Like modern public speaking, appearance before the television cameras requires a minimum of gestures and facial contortions. The speaker should play to the camera, the one with the red light, turning his head as indicated when one camera takes over from a different angle than the other or others.

On many major stations make-up is provided, but it is well to check on this, and where it is not, and make-up is important, to have it done elsewhere professionally. Television make-up lessons are available in major centers and advisable for women, and men too, who must make television appearances frequently whether or not make-up services are provided by the station. There are always emergencies. Sometimes with many people waiting to be made up, the job is cursory, to say the least.

On Camera Relaxation and naturalness are the keys to a good television appearance. Backstage before going on a series of relaxing exercises for the nervous guest can be of great help. A series of shoulder shrugs, bending forward and swinging the arms in limp fashion, going up and down on the toes, breathing deeply, smiling, all tend to dissipate nervousness. On camera the guest should try to behave as he naturally would in conversation, laughing or smiling as the situation calls for it, gesturing as he normally would. He should avoid, however, suddenly sitting bolt upright when he sees the camera coming toward him, or leaning sharply forward. The television camera before it is put into action is preceded by spot checking, changing of lights, and other technicalities. Abrupt movement—and especially standing up—on the part of a guest can throw all these preliminaries into a state of confusion. Women guests should not wear jangling bracelets and no guest should drum fingers on the table or on a glass, or touch a microphone when speaking. There should be quiet in the audience when the red light·on the camera is on. The microphone that is hung around the neck necessitates care when the show is over, so guests should not rise without unhooking it.

In leaving the studio while a show is still in progress, one should walk softly, avoid cables, and never walk in front of a camera. Even out of immediate range of the microphone one should speak softly if at all, otherwise his words may go right out over the air. For the same reason, it is best to ask permission before opening a heavy door to exit.

Chapter 61

SIMPLE PARLIAMENTARY PROCEDURE

Simple Parliamentary Procedure At one time or another most of us witness or take part in some meeting that is conducted by the ancient and formal form of English parliamentary procedure. The American method is slightly different from the original English one. This highly stylized form is used for the conduct of various clubs, societies, and church bodies as well as in ordinary business. Anyone asked to serve on a board of directors or who is elected to club or other office needs to know in greater detail than I shall set forth now the exact functioning of parliamentary procedure. The standard work on the subject is *Robert's Rules Of Order,* obtainable in any library, but many meetings, particularly smaller ones, follow a simplified version of the procedure set forth in this technical reference work.

The chairman of a meeting, sometimes in religious or debating assemblages called the moderator, must keep it in order and conduct its business. All members of the assembly are subject to the rulings of the chair. The chairman may not, himself, take part in debate unless he temporarily relinquishes the chair in order to do so.

Meetings conducted by means of parliamentary procedure may not transact any business unless a quorum is present, that is, a sufficient number of voting members to pass a resolution put to vote—normally a simple majority. The meeting is called to order by the chairman, who, if the secretary reports a quorum to be present, directs the secretary to read the minutes of the last meeting. The minutes are then approved as read, or corrected. Alternatively, the chairman may invite a motion to dispense with the reading of the minutes. The chairman then proceeds, according to the agenda for the meeting (usually prepared by the secretary), asking first for the officers' reports and thereafter for the various committee reports. These are followed by discussion, with each member who wishes to speak attracting the chairman's attention, usually by rising, and saying, "Mr. Chairman" or "Madam Chairman," sometimes "Mr. President" or "Madam President" (even in the case of an unmarried woman). In small meetings the members often do not rise, especially if they are sitting around a table in a board room, but no matter how well the members are known to each other they are formally correct in reference to one another. "I am informed by Mr. Burns, etc.," instead of "Joe tells me, etc." The chairman, who may have known a member all her life, will still recognize her by saying, "The chair recognizes Mrs. Carlson," when she takes the floor, not "Yes, Mae." Since minutes of the meeting are recorded, it is important that the secretary have the correct names and, where appropriate the identity, of the speakers. In taking the floor, a woman identifies herself if she is not identified by the chair by saying, "I am Mrs. John Brown (not "I am Mary Brown") and I wish to speak in behalf of—." It is better to err in the direction of overidentification than to assume that everyone in the room knows who you are and what you represent. A single woman would say, "Miss Mary Brown." A man identifies himself as "John Brown" not "Mr. Brown" or "Mr. John Brown."

Sometimes acrimonious exchanges take place in board and other meetings, and keeping matters on a formal level in proper parliamentary style helps to foster the necessary objectivity, especially between chairman and assemblage.

In order to permit everyone who wishes to speak to be heard within the time available, it may be desirable for the chairman to limit in advance the amount of time to be permitted each speaker, and not to permit any speaker to speak more than twice on a given subject, except in clarification of remarks previously made, until all persons who wish to speak have been heard. No person may speak without being recognized by the chairman. The person who first rises to speak is entitled to recognition. The chairman should ask the person recognized to state his name for the record.

If disorder should occur, the chairman, in his discretion, can quit the chair and adjourn the meeting at any time. By common practice, the chairman is also entitled to recess the meeting at any time he feels it necessary or desirable to consult with his advisers in respect to any issue which may have been raised.

The main or principal question is the matter that is up for discussion. It is presented in the form of a motion or resolution. Except in the case of formal motions, such as to adjourn, motions and resolutions must be given to the chairman in writing if the chairman or secretary so requests. No motion may be proposed which is the same in substance as a motion which has previously been voted on. If a motion fails to receive a second, the chairman may refuse to permit discussion or a vote on it on the ground that the motion obviously could not pass. After a motion has been made and seconded the chairman customarily repeats the motion to the meeting and then asks, "Are you ready for the question?" This is an invitation for discussion. After discussion has been concluded the chairman then puts the question to the meeting, i.e., states, "The question is on the adoption of the resolution (reading the resolution)" or "It has been moved and seconded, etc.," and conducts the vote. Except in the case of formal motions, such as to adjourn, the vote in large meetings should be by ballot. In smaller meetings, business is usually conducted by a voice vote, except for the election of officers or directors. After the voting, the chairman announces the results, saying, "The motion is carried," or "The resolution is adopted."

An amendment to a motion, like the motion itself, should be given to the chairman in writing, if requested, and should indicate clearly how the motion, as amended, will read. It should, of course, be seconded. An amendment to a motion must be relevant to the subject to be amended, and is not in order if it merely makes the affirmative of the amended question equivalent to the negative of the original question, or is identical with the question previously decided, or is a mere change in form. Discussion and vote on an amendment must be taken before discussion is resumed, and a vote taken, on the original motion.

A member of a board or committee should remain until the end of the meeting unless excused by the chair. If he has explained to the chairman before the start of the meeting that at some point he must leave, he may make his departure after catching the chair's eye at an opportune time and bowing. Sometimes in the case of an important member the chair makes some explanation, "Mr. Pryn has another meeting, gentlemen, and has asked to be excused at this time." The departing member then leaves without farewells, merely nodding to various members and the chair as he leaves. If in the middle of a meeting he is called to the phone, he may leave quietly without the chair's permission, unless a vote is about to be taken and his presence is necessary for a quorum.

When all items on the agenda have been covered, the chairman customarily asks, "Is there any further business to come before the meeting?" If he receives no reply, he may entertain a motion to adjourn or may say, after a suitable pause, "The meeting is adjourned." One then takes farewell of one's fellow board members or others in the meeting in a pleasant manner, even after heated and perhaps unpleasant discussion.

Chapter 62

YOUR APPEARANCE AT
PUBLIC FUNCTIONS

The Opera

Dressing for the Opera As with many other social customs there has been an increasing trend toward less formality at the opera. It was once unthinkable for a man or woman sitting in a box or in the orchestra to appear in anything but full evening dress. It is rarely seen now even on the fashionable Monday night in New York. Dinner jackets and a wide variety of male costumes from the acceptable dark blue or oxford gray complete with white shirt to tweeds and even sweaters are now seen in the orchestra while dinner jackets are still the rule in the boxes. Even there you see an occasional dark suit. Women in the orchestra accompanied by men in dinner jackets or occasionally in white tie wear anything from full evening dress to theater suits or cocktail dresses. If their escorts are not dressed, women wear dark or light street dresses such as they might wear to a concert, or possibly a cocktail dress depending on the degree of formality of their escorts. Evening pants suits and evening pajamas are also seen at the opera now. Women in boxes accompanied by dinner-jacketed men for the most part wear theater suits, cocktail dresses or if their escorts are formally dressed sometimes full decolletage. Women alone in the orchestra dress inconspicuously, often in a "little black dress" with or without a hat, usually without.

In the balconies all manner of clothes are now seen on both men and women. I like, however, the rule that says that in the balconies dark suits are usually worn by the men and street dresses or suits by the women, depending on what their later plans are. As in the theater, the balcony is a "don't dress" section, unless a couple is going on to some other function where evening dress is expected. A couple in evening dress but sitting in the balcony might seem to be slumming, though it is true that those who know music and the dance prefer the vantage point of the first balcony to the more fashionable orchestra.

Seating in Opera Boxes Promptness at the opera is only decent courtesy to the performers and to the rest of the audience. Conservative hostesses arrive at their boxes at least fifteen minutes before curtain time and seat themselves in the first row in the seat farthest from the stage (in a centrally located box the hostess is at the right). As guests arrive older women guests are seated with the hostess in the front row, the younger women sit in the second row with the older men, and the young men sit in the last row with the host.

Between the acts box holders and guests may repair for refreshments, now generally offered in most opera houses, and for the fascinating promenade on the stairs, hallways, and lobby. If the hostess or any older women wish to remain in the box during intermission, some male guest (or guests) stays with them. Any woman guest wishing to visit friends during intermission excuses herself to her hostess and visits, briefly, accompanied if possible by some male guest in the box. All should return to the box as soon as the "curtain rising" signal is given. Those who must leave before the end of an act excuse themselves before the act begins and slip out from a rear seat as quickly as possible.

Applauding at the Opera and at Concerts It is proper at the opera to applaud after arias—the "claque" (a group hired by a singer to applaud loudly at the right time) usually indicates when—and of course at each curtain. Entrances should not be applauded—but sometimes are by the over-enthusiastic who thus break the spell of the introductory measures.

Opera programs usually have a line indicating that applause should be held until the end of acts. Applause during the course of the opera prolongs the performance and in the view of very serious music lovers disrupts it. The exception to this, however, is the Italian opera at which applause for arias is virtually built in by the composer and performers pause significantly awaiting the tribute.

At concerts applause is held, even after a solo, until the conductor, by turning on the podium toward the audience, indicates that the selection is over. Even at the end of a program the enchantment should never be broken by applause until the conductor has turned for his bow to the audience. His each appearance from the wings is applauded, however, but the house becomes quiet the minute he turns to face the orchestra.

The Theater

It is not fashionable to be late for the theater at any time. On important opening nights (often with an earlier curtain than the regular performance nights), with everyone vying to be later than the next celebrity so as to steal the spotlight, such showing-off often delays the curtain interminable minutes, thus penalizing those courteous enough to be prompt and modest in their behavior. Anyone late for the first act should be considerate enough to stand at the back of the theater until the act is over, even if an usher is permitted to seat late-comers. An exception might be the holder of an aisle seat who could slip into it with the minimum of disturbance to others. In this country people entering a theater row, passing others already seated, excuse themselves and pass facing the stage. The seated patrons rise or half-rise if necessary. In Europe, by the way, those passing face those seated—a procedure we consider too intimate.

Seating The host (or hostess in a party of women) produces the tickets at the door and stands back to let guests file in. Guests then wait until the host or hostess may precede them with the usher to their seats. The hostess in a mixed group places a man first in a line of seats so a woman guest need not sit next to a stranger. She also places a man, usually the host, on the aisle. If two women must sit together in such an arrangement, one is the hostess.

Although there is no rule to this effect in this country, the woman accompanied by an escort who is European enters the theater row in such a way that she will be seated to her escort's right, he, if necessary, passing in front of her to seat himself on her left, although this may sometimes mean that she is seated on the aisle—a seating arrangement Americans try to avoid as the aisle-sitter may be brushed by passing patrons. Even the most formal European thus might decide to make an exception and permit the lady to be seated to his left.

The host sees to it that each guest has a program, and he also offers to secure cold drinks during the intermission.

Men and women may file out together during intermission to smoke in the lobby, or the women may stay together in their seats while the men go out after asking to be excused. No one woman is left alone, however, except in the case of a couple, and then the man may ask to be excused briefly after seeing that his companion is comfortable.

Talking Talking during the progress of a play, concert, or opera, is very bad manners and usually brings down well-deserved shushing from neighboring seats.

Eating Candy or other things should not be noisily passed or eaten during a performance. Even the rattle of candy papers can disturb others, and the bending forward of heads over a candy box can obscure the view of those behind. Candy may be passed during intermissions.

Hats It is always courteous for a woman who has on even a small theater hat to ask those in front of whom she is seated if they would like her to remove it. Hair combing is taboo and any replenishing of make-up should be done as discreetly as it would be done at a restaurant table.

Chapter 63

YOU AND CELEBRITIES

How Not to Treat a Celebrity

Fame sits uncomfortably on many celebrities. It is safer to assume that they do not wish to appear unduly conspicuous than to behave as if they desired public attention. Perhaps it depends very much on the kind of activity that has brought fame. A movie star or actor who can go with impunity into a restaurant or other public place and have people pay little or no attention to him is undoubtedly not buoyed up by the well-bred lack of stir he creates. On the other hand, a Jonas Salk or a Heifetz hopes to live a normal life among others, without being forever pointed out and approached by autograph hunters. And certainly not even the most publicity-loving movie star can enjoy having the clothes torn literally off his back. Physical discomfort—even danger—and continual lack of privacy are a high price to pay for so ephemeral a thing as fame in the entertainment field.

Asking for Autographs

The autograph of a really famous person, even if he is still alive, has a financial value—it can be bought and sold like a commodity. The more autographs such a person gives, the lower the market value of the autograph. You may desire an autograph for a serious collection of your own or for one you may be starting for a child, but you may be quickly rebuffed if the object of your interest is someone who rarely, if ever, gives an autograph because he knows that those that exist are bought and sold. Why should he stop and hand you, a stranger, the equivalent of a few dollars? On the other hand, even hardened cynics, George Bernard Shaw and Picasso for example, in the matter of autographs have been known to respond to a really sincere appeal from someone who seems moved by admiration rather than the profit motive in making such a request. Remember, autographs given freely to all and sundry have no value either historically or monetarily (if that interests you). The rare ones are the good ones, if the person who gives them is of the stuff that makes for more than transitory fame.

If you are really interested in the subject, study it and be an intelligent collector—not just a grabber of meaningless signatures in an autograph book. I'd rather encourage a child to ask grown-up friends to save important signatures for him from their own mail or collect them for him as a result of their connections, than have him turn into a little autograph-pest with no ability to discriminate between the worthwhile and the meretricious. To ask a really important person to sign an autograph book full of the names of nobodies is to insult him, no matter how graciously he may rise to the occasion in his acceptance of the request—or more probably, in his refusal. An autograph, by the way includes the full name of the author as it appears on the title page of his book. William Shakespeare, not "Will."

Entertaining the Celebrity

If you had a banker in to dinner, you'd hardly ask him to set up a cashier's desk and put on a little demonstration after dinner of how the bank handles money. Why, then, ask a famous singer who innocently enough has accepted your invitation to dinner, to literally sing for his supper? Would you ask a famous designer to run you up a dress? I can cite an actual case of a high-priced hat designer, though, who, having been invited to dinner—and a none-too-good home-cooked meal it was, she says—was presented with a lapful of the hostess's old hats immediately after dinner, with the request she retrim them, then and there.

Be very diffident indeed about requesting any of these professional people to render their services to you without pay. They need recreation, too. As a matter of fact, whether they are guests in your home or not, never ask authors to read your manuscript, playwrights to go over your play, singers to appraise your voice unless they maintain such advisory service on a professional basis—in which case they should be approached in their offices, not in your own home.

Don't invite celebrities to your home and then surround them with numerous uncongenial people whom you wish to impress by the fact that you have snared a literary or other lion. Treat a celebrity as you would any other honored guest. Provide him with good talk, good food, good company, decent privacy. Don't expect him to repay your hospitality with a free performance of his specialty.

Lo, the Poor Author

The general public is under the misapprehension that authors get limitless numbers of free copies of their books to dispense to friends and acquaintances. Many think the most flattering thing you can say to an author is, "Will you be sure to give me an autographed copy the minute the book comes out?"

Actually, in standard contracts, an author usually receives ten free copies of his book as *part of his remuneration*. If he wants to sell them, that's between him and the Bureau of Internal Revenue. But his agent, his mother, his wife, his mother-in-law, and his closest friends all expect one of these precious copies. And he needs one or two for his reference library. He is acutely embarrassed by requests for copies of his books, for he can't fill them except by paying his publisher for the books—at a discount, possibly, but nevertheless, it is money out of pocket and he must do bookkeeping on the matter.

It is, of course, all right to request an author to put you on the mailing list for information concerning the publication of the book. Publishers like to have lists of interested people and sometimes take advance orders by mail for the first edition of a book from those people who have put themselves on record as especially eager concerning it.

It isn't fair, however, to ask an author to get his own or other books from his publisher for you at the trade discount. Such little transactions always mean extra bookkeeping and are a real nuisance to all involved.

Impossible Questions Authors, among other professional people, are often subjected to somewhat impertinent questions by lay people who usually have no idea how tactless they are. A man who would never ask his doctor "How much did you get for taking out Mrs. Butler's appendix?" will say without a qualm to an author, "How much did you make on your first book? What's your royalty per copy? How much did your publisher spend on advertising it?" These are acutely personal questions an author, as a sensitive individual, too often seems bound to answer. He need not and should not. He should counter courteously with "I am not permitted to say" and put the burden of his refusal to disclose his financial affairs upon his publisher or his agent or another convenient whipping boy. He should avoid feeling offended, for the public is, fortunately, interested in everything concerning a celebrity and does not feel that such matters are any more sacrosanct than, say, the color of his eyes or what he eats for breakfast, subjects usually freely discussed in the public prints.

Part Eight

OFFICIAL ETIQUETTE FOR CIVILIANS

OFFICIAL ETIQUETTE FOR CIVILIANS

The civilian once under the mantle of officialdom, wherever it may be, is subject to the rules governing civilian behavior under official circumstances. The flag, for example, is our official emblem and a designer should not turn it into an evening wrap, however high her motive may be. A father visiting his son at Annapolis is subject to regulations even in respect to his son. He should not, for example, offer him a drink on or off the Reservation.

Transatlantic passengers are civilians subject to the captain, whose law is final aboard his ship. Visitors to military posts and installations, to government buildings and monuments, to national airports, and many other public places are subject to official regulations governing them.

In Washington, especially in time of war or during periods of great defensive preparation, protocol changes very rapidly. Armed with basic information on Washington's social pattern, the newcomer may consult his representatives for recent changes in procedure. Anyone planning to move to the capital and to entertain diplomatic and government representatives virtually requires the services of a social secretary on a regular basis or as needed, depending on the extent to which the new resident hopes to enter into his life so concerned with protocol. But even the casual visitor to Washington often needs to know something of its social requirements.

Each of us, at one time or another, will very likely find himself in a situation that calls for at least a modicum of knowledge of official etiquette. The section following endeavors to give the salient points of official protocol and to reassure the civilian who is frequently appalled and sometimes frightened by the official mind at work.

Chapter 64

ATTENDING ANNAPOLIS HOPS

A date at Annapolis is a coveted one for any girl and one, I hope, she has at least once in her lifetime if she can possibly arrange it. Annapolis means, of course, the United States Naval Academy at Annapolis, capital of Maryland, the naval equivalent of the Army's West Point. Its four-year course of college study, with accent on things naval, leads to a Bachelor of Science degree.

A man to be admitted to Annapolis or to West Point must be an excellent physical and mental specimen. Although most students (called midshipmen at Annapolis, cadets at West Point) are appointees by Senators, Congressmen, and President and all get college education free, they may come from any family, rich or poor. Even though Uncle Sam gives the midshipman his training, he must fulfill certain rigid standards of intelligence, of moral and physical fitness. A girl who accepts an invitation to Annapolis for the weekend pays for her transportation there and back and for her hotel or other accommodations. However, her escort can quite correctly make her reservations for her at one of the approved guest houses run, more out of civic duty than for possible revenue, by some of the fine old families of Annapolis. Twenty or twenty-five dollars is about as much as any girl can possibly use once she is at Annapolis and this will even include modest bus transportation costs from nearby Washington or Baltimore. Most girls arrive by public conveyance. During June Week the entire "brigade" may ride in cars and first classmen may even drive their own cars beginning the weekend before Army-Navy game.

No Saturday bus arriving in Annapolis before one o'clock may be met, as midshipmen are confined to the Reservation in the morning. If you arrive before that time—and, of course, all the arrangements for this big weekend have been made weeks, maybe months, in advance—you take a taxi to your hotel or the approved private home where you are to stay. For example, a fourth year man is allowed no more than sixty minutes to get you home from the hop. Infractions of rules mean demerits for your escort. Unbecoming behavior, or even unthinking behavior on your part, that brings censure on him—unspoken or not—means no future weekends at Annapolis for you.

The Navy is no place for individualism. That goes for the girl who is the guest of the Navy, and that is the way you should think of yourself. You are the guest of the Navy and subject to strict naval etiquette, not just the guest of an individual member of the Navy—for though your man is still in Annapolis, he is considered to be very much a part of the Navy. Your date will probably be a third, second, or first year man, for fourth year men, or plebes, are permitted to "drag" on few occasions.

If you are met—and never be later than one o'clock—you will be starting off right if you have brought a minimum of luggage, preferably one light bag. You will need neither golf clubs nor riding clothes. You don't need a bathing suit. All social activities are within prescribed limits so don't plan on taking your man for a little run down to Chevy Chase to see Aunt Prue.

Mrs. Grundy may have retired in the big cities, but at Annapolis she is omnipotent. Midshipmen are not allowed above the first level in drag houses except to carry your bag. Even then he is expected to return immediately to the living room. And even if you are engaged, don't try to hold hands with him in public, don't take his arm on limits, or expect him to walk arm-in-arm or with his arms around your waist—"Lollygagging" is the Navy term for such relaxed behavior.

It is, literally, a felony for a midshipman to take a drink within seven miles of the Academy Chapel Dome—and he isn't allowed to go beyond that seven-mile limit! So for a girl to take liquor with her, even for her own use in her room, is poor form, to say the least. And it is against the rules for her to take it there if her room is in a hotel. Even beer may not be served to midshipmen in public restaurants in Annapolis, and for their "drags" to take it when they can't is certainly impolite.

On the usual Annapolis weekend, never depend on receiving flowers from your escort as it is frowned on—some Mids can afford flowers—others can't—so the policy is "no corsages." Everyone understands the economics of this, and for a moneyed "drag" to bedeck herself in orchids is to proclaim that she has bought them for herself—or accepted them from a non-Annapolis admirer, an unpardonable sin. Flowers are, however, provided for all young girls at Ring Dance during June week.

The naval reservation is referred to as the "Yard." Within its confines you are subject to strict naval rules. You smoke in "Smoke Hall" (the recreation room in Bancroft Hall) but not on the street (I hope you won't do that anywhere) or on the dance floor. Your midshipman may not chew gum in public, and you should not either while you are with him.

The Navy man has conservatism drilled into him in all things touching on social and naval behavior. If you do anything to make a big splash, by wearing too sophisticated clothes or too conspicuous and expensive jewelry, by drinking, or by any attention-drawing behavior, you embarrass him, to say the least. He will wonder why he ever risked inviting you.

Necessary Clothes

Saturday noon to Sunday afternoon doesn't call for a very extensive wardrobe. If you try to ring in numerous changes, you will be wasting the time and temper of your escort and very probably infuriating the dates of his classmates. Here's the maximum you'll need, in addition to underclothing:

1. Traveling suit, sports dress (you'll arrive in one and wear it Saturday afternoon, for the game or a walk, and leave in it), or attractive pants suit.
2. Comfortable walking shoes—one pair for suit, one pair for dress (high heels would be murder on those cobblestones).
3. Sneakers or rubber-soled saddle oxfords in summer for possible sailing. (Never wear leather-heeled shoes on a sailboat.)
4. Warm, carefully-tailored slacks, socks, and sweaters for sailing. (It gets mighty cold if you have a long beat in.) Shorts are not permitted in some sections of Annapolis.
5. A waterproof topcoat because you'll walk, no matter what the weather, even in evening clothes.
6. A becoming but not too spectacular evening dress, short or long, and accessories for dancing Saturday night. Long ball gown or the formal pants dress (divided long skirt) usually worn at formal hops are a must for Ring Dance and Formal Ball.
7. An evening wrap or, in winter, a fur coat or jacket (but the men hate shedable "bunny" fur because it comes off on their blues). The right kind of rather dressy raincoat can serve as topcoat, evening wrap, and raincoat. You'll be better off with it than with a perishable evening wrap, because it's better not to ask a midshipman to carry an umbrella.
8. Those zip-up plastic and packable boots that can be worn over evening shoes in case of bad weather.
9. A scarf or hood to keep your head dry.
10. A daytime dress for church and for Sunday dinner.
11. A hat or veil for church is optional (most drags don't wear them) and white gloves. Short white gloves are often worn at Sunday afternoon tea dances but are not obligatory.

The Hop Itself

There are formal and informal hops on Saturday evenings during the Academic Year and rock-and-roll dances every Sunday afternoon from two to four in Smoke Hall. At the Homecoming Ball in the fall and the Graduation Hop in June Week either the "First Lady," wife of the superintendent or the wife of the commandant receives. She is assisted by the chairman of the hop committee, who introduces those approaching the receiving line to the hostess, after first being presented to the guests himself by their escorts.

The superintendent or the commandant usually receives with his wife, as do various of the senior officers and their wives. It is, of course, necessary to go through the line as soon as you arrive. In greeting, look cordial, smile, and say, "How do you do," taking the proffered hand of hostesses and hosts. Never hold up the receiving line, even if you know a host or hostess well and this is your first encounter since your arrival. Conduct yourself with dignity and nicely adjusted dispatch. Remember, a lady does not remove her gloves to shake hands (but see "Being Received at the White House"). This is a man's gesture.

Midshipmen come and go as they please at hops but most remain until "The Star-Spangled Banner" and "Navy Blue and Gold" are played at midnight.

Entertainment of Midshipmen

If this is your first invitation from a midshipman, it is usual for him to do whatever modest entertaining is possible for him. On successive trips— assuming you're lucky—you may in all propriety invite him to Sunday dinner at your hotel, where his check can be put on your bill without embarrassment to him. Taking him to any of the little, inexpensive tearooms in the area changes the situation, unless you can arrange beforehand for payment of your bill so that it won't be handed to him.

Gifts for Midshipmen

If a young lady wishes to send a midshipman a gift perhaps for Christmas or his birthday, it is helpful for her to know something of his personal habits. Does he smoke a pipe, is he an ardent bridge player, or is chess his game? The best practical suggestion (straight from Annapolis) is a box of *homemade* cookies. You know, "the way to a man's heart . . ." and all that!

The Souvenir Hunter

All the gilt accessories a naval man wears cost money—cost him money, I should say, if they have to be replaced—as do buttons, buckles, and the gold-thread insignia. One such replacement for a midshipman might mean the loss of his spending money for the month. Asking for a miniature of his ring is actually proposing marriage. The ring in miniature is worn insignia-in as an engagement ring. The insignia is turned out after the marriage has taken place. Collecting fraternity pins may be considered fair sport by some, but the wearing of a Navy ring is a serious matter. Don't put on a midshipman's hat, either, unless, of course, you want him to kiss you. For him to refuse to do so under the circumstances would be for him to be guilty of behavior unbecoming to a Navy man.

Chapter 65

VISITING WEST POINT

Many a teen-ager dreams of being invited to a West Point Hop but, should the coveted invitation come, a girl hates to ask her escort what's expected of her. She likes to pretend at least that she knows all about the Point, that she has been invited there before, though unable to accept.

The cost of a West Point weekend is very modest, even though the girl pays her own way some of the time. She is responsible for getting herself to the Point and back by bus or her own car. Her cadet makes a dormitory room reservation for her, if possible at the U. S. Hotel Thayer, the hotel on the Reservation. The room cost is three dollars per person per night and meals are available at moderate prices. If the Thayer is filled, the cadet makes arrangements for his drag to stay in the village of Highland Falls. A list of approved housing is available through the Office of the Cadet Hostess.

The weekend guest is not met at the bus that took her to the Point but taxies to her designated quarters sometime Saturday morning. West Pointers have classes half a day Saturday but expect their dates to be available by 2 P.M. When there are home football games cadets are free at 1:30 P.M.

As at Annapolis, there are strict rules concerning transportation and other matters. At the Point a cadet may not drive a car but may be driven in his guest's car or in his family's car. So a girl with a car will prove popular with her escort and will not have to pay taxi fares (fifty cents, point to point) to the dress parade or chapel (a Sunday morning must for cadets—and the considerate guest goes, too).

As at West Point a cadet is not permitted to drink at all, not even beer, a considerate guest does not drink in his presence and, of course, does not bring liquor of any kind into the Reservation itself, even for personal use.

Necessary Clothes

There is usually a Hop or other entertainment on Saturday night at the Post, for which cadets make all arrangements. Casual dresses or skirts and blouses are worn.

A cadet is conditioned to walking and expects his girl to be able to get around on her own two feet without wincing. A good pair of walking shoes is essential. A nicely tailored suit or a sweater and skirt is expected for sports or an afternoon walk. Slacks and shorts are not considered appropriate.

There is no riding for guests at the Point, but there is swimming in summer and ice skating in winter. A sweater and skirt is the usual dress at the skating rink although slacks and ski pants are permissible for this sport.

For Sunday chapel you will probably wear what you arrived in—a soft suit or dress and coat.

It is poor taste at any time for a girl to smoke on the street, so don't smoke while walking with your cadet, who is not allowed to smoke on main roads and sidewalks. Don't take his arm or kiss him in public—don't even attempt to hold hands while on the Reservation, except on Flirtation Walk where a little romantic leeway is permitted. And, of course, you wait to be invited there.

The Hop Itself

At a formal Hop, guests and cadets all pass down the receiving line before beginning to dance. The line consists of, first, the Hop manager, then the receiving officer and his lady and the Cadet Hostess. The cadet gives the name of his guest and his own name to the Hop manager who presents them to the receiving officer. He, in turn presents them to the Cadet Hostess. The line does not re-form after the dance.

After a Hop cadets may escort guests to their living quarters on the Post, but they are not permitted to leave the Post unless they have weekend privileges.

As West Point is near New York, it is possible for a cadet to get to town for dates.

Granting of weekends is progressive with each class. First classmen are allowed twelve weekends a year; second classmen are allowed six; third classmen are allowed three and plebes none. Additional weekends are available based on outstanding performances by individual cadets and units.

Chapter 66

HOW TO TELL MILITARY RANK

How to Tell Military Rank

Our armed forces, organized under the Department of Defense, consists of the Army, the Navy, and the Air Force. The Department of the Navy consists of two separate military services, the U. S. Navy and the U. S. Marine Corps. In time of war the Coast Guard is under the jurisdiction of the Navy but in time of peace operates under the Department of Transportation.

In all services staff officers, or non-combatant officers, are distinguished from line officers by a device signifying their staff corps. Line officers, generally speaking, are those entitled to command combat forces. There are certain specialists, however, who though technically line officers, do not command combat forces.

In the Army, devices signifying the corps in which men serve—the caduceus of the doctor, the cross of the chaplain, etc.— are worn on the lapel. In the Navy these staff officer devices are worn on the sleeve above the stripes indicating rank.

The positions of General of the Army and Navy Fleet Admiral were created to give the highest-ranking American military leaders acting on international joint staff during wartime a rank equivalent to the foreign position of Field Marshal. While the men holding this rank may not be actively engaged in military activities in peacetime, they are subject to call by the President if required.

The Army
Cap device—eagle clutching two arrows

In order of rank the officer personnel of the Army are:

GENERAL OF THE ARMY—Five silver stars
GENERAL—Four silver stars
LIEUTENANT GENERAL—Three silver stars

MAJOR GENERAL—Two silver stars

BRIGADIER GENERAL—One silver star

COLONEL—Silver eagle

LIEUTENANT COLONEL—Silver oak leaf

MAJOR—Gold oak leaf

CAPTAIN—Two silver bars

FIRST LIEUTENANT—One silver bar

SECOND LIEUTENANT—One gold bar

CHIEF WARRANT OFFICER—One gold bar, brown enamel top, gold longitudinal center

WARRANT OFFICER, JUNIOR GRADE—Same as above except gold center is latitudinal

The Navy
Cap device—crossed anchors, shield and eagle

On blue uniforms rank is indicated by gold stripes on sleeves, on white or dress khaki uniforms rank is indicated on detachable shoulder boards.

In order of rank the officer personnel of the Navy are:

FLEET ADMIRAL—Five silver stars, one 2″ stripe and four ½″ sleeve stripes with star of line officer

ADMIRAL—Four silver stars, one 2″ stripe and three ½″ sleeve stripes, with star of line officer, or corps device

VICE-ADMIRAL—Three silver stars, one 2″ stripe and two ½″ sleeve stripes, star of line officer or corps device

REAR ADMIRAL—Two silver stars, one 2″ stripe and one ½″ sleeve stripe, star of line officer or corps device

COMMODORE—One silver star, one 2″ sleeve stripe, star of line officer or corps device

CAPTAIN—Silver spread eagle, four ½″ stripes, star of line officer or corps device

COMMANDER—Silver oak leaf, three ½″ stripes, star of line officer or corps device

LIEUTENANT COMMANDER—Gold oak leaf, two ½″ stripes with ¼″ one between, star of line officer or corps device

LIEUTENANT—Two silver bars, two ½″ stripes, star of line officer or corps device

LIEUTENANT, JUNIOR GRADE—One silver bar, one ½″ stripe with ¼″ one above and star of line officer or corps device

ENSIGN—One gold bar, one ½″ gold stripe and star of line officer or corps device

CHIEF WARRANT OFFICER—One ½″ broken gold stripe and specialty device

WARRANT OFFICER—Onc ¼″ broken gold stripe and specialty device

The Marine Corps
Cap device—eagle, globe, and anchor

The top rank in the Marine Corps is general. He wears the four stars and shoulder rank of the Army. Other insignia in the Marine Corps are the same as those in the Army.

The Air Force
Cap device—wings flanking U.S.

The top rank in the Air Force is general. All insignia in the Air Force are the same as those in the Army.

The Coast Guard
Cap distinguished by single anchor, eagle, and shield

The top rank in the Coast Guard is admiral. All insignia are the same as those in the Navy.

The Women's Services
Each branch of the service has its women's division. Nurses in the service are commissioned officers ranging from second lieutenant to colonel in the Army and from ensign to captain in the Navy. The other women's corps are the Army's WACS with ranks up to that of Brigadier General, the Navy's WAVES with ranks up to that of captain, the Women Marines with ranks up to that of colonel, the Coast Guard's SPARS with ranks up to that of captain, the Air Corps WAFS with ranks up to that of Brigadier General. They all compare with men of the same rank in pay, privileges, and precedence.

Chapter 67

VISITING A NAVAL VESSEL

Visiting a Naval Vessel

If you are "in the Navy" as wife, mother, or fiancée, you will certainly be well schooled in the many visiting regulations. But the untutored civilian planning to visit one of our ships needs to know the accepted Navy way of doing these things.

Embarking When you go aboard a naval vessel at anchor, you embark in a small boat which takes you out to the ship. The trip may be choppy and the seats uncomfortable. Even when the small boat is still fast to the dock it may heave and rock menacingly—from the standpoint of the less sure-footed or the queasy. The idea, therefore, is for the youngest women to go aboard first, taking the seats up forward, leaving seats between them for younger officers or younger men civilians. Older and distinguished visitors are last to embark, take seats in the stern. When the small boat is alongside the ship it is the senior officers and their wives who disembark first— wives first unless there is no one at the foot of the ladder to assist them and the sea is rough, then a younger officer or two may disembark first to help the ladies. Very young women hold back until older women or the wives of dignitaries disembark, then dignitaries and high-ranking officers leave before the younger men and women. It is an honor to be last or among the last into a boat, barge, gig, or any such ship's boats and first or among the first to leave. Children, therefore, should not be allowed in their enthusiasm to clamber up the ladder, perhaps past the captain himself, although in a rough sea a very old person or mother and small baby would probably be granted precedence.

Stepping from a small boat to a ship's gangway is sometimes quite an athletic undertaking even when the weather on shore looks perfectly calm. Adequate underthings are a requisite, also a skirt that allows for a wide step and heels that won't be perilous. A visit to the engine room, when allowed, requires a perpendicular descent on steel ladders with blasts of air coming from beneath, so be forewarned (and take an extra pair of pantyhose and white gloves). Descents on the ordinary ladders between weather decks are steep, too, and the wind seems to find them even when a ship is tied snugly up to the dock.

Making a Call Aboard a Naval Vessel Suppose you have been invited aboard the USS *Monsoon* by an officer you've met. In wartime you need a pass and your host will arrange to furnish it for presentation to the boat officer for a specific day and time. You will, of course, have to fulfill the usual precautionary requirements. Otherwise, calls on ship take place conveniently, as they do on land, during afternoon naval calling hours, between three-thirty or four and six, unless you have been asked to a party (usually by formal invitation) that takes place at a stated time.

If you are expected aboard by your host at a certain hour, he will probably be on deck to meet you, but, even if you see him standing there as you come over the side, you first greet the officer of the deck stationed on the quarter-deck at the head of the ladder. You recognize him by the binoculars he always carries (or by an armband on some ships)—the officer of the deck glass (O.O.D. glass in seaman's terminology)—and by the gloves he must wear, white with whites, gray with his blue uniform. He is, during his watch, anyhow, in charge of the ship, the captain's surrogate on the quarter-deck. To you he is the official host, of whom you take cognizance the minute you arrive by saying, "How do you do," or "Good afternoon," (shaking hands after his salute, if you wish, if you are a civilian man) and of whom you take polite official leave. Your navy escort, if you have one, the captain excepted, must say to the O.O.D. as he leaves, "I have permission to leave the ship, Sir."

If your naval host has come out with you in the boat, you precede him up the gangway, greet the O.O.D., and step aside to await your host before joining any groups already formed on deck, even when you know members of them, although you may bow in recognition, of course. But you don't rush aboard and take charge of the ship, leaving your confused or angry escort to his own devices while you play the belle. Remember, almost any woman aboard ship looks good to men who have restricted shore leave.

Boarding The quarter-deck is a small area of deck located at that section of the ship where it is convenient to rig a sea ladder or gangway. In ancient times it consisted of the small raised deck in the stern of the ship where sacred images of the altar were kept, later the flags of kings. In deference to tradition, sacred in all the navies of the world, uniformed men, as they reach the upper gangway platform, face aft and salute the colors and, thereafter, the officer of the deck. Civilian men show correct deference by facing the colors and holding their hats, if they have them, or placing their hands over their hearts before stepping aboard, although with them the gesture is one of courtesy and not, as with the armed forces, obligatory.

Honors to Civilians The President or some other official might receive special honors as he boards—a salute from the guns or the running up of his flag. If so, he remains on the gangway platform with his hat over his heart, in the civilian flag salute until the honors have been completed. He then greets the O.O.D. by shaking hands before accepting the welcome of the captain and other officers.

Prohibitions Concerning Naval Vessels

It is not permissible for a civilian to transport liquor to a naval vessel either for his own use there or as a gift to his host. No one, even in peacetime, may take aboard a camera or a pet. No one may go aboard in an intoxicated condition, either, and part of the O.O.D.'s job is to prevent the boarding of such unwelcome guests.

Meals aboard are in the wardroom—enlisted men may not entertain aboard, except on specifically designated occasions such as Christmas or Thanksgiving, or in the chief petty officer's mess—or possibly in the captain's cabin, but the wardroom is run like a men's club with meals billed—to each officer on a monthly basis. Do not invite yourself to meals aboard under the mistaken assumption that they will be on Uncle Sam. Your entertainment is provided by the members of the mess. If you do eat there, the senior officer of the wardroom and president of the mess is your official host. Excuse yourself to him if you must leave before others.

Two topics are traditionally never mentioned in the wardroom—religion and women, presumably so the men can eat or relax in relative peace as they might in a well-ordered club. If you are taken through or to the wardroom, conduct yourself as you would in a club lounge—observe relative quiet and impeccable deportment. You may smoke there if invited to do so, but you may not smoke on deck or in passageways.

Officers' Staterooms

With the exception of the captain and senior officers, other officers generally share their rooms with one or more other officers. While a lady making a tour of a ship may be asked to inspect these quarters, she must treat them as the communal rooms they are, even if it's her husband's room that interests her particularly. Doors must be left open—even when wives are inspecting the rooms—and congregating must take place on deck or in the wardroom, not in the individual rooms. Tender moments, if any, aboard a ship are best arranged by your host. He may be "off duty" officially, but he is under constant surveillance while he's on his ship. Don't try to break down his very necessary dignity and decorum.

Nautical Terms

The layman often makes mistakes in referring to nautical matters, thereby unintentionally insulting serious followers of the sea. Never, by any chance, refer to a ship or a boat as anything but "she." Only small craft, pulling boats, dories, and small power boats of various kinds are "boats." Anything from a patrol craft up is a "ship."

Aboard a man-of-war there is no saloon, as on an ocean liner. Instead there is the wardroom for the officers' mess (dining) and recreation, the junior officers' mess, the warrant officers' mess, the chief petty officers' mess, and the enlisted men's mess. On large ships the captain's cabin is his mess hall but on smaller ships he eats with the other officers in the wardroom. There are no companionways on a battleship. Instead, the ladders leading from deck to deck are simply ladders. The hurricane deck becomes the main deck. Topside is any exposed deck, and below deck is any covered deck. Officers have rooms, not staterooms, and enlisted men are quartered in compartments.

Chapter 68

THE NEW RESIDENT IN WASHINGTON

Receiving a White House Invitation

An invitation to the White House should be answered in person or by messenger within twenty-four hours if one is in Washington, by wire or by special delivery if one is out-of-town. If the recipient is to be away or some personal or business matter prevents his attending, his excuse must be clearly stated:

Mr. and Mrs. Jonathan Streeter
regret that owing to Mr. Streeter's
absence in London
they will be unable to accept
the very kind invitation of
The President and Mrs. Jefferson
to dine
on Monday, the tenth of February

Recent death in the family, illness, absence at a great distance from Washington are all tenable excuses. An invitation from the White House always used to take precedence over any other social invitation, even a formal one that had already been accepted. There is much more leeway on this today, however, and a family wedding for example would be a valid excuse. If none of the above acceptable excuses hold true, a regret to one's hostess reads:

Mr. and Mrs. Jonathan Streeter
regret exceedingly that an invitation to
the White House
prevents their keeping
their engagement to dine
on Monday, the tenth of February

An acceptance to a formal White House invitation follows the usual formal acceptance. Informal invitations, usually sent by the President's secretary or his wife's secretary, are answered in the form in which they are sent —by note, by phone, or by wire, with the acceptance or regrets addressed to the secretary. Where husband and wife receive the invitation, the wife replies. A man alone replies in his own name, not through his secretary. The forms are:

Tuesday

Dear Miss Metcalfe,

My husband and I accept with great pleasure the kind invitation of the President and Mrs. Jefferson to dine at the White House on Monday, the tenth of February, at eight o'clock.

Sincerely,
Louise Streeter

or

Tuesday

Dear Miss Metcalfe,

Because I am sailing for France on February the ninth, I regret that I shall be unable to accept the President and Mrs. Jefferson's kind invitation to dine on February 10th.

Sincerely,
Luis Dávila

Being Received at the White House

All reception guests and dinner guests at the White House usually enter through the Diplomatic Entrance at *least* fifteen minutes prior to the time given in the invitation, as all the guests must be assembled before the President appears to greet them. When there is a large party of five hundred or so, guests usually enter through the East Gate. The President and his wife greet guests in any one of a number of rooms in the White House. When there is a receiving line, an aide makes the presentations, with gentlemen preceding their ladies down the line where they are greeted first by the President, then by the First Lady. Women do not now necessarily wear gloves, but if they do, the right glove should be removed when one is shaking hands with the President. The President is "Mr. President," (to men in prolonged conversation occasionally, "Sir") his wife is "Mrs. Monroe." The guest says merely, "Good evening, Mr. President" and passes on immediately unless the President stops him briefly to say a few words. But the guest does not engage in conversation in the line, no matter how well he may know the President.

Many rooms in the White House are used now for large receptions, with the East Room usually chosen for entertainment and with dancing often taking place in the Grand Hall. Some receptions are so small that all guests are greeted in the Diplomatic Reception Room. The rest rooms are downstairs and quite some distance from where the majority of social functions take place. And as a long time may be spent on line, the wise guest will take care of such needs beforehand.

Not all reception invitations require an answer, but it is courteous to give one anyhow.

When cards are left at all on diplomats—some Europeans still follow the custom—Friday is the usual day for doing it. No woman ever leaves cards on a single man.

The Ranking Guest

In Washington, rank is the all important thing considered in planning seating arrangements for official luncheons or dinners. Protocol can never be relaxed and should be followed just as strictly even when a diplomat is visiting in another city. Someone with official rank, such as an ambassador, may outrank the guest of honor at a function and therefore take his place on the hostess's right at the table. No guest ever leaves a luncheon, dinner, or ball before the ranking guest.

Business Calls on the President

Make Your Call Brief If you are given an appointment in business hours to see the President, present yourself at the White House executive office a few minutes before the stated time. Gentlemen usually wear conservative business suits or in the summer the usual tropicals or lightweight suits. A woman wears a simple street dress or suit and optionally, now, a hat, and gloves. She removes her right glove, as I've said above, when shaking hands with the President. If she is being received as a delegate, say, or as Somebody of the Year, and will be photographed with him, she may possibly wear a small corsage. Whatever your business, you will usually be told the maximum amount of time the President can give you. Keep your call within that limit and leave sooner, if possible.

There is an important thing to remember. Don't take a gift to the President without clearing it through his aide or secretary. A small package carried in a handbag or pocket and produced during the call might precipitate an assassination scare as, of course, the President is at all times guarded by Secret Service men, one or more of whom will be present during your interview.

Warning Buzzer If you are in the White House hallways at the moment when special buzzers sound, this indicates that the President or members of his family are about to enter or leave the White House. You will be required by your attendant to step out of the hallway and into a closed room until the passage has been effected. This, too, is for the President's and his family's safety.

The White House is the President's home rather than a public building. A gentleman removes his hat the minute he enters the portico. No visitor smokes unless smoking is suggested by the person he has gone to see.

Gifts to the White House

Don't send a gift to the President without receiving permission from his secretary or aide or from other members of the White House staff. There is a Presidential policy precluding the acceptance of personal gifts of value —items of $25.00 or over. There is also a strict policy against the acceptance of animals. Exceptions to this rule are made only when there is a question of a State gift. If you are an admirer of the President and decide to send him one of your home-grown geese, he'll never taste it unless it has been ascertained beforehand that the acceptance of such a gift from you is safe. The White House housekeeper is responsible for any gifts of food for the White House and must vouch for the safety of any accepted.

Chapter 69

THE FLAG AND OUR NATIONAL ANTHEM

Regulations for Displaying the Flag

Many homes and most business houses, fraternal organizations, and all public buildings own and from time to time display the flag. Some in doing so do not realize that there are definite rules concerning the proper display of the flag which protect it from desecration. It can't be used, for example, as a trademark or part of a coat of arms, even in slightly altered form. There are state and federal statutes to enforce this ruling and others concerning the respectful use and display of the flag, although some are or will be relaxed.

Here are the major regulations concerning display of the flag:

1. Never fly it upside down except as a distress signal.
2. Don't let it trail on the ground—or even touch it—or in the water.
3. Display the flag only from sunrise to sunset out of doors and lower it promptly if it rains. Flags flown at night must be lighted.
4. Hoist the flag briskly but lower it slowly and reverently.
5. City and State flags or those of organizations flown from the same staff as the United States flag should be placed below the flag. No other flag is ever flown above it.
   On boats signal and flag officers' flags are flown from the mast considerably above the national flag flown from the aft deck.
6. When organization or other flags are flown in conjunction with the U.S. flag on adjacent flagstaffs, the U.S. flag is always hoisted first and is last to come down (except in case of rain). Flags flown on adjacent flagpoles should always be placed on the left of the flag itself. No other flag is ever placed to the flag's right (observer's left).
7. When other nations' flags are flown with ours, they should be on separate standards, should be the same size as the U.S. flag and flown at the same height. In times of peace, no nation's flag takes precedence in an arrangement of flags, but it is usual for the U.S. flag flown on U.S.

soil, on its ships or bases, to have the central position in such a grouping of flags. In wartime, no immediately adjacent flag is ever flown at the U.S. flag's own right, even in a grouping of allies' flags.

8. A flag flown from a staff fastened to a window sill or balcony or fixed to the front of a building must be flown with the union, or blue field, at the peak of the staff unless the flag is at half-mast. Flags are flown at half-mast only by official state, federal, or city order, never flown in such a manner to indicate personal loss to a family or to a business or other organization. In the last case, the deceased is so honored occasionally but then only by official decree if he has been of civic importance.

9. When a flag is suspended over a sidewalk on a cord from the building to a pole on the sidewalk, the flag is hoisted from the building to the pole, union first (so it may be taken in quickly in a storm).

10. When a flag is displayed without a staff, it should lie flat against an upright support, indoors or out, never draped or festooned. (Use bunting for this purpose.) When it is displayed horizontally or vertically against a wall, the union or field is uppermost, to the flag's own right. When the flag is displayed from a window it is always shown with the union to the left of the observer in the street.

11. A flag displayed over the middle of the street should hang vertically with the union to the north in an east and west street or east in a north and south one.

12. In displaying the flag on a speaker's platform, place it above and behind the speaker, flat, union to the flag's right, observer's left. If it is flown from a staff on the platform, it should be flown to the speaker's right, in the place of honor. It must never be used to cover a table or desk. Never drape it over the platform.

13. Flags carried in a mourning parade or procession are never put at half-mast but may display a black crepe bow knot with or without two black crepe streamers at the fastening points by order of the President. It may not be used in this way for private funeral processions.

14. When the flag is to be flown at half-mast, it is first hoisted to the peak, then put at half-mast. Before lowering it for the night, hoist it again to the peak.

15. On Memorial Day the flag is flown at half-mast only from sunrise until noon, when it is hoisted to full staff.

16. Don't use the flag to unveil even a patriotic statue or monument, although it is properly used in the attendant ceremonies.

17. The only exception in the draping of the flag occurs when it is used to cover a casket, union at the head and over the deceased's left shoulder. The flag must not touch the ground nor be lowered into the grave. The casket is carried foot first. The flag is used for this honor only for members of the armed services, for cabinet officers of the federal and state

governments, and for others of national importance for whom the President decrees official mourning.

18. When a flag becomes torn, tattered, or otherwise unfit for display it is never heedlessly discarded. If it is beyond mending and cleaning it should be destroyed in one piece, privately, by burning. Its fabric may not be reused for some other purpose. An old flag, faded, worn, and torn beyond restitution, deserves and must receive respectful destruction so it will never fall into vicious or thoughtless hands.

19. The flag must never be dipped to any person or thing. Only personal, state, regimental or other flags may be used to render this honor.

20. Never place any object or emblem on or above the U.S. flag with the exception of the American eagle.

21. Never fasten the flag in a way that it can be easily torn.

22. The flag may not be draped on any vehicle. If it is to be displayed on a train, boat, or car it must be firmly fixed to a staff.

23. The flag must not be displayed from a parade float except from a staff.

24. The flag may not be used to cover the ceiling.

25. The flag may not be carried horizontally in a procession, but must be aloft and waving.

26. The flag should never be used as decoration for civilian clothing, pillows, furniture, or athletic uniforms. It may not be printed on paper napkins, tablecloths, or boxes. It is used only on official U.S. stationery, never on personal stationery. The rules are or have been relaxed. When in doubt check The United States Flag Foundation, 115 E. 86th St. N.Y., N.Y. 10028.

27. No lettering of any kind may be placed on the flag.

28. The pole from which the flag flies must never carry advertising signs or pennants. It may not be used in any form of display advertising, except that placed for the United States Government.

29. A flag displayed in the body of the church is flown from a staff, to the congregation's right as it faces the pulpit. Service, state, or other special flags are flown to the left of the congregation. If the flag is to be displayed from the chancel or the platform it is placed on the clergyman's right, to the congregation's left. Other flags are flown from the clergyman's left.

30. Store the flag in such a way that it will be protected from moths and other damage. Never place it on the floor even for a moment, and never permit anyone to step on it or show it any disrespect, unwitting or not. Most cleaners will dry clean the flag free of charge throughout the year or at least between June 1 and June 12. (Flag Day is June 14).

Invocation and Salute to the Flag

At a public dinner or luncheon meeting, or any other occasion where an invocation and a salute to the flag are given, the invocation precedes the salute—God, then country.

When the occasion arises for one to salute the flag, a lady does not remove her gloves indoors or out since they are part of her costume. Neither does a military man remove his gloves to salute.

The Singing of Our National Anthem

In times of national emergency very strict attention must be paid to any playing of the National Anthem. During wartime it is usually played before the beginning of such public performances as concerts, plays, sports events. In fact, in time of war it *must* be played at certain designated gatherings. You may have seated yourself at the opera after an impressive entrance, but you must rise promptly when the Anthem is played, unless you are exceedingly infirm or very, very old, or else so young that you cannot be expected to understand the significance of rising to your feet at the sound of this music. Even then, quite young children should be taught to stand quietly and respectfully when they hear "The Star-Spangled Banner" and, like the rest of us, they should, as soon as possible, learn the words of at least the first and last stanzas.

The National Anthem is not easy to sing, but most people can transpose the high notes an octave lower, as they go along, into something they can manage. Don't stand mute because you are afraid of those high notes. If you can't transpose, sing everything *but* the high notes and let the sopranos reach for them. It is shameful that so few of us can sing the words accurately, although I can sympathize with anyone's difficulty with the range. The idea behind the mass singing of the Anthem is to stir a feeling of patriotism and unity. Fine voices aren't essential. Enthusiastic, heart-warming, not half-hearted, singing by everybody does proper honor.

When the Anthem strikes up in any public place men, women, and children should stand at complete attention and should sing if they possibly can. If they can't sing they should stand quietly and respectfully without whispering, talking, or fidgeting until the Anthem is finished. Civilian men and boys remove their hats, hold them with the right hand over their hearts. Women stand at attention or place the right hand over the heart. It is usual if more than the first stanza is to be sung for the assemblage to go right into the last stanza, omitting the second and third unless the words appear on printed programs. Memorization of the first and last stanzas should be sufficient.

"The Star-Spangled Banner"

O say, can you see, by the dawn's early light,
    What so proudly we hailed at the twilight's last gleaming?
Whose broad stripes and bright stars, through the perilous fight,
    O'er the ramparts we watched were so gallantly streaming?
And the rockets' red glare, the bombs bursting in air,
    Gave proof through the night that our flag was still there.
O say, does that star-spangled banner yet wave
O'er the land of the free and the home of the brave?

LAST STANZA

O thus be it ever, when freemen shall stand
   Between their loved homes and the war's desolation!
Blest with vict'ry and peace, may the heav'n-rescued land
   Praise the Power that hath made and preserved us a nation.
Then conquer we must, when our cause it is just,
   And this be our motto: "In God is our trust."
And the star-spangled banner in triumph shall wave
O'er the land of the free and the home of the brave.

—Francis Scott Key

Don't chew gum, eat, or smoke during the playing of the Anthem in public places. Don't continue making your way to your seats, even if you are in an aisle when the music starts. If any confusion arises anywhere in the assemblage, all those except the individuals immediately involved continue their singing and their attitude of attention as if nothing untoward had occurred. As with many other such ceremonies, the singing of the Anthem (which you may not like as music or for what are called, by some, its chauvinistic lyrics) is a mark of respect for one's country and flag. There are other patriotic songs—"America the Beautiful," "Columbia the Gem of the Ocean," "God Bless America," "Yankee Doodle," etc.—but they do not require the respectful response which must be given "The Star-Spangled Banner," designated as our official National Anthem.

The hearing of the National Anthem at home over radio or television does not require the rising of those present if they are gathered informally together in a small group. If a large dance or ball is being given in a private home and the orchestra for some reason opens the entertainment with the Anthem, then, of course, everyone rises.

The Anthem is never played even in private homes merely for entertainment, is never improvised upon for dance purposes.

Every public appearance of the President is preceded by the rendition of Ruffles and Flourishes, a signal for all to stand at attention. The march "Hail to the Chief" is the signal for all to stand at attention and *applaud*. Before the opening of ceremonies at which the President is to speak, "The Star-Spangled Banner" is played. It is played directly after a public toast to the President (on the rare occasions when one is proposed). Usually only the first stanza is played, and singing accompaniment is not expected, although it is not incorrect to sing. The singing or playing of the Anthem is never applauded.

In an Orthodox synagogue it is not only proper but required that in any salute to the flag or singing of the National Anthem the men's heads remain covered. It is forbidden in an Orthodox synagogue for men's heads to be uncovered at any time.

Anthems of Other Nations

In America public gatherings often open with the playing of our National Anthem. If another country's representatives are present, as, for example, members of the cavalry teams from various countries in the National Horse Show, or a great pianist from another country at, say, a White House musicale, the visitors' national anthem is played first, ours second. For all national anthems, everyone stands at attention and all civilians place the right hand over the heart in salute (except indoors where no salute is given). Outdoors, if the flag is *not* displayed, men merely uncover their heads and stand at attention. They may sing the anthem if they wish—many Americans seem to know the "Marseillaise" and "God Save the Queen" (whose music is the same as that of "America")—but they need not actually salute any but their own flag. Abroad they never pledge allegiance to another flag, just as no non-American ever repeats the words of our Pledge.

Part Nine

TRAVEL ETIQUETTE AT HOME
AND ABROAD

TRAVEL ETIQUETTE AT HOME
AND ABROAD

If you wish to be at ease under any circumstance with any kind of person, by all means travel as much as your time and pocketbook permit. Travel is broadening if you undertake it with an open mind and a receptive heart.

Even though English is now virtually an international language, the knowledge of English alone is limiting to the traveler. Knowing at least a little of the language of the country or countries you are to visit not only is courteous to the people there but adds to your own pleasure and convenience. It is so easy to pick up the basic vocabulary of almost any language these days through the study-methods offered. You don't even have to be a linguist to become amazingly proficient in a relatively short time. Studying a new language in preparation for a trip can give your travels a breadth and interest they would never have had without this new, exciting stimulus. It helps, along with knowledge of what is expected, to make travel more enjoyable. Perhaps the best advice to the traveler is—

Go to new countries and new places as if you had no set tastes and standards by which you could judge what you are about to see and experience, even what you are about to eat.

Do not seek out your own countrymen exclusively in foreign lands, stay away from so-called American restaurants and tourist traps. Do not demand American-style efficiency, sanitation, manners, and service.

Accept your surroundings with grace and tact. Relax and learn to enjoy the new and different life without making invidious comparisons. You may be as American as you wish when you get back home.

Chapter 70

TRAVELING BY SHIP, PLANE, TRAIN, AND BUS

Before You Go

Whether you are off to Europe, the South Seas, or merely on a weekend in the country, you will certainly want to leave your house and belongings as safe as possible. You think it will never happen to you, but boilers blow up, pipes burst, burglars break in, electric wires come down, fires break out. Here are some of the things that you should do: Tell your neighbors where you are going and how you may be reached in an emergency. If your absence is going to be extended, tell the police and give them the necessary information. Give someone you trust a key to your house and let the police or your neighbors know who has it. Although your local paper may very well be interested in your comings and goings, such items are favorite reading material for burglars, especially during vacation periods. It will be safer for you and still be news if you will permit the report of your trip only after your return.

When you leave your house, make it a rule to check that all lights you want off are off, that all gas jets are shut, all small household appliances are disconnected. When you will be away for some time, valuable jewelry, clothing, papers, and securities should be left in a safe deposit box or insured storage. Locked closets and drawers in empty houses are an open invitation to pilferage. You might well lose your property, have your furniture damaged to boot.

Look at the locks on your windows and doors very critically. There are special safety locks that can be attached to window frame sides that make an ordinary window lock much safer and which cannot be manipulated from the outside. Extra strong, modern, double-cylinder dead door locks are a fine investment and so are the expensive new locks whose keys may not be duplicated except by the manufacturer. Remember, second-story artists can easily get to attic windows and upstairs porches. Cellar doors, dumbwaiter and service doors should be checked. Padlocks are an open announcement that you are gone and an invitation to lock pickers. Don't imagine either that you really can hide your key from a burglar—he knows all the favorite spots.

Leave your empty house or apartment with a lived-in look. An electronic eye that lets one or more lamps go on at dusk is an excellent investment. Shades should be left undrawn. Mail and newspaper deliveries should be stopped, or at least not permitted to accumulate. If these services go on for a brief period while you are away, a neighbor or friend who is in your confidence should pick up these telltale evidences of your absence. Of course, milk deliveries should be stopped.

And never, never, of course, leave notes around saying when you will return or where messages or packages are to be left for you. On the other hand, a few boldly printed or written notes left in such places as the kitchen, presumably to someone you expect to come into the house, might just deter someone who has managed to break in. Something like, "Joe, Bill and the others will be back in a few minutes. Uncle Ned is asleep so be quiet—he hears the *slightest* sound!"

Even all these precautions are of course not foolproof, no lock is secure against a broken window, a smashed door, but burglars like houses that are easy to break into, so the least you can do is make the matter difficult. And, of course, if you are fully insured that, too, helps your peace of mind when you are away from home.

Travel Courtesy

It is perhaps a human failing to think that just because you are away from home, away from your normal community, you need not practice your customary good manners. The matter is very sensitive indeed when you go abroad for there you are the foreigner and it seems as if a thousand critical eyes are upon you. While most countries are hospitable and friendly to the largesse-dispensing American traveler, there are always people everywhere who look upon the foreigner with a certain amount of suspicion. Our government warns of this and asks that you be particularly sensitive to the manners and mores of the countries you visit. Here are some of the points you should remember when you travel abroad.

Be dignified   It is perfectly normal to want to let loose when away from home as part of the release you seek in travel, but what you do, the way you behave, should come within tasteful limits. It is easy to label fun-loving, lazy vacationers as boors and, as a matter of fact, at home they might never behave in such a fashion. The good rule taught children is one to remember when you are in foreign countries—ladies and gentlemen never do anything in public that calls undue attention to themselves.

Be understanding and tolerant   Why should you expect the coffee to be exactly like that at home? The Frenchman probably considers our coffee miserable. Customs vary. If they didn't, what fun would travel be? Don't expect to take America, its dress, its customs, its manners with you. Find out what manners, what mode of dress is expected of people in the countries you are going to visit and then, within reason, conform in the matter of courtesy and consideration. It's the other fellow's country, remember.

Be friendly Of course you are paying your way and probably generously, but nevertheless you are a guest. It's an old saw, but to make a friend you must be a friend. An open, inquiring mind helps you communicate with people in strange lands. Sticking like American gum to your own group has the effect of shutting out enriching experiences.

Be modest You come from a big prosperous country whose history is short. In other parts of the world if Americans seem bumptious, it is only human for people to want to take them down a peg. Sheer bigness is no substitute for quality and culture. Our country has all three, of course, but by being boastful we sometimes seem lacking in these enviable qualities.

Open your mind to other languages I have seen Americans really indignant under some particular situation because no one in a foreign country spoke English. Why should they, even though it seems that English is rapidly becoming *the* international language? It is very flattering to people abroad if you know at least a few courteous words in their language, if you handle their money with knowledge and respect, making no invidious comparisons of its style, size, purchasing power, or anything else in comparison with American coin of the realm.

Be generous but not foolish American-scale tipping abroad is often not appreciated by foreign governments. Don't believe everything you hear about the necessity for haggling in shops and markets. To some this may be sport, but you should remember it is often very hard to earn a living this way in some countries where profits are tiny. Try to pay a fair price without argument.

Take health precautions You should be cautious about your health but not to the point of insulting the people. Before going, consult your doctor for all necessary inoculations and injections. Get his advice on what proprietary and other drugs to take along. Inform yourself by reading the available travel information on where water and milk are potable and quietly avoid them where there is any doubt. Remember, in many cases residents can drink and eat germ-ladened things to which we, in our protected state, have not developed an immunity so our very cautious behavior may seen eccentric to people who have been eating and drinking these things, evidently with no harm, perhaps for centuries. If you are being cautious, be consistent. Remember that if you were told to avoid water, you should also avoid ice unless you are absolutely certain it has been made under hygienic circumstances as it nearly always is at the great national restaurants and hotels. Remember that alcohol in your drink is no protection against impure water or unclean glasses, but on the other hand we have to take some chances in life everywhere.

Remember your social obligations In many countries, those we meet are very generous indeed in their entertainment of us, in their sending of gifts and flowers. Too often Americans, casual about these matters at home, do not realize that they should be punctilious in their thanks and that notes are expected, that there are certain courtesies toward hosts and hostesses that should be carefully followed. And remember that nowadays all the world is increasingly coming to us, so extend invitations to your own home. Keep up the line of communication at Christmas and at other times, don't be just a taker, be generous in your giving and your interest.

If You Go by Ship

Bon Voyage Parties One of the pleasures of sailing is the bon voyage party. Let your friends know your sailing time and suggest that if they wish they may see you off. Arrange, as the host or hostess, to be on board at least an hour or more before departure time. Consult with the cabin steward about necessary supplies—ice cubes, soda water, soft drinks, and glasses. You must arrange to bring liquor on board—if you plan to serve it—because liquor is not sold aboard ship while it is in port. The steamship line will tell you what time to be aboard and what time guests must leave the ship.

Behavior Aboard Ship A ship may be compared to a country hotel. It is good manners to greet other passengers in a friendly fashion without, however, making presumptuous overtures. You speak to the people next to you in deck chairs, but you do not force conversation upon them. In general, as in a friend's house, the roof is the introduction, but this does not mean you are expected to do more than bow in greeting to fellow passengers as you encounter them during the day. Congenial people usually introduce themselves to one another in short order aboard ship, except on the biggest transatlantic liners, but it should be kept in mind that shipboard friendships, like shipboard romances, usually end when the boat docks, despite many protestations to the contrary. The passenger who bares his soul to all who will listen to him within the first hour or two of embarkation looks very silly to sophisticated travelers. Neither should you air your complaints to those around you. This only makes it seem that you are unaccustomed to such luxury and are trying to achieve superiority. Legitimate complaints should go to the chief purser, who acts for the captain as your host aboard ship.

Deck Chairs In order to insure yourself of a deck chair for your voyage, you must reserve one through the deck steward. Also, there is a charge for each deck chair. An empty deck chair may be used, though, until its owner appears. Deck chair reservations may also be made in writing to the line or through your travel agent in advance of sailing in some instances. This eliminates the necessary standing in line just after sailing time. It seems ships never have enough deck chairs for all passengers who desire them and application must be made promptly. These reservations must then be confirmed immediately after embarking with the chief deck steward.

The Captain The captain of your ship should be treated with the greatest respect, both socially and professionally. Any invitation from him either to dine with him or to be a guest with others in his cabin should never if possible be refused. During each voyage he usually entertains at two general cocktail parties—one for first-class passengers and one for cabin class. Any invitation from him would probably be formal:

Captain Robert Cartier
and
Chief Purser Rene Dubois
request the honour of
Mr. and Mrs. Peter Rossi's company
for cocktails on
Sunday, May 3rd, 1970
at seven-fifteen
in the Salon Monaco, Verandah Deck

If you cannot go, leave word with the Purser's office to that effect, or if you wish, you may send a formal third person reply on suitable stationery supplied by the ship, leaving it at the Purser's office or, if you prefer, sending it by cabin boy, tipping him twenty-five cents or the foreign currency equivalent for his service.

Mr. and Mrs. Peter Rossi
regret exceedingly (or simply "regret")
that they are unable to accept
Captain Cartier's and Chief Purser Dubois'
kind invitation for
Sunday, May 3rd

Other officers sometimes act as hosts at various tables in the dining room. They also often invite passengers at their tables for cocktails in their own reception room. These invitations should be accepted or refused just as courteously as the captain's.

All officers except the captain should be addressed as "Mr." Ship's doctors are officers, too, but are called "Doctor."

Seating in the Dining Room Prior to the ship's departure it is desirable to see the second steward about your table reservations, unless you have made application in advance from the steamship company.

People with small children are expected to take the first sitting, unless the children are to eat with their nurse and the parents eat alone at a later hour. If you are seated at a table with any of the ship's officers, bear in mind that the officer acts as the table's host and passengers await his appearance before ordering. If he is unavoidably detained, he sends a message to that effect. If a lady seated with several gentlemen and perhaps another lady does not wish to come to a meal, it is courteous of her to send word to the table with her steward so the others will not wait. A passenger arriving early at his table for lunch or dinner (but not at breakfast) where no officer is host, is courteous to wait until at least the majority of the others arrive before ordering. Or, if he orders, he may ask the steward to refrain from serving him until at least some of the others have arrived.

Dress Aboard Transatlantic Ships   Clothing aboard ship is casual during the daytime—the sort of clothes worn at a country club in any good resort. At best they are conservative, with shorts and bathing apparel confined to the swimming and sports area. Slacks and pants suits on women are seen on all decks, to some extent in the dining room for breakfast and, to a lesser extent, at lunch. Men wear coats at all meals, too, on first-class liners except when costumes are called for. This information is given in the ship's bulletin. They do not wear sport clothes at night in the public rooms or dining room except on embarkation and debarkation nights. Women may or may not wear sport hats, as they please, on deck or at daytime meals. In the evening, except in tourist and cabin class, there is some attempt at formality, depending, of course, on the ship on which one travels. On the great transatlantic liners dinner jackets are the general, though not obligatory, rule. Sunday is now a dress night aboard ship unless Sunday falls on the night of departure or the eve of arrival (both traditionally, nondress nights). Gloves should not be worn below deck, but they should be worn on deck if the weather is cold. It is never bad taste to appear in dinner dress, and on ships where a Captain's or Gala Dinner is given, formality is expected, with men wearing dinner jackets and women appearing, if they wish, in full evening dress. On some ships this special night is made into a fancy dress affair, which permits considerable leeway in costumes. These are usually available from the ship's stores, but if you know a costume affair to be the ship's custom you may take along your own. The costumes that win the prizes, however, are usually the ones that are extemporized out of whatever happens to be on hand in one's baggage. But quite a few diehards attend such evenings in their usual clothes and enjoy themselves nonetheless, with perhaps a paper hat added to give the right festive note.

When One Doesn't Dress   On the first and last nights out it is customary for passengers to wear their ordinary travel clothes. Presumably the exigencies of packing and unpacking are too great for any degree of formality to be expected on these nights. But many women do change into something else such as the ubiquitous "little black dress" preferably in a fabric that travels so well that the dress won't need pressing on these hectic evenings. There can be great confusion below decks.

Behavior at Table   Other passengers at your table are treated exactly as if you were with them in your own home. Conversation is expected, gentlemen rise when ladies are seated and wait until ladies' orders are taken before ordering themselves. On ships where wine or cocktails are not included in the meal it is usual for a guest at the table who wishes either or both of these to include the others at the table in an invitation to join him, an invitation which may be refused, of course, with proper courtesy. Such invitations, by the way, are reciprocated by others at the table from time to time, even by a woman traveling alone who has enjoyed such invitations from men at the table or from couples. She may reciprocate by buying wine for the table and she usually announces that she will do so perhaps the night before, remembering that on gala nights wine (usually champagne) is furnished by the captain.

When passengers are assigned to various tables in the dining room by the second steward, a table for the captain and other tables for the ship's officers are made up from the passenger list, although on some ships officers sit by themselves without guests. On other ships distinguished personages, presumably, occupy these coveted seats and often arrangements have been made through special introductions to the line long before sailing. Sometimes these "distinguished" personages are just people the line wishes to cultivate for some reason or other, perhaps are merely passengers who have sailed for many years with the same line, but may well be not the most interesting company, although the captain nearly always is. To be invited to sit with the captain is always an honor. It is possible to refuse to sit at the captain's table, or elsewhere in a place of honor, if one has a very good excuse. During the trip it is permissible to shift seats at table in order to join friends only with the consent of the chief steward.

Entertaining on Board   On both transatlantic liners and cruises, it is a popular custom for passengers to arrange individual private cocktail parties either in their staterooms or in some of the public rooms. For an extensive party in one of the lounges or in the bar or elsewhere, speak to the chief steward. Your room steward will take care of hors d'oeuvres, glasses, and ice (if you want to supply your own liquor) or complete setups in your own stateroom. There is no charge for ice or hors d'oeuvres, and you may find that you must arrange some kind of party to pay off your numerous social obligations aboard ship, on cruises particularly, drink checks picked up, other people's cocktail parties, entertainment ashore, and so forth. As ships at sea are free of liquor taxes, you will find it a delightfully inexpensive way to entertain even if you choose the finest champagne. (Incidentally, passengers usually aren't allowed to bring their own wines and liquors into the public rooms on ships.) Stewards serving such parties in the lounges are tipped at the time, approximately 15 per cent of your bill for the party.

Tipping Aboard Ship Just before debarking, a passenger tips the following personnel: room steward, table steward, head dining steward, wine steward, if he's been used, and deck and bath stewards. The steward who has taken care of your cabin receives ten dollars per person as do the table steward and headwaiter. Ladies are attended by both steward and stewardess. The tip of ten dollars is divided between them at the end of the voyage for first-class quarters.

Deck stewards receive two or three dollars, depending on the amount of service they have rendered. Passengers without private baths tip the bath steward one dollar at the end of the voyage, and the "boots" receives one dollar to three dollars depending on how many shoes he has kept shined. Cabin boys are usually tipped twenty-five cents or the foreign currency equivalent at the time they perform their small services, if at all. Bar attendants are usually tipped 10 to 15 per cent of the bill at the time of service if the bill is settled at the time. If the check is signed by a regular frequenter of the smoke room, he might prefer to tip at the end of the voyage. On some ships the card-signing custom prevails, on others payment is required at the time of ordering.

On most ships the chief steward is classed as a ship's officer and, as such, is never tipped.

Tipping Stevedores Despite large signs on the piers stating that tipping stevedores supplied by the line is not necessary, I find that stevedores not only expect a tip but frequently tell you what to tip, often before they move your baggage. The suggested amount, depending on the amount of baggage, can be anywhere from three to five to even ten dollars unless you want to be ignored for a long time. Never make any attempt to tip a Customs officer. It is against the law.

Traveling by Freighter

Freighter vacations are so popular that there are many books about this phase of travel alone. Freighter trips are usually limited to twelve passengers, since if more passengers are aboard, a doctor is required. They are always informal, the captain never wearing dress uniform. Most frequently, passengers wear the same clothes throughout the day, including dinner with officers and passengers all dining together in a common room. Most freighters are comfortable, some—such as the Norwegian and the French —relatively luxurious, particularly in relation to the food. On most, however, the food is quite plain, often good, with entertainment limited to what the passengers choose for themselves such as cards and reading. Freighter trips can be lonely or rewarding, depending on whether or not you need rest or companionship, which, aboard freighters, is never predictable any more than are the times of arrival and departure. Freighters must wait for loading to be completed and fixed schedules are difficult to follow. The freighter passenger must be somewhat of an adventurer, ready to leave on a few hours' notice, never quite sure exactly when he will return. Many people, however, prefer to travel this way and dream of freighter trips in their future.

You certainly don't have to worry about clothes aboard a freighter. Sweaters and skirts, pants suits, slacks, knits, shorts, all are usual wear. For men, any sports clothes they choose to wear day and night are acceptable. If you figure approximately 15 per cent of the cost of the trip for tips, you will be in line. Divide this amount among the people who serve you. Freighter travel is, of course, much lower in cost than travel by luxury liner and is a wonderful way to transport children if you can find a freighter going at the time that they are free. Few children are bored on a ship or boat even when there is no dancing or a swimming pool or official entertainment. The French Line freighters, however, do have air conditioning and swimming pools of a sort (of canvas). Norwegian freighters, calling only at ports of Norway, need no air conditioning.

Cruises

Cruises are becoming more and more popular ways to spend vacations. They go north and south, to the North Cape, the Mediterranean, the Caribbean, and the Pacific. But wherever you go, remember it is best to dress and act inconspicuously.

If you are planning a lengthy cruise you can easily get from the line a listing of your itinerary so that you can receive mail and cables at the various ports. This list of addresses also gives postage rates.

Dress Cruises are always less formal than transatlantic crossings and require a larger wardrobe of informal and sports clothes. On a southern cruise, summer sports clothes are in order. Bathing suits and shorts are worn around the pool and with some covering are often permitted in the dining room for breakfast and lunch. Usually very simple cocktail dresses, summer silk, dressy cottons, or linen are worn to dinner. The night of the captain's dinner may be slightly dressier. Gentlemen usually take a white dinner jacket, sometimes two (there may be no dry cleaning aboard) but tropical-weight black is also worn as are colored dinner jackets, madras, etc.— especially by the young. These are sometimes worn ashore to night clubs, although a white linen or light-colored miracle fabric suit will do just as well. A jacket and tie is proper for dinner on all but special nights.

Fur stoles are sometimes worn on southern cruises, but I think they often look out of place. In the warm months I prefer pretty cashmere sweaters, short jackets suitable for covering cocktail dresses, or silk or wool stoles.

In Nassau and the Bahamas the spring and summer seasons are less formal than the winter one. Dinner jackets are expected at least on Saturday night and are never out of place. White, madras, and pastel jackets are common. Black or white dinner jackets—never the less formal colored ones—are worn to Government House functions in which many Americans may be included during the winter season. Dark or light business suits and white shirts are worn there during the day, however. Buttoned sports shirts with no tie are not correct.

For dining in fashionable hotels and in private homes, gentlemen wear dark suits (not brown), conservative ties, and either white or black shoes to the Government House or to church. Hats or some headcovering are required in church and most people do wear gloves for these dress-up occasions, even the tourists. In the exclusive resort areas, women are expected to wear stockings after six o'clock. Men must wear jackets and ties. Evening pajamas are of course worn formally and informally at night in the top hotels, but sports pants of any kind are not.

Don't overdress in the islands. Simple cottons and linens, simple jewelry (the native variety is delightful) look best for daytime excursions into town. Dresses may be sleeveless, but watch those too-low necklines. Bermuda shorts are permissible, but leave the short shorts and halters on the ship for your return voyage. Men also may wear Bermuda shorts but when in town should wear the proper dark long socks. White wool short socks are all right for active sports. Much sightseeing is done on foot, so wear comfortable summer shoes or sandals. Stockings and gloves are not necessary except on visits to Government House or to church. Hats and gloves are required in both of these places. Pick up one of the island's famous straw hats to shade you from the tropical sun during play hours. And don't forget your sun glasses. A light-weight all-purpose raincoat is always a good thing to have, too. Tropical showers soon pass but they can be frequent and sometimes drenching.

The tipping scale in the islands is approximately the same as in the United States, 10 to 20 per cent. The big hotels usually have a weekly rate of which you may take advantage. If so, tip your waiter in the dining room 15 to 20 per cent of the bill at the end of every week. Leave only a dollar for the chambermaid unless she has performed some special services.

If your cruise takes you north, leave the summer play clothes behind and take instead spring wools and warmer clothes such as knits and pants suits. It is still quite cool in Alaska during May and June and summer in Scandinavia is, for us, spring clothes weather. The local belles, however chilly they may look, do wear pastel cottons, however.

On a North Cape cruise, weather may be warm crossing the Atlantic if you go in midsummer, but sightseeing is likely to be cool. Sweaters, skirts, and wool suits and pants suits are recommended for women and slacks and wool sport coats for men. Take conservative cocktail clothes, maybe separates, and always have a stole, preferably wool, or sweater handy. Nights may often be cool enough for a topcoat, and don't forget walking shoes, a raincoat, and a rain hat. An all-purpose raincoat with supplementary wool sweaters or scarves is a sensible solution.

People do not dress formally for dinner when going ashore unless their plans specifically call for evening dress, for example at certain casinos in Puerto Rico. When in doubt, ask the cruise director's staff.

Tipping On cruises it is customary, depending on the quarters one occupies, to plan to distribute as tips anywhere from 10 to 20 per cent of the total passage fare, depending on the amount of service required and its quality. The tips to the ship's staff include the following: Table steward—this works out to about ten dollars per person and be sure to count the children in your party in this calculation. Room steward or stewardess—approximately ten dollars apiece or if they share the responsibility, the sum divided. Boots—two to three dollars, depending on the amount of service. Deck steward—five dollars. Wine steward—two dollars if you have used his services. Chief steward—five to ten dollars (he is equivalent to a maître d' in a restaurant) and his assistant three to five dollars, in both cases depending on the amount of service you have demanded in the preparation of special foods such as crêpes suzette and other flaming dishes, for example. Small tips of a dollar or two may be given to lounge stewards, for example in the library if you have patronized it considerably. On cruises, tips are divided so that they are paid one-half halfway through the voyage, just before a port of call and the other half just before debarkation, usually the night before. Tips are given in cash—in dollars—preferably in sealed envelopes where larger amounts are involved. The cruise staff is not tipped, but often passengers who have enjoyed their helpful activities give them gifts of liquor, perfume, and so forth, but this is not obligatory. Officers and sailors are not tipped.

Beauty Salons Aboard Ship Major cruise ships and transatlantic liners have beauty parlors—some of them elaborate and run by world-famous firms as concessions. If you want a regular appointment as you would ashore, you must go immediately to the beauty parlor on the day of embarkation or as soon afterward as possible to set up your appointments, otherwise you may find on cruise ships, particularly, that part of your valuable shoretime will be taken up having manicures and your hair done as the ships' beauty parlors are closed when the ship is in port. Experienced women travelers know that on cruises they need more than one hairdressing appointment a week because of swimming, tropical climates, and sports activities. Many carry wigs to cut down on appointments. Often women who are sophisticated travelers will arrange for comb-outs at the same time each night while at sea. Others lead a free life by depending on one or more wigs. Sometimes the wash and wear variety is easy to manage without professional help. Hairdressers and barbers aboard ship are tipped on the same basis that they are perhaps ashore—about one dollar to an operator who sets your hair and perhaps washes it too (twenty-five cents, more if you wish, to the girl who shampoos your hair if this is done separately), twenty-five cents or more to the manicurist, depending on the price of the manicure at least 10 per cent, perhaps 15 per cent. Special services—touch-ups, dyeing, permanents—are best, under most circumstances, not entrusted to ship beauty parlors, but if you are gone long enough and must have the services consult your own hairdresser on whatever supplies or formulas you may need to take along. Remember, in very rough weather, the beauty parlor usually closes down, so take along curlers, shampoo, bobby pins, nets, and so forth, in case you have to perform these services for yourself, and you will probably have to at some stage of a cruise at least.

Plane Travel

Before Leaving The very fact that airplanes have rapidly become the most popular and most convenient way to travel makes the practice of utmost courtesy essential in crowded airports and in the air. At airports allow at least half an hour to check in on domestic flights, an hour or more before international flights. Consider that you may have long distances to walk within the airport, so keep hand luggage to a minimum. There may be no carts, and porters are often impossible to find. Determine if possible in advance the weight of your luggage for international travel. A flight bag is weighed even if carried into the cabin, but a reasonable number of books, an umbrella, your handbag, a coat, and a camera are not. Two pieces of luggage are checked without charge on domestic flights, and any small items are free if they will fit under your seat. Luggage restrictions differ between economy-flight and first-class tickets, between domestic and overseas travel. Learn to travel light. Avoid luggage that is heavy in itself. All luggage now takes hard punishment in air travel and the most expensive is not always the best for your purposes. I have found that molded, lightweight airplane luggage without any soft sides and with sturdy locks is best for international travel.

"Transportation" covers airport to airport, not transportation from terminals to planes. The airlines provide optional limousine service at extra cost to the passenger. Sky-caps at the terminal entrances who assist you to check-in desks are tipped in a nominal fashion as are those who carry any luggage for you beyond baggage-claim areas (twenty-five cents, fifty cents, seventy-five cents—even a dollar—might be the tip depending on the amount of luggage involved, and the distances are usually short to limousines or cabs). Reservations clerks and the personnel aboard the planes are not tipped.

On long trips a passenger may wish to take with him to his seat a small bag for overnight things, along with his wraps. The rest of his baggage is stowed before the takeoff, to be reclaimed with his baggage stub at the terminal.

Upon checking in note the number of pieces of baggage you are having shipped through and the number of articles (limited) you are taking with you to your seat. Keep your belongings together. On some jets small bags are put in the baggage rack as you enter the plane. In others you must fit them under the seat. No heavy or pointed object (such as your umbrella) may be put in the overhead racks. Check the passenger behind you before you lower your seat. Return it to the erect position before take-off and landing. On takeoff and on landing return your tray to its proper position. Replace magazines in racks when you finish with them or hand them to passing stewardesses who are not otherwise occupied. On overseas flights and on returning flights from Miami, be sure to reconfirm your reservations within the time limit indicated on your ticket. This is done from your destination point. It is best done in the airport as you leave your plane.

Jet flight is so rapid these days that passengers barely have time to exchange courtesies let alone settle down for the night on an overseas trip. However, some chartered overseas flights continue to use prop planes.

On Board On entering a plane, the passenger is greeted by a steward or stewardess. There is sometimes a plaque with the name of this employee, who then is referred to as "Stewardess" or "Miss James," "Steward," or "Mr. Benson." The stewardess' job, or the steward's (one or the other serves, sometimes both), is to check aboard the passengers, to take coats and hang them up before or, usually, after the takeoff, serve meals, heat baby bottles, attend any airsick passengers (usually an academic matter on jet flights), offer reading material and gum or hard candies. Chewing gum helps reduce pressure on eardrums as the plane loses altitude in the landing operation, but again on jet flights there is much less need for this aid if any as cabins are fully pressurized. With regard to baby feeding and baby care, some few people imagine that a stewardess is available to take over full care and feeding of an infant. The airlines, however, are limited in what they can do. They do supply baby foods, a bassinet, a diaper kit with disposable diapers, and other comforts. The stewardesses are allowed to warm the formula but may not mix it. Only when their time permits—and this is rarely on the busy jets—may they help with the care of an infant. A stewardess is also there to keep the passengers at ease and should not have her time monopolized by any one passenger (usually male) who wants merely to be entertained. You need never exchange a single word with your seat mate, but conversation is permissible and is usual at mealtimes.

Regulations on various airlines differ concerning the showing of tickets. On some they are shown only at the gate, on others they are shown at the gate and upon entrance into the plane. On still others it may be requested by the steward or stewardess after the passenger is seated, and on still others there is no further request to see tickets once the passenger has embarked. It's wise to keep your tickets handy until the plane is in flight.

Regulations regarding seats differ on different lines, according to the type of plane. Sometimes a passenger selects his own seat before he boards the plane, sometimes afterward. On certain luxury flights seats are reserved. Once seated, he fastens his seat belt immediately and waits for the steward or stewardess to take his coat as soon as she is free to do so, if she hasn't taken it at the door. But first she must see that everyone is aboard, in his seat, and with the safety belt properly fastened. The door must be bolted shut and the signal given to the pilot. Passengers do not smoke at the takeoff when a sign above the pilot's compartment is lighted in the no-smoking warning. Smoking may be resumed when the light goes off.

The stewardess has all kinds of little remedies for airsickness and keeps on hand a medicine cabinet to cover any emergency. On overseas planes there is a life preserver under each seat, and instruction is usually given at the beginning of the trip by stewardess, steward, co-pilot, or flight officer on its use. On jets the oxygen mask is demonstrated before takeoff though its use is very rarely necessary. Electronic equipment such as tape recorders are permitted, but it is well to ask permission of the stewardess before using them. Music cassettes should be played very softly if at all, or with the use of earphones. Radios should not be used at all.

Meals Depending on the time you are traveling, the accommodations you have, the length of the flight and other factors, you may or may not get a meal on a plane. In picking up your ticket or making a reservation it is always wise to ask, "Is this a luncheon, breakfast, dinner (or whatever the meal hours happen to be) flight?" Sometimes on short flights between cities there is no time for the service of anything other than coffee or soft drinks. On the Continental flights, depending on where you board and where you are going, you may find yourself consuming two breakfasts, two dinners. Sometimes on a short domestic flight you may find yourself picking up a box lunch at nominal prices at the gate as you board, or waiting until your arrival before another meal. It is also perfectly permissible for a passenger to take along his own box lunch, which may well be more attractive than food offered. In addition, most airline terminals usually provide some eating facilities.

Alcoholic beverages are served free to first-class passengers. On economy and coach flights there is a charge of a dollar in the United States and internationally fifty cents per drink, but here again the service of drinks depends on the amount of time the flight takes. In all classes soft drinks are available without charge. On charter and other special flights arrangements may have been made to serve them to all passengers who want them. Technically passengers are limited to two drinks and even this can mean trouble if someone has come aboard pre-fortified. Stewardesses are not permitted to serve or sell alcohol to anybody obviously inebriated, or as a matter of fact, to accept a passenger aboard who is under the influence of liquor. No alcohol may be carried aboard a plane.

Lavatories on Planes Lavatories on planes are of course limited with usually two fore and two aft, which means that they may be serving hundreds of people depending on the size of the plane. If you have been waiting in the airport to board, it is wise, especially if you have children with you, to use the airport facilities before getting on the plane. In rough weather if the pilot requests that passengers and personnel all take their seats and fasten their seatbelts, passengers may not be permitted to use the lavatories. "Burp" bags are provided in the compartment in front of your seat. If you are in the lavatory and the "Return to your seat" light goes on, you must go back to your seat as soon as possible. Try to schedule your trips to the lavatory at times when meals are not being served as this is a difficult time for personnel and sometimes service carts in the aisle make it difficult to pass. Once the descent has been announced, do not tarry in the lavatory but return to your seat and fasten your seatbelt. Make your visit as brief as possible when people are waiting in line. You can always repair your make-up at your seat (but don't comb your hair there).

Unless it is absolutely necessary, don't enter the lavatory as others are entering the plane. Instead seat yourself as soon as possible. For the same reason, to avoid confusion, don't use it once passengers have begun to debark. Instead use the facilities at the airport. The lavatories of commercial planes have electrical outlets for 110-volt electric razors. In addition the plane will supply its own 24-volt razors for use on a special outlet.

Night Flights Long night flights are mainly restricted to international travel these days, but the sophisticated traveler knows just how to make himself comfortable for them. On a very long flight, for example Japan Air Lines non-stop flight from Moscow to Tokyo, the wise woman passenger after dinner unhooks her bra or removes it, takes off her girdle if she is wearing one, dons her own or the plane's slippers, accepts the eye shade and the Happi-coat offered her in first class (the Happi-coat is on loan) and settles down to sleep with perhaps stoppers in her ears if other passengers prefer to stay awake. The more you can sleep on these long flights, the better you will be able to go through the time zones. In your waking time, you should elevate your legs frequently, get up and walk around. It is unwise to drink anything but a moderate amount of alcohol, and tempting though the meals are, the wise travelers eat moderately.

Knits are the most comfortable for air travel especially on long flights. You may sleep in them in your reclining seat, knowing they will emerge looking relatively fresh. Feet swell at these altitudes very frequently, and your shoes should be very comfortable indeed and are replaced even during daytime flights if you wish with the socks the line may furnish you, or with your own slippers. Also, it isn't poor etiquette just to remove your shoes, but remember that on jet flights the floor is often cold and wool shoe-socks or warm slippers of some kind are very welcome. For the same reason, too, thin clothing should not be worn even in the summer on jet flights.

When the lights are lowered in the plane, those not wishing to settle down for rest should avoid loud talking that might keep others awake.

Men passengers remove suit coats and ties for night flights and some-times don sports shirts. They either accept the sleeping socks the airline usually provides at least to first-class passengers or put on their own slippers. Blankets and pillows are furnished to each passenger.

Tipping No member of a plane's personnel is ever tipped. One says good-by to the steward or stewardness in attendance at the gangplank when debarking.

Train Travel

Baggage When traveling by train one should take as little baggage as possible, for storage space is limited. The passenger who must have his numerous belongings piled on the platform, where they obstruct passage from car to car, is a nuisance. When much luggage is necessary for a trip part of it should be sent ahead by express or else shipped through in the baggage car on the ticket—150 pounds go free. In the latter case, how-ever, it is important to know that baggage cannot be shipped on the pas-senger's ticket beyond the point of his descent, and there is often a wait while the freight car is unloaded and baggage sorted out.

In a Pullman large bags are usually placed on the platform by the porter, unless they fit under the seat. They should be locked, of course. A small bag may go to a seat, but not if it is likely to be in the way of a seat mate. At night such a bag should be small enough to fit in the hammock above the berth. In a roomette or compartment all hand baggage is stored by the porter in the allotted space.

Seating The occupant of a lower berth is entitled to the forward seat of a Pullman section. It is courteous of anyone occupying this preferred place to offer to share it with the passenger riding backwards. If the occupant of the lower is a gentleman he usually cedes the seat during the daytime to a lady if she is the occupant of the less desirable seat. If he wishes, he may even offer to take the upper berth at night, especially if she is elderly, preg-nant, or ill, but, of course, having bought the preferred lower he is in no way actually obliged to give it up, especially if the other passenger is rea-sonably young and healthy. An elderly or infirm man, of course, might also be offered the lower berth. An upper-berth passenger should be sound and spry enough to negotiate the ladder.

Occupying a Section Occupants of a section consult each other cour-teously as to when the berths are to be made up for the night. Usually the porter likes to complete the work of bedmaking by ten or, at the latest, ten-thirty, doing the berths of those who have rung for him first. In order not to impede his work, those who wish to retire late usually go into the observation car until they are ready for bed.

Dressing and Undressing Attached to the curtains of each berth are hangers for clothes, and the hammock-rack for hats, shoes, bags, etc., is put in place after the berths are made up. The adept traveler, therefore, dresses and undresses completely in his berth, after preparing for the night in the dressing room. A toilet kit or bag for use in the dressing room is necessary. Women who prefer to cope with their girdles and to put on their dresses or suits after washing and making-up in the morning, make the trek to the dressing room in a dark tailored robe, having neatly combed their hair, if not finally arranged it, before their emergence from the berth. In the dressing room they occupy a minimum of shelf space for their belongings and complete their toilette as speedily as possible, unless most of the other passengers have already dressed. Men using the dressing room clean the basin for others after shaving.

Use of the Ladder Passengers occupying the upper berth must ring for the porter when they need the ladder. They are not permitted to put it in place themselves. Before going to bed the occupant of an upper should wash and be prepared to stay in his berth once he has been assisted into it. If he must descend during the night he rings for the porter—he never attempts to clamber down himself.

The Roomette and the Compartment The occupant of a roomette can easily operate the berth himself. The bed is made up before the passenger takes possession of the space and is out of sight in the wall. A lever lowers it into place, but, as it occupies the full length of the roomette once it's down, washing and undressing is done before the lever is pulled. Then the curtain is fastened over the door so the passenger in nightclothes will have privacy while he negotiates the bed. Once in, he reaches over and slides and locks the door.

Beds in a compartment are made up by the porter when he is summoned for the purpose.

Occupants of roomettes or compartments may have meals served in privacy if they wish, but occupants of Pullman and parlor car seats should go to the diner or to the observation car for refreshment.

The Diner A train that has been made up in the station has the diner ready for service if the train is pulling out at mealtime. A passenger may go to the diner at any convenient time during the normal service of meals. On going to the diner, he should always take his ticket or his ticket stub with him. He waits at the door until the chief steward, or in some cases, the headwaitress assigns him to a table. A lady alone takes something to read.

On a long trip dining car occupants usually greet each other when seated vis-à-vis and may carry on conversation, if they wish. But on a trip requiring but one or perhaps two meals in a diner, table mates rarely speak. (But see "Talking to Strangers While Traveling," page 853.)

After the meal is over, passengers should not linger in the dining car, even if they are among the last to dine. If other passengers are not waiting to be seated, the dining car crew usually is waiting to clean up.

Tipping A dining car steward is tipped 15 per cent of the bill, never less than a quarter per person if a meal has been served. An observation car steward who has served drinks is tipped 15 per cent of the total bar bill, not less than a quarter.

Station porters usually receive a fixed amount per bag. This may be anywhere from twenty-five to thirty-five cents. In addition to the fixed service charge, the porter generally expects a tip, but this is left to the discretion of the passenger. If he has handled two or three pieces of luggage, about a quarter is sufficient. If there is more luggage, the tip might be fifty cents or over depending upon luggage weight, distance, and difficulty of handling. In some places there is no definite charge per bag and the porters depend entirely on their tips for salary.

Pullman porters on overnight trips receive a minimum of one dollar per passenger. Possibly the tip is more if a great deal of service such as the fetching of food and drinks has been demanded, and if the porter has been particularly helpful.

Train Manners Occupants of private quarters may, of course, play portable radios with the door closed, have gatherings of friends, serve drinks, and smoke. But Pullman and parlor car occupants must maintain quiet, speak in low tones so as not to disturb others, drink and smoke only in areas set aside for the purpose. They keep their belongings in the space they occupy and do not litter the floor with papers or food.

Passengers on long trips who descend at stops to walk on the platform conduct themselves inconspicuously and return at the conductor's first warning.

Hotels

To be assured of getting desirable accommodations, it is better to make hotel reservations in advance. This may be done through your travel agent, a hotel in your own city, or by your writing or wiring. For information on making reservations and registering at a hotel see page 568. If, however, you have not made reservations in a hotel, ask at the desk for the kind of room you want. You may ask for something less expensive if the quoted price seems high, and you may politely ask to see the room or one like it.

When you are ready to check out, call the bell captain and tell him you are leaving. He will send up a boy to get your bags. If you are in a hurry, you may carry your own bags, but be obvious about leaving them with the bell captain as you check out. The house detective has his eye on you.

The Concierge There is no real equivalent to the European concierge in the United States, sad to say. In Europe he goes under several names, concierge, of course, in France. In Italy he is known as the *portiere*. In German the title is pronounced *con-cerge* and in England, of course, he is the Hall Porter. But whatever way his title is pronounced, the great man is in very small hotels virtually an entire executive staff—no mere American-style desk clerk. In more pretentious hotels you will be confronted by two desks, one where you register and pay your hotel bill yourself and often across the lobby the concierge's desk where you leave your key and get your mail. You can also leave all of your problems to this genial fellow—and sometimes he is twins or triplets. He speaks English, generally well or well enough, and in addition French, Spanish, and Italian, probably German, perhaps even another language or two—enough to get along. The concierge's desk will help you cope with the telephone, making your calls, and arranging your appointments. He will get you theater tickets and have a boy pick them up at the box office price. Of course at the end of your stay you take this into consideration, adding an appropriate amount to the concierge's bill which has gone to you separately. Even if you lose a heel from your shoe, you may take your shoe to the concierge and in no time it will be back in your room, repaired. In fact, he takes care of all repairs, the big ones and the small ones. If you don't find stationery in your room (very likely) the concierge will gladly give you some. He will sell you stamps and accept C.O.D. parcels for you. Of course the amount goes on his bill.

The concierge knows all about the best places to eat. He will watch over you like a mother hen, even suggesting to you some morning that you need your umbrella or your overshoes. He has medical prescriptions filled for you and will act as a mediator between you and a shop that in some way has caused you displeasure.

Don't think for a minute, however, that you can check out of your hotel in ten minutes. Even where computer systems are used, the concierge must be given a little time to present his bill, too. I like to allow half to three-quarters of an hour for checking out of a European hotel. You will be paying two bills and dealing probably with foreign currency. The bill at the main desk, if there are two desks, will cover ordinary hotel expenses, for example, meals, beverages, laundry, dry cleaning and pressing, usually, and telephone calls. The concierge's bill separately presented will include all the postcards you picked up in passing, your newspapers, theater tickets, C.O.D. packages. In fact a concierge prefers that you not pay him cash for the postcards or the papers, but ask him to charge it because this helps to make a nice well-rounded bill for him to present and get his tip on (never less than the equivalent of a dollar, but of course it can go to five dollars or more).

Has he not acted as moderator, purchasing agent, father confessor and travel agent? In fact, if the bill has really mounted up, you should figure anywhere from 10–15 per cent of it as his share. You will give it gladly, wishing he would move with all his talents to hotels and motels at home.

Hotel Tipping

Doorman The quality of the hotel, the amount of baggage one has, and the service expected, all have bearing on the size of the tips dispensed in hotels.

The man who opens the door of the cab and sets bags on the curb usually does no more than call a bellhop to take over. If he performs no service, no tip is required. If, on the other hand, he helps unload heavy and extensive baggage or assists anyone into the hotel itself, or at some other time summons a taxi, tipping is expected. For summoning a taxi from the stand in front of the hotel and merely opening its door for a passenger, a doorman usually gets a quarter. If he must fare forth in the rain and find one in the midst of traffic, the tip is gauged by the amount of trouble he has had—twenty-five cents or fifty cents or, perhaps in a bad storm late at night for guests in evening clothes, as much as a dollar. People who seek shelter under a hotel marquee in the rain and ask the doorman to find them a cab should always tip him a quarter. If you are going to be a guest for some time, you may find it easier to give the doorman an occasional quarter, and then when you leave hand him a dollar or possibly more if you feel that he has performed sufficient services to deserve it.

Bellhop The standard tip for a bellhop carrying up luggage for a newly registered guest or couple is a quarter if he does nothing but perhaps carry a light bag, turn on the air-conditioning and check the bath in one trip. If a large amount of luggage is involved the tip may be a dollar (about twenty-five cents a bag is expected but usually not more than a dollar). Bellhops who deliver telegrams, a newspaper, or other small things to the room receive a quarter. A large bulky package or armful of clothes from the valet should bring him a quarter, but if the valet himself delivers the clothes that have been pressed or cleaned he is not tipped, for he operates a concession. (See "Valets" on page 852.)

Pages Page boys usually receive a tip of a quarter from the person paged.

Chambermaid The proliferation of motels has changed America's tipping customs insofar as hotels are concerned. Today it is unusual for a guest to tip a chambermaid in a commercial hotel. Even in first-class hotels transients rarely tip, although the guest staying two or three nights is certainly considerate to leave the once customary twenty-five cents per person for each night, and more for a suite, with the amount depending of course on the quality of the hotel. Such tips are best given directly to the chambermaid, who may be sought out on the floor or found in the linen room. Money left under the pillow or on the bureau is often picked up by bellhops and doesn't reach the chambermaid at all. The best procedure is to place the tip for a chambermaid in a sealed envelope with the room number on it and give it to the housekeeper or leave it at the desk, asking that it be given to the maid involved. Guests in a residential hotel giving five dollars a week may insure good service, but again the amount depends on the quality of the hotel and local custom in the matter.

Beauty Operator Tipping in hotel beauty salons is the same as at home— 15 per cent–20 per cent, not less than fifty cents for a manicure and as much as a dollar and seventy-five cents or one dollar for a shampoo and hair set or more depending on the operator. Shop owners are not tipped. When in doubt, ask.

Barber Thirty-five cents is a minimum tip for a haircut in large cities and fifty cents is more common in a good shop. For services in addition to the haircut such as sunlamp, shampoo, or shave, as much as two dollars is customary. Some fashionable barbers that you find in big cities who style your hair and can charge as much as twenty-five dollars, are the owners of the emporium and might expect a gift at Christmas rather than a money tip. When in doubt ask at the desk. The manicurist in a big city shop receives seventy-five cents to a dollar tip. The shoeshine boy fifteen cents to twenty-five cents, the porter expects a quarter.

Porter A hotel porter receives fifty cents per trunk carried up to a room. If there is other heavy baggage as well, a dollar or more, depending on the amount and difficulty involved.

If he performs special services, such as making reservations or securing theater tickets, he receives anything from fifty cents to two or three dollars, depending again on the amount of trouble to which he has been put.

Checkroom Attendant At any checkroom in a hotel specially set up to serve a special affair such as a dance or ball, the attendant receives a quarter per person. However, many organizations arrange to take care of these gratuities and post a notice to that effect in the checkroom. Restaurant checkrooms usually have decoy quarters on the plate to indicate what is expected. Better take the hint. However, in private clubs there is no tipping, for members take care of this for themselves and their guests on a regular basis.

Elevator Starter A long-time guest in a hotel usually tips the elevator starter, if any, a dollar or more on leaving if he has been helpful and another dollar or more to elevator men who have served him. A resident in a hotel tips elevator men regularly serving him a dollar a month approximately and remembers the starter, too, at regular intervals.

Desk Clerks, Hotel Managers, Telephone Operators Hotel managers, as executives, are not tipped. Desk clerks, if they are asked for special services by residents, do expect to be remembered from time to time. Usually tips are given during the holidays. They may range from two to three dollars to five dollars for them and for telephone operators on such special occasions depending upon the amount of mail and calls handled. Guests usually ask the hotel manager for a list of the people who have regularly served them.

Room Waiters Many hotels make a charge for room service, but on top of this the waiter expects a tip. This is never less than a quarter for an individual small order such as a setup or a pot of tea and toast. For a dinner order, 15 to 20 per cent of the bill is expected depending on the quality of the hotel. If champagne has been served there should be an extra tip for the handling and serving of it, but many hotels have a "corkage" charge as well, if liquor is supplied by the guest. Guests may add a notation at the bottom of the bill concerning the amount of the tip they wish given the room waiter. Resident guests tip room waiters for each service, too, but usually see that head room waiters receive a tip about twice a year, the tip depending on the amount of room service the guest requires—a minimum of five dollars each time and possibly as much as ten.

Dining Room Waiters The dining room waiter is the man in charge of the service in the dining room of a hotel. He takes over from the headwaiter or, in some cases, the hostess, and ushers guests to their seats. Transients tip the dining room waiter sometimes, especially if they want to be sure of a good table on their next visit. Such tips are always given after the meal. A dollar is usual every third or fourth visit. Hotel residents tip the dining room waiter the same way as transients do, but they give the headwaiter, not normally tipped in hotels by transients, three to five dollars once a month depending on the hotel.

Valets Hotel valets, usually operating their own shops within a hotel do not expect tips, except for rush jobs or those done outside of the usual hours.

Motel Tipping One of the attractions of motels is that tipping is not expected unless you have asked for some very special service. As motels do not normally have cleaning and pressing services on the premises, it is advisable to carry your own iron or so pack your clothes that they do not need pressing. If you are able to find someone to send to a nearby tailor to have something pressed in a hurry, that service of course deserves a tip—between fifty cents to one dollar depending on the length of time the service has taken. In most motels ice is available in the hallways for guests to pick up, and in many there are facilities for making coffee in the rooms with supplies furnished at no extra charge. In those instances where meals can be delivered to the rooms, the normal tipping procedure takes place—15 per cent to 20 per cent of the bill, but not less than twenty-five cents.

Motor lodges, a development of the motel, are often many-storied and have many of the services that hotels offer including usually a coffee shop at least, but often a restaurant. These do offer such services as bell hops, room service, etc., and tipping in them is at the same level as it is in moderate-priced hotels.

Talking to Strangers While Traveling

Americans are gregarious people, and, while our social customs are much based on those of the English, we never did care for the rule that says one does not speak to strangers without introduction or permit strangers to open conversations except for some valid reason—to ask a direction, say.

A young teen-age girl traveling alone on a train might reply courteously to a man in the next seat who tried to open a conversation, "I am sorry, but I am not allowed to talk to strangers." She is too young to have discretion about such things, too inexperienced to be able to distinguish between the forwardness of a man attracted by her youth and charm and the friendliness of another person who merely wants someone to talk to on a journey of several hours. Her answer is the only possible one and the one her mother insists on for her self-protection. If the stranger persists in his attentions, she should change her seat or if there are no other seats and he is really offensive, as sometimes happens, say to the conductor as he comes through, "I wonder if you will arrange to change my seat." The conductor knows immediately what the trouble is and acts accordingly. If there is no conductor immediately available, any girl or woman being annoyed is justified in turning to another passenger, man or boy, and saying quietly, "I wonder if you will change seats with me." This is easily done and the annoyer properly chastened—often to a degree that he leaves the car.

A woman of more sophistication is usually able to appraise strangers and their motives for speaking without introduction. In the subway, on buses, in shared taxis, where this is necessary, on ferryboats, and on suburban trains, it is relatively unusual for strangers to try to engage others in conversation, though it does happen, often from the most innocent motives.

I can remember getting on a Fifth Avenue bus in New York at Thirty-fourth Street, having my fare paid by a perfectly strange old gentleman, having a few words with him, and being given his card—all within eight blocks. I had been waiting for a taxi in the rain, then in desperation had boarded a bus without first having the fare in hand. I stood, swaying, trying to reach my change in the depths of my bag, when a gentleman behind me reached forward and put the coin in the box for me. "Do permit me," he said. I found my fare as I made my way down the aisle and, turning, offered it to him. It so happened that the only seats were two next to each other, so we sat down together. He refused to take the money, but he was such a decorous old gentleman that I could hardly be offended.

"I am the Mayor of ———" he said, naming a western town. "Here's my card. Now when you come to our town you just look me up and repay that fare if it bothers you. My wife will be glad to meet you. So remember." I realized that out West his friendly gesture would seem the most natural thing in the world, while here, at first thought, it did seem embarrassing.

On long train, bus, or plane rides it is almost axiomatic that other travelers seated vis-à-vis or alongside a woman will try to open a conversation sooner or later, usually when meals are served. They should not be rudely snubbed, though if they seem hopelessly unattractive people or obviously impertinent, they are usually shut off by a murmured "Uh-um" in answer to some obvious question such as, "You bound for Chicago?" A book or paper is always a safe refuge, and boorish indeed is the person who persists in trying to maintain a conversation with someone who buries her nose in the printed page or one who answers everything in monosyllables.

In talking with strangers, it is unwise to volunteer information about oneself except in the vaguest manner. One rarely exchanges names or tells one's plans or home address. Conversation, if any, should be kept on impersonal topics—the weather, the scenery, perhaps the daily news. Certainly a woman never accepts the hospitality of a strange man, by allowing him to pay for refreshments or a meal en route or by accepting an invitation to lunch or dine when both reach a common destination. A woman accepting such an invitation, even from a man who has established that they have friends or acquaintances in common and who has carefully identified himself, makes a serious mistake. If the interest is really mutual and she wishes to see him after the trip, she can arrange for him to call when she will be with friends or relatives who can help appraise him. Otherwise, she may find herself in a position with which it is difficult to cope. A man may easily leap to conclusions if his invitation to a woman to whom he has not really been properly introduced is unquestioningly accepted.

It is, of course, possibly dangerous for a woman to accept an invitation even from another woman encountered during travel. Yet, again, there are always exceptions, and one usually learns to recognize motives. I once found it absolutely necessary when I was very young, because of an undelivered cable, to share a room in a crowded Basle hotel with an English girl whom I had talked to on the train but about whom I knew nothing, except her name. It was that or sit up all night in the lobby—and we both decided to risk being roommates. I put my money under my pillow and said my prayers. She was up before me and off to Italy, but I never forgot her kindness in letting me have part of the room that was really hers—for it was my reservation that had gone wrong.

Bus Travel

If your bus travel has been confined to intra-city busing, you have no idea of the delights in store for you on many of the cross-country bus systems in the United States or on the luxurious and comfortable ones in Europe.

In the United States inter-city or transcontinental bus travel is sometimes the only way to get to your destination aside from driving yourself. A bus may be much more comfortable and allow you to arrive fresh and relaxed. If you go in daylight you see the countryside. Your reclining seat (on a good line) allows you to take a nap or sleep through the night, as the case may be. Wide windows permit you to see the countryside. Long-distance buses and some of the short-haul ones, too, will be air-conditioned. There will be toilets and washbasins. On the charters there may be bar service if you want it. Sometimes there is music and always air conditioning. You are generally limited to 150 pounds of luggage on the inter-city lines, but you may carry more and pay an extra charge. On the American lines there is no place to hang coats and such garments plus hand luggage are stowed in racks above the seats with the driver, or a supervisor, the final authority on whether or not luggage is too large to go in the overhead racks.

The driver and the supervisor have the final say on whether or not a passenger has had too much to drink to be acceptable on board. The official limitation on the transportation of unaccompanied children is age twelve but there are many instances where children younger than this who are obviously mature enough to take care of themselves have been carried. It is always possible to ask for special attention for any elderly person traveling alone. Meals are available at meal stops which last between thirty and forty minutes, or at rest stops which last about fifteen minutes. Snacks are always available and so are box lunches. Many people wisely take their own.

Charter arrangements should be made as long in advance as possible on the major lines for group travel, for example, by a garden club to a spot such as Williamsburg or Winterthur. Many of the big bus lines such as Greyhound make buses available for charter for school outings and company picnics, as well as for dinner party hostesses entertaining prior to a charity theater party or ball, with such transportation included in the cost of the ticket or as part of the host and hostess's entertainment of their guests.

Friendliness On inter-city and transcontinental bus trips it is not actually expected that you carry on a conversation with your seatmate, who may be the same throughout the trip, but many people do strike up a conversation much more readily than they might on a train. If you wish to rest, or sleep or read, you need not, of course, talk, but the polite person indicates his desire for privacy by answering politely enough in monosyllables, then turning back to his book, looking out the window or closing his eyes. When this fails and the other person is a chatterbox, you can always say, "If you don't mind, I'd rather not talk just now, I'm very tired." If the person in the next seat is literally a pest, the passenger can always change his seat if other seats are available, as bus seats are not assigned (but once a seat has been chosen by a passenger it remains "his" even if he disembarks temporarily). In the rarer cases of unpleasantness of any kind, the passenger should appeal to the driver or perhaps ask another passenger if he minds changing seats. (Such a move might be necessary if a woman is being annoyed. The need for the request is usually quickly understood by the male passenger to whom she appeals.)

Annoyances Sometimes on a bus someone will play a transistor radio too loudly, or a group of young people will talk loudly, or "horse around" in a way that is annoying to other passengers. It is important to avoid unpleasant situations, especially when you may have many, many hours of travel ahead of you, but such situations should be handled with tact and consideration. Very often the offenders don't realize that they are offending and will quiet down, or turn down their radios when requested in a pleasant way. If this fails, then again the bus driver must be appealed to.

Small Comforts On long domestic bus trips it is certainly comfortable to have good-quality dark glasses, possibly a small throw for the knees as blankets are not provided as they are on airlines, and perhaps even an eyeshade and ear stoppers if you want to sleep. Lights are lowered at night, of course, but will come on at bus stops to let people on or off—it's a safety factor. Individual lights at each seat, however, are completely controlled by the passenger. The avoidance of alcohol, heavy rich food, large quantities of liquids helps in the prevention of car sickness. When traveling with small children, it may be wise to have some approved medication from your doctor against motion sickness, and carry small plastic bags in case of emergency (these are useful also in the collection of such things as apple cores, candy wrappers, etc., to avoid littering).

Bus Travel Abroad Inter-city and inter-country bus travel abroad is often much more familiar to American travelers than is the same kind of travel at home where they are more likely to go by car or plane, or possibly train. Luxury bus travel in Europe and also in Japan can be such a pleasure that many people prefer it to any other method of travel.

The use of these buses is particularly good for people who feel that they can't cope with foreign languages enough to drive themselves, but want the mobility of motor travel. There is no language problem because most of the tour buses do have guides who speak a variety of languages, always English. Even in Japan tour buses in the major areas, for example, Tokyo to Osaka, have English-speaking hostesses. Charters are available with English-speaking guides either men or women. The Japanese buses do not have toilets, but there are many rest stops. Delicious Japanese box lunches are everywhere available, as well as European-style food.

Europe is covered by a network of excellent tour buses such as Europabus and Linjebuss, equipped not only with lavatories but refrigerators and a place to hang your coats in many cases. Some even have bar service as well as music. In many cases there are pretty, linguistic hostesses. American tourists have taken to these luxury buses abroad with great enthusiasm. They are speedy, efficient, and inexpensive. They are a great way to travel with children, and drivers who might be hesitant to attempt driving in the Swiss Alps themselves lean back and enjoy expert driving the Swiss PTT motorcoaches offer them on Alpine tours in spring and early fall. Foreign bus trips may be booked in the country when you get there, but are better booked from home through your travel agent, as the tours are increasingly popular and some may be filled as much as a year in advance.

Ease and Comfort Abroad, buses save a great deal of strain. Taking them, you don't have to handle your luggage. If you are staying in a major hotel, the bus may pick you up there or at some other central point such as an airline terminal, bus terminal, or dockside. The rules about luggage differ. Some foreign tour buses permit as much as 110 pounds of luggage (especially on charters), others limit luggage to no more than 44 pounds. But why burden yourself. Clothing for bus travel should be simple and comfortable. Knits, pants suits or even slacks and sweaters, and easy shoes are the rule for women, and sports jackets and slacks (or even sweaters and slacks) the rule for men. The really wise traveler takes a flight bag and sends ahead other things he needs at his destination.

Bus tours abroad are likely to be much more friendly than are transcontinental trips at home. The majority of the people are on vacation and interested in meeting each other, talking, and sharing their experience. The presence of a hostess or a guide able to speak several languages gives cohesiveness to the group. Be friendly and communicative if you wish, but if you would prefer to be quiet, indicate this in a pleasant way. I once traveled from Helsinski to Leningrad on a bus with a lovely Finnish, English-speaking guide. Some of the friends I made on that trip I still have. Our bus soon became a little community although there were people from many lands. You need never fear you will be lonely on an actual bus tour anywhere. It is wise always, however, if you are quite young, not to tell too much about yourself and not give very personal information. One of the joys of maturity is that you can be freer with strangers than if you are a young person in great need of careful protection.

The Use of Postcards

Wise travelers buy postcards in the course of their travels and do not send them until they get home, not necessarily immediately. They find that their friends enjoy them just as much and they have not taken up valuable travel time for the sometimes irksome chore of sending postcards to myriad friends. I remember in Nice seeing a poor young girl who complained that she had not been able to sleep all night—she had been sitting up addressing postcards. And I feel that she was very confused about Nice.

Very efficient travelers frequently type up or have typed up address stickers with names and complete addresses of friends to whom they plan to send postcards in the course of their trips. This procedure requires only a "Love, Mary" or a word or two. I know many people do it, but it always seems a little bit too efficient to me, too impersonal. In many cases, however, it may be much kinder to the post office if one's handwriting is poor.

While joint signatures on social correspondence always seem provincial (they may be used on telegrams and greeting cards, however), names may be jointly inscribed on a postcard. No salutation is really necessary, just perhaps: This is the place! Wish we'd planned to stay longer. See you soon. Love, Gen and Al.

Remember in sending postcards from abroad that it is considered disrespectful to place the stamp so the head of state is standing on his head— just as we should not use our lovely flag stamp in this upside down way. We have all noted the line "This side for address only" but in some countries this interdiction is taken very seriously and the recipient may be charged extra postage if one line of writing drifts over to the address side. It is a good practice to confine oneself to the message area. Postcards may be addressed and written in pencil because they are often written on the fly, but ink is really better, and better too than felt-tipped pens, which may be difficult to read when used in such circumscribed space. The Post Office Department likes return addresses on everything, but of course they are impractical on postcards from abroad unless you are going to be in residence for some time.

Know that unfortunately in some countries the hotel concierge cannot be trusted to affix stamps. It is wise to buy your stamps from him and then put them on yourself before dropping the mail in the box or entrusting it to his tender mercies. In some very poor countries I have even known trusted messengers to soak off the stamps even when the reselling of them may net only a few pennies. When it doubt ask other experienced travelers or your tour guide, if you have one. Where necessary, take your mail to the post office, stamp it, and drop it into the correct slots yourself. Even this sometimes is no guarantee that it will reach its destination.

Chapter 71

TIPS TO THE STAY-AT-HOME

Suitable Bon Voyage Gifts

In seeing off friends use good sense in your gift-giving. It is wiser, if you have some particular gift in mind, to present it well in advance so it may be a planned part of the luggage. Things to wear come under this category, of course, for the pair of travel slippers and the traveling iron given as train pulls out or ship embarks may have to be carried as a separate package.

The new light steam irons are very good insurance on any kind of travel in or out of this country. The good ones are so constructed that they will press even a heavy uniform. Pressing services, even in luxury hotels, can be very unreliable. One Metropolitan Opera star told me that she always carries such an iron and does all of the pressing of important gowns herself while traveling, rather than take a chance on something not getting back in time, or perhaps having a hem that should have been rolled, pressed in by someone not competent to handle fine things. The five pounds (or less) that such travel irons weigh are worth the trouble and they can always be carried in a commodious handbag or in a flight bag if necessary. They should convert by means of a built-in switch from AC to DC. It is easy enough to carry a variety of plugs. (I even take my iron on weekend trips to people's houses so that I don't have to bother the hostess when I need to press a dress.)

Air passengers should receive nothing at point of embarkation that will add to the weight of their baggage.

Bon voyage gifts for a shipboard passenger should be suitable for the quarters he is to occupy. A woman sharing a small cabin with a stranger will not be popular if the space is so crowded with her flowers that the two can't move around. Since very few women wear corsages today, it is wise to resist sending them as bon voyage gifts. As passengers are very generously fed indeed during the course of a voyage, baskets of fruit, and boxes of candy, may well be an embarrassment, although packets of gum, rolls of hard candy and digestives might be very welcome in the traveler's handbag or pocket. Some of the big liners have their own flower shops and you may arrange on sailing day or before for gifts of flowers to be delivered during the voyage. If a woman does receive too many flowers, she can always arrange to have them sent to her table in the dining room, the chapel, or public rooms so other passengers may enjoy them.

Magazines, pantyhose or nylons, gloves, handkerchiefs, cosmetics (cold cream in unbreakable tubes, purse-size perfume spray), purse-size hair spray, scarves, cigarettes, underwear (especially drip-dry), plastic shoe socks, film, and for young people money, compact kits of various kinds are always welcome. But one of the most welcome gifts is an arrangement with the steamship company to serve a bottle of wine or champagne during the voyage with the compliments of the donor. This may be arranged with the wine steward when you see your friends off, or by mail with the line.

Current best-selling books are excellent gifts. Paperbacks are especially nice since they may be, without too great loss, left on the ship as an addition to its library or be given to other passengers. Choose bon voyage books for entertainment rather than valuable additions to your friend's collection as he may well pass them along to friends before returning home. Standard books are hard to pack or carry.

One might also arrange for credit at the bar, the beauty salon, or the masseur's.

Another rather unusual gift is to have flowers waiting in the traveler's hotel quarters. This may be done abroad through a service called Interflora. Through your own florist, flowers may be sent almost anywhere in the world. Incidentally, this is also a good way for Americans who have been entertained abroad to extend their thanks upon arriving home. Another interesting service through which you can actually entertain your friends in a distant city or abroad, is Be My Guest, available through American Express and chargeable to your credit card. This is a way also that American travelers arriving home can entertain their hosts abroad at any one of a long list of recommended restaurants.

Going Aboard to Say Good-by

In seeing friends off a ship, check with the steamship company as to permissible visiting hours. After bidding farewell, leave the ship at the warning gong. If you can't see your friends off, you may write them a bon voyage note addressed to the ship in time for it to be aboard to welcome passengers when they receive their mail. Or you may send a telegram addressed to them aboard ship. For example, Mr. and Mrs. Joshua Bodwin, S.S. *Michelangelo,* Pier 90 North River, New York, N.Y. 10019. For sailing New York May 12th (sailing date). Sailings are listed on the maritime news page in coastal metropolitan newspapers.

Train and Plane Farewells

It is less usual to see friends off on planes, as visitors are rarely allowed beyond the gate and farewells are of the briefest sort. Train farewells are equally unsatisfactory, as good-bys are usually said at the gate in large stations. Gifts (preferably not flowers, which can be a nuisance on a train) and telegrams may be delivered to trains if you know the seat, car, or compartment numbers and the hour of departure. You address a telegram (even after the train is en route it is possible for a passenger to receive a wire in this country): Miss Jessie De Groot, Aboard the *Linet* leaving Los Angeles at 2 P.M. Tuesday, June 6th, Seat 43, Car 1166.

Chapter 72

HOW CUSTOMS DIFFER ABROAD

Taking Baths

Rooms with baths are standard in first-class hotels around the world for the most part now. In second-class or other hotels the traveler frequently encounters rooms with washing facilities only and not necessarily running water. It is a European custom to take sponge baths daily and tub baths perhaps not oftener than once a week. Showers, where provided, are usually of the hand variety, and many Americans have come to enjoy this facility so much that hand showers are being attached to standard American showers by many people.

As there may be only one or two public bathrooms to a floor in a European hotel, the patron desiring to take a bath goes through a certain ritual. In most cases he rings for the maid and makes an appointment for his bath-time. When the hour arrives the bathroom will be vacant and ready for him and his bath drawn for him at the temperature he requests. In a small Paris hotel he may find a clean linen sheet lining the carefully scrubbed bathtub and a clean bath towel laid out for him, but, as elsewhere on the Continent, he may well be expected to furnish his own soap. There is, in addition, usually an extra charge for a bath, or at least the maid expects an extra *pourboire* (tip) for her trouble. Why can't these Americans get themselves clean in a sponge bath and *bidet* like normal people?

In the Orient, Japan, for example, the American proclivity for taking baths is not regarded as an aberration. Eager bath takers themselves, the Japanese consider bathing not only a method for keeping clean but a fine way to relax and enjoy one's family and friends. There are, however, certain bath customs and if you stay at one of the charming and excellent Japanese inns, *ryokans,* or if you are visiting a Japanese home, you will be expected to observe the following procedure. Before entering the bathroom it is necessary to take off the slippers you have been wearing on the *tatami* (the soft mat floor covering) and put on the slippers provided for you for entering the bathroom. Incidentally, shoes are removed before entering any Japanese home, inn, temple, or shrine. Japanese bathtubs are for soaking only and many people use the same water. Therefore, it is most important to get thoroughly clean *before* getting into the tub. You get washed by ladling out some of the hot water from the tub with the ladle or wooden bucket provided and soaping yourself down, or using the basin if there is one. The tile floor contains a drain of course. When you are clean, get into the tub and soak blissfully. At a Japanese inn, especially in the hot spring resorts, the bathrooms contain large pools, many of which are elaborately and beautifully decorated and can accommodate a number of people. The Japanese are aware that mixed nude bathing is not a Western custom and anyone desiring privacy can make arrangements with the maid to reserve one of the small family baths.

Massage is part of oriental culture, too. Almost any good Japanese hotel has masseuses on duty sometimes as late as one o'clock in the morning for weary travelers. The massage takes an hour and is usually a "dry" massage done with talcum powder in the guest's room. The cost is so small (about $2.50 with no tip expected) that the traveler to Japan quickly makes it a way of life with him as well. Major hotels have English-speaking operators who can get you a masseuse usually in a matter of minutes.

The Bidet

Americans until recently have looked at the bidet found in bathrooms abroad with a sideways, somewhat embarrassed, gaze, wondering what it was for and being afraid to ask. Those who found out sometimes went to the expense and trouble of installing them in their American ranch houses and apartments, so utilitarian did they find them.

The initial use for the bidet is as an adjunct to personal hygiene after use of the toilet. If it is thought of as a minuscule bathtub it doesn't seem so outlandish. It may be sat upon forward or aft. It may be used for soaking the feet, giving a small child a sponge bath. A friend of mine always puts her stockings to soak in it, or uses it as a temporary depository for flowers she hasn't time to arrange. Small children find the spout easy to use for hand washing. Small boys like to float boats in it. People with ills of various kinds have used it for centuries as a sitz bath. Sophisticated people all over the world now use it. Near the bidet is usually a row of small towels meant for use with this appliance.

The W.C.

All over Europe and the British Isles the letters "W.C." are to be found posted in public places, on signs, or on doors. This is the English abbreviation for "water closet," lavatory to us. Often there is just one door marked "W.C.," in which case the lavatory is for the use of both men and women. If there are two doors, there may be the "W.C." sign but on each door will be written the native equivalent of "Men" and "Women" and these foreign words, at least, must be understood by the traveler. As almost no one travels abroad without a pocket dictionary, it is easy enough to determine these words for each country to be visited. In pronouncing the letters

"W.C." in France one says "dooble-vay-say," in Germany and Holland "vay-say"; in Latin countries the word is some easily recognized variation of our "lavatory" or "toilet." In Dutch-speaking countries the word is "retirade." In Russia the symbol for the ladies room looks something like a spider. It is well to know that in Vienna in some places there is a common washroom for men and women with lavatories, undifferentiated, opening off this room.

The word "lavatory" in England has come to mean the toilet, itself, and never the washbasin, the bathroom, or restroom as in our inclusive use of the term. A friend of mine who spent much time in England says that the English are shocked, therefore, at such a bald American statement as "I'll just rinse out my stockings in the lavatory." To be really polite, in England you use that euphemism "Where may I wash my hands?" when in search of a bathroom.

The Pourboire

Many an American unused to the French language finds himself muttering "What?" to the mumbled *"Pourboire?"* he gets from the usher in a cinema as he is shown to his seat. A *pourboire* (literally, "for a drink") is a tip. Most European servitors have mastered the English word by now and use it freely, but *pourboire* is still the most common word an American will hear, and, unaccustomed as he is to anyone's actually asking for a tip or being obvious about the outstretched palm, he is sometimes deaf to that insistent, soft *"Pourboire?"*

The tipping system, which is expected to make up the difference between base pay, if any, and a living wage, is even more widespread in Europe than it is here. It is a Continental custom to tip the theater usher—even the cinema usher. In the British Isles theater ushers are not tipped, but where there is a program, there is a charge for it. The equivalent of about twenty or twenty-five cents, usually a coin about the size of our quarter—a franc, 150 lira, half a guilder, etc.—is a generous tip in Europe for anything other than a meal, the tip for which is, roughly, 10 to 15 per cent in round numbers, as it is here—20 per cent where lavish tipping seems expected but part of which is usually in your bill for "service." For small services, the equivalent of ten cents of so—5 pence, in the British Isles, for example—is considered usual.

Americans are known everywhere abroad as excessive tippers. This is viewed less as a matter of generosity than as an insult to the economy of the particular country. It is best to tip in the same manner as the most prosperous residents. I find indispensable *Richard Joseph's World Wide Money Converter and Tipping Guide,* published annually.

The "Boots"

A British stand-by is the "boots," who expects to find your shoes outside your hotel door each night for him to clean and put back silently. The "boots" by some other name is sometimes found on the Continent, but it is safer to be sure before putting out your footwear. Usually the cleaning of shoes—men's and women's—is a complimentary service on the part of the hotel, but even if there is some charge on the bill the "boots" receives a tip —about ten cents per night, a shilling in Great Britain—or if there is no billed charge for the cleaning roughly 10 per cent of the cost of the room, put out for him weekly in the shoes, as the "boots" is a nightworker whose face you may never see.

Train Travel

One may not even pass through some foreign countries on the train without a visa for each country, although much has been done recently to simplify travel, especially in the Common Market countries, where visas are now no longer necessary. While you may have had the matter of visas taken care of at home when you purchased your tickets, be sure, if your plans change, that any passage through a country not previously in your itinerary is covered by visas, wherever they are still necessary, as the lack of them may be a serious matter at borders. Visas are not requested when a traveler boards a train but only after he has passed through the territory in question and has been through customs. Scandinavia has simplified a traveler's problems by requiring that passports be shown only once as the traveler crosses into Scandinavia.

In the British Isles train travel has a strict formality, which even visiting Americans are expected to follow. In a big station like Waterloo, after buying your ticket, you line up in the queue at the gate. There is no mass frontal attack on the gates when the train is ready to load, with women and children trampled underfoot, as happens here. The British queue is respected at all bus stops, cinemas, fish markets, and bargain counters. It makes for better tempers and saves time in the end.

Trains in England usually carry two classes of accommodation, first and third. These accommodations, which are divided into compartments, open onto a corridor on longer journeys. On short runs, one car may be first-class, or one car may be divided into first- and second-class and there is no connecting corridor. It is important to locate the accommodations called for on your ticket and then to hold on to the ticket until you are safely through the turnstile at the end of your trip. A British train ticket is punched only by the conductor and is taken up finally at the station at which you detrain.

In European dining cars meals are served as they are on boats—first, second, third sitting often although I have known trains to have only one or two depending on the traffic. On boarding a train with dining facilities, one makes a reservation for a sitting with the steward in charge, giving one's name and seat number. The passenger is then assigned to a particular service and listens for the announcement called out for it during the dining hours. In many places on the Continent, as on small railroads here, it is expected that passengers will stop over for meals at the station restaurants provided and that is what the (to us) interminable wait-overs are for—so passengers can alight and eat.

On the Continent the trains are usually divided into first-class, second-class, and third-class, the last frequently equipped with hard wooden benches and replete with large families who do everything but the family wash en route. Except on overnight trips, however, the experienced traveler usually goes second-class rather than first.

As American train service rapidly deteriorates in many areas, train service and equipment on the Continent rapidly improves. Spain with its wonderful Talgo train running from Madrid to San Sebastian and Madrid to Barcelona is one of the fastest trains in the world (it is made of aluminum) and, like airliners, serves meals on trays. In Sweden the Sunlit Nights Land Cruiser going from Stockholm to Norway via the Arctic Circle is the most luxurious train imaginable—showers, a drip-dry laundry, piped music, a cruise staff, and stopovers at various points of interest.

In the Far East, Japan maintains an excellent railway system which spans all of the islands. Japanese trains no longer have clear-cut classes, but the green car for which a special ticket is needed is equivalent to first-class. They are all certainly among the finest and most efficient trains in the world. Dining cars are well managed and clean. On the luxurious stream-liners, the Asakaze (Morning Breeze), Sakuna (Cherry Blossom) and Fuji which link Tokyo with Osaka and Kobe and beyond to the southern island of Kyushu, for example, some of the restaurant cars are serviced by Tokyo's Imperial Hotel. Tipping is not customary unless some special service has been performed. Keep your train stubs. They will be collected at the end of your trip. Stops are very brief, so organize yourself to leave the train promptly. The station name will be in both Japanese and English. Indicated also will be the station you have just left and the station to which the train is going. There are also directions in English prominently posted in every station. The girls in the buffet cars are English-speaking and most stations have offices of the Japanese Travel Bureau to aid travelers.

The famous bullet train "Hikari," a super express, *averages* 100 miles an hour, but goes as fast 130 miles an hour. It has reclining seats like an airliner. In the "green car" (equivalent to first-class) there are carpeted aisles. It has a buffet car where Japanese snacks are sold—and very good, too—dried cuttle fish and squid, for example, and interesting small Japanese cakes filled with sweetened chestnut or bean purée as well as coffee cakes and even spaghetti. The clean, wide-view windows permit you to see the countryside. Seats in the super-express-Hikari "green car" (green ticket) are reserved and no standees are permitted. On the rest of the train, standees are permitted only when there is an unexpected demand as on a holiday weekend, and two tickets are issued—one red and one the rail ticket and these are collected also at the end of the trip. If you are traveling on the general part of the train, it is wise to arrive at any main station approximately three quarters of an hour early for a choice of seats.

Eating Customs

On the Continent, the meat knife is always steel-bladed. It is, by the way, quite incorrect in Europe to use the meat knife on potatoes, which should always be cut with a fork (a steel blade would turn them an unappetizing black). Fish is always eaten with a special, non-steel fish knife and fork, so that the fish will not have a metallic taste.

Chopsticks are used in Japan of course and they may be anything from simple wooden ones to those elegantly made of ivory. In Western-style restaurants, knives and forks are used, but even in Japanese inns and in many Japanese-style restaurants, knives and forks are available on request. It's a great deal of fun to try chopsticks, but unless you're really proficient don't try to tackle a whole meal using them. You may starve to death or at least be fairly sloppy in trying to manage them. Better pocket your pride and ask for knife and fork. (But see use of chopsticks, page 352.)

Another Japanese custom is the serving of hot towels before eating so that the diner may clean his hands. When the maid passes the tray or basket of hot towels, take one and pat your hands with it. You may also use it on your face and neck. She will be around in a moment or so to pick it up and you then drop the towel onto the tray or into the basket.

Smoking at Table   In England at public dinners there is no smoking before the "Queen's Toast," the first toast offered. This is a rule foreigners are certainly expected to know and must observe. In fact, there is much less smoking at meals abroad than there is here, and it is wise, even in a group of young people, to let the hostess make the first move toward offering cigarettes.

Presentation of Flowers   In Europe and Scandinavia, when one is invited to dinner it is considered almost mandatory to take flowers to the hostess. In Scandinavia the number of flowers should be uneven as they are thus considered easier to arrange. In France never take carnations to your hostess. Many people think they are bad luck. In Germany and countries with a Germanic culture, it is customary for a gentleman to take three flowers to his hostess. I have seen this custom followed by a mannerly Pole who gave me some romantic explanation of the number three to the effect that a male guest delicately suggests to his hostess with the gift that were it not for her husband, he would like to be her heart interest.

Is the Woman Always Placed to the Right of the Man?

On the Continent a gentleman is careful to seat a lady on his right. In Victorian and earlier times any lady a man seated on his left was no lady. He so proclaimed the fact to prevent any passing male friend from introducing her to his wife. Among younger people, this convention certainly no longer holds, except in Latin countries, but it is just as well for a lady to sit at a man's right even in a car or taxi. The theater is excepted, if to sit on a man's right would place the woman in an aisle seat. On the street, especially in Latin countries, the lady is always on the man's right whether or not this places her on the curb side temporarily. In olden times, in fact, it was considerably safer, especially in London's narrow, congested streets, with the many dark alleys and people's habit of dumping refuse in the street, for the man to cede the safer curb side to the woman. Generally speaking, we cling to the opposite convention here, because in our early days alleys were not a menace but the flying mud from unpaved streets was.

In the Scandinavian countries the place of honor is always on the left, or heart side, whether a gentleman is walking with a lady or a hostess is seating a guest of honor.

Shaking Hands and Hand Kissing

Europeans shake hands more frequently than we do, and it is well to remember this and anticipate it. Women customarily rise to shake hands with either men or women, and there are handshakes all around when one meets or leaves someone. I have noticed in most Continental society and in Latin America that it is the man who takes the initiative in handshaking. In England and France it is the woman who offers to shake hands or not. The gesture is almost a spontaneous one with the man slightly in the lead in taking the initiative.

In the most formal Continental society (except in France), particularly among older people, it is still correct for women to remove the right glove before shaking hands or, if there is time, before extending the hand to be kissed. It is the English convention, however, for the woman to leave on her gloves for handshaking for in England there is no hand kissing. Exception: the right glove is removed when a woman is being presented to reigning royalty unless she has received directions to the contrary, and also to a head of church. In these things we follow the British tradition. I have found in Spain, France, Scandinavia, and Holland, however, especially among the younger women, that there is now less removing of the glove for introductions unless the gloves are heavy ones. They now tend to follow the English convention in this matter, too.

From the American woman's standpoint, it is well for you to be attentive during introductions and to be prepared to extend your hand gracefully if the man who is being introduced bows and extends the palm of his hand. It is awkward to offer to shake a hand in this position.

In Italy, France, and Spain, hand kissing is becoming more and more a rather impersonal gesture. The man's lips properly never touch the lady's hand, and in Roman society the hand is barely lifted as the man bows perfunctorily over it, despite the kind of kiss-implanting motions you see in Italian movies. As an Italian said to me, "In our own society we kiss hands less and less. It's just a gesture. But with American women we go to some lengths because they seem to expect it and like it and we want to please."

There is very little hand kissing in Holland and the Scandinavian countries, much in Austria (it is a pretty gesture for your dancing partner to kiss your hand as the music ends), and still fairly customary in German social circles.

In Japan there is much more handshaking than there used to be but this is mainly among people who have considerable contact with foreigners, perhaps in business. The Japanese have various degrees of bows but you are safer bowing slightly in the Western style so as not to lose "face" in trying to imitate a style whose intricacies you don't really understand. A bow is always safe in Japan. Young people frequently shake hands with Western guests quite spontaneously but with others let the bow suffice unless a hand is offered. The Western "kiss of greeting" is taboo. For centuries kissing even privately was outside of the Japanese culture. It now does occur but mainly in private even among young people. When they follow the Western custom and kiss publicly, they encounter shocked responses from older people. It is wise to refrain from too-public expression of hugs and kisses even with Western friends in any oriental culture, particularly in Japan.

Visiting in a Continental Home

It is not considered good manners on the Continent for guests to be complimentary about the house they are entering. Instead, you go in quietly and say nothing about your surroundings unless you are asked to comment. Your hostess might say, "I'd like you to see our garden. I spend a great deal of my time there as flowers are my hobby." The reason for this reticence on the part of guests is that it is assumed that people of good taste come from similar backgrounds.

Also on the Continent women guests are rarely shown to their hostess's bedroom and should not ask to see private living quarters of the house. Instead, coats are often taken by a maid or other servant and bathroom facilities are usually provided near the entrance hall.

American Women in Latin Countries

Urban Latins are getting used to us, but to the less sophisticated the behavior and appearance of American girls and women abroad is an open invitation to unwelcome advances.

I have seen young American girls in Mexico City run in and out of the lobby of the Reforma in the shortest of shorts and bra tops. Had they been able to understand the comments of the guides and the peddlers on the corner, they would have gone to their rooms and stayed there in humiliation.

On the Continent and in Latin America there is never the kind of drinking among women that goes on sometimes in the United States. Any woman or group of women entering a bar for the purpose of drinking, especially drinking hard liquor, can expect "incidents." In fact, right in the United States, unescorted women in bars, if indeed they are admitted, can expect trouble and a lone woman drinker in a bar is frankly suspect.

In some Latin countries one or two young, or even not-so-young, women traveling alone must be circumspect to the point of prudery or else develop a keen parrying power. Two college girls on a summer trip to Rome were plagued by a pair of Italian boys who, misunderstanding their free American manners, followed them openly through several streets. Finally the older of the two girls, knowing how quickly the Italian "gentleman" takes offense, turned around and calmly tossed their pursuers a lira. What an insult for Roman Romeos to be taken for mere beggars! They were gone in an instant.

It is better sense for American women to fare forth at night in Latin countries in groups or with male escorts. If they must go alone, they should summon a taxi from a public stand. Latin women are so carefully protected that the woman who goes out alone, especially at night, is fairly sure to be accosted, if only verbally. And even if she knows the language, a woman in a foreign land spoken to impertinently by a passing stranger does just what she does at home—pretends she has heard nothing and goes quickly and quietly on her way.

Anklets, which used to be *déclassé* here but are now occasionally seen on quite respectable women, have a homosexual connotation in Europe. American women who ordinarily wear a gold anklet, if only for identification purposes, might do well to remove it before going abroad.

In all Latin countries it is mere social technique for men to indulge in the wildest hyperbole, quite publicly, concerning the women they accompany. Such remarks as "You are absolutely magnificent!" or "The angels should have such eyes!" should be taken with a grain of salt and an unstartled "Thank you." In Latin etiquette all social intercourse has a very personal connotation but its very personalness is stylized. Not every man is madly in love, or about-to-be-madly-in-love, with every woman to whom he is presented. But the very fact that, for social reasons, it almost seems he is makes for warmth and gaiety in Latin gatherings. Everyone knows it is just a graceful social game with all holds barred, but the atmosphere is certainly more conducive to conversation than that of a restrained English or German group. Perhaps this is because, in Latin etiquette, the extravagant, admiring phrases are directed as frequently to the old as to the young and tempting.

It is our cold, English culture, of course, that makes us, if not suspicious of the stranger, at least most restrained and impersonal in our casual contact with him. The Latins do not place courtesy on two separate levels —the embarrassed, eyes-averted kind for strangers and another warmer kind for friends and acquaintances. The warmth of the Latin is in everything he does and must not be misconstrued. He will speak to an unaccompanied woman with no encouragement whatsoever, whether or not he has performed some routine service for her. His motives are not necessarily ulterior. If they should turn out to be, it is quite easy to rebuff him politely.

The Latin's personal brand of courtesy extends to people who serve him (in shops, particularly) as well as to those he serves. A little polite conversation precedes the purchase of a bunch of bananas in the *mercado,* a little passing of the time of day. Latin purveyors find time to greet the customer, serve her in a leisurely manner, and bid her farewell, to which the customer replies in kind. In even the busiest shop in France each customer greets the sales person with a *"Bonjour, madame"* (or mademoiselle, or monsieur), or the equivalent in other countries, and the sales person returns the greeting before the transaction begins. Americans who cannot give these greetings in the language of the country should remember at least to give them in English, adding the polite "madame" or other title, as is always done in Latin countries. When we omit these little ceremonies we are adjudged boorish.

In all Latin countries funerals are shown great respect. Often the procession is on foot, and if it passes us, we should do whatever others on the sidewalk are doing. Women usually bow the head or, if Catholics, make the sign of the cross and, if possible, wait until the funeral has passed before continuing on their way.

And, of course, women as well as men should be able to recognize the national anthem of any country they are visiting and should rise (men should uncover their heads) with others in public places whenever it is played.

American Men in Latin Countries

Italian, Austrian, and French men sometimes embrace and kiss on both cheeks their male relatives and close men friends on meeting. Spaniards do little of this, and Latin-American men don't do it at all. A ceremonial kiss, when an honor is bestowed, may be preceded by the usual handclasp in France, Spain, and Italy. The bestower of the honor, some dignitary, places the ribbon or medal on the recipient, clasps his hand briefly, then leans forward and kisses him first on one cheek, then on the other. They then shake hands, and the ceremony is over.

American men must be very chary indeed with their attentions toward unmarried Latin women. Any attention is frequently construed by wary parents as serious *intention.* Chaperones, in some countries, are required for all girls of good family after 6 P.M. and on some occasions even in the daytime, although in the more modern countries groups of boys and girls often go out together, especially if the girls' brothers are in the party. A Latin brother is trained to be even more careful of his sister's honor than is the most fusty chaperone. The "date" as it exists in America is unknown in most Latin countries, where all upper-class girls are protected. The system is breaking down in sections of some modern Latin countries, particularly Mexico, Colombia, Brazil, and Peru, but American-style freedom between upper-class single men and women is unusual still. Unmarried young women of good families, for example, don't have apartments by themselves or even with other girls.

Once you have been presented to a girl under proper auspices, it is correct to ask if you may call. A first call always takes place in the presence of a chaperone or the family and is very formal. Later, without prior arrangement, a young man may present himself at the young lady's grilled window, in those countries where this is the custom (now pretty much confined to small towns—mostly in Spain) and talk to her or serenade her. She is permitted to chat through the grille, unchaperoned, far into the night if she is so disposed, but it is not only futile but dangerous for a suitor to try to get into her apartment.

A popular girl may have more than one suitor beneath her window at a time. It is for them to work out whether they will both stay or whether the one there first will have the evening to himself. About nine o'clock is suitable for calling on a Latin beauty at her window, but if she does not come to the grille within a few minutes it is considered poor taste to stay, as she may be waiting for some more welcome caller.

Some Latin married women are given considerable freedom. They do not herd together as American women do at luncheon and tea spots, but often lunch with men, their husbands, or their husbands' friends—with the husbands' knowledge. It is considered quite correct for a man who has been entertained in someone's home to ask his hostess to luncheon or tea without her husband—especially in France. He may call also upon her at her home in the afternoon hours. In America, if a businessman left his office to call on the wife of a friend at four o'clock, it might not seem exactly cricket to an absent husband when no one else but servants was present, but in France particularly such calls are quite usual. In Latin America such calling is much less usual except perhaps on a special occasion.

Dancing Abroad

The American system of "cutting in" is a holdover from pioneer days, when at any dance there were never enough women to go around. We try to maintain this situation artificially, in New York especially, by having a large stag line or, at subscription dances, requiring each girl to bring more than one partner. This is supposed to ensure that all the girls will be constantly awhirl—but doesn't. Good dancers and popular girls enjoy the cutting in of eager gentlemen, but the shy girl hates the system. Rarely is her partner cut in on, and the boys avoid her for fear of being "stuck." Short of breaking an ankle, her partner must stay with her until he can unload her on someone else or she has sense enough to plead fatigue and retreat to the ladies room. "Cutting back" is frowned upon.

In Europe and Latin America dances are never the social agony they often are for the young here. In the first place, the chaperone system guarantees that the girl will have a place to go when the music stops, and her partner is always expected to return her to her chaperone or to the spot where he claimed her, where she was standing or seated with friends. A bow and thanks and her partner is gone. There is no cutting in, or virtually none, or when it does occur it is most unusual. For example in Holland it might occur in some small community or college dance, but then only when it is announced by the master of ceremonies probably on some special festival occasion. A girl can relax and enjoy her dance with one partner throughout the musical selection and not have to keep a weather eye out for the stag line.

Furthermore, Continental style, the young men at a dance do not concentrate their dancing attention on the eligible girls alone but do considerable duty dancing with their parents' friends. And because the married women are kept dancing, older men have plenty of opportunity of dancing with their friends' daughters, an expected thing. In this country an older man trying to compete with the stag line is considered a silly old "wolf," and the older woman dancing with a twenty-year-old is either pitiable or suspect.

Taking Pictures

Our country is very large and the number of tourists descending upon it yearly and bent on picture-taking is relatively small. Have you ever been stopped on the street and asked to pose—as a local curiosity—for a foreigner's box camera? Probably not, but Americans abroad always think in terms of people-in-their-pictures and are pretty abrupt in their posing orders, at that. Think how it must be on, say, an island like Jamaica for a whole boatload of tourists to descend all at once, all focusing their cameras on the passing citizenry without, usually, even a "by-your-leave."

Strange as it may seem, many people are not pleased at being camera subjects. Unless you have the kind of camera that can take action shots inconspicuously, always ask people to pose (if you must) and with great politeness in the sign language, if necessary. And where the practice seems acceptable, give tips to your models. In countries where national costumes are worn many working people are plagued to death by camera addicts during the tourist season. Some dress only on Sunday and holidays and hope for tips. It is only fair to offer them some compensation for the time all this posing takes.

The Chinese—about one fourth of the world's population—inhabit many other places than the mainland of China of course. In general, older people among them particularly do not like to have their pictures taken. The procedure can, in their way of thinking, "take their souls." Don't, therefore, heedlessly take a picture of a Chinese. At least attempt to get his permission. The Japanese evidently have no such feeling. They enjoy having tourists take pictures, particularly when they are with their children. It is always courteous to ask, however. You will find a mother and father very often bowing low in acquiescence and smiling widely. You may get a little shock when they ask to take *your* picture, on their home territory, as they are all great camera bugs, but you look just as exotic to them as they to you.

Chapter 73

AN AUDIENCE WITH THE POPE

Requesting an Audience

Visitors to Rome, Catholics and non-Catholics, usually desire to visit the historic and beautiful Vatican City and have an audience with the Pope, head of the Roman Catholic Church.

The etiquette concerning an audience with the Pope is very rigid. Requests by Americans are cleared through the North American College in Rome and are presented to a papal secretary by means of introductory letters from your parish priest. The greatly sought-after audiences cannot be quickly arranged, so letters should be written much in advance of arrival in Rome, and should be sent to the Office of the Papal Audience, Casa S. Maria dell'Umilta, Via dell'Umilta 30, Rome, 00187. Upon reaching Rome with the reply from the audience office in hand, you should call them immediately to arrange the time of the audience. If you do not arrive with an invitation, you should present yourself in person to the office, which is open from 9 to 1 and from 4 to 7 P.M.

Non-Catholics should use the same procedure for getting an audience. See your local parish priest and generally he will write to the audience office on Via dell'Umilta giving your name and the date of your stay in Rome. Take a carbon of this letter with you to Rome for reference.

Needless to say, once an audience has been granted you do not refuse it for any reason save illness. In the case of illness, an explanatory note in English or Italian (if you are letter-perfect) should be sent by hand in ample time to the office for audiences, but holders of general admission invitations (no reserved seats) need not go through the formality of sending their regrets, for in the big crowd their absence will not be noted.

If you cannot decipher the details of the audience as they appear on the Italian summons, discuss it with your hotel concierge, who is very familiar with the procedure at the Vatican. Special annotations on the invitations for general audiences—or their color—may denote special places in the hall for these audiences. Perhaps the tickets you receive may be those indicated for diplomats and others of considerable importance. They permit their holders to seat themselves on the benches placed in a single row on the dais and facing the great gold color wooden throne of His Holiness. Or they may be marked in another way to indicate that you are to be seated in the front row of seats on the floor of the hall or in adjoining boxes. Holders of invitations to a general audience crowd into the remaining space, some seated, some standing. These general audiences take place on Wednesday at 11 A.M. at St. Peter's. Even if you have reserved seats (the favored seats are considered to bestow upon you the honor of a semiprivate audience), be very early. Otherwise you may not be able to get through the crush to them.

During the time when the Pope is at his summer residence at Castel Gandolfo, the audiences usually take place at 10 A.M. At present, private audiences held in the Vatican apartments are generally limited to heads of state, the diplomatic corps, cardinals, bishops, and those who have business affairs with the Vatican State.

Incidentally, for those unable to arrange an audience with the Pope, it may be of interest to know that he comes to his apartment window on Sunday at noon, gives a short talk, says the Angelus (the noonday prayer), and gives his Papal Blessing to all assembled in St. Peter's Square below. At this time visitors may have their religious articles blessed by the Pope in the general blessing.

What Clothes to Wear

The dress for general papal audiences today is very relaxed. Some of the women in the reserved seats (especially those on the dais) wear the long black, long-sleeved, high-necked gowns that used to be *de rigueur* for semiprivate audiences but which are required now only at the semiprivate audiences in the Vatican apartments. They also wear mantillas on their heads as most of the Roman women do, and none but functional jewelry. While gloves may be worn en route to and from the audience, no gloves whatever are worn during the audience. It is incorrect to remove only the right glove. Some of the men are in uniform, others in formal daytime wear, but still others wear ordinary dark business suits and white shirts. There are also women (probably non-diplomatic) in the ordinary clothes a traveler wears, but with hats, scarves, or mantillas on their heads. The colors they choose are quiet and none but religious emblems are worn by both men and women. Black stockings are no longer required (and few wear them), but sleeveless or décolleté dresses even in black are not permitted.

Those with general admission tickets (no reserved seats) now wear ordinary travel clothes. Although head covering for women is still a requirement, the rule is not always observed, even among some of the Italian women present. This covering of the heads is an ancient tradition and is, in my opinion, better not breached at an audience or at St. Peter's, which is still rigid in the matter of impropriety in dress. A woman in a sleeveless dress would not be permitted to enter St. Peter's without something to cover her arms. Pants suits are now permitted but slacks or shorts are not.

Private Audiences For the very few private audiences granted, men must wear either dark blue or Oxford-gray suits (if they are not in uniform), but if neither of these is available, then formal evening clothes are worn even in daytime hours or (and a man would feel more comfortable) formal morning clothes. No boutonnieres are ever worn, although orders, such as the ribbon of the Chevalier of the Legion of Honor or the sash of some important official order, are encouraged. No fraternal emblems are allowed and other jewelry should be as inconspicuous as possible.

For these rare private audiences, women who are not in uniform wear black. The neck of the costume must be high, the sleeves to the wrist, the skirt long and the head covered by a black mantilla. Shoes and stockings should be black. Any jewelry must be strictly functional. Wedding and engagement rings are, of course, permitted, but bracelets and decorative pins should be removed, although a pin actually needed to hold together a neckline is allowed but should be preferably of dull gold, pearl, platinum, silver, or jet—not brightly colored stones. A simple strand of pearls is allowable, but earrings are usually removed as too frivolous.

Children's Clothes for Audiences Children at a private audience may wear white. A small boy is acceptable in gray with a white shirt, black shoes and socks, and a black or gray tie, but even in winter a white summer suit for a boy who is not old enough for a dinner jacket is quite usual. Girls must cover their heads, too, with white veils or with black veils to match black or white costumes.

For semiprivate or general audiences, conservative church-going clothes for children—as for adults—are best.

Taking Religious Objects to Be Blessed

Catholics usually go to the Vatican with a few rosaries, a sacred statuette, or missal for the papal blessing (as gifts for their family and friends). Protestants who wish to make such gifts to Catholic friends do the same, buying the things to be blessed in the various shops in Rome which sell religious articles or bringing their friends' own rosaries or other religious possessions with them for the blessing. Rosaries are usually draped over the left wrist. The benediction is mentioned as extending to such objects as the pilgrim brings with him to the audience.

Procedure During the Audience

There are three classes of papal audience—private, semiprivate, and general. The second is given to people who have given outstanding service to the Church in one form or another. The third is for the many pilgrims to the Vatican who from time to time have the privilege of attending audiences and services conducted by the Pope in the Eternal City.

In private audiences those who are to receive the papal benediction are instructed to get on both knees at the entrance of the Pope. As the Pope enters the room, he addresses each pilgrim separately, stepping in front of him. The pilgrim receives the benediction kneeling with bowed head. The Pope then extends his hand. The proper procedure is to place your hand under his and kiss the ring, symbol of the churchly office. Upon certain circumstances, if some aspect of this very special formality conflicts in any way with his own convictions, the non-Catholic, if necessary, discusses with the authorities what modification may be possible in his case. The Vatican feels that the kneeling of the audience-seeker is properly courteous and traditional and can in no way compromise any religious conviction. It would seem better, if one feels strongly about this, to forgo the audience entirely rather than to ask that exceptions be made in one's case.

The Pope's Entrance   At a general audience the Pope is borne into the Benediction Hall in low season and into St. Peter's in high season on the stroke of eleven on a sedan chair in red damask (a *sedia*) by the "Sediari." As he approaches, the assemblage stands clapping and cheering. He proceeds slowly up the roped-off aisle. Those near him thrust rosaries and religious articles toward him for his blessing. As the chair reaches the dais and the waiting array of Swiss Guards, the Pope descends and mounts the throne. As he sits, those with seats sit also.

The Papal Address   On the throne, the Pope addresses his audience in Italian and other languages. He extends his personal greeting to various groups there from all over the world. Those so greeted respond with cheers and hand clapping. At the moment of benediction, the audience kneels and the Pope gives his benediction in Latin, first explaining that his blessings extend to all religious articles his hearers have with them.

Recessional   At the conclusion of the blessing, the Pope descends the throne (the assemblage rises, then kneels for a final benediction). If his time and health permit, he then approaches in turn each visitor in the special area. As he extends his hand, each sinks briefly on his right knee as instructed by the monsignors attending the Pope. Those with some compunction against following this formality merely bend the knee in the prescribed fashion as the Pope lays his hand in theirs. He then speaks briefly to each visitor, often in his own language, before mounting to his chair again and being borne slowly down the aisle. No one, of course, leaves before he does.

Making the Sign of the Cross   Although the rest of the procedure is rigidly prescribed, no one who does not ordinarily make the sign of the cross in his devotions is expected to do so during an audience with the Pope.

Taking Leave   At a private audience while the Pope is present those in the room, with the exception of his retinue, remain on their knees. Those who have received the benediction remain on their knees until the Pope has left the room or has signaled that those present may stand. Anyone leaving the papal presence backs away a few steps, then moves to the side before turning around, as with royalty, on whom one must never turn the back.

When Interviews Are Arranged   Again as with royalty, one must not open the conversation but must wait for the Pope to speak first. One leaves only after permission to leave has been granted or if the Pope rises to indicate that the interview is at a close.

Chapter 74

TRAVELING BY CAR

Taking Taxis

When you hail a taxi that carries a meter, be sure the driver pushes the flag up to start the meter again. Otherwise, the previous passenger's fare will be added to yours. The minute the cab pulls to a stop the meter should be stopped by the driver's pushing the flag down. The driver is not supposed to let the meter run while he makes change. If you are careful to insist upon this you protect the next passenger. It is against the law for a metered taxi to proceed with the flag down while carrying a passenger, unless the taxi has been engaged for a trip out of town at a flat rate. A passenger may not make such a flat rate with a company driver. Such a driver must phone his company to get permission to leave city limits and get the flat rate. The driver of an independent cab may fix his own flat rates but not within city limits if he has a metered cab. If you ask any driver of a metered taxi to set you a flat rate within the city limits—perhaps late at night when the police may be less alert—you are asking him to break the law, and, if caught, he can lose his license. If the trip takes a metered taxi outside city limits and you have neglected to ask for a flat rate, you can be held responsible for the metered cost of the return trip if the car breaks down.

Protection When you enter a cab, look immediately at the license in the back and be sure the driver's face corresponds with that in the picture on the license. These pictures are in most cities taken with the driver wearing a cap, not a hat, to make identification easier for the passenger. If you entrust a woman or child to a taxi, make a notation of the driver's license and that of the car. For safety's sake, in the case of a child or sick person, have someone phone you on his arrival. All taxi drivers must be licensed and fingerprinted. To ride in a cab not driven by its proper driver as indicated on the posted license is to risk accident, robbery, attack, and even death.

You and the Taxi Driver Many people behave in cabs as if the drivers were wooden Indians. It is quite possible for drivers to hear all conversation in the back of the cab and many cabs have strategically placed rear-view mirrors that permit the driver a full view of the back of the cab. A taxi, therefore, is as public as the library, about as private as the back seat of a bus.

Taximen are a philosophical, often cynical crew. They must drive all day, relatively unprotected from the weather for eight hours—sometimes longer, if they have the stamina to work for overtime pay. To pass the time they often open conversations with passengers—if the passengers don't get the conversational drop on them first. Such conversations should be kept impersonal. Why take violent issue—say on politics—with a taximan whom you will probably never see again. He needs to blow off a little steam from his tiresome spot behind the wheel. Listen and sometimes learn, but never, if you're a woman, permit remarks that seem too personal or prying. It is easy enough to be monosyllabic in your replies, if any, if you don't want to talk or if his remarks get out of hand. The law says, that, with or without conversation, he must deliver you where you want to go within the area in which his cab operates.

Most taxi drivers are agreeable, but occasionally there are exceptions. If a driver without an "off duty" plaque on his car refuses to pick you up for some quixotic reason known only to himself, you can take the number of his cab and report him to your local division of licenses. Taxi cab drivers generally are not supposed to smoke while on duty, at least if the passenger objects. If, for example, the smoke of a cigar is offensive to you in such small confines as it is to many, you are perfectly free to ask the driver to refrain. If he refuses, or suggests you take another cab (I have had this happen), again you should report him to the complaint desk at your local division of licenses, giving the time and the date of the occurrence, the number of the cab, and the driver's number also if you have had a chance to get it and expect to appear against him.

Interestingly enough, you may even see a sign in the cab which says "No smoking please." This means that the driver doesn't enjoy the odor of cigars and cigarettes and you should be courteous enough to comply with his request and not smoke.

Losing Articles in Taxis In all big cities drivers must keep a log of each trip they make. You have seen them filling the log or trip sheet out as you enter and leave the cab or sometimes when they must stop for a light. These cards note where the passenger—or passengers—were picked up, the number of passengers, and where they alighted, together with the meter reading for the trip. The cards must be kept over quite a long period of time in case of police check-up. If you leave something in a cab and do not remember what company operated it, it is still possible to trace your property. Notify the police at once and tell them where and at what time you took the cab and how many passengers were in the car. If the article has not been turned in to police headquarters, a fairly quick check on your driver can be made. Most cab drivers are honest, and there are many regulations they have to observe. They must, for example, check the cab for forgotten articles as you leave, for they can be held responsible if a subsequent passenger appropriates lost property.

Where a taxi driver does turn in something of impressive value left in his cab, it is usual to give a reward of at least 10 per cent of the actual value of the article.

Tipping

Tipping in Taxis For rides under fifty cents, never give less than a fifteen or twenty cent tip. If the meter reads thirty or thirty-five cents, do not expect change from a dollar. Trips totaling about a dollar call for twenty to twenty-five cents in tip. Drivers work on a base salary plus tips. Every time you undertip or—as some parsimonious people do—fail to tip at all, you cut their salary. For longer rides 15 per cent of the total is fair. As women tend to undertip, don't be surprised if your driver looks less than cordial when you start counting out your money. He expects the worst. If you think of the tip as part of your fare, not as gratutity, it will be easier to endure the usual stony silence when you give even a generous tip. If you tip what you consider an adequate or even generous amount and get no "thank you," you can always do what one famous male columnist did under the circumstances—leave the door open as you depart.

Tipping Chauffeurs Tips to the drivers of hired limousines are handled in cash with 10 to 15 per cent of the total bill the usual amount. Or, you may ask that this amount be added to the bill to be tendered by the company. Private chauffeurs are not tipped unless they have performed some very special service such as handling a large amount of luggage, particularly for a weekend guest. The tip—a dollar or two—is folded up and handed to the chauffeur quietly without discussion of the matter with the owner of the car.

Drivers of airline limousines, even though they handle luggage, are not tipped, nor are the drivers of privately rented buses.

Garage Tipping In public parking garages and lots, tipping is unusual unless some special service is performed. In a public garage, however, special services may be tipped for from time to time. Delivery of the car, however, is covered by the monthly rent. In many garages employees do expect to be tipped at Christmas. The wise car owner leaves approximately five dollars per employee for the kitty at that time, but the amount depends on the location of the garage and the rental paid. It could be more or it could be less. Ask the manager or another user of the garage. The amount of service, of course, determines the tip as well. People who take their cars out daily would of course tip substantially more than those who take the car out once a week or even less.

Good Manners and Your Car

Nowhere in the world are there so many privately owned automobiles as there are in America. Or such widely practiced bad car manners.

If you are really observant, you can learn more about a person's poise, considerateness (or lack of it), probity, and judgment by riding with him at the wheel of his car than you can by studying him long hours in his living room. You will see the timid man, or woman, grow bullying and bellicose behind the wheel. You will note the neighbor's fender scraped as your man pulls heedlessly out of the parking spot, the pedestrian narrowly missed and roundly cursed although he has the right of way. You will experience the senseless weaving in and out of traffic with the many accidents and near-accidents it causes.

The established rules of driving are for the protection of other drivers and the non-driving public, but they are also related to good manners. If you do scrape someone else's fender in leaving a parking space, you should, as a well-mannered person, leave your car and arrange to make good the damage, even if the law didn't hold you responsible under the circumstances. Most careful people carry liability and property damage even in states where it is not actually required, but most insurance doesn't cover such slight property damage as is occasioned by the scraping of a fender. The owner of the car must pay for that himself. You who inflicted the damage may find your own insurance will cover even such minor damage to someone else's car, but even if it doesn't, you should make yourself responsible. If no one is in the other car, leave a card or note with your name and address so that matters may be arranged between you. In some states any damage over a certain amount to another car or to your own—even, in the latter case, if you inflicted it yourself—must be reported to police. Elsewhere, adjustments of this kind are a matter of good manners.

Hand Signals While hand signals are almost everywhere obligatory, there is usually no policeman behind a car to check on whether the driver uses them consistently. Hand signals or the use of directional lights should be second nature to the good driver, which means he should use them automatically even when they don't seem strictly necessary as, for example, on a country road. It is much too easy if you do a lot of country driving to get out of the habit of using hand signals. Yet forgetfulness of them in even slightly heavy town or city traffic can cause accidents or at least inconvenience to other drivers.

Your state's Department of Motor Vehicles probably issues a pamphlet which shows, usually graphically, all accepted hand signals and all state driving regulations. If you have been driving many years without having had to take additional driving tests, it is possible that you are not properly informed about local and state driving ordinances and that your driving may eventually bring you into conflict with ever-toughening state laws.

Thoughtless Acts The innocent bystander who is mud-spattered because you didn't avoid or proceed more slowly through the mud puddle in the road doesn't have recourse to law, but he does have his opinion of your manners. The householder who finds his driveway blocked by your car can call the police, but usually he just fumes until you turn up to move your vehicle. In some places citizens aroused by the noise of your unmuffled muffler can do something about it, but in other communities it's up to you to see that you are not creating a nuisance.

The Good Driver A really good driver has been taught to drive by another really good driver. He learns that he touches the foot brake as little as possible if he would avoid jerks and sudden stops. He lets the engine brake the car. He never grinds his gears or slips backward on a hill before starting up. He sounds his horn only as necessary and never when the traffic is held up and other drivers are stupidly leaning on their horns on the assumption that they will thus speed things along. As a matter of fact, this particular action in most metropolitan areas may bring arrest. Know your local ordinances concerning any sounding of the horn.

No considerate person ever sounds his horn outside another's home in summons if he can possibly leave the wheel or send someone in with a message. And when he takes to the road he has with him any necessary repair tools, so as not to annoy passing motorists by asking to borrow a jack or a wrench in the case of a blowout.

In cold climates the considerate motorist carries in winter a shovel or trowel and some sand in his car and, if possible, a tow line, not only for his own car's probable use but to help others stuck on the road. At all times he carries a flashlight and a first-aid kit (which he knows how to use). If he's really sensible, he has a fire extinguisher—the kind with carbontetrachloride or with CO_2—or at least knows enough to put out an engine fire with sand or earth.

The Welcome Passenger A passenger should know, above all else, when to keep quiet. He should not chatter when the car is in heavy traffic, and he should abstain from giving gratuitous advice in times of difficulty. He should sit as still as possible and not distract the driver by reaching into the back of the car, bouncing around on the seat, or opening the door while the car is in motion. Let the passenger keep his hands and belongings well inside the car, too, to avoid confusing drivers behind him.

It is the driver, not the passenger, too, who must determine whether or not the car radio is to be on or whether or not smoking will disturb him.

No one leaving a car should fail to close all doors carefully.

Double Parking In some towns and cities even momentary double parking, while the boy runs out with your groceries or you call a greeting to a neighbor, may get you a ticket. Elsewhere it's a matter of manners. If no one is trying to pass you, there is nothing against a brief double parking (if it's legal), but keep your motor running so you can make way if you find yourself blocking free passage.

Is the Slow Driver the Best Driver?   It takes constant exercise of judgment to make the good driver. Sometimes slow driving is the best driving. In other cases a fast clip, evenly sustained, is sometimes required. Never, for example, keep your car in the left-hand lane of a through route, if you do not plan to maintain the maximum speed. By doing so you hold up the drivers behind you, who will be irritated—probably noisily so—by your refusal to let them pass. On a narrow road, especially at night, if you prefer to proceed at a very moderate rate—which is your privilege—and another car is forced to tail you at your speed, although he obviously would like to overtake you, pull up to the side of the road to let him pass, unless you know the road will soon widen enough to let him go by.

You and the Law

It is curious how so many otherwise law-abiding people feel they can break traffic laws with impunity. When they are occasionally caught up with for their infractions, they tend to become abusive to the arresting officer, or at least show indignation.

If you are picked up for speeding or some other flouting of the traffic laws, treat the officer, who must caution you, serve you with a ticket, or take you in, as the representative of the public (and of you yourself) that he is, not as an archenemy. Hand him the papers he asks for—your license, the car registration. Answer his questions quietly. You may be quite in the right, but abusive language now will nullify any chance you might have to avoid this mark against your record. Above all, never threaten to try to bribe a traffic officer or state policeman. Trying to do such a thing may land you in even hotter water.

Policemen are human, too. If you have been in the wrong, an immediate admission of the fact instead of an argument may get you off with a warning instead of a ticket.

In case of any serious accident involving your car, do not leave the scene until the police have arrived and taken all information. Do not move anyone with possible back or bone injury until a doctor has arrived.

Hitchhikers

In all states it is against the law for people to hitchhike. Everywhere the motorist himself takes a real chance from a liability standpoint when he picks up someone at the side of the road, even if that person is known to him. Every car should carry liability insurance to protect car owners against possible suit by passengers, hitchhikers or not.

Selecting an Automobile

Can You Live Up to Your Car? It is certainly not unheard of for a man, usually a young one, to invest his all in a car that he can't possibly live up to. A five- or ten-thousand-dollar imported car—even though it cost considerably less secondhand—can bring its owner much embarrassment if he lives in a neighborhood out of tune with such luxuries. If he's not careful, the car, not he, will be the master, dictating where he must go, what he should spend, and how he must dress, even though his income is nowhere in line with what the possession of such a car would indicate.

I once knew a promising young man, whose name was on all the social lists, who, although he had a very modest job, strained every nerve to keep up a front, however false. On his small salary he supported a secondhand Rolls-Royce, an extravagance that forced him to share a little walk-up apartment with two other boys. He missed many a meal and often had to abandon his car to possible street vandals for lack of gas to get it home. Yet he felt he was investing in his future. I often wonder what happened to him.

People with money do not necessarily have expensive cars, and the old snobbishness about the price of a car is gone. Many who could afford super-elegant cars prefer simple small ones in sufficient number to accommodate a busy family that, very probably, chauffeurs itself.

The Station Wagon Station wagons, originally thought of as estate trucks to be used for humble purposes such as hauling the family baggage and groceries, have risen in the social scale to such a degree that they often replace other vehicles entirely and fulfill all the family needs. One need never apologize for meeting even the most distinguished guest in a station wagon. City families, especially those with weekend places and several children, frequently have station wagons because of their size and flexibility.

Marking the Station Wagon Many estates have place names instead of street numbers. In that case it is perfectly proper to have the name of the estate and its address, if you wish, on the front doors of the wagon, just below the windows or in the panel beneath them. This lettering usually matches or blends with the color trim of the station wagon or is of the colors favored by the estate or farm. Usually the lettering is outlined in gold paint or in black, to make for better visibility. Whatever appears should be in modest-size lettering and kept simple. Use capitals instead of quotes and, preferably, avoid any, probably coy, illustrations.

Some marking of a station wagon, if only with the owner's initials (never his name, as this seems commercial), is useful when you direct people to it. In the country many station wagons are used. There are relatively few makes and the colors are limited in those manufactured.

INDEX

Cigarettes, 401, 420, 426–27. *See also* Smoking
  lighting and offering, 241
Cigars, 249, 315–16
  on elevators, 317
  at formal dinners, 420
  at formal luncheons, 426
  never on street, 243
  in offices, 317
Cities,
  clothing for sports, 302–3
  single women in, 277ff.
  women smoking on streets, 317
Citizenship, new, 362–72
  and changing names, 368–70
  and differences in manners, 364–68
  obtaining, 363–64
  what new citizens think of us, 364
Civil marriages, 141–42
  and elopement, 141
  Mormon, 137
Clams, 348
  and finger bowls, 435
  on half shell, 349–51
Claques, 793
Claret wines, 444, 447
Clay pigeon shoots, 301
Cleaning. *See* House cleaning; specific areas
Cleanliness. *See also* Grooming
  babies and, 662
  children and, 690–91
  for medical exams, 777
  teen-age, 703
    and dating, 704
Clergymen (ministers; priests),
  addressing, 594–601
    chaplains, 613
  and christenings, 8
  dress, 361
  at engagement parties, 21
  and funerals, 178, 181, 185
    acknowledgments to, 188
    fees, 186
  introductions to church heads, 312
  and marriage counseling, 732
  respect for, 249
  rising for, 229
  and saying grace, 339, 340
  and weddings. *See also* Weddings
    fees, 90, 104, 138
    photos in church, 108
    post-wedding calls, 169
    reaffirmation of marriage vows, 175–76
    at receptions, 148, 149
    at rehearsals, 103, 119, 120, 121
    their own, 138–40
    visiting before, 78–79
    visiting before second marriage, 163
    wear spare rings, 115
Clichés, in public speaking, 781
Cloakrooms. *See also* Checkrooms
  guests' rooms as, 472
  and tips at wedding receptions, 148
Closing doors, children and, 672
Closing jars, bottles, etc., habit of, 652–53
Clothes (dress),
  for Annapolis weekend, 805
  for audience with Pope, 876–77
  for baby showers, 658
  burial, 178–79
  for bus travel, 857

for calls on President, 818
children's, 660–64. *See also* specific occasions
  baby, 660–62
  choosing own, 664
  hand-me-downs and made-overs, 663
  pre-school and older, 662–64
for christenings, 5–6
clerical, 361
for coffee parties, 406–7
college, 725–26
for debuts, 11, 12
flag on, 822
foreign guests and, 372–73
for golf, 283–84
for hunting and shooting, 300–1
for informal teas, 405
for memorial services, 185
men's, 199–222. *See also* specific
  functions, occasions
  bad-weather, 219
  city wear, 220
  dinner jackets and accessories, 205–7
  hatless and gloveless men, 218
  hats, formal, 208–9
  morning coats or cutaways and accessories, 203–4
  overcoats, daytime, 219
  overcoats, formal, 208–9
  suits, 199–203
  tail coats and accessories, 207–8
  tieless men, 218–19
  ties, handkerchiefs, jewelry, 209–16
  turtlenecks, 219
  vests, socks, shoes, 216–18
  wearing decorations, 221–22
  what to wear when, 220–21
  when not to wear evening clothes, 209
mourning, 190–92
for opera, 792
for plane travel, 845–46
at public dinners, 755
for public speaking, 784–85
for riding, 292, 295–96
servants', 524–25ff. *See also* specific servants
for ship travel, 836–37
  cruises, 839–41
  freighters, 838, 839
for skating, 297
for sports. *See also* specific sports
  don't be too casual, 302–3
and teen-age grooming, 702
and teen-age job interviews, 719
for television appearances, 787
for tennis and badminton, 287–88
on trains, dressing, 847
wedding, 106–18, 203, 204, 207, 209, 218
  best man's, 89, 109–10ff., 165
  bridal attendants', 111–16, 128, 165
  brides', 106–9. *See also* Brides; Gowns: wedding
  for civil marriages, 141
  for double weddings, 128
  grooms', 89, 109–10ff. *See also* Grooms
  guests', 118, 156, 165
  for home weddings, 137
  Jewish weddings. *See* Jews: weddings
  parents', 117–18
  for rectory weddings, 138
  for second weddings, 165
  ushers', 89, 110ff., 128

hand-shaking and kissing, 868
W.C.s, 864
Franciscans, addressing Episcopal, 596n–97n
Frankenthaler, Helen (Mrs. Robert Motherwell), 325
Fraternity houses, 724
Freighter travel, 838–39
French, the. *See* France and the French; French language
French language,
menus, 744–46
words and phrases, 622–25
French Line, 839
Friendliness, when traveling, 833
on buses, 855–56
Friends. *See also* Calls; Guests; specific occasions
descending on, while traveling, 698
interference in parent-child relations, 690–91
meeting man's, during courtship, 14–15
single women and city, 277
Friends, Society of. *See* Quakers
Frock coats, for fox hunting, 295
Frogs' legs, 341
Fruit. *See also* Dessert
breakfast, 495ff.
cake,
eating, 341
wedding, 152–53
at formal dinner, 422
how to eat various kinds, 344–46
Funerals, 176–93
acknowledging flowers, 187
acknowledgments to clergy, pallbearers, ushers, 188
arranging, 178
attending, 181
boutonnieres for, 208
calls, 183, 773
and clothing, 204, 208
for burial, 178–79
mourning dress, 190–92
patent shoes unsuitable, 208
ties with cutaways, 204
and cremation, 185
death notices, 179–80
eulogies, 181
flag in processions, 821
food after, 190
hanging the bell, 179
immediate procedures, 177–78
in Latin countries, 871
letters of condolence, 188–89, 551
mass cards, 182–83
memorial services, 185
printed sympathy cards, 189
restriction of activities, 192
services, 183–85
ushers and seating, 184–85
where funerals take place, 179
Furnishings, 499–509. *See also* Furniture; specific rooms
china, 504
choose furniture to fit individuals, 500
colors for, 500–1
forming taste, 499
glass, 504–9
linens, 501–4
planning rooms, 500
Furniture, 499–501. *See also* specific items

choose to fit individual, 500
cleaning, 531
colors, 500–1
the flag on, 822
forming tastes, 499
planning rooms, 500
standing on, 482
Furs, 252, 258
hats, 254
stoles for cruises, 839
Fuse boxes, emergency instructions for, 474

Gambling, 456
"Game, The," 453
Games. *See also* Sports
indoor, 451, 452
"Garage," pronouncing, 371
Garages, tipping in, 882
Garbage, 327
disposal on boats, 289
taking out, 648
Gardeners, addressing, 480
Garden weddings,
flowers for, 16
invitations to, 43–44
men's clothes for, 110–11
Garnishes, 439–40
cocktail, 443
eating, 346–47. *See also* specific kinds
Garters,
bride's, 154
with morning coats, 204
with tail coats, 208
Gas jets, checking before traveling, 831
General Federation of Women's Clubs, 323
General houseworkers, 523–24
Generals, 809–10, 811
"Gentleman," use of, 368
Germany,
concierges, 849
and hand-kissing, 869
taking flowers to hostesses, 867
W.C.s, 864
words and phrases from, 627
Get-well cards, 555
"Ghosts" (game), 453
Gibson cocktails, 442
Gifts,
for adopted children, 695
for Annapolis midshipmen, 806
for baby showers, 658
baptismal, 5
birthday, children's, 677, 678
birthday, Sweet Sixteen, 711
bon voyage, 859–60, 861
cards with, 757. *See also* specific occasions
christening, 6
Christmas, after bereavement, 193
college graduation, 729, 730
to cruise staffs, 841
debutante, 13
to doctors, 778
engagement, 21
returning, 29
guests and, 475–78, 553
foreign, 476
for servants from, 483
high school graduation, 716
to hospitals, 774–75
nurses, 776
housewarming, 411

Punch,
glass for, 506
at informal dances, 409
at wedding receptions, 150
Punctuation, for business letters, 565–66
Punishment,
and children's allowances, 665–66
children and threats of, 689
Purim, 357

Quail, eating, 341
Quakers,
christenings, 359
use of "thee" and "thou," 359
weddings, 136
Queen, addressing British, 602–3
Questions,
children and answering, 672
impossible, to authors, 797
personal, 307–10
Quilts, in bed-making, 489
Quotation marks, use in letters, 565
Quotations. *See* Language

Rabats, 361
Rabbis, 131ff., 185
addressing, 596–97
no clerical collar, 361
Raccoon fur, 252
Race, criticizing another's, 249
Radio appearances, 785–87
Radios, 326
on buses, 856
car, 884
in hospitals, 776
national anthem on, 824
on planes, 844
for servants, 525
on trains, 848
Radishes, 347
Rain, and outdoor weddings, 43–44
Raincoats, 219, 252, 253
at Annapolis, 805
and cruises, 840, 841
yachting, 290
Ramadan, 357
Ranch mink, 252
Razors,
leaving clean, 653
on planes, 845
Reading,
over someone's shoulder, 273
on radio appearances, 785, 786
speeches, 782
Reaffirmation of marriage vows, 175–76
Rear admirals, 810
addressing, 614
Receiving lines, 268, 430, 755
at Annapolis hop, 805–6
at college functions, 723
at debuts, 12
at wedding anniversaries, 171
at wedding receptions, 142, 143, 144–47
addressing bride, 146
civil weddings, 142
complications, 144, 155
conversation, 144–46
fathers in, 144
home weddings, 138
kissing bride, 127
music, 153

palms for, 147
second marriages, 166
what bride and groom say, 146–47
who receives in place of bride's mother, 144
at West Point, 808
at White House, 817
Receptions. *See also* At home; Receiving lines; Teas
college, 723
debut, 11, 574
engagement parties, 20, 21
for guests of honor at public dinners, 754–55
pre-nuptial, 104–5
wedding, 31, 84, 91, 143–59
addressing bride, 146
bride's table, 149–50
children at, 115, 164. *See also* specific attendants
Christian Scientists and, 135
civil marriages and, 142
clergyman's wedding, 139–40
and complications in family, 154–55
complications in receiving line, 144, 155
conduct of guests, 157
congratulatory telegrams, 56, 91, 158
conversation in receiving line, 144–46
divorced and remarried father giving, 86
fathers in receiving line, 144
flowers, 147
gifts at, 63–64
gratuities, 148
guest book, 147–48
home weddings, 137, 138
invitations, 36, 38, 44–46ff., 50, 52–54, 158ff.
Jewish, 134, 135
Mormon, 137
music, 83
parents' table, 148–49
photos, 147
rectory weddings, 138
second or delayed, 158–59
second marriages, 158, 161–62ff.
throwing bride's bouquet, 154
transportation to, 90, 142
ushers and, 94–95
wedding breakfast, 148
who receives in place of bride's mother, 144
White House, 817–18
Recessional, wedding, 94, 115, 126
double weddings, 128, 129
Jewish, 131, 133
military weddings, 95, 96
music, 82
rehearsal, 120–21, 122
second marriages, 164
Recipe files, 400
Recommendation, letter of, and college application, 721–22
Records. *See* Phonograph records
Rectory weddings, 138
Red (color), and hunting, 300–1
Red Cross, teen-age work with, 717
Red wine. *See* Wine
References,
giving for servants, 520–22
in hiring servants, 513
social letters of reference, 557–59